LEADING ORGANIZATIONS

SECOND EDITION

LEADING ORGANIZATIONS

PERSPECTIVES FOR A NEW ERA

SECOND EDITION

GILL ROBINSON HICKMAN, EDITOR
University of Richmond

Los Angeles | London | New Delhi
Singapore | Washington DC

For information:

SAGE Publications, Inc.
2455 Teller Road
Thousand Oaks, California 91320
E-mail: order@sagepub.com

SAGE Publications Ltd.
1 Oliver's Yard
55 City Road
London EC1Y 1SP
United Kingdom

SAGE Publications India Pvt. Ltd.
B 1/I 1 Mohan Cooperative Industrial Area
Mathura Road, New Delhi 110 044
India

SAGE Publications Asia-Pacific Pte Ltd
33 Pekin Street #02-01
Far East Square
Singapore 048763

Printed in the United States of America

Library of Congress Cataloging-in-Publication Data

Leading organizations : perspectives for a new era/editor, Gill Robinson Hickman. — 2nd ed.
    p. cm.
Includes bibliographical references and index.
ISBN 978-1-4129-3908-9 (pbk.: acid-free paper)
  1. Organizational behavior. 2. Organizational effectiveness. 3. Leadership. I. Hickman, Gill Robinson.

HD58.7.L4 2010
658.4′092—dc22
                         2009035798

This book is printed on acid-free paper.

09   10   11   12   13   10 9 8 7 6 5 4 3 2 1

Acquisitions Editor:	Lisa Cuevas Shaw
Editorial Assistant:	MaryAnn Vail
Production Editor:	Catherine M. Chilton
Typesetter:	C&M Digitals (P) Ltd.
Proofreaders:	Annette Van Deusen, Annie Lubinsky, and World Wise Webb Editorial Services
Indexer:	Molly Hall
Cover Designer:	Gail Buschman
Marketing Manager:	Carmel Schrire

Contents

Preface

My intent for the design and content of this book is to increase the reader's understanding of concepts and practices that facilitate *shared responsibility* for leadership and fluid roles among leaders and participants in new era organizations. The second edition of *Leading Organizations* has been restructured and updated to include many new and revised chapters throughout the book.

The central organizing feature of the book is an overarching framework (depicted in the Introduction) that outlines the components of leadership in organizations. This framework is repeated at the beginning of each Part with highlighted sections that indicate the focus of a section. The book features current chapters by many prominent scholars in the field of leadership studies and a variety of other disciplines.

This edition begins with all new chapters on the environment of new era organizations. Classic leadership theories remain in the volume and a new section has been added on concepts and theories that contribute to shared responsibility for leadership. This section emphasizes the increasing need for leadership by participants throughout an organization. It also contains chapters on dysfunctional leadership.

There is more emphasis on culture as the internal life force of the organization, with several new chapters added to this section. A completely new section has been incorporated in this edition on inclusion of leaders and participants in organizations that represent a wide range of backgrounds and experiences. Vision, mission, and structure are still central to the book, and chapters in these sections have been updated. Sections on capacity building and social responsibility remain in this edition with new articles in each category.

The book is intended for both those who study leadership in organizations and those who serve in the roles of leaders and participants. These are the individuals who can make a difference in the processes and outcomes of organizations now and in the future.

Acknowledgments

I wish to thank the many colleagues, students, and family members who have contributed to the completion of this book. I am especially grateful to Tammy Tripp, the Academic Coordinator in the Jepson School of Leadership Studies, for her expert editing, persistent requests for the numerous permissions required for this book, infinite patience, and wonderful temperament.

I am thankful to the editors and staff of SAGE Publications for their expertise and support during the editing and publication of the book, especially Lisa Cuevas Shaw, MaryAnn Vail, and the late Al Bruckner. I want to thank Charles (Chuck) Metzgar for his sage counsel on changes to the second edition and his dedication to teaching the course Leadership in Organizations at the Jepson School. I am also grateful to Wang Fang, who read every chapter and offered her insight and advice on this edition of the book. I will miss her deeply when she returns to Shanghai. Finally, I owe deep gratitude to my husband, Garrison Michael Hickman, who kept me going so that I could complete this second edition of *Leading Organizations*.

SAGE Publications would like to thank the following reviewers: Daniel Huck, Marietta College; James E. Henderson, Duquesne University; Carmen L. McCrink, Barry University; Anthony Marchese, University of Charleston; Dayle M. Smith, University of San Francisco; Michael K. McLendon, Vanderbilt University; and Patrice M. Buzzanell, Purdue University.

Introduction

The fast pace and rapidly changing environment in which new era or postindustrial organizations function require leadership that is substantially different from Max Weber's solitary executive at the top of a bureaucratic hierarchy. Organizations require leadership that is fluid, not simply positional, dispersed rather than centralized, and agile not inflexible. Current organizational leaders know this mantra well, but are often reluctant in practice to distribute genuine leadership below managerial levels. Despite this reluctance, the external environment and continuous advancements in technology are major driving forces underlying change in organizational leadership. A single leader or leadership team rarely has enough knowledge, information, expertise, or ability to understand and respond quickly, effectively, and ethically to the dynamic changes in the environment and adapt or transform the organization and its participants.

This book focuses on concepts and practices that facilitate shared responsibility for leadership and fluid roles among leaders and participants (employees, followers, or associates) in organizations. A primary assumption underlying the book is that new era organizations can become better able to meet the challenges of their environment by developing the capacity of participants to share responsibility for leadership of the organization and implementation of its mission. A further assumption is that leadership of these organizations can become increasingly more trustworthy, concerned about the effect of their decisions or actions on others, and more resilient when leaders and participants base their decisions and actions on a foundation of ethics and shared values. A final assumption is that organizations will need to align their leadership, vision, mission, values, and social responsibility to respond effectively to changes in the external and internal environment.

Given these assumptions, organizational participants will need to choose and cultivate their leadership philosophy thoughtfully and deliberately. An organization's leadership philosophy is more than a style. It is the essence of the organization's integrity—a clear demonstration of its beliefs in action. Determining the tenets of organizational philosophy requires the combined efforts of leaders and participants. Accordingly, leadership concepts and theories are incorporated in the book to advance purposeful creation of leadership philosophy and beliefs.

Figure 1 depicts a holistic framework for understanding and analyzing the role of leadership in new era organizations. The first two components of the framework identify the leadership role with regard to accessing changes in the external environment and adapting the organization to these changes. The center of the Venn diagram represents core leadership processes and actions that permeate and guide all components of organizational life. As depicted in the framework, shared responsibilities for leadership by organizational participants consist of generating and advancing the organization's vision, ethics/values, culture, inclusion, change, capacity building, and social responsibility, among other aspects. The content, processes, and practices of these areas shape how participants implement and adapt the organization's mission, management functions, and structure.

Robert Kelley points out that leaders and participants play different but equal roles in carrying out these core processes and actions; yet both leaders and participants do leadership.[1] Though executive leaders are

Figure 1 Leading Organizations Framework

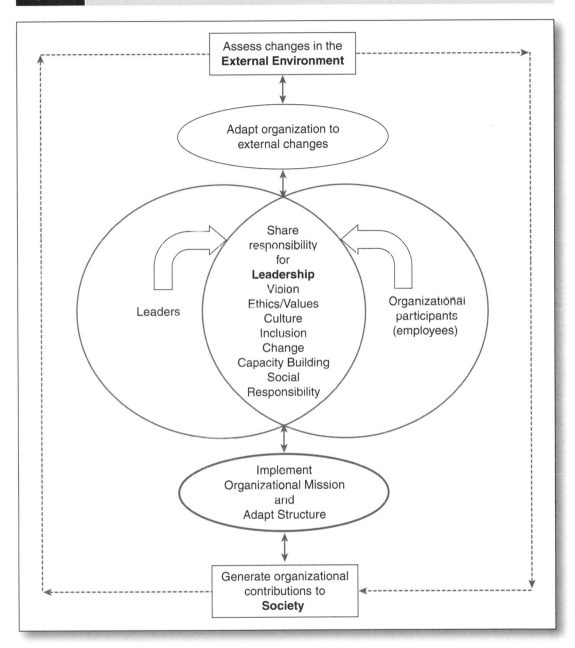

designated formal responsibility and authority by a board of directors or government regulations—that is, legitimate power to act on behalf of the organization, responsibility for accomplishing the organization's purpose, accountability for performance of its members to meet organizational goals, financial and resource accountability, and organizational structure or design—the complex realities of contemporary organizations call for leadership roles that are more fluid than in past eras. The fluidity of these roles is a fundamental shift in the philosophy and functioning of leadership in organizations. The concept of leadership as a process of initiation and involvement does not negate formal authority. Participants share formal authority broadly in contemporary structures. Individuals move from participant to leader or leader to participant based on capabilities, expertise, motivation, ideas, and circumstances, not solely on position or formal authority. In new era organizations, leadership can start with formal leaders (appointed authorities) in concert with other organizational participants and stakeholders, *and* leadership can originate with participants without formal authority.

The next component of the framework—implementing the mission—is the primary reason for an organization's existence. Leadership processes, functions, and actions are directed toward identifying and achieving this ultimate purpose. To accomplish the mission, leaders and participants must design and adapt new organizational forms or structures that facilitate maximum performance, foster knowledge sharing, and increase interaction. The final component of the framework emphasizes the organization's responsibility to contribute to the well-being of society.

In its entirety, the framework provides an approach to conceptualizing and guiding leadership in new era organizations. The book follows this framework throughout and the selected readings provide meaning and depth to each component. The text contains several parts with an overview by the editor on leadership and organizational issues for each segment. Part I examines the impact of major changes in the external environment on new era organizations and features several approaches used by organizations to deal with these changes including peering or collaboration and alliances. Part II examines classic theories of leadership that remain viable in many contemporary organizations. Part III begins with a historical perspective on one of the primary themes of this text—shared leadership. Chapters in this section examine issues of responsibility for shared leadership in new era organizations. Part IV emphasizes the influence of vision and mission on the passion and engagement of organizational leaders and participants and the importance of effective organizational design on implementation of the organization's purpose. Part V considers the essence of an organization—its culture. This section examines the effect of leadership on culture and the vital component of ethics and shared values. Additionally,

various ethical leadership challenges are assessed in an effort to discourage harmful or damaging forms of organizational leadership. Part VI explores inclusion of leaders and participants in organizations that represent a wide range of cultural, national, gender, racial, religious, and generational pluralism, among others. It also examines issues of work-life balance as a component of inclusiveness. Part VII looks at capacity building as a means of developing organizational members' abilities to adapt, change, collaborate, cultivate democratic processes, and use conflict constructively. Finally, Part VIII explores the new responsibility of organizational leadership to contribute to society through social activism. Even though organizations in previous eras were expected to generate contributions to society, the expectations of new era organizations are more challenging. Society requires more than job creation and employment. People want organizations to give time, human capital, and monetary resources to advance the well-being of society. Organizational leaders and participants are expected to take activist roles to tackle issues such as education, the environment, health, and housing in addition to traditional forms of philanthropy. They are in highly advantageous positions to facilitate unprecedented advances for society and resolve complex problems based on their collective capacity to mobilize human, technical, and economic resources.

Most of us spend a large portion of our lives in organizations. Face-to-face or electronically, we are educated in and work for organizations that matter a great deal. Leadership makes a meaningful difference in every aspect of these organizations. We want and expect leadership that is purposeful and intelligent, effective and competent, caring and moral. This book strives to provide more than a collection of engaging readings. Its intent is to provide an integrated perspective for facilitating good leadership of organizations so that they are well suited to meet our expectations and the demands of a highly complex and changing environment.

Note

1. Kelley, R. (1988). In praise of followers. *Harvard Business Review, 88*(6), 142–148.

PART I

The Environment of New Era Organizations

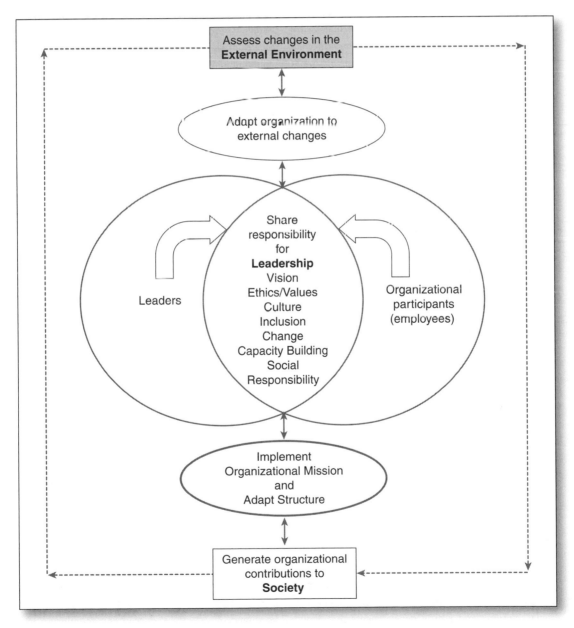

Overview

The dynamic external environment is one of the major forces in the existence of organizations. Organizations can thrive in this environment if leaders and participants identify emerging patterns and seize opportunities presented by environmental changes. The chapters in this section describe some of the characteristics of this environment and propose processes that organizational participants can use to recognize signals and impending changes, and gain advantage in this context.

Peter Schwartz (Chapter 1) characterizes the current period as civilization's third Great Transformation. He describes the first transformation as distinguished by the earth's warming and climate stabilization accompanied by the birth of agriculture and village life, and the second transformation as symbolized by the industrial revolution, new technologies, an increasingly integrated world economy, and a polity with larger, more complex organizations. In the third Great Transformation, people witness many more individuals living far longer, a deceleration of population growth, revolutionary advances in science and technology, especially in the life sciences, the economic potential to lift billions of people out of poverty, a new kind of political order, and the challenge of abrupt climate change, among other changes.

Schwartz stresses that these individual changes are significant but even more consequential is the way in which all these changes will interact together. The cumulative effect will produce the most important inevitable surprises that are capable of making the world radically different from the previous era. Since we cannot predict the chaos and turbulence to come, he provides guidance for organizational participants to prepare them for the inevitable surprises of the future including building and maintaining sensory and intelligence systems, identifying early-warning indicators that signal rapidly approaching change, and placing a very high premium on learning, among others.

Globalization is one of the major components of a complex, dynamic environment that organizational participants must recognize and factor into their planning and actions. Douglas Hicks (Chapter 2) describes globalization as a set of processes—sometimes competing, sometimes complementary—that incorporate the global level into economic, political, technological, social, cultural, and ethical developments that would otherwise remain local, national, or regional in scope. Economic globalization, which is a factor in many private sector organizations, concerns the expansion of production, trade, consumption, savings, and investment to markets beyond national and regional borders. Hicks indicates that technological innovations in the telecommunications and computer industries are major components of globalization and make immediate, coordinated, and sustained communication possible among multiple geographic locations in the world.

Though globalization is not a wholly new phenomenon, the level of international trade, economic investments, technological enhancements, and emerging global infrastructure have greatly accelerated the rate and growth of globalization. It is a major factor reshaping society in the new era or third Great Transformation, portrayed by Schwartz. Part of the complexity for organizational participants is that globalization is not considered a positive circumstance by all groups. Hicks points out that some activists, scholars, and citizens oppose and protest certain dimensions of globalization, especially when it is based on, contributes to, or perpetuates disparities of economic wealth and political power. These concerns about perpetuating disparities or inequality require more vigilance and greater social consciousness and actions by organizations that participate in globalization.

How do organizational participants recognize and plan for factors in the external environmental? Gregory Dess, G. T. Lumpkin, and Alan Eisner (Chapter 3) advocate several processes to create an environmentally aware organization—scanning, monitoring, gathering competitive intelligence, and forecasting. Scanning involves surveillance of an organization's external environment to predict environmental changes and detect changes already underway. Monitoring tracks the evolution of environmental trends, sequences of events, or streams of activities. Competitive intelligence helps organizations define and understand their industry and identify rivals' strengths and weaknesses, and environmental forecasting involves the development of plausible projections about the direction, scope, speed, and intensity of environmental change in order to predict change. Scenario planning is one form of environmental forecasting, which is used for coping with uncertainty over medium- to long-term horizons. This method uses data collected through scanning, monitoring, and gathering competitive intelligence to create scenarios of possible outcomes and project how trends or forecasts could be upset by events and their outcomes.

Paul Schoemaker and George Day (Chapter 4) focus on how organizations can identify, interpret, and use "weak signals" to recognize impending change in the environment. They suggest that personal and organizational biases (such as filtering and groupthink) of participants may cause them to be unaware of critical information on the periphery, even in organizations with active scanning processes. They identify a three-stage process—scanning for weak signals, sense-making, and probing and acting—to help organizational participants interpret weak signals and turn them into useful information for decision making.

How do new era organizations innovate and succeed in a dynamic and uncertain environmental context? The final chapters in this section examine two approaches to collaboration beyond organizational boundaries to increase an organization's chances of success. Don Tapscott and Anthony Williams (Chapter 5) explain an approach to innovation and value creation called "peer production" or "peering," which describes a process that occurs when masses of people and firms collaborate openly to drive innovation and growth in their industries. Organizations invite anyone from professional to amateur creators to join them in innovating and problem solving using low-cost, technology-driven collaborative infrastructures. They typically provide monetary rewards to collaborators who are successful in generating new breakthroughs or solutions. In other cases, such as contributions to Wikipedia, people make voluntary contributions to knowledge creation.

Tapscott and Williams use the term "wikinomics" (based on *wiki*) as a metaphor for a new era of collaboration and participation. They indicate that with the right approach, companies can obtain higher rates of growth and innovation by learning how to engage and cocreate with a dynamic and increasingly global network of peers that include and go beyond organizational participants.

Assessing the environment and adapting the organization to changes in the context are essential components of leadership in new era organizations. Leaders and participants must imagine and experiment with new ways to innovate and create value beyond the organization's usual boundaries. Dynamic changes in the environmental context are challenging organizations to consider new functions and roles for leaders and engage different participants in the process of leadership.

CHAPTER 1

Inevitable Strategies

Peter Schwartz

Global Business Network

In 1993, the University of San Diego mathematician and science fiction writer Vernor Vinge proposed that humanity was entering a no-return transition point that he called the "singularity"[1]: a point after which human experience would change forever. Or, as Vinge put it: "a point where our old models must be discarded and a new reality rules." Vinge (and others, like the computer scientist Raymond Kurzweil) have posited that the tipping point will come when computers are developed with processing power on a par with human intelligence. From there machines will begin to design and build their own machines, outpace the human ability to understand their purpose and processes, and direct the course of progress ever after. "Any intelligent machine would not be humankind's 'tool,'" wrote Vinge, "any more than humans are the tools of rabbits or robins or chimpanzees."

I don't think the evolution of computers beyond human capability is inevitable. It's certainly plausible, but I don't think it's predetermined to take place sooner than 2030, as Vinge does.

And in a sense it doesn't matter. Whether or not that specific technology is realized, a singularity is approaching anyway. It is the third such singularity in human history, and it will be upon us within the next twenty-five to thirty years.

The first such singularity occurred about eleven thousand years ago, and took several millennia to travel around the Earth. It was a Great Transition for humanity: the advancement of the species from a survival strategy of hunting and gathering, to a state of civilization based on agriculture. That civilization, by the time of Jesus Christ, was characterized by centralized authority (often in the form of a monarch), slaveholding (just about every agricultural civilization had slaves of one form or another), commerce (often in the form of markets), and literacy for the elites.

Beginning with the Europeanization of movable type, and ending with the technologies of the mid-twentieth century, there was another singularity: the industrial revolution. This Great Transition might perhaps be described by a simple listing of inventions:

Source: "Inevitable Strategies": from *Inevitable surprises: thinking ahead in a time of turbulence* by Peter Schwartz, copyright © 2003 by Peter Schwartz & Monitor Company Group LP. Used by permission of Gotham Books, an imprint of Penguin Group (USA) Inc.

clocks, telescopes, guns, motors, steam engines, telegraphy, railroads, electricity, automobiles, telephony, radio, the submarine, the airplane, the rocket, the television, the computer, and the atom bomb. But there was much more to this Great Transition than technology.

It took several hundred years for the mutual interaction among technology, economics, local politics, geopolitics, media, culture, agriculture, medicine, religion, and patterns of community development to interact and produce the kind of civilization that we think of as "modern": distributed authority (with many large-scale democracies), machine automation, large-scale organizations as commercial entities, relatively widespread education, a shift in attitude about wilderness (no longer a threat to humankind, it was a resource that needed protection), the birth of modern medicine, and ultimately the terrors of fascism and communism. The world in 1925 was a very different place from that of 1850 —and even more radically different from that of 1650. But someone looking back from 1925 could see, in effect, how the pattern of civilized change had progressed.

The period since World War II, for all its change, has been a time of relative stability. Alvin Toffler's *Future Shock* suggested that the pace of change was speeding up; but in truth it seemed to level off compared with political and cultural upheavals in the years between, say, 1850 and 1930. Space travel, the personal computer, and the cellular phone are civilization-changing technologies; but they cannot compare with the impact the development of the electric light, the broadcast signal, and the automobile had on the average person. Nor can the breakup of the Soviet Union, for all its significance, compare in impact with the rise of democracy two hundred years earlier.

Each of these great transformations has followed a similar pattern based largely on demographic and scientific-technical factors: how many of us there are, our age distribution, where and how densely we live, what we know, and what we know how to do. These are the human dimensions and capabilities that lead to the economic and political process of development and transformation. These fundamental transformations are often linked to huge ecological changes as well.

In the first "Great Transformation," for example, we saw the warming and stabilization of the Earth's climate accompanied by the birth of agriculture and village life. As greater numbers of people survived and lived longer and more securely, civilization began to develop. During the second Great Transformation, which may have been linked to the beginning and end of the Little Ice Age, we developed a new world view, new technologies, and an increasingly integrated world economy and polity characterized by larger and more complex organizations. Population took off after 1890 with the advance of agricultural science and a warming planet.

Looking ahead to the third Great Transformation we see many more people living far longer and global population growth decelerating to its peak in the mid-twenty-first century. The revolutionary advance of science and technology, especially in the life sciences, will create new, fundamental, and controversial possibilities for our species. The economic potential to lift billions out of poverty will be within our grasp. And a new kind of political order will result. Yet, as in the past, we are increasingly likely to find ourselves challenged by climate change—this time of a very abrupt nature. During the next twenty years, there may well be as many disruptive and overwhelming changes for civilization as there were in the first two Great Transformations.

Why would this happen? Because of the magnitude of changes in a variety of arenas:

- A dramatically increased life span, and its effect on human identity, capability, and community
- New patterns of human migration, which either fragment or unite humanity in new ways
- The return of a reliable "Long Boom" with global investment, expanded productivity, and the unprecedented opportunity for people around the world
- A dominant global military and economic superpower—the United States, with unchecked reach and a potential for political capriciousness—such as has not been seen since the Roman Empire
- A consortium of nations bound together not just by their intentions but by their common need for lawful collaboration
- A set of disorderly nations with the capacity to unleash terror, disease, and disruption on the rest of the world

- Technological capabilities that include new materials and machines, which could expand the power of computers by orders of magnitude, and permit people to reprogram reality
- Pollution-free and inexpensive energy sources that release humanity from its addiction to fossil fuels
- A restoration of nature under human steward-ship, alongside extreme and unavoidable danger from a new plague and global climate crises

Any of these in itself would be a significant change. But the greater significance comes from the ways in which all these changes will interact together.

Anticipating the Cumulative Effects

Imagine reading a book like this in, say, the year 1895. It includes details on the nascent science of electromagnetic transmission, and informs you that an Italian named Guglielmo Marconi has just transmitted a form of telegraphic code through the air. Someday, it says, we may do the same with sounds and pictures.

Then it lists other inevitable surprises in the works: electric lights, motion pictures, automobiles, and even the airplane. Less than fifteen years from now the Wright brothers will be launching their airplane-constructing business. Perhaps the book might even describe the inevitable results of new infrastructures under construction now: subways, sewage systems, and water supply systems, as well as the even newer infra-structures needed for electric power transmission, tele-phony, and the automobile. Perhaps it would even be prescient enough to recognize those technologies that will turn out to be insignificant (the Zeppelin) or short lived (the telegraph and the steam engine).

And the book would not stop with technology. It would contain the result of conversations with political leaders, military leaders, financial leaders like J. P. Morgan, and perhaps social pioneers like W.E.B. Du Bois and Susan B. Anthony. It would explore the grow-ing phenomenon of international trade, the opening of a canal across the Isthmus of Panama, and the explo-ration of the North and South polar regions. It would

describe advances being made in cure for malaria, and the changes in education and longevity for wealthy people in London, Paris, and New York. It would talk about the radical concept of world government, and foreshadow how all nations could come together in a global league—not in a reaction to war (for that wouldn't be foreseen yet), but perhaps because of world trade and the well-established peace.

There were, in fact, a number of such books. (One of the most famous was titled *Looking Backward,* by Edward Bellamy.) They were so popular that a publish-ing genre was named to describe them: Utopian fiction. They varied quite a bit in their prescience and approach. But even the best of them missed a great deal of the future.

It was difficult to foresee, for instance, how the auto-mobile would affect disease control by reducing the num-ber of animals in cities. No one could have identified the way in which modern bookkeeping techniques, the tele-phone, and the airplane would empower the rise of multi-national corporations; or the impact of industrialization on climate change, or the relationship between the com-puter and the science of genetics, or the end of European colonies and the surge in population growth in what was then called the "colonial" world. Few could have imagined the ways in which the peace of the Edwardian era helped create a cultural readiness for war, and the ways in which the brutal experiences of World War I ensured that the peace that followed would be incomplete.

In short, no matter how skilled a book of 1890 might have been at extrapolating and foreseeing individual inevitable surprise, it would have been almost impossi-ble to delineate the most important inevitable surprise of all: the second-order effects that naturally occur as these changes reinforce and affect each other in dynamic, cumulative, self-reinforcing ways. So they were not just individual developments, but fundamen-tal shifts that made the world of 1930 radically different from the world of 1900.

What, then, are the cumulative effects of the inevitable surprises that have been described in this book? What are the ways in which these "first-order effects" will influence and reinforce each other? What are the inevitable second-order effects?

First, the more extreme the first-order effects become, the more explosive the second-order effects will be. That is the reason, in fact, that the transition of the next few years will be as significant and world changing as the transition from 1650 to 1950.

Second, the next transition will take place over a much shorter time than the last one—perhaps over the course of thirty years instead of three hundred. If this is the case, by the end of the lifetime of most people reading this book, it will have happened.

Third, the stability we feel today is rapidly going to disappear. Utopian authors at work in 1890 were writing in the midst of the "Gilded Age": a time of great stability; when it seemed peace and prosperity could go on forever. Looking at the changes ahead of them, they might have written, "The world seems stable now, but it will be a surprise if that stability continues." And they would have been right. The next sixty years would bring two world wars, a massive depression, an end to European colonial empires, and many other changes.

The same is true of the next sixty years ahead of us today. The magnitude of change will be so large and disruptive that, if there should be economic and political stability in the world, it will be a great surprise. The potential for progress is enormous, but the potential for disruption is equally great.

The World of Maximum Surprise

Let's consider what it will be like to live in the year 2030 if nearly all the surprises in this book come to pass before then.

As you walk down a typical street in a city of 2030 you will see far more older people, at much more advanced ages, than you would ever have seen in 2003. You might see men and women of seventy doing things that formerly only people in their twenties and thirties did, such as holding hands in public, or pushing baby carriages containing their own children. Some of these people might have a kind of synthetic strength, youthfulness, or other physical attributes that would have looked distinctly peculiar in 2003, but which are now taken for granted. This is because of the more radical and interactive impacts of the new biomedicine. Will this lead to a large number of significantly modified human beings? If so, they would probably include some

people who have undergone genetic treatment as adults, and others, younger people, whose genetic code was modified while they were still embryos. They may be smarter, bigger, stronger, longer lived, and more disease resistant than their parents. Some of them may be bioenhanced warriors, fighting against terrorists and shock troops from the disorderly parts of the world.

With each passing year the aged will be getting younger, so that the centenarian of 2030 (including some readers of this book) will resemble a sixty-year-old of 2003. If you are one of these people, you will find a variety of genetic therapies available for you; diseases like Alzheimer's, diabetes, heart disease, arthritis, and many more will claim fewer and fewer victims.

Will only a wealthy few benefit? Or will the cost continue to fall, making the new technologies and remedies available to an ever-increasing number of those who need it? The answer may well vary in different parts of the world. If Europe can hold off the demographic tensions that threaten its unity, and preserve its social welfare ethic, then it may come to finance that ethic, in part, by recreating itself as a center of new therapies. Doctors and patients alike would be drawn there by not just the high quality of life, but by the secular nature of its society; religious opposition to many of the therapies could make Europe the center for the new medicine.

This is an especially plausible prospect if the migrants to Europe, from the Middle East, India, and Russia in particular, include people with the will and talent to work in this field. Certainly the number of aging people there would provide some impetus; by 2030 the number of centenarians will be growing fast especially in Europe, the U.S., and Japan. And they will be younger and more vigorous than the few who feebly stumbled over the century finish line in the past. All of this might help energize the European economy, particularly if Europe's proactive leaders, emboldened by their success with European union, recognize the potential benefit of investing in their population. They might see high-tech biotechnology as one arena where private enterprise (starting with the Swiss biotech industry of 2003) and public government (starting with the European Union bureaucracy) can work together to manage the necessary institutions effectively and still promote research and development. We might then see a high-tech bioentrepreneurial revolution in Europe.

At the same time, we might see whole European cities evolve into ghettoes for Muslim and African immigrants, virtually walled off from the rest of the continent, and festering with crime, disease, and random violence like the American ghettos of the 1970s and 1980s. If that happens, then the ship of European integration might founder on this rock of immigrant-related tension. Unquestionably, the faces on the street in any European city will be increasingly more multiracial. But will they be prosperous and content or impoverished and angry? The answer is not certain. We know that the typical city in the United States will be similarly diverse, but we also know that it will not have nearly the same levels of ethnic tension. We'll already be accustomed to seeing the American way of life as a culture with widespread Hispanic and Asian components, so much so that we won't always recognize them as such. Fajitas and lo mein will be long-standing American food staples in 2030, just as bagels and pasta were in 2003.

In the "disorderly world" the falling birthrates will lead to an ever higher proportion of elderly there as well. Foreign aid to developing countries will have shifted toward new problems, including the needs of a generation of AIDS orphans now entering their thirties and forties. Will there be any feasible way for countries that have endured thirty years or more of disorder to climb out of that hole? If not, one can imagine the future that many people fear coming to pass: islands of prosperity in a sea of poverty and despair. Gated communities in the rich world will hold back the tides of crime and misery, while more and more countries lose ground.

Or perhaps the gathering wave of prosperity that exists in the wealthier parts of the world will be enough to lift up all of humanity. If the current growth rates are sustained, then the world will be about one and a half times richer than it is today. The three big drivers of wealth—new productivity, new globalization, and new infrastructure—are all likely to increase, with varying rates of development. In the traditional dynamics of creative destruction we will transform old industries and create entirely new ones. The new older and more experienced workforce will be enabled, with ever more powerful technologies, to be increasingly more productive. If there is a political will (or a philanthropic way) to ensure that this wealth is distributed more broadly,

then we might see an ever-widening circle of prosperity. More and more poor countries could begin to develop a significant middle class, while the rich countries would make great progress in reducing poverty within their boundaries. It won't happen on its own, but we know that the necessary ingredients for such a future, including the political will, will exist.

Prosperity will depend, in part, on bioelectronics and bioindustrial processes that will spark a new computing and industrial revolution. Imagine building things the way that nature does. And of course, these new life-science-based technologies will contribute to making the earth greener and slowing the use of nonrenewable resources. If the new scientific revolution is as broad and deep as I believe it will be, then it will also include far more powerful computers, based on "quantum information sciences" (as we'll call it). This, too, will be a much more global enterprise—based in part in American research universities, but with outposts and researchers all over the world, especially in Russia, China, and India. Any accomplishments in this realm will accelerate accomplishments in all other fields—for instance, it would enable us to manage the complexity of intelligent highways, with computers that map and control the position of every vehicle in real time. Or it would enable biologists to model the unimaginably complex folding of protein molecules, leading to still faster advances in medicine. Ultimately, it might signal the arrival of artificial intelligence.

That would be enough to propel us into the "days of miracles and wonders," as Paul Simon put it. But science and technology could take us farther still. If a new synthesis emerges in physics, we will begin to see new technology that operates on new physical principles. This could include new ways of generating energy, new modes of propulsion and travel (including space travel), new methods of computing and storing information, new modes of communication, and new kinds of sensors. Perhaps the future of energy does not lie with any of today's technologies and fuels but with entirely new domains of science such as dark energy. Perhaps the future of aviation lies not with the aerodynamics of lift, but rather with the physics of antigravity. We may think of these as fantastic ideas now, but if any of them come to pass, it will dramatically accelerate the shift in all aspects of society, if only because each of these new technologies will require new infrastructure, new financing, new cultural adaptation, and new corporate and government sponsorship. If China, for example, becomes the center of research in the new physics, that could mean the first serious challenge to the American political hegemony of this new era.

Geopolitics may well be the hardest domain to envision for 2030. It is virtually certain that the United States will still be the single strongest nation on earth in both economic and military terms. But will it be a more peaceful or a more troubled world? Perhaps the Bush administration is right. What the world needs is "tough love." The U.S. thus becomes a reluctant but conscientious sheriff, shielding the orderly nations from destructive forces emanating from the chaotic and failed parts of the world. In such a future the U.S. would naturally become more adept in cultivating the support developing and imprimatur of the other nations, especially the great powers and major international institutions. As that happens the other nations, even some of those currently opposed, might come gradually to support the U.S. role as the peacekeeper and guarantor of the new order.

Such a benign, stable, and peaceful outcome relies on two key assumptions; that problems are actually addressable and the United States is competent in the execution of its aims. A wealthier world may not be sufficient to overcome the passions inflamed by a battle of theologies. We may by then be enduring the 25th year of a new Thirty Years' War, exacerbated by the spread of biotechnology that could arm new forms of terrorism. Indeed, though the U.S. military has had mostly a solid string of success since Vietnam, that is not predetermined to continue—especially because we are confronting new and uncomfortable terrain in the war on terror. Success is not guaranteed and a protracted and widening conflict is not implausible.

Even if this war between Christianity and Islam does not materialize, there are still plenty of hot spots to create trouble and many competing interests to create tensions. It is not hard to image a turbulent world of 2030 in which the U.S. is powerful but isolated. Now in its thirtieth year of "rogue superpowerdom," America could face skilled coalitions of denial (perhaps *still* led by French and German leaders, perhaps by other Europeans or non-Europeans) who have learned to use

their soft power and the international rule of law to block U.S. interests. In such a world there will often be hot spots needing attention. It is in these poor benighted countries that the U.S. will play out its conflicts with the other great nations. In this sense it will resemble the Cold War surrogate struggles between the Soviet Union and the United States in places like Africa, Southeast Asia, and Latin America. If the world of 2030 is dominated by chaos and conflict, then poverty and violence will feed on each other in a downward spiral of self-destruction.

Here lies the challenge, and the choice, of the world ahead. Will the world be more like China, in which a one-party state creates stability and prosperity that go hand in hand? Or like India, in which a disorderly democracy has produced a mixed record of economic progress? Or will other models for effective political economy evolve? We still don't quite know how to generate economic stability in a world of turbulence and inevitable surprises—but there is some reason to think we may be able to pull that rabbit out of the hat after all.

Preparing for the Future

The next logical question is the same that a reasonable reader of a book about the future might have wanted to ask those imaginary authors of 1890:

> As someone who cares about my business, my locale, my community, my country, or my family, what are the precautions I would want to have in place?

In other words, you can't predict the chaos and turbulence to come. But how can you best prepare? What foresight can you cultivate, so that when this level of instability comes, you, and the people you care about, are ready for it? How can we learn from the last Great Transition to be better prepared for this new one?

I have learned that several answers are available from years of helping organizations anticipate the future in scenario practice.

Build and maintain your sensory and intelligence systems. That doesn't just mean technological systems. It means the continued kinds of "strategic conversations" in which you and your cohorts and colleagues keep looking around to observe and interpret the interaction of forces that might affect you, your enterprises, and your communities.

This seems obvious, but it's surprising how many politicians, educators, and businesspeople I have met who do not make time for it. Over the years their ability to observe and interpret the world around them atrophies. In a singularity like the one approaching us, fine-grained awareness of the world outside your own organizational boundaries will be a paramount aid to survival.

Cultivate a sense of timing. When you see an event approaching, make a point of asking: How rapidly is it approaching? When could it occur? How far in the future?

Identify in advance the kinds of "early-warning indicators" that would signal that a change is rapidly upon you. For instance, if you are a foreign investor, what are the early signals of potential financial crises? You know they will occur in China and India—what do you look for there? If you are a technologist, what kind of funding will be evident in your arena first, before it attracts financing from elsewhere? If you are concerned about climate change, what represents the next big warning sign? And how do you distinguish it from run-of-the-mill climate variation?

Once you've identified these signals, keep an eye out for them and be prepared to act when you observe them. This is one place where my colleagues and I use short-term scenario exercises: "If we saw such a signal, what could it mean? And what would we do in response to it?" In 1997, when the financial crisis hit Southeast Asia, the U.S. Treasury had already undergone the kind of firewall-building exercise necessary in Mexico in 1994—which made it possible to move rapidly to contain the crisis, so that it did not ripple into China, Korea, and Japan.

Put in place mechanisms to engender creative destruction. The institutions, companies, agencies, political parties, and values of the past may turn out to be moribund and counterproductive in a new historical environment. Are you prepared to discard them? More importantly, have you practiced discarding them? What processes, practices, and organizations have you actually dismantled in the last year or two? If the answer is none, perhaps it's time to get some practice in *before* urgency strikes.

Creative destruction is not simply a matter of getting rid of old baggage. It means learning how to mitigate the costs. There is inevitably a fair amount of disruption to communities, the abandonment of secure livelihoods, and the severing of deep relationships. You cannot keep those old institutions for the sake of convenience; you need the creativity that comes from releasing them. But unless you can ease the pain of disruption, you will engender fierce resistance. Moreover, the pain of disruption tends to fall disproportionately on the "20% to 40% group": the hidden population of lower-level employees on whom the revival of the economy depends. Unless you can help them bear the consequences of disruption, you may cripple your ability to recover.

Note how many of the most successful businesspeople and politicians of the past twenty years have been successful at this, including the last two American presidents (both of whom arguably rode to success by largely discarding the previous identities of their political parties).

Try to avoid denial. When an "inevitable surprise" comes along that makes life difficult for you or your organization, do not pretend that it isn't happening. There are many examples where leaders exacerbated a problem by trying to deny its significance: AIDS in Africa and Russia, the telecommunications "last mile" problem, and the potential severity of global climate change.

Unfortunately, most standard corporate or government planning is a recipe for denial. The standard operating procedure is to talk about the various futures that might lie ahead, pick the one that seems most likely to happen, plot the course accordingly, and maybe build in a few exigencies. Having done this, the planners (being, after all, human beings) are naturally prone to discount any signals from the outside world that contradict the outcome they expected. The very fact that a future feels "likely" should make us skeptical of it. Chances are, we are drawn by our own limited worldview and predisposition to assume that what we expect to happen, will.

By contrast, when a future feels particularly wrong or discomfiting, and your first impulse is to say, "That would hurt us if it happened, but it won't happen," that's a signal to pay closer attention to it. Something about that future is trying to break through your mental blinders, and if you deny it or ignore it, you may well inadvertently help to bring it to pass. Indeed that kind of denial may have caused the NASA leadership to deny the potential for catastrophic failure despite contrary evidence on the *Columbia*.

As a resident of California, I'm seeing this take place now with my own state government. During the dot-com boom, tax revenues poured in, as both companies and individuals grew rich. The governor and the legislature piled on services and spending accordingly. They didn't plan for the day when the revenues would drop, and they must therefore now deal with a $45 billion budget shortfall.

Traditional commodity companies understand this temptation very well. They know that there will be fat years and lean years and the surplus from the growth periods allows you to survive the deficits of the down years.

Be aware of the competence of your judgment and the level of judgment that new situations require, and move deliberately and humbly into new situations that stretch your judgment. Every successful individual and organization has an integrated core of judgment—not just knowledge, but the ability to make wise decisions quickly in a particular field—that lies at the heart of success. When times are turbulent, the temptation to move outside that knowledge to take advantage of outside opportunities is great. Those are the risks that often get you into trouble.

My own education-by-fire in this principle came at Royal Dutch/Shell. In the mid-1980s Shell was flush with cash: $13 billion of it, a legacy of a decade of high oil prices. Along with a brilliant young Shell treasurer named David Welham, I proposed risking some of it in international currency arbitrage in what seemed a very low-risk way of using our short-term funds more efficiently. We could lend it to big banks like Citicorp at a favorable rate, and they could use it for currency arbitrage—for which they needed huge piles of cash. We would make a tenth of a point per day, and they'd make a half a point; on a few billion dollars this would provide an income of hundreds of millions of dollars at virtually no risk.

The decision went up the hierarchy to Bill Thompson, the managing director of Royal Dutch/Shell for finance at the time, who was David's and (indirectly) my boss. Bill vetoed the idea. "We're not a bank," he said. "We've got to manage our money appropriately, but our business is not making money with our money. We are, as management, incompetent to make the necessary judgments."

I was extremely disappointed. But I didn't realize the wisdom of that decision until a number of years later. At that point a failure of control had opened the door to strategies similar to those Bill had rejected. And a Shell currency trader working in Tokyo lost $900 million in one day. It was the biggest currency trading loss of any sort for any company in history. It happened because the controls and judgment were simply not in place as they would have been in an experienced bank.

Bill was right. I was wrong. Because we had figured out our oil strategy so well, I was supremely confident. I thought we could do anything. I'm not saying that I would have lost $900 million, but I am certain that I didn't know enough about playing the currency game to set up the necessary controls. And I've observed, all too many times since, that would-be innovators get their way too often, without someone as smart and wise as Bill Thompson to stop a foolish new idea.

Place a very, very high premium on learning. Most failures to adapt are, in effect, failures to learn enough in time about the changing circumstances. And there will be more to learn in the future. If advances in science and technology are any indication, work will be increasingly knowledge intensive, and the value of scientific knowledge in particular will be all the greater.

Unfortunately, most Western societies have approached education ideologically. There has not yet been a genuine consensus, among educators and budget-setting politicians, about how children and adults learn, and about how best to set up schools. Until such a consensus is reached in the most pragmatic, nonideo-logical way, we are unlikely to see a functional education system in most countries. Instead, we will have what we have now: various splinter groups arguing that their favored approach is best for schools, and no solid way to compare the results. (Standardized tests measure only a very small part of the capabilities that people need edu-cation to gain.) This is an extremely dysfunctional way to deal with the future.

Place a very high premium on environmental and eco-logical sustainability. This is not just a global political and environmental issue; it is a vehicle for high-quality integration and development. You almost have to run an organization that follows this path to recognize how valuable it is; it focuses attention on the "side effects" of your actions, in ways that are extremely useful.

Place a very high premium on financial infrastructure and support. Individuals need safety nets and insurance against crises. Organizations need to build in safe-guards and help individuals build the financial infra-structure they need. And society as a whole will need to watch out for the interests of the "20-40-percent" group, for whom no one else typically is.

The risks are greater than we think. In the future, people at all three levels will need safety nets in a way that hasn't been true before. And organizations will need to muster profits and use them wisely. Do you have the kind of portfolio of income and assets that will help you weather the storms to come? Do you have enough profits to fund your transition into the next stage of your evolution, whatever that turns out to be?

Cultivate connections. In the world of 2025 people will be inevitably in contact far more regularly and compre-hensively than they are today. Quantum computing, universal broadband, longer lives, globalization, and clean, green energy will reshape our world toward far greater interconnection. Are you prepared for this? Do you have the kinds of deep, candid connections that will help you ride through the next transition without hav-ing to ride alone?

Taking the Long View

Perhaps sailing is the best metaphor. One wave after another is going to hit your ship, and you have to be able to react immediately to them. But are you merely stum-bling from one wave—one crisis—to the next? Or are you the master of your fate, moving toward a point that is a long-term vision of your own?

The world will not make those decisions for you. The future will almost certainly be a prosperous world, with lots of new technology. But it will not have solved the problems of poverty and "haves and have-nots"; indeed, those problems may be more extreme than they have ever been before. It will have quantum computers and remarkable new forms of infrastructure, but it will also be struggling against outmoded infrastructure and a capital base that will not inhibit the old infrastructure giving way to the new. It will have broken the barriers of aging and genetic engineering, but it will also have ram-pant plagues, either naturally developed or spread through terrorism, that could be as bad as any in human history. It may fall to you and your organizations to help solve some of these problems, or others. Or you may simply seek to thrive and keep yourself and family afloat. But you will achieve neither easily unless you choose where you are going.

Consider the difference between a trading company and an investment company. A trading company counts itself successful if it just comes out ahead, day by day, in its accounts. An investment company knows that success depends on being able to reach a significant long-term goal: building cars, opening a market, or creating some kind of new infrastructure (or whatever it may be). Trading companies are often more comfortable to be part of the present moment. But they invariably get wiped out. The investment companies, just by virtue of pursuing a long-term goal, have been building the capabilities, protec-tions, and judgments they need to survive; while those who live by immediate circumstances, die by them as well.

The great risk of our time is being overtaken by inevitable surprises. When we don't have a sense of direction and purpose, we can easily be swept away by events. We have an example in recent history to consider: it's the first half of the twentieth century. Had leaders of the world been willing to think ahead more, they might have avoided two world wars, a depression, millions of deaths, and a half century of global disruption. Arguably, had that happened, we wouldn't be facing the kinds of challenges that daunt us today.

The second half of the twentieth century indicates that we may have learned that the cycle of progress and disruption is not predetermined. It is possible to break it. It is possible to see beyond immediate events, hold fast to long-term directions, and maintain the resources to manage the consequences of disruption. We can't stop disruptions from happening, but we can cope with them far better than we have in the past.

There is no recipe or playbook for doing this. There is only the ongoing knot of life to unravel. Perhaps the string that is the easiest to pull first is the string of inevitable surprises.

Note

1. Vernor Vinge, "Technological Singularity," presented at the VISION-21 Symposium sponsored by NASA Lewis Research Center and the Ohio Aerospace Institute, March 30–31, 1993. A version of this presentation is available at http://singularity.manilasites.com/stories/story Reader$35.

CHAPTER 2

Globalization

Douglas A. Hicks

University of Richmond

Few current topics are more contested than globalization—its definition, causes, and economic, political, social, and moral implications. Some critics maintain that globalization is a faddish term that encompasses too many ideas to be coherent. Yet it is hard to deny that some kinds of global interaction are taking place that are significantly reshaping life for many human beings. Debates swirl around how globalization can be most efficiently and equitably steered or constrained, if indeed it can be guided in some way. At whatever level (local, national, and international), leaders in various sectors face effects of globalization.

Globalization is better understood as a set of processes—sometimes competing; sometimes complementary—than as a unified process. It refers to economic, political, technological, social, cultural, and ethical developments. The term is most often employed in relation to developments after 1980, even though many scholars now assert that earlier periods of history also contained elements of globalization. In general, globalization refers to the incorporation of the global level into activities or frames of reference that would otherwise remain local, national, or regional in scope.

Economic Aspects

Although globalization can and does entail a variety of dimensions, the term commonly refers to economic links and processes. Economic globalization concerns the expansion of production, trade, consumption, savings, and investment to markets beyond national and regional ones. Although trade has always crossed national boundaries, from spice routes to the East, to trade in the Roman Empire, to international shipping between Europe, Africa, and the Americas, the level of international trade has skyrocketed since about 1980.

With strong encouragement from leaders in private enterprise, political leaders have pushed for the reduction in tariffs on the trade of goods and service across national lines. The Uruguay round of trade talks (1986–1994) of the General Agreement on Tariffs and Trade (GATT, established in 1947), created the World Trade Organization (WTO). The WTO, which began officially in 1995, is an international institution consented to by various partner countries. It has the power to enforce agreed-upon treaties and to mediate trading disagreements among member countries.

Source: From G. R. Goethals, G. J. Sorenson, and J. M. Burns (Eds.), *Encyclopedia of leadership* (pp. 570–577). Thousand Oaks, CA: Sage. © 2004 Sage Publications, Inc. Used by permission.

Critics maintain that the WTO governance is not democratic and privileges an ideology of the free market over social values. In this view, economic globalization that promotes free trade and growth of production comes at the expense of weaker economies and nations (who consent to membership out of a very limited set of options), the rights and protections of laborers, and environmental health.

The increased international flow of commodities is a visible form of globalization, but the rise in global financial markets dwarfs the markets in goods. With the technological developments discussed below, trillions of dollars change hands every day electronically. In unprecedented ways, global capital and currency markets have reshaped economic investment. This is not to say that investment across national lines is new; foreign investment as a share of total investment is not larger today than it was in the pre-World War I period. Concerned about speculation as well as seeking to finance a global infrastructure, some economists, activists, and policymakers have called for a tax (like the so-called Tobin tax) to be levied upon global financial transactions.

Globalization has not occurred as readily for human labor as it has for capital. On the labor front, political questions of national sovereignty confront globalizing economic trends. A number of nations have addressed the labor issue through legalized migrant- and guest-worker programs. Some permit immigration and offer citizenship to persons who can fill certain kinds of gaps in the national labor force. Yet, the majority of persons are not able readily to move their labor power across national lines, as they would be able to do in a fully globalized society.

Technological Changes

Late-twentieth-century technological innovations are a major component of globalization. A series of developments in the telecommunications and computer industries has made immediate, coordinated, and sustained communication possible among multiple geographic locations in the world. The cost of a one-minute phone call from New York to London has dropped precipitously, by about 99 percent, over the past seven decades (United Nations Development Programme 1999, 30). Cell phone technology promises to make communication to remote areas affordable; entire nations appear poised to skip a generation of wired technology and adopt wireless communication systems.

The Internet, developed as a way of communication within the military and university sectors, has made instant interaction and a common pool of information potentially available to persons around the world. Internet access and usage vary by country and socioeconomic status, but at its best, the Internet promises a cheap and reliable medium for global interaction. Critics call attention to the downfalls of this sort of interaction, including inequalities of access and influence, the over-commercialized use of the World Wide Web, and the lack of genuine, personal human-to-human communication.

The decline of prices of international air travel, in addition to contributing to the global trade of time-sensitive products, has increased international tourism. Persons who can afford this form of travel comprise a global tourist industry. Yet, the cost of a standard coach-class seat on a round-trip transatlantic flight exceeds the average annual per capita income of almost half of the world's nations.

An Emerging Global Infrastructure

A different kind of globalization, of a political nature, has taken place more slowly and less directly than the economic and technological dimensions. Market structures can readily transform themselves from a national to an international level, but a political system based on national sovereignty will, by definition, face structural issues in international contexts. The founding of the United Nations (UN) in 1945 offered the promise of a global community of nations working together to address the social ills and, at a minimum, to reduce the probability of conflict on a global scale. The UN charter did not usurp national sovereignty—indeed, it was built upon it. Although the Security Council, whose five permanent countries hold veto power, ensures that a set of dominant countries has undue influence, the UN structure is still more democratic and participatory than international financial institutions such as the World

Bank, International Monetary Fund, and World Trade Organization. The UN's efforts to forge global peacekeeping alliances and to avoid political-military conflict have had mixed results. The current Secretary General, Kofi Annan, of Ghana, has questioned the absolute right of national sovereignty when it comes to issues of the violation of human rights within national boundaries. The degree to which his leadership efforts will erode national sovereignty, however, remains to be seen.

The UN has had some success in its promotion of human rights. The UN Universal Declaration of Human Rights, adopted by the Security Council in 1948 and now ratified by at least 140 countries, set the stage for a series of human rights conventions and treaties, including international statements on civil and political rights; economic, social and cultural rights; and the rights of women, racial minority groups, and children. A group of nongovernmental human rights organizations, including Amnesty International and Human Rights Watch, endeavors to protect human rights around the world. Scholars now discuss the emergence of a global culture and structure of human rights.

Other multinational efforts have contributed to a global political and juridical order. The formation of an International Criminal Court, despite objections by the United States, is reshaping the understanding of justice across national boundaries. International treaties and protocols, relating to the environment, military weapons, fishing, and so on, contribute to a global order. Some of these international efforts have resulted not from a formal political structure, but through the leadership of persons in nongovernmental organizations that are committed to addressing a particular issue. The awarding of the Nobel Peace Prize to Jody Williams and the International Campaign to Ban Landmines is a recent example of such citizen leadership that seeks to create a global order.

The globalization of human rights and international treaties is distinct from economic understandings of globalization that focus on the growth of production and the expansion of trade and investment. Yet a set of economic institutions has played a prominent role in an emerging global infrastructure. The International Bank for Reconstruction and Development, or the World Bank, and the International Monetary Fund (IMF) have become highly influential international financial institutions (IFIs) in the emerging international order. These institutions were envisioned at the Bretton Woods Conference in 1944 (and organized the following year), under enlightened leadership of the economist John Maynard Keynes, who believed in the importance of building an improved economic system in the postwar period.

The World Bank is charged to provide development assistance through loans for development projects and the IMF is directed to provide emergency assistance to national governments for macroeconomic stability and structural adjustment loans to make national economies more market oriented. Even beyond these important roles, these IFIs wield significant power in the shaping of national economic development strategies, and their evaluations influence commercial banks in their own lending decisions. As mentioned in the discussion of economic globalization above, the World Trade Organization also has become increasingly significant as an IFI; its critics point out that its policies affect not only production and trade of goods and services, but also environmental, labor, and social policies.

One intentional leadership effort to shape a global economy has been the World Economic Forum (WEF), an independent organization that brings together elite financial, political, and social leaders to address issues related to globalization that arise because of the discontinuities, gaps, and flaws in the global order. This organization does not claim to be representative or democratic in its processes; rather, it provides a forum for discussion among persons who are powerful in their own sphere but might otherwise not communicate with one another. Some observers are critical (or suspicious) of the very effort of economic and political elites to get together, since they might create a global infrastructure that favors persons already in power and give corporations additional public influence. In intentional opposition to the WEF's elite approach, the Forum Social Mundial, or World Social Forum (WSF), has organized open international meetings in Porto Alegre, Brazil, for scholars, activists, and policymakers who see the economic dimensions of globalization as a process of exclusion of poor and marginalized persons.

Cultures and Globalization

Some commentators understand cultural difference to be a significant barrier to any form of global community.

Samuel Huntington's thesis about a clash of civilizations has received significant attention. Huntington asserts that a set of civilizations—no longer national boundaries or Cold War alliances—has created and will maintain the fault lines of the global order. These so-called civilizations—the West, Islam, Confucianism, and so on—are not easily reconciled, integrated, or transcended via any global political or economic process. A particularly important tension, Huntington maintains, is between the West and Islam. Respondents have questioned his framework, particularly the simple categorizations of civilizations, the assumption that cultural difference necessitates (often violent) conflicts, and the thinly veiled preference for "Western" civilization.

A second significant discussion of culture and globalization centers around Benjamin Barber's thesis that two forces—"McWorld" and "Jihad"—are undermining democracy around the world. McWorld, as Barber describes it, is the process of creating a global "monoculture" based upon consumer values and practices. McWorldization is driven by U.S. commercialism, including the tremendous global influence of multinational corporations like Coca-Cola and Nike, the Hollywood film industry, and media-entertainment conglomerates like Disney and AOL-Time Warner. McWorld threatens the richness and diversity of less powerful cultures around the world. Barber defines Jihad as those movements away from multicultural, multiethnic democracies toward ethnic or religious enclaves of self-determination. Such efforts are aided by the global communications and media technologies of McWorld. Barber thus asserts that globalization, paradoxically, is aiding both Western economic dominance and balkanizing movements around the world, both to the detriment of democratic participation.

Global Citizenship?

In addition to tangible transformations on economic, technological, political, and cultural fronts, globalization entails a less visible transition in persons' frames of reference, or ways of thinking, concerning identity and affiliation, time, and geography. The concept of *neighbors* changes as technology and communication make people who are geographically far away become, in real senses, proximate. For many persons, an international or even truly global perspective is added to other frameworks such as family, neighborhood, city, and nation. As leaders seek to address problems—even apparently very local ones—it is important to understand the ways in which the relevant issues have global dimensions. The popular activist slogan, "Think Globally, Act Locally," captures only some of the complexities of thinking and acting at various levels (see Robertson 1992).

Since the 1970s, moral and political philosophers have renewed an interest in global justice and the rights and responsibilities of a global community. The philosopher John Rawls adapted his famous work *A Theory of Justice* (1971) to identify certain limited transnational duties that are contained in a "law of peoples" (Rawls 1999). Marxist and post-colonial scholars have emphasized the need to understand struggles in various parts of the world as part of a common fight against forces of oppression and for human dignity. Hardt and Negri's book, *Empire* (2000), portrays globalization as a complex movement that creates a hegemonic global order but that also provides opportunities for mass resistance to it. Other scholars, including Martha Nussbaum (1996), Peter Singer (2002), and Hans Küng (1998), have offered "cosmopolitan" visions of moral obligation and global community. In cosmopolitanism, national citizenship has very little relevance to the rights and duties that humans share with and toward one another. Some analysts have retorted that global citizenship is an interesting concept, and perhaps a worthy ideal, but it is only the "global class"—those who can afford to debate such ephemeral topics—who have the privilege to dream of such a condition.

Protesters of Globalization

Some activists, scholars, and citizens oppose various dimensions of globalization. The most highly visible protests reject current economic processes and, specifically, those international financial institutions seen to be pushing for it—the IMF, the World Bank, and the WTO. High-profile demonstrations have taken place since 1999, outside meetings of IFIs in Seattle, Prague, Quebec City, and Washington, DC. Other protests have disrupted meetings of leaders of the most powerful economies, such as the G-8, or Group of Eight, meetings in Genoa, Italy, in 2001.

These protests, like globalization itself, are multivocal events, bringing together citizens concerned about labor practices, poverty, and the environment. The vast majority of efforts to place social concerns on the public agenda have been nonviolent. At almost every protest, however, a few protesters gain the attention of the media by using violence. Leadership within the "antiglobalization" movement struggles to unite disparate voices concerned about developments that accompany globalization in its current forms. Organizations that are pro-labor, pro-environment, and advocates of impoverished people face the challenge of working together when their short-term interests might not be aligned completely. Although it is difficult to assess directly the success of such efforts, all three of the IFIs have recently (if gradually and to varying degrees) shifted their discourse to incorporate concern for poor persons, social policies, and environmental protection.

Paradoxically, the successful organizing efforts against economic globalization tend to be highly global in terms of technology and communication. That is, leaders in the anti-globalization movement employ the Internet and international networking as principal means for organizing. While some groups of genuine anti-globalizers prefer communal separatism, or autonomy, the majority of organizations embracing the term *anti-globalization* are actually protesting specific forms of globalization (viz., models that are based upon, or perpetuate, existing disparities of economic wealth and political power).

It is important to note an additional aspect of globalization in the current international arena. Terrorist networks such as al-Qaeda purport to be fighting the hegemonic political and economic power of the United States (and its allies). Its leaders claim to resist a global economic system that imposes Western values upon all persons and cultures in the world. The terrorist attack of 11 September 2001, against the World Trade Center in New York City and the Pentagon, targeted the global economy. Yet, even as al-Queda fights the forces of globalization, it is itself a profoundly globalized institution, dependent upon the electronic media for its internal communication and dissemination of its message. Thus, even the most radical forms of protest against globalization are also affected by the realities of the phenomenon.

Inequality and Inclusion

One of the central issues in globalization debates is the relation of globalization to inequality. Economists debate the question of whether and by how much the process of globalization—specifically, in this case, the expansion of international trade and capital movement—has increased inequality. Although there is no broad consensus, scholars generally agree that technological changes have had at least as significant an impact on inequality as trade. Many economists agree that the level of global inequality increased during the 1970s and 1980s, but the degree of that rise turns on a number of technical factors, including currency conversion rates. There is no consensus about the more recent period—or, importantly, the causal relationship(s) between globalization and equality or inequality.

SELECTION FROM THE MARRAKESH AGREEMENT ESTABLISHING THE WORLD TRADE ORGANIZATION, 1994

The *Parties* to this Agreement,

Recognizing that their relations in the field of trade and economic endeavour should be conducted with a view to raising standards of living, ensuring full employment and a large and steadily growing volume of real income and effective demand, and expanding the production of and trade in goods and services, while allowing for the optimal use of the world's resources in accordance with the objective of sustainable development, seeking both to protect and preserve the environment and to enhance the means for doing so in a manner consistent with their respective needs and concerns at different levels of economic development,

Recognizing further that there is need for positive efforts designed to ensure that developing countries, and especially the least developed among them, secure a share in the growth in international trade commensurate with the needs of their economic development,

Being desirous of contributing to these objectives by entering into reciprocal and mutually advantageous arrangements directed to the substantial reduction of tariffs and other barriers to trade and to the elimination of discriminatory treatment in international trade relations,

Resolved, therefore, to develop an integrated, more viable and durable multilateral trading system encompassing the General Agreement on Tariffs and Trade, the results of past trade liberalization efforts, and all of the results of the Uruguay Round of Multilateral Trade Negotiations,

Determined to preserve the basic principles and to further the objectives underlying this multilateral trading system,

Agree as follows: [The sixteen articles of agreement follow.]

Source: World Trade Organization. Retrieved October 15, 2003, from http://www.wto.org/english/docs_e/legal_e/04-wto.doc

At least one additional relationship is frequently overlooked in these discussions. Even if global inequality did not increase in the past two or three decades, communications and media innovations have broadened the "frame of reference" beyond national borders to see global inequality as a more relevant and pressing issue. Currently, the level of income inequality in the world stands at least as high as inequality in the most unequal nations. Although in earlier eras this fact may not have been acknowledged, today's increasingly interconnected citizens are more likely to take note of inequality, and its implications, at the global level (Hicks 2001).

One key question of globalization and inequality concerns who the agents of globalization are. Do common local citizens in the United States, Australia, Venezuela, or India have the ability to influence, even in a small way, the globalizing world in which they increasingly live? The vastness of a global process makes any individual agency seem remote at best, and this is a fact unlikely to increase a person's leadership initiative. To the extent that globalization is disproportionately shaped by political and economic elites, it can neglect (at best) or diminish the agency of local citizens.

Movements on behalf of labor, the poor, and the environment share a concern about the loss of agency by non-elites in the globalization process. Scholars and advocates now speak about *glocalization*, a term that once referred to a kind of marketing (Robertson 1992, 173–174) but now also denotes a process whereby actors at the local level are able to shape their own experience of globalization. "Glocal" leadership, in other words, helps individuals and groups to influence their context, given the wider situational realities of globalization.

Leadership for, Against, and Amid Globalization

Few leaders in political or economic sectors claim to be pursuing (or, for that matter, resisting) globalization intentionally as one of their direct ends. (Exceptions are individuals and organizations such as the WEF and the WSF.) Rather, globalization is a systemic outcome of various actors who are seeking their more limited ends to benefit themselves, their institution, or their constituency. The vast majority of leaders confront global and globalizing realities as contextual factors that they must negotiate in their work: Business leaders adopt an international horizon on their would-be customers, competitors, investors, and potential labor force; political leaders carve out their place in the international order as a piecemeal global infrastructure develops;

and leaders of civil society expand their mission to new countries and contexts.

Even as leaders focus on the needs of their followers and constituents, intentional efforts are needed, however, to develop globalization, as possible, in directions that are effective and ethical. It is clear that the interactions between and among the peoples of all parts of the world will increase in the decades ahead, but it is not clear what the quality of those relationships will be. It remains to be seen whether the leadership processes associated with globalization will be top-down and exclusive or, rather, will include the voice and contribution of many persons and organizations around the world. Determining the meanings of globalization is more than an academic debate about definitions; it requires multifaceted leadership efforts on financial, political, social, and cultural fronts to shape a world in which all persons have the opportunity to be agents of their own lives.

Further Reading

Barber, B. R. (1995). *Jihad vs. McWorld: How globalism and tribalism are reshaping the world.* New York: Ballantine.

Berger, P. (1997). Four faces of global culture. *The National Interest, 49,* 23–29.

Finn, D. (1996). *Just trading: On the ethics and economics of international trade.* Nashville, TN: Abingdon Press.

Friedman, T. L. (1999). *The Lexus and the olive tree: Understanding globalization.* New York: Anchor Books/ Random House.

Gilpin, R., & Gilpin, J. M. (2001). *Global political economy.* Princeton, NJ: Princeton University Press.

Hardt, M., & Negri, A. (2000). *Empire.* Cambridge, MA: Harvard University Press.

Hicks, D. A. (2001). Inequality, globalization, and leadership: "Keeping up with the Joneses" across national boundaries. *Annual of the Society of Christian Ethics, 21,* 63–80.

Huntington, S. (1996). *The clash of civilizations and the remaking of world order.* New York: Simon & Schuster.

Küng, H. (1998). *A global ethic for global politics and economics.* New York: Oxford University Press.

Micklethwait, J., & Wooldridge, A. (2000). *A future perfect: The essentials of globalization.* New York: Crown Books.

Nussbaum, M., and respondents. (1996). *For love of country: Debating the limits of patriotism.* J. Cohen (Ed.). Boston: Beacon Press.

Rawls, J. (1971). *A theory of justice.* Cambridge, MA: Harvard University Press.

Rawls, J. (1999). *The law of peoples, with "The idea of public reason revisited."* Cambridge, MA: Harvard University Press.

Robertson, R. (1992). *Globalization: Social theory and global culture.* London: Sage.

Rodrik, D. (1999). *The new global economy and developing countries: Making openness work.* Washington, DC: Overseas Development Council/ Johns Hopkins University Press.

Sassen, S. (1998). *Globalization and its discontents: Essays on the new mobility of people and money.* New York: The New Press.

Singer, P. (2002). *One world: The ethics of globalization.* The Terry Lectures. New Haven, CT: Yale University Press.

Stiglitz, J. E. (2002). *Globalization and its discontents.* New York: W. W. Norton and Co.

Streeten, P. (2001). *Globalisation: Threat or opportunity?* Copenhagen, Denmark: Copenhagen Business School Press.

The World Bank. (2002). *Globalization, growth, and poverty: Building an inclusive world economy. A World Bank Policy Research Report.* Washington, DC: World Bank and Oxford University Press.

Yergin, D., & Stanislaw, J. (1998). *The commanding heights: The battle for the world economy.* New York: Touchstone/Simon and Schuster.

CHAPTER 3

Creating the Environmentally Aware Organization

Gregory G. Dess
University of Texas at Dallas

G. T. Lumpkin
Texas Tech University

Alan B. Eisner
Pace University

So how do managers become environmentally aware?[1] We will now address three important processes—scanning, monitoring, and gathering competitive intelligence—used to develop forecasts. Exhibit 3.1 illustrates relationships among these important activities. We also discuss the importance of scenario planning in anticipating major future changes in the external environment and the role of SWOT analysis.[2]

The Role of Scanning, Monitoring, Competitive Intelligence, and Forecasting

Environmental scanning. **Environmental scanning** involves surveillance of a firm's external environment to predict environmental changes and detect changes already underway.[3] Successful environmental scanning alerts the organization to critical trends and events

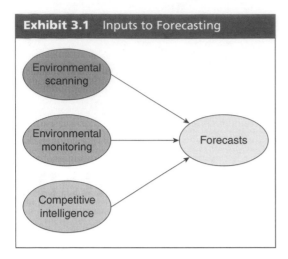

Exhibit 3.1   Inputs to Forecasting

• *Market.* Despite recent improvements, there's still a gap between product development cycles in the United States and Europe compared to Japan. This gap may be widening as Japanese companies continue to make improvements.
• *Shifting Roles and Responsibilities.* Design responsibility, purchasing, and even project management and systems engineering are shifting from original equipment manufacturers to integrators/suppliers.

Consider how disadvantaged you would be as an executive in the global automobile industry if you were unaware of such trends.

before the changes have developed a discernible pattern and before competitors recognize them.[4] Otherwise, the firm may be forced into a reactive mode.[5]

Sir John Browne, former chief executive officer of petroleum company BP Amoco, described the kind of environmental changes his company was experiencing.

The next element of the change we've experienced is the growth in demand, and the changing nature of that demand. The world uses eight million more barrels of oil and 30 billion more cubic feet of natural gas every day than it did in the spring of 1990. The growth of natural gas in particular has been and continues to be spectacular, and I believe that change can legitimately be seen as part of a wider, longer-term shift to lighter, cleaner, less carbon-intensive fuels.[6]

Consider how difficult it would be for BP Amoco to develop strategies and allocate resources if it did not scan the external environment for such emerging changes in demand.

At times, your company may benefit from studies conducted by outside experts in a particular industry. A. T. Kearney, a large international consulting company, identified several key issues in the automobile industry, including[7]

• *Globalization.* This is not a new trend but it has intensified, with enormous opportunities opening up in Asia, central and eastern Europe, and Latin America.

Environmental Monitoring. **Environmental monitoring** tracks the evolution of environmental trends, sequences of events, or streams of activities. They may be trends that the firm came across by accident or ones that were brought to its attention from outside the organization. Consider the automobile industry. While environmental scanning may make you aware of the trends, they require close monitoring, which involves closer ongoing scrutiny. For example, you should closely monitor sales in Asia, central and eastern Europe, and Latin America. You should observe how fast Japanese companies and other competitors bring products to market compared with your firm. You should also study trends with your own suppliers/integrators in purchasing, project management, and systems engineering. Monitoring enables firms to evaluate how dramatically environmental trends are changing the competitive landscape.

One of the authors of this text has conducted on-site interviews with executives from several industries to identify indicators that firms monitor as inputs to their strategy process. Examples of such indicators included:

• *A Motel 6 executive.* The number of rooms in the budget segment of the industry in the United States and the difference between the average daily room rate and the consumer price index (CPI).
• *A Pier 1 Imports executive.* Net disposable income (NDI), consumer confidence index, and housing starts.

- *A Johnson & Johnson medical products executive.* Percentage of gross domestic product (GDP) spent on health care, number of active hospital beds, and the size and power of purchasing agents (indicates the concentration of buyers).

Such indices are critical for managers in determining a firm's strategic direction and resource allocation.

Competitive Intelligence **Competitive intelligence** (CI) helps firms define and understand their industry and identify rivals' strengths and weaknesses.[8] This includes the intelligence gathering associated with collecting data on competitors and interpreting such data. Done properly, competitive intelligence helps a company avoid surprises by anticipating competitors' moves and decreasing response time.[9]

Examples of competitive analysis are evident in daily newspapers and periodicals such as *The Wall Street Journal, Business Week,* and *Fortune.* For example, banks continually track home loan, auto loan, and certificate of deposit (CD) interest rates charged by peers in a given geographic region. Major airlines change hundreds of fares daily in response to competitors' tactics. Car manufacturers are keenly aware of announced cuts or increases in rivals' production volume, sales, and sales incentives (e.g., rebates and low interest rates on financing). They use this information to plan their own marketing, pricing, and production strategies. Exhibit 3.2 provides some insights on what CI is (and what it isn't).

The Internet has dramatically accelerated the speed at which firms can find competitive intelligence. Leonard Fuld, founder of the Cambridge, Massachusetts, training and consulting firm Fuld & Co., specializes in competitive intelligence.[10] His firm often profiles top company and business group managers and considers these issues: What is their background? What is their style? Are they marketers? Are they cost cutters? Fuld has found that the more articles he collects and the more biographies he downloads, the better he can develop profiles.

Ethical Guidelines on Competitive Intelligence: United Technologies

United Technologies (UT) is a $28 billion global conglomerate composed of world-leading businesses with rich histories of technological pioneering, such as Otis Elevator, Carrier Air Conditioning, and Sikorsky (helicopters). It was founded in 1853 and has an impressive history of technological accomplishments. UT built the first working helicopter, developed the first commercially available hydrogen cells, and designed complete life support systems for space shuttles. UT believes strongly in a robust code of ethics. In the last decade, they have clearly articulated their principles governing business conduct. These include an antitrust guide, an ethics guide when contracting with the U.S. government and foreign governments, a policy on accepting gifts from suppliers, and guidelines for proper usage of e-mail. One such document is the Code of Ethics Guide on Competitive Intelligence. This encourages managers and workers to ask themselves these five questions whenever they have ethical concerns.

1. Have I done anything that coerced somebody to share this information? Have I, for example, threatened a supplier by indicating that future business opportunities will be influenced by the receipt of information with respect to a competitor?

2. Am I in a place where I should not be? If, for example, I am a field representative with privileges to move around in a customer's facility, have I gone outside the areas permitted? Have I misled anybody in order to gain access?

3. Is the contemplated technique for gathering information evasive, such as sifting through trash or setting up an electronic "snooping" device directed at a competitor's facility from across the street?

4. Have I misled somebody in a way that the person believed sharing information with me was required or would be protected by a confidentiality agreement? Have I, for example, called and misrepresented myself as a government official who was seeking some information for some official purpose?

5. Have I done something to evade or circumvent a system intended to secure or protect information? (Sources: Nelson, B. 2003. The thinker. *Forbes,* March 3: 62–64, and The Fuld war room—Survival kit 010. Code of Ethics, printed 2/26/01)

Exhibit 3.2 What Competitive Intelligence Is and Is Not	
Competitive Intelligence Is . . .	*Competitive Intelligence Is Not . . .*
1	**Information** that has been analyzed to the point where you can make a decision	**Spying.** Spying implies illegal or unethical activities. It is a rare activity, since most corporations do not want to find themselves in court or to upset shareholders.
2	A **tool** to alert management to early recognition of both threats and opportunities.	A **crystal ball**. CI gives corporations good approximations of short- and long-term reality. It does not predict the future.
3	A **means to deliver reasonable assessments**. CI offers approximations of the market and competition. It is not a peek at a rival's financial books. Reasonable assessments are what modern entrepreneurs need and want on a regular basis.	**Database search.** Databases offer just that—data. They do not massage or analyze the data in any way. They certainly don't replace human beings who make decisions by examining the data and applying their common sense, experience, and intuition.
4	A **way of life**, a process. If a company uses CI the way it should be used, it becomes everyone's job, not just the strategic planning or marketing staff's. It is a process by which critical information is available to those who need it.	A **job** for one smart person. A CEO may appoint one person as the CI ringmaster, but one person cannot do it all. At best! the ringmaster can keep management informed and ensure that others become trained to apply this tool with their business units.

Sources: Imperato, G. 1998. Competitive intelligence—Get smart! *Fast Company,* April: 26-29; and Fuld, F. M. What competitive intelligence is and is not! www.fuld.com/whatCI.html.

One of Fuld & Co.'s clients needed to know if a rival was going to start competing more aggressively on costs. Fuld's analysts tracked down articles from the Internet and a local newspaper profile of the rival firm's CEO. The profile said the CEO had taken a bus to a nearby town to visit one of the firm's plants. Fuld claimed, "Those few words were a small but important sign to me that this company was going to be incredibly cost-conscious." Another client retained Fuld to determine the size, strength, and technical capabilities of a privately held company. Initially, it was difficult to get detailed information. Then one analyst used Deja News (www.dejanews.com), now part of Google, to tap into some online discussion groups. The analyst's research determined that the company had posted 14 job openings on one Usenet group. That posting was a road map to the competitor's development strategy.

At times, a firm's aggressive efforts to gather competitive intelligence may lead to unethical or illegal behaviors.[11] As discussed earlier, United Technologies has set clear guidelines to help prevent unethical behavior.

A word of caution: Executives must be careful to avoid spending so much time and effort tracking the actions of traditional competitors that they ignore new competitors. Further, broad environmental changes and events may have a dramatic impact on a firm's viability. Peter Drucker, often considered the father of modern management, wrote:

Increasingly, a winning strategy will require information about events and conditions outside the institution: noncustomers, technologies other than those currently used by the company and its present competitors, markets not currently served, and so on.[12]

Consider the fall of the once-mighty *Encyclopaedia Britannica.*[13] Its demise was not caused by a traditional competitor in the encyclopedia industry. It was caused by new technology. CD-ROMs came out of nowhere and devastated the printed encyclopedia industry. Why? A full set of the *Encyclopaedia Britannica* sells for about $2,000, but an encyclopedia on CD-ROM, such as Microsoft *Encarta,* sells for about $50. To make matters worse, many people receive *Encarta* free with their personal computers.

Environmental Forecasting. Environmental scanning, monitoring, and competitive intelligence are important inputs for analyzing the external environment. However, they are of little use unless they provide raw material that is reliable enough to help managers make accurate forecasts. **Environmental forecasting** involves the development of plausible projections about the direction, scope, speed, and intensity of environmental change.[14] Its purpose is to predict change. It asks: How long will it take a new technology to reach the marketplace? Will the present social concern about an issue result in new legislation? Are current lifestyle trends likely to continue?

Some forecasting issues are much more specific to a particular firm and the industry in which it competes. Consider how important it is for Motel 6 to predict future indicators, such as the number of rooms, in the budget segment of the industry. If its predictions are low, it will build too many units, creating a surplus of room capacity that would drive down room rates. Similarly, if Pier 1 Imports is overly optimistic in its forecast of future net disposable income and U.S. housing starts, it will order too much inventory and later be forced to discount merchandise drastically.

A danger of forecasting is that managers may view uncertainty as black and white and ignore important gray areas. Either they assume that the world is certain and open to precise predictions, or they assume it is uncertain and completely unpredictable.[15] The problem is that underestimating uncertainty can lead to strategies that neither defend against threats nor take advantage of opportunities. In 1977 one of the colossal underestimations in business history occurred when Kenneth H. Olsen, then president of Digital Equipment Corp., announced, "There is no reason for individuals to have a computer in their home." The explosion in the personal computer market was not easy to detect in 1977, but it was clearly within the range of possibilities that industry experts were discussing at the time. And, historically, there have been underestimates of the growth potential of new telecommunication services. The electric telegraph was derided by Ralph Waldo Emerson, and the telephone had its skeptics. More recently, an "infamous" McKinsey study in the early 1980s predicted that there would be fewer than 1 million cellular users in the United States by the year 2000. Actually, there were nearly 100 million.[16] As humorously noted by Jane Bryant Quinn, a business writer: "The rule on staying alive as a forecaster is to give 'em a number or give 'em a date, but never give 'em both at once."[17]

At the other extreme, if managers assume the world is unpredictable, they may abandon the analytical rigor of their traditional planning process and base strategic decisions on gut instinct. Such a "just do it" approach may cause executives to place misinformed bets on emerging products or markets that result in record write-offs. Entrepreneurs and venture capitalists who took the plunge and invested in questionable Internet ventures in the late 1990s provide many examples.

A more in-depth approach to forecasting involves scenario analysis. **Scenario analysis** draws on a range of disciplines and interests, among them economics, psychology, sociology, and demographics. It usually begins with a discussion of participants' thoughts on ways in which societal trends, economics, politics, and technology may affect the issue under discussion.[18] For example, consider Lego. The popular Danish toy manufacturer has a strong position in the construction toys market. But what would happen if this broadly denned market should change dramatically? After all, Lego is competing not only with producers of similar products but also on a much broader canvas for a share of children's playtime. In this market, Lego has a host of competitors, many of them computer based; still others have not yet been invented. Lego may end up with an increasing share of a narrow, shrinking market (much like IBM in the declining days of the mainframe computer). To avoid such a fate, managers must consider their future in a wider context than their narrow, traditional markets. They need to lay down guidelines for at least 10 years in the future to anticipate rapid change. An example of scenario planning at Shell Oil Company follows.

Scenario Planning at Shell Oil Company

Preparing to cope with uncertainty is one of the biggest strategic challenges faced by most businesses. There are few tools for coping with strategic uncertainty, especially over medium- to long-term horizons. One technique that has proved its usefulness is scenario planning.

Scenario planning is different from other tools for strategic planning such as trend analysis or high and low forecasts. The origins of scenario planning lie with the military, which used it to cope effectively with multiple challenges and limited resources.

In the 1960s and 1970s, Shell combined analytical tools with information to create scenarios of possible outcomes. The result of the 1973 oil embargo was a sharp increase in crude oil prices, short supplies of gasoline for consumers, and a depressed world economy. However, Shell's strategic planning, including the use of scenarios, had strongly suggested that a more unstable environment was coming, with a shift of power from oil companies to oil producers. As a result of the precautionary actions it took, Shell was in a better position than most oil companies when the 1973 embargo occurred. Shell also uses scenario planning to plan major new oil field investments because elements of risk can be identified and explored over a considerable period of time.

The Shell process of scenario planning involves the following stages:

1. Interviews with people both inside and outside the business, using an open-ended questioning technique to encourage full and frank answers.

2. Analysis of interviews by issue in order to build a "natural agenda" for further processing.

3. Synthesis of each agenda to draw out underlying areas of uncertainty/dispute and possible interrelationships among issues.

4. A small number of workshops to explore key issues to improve understanding and identify gaps for further research. These generate a wide range of strategy options.

5. A workshop to identify and build a small number of scenarios that may occur in the next 10 to 15 years or even later.

6. A testing of strategy options against the scenarios in order to assess robustness (i.e., whether or not a given strategy is effective under more than one scenario).

Other practitioners of scenario planning include Levi Strauss, which uses scenario planning to consider potential impacts of everything from cotton deregulation to the total disappearance of cotton from this planet. Also, a German insurance company anticipated the fall of the Berlin wall and made plans to expand in central Europe. And in 1990 when Nelson Mandela was released from a South African prison, he met with a panel that helped him create scenarios to chart out the country's future. Scenario planning helps by considering not just trends or forecasts but also how they could be upset by events and the outcomes that may result.

(Sources: Martin, R. 2002. The oracles of oil. *Business 2.0,* January: 35-39; www.touchstonerenard.co.uk/ Expertise/Strategy/Scenario_Planning/scenario_planning .htm; and Epstein, J. 1998. Scenario planning: An introduction. *The Futurist,* September: 50-52).

SWOT Analysis

To understand the business environment of a particular firm, you need to analyze both the general environment and the firm's industry and competitive environment. Generally, firms compete with other firms in the same industry. An industry is composed of a set of firms that produce similar products or services, sell to similar customers, and use similar methods of production. Gathering industry information and understanding competitive dynamics among the different companies in your industry is key to successful strategic management.

One of the most basic techniques for analyzing firm and industry conditions is **SWOT analysis.** SWOT stands for strengths, weaknesses, opportunities, and threats. SWOT analysis provides a framework for analyzing these four elements of a company's internal and external environment. It provides "raw material"—a basic listing of conditions both inside and surrounding your company.

The Strengths and Weaknesses portion of SWOT refers to the internal conditions of the firm—where your firm excels (strengths) and where it may be lacking relative to competitors (weaknesses). Opportunities and Threats are environmental conditions external to the firm. These could be factors either in the general environment or in the competitive environment. In the general environment, one might experience developments that are beneficial for most companies such as improving economic conditions, that cause lower borrowing costs or trends that benefit some companies and harm others. An example is the heightened concern with fitness, which is a threat to some companies (e.g., tobacco) and an opportunity to others (e.g., health clubs). Opportunities and threats are also present in the competitive environment among firms competing for the same customers.

The general idea of SWOT analysis is that a firm's strategy must:

- build on its strengths,
- try to remedy the weaknesses or work around them,
- take advantage of the opportunities presented by the environment, and,
- protect the firm from the threats.

Despite its apparent simplicity, the SWOT approach has been immensely popular for a number of reasons. First, it forces managers to consider both internal and external factors simultaneously. Second, its emphasis on identifying opportunities and threats makes firms act proactively rather than reactively. Third, it raises awareness about the role of strategy in creating a match between the environmental conditions and the firm's internal strengths and weaknesses. Finally, its conceptual simplicity is achieved without sacrificing analytical rigor.

We discuss the analysis of the external environment in the following sections of this chapter.

The General Environment

The **general environment** is composed of factors that can have dramatic effects on firm strategy.[19] Typically, a firm has little ability to predict trends and events in the general environment and even less ability to control them. When listening to CNBC, for example, you can hear many experts espouse totally different perspectives on what action the Federal Reserve Board may take on short-term interest rates—an action that can have huge effects on the valuation of entire economic sectors. Also, it's difficult to predict future political events such as the ongoing Middle East peace negotiations and tensions on the Korean peninsula. In addition, who would have guessed the Internet's impact on national and global economies in the past decade or two? Such dramatic innovations in information technology (e.g., the Internet) have helped keep inflation in check by lowering the cost of doing business in the United States at the beginning of the 21st century.

We divide the general environment into six segments: demographic, sociocultural, political/legal, technological, economic, and global. First, we discuss each segment and provide a summary of the segment and examples of how events and trends can impact industries. Second, we address relationships among the general environment segments. Third, we consider how trends and events can vary across industries. Exhibit 3.3 provides examples of key trends and events in each of the six segments of the general environment.

The Demographic Segment

Demographics are the most easily understood and quantifiable elements of the general environment. They are at the root of many changes in society. Demographics include elements such as the aging population,[20] rising or declining affluence, changes in ethnic composition, geographic distribution of the population, and disparities in income level.

Exhibit 3.3   General Environment: Key Trends and Events

Demographic

- Aging population
- Rising affluence
- Changes in ethnic composition
- Geographic distribution of population
- Greater disparities in income levels

Sociocultural

- More women in the workforce
- Increase in temporary workers
- Greater concern for fitness
- Greater concern for environment
- Postponement of family formation

Political/Legal

- Tort reform
- Americans with Disabilities Act (ADA) of 1990
- Repeal of Glass-Steagall Act in 1999 (banks may now offer brokerage services)
- Deregulation of utility and other industries
- Increases in federally mandated minimum wages
- Taxation at local, state, federal levels
- Legislation on corporate governance reforms in bookkeeping, stock options, etc. (Sarbanes-Oxley Act of 2002)

Technological

- Genetic engineering
- Emergence of Internet technology
- Computer-aided design/computer-aided manufacturing systems (CAD/CAM)
- Research in synthetic and exotic materials
- Pollution/global warming
- Miniaturization of computing technologies
- Wireless communications
- Nanotechnology

Economic

- Interest rates
- Unemployment rates
- Consumer Price Index
- Trends in GDP
- Changes in stock market valuations

Global

- Increasing global trade
- Currency exchange rates
- Emergence of the Indian and Chinese economies
- Trade agreements among regional blocs (e.g., NAFTA, EU, ASEAN)
- Creation of WTO (leading to decreasing tariffs/free trade in services)

The impact of a demographic trend, like all segments of the general environment, varies across industries. The aging of the U.S. population has had a positive effect on the health care industry but a negative impact on the industry that produces diapers and baby food. Rising levels of affluence in many developed countries bode well for brokerage services as well as for upscale pets and supplies. However, these same trends may have an adverse effect on fast food restaurants because people can afford to dine at higher-priced restaurants. Fast-food restaurants depend on minimum-wage employees to operate efficiently, but the competition for labor intensifies as more attractive employment opportunities become prevalent, thus threatening the employment base for restaurants. Let's look at the details of one of these trends.

The aging population in the United States and other developed countries has important implications. The U.S. Bureau of Statistics states that only 14 percent of American workers were 55 and older in 2002.[21] However, by 2012 that figure will increase to 20 percent, or one in five, of all U.S. workers. At the same time, the United States is expected to experience a significant drop in the percentage of younger workers aged 25 to 44, making it increasingly important for employers to find ways to recruit and retain older workers. Similarly, the National Association of Manufacturing estimates that as baby boomers continue retiring and the economy grows, the United States will have 7 million more jobs than workers by 2010.

The Sociocultural Segment

Sociocultural forces influence the values, beliefs, and lifestyles of a society. Examples include a higher percentage of women in the workforce, dual-income families, increases in the number of temporary workers, greater concern for healthy diets and physical fitness, greater interest in the environment, and postponement of having children. Such forces enhance sales of products and services in many industries but depress sales in others. The increased number of women in the workforce has increased the need for business clothing merchandise but decreased the demand for baking product staples (since people would have less time to cook from scratch). A greater concern for health and fitness has had differential effects. This trend has helped industries that manufacture exercise equipment and healthful foods but harmed industries that produce unhealthful foods.

The trend toward increased educational attainment by women in the workplace has led to an increase in the number of women in upper management positions. U.S. Department of Education statistics show that women have become the dominant holders of college degrees. Based on figures of a recent graduating class, women with bachelor's degrees will outnumber their male counterparts by 27 percent. By the class of 2006-2007, the gap should surge to 38 percent. Additionally, throughout the 1990s the number of women earning MBAs increased by 29 percent compared to only 15 percent for men.[22] Given these educational attainments, it is hardly surprising that companies owned by women have been one of the driving forces of the U.S. economy; these companies (now more than 9 million in number) account for 40 percent of all U.S. businesses and have generated more than $3.6 trillion in annual revenue. In addition, women have a tremendous impact on consumer spending decisions. Not surprisingly, many companies have focused their advertising and promotion efforts on female consumers. Consider, for example, Wilkesboro (North Carolina)-based Lowe's efforts to attract female shoppers: Lowe's has found that women prefer to do larger home-improvement projects with a man—be it a boyfriend, husband, or neighbor.[23] As a result, in addition to its "recipe card classes" (that explain various projects that take only one weekend), Lowe's offers co-ed store clinics for projects like sink installation. "Women like to feel they're given the same attention as a male customer," states Lowe's spokespersons Julie Valeant-Yenichek, who points out that most seminar attendees, whether male or female, are inexperienced.

Not surprisingly, Home Depot has recently spent millions of dollars to add softer lighting and brighter signs in 300 stores. Why? It is an effort to match rival Lowe's long-standing appeal to women.

The Sarbanes-Oxley Act: A Boon for Accountants

Government regulation is often prompted as elected officials respond to voters' expectations. When faced with a crisis, voters often demand a solution and expect elected officials to provide one. If the politicians fail to deliver, they suffer in the next election. Consider some of the historical examples of how the U.S. government has reacted to ethical disasters with the blunt force of increased legislation.

- The creation of the Securities and Exchange Commission (SEC) and other legislation following the stock market crash of 1929.
- The Foreign Corrupt Practices Act of 1977, which followed Lockheed's bribes to government officials.
- In the wake of the Enron, WorldCom, and Andersen debacles, Congress passed the Sarbanes-Oxley Act on July 30, 2002. (The law was passed just 35 days after WorldCom announced that it had overstated its revenues by at least $3.8 billion.)

Accounting firms have really benefited from the Sarbanes-Oxley Act. They had lobbied hard to keep the act from being passed. But, fortunately for them, they lost!

Companies are working hard to comply with Section 404 of the act. The provision requires publicly traded corporations to vouch for internal financial controls and remedy problems. A recent survey by Financial Executives International (FEI) finds that, on average, companies will spend $3.1 million and 30,700 hours to comply—nearly double the estimates of an earlier poll.

Much of that expense goes to privately held accounting firms. Audit fees are expected to surge more than 50 percent, according to FEI. To deal with the increased business, the Big Four accounting firms are in a hiring frenzy and logging lots of overtime. For example, KPMG has added 850 auditors in 2004, while PricewaterhouseCoopers (PWC) has hired 400 people from English-speaking foreign countries as temporary employees. "It's a scramble," say Dennis Nally, PWC's U.S. senior partner. It seems every cloud has a silver lining.

(Sources: Arndt, M. 2004. A noon for bean counters. *Business Week,* November 22:13; and Thomas, T., Schermerhorn, R. R, Jr., & Dienhart, J. W. 2004. Strategic leadership of ethical behavior in business. *The Academy of Management Executive,* 18[2]: 55-68.)

The Political/Legal Segment

Political processes and legislation influence the environmental regulations with which industries must comply.[24] Some important elements of the political/legal arena include tort reform, the Americans with Disabilities Act (ADA) of 1990, the repeal of the Glass-Steagall Act in 1999 (banks may now offer brokerage services), deregulation of utilities and other industries, and increases in the federally mandated minimum wage.

Government legislation can also have a significant impact on the governance of corporations. The U.S. Congress passed the Sarbanes-Oxley Act in 2002, which greatly increases the accountability of auditors, executives, and corporate lawyers. This act was a response to the widespread perception that existing governance mechanisms have failed to protect the interests of shareholders, employees, and creditors. Perhaps it is not too surprising that Sarbanes-Oxley has also created a tremendous demand for professional accounting services.

Legislation also helps companies in the high-tech sector of the economy by expanding the number of temporary visas available for highly skilled foreign professionals. For example, a bill passed in October 2000 allows 195,000 H-1B visas in each of the next three years, up from the cap of only 115,000 in 2000. The allotment for the year 2000 was used up by March, and the cap decreased to 107,500 for 2001 and a mere 65,000 each year thereafter. Almost half of the visas are for professionals from India, and most of them are computer or software specialists.[25] For U.S. labor and workers' rights groups, however, the issue was a political hot potato.

The Technological Segment

Developments in technology lead to new products and services and improve how they are produced and delivered to the end user. Innovations can create entirely new industries and alter the boundaries of existing industries.[26] Examples of technological developments and trends are genetic engineering, Internet technology, computer-aided design/computer-aided manufacturing (CAD/CAM), research in artificial and exotic materials, and, on the downside, pollution and global warming. Firms in the petroleum and primary metals industries incur significant expenses to reduce the amount of pollution they produce. Engineering and consulting firms that work with polluting industries derive financial benefits from solving such problems.

Another important technological development is the combination of information technology (IT) and the Internet, which has played a key role in productivity improvement.[27] In the United States, for example, improvement in productivity rates is running at an all-time high. For the 20-year period ending in 1990, U.S. worker productivity grew at less than 1.7 percent annually. In contrast, from 2001 to 2005, it grew at an annual rate of 3.6 percent. In recent years, productivity around the world has also increased by, for example, nearly 6 percent in Taiwan and nearly 10 percent in South Korea. Better productivity means that more work can be done by fewer people.

Nanotechnology is becoming a very promising area of research with many potentially useful applications.[28] Nanotechnology takes place at industry's tiniest stage: one billionth of a meter. Remarkably, this is the size of 10 hydrogen atoms in a row.

Researchers have discovered that matter at such a tiny scale behaves very differently. While some of the science behind this phenomenon is still shrouded in mystery, the commercial potential is coming sharply into focus. Familiar materials—from gold to carbon soot—display startling and useful new properties. Some transmit light or electricity. Others become harder than diamonds or turn into potent chemical catalysts. What's more, researchers have found that a tiny dose of nanoparticles can transform the chemistry and nature of far bigger things, creating everything from stronger fenders to superefficient fuel cells. Exhibit 3.4 lists a few of the potential ways in which nanotechnology could revolutionize industries.

There are downsides to technology. In addition to ethical issues in biotechnology, there are threats to our environment associated with the emission of greenhouse gases. In response, some firms have taken a proactive approach. BP Amoco plans to decrease its greenhouse gas emissions by giving each of its 150 business units a quota of emission permits and encouraging the units to trade them. If a unit cuts emissions and has leftover permits, it can sell them to other units that are having difficulty meeting their goals. For example, Julie Hardwick, manager at the Naperville, Illinois, petrochemical division, saved up permits by fast-tracking a furnace upgrade that allowed elimination of a second furnace.[29]

The Economic Segment

The economy has an impact on all industries, from suppliers of raw materials to manufacturers of finished goods and services, as well as all organizations in the service, wholesale, retail, government, and nonprofit sectors. Key economic indicators include interest rates, unemployment rates, the Consumer Price Index, the gross domestic product, and net disposable income. Interest-rate increases have a negative impact on the residential home construction industry but a negligible (or neutral) effect on industries that produce consumer necessities such as prescription drugs or common grocery items.

Other economic indicators are associated with equity markets. Perhaps the most watched is the Dow Jones Industrial Average (DJIA), which is composed of 30 large industrial firms. When stock market indexes increase, consumers' discretionary income rises and there is often an increased demand for luxury items such as jewelry and automobiles. But when stock valuations decrease, demand for these items shrinks.

The Global Segment

There is an increasing trend for firms to expand their operations and market reach beyond the borders of their "home" country. Globalization provides both opportunities to access larger potential markets and a broad base of production factors such as raw materials,

---

Exhibit 3.4   How Nanotechnology Might Revolutionize Various Industries

- **To fight cancer,** sensors will be able to detect a single cancer cell and will help guide nanoparticles that can burn tumors from the inside out, leaving healthy cells alone.
- **To transform energy,** nano-enhanced solar panels will feed cheap electricity onto superconducting power lines made of carbon nanotubes.
- **To replace silicon,** carbon nanotubes will take over when silicon peters out, leading to far faster chips that need less power than today's chips.
- **For space travel,** podlike crawlers will carry cargo thousands of miles up a carbon-nanotube cable to a space station for billions less than rocket launches.

Source: Baker, S. & Aston, A. 2004. Universe in a grain of sand. *BusinessWeek,* October 11: 139-140.

---

labor, skilled managers, and technical professionals. However, such endeavors also carry many political, social, and economic risks.

Examples of key elements include currency exchange rates, increasing global trade, the economic emergence of China, trade agreements among regional blocs (e.g., North American Free Trade Agreement, European Union), and the General Agreement on Tariffs and Trade (GATT) (lowering of tariffs). Increases in trade across national boundaries also provide benefits to air cargo and shipping industries but have a minimal impact on service industries such as bookkeeping and routine medical services. The emergence of China as an economic power has benefited many industries, such as construction, soft drinks, and computers. However, it has had a negative impact on the defense industry in the United States as diplomatic relations between the two nations improve.

Few industries are as global as the automobile industry. Consider just a few examples of how some of the key players expanded their reach into Latin America during the 1990s. Fiat built a new plant in Argentina, Volkswagen retooled a plant in Mexico to launch the New Beetle, DaimlerChrysler built a new plant as a joint venture with BMW to produce engines in Brazil, and General Motors built a new car factory in Brazil. Why the interest? In addition to the region's low wage rates and declining trade barriers, the population of 400 million is very attractive. But the real bonus lies in the 9-to-1 ratio of people to cars in the region compared to a 2-to-1 ratio in developed countries. With this region's growth expected to be in the 3 to 4 percent range for the first part of the century, sales should increase at a healthy rate.[30]

Finally, consider the cost of terrorism. A recent survey indicates that for S&P 500 firms, the threat has caused direct and indirect costs of $107 billion a year. This figure includes extra spending (on insurance and redundant capacity, for instance) as well as lost revenues (from fearful consumers' decreased activity). Another finding in a 2006 survey of CFOs: Some 21 percent of U.S. companies have reduced employees' air travel since September 11 (as have 17 percent of European companies).[31]

Relationships Among Elements of the General Environment

In our discussion of the general environment, we see many relationships among the various elements.[32] For example, a demographic trend in the United States, the aging of the population, has important implications for the economic segment (in terms of tax policies to provide benefits to increasing numbers of older citizens). Another example is the emergence of information technology as a means to increase the rate of productivity gains in the United States and other developed countries. Such use of IT results in lower inflation (an important element of the economic segment) and helps offset costs associated with higher labor rates.

The effects of a trend or event in the general environment vary across industries. Governmental legislation (political/legal) to permit the importation of prescription drugs from foreign countries is a very positive development for drugstores but a very negative event for U.S. drug manufacturers. Exhibit 3.5 provides

Exhibit 3.5				
Segment/Trends and Events	*Industry*	*Positive*	*Neutral*	*Negative*
Demographic				
Aging population	Health care	✓		
	Baby products			✓
Rising affluence	Brokerage services	✓		
	Fast foods			✓
	Upscale pets and supplies	✓		
Sociocultural				
More women in the workforce	Clothing	✓		
	Baking products (staples)			✓
Greater concern for health and fitness	Home exercise equipment	✓		
	Meat products			✓
Political/legal				
Tort reform	Legal services			✓
	Auto manufacturing	✓		
Americans with Disabilities Act (ADA)	Retail			✓
	Manufacturers of elevators, escalators, and ramps	✓		
Technological				
Genetic engineering	Pharmaceutical	✓		
	Publishing		✓	
Pollution/global warming	Engineering services	✓		
	Petroleum			✓
Economic				
Interest rate increases	Residential construction			✓
	Most common grocery products		✓	

(Continued)

Exhibit 3.5 (Continued)

Segment/Trends and Events	Industry	Positive	Neutral	Negative
Global				
Increasing global trade	Shipping	✓		
	Personal service		✓	
Emergence of China as an economic power	Soft drinks	✓		
	Defense			✓

other examples of how the impact of trends or events in the general environment can vary across industries.

The Internet and Digital Technologies: Affecting Many Environmental Segments

The Internet has dramatically changed the way business is conducted in every corner of the globe. According to digital economy visionary Don Tapscott:

> The Net is much more than just another technology development; the Net represents something qualitatively new—an unprecedented, powerful, universal communications medium. Far surpassing radio and television, this medium is digital, infinitely richer, and interactive. . . . Mobile computing devices, broadband access, wireless networks, and computing power embedded in everything from refrigerators to automobiles are converging into a global network that will enable people to use the Net just about anywhere and anytime.

The Internet provides a platform or staging area for the application of numerous technologies, rapid advances in knowledge, and unprecedented levels of global communication and commerce. Even technologies that don't require the Internet to function, such as wireless phones and GPS, rely on the Internet for data transfer and communications.

Growth in Internet usage has surged in recent years both among individual users as well as businesses. Exhibit 3.6 illustrates current usage levels as well as worldwide growth trends in Internet use. Business use of the Internet has become nearly ubiquitous throughout the economy. Major corporations all have a Web presence, and many companies use the Internet to interact with key stakeholders. For example, some companies have direct links with suppliers through online procurement systems that automatically reorder inventories and supplies. Companies such as Cisco Systems even interact with their own employees using the Internet to update employment records, such as health care information and benefits.

Small and medium-sized enterprises (SMEs) are also relying on the Internet more than ever. A recent study found that 87 percent of SMEs are receiving monthly revenue from their Web site, and 42 percent derive more than a quarter of their monthly revenue from their Internet presence. According to Joel Kocher, CEO of Interland, "We are getting to the point in most small-business categories where it will soon be safe to say that if you're not online, you're not really serious about being in business."

Despite these advances, the Internet and digital technologies still face numerous challenges. For example, international standards for digital and wireless communications are still in flux. As a result, cell phones and other devices that work in the United States are often useless in many parts of Europe and Asia. And, unlike analog systems, electronic bits of data that are zooming

Exhibit 3.6 Growth in Internet Activity		
	Internet Users (in millions)	
Geographic Region	2005	2010 (estimated)
North America	219,650	259,390
Western Europe	215,734	319,528
Eastern Europe/Russia	70,381	130,888
Asia-Pacific	420,999	745,421
South/Central America	83,724	155,590
Middle East/Africa	64,245	146,624
Total Internet Users	1,074,733	1,785,941

Source: Computer Industry Almanac.

through space can be more easily lost, stolen, or manipulated. However, even with these problems, Internet and digital technologies will continue to be a growing global phenomenon. As Andy Grove, former chairman of Intel, stated, "The world now runs on Internet time."

(Sources: Anonymous. 2005. SMBs believe in the Web. *eMarketer.com*, www.emarketer.com, May 16. Downes, L. & Mui, C. 1998. *Unleashing the killer app.* Boston: Harvard Business School Press. Green, H. 2003. Wi-Fi means business. *BusinessWeek*, April 28: 86-92; McGann, R. 2005. Broadband: High speed, high spend. *ClickZ Network*, www.clickz.com, January 24. Tapscott, D. 2001. Rethinking strategy in a networked world. *Strategy and Business,* Third Quarter: 34-41. Yang, C. 2003. Beyond Wi-Fi: A new wireless age. *BusinessWeek*, December 15: 84-88.)

Notes

1. For an insightful discussion on managers' assessment of the external environment, refer to Sutcliffe, K. M., & Weber, K. 2003. The high cost of accurate knowledge. *Harvard Business Review*, 81(5): 74–86.

2. Charitou, C. D., & Markides, C. C. 2003. Responses to disruptive strategic innovation. *MIT Sloan Management Review*, 44(2): 55–64.

3. Our discussion of scanning, monitoring, competitive intelligence, and forecasting concepts draws on several sources. These include Fahey, L., & Narayanan, V. K. 1983. *Macroenvironmental analysis for strategic management.* St. Paul, MN: West; Lorange, P., Scott, F. S., & Ghoshal, S. 1986. *Strategic control.* St. Paul, MN: West; Ansoff, H. I. 1984. *Implementing strategic management.* Englewood Cliffs, NJ: Prentice Hall; and Schreyogg, G., & Stienmann, H. 1987. Strategic control: A new perspective. *Academy of Management Review,* 12: 91–103.

4. Elenkov, D. S. 1997. Strategic uncertainty and environmental scanning: The case for institutional influences on scanning behavior. *Strategic Management Journal,* 18: 287–302.

5. For an interesting perspective on environmental scanning in emerging economies see May, R. C., Stewart, W. H., & Sweo, R. 2000. Environmental scanning behavior in a transitional economy: Evidence from Russia. *Academy of Management Journal,* 43(3): 403–27.

6. Browne, Sir John. The new agenda. Keynote speech delivered to the World Petroleum Congress in Calgary, Canada, June 13, 2000.

7. Bowles, J. 1997. Key issues for the automotive industry CEOs. *Fortune,* August 18: S3.

8. Walters, B. A., & Priem, R. L. 1999. Business strategy and CEO intelligence acquisition. *Competitive Intelligence Review,* 10(2): 15–22.

9. Prior, V. 1999. The language of competitive intelligence, Part 4. *Competitive Intelligence Review,* 10(1): 84–87.

10.   Zahra, S. A., & Charples, S. S. 1993. Blind spots in competitive analysis. *Academy of Management Executive* 7(2): 7–27.

11.   Wolfenson, J. 1999. The world in 1999: A battle for corporate honesty. *The Economist* 38: 13–30.

12.   Drucker, P. F. 1997. The future that has already happened. *Harvard Business Review*, 75(6): 22.

13.   Evans, P. B., & Wurster, T. S. 1997. Strategy and the new economics of information. *Harvard Business Review*, 75(5): 71–82.

14.   Fahey & Narayanan, op. cit., p. 41.

15.   Courtney, H., Kirkland, J., & Viguerie, P. 1997. Strategy under uncertainty. *Harvard Business Review*, 75(6): 66–79.

16.   Odlyzko, A. 2003. False hopes. *Red Herring*, March: 31.

17.   Rosne, B. 2007. The little guy. abcnews.com. January 12:4.

18.   For an interesting perspective on how Accenture practices and has developed its approach to scenario planning, refer to Ferguson, G., Mathur, S., & Shah, B. 2005. Evolving from information to insight. *MIT Sloan Management Review*, 46(2): 51–58.

19.   Dean, T. J., Brown, R. L., & Bamford, C. E. 1998. Differences in large and small firm responses to environmental context: Strategic implications from a comparative analysis of business formations. *Strategic Management Journal*, 19: 709–728.

20.   Colvin, G. 1997. How to beat the boomer rush. *Fortune*, August 18: 59–63.

21.   Guntner, T. 2006. Still working and loving it. *BusinessWeek*, October 16: 108; Warner, M. 2004. Home Depot goes old school. *Business 2.0*, June: 74; and, O'Brien, S. 2005. Over 50 and looking for work? *www.seniorliving.about.com*.

22.   Challenger, J. 2000. Women's corporate rise has reduced relocations. *Lexington* (KY) *Herald-Leader*, October 29: Dl.

23.   Tsao, A. 2005. Retooling home improvement, Businessweek.com, February, 14; and, Grow, B. 2004. Who wears the wallet in the family? *BusinessWeek*, August 16:10.

24.   Watkins, M. D. 2003. Government games. *MIT Sloan Management Review* 44(2): 91–95.

25   Davies, A. 2000. The welcome mat is out for nerds. *BusinessWeek*, October 16: 64.

26.   Anonymous. Business ready for Internet revolution. 1999. *Financial Times*, May 21: 17.

27.   Lataif, L. E. 2006. B-Schools and the common good. *BizEd*, March/April: 36–39.

28.   Baker, S., & Aston, A. 2005. The business of nanotech. *BusinessWeek*, February 14: 64–71.

29.   Ginsburg, J. 2000. Letting the free market clear the air. *BusinessWeek*, November 6: 200, 204.

30.   Smith, G., Wheatley, J., & Green, J. 2000. Car power. *BusinessWeek*, October 23: 72–80.

31.   Byrnes, N. 2006. The high cost of fear. *BusinessWeek*, November 6: 16.

32.   Goll, I., & Rasheed, M. A. 1997. Rational decision-making and firm performance: The moderating role of environment. *Strategic Management Journal*, 18: 583–591.

CHAPTER 4

How to Make Sense of Weak Signals

Paul J. H. Schoemaker
George S. Day

Wharton School of the University of Pennsylvania

When people stumble onto the truth, they usually pick themselves up and hurry about their business.

—attributed to Winston Churchill

The Leading Question: How can managers develop their peripheral vision to see what's ahead more sharply?

Findings

- Managers who can identify and minimize both their personal and organizational biases are less likely to get blindsided.

- Catching and capturing distant threats and opportunities means applying different search methods—and looking for overlapping results.
- Teasing out the implications of any finding requires fitting it into different frameworks.

It's the question everyone wants answered: Why did so many smart people miss the signs of the collapse of the subprime market? As early as 2001, there were many

---

danger signals about the impending housing bubble and the rampant use of derivatives. Yet these signals were largely ignored by such financial players as Northern Rock, Countrywide, Bear Stearns, Lehman Brothers and Merrill Lynch until they all had to face the music harshly and abruptly. Some players were more prescient, however, and sensed as well as acted on the early warning signals. In 2003, investment guru Warren Buffett foresaw that complex derivatives would multiply and mutate until "some event makes their toxicity clear." In 2002, the derided derivatives as financial weapons of mass destruction. Likewise, Edward Gramlich, a governor of the Federal Reserve, warned in 2001 about a new breed of lenders luring buyers with poor credit records into mortgages they could not afford.[1]

Some business leaders also noticed. Hedge-fund honcho John Paulson spotted "overvalued" credit markets in 2006 and made $15 billion in 2007 by shorting subprime. In July 2006, the chief U.S. economist at The Goldman Sachs Group Inc. warned that "nominal U.S. home prices may be headed for an outright decline in 2007. It would be the first decline in national home-prices ever recorded, at least in nominal terms." And in early 2007, his colleague further warned that "there are signals of a decrease in mortgage lending criteria and initial signals of financial troubles from subprime lenders."[2] Likewise, the board of the Dutch bank ABN AMRO Holding N.V. recognized the looming problems facing the banking sector, and sold itself. Shareholders did very well, collecting about $100 billion before it all fell apart, with Fortis SA/NV and others in the syndicate in ruin.[3]

So, what separates the prescient few from the hapless horde? Did the siren call of outsize profits and bonuses, coupled with the delusional promises of manageable risk, dull the senses? Was the ability to see sooner and more clearly compromised by information overload, organizational filters and cognitive biases that afflict sense making in all organizations? Economist Robert Shiller of Yale University, a leading housing expert, recently invoked "groupthink" to explain why the Federal Reserve didn't take the early warning signs of a looming housing bubble more seriously.[4]

All managers are susceptible to the distortions and biases we saw in the credit crunch of 2008.

Organizations get blindsided not so much because decision makers aren't seeing signals, but because they jump to the most convenient or plausible conclusion. Our own research suggests that fewer than 20% of global companies have sufficient capacity to spot, interpret and act on the weak signals of forthcoming threats and opportunities.

The purpose of this chapter is to provide leaders and management teams with proven ways of reducing the chance that they will be ambushed from left or right field by an upstart rival, say, or a destabilizing technology. Our approach addresses the *cognitive* biases organizations may not be aware of, yet need to overcome.

Signals in Pearl Harbor

On the morning of December 7, 1941, the captain of the destroyer USS Ward heard muffled explosions corning from Pearl Harbor on the mainland. This captain had dropped depth charges on an enemy submarine moving into the harbor and had apparently sunk it. Yet when the captain heard the explosions while sailing back to port, he turned to his lieutenant commander and said, " I guess they are blasting the new road from Pearl Harbor to Honolulu." Despite his unusual encounter with a foreign submarine that morning, he made sense of the exploding sound using his peacetime mind-set and failed to notice the signs of the first hostilities between the United States and Japan.

The Shocking Truth About Surprise Attacks

There are various *individual* biases that may cause managers to be taken unaware. In addition, there are *organizational* biases —such as groupthink or polarization—that may keep much of the periphery-dwelling enemy in the shadows, even in organizations with an active scanning process. The decision-making literature identifies many of the human weaknesses that impair our sense-making skills.[5] Even for scholars, however, it is difficult at times to untangle the knot of factors that clogged a decision-making process. For example, academics have attributed NASA's ill-fated decision to launch the space shuttle Challenger in 1986—despite multiple warnings from its own engineers about risky O-ring seals—to multiple causes. Among them: incomplete data analysis by key engineers (a cognitive failure); stress-induced groupthink—a bias that values consensus above independent thinking—caused by deadlines and isolation (a group-dynamic explanation); and organizational values that gradually normalized danger beyond the point of prudence (a cultural or institutional explanation).[6]

Once managers lock in on a certain picture, they will often reshape reality to fit into that familiar frame.[7] Humans tend to judge too quickly when presented with ambiguous data; we have to work extra hard to consider less familiar scenarios.

Whenever multiple pieces of evidence point in opposite directions, or when crucial information is missing, our minds naturally shape the facts to fit our preconceptions.

Personal Biases: An Objective View

Although complete objectivity is elusive, managers need to be aware of well-established traps that underlie human inference and judgment. The major ones are described below in terms of how information is filtered, interpreted and often bolstered by seeking additional information aimed at confirming prior leanings.[8] The net effect of these biases is that we frame a complex or ambiguous issue in a certain way—without fully appreciating other possible perspectives—and then become overconfident about that particular view.

Filtering. What we actually pay attention to is very much determined by what we expect to see. Psychologists call this *selective perception.* If something doesn't fit our mental model, we often distort reality to make it fit rather than challenge our fundamental assumptions. A related phenomenon is *suppression* or the refusal to acknowledge an unpleasant reality because it is too discordant.

Distorted Inference. Whatever information passes through our cognitive and emotional filters may be subject to further distortion. One well-known bias is *rationalization:* interpreting evidence in a way that sustains a desired belief. We fall victim to this when trying to shift blame for a mistake we made to someone else or to external circumstances. *Wishful thinking* leads us to see the world only in a pleasing way, denying subtle evidence that a child is abusing drugs or a spouse is being unfaithful. Another common interpretation bias is *egocentrism,* according to which we overemphasize our own role in the events we seek to explain. This self-serving tendency is related to the *fundamental attribution bias,* which causes us to ascribe more importance to our own actions than to those of others or the environment. We often view our organization as a more central actor than it really is.

Bolstering. Not only do we heavily filter the limited information that we pay attention to, but also we may seek to bolster our case by searching for additional evidence that confirms our view. We might disproportionately talk to people who already agree with us. Or we may actively look for new evidence that confirms our perspective, rather than pursuing a more balanced search strategy. Over time, our opinions may become frozen and our attitudes hardened as we immunize ourselves from contradictory evidence. Indeed, we may even engage in *selective memory* and forget those inconvenient facts that don't fit the overall picture. The *hindsight bias* similarly distorts our memories such that our original doubts are erased. A vicious circle is created in which we exacerbate the earlier biases and get trapped in a self-sealing echo chamber.

Organizational Bias: Getting Along, Getting It Wrong

In addition to our personal biases, we function in organizations as well and may end up suffering from what social psychologist Irving Janis termed *groupthink.*[9] In principle, groups should be better than individuals at detecting changes and responding to them. But often a group can fall victim to narrow-minded analysis, tunnel vision, a false sense of consensus and poor information gathering, resulting in groupthink. The true relevance of various snippets of information often can be fully appreciated only when they are debated with others and merged into a larger mosaic.

The organizational problems caused by dispersed memory and varying perceptions can only be overcome when information flows freely across departmental boundaries.[10] During the five months preceding the terrorist attacks of September 11, 2001, for example, the U.S. Federal Aviation Administration received a total of 105 intelligence reports, in which Osama bin Laden or Al Qaeda were mentioned 52 times.[11] These reports, from the CIA, FBI and U.S. State Department, were streaming into various parts of the government bureaucracy, which did not have the necessary means to make sense of it all. Some signals were dismissed at the local level and simply not transmitted; some were shared as fragments that remained unconnected to other pieces of the puzzle. The end result was that the full magnitude of the terrorist threat facing the United States was not seen in time, even when the signals were there.

Organizational sense making occurs in a complex social environment in which people are not just sensitive to what is being said, but also to who is speaking. We judge both the signal and the source when we assess the meaning of information. Source credibility is influenced by many factors, including status, past experience, politics, and the like. Since most managers receive information from multiple sources, they need to be aware of such biases. These social biases will be especially strong when the information is weak or incomplete.

The individual and organizational biases discussed above underscore why it is important to bring together different perspectives on the same issue. But *how* these different perspectives are cultivated and connected will greatly affect the ability of the organization to make sense of the weak information it receives.[12]

Start Making Sense

Sense making or interpretation is usually the weakest link in the process of capturing weak signals and eventually making a sound decision. How can management learn to overcome biases to improve their sense making? There are nine proven approaches that managers can use actively to reveal, amplify and clarify potentially important weak signals.

Actively Reveal Weak Signals

1. Tap local intelligence. Insects use a compound lens system, where most of what they see and notice occurs in the eye itself as opposed to in the brain. They rely on "localized intelligence" at the level of each eyelet and respond accordingly, likewise, organizations may wish to drive more of their sense making to local levels. Terrorist networks have demonstrated the deadly power and resiliency of such an approach, using nearly autonomous cells that see and think locally. Or, in a more positive vein, Linux and the open-source movement have used local design to build an ongoing global software project.[13] From fighter plane cockpits to nuclear power plant control rooms, the key to safety and reliability is to spot problems early and share them among well-trained personnel. This requires procedures for real-time cognition and constrained improvisation to bring about flexibility and promptness in highly complex, volatile environments. Accessing distributed intelligence takes a culture of alertness and information sharing across multiple social networks.[14]

2. Leverage extended networks. A valuable but frequently overlooked way actively to reveal weak signals is for executives to query their extended networks to partners, suppliers, customers and others in the company's ecosystem. The common element of all these networks is that they extend the eyes and ears of the company. Different networks tap different zones of the periphery in diverse ways. For example, the research and development departments of Royal Philips Electronics N. V. and General Electric Co. were greatly helped in their early days by being deeply embedded in external government, academia and customer networks, as well as connected to other parts of the organization internally.[15] Similar results were found in a historical study of Merck & Co. Inc., showing how

| Figure 4.1 | Signal Stages |

Finding a Purpose of Sense

There's no sense in denying it: interpreting weak signals into useful decision making takes time and focus. The three stages shown here can help you see what's on the periphery—and act with much *more* confidence.

Scanning for Weak Signals	Sense-Making	Probing and Acting
Actively surface weak signals	*Amplify interesting weak signals*	*Probe further and clarify*
• Tap local intelligence • Leverage extended networks • Mobilize search parties	• Test multiple hypotheses • Canvass the wisdom of the crowd • Develop diverse scenarios	• Confront reality • Encourage constructive conflict • Trust seasoned intuition

its innovations in biological compounds were related to a "series of complex, evolving networks of scientific, governmental and medical institutions."[16] One consequence of greater organizational participation in extended networks—where many nodes in the network are connected to other networks—is a rapid increase in the number of weak signals received. This problem is intensified within Internet-enabled networks, which virtually eliminate signal transmission time and cost. Thus, managers must be selective about which signals to pay attention to and stay within the boundaries of the company's absorption capacity.

3. Mobilize search parties. Senior leaders can identify weak signal areas that merit separate task forces to canvass further. For example, IBM Corp. has an ongoing capability called "Crow's Nest" to scan specific zones of the periphery and share insights with top management. The zones include time compression, customer diversity, globalization and networks. The responsibility of the group is to rise above functional and product blinders, like a "crow's nest" on a ship, where lookouts watch for new land, pirates and dangerous reefs ahead.

Scanning activities are most valuable when used in combination. For example, the CIA has brought together a crow's nest-type group and a venture fund to find and assess emerging technologies that could be used to fight terrorism. The agency tasked a sensing group with identifying and assessing these technologies. The primary activity of the sensing group is to be the link between the agency and In-Q-Tel Inc., an internal but separate venture fund that invests in startups with technologies that could address an agency priority. Because In-Q-Tel has access to the deal streams of tier 1 venture capital companies, it allows the CIA to get involved early, when the technology can be shaped to address an agency problem.

Amplifying Interesting Signals

4. Test multiple hypotheses. Organizational sense making is usually driven toward a single interpretation, so new data are force-fit into the existing mental model.[17]

Managers often have limited tolerance for ambiguity and may be reluctant to devote additional time to develop alternative hypotheses. However, organizations need competing hypotheses to escape the trap of getting stuck on a simple, single view that is wrong. The British Armed Forces and other organizations deploy so-called red teams to accomplish this. The red team is a parallel task force, made up of senior leaders and support staff, whose only mission is to collect and synthesize information to prove that the current plan is wrong and needs to be changed.[18] This team plays the role of the loyal opposition, in the spirit of Alexander the Great, who would periodically ask himself how much evidence it would take for him to abandon the current plan.

As was recognized so painfully after the initial, short-lived U.S. military victory in Iraq, such contrarian information is usually dispersed, unreliable and ambiguous at first. Unless a concerted effort is made by credible and trusted parties to show that the combined evidence from many sources calls for a change of course, leaders may pursue a flawed strategy for too long. The red team approach requires a judicious balance between the doubt necessary to challenge false assumptions and the conviction or courage needed to pursue a bold course of action in the face of challenge and opposition. This balance can occur only if the underlying theme is that strategic surprise is inevitable and midcourse corrections are often necessary when facing the unknown. In the pithy phrase of Prussian General Helmuth von Moltke, "No plan survives contact with the enemy."

5. *Canvass the wisdom of the crowd.* To handle the dangers of groupthink or the problem of distributed intelligence (where key information is dispersed around the organization), managers may wish to pay more attention to the grapevine. James Surowiecki, author of *The Wisdom of Crowds,* summarizes research showing that groups or markets often make far better judgments than individuals. This is particularly true if companies can create forecasting methods (such as Delphi polling) to pool the collective wisdom of an organization without fostering undue conformity. Information flows quickly through the grapevine when Big Brother is not watching. One way to avoid collective myopia is to cre-

ate anonymous opinion markets. For example, in the 1990s, Hewlett-Packard Co. asked employees to participate in a newly created opinion market to forecast its sales. Employees would bet in this market at lunch or in the evenings, revealing through their investments where they thought the sales trend was headed. This market's forecast beat traditional company forecasts 75% of the time. More recently, a division of Eli Lilly and Co. asked employees to assess whether drug candidates would be approved by the FDA based on profiles and experimental data, and the internal company market correctly identified the winners from a set of six candidates.[19]

6. *Develop diverse scenarios.* Unfortunately, no method is perfect, and uncertainty can never be fully tamed or conquered. The consensus can be badly mistaken, as Charles Mackay vividly chronicled in his classic 1841 book, *Extraordinary Popular Delusions and the Madness of Crowds.* To challenge the dominant view in your organization, it may be wise to create multiple scenarios about the issues under debate. For example, when a Houston credit union was going gang busters thanks to Enron Corp.'s meteoric rise, one of our colleagues asked senior managers to imagine a scenario where they could no longer rely on Enron for growth and deposits. At first, there was reluctance to develop such an unrealistic and negative view, especially because Enron was the company's single corporate sponsor. But then some interesting scenarios emerged, ranging from an Enron takeover to more dire scenarios involving trouble for either Enron or the credit union. Later, when Enron suddenly collapsed, the credit union was saved—against the odds, according to regulators—because managers had taken pragmatic actions to be less dependent on Enron.[20] They had launched their own e-mail system to communicate with members rather than using Enron's system. And they had opened branches outside the Enron building and started to admit non-Enron employees into the credit union.

By considering multiple scenarios at the same time, the organization can keep from being locked into one view of what future might emerge and yet share a common set of frameworks for discussing new signals,[21] Royal Dutch Shell PLC, which pioneered scenario planning in the corporate sector, viewed it as "the gentle art of re-perceiving."[22] The aim of scenario planning at Shell was not so much to plan as to challenge people's mental models. Scenario planning systematizes the hunt for weak signals that may foreshadow fundamental shifts in the marketplace and society at large—scenarios seek to magnify "postcards from the edge" so that they are readable by more eyes.

Probing and Clarifying

7. Seek new information to "confront reality." As Larry Bossidy and Ram Charan emphasize in their book *Confronting Reality,* the greatest business failures are usually not due to poor management but rather reflect failure to "confront reality."[23] Bossidy and Charan write about how data-storage company EMC Corp. missed key changes in its environment that caused a rapid decline in sales in 2001. EMC's sales force, speaking mostly with CIOs, was confident that orders were only being delayed. They interpreted the downturn as a temporary blip. But when Joe Tucci was named CEO in early 2001, he began speaking to CEOs and CFOs at customer companies and found that they were not interested in paying a premium for top performance. Also, they wanted software that wasn't proprietary, since IBM and Hitachi Ltd. were selling machines comparable to EMC's at a lower price. As EMC's market share slipped, Tucci rapidly transformed EMC's business model to focus more on software and services than on hardware, which was becoming commoditized. Once Tucci recognized the new reality, he understood how the company needed to transform.

8. Encourage constructive conflict. A statue in Helsinki, honoring former Finland president J.K. Paasikivi (1870-1956), is engraved with his motto that "All wisdom starts by recognizing the facts." This is especially difficult when not all the facts are known and subject to interpretation. Wisdom requires constructive conflict to ascertain and interpret the facts as they are. But the conflict must be among ideas, not people, and remain within reason. Several academic studies show that *moderate,* as opposed to little or extreme conflict, leads

to the best decisions.[24] This results in better intelligence gathering, a wider exploration of options and a deeper examination of the issues. Unfortunately, the opposite often happens, as one insider at Merrill Lynch & Co. Inc. observed about the leadership team under CEO Stanley O'Neal: "There was no dissent. So, information never really traveled."[25] Leaders can play a key role in managing conflict well; they must allow peripheral observations by team members to enter the discussion.

9. Trust seasoned intuition. Experienced managers often possess far more knowledge than they realize, especially when operating within their domains of expertise. If so, they should learn when and how to trust their hunches. Scientist Gary Klein has studied the power of intuition in fast-moving environments such as firefighting, medical emergencies and military combat.[26] In one study he found that experienced nurses picked up the onset of septic shock in premature infants at least a day before the textbook symptoms appeared and a blood test could confirm the presence of the deadly bacterium. These nurses had learned to be sensitive to weak signals even if the cues varied and the symptoms were not strong. It takes many years of experience, with good feedback, to develop reliable intuition. But once it has been honed, intuitive hunches should be viewed as valuable inputs, along with more analytical ones, for the judgment process.

Broadening Your Perspective

Just as having two eyes allows humans to use triangulation and parallax for depth perception, organizations should use *multiple* perspectives to provide greater peripheral vision. Unlike humans, organizations can draw upon more than two eyes to make sense of what they're seeing. Each single view may have its biases, but several views together allow organizations to see what's really going on and identify new opportunities.

When General Motors Corp. developed OnStar, it drew on expertise in both technology and marketing to identify an emerging market opportunity. The carmaker launched the OnStar service in its 1997 Cadillac line, using "telematics," the integration of wireless communications, vehicle monitoring systems and location devices. This new venture was far out on the periphery of the automobile market. OnStar had nothing to do with automobile design and production. Telematics had little to do with price, reliability or comfort—the industry's traditional bases of competition. Finally, the market was minus-cute. In the early days, OnStar set a goal of bringing in 50 new customers a day in an organization that's used to counting its buyers by the millions.

How did General Motors manage to get this peripheral opportunity rolling? GM's acquisition of Hughes Electronics Corp. (and later EOS Corp.) gave it an early window on telematics technology, and the company had reason to believe that there was a market for it. In 1995, GM had commissioned a study to look at the key factors influencing consumers' decisions to purchase an automobile. The study revealed 26 factors, which were ranked according to their importance to customers' current satisfaction.[27] GM found that while customers were very satisfied with how its products met their need for "mobility," four factors revealed important unmet consumer needs: (1) personal attention, (2) limited time and energy, (3) privacy and (4) personal safety.[28] With insights into the desire of customers for personal attention and safety, as well as an understanding of the emerging technology, GM managers were able to spot an opportunity at the intersection. By 2004, OnStar controlled 70% of the market with 2.5 million subscribers, generating an estimated $1 billion in revenue.

Seeing the Biggest Picture Possible

No single technique will suffice in revealing the whole picture, since all methods are flawed or limited in some important respect. Managers seeking to understand an emerging technology might use analogies to markets for technologies with similar characteristics. But these analogies distort, because the situations may not be comparable in critical but unknown respects. A combination of methods is ideal.

Deploy Multiple Lenses. One way to systematize the triangulation process is to look at weak signals through various scenario lenses. More than a decade ago, we worked with a major U.S. newspaper company that used scenario planning to look at a single technological innovation from different perspectives. Xerox Corp. had just introduced a new service to deliver customized newspapers electronically to hotels and other locations, allowing users to print out tailor-made content. Travelers to foreign cities for example, could get their local news delivered or read the leading national newspaper in their native language.[29]

How important was this signal? Would it mean that hotel guests would never again hear the familiar thump of a newspaper outside their doors, or would it be a nonstarter? It depends on the scenario. In a scenario of "business as usual," this new service would represent a niche market (the traveler's market) and a welcome alternative channel of distribution besides the physical delivery of newspapers. It might create new opportunities for newspapers to move beyond their natural geographic area as well as enhancing customer loyalty. In another scenario, called "cyber-media," where electronic channels would be adopted rapidly, this initial foray into customized printing in hotels might lead to customized home printing of newspapers. Such a development could render the company's physical assets (such as expensive printing presses) obsolete.

By looking at this single weak signal through multiple lenses, the managers were better able to explore its potential implications. Considering the high ambiguity surrounding the signal, the company decided to track the development of remote electronic printing of newspapers. While such scenario-based analysis doesn't eliminate the uncertainty about either the development of the technology or consumer acceptance, it can help managers make better sense when one small piece of information is added to the puzzle (such as Xerox's minor announcement about remote printing options).

Talk to Customers and Competitors. Companies often suffer from focusing too narrowly on either customers or competitors, rather than looking at both. An exclusive focus on one or the other creates dangerous blind spots.[30]

By looking closely at its customers *and* competitors, a company that owned a major carpet manufacturing business forced its management team to face up to so many unpleasant realities that it walked away from the business.

These are just a few examples of how multiple perspectives and methods can aid in the interpretation of weak signals from the periphery. Overlaps in scanning may seem inefficient, but they serve an important purpose. They verify a weak signal's strategic import, and help to compensate for known deficiencies in our individual and collective vision.

Conclusions

There is a major difference between taking in signals and realizing what they mean. Managers as well as organizations tend to see the world in a certain way and confuse their mental maps with the territory. Weak signals that don't fit are often ignored, distorted or dismissed, leaving the company exposed.

In any given week—especially lately—the popular press is full of examples of managers missing weak signals. The major problem is that managers are insufficiently aware of cognitive and emotional biases that can cloud their judgment when interpreting weak signals. When ambiguity is high, we can easily torture the weak data until it confesses to whatever we want to believe. Countering these insidious tendencies requires leadership as well as the mastery of various tools to combat the pernicious filters that obscure and distort important weak signals. In a fast-moving marketplace, none of us can afford to miss what we are seeing.

Notes

1. E.L. Andrews, "Fed Shrugged as Subprime Crisis Spread," New York Times, Dec. 18, 2007; P. Barrett, "Wall Street Staggers," Business Week, Sept. 29, 2008, 28-31; and N.D. Schwartz and V. Bajaj, "How Missed Signs Contributed to a Mortgage Meltdown." New York Times, Aug. 19, 2007.

2. These and other warnings were sounded by Jan Hatzius, chief U.S. economist at Goldman Sachs, July 30, 2006;

Dan Sparks, mortgage department, Goldman Sachs, The Times, Jan. 2007; and again by Jan Hatzius on Feb. 12, 2007, at a Goldman Sachs housing conference.

3. Board member interview with authors; see also a detailed account in Dutch by P. Battes and P. Elshout, "De va van ABN AMRO" (Amsterdam: Business Contact, 2008).

4. R.J. Shriller, "Challenging the Crowd in Whispers, Not Shouts," New York Times, Nov. 2, 2008. p. 5.

5. For a managerial overview of the extensive field of decision making, see J.E. Russo and R.J.H. Schoemaker, "Winning Decisions" (New York: Doubleday Publishing Co., 2001).

6. The space shuttle data oversights are discussed in S.R. Dalai, E.B. Fowlkes and B. Hoadley, "Risk Analysis of the Space Shuttle: Pre-Challenger Prediction of Failure," Journal of the American Statistical Association 84, no. 408 (December 1939): 945-957; and E.R. Tufte, chap. 2 in "Visual and Statistical Thinking: Displays of Evidence for Making Decisions" (Cheshire, Connecticut: Graphics Press, 1997). The groupthink explanation of the Challenger case, and the associated tendency toward excessive risk taking, are examined in J.K. Esser and J.S. Lindoerfer, "Groupthink and the Space Shuttle Challenger Accident: Towerd a Quantitative Case Analysis," Journal of Behavioral Decision Making 2, no. 3 (1989): 167-177. An organizational and cultural account is offered in an excellent field study by D. Vaughn, "The Challenger Launch Decision" (Chicago: University of Chicago Press. 1996).

7. R. Wohlstetter, "Pearl Harbor: Warning and Decisions" (Stanford, California: Stanford University Press, 1962); and G. Prange, "At Dawn We Slept" (New York: Penguin Books, 1981).

8. The biases mentioned here reflect multiple research streams that are too broad to cite fully. We suffice by listing some of the classic references, such as L. Festinger, "Conflict, Decision and Dissonance" (Stanford, California: Stanford University Press, 1964); I. Janis, "Groupthink: Psychological Studies of Policy Decisions and Fiascos," 2nd ed. (Boston: Houghton Mifflin, 1982); I.L. Janis and L. Mann, "Decision Making: A Psychological Analysis of Conflict, Choice and Commitment" (New York: Free Press, 1977); and H.H. Kelley and J.L Michela, "Attribution Theory and Research," Annual Review of Psychology 31 (1980): 457-501.

9. The original and classic reference on groupthink is I. Janis, "Groupthink: Psychological Studies of Policy Decisions and Fiascos." 2nd ed. (Boston: Houghton Mifflin, 1982). For a critical review of groupthink as a psychological model, see W.W. Park, "A Review of Research on Groupthink," Journal of Behavioral Decision Making 3 (1990):229-245.

10. The special challenges of organizational coordination and distortion are addressed in C.A. Heimer, "Social Structure. Psychology and the Estimation of Risk." Annual Review of Sociology 14 (1988): 491-519; E. Hutchins and T. Klausen, "Distributed Cognition in an Airline Cockpit," in "Cognition and Communication at Work," eds. D. Middleton and Y. Engstrom (Cambridge, U.K.: Cambridge University Press, 1996); and K.E.Weick and K.H.Roberts. "Collective Wind in Organizations: Heedful Interrelating on Flight Decks," Administrative Science Quarterly 38 (1993): 357-381.

11. "A Vital Job Goes Begging," New York Times, Feb. 12, 2005, Sec. A, p. 30.

12. Some classic sociological studies on organizational sense making include C. Perrow, "Normal Accidents: Living with High-Risk Technologies" (Princeton, New Jersey; Princeton University Press, 1999); and M. Douglas, "How Institutions Think," (Syracuse, New York: Syracuse University Press. 1985). See also L.B. Clarke and J.F. Short Jr., "Social Organization and Risk: Some Current Controversies," Annual Review of Sociology 19 (1993): 375-99; and L.B. Clarke, "Mission Improbable: Using Fantasy Documents to Tame Disaster" (Chicago: University of Chicago Press, 2001).

13. How organizations can maintain high reliability of performance in complex environments is addressed in E. Roth, J. Multer and T. Raslear, "Shared Situation Awareness as a Contributor to High Reliability Performance in Railroad Operations," Organization Studies 27, no. 7 J20Q6I: 967-987: see also K.H. Roberts, "Some Characteristics of One Type of High Reliability Organization," Organization Science 1, no. 2 (1990): 160-176.

14. K.H. Roberts, "Managing High Reliability Organizations," California Management Review 32 (1990): 101-113; G.A. Bigfey and K.H. Roberts, "The Incident Command System: High-Reliability Organizing for Complex and Volatile Task Environments," Academy of Management Journal 44, no. 61 (2001): 1281-1299; E. Hutchins and T. Klausen, "Distributed Cognition in an Airline Cockpit," in "Cognition and Communication at Work," eds. D. Middleton and Y. Engstrom (Cambridge, U.K.: Cambridge University Press, 1996); and K.E. Weick and K.H. Roberts, "Collective Mind in Organizations: Heedful Interrelating on Flight Decks," Administrative Science Quarterly 38 (1993): 357-381.

15. F.K. Boersma, "The Organization of Industrial Research as a Network Activity: Agricultural Research at Philips in the 1930s," Business History Review 78, no. 2 (2004): 255-72; F.K. Boersma, "Structural Ways to Embed a Research Laboratory Into the Company: A Comparison Between Philips end General Electric 1900-1940," History and Technology 19, no. 2 (2003): 109-126.

16. M.W. Dupree, book review of L. Galambos and J.E. Sewell, "Networks of Innovation: Vaccine Development at Merck, Sharp & Dohme, and Mulford, 1895-1995," Business History, Oct. 1, 1997.

17. A classic philosophical treatment of different approaches to gathering and interpreting information is C.W. Churchman's book "The Design of Inquiring Systems" (New York Basic Books, 1971).

18. Sir Kevin Tebbit, interview with authors; also, see P. Bose, "Alexander the Great's Art of Strategy" (New York: Gotham Books, Penguin Group [USA] Inc., 2003).

19. From a brief discussion of the book in Wired, www.wired.com/wired/archive/12.06/pr.html.

20. For more detail on the case, see PJ.H. Schoemaker, "Profiting from Uncertainty" (New York: Free Press, 2002)

21. Royal Dutch Shell used scenario planning as a learning process to help reveal the implicit mental models in its organization. This form of institutional learning can be seen as a way for management teams to "change their shared models of their company, their markets and their competitors." A.P. de Geus, "Planning as Learning," Harvard Business Review 66 (March-April 1988): 70-74.

22. This was the original title of an internal Shell paper by Pierre Wack, the main founder of Shell's approach to scenario planning. The paper was later revised and published as two articles: P. Wack, "Scenarios: Uncharted Waters Ahead," Harvard Business Review 63, no. 5 (September-October 1985): 73-89; and P. Wack, "Scenarios: Shooting the Rapids," Harvard Business Review 63, no. 6 (November-December 1985): 139-150.

23. L. Bossidy and R. Charan. "Confronting Reality, " Fortune, Oct. 18, 2004, 225-229, excerpted from "Confronting Reality; Doing What Matters to Get Things Right" (New York: Crown Business, 2004).

24. K.A. Jehn, "A Multimethod Examination of the Benefits and Detriments of Intragroup Conflict," Administrative Science Quarterly 40, no. 2 (June 1995): 256-282. For an excellent discussion of management conflict and performance, see K.M. Eisenhardt, J.L. Kahwajy and L.J. Bourgeois III, "Conflict and Strategic Choice: How Top Management Teams Disagree," California Management Review 39, no. 2 (winter 1997): 42-62.

25. G. Morgenson "How the Thundering Herd Faltered and Fell," New York Times, Sunday, Nov. 9, 2008.

26. G. Klein, "Sources of Power" (Cambridge, Massachusetts: MIT Press, 1998); also see R.M. Hogarth,

"Educating Intuition" (Chicago: University of Chicago Press, 2001).

27. V. Barabba, "Surviving Transformation: Lessons from GM's Surprising Turnaround" (New York: Oxford University Press, 2004).

28. These unmet needs were identified in a study by Wirthlin Worldwide Inc. through two measures—the importance consumers placed on key factors that influenced their buying decisions and their current level of satisfaction with these factors.

29. This example is more fully discussed in P.J.H. Schoemaker and MV. Mavaddat "Scenario Planning for Disruptive Technologies," chap. 10 in eds. G. Day and P.J.H. Schoemaker. "Wharton, on Managing Emerging Technologies" (New York: Wiley, 2000).

30. See M. Neugarten, "Seeing and Noticing: An Optical Perspective on Competitive Intelligence," Journal of Competitive Intelligence and Management 1, no. 1 (spring 2003): 93-104.

CHAPTER 5

Wikinomics

The Art and Science of Peer Production

Don Tapscott

University of Toronto

Anthony D. Williams

London School of Economics

Don Tapscott

University of Toronto

Anthony D. Williams

London School of Economics

I t was late in the afternoon, on a typically harsh Canadian winter day, as Rob McEwen, the CEO of Goldcorp Inc., stood at the head of the boardroom table confronting a room full of senior geologists. The news he was about to deliver was not good. In fact it was disastrous, and McEwen was having a hard time shielding his frustration.

The small Toronto-based gold-mining firm was struggling, besieged by strikes, lingering debts, and an exceedingly high cost of production, which had caused them to cease mining operations. Conditions in the marketplace were hardly favorable. The gold market was contracting, and most analysts assumed that the company's fifty-year-old mine in Red Lake, Ontario, was dying. Without evidence of substantial new gold deposits, the mine seemed destined for closure, and Goldcorp was likely to go down with it.

Tensions were running at fever pitch. McEwen had no real experience in the extractive industries, let alone in gold mining. Nevertheless, as an adventurous young mutual fund manager he had gotten involved in a takeover battle and emerged as Goldcorp Inc.'s majority owner. Few people in the room had much confidence that McEwen was the right person to rescue the company. But McEwen just shrugged off his critics.

He turned to his geologists and said, "We're going to find more gold on this property, and we won't leave this room tonight until we have a plan to find it." At the conclusion of the meeting he handed his geologists $10 million for further exploration and sent them packing for Northern Ontario.

Most of his staff thought he was crazy but they carried out his instruction, drilling in the deepest and most remote parts of the mine. Amazingly, a few weeks later they arrived back at Goldcorp headquarters beaming with pride and bearing a remarkable discovery: Test drilling suggested rich deposits of new gold, as much as thirty times the amount Goldcorp was currently mining!

The discovery was surprising, and could hardly have been better timed. But after years of further exploration, and to McEwen's deep frustration, the company's geologists struggled to provide an accurate estimate of the gold's value and exact location. He desperately needed to inject the urgency of the market into the glacial processes of an old-economy industry.

In 1999, with the future still uncertain, McEwen took some time out for personal development. He wound up at an MIT conference for young presidents when coincidentally the subject of Linux came up. Perched in the lecture hall, McEwen listened intently to the remarkable story of how Linus Torvalds and a loose volunteer brigade of software developers had assembled the world-class computer operating system over the Internet. The lecturer explained how Torvalds revealed his code to the world, allowing thousands of anonymous programmers to vet it and make contributions of their own.

McEwen had an epiphany and sat back in his chair to contemplate. If Goldcorp employees couldn't find the Red Lake gold, maybe someone else could. And maybe the key to finding those people was to open up the exploration process in the same way Torvalds "open sourced" Linux.

McEwen raced back to Toronto to present the idea to his head geologist. "I'd like to take all of our geology, all the data we have that goes back to 1948, and put it into a file and share it with the world," he said. "Then we'll ask the world to tell us where we're going to find the next six million ounces of gold." McEwen saw this as an opportunity to harness some of the best minds in the industry. Perhaps understandably, the in-house geologists were just a little skeptical.

Mining is an intensely secretive industry, and apart from the minerals themselves, geological data is the most precious and carefully guarded resource. It's like the Cadbury secret—it's just not something companies go around sharing. Goldcorp employees wondered whether the global community of geologists would respond to Goldcorp's call in the same way that software developers rallied around Linus Torvalds. Moreover, they worried about how the contest would reflect on them and their inability to find the elusive gold deposits.

McEwen acknowledges in retrospect that the strategy was controversial and risky. "We were attacking a fundamental assumption; you simply don't give away proprietary data," he said. "It's so fundamental," he adds, "that no one had ever questioned it." Once again, McEwen was determined to soldier on.

In March 2000, the "Goldcorp Challenge" was launched with a total of $575,000 in prize money available to participants with the best methods and estimates. Every scrap of information (some four hundred megabytes worth) about the 55,000-acre property was revealed on Goldcorp's Web site. News of the contest spread quickly around the Internet, as more than one thousand virtual prospectors from fifty countries got busy crunching the data.

Within weeks, submissions from around the world came flooding in to Goldcorp headquarters. As expected, geologists got involved. But entries came from surprising sources, including graduate students, consultants, mathematicians, and military officers, all seeking a piece of the action. "We had applied math, advanced physics, intelligent systems, computer graphics, and organic solutions to inorganic problems. There were capabilities I had never seen before in the industry," says McEwen. "When I saw the computer graphics I almost fell out of my chair." The contestants had identified 110 targets on the Red Lake property, 50 percent of which had not been previously identified by the company. Over 80 percent of the new targets yielded substantial quantities of gold. In fact, since the challenge was initiated an astounding eight million ounces of gold have been found. McEwen estimates the collaborative process shaved two to three years off their exploration time.

Today Goldcorp is reaping the fruits of its open source approach to exploration. Not only did the contest yield copious quantities of gold, it catapulted his underperforming $100 million company into a $9 billion juggernaut while transforming a backward mining site in Northern Ontario into one of the most innovative and profitable properties in the industry. Needless to say McEwen is one happy camper. As are his shareholders.

One hundred dollars invested in the company in 1993 is worth over $3,000 today.

Perhaps the most lasting legacy of the Goldcorp Challenge is the validation of an ingenious approach to exploration in what remains a conservative and highly secretive industry. Rob McEwen bucked an industry trend by sharing the company's proprietary data and simultaneously transformed a lumbering exploration process into a modern distributed gold discovery engine that harnessed some of the most talented minds in the field.

McEwen saw things differently. He realized the uniquely qualified minds to make new discoveries were probably outside the boundaries of his organization, and by sharing some intellectual property he could harness the power of collective genius and capability. In doing so he stumbled successfully into the future of innovation, business, and how wealth and just about everything else will be created. Welcome to the new world of wikinomics, where collaboration on a mass scale is set to change every institution in society.

The New World of Wikinomics

Due to deep changes in technology, demographics, business, the economy, and the world, we are entering a new age where people participate in the economy like never before. This new participation has reached a tipping point where new forms of mass collaboration are changing how goods and services are invented, produced, marketed, and distributed on a global basis. This change presents far-reaching opportunities for every company and for every person who gets connected.

In the past, collaboration was mostly small scale. It was something that took place among relatives, friends, and associates in households, communities, and workplaces. In relatively rare instances, collaboration approached mass scale, but this was mainly in short bursts of political action. Think of the Vietnam-era war protests or, more recently, about the raucous antiglobalization rallies in Seattle, Turin, and Washington. Never before, however, have individuals had the power or opportunity to link up in loose networks of peers to produce goods and services in a very tangible and ongoing way.

Most people were confined to relatively limited economic roles, whether as passive consumers of mass-produced products or employees trapped deep within organizational bureaucracies where the boss told them what to do. Even their elected representatives barely concealed their contempt for bottom-up participation in decision making. In all, too many people were bypassed in the circulation of knowledge, power, and capital, and thus participated at the economy's margins.

Today the tables are turning. The growing accessibility of information technologies puts the tools required to collaborate, create value, and compete at everybody's fingertips. This liberates people to participate in innovation and wealth creation within every sector of the economy. Millions of people already join forces in self-organized collaborations that produce dynamic new goods and services that rival those of the world's largest and best-financed enterprises. This new mode of innovation and value creation is called "peer production," or *peering*—which describes what happens when masses of people and firms collaborate openly to drive innovation and growth in their industries.[1]

Some examples of peer production have recently become household names. As of August 2006, the online networking extravaganza MySpace had one hundred million users—growing a half a million a week—whose personal musings, connections, and profiles are the primary engines of value creation on the site. MySpace, YouTube, Linux, and Wikipedia—today's exemplars of mass collaboration—are just the beginning; a few familiar characters in the opening pages of the first chapter in a long-running saga that will change many aspects of how the economy operates.

Age of Participation

Call them the "weapons of mass collaboration." New low-cost collaborative infrastructures—from free Internet telephony to open source software to global outsourcing platforms—allow thousands upon thousands of individuals and small producers to cocreate products, access markets, and delight customers in ways that only large corporations could manage in the past. This is giving rise to new collaborative capabilities and business models that will empower the prepared firm and destroy those that fail to adjust.

The upheaval occurring right now in media and entertainment provides an early example of how mass collaboration is turning the economy upside down Once a bastion of "professionalism," credentialed knowledge producers share the stage with "amateur" creators who are disrupting every activity they touch. Tens of millions of people share their news, information, and views in the blogosphere, a self-organized. network of over 50 million personal commentary sites that are updated every second of the day.[2] Some of the largest weblogs (or blogs for short) receive a half a million daily visitors,[3] rivaling some daily newspapers. Now audioblogs, podcasts, and mobile photo blogs are adding to a dynamic, up-to-the-minute stream of person-to-person news and information delivered free over the Web.

Individuals now share knowledge, computing power, bandwidth, and other resources to create a wide array of free and open source goods and services that anyone can use or modify. What's more, people can contribute to the "digital commons" at very little cost to themselves, which makes collective action much more attractive. Indeed, peer production is a very social activity. All one needs is a computer, a network connection, and a bright spark of initiative and creativity to join in the economy.

These new collaborations will not only serve commercial interests, they will help people do public-spirited things like cure genetic diseases, predict global climate change, and find new planets and stars. Researchers at Olson Laboratory, for example, use a massive supercomputer to evaluate drug candidates that might one day cure AIDS. This is no ordinary supercomputer, however. Their FightAIDS@home initiative is part of the World Community Grid, a global network where millions of individual computer users donate their spare computing power via the Internet to form one of the world's most powerful computing platforms.

These changes, among others, are ushering us toward a world where knowledge, power, and productive capability will be more dispersed than at any time in our history—a world where value creation will be fast, fluid, and persistently disruptive. A world where only the connected will survive. A power shift is underway, and a tough new business rule is emerging: Harness the new collaboration or perish. Those who fail to grasp this will find themselves ever more isolated—cut off from the networks that are sharing, adapting, and updating knowledge to create value.

This might sound like hyperbole, but it's not. Consider some additional ways ordinary citizens can now participate in the global body économique.

Rather than just read a book, you can write one. Just log on to Wikipedia—a collaboratively created encyclopedia, owned by no one and authored by tens of thousands of enthusiasts. With five full-time employees, it is ten times bigger than *Encyclopedia Britannica* and roughly the same in accuracy.[4] It runs on a *wiki*, software that enables users to edit the content of Web pages. Despite the risks inherent in an open encyclopedia in which everyone can add their views, and constant battles with detractors and saboteurs, Wikipedia continues to grow rapidly in scope, quality, and traffic. The English-language version has more than a million entries, and there are 92 sister sites in languages ranging from Polish and Japanese to Hebrew and Catalan.

Or perhaps your thing is chemistry. Indeed, if you're a retired, unemployed, or aspiring chemist, Procter & Gamble needs your help. The pace of innovation has doubled in its industry in the past five years alone, and now its army of 7,500 researchers is no longer enough to sustain its lead. Rather than hire more researchers, CEO A. G. Lafley instructed business unit leaders to source 50 percent of their new product and service ideas from outside the company. Now you can work for P&G without being on their payroll. Just register on the InnoCentive network where you and ninety thousand other scientists around the world can help solve tough R&D problems for a cash reward. InnoCentive is only one of many revolutionary marketplaces matching scientists to R&D challenges presented by companies in search of innovation. P&G and thousands of other companies look to these marketplaces for ideas, invention, and uniquely qualified minds that can unlock new value in their markets.

Media buffs are similarly empowered. Rather than consume the TV news, you can now create it, along with thousands of independent citizen journalists who are turning the profession upside down. Tired of the familiar old faces and blather on network news? Turn off your TV, pick up a video camera and some cheap editing software, and create a news feature for Current TV, a new national cable and satellite network created almost entirely by amateur contributors. Though the contributors are unpaid volunteers, the content is surprisingly good. Current TV provides online tutorials for camera operation and storytelling techniques, and their guidelines for creating stories help get participants started. Viewers vote on which stories go to air, so only the most engaging material makes prime time.

Finally, a young person in India, China, Brazil, or any one of a number of emerging Eastern European countries can now do what their parents only dreamed of by joining the global economy on equal footing. You might be in a call center in Bangalore that takes food orders for a drive-through restaurant in Los Angeles. Or you could find yourself working in Foxconn's new corporate city in the Schenzen province of China, where a decade ago farmers tilled the land with oxen. Today 180,000 people work, live, learn, and play on Foxconn's massive high-tech campus, designing and building consumer electronics for teenagers around the globe.

For incumbents in every industry this new cornucopia of participation and collaboration is both exhilarating and alarming. As New Paradigm executive David Ticoll argues, "Not all examples of self-organization are benign, or exploitable. Within a single industry the development of opportunities for self-organized collaboration can be beneficial, neutral, or highly competitive to individual firms, or some combination of at least two of these." Publishers found this out the hard way. Blogs, wikis, chat rooms, search engines, advertising auctions, peer-to-peer downloading, and personal broadcasting represent new ways to entertain, communicate, and transact. In each instance the traditionally passive buyers of editorial and advertising take active, participatory roles in value creation. Some of these grassroots innovations pose dire threats to existing business models.

Publishers of music, literature, movies, software, and television are like proverbial canaries in a coal mine—the first casualties of a revolution that is sweeping across all industries. Many enfeebled titans of the industrial economy feel threatened. Despite heroic efforts to change, they remain shackled by command-and-control legacies. Companies have spent the last three decades remolding their operations to compete in a hyper-competitive economy—ripping costs out of their businesses at every opportunity; trying to become more "customer-friendly"; assembling global production

networks; and scattering their bricks-and-mortar R&D organizations around the world.

Now, to great chagrin, industrial-era titans are learning that the real revolution is just getting started. Except this time the competition is no longer their arch industry rivals; it's the uberconnected, amorphous mass of self-organized individuals that is gripping their economic needs firmly in one hand, and their economic destinies in the other. "We the people" is no longer just a political expression—a hopeful ode to the power of "the masses"—it's also an apt description of how ordinary people, as employees, consumers, community members, and taxpayers now have the power to innovate and to create value on the global stage.

For smart companies, the rising tide of mass collaboration offers vast opportunity. As the Goldcorp story denotes, even the oldest of old economy industries can harness this revolution to create value in unconventional ways. Companies can reach beyond their walls to sow the seeds of innovation and harvest a bountiful crop. Indeed, firms that cultivate nimble, trust-based relationships with external collaborators are positioned to form vibrant business ecosystems that create value more effectively than hierarchically organized businesses.

For individuals and small producers, this may be the birth of a new era, perhaps even a golden one, on par with the Italian renaissance or the rise of Athenian democracy. Mass collaboration across borders, disciplines, and cultures is at once economical and enjoyable. We can peer produce an operating system, an encyclopedia, the media, a mutual fund, and even physical things like a motorcycle. We are becoming an economy unto ourselves—a vast global network of specialized producers that swap and exchange services for entertainment, sustenance, and learning. A new economic democracy is emerging in which we all have a lead role.

Promise and Peril

Experience shows that the first wave of Internet-enabled change was tainted by irrational exuberance, A sober analysis of today's trends reveals that this new participation is both a blessing and a curse. Mass collaboration can empower a growing cohort of connected individuals and organizations to create extraordinary wealth and reach unprecedented heights in learning and scientific discovery. If we are wise, we will harness this capability to create opportunities for everyone and to carefully steward the planet's natural resources. But the new participation will also cause great upheaval, dislocation and danger for societies, corporations, and individuals that fail to keep up with relentless change.

As with all previous economic revolutions, the demands on individuals, organizations, and nations will be intense, and at times traumatic, as old industries and ways of life give way to new processes, technologies, and business models. The playing field has been ripped wide open, and the recurrent need to reconfigure people and capabilities to serve an ever changing market will require individuals to embrace constant change and renewal in their careers.

As recent events foretell, a smaller, more open and interdependent world has the potential to be dynamic and vibrant, but also more vulnerable to terrorism and criminal networks. Just as the masses of scientists and software coders can collaborate on socially beneficial projects, criminals and terrorists can conspire over the Internet to wreak havoc on our daily existence.

Even with good intentions, mass collaboration is certainly no panacea. When people organize en masse to create goods, services, and entertainment they create new challenges as well as opportunities. Renowned computer scientist, composer, and author Jaron Lanier worries that collaborative communities such as flickr, MySpace, and Wikipedia represent a new form of "online collectivism" that is suffocating authentic voices in a muddled and anonymous tide of mass mediocrity. Lanier laments the idea that "the collective is all-wise," or as he put it, "that it is desirable to have influence concentrated in a bottleneck that can channel the collective with the most verity and force." He rightly points out that such ideas have had terrible consequences when imposed by ruthless dictators like Stalin or Pol Pot. But his argument runs afoul when he attributes the same kind of "collective stupidity" to the emerging forms of mass collaboration on the Web.

Other wise and thoughtful people such as Microsoft's Bill Gates, meanwhile, complain that the incentives for knowledge producers are disappearing in a world where individuals can pool their talents to create free goods that compete with proprietary marketplace offerings. Gates cites the movement to assemble a global "creative commons" that contains large bodies of scientific and cultural content as a potential threat to the ability to make profits in knowledge-based industries such as software. Many top executives are lining up alongside Gates to harpoon what they see as newfangled "communists" in various guises.

Reactionary sentiments are hardly surprising, given the circumstances. The production of knowledge, goods, and services is becoming a collaborative activity in which growing numbers of people can participate. This threatens to displace entrenched interests that have prospered under the protection of various barriers to entry, including the high costs of obtaining the financial, physical, and human capital necessary to compete. Companies accustomed to comfortably directing marketplace activities must contend with new and unfamiliar sources of competition, including the self-organized masses, just as people in elite positions (whether journalists, professors, pundits, or politicians) must now work harder to justify their exalted status. As the global division of labor becomes ever more complex, variegated, and dynamic, the economy is spinning out of the control of the usual suspects. There will be casualties, but the winners will outnumber the losers. Indeed, we believe the new era heralds more economic opportunity for individuals and businesses, and greater efficiency, creativity, and innovation throughout the economy as a whole.

Though we disagree with Lanier and Gates, they do raise important issues that need to be addressed. For now it must be said that mass collaboration and peer production are really the polar opposites of the communism that Gates and Lanier despise. Digital pioneer Howard Rheingold points out, "Collectivism involves coercion and centralized control; collective action involves freely chosen self-selection and distributed coordination." Whereas communism stifled individualism, mass collaboration is based on individuals and companies employing widely distributed computation and communication technologies to achieve shared outcomes through loose voluntary associations.

What's more, the participation revolution now underway opens up new possibilities for billions of people to play active roles in their workplaces, communities, national democracies, and the global economy at large. This has profound social benefits, including the opportunity to make governments more accountable and lift millions of people out of poverty.

Moreover, it is wrong to assume that the new collective action represents only a threat to established businesses. While some fear mass collaboration will reduce the proportion of our economy that is available for profitable activity and wealth creation, we will show the opposite. New models of peer production can bring the prepared manager rich new possibilities to unlock innovative potential in a wide range of resources that thrive inside and outside the firm. With the right approach, companies can obtain higher rates of growth and innovation by learning how to engage and cocreate with a dynamic and increasingly global network of peers, Rather than conceding defeat to the most powerful economic force of our times, established companies can harness the new collaboration for unparalleled success.

A new art and science of collaboration is emerging—we call it *wikinomics*. We're not just talking about creating online encyclopedias and other documents. A wiki is more than just software for enabling multiple people to edit Web sites. It is a metaphor for a new era of collaboration and participation, one that, as Dylan sings, "will soon shake your windows and rattle your walls." The times are, in fact, a changin'.

The New Promise of Collaboration

Word association test: What's the first thing that comes to mind when you hear the word *collaboration?* If you're like most people, you conjure up images of people working together happily and productively. In everyday life, we collaborate with fellow parents at a PTA meeting, with other students on a class project, or with neighbors to protect and enhance our communities. In business we collaborate with coworkers at the office, with partners in the supply chain, and within teams that traverse departmental and organizational silos. We collaborate on research projects, work together to make a big sale, or plan a new marketing campaign.

Google CEO Eric Schmidt says, "When you say 'collaboration,' the average forty-five-year-old thinks they know what you're talking about—teams sitting down, having a nice conversation with nice objectives and a

nice attitude. That's what collaboration means to most people."

We're talking about something dramatically different. The new promise of collaboration is that with peer production we will harness human skill, ingenuity, and intelligence more efficiently and effectively than anything we have witnessed previously. Sounds like a tall order. But the collective knowledge, capability, and resources embodied within broad horizontal networks of participants can be mobilized to accomplish much more than one firm acting alone. Whether designing an airplane, assembling a motorcycle, or analyzing the human genome, the ability to integrate the talents of dispersed individuals and organizations is becoming the defining competency for managers and firms. And in the years to come this new mode of peer production will displace traditional corporation hierarchies as the key engine of wealth creation in the economy.

A variety of social, economic, and demographic forces are fueling the rising tide of mass collaboration. More than anything, however, the evolution of the Internet is driving this new age. From the stunning increases in computing power, network capability, and reach, to the growing accessibility of the tools required to get organized, create value, and compete, this new Web has opened the floodgates to a worldwide explosion of participation.

There are many names for this new Web: the Web 2.0, the living Web, the Hypernet, the active Web, the read/write Web.[5] Call it what you like—the sentiment is the same. We're all participating in the rise of a global, ubiquitous platform for computation and collaboration that is reshaping nearly every aspect of human affairs. While the old Web was about Web sites, clicks, and "eyeballs," the new Web is about the communities, participation, and peering. As users and computing power multiply, and easy-to-use tools proliferate, the Internet is evolving into a global, living, networked computer that anyone can program. Even the simple act of participating in an online community makes a contribution to the new digital commons—whether one's building a business on Amazon or producing a video clip for YouTube, creating a community around his or her flickr photo collection or editing the astronomy entry on Wikipedia.

This new Web already links more than a billion people directly and (unlike Web 1.0) is reaching out to the physical world, connecting countless invert objects, from hotel doors to cars. It is beginning to deliver dynamic new services—from free long-distance video telephony to remote brain surgery. And it covers the planet like a skin, uniting a machine soldering chips onto circuit boards in Singapore with a chip warehouse in Denver, Colorado.

Twenty years from now we will look back at this period of the early 21st century as a critical turning point in economic and social history. We will understand that we entered a new age, one based on new principles, worldviews, and business models, where the nature of the game was changed.

The pace of change and the evolving demands of customers are such that firms can no longer depend only on internal capabilities to meet external needs. Nor can they depend only on tightly coupled relationships with a handful of business partners to keep up with customer desires for speed, innovation, and control. Instead, firms must engage and cocreate in a dynamic fashion with everyone—partners, competitors, educators, government, and, most of all, customers.

To innovate and succeed, the new mass collaboration must become part of every leader's playbook and lexicon. Learning how to engage and cocreate with a shifting set of self-organized partners is becoming an essential skill, as important as budgeting, R&D, and planning.

The Principles of Wikinomics

The new mass collaboration is changing how companies and societies harness knowledge and capability to innovate and create value. This affects just about every sector of society and every aspect of management. A new kind of business is emerging—one that opens its doors to the world, co-innovates with everyone (especially customers), shares resources that were previously closely guarded, harnesses the power of mass collaboration, and behaves not as a multinational but as something new, a truly global firm. These companies are driving important changes in their industries and rewriting many rules of competition.

Now compare this to traditional business thinking. Conventional wisdom says companies innovate, differentiate, and compete by doing certain things right: by having superior human capital; protecting their intellectual property fiercely; focusing on customers; thinking globally but acting locally, and by executing well (i.e., having good management and controls). But the new business world is rendering each of these principles insufficient, and in some cases, completely inappropriate.

The new art and science of wikinomics is based on four powerful new ideas: openness, peering, sharing, and acting globally. These new principles are replacing some of the old tenets of business.

Being Open

If you consider the vernacular, the term *open* is loaded—rich with meaning and positive connotations. Among other things, openness is associated with candor, transparency, freedom, flexibility, expansiveness, engagement and access. Open, however, is not an adjective often used to describe the traditional firm, and until recently, open would not have appropriately described the inner workings of the economy either. Recently, smart companies have been rethinking openness, and this is beginning to affect a number of important functions, including human resources, innovation, industry standards, and communications.

Companies were closed in their attitudes toward networking, sharing, and encouraging self-organization, in large part because conventional wisdom says that companies compete by holding their most coveted resources close to their chest. When it came to managing human resources, firms were exhorted to hire the best people, and to motivate, develop, and retain them, since human capital is the foundation of competitiveness. Today, companies that make their boundaries porous to external ideas and human capital outperform companies that rely solely on their internal resources and capabilities.

Rapid scientific and technological advances are among the key reasons why this new openness is surfacing as a new imperative for managers. Most business can barely manage to research the fundamental disciplines that contribute to their products, let alone retain the field's most talented people within their boundaries. So to ensure they remain at the forefront of their industries, companies must increasingly open their doors to the global talent pool that thrives outside their walls.[6]

Standards are another area where openness is gaining momentum. In today's complex and fast-moving economy, the economic deficiencies and liabilities caused by the lack of standardization surface faster, and they are more jarring and consequential than in the past. For years the information technology (IT) industry fiercely fought concepts like open systems and open source. But in the last decade there has been a stampede toward open standards, in part because customers are demanding them. Customers were fed up with being locked into each vendor's architecture, where applications were islands and not portable to another vendor's hardware. Microsoft reaped huge revenues as the provider of a standard platform on which software companies could build their applications, regardless of the brand name on the computers. The shift to openness gained momentum as IT professionals began to collaborate on a wide range of open software platforms. The result was Apache for Web servers, Linux for operating systems, MySQL for databases, Firefox for browsers, and the World Wide Web itself.

Yet another kind of openness is exploding: the communication of previously secret corporate information to partners, employees, customers and shareholders, and other interested participants. Transparency— the disclosure of pertinent information—is a growing force in the networked economy. This goes far beyond the obligation to comply with laws regarding the disclosure of financial information. This is not about the Securities and Exchange Commission (SEC), Sarbanes-Oxley, Eliot Spitzer, or avoiding the "perp walk." Rather, people and institutions that interact with firms are gaining unprecedented access to important information about corporate behavior, operations, and performance. Armed with new tools to find out, inform others, and self-organize, stakeholders are scrutinizing the firm like never before.

Customers can see the true value of products better. Employees have previously unthinkable knowledge about their firm's strategy, management and challenges. Partners must have intimate knowledge about each other's operations to collaborate. Powerful institutional investors who now own or manage most wealth are developing x-ray vision. And in a world of instant communications, whistle-blowers, inquisitive media, and Googling, citizens and communities can easily put firms under the microscope.

Leading firms are opening up pertinent information to all these groups—because they reap significant benefits from doing so. Rather than something to be feared, transparency is a powerful new force for business success. Smart firms embrace transparency and are actively open. Our research shows that transparency is critical to business partnerships, lowering transaction costs between firms and speeding up the metabolism of business webs. Employees of open enterprises have higher trust among each other and with the firm, resulting in lower costs, better innovation, and loyalty. And when companies like Progressive Insurance are open with customers—honestly sharing both their prices and their competitors even when they are not as good—customers respond by giving their trust.[7]

Finally, it's worth noting that the economy and society are open in new ways too. Falling trade barriers and information technologies are often cited as key reasons why dozens of highly competitive countries have entered the global economy for the first time, but take education as another important example. Today an aspiring student in Mumbai who has always dreamed of going to MIT can now access the university's entire curriculum online without paying a penny in tuition fees. She can just log on to ocw.mit.edu, and she will read "Welcome to MIT's OpenCourseware: a free and open educational resource (OER) for educators, students, and self-learners around the world. MIT OpenCourseWare (MIT OCW) supports MIT's mission to advance knowledge and education, and serve the world in the 21st century." She can engage with the content and faculty of one of the world's leading universities, studying everything from aeronautics to zoology. Download the readings and assignments for courses. Share her experiences in one of the community forums. Become part of MIT, participating in lifelong learning for the global knowledge economy.

Peering

Throughout most of human history, hierarchies of one form or another have served as the primary engines of wealth creation and provided a model for institutions such as the church, the military, and government. So pervasive and enduring has the hierarchical mode of organization been that most people assume that there are no viable alternatives. Whether the ancient slave empires of Greece, Rome, China, and the Americas, the feudal kingdoms that later covered the planet, or the capitalist corporation, hierarchies have organized people into layers of superiors and subordinates to fulfill both public and private objectives. Even the management literature today that advocates empowerment, teams, and enlightened management techniques takes as a basic premise the command modus operandi inherent in the modern corporation. Though it is unlikely that hierarchies will disappear in the foreseeable future, a new form of horizontal organization is emerging that rivals the hierarchical firm in its capacity to create information based products and services, and in some cases, physical things. As mentioned, this new form of organization is known as peering.

The quintessential example of peering is Linux, which we introduced briefly during the Goldcorp story. While the basic facts of Linux are well known in the technology community, they are not known by all, so allow us to briefly recap the story. In 1991, before the World Wide Web had even been invented, a young programmer from Helsinki named Linus Torvalds created a simple version of the Unix operating system. He called it Linux and shared it with other programmers via an online bulletin board. Of the first ten programmers who corresponded with him, five made substantive changes. Torvalds eventually decided to license the operating system under a general public license (GPL) so that anyone could use it for free, provided they made their changes to the program available to others. Over time an informal organization emerged to manage ongoing development of the software that continues to harness inputs from thousands of volunteer programmers. Because it was reliable and free, Linux became a useful operating system for computers hosting Web servers, and ultimately databases, and today many companies consider Linux an enterprise software keystone.

Today the growing ease with which people can collaborate opens up the economy to new Linux-like projects everyday. People increasingly self-organize to design goods or services, create knowledge, or simply produce dynamic, shared experiences. A growing number of examples suggest that peer-to-peer models of organizing economic activity are making inroads into areas that go well beyond creating software. Take two examples for starters.

Researchers at the Australian biotech institute CAMBIA worry that patents owned by multinational firms such as Monsanto are compromising billions of people who can't afford the licensing fees to exploit genetically modified crops. So CAMBIA researchers who are working on solutions to the challenges of food security and agricultural productivity release their results publicly under BiOS (Biological Open Source Licenses). This way they engage a much wider pool of talented scientists in the process of getting solutions to farmers who need them.

Marketocracy employs a similar form of peering in a mutual fund that harnesses the collective intelligence of the investment community. It has recruited seventy thousand traders to manage virtual stock portfolios in a competition to become the best investors. Marketocracy indexes the top one hundred performers, and their trading strategies are emulated in a mutual fund that consistently outperforms the S&P 500. Though not strictly open source, it is an example of how meritocratic, peer-to-peer models are seeping into an industry where conventional wisdom favors the lone superstar stock adviser.

These cases are tangible examples of a new mode of production that is emerging in the heart of the most advanced economies in the world—producing a rich new economic landscape and challenging our basic assumption about human motivation and behavior. In some cases, self-organized "nonmarket" production is moving into arenas that used to be dominated by profit-making firms. Wikipedia, with its free online encyclopedia, is one example where a once vibrant publishing industry is suffering. At the same time, powerful new economic ecosystems are forming on top of shared infrastructures and resources like Linux. Though Linux is free to use or modify, it has been embedded in all kinds of profitable products and services developed by large companies like BMW, IBM, Motorola, Philips, and Sony.

Participants in peer production communities have many different motivations for jumping in, from fun and altruism to achieving something that is of direct value to them. Though egalitarianism is the general rule, most peer networks have an underlying structure, where some people have more authority and influence than others. But the basic rules of operation are about as different from a corporate command-and-control hierarchy as the latter was from the feudal craft shop of the preindustrial economy.

Peering succeeds because it leverages self-organization—a style of production that works more effectively than hierarchical management for certain tasks. Its greatest impact today is in the production of information goods—its initial effects are most visible in the production of software, media, entertainment, and culture—but there are few reasons for peer production to stop there. Why not open source government? Could we make better decisions if we were to tap the insights of a broader and more representative body of participants? Or perhaps we could apply peer production to physical objects like cars, airplanes, and motorcycles. As we will discover in later chapters, these are not idle fantasies, but real opportunities that the new world of wikinomics makes possible.

Sharing

Conventional wisdom says you should control and protect proprietary resource and innovation—especially intellectual property—through patents, copyright and trademarks. If someone infringes your IP, get the lawyers out to do battle. Many industries still think this way. Millions of technology-literate kids and teenagers use the Internet to freely create and share MP3 software tools and music. Digital music presents a huge opportunity to place artists and consumers at the center of a vast web of value creation. But rather than embrace MP3 and adopt new business models, the industry has adopted a defensive posture. Obsession with control, piracy, and proprietary standards on the part of large industry players has only served to further alienate and anger music listeners.

No doubt digitization introduces tough new appropriation problems for the creators of digital content. Digital inventions are easy to share, remix, and repurpose, and just as easy to replicate. On the plus side, this means industries with zero marginal cost (i.e., software and digital entertainment) can gain incredible economies of scale. But if your invention can be replicated at no cost, why should anyone pay? And if no one pays, how do you recoup your fixed-cost investment?

Hollywood's proposed solution is to expand the scope and vigor of IP protection. New digital rights management technologies make knowledge and content more excludable—information can be metered, consumer behavior can be controlled, and owners of intellectual property can extract a fee for access. Walled gardens of content, proprietary databases, closed-source software: They all promise healthy returns for knowledge producers. But at the same time, they all restrict access to the essential tools of a knowledge-based economy. And worse, they shut out the real opportunities for customer-driven innovation and creativity that could spawn new business models and industries.

Today, a new economics of intellectual property is prevailing. Increasingly, and to a degree paradoxically, firms in electronics, biotechnology, and other fields find that maintaining and defending a proprietary system of intellectual property often cripples their ability to create value. Smart firms are treating intellectual property like a mutual fund—they manage a balanced portfolio of IP assets, some protected and some shared.

For example, starting in 1999, more than a dozen pharmaceutical firms—hardly what one would call modern-day communists—abandoned their proprietary R&D projects to support open collaborations such as the SNP Consortium and the Alliance for Cellular Signaling. Both projects aggregate genetic information culled from biomedical research in publicly accessible databases. They also use their shared infrastructures to harness resources and insights from the for-profit and not-for-profit research worlds. These efforts are speeding the industry toward fundamental breakthroughs in molecular biology—breakthroughs that promise an era of personalized medicine and treatments for intractable disorders. Nobody gives up their potential patent rights over new end products, and by sharing some basic intellectual property the companies bring products to market more quickly.

This logic of sharing applies in virtually every industry. "Just as it's true that a rising tide lifts all boats," says Tim Bray, director of Web technologies at Sun Microsystems, "we genuinely believe that radical sharing is a win-win for everyone. Expanding markets create new opportunities." Under the right condition, the same could be said of most industries, whether automobiles or other consumer products.

Of course companies need to protect critical intellectual property. They should always protect their crown jewels, for example. But companies can't collaborate effectively if all of their IP is hidden. Contributing to the commons is not altruism; it's often the best way to build vibrant business ecosystems that harness a shared foundation of technology and knowledge to accelerate growth and innovation.

The power of sharing is not limited to intellectual property. It extends to other resources, such as computing power, bandwidth, content and scientific knowledge. Peer-to-peer sharing of computing power, for example, is bringing the telecommunications business to its knees. The cofounder and CEO of Skype, Niklas Zennstrom, says, "The idea of charging for telephone calls belongs to the last century." His company's software harnesses the collective computing power of peers, allowing them to speak with each other free of charge via the Internet. The result is a self-sustaining phone system that requires no central capital investment— just the willingness of its users to share.

The sky seems the limit for Skype. The Luxemberg-based company went from one hundred thousand to one hundred million registered users in two years, and was acquired by eBay for $2.6 billion in September 2005. The first time Michael Powell, then chairman of the Federal Communication Commission, used Skype, he concluded: "It's over. The world will change now inevitably."

Acting Globally

Consider life on the Galapagos Islands. Its separation from the rest of the world has resulted in a diverse collection of species, many found nowhere else on earth, yet each uniquely tailored to its environment. Now imagine what would happen if a teleportation device appeared on the Galapagos, thereby enabling resident animals to intermingle and roam freely among the islands. Surely the Galapagos would never be the same.

This thought experiment illustrates the consequences of the new era of globalization. The barriers between the Galapagos and the mainland are analogous to geographic and economic barriers that insulate firms and nations. When the insulation is removed, it cannot help but produce disruptive effects on business strategy, enterprise structures, the competitive landscape, and the global social and political order.

Thomas Friedman's book *The World Is Flat* brought the significance of the new globalization to many. But the quickening pace and deep consequences of globalization for innovation and wealth creation are not yet fully understood. In the last twenty years of globalization we have seen Chinese and Indian economic liberalization, the collapse of the Soviet Union, and the first stage of the worldwide information technology revolution. The next twenty years of globalization will help sustain world economic growth, raise world living standards, and substantially deepen global interdependence. At the same time, it will profoundly shake up the status quo almost everywhere—generating enormous economic, cultural, and political convulsions.[8]

On the economic front, the ongoing integration of national economies into a borderless world and the surprisingly fast and furious rise of new titans such as China, India, and South Korea will continue to broaden and flatten the playing field. Two billion more people from Asia and Eastern Europe are already joining the global workforce. And while developed countries worry about growing dependency ratios, most of the increase in world population and consumer demand will take place in today's developing nations—especially in China, India, and Indonesia.

The new globalization is both causing and caused by changes in collaboration and the way firms orchestrate capability to innovate and produce things. Staying globally competitive means monitoring business development internationally and tapping a much larger global talent pool.

Global alliances, human capital marketplaces, and peer production communities will provide access to new markets, ideas, and technologies. People and intellectual assets will need to be managed across cultures, disciplines, and organizational boundaries. Winning companies will need to know the world, including its markets, technologies, and peoples. Those that don't will find themselves handicapped, unable to compete in a business world that is unrecognizable by today's standards.

To do all this, it makes sense to not only *think* globally, as the mantra says, but to *act* globally as well. Managers in the trenches are finding out that acting globally is a tremendous operational challenge, especially when you're buried in legacy systems and processes. Ralph Szygenda, CIO of General Motors, says, "Most big companies are multinationals, not global, and increasingly that's a big problem for all of us."

Szygenda describes how GM grew up as a collection of separate companies. Each major brand, including Cadillac, Oldsmobile, and Buick, had separate staff, procedures, and agendas, and there was very little coordination among them. They might have found shelter under the same umbrella, but they were about as friendly as a group of strangers standing on a New York City sidewalk.

Like many multinationals, GM also was divided into geographically demarcated fiefdoms. Regional divisions had power and autonomy to develop, manufacture, and distribute cars according to local needs and by sourcing from local suppliers. For GM as a whole this federated structure came with immense and costly redundancies, as each division employed a full roster of local workers to take care of everything from manufacturing to human resources. Bob Lutz, GM's vice chairman of global product development, says that duplication of effort cost the company billions of dollars a year and prevented it from leveraging its size and scale.

In an increasingly global and competitive economy such redundancies are swiftly punished. So it pays to have global capabilities—including truly global workforces, unified global processes, and a global IT platform to enhance collaboration among all of the parts of the business as well as the company's web of external partners.

By definition, a truly global company has no physical or regional boundaries. It builds planetary ecosystems for designing, sourcing, assembling, and distributing products on a global basis. The emergence of open IT standards makes it considerably easier to build a global business by integrating best-of-breed components from various geographies.[9] Szygenda envisions how such unity might play out for GM. "Whether we're developing a product, manufacturing, sourcing, or distributing," he says, "we'll be able to link up all of our activities in a seamless global operation." Or as Bob

Lutz says, "My vision would be a corporation operating on a truly global basis—no U.S. dominance. We will have global budgets that will be administered optimally, be it the allocation of capital, the allocation of design resources, engineering resources, purchasing, manufacturing. We will treat the whole world as if it were one country." GM has already taken large steps toward this vision, which may well be the company's ticket to recovery.

If companies can go global, how about individuals? In fact, it turns out they can. When we went to see Steve Mills, who runs IBM's software operation, he was immersed in twenty different instant messaging sessions with clients and colleagues around the world. He says, "When computers run fast enough, and the bandwidth is there, everything that is remote feels local—in fact, the whole world feels local to me. I don't need to be present in the room to participate." The new global platform for collaboration opens up myriad new possibilities for individuals like Mills to act globally. The world is teeming with possibilities for education, work, and entrepreneurship—one just needs the skills, motivation, the capacity for lifelong learning, and a basic income level to get connected.

Thriving in a World of Wikinomics

These four principles—openness, peering, sharing, and acting globally—increasingly define how twenty-first-century corporations compete. This is very different from the hierarchical, closed, secretive, and insular multinational that dominated the previous century.

One thing that has not changed is that winning organizations (and societies) will be those that tap the torrent of human knowledge and translate it into new and useful applications. The difference today is that the organizational values, skills, tools, processes, and architectures of the ebbing command-and-control economy are not simply outdated; they are handicaps on the value creation process. In an age where mass collaboration can reshape an industry overnight, the old hierarchical ways of organizing work and innovation do not afford the level of agility, creativity, and connectivity that companies require to remain competitive in today's environment. Every individual now has a role to play in the economy, and every company has a choice—commoditize or get connected.

Changes of this magnitude have occurred before. In fact, human societies have always been punctuated by periods of great change that not only cause people to think and behave differently, but also give rise to new social orders and institutions. In many instances these changes are driven by disruptive technologies, such as the printing press, the automobile, and the telephone, that penetrate societies to fundamentally change their culture and economy.

The new Web—which is really an internetworked constellation of disruptive technologies—is the most robust platform yet for facilitating and accelerating new creative disruptions. People, knowledge, objects, devices, and intelligent agents are converging in many-to-many networks where new innovations and social trends spread with viral intensity. Organizations that have scrambled to come up with responses to new phenomena like Napster or the blogosphere should expect much more of the same—at an increasing rate—in the future.

Previous technology-driven revolutions, like the electrification of industry, took the better part of a century to unfold.[10] Today the escalating scope and scale of the resources applied to innovation means that change will unfold more quickly. Though we are still just beginning a profound economic institutional adjustment, incumbents should not expect a grace period. The old, hardwired "plan and push" mentality is rapidly giving way to a new, dynamic "engage and cocreate" economy. A hypercompetitive global economy is reshaping enterprises, and political and legal shift loom.

As organizations, and indeed societies, confront this changing reality, they must ensure that they can continue to be innovative. The "who, where, what, how, and why" of innovation are in flux, across geography and economic sectors. The speed and scope of change is intensifying.

A perfect storm is gathering force and shipwrecking the old corporation in wave after wave of change. The "publish and browse," read-only Internet of yesterday is becoming a place where the knowledge, resources, and computing power of billions of people are coming together into a massive collective force. Energized through blogs, wikis, chat rooms, personal broadcasting, and other forms of peer-to-peer creation and communication, this utterly decentralized and amorphous force increasingly self-organizes to provide its own news, entertainment, and services. As these effects permeate out through the economy and intersect with deep structural changes like globalization, we will witness the rise of an entirely new kind of economy where firms coexist with millions of autonomous producers who connect and cocreate value in loosely coupled networks. We call this the collaboration economy.

A tour of the collaboration economy would include seven new models of mass collaboration that are successfully challenging traditional business designs.

1. The journey begins with the "Peer Pioneers"—the people who brought you open source software and Wikipedia while demonstrating that thousands of dispersed volunteers can create fast, fluid, and innovative projects that outperform those of the largest and best-financed enterprises.

2. An emerging marketplace for ideas, inventions, and uniquely qualified minds enables companies like P&G to tap global pools of highly skilled talent more than ten times the size of its own workforce.

3. In the increasingly dynamic world of customer innovation, a new generation of producer consumers considers the "right to hack" its birthright. This is good news.

4. A new science of sharing will rapidly accelerate human health, turn the tide on environmental damage, advance human culture, develop breakthrough technologies, and even discover the universe—all while helping companies grow wealth for their shareholders.

5. Smart companies are opening up their products and technology infrastructures to create an open stage where large communities of partners can create value and, in many cases, create new businesses.

6. Even manufacturing-intensive industries are giving rise to planetary ecosystems for designing and building physical goods, marking a new phase in the evolution of mass collaboration.

7. Mass collaboration is taking root in the workplace and creating a new corporate meritocracy that is sweeping away the hierarchical silos in its path and connecting internal teams to a wealth of external networks.

For individuals and small businesses this is an exciting new era—an era where they can participate in production and add value to large-scale economic systems in ways that were previously impossible. For large companies, the seven models of mass collaboration provide myriad ways to harness external knowledge, resources, and talent for greater competitiveness and growth. For society as a whole, we can harness the explosion of knowledge, collaboration, and business innovation to lead richer, fuller lives and spur economic development for all.

Take heed. Whenever such a shift occurs, there are always realignments of competitive advantage and new measures of success and value. To succeed in this new world, it will not be enough—indeed, it will be counterproductive—simply to intensify current policies, management strategies, and curricular approaches. Remaining innovative requires us to understand both the shifts and the new strategy agenda that follows. We must collaborate or perish—across borders, cultures, disciplines, and firms, and, increasingly, with masses of people at one time.

Notes

1. The term "peer production" was coined by Yale professor Yochai Benkler. See Yochai Benkler, "Coase's Penguin, or, Linux and the Nature of the Firm," *Yale Law Journal*, vol. 112 (2002–2003). Throughout the book we use peer production and mass collaboration interchangeably.

2. According to Technorati.com, which monitors registered blogs. The actual number including unregistered blogs is much higher.

3. At the time of writing, Boing Boing was receiving 750,000 visits per day.

4. Jim Giles, "Internet encyclopedias go head to head," *Nature,* vol. 438 no. 531 (December 15, 2005) www.nature.com/news/2005/051212/full/438900a.html.

5. The term "Web 2.0" was coined by O'Reilly vice president Dale Dougherty in 2004. Tim O'Reilly, "What Is Web 2.0?" oreillynet.com (September 30, 2005).

6. For example, as global complexity increases so does the list of challenges we face that are unsolvable by individual organizations acting alone. Tackling global warming. Defeating poverty and disease. Finding new energy sources. Building nano-size supercomputers. Not just sequencing the human genome, but genuinely understanding it. There is simply no end to the requirements or possibilities for innovation. These complex problems demand cross-disciplinary and interorganizational solutions. Even comparatively simple products are becoming more complex. All of this complexity is fueling an increase in the requirement for openness and boundary-spanning collaborations.

7. Don Tapscott and Anthony Williams, "Creating Value in the Age of Transparency," Conference Board (2003). Don Tapscott and David Ticoll, *The Naked Corporation: How the Age of Transparency Will Revolutionize Business* (New York: Simon & Schuster, 2003).

8. National Intelligence Council, "Mapping the Global Future: Report of the National Intelligence Council's 2020 Project" (December 2004).

9. James W. Cortada and David Ticoll, "On Using IT Standards As a Competitive Tool in a Global Economy," New Paradigm's IT & CA Research Program, Big Idea Series (2005).

10. The electric dynamo (a device for converting mechanical energy into electricity) was invented in 1832, but the diffusion of electric motors in U.S. industry was a protracted process, and the anticipated leaps in productivity were long delayed. Much of the delay reflected the fact that both public and private organizations needed time to absorb the new technologies and their impacts. When a new technoeconomic paradigm finally matured, we experienced over half a century of sustained growth and productivity during the post–World War II period. See Stanford economist Paul David's work for a fascinating look at how technology figures in recent economic history.

PART II

Leadership Concepts and Theories

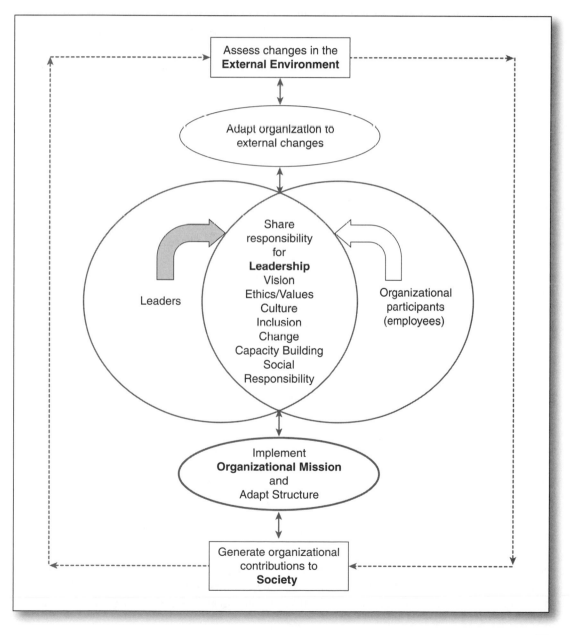

Overview

Part II presents several leadership theories that were developed in the late 20th century and remain in use in many contemporary organizations. James MacGregor Burns (Chapter 6) sparked a new era of study and practice of leadership with his groundbreaking book *Leadership*. His classic conceptualization of *transactional* and *transforming* leadership provided the foundation for revolutionary thinking about the role and purpose of leadership. Burns explains that transactional leadership takes place when one person takes the initiative in making contact with others for the purpose of an exchange of valued things. Clearly, transactional leadership can exist between leaders of two or more organizations or between leaders and members within the same organization.

Burns contrasts this form of leadership with *transforming* leadership, which occurs when one or more persons engage with others in such a way that leaders and followers raise one another to higher levels of motivation and morality. Although Burns feels that transforming leadership cannot work in bureaucratic organizations, it is possible that this form of leadership can exist where organizational leaders and participants aspire to generate collective purpose and transforming processes that are ultimately linked to social change. Looking ahead to the chapters in Part VIII, many organizational leaders mobilize participants and resources to work on community, social, and environmental problems outside the organization, often partnering with nonprofit, business, or government agencies. Implementing this social mission, together with the organization's business mission, is becoming a standard leadership commitment and responsibility in many new era organizations. If this trend continues and leaders effect real change in social conditions, then transforming leadership can become a viable form of leadership in organizations.

Bernard Bass (Chapter 7) was the first scholar to import Burns's concepts from the political and social movement arena into the context of organizations. Bass separated Burns's link to social change from the theory of transforming leadership and adopted Burns's definition of transactional leadership to shape what he termed *transformational* leadership. Table II.1 illustrates the differences in Burns's and Bass's concepts. Bass and colleagues found that a qualitative change in performance and relationships occurs in transformational leadership to the benefit of the individual and the organization. Four critical factors, called the "Four I's," comprise this form of leadership: idealized influence, inspirational motivation, intellectual stimulation, and individualized consideration.

Robert Greenleaf's (Chapter 8) concept of *servant* leadership characterizes the leader as *steward* or *servant-first*. The needs of participants are the foremost priority for servant leaders, whose role is to pave the way and provide support for participants to function at their best. Greenleaf provides several criteria for evaluating successful servant leadership: Do those served grow as persons? Do they, while being served, become healthier, wiser, freer, more autonomous, more likely themselves to become servants? And what is the effect on the least privileged in society? Will they benefit or at least not be further deprived?

Charismatic leadership is a constellation of behaviors that leads to individuals being judged as charismatic, according to Jay Conger (Chapter 9). These behaviors entail sensitivity to the environmental context (especially shortcomings or deficiencies that these leaders can see as platforms for action or strategic opportunities), accompanied by sensitivity to the abilities and emotional needs of participants; the ability to form and articulate an idealized future vision filled with opportunity; the ability to evoke this idealized vision in the imagination of participants; and the capacity to inspire participants with confidence in the leader's abilities and to demonstrate clearly the tactics and behaviors required to achieve the shared goal.

Richard Hughes, Robert Ginnett, and Gordon Curphy (Chapter 10) present an overview of *contingency* theories of leadership. They examine several different contingency theories, including the situational model, contingency model, and path-goal theory. In general, these theories state that leadership effectiveness is maximized when leaders correctly make their behavior "contingent" on certain situational and follower characteristics.

Finally, *strategic* leadership focuses on senior executive leaders at the top of organizations, including CEOs, top management/leadership teams, and business unit

Table II.1 Differences Between Transforming and Transformational Leadership Theories

	Transforming Leadership (Burns)	*Transformational Leadership (Bass)*
Purpose	To enhance the well-being of human existence	To motivate others to do more than they originally intended and often more than they thought possible
Context	Political and societal	Organizational
Influence process	Two-way (leader ◄──► follower)	One-way (leader ──► follower)
Requirement for social change	Yes ("real, intended change")	No

or division heads, who make substantive decisions concerning the direction and positioning of the overall organization. Strategic leadership is defined as

a person's [or executive team's] ability to anticipate, envision, maintain flexibility, think strategically, and work with others to initiate changes that will create a viable future for the organization.[1]

The chapter by Sydney Finkelstein, Donald Hambrick, and Albert Cannella, Jr. (Chapter 11) examines top management teams (TMTs) and their role in strategic decision making. Many organizations use TMTs in the strategic decision-making process because the complexity and uncertainty of the external environment, discussed in Part I, make it almost impossible for a single executive leader to be fully informed on every issue or to make strategic decisions without the contributions and perspectives of other well-informed individuals. The researchers present a framework for understanding the composition, structure, and process of top teams and delineate three main research questions that shape the chapter: What is the nature of top management team interaction? What are the characteristics of top management

teams? How do top management teams affect strategic decision-making processes and organizational outcomes? The discussion of TMTs provides a transition to Part III, as these teams represent a form of shared leadership; however, participation in decision making is confined to a small number of executive leaders.

The concepts and theories in this section focus primarily on what leaders, often top-level or positional leaders, need to do to accomplish effective and/or moral leadership. These forms of leadership have great value for organizations, although they comprise only part of the leadership that organizations need now and in the future. These forms of leadership need to be added to the concepts and practices of multilevel, shared leadership, described in Part III, to meet the challenges of organizations in a new era.

Note

1. Ireland, R. D., & Hitt, M. A. (2005). Achieving and mantaining strategic competitiveness in the 21st century: The role of strategic leadership. *Academy of Management Executive Journal, 19*(4), 63.

CHAPTER 6

Leadership

(Excerpts)

James MacGregor Burns

Williams College and University of Maryland

One of the most serious failures in the study of leadership has been the bifurcation between the literature on leadership and the literature on followership. The former deals with the heroic or demonic figures in history, usually through the medium of biography and with the inarticulated major premise that fame is equated with importance. The latter deals with the audiences, the masses, the voters, the people, usually through the medium of studies of mass opinion or of elections; it is premised on the conviction that in the long run, at least, leaders act as agents of their followers. The leadership approach tends often unconsciously to be elitist; it projects heroic figures against the shadowy background of drab, powerless masses. The followership approach tends to be populistic or anti-elitist in ideology; it perceives the masses, even in democratic societies, as linked with small, overlapping circles of conservative politicians, military officers, hierocrats, and businessmen. I describe leadership here as no mere game among elitists and no mere populist response but as a structure of action that engages persons, to varying degrees, throughout the levels and among the interstices of society. Only the inert, the alienated, and the powerless are unengaged.

Surely it is time that the two literatures are brought together, that the roles of leader and follower be united conceptually, that the study of leadership be lifted out of the anecdotal and the eulogistic and placed squarely in the structure and processes of human development and political action. I hope to demonstrate that the processes of leadership must be seen as part of the dynamics of conflict and of power; that leadership is nothing if not linked to collective purpose; that the effectiveness of leaders must be judged not by their press clippings but by actual social change measured by intent and by the satisfaction of human needs and expectations; that political leadership depends on a

---

long chain of biological and social processes, of interaction with structures of political opportunity and closures, of interplay between the calls of moral principles and the recognized necessities of power; that in placing these concepts of political leadership centrally into a theory of historical causation, we will reaffirm the possibilities of human volition and of common standards of justice in the conduct of peoples' affairs.

I will deal with leadership as distinct from mere power-holding and as the opposite of brute power. I will identify two basic types of leadership: the *transactional* and the *transforming*. The relations of most leaders and followers are *transactional*—leaders approach followers with an eye to exchanging one thing for another: jobs for votes, or subsidies for campaign contributions. Such transactions comprise the bulk of the relationships among leaders and followers, especially in groups, legislatures, and parties. *Transforming* leadership, while more complex, is more potent. The transforming leader recognizes and exploits an existing need or demand of a potential follower. But, beyond that, the transforming leader looks for potential motives in followers, seeks to satisfy higher needs, and engages the full person of the follower. The result of transforming leadership is a relationship of mutual stimulation and elevation that converts followers into leaders and may convert leaders into moral agents.

This last concept, *moral leadership,* concerns me the most. By this term I mean, first, that leaders and led have a relationship not only of power but of mutual needs, aspirations, and values; second, that in responding to leaders, followers have adequate knowledge of alternative leaders and programs and the capacity to choose among those alternatives; and, third, that leaders take responsibility for their commitments—if they promise certain kinds of economic, social, and political change, they assume leadership in the bringing about of that change. Moral leadership is not mere preaching, or the uttering of pieties, or the insistence on social conformity. Moral leadership emerges from, and always returns to, the fundamental wants and needs, aspirations, and values of the followers. I mean the kind of leadership that can produce social change that will satisfy followers' authentic needs. I mean less the Ten Commandments than the Golden Rule. But even the Golden Rule is inadequate, for it measures the wants and needs of others simply by our own.

I propose, in short, to move from the usual "practical" questions to the most exacting theoretical and moral ones. Assuming that leaders are neither "born" nor "made," we will look for patterns in the origins and socializing of persons that account for leadership. Using concepts that emphasize the evolving structures of motivations, values, and goals, we will identify distinctive leadership roles and qualities. We will note the interwoven texture of leadership and followership and the vital and concentric rings of secondary, tertiary, and even "lower" leadership at most levels of society, recognizing nevertheless the role of "great leaders," who exercise large influences on the course of history. Searching always for the moral foundations of leadership, we will consider as truly legitimate only those acts of leaders that serve ultimately in some way to help release human potentials now locked in ungratified needs and crushed expectations.

Do skill and genius still matter? Can we distinguish *leaders* from mere power holders? Can we identify forces that enable leaders to act on the basis of common, non-culture-bound needs and values that, in turn, empower leaders to demonstrate genuine moral leadership? Can we deal with these questions across polities and across time? Can we, therefore, apply these concepts of political leadership to wider theories of social change and historical causation?

If we can do these things, we can hope to fashion a general theory of political leadership. And, when we return from moral and causal questions to ways of practical leadership, we might find that there is nothing more practical than sound theory, if we can fashion it.

* * *

Leadership and Followership

Leadership is an aspect of power, but it is also a separate and vital process in itself.

Power over other persons, we have noted, is exercised when potential power wielders, motivated to achieve certain goals of their own, marshal in their power base resources (economic, military, institutional, or skill) that enable them to influence the behavior of respondents by activating motives of respondents relevant to those resources and to those goals. This is done in order to realize the purposes of the *power wielders, whether or not these are also the goals of the respondents.* Power wielders also exercise influence by mobilizing their own power base in such a way as to establish direct physical control over others' behavior, as in a war of conquest or through measures of harsh deprivation, but these are highly restricted exercises of power, dependent on certain times, cultures, and personalities, and they are often self-destructive and transitory.

Leadership over human beings is exercised when persons with certain motives and purposes mobilize, in competition or conflict with others, institutional, political, psychological, and other resources so as to arouse, engage, and satisfy the motives of followers. This is done in order to realize goals mutually held by *both* leaders and followers, as in Lenin's calls for peace, bread, and land. In brief, leaders with motive and power bases tap followers' motives in order to realize the purposes of both leaders and followers. Not only must motivation be relevant, as in power generally, but its purposes must be realized and satisfied. Leadership is exercised in a condition of *conflict* or *competition* in which leaders contend in appealing to the motive bases of potential followers. Naked power, on the other hand, admits of no competition or conflict—there is no engagement.

Leaders are a particular kind of power holder. Like power, leadership is relational, collective, and purposeful. Leadership shares with power the central function of achieving purpose. But the reach and domain of leadership are, in the short range at least, more limited than those of power. Leaders do not obliterate followers' motives though they may arouse certain motives and ignore others. They lead other creatures, not things (and lead animals only to the degree that they recognize animal motives—i.e., leading cattle to shelter rather than to slaughter). To control *things*—tools, mineral resources, money, energy—is an act of power, not leadership, for things have no motives. Power wielders may treat people as things. Leaders may not.

All leaders are actual or potential power holders, but not all power holders are leaders.

These definitions of power and of leadership differ from those that others have offered. Lasswell and Kaplan hold that power must be relevant to people's valued things; I hold that it must be relevant to the *power wielder's* valued things and may be relevant to the *recipient's* needs or values only as necessary to exploit them. Kenneth Janda defines power as "the ability to cause other persons to adjust their behavior in conformance with communicated behavior patterns." I agree, assuming that those behavior patterns aid the purpose of the power wielder. According to Andrew McFarland, "If the leader causes changes that he intended, he has exercised power; if the leader causes changes that he did not intend or want, he has exercised influence, but not power." I dispense with the concept of influence as unnecessary and unparsimonious. For me the leader is a very special, very circumscribed, but potentially the most effective of power holders, judged by the degree of intended "real change" finally achieved. Roderick Bell et al. contend that power is a relationship rather than an entity—an entity being something that "could be smelled and touched, or stored in a keg"; while I agree that power is a relationship, I contend that the relationship is one in which some entity—part of the "power base"—plays an indispensable part, whether that keg is a keg of beer, of dynamite, or of ink.

The crucial variable, again, is *purpose.* Some define leadership as leaders making followers do what *followers* would not otherwise do, or as leaders making followers do what the *leaders* want them to do; I define leadership as leaders inducing followers to act for certain goals that represent the values and the motivations—the wants and needs, the aspirations and expectations—*of both leaders and followers.* And the genius of leadership lies in the manner in which leaders see and act on their own and their followers' values and motivations.

Leadership, unlike naked power-wielding, is thus inseparable from followers' needs and goals. The essence of the leader-follower relation is the interaction of persons with different levels of motivations and of power potential, including skill, in pursuit of a common or at least joint purpose. That interaction, however, takes two fundamentally different forms. The first I will call *transactional* leadership. Such leadership occurs when one person takes the initiative in making contact with others for the purpose of an exchange of valued things. The exchange could be economic or political or psychological in nature: a swap of goods or of one good for money; a trading of votes between candidate and citizen or between legislators; hospitality to another person in exchange for willingness to listen to one's troubles. Each party to the bargain is conscious of the power resources and attitudes of the other. Each person recognizes the other as a *person*. Their purposes are related, at least to the extent that the purposes stand within the bargaining process and can be advanced by maintaining that process. But beyond this the relationship does not go. The bargainers have no enduring purpose that holds them together; hence they may go their separate ways. A leadership act took place, but it was not one that binds leader and follower together in a mutual and continuing pursuit of a higher purpose.

Contrast this with *transforming* leadership. Such leadership occurs when one or more persons *engage* with others in such a way that leaders and followers raise one another to higher levels of motivation and morality. Their purposes, which might have started out as separate but related, as in the case of transactional leadership, become fused. Power bases are linked not as counterweights but as mutual support for common purpose. Various names are used for such leadership, some of them derisory: elevating, mobilizing, inspiring, exalting, uplifting, preaching, exhorting, evangelizing. The relationship can be moralistic, of course. But transforming leadership ultimately becomes *moral* in that it raises the level of human conduct and ethical aspiration of both leader and led, and thus it has a transforming effect on both. Perhaps the best modern example is Gandhi, who aroused and elevated the hopes and demands of millions of Indians and whose life and personality were enhanced in the process. Transcending leadership is dynamic leadership in the sense that the leaders throw themselves into a relationship with followers who will feel "elevated" by it and often become more active themselves, thereby creating new cadres of leaders. Transcending leadership is leadership *engagé*. Naked power-wielding can be neither transactional nor transforming; only leadership can be.

Leaders and followers may be inseparable in function, but they are not the same. The leader takes the initiative in making the leader-led connection; it is the leader who creates the links that allow communication and exchange to take place. An office seeker does this in accosting a voter on the street, but if the voter espies and accosts the politician, the voter is assuming a leadership function, at least for that brief moment. The leader is more skillful in evaluating followers' motives, anticipating their responses to an initiative, and estimating their power bases, than the reverse. Leaders continue to take the major part in maintaining and effectuating the relationship with followers and will have the major role in ultimately carrying out the combined purpose of leaders and followers. Finally, and most important by far, leaders address themselves to followers' wants, needs, and other motivations, as well as to their own, and thus they serve as an *independent force in changing the makeup of the followers' motive base through gratifying their motives*.

Certain forms of power and certain forms of leadership are near-extremes on the power continuum. One is the kind of absolute power that, Lord Acton felt, "corrupts absolutely." It also coerces absolutely. The essence of this kind of power is the capacity of power wielders, given the necessary motivation, to override the motive and power bases of their targets. Such power objectifies its victims; it literally turns them into objects, like the inadvertent weapon tester in Mtésa's court. Such power wielders, as well, are objectified and dehumanized. Hitler, according to Richard Hughes, saw the universe as containing no persons other than himself, only "things." The ordinary citizen in Russia, says a Soviet linguist and dissident, does not identify with his government. "With us, it is there, like the wind, like a wall, like the sky. It is something permanent, unchangeable. So the individual acquiesces, does not dream of changing it— except a few, few people."

At the other extreme is leadership so sensitive to the motives of potential followers that the roles of leader and follower become virtually interdependent. Whether the leadership relationship is transactional or transforming, in it motives, values, and goals of leader and led have merged. It may appear that at the other extreme from the raw power relationship, dramatized in works like Arthur Koestler's *Darkness at Noon* and George Orwell's *1984*, is the extreme of leadership-led merger dramatized in novels about persons utterly dependent on parents, wives, or lovers. Analytically these extreme types of relationships are not very perplexing. To watch one person absolutely dominate another is horrifying; to watch one person disappear, his motives and values submerged into those of another to the point of loss of individuality, is saddening. But puzzling out the nature of these extreme relationships is not intellectually challenging because each in its own way lacks the qualities of complexity and conflict. Submersion of one personality in another is not genuine merger based on mutual respect. Such submersion is an example of brute power subtly applied, perhaps with the acquiescence of the victim.

More complex are relationships that lie between these poles of brute power and wholly reciprocal leadership-followership. Here empirical and theoretical questions still perplex both the analysts and the practitioners of power. One of these concerns the sheer measurement of power (or leadership). Traditionally we measure power resources by calculating each one and adding them up: constituency support plus access to leadership plus financial resources plus skill plus "popularity" plus access to information, etc., all in relation to the strength of opposing forces, similarly computed. But these calculations omit the vital factor of motivation and purpose and hence fall of their own weight. Another controversial measurement device is *reputation*. Researchers seek to learn from informed observers their estimates of the power or leadership role and resources of visible *community* leaders (projecting this into national arenas of power is a formidable task). Major questions arise as to the reliability of the estimates, the degree of agreement between interviewer and interviewee over their definition of power and leadership, the transferability of power from one area of decision-making to another. Another device for studying power and leadership is *linkage theory*, which requires elaborate mapping of communication and other interrelations among power holders in different spheres, such as the economic and the military. The difficulty here is that communication, which may expedite the processes of power and leadership, is not a substitute for them.

My own measurement of power and leadership is simpler in concept but no less demanding of analysis: *power and leadership are measured by the degree of production of intended effects.* This need not be a theoretical exercise. Indeed, in ordinary political life, the power resources and the motivations of presidents and prime ministers and political parties are measured by the extent to which presidential promises and party programs are carried out. Note that the variables are the double ones of *intent* (a function of motivation) and of *capacity* (a function of power base), but the test of the extent and quality of power and leadership is the degree of *actual accomplishment* of the promised change.

Other complexities in the study of power and leadership are equally serious. One is the extent to which power and leadership are exercised not by positive action but by *inaction* or *nondecision*. Another is that power and leadership are often exercised not directly on targets but indirectly, and perhaps through multiple channels, on multiple targets. We must ask not only whether P has the power to do X to R, but whether P can induce or force R to do Y to Z. The existence of power and leadership in the form of a stream of multiple direct and indirect forces operating over time must be seen as part of the broader sequences of historical causation. Finally, we must acknowledge the knotty problem of events of history that are beyond the control of identifiable persons capable of foreseeing developments and powerful enough to influence them and hence to be held accountable for them. We can only agree with C. Wright Mills that these are matters of fate rather than power or leadership.

We do well to approach these and other complexities of power and leadership with some humility as well as a measure of boldness. We can reject the "gee whiz" approach to power that often takes the form of the automatic presumption of "elite control" of communities, groups, institutions, entire nations. Certain concepts and techniques of the "elitist" school of power are indispensable in social and political analysis, but "elitism" is often used as a concept that *presupposes* the existence of the very degree and kind of power that is to be estimated and analyzed. Such "elite theorists" commit the gross error of equating power and leadership with the assumed power bases of preconceived leaders and power holders, without considering the crucial role of *motivations* of leaders and followers. Every good detective knows that one must look for the motive as well as the weapon.

* * *

The Test: Real, Intended Change

Most of the world's decision makers, however powerful they may appear in journalistic accounts, must cope with the effects of decisions already made by events, circumstances, and other persons and hence, like Khrushchev and Kennedy, must act within narrow bounds. Decision-making opportunities typically come to them in the form of a few limited options. The advisers and institutions and procedures that once upon a time might have been organized to empower them often turn out to have become sources of restraint. The main function—even of those labeled radicals or reformers or revolutionaries—is often to maintain existing political arrangements and hence to contribute to continuity, equilibrium, and stability. Such decision makers are defensive and palliative rather than creative. Occasionally they act at such critical turning points in the great affairs of nations that their tiny leverage tips affairs toward one course of action rather than another or holds matters in balance or in suspension until decisions can be made at a later time. But those later decisions may be even more constrained as a result of intervening events.

Napoleon, it is said, could look upon a battle scene of unimaginable disorder and see its coherence for his own advantage. If some decision makers seem to have enormous influence on history and are thrust into the pantheon of world heroes, this may be in part the result of miscalculation by the chroniclers of their actual impact on the shank of history and their glorification as heroes by panegyrists. Even more the reason may be a faulty or inadequate conception of the nature of change. Dramatic decision-making may lead only to cosmetic change, or to temporary change, or to the kind of change in symbols and myths that will preserve the existing order rather than transform or undermine it. Such seemed to be true of de Gaulle's regime. A realistic and restricted definition of policy and decision leadership is necessary to a serviceable concept of social change.

By social change I mean here *real change*—that is, a transformation to a marked degree in the attitudes, norms, institutions, and behaviors that structure our daily lives. Such changes embrace not only "new cultural patterns and institutional arrangements" and "new psychological dispositions," in the terms used by Herbert Kelman and Donald Warwick, but changes in material conditions, in the explicit, felt existence, the flesh and fabric of people's lives. Such changes may be a far cry from the "changes" that legislative, judicial, and executive decisions are supposed to bring automatically. The leadership process must be defined, in short, as carrying through from the decision-making stages to the point of concrete changes in people's lives, attitudes, behaviors, institutions. Even the sweep of this process is not enough, however, for we must include another dimension: *time*. Attitude and behavior can change for a certain period; as in a war, popular fads and emotional political movements change only to revert later. Real change means a continuing interaction of attitudes, behavior, and institutions, monitored by alterations in individual and collective hierarchies of values.

Leadership brings about real change that leaders *intend*, under our definition. Leaders may seem to cause the most titanic of changes—such as the human and physical wreckage left in the wake of civil war—but that wreckage itself presumably was not the central purpose of the leaders. It would be idle here to measure the extent and character of social change unless we also examine the intentions of those who make the decisions that were intended to bring about change. Such an examination is necessary if we are to find purpose and meaning, rather than sheer chance or chaos, in the unfolding of events. A definition that demands so much from leadership also requires that we consider the totality of decision-making by leaders at all levels and in all the interstices of the polity. For actions or changes that might seem errant or vagrant in relation to visible leaders may be the planned outcome of decisions by less conspicuous and less "legitimate" leaders far down the line. The test is purpose and intent, drawn from values and goals, of leaders, high and low, resulting in policy decision and real, intended change.

Social change is so pervasive and ubiquitous in the modern world, and often so dramatic and menacing, as to attract intensive scholarly investigation. It has become an intellectual growth industry. Hegel and Marx are not the only celebrated theorists who have dealt with it as a central phenomenon in social analysis and historical fact. In surveying the vast literature on change, one remarks once again on the absence of a clear concept of the role of artistic or intellectual or political or social leadership in the processes of change, on the absence in most works of references to leadership in theory or practice. Often the process of *innovation* is explored but not in a broad framework of the leadership motivations, goals, and processes within which innovation takes on meaning and direction. It is as though change took place mechanically, apart from human volition or participation. What then, in a preliminary way, can be said about the role of policy and decision-making leadership in the process of real social change?

This question can be answered only in the context of the conditions of stability, continuity, persistence, and inertia that grip most of humankind. We of the modern era hear and see so much of what is called dizzying change—the rise and fall of leaders, dynasties, and whole nations, the continuing eruptions and disruptions of technology, massive migrations, the "population explosion," rapid alterations in economic conditions, the flux of artistic, literary, and other fashions—that we tend to underplay the fixity in human affairs. "Social interaction is to be found in social fixity and persistence as well as in social change," Robert Nisbet observes. "That is why, if we are to answer the question of causation in change, we are obliged to deal with, first, *the nature of social persistence* and, then, with *variables, not constants,* when we turn to the matter of what causes the observed change in structure, trait, or idea." Systems, once established, generate countless forces and balances to perpetuate themselves.

Our very assumption of change is culture-bound. "For most of the world's people, who have known only the changelessness of history, such stress on the difficulty of change would not be necessary," according to Robert Heilbroner. "But for ourselves, whose outlook is conditioned by the extraordinary dynamism of our unique historical experience, it is a needed caution. Contrary to our generally accepted belief, change is not the rule but the exception in life." And Leonard Meyer says, at the start of a chapter headed "The Probability of Stasis": "The presumption that social-cultural development is a necessary condition of human existence is not tenable. The history of China up to the nineteenth century, the stasis of ancient Egypt, and the lack of

cumulative change in countless other civilizations and cultures make it apparent that stability and conservation, not change, have been the rule in mankind generally."

What then is all the activity? Much of it is the appearance of multitudinous readjustments as the system absorbs small variations in the basic pattern and maintains its own pace and direction. The anthropologist Alfred R. Radcliffe-Brown noted the changes within structures that did not affect the structural form of society. He made a sharp distinction between *system maintenance*, the kind of readjustment that was essentially an adjustment of the equilibrium of a social structure, and what he called *system change* or "change of type," which he defined as "a change such that when there is sufficient of it, the society passes from one type of social structure to another." The vast proportion of the decisions of decision makers, high and low, is readjustment that maintains the equilibrium of the social structure.

A system can appear dynamic in guarding its own statics. A leader who departs from system or group norms in some decision will suffer undue attention, pressure, sanctions, and perhaps rejection or exclusion. To cite one of innumerable laboratory experiments, F. Merei demonstrated that a child with evident leadership qualities was nevertheless forced to abide by the established play norms of a small kindergarten group. If a change in one part of a system seems to threaten other parts, it is sealed off; at most it is not allowed to change much faster than the others. A host of institutional safeguards, some of them vested with sacrosanct status or mystification, is built around stabilizing decision-making processes. Outsiders and outside ideas are smoothly rejected. One of the most common tendencies in the history of arms development and change has been the resistance of military decision makers to weapons innovations that much later, after being adopted in crisis or catastrophe, took on their own institutional protection.

A number of strategies have been developed to overcome resistance to change: coercive strategies, normative strategies (achieving compliance by invoking values that have been internalized), utilitarian strategies (control over allocation and deprivation of rewards and punishments), empirical-rational strategies (rational justification for change), power-coercive strategies (application of moral, economic, and political resources to achieve change), and reeducative strategies (exerting influence through feeling and thought). Coercive strategies need not detain us here, since we exclude coercion from the definition of leadership; the majority of the other strategies provide for deprivation of group support for the beliefs, attitudes, values, and concepts of self that combine to tie a person to the status quo. A common thread—perhaps the only common thread—running through these diverse strategies is their difficulty. Most seem to be aimed not so much at altering the attitudes and behavior of the ultimate targets of change—citizens in their daily lives—but at the subordinate decision makers in government or business or other collectivities who are supposed to *administer* the change. Even if top policy makers were able to exert control down the line over subordinate policy makers, a huge gap remains between their operating decisions and real change in the behavior of the greater public. "In here" is still sharply different from "out there." All this simply confirms in theory what decision-making leaders find in practice: that breaks and erosions and disturbances in the "line of command" produce attenuation of purpose and of action at the grass roots and that, even when they do not, the target publics may not respond. Decisions are rarely self-implementing. Many of the administrative devices intended to communicate command and direction from the top become means for blunting or distorting the chain of decision.

Grand policy-making and decision-making leadership, in short, can wither at the most crucial phase—that of influence over popular attitudes and behavior. Is there any way out of this dilemma?

The answer to this question ultimately turns on the nature of the goals of decision-making leadership. These, of course, vary enormously. On the most personal and individual level policy makers may seek small changes that affect only themselves. This may be a service from a government bureau, exemption from a regulation, some honor or special recognition from the state. Frustrated by the regular bureaucratic decision-making machinery, they may "walk their papers" through the administrative labyrinth. In realizing their own specific and perhaps narrow goal, in effecting a small change for themselves, they leave the decision-making process itself hardly touched. They have "beaten the system," but the system in the long run

beats them, for their very success lowers pressure to improve the machinery—at least on their part and for the short run—hence it may continue to operate poorly for the great number of persons it services. Some individual efforts, however narrowly and self-servingly motivated, may implicate others in a beneficial way, but those benefits will rarely rise above the "satisficing" level.

At the general or collective level, on the other hand, the goal of a leader may be such comprehensive social change that the existing social structure cannot accommodate it. Hence, in the eyes of certain leaders, that structure must be entirely uprooted and a whole new system substituted, probably through revolutionary means. Revolutions do not always succeed, however, and when they do succeed, revolutionary action, in disrupting existing structures and mobilizing new social forces, incidentally arouses new needs and establishes new goals. Real change may take forms very different from the revolutionary goals originally sought. The most violent revolution, no matter how far-reaching its professed desire for reconstructing society, typically falls short of complete real change. The notion of "a *complete* change in the structural form of a society is . . . incoherent," Ernest Nagel says.

Between the extremes of planning discrete individual change and planning comprehensive and drastic change lies *middle-range* planning, responding to shared needs and other motivations and aimed at collective goals that represent the main planning effort of political leadership in most societies. This kind of *planning leadership* seeks genuine social change for collective purposes, though not necessarily at the same pace, or on so wide a front, as that of revolutionary action. The task of this kind of leadership is political and governmental planning for real social change.

The critical problem concerns the implication of planned ends for planning ways and means, the demands that comprehensive real change puts on existing social and political systems (which we will label here "social structures"). We are defining planning here not only as the establishment of definite social and economic goals to meet popular wants, needs, and expectations, but as the considered and deliberate reshaping of means necessary for the realization of comprehensive real change. Lewis Coser, like Radcliffe-Brown, has made a useful distinction between changes *of* systems and changes *in* systems. He refers to a change *of* system "when all major structural relations, its basic institutions, and its prevailing value system have been drastically altered." Changes *in* system take place more slowly and affect smaller sectors of a system. Given enough time, however, changes in system, through mutual stimulation and adjustment, can produce extensive change if not fundamental transformation of system. The accumulated changes in the British political system over the past two centuries have substantially altered the political structure, but these changes (such as extension of the suffrage) appeared at the time to be changes within the system.

Changes *in* system would seem far more system-transforming than changes *of* systems, if only because the latter type of change comes so hard. Yet the extent of change *of* political systems since 1800 has been remarkable. Ted Gurr has found that the incidence of "system-transforming political change" has been high and pervasive both in the Third World and in the European zone of influence. The median duration of historical Latin and Afro-Asian polities and of European nations during that period was about the same: twelve years. The incidence of abrupt political change had increased markedly from the nineteenth to the twentieth centuries, Gurr found. "Of the 150 historical polities in the sample which were established before 1900," according to Gurr, "half survived for 20 years; but for the 117 historical polities established after 1900, the 'half-life' was only nine years." The extent to which these transformations took place as a result of collective and comprehensive planning by leaders varied widely, but these findings underline the vulnerability and impermanence of social structures that may appear to be well established.

Planning for structural change, whether of the system or in the system, is the ultimate moral test of decision-making leadership inspired by certain goals and values and intent on achieving real social change; it is also the leader's most potent *weapon*. It is a test in that planning calls for thinking and acting along a wide battlefront of complex forces, institutions, and contingencies; if the planners really "mean it," they must plan for the reshaping of means as required by the ends to which they are committed. It is a weapon in that a well-conceived plan, along with available planning technology, supplies leaders with an estimate of the human, material, and intellectual resources necessary to draw up and drive through a plan for substantial social change. Planning is designed to anticipate and to counter the myriad factors that impair the line of decision and action between the policy-making of planning leaders and real change in the daily lives of great numbers of people.

Still, the best laid plans of mice and men go aft agley. Why? In part because the plans are poorly drawn or badly executed. In part because plans encounter "chance" developments no mortal could possibly predict. And in large part because most planners focus on technical and administrative factors, minimizing the psychological and the structural forces. At a certain point following the Bolshevik revolution, Alex Inkeles observes, the "political and economic development of the revolution had now run far ahead of the more narrowly 'social.' In the haste of revolutionary experiment, no systematic attention had been given to the congruence of the newly established institutional forms with the motivational systems, the patterns of expectation and habitual behavior, of the population. Furthermore, as the new institutions began to function they produced social consequences neither planned nor anticipated by the regime." The problem was exacerbated for the Bolsheviks, Inkeles adds, by a Marxist ideology that predisposed leaders to assume that basic changes in the pattern of human relations, which they viewed only as part of the "dependent" superstructure of society, must automatically follow from changes in the political and economic system.

Planners elsewhere have encountered similar problems of human motivation. A British Labour government, in nationalizing the coal mines, misconceived the reactions of the very miners whose lot it was mainly designed to ameliorate. For many miners the change seemed to amount to the substitution of one bureaucracy for another. Indian population planners miscalculated the principal motive of Indian villagers, which was to raise children who would be available for labor and for family income—a motive that overrode the effect of propaganda in favor of limited families for the sake of other goals. American political planners in 1787 shaped a superb political structure for pitting faction against faction and thus breaking the force of faction in government, but they underestimated the popular and egalitarian forces that would threaten such balanced and stabilized government from outside. In the light of planning mishaps, it is not surprising that planners often seek to isolate their new structures from unpredictable psychological forces operating through a political system. Thus the leaders of the Tennessee Valley Authority established their own planning mechanism "in the field" and resented efforts by Washington decision makers to intervene. Autonomy was a two-bladed sword, however; it protected sectoral planners against bureaucratic aggression in the central government, but it did so at the expense of contracting the scope and power of leadership planning.

To note that effective planning must consider motives and values is to return to our central emphasis on a general theory of political leadership. Planning leaders, more than other leaders, must respond not simply to popular attitudes and beliefs but to the fundamental wants and needs, aspirations and expectations, values and goals of their existing and potential followers. Planning leadership must estimate not only initial responses from the public but the extent to which successful plans will arouse new wants and needs and aims in the second and succeeding "rounds" of action. Planning leaders must perceive that consensus in planning would be deceptive and dangerous, that *advocacy and conflict* must be built into the planning process in response to pluralistic sets of values. Planning leaders must recognize *purpose*—indeed, planning is nonexistent without goals—and recognize that different purposes will inform the planning process. Plans must recognize means or modal values too, especially in procedures providing for expression of majority attitudes without threatening rights of privacy and self-expression. And planning must recognize the many faces of power; ultimately the authority and credibility of planning leadership will depend less on formal position than on the capacity to recognize basic needs, to mobilize masses of persons holding sets of values and seeking general goals, to utilize conflict and the adversary process without succumbing to it, and to bring about real social change either through existing social structures or by altering them.

"Increasingly," Karl Mannheim wrote shortly before his death, "it is recognized that real planning consists in coordination of institutions, education, valuations and psychology. Only one who can see the important ramifications of each single step can act with the responsibility required by the complexity of the modern age." It is the leaders who preeminently must see in this way. But to *see* alone is insufficient; they must *act* too, and of all the tasks proposed by Mannheim, the changing of institutions is the most difficult. For institutions are encapsulated within social structures that are themselves responses to earlier needs, values, and goals. In seeking to change social structures in order to realize new values and purposes, leaders go far beyond the politicians who merely cater to surface attitudes. To elevate the goals of humankind, to achieve high moral purpose, to realize major intended change, leaders must thrust themselves into the most intractable processes and structures of history and ultimately master them.

CHAPTER 7

The Transformational Model of Leadership

Bernard M. Bass

Binghamton University

Ronald E. Riggio

Claremont McKenna College

A new paradigm of leadership has captured widespread attention. James MacGregor Burns (1978) conceptualized leadership as either transactional or transformational. Transactional leaders are those who lead through social exchange. As Burns (1978) notes, politicians, for example, lead by "exchanging one thing for another: jobs for votes, or subsidies for campaign contributions" (p. 4). In the same way, transactional business leaders offer financial rewards for productivity or deny rewards for lack of productivity. Transformational leaders, on the other hand, are those who stimulate and inspire followers to both achieve extraordinary outcomes and, in the process, develop their own leadership capacity. Transformational leaders help followers grow and develop into leaders by responding to individual followers' needs by empowering them and by aligning the objectives and goals of the individual followers, the leader, the group, and the larger organization. More evidence has accumulated to demonstrate that transformational leadership can move followers to exceed expected performance, as well as lead to high levels of follower satisfaction and commitment to the group and organization (Bass, 1985,1998a).

Although early research demonstrated that transformational leadership was a particularly powerful source in military settings (e.g., Bass, 1985; Boyd, 1988; Curphy, 1992; Longshore, 1988; O'Keefe, 1989; Yammarino & Bass, 1990), more recent research has accumulated that demonstrates that transformational leadership is important in every sector and in every setting (Avolio & Yammarino, 2002). We soon review the components of transformational leadership, examine transactional leadership, and present the Full Range of Leadership

Source: The Transformational Model of Leadership, by Bernard M. Bass and Ronald E. Riggio, pp. 3-16. In *Transformational Leadership*, 2nd ed. by Bernard M. Bass and Ronald E. Riggio (2006). Copyright © Lawrence Erlbaum Associates, Inc.

model, which incorporates all of these aspects of leadership. But first, we provide a brief discussion of the roots of transformational leadership.

Historical Background of Transformational Leadership

Historians, political scientists, and sociologists have long recognized leadership that went beyond the notion of a social exchange between leader and followers. Weber's (1924/1947) examination of charisma epitomized such study. However, both psychology and economics supported contingent reinforcement—offering a reward or compensation for a desired behavior—as the underlying concept for the study of leadership. Leadership was seen primarily as an exchange relationship (e.g., Homans, 1950). Research exemplified by Podsakoff and Schriescheim (1985), as well as much of the research with the Full Range of Leadership (FRL) model (Avolio & Bass, 1991) to be described subsequently, indicated that contingent reward is reasonably effective under most circumstances. In addition, active management-by-exception (corrective leadership for failure of a follower to comply) is more varied in effects, and passive management-by-exception ("if it ain't broke, don't fix it") is contraindicated as an effective act of leadership, for, as Levinson (1980) suggested, if you limit leadership of a follower to rewards with carrots for compliance or punishment with a stick for failure to comply with agreed-on work to be done by the follower, the follower will continue to feel like a jackass. Leadership must also address the follower's sense of self-worth to engage the follower in true commitment and involvement in the effort at hand. This is what transformational leadership adds to the transactional exchange.

Transformational leaders motivate others to do more than they originally intended and often even more than they thought possible. They set more challenging expectations and typically achieve higher performances. Transformational leaders also tend to have more committed and satisfied followers. Moreover, transformational leaders empower followers and pay attention to their individual needs and personal development, helping followers to develop their own leadership potential.

Transformational leadership is in some ways an expansion of transactional leadership. Transactional leadership emphasizes the transaction or exchange that takes place among leaders, colleagues, and followers. This exchange is based on the leader discussing with others what is required and specifying the conditions and rewards these others will receive if they fulfill those requirements. Transformational leadership, however, raises leadership to the next level. Transformational leadership involves inspiring followers to commit to a shared vision and goals for an organization or unit, challenging them to be innovative problem solvers, and developing followers' leadership capacity via coaching, mentoring, and provision of both challenge and support.

Early social science perspectives on leadership focused on the dichotomy of directive (task-oriented) versus participative (people-oriented) leadership. As we soon show, transformational leadership can be either directive or participative and is not an either-or proposition.

Transformational leadership has much in common with charismatic leadership, but charisma is only part of transformational leadership. The Weberian notion of charismatic leadership was, in fact, fairly limited. More modern conceptions of charismatic leadership take a much broader perspective (e.g., Conger & Kanungo, 1998; House & Shamir, 1993), however, and have much in common with transformational leadership.

A critical concern for theories of both transformational and charismatic leadership involves what many refer to as the dark side of charisma—those charismatic leaders who use their abilities to inspire and lead followers to destructive, selfish, and even evil ends. Most often coming to mind are international leaders who wreaked havoc, death, and destruction on thousands and even millions—Adolf Hitler, Pol Pot, Josef Stalin, Osama Bin Laden. But these leaders are those who can be called pseudotransformational. They exhibit many elements of transformational leadership (the charismatic elements particularly) but have personal, exploitative, and self-aggrandizing motives. Thus, we speak at length near the end of this chapter about the notions of authenticity and authentic transformational leaders.

Components of Transformational Leadership

Transformational leaders do more with colleagues and followers than set up simple exchanges or agreements. They behave in ways to achieve superior results by employing one or more of the four core components of transformational leadership described later.

To some extent, the components of transformational leadership have evolved as refinements have been made in both the conceptualization and measurement of transformational leadership. Conceptually, leadership is charismatic, and followers seek to identify with the leader and emulate him or her. The leadership inspires followers with challenge and persuasion, providing both meaning and understanding. The leadership is intellectually stimulating, expanding the followers' use of their abilities. Finally, the leadership is individually considerate, providing the follower with support, mentoring, and coaching. Each of these components can be measured with the Multifactor Leadership Questionnaire (MLQ). Factor analytic studies from Bass (1985) to Howell and Avolio (1993), and Bycio, Hackett, and Allen (1995) to Avolio, Bass, and Jung (1997) have identified the components of transformational leadership.

Descriptions of the components of transformational leadership are presented in the following sections.

Idealized Influence (II). Transformational leaders behave in ways that allow them to serve as role models for their followers. The leaders are admired, respected, and trusted. Followers identify with the leaders and want to emulate them; leaders are endowed by their followers as having extraordinary capabilities, persistence, and determination. Thus, there are two aspects to idealized influence: the leader's behaviors and the elements that are attributed to the leader by followers and other associates. These two aspects, measured by separate subfactors of the MLQ, represent the interactional nature of idealized influence—it is both embodied in the leader's behavior and in attributions that are made concerning the leader by followers. A sample item from the MLQ that represents idealized influence behavior is "The leader emphasizes the importance of having a collective sense of mission." A sample item from the

idealized influence attributed factor is "The leader reassures others that obstacles will be overcome."

In addition, leaders who have a great deal of idealized influence are willing to take risks and are consistent rather than arbitrary. They can be counted on to do the right thing, demonstrating high standards of ethical and moral conduct.

Inspirational Motivation (IM). Transformational leaders behave in ways that motivate and inspire those around them by providing meaning and challenge to their followers' work. Team spirit is aroused. Enthusiasm and optimism are displayed. Leaders get followers involved in envisioning attractive future states; they create clearly communicated expectations that followers want to meet and also demonstrate commitment to goals and the shared vision. A sample MLQ item for IM is "The leader articulates a compelling vision of the future."

Idealized influence leadership and inspirational motivation usually form a combined single factor of charismatic-inspirational leadership. The charismatic-inspirational factor is similar to the behaviors described in charismatic leadership theory (Bass & Avolio, 1993; House, 1977).

Intellectual Stimulation (IS). Transformational leaders stimulate their followers' efforts to be innovative and creative by questioning assumptions, reframing problems, and approaching old situations in new ways. Creativity is encouraged. There is no public criticism of individual members' mistakes. New ideas and creative problem solutions are solicited from followers, who are included in the process of addressing problems and finding solutions. Followers are encouraged to try new approaches, and their ideas are not criticized because they differ from the leaders' ideas. A sample item from the MLQ that represents intellectual stimulation is "The leader gets others to look at problems from many different angles."

Individualized Consideration (IC). Transformational leaders pay special attention to each individual follower's needs for achievement and growth by acting as a coach or mentor. Followers and colleagues are developed to successively higher levels of potential. Individualized consideration is practiced when new learning opportunities are created along with a supportive climate. Individual differences in terms of needs and desires are recognized. The leader's behavior demonstrates acceptance of individual differences (e.g., some employees receive more encouragement, some more autonomy, others firmer standards, and still others more task structure). A two-way exchange in communication is encouraged, and "management by walking around" workspaces is practiced. Interactions with followers are personalized (e.g., the leader remembers previous conversations, is aware of individual concerns, and sees the individual as a whole person rather than as just an employee). The individually considerate leader listens effectively. The leader delegates tasks as a means of developing followers. Delegated tasks are monitored to see if the followers need additional direction or support and to assess progress; ideally, followers do not feel they are being checked on. A sample MLQ item from the individualized consideration scale is "The leader spends time teaching and coaching."

The Full Range of Leadership Model

In addition to the four components of transformational leadership, the Full Range of Leadership model also includes several components of transactional leadership behavior, along with laissez-faire (or nonleadership) behavior.

Transactional leadership occurs when the leader rewards or disciplines the follower, depending on the adequacy of the follower's performance. Transactional leadership depends on contingent reinforcement, either positive contingent reward (CR) or the more negative active or passive forms of management-by-exception (MBE-A or MBE-P).

Contingent Reward (CR). This constructive transaction has been found to be reasonably effective in motivating others to achieve higher levels of development and performance, although not as much as any of the transformational components. Contingent reward leadership involves the leader assigning or obtaining follower agreement on what needs to be done with promised or actual rewards offered in exchange for satisfactorily carrying out the assignment. A sample contingent reward item is "The leader makes clear what one can expect to receive when performance goals are achieved." Contingent reward is transactional when the reward is a material one, such as a bonus. Contingent reward can be transformational, however, when the reward is psychological, such as praise (Antonakis, Avolio, & Sivasubramaniam, 2003).

Management-by-Exception (MBE). This corrective transaction tends to be more ineffective than contingent reward or the components of transformational leadership. The corrective transaction may be active (MBE-A) or passive (MBE-P). In active MBE, the leader arranges to actively monitor deviances from standards, mistakes, and errors in the follower's assignments and to take corrective action as necessary. MBE-P implies waiting passively for deviances, mistakes, and errors to occur and then taking corrective action. Active MBE may be required and effective in some situations, such as when safety is paramount in importance. Leaders sometimes must practice passive MBE when required to supervise a large number of subordinates who report directly to the leaders. Sample MLQ items for management-by-exception are "The leader directs attention toward failures to meet standards" (active) and "The leader takes no action until complaints are received" (passive).

Laissez-Faire Leadership (LF). As mentioned, laissez-faire leadership is the avoidance or absence of leadership and is, by definition, most inactive, as well as most ineffective according to almost all research on the style. As opposed to transactional leadership, laissez-faire represents a nontransaction. Necessary decisions are not made. Actions are delayed. Responsibilities of leadership are ignored. Authority remains unused. A sample laissez-faire item is "The leader avoids getting involved when important issues arise."

Fundamental to the FRL model is that every leader displays each style to some amount. An optimal profile is shown in Figure 7.1. The third dimension of this model (depth) represents how frequently a leader displays a particular style of leadership. The horizontal active dimension is by self-evident definition; the vertical effectiveness dimension is based on empirical findings.

| **Figure 7.1** | The Model of the Full Range of Leadership: Suboptimal Profile |

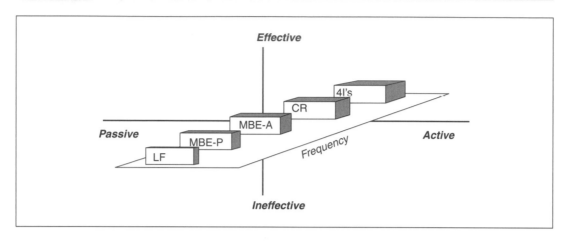

In Figure 7.1, the person with an optimal profile infrequently displays (LF) leadership. This individual displays successively higher frequencies of the transactional leadership styles of MBE-P, MBE-A, and CR and displays the transformational components most frequently. In contrast, as shown in Figure 7.2, the poorly performing leader tends toward inactivity and ineffectiveness, exhibiting LF most frequently and the transformational components least frequently.

The Effectiveness of Transformational Leadership

There is a large and growing body of evidence that supports the effectiveness of transformational leadership over transactional leadership and the other components in the Full Range of Leadership model.

The research evidence that supports this claim begins with meta-analytic findings. Transformational leadership can lead to more committed, loyal, and satisfied followers; in fact, the results suggest a hierarchy, with the four *Is*—the components of transformational leadership—at the top, followed by contingent reward, then active and passive management-by-exception, respectively, with laissez-faire leadership at the bottom as a style generally proving to be ineffective.

Clearly, there is nothing wrong with transactional leadership. It can, in most instances, be quite effective.

Likewise, active, and even passive, management-by-exception can work depending on the circumstances. However, Bass (1985) proposed an augmentation relationship between transformational and transactional leadership. It was suggested that transformational leadership augments transactional in predicting effects on follower satisfaction and performance. Specifically, in statistical terms, transformational leadership should and does account for unique variance in ratings of performance (or other outcomes) over and above that accounted for by active transactional leadership.

Waldman, Bass, and Yammarino (1990) reported evidence for the augmentation effect among various samples of industrial managers and military officers, and Elenkov (2002) found it with Russian managers. The augmentation effect was also obtained by Seltzer and Bass (1990) for a sample of 300 part-time MBA students, each describing their superiors at their full-time working settings. For another sample of 130 MBAs, who each asked three of their followers to complete MLQs about them, the augmentation effect held when one follower's leadership ratings and a second follower's outcomes were correlated. The same augmentation effect occurred when initiation and consideration, as measured by the Leader Behavior Description Questionnaire (LBDQ), were substituted as the measure of transactional leadership. These results demonstrate a fundamental point emphasized in the Bass (1985) theory of leadership: Transactional leadership, particularly

Figure 7.2	The Model of the Full Range of Leadership: Optimal Profile

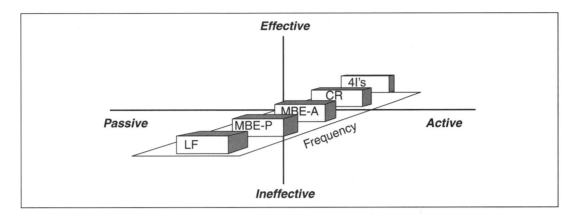

contingent reward, provides a broad basis for effective leadership, but a greater amount of effort, effectiveness, and satisfaction is possible from transactional leadership if augmented by transformational leadership. Finally, as reported earlier by Avolio and Howell (1992), transformational leadership also augments transactional in predicting levels of innovation, risk taking, and creativity.

Transformational Leadership: Directive or Participative?

Critics perceive transformational leadership as elitist and antidemocratic. Indeed, particularly when dealing with charisma, Weber (1947) and his successors emphasized the extent that the charismatic leader directed dependent followers out of crises with radical solutions to deal with their problems; inspirational leaders were seen to be highly directive in their means and methods. The intellectually stimulating leader challenged his followers, and the individually considerate leader could rise above the demands for equality from his followers to treat them differently according to their different needs for growth. At the same time, however, such transformational leaders could share the building of visions and ideas that could be a democratic and collective enterprise. They could encourage follower participation in the change processes involved. In the same way, transactional leadership can be either directive or participative.

Table 7.1 illustrates formulaic statements illustrating that transformational and transactional leadership can be either directive or participative, authoritarian or democratic. This theory has been found useful and essential in convincing trainees that transformational leadership is not a veiled attempt at resurrecting participative leadership. It can be participative as well as more directive in orientation (Avolio & Bass, 1991).

Authentic Versus Inauthentic (Pseudotransformational) Transformational Leadership

A crucial element for James MacGregor Burns's conception of transformational leadership was his firm belief that to be transforming leaders had to be morally uplifting. Bass (1985) originally expected the dynamics of transformational leadership to be the same whether beneficial or harmful to others. As noted earlier, this notion of morally "good" and "evil" leaders has also been a dilemma for charismatic leadership theories.

Charismatic leadership has been differentiated as socialized or personalized. Socialized charismatic leadership is based on egalitarian behavior, serves collective interests, and develops and empowers others. Socialized leaders tend to be altruistic and to use legitimate established channels of authority (House & Howell, 1992; McClelland, 1975). Personalized charismatic leadership is based on personal dominance and authoritarian

Table 7.1 Descriptions of Participative Versus Directive Leadership and the Components of the Full Range of Leadership Model

	Participative	*Directive*
Laissez-faire	"Whatever you think is the correct choice is okay with me."	"If my followers need answers to questions, let them find the answers themselves."
Management-by-exception	"Let's develop the rules together that we will use to identify mistakes."	"These are the rules, and this is how you have violated them."
Contingent reward	"Let's agree on what has to be done and how you will be rewarded if you achieve the objectives."	"If you achieve the objectives I've set, I will recognize your accomplishment with the following reward. . . ."
Individualized consideration	"What can we do as a group to give each other the necessary support to develop our capabilities?"	"I will provide the support you need in your efforts to develop yourself in the job."
Intellectual stimulation	"Can we try to look at our assumptions as a ground without being critical of each other's ideas until all assumptions have been listed?"	"You must reexamine the assumption that a cold fusion engine is a physical impossibility. Revisit this problem and question your assumption."
Inspirational motivation	"Let's work together to merge our aspirations and goals for the good of our group."	"You need to say to yourself that every day you are getting better. You must look at your progression and continue to build upon it over time."
Idealized influence	"We can be a winning team because of our faith in each other. I need your support to achieve our mission."	*Alea icta ist* (i.e., "I've made the decision to cross the Rubicon, so there's no going back"). You must trust me and my direction to achieve what we have set out to do."

Note: From *The Full Range of Leadership Development: Basic and Advanced Manuals* (pp. 5.5-5.6), by B. J. Avolio and B. M. Bass, 1991, Binghamton, NY: Bass, Avolio, and Associates. Copyright 1991 by Bass, Avolio, and Associates. Reprinted with permission.

behavior, is self-aggrandizing, serves the self-interest, and is exploitative of others (McClelland, 1975). Personalized leaders rely heavily on manipulation, threat, and punishment and show disregard for the established institutional procedures and for the rights and feelings of others. They are impulsively aggressive, narcissistic, and impetuous (House & Howell, 1992; Popper, 2002). For Howell and Avolio (1993) authentic charismatic/transformational leaders must be socialized leaders.

This notion of personalized versus socialized leaders can apply to both charismatic and noncharismatic leaders. The defining issue is whether the leader works primarily toward personal gains as opposed to focusing also on the outcomes for followers (i.e., costs and benefits for self vs. costs and benefits for others; Bass & Steidlmeier, 1999). For example, Tyco's CEO, Dennis Kozlowski, who was prosecuted for raiding his company of $600 million to support his lavish lifestyle, represents the extreme of a personalized leader. However, a socialized leader can both achieve personal gains as well as enrich followers. An example is Bill Gates, whose Microsoft Corporation is regularly considered one of the best companies to work for and a company that made many of its employees into millionaires via generous stock options. It is important to note that for most leaders it is not clear-cut. Being personalized or socialized is usually a matter of degree, being more or less selfish or selfless in one's actions (Bass, 1998b).

Originally, the dynamics of transformational leadership were expected to be the same, whether beneficial or harmful to followers (Bass, 1985), although Burns (1978) believed that to be transforming, leaders had to be morally uplifting. Since those early writings, Bass (1998b) has come to agree with Burns. Personalized transformational leaders are pseudotransformational, or inauthentic transformational leaders. They may exhibit many transforming displays but cater, in the long run, to their own self-interests. Self-concerned, self-aggrandizing, exploitative, and power oriented, pseudotransformational leaders believe in distorted utilitarian and warped moral principles. This is in contrast to the authentic transformational leaders, who transcend their own self-interests for one of two reasons: utilitarian or moral. If utilitarian, their objective is to benefit their group or its individual members, their organization, or society, as well as themselves, and to meet the challenges of the task or mission. If a matter of moral principles, the objective is to do the right thing, to do what fits principles of morality, responsibility, sense of discipline, and respect for authority, customs, rules, and traditions of a society. There is belief in the social responsibility of the leader and the organization. Thomas Paine's writings illustrated the authentic transforming leader in his appeals to reason in "Common Sense" and "Age of Reason," his appeals to principle in "Rights of Man," and his often quoted need for transcendence: "These are the times that try men's souls."

Each of the components of transformational leadership (as well as the elements of transactional leadership) can be scrutinized to determine whether they indicate authentic or inauthentic leadership. For example, the transformational components of idealized influence and inspirational motivation can be used authentically to create follower commitment and motivation to a noble cause that benefits all, or they can be used to manipulate followers and produce an unhealthy dependence on the leader. Table 7.2 displays some of the moral elements associated with components of transformational and transactional leadership to demonstrate how these can lead to authentic or inauthentic transformational leadership.

The element of transformational leadership that usually best distinguishes authentic from inauthentic leaders is individualized consideration. The authentic transformational leader is truly concerned with the desires and needs of followers and cares about their individual development. Followers are treated as ends not just means (Bass & Steidlmeier, 1999).

In recent years, scholars have begun to examine the relationship between transformational leadership and ethical leadership behavior or perceptions of leader authenticity. For example, one study examined the relationship between transformational leadership and the perceived integrity of New Zealand managers, as rated by subordinates, peers, and superiors (Parry & Proctor-Thompson, 2002). The results showed that transformational leaders were rated as having more integrity and being more effective than were nontransformational leaders. An interesting study of marketing managers from multinational companies in India presented these leaders with vignettes depicting certain unethical business situations (e.g., bribery, endangerment of the physical environment, personal gain, displays of favoritism) and asked the leaders how they might act in these situations. Transformational leaders, particularly those high on inspirational motivation and intellectual stimulation, were more likely to behave ethically in the tempting scenarios (Banerji & Krishnan, 2000).

In an important study, Turner, Barling, Epitropaki, Butcher, and Milner (2002) found that managers/leaders

Table 7.2   Moral Elements of Transformational and Transactional Leadership

Leadership Dynamic	Transactional Leadership Ethical Concern
Task	Whether what is being done (the end) and the means employed to do it are morally legitimate
Reward system	Whether sanctions or incentives impair effective freedom and respect conscience
Intentions	Truth telling
Trust	Promise keeping
Consequences	Egoism versus altruism—whether the legitimate moral standing and interests of all those affected are respected
Due process	Impartial process of settling conflicts and claims
	Transformational Leadership
Idealized influence	Whether "puffery" and egoism on part of the leader predominate and whether the leader is manipulative or not
Inspirational motivation	Whether providing for true empowerment and self-actualization of followers or not
Intellectual stimulation	Whether the leader's program is open to dynamic transcendence and spirituality or is closed propaganda and a "line" to follow
Individualized consideration	Whether followers are treated as ends or means, whether their unique dignity and interests are respected or not

Note: From "Ethics, Character, and Authentic Transformational Leadership Behavior," by B. M. Bass and P. Steidlmeier, 1999, *Leadership Quarterly,* 10(2), p. 185. Copyright by Elsevier. Reprinted with permission.

from a Canadian university and a British telecommunications company who had higher levels of moral reasoning, as assessed by a self-report, pencil-and-paper measure, were rated by their subordinates as being more transformational. Finally, Brown and Trevino (2003) found that employees of transformational leaders engaged in less employee deviant behavior than followers of leaders who were well liked but not transformational.

Clearly, and as Burns (1978) emphasized, the morality of transformational leadership is critical. Throughout our discussion of transformational leadership, we assume for the most part that we are speaking of authentic transformational leadership. Yet it is clear that much work needs to be done to better understand the dynamics of authentic leadership, in general, and authentic transformational leadership in particular.

The Universality of Transformational Leadership

Bass (1997) argued that transactional and transformational leadership can be found in all parts of the globe and in all forms of organizations. Indeed, research on transformational leadership, including the use of the

MLQ has taken place in every continent and in nearly every industrialized nation. Research from the Global Leadership and Organizational Behavior Effectiveness (GLOBE) research program supports earlier notions that elements of charismatic-transformational leadership are valued leader qualities in all countries and cultures (Den Hartog, House, Hanges, Ruiz-Quintanilla, & Dorfman, 1999; Dorfman, Hanges, & Brodbeck, 2004).

Research evidence from around the world suggests that transformational leadership typically provides a positive augmentation in leader performance beyond the effects of transactional leadership. Furthermore, transformational leadership should be a more effective form of leadership globally because the transformational leader is consistent with people's prototypes of an ideal leader (Bass, 1997). Of course, there are cultural contingencies, as well as organizational factors, that can affect the impact of transformational leadership in particular instances. However, authentic transformational leadership has an impact in all cultures and organizations because transformational leaders have goals that transcend their own self-interests and work toward the common good of the followers (Burns, 1978).

References

Antonakis, J., Avolio, B. J., & Sivasubramaniam, N. (2003). Context and leadership: An examination of the nine-factor full-range leadership theory using the Multifactor Leadership Questionnaire. *The Leadership Quarterly, 14*(3), 261-295.

Avolio, B. J., & Bass, B. M. (1991). *The full range of leadership development: Basic and advanced manuals*. Binghamton, NY: Bass, Avolio, & Associates.

Avolio, B. J., Bass, B. M., & Jung, D. I. (1997). *Replicated confirmatory factor analyses of the Multifactor Leadership Questionnaire*. Binghamton, NY: Center for Leadership Studies, Binghamton University.

Avolio, B. J., & Howell, J. M. (1992). The impact of leader behavior and leader-follower personality match on satisfaction and unit performance. In K. E. Clark, M. B. Clark, & D. R. Campbell (Eds.), *Impact of leadership* (pp. 225-247). Greensboro, NC: The Center for Creative Leadership.

Avolio, B. J., & Yammarino, F. J. (Eds.). (2002). *Transformational and charismatic leadership: The road ahead*. Boston: JAI.

Banerji, P., & Krishnan, V. R. (2000). Ethical preferences for transformational leaders: An empirical investigation. *Leadership and Organization Development Journal, 21*, 405-413.

Bass, B. M. (1985). *Leadership and performance beyond expectations*. New York: Free Press.

Bass, B. M. (1997). Does the transactional/transformational leadership paradigm transcend organizational and national boundaries? *American Psychologist, 52*, 130-139.

Bass, B. M. (1998a). *Transformational leadership: Industrial, military, and educational impact*. Mahwah, NJ: Lawrence Erlbaum Associates.

Bass, B. M. (1998b). The ethics of transformational leadership. In J. Ciulla (Ed.), *Ethics: The heart of leadership* (pp. 169-192). Westport, CT: Praeger.

Bass, B, M., & Avolio, B. J. (1993). Transformational leadership: A response to critiques. In M. M. Chemers & R. Ayman (Eds.), *Leadership theory and research: Perspectives and directions* (pp. 49-80). New York: Academic Press.

Bass, B. M., & Steidlmeier, P. (1999). Ethics, character, and authentic transformational leadership. *The Leadership Quarterly, 10*, 181-217.

Boyd, J. T., Jr. (1988). *Leadership extraordinary: A cross-national military perspective on transactional versus transformational leadership*. Unpublished doctoral dissertation. Nova University, Boca Raton, FL.

Brown, M. E., & Trevino, L. K. (2003, August). *The influence of leadership styles on unethical conduct in work groups: An empirical test*. Paper presented at the meeting of the Academy of Management, Seattle, WA.

Burns, J. M. (1978). *Leadership*. New York: Harper & Row.

Bycio, P., Hackett, R. D., & Allen, J. S. (1995). Further assessments of Bass's (1985) conceptualization of transactional and transformational leadership. *Journal of Applied Psychology, 80*, 468-478.

Conger, J. A., & Kanungo, R. N. (1988). *Charismatic leadership: The elusive factor in organization effectiveness*. San Francisco: Jossey-Bass.

Curphy, G. J. (1992). An empirical investigation of the effects of transformational and transactional leadership on organizational climate, attrition and performance. In K. E. Clark, M. B. Clark, & D. R. Campbell (Eds.), *Impact of leadership* (pp. 177-187). Greensboro, NC: The Center for Creative Leadership.

Den Hartog, D. N., House, R. J., Hanges, P. J., Ruiz-Quintanilla, S. A., & Dorfman, P. W. (1999). Culture specific and cross-cultural generalizable implicit leadership theories: Are attributes of charismatic/transformational leadership universally endorsed? *The Leadership Quarterly, 10*, 219-256.

Dorfman, P. W., Hanges, P. J., & Brodbeck, F. C. (2004). Leadership and cultural variation: The identification of culturally endorsed leadership profiles. In R. J. House, P. J. Hanges, M. Javidan, P. W. Dorfman, & V. Gupta (Eds.), *Culture, leadership, and organizations: The GLOBE study of 62 societies* (pp. 669-719). Thousand Oaks, CA: Sage.

Elenkov, D. S. (2002). Effects of leadership on organizational performance in Russian companies. *Journal of Business Research*, 55, 467-480.

Homans, G. C. (1950). *The human group*. New York: Harcourt, Brace.

House, R. J. (1977). A 1976 theory of charismatic leadership. In J. G. Hunt & L. L. Larson (Eds.), *Leadership: The cutting edge* (pp. 189-207). Carbondale: Southern Illinois University Press.

House, R. J., & Howell, J. M. (1992). Personality and charismatic leadership. *The Leadership Quarterly*, 3, 81-108.

House, R. J., & Shamir, B. (1993). Toward the integration of transformational, charismatic and visionary theories. In M. M. Chemers & R. Ayman (Eds.), *Leadership theory and research: Perspective and directions* (pp. 81-107). New York: Academic Press.

Howell, J. M., & Avolio, B. J. (1993). Transformational leadership, transactional leadership, locus of control, and support for innovation: Key predictors of consolidated business-unit performance. *Journal of Applied Psychology*, 78, 891-902.

Levinson, H. (1980). Power, leadership, and the management of stress. *Professional Psychology*, 11, 497-508.

Longshore, J. M. (1988). *The associative relationship between transformational and transactional leadership styles and group productivity*. Unpublished doctoral dissertation, Nova University, Boca Raton, FL.

McClelland, D. C. (1975). *Power: The inner experience*. New York: Irvington.

O'Keeffe, M. J. (1989). *The effects of leadership style on the perceived effectiveness and satisfaction of selected Army officers*. Unpublished doctoral dissertation, Temple University, Philadelphia.

Parry, K. W., & Proctor-Thomson, S. B. (2002). Perceived integrity of transformational leaders in organizational settings. *Journal of Business Ethics*, 35, 75-96.

Podsakoff, P. M., & Schriescheim, C. A. (1985). Leader reward and punishment behavior: A methodological and substantive review. In B. Staw & L. L. Cummings (Eds.), *Research in organizational behavior*. San Francisco: Jossey-Bass.

Popper, M. (2002). Narcissism and attachment patterns of personalized and socialized charismatic leaders. *Journal of Social and Persona! Relationships*, 19, 797-809.

Seltzer, J., & Bass, B. M. (1990). Transformational leadership: Beyond initiation and consideration. *Journal of Management*, 16, 693-703.

Turner, N., Barling, J., Epitropaki, O., Butcher, V., & Milner, C. (2002). Transformational leadership and moral reasoning. *Journal of Applied Psychology*, 87, 304-311.

Waldman, D. A., Bass, B. M., & Yammarino, F. J. (1990). Adding to contingent-reward behavior: The augmenting effect of charismatic leadership. *Group and Organizational Studies*, 15, 381-394.

Weber, M. (1947). *The theory of social and economic organizations* (T. Parsons, Trans.). New York: Free Press. (Original work published in 1924)

Yammarino, F. J., & Bass, B. M. (1990). Long-term forecasting of transformational leadership and its effects among naval officers: Some preliminary findings. In K. E. Clark & M. R. Clark (Eds.), *Measures of leadership* (pp. 151-169). Greensboro, NC: Center for Creative Leadership.

CHAPTER 8

Servant Leadership

Robert K. Greenleaf

Greenleaf Center for Servant Leadership and Indiana State University

Servant and leader—can these two roles be fused in one real person, in all levels of status or calling? If so, can that person live and be productive in the real world of the present? My sense of the present leads me to say yes to both questions. This chapter is an attempt to explain why and to suggest how.

The idea of the servant as leader came out of reading Hermann Hesse's *Journey to the East.* In this story we see a band of men on a mythical journey, probably also Hesse's own journey. The central figure of the story is Leo, who accompanies the party as the *servant* who does their menial chores, but who also sustains them with his spirit and his song. He is a person of extraordinary presence. All goes well until Leo disappears. Then the group falls into disarray and the journey is abandoned. They cannot make it without the servant Leo. The narrator, one of the party, after some years of wandering, finds Leo and is taken into the Order that had sponsored the journey. There he discovers that Leo, whom he had known first as *servant*, was in fact the titular head of the Order, its guiding spirit, a great and noble *leader.*

One can muse on what Hesse was trying to say when he wrote this story. We know that most of his fiction was autobiographical, that he led a tortured life, and that *Journey to the East* suggests a turn toward the serenity he achieved in his old age. There has been much speculation by critics on Hesse's life and work, some of it centering on this story which they find the most puzzling. But to me, this story clearly says that *the great leader is seen as servant first*, and that simple fact is the key to his greatness. Leo was actually the leader all of the time, but he was servant first because that was what he was, *deep down inside.* Leadership was bestowed upon a person who was by nature a servant. It was something given, or assumed, that could be taken away. His servant nature was the real man, not bestowed, not assumed, and not to be taken away. He was servant first.

I mention Hesse and *Journey to the East* for two reasons. First, I want to acknowledge the source of the idea of the servant as leader. Then I want to use this reference as an introduction to a brief discussion of prophecy.

Fifteen years ago when I first read about Leo, if I had been listening to contemporary prophecy as intently as I do now, the first draft of this piece might have been written then. As it was, the idea lay dormant for eleven years until, four years ago, I concluded that we in this country were in a leadership crisis and that I should do what I could about it. I became painfully aware of how dull my sense of contemporary prophecy had been. And I have reflected much on why we do not hear and heed the prophetic voices in our midst (not a new question in our times, nor more critical than heretofore).

I now embrace the theory of prophecy, which holds that prophetic voices of great clarity, and with a quality of insight equal to that of any age, are speaking cogently all of the time. Men and women of a stature equal to the greatest of the past are with us now addressing the problems of the day and pointing to a better way and to a personality better able to live fully and serenely in these times.

The variable that marks some periods as barren and some as rich in prophetic vision is in the interest, the level of seeking, the responsiveness of the hearers. The variable is not in the presence or absence or the relative quality and force of the prophetic voices. Prophets grow in stature as people respond to their message. If their early attempts are ignored or spurned, their talent may wither away.

It is *seekers*, then, who make prophets, and the initiative of any one of us in searching for and responding to the voice of contemporary prophets may mark the turning point in their growth and service. But since we are the product of our own history, we see current prophecy within the context of past wisdom. We listen to as wide a range of contemporary thought as we can attend to. Then we *choose* those we elect to heed as prophets—*both old and new*—and meld their advice with our own leadings. This we test in real-life experiences to establish our own position.

Some who have difficulty with this theory assert that their faith rests on one or more of the prophets of old having given the "word" for all time and that the contemporary ones do not speak to their condition as the older ones do. But if one really believes that the "word" has been given for all time, how can one be a seeker? How can one hear the contemporary voice when one has decided not to live in the present and has turned that voice off?

Neither this hypothesis nor its opposite can be proved, but I submit that the one given here is the more hopeful choice, one that offers a significant role in prophecy to every individual. One cannot interact with and build strength in a dead prophet, but one can do it with a living one. "Faith," Dean Inge has said, "is the choice of the nobler hypothesis."

One does not, of course, ignore the great voices of the past. One does not awaken each morning with the compulsion to reinvent the wheel. But if one is *servant*, either leader or follower, one is always searching, listening, expecting that a better wheel for these times is in the making. It may emerge any day. Any one of us may find it out from personal experience. I am hopeful.

I am hopeful for these times, despite the tension and conflict, because more natural servants are trying to see clearly the world as it is and are listening carefully to prophetic voices that are speaking *now*. They are challenging the pervasive injustice with greater force, and they are taking sharper issue with the wide disparity between the quality of society they know is reasonable and possible with available resources, and, on the other hand, the actual performance of the whole range of institutions that exist to serve society.

A fresh critical look is being taken at the issues of power and authority, and people are beginning to learn, however haltingly, to relate to one another in less coercive and more creatively supporting ways. A new moral principle is emerging, which holds that the only authority deserving one's allegiance is that which is freely and knowingly granted by the led to the leader in response to, and in proportion to, the clearly evident servant stature of the leader. Those who choose to follow this principle will not casually accept the authority of existing institutions. *Rather, they will freely respond only to individuals who are chosen as leaders because they are proven and trusted as servants.* To the extent that this principle prevails in the future, the only truly viable institutions will be those that are predominantly servant led.

I am mindful of the long road ahead before these trends, which I see so clearly, become a major society-shaping force. We are not there yet. But I see encouraging movement on the horizon.

What direction will the movement take? Much depends on whether those who stir the ferment will come to grips with the age-old problem of how to live in a human society. I say this because so many, having made their awesome decision for autonomy and independence from tradition, and having taken their firm stand against injustice and hypocrisy, find it hard to convert themselves into *affirmative builders* of a better society. How many of them will seek their personal fulfillment by making the hard choices and by undertaking the rigorous preparation that building a better society requires? It all depends on what kind of leaders emerge and how they—we—respond to them.

My thesis, that more servants should emerge as leaders, or should follow only servant-leaders, is not a popular one. It is much more comfortable to go with a less demanding point of view about what is expected of one now. There are several undemanding, plausibly argued alternatives to choose. One, since society seems corrupt, is to seek to avoid the center of it by retreating to an idyllic existence that minimizes involvement with the "system" (with the "system" that makes such withdrawal possible). Then there is the assumption that since the effort to reform existing institutions has not brought instant perfection, the remedy is to destroy them completely so that fresh new perfect ones can grow. Not much thought seems to be given to the problem of where the new seed will come from or who the gardener to tend them will be. The concept of the servant-leader stands in sharp contrast to this kind of thinking.

Yet it is understandable that the easier alternatives would be chosen, especially by young people. By extending education for so many so far into the adult years, normal participation in society is effectively denied when young people are ready for it. With education that is preponderantly abstract and analytical it is no wonder that there is a preoccupation with criticism and that not much thought is given to "What can I do about it?"

Criticism has its place, but as a total preoccupation it is sterile. In a time of crisis, like the leadership crisis we are now in, if too many potential builders are taken in by a complete absorption with dissecting the wrong and by a zeal for instant perfection, then the movement so many of us want to see will be set back. The danger, perhaps, is to hear the analyst too much and the artist too little.

Albert Camus stands apart from other great artists of his time, in my view, and deserves the title of *prophet* because of his unrelenting demand that each of us confront the exacting terms of our own existence, and, like Sisyphus, *accept our rock and find our happiness in*

dealing with it. Camus sums up the relevance of his position to our concern for the servant as leader in the last paragraph of his last published lecture, entitled "Create Dangerously":

One may long, as I do, for a gentler flame, a respite, a pause for musing. But perhaps there is no other peace for the artist than what he finds in the heat of combat. "Every wall is a door," Emerson correctly said. Let us not look for the door, and the way out, anywhere but in the wall against which we are living. Instead, let us seek the respite where it is—in the very thick of battle. For in my opinion, and this is where I shall close, it *is* there. Great ideas, it has been said, come into the world as gently as doves. Perhaps, then, if we listen attentively, we shall hear, amid the uproar of empires and nations, a faint flutter of wings, the gentle stirring of life and hope. Some will say that this hope lies in a nation, others, in a man. I believe rather that it is awakened, revived, nourished by millions of solitary individuals whose deeds and works every day negate frontiers and the crudest implications of history. As a result, there shines forth fleetingly the ever-threatened truth that each and every man, on the foundations of his own sufferings and joys, builds for them all.

One is asked, then, to accept the human condition, its sufferings and its joys, and to work with its imperfections as the foundation upon which the individual will build wholeness through adventurous creative achievement. For the person with creative potential there is no wholeness except in using it. And, as Camus explained, the going is rough and the respite is brief. It is significant that he would title his last university lecture "Create Dangerously." And, as I ponder the fusing of servant and leader, it seems a dangerous creation: dangerous for the natural servant to become a leader, dangerous for the leader to be servant first, and dangerous for a follower to insist on being led by a servant. There are safer and easier alternatives available to all three. But why take them?

As I respond to the challenge of dealing with this question in the ensuing discourse, I am faced with two problems.

First, I did not get the notion of the servant as leader from conscious logic. Rather, it came to me as an intuitive insight as I contemplated Leo. And I do not see what is relevant from my own searching and experience in terms of a logical progression from premise to conclusion. Rather, I see it as fragments of data to be fed into my internal computer from which intuitive insights come. Serving and leading are still mostly intuition-based concepts in my thinking.

The second problem, related to the first, is that, just as there may be a real contradiction in the servant as leader, so my perceptual world is full of contradictions. Some examples: I believe in order, and I want creation out of chaos. My good society will have strong individualism amid community. It will have elitism along with populism. I listen to the old and to the young and find myself baffled and heartened by both. Reason and intuition, each in its own way, both comfort and dismay me. There are many more. Yet, with all of this, I believe that I live with as much serenity as do my contemporaries who venture into controversy as freely as I do but whose natural bent is to tie up the essentials of life in neat bundles of logic and consistency. But I am deeply grateful to the people who are logical and consistent because some of them, out of their natures, render invaluable services for which I am not capable.

My resolution of these two problems is to offer the relevant gleanings of my experience in the form of a series of unconnected little essays, some developed more fully than others, with the suggestion that they be read and pondered separately within the context of this opening section.

Who Is the Servant-Leader?

The servant-leader *is* servant first—as Leo was portrayed. It begins with the natural feeling that one wants to serve, to serve *first*. Then conscious choice brings one to aspire to lead. That person is sharply different from one who is *leader* first, perhaps because of the need to assuage an unusual power drive or to acquire material possessions. For such, it will be a later choice to serve—after leadership is established. The leader-first and the servant-first are two extreme types. Between them there are shadings and blends that are part of the infinite variety of human nature.

The difference manifests itself in the care taken by the servant-first to make sure that other people's highest priority needs are being served. The best test, and difficult to administer, is this: Do those served grow as persons? Do they, *while being served*, become healthier, wiser, freer, more autonomous, more likely themselves to become servants? *And*, what is the effect on the least privileged in society? Will they benefit or at least not be further deprived?

As one sets out to serve, how can one know that this will be the result? This is part of the human dilemma; one cannot know for sure. One must, after some study and experience, hypothesize—but leave the hypothesis under a shadow of doubt. Then one acts on the hypothesis and examines the result. One continues to study and learn and periodically one reexamines the hypothesis itself.

Finally, one chooses again. Perhaps one chooses the same hypothesis again and again. But it is always a fresh, open choice. And it is always a hypothesis under a shadow of doubt. "Faith is the choice of the nobler hypothesis." Not the *noblest*; one never knows what that is. But the *nobler*, the best one can see when the choice is made. Since the test of results of one's actions is usually long delayed, the faith that sustains the choice of the nobler hypothesis is psychological self-insight. This is the most dependable part of the true servant.

The natural servant, the person who is *servant-first*, is more likely to persevere and refine a particular hypothesis on what serves another's highest priority needs than is the person who is *leader-first* and who later serves out of promptings of conscience or in conformity with normative expectations.

My hope for the future rests in part on my belief that among the legions of deprived and unsophisticated people are many true servants who will lead and that most of them can learn to discriminate among those who presume to serve them and identify the true servants whom they will follow.

Everything Begins With the Initiative of an Individual

The forces for good and evil in the world are propelled by the thoughts, attitudes, and actions of individual beings. What happens to our values, and therefore to the quality of our civilization in the future, will be shaped by the conceptions of individuals that are born of inspiration. Perhaps only a few will receive this inspiration (insight) and the rest will learn from them. The very essence of leadership, going out ahead to show the way, derives from more than usual openness to inspiration. Why would anybody accept the leadership of another except that the other sees more clearly where it is best to go? Perhaps this is the current problem: too many who presume to lead do not see more clearly, and in defense of their inadequacy, they all the more strongly argue that the "system" must be preserved—a fatal error in this day of candor.

But the leader needs more than inspiration. A leader ventures to say, "I will go; come with me!" A leader initiates, provides the ideas and the structure, and takes the risk of failure along with the chance of success. A leader says, "I will go; follow me!" while knowing that the path is uncertain, even dangerous. One then trusts those who go with one's leadership.

Paul Goodman, speaking through a character in *Making Do*, has said, "If there is no community for you, young man, young man, make it yourself."

What Are You Trying to Do?

"What are you trying to do?" is one of the easiest to ask and most difficult to answer of questions.

A mark of leaders, an attribute that puts them in a position to show the way for others, is that they are better than most at pointing the direction. As long as one is leading, one always has a goal. It may be a goal arrived at by group consensus, or the leader, acting on inspiration, may simply have said, "Let's go this way." But the leader always knows what it is and can articulate it for any who are unsure. By clearly stating and restating the goal the leader gives certainty to others who may have difficulty in achieving it for themselves.

The word *goal* is used here in the special sense of the overarching purpose, the big dream, the visionary concept, the ultimate consummation that one approaches but never really achieves. It is something presently out of reach; it is something to strive for, to move toward, to become. It is so stated that it excites the imagination and challenges people to work for something they do not yet know how to do, something they can be proud of as they move toward it.

As a generalization, I suggest that human service that requires love cannot be satisfactorily dispensed by specialized institutions that exist apart from community, that take the problem out of sight of the community. Both those being cared for and the community suffer.

Love is an undefinable term, and its manifestations are both subtle and infinite. But it begins, I believe, with one absolute condition: unlimited liability! As soon as one's liability for another is qualified *to any degree*, love is diminished by that much.

Institutions, as we know them, are designed to limit liability for those who serve through them. In the British tradition, corporations are not "INC" as we know them, but "LTD"—Limited. Most of the goods and services we now depend on will probably continue to be furnished by such limited liability institutions. But any human service where the one who is served should be loved in the process requires community, a face-to-face group in which the liability of each for the other and all for one is unlimited, or as close to it as it is possible to get. Trust and respect are highest in this circumstance, and an accepted ethic that gives strength to all is reinforced. Where community doesn't exist, trust, respect, and ethical behavior are difficult for the young to learn and for the old to maintain. Living in community as one's basic involvement will generate an exportable surplus of love that we may carry into our many involvements with institutions that are usually not communities: businesses, churches, governments, schools.

Out of the distress of our seeming community-less society, hopeful new forms of community are emerging: young people's communes, Israeli kibbutzim, and therapeutic communities like Synanon. Seen through the bias of conventional morality, these communities are sometimes disturbing to the older generation. But whatever happens with these specific examples, they show a genuine striving for community and represent a significant new social movement that may foretell the future.

The opportunities are tremendous for rediscovering vital lost knowledge about how to live in community while retaining as much as we can of the value in our present urban, institution-bound society.

All that is needed to rebuild community as a viable life form for large numbers of people is for enough servant-leaders to show the way, not by mass movements, but by each servant-leader demonstrating his or her own unlimited liability for a quite specific community-related group.

Institutions

We differ from the primitives in that it is our task to rediscover the elementary knowledge of community while we refine and radically improve much of the vast non-community institutional structure on which we depend and without which we could not survive. A hopeful sign of the times, in the sector of society where it seems least expected—highly competitive business—is that people-building institutions are holding their own while they struggle successfully in the marketplace. It is not a great revolutionary movement, but it is there as a solid fact of these times. And it is a very simple approach. The first order of business is to build a group of people who, under the influence of the institution, grow taller and become healthier, stronger, more autonomous.

Some institutions achieve distinction for a short time by the intelligent *use* of people, but it is not a happy achievement, and eminence, so derived, does not last long. Others aspire to distinction (or the reduction of problems) by embracing gimmicks: profit sharing, work enlargement, information, participation, suggestion plans, paternalism, motivational management. There is nothing wrong with these in a people-building institution. But in a people-using institution they are like aspirin—sometimes stimulating and pain relieving, and they may produce an immediate measurable improvement of sorts. But these are not the means whereby an institution moves from people-using to people-building. In fact, an overdose of these nostrums may seal an institution's fate as a people-user for a very long time.

An institution starts on a course toward people-building with leadership that has a firmly established context of *people first*. With that, the right actions fall naturally into place. And none of the conventional gimmicks may ever be used.

Trustees

Institutions need two kinds of leaders: those who are inside and carry the active day-to-day roles, and those who stand outside but are intimately concerned, and who, with the benefit of some detachment, oversee the active leaders. These are the *trustees*.

Trustees are what their title implies, persons in whom ultimate trust is placed. Because institutions inevitably harbor conflict, trustees are the court of last resort if an issue arises that cannot be resolved by the active parties. If tangible assets are involved, trustees legally hold them and are responsible to all interested parties for their good use. They have a prime concern for goals and for progress toward goals. They make their influence felt more by knowing and asking questions than by authority, although they usually have authority and can use it if need be. If, as is usual, there are several trustees, their chairperson has a special obligation to see that the trustees as a group sustain a common purpose and are influential in helping the institution maintain consistent high-level performance toward its goals. The board chair is not simply the presider over meetings but also must serve and lead the trustees as a group and act as their major contact with the active inside leadership. Although trustees usually leave the "making of news" to active persons in the enterprise, theirs is an important leadership opportunity.

So conceived, the role of trustees provides a great opportunity for those who would serve and lead. And no one step will more quickly raise the quality of the total society than a radical reconstruction of trustee bodies so that they are predominantly made up of able, dedicated servant-leaders. Two disturbing questions: Is there now enough discerning toughness strategically placed to see that this change takes place, in the event that able, dedicated servant-leaders become available in sufficient numbers to do it? And are enough able people now preparing themselves for these roles so that this change *can* be made in the event that it is possible to make it?

Power and Authority—The Strength and the Weakness

In a complex institution-centered society, which ours is likely to be into the indefinite future, there will be large and small concentrations of power. Sometimes it will be a servant's power of persuasion and example. Sometimes it will be coercive power used to dominate and manipulate people. The difference is that, in the former, power is used to create opportunity and alternatives so that individuals may choose and build autonomy. In the latter, individuals are coerced into a predetermined path. Even if it is "good" for them, if they experience nothing else, ultimately their autonomy will be diminished.

Some coercive power is overt and brutal. Some is covert and subtly manipulative. The former is open and acknowledged; the latter is insidious and hard to detect. Most of us are more coerced than we know. We need to be more alert in order to know, and we also need to acknowledge that, in an imperfect world, authority backed up by power is still necessary because we just don't know a better way. We may one day find one. It is worth searching for. Part of our dilemma is that all leadership is, to some extent, manipulative. Those who follow must be strong!

The trouble with coercive power is that it only strengthens resistance. And, if successful, its controlling effect lasts only as long as the force is strong. It is not organic. Only persuasion and the consequent voluntary acceptance are organic.

Since both kinds of power have been around for a long time, an individual will be better off by at some point being close enough to raw coercion to know what it is. One must be close to both the bitterness and goodness of life to be fully human.

Servants, by definition, are fully human. Servant-leaders are functionally superior because they are closer to the ground—they hear things, see things, know things, and their intuitive insight is exceptional. Because of this they are dependable and trusted. They know the meaning of that line from Shakespeare's sonnet, "They that have power to hurt and will do none."

How Does One Know the Servant?

For those who follow—and this is everyone, including those who lead—the really critical question is: Who is this moral individual we would see as leader? Who is the servant? How does one tell a truly giving, enriching servant from the neutral person or the one whose net influence is to take away from or diminish other people?

Rabbi Heschel had just concluded a lecture on the Old Testament prophets in which he had spoken of true prophets and false prophets. A questioner asked him how one tells the difference between the true and the false prophets. The rabbi's answer was succinct and to the point. "There is no *way!*" he said. Then he elaborated, "If there were a *way*, if one had a gauge to slip over the head of the prophet and establish without question that this prophet is or isn't a true prophet, there would be no human dilemma and life would have no meaning."

So it is with the servant issue. If there were a dependable way that would tell us "these people enrich by their presence, these are neutral, or these take away," life would be without challenge. Yet it is terribly important that one *know*, both about oneself and about others, whether the net effect of one's influence on others enriches, is neutral, or diminishes and depletes.

Since there is no certain way to know this, one must turn to the artists for illumination. Such an illumination is in Hermann Hesse's idealized portrayal of the servant Leo, whose servant-hood comes through in his leadership. In stark, modern terms it can also be found in the brutal reality of the mental hospital where Ken Kesey (in *One Flew over the Cuckoo's Nest*) gives us Big Nurse—strong, able, dedicated, dominating, authority-ridden, manipulative, exploitative—the net effect of whose influence diminished other people, literally destroyed them. In the story she is pitted in a contest with tough, gutter-bred MacMurphy, a patient, the net effect of whose influence is to build up people and make both patients and the doctor in charge of the ward grow larger as persons, stronger, healthier—an effort that ultimately costs MacMurphy his life. If one will study the two characters, Leo and MacMurphy, one will get a measure of the range of possibilities in the role of servant as leader.

In Here, Not Out There

A king once asked Confucius's advice on what to do about the large number of thieves. Confucius answered, "If you, sir, were not covetous, although you should reward them to do it, they would not steal." This advice places an enormous burden on those who are favored by the rules, and it establishes how old is the notion that the servant views any problem in the world as *in here*, inside oneself, not *out there*. And if a flaw in the world is to be remedied, to the servant the process of change starts *in here*, in the servant, not *out there*. This is a difficult concept for that busybody, modern man.

So it is with joy. Joy is inward, it is generated inside. It is not found outside and brought in. It is for those who accept the world as it is, part good, part bad, and who identify with the good by adding a little island of serenity to it.

Hermann Hesse dramatized it in the powerful leadership exerted by Leo, who ostensibly served only in menial ways but who, by the quality of his inner life that was manifest in his presence, lifted others up and made the journey possible. Camus, in his final testament quoted earlier, leaves us with: "Each and every man, on the foundations of his own sufferings and joys, builds for them all."

Who Is the Enemy?

Who is the enemy? Who is holding back more rapid movement to the better society that is reasonable and possible with available resources? Who is responsible for the mediocre performance of so many of our institutions? Who is standing in the way of a larger consensus on the definition of the better society and paths to reaching it?

Not evil people. Not stupid people. Not apathetic people. Not the "system." Not the protesters, the disrupters, the revolutionaries, the reactionaries.

Granting that fewer evil, stupid, or apathetic people or a better "system" might make the job easier, their removal would not change matters, not for long. The better society will come, if it comes, with plenty of evil, stupid, apathetic people around and with an imperfect, ponderous, inertia-charged "system" as the vehicle for change. Liquidate the offending people, radically alter or destroy the system, and in less than a generation they will all be back. It is not in the nature of things that a society can be cleaned up once and for all according to an ideal plan. And even if it were possible, who would

want to live in an aseptic world? Evil, stupidity, apathy, the "system" are not the enemy even though society building forces will be contending with them all the time. The healthy society, like the healthy body, is not the one that has taken the most medicine. It is the one in which the internal health-building forces are in the best shape.

The real enemy is fuzzy thinking on the part of good, intelligent, vital people, and their failure to lead, and to follow servants as leaders. Too many settle for being critics and experts. There is too much intellectual wheel spinning, too much retreating into "research," too little preparation for and willingness to undertake the hard and high-risk tasks of building better institutions in an imperfect world, too little disposition to see "the problem" as residing *in here* and not *out there*.

In short, the enemy is strong natural servants who have the potential to lead but do not lead, or who choose to follow a nonservant. They suffer. Society suffers. And so it may be in the future.

Implications

The future society may be just as mediocre as this one. It may be worse. And no amount of restructuring or changing the system or tearing it down in the hope that something better will grow will change this. There may be a better system than the one we now have. It is hard to know. But, whatever it is, if the people to lead it well are not there, a better system will not produce a better society.

Many people finding their wholeness through many and varied contributions make a good society. Here we are concerned with but one facet: *Able servants with potential to lead will lead, and, where appropriate, they will follow only servant-leaders*. Not much else counts if this does not happen.

This brings us to that critical aspect of realism that confronts the servant-leader, that of *order*. There must be some order because we know for certain that the great majority of people will choose some kind of order over chaos even if it is delivered by a brutal non-servant and even if, in the process, they lose much of their freedom. Therefore the servant-leader will beware of pursuing an idealistic path regardless of its impact on order. The big question is: What kind of order? This is the great challenge to the emerging generation of leaders: Can they build better order?

Older people who grew up in a period when values were more settled and the future seemed more secure will be disturbed by much they find today. But one firm note of hope comes through loud and clear; we are at a turn of history in which people are growing up faster and some extraordinarily able, mature, servant-disposed men and women are emerging in their early and middle twenties. The percentage may be small, and again, it may be larger than we think. Moreover, it is not an elite; it is all sorts of exceptional people. Most of them could be ready for some large society-shaping responsibility by the time they are thirty if they are encouraged to prepare for leadership as soon as their potential as builders is identified, which is possible for many of them by age eighteen or twenty. Preparation to lead need not be at the complete expense of vocational or scholarly preparation, but it must be the *first priority*. And it may take some difficult bending of resources and some unusual initiatives to accomplish all that should be accomplished in these critical years *and* give leadership preparation first priority. But whatever it takes, it must be done. For a while at least, until a better-led society is assured, some other important goals should take a subordinate place.

All of this rests on the assumption that the only way to change a society (or just make it go) is to produce people, enough people, who will change it (or make it go). The urgent problems of our day—the disposition to venture into immoral and senseless wars, destruction of the environment, poverty, alienation, discrimination, overpopulation—are here because of human failures, individual failures, one person at a time, one action at a time failures.

If we make it out of all of this (and this is written in the belief that we will make it), the "system" will be whatever works best. The builders will find the useful pieces wherever they are and invent new ones when needed, all without reference to ideological coloration.

"How do we get the right things done?" will be the watchword of the day, every day. And the context of those who bring it off will be this: all women and men who are touched by the effort grow taller, and become healthier, stronger, more autonomous, *and* more disposed to serve.

Leo the *servant*, and the exemplar of the *servant-leader*, has one further portent for us. If we may assume that Hermann Hesse is the narrator in *Journey to the East* (not a difficult assumption to make), at the end of the story he establishes his identity. His final confrontation at the close of his initiation into the Order is with a small transparent sculpture, two figures joined together. One is Leo, the other is the narrator. The narrator notes that a movement of substance is taking place within the transparent sculpture.

I perceived that my image was in the process of adding to and flowing into Leo's, nourishing and strengthening it. It seemed that, in time . . . only one would remain: Leo. He must grow, I must disappear.

As I stood there and looked and tried to understand what I saw, I recalled a short conversation that I had once had with Leo during the festive days at Bremgarten. We had talked about the creations of poetry being more vivid and real than the poets themselves.

What Hesse may be telling us here is that Leo is the symbolic personification of Hesse's aspiration to serve through his literary creations, creations that are greater than Hesse himself; and that his work, for which he was but the channel, will carry on and serve and lead in a way that he, a twisted and tormented man, could not—except as he created.

Does not Hesse dramatize, in extreme form, the dilemma of us all? Except as we venture to create, we cannot project ourselves beyond ourselves to serve and lead.

To which Camus would add: *Create dangerously!*

CHAPTER 9

Charismatic Theory

Jay A. Conger

Claremont McKenna College

Certain leaders, such as Winston Churchill, Mohandas Gandhi, Martin Luther King, Jr., and Franklin Delano Roosevelt, inspired their followers to throw heart and soul into creating a better world. Other leaders led their followers down paths of destruction and disaster—perhaps the most notable being Adolf Hitler. Whatever history's judgment on their goals and the outcome of their efforts, these leaders all share the quality of charisma. Defined as a special power to attract and inspire followers through a compelling vision and perceptions of extraordinary capabilities, the phenomenon of charisma is based in followers' perceptions, as described below.

The German sociologist Max Weber (1864–1920) was the first to apply the adjective *charismatic* to leaders. He posited three forms of authority in society (the traditional, the rational-legal, and the charismatic), with charismatic authority being based on people's collective perception that a given individual is extraordinary and therefore worthy of leading. In contrast to leaders whose authority derives from tradition or rules or elections, leaders whose authority derives from charisma are "set apart from ordinary men and . . . treated as endowed with . . . exceptional powers and qualities . . . [which] are not accessible to the ordinary person but are regarded as of divine origin or as exemplary" (Weber 1947, 358–359).

While Weber did not give a detailed explanation of the behaviors associated with this form of leadership, his writings do provide us with elements of the character and the course of charismatic leadership. Weber describes the condition under which it typically arises (distress), one requirement for its maintenance (success), its likely outcome over time (institutionalization), and some of the means by which charismatic leaders exercise their authority (powers of vision, speech, heroism). Because of Weber's sociological perspective, however, he largely overlooked the issues of personal attributes and relational dynamics between the leader and followers. Only later in the twentieth century did organizational theorists turn their attention to those particular gaps in our understanding.

The Distinguishing Behaviors of Charismatic Leaders

Most social psychological theories consider leadership to be a by-product of the interaction between members

Source: From G. R. Goethals, G. J. Sorenson, and J. M. Burns (Eds.), *Encyclopedia of leadership* (pp. 162–167). Thousand Oaks, CA: Sage. © 2008 Sage Publications, Inc. Used by permission.

of a group. As members work together to attain group objectives, they begin to realize their status in the group as either a leader or a follower. This realization is based on observations of their relative influence within a group. The individual who exerts maximum influence is perceived to be playing the leadership role. That leadership is affirmed by group members' continuing interactions with and deference to that person. In other words, leadership qualities are attributed to an individual on the basis of his or her influence.

Similarly, followers characterize a leader as either charismatic or not charismatic on the basis of his or her behavior. But what are the behavioral components responsible for such an attribution? What attributes are charismatic and what attributes are not? A simple process model of leadership allows us to highlight the distinctions.

To learn the distinguishing behaviors of charismatic leaders, we can examine how leaders approach and solve a problem. In the initial stage, the leader must evaluate the existing situation or status quo critically. Deficiencies in the status quo or poorly exploited opportunities in the environment lead to formulation of future goals. Before devising those goals, however, the leader must assess what resources are available and what constraints he or she faces. In addition, the leader must assess the inclinations, the abilities, the needs, and the level of satisfaction experienced by his or her followers. Having completed this evaluation, the leader formulates the goals. Finally, in stage three, the leader demonstrates how the goals can be achieved. As leaders move through these three stages, we can identify behavioral components unique to charismatic leaders.

Stage One: Sensitivity to the Environmental Context

We can distinguish charismatic leaders from non-charismatic leaders in stage one by their sensitivity to environmental constraints and by their heightened sensitivity to deficiencies and poorly exploited opportunities in the status quo. For this reason, we find that entrepreneurs are often charismatic leaders. Entrepreneurs are very critical of the status quo. They tend to be highly sensitive to the social and physical

environments in which they operate. Charismatic leaders also tend to be highly sensitive to the abilities and the emotional needs of their followers—who are the most important resource for attaining the leaders' goals. This is especially true of leaders of social movements, such as Gandhi, Martin Luther King, and César Chávez. A non-charismatic leader is less likely to pay a great deal of attention to the shortcomings in their environment and to see these as platforms for action.

In the business context, a charismatic leader's increased sensitivity to deficiencies in the environment lets him or her perceive strategic opportunities. For example, a charismatic entrepreneur can see the retail potential of the Internet, as did Jeff Bezos, the founder of Amazon.com, the online bookstore that grew into an online department store. The charismatic business leader may also recognize internal organizational deficiencies and advocate radical internal change. During periods of relative tranquility, charismatic leaders often foster a need for change by actually creating the deficiencies or exaggerating existing minor ones. A non-charismatic leader, by comparison, is more likely to accept and work within the status quo—making improvements but not fundamentally challenging the system.

Because of their emphasis on deficiencies in the system and their high levels of intolerance for them, charismatic leaders always act as agents of innovative and radical change. The attribution of charisma is dependent not on the outcome of change but simply on the fact that the leader demands that action be taken to bring about that change.

Stage Two: The Future Vision

After assessing the environment, a leader will formulate goals for achieving the organization's objectives. Charismatic leaders can be distinguished from others by the nature of these goals and by the manner in which they articulate them. For example, charismatic leaders tend to aim for an idealized future. In stage two, it is their formulation of that idealized future vision, their ability to evoke it in the imagination of their followers, that sets them apart from other leaders. Steven Jobs, founder of Apple Computer, and Fred Smith, founder of

Federal Express, are two examples of charismatic leaders who articulated compelling visions of a future filled with opportunity.

The more idealized or utopian the future goal advocated by the leader, the greater the discrepancy with the status quo, and the greater the discrepancy between the goal and the status quo, the more likely followers are to attribute the leader with extraordinary vision. Moreover, by presenting a very discrepant and idealized goal to followers, a leader provides a sense of challenge and a motivating force for change. Psychologists have suggested that within a certain latitude of acceptance, the greater the discrepancy between reality and the goal, the greater the pressure on followers to shed their resistance and accept the advocated change. Since the idealized goal promises to meet followers' hopes and aspirations, it tends to be within this latitude of acceptance in spite of its extreme discrepancy. Leaders become charismatic as they succeed in winning followers' support for the advocated vision. They are charismatic when their vision is an idealized embodiment of a perspective shared by followers.

It is the fact that they can articulate a shared vision with the potential for satisfying followers' needs that make charismatic leaders so attractive. Furthermore, the fact that the vision is idealized (and therefore discrepant) makes the leader who champions it an admirable person in the eyes of the followers, one deserving of respect and worthy of identification and imitation.

To be charismatic, leaders not only need to have visions and plans for achieving them, they must also be able to articulate their visions and plans effectively so as to influence their followers. Here articulation involves two separate processes: articulation of the context and articulation of the leader's motivation for leading. Articulating the context involves explaining the nature of the status quo and its shortcomings, describing the vision of the future, and explaining how, when realized, the new reality will have eliminated existing deficiencies and fulfilled the hopes of followers. Finally, articulating the context means articulating the leader's plans for realizing the vision.

In articulating the context, the charismatic leader is careful to emphasize only the positive features of the future vision and only the negative features of the current status quo. The status quo is usually presented as unacceptable, while the vision is presented in clear, specific terms as the most attractive alternative and, though deeply challenging, attainable. The charismatic leader attempts to create among followers disenchantment or discontentment with the status quo, a strong identification with future goals, and a compelling desire to be led in the direction of the goal in spite of obstacles.

In articulating their motivation for leading, charismatic leaders are highly expressive. They convey strong conviction, emotions, self-confidence when communicating. They use colorful phrases and descriptions along with engaging gestures. As masters of rhetoric, charismatic leaders choose words that convey assertiveness, confidence, expertise, and concern for followers' needs. These same qualities may also be expressed through their dress (for example, Gandhi's *dhoti,* or loincloth, which conveyed simplicity and unity with the common people of India), their appearance, and their body language. Charismatic leaders' use of rhetoric, their high energy, persistence, unconventional and risky behavior, heroic deeds, and personal sacrifices all serve to articulate their high motivation and enthusiasm, which then become contagious among their followers.

Stage Three: Achieving the Vision

In the final stage of the leadership process, an effective leader inspires followers with confidence in his or her abilities and clearly demonstrates the tactics and behaviors required to achieve the shared goal. The charismatic leader does this by building trust through personal example and risk taking, and through unconventional or innovative expertise (for example, Steven Jobs's success with the personal computer in an era dominated by mainframe computers). It is critical that followers trust the leader's vision, otherwise they will not follow. Generally, leaders are perceived as trustworthy when they advocate their position in a disinterested manner and demonstrate a concern for followers' needs. However, in order to be charismatic, leaders must make these qualities appear extraordinary. They must transform their concern for followers' needs into a total dedication; they must engage in exemplary acts that are perceived as involving great personal risk—for example, the possible loss of personal finances, the possibility of being fired or (in a political context) jailed, and the potential loss of formal or informal status, power, authority, and credibility. The higher the manifest personal cost or sacrifice for the common goal, the greater is the trustworthiness of a leader. The more leaders are able to demonstrate that they are indefatigable workers prepared to champion the shared vision regardless of cost to themselves, the more they are perceived as charismatic.

Finally, charismatic leaders must appear to be knowledgeable and experts in their areas of influence. Some degree of demonstrated expertise, as reflected in successes in the past, may be a necessary condition for the attribution of charisma. For example, Steven Jobs's success with the Apple I personal computer and Lee Iacocca's responsibility for the Ford Mustang made them both more credible with employees at Apple Computer and Chrysler Corporation, respectively. First, charismatic leaders use their expertise to demonstrate the inadequacy of the traditional technology, rules, and regulations of the status quo. Then they use their expertise to devise effective but unconventional strategies and plans of action. We can say that leaders are perceived as charismatic when they expertly transcend the existing order through unconventional or countercultural means. For instance, Gandhi chose to use nonviolent actions to lead his revolution in sharp contrast to the conventions of a revolution using combat.

As hinted at above, the attribution of charisma to leaders also depends on followers' perceptions of their leaders as revolutionary or countercultural. The countercultural qualities of leaders are partly manifested in their discrepant idealized visions. But more important, charismatic leaders adopt unconventional, countercultural, and therefore innovative plans and strategies for achieving desired changes, and their exemplary acts of heroism involving personal risks or self-sacrifice are novel and unconventional. Their uncommon behavior, when successful, evokes in their followers emotional responses of surprise and admiration—and the attribution of charisma.

The Charisma Constellation

Charismatic leadership is not a mysterious force. It is the product of a distinct collection of behaviors and activities on the part of the leader. While we have identified many of the critical dimensions that distinguish this remarkable form of leadership, it is important to note that charismatic leadership is a constellation of behaviors. In other words, as a leader manifests a growing number of the behaviors described above, the likelihood of an attribution of charisma increases. Thus, a leader who is only skillful at detecting deficiencies in the status quo is less likely to be seen as charismatic than one who not only detects deficiencies but also formulates future visions, articulates them, and devises unconventional means for achieving them.

Besides the total number of manifested behavioral components, leaders may differ in the intensity or frequency (or both) with which they exhibit a given behavioral component. The greater the intensity or frequency of a behavior, the more likely it is to reflect charisma. Finally, certain behaviors are critical and effective sources of charisma in some organizational or cultural contexts, but not in others. For example, in some contexts, unconventionality may be less valued as an attribute of charisma than articulation skills, while in other contexts it may be more valued. For example, in highly individualistic organizations or societies, unconventionality might be more the norm and so would be less appealing. The constellation of behaviors and their relative importance as determinants of charisma will differ from one organization to another and from one culture to another.

Further Reading

Bass, B. M., & Avolio, B. (1993). Transformational leadership: A response to critiques. In M. M. Chemers & R. Ayman (Eds.), *Leadership theory and research: Perspectives and directions.* New York: Academic Press.

Berlew, D. E. (1974). Leadership and organizational excitement. *California Management Review, 17*(2), 21–30.

Boal, K. B., & Bryson, J. M. (1988). Charismatic leadership: A phenomenological and structural approach. In J. G. Hunt, B. R. Baliga, H. P. Dachler, & C. A. Schriesheim (Eds.), *Emerging leadership vistas* (pp. 11–28). Lexington, MA: Lexington Books.

Byrne, D. (1977). *The attraction paradigm.* New York: Academic Press.

Conger, J. A. (1989) *The charismatic leader: Beyond the mystique of exceptional leadership.* San Francisco: Jossey-Bass.

Conger, J. A., & Kanungo, R. N. (1998). *Charismatic leadership in organizations.* Thousand Oaks, CA: Sage.

Friedland, W. H. (1964). For a sociological concept of charisma. *Social Forces, 43*(1), 18–26.

House, R. J. (1977). A 1976 theory of charismatic leadership. In J. G. Hunt & L. L. Larson (Eds.), *Leadership: The cutting edge* (pp. 189–207) Carbondale: Southern Illinois University Press.

House, R. J. (1995). Leadership in the twenty-first century: A speculative inquiry. In A. Howard (Ed.), *The changing nature of work* (pp. 411–450). San Francisco: Jossey-Bass.

House, R. J., Spangler, W. D., & Woycke, J. (1991). Personality and charisma in the U.S. presidency: A psychological theory of leader effectiveness. *Administrative Science Quarterly, 36*(3), 364–396.

Hovland, C. I., & Pritzker, H. A. (1957). Extent of opinion change as a function of amount of change advocated. *Journal of Abnormal Psychology, 54,* 257–261.

Kanter, R. M. (1967). Commitment and social organization: A study of commitment mechanisms in utopian communities. *American Sociological Review, 33*(4), 499–517.

Kanter, R. M. (1979). Power failures in management circuits. *Harvard Business Review, 57*(4), 65–75.

Katz, J., & Kahn, R. L. (1978). *The social psychology of organizations.* New York: Wiley.

Kirkpatrick, S. A. & Locke, E. A. (1996). Direct and indirect effects of three core charismatic leadership components on performance and attitudes. *Journal of Applied Psychology, 81(1),* 36–51.

Kouzes, J. M., & Posner, B. Z. (1987). *The leadership challenge.* San Francisco: Jossey-Bass.

Locke, E., Kirkpatrick, S., Wheeler, J. K., Schneider, J., Niles, K., Goldstein, H., et al. (1991). *The essence of leadership.* New York: Lexington Books.

McClelland, D. C. (1985). *Human motivation.* Glenview, IL: Scott Foresman.

Neilson, E. (1986). Empowerment strategies: Balancing authority and responsibility. In S. Srivastra (Ed.), *Executive power* (pp. 78–110). San Francisco: Jossey-Bass.

Petty, R. E., & Cacioppo, J. T. (1981). *Attitudes and persuasion: Classic and contemporary approaches.* Dubuque, IA: Brown.

Puffer, S. M. (1990). Attributions of charismatic leadership: The impact of decision style, outcome, and observer characteristics. *Leadership Quarterly, 1*(3), 177–192.

Salancik, G. R. (1977). Commitment and the control of organizational behavior and belief. In B. M. Staw & G. R. Salancik (Eds.), *New directions in organizational behavior* (pp. 1–54). Chicago: St. Clair.

Shamir, B. (1992). Attribution of influence and charisma to the leader: The romance of leadership revisited. *Journal of Applied Social Psychology, 22*(5), 386–407.

Walster, E., Aronson, D., & Abrahams, D. (1966). On increasing the persuasiveness of a low prestige communicator. *Journal of Experimental Social Psychology, 2,* 325–342.

Weber, M. (1947). *The theory of social and economic organizations* (A. M. Henderson & T. Parsons, Trans.). New York: Free Press.

Willner, A. R. (1984). *The spellbinders: Charismatic political leadership.* New Haven, CT: Yale University Press.

Zaleznik, A., & Kets de Vries, M. (1975). *Power and the corporate mind.* Boston: Houghton Mifflin.

CHAPTER 10

Contingency Theories of Leadership

Richard L. Hughes

U.S. Air Force Academy

Robert C. Ginnett

Impact Leadership Development Group

Gordon J. Curphy

Curphy Consulting Corporation

Introduction

This chapter reviews four of the more well-known contingency theories of leadership. All four address certain aspects of the leader, the followers, and the situation. These four theories also share several other similarities: First, because they are theories rather than someone's personal opinions, these four models have been the focus of a considerable amount of empirical research over the years. Second, these theories implicitly assume that leaders are able to accurately diagnose or assess key aspects of the followers and the leadership situation. Third, with the exception of Fiedler's contingency model,[1] leaders are assumed to be able to act in a flexible manner In other words, leaders can and should change their behaviors as situational and follower characteristics change. Fourth, a correct match between situational and follower characteristics and leaders' behaviors is assumed to have a positive effect on group or organizational outcomes. . . .

HOW MUCH TIME DO I HAVE?

In a world of instant messages that require lightning-fast responses, Steven B. Sample, president of the University of Southern California, is touting the benefits of "artful procrastination." In his course on leadership and his book. *The Contrarian's Guide to Leadership, a* key lesson is never make a decision today that can reasonably be put off to tomorrow:

> With respect to timing, almost all great leaders have understood that making quick decisions is typically counterproductive. I'm not talking about what to have for breakfast or what tie to wear today. President Harry Truman almost personified this concept. When anyone told him they needed a decision, the first thing he would ask is "How much time do I have—a week, 10 seconds, six months?" What he understood was that the nature of the decision that a leader makes depends to a large extent on how much time he has in which to make it. He also understood that delaying a decision as long as reasonably possible generally leads to the best decisions being made.

Other lessons from Sample include:

- Think gray. Don't form opinions if you don't have to.
- Think free. Move several steps beyond traditional brainstorming.
- Listen first, talk later. And when you listen, do so artfully.
- You can't copy your way to the top.

Sources: http://www.usc.edu/president/book/; http://www.refresher.com/!enescontrarian.html; http://bottomlinesecrets.com/blpnet/artide.html?artide_id=33302.

The Situational Leadership® Model

It seems fairly obvious that leaders do not interact with all followers in the same manner. For example, a leader may give general guidelines or goals to her highly competent and motivated followers but spend considerable time coaching, directing, and training her unskilled and unmotivated followers. Or leaders may provide relatively little praise and assurances to followers with high self-confidence but high amounts of support to followers with low self-confidence. Although leaders often have different interactional styles when dealing with individual followers, is there an optimum way for leaders to adjust their behavior with different followers and thereby increase their likelihood of success? And if there is, then what factors should the leader base his behavior on—the follower's intelligence? Personality traits? Values? Preferences? Technical competence? A model called *Situational Leadership* offers answers to these two important leadership questions.

Leader Behaviors

The Situational Leadership model has evolved over time. Its essential elements first appeared in 1969,[2] with roots in the Ohio State studies, in which the two broad categories of leader behaviors, initiating structure and consideration, were initially identified. As Situational Leadership evolved, so did the labels (but not the content) for the two leadership behavior categories. Initiating structure changed to task behaviors, which were defined as the extent to which the leader spells out the responsibilities of an individual or group. Task behaviors include telling people what to do, how to do it, when to do it, and who is to do it. Similarly, consideration changed to relationship behaviors, or how much the leader engages in two-way communication. Relationship behaviors include listening, encouraging, facilitating, clarifying, explaining why the task is important, and giving support.

When the behavior of actual leaders was studied, there was little evidence to show these two categories of leader behavior were consistently related to leadership success; the relative effectiveness of these two behavior dimensions often depended on the situation. Hersey's Situational Leadership model explains why leadership effectiveness varies across these two behavior dimensions and situations. It arrays the two orthogonal dimensions as in the Ohio State studies and then divides each of them into high and low segments (see Figure 10.1). According to the model, depicting the two leadership dimensions this way is useful because certain combinations of task and relationship behaviors may be more effective in some situations than in others.

For example, in some situations high levels of task but low levels of relationship behaviors are effective; in other situations, just the opposite is true So far, however, we have not considered the key follower or situational characteristics with which these combinations of task and relationship behaviors were most effective. Hersey says that these four combinations of task and relationship behaviors would increase leadership effectiveness if they were made contingent on the readiness level of the individual follower to perform a given task.

Follower Readiness

In Situational Leadership, *follower readiness* refers to a follower's ability and willingness to accomplish a particular task. Readiness is not an assessment of an individual's personality, traits, values, age, and so on. It's not a personal characteristic, but rather how ready an individual is to perform a particular task. Any given follower could be low on readiness to perform one task but high on readiness to perform a different task. An experienced emergency room physician would be high in readiness on tasks like assessing a patient's medical status, but

could be relatively low on readiness for facilitating an interdepartmental team meeting to solve an ambiguous and complex problem like developing hospital practices to encourage collaboration across departments.

Prescriptions of the Model

Now that the key contingency factor, follower readiness, has been identified, let us move on to another aspect of the figure—combining follower readiness levels with the four combinations of leader behaviors described earlier. The horizontal bar or arrow in Figure 10.3 depicts follower readiness as increasing from right to left (not in the direction we are used to seeing). There are four segments along this continuum, ranging from R1 (the lowest) to R4 (the highest). Along this continuum, however, the assessment of follower readiness can be fairly subjective. A follower who possesses high levels of readiness would clearly fall in the R4 category, just as a follower unable and unwilling (or *too* insecure) to perform a task would fall in R1.

To complete the model, a curved line is added that represents the leadership behavior that will most likely be effective given a particular level of follower readiness. In order to apply the model, leaders should first assess the readiness level (R1-R4) of the follower relative to the task to be accomplished. Next, a vertical line should be drawn from the center of the readiness level up to the point where it intersects with the curved line in Figure 10.3. The quadrant in which this intersection occurs represents the level of task and relationship behavior that has the best chance of producing successful outcomes. For example, imagine you are a fire chief and have under your command a search-and-rescue team. One of the team members is needed to rescue a backpacker who has fallen in the mountains, and you have selected a particular follower to accomplish the task. What leadership behavior should you exhibit? If this follower has both substantial training and experience in this type of rescue, you would assess his readiness level as R4. A vertical line from R4 would intersect the curved line in the quadrant where both low task and low relationship behaviors by the leader are most apt to be successful. As the leader, you should exhibit a low level of task and relationship behaviors and delegate

Figure 10.1 Situational Leadership

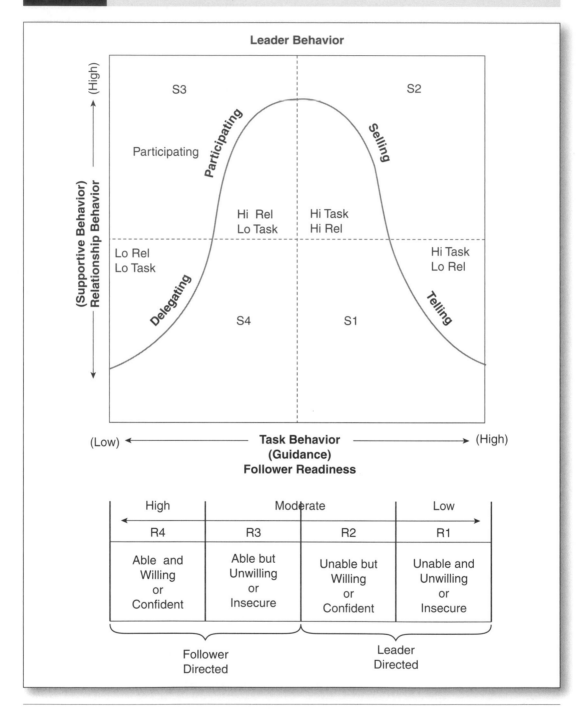

this task to the follower. On the other hand, you may have a brand-new member of the fire department who still has to learn the ins and outs of fire-fighting. Because this particular follower has low task readiness (R1), the model maintains that the leader should use a high level of task and a low level of relationship behaviors when initially dealing with this follower.

Hersey suggests one further step leaders may wish to consider. The model described above helps the leader select the most appropriate behavior given the current level of follower readiness. However, there may be cases when the leader would like to see the followers increase their level of readiness for particular tasks by implementing a series of *developmental interventions* to help boost follower readiness levels The process would begin by first assessing the follower's current level of readiness and then determining the leader behavior that best suits that follower in that task. Instead of using the behavior prescribed by the model, however, the leader would select the next higher leadership behavior. Another way of thinking about this would be for the leader to select the behavior pattern that would fit the follower if that follower were one level higher in readiness. This intervention is designed to help followers in their development, hence its name (see box on developmental interventions).

A DEVELOPMENTAL INTERVENTION USING SLT

Dianne is a resident assistant in charge of a number of students in a university dorm. One particular sophomore, Michael, has volunteered to work on projects in the past but never seems to take the initiative to get started on his own. Michael seems to wait until Dianne gives him explicit direction, approval, and encouragement before he will get started. Michael can do a good job, but he seems to be unwilling to start without some convincing that it is all right, and unless Dianne makes explicit what steps are to be taken. Dianne has assessed Michael's readiness level as R2, but she would like to see him develop, both in task readiness and in psychological maturity. The behavior most likely to fit Michael's current readiness level is selling, or high task, high relationship. But Dianne has decided to implement a developmental intervention to help Michael raise his readiness level. Dianne can be most helpful in this intervention by moving up one level to participating, or low task, high relationship. By reducing the amount of task instructions and direction while encouraging Michael to lay out a plan on his own and supporting his steps in the right direction, Dianne is most apt to help Michael become an R3 follower. This does not mean the work will get done most efficiently, however. Just as we saw in the Vroom and Yetton model earlier, if part of the leader's job is development of followers, then time may be a reasonable and necessary trade-off for short-term efficiency.

Concluding Thoughts About the Situational Leadership Model

In Figure 10.2, we can see how the factors in Situational Leadership fit within the L-F-S framework. In comparison to the Vroom and Yetton model, there are fewer factors to be considered in each of the three elements. The only situational consideration is knowledge of the task, and the only follower factor is readiness. On the other hand, the theory goes well beyond decision making, which was the sole domain of the normative decision model.

Situational Leadership is usually appealing to students and practitioners because of its commonsense approach as well as the ease of understanding it. Unfortunately, there is little published research to support the predictions of Situational Leadership in the workplace.[3,4] A great deal of research has been done within organizations that have implemented Situational Leadership, but most of those findings are not available

Figure 10.2   Factors From the Situational Leadership Model and the Interactional Framework

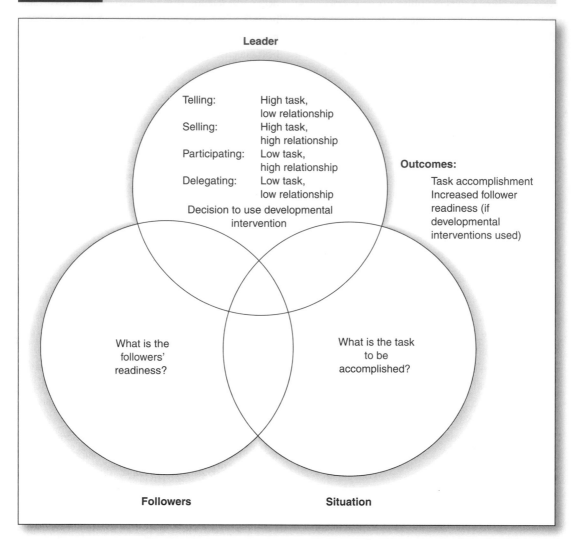

for public dissemination. Nevertheless, even with these shortcomings, Situational Leadership is a useful way to get leaders to think about how leadership effectiveness may depend somewhat on being flexible with different subordinates, not on acting the same way toward them all.

The Contingency Model

Although leaders may be able to change their behaviors toward subordinates, leaders also have dominant behavioral tendencies. Some leaders may be generally more supportive and relationship-oriented, whereas others may be more concerned with task or goal accomplishment. The contingency model[5] recognizes that leaders have these general behavioral tendencies and specifies situations where certain leaders (or behavioral dispositions) may be more effective than others.

Fiedler's[6] contingency model of leadership is probably the earliest and most well-known contingency theory, and is often perceived by students to be almost the opposite of SLT. Compared to the contingency models, SLT emphasizes flexibility in leader behaviors, whereas the contingency model maintains that leaders are much more consistent (and consequently less flexible) in their behavior. Situational leadership theory maintains that leaders who *correctly base their behaviors* on follower maturity will be more effective, whereas the contingency model suggests that leader effectiveness is primarily determined by *selecting the right kind of leader for a certain situation or changing the situation* to fit the particular leader's style. Another way to say this is that leadership effectiveness depends on both the leader's style and the favorableness of the leadership situation. Some leaders are better than others in some situations but less effective in other situations. To understand contingency theory, therefore, we need to look first at the critical characteristics of the leader and then at the critical aspects of the situation.

The Least Preferred Co-worker Scale

In order to determine a leader's general style or tendency, Fiedler developed an instrument called the *least preferred co-worker (LPC) scale*. The scale instructs a leader to think of the single individual with whom he has had the greatest difficulty working (i.e., the least-preferred co-worker) and then to describe that individual in terms of a series of bipolar adjectives (e.g., friendly-unfriendly, boring-interesting, sincere-insincere). Those ratings are then converted into a numerical score.

In thinking about such a procedure, many people assume that the score is determined primarily by the characteristics of whatever particular individual the leader happened to identify as his least-preferred co-worker. In the context of contingency theory, however, it is important to understand that the score is thought to *represent something about the leader, not the specific individual the leader evaluated.*

The current interpretation of these scores is that they identify a leader's motivation hierarchy.[7] Based on their LPC scores, leaders are categorized into two groups: *low-LPC leaders* and *high-LPC leaders*. In terms of their motivation hierarchy, low-LPC leaders are primarily motivated by the task, which means that these leaders primarily gain satisfaction from task accomplishment. Thus, their dominant behavioral tendencies are similar to the initiating structure behavior described in the Ohio State research or the task behavior of SLT. However,

if tasks are being accomplished in an acceptable manner, then low-LPC leaders will move to their secondary level of motivation, which is forming and maintaining relationships with followers. Thus, low-LPC leaders will focus on improving their relationships with followers *after* they are assured that assigned tasks are being satisfactorily accomplished. As soon as tasks are no longer being accomplished in an acceptable manner, however, low-LPC leaders will refocus their efforts on task accomplishment and persist with these efforts until task accomplishment is back on track.

In terms of motivation hierarchy, high-LPC leaders are primarily motivated by relationships, which means that these leaders are primarily satisfied by establishing and maintaining close interpersonal relationships. Thus, their dominant behavioral tendencies are similar to the consideration behaviors described in the Ohio State research or the relationship behaviors in SLT. If high-LPC leaders have established good relationships with their followers, then they will move to their secondary level of motivation, which is task accomplishment. As soon as leader-follower relations are jeopardized, however, high-LPC leaders will cease working on tasks and refocus their efforts on improving relationships with followers.

You can think of the LPC scale as identifying two different sorts of leaders, with their respective motivational hierarchies depicted in Figure 10.3. Lower-level needs must be satisfied first. Low-LPC leaders will move "up" to satisfying relationship needs when they are assured the task is being satisfactorily accomplished. High-LPC leaders will move "up" to emphasizing task accomplishment when they have established good relationships with their followers.

Because all tests have some level of imprecision, Fiedler[8] suggested that the LPC scale cannot accurately identify the motivation hierarchy for those individuals with certain intermediate scores. Research by Kennedy[9] suggested an alternative view. Kennedy has shown that individuals within the intermediate range of LPC scale scores may more easily or readily switch between being task- or relationship-oriented leaders than those individuals with more extreme scale scores. They may be equally satisfied by working on the task or establishing relationships with followers.

Situational Favorability

The other critical variable in the contingency model is *situational favorability*, which is the amount of control the leader has over the followers. Presumably, the more control a leader has over followers, the more favorable the situation is, at least from the leader's perspective. Fiedler included three subelements in situation favorability. These were leader-member relations, task structure, and position power.

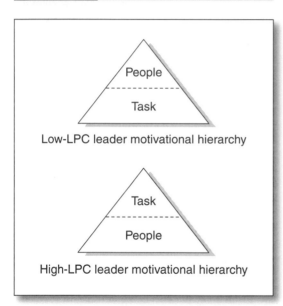

| **Figure 10.3** | Motivational Hierarchies for Low- and High-LPC Leaders |

Low-LPC leader motivational hierarchy

High-LPC leader motivational hierarchy

Leader-member relations is the most powerful of the three subelements in determining overall situation favorability. It involves the extent to which relationships between the leader and followers are generally cooperative and friendly or antagonistic and difficult. Leaders who rate leader-member relations as high would feel they had the support of their followers and could rely on their loyalty.

Task structure is second in potency in determining overall situation favorability. Here the leader would objectively determine task structure by assessing whether there were detailed descriptions of work products, standard operating procedures, or objective indicators of how well the task is being accomplished. The

more one could answer these questions affirmatively, the higher the structure of the task.

Position power is the weakest of the three elements of situational favorability. Leaders who have titles of authority or rank, the authority to administer rewards and punishments, and the legitimacy to conduct follower performance appraisals have greater position power than leaders who lack them.

The relative weights of these three components, taken together, can be used to create a continuum of situational favorability. When using the contingency model, leaders are first asked to rate items that measure the strength of leader-member relations, the degree of task structure, and their level of position power. These ratings are then weighted and combined to determine an overall level of situational favorability facing the leader.[10] Any particular situation's favorability can then be plotted on a continuum Fiedler divided into octants representing distinctly different levels of situational favorability. The relative weighting scheme for the subelements and how they make up each of the eight octants can be seen in Figure 10.4.

You can see that the octants of situational favorability range from 1 (highly favorable) to 8 (very unfavorable). The highest levels of situational favorability occur when leader-member relations are good, the task is structured, and position power is high. The lowest levels of situational favorability occur when there are high levels of leader-member conflict, the task is unstructured or unclear, and the leader does not have the power to reward or punish subordinates. Moreover, the relative weighting of the three subelements can easily be seen by their order of precedence in Figure 10.4, with leader-member relations appearing first, followed by task structure, and then position power. For example, because leader-member relations carry so much weight, it is impossible for leaders with good leader-member relations to have anything worse than moderate situational favorability, regardless of their task structure or position power. In other words, leaders with good leader-member relations will be in a situation that has situational favorability no worse than octant 4; leaders with poor leader-member relations will be facing a leadership situation with situational favorability no better than octant 5.

| Figure 10.4 | Contingency Model Octant Structure for Determining Situational Favorability |

High	← Overall situation favorability					Low	
Leader-member relations	Good				Poor		
Task structure	Structured		Unstructured		Structured		Unstructured	
Position power	High	Low	High	Low	High	Low	High	Low
Octant	1	2	3	4	5	6	7	8

Prescriptions of the Model

Fiedler and his associates have conducted numerous studies to determine how different leaders (as described by their LPC scores) have performed in different situations (as described in terms of situational favorability). Figure 10.5 describes which type of leader (high or low LPC) Fiedler found to be most effective, given different levels of situation favorability The solid dark line represents the relative effectiveness of a low-LPC leader, and the dashed line represents the relative effectiveness of a high LPC leader. It is obvious from the way the two lines cross and recross that there is some interaction between the leader's style and the overall situation favorability. If the situational favorability is moderate (octants 4, 5, 6, or 7), then those groups led by leaders concerned with establishing and maintaining relationships (high-LPC leaders) seem to do best. However, if the situation is either very unfavorable (octant 8) or highly favorable (octants 1, 2, or 3), then those groups led by the task-motivated (low-LPC) leaders seem to do best.

Fiedler suggested that leaders will try to satisfy their primary motivation when faced with unfavorable or moderately favorable situations. This means that low-LPC leaders will concentrate on the task and high-LPC leaders will concentrate on relationships when faced with these two levels of situational favorability. Nevertheless, leaders facing highly favorable situations know that their primary motivations will be satisfied and thus will move to their secondary motivational state. This means that *leaders will behave according to their secondary motivational state only when faced with highly favorable situations* (see box below).

HIGH- AND LOW-LPC LEADERS AND THE CONTINGENCY MODEL

Suppose we had two leaders, Tom Low (a low-LPC or task-motivated leader) and Brenda High (a high-LPC or relationship-motivated leader). In unfavorable situations, Tom will be motivated by his primary level and will thus exhibit task behaviors. In similar situations, Brenda will also be motivated by her primary level and as a result will exhibit relationship behaviors. Fiedler found that, in unfavorable situations, task behavior will help the group to be more effective, so Tom's behavior

(Continued)

(Continued)

would better match the requirements of the situation. Group effectiveness would not be aided by Brenda's relationship behavior in this situation.

In situations with moderate favorability, both Tom and Brenda are still motivated by their primary motivations, so their behaviors will be precisely the same as described: Tom will exhibit task behaviors and Brenda will exhibit relationship behaviors, Because the situation has changed, however, group effectiveness no longer requires task behavior. Instead, the combination of situational variables leads to a condition where a leader's relationship behaviors will make the greatest contribution to group effectiveness. Hence, Brenda will be the most effective leader in situations of moderate favorability.

In highly favorable situations, the explanation provided by Fiedler gets more complex. When leaders find themselves in highly favorable situations, they no longer have to be concerned about satisfying their primary motivations. In highly favorable situations, leaders switch to satisfying their secondary motivations. Because Tom's secondary motivation is to establish and maintain relationships, in highly favorable situations he will exhibit relationship behaviors. Similarly, Brenda will also be motivated by her secondary motivation, so she would manifest task behaviors in highly favorable situations. Fiedler believed that leaders who manifested relationship behaviors in highly favorable situations helped groups to be more effective. In this case, Tom is giving the group what they need to be more effective.

| **Figure 10.5** | Leader Effectiveness Based on the Contingency Between Leader LPC Score and Situation Favorability |

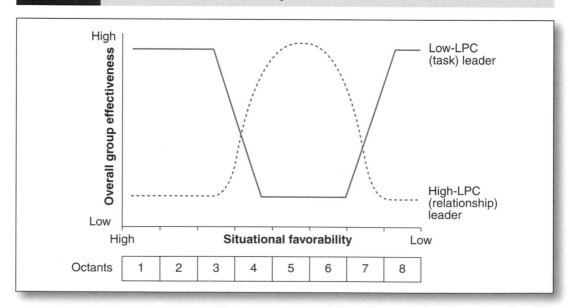

There are several interesting implications of Fiedler's[11] model worthy of additional comment. Because leaders develop their distinctive motivation hierarchies and dominant behavior tendencies through a lifetime of experiences, Fiedler believed these hierarchies and tendencies would be difficult to change through training. Fiedler maintained it was naive to believe that sending someone to a relatively brief leadership training program could substantially alter any leader's personality or typical way of acting in leadership situations; after all, such tendencies had been developed over many years of experience. Instead of trying to change the leader Fiedler concluded, training would be more effective if it showed leaders how to recognize and change key situational characteristics to better fit their personal motivational hierarchies and behavioral tendencies. Thus, according to Fiedler, the content of leadership training should emphasize situational engineering rather than behavioral flexibility in leaders. Relatedly, organizations could become more effective if they matched the characteristics of the leader (in this case LPC scores) with the demands of the situation (i.e., situational favorability) than if they tried to change the leader's behavior to fit the situation. These suggestions imply that high- or low-LPC leaders in mismatched situations should either change the situation or move to jobs that better match their motivational hierarchies and behavioral patterns.

Concluding Thoughts About the Contingency Model

Before reviewing the empirical evidence, perhaps we can attain a clearer understanding of the contingency model by examining it through the L-F-S framework. As seen in Figure 10.6, task structure is a function of the situation and LPC scores are a function of the leader. Because position power is not a characteristic of the leader but of the situation the leader finds him- or herself in, it is included in the situational circle. Leader-member relations is a joint function of the leader and the followers; thus, it best belongs in the overlapping intersection of the leader and follower circles.

As opposed to the dearth of evidence for Hersey and Blanchard's[12-13] situational theory, Fiedler and his fellow researchers have provided considerable evidence that the predictions of the model are empirically valid, particularly in laboratory settings.[14-18] However, a review of the studies conducted in field settings yielded only mixed support for the model,[19] Moreover, researchers have criticized the model for the uncertainties surrounding the meaning of LPC scores,[20-22] the interpretation of situational favorability,[23-24] and the relationships between LPC scores and situational favorability.[25-27] Despite such questions, however, the contingency model has stimulated considerable research and is the most validated of all leadership theories.

The Path-Goal Theory

Perhaps the most sophisticated (and comprehensive) of the four contingency models is path-goal theory. The underlying mechanism of *path-goal theory* deals with expectancy, a cognitive approach to understanding motivation where people calculate effort-to-performance probabilities (If I study for 12 hours, what is the probability I will get an A on the final exam?), performance-to-outcome probabilities (If I get an A on the final, what is the probability of getting an A in the course?), and assigned valences or values to outcome (How much do I value a higher GPA?). Theoretically at least, people were assumed to make these calculations on a rational basis, and the theory could be used to predict what tasks people would put their energies into, given some finite number of options.

Path-goal theory uses the same basic assumptions as expectancy theory. At the most fundamental level, the effective leader will provide or ensure the availability of valued rewards for followers (the "goal") and then help them find the best way of getting there (the "path"). Along the way, the effective leader will help the followers identify and remove road-blocks, and avoid dead ends; the leader will also provide emotional support as needed. These "task" and "relationship" leadership actions essentially involve increasing followers' probability estimates for effort-to-performance and performance-to-reward

Figure 10.6	Factors From Fiedler's Contingency Theory and the Interactional Framework

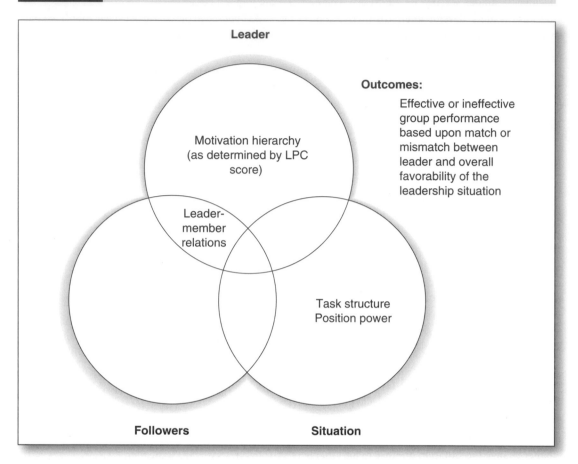

expectancies. In other words, the leader's actions should strengthen followers' beliefs that if they exert a certain level of effort, then they will be more likely to accomplish a task, and if they accomplish the task, then they will be more likely to achieve some valued outcome.

Although not very complicated in its basic concept, the model added more variables and interactions over time. Evans[28] is credited with the first version of path-goal theory, but we will focus on a later version developed by House and Dressier.[29] Their conceptual scheme is ideally suited to the L-F-S framework because they described three classes of variables, which include leader behaviors, followers, and the situation. We will examine each of these in turn.

Leader Behaviors

The four types of leader behavior in path-goal theory can be seen in Table 10.1. Like SLT, path-goal theory assumes that leaders not only may use varying styles with different subordinates but might very well use differing styles with the same subordinates in different situations. Path-goal theory suggests that, depending on the followers and the situation, these different leader behaviors can increase followers' acceptance of the leader, enhance their level of satisfaction, and raise their expectations that effort will result in effective performance, which in turn will lead to valued rewards (see box below).

SHIFTING BEHAVIORS AT CATERPILLAR

James Despain was a leader with a very directive leadership style. He began his career at Caterpillar Inc., as a young man, sweeping up the factory floor. He followed the lead of others of his generation—the 1950s were a time when leaders were the ultimate authority and words like *participative* and *consultative* were unheard of. Despain worked his way into supervisory positions and finally was named vice president of the track-type tractor division. Despain claims he "spent much of [his] career as a manager focusing on what employees were doing wrong." He focused on the tasks at hand and little else. But in the early 1990s Despain had to face some hard facts: His $1.2 billion division was losing millions of dollars per year, his management team was getting hundreds of grievances from their employees, and morale at the Caterpillar plant was extremely low.

Despain and his leadership group identified the need for a strategic plan to transform the working culture. Key to the plan was to determine a strategy for dealing with employee attitudes and behavior, Despain and his transformation team identified nine behaviors or "Common Values" that they wanted every employee to emulate every day—trust, mutual respect, customer satisfaction, a sense of urgency, teamwork, empowerment, risk taking, continuous improvement, and commitment. Employee evaluations were then based on the manifestation of these behaviors. Above and beyond those behaviors, top executives and management were expected to lead by example and commit themselves to practice 100 positive leadership traits. Statements such as "I will know every one of my employees by name . . . will recognize their accomplishments with praise . . . will trust my employees to do their work" became the new mantras for those in charge.

Through this process, Despain came to understand that "the most important thing for employees in the workplace is to achieve self-worth." The principal change he was striving to achieve was to make employees accountable for how their jobs got done—for workers that meant stretching a little more every day, to achieve their full potential. For managers it meant shifting away from achieving traditional metrics and toward drawing desired behavior from workers. "And we found that the more we focused on behavior, the better the metrics got." The result: Despain's division cut its break-even point in half within five years of launching the transformation.

Sources: http://www.tribuneindia.com/20040509/spectrum/book2.htm; http://www.sodexho-usa.com/printer_friendly.htm; http://www.stchas.edu/press/despain.shtml.

The Followers

Path-goal theory contains two groups of follower variables. The first relates to the *satisfaction of followers*, and the second relates to *the followers' perception of their own abilities* relative to the task to be accomplished. In terms of followers' satisfaction, path-goal theory suggests that leader behaviors will be acceptable to the followers to the degree followers see the leader's behavior either as an immediate source of satisfaction or as directly instrumental in achieving future satisfaction. In other words, followers will actively support a leader as long as they view the leader's actions as a means for increasing their own levels of satisfaction. However, there is only so much a leader can do to increase followers' satisfaction levels, as satisfaction also depends on characteristics of the followers themselves.

Table 10.1	The Four Leader Behaviors of Path-Goal Theory

- *Directive leadership.* These leader behaviors are. very similar to the task behaviors from SLT. They include telling the followers what they are expected to do, how to do it, what it is to be done, and how their work fits in with the work of others. This behavior would also include setting schedules, establishing norms, and providing expectations that followers will adhere to established procedure and regulations.
- *Supportive leadership.* Supportive leadership behaviors include having courteous and friendly interactions, expressing genuine concern for the followers' well-being and individual needs, and remaining open and approachable to followers. These behaviors, which are very similar to the, relationship behaviors in SLT, also are marked by attention to the competing demands of treating followers equally while recognizing status differentials between the leader and the followers.
- *Participative leadership.* Participative leaders engage in the behaviors that mark the consultative and group behaviors described by Vroom and Yetton.[31] As such they tend to share work problems with followers; solicit their suggestions, concerns, and recommendations; and weigh these inputs in the decision-making process.
- *Achievement-oriented leadership.* Leaders exhibiting these would be seen as both demanding and supporting in interactions with their followers. In the first place, they would set very challenging goals for group and follower behavior, continually seek ways to improve performance en route, and expect the followers to always perform at their highest levels. But they would support these behaviors by exhibiting a high degree of ongoing confidence that subordinates can put forth the necessary effort, will achieve the desired results; and, even further, will assume even more responsibility in the future.

A frequently cited example of how followers' characteristics influence the impact of leader behaviors on followers' levels of satisfaction involves the trait of locus of control. People who believe they are "masters of their own ship" are said to have an internal locus of control; people who believe they are (relatively speaking) "pawns of fate" are said to have an external locus of control. Mitchell, Smyser, and Weed[30] found that follower satisfaction was not directly related to the degree of participative behaviors manifested by the leader (i.e., followers with highly participative leaders were not any more satisfied than followers with more autocratic leaders). However, when followers' locus-of-control scores were taken into account, a contingency relationship was discovered. As can be seen in Figure 10.7, internal-locus-of-control followers, who believed outcomes were a result of their own decisions, were much more satisfied with leaders who exhibited participative behaviors than they were with leaders who were directive. Conversely, external-locus-of-control followers were more satisfied with directive leader behaviors than they were with participative leader behaviors.

Followers' perceptions of their own skills and abilities to perform particular tasks can also affect the impact of certain leader behaviors. Followers who believe they are perfectly capable of performing a task are not as apt to be motivated by, or as willing to accept, a directive leader as they would a leader who exhibits participative behaviors. Using the same rationale as for locus of control, one can predict the opposite relationship for followers who do not perceive they have sufficient abilities to perform the task. Once again, the acceptability of the leader and the motivation to perform are in part determined by followers' characteristics. Thus, path-goal theory suggests that both leader behaviors and follower characteristics are important in determining outcomes.

The Situation

Path-goal theory considers three situational factors that impact or moderate the effects of leader behavior on follower attitudes and behaviors. These

Figure 10.7	Interaction Between Followers' Locus of Control Scores and Leader Behavior in Decision Making

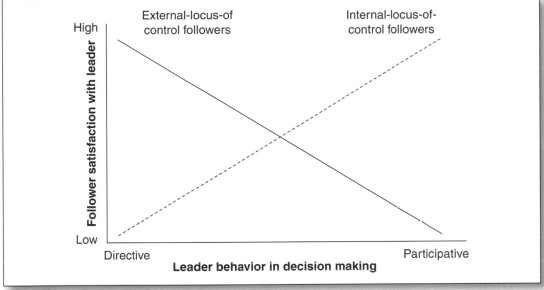

Source: Adapted from T. R. Mitchell, G M. Smyser, and S. E. Weed, "Locus of Control: Supervision and Work Satisfaction." Academy *of Management Journal* 18 (1975), pp. 623-30.

include *the task, the formal authority system,* and *the primary work group.* Each of these three factors can influence the leadership situation in one of three ways. These three factors can serve as an independent motivational factor, as a constraint on the behavior of followers (which may be either positive or negative in outcome), or as a reward.

However, it should also be increasingly apparent that these variables can often affect the impact of various leader behaviors. For example, if the task is very structured and routine, the formal authority system has constrained followers' behaviors, and the work group has established clear norms for performance, then leaders would be serving a redundant purpose by manifesting directive or achievement-oriented behaviors. These prescriptions are similar to some of those noted in substitutes for leadership theory,[32] as everything the follower needs to understand the effort-to-performance and performance-to-reward links is provided by the situation. Thus, redundant leader behaviors might be interpreted by followers as either a complete lack of understanding or empathy by the leader, or an attempt by the leader to exert excessive control. Neither of these

interpretations is likely to enhance the leader's acceptance by followers or increase their motivation.

Although we have already described how follower characteristics and situational characteristics can impact leader behaviors, path-goal theory also maintains that follower and situational variables can impact each other. In other words, situational variables, such as the task performed, can also impact the influence of followers' skills, abilities, or personality traits on followers' satisfaction. Although this seems to make perfect sense, hopefully you are beginning to see how complicated path-goal theory can be when one starts considering how situational variables, follower characteristics, and leader behaviors interact in the leadership process.

Prescriptions of the Theory

In general, path-goal theory maintains that leaders should first assess the situation and select a leadership behavior appropriate to situational demands. By manifesting the appropriate behaviors, leaders can increase followers' effort-to-performance expectancies,

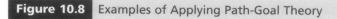

Figure 10.8   Examples of Applying Path-Goal Theory

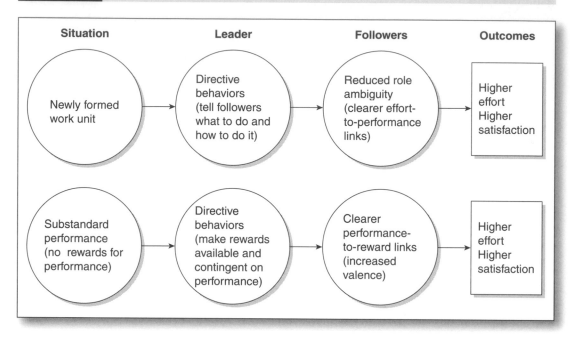

performance-to-reward expectancies, or valences of the outcomes. These increased expectancies and valences will improve subordinates' effort levels and the rewards attained, which in turn will increase subordinates' satisfaction and performance levels and the acceptance of their leaders. Perhaps the easiest way to explain this fairly complicated process is through the use of an example. Suppose we have a set of followers who are in a newly created work unit and do not have a clear understanding of the requirements of their positions. In other words, the followers have a reasonably high level of role ambiguity. According to path-goal theory, leaders should exhibit a high degree of directive behaviors in order to reduce the role ambiguity of their followers. The effort-to-performance link will become clearer when leaders tell followers what to do and how to do it in ambiguous situations, which in turn will cause followers to exert higher effort levels. Because role ambiguity is assumed to be unpleasant, these directive leader behaviors and higher effort levels should eventually result in higher satisfaction levels among followers. Figure 10.8 illustrates this process. Similarly, leaders may look at the leadership situation and note that followers' performance levels are not acceptable. The leader may also conclude that the current situation offers few, if any, incentives for increased

performance. In this case, the leader may use directive behaviors to increase the value of the rewards (or valence), which in turn will increase followers' effort levels and performance.

Concluding Thoughts About the Path-Goal Theory

Before getting into the research surrounding path-goal theory, you may wish to examine the theory using the L-F-S framework. As seen in Figure 10.9, the components of path-goal theory fit quite nicely into the L-F-S model. The four leader behaviors fit nicely in the leader circle, the characteristics of the followers fit into the follower circle, and the task and the formal authority system fit into the situation circle. Of all the components of path-goal theory, the only "mismatch" with the L-F-S model deals with the primary work group. The norms, cohesiveness, size, and stage of development of groups is considered to be part of the follower function in the L-F-S model but is part of the situation function in path-goal theory. In that regard, we hasten to note we use the L-F-S framework primarily for heuristic purposes. Ultimately, the concepts described in these four theories

Figure 10.9 Factors From Path-Goal Theory and the Interactional Framework

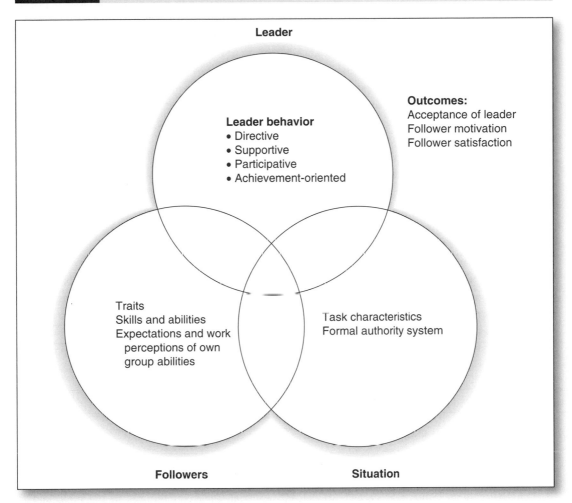

are sufficiently complex and ambiguous that there probably is no right answer to any single depiction.

In terms of research, the path-goal theory has received only mixed support to date.[33-36] Although many of these mixed findings may be due to the fact that the path-goal theory excludes many of the variables found to impact the leadership process, that may also be due to problems with the theory. Yukl[37] maintained that most of these criticisms deal with the methodology used to study path-goal theory and the limitations of expectancy theory. Moreover, the path-goal theory assumes that the only way to increase performance is to increase followers' motivation levels. The theory ignores the roles leaders play in selecting talented followers, building their skill levels through training, and redesigning their work.[38]

Nonetheless, path-goal theory is useful for illustrating two points. First, as noted by Yukl,[39] "path-goal theory has already made a contribution to the study of leadership by providing a conceptual framework to guide researchers in identifying potentially relevant situational moderator variables." Path-goal theory also illustrates that, as models become more complicated, they may be more useful to researchers and less appealing to practitioners. Our experience is that pragmatically oriented students and in-place leaders want to take something from a model that is understandable and can be applied in their work situation right away. This does not mean they prefer simplicity to validity—they generally appreciate the complexity of the leadership process. But neither do they want a model that is so complex as to be indecipherable.

Summary

This chapter is designed to provide an overview of four of the more well-known contingency theories of leadership, which include the normative decision model,[40] the Situational Leadership model, the contingency model,[41] and the path-goal theory.[42] All four models are fairly similar in that they specify that leaders should make their behaviors contingent on certain aspects of the followers or the situation in order to improve leadership effectiveness. In addition, all four theories implicitly assume that leaders can accurately assess key follower and situational factors. However, it is entirely possible that two leaders in the same situation may reach very different conclusions about followers' levels of knowledge, the strength of leader-follower relationships, the degree of task structure, or the level of role ambiguity being experienced by followers. These differences in perception could lead these two leaders to reach different conclusions about the situation, which may in turn cause them to take very different actions in response to the situation. Furthermore, these actions may be in accordance or in conflict with the prescriptions of any of these four theories. Also, the fact that leaders' perceptions may have caused them to act in a manner not prescribed by a particular model may be an underlying reason why these four theories have reported conflicting findings, particularly in field settings.

Another reason these theories have generally found mixed support in field settings concerns the fact that they are all fairly limited in scope. Many of the factors that affect leader and follower behaviors in work-group, team, or volunteer committee settings are not present in laboratory studies but often play a substantial role in field studies. For example, none of the models take into account how levels of stress, organizational culture and climate, working conditions, technology, economic conditions, or types of organizational design affect the leadership process. Nevertheless the four contingency theories have been the subject of considerable research, and even if only mixed support for the models has been found, this research has succeeded in adding to our body of knowledge about leadership, and has given us a more sophisticated understanding of the leadership process.

MINICASE

Big Changes for a Small Hospital

As F. Nicholas Jacobs toured the Windber Medical Center facility, he was dismayed by the industrial pink painted walls, the circa 1970 furniture, and the snow leaking through the windows of the conference room. Employees earned 30 percent less than their counterparts in the area, and turnover was steep. As Windber's newest president, Jacobs knew he was the facility's last hope—if he couldn't successfully turn around the aging facility, it would mean closing the doors forever.

Coming to Windber Medical Center in 1997, Jacobs was keenly aware that the hospital could be the next in a series of small hospitals that had fallen victim to a struggling economy. Determined to see that not happen, he began by making connections with the employees of the hospital and the community at large. Jacobs's first step was to interview each of the employees to find out firsthand what they wanted for the Windber community and the medical center. He also looked to members of local community groups like the local library, the Agency on Aging, and local politicians and asked these groups what they wanted from their local medical facility. When Jacobs realized that octogenarians made up a larger percent of the population in Windber, Pennsylvania, than in all of Dade County, Florida, he made it a priority to provide more options to seniors for improving their health and quality of life. He set forth a vision of a medical center that was more of a community center—a center that would allow members of the community to exercise in a state-of-the-art facility while having access to professionals to answer health-related questions. Jacobs realized that keeping people in the community both physically and mentally healthy also meant keeping the hospital financially healthy. He made the center's new preventive-care philosophy clear to the public: "Work out at our hospital so you can stay out of our hospital."

Jacobs's efforts have paid off—in an era when small hospitals are closing left and right, Windber Medical Center is thriving. Under Jacobs's leadership Windber has established an affiliation with the Planetree treatment system, which integrates meditation, massage, music, and other holistic methods into traditional health care. Windber's wellness center, which offers fitness training, yoga, and acupuncture, among other treatments, opened in January 2000 and now generates over $500,000 annually. Gone are the pink walls and dated furniture—replaced with fountains, plants, and modern artwork. Jacobs recruited a former hotel manager to oversee food service. And, despite the dismissal of about 32 employees (those used to a more traditional hospital setting had a tough time in the new environment), the staff has nearly doubled to 450 employees, and pay has improved. Windber has raised more than $50 million in public and private funding and has forged research partnerships with the Walter Reed Army Health System and the University of Pittsburgh, among others. The Windber Research Institute, Windber's heart-disease-reversal program, has treated about 250 patients.

Exercises

1. Consider the factors from the situational leadership theory outlined in Figure 12.2. Apply these factors to Jacobs and Windber.

2. How do you think Jacobs would score on the least preferred co-worker (LPC) scale? Why?

3. Based on the success of Windber, in what range would you guess the overall situational favorability might fall for Jacobs on the continuum illustrated in Figure 12.4?

Sources: http://www.careerjournaleurope.com/columnists/inthelead/20030827-inthelead.html; http://www.haponline.org/ihc/hospitalshealthsystems/models2.asp; http://www.post-gazette.com/pg/04013/260747.stm.

Notes

1. Fiedler, F. E. "Reflections by an Accidental Theorist." *Leadership Quarterly* 6, no. 4 (1995), pp. 453-61;———. *A Theory of Leadership Effectiveness.* New York McGraw-Hill, 1967.

2. Hersey, P., and K H. Blanchard. "Life Cycle Theory of Leadership." *Training and Development Journal* 23 (1969), pp. 26–34.

3. Vecchio, R. P. "Situational Leadership Theory: An Examination of a Prescriptive Theory." *Journal of Applied Psychology* 72 (1987), pp. 444–51.

4. Yukl, G. A., and D. D. Van Fleet. "Theory and Research on Leadership in Organizations." In *Handbook of Industrial Organizational Psychology.* Vol. 3. Eds. M. D. Dunnette and L. M. Hough. Palo Alto, CA: Consulting Psychologists Press, 1992, pp. 1–51.

5. Fiedler, F. E. "Reflections by an Accidental Theorist." *Leadership Quarterly* 6, no. 4 (1995), pp. 453–61 ———. *A Theory of Leadership Effectiveness.* New York: McGraw-Hill, 1967.

6. Fiedler, F. E. "Reflections by an Accidental Theorist." *Leadership Quarterly* 6, no. 4 (1995), pp. 453–61. ———. *A Theory of Leadership Effectiveness.* New York: McGraw-Hill, 1967.

7. Fiedler, F. E. "The Contingency Model and the Dynamics of the Leadership Process." In *Advances in Experimental Social Psychology.* Ed. L. Berkowitz. New York: Academic Press, 1978.

8. Fiedler, F. E. "The Contingency Model and the Dynamics of the Leadership Process." In *Advances in Experimental Social Psychology.* Ed. L. Berkowitz. New York: Academic Press, 1978.

9. Kennedy, J. K. "Middle LPC Leaders and the Contingency Model of Leader Effectiveness." *Organizational Behavior and Human Performance* 30 (1982), pp. 1–14.

10. Fiedler, F. E., and M. M. Chemers. *Improving Leadership Effectiveness: The Leader Match Concept.* 2nd ed. New York: John Wiley, 1982.

11. Fiedler, F. E. "Reflections by an Accidental Theorist." *Leadership Quarterly* 6, no. 4 (1995), pp. 453–61 ———. *A Theory of Leadership Effectiveness.* New York: McGraw-Hill, 1967.

12. Hersey, P., and K. H. Blanchard. "Life Cycle Theory of Leadership." *Training and Development Journal* 23 (1969), pp. 26–34.

13. Hersey, P., and K. H. Blanchard. *Management of Organizational Behavior: Utilizing Human Resources*. 4th ed. Englewood Cliffs, NJ: Prentice Hall, 1982.

14. Fiedler, F. E. "The Contingency Model and the Dynamics of the Leadership Process." In *Advances in Experimental Social Psychology*. Ed. L. Berkowitz. New York: Academic Press, 1978.

15. Fiedler, F. E. "Cognitive Resources and Leadership Performance." *Applied Psychology: An International Review* 44, no. 1 (1995), pp. 5–28.

16. Fiedler, F. E., and M. M. Chemers. *Improving Leadership Effectiveness: The Leader Match Concept*. 2nd ed. New York: John Wiley, 1982.

17. Peters, L. H., D. D. Hartke, and J. T. Pohlmann. "Fiedler's Contingency Theory of Leadership: An Application of the Meta-analytic Procedures of Schmidt and Hunter." *Psychological Bulletin* 97 (1985), pp. 274–85.

18. Strube, M. J., and J. E. Garcia. "A Meta-analytic Investigation of Fiedler's Contingency Model of Leadership Effectiveness." *Psychological Bulletin* 90 (1981) pp. 307-21.

19. Peters, L. H., D. D. Hartke, and J. T. Pohlmann. "Fiedler's Contingency, Theory of Leadership: An Application of the Meta-analytic Procedures of Schmidt and Hunter." *Psychological Bulletin* 97 (1985), pp. 274–85.

20. Kennedy, J. K. "Middle LPC Leaders and the Contingency Model of Effectiveness." *Organizational Behavior and Human Performance* 30 (1982), pp. 1–14.

21. Rice, R. W. "Construct Validity of the Least Preferred Co-Worker Score." *Psychological Bulletin* 85 (1978), pp. 1199–1237.

22. Schriesheim, C. A., and S. Kerr. "Theories and Measures of Leadership: A Critical Appraisal of Current and Future Directions." In *Leadership: The Edge*. Eds. J. G. Hunt and L. L. Larson. Carbondale, IL: Southern Illinois University Press, 1977.

23. Jago, A. G., and J. W. Ragan. "The Trouble with Leader Match Is That It Dosn't Match Fiedler's Contingency Model." *Journal of Applied Psychology* 71 (1986a), pp. 555–59.

24. Jago, A. G., and J. W. Ragan. "Some Assumptions Are More Troubling than Others: Rejoinder to Chemers and Fiedler." *Journal of Applied Psychology* 71 (1986b), pp. 564–65.

25. Jago, A. G., and J. W. Ragan. "The Trouble with Leader Match Is That It Doesn't Match Fiedler's Contingency Model." *Journal of Applied Psychology* 71 (1986a), pp. 555–59.

26. Jago, A. G., and J. W. Ragan. "Some Assumptions Are More Troubling than Others: Rejoinder to Chemers and Fiedler." *Journal of Applied Psychology* 71 (1986b), pp. 564–65.

27. Vecchio, R. P. "Assessing the Validity of Fiedler's Contingency Model of Leadership Effectiveness: A Closer Look at Strube arid Garcia." *Psychological Bulletin* 93 (1983), pp. 404–08.

28. Evans, M. G. "The Effects of Supervisory Behavior on the Path-Goal Relationship." *Organizational Behavior and Human Performance* 5 (1970), pp. 277–98.

29. House, R. J., and G., Dressier, "The Path-Goal Theory of Leadership: Some Post Hoc and A Priori Tests." In *Contingency Approaches to Leadership*. Eds. J. G. Hunt and L.L. Larson. Carbondale, IL: Southern Illinois University Press, 1974.

30. Mitchell, T. R., C. M. Smyser, and S. E. Weed, "Locus of Control: Supervision and Work Satisfaction." *Academy of Management Journal* 18 (1975), pp. 623–30.

31. Vroom, V. H., and P. W. Yetton. *Leadership and Decision Making*. Pittsburgh, PA: University of Pittsburgh Press, 1973.

32. Kerr, S., and J. M. Jermier. "Substitutes for Leadership: Their Meaning and Measurement." *Organizational Behavior and Human Performance* 22 (1978), pp. 375–403.

33. Schriesheim, C. A., and A. S. DeNisi. "Task Dimensions as Moderators of the Effects. of Instrumental Leadership: A Two Sample Replicated Test of Path-Goal Leadership Theory." *Journal of Applied Psychology* 66 (1981), pp. 589–97.

34. Schriesheim, C. A., and S. Kerr. "Theories and Measures of Leadership: A Critical Appraisal of Current and Future Directions." In *Leadership: The Cutting Edge*. Eds. J. G. Hunt and L. L. Larson. Carbondale, IL: Southern Illinois University Press, 1977.

35. Yukl, G. *Leadership in Organizations*. 2nd ed. Englewood Cliffs, NJ: Prentice Hall, 1989.

36. Schriesheim, C. A., S. L. Castro, X. Zhou, and. L. A. DeChurch. "An Investigation of Path-Goal and Transformational Leadership Theory Predictions at the Individual Level of Analysis." *Leadership Quarterly* 17 (2006), pp. 21–38.

37. Yukl, G. *Leadership in Organizations*. 2nd ed. Englewood Cliffs, NJ: Prentice Hall, 1989.

38. Yukl, G. A., and D. D. Van Fleet. "Theory and Research on Leadership in Organizations." In *Handbook of Industrial & Organizational Psychology*. Vol. 3. Eds. M. D. Dunnette and L. M. Hough. Palo Alto, CA: Consulting Psychologists Press, 1992, pp. 1–51.

39. Yukl, G. *Leadership in Organizations.* 2nd ed. Englewood Cliffs, NJ: Prentice Hall, 1989, p. 104.

40. Vroom, V. H., and P. W. Yetton. *Leadership and Decision Making.* Pittsburgh, PA: University of Pittsburgh Press, 1973.

41. Fiedler, F. E. "Reflections by an Accidental Theorist." *Leadership Quarterly* 6, no. 4 (1995), pp. 453–61.

42. House, R. J., and G. Dressler. "The Path-Goal Theory of Leadership: Some Post Hoc and A Priori Tests." In *Contingency Approaches to Leadership.* Ed. J. G. Hunt and L. L. Larson. Carbondale, IL: Southern Illinois University Press, 1974.

CHAPTER 11

Strategic Leadership

Top Management Teams

Sydney Finkelstein

Dartmouth College

Donald C. Hambrick

Pennsylvania State University

Albert A. Cannella, Jr.

Tulane University

Although the pyramid headed by an all-powerful individual has been a symbol of organizations, such omnipotence is possible only in simple situations where perfected technologies and bland task environments make computational decision processes feasible. Where technology is incomplete or the task environment heterogeneous, the judgmental decision strategy is required and control is vested in a dominant coalition.

—Thompson (1967, p. 143)

One of the most enduring ideas in organization theory is that environments impose constraints on individuals (Lawrence and Lorsch 1967), making it exceedingly difficult for any one person to control all aspects of organizational life. The conditions for omnipotence noted by Thompson

Source: Top Management Teams by Sydney Finkelstein, Donald C. Hambrick, and Albert A. Cannella Jr. (2008). Pp. 121-163 in *Strategic Leadership: Theory and Research on Executives, Top Management Teams, and Boards* by Finkelsein, Hambrick, & Cannella. Used by permission of Oxford University Press, Inc.

(1967) are rare, for they imply the absence of decision-making uncertainty. Rather, given the great ambiguity and complexity inherent in strategic decision making (Mintzberg 1973), the formation of a coalition at the top is more plausible. As a result, when modeling how strategic leaders make strategic decisions, it seems that we are "left with something more complicated than an individual entrepreneur" (Cyert and March 1963, 30).

Scholars have been drawn to the study of top management teams (TMTs) for five main reasons. First, as an aggregation of subunits and individuals, organizations have multiple goals that are often in conflict (Cyert and March 1963; Weick 1979). The existence of these multiple goals, and hence of multiple preferences, at the top of organizational hierarchies is likely to affect how organizations strive toward organizational outcomes, as well as the characteristics of those outcomes. Second, almost all descriptions of strategic decision-making processes typically emphasize the relevance of stages, sequences, and processes that involve a group of top managers interacting toward desired ends (Pettigrew 1973; Mintzberg, Raisinghani, and Theoret 1976; Nutt 1984; Roberto 2003). Indeed, the top management team is at the strategic apex of an organization (Mintzberg 1979); it is the executive body most responsible for strategic decision making and, by extension, for such fundamental organizational outcomes as firm strategy, structure, and performance. Third, the interactions among top managers, including power distributions, decision processes and integration, and fragmentation, create outcomes of interest to strategy research.

Fourth, there is clearly some amount of role differentiation in most, if not all, top management groups. For example, Sarbanes-Oxley requires that a chief financial officer, along with the CEO, personally certifies accounting statements prior to sending them to shareholders and filing them with the Securities and Exchange Commission (SEC).[1] Thus, some specific responsibilities of executives other than the CEO have been legally mandated for public companies.

Fifth, and most important, evidence suggests that studying TMTs, rather than CEOs alone, provides better predictions of organizational outcomes (Hage and Dewar 1973; Tushman, Virany, and Romanelli 1985; Finkelstein 1988; Ancona 1990; O'Reilly, Snyder, and Boothe 1993; Tushman and Rosenkopf 1996). For example, in a series of tests of upper-echelons hypotheses, Finkelstein (1988) reported far stronger results using the TMT, rather than the CEO, as the level of analysis. Other studies have similarly demonstrated that significant variance in organization-level outcomes can be explained by examining the attributes of executives beyond the CEO (Bertrand and Schoar 2003; Reutzel and Cannella 2004; Zhang and Rajagopalan 2004; Bigley and Wiersema 2002).

For these reasons, whether one refers to such groups as dominant coalitions (Cyert and March 1963; Bourgeois 1980), "inner circles" (Thompson 1967; Finkelstein 1992), top management groups (Hambrick 1994), or top management teams[2] (Bourgeois 1980; Hambrick and Mason 1984; Carpenter, Geletkanycz, and Sanders 2004), there is much to gain from focusing on the relatively small constellation of executives at the top of an organization.

We should acknowledge, however, that the inclination to consider TMTs, rather than just CEOs, is not universal. For example, Hambrick (1994) suggested that many groups of top managers do not act as teams and may interact hardly at all. Similar questions about the examination of teams as an appropriate level of analysis are evident in Carpenter (2002), O'Reilly, Snyder and Boothe (1993), and Simsek, Veiga, Lubatkin, and Dino (2005). Cannella and Holcomb (2005) describe a number of complexities that are introduced when teams are used as the level of analysis in upper-echelons research. Further, Cannella and Holcomb describe several situations in which the team is probably not the appropriate level of analysis. For example, in situations characterized by an autocratic CEO, or a CEO who does not permit open debate and discussion of strategic issues, or situations in which the CEO has a very clear and powerful vision, the team may be relatively unimportant to organizational outcomes. When the influence of the team is muted relative to the CEO, it might be best to simply consider the CEO alone. Perhaps the strongest criticism of focusing on the TMT as the level of analysis in upper-echelons research comes from Dalton and Dalton (2005), who put forth two arguments. First, they believe that the measures and analytical strategies in use at the team level are inadequate, reducing the appeal of the team as the level of analysis. Second, they simply believe that teams are much less important than CEOs and that, absent strong evidence to the contrary, the CEO should be the unit of analysis in upper-echelons research. Despite these doubts and caveats, we believe there is substantial evidence, as noted above, that scholarly attention to TMTs has been and will be fruitful.

Hence, this chapter focuses on TMTs in the context of the strategic decision-making process, and it models the interactions among TMT members as a central construct in that process. Viewed in this way, TMTs present many possible research questions. TMTs are not only a central component in the strategic decision-making process and in postdecision implementation; they may also be viewed as a basic organizational attribute, worthy of exploration in their own right. A dual emphasis, encompassing an interest in both the antecedents and consequences of TMT characteristics, is adopted in this chapter.

We need to note an important matter of scope, however. The strategic decision-making literature is vast and involves numerous sets of relationships among determinants, decision-specific factors, process characteristics, process outcomes, and consequences (Carpenter, Geletkanycz, and Sanders 2004; Eisenhardt and Zbaracki 1992; Rajagopalan, Rasheed, and Datta 1993; Cannella and Holcomb 2005). It is clearly impossible in a single chapter to address each facet of the strategic decision-making process. Rather, our interest is in the role of TMTs in strategic decision making and decision implementation, and more specifically in the nature and effects of social relations among top team members as they develop and implement strategies for their organizations.

The Conceptual Elements of Top Management Teams

Although the term *top management team* is now widely used, it is not uncommon for individual pieces of research to emphasize different aspects of what is, in essence, a multidimensional construct. A top management team has three central conceptual elements: composition, structure, and process. Composition refers to the collective characteristics of top team members, such as their values, cognitive bases, personalities, and experiences. Although these characteristics can be considered in terms of both the central tendency of the

team and the heterogeneity of the team, most researchers have focused on the latter.[3] In addition, our conceptualization of TMT heterogeneity encompasses both psychological factors (values, beliefs, cognitions) and aspects of executive experiences (age, tenure, functional background, education).

The structure of a top team is defined by the roles of members and the relationships among those roles. Central to this definition is the role interdependence of team members, an important construct that surely has significant consequences for how strategic decisions are made (Michel and Hambrick 1992; Hambrick 1994). We define role interdependence as the degree to which the performance of the firm depends on information- and resource-sharing, as well as other forms of coordination within the TMT. For example, a TMT consisting of heads of functional areas typically has more role interdependence than one made up of heads of autonomous business units. Beyond the nature of executive roles, the actual size of a team is also a fundamental aspect of structure (Merton 1968; Keck 1990).

The third major conceptual element of a TMT is its processes. By processes, we mean the nature of interaction among top managers as they engage in strategic decision making. We limit our focus to two process dimensions: social integration and consensus.[4] Social integration is defined as "the attraction to the group, satisfaction with other members of the group, and social interaction among the group members" (O'Reilly, Caldwell, and Barnett 1989, 22) and is one of the most studied of process constructs. Consensus within a TMT is "the [extent of] agreement of all parties of a group decision" (Dess and Origer 1987, 313).

All three conceptual elements—composition, structure, and process—are related to the social makeup and interactions of the top team in the process of making strategic decisions. Strategic decisions are not made in a vacuum; rather, they emanate from a group of top managers interacting as social and political creatures. The nature of these interactions and their effects on both strategic decision making and organizational outcomes are of central importance. Beyond the complex set of interactions at the top, strategic decision making is also heavily influenced by activities in the organization and its environment. Hence, we are also interested in the contextual conditions that give rise to particular TMT configurations.

We believe these issues can be best understood by adopting the framework shown in Figure 11.1. At the center of this framework is the TMT, characterized in terms of a set of conceptual constructs: heterogeneity (TMT composition); role interdependence and team size (TMT structure); and social integration and consensus (TMT process). We focus on these constructs, in particular, because they are central to both strategic decision making and social relations within TMTs, and they have been the subject of considerable theoretical interest among scholars for some time. Other aspects of TMTs are certainly important and worthy of study, but the goals of this chapter call for a circumscribed scope.

The framework suggests ways in which each of these facets of TMTs are interrelated. The model also encompasses the effects of contextual conditions on TMTs. These contextual factors include the environment, the organization, and the CEO. Finally, Figure 11.1 shows how TMTs are associated with the strategic decision-making process and the organizational outcomes that arise from this process. A primary goal of this framework is to highlight three key research questions on TMTs: (1) What is the nature of the interaction within TMTs? (2) How do contextual conditions affect TMTs? (3) What are the consequences of TMTs for both strategic decision making and organizational outcomes? These questions establish the scope of the major sections of this chapter.

How the Conceptual Elements of TMTs Are Related

There is a long history of work in social psychology on the composition of groups and the nature of their interactions (Jackson 1992). Much of this research has been conducted on ad hoc "groups" (via lab experiments on college students) or on lower-level employee work groups. However, in recent years, a growing number of studies have directly gauged TMT process constructs using samples of actual TMTs (Glick, Miller, and Huber 1993; Barsade et al. 2001; Athanassion and Nigh 1999; Bunderson and Sutcliffe 2002; Pitcher and Smith 2001; Chatman and Flynn 2001; O'Reilly, Snyder, and Boothe 1993; Smith et al. 1994; Amason 1996; Amason and

Sapienza 1997). Virtually all TMT researchers agree that the dynamics of TMT interaction affect the extent of social integration and consensus, both of which have been conceptually and empirically linked to a wide set of organizational outcomes (e.g., Wiersema and Bantel 1992; Pitcher and Smith 2001; Amason and Sapienza 1997; Amason 1996; Cannella and Holcomb 2005). Unfortunately, team processes are seldom directly measured.[5] Instead, most researchers simply assume that team demography influences team processes, and that team processes mediate the relationship between team demography and organizational outcomes (Smith et al. 1994; Carpenter 2002; Carpenter and Fredrickson 2001; Richard et al. 2004; Sambharya 1996; Cannella, Park, and Lee 2008).

A large number of potential intervening processes exist between TMT composition and organizational outcomes. For example, the strategic decision-making process has many steps, including generation and evaluation of alternatives, selection, implementation, and evaluation. Before a decision can affect organizational outcomes, it must go through each of these stages[6]— with TMT members interacting throughout the process. A substantial body of work documents linkages between TMT characteristics and outcomes. Our goal in this section is to shed light on some of the intervening processes that define the "black box" in much of this work. We do so by considering interrelationships among TMT composition, structure, and process and by focusing on how these factors affect the strategic decision-making process.

Teams Versus Groups

It is at once problematic and self-evident that top management "teams" are really top management "groups."[7] It is problematic because virtually all published research on the constellation of executives at the top characterizes these managers as a team, irrespective of whether they are cohesive or cooperative. For example, consider how the executive vice president of marketing in a large firm described the TMT of which he was a member:

Team? How do you define "team"? When I think of a team, I think of interaction, a lot of give-and-take,

Figure 11.1   A Model of Top Management Teams

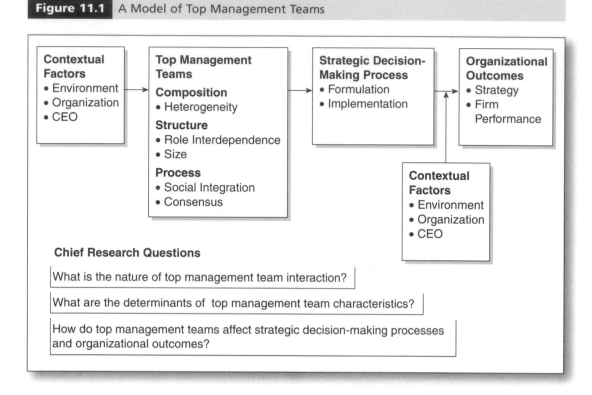

and shared purpose. In our company, we're a collection of strong players, but hardly a "team." We rarely meet as a team—rarely see each other, in fact. We don't particularly share the same views. I wouldn't say we actually work at cross-purposes, but a lot of self-centered behavior occurs. Where's the "team" in all this? (Hambrick 1994, 172)

It is also self-evident that TMTs are really top management groups because virtually all of the underlying theoretical support for proposed relationships on TMTs is based on research on work groups in social psychology. As Jackson notes, "Most of the relevant studies have been conducted by psychologists interested in understanding group processes and group performance. After fifty years of psychological research on groups, a large body of findings has accumulated" (Jackson 1992, 354). Several important conclusions follow: (1) definitions of top management teams or groups need to make clear which executives are included and why; (2) the importance of power dynamics among the group of executives at the top

becomes more central; and (3) relationships among different facets of TMTs need to be empirically investigated. We elaborate on each of these points below.

Who Is in the Top Group?

The question of who actually constitutes the TMT[8] is an interesting and important issue, as evidenced by the surprisingly wide array of operational definitions used in the literature. TMT boundaries take on additional significance, because TMT size is increasingly being examined as a meaningful construct in empirical work (e.g., Haleblian and Finkelstein 1993; Forbes and Milliken 1999; Snow et al. 1996).

The top management team is the relatively small group of executives at the strategic apex of an organization. Hence, a TMT is the group of top executives with "overall responsibility for the organization" (Mintzberg 1979, 24). As simple as this definition appears, there is no consensus among researchers regarding an appropriate operational definition of TMT membership, and definitional concerns have been largely ignored in published research (Roberto 2003; Cannella and Holcomb 2005). Among the different measures used to identify TMT members are: (1) all managers identified by the CEO as belonging to the TMT (e.g., Bantel and Jackson 1989; Glick, Miller, and Huber 1993; O'Reilly, Snyder, and Boothe 1993; Smith et al. 1994; Sutcliffe 1994); (2) inside board members (e.g., Finkelstein and Hambrick 1990; Haleblian and Finkelstein 1993); (3) all managers at the vice-president level and higher (e.g., Wagner, Pfeffer, and O'Reilly 1984; Hambrick and D'Aveni 1992; Michel and Hambrick 1992; Keck and Tushman 1993); (4) the two highest executive levels (e.g., Wiersema and Bantel 1992); (5) all founders of the organization (Eisenhardt and Schoonhoven 1990); and (6) the five highest paid executives (Carpenter, Sanders, and Gregersen 2001; Carpenter, Pollock, and Leary 2003). A few studies have defined the TMT depending on the outcome under study (e.g., Amason 1996; Knight et al. 1999; Smith et al. 1994). (See also Carpenter, Geletkanycz, and Sanders 2004.)

On an a priori basis, it is not possible to unequivocally favor one operationalization over another.[9] Rather, the operationalization used should correspond to the research questions that guide a particular study[10] (O'Reilly, Snyder, and Boothe 1993; Cannella and Holcomb 2005). For example, it would not be appropriate for most studies to define TMTs in terms of founders, but that might be a suitable definition when studying entrepreneurial firms (Eisenhardt and Schoonhoven 1990; Ruef, Aldrich, and Carter 2003; Watson, Ponthieu, and Critelli 1995).

Also, there is a need to study the sensitivity of findings to different operationalizations of TMTs. The ability to gradually develop more generalizable theory on strategic leadership may be enhanced if results are found to differ systematically according to TMT definition. For example, in a study of TMT demography and organization innovation, Flatt (1992) compared results using alternative definitions of the TMT and found that they differed significantly. (See also Carpenter and Fredrickson 2001; Jensen and Zajac 2004.) Developing varying operationalizations of TMTs in a given data set is often feasible, and thus sensitivity analysis would be possible in many studies. Stronger theory may arise from this type of analysis, for it could enable greater

understanding of which executives are influential in a particular setting. Moreover, meta-analysis of research that examines the effects of alternative TMT definitions may be warranted.

The appropriate definition of a TMT may depend on the strategic issue under consideration, with a different set of executives included depending on the issue (Dutton, Fahey, and Narayanan 1983; Roberto 2003; Cannella and Holcomb 2005). Such a "strategic issue processing" perspective assumes that the top decision-making body is not constant (though it may have a handful of stable core members) and implies that the appropriate definition of the relevant group is that set of executives who are most involved in a particular issue (Jackson 1992; Roberto 2003). For example, if we were trying to predict the propensity of a company to increase its investment in R&D, we might consider the relevant decision body to consist of the CEO, CFO, VP of R&D, and VP of marketing, but we would exclude consideration of other executives, such as the VP of human resources and the general counsel. Obviously, such an approach either requires firsthand data about the involvement of various executives in specified decision domains, or it requires some relatively coarse judgments (perhaps aided by expert panels) about the selective involvement of executives in different types of decisions. See Roberto (2003) for a more complete discussion of these issues.

Power Dynamics at the Top

One answer to the question of "Who constitutes the TMT?" is that it consists of those executives with the greatest power to affect the overall strategic direction of an organization. This is precisely the point made by Finkelstein (1992), when he argued that the distribution of power among top executives is usually unequal, and therefore a consideration of power differences may go a long way toward better predictions of TMT effects. Hence, it may make sense to evaluate the power of a wide set of top managers and then focus on the subset that appears most influential. This approach is analogous to Thompson's (1967) concept of the inner circle—the group of individuals with the greatest decision-making influence in an organization.

For example, in a study of 102 companies, Finkelstein (1988) asked top managers to rate the influence of themselves and others within their firms on specific strategic decisions. Using these data, it was possible to gauge the relative power of members of each executive group. Data were collected on a total of 444 top managers, consisting of 283 inside board members and 161 executives who held other top managerial positions but did not sit on the board. The average rating of managerial power for executives who were board members was 13.99,[11] while the average score for "nonboard" executives was 9.80, a statistically significant difference (p < .001). Even when CEOs were excluded from the analysis (and power scores for other executive board members dropped to 12.00), the difference remained very significant (p < .001). Hence, top managers identified a sizable gap between the power of inside board members and other executives, providing support for the use of inside board members as an operational definition of TMT. Since 1992, however, the average number of inside board members has steadily declined, and Sarbanes-Oxley requirements have accelerated this process. Hence, inside board membership is no longer a meaningful criterion to use, but the Finkelstein study highlights more broadly the importance of distinguishing the power differentials within TMTs.

Research on the distribution of power among top managers is important for several reasons. First, and perhaps foremost, power is central to strategic choice (Child 1972; Finkelstein 1992). It is generally well-established that strategic decisions are unstructured and ambiguous (Mintzberg, Raisinghani, and Theoret 1976) and, hence, invite the use of power (Mintzberg 1983b). Numerous examples exist of the important role of power in the strategic decision-making process (Allison 1971; Carter 1971; Pettigrew 1973; Hinings et al. 1974; Bourgeois and Eisenhardt 1988). Second, as we discussed earlier, the distribution of power within TMTs affects which executives are influential and, as a result, the impact of executive experiences and personality on organizational outcomes (Finkelstein 1992; Pitcher and Smith 2001). Finally, studying top managerial power makes clear that TMTs are really groups of individuals—each with their own goals and preferences—and are not necessarily cooperative teams with unitary goals and preferences (Cyert and March 1963).

It is also important to use a broad definition of power and to consider a full range of power sources when measuring the power of TMT members individually. For example, Finkelstein (1992) describes four sources of power: structural, prestige, ownership, and expertise. Of these, structural, prestige, and ownership will tend to be concentrated in the CEO position. For example, when comparing the ownership positions of CEOs and other members of the TMT, both Cannella and Shen (2001) and Reutzel and Cannella (2004) measured the ownership power of heirs apparent and CFOs, respectively. In both cases, ownership power did have significant effects, but the ownership positions of these two very senior executive positions were small relative to those held by CEOs. For these reasons, we expect that expertise power will have the most predictive power among TMT members, though as Bunderson (2003) describes, these effects may be quite complex. Unfortunately, expertise power is more difficult to measure than power deriving from ownership or prestige. Most attempts to examine expertise power have relied on functional backgrounds, as Finkelstein (1992) did, typically by positing an optimal match between functional experiences and strategic contingencies (Carpenter and Wade 2002; Guthrie and Datta 1997; Hambrick 1981). See Bunderson (2003) for perhaps the most sophisticated measurement strategy.[12]

A study by Pitcher and Smith (2001) focuses on the role of power in affecting the association between TMT attributes and both decision-making processes and organizational outcomes. Using an in-depth case methodology, the authors provide rich insights into the issues of TMT member power and team process. The authors studied the changes in a single organization's TMT over three eras, with the intent of understanding how TMT heterogeneity influenced both team processes and outcomes. In the first era, the CEO was very participative and held frequent team meetings and open discussions. Members all had some power and influence, and every member's opinion was sought out. Under these conditions, team member heterogeneity explained intermediate outcomes and organizational performance quite well. In the second era, only the CEO changed, and the new CEO was one of the team members from the previous era. The new CEO, however, disdained input from TMT members. The only powerful TMT members in the second era were the CEO and his CFO. The new CEO held few team meetings, preferring one-on-one exchanges with executives. TMT members began to avoid visits to headquarters and soon gave up trying to make a difference in strategy, as their opinions and suggestions were ignored or ridiculed. In this second era, *even though the composition of the team was nearly identical to the first era,* the team's heterogeneity did not affect team outcomes or organizational performance. This evidence, though limited, suggests that unless all team members have at least moderate power, team-level heterogeneity will provide few clues to team decisions, intermediate organizational outcomes, or organizational performance.

Another way to interpret Pitcher and Smith would be to assert that the TMT changed considerably in makeup over the first two eras, although the titles and identities of the individuals in senior positions stayed largely the same. In the first era, the team could be described as meeting the basic assumptions of most TMT researchers, as well as Hambrick and Mason's (1984) original conceptualization. That is, the team consisted of a number of senior executives who were influential in determining the strategic direction of the firm. In the second era, however, it could easily be argued that the TMT consisted of only two members—the CEO and his CFO. This interpretation aligns with our discussion of power, but it also illustrates that the CEO may exert a strong influence over who has power among the other executives.

In summary, it seems imperative to consider the relative power of individual executives in the strategic decision-making process (Pitcher and Smith 2001). As Finkelstein has argued:

> Power is ... central to research on top management teams. In fact, the choice of unit of analysis in research on top managers and the issue of managerial power are two sides of the same coin. That is, adoption of a unit of analysis rests on an implicit assumption about the distribution of power among top managers. For example, in an organization in which the CEO wields dominant power, studying only the CEO may provide sufficient information with which to test propositions. However, in organizations in which power is less polarized,

consideration of a coalition of top managers is necessary to fully capture the range of managerial orientations prevailing. Hence, consideration of the distribution of power among top managers seems an essential ingredient for research on top management teams. (1992, 505)

We now turn our attention to the dynamics of TMT interactions. In particular, we consider how TMT composition, structure, and process are interconnected and how the distribution of power within TMTs affects these important facets of executive interaction. While the first part of our analysis leaves the role of power to the side so we can more easily crystallize the relevant research on TMT composition, structure, and process, this choice in exposition should not be construed as indicating that power can be omitted from conceptual and empirical work on this topic. We return again to this point shortly.

Interactions Within TMTs

Figure 11.2 elaborates on Figure 11.1 by depicting relationships among TMT composition, structure, and process. In this section, we develop the rationale for the associations proposed by drawing on work in social psychology, organizational demography, and strategic management. Because much of the relevant research comes from conceptual articles or empirical studies based on samples of people who are not executives, these ideas constitute unfinished business for a research agenda on strategic leadership.

To help understand how senior executives interact as a group, it is useful to carefully consider one of the most studied facets of TMTs—demographic heterogeneity. Referring to the extent to which TMT members have had a wide variety of experiences, demographic heterogeneity is one of the most studied characteristics of TMTs, though it remains among the most ambiguous. Its popularity among researchers is owed to a fair degree to the accessibility, objectivity, and reliability of demographic data (Hambrick and Mason 1984), but critics have questioned the underlying meaning of such data (e.g., Smith et al. 1994; Lawrence 1997; West and Schwenk 1996; Priem, Lyon, and Dess 1999).

Figure 11.2 Top Management Team Interaction

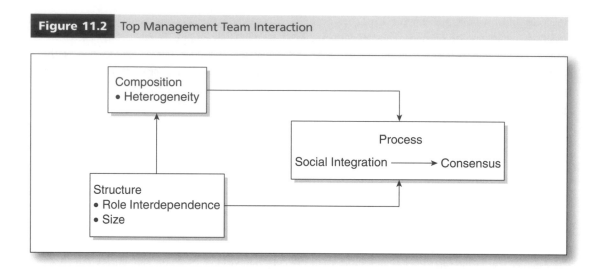

At one level, demographic heterogeneity may be seen as a proxy for cognitive heterogeneity (Hambrick and Mason 1984), representing innovativeness (Bantel and Jackson 1989; Murray 1989), problem-solving abilities (Nemeth 1986; Hurst, Rush, and White 1989), creativity (Triandis, Hall, and Ewen 1965; Shaw 1981; Wanous and Youtz 1986; Bantel and Jackson 1989), diversity of information sources and perspectives (Jackson 1992; Geletkanycz and Hambrick 1997; Wiersema and Bantel 1992; Sutcliffe 1994; Carpenter 2002; Carpenter and Fredrickson 2001; Sambharya 1996), openness to change (Katz 1982; Dutton and Duncan 1987; Virany, Tushman, and Romanelli 1992; Glick, Miller, and Huber 1993; Bertrand and Schoar 2003), and willingness to challenge and be challenged (Hoffman and Maier 1961; Sorenson 1968; Janis 1972; Gladstein 1984; Eisenhardt and Schoonhoven 1990). Although it is often argued that these positive features lead to superior organizational performance, for now we restrict ourselves to a more limited proposition:

Proposition 1A: The greater the demographic heterogeneity within TMTs, the greater the cognitive heterogeneity within TMTs.

Alternatively, there is also considerable support for the idea that demographic heterogeneity has drawbacks for team functioning, reducing social integration within TMTs (and by implication group and organizational performance), increasing conflict (Amason 1996; Amason and Sapienza 1997; Ferrier 2001; Williams and O'Reilly 1998; Simons, Pelled, and Smith 1999; Schmidt 1974; Chatman and Flynn 2001; Reed 1978; Pfeffer 1981a; Deutsch 1985; Nemeth and Staw 1989; O'Reilly, Snyder, and Boothe 1993; Barsade et al. 2001), increasing coordination costs (Pfeffer 1983; Smith et al. 1994), reducing communication frequency (Roberts and O'Reilly 1979; Bunderson and Sutcliffe 2002; McCain, O'Reilly, and Pfeffer 1983; Wagner, Pfeffer, and O'Reilly 1984; O'Reilly, Caldwell, and Barnett 1989; Zenger and Lawrence 1989; Stasser 1993), reducing attentional focus (Bertrand and Schoar 2003; Cho, Hambrick, and Chen 1994), and reducing group identification and cohesiveness (Lott and Lott 1965; Zander 1977; Ancona and Caldwell 1992; Michel and Hambrick 1992).

Despite these arguments for negative effects from TMT heterogeneity, studies have varied somewhat. For instance, research by O'Reilly and colleagues (1993) is supportive; a study by Glick, Miller, and Huber (1993) reports mixed results; and research by Smith and colleagues (1994) is not supportive. Further, two other issues arise and can be quite important. First, while diversity negatively impacts team process early in the team's life, the negative effects appear to decline over time, as norms for group interaction become established (Chatman and Flynn 2001). Therefore, the life stage of the group under consideration may have important implications for the effects of team heterogeneity on team functioning.

Second, research has been widely inconsistent in how group-level heterogeneity has been conceptualized and measured (Bunderson and Sutcliffe 2002). Future research will need very careful conceptualization and measurement if we are to develop a better understanding of the effects of group-level diversity (Harrison and Klein 2007). (See also Cannella, Park, and Lee 2008; Ferrier 2001; Carpenter, Geletkanycz, and Sanders 2004; Polzer et al. 2006.) Thus, the question of how demographic heterogeneity affects social integration remains an open one. But this is the most promising proposition:

Proposition 1B: The greater the demographic heterogeneity within TMTs, the less the degree of social integration within TMTs.

The theory behind cognitive heterogeneity and social integration imply that they should be negatively associated as well. Indeed, social integration is facilitated when group members are more similar (Byrne 1961; Chatman and Flynn 2001; Pfeffer 1981a), while many of the effects of demographic heterogeneity, such as greater diversity of perspectives and willingness to challenge others (Eisenhardt and Schoonhoven 1990; Amason 1996; Barsade et al. 2001; Glick, Miller, and Huber 1993), can create conflict that detracts from team cohesiveness and social integration. Hence, we propose the following:

Proposition 1C: The greater the cognitive heterogeneity within TMTs, the less the degree of social integration within TMTs.

Most research that links TMT heterogeneity to factors such as social integration relies upon fixed characteristics of executives, such as race and gender (Chatman and Flynn 2001; Richard et al. 2004; Westphal and Milton 2000), personality (Barsade et al. 2001; Peterson et al. 2003), functional background (Chattopadhyay et al. 1999; Cronin and Weingart 2007), experience (Carpenter and Fredrickson 2001; Sambharya 1996; Richard et al. 2004; Tihanyi et al. 2000; Carpenter, Pollock, and Leary 2003) or co-location (the extent to which the members

are physically located near each other) (Cannella, Park, and Lee 2008; see also Carpenter, Geletkanycz, and Sanders 2004; Polzer et al. 2006). However, there are also some sources of heterogeneity that are more time-dependent or context-dependent. For example, as the incumbent CEO nears retirement age, members of the TMT may begin to compete with each other as each strives to be selected as the next CEO (Vancil 1987). The selection of an heir apparent may reduce this competition somewhat (Cannella and Shen 2001); but even in the presence of a clear heir apparent, team members are still likely to compete for favorable positions following the expected change in leadership. Thus, friction among TMT members should be expected in the succession context (Shen and Cannella 2002a), and it seems natural to expect that this friction will spill over into team processes. This remains a fertile area for future research.

Demographic (and cognitive) homogeneity and social integration may increase TMT consensus. Homogeneous teams develop greater cohesiveness over time (Pfeffer 1983), which promotes greater agreement about the organization and its goals (Tushman and Romanelli 1985). Hence, consensus is formed, as TMT members are able to coalesce around a shared understanding of what the organization seeks to accomplish (Dutton and Duncan 1987; Wiersema and Bantel 1992) and members establish norms of interaction (Chatman and Flynn 2001). To the extent that TMT homogeneity promotes a "dominant logic" (Prahalad and Bettis 1986) among a group of top managers, consensus is more likely (Dess and Keats 1987). Shared understandings are also engendered through cooperation, frequent communication, and group identification, all of which are attributes of socially integrated groups (Lott and Lott 1965; O'Reilly, Caldwell, and Barnett 1989). Finally, TMT heterogeneity may weaken consensus on goals and perceptions (Cyert and March 1963; Bunderson and Sutcliffe 2002; Richard et al. 2004; Snow et al. 1996; Grinyer and Norburn 1975; Bettenhausen and Murnighan 1985; Bourgeois 1985; Priem 1990; Amason and Schweiger 1992). In all, TMT consensus is expected to be positively related to TMT homogeneity and integration.[13]

Proposition 1D: The greater the heterogeneity within TMTs, the less the degree of consensus within TMTs.

Proposition 1E: The greater the social integration within TMTs, the greater the degree of consensus within TMTs.

The number of individuals within a TMT (its size) is also expected to affect cognitive heterogeneity, social integration, and consensus for many of the same reasons already discussed. To some extent, this may be definitional, because the larger the team, the stronger the likelihood that executives will be demographically heterogeneous (Haleblian and Finkelstein 1993). Nevertheless, we can add two more rationales: (1) larger groups have greater capabilities and resources upon which to rely in the strategy-making process (Hambrick and D'Aveni 1992; Haleblian and Finkelstein 1993), increasing the variety of perspectives that they can bring to a problem and thus promoting greater cognitive heterogeneity but less consensus at the top; and (2) larger groups create coordination and communication problems that smaller groups do not have (Blau 1970; Shaw and Harkey 1976), curtailing member cohesiveness, cooperation (Wagner 1995), social integration (Shaw 1981), and consensus (Shull, Delbecq, and Cummings 1970).

Proposition 1F: The larger the size of TMTs, the greater the degree of cognitive heterogeneity within TMTs.

Proposition 1G: The larger the size of TMTs, the less the degree of social integration within TMTs.

Proposition 1H: The larger the size of TMTs, the less the degree of consensus within TMTs.

Recently, evidence and theory has pointed to the role that TMT tenure can play in team processes. For example, Chatman and Flynn (2001) demonstrated that after a few months of working together, norms of interaction become established, reducing conflict and friction even in very diverse teams. However, while most studies of TMT tenure consider the average tenure across members (Carpenter, Geletkanycz, and Sanders 2004), there are reasons to expect that the tenure of the most recent addition to the team might also be important. Team situations characterized by several long-tenured members and fewer short-term members has long been known to cause interpersonal friction and conflict (Wagner, Pfeffer, and O'Reilly 1984). Even one or two very short-tenured members might be enough to disrupt team norms of functioning, especially if those members are high-ranking (say the CFO or COO). Future research should consider the implications of adding a single new member to a team (e.g., Tushman and Rosenkopf 1996) and should especially consider the implications of the new member or members for established norms and patterns of interaction. If one new member can disrupt the established norms of interaction (which seems likely), then the tenure of the most recent addition might be much more informative than average team tenure.

Although we draw on research in social psychology to develop propositions on the interrelationships among TMT characteristics, there are important differences between TMTs and other groups. Indeed, one of the problems in interpreting the meaning of TMT heterogeneity is that researchers often tend not to specifically describe how top management groups are different from other groups (upon which much of the supporting literature on TMT heterogeneity typically cited is based).[14] Perhaps of greatest importance is the role of power in TMTs (Keck 1990; Pitcher and Smith 2001; Finkelstein 1992; O'Reilly, Snyder, and Boothe 1993). In contrast to most work groups, one of the major functions of TMTs is to direct the behavior of others, an activity that both generates and uses power for each executive. In addition, top managers are expected to have a functional impact on organizations (Mintzberg 1979); but without the power to make decisions and direct others, they are unable to do so. Hence, it seems particularly important to incorporate power in models of TMT interaction. Nevertheless, such a focus is rare in the literature to date.

One of the most promising efforts along these lines has been the work of Eisenhardt and Bourgeois (1988). Through interviews and surveys, these authors investigated the "politics of strategic decision making" in eight microcomputer companies, developing a series of propositions on power and politics within TMTs. For example, they linked power and politics to TMT centralization, coalition formation, and demography. Unfortunately, their ideas have yet to be formally studied in any large-scale empirical investigation.

We suggest a different perspective on power in TMTs, which builds on research by Finkelstein (1992).

He suggested that research on TMTs requires a "recognition of the role of power in strategic choice and a means of incorporating power" if stronger predictions of executive effects are to be found (1992, 532). The basic logic of this approach can be applied to TMT interaction. For example, the effects of TMT heterogeneity on TMT process should be stronger when the relative power of each top manager is taken into consideration. In a typical test of TMT heterogeneity, the dispersion of an attribute among different executives (such as tenure or tolerance for ambiguity) is calculated for the overall group. The impact of each executive on the top team is considered equal to that of any other executive, when in fact this seems unlikely (Mintzberg 1979; Finkelstein 1992; Cannella and Holcomb 2005). Because CEOs are generally more influential than others, an accurate assessment of the real level of heterogeneity in a TMT should take this into consideration. Additionally, the CEO's role in establishing and maintaining team processes seems critical to future research on TMT heterogeneity (Pitcher and Smith 2001; Cannella and Holcomb 2005). Virtually all of the research linking TMT heterogeneity to team process and/or organizational outcomes assumes that the team meets, thinks, and acts like a team. However, as we have noted, this assumption needs to be substantiated. Relatedly, the CEO's leadership style will be very important to team processing. If the CEO does not encourage open debate, is autocratic, or does not tolerate dissent, then TMT heterogeneity would seem largely irrelevant.

Power issues are not limited to CEOs. In many situations, managers with particular expertise, prestige, or ownership position may be more powerful (Finkelstein 1992; Roberto 2003). For example, when decisions regarding financial policy are considered, the CFO's role (or power) in the decision is likely to be enhanced (Reutzel and Cannella 2004), and similar effects can be expected to the extent that there is role differentiation among TMT members (Cannella and Holcomb 2005; Roberto 2003). Further, as illustrated by Pitcher and Smith (2001), sometimes only one or two TMT members have any real influence. In situations such as these, taking the coefficient of variation of tenure within a TMT and suggesting that this accurately assesses the heterogeneity of that team is potentially misleading. The most powerful managers have the greatest impact on strategic choices (Child 1972), and thus it seems important to factor this into the analysis of TMT interaction.

One way to do this is to measure the relative power of each member of a TMT and adjust the demographic or cognitive makeup of the team by weighting each executive's characteristics by his or her power before computing heterogeneity measures. Such an analysis would yield more precise (and accurate) measures of heterogeneity and would perhaps help establish more consistent and stronger relationships between TMT composition, structure, and process than has been evident in the literature to date. The following proposition is representative:

Proposition 1i: The effects of TMT heterogeneity on other characteristics of TMTs are stronger when the relative power of each member of the TMT is factored into the computation of heterogeneity.

The CEO and Team Process

The CEO plays an important role in team processes in several ways. First, as noted above, the CEO sets the stage for the team's interactions. If the CEO encourages open discussion and dispute resolution and treats the TMT as if it is a central component of both strategy formulation and strategy implementation, then team processes will be enhanced. By enhanced, we mean that team processes will approach what are commonly believed to be those that lead to effective functioning—broad consideration of alternatives, widespread information gathering, effective dispute resolution, and the development of strong commitment to the decisions made (Cannella and Holcomb 2005; Pitcher and Smith 2001). Second, if the CEO has a strong vision for the company and communicates that vision effectively to TMT members, then decisions and actions will come to be framed by that vision. In this setting, there will be less comprehensive consideration of strategic issues, and those issues noticed and acted upon are likely to be directly related to the CEO's vision. Additionally, issues raised for reasons peripheral to the vision are likely to be framed in the words and terms of the vision, in order to gain CEO support for action (Cannella and Holcomb

2005). Finally, the CEO's degree of charisma will have an important impact on team functioning (Waldman and Yammarino 1999), as charismatic CEOs are able to secure extraordinary effort and commitment from their followers, especially through direct reports. The research on charisma is highly relevant for scholars who seek to understand TMT dynamics (Klein and House 1995; House, Spangler, and Woycke 1991; Colbert et al. 2008).

In summary, significant interrelationships exist among the major facets of TMT interaction. Although they are sometimes recognized in the literature, we believe it is important to make these associations explicit. We have suggested several basic propositions that, with a few exceptions, have not been directly tested in an empirical setting. In addition, the idea that power is central to processes within a TMT is generally accepted but has seen only limited application in published research (e.g., Eisenhardt and Bourgeois 1988; Carpenter and Sanders 2002; Pitcher and Smith 2001). Armed with this understanding of the nature of TMT interaction, we are now in a position to analyze both the determinants and consequences of TMTs. We turn first to the contextual conditions that help explain TMT characteristics.

Determinants of TMT Characteristics

Contextual conditions arising from environmental, organizational, and CEO factors may have pervasive effects on TMTs. In fact, there is a real "need to treat team characteristics as a dependent variable—why do teams look the way they do?" (Pettigrew 1992, 176). Hence, in this section, we develop propositions on how contextual conditions affect TMTs. Although research on the major contextual conditions we focus on is abundant, relatively little of this work has been specifically directed toward TMTs.

Environment

An organization's environment constrains and shapes activities and behaviors within the boundaries of the firm (Duncan 1972; Aldrich 1979; Dess and Beard 1984). Research has indicated the pervasiveness of environmental effects by showing how they affect such major facets of organizational life as strategy (Porter 1980; Miller, Droge, and Toulouse 1988), structure (Lawrence and Lorsch 1967; Keats and Hitt 1988), organizational processes (Rajagopalan and Finkelstein 1992), and firm performance (Hannan and Freeman 1977). Although few studies have directly examined how TMTs are shaped by environmental influences, such forces likely are important here as well. To help guide our discussion, we consider three fundamental dimensions of the environment: complexity, instability, and munificence (Dess and Beard 1984). Environmental complexity refers to the number of environmental factors that impinge on an organization (Thompson 1967); environmental instability is defined by the rate of change in these factors (Thompson 1967); and environmental munificence refers to the extent to which the environment supports sustained growth (Starbuck 1976). We now consider the effects of each of these dimensions on TMTs.

Environmental Complexity

Organizations in complex environments are typically confronted with conflicting demands from multiple constituencies (Thompson 1967). Managing each of these stakeholders may require a different set of skills or competencies that force organizations to develop greater structural differentiation to cope (Pfeffer and Salancik 1978). As Gupta asserts, drawing from Lawrence and Lorsch (1967) and Arrow (1974), "The more diverse an organization's environment, the more necessary it becomes to have a differentiated top management team in order to appropriately monitor the diversity of the environment" (1988, 160). Indeed, environmental complexity has often been operationalized as heterogeneity in the environment (e.g., Dess and Beard 1984; Keats and Hitt 1988).

Although these ideas have been subject to only limited empirical investigation (Wiersema and Bantel 1993), they seem worth pursuing. Firms in complex environments often face ill-defined and novel problem-solving situations, suggesting that larger, more heterogeneous TMTs may be more common under these conditions (Janis 1972). Such teams have a broader range of skills represented among their members (Steiner 1972), are more likely to develop diverse interpretations and perspectives (Wanous and Youtz 1986), and tend to engender more debate and questioning among team members (Hoffman and Maier 1961). In simpler, less complex environments, such heterogeneity is not required and indeed may be dysfunctional to the extent that it engenders poor communication (Zenger and Lawrence 1989) and conflict (Ebadi and Utterback 1984). In addition, as Thompson (1967) has argued, to the degree that environmental complexity creates additional challenges for top management, the dominant coalition will be larger. As a result, we offer the following propositions:

Proposition 2A: The more complex the environment, the greater the heterogeneity within TMTs.

Proposition 2B: The more complex the environment, the larger the size of TMTs.

Sanders and Carpenter (1998) provided evidence in support of Proposition 2B. They argued (and provided supporting empirical evidence) that complexity arising from a firm's degree of internationalization leads to such outcomes as larger TMTs and the separation of the CEO and Chair position.

A related argument can be offered for role interdependence. Environmental complexity promotes greater differentiation within the top team and reduces the opportunity for executives to interact, share resources, and operate in a cohesive manner. The greater environmental demands characteristic of this setting force greater task specialization (role differentiation) and make coordination more difficult (Mintzberg 1979). While these circumstances may call for *greater integration* (Lawrence and Lorsch 1967), the demands on top team members from disparate environmental constituencies may make such integration difficult to achieve. As Galbraith (1973) has argued, complexity forces greater specialization and decentralization, reducing opportunities for coordination and increasing both the number of individuals involved in decision making and their decision-making independence.

Proposition 2C: The more complex the environment, the less the role interdependence within TMTs.

Finally, environmental complexity is expected to have a direct effect on TMT social integration and consensus. Arguing that environmental complexity requires greater division of labor, which in turn increases differences in interpersonal orientation and time orientation within TMTs (Lawrence and Lorsch 1967), Dess and Origer suggest that "such divergence in perspectives makes consensus on the strategic direction of the firm difficult" (1987, 326). The same logic also suggests that environmental complexity reduces social integration by forcing TMTs to attend to multiple stimuli and demands that highlight differences within the top team. At the same time, the added demands of complex environments also reduce opportunities for team building and cohesion. Consistent with Bourgeois's (1980) contention that complexity promotes conflict, as well as with work by Dess and Origer (1987), we expect the following:

Proposition 2D: The more complex the environment, the less the degree of social integration within TMTs.

Proposition 2E: The more complex the environment, the less the degree of consensus within TMTs.

Environmental Instability

Environments vary in the degree to which they are characterized by unpredictability and unexpected change (Mintzberg 1979). Such environmental instability can have a dramatic impact on how organizations are structured and operate (Duncan 1972) and, of primary importance here, on the nature of TMT composition, structure, and even process. Environmental instability may refer to the "steady-state" rate of change in environmental factors affecting organizations (Thompson 1967) or to the extent of discontinuous change in the environment (Tushman and Romanelli 1985). Using either definition, few studies have probed the effects of environmental instability on TMTs. Nevertheless, as we discuss below, important relationships may exist.

In a manner analogous to our argument above on environmental complexity, environmental instability may affect TMT heterogeneity and size. Such environments increase the variation and fragmentation of managerial work (Mintzberg 1973), enlarging the information-processing demands on the top team (Daft, Sormunen, and Parks 1988). As Galbraith argued, "The greater the task uncertainty, the greater the amount of information that must be processed among decision makers during task execution" (1973, 4). The greater information-processing requirements characteristic of unstable environments have two effects on top teams: greater heterogeneity and greater size. Both effects arise from the need for TMTs to increase the quantity and range of (1) information absorbed and recalled, (2) perspectives brought to bear on a problem, and (3) potential solutions considered (Hoffman and Maier 1961; Harrison 1975; Shaw 1981), as environments become more unstable. Hence, the greater information-processing capabilities of larger and more heterogeneous teams (e.g., Steiner 1972) are needed to help firms adapt to the greater information-processing requirements of unstable environments (Haleblian and Finkelstein 1993).

> *Proposition 3A:* The more unstable the environments, the greater the heterogeneity within TMTs.

> *Proposition 3B:* The more unstable the environment, the larger the size of TMTs.

Environmental instability may affect other aspects of TMTs as well. Challenging environments create large demands on TMT members to cope with external requirements (Pfeffer and Salancik 1978; Hambrick, Finkelstein, and Mooney 2005). As with complex environments, when environmental instability is high, TMTs face greater information-processing and decision-making demands (Kotter 1982) and greater time pressures to reach decisions (Eisenhardt 1989). The result is less opportunity for role interdependence and, by implication, less social integration. We would also expect TMT consensus to be more difficult to attain, because instability and change promote multiple perspectives (Khandwalla 1977) and uncertainty about both means-ends relationships and outcome preferences (Thompson 1967). The resulting diversity of opinions creates conflict and makes consensus elusive (Amason

and Sapienza 1997; Amason 1996). In contrast, higher levels of consensus may be relatively more achievable in stable environments (Priem 1990).

> *Proposition 3C:* The more unstable the environment, the less the degree of role interdependence within TMTs.

> *Proposition 3D:* The more unstable the environment, the less the degree of social integration within TMTs.

> *Proposition 3E:* The more unstable the environment, the less the degree of consensus within TMTs.

These arguments are expected to hold when environments change more dramatically as well. For example, technological discontinuities (Tushman and. Anderson 1986; Tushman and Rosenkopf 1996), changing competitive conditions, and regulatory changes are all expected to affect TMTs. As Keck and Tushman noted, "Organizations in jolted environments may require substantially altered executive teams to allow firms to develop the competencies and internal processes that will make it possible for them to cope with altered competitive requirements" (1993, 1317). For example, Smith and Grimm (1987) found that deregulation caused railroads to alter their TMTs toward younger, shorter-tenured, and more highly educated executives. And Cho and Hambrick (2006) found that top management teams characterized by a greater proportion of output-oriented functional backgrounds and shorter industry tenures emerged in the years after deregulation in the airline industry. In the interests of space, however, we only offer an illustrative proposition for environmental discontinuities, rather than repeating each proposition just presented.

> *Proposition 3F:* Environmental discontinuities increase the degree of heterogeneity within TMTs.

Environmental Munificence

Munificent environments help buffer organizations from external threats and enable them to accumulate slack resources (Cyert and March 1963). In addition, munificence confers flexibility and growth opportunities on organizations (Aldrich 1979). This cushion allows TMTs to operate with less constraint than otherwise might exist. As a result, predicting the consequential effects on TMTs is difficult. On the one hand, TMT consensus may be greater in munificent environments, because the generally nonthreatening conditions facilitate agreement and cooperation. On the other hand, because environmental munificence offers TMTs a wider breadth of choices, there may be more diversity of opinion and, hence, disagreement (Dess and Origer 1987).[15]

The only proposition we offer here relates to TMT size. As noted, greater organizational slack often accompanies environmental munificence, creating the "problem" of how to use it. Williamson (1963) has suggested that firms with slack resources tend to hire more staff than needed—especially at the executive level. This argument is analogous to a related point by Jensen (1986), who held that top managers with "free cash flow" may have an incentive to engage in such profit-damaging behavior as empire building. In contrast, firms in more challenging contexts often focus on cost containment (Hofer 1980), including by reducing executive and other staff. Hence, environmental munificence may have a direct effect on TMT size (Keats and Hitt 1988; Bantel and Finkelstein 1995).

> *Proposition 4:* The more munificent the environment, the larger the size of TMTs.

Organization

Numerous aspects of organizations may affect TMTs. As with environment, however, the empirical work on this question has been quite limited. As a result, we will focus on only two characteristics of organizations—strategy and performance—in developing propositions on the determinants of TMT composition, structure, and process. Firm strategy and performance are emphasized here because they (1) are central to the study of strategic leadership; (2) are fundamental organizational attributes of interest to a wide set of scholars, and (3) appear particularly promising as antecedents to TMTs. This latter concern is important, given our interest in encouraging future investigations of the relationships we discuss.

Strategy

Of all potential antecedents of TMT characteristics, the strategy of a firm may be the most important, yet

equivocal, factor. On the one hand, according to the old maxim that "structure follows strategy" (Chandler 1962), organizational characteristics such as the TMT should at least partially be a function of the organization's strategy. For example, Porter argued that his "generic strategies [implied] differing organizational arrangements, control procedures, and incentive systems" (1980, 40) all of which affect the TMT. Hence, the effects of strategy on TMTs may be pervasive. On the other hand, organizations and the strategies they follow may be a reflection of their top managers (Hambrick and Mason 1984). Thus, disentangling causal direction in these relationships seems to be a fundamental requirement for future work.

Interestingly, Westphal and Fredrickson (2001) turn the "structure follows strategy" theme on its head, as they illustrate how the board of directors can take actions that lead to both changes in CEOs and changes in strategy. In their study, powerful members of the board of directors, who were CEOs of other firms, initiated succession events and selected successors who tended to initiate strategies similar to those of the outside director's home firm. While not a central source of CEO successions, the study demonstrates that the preferences and experiences of outside directors can shape company strategies and, indirectly, TMT characteristics.

A firm's corporate strategy, or the mix of businesses in which the firm competes, may have important implications for TMTs. Michel and Hambrick (1992) tested a series of hypotheses linking corporate strategy with TMT characteristics by developing theory on how the interdependence of diversification postures varies from low to high in the following order: unrelated, related-linked, related-constrained, and vertically integrated.

The same logic can be used to make predictions about TMT composition, structure, and process. For example, in firms with highly interdependent diversification postures, such as those that are vertically integrated, "there is need for abundant inter-unit negotiation, compromise, and collaboration. This process is greatly aided if corporate managers have a well-developed rapport and a common outlook and language" (Michel and Hambrick 1992, 17). Similarly, Athanassiou and Nigh (1999) showed that the extent of a multinational firm's internationalization was directly related to the TMT's advice network density, and greater interdependence among subunits across national borders increased advice network density. As a result, firms with highly interdependent operations should have TMTs with the following characteristics: low heterogeneity, high social integration, and high consensus. Role interdependence within TMTs is related almost by definition to the interdependence of diversification postures (whether product-based or geographic) as well.

The following propositions summarize this discussion:

Proposition 5A: The greater the interdependence of a firm's diversification posture, the less the heterogeneity within its TMT.

Proposition 5B: The greater the interdependence of a firm's diversification posture, the greater the degree of role interdependence within its TMT.

Proposition 5C: The greater the interdependence of a firm's diversification posture, the greater the degree of social integration within its TMT.

Proposition 5D: The greater the interdependence of a firm's diversification posture, the greater the degree of consensus within its TMT.

One final proposition concerns team size. Managing firms with unrelated diversification postures has been likened to managing a financial portfolio (Berg 1969; Rumelt 1974). Top teams are more concerned with buying and selling businesses than with actively managing the operations of each business. Because the task of operating each business is decentralized to general managers at the individual level, the corporate offices of highly diversified firms tend to be quite small (Pitts 1976). In contrast, corporate management of firms with more interdependent diversification postures may be larger because they "typically retain responsibility for overall product-market strategy and initiate investment projects (Ackerman 1970)" (Michel and Hambrick 1992, 12). These firms tend to rely on strategic controls instead of financial controls (Hoskisson and Hitt 1988, 1994) and promote coordination among business units by use of specialized incentives based on corporate as well as divisional performance (Hoskisson, Hitt, and Hill 1993). The ability to enact strategic controls and to effectively manage the greater information-processing demands that arise from corporate-based incentives adds complexity and, hence, staffing needs to corporate offices. Therefore, we propose the following:

Proposition 5E: The greater the interdependence of the diversification posture, the larger the size of the TMT.

A firm's competitive, or business, strategy is also likely to affect the composition, structure, and process of its TMT. To help structure our discussion, we contrast how the strategies of Prospector (growth, innovation, and the search for new opportunities) and Defender (cost control, stability, and efficiency) firms call for different TMT characteristics (Miles and Snow 1978).

Compared to Prospectors, the greater stability in Defender firms suggests that they face fewer strategic contingencies (Hambrick 1981) and do not require larger, more differentiated TMTs. Firms following Defender strategies generally exhibit lower growth, constraining internal labor markets by limiting promotion opportunities for top managers (Pfeffer 1983). Prospectors are not only more growth-oriented, they are also more innovative and forward-looking.

These differences between Prospectors and Defenders have several implications for TMTs. First, it is likely that TMTs of Defenders will be smaller and less heterogeneous, given the importance of maintaining existing domains. As Miles and Snow note, "It is more advantageous for the dominant coalition to know the strengths and capacities of 'our company' than it is for them to know the trends and developments in 'our industry'" (1978, 42). Such internally focused TMTs do not require the same breadth and diversity that TMTs with Prospector strategies might need.

Second, top management teams in Prospector firms need to be receptive to change and innovation—searching for new opportunities may require new perspectives and approaches that are more likely to exist when TMTs are heterogeneous (Wiersema and Bantel 1992). In contrast, TMTs in firms with Defender strategies have already coalesced around a specific product market and a narrow range of competitive weapons to defend their firm's position in that product market. In addition, Defenders face much less uncertainty (Miles and Snow 1978). Hence, TMTs of Defenders are more likely to have similar mind-sets, exhibit greater cohesiveness, and develop congruent beliefs about their firm and how it operates, making it easier for them to reach agreement (Dutton and Duncan 1987). Indeed, both means-ends relationships and desired outcomes are fixed to a much greater extent in these firms.

> *Proposition 6A:* Firms pursuing Defender strategies exhibit less TMT heterogeneity than do Prospector firms.

> *Proposition 6B:* Firms pursuing Defender strategies have fewer members in their TMTs than do Prospector firms.

> *Proposition 6C:* Firms pursuing Defender strategies exhibit more social integration within their TMTs than do Prospector firms.

> *Proposition 6D:* Firms pursuing Defender strategies exhibit more consensus within their TMTs than do Prospector firms.

A final characteristic of a firm's strategy considered here is the extent to which it is relatively constant or changing. Strategic change creates ripple effects throughout an organization, including within the TMT (Wiersema and Bantel 1992; Tushman and Rosenkopf 1996; Keck and Tushman 1993). Changes in firm strategy often disrupt existing ways of doing business, involve shifts to new domains or new tactics within the same domain, and create new power bases within the firm (Starbuck, Greve, and Hedberg 1978; Tushman and Romanelli 1985). These changes have significant implications for the functioning of the TMT. Established communication patterns (Zenger and Lawrence 1989), knowledge structures (Gersick and Hackman 1990), needed competencies and process (Ancona 1990), and patterns of interaction (O'Reilly, Caldwell, and Barnett 1989) all shift. To the extent that the strategic changes are severe, threatening the integrity of the organization or the positions of top managers, constriction of power and control may also result (Staw, Sandelands, and Dutton 1981). Under these conditions, we would expect to see several changes in the TMT: greater heterogeneity and size to try to cope with the changes; less role interdependence as it becomes more difficult for top managers to coordinate activities, at least in the short term;

less social integration as a consequence of disrupted patterns of interaction; and greater difficulty in reaching consensus because the rules of the game are in flux.

> *Proposition 7A:* The greater the amount of strategic change, the greater the heterogeneity within TMTs.

> *Proposition 7B:* The greater the amount of strategic change, the less the degree of role interdependence within TMTs.

> *Proposition 7C:* The greater the amount of strategic change, the larger the size of TMTs.

> *Proposition 7D:* The greater the amount of strategic change, the less the degree of social integration within TMTs.

> *Proposition 7E:* The greater the amount of strategic change, the less the degree of consensus within TMTs.

Organizational Performance

The effects of few organizational attributes are as immediately felt as those of recent performance. These effects are observed by numerous stakeholders, both within and outside an organization, leading one to expect that organizational performance may have important consequences for TMTs as well. Nevertheless, as is the case for the other contextual conditions we have discussed, research on how performance affects TMT configurations is lacking. Hence, in this section, we build on theories of threat rigidity and organizational slack to help develop some testable propositions on how recent organizational performance affects TMTs.

High-performing firms are characterized by excess organizational slack and, by extension, a multitude of strategic options. Organizational slack is defined as "the difference between the resources of the organization and the combination of demands made on it" (Cohen, March, and Olson 1972, 12). In a sense, performance and slack create additional opportunities that might be foreclosed in firms with less abundant resources. For example, decisions to enter new markets or develop new products are possible only when adequate resources exist. When resource constraints are tighter, fewer options exist, and the organization must be more reactive than proactive in dealing with environmental and strategic contingencies (Pfeffer and Salancik 1978). What is more, when performance is very poor, organizations tend to constrict control at the top, restricting intragroup information flows and promoting dissension (Staw, Sandelands, and Dutton 1981).

These effects have several important consequences for TMTs. Specifically since high-performing firms have abundant slack and opportunity, while low-performing firms are constrained and constricted, we expect a curvilinear relationship between organization performance and several attributes of TMTs. For example, TMTs are larger in both the highest performers (because their excess slack facilitates expenditures on staff; Williamson 1963) and lowest performers (because centralized control at the top creates a need for additional senior executives to take over responsibilities that were previously delegated).[16]

Proposition 8A: Under conditions of very low and very high organization performance, TMT size is larger; when organization performance is at a moderate level, TMTs have fewer members.

The same effects of very high and very low organization performance are expected to affect several other dimensions of TMTs: role interdependence, social integration, and consensus. As we have described, resources are so plentiful in very high-performing firms that TMTs do not have to deal with trade-offs or elaborate coordination. Under these conditions, TMT members need not engage in intensive interchange, because abundant slack allows "the unchecked pursuit of subunit goals" (Bourgeois 1981, 33), Moreover, the TMTs of successful firms may become less interactive and collaborative over time, as the resource constraints that force careful orchestration and collective attention to external contingencies dissipate (Hambrick 1995). Hence, we would expect less emphasis on role interdependence, a breakdown of social integration, and more disagreement on means and ends.

But, at the other extreme, these same TMT effects occur in organization: where performance is dire. A dominant individual or inner circle at the top takes charge, forcing changes without the same degree of

collaboration and consultation that may have previously existed (Staw, Sandelands, and Dutton 1981). Time pressures force immediate actions, reducing role interdependence; conflict and self-seeking behavior abound (Bourgeois and Eisenhardt 1988). It is only when firm performance is not at an extreme that social interactions within TMTs can be achieved and sustained. Thus, we offer the following propositions:

Proposition 8B: Under conditions of very low and very high organization performance, role interdependence within TMTs is low; when organization performance is at a moderate level, role interdependence is greatest.

Proposition 8C: Under conditions of very low and very high organization performance, social integration within TMTs is low; when organization performance is at a moderate level, social integration is greater.

Proposition 8D: Under conditions of very low and very high organization performance, consensus within TMTs is low; when organization performance is at a moderate level, consensus is greatest.

CEO

Chief executive officers play a major role in the composition and functioning of TMTs. CEOs are central members of the TMT (Jackson 1992) who have a disproportionate impact on team characteristics and outcomes (Finkelstein 1992). Although the importance of CEO characteristics and behaviors to TMTs seems almost self-evident (Hambrick 1994), studies investigating the nature of this relationship are rare. Thus, it seems important to examine how a CEO's influence permeates TMTs, the topic to which we now turn.

We will consider the impact of CEOs in two related ways. First, extending Hambrick and Mason's (1984) core idea that organizations are a reflection of their senior executives, it seems sensible to consider the degree to which TMT characteristics reflect CEO biases and preferences.[17] Second, CEO power is variable and is likely to affect TMTs (Finkelstein 1992; Hambrick and D'Aveni 1992; Jackson 1992). Research on CEO power or dominance is not plentiful; we are aware of only one study focused on its effects on TMTs (Pitcher and Smith 2001). Thus, there are important reasons to examine how CEO dominance affects TMTs[18] (Cannella and Holcomb 2005).

CEO dominance can take many forms. The traditional view is that CEOs enforce their will through their power (e.g., Finkelstein 1992; Pfeffer 1981b). However, CEO influence can go beyond the common and traditional bases of power (e.g., prestige, expertise, and ownership). For example, CEOs can influence team processes, and through that influence can determine if the TMT has any real influence or not (Pitcher and Smith 2001). Further, through a strong and focused vision, CEOs can influence decision making throughout the firm, as organizational participants must frame their issues in terms of the CEO's vision in order to attract the resources and attention necessary to take action (Cannella and Holcomb 2005). Finally, through charisma, some CEOs can get extra effort and commitment from their employees, especially those who are in direct contact with the leader (Waldman and Yammarino 1999; Klein and House 1995).

Thus, a multitude of CEO characteristics and their effects on TMTs can be considered. In the interests of space, however, we only examine "CEO openness"—a composite of such facets of CEO personality as awareness of multiple perspectives, valuing discourse and debate, and openness to new ideas. CEO openness is a virtual prerequisite for adaptability to changing circumstances, and its absence has been associated with organizational turmoil (Finkelstein and Mooney 2003). Open-minded CEOs are not so committed to a paradigm that alternative perspectives are foreclosed; rather, they are willing to try new approaches (Hambrick and Fukutomi 1991). CEO openness may be gauged by an array of characteristics, including a broad educational background, a higher level of education, newness to the organization, and a high variety of work experience, such as in multiple functional areas and industries. CEOs with this type of background are more likely to value diversity of opinion for the intellectual discourse it promotes as much as for the more varied range of ideas generated.

Some related support exists for these ideas: highly educated CEOs, particularly those with MBAs, promote

administrative complexity and sophistication (Hambrick and Mason 1984), as well as innovativeness (Kimberly and Evanisko 1981; Bantel and Jackson 1989)—both of which may lead to inclusion and diversity (Bantel and Jackson 1989). For example, to the extent that large TMTs have greater information-processing and decision-making capabilities than small teams (Eisenhardt and Schoonhoven 1990; Haleblian and Finkelstein 1993), a wider set of opinions can be heard.

CEO openness may also be enhanced when the CEO is new to the organization. CEOs selected from outside the firm are not as beholden to the status quo and often bring new perspectives to the organization (Dalton and Kesner 1985). In addition, outsiders tend to replace more members of the TMT than do CEOs promoted from within (Helmich and Brown 1972; Gabarro 1987; Shen and Cannella 2002b). These changes are consistent with the idea that CEO openness, as gauged by newness to the organization, promotes TMT heterogeneity (Keck and Tushman 1993). Further, it is important to remember that team changes can involve exits of existing members or entries of new members, or both. Entries and exits may be independent events, and may be associated with very different outcomes (Tushman and Rosenkopf 1996).

Proposition 9A: The greater the level of CEO openness, the greater the heterogeneity within TMTs.

Proposition 9B: The greater the level of CEO openness, the larger the size of TMTs.

The effects of CEO openness are not expected to remain constant over time. Although CEO interest in discussion and debate promotes heterogeneity and inclusiveness, we expect that these effects will dissipate over time. Gradually, CEOs develop routinized procedures (Tushman and Romanelli 1985; Keck and Tushman 1993), stronger opinions on appropriate strategies and how to achieve them (Gabarro 1987), greater interest in perpetuating their power (Pfeffer 1981a; Shen and Cannella 2002a; Finkelstein and Hambrick 1989), and more concern for their legacy (Westphal and Zajac 1995). Whether referred to as "commitment to a paradigm" (Hambrick and Fukutomi

1991), "stale in the saddle" (Miller 1991), or "entrenchment" (Fama and Jensen 1983), long-tenured CEOs become less responsive to diverse perspectives (Katz 1982; Hambrick, Geletkanycz, and Fredrickson 1993). Long tenure not only attenuates the effects of CEO openness, but it also reduces TMT heterogeneity directly because shared understandings about decision making and strategy become progressively more refined and similar over time (Pfeffer and Salancik 1978; Shen and Cannella 2002a; Kiesler and Sproull 1982; Fredrickson and Iaquinto 1989; Keck and Tushman 1993).[19]

Proposition 9C: The longer a CEO's tenure, the weaker the relationships between CEO openness and TMT heterogeneity and size.

Proposition 9D: The longer a CEO's tenure, the less the heterogeneity within TMTs.

The second important characteristic of a CEO is his or her power within the TMT. With few exceptions (Hambrick 1981; Pitcher and Smith 2001; Bourgeois and Eisenhardt 1988; Finkelstein 1992), the distribution of power among senior executives has not been the subject of in-depth investigation. As we argued earlier, however, understanding who has power and who does not within the TMT seems essential for developing more complete models of strategic decision making. Our interest here is how CEO dominance affects TMTs, specifically their heterogeneity and consensus.

Responsibility for selecting a top team generally resides with the CEO (Kotter 1982). Nevertheless, his or her ability to make such selections without constraint depends to some extent on other stakeholders, such as the board of directors (Lorsch and MacIver 1989; West and Schwenk 1996), organizations and individuals on which a firm is dependent (Pfeffer and Salancik 1978), and even other top managers (Finkelstein 1988; Shen and Cannella 2002a). Thus, the more powerful or dominant the CEO, the greater his or her influence on the executive selection process. Dominant CEOs are likely to select top managers who are similar to themselves.[20] This belief is predicated on three related arguments: (1) individuals tend to prefer others who are similar to themselves (Byrne 1971; Boone and de Brabander

1993); (2) individuals may derive self-esteem by belonging to a group of similar individuals (Tsui, Egan, and O Reilly 1992); and (3) by selecting individuals with similar perspectives, CEOs can consolidate power at the top (Westphal and Zajac 1995).

Proposition 10A: The greater the CEO dominance, the less the heterogeneity within TMTs.

Although CEO dominance is expected to reduce heterogeneity within the top team, it is likely that the actual size of the team may grow. Several writers have noted the tendency for powerful individuals to add staff and personnel in an attempt to build a protective core around their positions (Williamson 1963; Mintzberg 1983a; Whisler et al. 1967). The more powerful the CEO, the greater the ability to institutionalize power within the organization (Pfeffer 1981b). The net effect of such empire building is a larger TMT.

Proposition 10B: The greater the CEO dominance, the larger the size of TMTs.

Finally, CEO dominance may also reduce the degree of consensus achieved in reaching strategic decisions. For example, Eisenhardt and Bourgeois found that power centralization (a notion akin to CEO dominance) was associated with a higher degree of political activity within TMTs. When CEOs were less dominant, there was greater sharing of information, and the decision process was described as "consensus style" (1988, 749). Eisenhardt and Bourgeois's description of strategic decision making at Alpha, one of the companies they studied, is informative:

The CEO (the president) was described as a "parent" and "benevolent dictator." His power score was 9.6, tied for highest in our cases. The next most powerful executive at Alpha scored only 5.8. The strategic decision we studied corroborated those data. For example, the VP Sales said of the decision process, "The decision was a Don Rogers edict—not a vote." The president agreed: "I made the decision myself, despite the objections of everyone. I said 'the hell with it, let's go with the PC interface.'" (1988, 748-749)

Proposition 10C: The greater the CEO dominance, the less the degree of consensus within TMTs, and the less relevant is consensus to organizational outcomes.

To conclude, this section has elaborated a model of the determinants of TMT characteristics. This model is based on the idea that the context within which a TMT operates significantly influences its composition, structure, and process. We focused on such important antecedents as environment, organization, and the CEO, the central player within the top team. Although our model is not meant to be exhaustive (other factors may also contribute to an explanation of TMTs), it is an important step toward opening up our investigative lenses to the factors that affect how a TMT comes to take on certain characteristics. An emphasis on antecedents is important not only because of the greater understanding of TMTs it affords, but also because of its implications for what TMTs actually do. That is, much of the interest in TMTs apparent in the literature is driven by a desire to learn more about how TMTs are involved in strategic decision making and how this involvement translates into actions that help determine organizational strategy and performance. It is to these issues that we now turn.

Consequences of TMTs' Interaction

Empirical research on TMTs and organizational outcomes has increased dramatically in the past several years. In this section, we review this research to assess what progress has been made and to suggest some new lines of inquiry. Although some studies have examined multiple organizational outcomes, we organize this discussion by the dependent variables of strategic decision-making process, strategic choices and changes, and firm performance.[21]

Consequences of TMTs on Strategic Decision Making

Research on strategic decision making is abundant. Numerous attributes of this process can be studied, including decision speed (Eisenhardt 1989), comprehensiveness (Fredrickson 1984), analytical techniques (Schweiger, Sandberg, and Rechner 1989), urgency (Pinfield 1986; Bourgeois and Eisenhardt 1988), extent of subunit involvement (see Duhaime and Baird 1987; Pitcher and Smith 2001; Rajagopalan, Rasheed, and Datta 1993), the decision to engage in illegal acts (Daboub et al. 1995), and the handling of cross-cultural issues (Snow et al. 1996; Richard et al. 2004). Here, we develop propositions that relate the major facets of TMTs examined in this chapter with the strategic decision-making process.

The strategic decision-making process is often depicted as a series of stages, beginning with the generation of alternative strategic choices and moving through evaluation of those alternatives, strategic choice, implementation, and finally, evaluation (Ansoff 1965; Hofer and Schendel 1978). Although there are important differences across each stage, strategists have adopted the analytical convention of viewing the process in terms of formulation and implementation (e.g., Andrews 1971). The strategy formulation process involves the generation and evaluation of alternatives, as well as the choice, while strategy implementation encompasses the organizational execution of that choice. While this bifurcation of the strategic decision-making process is somewhat artificial (Mintzberg 1978), it serves a valuable purpose in facilitating the more pointed consideration of potential relationships with TMT dynamics.

Strategy formulation requires an analysis of (1) external threats and opportunities, especially with respect to the competitive environment (Andrews 1971; Porter 1980) and (2) internal strengths and weaknesses within and across functional areas (Prahalad and Hamel 1990). The alternatives that arise from this analysis are assessed and debated before settling on a satisfying solution (Cyert and March 1963). Top management team members are active throughout this process, in part through direct participation and in part by setting agendas (Kotter 1982), by delegating to others (Mintzberg 1983a), and by signaling ideas and preferences (Pfeffer and Salancik 1978; Cannella and Holcomb 2005).

Our review of related research suggests that TMTs with certain characteristics, such as large size and heterogeneity, are likely to generate more alternatives, to evaluate those alternatives along more dimensions, and, as a consequence, to make higher-quality decisions than TMTs without these attributes. As we argued earlier, heterogeneous teams are more innovative, have greater problem-solving skills, and employ multiple perspectives (e.g., Bantel and Jackson 1989), all of which should increase the number and variety of alternatives under consideration. In addition, they can rely on their heterogeneous backgrounds to gather information from different internal and external contacts (Jackson 1992), which is much less likely in homogeneous teams. Moreover, evaluation of alternatives will tend to be comprehensive, given the propensity and willingness of heterogeneous team members to challenge and debate each other (e.g., Gladstein 1984; Schweiger, Sandberg, and Rechner 1989). To the extent that decision quality depends on analytical effectiveness, the resulting strategic choices may prove superior (Hoffman 1959; Amason 1996; Filley, House, and Kerr 1976; Shaw 1981; McGrath 1984).

In contrast, social integration within TMTs may have the opposite effect. Socially integrated teams value cooperation, are more cohesive, and are motivated by a desire to maintain cordial relations among members (O'Reilly, Caldwell, and Barnett 1989). What is more, highly cohesive groups tend to exert more pressure for conformity than less cohesive groups (Hackman 1976). For example, Lott and Lott (1965) found that cohesiveness was highly correlated with pressures for attitudinal conformity. In TMTs, this emphasis on cooperation and conformity may limit the quality of both alternative generation and evaluation.

Proposition 11A: The quality of strategic decisions (as defined by the generation of multiple feasible alternatives and the comprehensive evaluation of those alternatives) is positively associated with TMT heterogeneity and size and negatively associated with social integration within TMTs.

Strategy implementation involves mobilizing the resources needed to ensure that the strategic initiatives selected are appropriately executed. The implementation process typically requires significant integration of people and resources, takes considerable time, and depends on the cooperation of numerous individuals both in and out of the TMT (Galbraith and Kazanjian 1986; Waldman and Yammarino 1999; Cannella and Holcomb 2005). Effectively implementing strategic decisions is challenging because executives who find particular changes threatening or objectionable often have numerous opportunities to disrupt the process (Bardach 1977; Guth and MacMillan 1986). As a result, it becomes important to gain their acceptance and commitment to a strategic decision (Dess 1987; Amason 1996; Nutt 1987), especially in light of evidence that direct intervention, persuasion, and participation tactics are superior to the use of edicts (Nutt 1986).

The implications of these arguments for TMTs are twofold. First, as we have seen, some evidence suggests that heterogeneous teams engender conflict (O'Reilly, Snyder, and Boothe 1993; Cronin and Weingart 2007). Indeed, many of the positive features of heterogeneous TMTs, such as debate, multiple perspectives, and confrontation, also have negative side effects, including dissatisfaction and dissensus (Schweiger, Sandberg, and Rechner 1989; Priem 1990). These problems are particularly important for implementation because "successful installation . . . often depends on obtaining the involvement, cooperation, endorsement, or consent" (Nutt 1989, 145) of managers. When team members disagree with a decision, implementation becomes problematic (Hitt and Tyler 1991). Thus, "the ultimate value of high-quality decisions depends to a great extent on the willingness of managers to cooperate in implementing those decisions (Maier 1970; Guth and MacMillan 1986; Wooldridge and Floyd 1990)" (Korsgaard, Schweiger, and Sapienza 1995, 60).

If heterogeneity is disadvantageous for strategy implementation, social integration and consensus should be beneficial. We have already emphasized that social integration is associated with cooperation, frequent communication, and group identification (O'Reilly, Caldwell, and Barnett 1989), all of which may facilitate the implementation process (Guth and MacMillan 1986). And TMT consensus tends to engender greater feelings of satisfaction with the decision-making process, promoting decision acceptance and commitment (Dess 1987; Bowman and Ambrosini 1997; Fredrickson and Iaquinto 1989; Isabella and Waddock 1994). Hence, we propose:

Proposition 11B: The effectiveness of the strategy implementation process is positively associated with social integration and consensus within TMTs and negatively associated with TMT heterogeneity and size.[22]

Consequences of TMTs on Strategy

If TMT composition, structure, and process affect strategic decision making, these factors should also affect the types of strategic choices made. Over the past twenty years, a series of studies on this very point have examined organizational innovativeness, interdependence of diversification posture, and strategic change. Unfortunately, however, the findings reported in these studies generally have been inconsistent.

We will highlight two studies that have been conducted on the associations among demographic heterogeneity,[23] team size, and organizational innovation. Arguing that demographic heterogeneity proxies for cognitive heterogeneity within a TMT, Bantel and Jackson (1989) found that functional heterogeneity was positively associated with administrative innovation in a sample of 199 banks in the midwestern United States. But the heterogeneity of team members along other demographic dimensions, such as age, tenure, and educational specialization, did not significantly predict administrative innovations.

In another study on innovation, O'Reilly and Flatt (1989) used multiple measures of organization innovation (i.e., the score from a *Fortune* magazine survey on innovation and a metric based on articles in *F&S Predicasts)*, as well as both age and tenure heterogeneity of TMTs, to test related hypotheses. Of the eight different models tested, three yielded negative and significant results, indicating that homogeneous TMTs were more innovative.

No consistent pattern of results arises across the two studies. Of the sixteen different models tested across articles, one indicated that heterogeneity was a positive predictor of innovation and three suggested the opposite.[24] There were significant differences in the methods employed: Bantel and Jackson (1989) defined a TMT in terms of the number of individuals listed by the CEO in a survey, while O'Reilly and Flatt (1989) counted the number of vice presidents. These design choices will have an important impact on measures of heterogeneity. Both studies also used different operationalizations of innovation.[25]

More recently, Carpenter and Fredrickson (2001) examined the implications of TMT heterogeneity for a firm's global strategic posture (GSP; the degree to which a firm depends on foreign markets for customers and factors of production and the geographical dispersion of these markets and factors) and the moderating effects of environmental uncertainty on that relationship. The authors considered breadth of international work experience, educational heterogeneity, functional background heterogeneity, and tenure heterogeneity as predictive of a firm's GSP. All measures were significant, but two (functional heterogeneity and tenure heterogeneity) had negative coefficients. The authors interpreted this evidence as indicating that heterogeneity on these dimensions detracts from TMT cohesiveness and lessens the firm's global impetus.

Relatedly, Sambharya (1996) examined the foreign experience of TMT members and their association with international diversification strategy. The author predicted that the average number of years of TMT member international experience, the proportion of TMT members with international experience, and TMT heterogeneity of international experience would all be positively associated with international diversification. The authors report some support for all three predictions.

Several other recent studies have investigated the effects of TMTs on global diversification posture of companies (Carpenter, Geletkanycz, and Sanders 2004). For example, Tihanyi, Ellstrand, Daily, and Dalton (2000) examined the association between TMT characteristics and GSP (as did Sanders and Carpenter [1998]). Other studies in this stream include Carpenter, Pollock and Leary (2003), and Carpenter et al. (2001). All of these studies demonstrate that the characteristics of top management groups are important to the firm's internationalization strategy.

TMT composition may also influence the attentional orientation of the TMT, and through that, strategic choices. For example, Cho and Hambrick (2003) integrated upper-echelons with an attention-based perspective, arguing that TMT demographic composition will affect attentional orientation and, through that mediator, strategic choices. They examined deregulation as a trigger for the shift in attentional orientation, and specifically emphasized a shift from an engineering orientation (emphasis on efficiency, or throughput-oriented) to an entrepreneurial orientation (emphasis on customers and markets, more output-oriented). They predicted that greater recomposition of the TMT would lead to greater shifts in attention from engineering to entrepreneurial concerns. Specifically, they predicted that increases in TMT output function experience, decreases in TMT airline industry tenure, and increases in TMT heterogeneity would all lead to greater shifts in attention. And, greater shifts in attention were expected to result in greater movement toward an entrepreneurial strategy. Put differently, they expected that attention would mediate the relationship between TMT characteristics and strategy outcomes. Evidence from a sample of publicly traded airlines from 1976 to 1986 supported their predictions.

Another recent study provides important insights into the relationship between TMT composition and strategic choices. Ferrier and Lyon (2004) studied the extent to which firm performance derived from the simplicity of competitive repertoires and evaluated TMT heterogeneity as a moderator of that relationship. They concluded that TMT heterogeneity was an important moderator of the relationship between repertoire simplicity and firm performance.

Although there are differences across studies, the inconsistent results apparent in the articles above are troubling. One explanation may be that attempts to relate TMT heterogeneity and strategic choices directly are assuming a connection that is more distant than commonly recognized. In this chapter, we have argued that demographic heterogeneity is associated with cognitive heterogeneity, both of which increase the number of strategic alternatives considered by a TMT and the quality of the evaluation of those alternatives. Rigorous strategy formulation, in turn, is expected to lead to higher quality decisions. Using this logic to predict strategic outcomes is subject to three potential drawbacks.

First—and as is the case for predictions based on the central tendencies of TMTs—there are several logical stages between TMT composition and strategic choice that can disrupt or attenuate expected associations (Cannella and Holcomb 2005). For example, the

strategic decision-making process is complex and ambiguous, numerous contextual conditions can affect the process through which strategic choices are selected and implemented, and many of these same contextual factors are often direct determinants of strategic choices as well. Hence, while TMTs undoubtedly affect strategic outcomes, our ability to empirically detect this relationship may be limited.

Second, the logical sequence we outlined above does not link TMT heterogeneity to strategic choices as much as it relates heterogeneity to the quality of strategic decisions. There is a big difference between predicting rigorous strategy formulation and predicting specific strategic outcomes, which suggests that measures of cognitive heterogeneity should not be any better predictors of strategy, since heterogeneity—whether measured demographically or cognitively—is potentially far-removed from specific strategic outcomes.

Finally, there is a point that is seldom noted in the literature but may be quite telling. Logically, a significant difference exists between how TMT heterogeneity and TMT average tendencies are expected to affect strategy. Because the extent to which a TMT is characterized by a particular compositional attribute defines its orientation or preference set (Finkelstein 1988), this attribute can more easily be translated into specific strategic outcomes than is true for TMT heterogeneity. For example, TMTs dominated by executives with sales and marketing experience will perceive and interpret information in such a way that they will be more likely to prefer such strategies as product innovation and differentiation (Hambrick and Mason 1984). In contrast, and as we have seen, TMT heterogeneity affects the *process* of making strategic decisions much more than it does the *content* of those strategies. Hence, we should not necessarily expect heterogeneity to have a direct impact on strategy content.

These difficulties in studying the strategic effects of TMT heterogeneity are only partially ameliorated in studies of strategic change. However, two studies have employed virtually opposing theoretical rationales. Wiersema and Bantel (1992) argued that demographically heterogeneous TMTs will be more creative and will be able to rely on a wider set of information sources and perspectives during the decision-making process than more homogeneous TMTs. As a result, such teams will be more open to change. In addition, although these authors did not make this argument, it stands to reason that TMT heterogeneity should enhance the variety of strategic alternatives considered and the degree to which they are rigorously evaluated, increasing the likelihood that new strategic initiatives will be suggested. In contrast, O'Reilly, Snyder, and Boothe (1993) argued that TMT homogeneity promotes the cooperation that is needed to implement strategic changes. Hence, Wiersema and Bantel (1992) predicted a positive association and O'Reilly, Snyder, and Boothe (1993) a negative association between TMT heterogeneity and change.

Our analysis of TMTs and strategic decision making produces more equivocal expectations: that is, if TMT heterogeneity increases the breadth of strategy formulation (Proposition 11A) but detracts from the implementation process (Proposition 11B), the resulting effect on strategic change is uncertain.[26] The findings of these two studies are consistent with this interpretation. Wiersema and Bantel (1992) reported that one of four demographic measures of heterogeneity (educational specialization) was positively associated with change, while O'Reilly, Snyder, and Boothe (1993) found that TMT tenure heterogeneity was negatively associated with one of two measures of change. O'Reilly, Snyder, and Boothe also reported that a perceptual measure of TMT cooperation or consensus was not associated with organization change but was negatively related to political change.

Beyond heterogeneity, several studies link executive-level social capital to strategic choices. For example, Geletkanycz and Hambrick (1997) studied boundary-spanning relations between TMT members and others from both inside and outside the industry, arguing that strategic choices are affected by social ties. They concluded that social ties (i.e., trade association ties) are weakly linked to strategic conformity to industry averages, although ties to others outside the industry had no effect on strategic conformity. Collins and Clark (2003) examined whether human resource practices directed toward top managers would affect the social networks of the TMT. They documented that network-building practices influenced both external and internal network creation and had important implications for sales growth and stock prices.

In all, the findings we summarize here suggest that direct relationships between TMT heterogeneity and strategic choices are unlikely to be robust. Rather, it may be that TMT heterogeneity and social integration interact during strategic decision making, potentially affecting how the formulation and implementation processes develop. As a result, it seems important to study the relationships among TMT heterogeneity, social integration, and strategic decision making as a first step before attempting to predict strategic outcomes. Further, extending consideration to other aspects of TMT functioning, such as social capital networks, holds additional promise.

Consequences of TMTs on Firm Performance

Given some of the problems in empirically establishing linkages between TMT interaction processes and strategic choices, it would not be surprising if studies of the association between the distributional properties of TMTs and firm performance were even more problematic. To some extent, this is reflected in the often inconsistent findings that emerge from this work. In contrast to studies of strategic outcomes, however, several of the projects predicting firm performance have also incorporated contingency factors, such as industry change or turbulence, that have the potential to strengthen results. Although this work also has inconsistencies, it offers the potential for redirecting research on the consequences of TMTs on firm performance in the future.

In one of the first studies to examine these issues, Murray (1989) collected longitudinal data on TMT temporal heterogeneity (an index of age and tenure heterogeneity, and mean tenure in the firm [loading negatively]) and "occupational" heterogeneity (an index of two measures of functional heterogeneity) in eighty-four firms in the oil and food industries. He predicted that heterogeneous TMTs would do worse in the short run because they often disrupt established norms and procedures that promote efficiency, but better in the long term because of their superior adaptability. In a series of regressions, Murray (1989) reported that (1) temporal heterogeneity was positively associated with long-term performance (in two of four regressions), while occupational heterogeneity was not, and (2) occupational heterogeneity was negatively associated with short-term performance (in one of four models), while temporal heterogeneity was not.

The pattern of results reported by Murray (1989) provides only the most limited support for the effects of TMT heterogeneity on firm performance. However, this study is commendable for its consideration of multiple industries, independent measures of industry change and rivalry, and multiple measures of firm performance, and especially for its attempt to develop more complex theory that appreciates some of the subtleties of TMTs. Nevertheless, one tentative conclusion that emerges from this work, as well as from four other studies examining related ideas (O'Reilly and Flatt 1989; West and Schwenk 1996; Hambrick and D'Aveni 1992; Glick, Miller, and Huber 1993), is that the distributional properties of TMTs will not be predictive of firm performance in all circumstances.[27]

Of the other studies published on TMTs and firm performance, contingency factors were incorporated explicitly (Barrick et al. 2007; Michel and Hambrick 1992; Haleblian and Finkelstein 1993; Geletkanycz and Hambrick 1997; Keck 1997; Cannella, Park, and Lee 2008) or implicitly (Eisenhardt and Schoonhoven 1990; Smith et al. 1994; Kor 2003). In Michel and Hambrick (1992), the only study in this group to model strategy as a contingency factor, the interdependence of a firm's diversification posture did not moderate the TMT heterogeneity-firm performance relationship. However, Haleblian and Finkelstein's (1993) study of forty-seven firms in the computer and natural gas distribution industries found that environmental turbulence moderated the association between firm performance and both team size and CEO dominance. Specifically, they found that firms with larger teams and less dominant CEOs did better in turbulent environments, ostensibly because such TMTs had superior information-processing capabilities.

An interesting study that lifts the veil behind team processes sheds light on how top management teams may affect firm performance. Barrick and colleagues (2007) studied the relationship among team cohesion and communication (team mechanisms), interdependence, and both team and firm performance in ninety-four top management teams in credit unions. They found that the interaction of team mechanisms and team interdependence was positive related to team and firm performance, but in regressions without the interaction the main effects of team mechanisms on the dependent variables were not significant. The implications are important. First, the well-established finding in the small groups literature that interdependence moderates the relationship between cohesion and communication, as well as performance (e.g., Beal et al. 2003; Gully et al. 2002), was also supported in a sample of top management teams. And second, because the main effects were sometimes not related to performance, these results suggest that cohesion and communication may not necessarily be advantageous for top management teams. In the absence of interdependence among senior executives, such cohesion and communication may not play much of a role at all.

Four studies examined TMT characteristics and firm performance in rapidly changing, or "high-velocity," industries. Arguing that larger and more heterogeneous TMTs engaged in more constructive conflict (Eisenhardt and Schoonhoven 1990) and exhibited less social integration (Smith et al. 1994), two studies found a positive association between several measures of TMT heterogeneity and firm performance. Although not all associations were consistently positive, the overall pattern from these studies quite strongly indicates support for the authors' ideas.

Keck's (1997) study reported mixed results. She found that tenure heterogeneity and top management team fluctuation, among other measures, were positively related to firm performance in the turbulent computer industry, but also (unexpectedly) reported a similar result for tenure heterogeneity in the stable cement industry. Taking a somewhat different tack, Kor (2003) studied the relationship between TMT member experiences and the sustained growth of their companies. She concluded that heterogeneity in team, firm, and industry tenure each had important effects on firm-level growth among entrepreneurial firms. She tied her evidence to the notion that there are bundles of experience, and that particular configurations (e.g., bundles) of experiences are important to firm growth.

Cannella, Park, and Lee (2008) used a broad sample of industries that other authors had noted as either relatively certain or relatively uncertain to consider how physical co-location might impact the TMT diversity–firm performance association. Their evidence supported their predictions that when TMT members work at the same physical location, the implications of TMT member diversity for firm performance are positive, and even more positive in uncertain industries. These relationships held across measures of both TMT-level background diversity and TMT member intrapersonal functional diversity.

Finally, the study by Geletkanycz and Hambrick (1997), described above, also considered the implications of strategic conformity (as caused by social ties) for firm performance. They found that conformity was linked to better performance in the turbulent computer industry but not in the less turbulent branded foods industry.

In summary, while an empirical record on the association between TMT heterogeneity and firm performance has been established, it appears from this work that we are unlikely to uncover a strong direct relationship between the heterogeneity of TMTs and the success of the firms they manage.[28] Nevertheless, the positive effects of TMT heterogeneity on firm performance in "high velocity" or turbulent environments in several of these studies may help point the way to a clearer understanding of what heterogeneity among top managers really means. Recall our earlier discussion of how TMT heterogeneity promotes a more rigorous strategy formulation process by increasing the number of feasible strategic alternatives under consideration and the quality of their evaluation. In fast-changing, dynamic environments, managerial work becomes more fragmented (Mintzberg 1973), information-processing requirements increase (Hambrick, Finkelstein, and Mooney 2005), and new opportunities and crises necessitate greater adaptive capabilities (Galbraith 1973)—all of which place a higher premium on the generation of multiple and novel solutions. It is precisely in the most unstable environments that TMT heterogeneity is most valuable.

In contrast, consider Haleblian and Finkelstein's (1993) description of stable environments:

Information processing requirements are not as intense in stable environments (Ancona 1990). For example, Kotter found that top managerial information and decision making requirements

in stable environments were "more standardized and routine" than in turbulent environments (1982: 29). Stable environments tend to attenuate learning requirements (Tushman and Keck 1990), making problem solving more systematic than it is in turbulent environments (Eisenhardt 1989). (p. 847)

Under conditions of stability, we might expect strategy implementation to be more salient than strategy formulation, because the strategic challenge is less in developing new ideas than it is in preserving established procedures (Tushman and Romanelli 1985). As we discussed earlier, TMT cooperation and stability become more important when environments are more stable (Nutt 1987), suggesting that integrated TMTs may be preferred. Hence, in stable environments, TMT social integration, rather than heterogeneity, may be related to firm performance. The following two propositions summarize these arguments:

Proposition 12A: The more unstable the environment, the more positive the relationship between TMT heterogeneity and firm performance.

Proposition 12B: The more unstable the environment, the more negative the relationship between TMT social integration and firm performance.

Beyond the moderating role of organizational environments, other contingency factors may help explain how and when TMT heterogeneity affects firm performance. For example, the contextual conditions that give rise to difficult configurations of TMTs may themselves often operate as moderating forces on firm performance. The propositions on environmental instability above are cases in point. Earlier in this chapter, we argued that TMT heterogeneity is greater in unstable environments, to a large extent because such environments impose demands on how organizations should structure their TMTs. An implicit assumption in Proposition 3A was that organizations would respond to these environmental requirements in a variety of ways because these responses would enhance their position and performance. Thus, to the extent that organizations are responsive to environmental demands, firm performance should be greater. Restating this logic in terms of Proposition 3A suggests that firms promoting TMT demographic heterogeneity in unstable environments should do better, a prediction represented by Proposition 12A. Hence, an extension of the "fit" or alignment argument implicit in Proposition 3A gives rise to the contingency-based Proposition 12A.

Conclusion

This chapter has documented a large and growing body of work on TMTs and has outlined a number of robust conclusions as well as future directions. Still, significant problems remain in the study of TMTs, including how they come to have certain characteristics and what implications they have for firm performance and other outcomes. Robust work in this area will continue to require careful attention to issues such as the identification of TMT boundaries, specification of power relationships, and consideration of TMT processes. While we did not convert each of the propositions predicting TMT characteristics into propositions predicting firm performance, such propositions clearly represent viable and interesting research questions that often have received support in the literature, as we have documented. There may be other relevant contextual factors worthy of study as well. Several important issues pose particular challenges to TMT researchers and, if resolved, could move the area significantly forward. We discuss these areas briefly below.

First, the boundaries of TMTs need very clear explication and theoretical treatment. At present, there are empirically well-accepted means of identifying TMTs (e.g., Finkelstein 1992; Finkelstein and Hambrick 1990). However, there is a significant heterogeneity in how TMTs are identified, even in the empirical literature. Most frequently, TMTs are identified as the five highest paid officers, all inside directors, and all executives above the rank of executive vice president. Given a particular company, these three approaches might well identify quite different TMTs for that single company. Because we rely so much on processes and demographic heterogeneity, coming to a strong agreement about who is in and who is out seems critical. For example, Roberto (2003) has provided a theoretical alternative that has some appeal to the empirical approaches—a stable core and dynamic periphery. It will

be important, in future studies, to carefully specify and justify how the TMT is identified.

A second critical issue, mentioned earlier, is how to treat the CEO in the determination of TMT-level measures. Clearly, not all members of the TMT are equal, yet most empirical treatments weight each member as essentially equivalent in calculations of team-level heterogeneity. While we have discussed the moderating effects of team member power and other factors, clearly most prominent in this issue is the CEO, as his or her preferences, biases, habits, and capabilities may have very important effects for team-level functioning. As Cannella and Holcomb (2005) and Pitcher and Smith (2001) have discussed, the CEO is the guardian of TMT processes. Perhaps the notion of "control over process" will direct fruitful study of phenomena such as the CEO's impact on the TMT and the TMT's identity separate from the CEO.

A third issue revolves around capturing the heterogeneity of the TMT. Bunderson and Sutcliffe (2002) describe a somewhat unusual but potentially very valuable approach to TMT heterogeneity. The concept of intrapersonal functional heterogeneity, which they describe as the average within-member breadth of functional experience, holds a great deal of promise in our view. Intrapersonal functional diversity is different enough from more traditional forms of diversity to deserve separate treatment, often leading to different hypotheses than would arise from, say, dominant functional diversity among team members (see Bunderson 2003 and Cannella, Park, and Lee 2008 for empirical examples).

In sum, we need more complex frameworks of TMTs that recognize the role of senior executives in strategic decision making, along with the moderating role of such important contextual influences as the environment, the organization, and the CEO. In addition, much more work is needed on such basic aspects of TMTs as their boundaries and determinants. This chapter offers one model of these phenomena that we believe is particularly promising for future research.

Notes

1. As one example, in an intriguing analysis of the rise of CFOs in corporations, Zorn (2003) documents how regulatory changes enacted by the Federal Accounting

Standards Board (FASB) drove firms to create a new formal position—the chief financial officer—as a solution to an ill-defined problem.

2. We refer to the group of executives at the top of an organization as a "team" only for ease of presentation; we agree with Hambrick (1994) that this constellation of executives may not necessarily behave in a "team-like" fashion. Indeed, as we discuss below, the nature of the interactions among top managers composing a team is an issue that should be studied in its own right.

3. It is important to keep in mind that mean levels of psychological and demographic attributes of top management teams are consequential (Hage and Dewar 1973; Finkelstein and Hambrick 1990; see also Carpenter, Geletkanycz, and Sanders 2004).

4. Other dimensions of process have been considered. For example, Amason (1996) discusses affective and cognitive conflict, Waldman and Yammarino (1999) and Klein and House (1995) discuss charisma, and Shen and Cannella (2002a) and Bigley and Wiersema (2002) discuss politics. Colbert, Kristof-Brown, Bradley, and Barrick (2008) use "goal importance congruence," and Van der Vegt, Bunderson, and Oosterhof (2006) consider "interpersonal helping."

5. For some important exceptions, see Peterson et al. (2003), Amason and Sapienza (1997), Papadakis and Barwise (2002), and Athanassiou and Nigh (1999).

6. This is not meant to imply that all decisions proceed in such a linear, or complete, fashion. Moving toward quick decisions without in-depth analysis (Cohen, March, and Olson 1972), avoiding evaluation of failed strategies (Finkelstein and Mooney 2003), and shifting among the various stages of the process (Mintzberg 1978) are far from unknown. Our goal here is simply to point out that the "intervening processes," no matter how construed, are consequential.

7. The distinction between "team" and "group" is perhaps more subtle in the organizational behavior or organization theory literature than in the literature of the upper echelons. For example, Weick (1993) goes to some length to convince readers that the smoke jumpers he studied comprised a group. For more micro-oriented scholars the key concern is that the members of a "group" perceive themselves to be part of a group. When this is the case, the "group" becomes more like a "team." When we use the word "team" we mean that the members of the TMT perceive themselves to be part of a cohesive group, and have a psychological attachment to the group.

8. We continue to use the "TMT" label despite our call for greater attention to the "group" nature of top executive interaction simply for ease of reference and continuity and because essentially all of the research we review in this chapter also adopts this nomenclature.

9. It is critical to control for industry, however, because institutional arrangements within industries often affect structural arrangements, such as the hierarchy of positions at the top (DiMaggio and Powell 1983). For example, the number of vice presidents differs across industries, as does the meaning of the title "vice president." There are many more vice presidents in firms in the investment banking industry than in other industries, but not all are influential in strategic decision making. As a result, definitions of TMTs that are based on titles may be problematic in cross-industry studies.

10. This is true even when deciding which individual member of a TMT to study. For example; arguing that chief financial officers (CFOs) were central players in ethical dilemmas organizations confront, Stevens, Steensma, Harrison, and Cochran (2005) focused their study solely on CFOs. While one can easily imagine the same research issue also being directed toward a population of CEOs, Stevens and colleagues build an argument to support their design choice.

11. Respondents were asked to rate managerial power for three different strategic decisions (major resource allocations, organizational redesign, and domain changes), with each measured on a seven-point scale (from "no influence" to "total influence"). The reported rating of managerial power is the sum of the scores for each of the three strategic decisions.

12. We can apply Barney's (1991) four tests of resource value to evaluate the "fit" of executive experiences with the challenges faced by a firm. In the context of TMTs, this suggests that expertise power can be assessed relative to the expertise power of other top managers within the team, and relative to the expertise power of top executives in competitor firms. There are no studies to date, however, that have addressed this research idea.

13. Although some may suggest that role interdependence is related to TMT consensus, we have purposely refrained from arguing for such an association. When TMT roles are interdependent, there is a greater need for cooperation and resource sharing among senior executives. Nevertheless, a need for such activities does not necessarily translate into actual behavior, so it is not clear whether interdependent TMTs really do cooperate. By the same token, the relationship between role interdependence and social integration is imprecise, because it cannot necessarily be assumed that interdependent TMTs are cohesive (Schmidt and Kochan 1972).

14. A different problem sometimes noted, stemming from the paucity of studies directly examining the association between TMT demography and TMT interaction processes, is that demographic and process constructs may have no direct relationship.

15. In fact, in line with this latter argument, Rajagopalan and Datta (1996) reported that capital intensity was

negatively, and industry growth positively, related to CEO functional heterogeneity.

16. Of course, when performance reaches a minimal threshold, the interests of TMT members turns more to saving their own security and careers, and less to saving the company (Lane, Cannella, and Lubatkin 1998). In support of this notion, Hambrick and D'Aveni found in their study of bankrupts and survivors that in the year before bankruptcy, "the actual size of the bankrupt teams shrank appreciably" (1992, 1462). Additionally, Cannella, Fraser, Lee and Semadeni (2002) showed that as their sample firms spiraled toward bankruptcy, executives were more likely to "jump ship"—leaving the failing firm to join another company, often at significant personal cost.

17. Actually, we would expect CEO effects on TMTs to be more readily discernible empirically because CEOs can change the makeup of their team more easily than they can the organization's strategy and performance.

18. We define CEO dominance as the power of the CEO relative to the rest of the TMT (Hambrick and D'Aveni 1992; Haleblian and Finkelstein 1993), as well as the CEO's willingness to use that power to influence the behavior of others.

19. Although we do so in the context of a chapter on TMTs, it is also possible to offer a proposition on the negative association between CEO openness and CEO tenure.

20. Boone, Olffen, Witteloostuijn, and Brabander (2004) did not find support for their hypothesis that top management team power over the board increased the similarity of new executives entering the team.

21. Research has also been conducted on the association between TMTs and executive turnover (Wagner, Pfeffer, and O'Reilly 1984; Jackson et al. 1991; Wiersema and Bantel 1993; Wiersema and Bird 1993; Cannella and Shen 2001; Shen and Cannella 2002a, 2002b).

22. See West and Schwenk (1996) for a dissenting viewpoint.

23. Almost all of this work has focused on demographic heterogeneity as an independent variable.

24. Both studies included team size as a control variable but reported no significant associations with dependent variables.

25. In a study with a different focus, but of some relevance here, Elenkov, Judge, and Wright (2005) found that TMT heterogeneity moderated the relationship between transformational and transactional leadership behaviors and executive influence on innovation. The authors argued that because heterogeneity conveys cognitive diversity (Pitcher and Smith 2001), TMTs employing leadership behaviors will be more influential. The cognitive or processual mechanisms that link these factors were not clear from this study; however, it does suggest that some attention to TMT heterogeneity as a moderating variable may be warranted.

26. The operational definitions and methods of identifying change in the two studies are also very different and could account for some of the inconsistent results.

27. Neither Hambrick and Mason (1984) nor Pfeffer (1983) suggests direct associations between demographic heterogeneity and organization performance.

28. The theory and evidence from Cannella, Park, and Lee (2008) suggest that we are much more likely to observe a performance association for TMT member intrapersonal functional diversity (see Bunderson and Sutcliffe 2002) than for the more common measures of TMT-level background diversity or heterogeneity.

References

Aldrich, Howard E. 1979. *Organizations and environments.* Englewood Cliffs, NJ: Prentice-Hall.

Allison, Graham T. 1971. *Essence of decision: Explaining the Cuban missile crisis.* Boston: Little, Brown.

Amason, Allen C. 1996. Distinguishing the effects of functional and dysfunctional conflict on strategic decision making: Resolving a paradox for top management teams. *Academy of Management Journal* 39(1): 123–148.

Amason, Allen C., and Harry J. Sapienza. 1997. The effects of top management team size and interaction norms on cognitive and affective conflict. *Journal of Management* 23(4): 495–516.

Amason, Allen C., and David M. Schweiger. 1992. Toward a general theory of top management teams: An integrative framework. Paper presented at the Annual Meetings of the Academy of Management, Las Vegas, NV.

Ancona, Deborah G. 1990. Top management teams: Preparing for the revolution. In *Applied social psychology and organizational settings,* edited by John S. Carroll, 99–128. Hillsdale, NJ: Erlbaum.

Ancona, Deborah G., and David F. Caldwell. 1992. Demography and design: Predictors of new product team performance. *Organization Science* 3: 321–341.

Andrews, Kenneth R. 1971. *The concept of corporate strategy.* Homewood, IL: Dow Jones-Irwin.

Ansoff, H. Igor. 1965. *Corporate Strategy: An analytic approach to business policy for growth and expansion.* New York: McGraw-Hill.

Arrow, Kenneth J. 1974. *The limits of organization.* 1st ed. New York: Norton.

Athanassiou, Nicholas, and Douglas Nigh. 1999. The impact of U.S. company internationalization on top management team advice networks: A tacit knowledge perspective. *Strategic Management Journal* 20(1): 83–92.

Bantel, Karen A., and Sydney Finkelstein. 1995. The determinants of top management teams. In *Advances in group processes,* edited by Barry Markovsky, Jodi O'Brian, and Karen Heimer, 139–165. Greenwich, CT: JAI Press.

Bantel, Karen A., and Susan E. Jackson. 1989. Top management and innovations in banking: Does the composition of the top team make a difference? *Strategic Management Journal* 10: 107–124.

Bardach, Eugene. 1977. *The implementation game.* Cambridge, MA: MIT Press.

Barney, Jay B. 1991. Firm resources and sustained competitive advantage. *Journal of Management* 17(1): 99–120.

Barrick, Murray R., Bret Bradley, Amy L. Kristof-Brown, and Amy E. Colbert. 2007. The moderating role of top management team interdependence: Implications for real teams and working groups. *Academy of Management Journal* 50(3): 544–557.

Barsade, Sigal G., Andrew J. Ward, J. D. F. Turner, and Jeffrey A. Sonnenfeld. 2001. To your heart's content: A model of affective diversity in top management teams (vol. 45, p. 802, 2000). *Administrative Science Quarterly* 46(1): 174.

Beal, Daniel J., Robin R. Cohen, Michael J. Burke, and Christy L. McLendon. 2003. Cohesion and performance in groups: A meta-analytic clarification of construct relations. *Journal of Applied Psychology* 88(6): 989–1004.

Berg, Norman A. 1969. What's different about conglomerate management? *Harvard Business Review* 47(6): 112–120.

Bertrand, Marianne, and Antoinette Schoar. 2003. Managing with style: The effect of managers on firm policies. *Quarterly Journal of Economics* 118(4): 1169–1208.

Bettenhausen, Kenneth, and J. Keith Murnighan. 1985. The emergence of norms in competitive decision-making groups. *Administrative Science Quarterly* 30: 350–372.

Bigley, Gregory A., and Margarethe F. Wiersema. 2002. New CEOs and corporate strategic refocusing: How experience as heir apparent influences the use of power. *Administrative Science Quarterly* 47: 707–727.

Blau, Peter M. 1970. A formal theory of differentiation in organizations. *American Sociological Review* 35: 201–218.

Boone, Christophe, and Bert de Brabander. 1993. Generalized vs. specific locus of control expectancies of chief executive officers. *Strategic Management Journal* 14:619–625.

Boone, Christophe, Woody van Olffen, Arjen van Witteloostuijn, and Burt de Brabander. 2004. The genesis of top management team diversity: Selective turn-over among top management teams in Dutch newspaper publishing, 1970–1994. *Academy of Management Journal* 47(5): 633–656.

Bourgeois, L. Jay, III. 1980. Performance and consensus. *Strategic Management Journal* 1: 227–248.

———. 1981. On the measurement of organizational slack. *Academy of Management Review* 6: 29–39.

———. 1985. Strategic goals, perceived uncertainty, and economic performance in volatile environments. *Academy of Management Journal* 28: 548–573.

Bourgeois, L. Jay, III, and Kathleen M. Eisenhardt, 1988. Strategic decision processes in high velocity environments: Four cases in the microcomputer industry. *Management Science* 34(7): 816–835.

Bowman, Cliff, and Veronique Ambrosini. 1997. Perceptions of strategic priorities, consensus and firm performance. *Journal of Management Studies* 34(2): 241–258.

Bunderson, J. Stuart. 2003. Team member functional background and involvement in management teams: Direct effects and the moderating role of power centralization. *Academy of Management Journal* 46(4): 458–473.

Bunderson, J. Stuart, and Kathleen M. Sutcliffe. 2002. Comparing alternative conceptualizations of functional diversity in management teams: Process and performance effects. *Academy of Management Journal 45(5):* 875–893.

Byrne, Donn. 1961. Interpersonal attraction as a function of affiliation need and attitude similarity. *Human Relations* 14: 63–70.

———. 1971. *The attraction paradigm.* New York: Academic Press.

Cannella, Albert A., Jr., and Tim R. Holcomb. 2005. A multilevel analysis of the upper-echelons model. In *Research in Multi-Level Issues,* edited by Alfred Dansereau and Francis J. Yammarino, 197–237. Oxford, UK: Elsevier Ltd.

Cannella, Albert A., Jr., Jong-Hun Park, and Ho-uk Lee. 2008. Top management team functional background diversity and firm performance: Examining the roles of team member co-location and environmental uncertainty. *Academy of Management Journal 51(4):* In Press.

Cannella, Albert A., Jr., and W. Shen. 2001. So close and yet so far: Promotion versus exit for CEO heirs apparent. *Academy of Management Journal* 44(2): 252–270.

Carpenter, Mason A. 2002. The implications of strategy and social context for the relationship between top management team heterogeneity and firm performance. *Strategic Management Journal* 23(2): 275–284.

Carpenter, Mason A., and James W. Fredrickson. 2001. Top management teams, global strategic posture, and the moderating role of uncertainty. *Academy of Management Journal* 44(3): 533–545.

Carpenter, Mason A., Marta A. Geletkanycz, and William Gerard Sanders. 2004. The upper echelons revisited: Antecedents, elements, and consequences of top management team composition. *Journal of Management* 60(6): 749–778.

Carpenter, Mason A., Timothy G. Pollock, and Myleen M. Leary. 2003. Governance, the experience of principals and agents, and global strategic intent: Testing a model of reasoned risk-taking. *Strategic Management Journal* 24: 803–820.

Carpenter, Mason A., and William Gerard Sanders. 2002. Top management team compensation: The missing link between CEO pay and firm performance? *Strategic Management Journal* 23(4): 367–375.

Carpenter, Mason A., William Gerard Sanders, and Hal B. Gregersen. 2001. Bundling human capital with organizational context: The impact of international assignment experience on multinational firm performance and CEO pay. *Academy of Management Journal* 44(3): 493–511.

Carpenter, Mason A., and James B. Wade. 2002. Microlevel opportunity structures as determinants of non-CEO executive pay. *Academy of Management Journal* 45: 1085–1103.

Carter, E. Eugene. 1971. The behavioral theory of the firm and top-level corporate decisions. *Administrative Science Quarterly* 16: 413–428.

Chandler, Alfred D., Jr. 1962. *Strategy and structure: Chapters in the history of the American industrial enterprise.* Cambridge, MA: MIT Press.

Chatman, Jennifer A., and Francis J. Flynn. 2001. The influence of demographic heterogeneity on the emergence and consequences of cooperative norms in work teams. *Academy of Management Journal* 44(5): 956–974.

Chattopadhyay, Pirithviraj, William H. Glick, C. Chet Miller, and George P. Huber. 1999. Determinants of executive beliefs: Comparing functional conditioning and social influence. *Strategic Management Journal* 20(8): 763–789.

Child, John. 1972. Organization structure, environment and performance; The role of strategic choice. *Sociology* 6(1): 1–22.

Cho, Theresa S., and Donald C. Hambrick. 2006. Attention patterns as mediators between top management team characteristics and strategic change: The case of airline deregulation. *Organization Science* 17(4): 453–469.

Cho, Theresa S., Donald C. Hambrick, and Ming-Jer Chen. 1994. Effects of top management team characteristics on competitive behaviors of firms. *Academy of Management Best Papers Proceedings,* 12–16.

Cohen, Michael D., James G. March, and Johan P. Olson. 1972. A garbage-can model of organizational choice. *Administrative Science Quarterly* 17(1): 1–25.

Colbert, Amy E., Amy L. Kristof-Brown, Bret Bradley, and Murray R. Barrick. 2008. CEO transformational leadership: The role of goal importance congruence in top management teams *Academy of Management Journal* 51(1): 81–96.

Collins, Christopher J., and Kevin D. Clark. 2003. Strategic human resource practice, top management team social networks, and firm performance: The role of human resource practices in creative organizational competitive advantage. *Academy of Management Journal* 46(6): 720–731.

Cronin, Matthew A., and Laurie R. Weingart. 2007. Representational gaps, information processing, and conflict in functionally diverse teams. *Academy of Management Review* 32(3): 761–773.

Cyert, Richard M., and James G. March. 1963. *A behavioral theory of the firm.* Englewood Cliffs, NJ: Prentice-Hall.

Daboub, Anthony J., Abdul M. A. Rasheed, Richard L. Priem, and David A. Gray. 1995. Top management team characteristics and corporate illegal activity. *Academy of Management Review* 20(1): 138–170.

Daft, Richard L., Juhani Sormunen, and Don Parks. 1988. Chief executive scanning, environmental characteristics, and company performance: An empirical study. *Strategic Management Journal* 9(2): 123–139.

Dalton, Dan R., and Catherine M. Dalton. 2005. Upper echelons perspective and multi-level analysis: A case of the cart before the horse? In *Research in Multi-Level Issues,* edited by Alfred Dansereau and Francis J. Yammarino, 249–261. Oxford, UK: Elsevier Ltd.

Dalton, Dan R., and Idalene F. Kesner. 1985. Organizational performance as an antecedent of inside/outside chief executive succession: An empirical assessment. *Academy of Management Journal* 28(4): 749–762.

Dess, Gregory G. 1987. Consensus on strategy formulation and organizational performance: Competitors in a fragmented industry. *Strategic Management Journal* 8: 259–277.

Dess, Gregory G., and Donald W. Beard. 1984. Dimensions of organizational task environments. *Administrative Science Quarterly* 29: 52–73.

Dess, Gregory G., and Barbara W. Keats. 1987. Environmental assessment and organizational performance: An exploratory field study. *Academy of Management Best Papers Proceedings,* 21–25.

Dess, Gregory G., and Nancy K. Origer. 1987. Environment, structure, and consensus in strategy formulation: A conceptual integration. *Strategic Management Journal* 8:313–330.

Deutsch, Morton. 1985. *Distributive justice: A social psychological perspective.* New Haven, CT: Yale University Press.

DiMaggio, Paul J., and W. W. Powell. 1983. The iron cage revisited: Institutional isomorphism and collective rationality in organizational fields. *American Sociological Review* 48: 147–160.

Duhaime, Irene M., and Inga S. Baird. 1987. Divestment decision-making: The role of business unit size. *Journal of Management* 13(3): 483–498.

Duncan, Robert B. 1972. Characteristics of organizational environments and perceived environmental uncertainty. *Administrative Science Quarterly* 17: 313–327.

Dutton, Jane E., and Robert B. Duncan. 1987. The creation of momentum for change through the process of strategic issue diagnosis. *Strategic Management Journal* 8: 279–295.

Dutton, Jane E., Liam Fahey, and V. K. Narayanan. 1983. Toward understanding strategic issue diagnosis. *Strategic Management Journal* 4: 307–323.

Ebadi, Yar M., and James M. Utterback. 1984. The effects of communication on technological innovation. *Management Science* 30: 572–585.

Eisenhardt, Kathleen M. 1989. Making fast strategic decisions in high-velocity environments. *Academy of Management Journal* 32: 543–576.

Eisenhardt, Kathleen M., and L. Jay Bourgeois. 1988. Politics of strategic decision making in high-velocity environments: Toward a midrange theory. *Academy of Management Journal* 31: 737–770.

Eisenhardt, Kathleen M., and Claudia Bird Schoonhoven. 1990. Organizational growth: Linking founding team, strategy, environment, and growth among US semiconductor ventures, 1978–1988. *Administrative Science Quarterly* 35: 504–529.

Eisenhardt, Kathleen M., and Mark J. Zbaracki. 1992. Strategic decision making. *Strategic Management Journal* 13: 17–38.

Elenkov, Detelin S., William Q. Judge, Jr., and Peter Wright. 2005. Strategic leadership and executive innovation influence: An international multi-cluster comparative study. *Strategic Management Journal* 26(7): 665–682.

Fama, Eugene F., and Michael C. Jensen. 1983. Separation of ownership and control. *Journal of Law and Economics* 26: 301–325.

Ferrier, Walter J. 2001. Navigating the competitive landscape: The drivers and consequences of competitive aggressiveness. *Academy of Management Journal* 44: 858–877.

Ferrier, Walter J., and Douglas W. Lyon. 2004. Competitive repertoire simplicity and firm performance: The moderating role of TMT heterogeneity. *Managerial and Decision Economics* 25: 317–327.

Filley, Alan C., Robert J. House, and Steven Kerr. 1976. *Managerial process and organizational behavior.* Glenview, IL: Scott Foresman.

Finkelstein, Sydney. 1988. Managerial orientations and organizational outcomes: The moderating roles of managerial discretion and power. Unpublished Ph.D. dissertation, Columbia University, New York.

———. 1992. Power in top management teams: Dimensions, measurement, and validation. *Academy of Management Journal 35:* 505–538.

Finkelstein, Sydney, and Donald C. Hambrick. 1989. Chief executive compensation: A study of the intersection of markets and political processes. *Strategic Management Journal* 10: 121–134.

———. 1990. Top management team tenure and organizational outcomes: The moderating role of managerial discretion. *Administrative Science Quarterly* 35: 484–503.

Finkelstein, Sydney, and Ann C. Mooney. 2003. Not the usual suspects: How to use board process to make boards better. *Academy of Management Executive* 17(2): 101–113.

Flatt, Sylvia. 1992. A longitudinal study in organizational innovativeness: How top management team demography influences organizational innovation. Unpublished Ph.D. dissertation, University of California, Berkeley, CA.

Forbes, Daniel P., and Frances J. Milliken. 1999. Cognition and corporate governance: Understanding boards of directors as strategic decision-making groups. *Academy of Management Review* 24(3): 489–505.

Fredrickson, James W., and Anthony L. Iaquinto. 1989. Inertia and creeping rationality in strategic decision processes. *Academy of Management Journal* 32(3): 516–542.

Gabarro, John J. 1986. When a new manager takes charge. *Harvard Business Review* 64: 110–123.

———. 1987. *The dynamics of taking charge.* Boston, MA: Harvard Business School Press.

Galbraith, Jay R. 1973. *Designing complex organizations.* Reading, MA: Addison-Wesley.

Galbraith, Jay R., and Robert K. Kazanjian. 1986. *Strategy implementation: Structure, systems and processes.* St. Paul, MN: West.

Geletkanycz, Marta A., and Donald C. Hambrick. 1997. The external ties of top executives: Implications for strategic choice and performance. *Administrative Science Quarterly* 42(4): 654–681.

Gersick, Connie J. G., and Richard Hackman. 1990. Habitual routines in task-performing groups. *Organizational Behavior and Human Decision Processes* 47: 5–97.

Gladstein, Deborah. 1984. Groups in context: A model of task group effectiveness. *Administrative Science Quarterly* 29: 1–3.

Glick, William H., C. Chet Miller, and George P. Huber. 1993. The impact of upper-echelon diversity on organizational performance. In *Organizational change and redesign: Ideas and insights for improving performance,* edited by George P. Huber and William H. Glick, 176–214. New York: Oxford University Press.

Grinyer, Peter H., and David Norburn. 1975. Planning for existing markets: Perceptions of executives and financial performance. *Journal of the Royal Statistical Society* 138: 70–97.

Gully, Stanley M., Kara A. Incalcaterra, Aparna Joshi, and J. Matthew Beaubien. 2002. A meta-analysis of team-efficacy, potency, and performance: Interdependence and level of analysis as moderators of observed relationships. *Journal of Applied Psychology* 87(5): 819–832.

Guth, William D., and Ian C. MacMillan. 1986. Strategy implementation versus middle management seif-interest. *Strategic Management Journal* 7: 313–327.

Guthrie, James P., and Deepak K. Datta. 1997. Contextual influences on executive selection: Firm characteristics and CEO experience. *Journal of Management Studies* 34(4): 537–560.

Hackman, Judith R. 1976. Group influences on individuals. In *Handbook of industrial and organizational psychology,* edited by Marvin D. Dunnette, 1455–1525. Chicago: Rand McNally.

Hage, Jerald, and Roger Dewar. 1973. Elite values versus organizational structure in predicting innovations. *Administrative Science Quarterly* 18: 279–290.

Haleblian, Jerayr, and Sydney Finkelstein. 1993. Top management team size, CEO dominance, and firm performance: The moderating roles of environmental turbulence and discretion. *Academy of Management Journal* 36: 844–86.

Hambrick, Donald C. 1981. Environment, strategy, and power within top management teams. *Administrative Science Quarterly* 26: 253–276.

———. 1994. Top management groups: A conceptual integration and reconsideration of the "team" label. In *Research in organizational behavior,* edited by Barry M. Staw and Lawrence L. Cummings, 171–214. Greenwich, CT: JAI Press.

———. 1995. Fragmentation and the other problems CEOs have with their top management teams. *California Management Review* 37: 110–127.

Hambrick, Donald C., and Richard A. D'Aveni. 1992. Top team deterioration as part of the downward spiral of large corporate bankruptcies. *Management Science* 38: 1445–1466.

Hambrick, Donald C., Sydney Finkelstein, and Ann C. Mooney. 2005. Executive job demands: New insights for explaining strategic decisions and leader behaviors. *Academy of Management Review* 30(3): 472–491.

Hambrick, Donald C., and Gregory D. S. Fukutomi. 1991. The seasons of a CEO's tenure. *Academy of Management Review* 16(4): 719–742.

Hambrick, Donald C., Marta A. Geletkanycz, and James W. Fredrickson. 1993. Top executive commitment to the status quo: Some tests of its determinants. *Strategic Management Journal* 14(6): 401–418.

Hambrick, Donald C., and Phyllis Mason. 1984. Upper echelons: The organization as a reflection of its top managers. *Academy of Management Review* 9: 193–206.

Hannan, Michael T., and John H. Freeman. 1977. The population ecology of organizations. *American Journal of Sociology* 82: 929–964.

Harrison, David A., and Katherine J. Klein. 2007. What's the difference? Diversity constructs as separation, variety, or disparity in organizations. *Academy of Management Review* 32(4): 1229–1245.

Harrison, E. Frank. 1975. *The managerial decision-making process.* Boston, MA: Houghton Mifflin.

Helmich, Donald L., and Warren B. Brown. 1972. Successor type and organizational change in the corporate enterprise. *Administrative Science Quarterly* 17: 371–378.

Hinings, Christopher R., David J. Hickson, Johannes M. Pennings, and Rodney E. Schneck. 1974. Structural conditions of intraorganizational power. *Administrative Science Quarterly* 19(1): 22–44.

Hitt, Michael A., and Beverly B. Tyler. 1991. Strategic decision models: Integrating different perspectives. *Strategic Management Journal* 12(5): 327–351.

Hofer, Charles W. 1980. Turnaround strategies: An examination. *Journal of Business Strategy* 1(1): 19–31.

Hofer, Charles W., and Dan Schendel. 1978. *Strategy formulation: Analytical concepts.* St. Paul: West Pub. Co.

Hoffman, L. Richard. 1959. Homogeneity of member personality and its effect on group problem solving. *Journal of Abnormal and Social Psychology* 58: 27–32.

Hoffman, L. Richard, and Norman R. F. Maier. 1961. Quality and acceptance of problem solutions by members of homogeneous and heterogeneous groups. *Journal of Abnormal and Social Psychology* 62: 401–407.

Hoskisson, Robert E., and Michael A. Hitt. 1988. Strategic control systems and relative R&D investment in large multiproduct firms. *Strategic Management Journal* 9(6): 605–621.

———. 1994. *Downscoping: How to tame the diversified firm.* New York: Oxford University Press.

Hoskisson, Robert E., Michael A. Hitt, and Charles W. L. Hill. 1993. Managerial incentives and investment in R&D in large multiproduct firms. *Organization Science* 4: 325–341.

House, Robert J., William D. Spangler, and James Woycke. 1991. Personality and charisma in the U.S. presidency: A psychological theory of leader effectiveness. *Administrative Science Quarterly* 36(3): 364–396.

Hurst, David K., James C. Rush, and Roderick E. White. 1989. Top management teams and organizational renewal. *Strategic Management Journal* 10: 87–105.

Isabella, Lynn A., and Sandra A. Waddock. 1994. Top management team certainty: Environmental assessments, teamwork, and performance implications. *Journal of Management* 20: 835–858.

Jackson, Susan E. 1992. Consequence of group composition for the interpersonal dynamics of strategic issue processing. In *Advances in strategic management,* edited by Paul Shrivastava, Ann S. Huff, and Jane Dutton, 345–382. Greenwich, CT: JAI Press.

Janis, Irving L. 1972. *Victims of groupthink: A psychological study of foreign policy decisions and fiascoes.* Boston, MA: Houghton Mifflin.

Jensen, Michael C. 1986. Agency costs of free cash flow, corporate finance and takeovers. *American Economic Review* 76: 323–329.

Jensen, Michael, and Edward J. Zajac. 2004. Corporate elites and corporate strategy: How demographic preferences and structural position shape the scope of the firm. *Strategic Management Journal* 25(6): 507–524.

Katz, Ralph. 1982. The effects of group longevity on project communication and performance. *Administrative Science Quarterly* 27: 81–104.

Keats, Barbara W., and Michael A. Hitt. 1988. A causal model of linkages among environmental dimensions, macro organizational characteristics, and performance. *Academy of Management Journal* 31: 570–598.

Keck, Sara L. 1990. *Determinants and consequences of top executive team structure.* Unpublished Ph.D. dissertation, Columbia University, New York.

Keck, Sara L., and Michael L. Tushman. 1993. Environmental and organizational contextand executive team structure. *Academy of Management Journal* 36: 1314–1344.

Khandwalla, Pradip N. 1977. *The design of organizations.* New York: Harcourt Brace Jovanovich.

Kiesler, Sara B., and Lee Sproull. 1982. Managerial response to changing environments: Perspectives on problem sensing from social cognition. *Administrative Science Quarterly* 27: 548–570.

Kimberly, John R., and M. J. Evanisko. 1981. Organizational innovation: The influence of individual, organizational, and contextual factors on hospital adoption of technological and administrative innovations. *Academy of Management Journal* 24(4): 689–713.

Klein, Katherine J., and Robert J. House. 1995. On fire: Charismatic leadership and levels of analysis. *Leadership Quarterly* 6: 183–198.

Knight, Don, Craig L. Pearce, Ken G. Smith, Judy D. Olian, Henry P. Sims, Ken A. Smith, and Patrick Flood. 1999. Top management team diversity, group process, and strategic consensus. *Strategic Management Journal* 20(5): 445–465.

Korsgaard, M. Audrey, David M. Schweiger, and Harry J. Sapienza. 1995. Building commitment, attachment, and trust in strategic decision-making teams: The role of procedural justice. *Academy of Management Journal* 38: 60–84.

Kotter, John P. 1982. *The general managers.* New York: Free Press.

Lane, Peter J., Albert A. Cannella, Jr., and Michael H. Lubatkin. 1998. Agency problems as antecedents to unrelated mergers and diversification: Amihud and Lev reconsidered. *Strategic Management Journal* 19(6): 555–578.

Lawrence, Barbara S. 1997. The black box of organizational demography. *Organization Science* 8(1): 1–22.

Lawrence, Paul R., and Jay W. Lorsch. 1967. *Organization and environment.* Boston, MA: Harvard Business School Press.

Lorsch, Jay W., and Stephen A. Allen. 1973. *Managing diversity and interdependence.* Boston, MA: Harvard Business School Press.

Lorsch, Jay W., and Elizabeth MacIver. 1989. *Pawns or potentates: The reality of America's boards.* Boston, MA: Harvard Business School Press.

Lott, Bernice E., and Albert J. Lott. 1965. Group cohesiveness and interpersonal attraction: A review of relationships with antecedent and consequent variables. *Psychological Bulletin* 4: 259–309.

Maier, Norman R. F. 1970. *Problem solving and creativity in individuals and groups.* Belmont, CA: Brooks/Cole.

McCain, Bruce E., Charles A. O'Reilly, III, and Jeffrey Pfeffer. 1983. The effects of departmental demography on turnover. *Administrative Science Quarterly* 26(4): 626–641.

McGrath, Joseph E. 1984. *Groups: Interaction and performance.* Englewood Cliffs, NJ: Prentice-Hall.

Merton, Robert K. 1968. *Social theory and social structure.* New York: Free Press.

Michel, John G., and Donald C. Hambrick. 1992. Diversification posture and top management team characteristics. *Academy of Management Journal* 35: 9–37.

Miles, Raymond H., and Charles C. Snow. 1978. *Organizational strategy, structure, and process.* New York: McGraw-Hill.

Miller, Danny. 1991. Stale in the saddle: CEO tenure and the match between organization and environment. *Management Science* 37(1): 34–52.

Miller, Danny, Cornelia Droge, and Jean-Marie Toulouse. 1988. Strategic process and content as mediators between organizational context and structure. *Academy of Management Journal* 31(3): 544–569.

Mintzberg, Henry. 1978. Patterns in strategy formation. *Management Science* 24: 934–948.

———. 1979. *The structuring of organizations: The synthesis of the research.* Englewood Cliffs, NJ: Prentice-Hall.

———. 1983a. *Power in and around organizations.* Englewood Cliffs, NJ: Prentice-Hall.

———. 1983b. *Structure in fives: Designing effective organizations.* Englewood Cliffs, N.J.: Prentice-Hall.

Mintzberg, Henry, Duru Raisinghani, and Andre Theoret. 1976. The structure of unstructured decision processes. *Administrative Science Quarterly* 21: 246–275.

Murray, Alan I. 1989. Top management group heterogeneity and firm performance. *Strategic Management Journal* 10: 125–141.

Nemeth, Charlan J. 1986. Differential contributions of majority and minority influence. *Psychological Review* 91: 23–32.

Nemeth, Charlan J., and Barry M. Staw. 1989. The tradeoffs of social control and innovation in groups and organizations. In *Advances in Experimental Social Psychology,* edited by L. Berkowitz, 175–210. New York: Academic Press.

Nutt, Paul C. 1984. Types of organizational decision-processes. *Administrative Science Quarterly* 29: 414–450.

———. 1986. Tactics of implementation. *Academy of Management Journal* 29: 230–261.

———. 1987. Identifying and appraising how managers install strategy. *Strategic Management Journal* 8: 1–14.

———. 1989. Selecting tactics to implement strategic plans. *Strategic Management Journal* 10: 145–161.

O'Reilly, Charles A., III, David F. Caldwell, and William P. Barnett. 1989. Workgroup demography, social integration, and turnover. *Administrative Science Quarterly* 34: 21–37.

O'Reilly, Charles A., III, and Sylvia Flatt. 1989. Executive team demography, organizational innovation and firm performance. In *Working Paper.* University of California, Berkeley.

O'Reilly, Charles A., III, Richard C. Snyder, and Joan N. Boothe. 1993. Executive team demography and organizational change. In *Organizational change and redesign: Ideas and insights for improving performance,* edited by George P. Huber and William H. Glick, 147–175. New York: Oxford University Press.

Papadakis, Vassilis M., and. Patrick Barwise. 2002. How much do CEOs and top managers matter in strategic decision-making? *British Journal of Management* 13: 83–95.

Peterson, Randall S., D. Brent Smith, Paul V. Martorana, and Pamela D. Owens. 2003. The impact of chief executive officer personality on top management team dynamics: One mechanism by which leadership affects organizational performance. *Journal of Applied Psychology* 88(5): 795–808.

Pettigrew, Andrew M. 1973. *The politics of organizational decision making.* London: Tavistock.

———. 1992. On studying managerial elites. *Strategic Management Journal* 13(Special Issue): 163–182.

Pfeffer, Jeffrey. 1981a. Management as symbolic action: The creation and maintenance of organizational paradigms. In *Research in organizational behavior,* edited by Lawrence L. Cummings and Barry M. Staw, 1–52. Greenwich, CT: JAI Press.

———. 1981b. *Power in organizations.* Boston, MA: Pitman.

———. 1983. Organizational demography. In *Research in organizational behavior,* edited by Lawrence L. Cummings and Barry M. Staw, 299–357. Greenwich, CT: JAI Press.

Pfeffer, Jeffrey, and Gerald R. Salancik. 1978. *The external control of organizations: a resource dependence perspective.* New York: Harper & Row.

Pinfield, Lawrence T. 1986. A field evaluation of perspectives on organizational decision making. *Administrative Science Quarterly* 31: 365–388.

Pitcher, Patricia, and Anne D. Smith. 2001. Top management team heterogeneity: Personality, power, and proxies. *Organization Science* 12(1): 1–18.

Pitts, Robert A. 1976. Toward a contingency theory of multi-business organization design. *Academy of Management Review* 3: 203–210.

Polzer, Jeffrey T., C. Brad Crisp, Sirkaa L. Jarvenpaa, and Jerry W. Kim. 2006. Extending the faultline model to geographically dispersed teams: How colocated subgroups can impair group functioning. *Academy of Management Journal* 49 (4): 679–692.

Porter, Michael E. 1980. *Competitive strategy: Techniques for analyzing industry and competitors.* New York: Harper & Row.

Prahalad, C. K., and Richard A. Bettis. 1986. The dominant logic: A new linkage between diversity and performance. *Strategic Management Journal* 7(6): 485–501.

Prahalad, C. K., and Gary Hamel. 1990. The core competence of the corporation. *Harvard Business Review* 68: 79–93.

Priem, Richard L. 1990. Top management team group factors, consensus, and firm performance. *Strategic Management Journal* 11: 469–478.

Priem, Richard L., Douglas W. Lyon, and Gregory G. Dess. 1999. Inherent limitations of demographic proxies in top management team heterogeneity research. *Journal of Management* 25(6): 935–953.

Rajagopalan, Nandini, and Deepak K. Datta. 1996. CEO characteristics: Does industry matter? *Academy of Management Journal* 39(1): 197–215.

Rajagopalan, Nandini, and Sydney Finkelstein. 1992. Effects of strategic orientation and environmental change on senior management reward systems. *Strategic Management Journal* 13: 127–142.

Rajagopalan, Nandini, Abdul M. A. Rasheed, and Deepak K. Datta. 1993. Strategic decision processes: Critical review and future directions. *Journal of Management* 19(2): 349–384.

Reed, Richard L. 1978. Organizational change in the American foreign service, 1925–1965: The utility of cohort analysis. *American Sociological Review* 43: 404–421.

Reutzel, Christopher R., and Albert A. Cannella, Jr. 2004. A model of Chief Financial Officer promotion and exit. Paper presented at the Annual Meetings of the Academy of Management, New Orleans, LA.

Richard, Orlando C., Tim Barnett, Sean Dwyer, and Ken Chadwick. 2004. Cultural diversity in management, firm performance, and the moderating role of entrepreneurial orientation dimensions. *Academy of Management Journal* 47(2): 255–266.

Roberto, Michael A. 2003. The stable core and dynamic periphery in top management teams. *Management Decision* 41 (2): 120–131.

Roberts, Karlene H., and Charles A. O'Reilly, III. 1979. Some correlates of communication roles in organizations. *Academy of Management Journal* 22: 42–57.

Ruef, Martin, Howard E. Aldrich, and Nancy M. Carter. 2003. The structure of founding teams: Homophily, strong ties, and isolation among U. S. entrepreneurs. *American Sociological Review* 68(April): 195–222.

Rumelt, Richard P. 1974. *Strategy, structure and economic performance.* Boston, MA: Harvard University Press.

Sambharya, Rakesh B. 1996. Foreign experience of top management teams and international diversification strategies of U.S. multinational corporations. *Strategic Management Journal* 17(9): 739–746.

Sanders, William Gerard, and Mason A. Carpenter. 1998. Internationalization and firm governance: The roles of CEO compensation, top team composition, and board structure. *Academy of Management Journal* 41 (2): 158–178.

Schmidt, Stuart M., and Thomas A. Kochan. 1972. The concept of conflict: Toward conceptual clarity. *Administrative Science Quarterly* 17: 359–370.

Schmidt, Warren H. 1974. Conflict: A powerful process for (good or bad) change. *Management Review* 63: 4–10.

Schweiger, David M., William R. Sandberg, and Paula L. Rechner. 1989. Experiential effects of dialectical inquiry, devil's advocacy, and consensus approaches to strategic decision making. *Academy of Management Journal* 32: 745–772.

Shaw, Marvin E. 1981. *Group dynamics.* New York: McGraw-Hill.

Shaw, Marvin E., and Blaze Harkey. 1976. Some effects of congruency of member characteristics and group structure upon group behavior. *Journal of Personality and Social Psychology* 34(3): 412–418.

Shen, Wei, and Albert A. Cannella, Jr. 2002a. Power dynamics within top management and their impacts on CEO dismissal followed by inside succession. *Academy of Management Journal* 45: 1195–1208.

———. 2002b. Revisiting the performance consequences of CEO succession: The impacts of successor type, postsuccession senior executive turnover, and departing CEO tenure. *Academy of Management Journal* 45(4): 717–733.

Shull, Fremont A., Andre L. Delbecq, and Lawrence L. Cummings. 1970. *Organizational decision making.* New York: McGraw-Hill.

Simons, Tony, Lisa Hope Pelled, and Ken A. Smith. 1999. Making use of difference: Diversity, debate, and decision comprehensiveness in top management teams. *Academy of Management Journal* 42: 662–673.

Simsek, Zeki, John F. Veiga, Michael Lubatkin, and Richard N. Dino. 2005. Modeling the multilevel determinants of top management team behavioral integration. *Academy of Management Journal* 48: 69–84.

Smith, Ken G., and Curtis M. Grimm. 1987. Environmental variation, strategic change and firm performance: A study of railroad deregulation. *Strategic Management Journal* 8(4): 363–376.

Smith, Ken G., Ken A. Smith, Judy D. Olian, Henry P. Sims, Jr., Douglas P. O'Bannon, and Judith A. Scully. 1994. Top management team demography and process: The role of social integration and communication. *Administrative Science Quarterly* 39(3): 412–438.

Snow, Charles C. Scott A. Snell, Sue Canney Davison, and Donald C. Hambrick. 1996. Use transnational teams to globalize your company. *Organizational Dynamics* 24(4): 50–67.

Sorenson, Theodore. 1968. *Decision making in the White House.* New York: Columbia University Press.

Starbuck, William H. 1976. Organizations and their environments. In *Handbook of industrial and social psychology,* edited by Marvin D. Dunnette, 1069–1123. Chicago: Rand McNally.

Starbuck, William H., Arent Greve, and Bo L. T. Hedberg. 1978. Responding to crisis. *Journal of Business Administration* 9: 111–137.

Stasser, Garold. 1993. Pooling of unshared information during group discussions. In *Group process and productivity,* edited by Stephen Worchel, Wendy L. Wood and Jeffry A. Simpson, 48–86. Newbury Park, CA: Sage.

Staw, Barry M., Lloyd E. Sandelands, and Jane E. Dutton. 1981. Threat-rigidity effects in organizational behavior: A multi-level analysis. *Administrative Science Quarterly* 26: 501–524.

Steiner, Ivan D. 1972. *Group process and productivity.* New York: Academic Press.

Sutcliffe, Kathleen M. 1994. What executives notice: Accurate perceptions in top management teams. *Academy of Management Journal* 37: 1360–1378.

Thompson, James D. 1967. *Organizations in action: Social science bases of administrative theory.* New York: McGraw-Hill.

Tihanyi, Laszlo, Alan E. Ellstrand, Catherine M. Daily, and Dan R. Dalton. 2000. Composition of the top management team and firm international diversification. *Journal of Management* 26(1157–1177).

Triandis, Harry C., Eleanor R. Hall, and Robert B. Ewen. 1965. Member heterogeneity and dyadic creativity. *Human Relations* 18: 33–55.

Tsui, Anne S., Terri D. Egan, and Charles A. O Reilly, III. 1992. Being different: Relational demography and organizational attachment. *Administrative Science Quarterly* 37(4): 549–579.

Tushman, Michael L., and Philip Anderson. 1986. Technological discontinuities and organizational environments. *Administrative Science Quarterly* 31(3): 439–465.

Tushman, Michael L., and Sara L. Keck. 1990. Environmental and organization context and executive team characteristics: An organizational learning approach. In *Working Paper.* Columbia University.

Tushman, Michael L., and Elaine Romanelli. 1985. Organizational evolution: A metamorphosis model of convergence and reorientation. In *Research in organizational behavior,* edited by Lawrence L. Cummings and Barry M. Staw, 171–222. Greenwich, CT: JAI Press.

Tushman, Michael L., and Lori Rosenkopf 1996. Executive succession, strategic reorientation and performance growth: A longitudinal study in the U.S. cement industry. *Management Science* 42(7): 939–953.

Tushman, Michael L., Beverly Virany, and Elaine Romanelli. 1985. Executive succession, strategic reorientation, and organization evolution. *Technology In Society* 7: 297–314.

Van der Vegt, Gerben S., J. Stuart Bunderson, and Aad Oosterhof. 2006. Expertness diversity and interpersonal helping in teams: Why those who need the most help end up getting the least. *Academy of Management Journal* 49(5): 877–893.

Vancil, Richard F. 1987. *Passing the baton.* Boston, MA: Harvard Business School Press.

Virany, Beverly, Michael L. Tushman, and Elaine Romanelli. 1992. Executive succession and organization outcomes in turbulent environments: An organizational learning approach. *Organizational Science* 3: 72–91.

Wagner, John A., III. 1995. Studies of individualism-collectivism: Effects on cooperation in groups. *Academy of Management Journal* 38: 152–172.

Wagner, W. Gary, Jeffrey Pfeffer, and Charles A. O'Reilly III. 1984. Organizational demography and turnover in top-management groups. *Administrative Science Quarterly* 29: 74–92.

Waldman, David A., and Francis J. Yammarino. 1999. CEO charismatic leadership: Levels-of-management and levels-of-analysis effects. *Academy of Management Review* 24(2): 266–285.

Wanous, John P., and Margaret A. Youtz. 1986. Solution diversity and the quality of group decisions. *Academy of Management Journal* 29: 149–158.

Watson, Warren E, Louis D Ponthieu, and Joseph W Critelli. 1995. Team interpersonal process effectiveness in venture partnerships and its connection to perceived success. *Journal of Business Venturing* 10(5): 393–411.

Weick, Karl E. 1979. *The social psychology of organizing.* Reading, MA: Addison-Wesley.

———. 1983. Managerial thought in the context of action. In *The executive mind,* edited by Suredh Srivastava, 221–242. San Francisco: Jossey-Bass.

West, Clifford T., Jr., and Charles R. Schwenk. 1996. Top management team strategic consensus, demographic homogeneity and firm performance: A report of resounding nonfindings. *Strategic Management Journal* 17(7): 571–576.

Westphal, James D., and James W. Fredrickson. 2001. Who directs strategic change? Director experience, the selection of new CEOs, and change in corporate strategy. *Strategic Management Journal* 22(12): 1113–1137.

Westphal, James D., and Laurie P. Milton. 2000. How experience and network ties affect the influence of demographic minorities on corporate boards. *Administrative Science Quarterly* 45: 366–398.

Westphal, James D., and Edward J. Zajac. 1995. Who shall govern? CEO/board power, demographic similarity, and new director selection. *Administrative Science Quarterly* 40(1): 60–83.

Whisler, Thomas L., Harald Meyer, Bernard H. Baum, and Peter F. Sorensen, Jr. 1967. Centralization of organizational control: An empirical study of its meaning and measurement. *Journal of Business* 40: 10–26.

Wiersema, Margarethe F., and Karen A. Bantel, 1992. Top management team demography and corporate strategic change. *Academy of Management Journal* 35:91–121.

Wiersema, Margarethe F., and Allan Bird. 1993. Organizational demography in Japanese firms: Group heterogeneity, individual dissimilarity, and top management team turnover. *Academy of Management Journal* 36(5): 996–1025.

Williams, Katherine Y., and Charles A. O'Reilly, III. 1998. Demography and diversity in organizations: A review of 40 years of research. In *Research in Organizational Behavior,* edited by Barry M. Staw and Lawrence L. Cummings, 77–140. Greenwich, CT: JAI Press.

Williamson, Oliver E. 1963. Managerial discretion and business behavior. *American Economic Review* 53: 1032–1057.

Wooldridge, Bill, and Steven W. Floyd. 1990. The strategy process, middle management involvement, and organizational performance. *Strategic Management Journal* 11(3): 231–241.

Zander, Alvin. 1977. *Groups at work.* San Francisco, CA: Jossey-Bass.

Zenger, Todd R., and Barbara S. Lawrence. 1989. Organizational demography: The differential effects of age and tenure distributions on technical communication. *Academy of Management Journal* 32: 353–376.

Zhang, Yan, and Nandini Rajagopalan. 2004. When the known devil is better than an unknown God: An empirical study of the antecedents and consequences of relay CEO succession. *Academy of Management Journal* 47: 483–500.

Zorn, Dirk M. 2003. Here a chief, there a chief: The rise of the Chief Financial Officer in American corporations. Working paper, Princeton University.

PART III

Shared Responsibility for Leadership

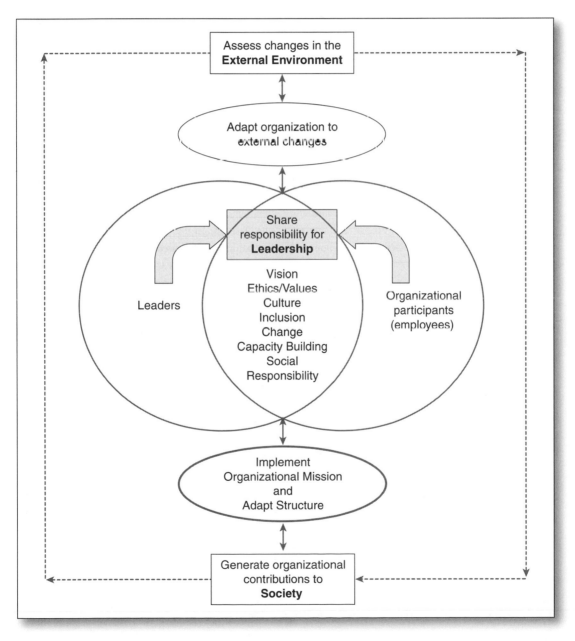

Overview

The chapters in Part III present concepts, theories, and practices that contribute to shared leadership. As indicated in the Introduction, a primary assumption underlying this volume is that new era organizations can become better able to meet the challenges of their complex and rapidly changing environment by developing the capacity of participants to share responsibility for leadership.

Craig Pearce and Jay Conger (Chapter 12) define shared leadership as a dynamic, interactive influence process among individuals in groups for which the objective is to lead one another to achieve group or organizational goals or both. The key distinction between shared leadership and traditional models of leadership, as identified by the authors, is that the influence process involves more than downward influence from leaders to participants; it emphasizes leadership that is broadly distributed *among* a set of individuals. Pearce and Conger demonstrate that scholars from Mary Parker Follet to Charles Manz and Henry Sims to Jean Lipman-Blumen have laid the groundwork for shared leadership in organizations, even though interest in this area of research has fluctuated throughout the years.

Organizations have entered an era where there is a sense of urgency to understand shared leadership because of the shift in how work is done—for instance, work is often accomplished in teams where there is an absence of hierarchical authority. Several other driving forces that contribute to an increase in shared leadership include the realization that senior leaders may not and often cannot possess sufficient and relevant information to make highly effective decisions, the requirement of a faster-paced environment to make high-speed decisions, and the complexity of the job held by the senior leader. Based on these factors, Pearce and Conger boldly proclaim that shared leadership is not just another blip on the radar screen of organizational science. Its time has arrived.

The next chapters focus on three concepts that Pearce and Conger identified in the existing body of

research on shared leadership—followership, empowerment, and leading teams. Robert Kelley's concept of *exemplary* or *star* followers began to pierce the leader-centric focus of leadership studies in 1988: His contention was that followership is on equal parity with leadership, and, in fact, that both leaders and followers engage in leadership. Kelley (Chapter 13) views "follower" and "leader" as *roles* that individuals assume at different times:

> Followership is not a person but a role, and what distinguishes followers from leaders is not intelligence or character but the role they play . . . effective followers and effective leaders are often the same people playing different parts at different hours of the day.[1]

He describes exemplary or star followership as active engagement in helping an organization or cause succeed while exercising independent, critical judgment of goals, tasks, potential problems, and methods. Star followers are self-motivated, responsible, self-confident, committed, and courageous team members who do not require supervision by leaders.

This idea of followers provides a stark contrast to the notion of followers as passive sheep. Exemplary followers work in cooperation with leaders to accomplish organizational goals.

Empowerment is another concept that alters traditional notions of leader-participant roles. According to Lynn Offermann (Chapter 14), empowerment typically involves sharing of power, whereby a hierarchically superior leader gives some of the authority and decision-making latitude previously in his or her purview to one or more followers, thus expanding the follower's sphere of influence. It involves redistributing authority so that the person closest to the work, with the most knowledge, can make decisions without checking with the leader. Offermann warns that individuals need to be ready for empowerment, in terms of both their skills and their motivation levels, and leaders need to develop staff to the point at which they are able to assume this increase in responsibility. Shared power does not simply change the

---

1. Kelley, R. (1988). In praise of followers. *Harvard Business Review, 88*(6), 146.

participant's job, it also changes the leader's job, so that leadership becomes less about direction and control and more about developing the participant's capabilities.

Joanne Ciulla (Chapter 15) distinguishes between authentic and bogus empowerment of organizational participants. Bogus empowerment involves inflated claims and undelivered promises to employees of shared power; this behavior neither shows respect for them nor demonstrates loyalty and commitment through good times and bad. She describes authentic empowerment as a reciprocal moral relationship that entails responsibility, trust, respect, and loyalty. Ciulla emphasizes that empowerment is more than discretion on the job. It requires freedom to choose and freedom from emotional manipulation. Leaders should decide whether they are ready and willing to practice authentic empowerment. If not, they should refrain from engaging in the practice.

Pearce and Conger note that the fastest growing unit in organizations is the team. Teams have several basic characteristics:

- *Interaction*: Teams create, organize, and sustain group behavior. Teams focus primarily on task-oriented activity, because they are based in workplaces, and their members are paid to address work-related concerns. Teams also promote relationship-sustaining interactions.
- *Interdependence*: Team members' interactions are cooperative and coordinated. Members work together, combining their individual inputs in a deliberate way.
- *Structure*: Teams are structured groups. Group norms, members' specific roles in the group, and communication patterns are often explicitly stated.
- *Goals*: Teams are goal oriented. Teammates' interdependence is based on the coordination of actions in pursuit of a common goal.
- *Cohesiveness*: Teams are typically cohesive, particularly in the sense that their members are united in their efforts to pursue a common goal.[2]

According to Richard Hackman (Chapter 16), the use of teams in current organizational settings has several worthwhile benefits:

Work teams have more resources, and a greater diversity of resources, than do individual performers. Teams have great flexibility in how to deploy and use their resources. Teams provide a setting in which members can learn from one another and thereby build an ever-larger pool of knowledge and expertise. Also, there is always the possibility that a team will generate magic—producing something extraordinary, a collective creation of previously unimagined quality or beauty.[3]

To accrue these benefits, team leadership must create conditions that enhance team performance by providing a compelling direction, enabling team structure, supportive organizational context, and team performance processes. The ultimate aim of team leadership is to build the team's capacity to manage itself well.

Another increasingly common form of team leadership in new era organizations is e-leadership or leadership of virtual teams. Surinder Kahai and Bruce Avolio (Chapter 17) define e-leadership as a process of social influence that takes place in an organizational context where a significant amount of work, including communication, is supported by information technology (IT). Although leadership in virtual teams is a relatively new area of study, early research indicates that effective e-leadership differs from traditional forms of face-to-face leadership with regard to leadership style and processes, culture, and organizational structure. The nature and context of virtual teams call for greater shared leadership, information dissemination, and participation in decision making or problem solving. Kahai and Avolio indicate that e-leadership, like other forms of shared leadership, opens a whole new area of inquiry and research.

Beyond leadership in teams, Kathleen Allen and colleagues (Chapter 18) outline the role of shared or collective leadership in organizations and society in general to carry out the purpose of leadership in this era. They maintain that the basic premise of shared or collaborative leadership is the recognition that no

---

2. Forsyth, D. R. (2006). *Group dynamics* (4th ed.). Belmont, CA: Thomson/Wadsworth.

3. Hackman, J. R. (2002). *Leading teams: Setting the stage for great performances.* Boston: Harvard Business School Press.

one person has the solutions to the multifaceted problems that a group or organization must address. Leadership in this context requires a set of principles that empowers all members to act and employs a process that allows collective wisdom to surface. Allen and colleagues suggest a set of core principles and accompanying practices to develop, nurture, and implement collective leadership. They suggest a threefold purpose for leadership in the 21st century and challenge each person to assume her or his role and responsibility for leading, participating in, and shaping organizations and other entities in society so that they become more supportive, sustainable, and caring.

CHAPTER 12

All Those Years Ago

The Historical Underpinnings of Shared Leadership

Craig L. Pearce

Claremont Graduate University

Jay A. Conger

Claremont McKenna College

Shared leadership can be defined as a dynamic, interactive influence process among individuals in groups for which the objective is to lead one another to the achievement of group or organizational goals or both. This influence process often involves peer, or lateral, influence and at other times involves upward or downward hierarchical influence. The key distinction between shared leadership and traditional models of leadership is that the influence process involves more than just downward influence on subordinates by an appointed or elected leader (see Pearce & Sims, 2000, 2002). Rather, leadership is broadly distributed among a set of individuals instead of centralized in hands of a single individual who acts in the role of a superior.

This conceptualization of leadership stands in stark contrast to traditional notions. Historically, leadership has been conceived around a single individual—*the leader*—and the relationship of that individual to subordinates or followers. This relationship between the leader and the led has been a vertical one of top-down influence. As a result, the leadership field has focused its attention on the behaviors, mind-sets, and actions of "the leader" in a team or organization. This paradigm has been the dominant one in the leadership field for many decades. In recent years, however, a few scholars have challenged this conception, arguing that leadership is an *activity* that can be shared or distributed among members of a group or organization. For example, depending on the demands of the moment,

Source: C. L. Pearce and J. A. Conger (Eds.), *Shared leadership: Reframing the hows and whys of leadership* (pp. 1–8). © 2003 Sage Publications, Inc. Used by permission.

individuals who are not formally appointed as leaders can rise to the occasion to exhibit leadership and then step back at other times to allow others to lead. This line of thinking is gaining attention among leadership scholars. Yet our understanding of the dynamics and opportunities for shared leadership remains quite primitive. At the same time, there is a sense of urgency to understand the dynamics of this phenomenon given growing demands for shared leadership within the world of organizations.

These demands have largely to do with shifts in how work is performed. For example, today the fastest growing organizational unit is the team and, specifically, cross-functional teams. What distinguishes these units from traditional organizational forms is the absence of hierarchical authority. Although a cross-functional team may have a formally appointed leader, this individual is more commonly treated as a peer. For example, outside the team, they often do not possess line authority over the individual members. Moreover, the formal leader is usually at a knowledge disadvantage. After all, the purpose of the cross-functional team is to bring a very diverse set of functional backgrounds together. The formal leader's expertise represents only one of the numerous functional specialties at the table. The leader is therefore highly dependent on the expertise of team members. Leadership in these settings is not determined by positions of authority or depth of expertise but rather by an individual's capacity to influence peers and by the leadership needs of the team in a given moment. In addition, each member of the team brings unique perspectives, knowledge, and capabilities to the team. At various junctures in the team's life, there are moments when these differing backgrounds and characteristics provide a platform for leadership to be distributed across the team.

In addition to organizational demands for team-based work arrangements, there is a parallel demand for leadership to be more equally distributed up and down the hierarchy. This need is being driven by a number of forces. The first is the realization that seniormost leaders may not possess sufficient and relevant information to make highly effective decisions in a fast-changing and complex world. In reality, managers down the line may be more highly informed and in a far better position to provide leadership. Second, speed of response is an organizational imperative given a faster-paced environment. Many companies, for example, have actually incorporated speed as one of their core values (General Electric being the most commonly cited example). This demand suggests that organizations cannot wait for leadership decisions to be pushed up to the top for action. Instead, leadership has to be distributed or shared across the organization to ensure speedier response times. The final force driving the need for shared leadership has to do with the complexity of the job held by the seniormost leader in an organization—the chief executive officer. Increasingly, this individual is hard-pressed to possess all the leadership skills and knowledge necessary to guide complex organizations in a dynamic and global marketplace. In response to this dilemma, there have been a growing number of experiments in which leadership is being shared at the very top. At Dell, for example, there is an office of the CEO where the responsibilities of the chief executive are distributed among several executives. In summary, a powerful set of forces within organizations is fostering greater demand for shared leadership across all levels.

Although the need and appreciation for shared leadership has been growing, our understanding of it lags seriously behind. In large part, this shortcoming is due to the leadership field's singular focus on the conception of an individual leader to the neglect of distributed forms of leadership. As a result, there have only been a small number of published studies examining shared forms of leadership. For example, until very recently, only two publications have indicated a clear interest in shared leadership as a potential mechanism for constructively engaging in integrated human effort. The first was in the 1920s, and the second occurred more than 40 years later in the mid-1960s. Shortly, we will describe in some detail these two instances.

The purpose of this chapter is to provide a historical backdrop for shared leadership. As Bass and Avolio (1993) have astutely noted, the field of leadership often reinvents itself without regard to previous theory. We hope to avoid falling into this selective memory trap and, rather, hope to illuminate the extensive historical underpinnings of the concept of shared leadership. Specifically, we wish to illustrate how our current conceptions of the phenomenon have been shaped by other contributions in the fields of leadership, organizational behavior, psychology, and teamwork (see Table 12.1). In so doing, we intend to craft the proper space for future research on the topic to be well-grounded and to advance the understanding and practice of teamwork and leadership in a deeper, more meaningful way.

The Emergence of the Scientific Study of Leadership: The Leader in a Command Role

Not until the Industrial Revolution was the task of leadership formally studied and documented in a scientific manner: At the beginning of the 1800s, leadership and management was formally recognized as a factor of production when Jean Baptiste Say (1803/1964), a French economist, claimed that entrepreneurs "must possess the art of superintendence and administration" (p. 330). Prior to this time, economists were primarily occupied with two factors of production—land and labor—and, to a lesser extent, capital. During the Industrial Revolution, however, the concept of leadership as important to economic endeavor was recognized. Nonetheless, the predominant role of leadership was command and control. It was not until much later that we observed slight acknowledgment of concepts related to the notion of shared leadership.

The emphasis on leadership centered on control or oversight—in other words, the "vertical model" of leading. For example, James Montgomery (1840) is credited as the first author to scientifically study industrial management and leadership. In 1840, he published a book that compared and contrasted cotton manufacturing in the United States and Great Britain. He concluded that the British organizations were more effective based on their enhanced level of managerial expertise. This expertise was largely focused on the establishment of control systems (Wren, 1994).

Throughout the 1800s, the literature on management focused primarily on organizational forms, structures, and manufacturing processes shaped in large part by the advent of the Industrial Age and the needs of an emerging new industry— the railroads. The advent of the railroads, the first of the large-scale American corporations, necessitated more systematic organizational and leadership approaches to coordinate

and control these vast organizations that were geographically dispersed, capital intensive, and employing large numbers of people (Chandler, 1965).

One of the early management thinkers in this arena was Daniel C. McCallum. He developed six principles of management, and this was perhaps the first articulation of management principles that could apply across industrial lines. One of McCallum's principles dealt specifically with the notion of leadership. Although this principle did not indicate what was appropriate leadership, it indicated that the organization should not interfere with supervisors' "influence with their subordinates" (Wren, 1994, p. 77). Thus, during the mid-1800s, we observe the beginnings of interest in the scientific study of leadership.

By the turn of the century, thinking on management and leadership had crystallized into what was ultimately termed "scientific management" (Gantt, 1916; Gilbreth, 1912; Gilbreth & Gilbreth, 1917; Taylor, 1903, 1911). The fundamental principle of scientific management was that all work could be studied scientifically and optimal procedures could be developed to ensure maximum productivity. An important component of scientific management was the separation of managerial and worker responsibilities, with managerial ranks having responsibility for identifying precise work procedures and workers following the dictates of management to the letter. Thus, scientific management perhaps went the furthest in clearly articulating a command-and-control perspective on the role of leaders in organizational life. The formally appointed leader was to oversee and direct those below. Subordinates were to follow instructions to the letter. The notion that leaders and their subordinates might mutually influence one another was largely unthinkable at the time.

During the period of the development of scientific management in the United States, two Europeans also made particularly noteworthy intellectual contributions to the formal study of leadership. Henri Fayol from France derived 14 flexible principles of management (Fayol, 1916/1949). Thus, one could credit him with early developments in contingency theory. The second, Max Weber from Germany, developed both a theory of organizational structure—bureaucracy (Weber, 1924/1947)—and a theory of authority or leadership (Weber, 1905/1958). Both individuals clearly articulated

Table 12.1   Historical Bases of Shared Leadership

Theory/Research	Key Issues	Representative Authors
Law of the situation	Let the situation, not the individual, determine the "orders."	Follett (1924)
Human relations and social systems perspective	One should pay attention to the social and psychological needs of employees.	Turner (1933) Mayo (1933) Barnard (1938)
Role differentiation in groups	Members of groups typically assume different types of roles.	Benne and Sheats (1948)
Co-leadership	Concerns the division of the leadership role between two people—primarily research examines mentor and protégé relationships.	Solomon, Loeffer, and Frank (1953) Hennan and Bennis (1998)
Social exchange theory	People exchange punishments and rewards in their social interactions.	Festinger (1954) Homans (1958)
Management by objectives and participative goal setting	Subordinates and superiors jointly set performance expectations.	Drucker (1954) Erez and Arad (1986) Locke and Latham (1990)
Emergent leadership	Leaders can "emerge" from a leaderless group.	Hollander (1961)
Mutual leadership	Leadership can come from peers.	Bowers and Seashore (1966)
Expectation states Theory and team member exchange	Team members develop models of status differential between various team members.	Berger, Cohen, and Zelditch (1972) Seers (1989)
Participative decision making	Under certain circumstances, it is advisable to elicit more involvement by subordinates in the decision-making process.	Vroom and Yetton (1973)
Vertical dyad linkage/leader member exchange	Examines the process between leaders and followers and the creation of in-groups and out-groups.	Graen (1976)
Substitutes for leadership	Situation characteristics (e.g., highly routinized work) diminish the need for leadership.	Kerr and Jermier (1978)
Self-leadership	Employees, given certain conditions, are capable of leading themselves.	Manz and Sims (1980)

Theory/Research	Key Issues	Representative Authors
Self-managing work teams	Team members can take on roles that were formerly reserved for managers.	Manz and Sims (1987, 1993)
Followership	Examines the characteristics of good followers.	Kelly (1988)
Empowerment	Examines power sharing with subordinates.	Conger and Kanungo (1988)
Shared cognition	Examines the extent to which team members hold similar mental models about key internal and external environmental issues.	Klimoski and Mohammed (1994) Cannon-Bowers, Salas, and Converse (1993) Ensley and Pearce (2001)
Connective leadership	Examines how well leaders are able to make connections to others both inside and outside the team.	Lipman-Blumen (1996)

influence or leadership processes centered on an individual leader whose authority was top-down and based on command and control. Thus, by the end of the Industrial Revolution, management and leadership had come to be scientifically studied. The consensus was one that emphasized a distinction between leaders and followers and rested on the principle of the unity of command. Orders should come from above and be followed by those below. In addition, these early thinkers on management also spent considerable time trying to figure out ways to prevent followers from shirking responsibilities and thus designed more and more elaborate methods for controlling the behavior of followers. The absolute control of worker behavior—down to the smallest detail—was defined as the prerogative of management.

The Management Field's Brief Flirtations With Concepts Related to Shared Leadership

Despite this strong historical emphasis on a command-and-control approach to leadership, alternative perspectives did appear in the 20th century—albeit briefly. In fact, in two instances, management thinkers pointed to the possibility of shared leadership

processes augmenting the strictly command and control orientation to leadership. These are reviewed below.

Flirtation Number One

Mary Parker Follett (1924) introduced the concept of the *law of the situation*. The law of the situation stated that rather than simply following the lead of the person with the formal authority in a situation, one should follow the lead of the person with the most knowledge regarding the situation at hand. Thus, Follett proposed a radically different leadership process in contrast to her contemporaries—one closely aligned with the concept of shared leadership.

Follett was a popular speaker and management consultant during the 1920s and was regarded as "the brightest star in the management firmament" of the times (Drucker, 1995, p. 2). Many of her ideas, however, were discounted and discarded by business leaders due to the socioeconomic realities of the late 1920s, 1930s, and 1940s. This period erased any notion that workers might actively shape the thinking and actions of management. Peter Drucker recalls a conversation he had with a member of the National Labor Relations Board

(NLRB) in the late 1940s that powerfully illustrates the attitudes of the times. Drucker (1995) explains that

> when I said something about both management and workers having "a common interest in the survival and prosperity of the company" (also one of Follett's arguments, although I did not know that at the time), my friend cut me short: "Any company that asserts such a common interest," he said, "is prima facie in violation of the law and guilty of a grossly unfair labor practice." (p. 5)

Thus, the common wisdom following the stock market crash and depression years was very much one of command and control: Leaders and subordinates in the modern industrial complex were to have separate roles and conflicting goals. Influence was to remain vertical and unidirectional—downward.

Flirtation Number Two

The second instance of historical interest in shared leadership-type concepts came with the Bowers and Seashore (1966) study of insurance offices. Interestingly enough, Bowers and Seashore did not cite Follett in their theoretical development of a concept they termed "mutual leadership."

What Bowers and Seashore (1966) empirically documented was that leadership influence processes could come from peers and that this source of leadership could positively affect organizational outcomes. As with Follett over 40 years earlier, however, the Bowers and Seashore study was a mere blip on the radar screen of scientific thought regarding leadership processes. Their concept of mutual leadership came and went much the same as did Follett's concept of the law of the situation.

Not until the late 1990s did scholars return to an examination of shared leadership in organizations. In reality, although the majority of scholars have not explicitly conceived of leadership as a shared phenomenon, there have been implicit links for some time. Important theoretical developments from the 1930s through the 1960s in the fields of leadership, psychology, and organizational behavior

laid historical roots that today inform the study of shared leadership.

Laying the Theoretical Groundwork for Shared Leadership: Organizational Research From the 1930s Through the 1960s

Between Follett's (1924) book and the Bowers and Seashore (1966) paper, the interest in topics related to shared leadership was not completely absent. At least six theoretical contributions have informed our current understanding of the concept of shared leadership. These are (a) the human relations and social systems perspective, (b) role differentiation in groups, (c) co-leadership, (d) social exchange theory, (e) management by objectives and later research on participative goal setting, and (f) emergent leadership theory (see Table 12.1).

Human Relations and Social Systems Perspectives

The major advance in the 1930s regarding the management of organizations was the adoption of a *social* view of organizational life. The relations between leaders and those led took on new significance with a newfound emphasis on interpersonal dynamics in the workplace (e.g., Barnard, 1938; Mayo, 1933; Roethlisberger & Dickson, 1939; Turner, 1933). This viewpoint did not characterize workers as shirkers who primarily required direction and control but, rather, suggested that leaders needed to understand the psychological bases of human motivation in order to more fully integrate employees into a productive system. Accordingly, this major advance—paying attention to the psychological needs of employees—was an important step toward the ultimate articulation of shared leadership as an organizational possibility. It opened the possibility that the act of leadership was not simply a unidirectional process of "leader to led" but, rather, a more complex one in which subordinates and their needs might influence the leader as well.

Role Differentiation in Groups

By articulating 19 distinct roles that members of a working group could serve, Benne and Sheats (1948) raised the possibility that group members played roles as critical as that of the group's leader. In addition, several of these roles could be considered leadership roles. Leadership was no longer unidirectional but was now a reciprocal process. Benne and Sheats subdivided their roles under two broad categories: task roles and socioemotional roles. Task roles included initiator/contributor, information seeker, opinion seeker, opinion giver, elaborator, coordinator, orienter, evaluator/critic, energizer, procedural technician, and recorder. Socioemotional roles included encourager, harmonizer, compromiser, gatekeeper/expediter, standard setter, group observer/commentator, and follower. The important contribution of this early work on role differentiation was that it identified the potential for different types of influence originating from different members of the group beyond the formally appointed leader. There was a growing realization that members of a group could be playing roles as influential as the leader him or herself. Many of these types of influence that Benne and Sheats describe fall squarely into the realm of the modern-day purview of leader behavior research (see Pearce & Sims, 2000, 2002). Thus, they opened the door to the study of shared leadership dynamics within groups through the notion of multiple roles.

Co-Leadership

Early writings on co-leadership research appeared in the early 1950s (Solomon, Loeffer, & Frank, 1953). This work focused primarily on situations in which two individuals simultaneously shared one leadership position. The literature, however, has been dominated by research in *group therapy settings* where co-leaders occupy mentor-protégé relationships (e.g., Mintz, 1963; Rittner & Hammons, 1992; Solomon et al., 1953; Winter, 1976). Much of it examines how co-leadership develops

(e.g., Winter, 1976) and the tactics for improving co-leadership effectiveness in these settings (e.g., Greene, Morrison, & Tischler, 1981; Herzog, 1981). Since this literature is primarily concerned with mentor-protégé relationships, it might be viewed as a special case of vertical leadership. In the last few years, there have also been explorations of co-leadership in the executive suite—most notably between the CEO and COO or between a company founder and his or her "right hand man," or woman, as the case may be (e.g., Heenan & Bennis, 1999). Under these circumstances, co-leadership can be considered a special case of shared leadership—the two-person case. Nonetheless, co-leadership, although a distinct concept, is clearly related to the concept of shared leadership.

Social Exchange Theory

Originating in the 1950s, social exchange theory (Festinger, 1954; Homans, 1958; Thibaut & Kelly, 1959) extends theories of economic exchange by claiming that people enter into social relationships expecting some type of social "gain" and some type of social "cost." This body of work is concerned with "the exchange of rewards and punishments that take place when people interact" (Berscheid, 1985, p. 429). Much of the work in social exchange theory has dealt with friendship groups and interpersonal attractiveness (Byrne, Ervin, & Lamberth, 1970; Festinger, 1954; Newcomb, 1960). The essence of this theory, as it relates to shared leadership, is that it suggests that influence processes are embedded in most, if not all, social interactions and, by extension, influence is not limited to appointed leaders but widely distributed among others.

Management by Objectives and Participative Goal Setting

Drucker (1954) identified management by objectives (MBO) as a useful technique for engaging individuals by tying their objectives to the larger organizational purpose. The essence of MBO is that subordinates and superiors actively engage in a process of articulating the objectives toward which subordinates will work and subsequently the ones they will be held accountable for achieving. Extensions to MBO followed under the rubric of participative goal-setting research (see Erez & Arad, 1986; Locke & Latham, 1990), in which subordinates participate in defining their objectives. The leader is no longer the sole source for defining the objectives of their subordinates; rather, this becomes a *shared* activity. MBO and participative goal setting therefore identify a role for subordinates in the articulation of performance expectations and thus inch us closer toward a model of shared leadership in organizations.

Emergent Leadership

Developed by Hollander (1961), the concept of emergent leadership refers to the phenomenon of leader selection by the members of a leaderless group (e.g., Bartol & Martin, 1986; Hollander, 1978; Stein & Heller, 1979). Whereas emergent leadership is typically concerned with the ultimate selection of an appointed leader, the concept of shared leadership is linked to the "serial emergence" of multiple leaders over the life of the team (Pearce, 1997, 2002). Thus, emergent leadership provides yet another theoretical base for shared leadership.

Building the Case for Shared Leadership: Organizational Research From the 1970s Through the Turn of the Millennium

As the preceding section suggests, the period of the 1930s through the 1960s witnessed several interesting developments in the scientific study of management and leadership. These developments culminated in the Bowers and Seashore (1966) study of mutual leadership. Following their study of mutual leadership, however, the field once again lost sight of shared leadership. Instead, scholars began work on several other theoretical concepts that help to provide a rich theoretical foundation for the emergence of the study of shared leadership today and in the future. The period of the

1970s through the turn of the millennium, not counting participative goal-setting research (which was discussed earlier), witnessed the development of at least 10 conceptual foundations related to the conceptualization of shared leadership: (a) expectation states theory, which later led to research on team member exchange; (b) participative decision making; (c) vertical dyad linkage theory (later termed leader-member exchange); (d) substitutes for leadership; (e) self-leadership; (f) self-managing work teams; (g) followership; (h) empowerment; (i) shared cognition; and (j) connective leadership (see Table 12.1). We review each of these, in turn, below.

Expectation States Theory and Team Member Exchange

Building on social exchange theory, Berger, Cohen, and Zelditch (1972) developed expectation states theory. Expectation states theory suggests that team members intuitively develop ideas regarding one another's status in the team. Later, elaborating on and integrating expectation states theory and leader member exchange, Seers (1989) introduced the team member exchange construct. Whereas leader member exchange focuses on the quality of the relationships between leaders and their followers, team member exchange focuses on the quality of the exchange relationships between the team members. Seers theorized that the quality of the exchange attributed to individuals was positively related to their respective status in the team. Thus, from a shared leadership perspective, this idea translates into the possibility of individual members (beyond the leader) gaining status to the point at which they are able to influence the team themselves. More important, this perspective suggests that different individuals may acquire high levels of status depending on the specific function or task being addressed, thereby permitting the transference of the influence process from one team member to the next.

Participative Decision Making

Vroom and Yetton (1973) articulated a model that prescribed when and how leaders should involve their subordinates in the decision-making process. Generally speaking, their model suggests that greater involvement is required under the following conditions: when there is a higher need for quality decision making; when subordinates have knowledge that augments the leader's knowledge; when subordinate acceptance of the decision is important; and when there is low potential conflict among subordinates regarding the potential decision. Thus, Vroom and Yetton's model identifies certain circumstances under which shared leadership is likely to be more or less efficacious than directive forms of vertical leadership.

Vertical Dyad Linkage/Leader-Member Exchange

Building on social network theory, Graen and colleagues (e.g., Graen, 1976; Graen & Scandura, 1987; Graen & Schiemann, 1978) introduced vertical dyad linkage/leader-member exchange (LMX) into the formal lexicon of leadership studies. These authors have discussed the importance of the leader-follower dyad in their work on leadership process. The theory suggests that leaders will need to vary their styles depending on different subordinates. In other words, subordinates influence how the leader behaves. Their work suggests that followers have a role in the leadership process, but do not go so far as to say that the source of leadership can be from the followers, as is the case with shared leadership.

Substitutes for Leadership

The substitutes for leadership literature (e.g., Kerr & Jermier, 1978) also provides a useful framework for understanding the concept of shared leadership. The literature on substitutes for leadership suggests that certain conditions, such as highly routinized work or professional standards, may serve as substitutes for social sources of leadership. In this sense, shared leadership may serve as a substitute for more formal appointed leadership. For example, if team members are actively involved in developing the vision for their team, it may be possible that a strong visionary leader is not necessary for the team to focus on its distal goals.

Therefore, the substitutes for leadership concept serves as another theoretical base of shared leadership.

Self-Leadership

Building on the substitutes for leadership framework, Manz and Sims (1980) identified self-management, or self-leadership, as a potential substitute for more formal leadership. To the extent that subordinates were knowledgeable about organizational needs, had appropriate skills for the tasks at hand, and were motivated to engage in productive activity, self-leadership could alleviate the need for close supervision, direction, and control. If we take their argument to the group level of analysis, we might see how shared leadership could operate in a similar manner. In fact, Pearce and Sims (2002) identified shared leadership as accounting for more variance in team performance than the leadership displayed by the appointed leaders of the teams in their study of 71 change management teams.

Self-Managing Work Teams

Recent work on self-managing work teams (SMWTs) has taken the boldest steps toward articulating the concept of shared leadership (e.g., Manz, Keating, & Donnellon, 1990; Manz & Sims 1987, 1993; Stewart & Manz, 1995). Although recognizing that team members can, and do, take on roles that were previously reserved for management, this literature focuses more on the role of the appointed leader and less on the role of the team members in the leadership process (see Stewart & Manz, 1995). Thus, although the self-managing work teams literature does acknowledge the role of team members in the leadership process, it does not go so far as to suggest a systematic approach to the examination of how, and to what effect, the process of leadership can be shared by the team as a whole.

Followership

Although followers have not been of central interest in leadership research, several scholars and practitioners from widely disparate fields have emphasized the role that followers play in the leadership process (e.g., Campbell & Kinion, 1993; Cooper, Higgott, & Nossal, 1991; Kelly 1988; Lundin & Lancaster, 1990; Nakamura, 1980; Nishigaki, Vavrin, Kano, Haga, Kunz, & Law, 1994; Rippy, 1990; R. Smith, 1991; W. Smith, 1994). The primary emphasis of this line of research is around the definition of what constitutes "good" followership. Kelly (1988) defined good followers as those who

> have the vision to see both the forest and the trees, the social capacity to work well with others, the strength of character to flourish without heroic status, the moral and psychological balance to pursue personal and corporate goals at no cost to either, and, above all, the desire to participate in a team effort for the accomplishment of some greater purpose. (p. 107)

Under conditions of shared leadership, followership is dynamically determined. Thus, the need for good followership skills in all team members is heightened: Team members need to be able to clearly recognize when they should be leading and when they should be following.

Empowerment

The topic of empowerment has received considerable attention in recent years (e.g., Blau & Alba, 1982; Conger & Kanungo, 1988; Manz, 1986; Manz & Sims, 1989, 1990; Mohrman, Cohen, & Mohrman, 1995; Pearce & Sims, 2000, 2002; Cox, Pearce, & Sims, in press). The central issue in the empowerment literature is that of power (e.g., Conger & Kanungo, 1988). Whereas traditional models of management emphasize power emanating from the top of an organization, the empowerment concept emphasizes the decentralization of power. The rationale behind empowering individual workers is that those dealing with situations on a daily basis are the most qualified to make decisions regarding those situations.

Although the vast majority of the empowerment literature focuses on the impact on the individual (e.g., Conger & Kanungo, 1988), some researchers have expanded the concept to the group level of analysis

(e.g., Mohrman et al., 1995). To empower, or share power with, members of a team, however, is not the same as observing shared leadership emanating from a group. Shared leadership only exists to the extent that the team actively engages in the leadership process. As such, empowerment is a necessary, but not sufficient, condition for shared leadership to be developed and displayed by teams.

Shared Cognition

Shared cognition in teams primarily refers to the extent to which the team members have similar "mental maps" regarding important aspects of their internal and external environment. As recently as 1991, shared cognition was viewed as "almost a contradiction in terms" (Resnick, 1991, p. 1). As more and more organizations are turning to team-based approaches to organizing (Aldag & Fuller, 1993), however, the study of teams has become increasingly important in recent years. With the focus on teams, organizational researchers have taken a strong interest in the role shared cognition may play in teams in an effort to develop a deeper understanding of team dynamics and team effectiveness (e.g., Cannon-Bowers, Salas, & Converse, 1993; Ensley & Pearce, 2001; Klimoski & Mohammed, 1994; Knight et al., 1999). Shared cognition theory advances our understanding of shared leadership by providing a cognitive framework through which leadership might be shared: Without similar mental models, it seems unlikely that team members would be able to accurately interpret influence attempts within the team, and the potential effectiveness of shared leadership would be seriously limited. Thus, shared cognition provides yet another conceptual foundation for shared leadership.

Connective Leadership

Lipman-Blumen (1996) introduced the concept of connective leadership. Connective leadership focuses on the ability of leaders to develop interpersonal connections both internal to the team and in external networks. Although most of the discussion of shared leadership is focused on the internal leadership dynamics within teams, connective leadership helps in further developing the external focus of leadership activity by the team. For example, it explores the necessity of leaders to connect their own visions with the visions of their constituents.

The "Arrival" of Shared Leadership and the Way Forward

From the 1970s to the mid-1990s, we have witnessed a multitude of theoretical and research developments that provide conceptual grounding for the concept of shared leadership. By the mid-1990s, several scholars began mining this fertile intellectual soil. These scholars, independently and simultaneously, developed models that directly addressed shared leadership (Avolio, Jung, Murry, & Sivasubramaniam, 1996; Pearce, 1997; Seers, 1996). Conditions were finally right for the acceptance of this seemingly radical departure from the traditional view of leadership as something imparted to followers by a leader from above. Additional publications on shared leadership have followed. For example, Pearce and colleagues have refined the articulation of a theory of shared leadership by developing a general theoretical model (Pearce & Sims, 2000) and context-specific models that address unique organizational contexts, such as sales teams (Perry, Pearce, & Sims, 1999), nonprofit organizations (Pearce, Perry, & Sims, 2001), entrepreneurial top management teams (Ensley, Pearson, & Pearce, in press), and cross-cultural implications for shared leadership (Pearce, in press).

At the same time, the empirical examination of this alternate source of leadership has remained relatively unexplored. There are four notable exceptions. First, Bowers and Seashore (1966) found what they termed "mutual leadership" between life insurance agents to be predictive of the types of insurance sold and the cost per unit of new policies. Second, Avolio et al. (1996) found shared leadership in teams of undergraduate students to be positively correlated with self-reported ratings of effectiveness. Third, Pearce and Sims (2002) found shared leadership to be a more useful predictor of change management team effectiveness than the leadership of

the appointed team leader. Fourth, Pearce, Yoo, and Alavi (in press), in a study of virtual teams, found shared leadership to be a more useful predictor of team dynamics and perceived effectiveness than vertical leadership. Nonetheless, very few empirical studies of shared leadership have appeared in the literature. Thus, we can confidently state the field is clearly still in its infancy.

One thing that is clear is that shared leadership will not merely be another blip on the radar screen of organizational science. Its time has arrived.

References

Aldag, R. J., & Fuller, S. R. (1993). Beyond fiasco: A reappraisal of the groupthink phenomenon and a new model of group decision processes. *Psychological Bulletin, 113(3),* 533–552.

Avolio, B. J., Jung, D., Murry, W., & Sivasubramaniam, N. (1996). Building highly developed teams: Focusing on shared leadership process, efficacy, trust, and performance. In M. M. Beyerlein, D. A. Johnson, & S. T. Beyerlein (Eds.), *Advances in interdisciplinary studies of work teams* (pp. 173–209). Greenwich, CT: JAI Press.

Barnard, C. I. (1938). *The functions of the executive.* Cambridge, MA: Harvard University Press.

Bartol, K. M., & Martin, D. C. (1986). Women and men in task groups. In R. D. Ashmore & F. K. Del Boca (Eds.), *The social psychology of female-male relations* (pp. 259–310). New York: Academic Press.

Bass, B. M., & Avolio, B. J. (1993). Transformational leadership: A response to critiques. In J. G. Hunt, B. R. Baliga, H. P. Dachler, & C. A. Schriesheim (Eds.), *Emerging leadership vistas* (pp. 29–40). Lexington, MA: D. C. Heath.

Benne, K. D., & Sheats, P. (1948). Functional roles of group members. *Journal of Social Issues, 4,* 41–49.

Berger, J., Cohen, B. P., & Zelditch, M. (1972). Status characteristics and social interaction. *American Sociological Review, 37,* 241–255.

Berscheid, E. (1985). Interpersonal attraction. In G. Lindzey & E. Aronson (Eds.), *Handbook of social psychology* (3rd ed., Vol. 2, pp. 413–484). New York: Random House.

Blau, J. R., & Alba, R. D. (1982). Empowering nets of participation. *Administrative Science Quarterly, 27,* 363–379.

Bowers, D. G., & Seashore, S. E. (1966). Predicting organizational effectiveness with a four factor theory of leadership. *Administrative Science Quarterly, 11,* 238–263.

Byrne, D., Ervin, C. R., & Lamberth, J. (1970). Continuity between the experimental study of attraction and real-life computer dating. *Journal of Personality and Social Psychology, 16*, 157–165.

Campbell, J. M., & Kinion, S. (1993). Teaching leadership/followership to RN-to-MSN students. *Journal of Nursing Education, 32*(3), 138–140.

Cannon-Bowers, J. A., Salas, E., & Converse, S. (1993). Shared mental models in expert team decision making. In N. J. Castellan Jr. (Ed.), *Individual and group decision making* (pp. 221–243). Hillside, NJ: Erlbaum.

Chandler, A. D., Jr., (Ed.). (1965). *The railroads: The nation's first big business, sources and readings.* New York: Harcourt Brace Jovanovich.

Conger, J. A., & Kanungo, R. N. (1988). The empowerment process: Integrating theory and practice. *The Academy of Management Review, 13*, 639–652.

Conger, J. A., & Kanungo, R. N. (1998). *Charismatic leadership in organizations.* Thousand Oaks, CA: Sage.

Cooper, A. E., Higgott, R. A., & Nossal, K. R. (1991). Bound to follow? Leadership and followership in the gulf conflict. *Political Science Quarterly, 106*(3), 391–410.

Cox, J. F., Pearce, C. L., & Sims, H. P., Jr. (in press). Toward a broader agenda for leadership development: Extending the transactional-transformational duality by development directive, empowering and shared leadership skills. In R. E. Riggio & S. Murphy (Eds.), *The Future of Leadership Development.* Mahwah, NJ: Lawrence Erlbaum.

Drucker, P. F. (1954). *The practice of management.* New York: Harper.

Drucker, P. F. (1995). *Management in a time of great change.* New York: Penguin Putnam.

Drucker, P. F. (2001). *The essential Drucker.* New York: Harper Collins.

Ensley, M. D., & Pearce, C. L. (2001). Shared cognition in top management teams: Implications for new venture performance. *Journal of Organizational Behavior, 22,* 145–160.

Ensley, M. D., Pearson, A., & Pearce, C. L. (in press). Top management team process, shared leadership and new venture performance: A theoretical model and research agenda. *Human Resource Management Review.*

Erez, M., & Arad, R. (1986). Participative goal-setting: Social, motivational, and cognitive factors. *Journal of Applied Psychology, 71,* 591–597.

Fayol, H. (1916/1949). *Administration industrielle et generale.* Storrs, London: Sir Isaac Pitman and Sons.

Festinger, L. (1954). A theory of social comparison processes. *Human Relations, 7,* 117–140.

Follett, M. P. (1924). *Creative experience.* New York: Longmans Green.

Gantt, H. L. (1916). *Industrial leadership.* New Haven, CT: Yale University Press.

Gilbreth, F. B. (1912). *Primer of scientific management.* New York: Van Nostrand Reinhold.

Gilbreth, F. B., & Gilbreth, L. M. (1917). *Applied motion study.* New York: Sturgis & Walton Co.

Graen, G. B. (1976). Role making processes within complex organizations. In M. D. Dunnette (Ed.), *Handbook of industrial and organizational psychology* (pp. 1201–1245). Chicago: Rand McNally.

Graen, G. B., & Scandura, T. A. (1987). Toward a psychology of dyadic organizing. In L. L. Cummings & B. M. Staw (Eds.), *Research in organizational behavior* (pp. 175–208). Greenwich, CT: JAI Press.

Graen, G. B., & Schiemann, W. (1978). Leader-member agreement: A vertical dyad linkage approach. *Journal of Applied Psychology, 63,* 206–212.

Greene, L. R., Morrison, T. L., & Tischler, N. G. (1981). Gender and authority: Effects on perceptions of small group co-leaders. *Small Group Behavior, 12*(4), 401–413.

Hennan, D.A., & Bennis, W. (1999). *Co-leadership: The power of great partnerships.* New York: Wiley.

Herzog, J. (1981). Communication between co-leaders: Fact or myth: A student's perspective. *Social Work with Groups,* 3(4), 19–29.

Hollander, E. P. (1961). Some effects of perceived status on responses to innovative behavior. *Journal of Abnormal and Social Psychology, 63,* 247–250.

Hollander, E. P. (1978). *Leadership dynamics: A practical guide to effective relationships.* New York: Free Press.

Hollenbeck, J. R., Ilgen, D. R., & Sego, D. J. (1994). Repeated measures regression and mediational tests: Enhancing the power of leadership research. *Leadership Quarterly,* 5, 3–23.

Homans, G. C. (1958). Social behavior as exchange. *American Journal of Sociology, 63,* 597–606.

Kelly, R. E. (1988). In praise of followers. *Harvard Business Review,* 66(6), 141–148.

Kerr, S., & Jermier, J. (1978). Substitutes for leadership: Their meaning and measurement. *Organizational Behavior and Human Performance, 22,* 374–403.

Klimoski, R., & Mohammed, S. (1994). Team mental model: Construct or metaphor. *Journal of Management, 20,* 403–437.

Knight, D., Pearce, C. L., Smith, K. G., Sims, H. P., Jr., Olian, J. D., Smith, K. A., et al. (1999). Top management team diversity, group dynamics, and strategic consensus:

An empirical investigation. *Strategic Management Journal, 20*(5), 445–466.

Lipman-Blumen, J. (1996). *The connective edge.* San Francisco: Jossey-Bass.

Locke, E. A., & Latham, G. P. (1990). *A theory of goal setting and task performance.* Englewood Cliffs, NJ: Prentice Hall.

Lundin, S. C., & Lancaster, L. C. (1990, May–June). Beyond leadership: The importance of followership. *The Futurist,* 19–22.

Manz, C. C. (1986). Self-leadership: Toward an expanded theory of self-influence processes in organizations. *Academy of Management Review, 11,* 585–600.

Manz, C. C., Keating, D., & Donnellon, A. (1990). Preparing for organizational changes in employee self management: The managerial transition. *Organizational Dynamics, 19,* 15–26.

Manz, C. C., & Sims, H. P., Jr. (1980). Self-management as a substitute for leadership: A social learning perspective. *Academy of Management Review, 5,* 361–367.

Manz, C. C., & Sims, H. P., Jr. (1987, March). Leading workers to lead themselves: The external leadership of self-managing work teams. *Administrative Science Quarterly, 32,* 106–128.

Manz, C. C., & Sims, H. P., Jr. (1989). *Super leadership: Leading others to lead themselves.* New York: Prentice Hall.

Manz, C. C., & Sims, H. P., Jr. (1990). *Superleadership: Leading others to lead themselves.* New York: Berkley Books.

Manz, C. C., & Sims, H. P., Jr. (1993). *Businesses without bosses: How self-managing teams are building high performance companies.* New York: Wiley.

Manz, C. C., & Sims, H. P., Jr. (2001). *The new superleadership: Leading others to lead themselves.* San Francisco: Berrett Koehler.

Mayo, E. (1933). *The human problems of an industrial civilization.* New York: Macmillan.

Mintz, E. (1963). Special value of co-therapists in group psychotherapy. *International Journal of Group Psychotherapy, 13,* 127–32.

Mohrman, S. A., Cohen, S. G., & Mohrman, A. M. (1995). *Designing team-based organizations: New forms for knowledge work.* San Francisco: Jossey-Bass.

Montgomery, J. (1840). *The cotton manufacture of the United States of America contrasted and compared with that of Great Britain* (p. 138). London: John N. Van.

Nakamura, R. T. (1980). Beyond purism and professionalism: Styles of convention delegate followership. *American Journal of Political Science, 24*(2), 207–232.

Newcomb, T. M. (1960). Varieties of inter-personal attraction. In D. Cartwright & A. Zander (Eds.), *Groupdynamics: Research and theory* (2nd ed., pp. 104–119). Evanston, IL: Row, Peterson.

Nishigaki, S., Vavrin, J., Kano, N., Haga, T., Kunz, J., & Law, K. (1994). Humanware, human error, and hiyari-hat: A template of unsafe symptoms. *Journal of Construction Engineering and Management, 120*(2), 421–432.

Pearce, C. L. (1997). The determinants of change management team effectiveness: A longitudinal investigation. Unpublished doctoral dissertation, University of Maryland.

Pearce, C. L. (2002). *Mas allá del liderazco heroico: Como el buen vino, el liderazco es algo para ser compartido.* Revista de empresa.

Pearce, C. L., Perry, M. L., & Sims, H. P., Jr. (2001). Shared leadership: Relationship management to improve NPO effectiveness. In T. D. Connors (Ed.), *The nonprofit handbook: Management* (pp. 624–641). New York: Wiley.

Pearce, C. L., & Sims, H. P., Jr. (2000). Shared leadership: Toward a multi-level theory of leadership. In M. M. Beyerlein, D. A. Johnson, & S. T. Beyerlein (Eds.), *Advances in interdisciplinary studies of work teams* (pp. 115–139). Greenwich, CT: JAI Press.

Pearce, C. L., & Sims, H. P., Jr. (2002). The relative influence of vertical vs. shared leadership on the longitudinal effectiveness of change management teams. *Group Dynamics: Theory, Research, and Practice, 6*(2), 172–197.

Pearce, C. L., Yoo, Y., & Alavi, M. (in press). Leadership, social work and virtual teams: The relative influence of vertical vs. shared leadership in the nonprofit section. In R. E. Riggio & S. Smith Orr (Eds.), *Nonprofit leadership.* San Francisco: Jossey-Bass.

Perry, M. L., Pearce, C. L., & Sims, H. P., Jr. (1999). Empowered selling teams: How shared leadership can contribute to selling team outcomes. *Journal of Personal Selling and Sales Management, 19,* 33–52.

Resnick, L. A. (1991). Shared cognition: Thinking as social practice. In L. B. Resnick, J. M. Levine, & S. D. Teasley (Eds.), *Perspectives on socially shared cognition* (pp. 1–19). Washington, DC: American Psychological Association.

Rippy, K. M. (1990, September). Effective followership. *The Police Chief,* 22–24.

Rittner, B., & Hammons, K. (1992). Telephone group work with people with end stage AIDS. *Social Work With Groups, 15*(4), 59–72.

Roethlisberger, F. J., & Dickson, W. J. (1939). *Management and the worker.* Cambridge, MA: Harvard University Press.

Say, J. B. (1803/1964). *A treatise on political economy* (pp. 330–331). New York: Augustus M. Kelley.

Seers, A. (1989). Team-member exchange quality: A new construct for role-making research. *Organizational Behavior and Human Decision Processes, 43,* 118–135.

Seers, A. (1996). Better leadership through chemistry: Toward a model of shared team leadership. In M. Beyerlein (Ed.), *Advances in interdisciplinary studies of work teams* (pp. 145–172). Greenwich, CT: JAI Press.

Smith, R. (1991, October/November). Principals need to be good followers. *High School Journal,* 24–27.

Smith, W. (1994). Followership: The art of working together. *Principal,* 74(2), 22–24.

Solomon, A., Loeffer, F. J., & Frank, G. H. (1953). An analysis of co-therapist interaction in group psychotherapy. *International Journal of Group Psychotherapy, 3,* 171–180.

Stein, R. T., & Heller, T. (1979). An empirical analysis of the correlations between leadership status and participation rates reported in the literature. *Journal of Personality and Social Psychology, 37,* 1993–2002.

Stewart, G. L., & Manz, C. C. (1995). Leadership for self-managing work teams: A typology and integrative model. *Human Relations, 48,* 347–370.

Taylor, F. W. (1903). *Shop management.* New York: Harper & Row.

Taylor, F. W. (1911). *Principles of scientific management.* New York: Harper & Brothers.

Thibaut, J., & Kelley, H. H. (1959). *The social psychology of groups.* New York: Wiley.

Turner, C. E. (1933, June). Test room studies in employee effectiveness. *American Journal of Public Health, 23,* 577–584.

Vroom, V. H., & Yetton, P. W. (1973). *Leadership and decision-making* (Rev. ed.). New York: Wiley.

Weber, M. (1905/1958). *The Protestant ethic and the spirit of capitalism.* New York: Scribner's.

Weber, M. (1924/1947). *The theory of social and economic organization.* (T. Parsons, Trans.). New York: Free Press.

Winter, S. (1976). Developmental stages in the roles and concerns of group co-leaders. *Small Group Behavior, 7*(3), 349–362.

Wren, D. A. (1994). *The evolution of management thought* (4th ed.). New York: John Wiley.

CHAPTER 13

Followership

Robert E. Kelley

Carnegie Mellon

The concept of followership and its relationship to leadership was popularized by the business professor and management consultant Robert Kelley in his 1988 *Harvard Business Review* article "In Praise of Followers" and his 1992 book *The Power of Followership*. These works thrust followership center stage into what had previously been a leader-centric world.

Definition

Followership is active engagement in helping an organization or a cause succeed while exercising independent, critical judgment of goals, tasks, potential problems, and methods. In an organization, star followers have the ability to work cooperatively with a leader to accomplish goals even when there are personality or workplace differences. They are key players both in planning courses of action and in implementing them in the field. Followers as thus defined contrast sharply with the common negative stereotype of followers as passive sheep in need of a strong leader to motivate and direct them.

The word *follower* has its etymological roots in Old High German *follaziohan*, which meant "to assist, help, succor, or minister to." This parallels the Old High German root of *leader*, which meant "to undergo, suffer, or endure." In the original meaning, followers helped take care of leaders; the relationship between them appears to have been a symbiotic one between equals.

Over time, *follower* came to mean "to go or be full in number," as in a crowd. If someone, a leader perhaps, was issuing an edict, appearing in a public forum, or traveling a distance, the people in attendance were called followers. This did not denote any inferior standing; on the contrary, to be a follower was an honor. Christ chose his disciples, just as King Arthur chose the knights for his Round Table. In these cases, the follower gained prestige rather than lost it.

Only in the last hundred years or so have the terms *leader* and *follower* taken on their current connotations.

Source: From G. R. Goethals, G. J. Sorenson, and J. M. Burns (Eds.), *Encyclopedia of leadership* (pp. 504–513). Thousand Oaks, CA: Sage. © 2008 Sage Publications, Inc. Used by permission.

Kelley ascribed the "great person" leadership notion to the British philosopher Thomas Carlyle (1795–1881). He and other proponents of a leadership-centric world believe that leaders create or shape the events and institutions that define society. Without leaders, the (negative) status quo would continue until entropy pushed society into chaos.

As for the negative stereotype of the follower, it is attributed to social Darwinism. Survival of the fittest pits contenders against one another; to struggle and compete is natural, good, and right. The winners, by definition, are leaders; the losers are everyone else. For example, Kelley found that when he asks training seminar participants whether they would rather be a follower or a leader, most quickly choose leadership. The result is a hierarchical social topography, as if only leaders matter, while the remaining 90 to 99 percent of the world is inferior and not worth mapping.

And yet, that assessment makes no sense when one considers that followership and leadership are a dialectic. Just as there can be no front of an object without a back, there can be no leaders without followers and no followers without leaders. Each depends on the other for existence and meaning. They can never be independent. But unlike front and back, it is not always so easy to sort out who is leading and who is following.

Followership Styles

Just as there are different leadership styles, there are different followership styles. In Kelley's model, illustrated in Figure 13.1, followership style is determined by how one performs in two behavioral dimensions. The first is independent, critical thinking; the second is a ranking on an active-positive, passive-negative scale. Depending on a person's performance, he or she will fall into one of five separate styles of followership. Keep in mind that these labels categorize how one carries out the followership role, not one's personality traits. A person may use one followership style in one situation and different style in another.

Star Followers

These followers think for themselves and actively engage with the leader to make the organization a success. Star followers do not follow blindly, but when they disagree with the leader, they do so constructively, with the organization's best interest at heart. They carry out their assignments with great energy, paying attention to the implications current actions have for the future and to the details of implementation. Star followers are self-starters and creative problem solvers; they use their

---

Figure 13.1 Followership Styles

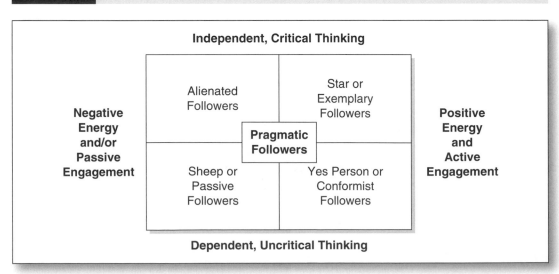

Source: Robert E. Kelley; used with permission.

talents for the benefit of the organization even when confronted with bureaucratic inanities or nonproducing colleagues. Because they have these qualities, they get consistently high ratings from peers as well as leaders.

Star followership brings enthusiasm, intelligence, and self-reliance to the implementation of an organizational goal, while less effective followers are more passive, withholding their best thinking or efforts. Star followers are those who can take on a project with minimal preparation. Leaders trust them enough to turn their attention elsewhere; they rely on star followers to do the job in the best way possible (even if it's not the way the leader originally had in mind). A leader who has a star follower on staff doesn't need to worry about hands-on supervision, time-consuming explanation of assignments, or being visited with problems along the way to implementation. Star followers are independent and responsible members of the team, and they recognize that they add as much value to the organization as anyone in upper management.

Alienated Followers

These followers are critical thinkers and very independent in relations with leaders, but they are passive or negative in the workplace. They have a personal dislike for leaders in the organization or they are unhappy with their work situation. Alienated followers are often cynical and skeptical. They tear down what the leader is trying to build up. Their energy is channeled into fighting against the leader or organization rather than toward their work or a mutually desired future.

Kelley found that many alienated followers begin as star followers. Some negative experience or event alienates them; they become angry and withdraw from those around them. Some see themselves as victims; others project themselves as the conscience of the group battling against unfair organizations, power-hungry leaders, mindless yes-followers, and stupid ideas. However, their negative attitudes and actions often create a cycle of resentment or retaliation that engenders further negativity.

Sheep, or Passive Followers

These followers are passive and rely on others to think for them. These people are often viewed as rudderless and mindless; they need to latch on to a leader. In the extreme, passive followers may have a herd instinct, like sheep. However, unlike sheep, passive followers can require substantial motivation and direction from their leader.

Yes-People, or Conformist Followers

These followers are also in the negative section of the critical-thinking chart. They are more enthusiastic and involved than their sheep coworkers, but they are aggressively dependent on leaders for direction. They will do whatever the leader says, but they need the leader to say it.

Yes-followers are all too eager to take orders, to defer to the leader's authority, and to yield to the leader's views or judgment. They assume that the leader's position of power entitles her or him to obedience and accommodation from the subordinate. Yes-followers know their place and do not question the social order. They find comfort in structure and in having someone above them. This can create a follower-leader dynamic in which followers tell leaders what they want to hear, not what they need to know. Although in some cultures (both outside of and within the United States), this style of followership is emphasized, expected, and rewarded, it has led to many fiascoes when the followers give up their capacity for independent, critical thinking.

Pragmatic Followers

In the center of Figure 13.1 are the pragmatic followers. Sometimes these are capable subordinates who eschew their independence for political expediency. Sometimes they are system bureaucrats who carry out directives to the letter, even though they might have valuable ideas for improving them. Sometimes they are gamespeople who manipulate others and the system to their benefit. They avoid taking a strong position that crosses powerful people. They are constantly monitoring the wind direction, and their motto is "better safe than sorry." They keep conflict to a minimum and always have a ready excuse with a corresponding paper trail for any failure. They manage to survive even the most sweeping changes in the workplace.

Choosing Followership: The Various Paths

Why would anyone of perseverance, spirit, and intelligence slow a career before reaching the top or choose not to strive for the top in the first place? How did Aristotle (384–322 BCE) choose to follow Plato (c. 428–348 BCE)? What led Ellen Gates Starr (1859–1940) to follow the social reformer Jane Addams (1860–1935) in the establishment of Hull House, an internationally recognized achievement as a settlement center for Chicago's poor immigrants?

FRANCIS BACON ON FOLLOWERS

In this excerpt from his essay "Of Followers and Friends"—written in the late sixteenth century—Francis Bacon alerts his readers to be watchful of certain types of followers.

Costly *Followers* are not to be liked; Lest while a Man maketh his Traine Longer, hee make his Wings Shorter. I reckon to bee Costly, not them alone, which charge the Purse, but which are Wearisome and Importune in Sutes. Ordinary *Followers* ought to challenge no Higher Conditions, then Countenance, Recommendation, and Protection from Wrongs. Factious *Followers* are worse to be liked, which Follow not upon Affection to him, with whom they range Themselves, but upon Discontentment Conceived against some Other: Whereupon commonly ensueth, that Ill Intelligence, that we many times see betweene Great Personages. Likewise Glorious *Followers,* who make themselves as Trumpets, of the Commendation of those they Follow, are full of Inconvenience; For they taint Businesse through Want of Secrecie; And they Export Honour from a Man, and make him a Returne in Envie. There is a Kinde of *Followers* likewise, which are Dangerous, being indeed Espials; which enquire the Secrets of the House, and beare Tales of them to Others. Yet such Men, many times, are in great Favour; For they are Officious, And commonly Exchange Tales. The *Following* be certaine *Estates* of *Men,* answerable to that, which a Great Person himselfe professeth, (as of Soldiers to him that hath been employed in the Warres, and the like,) hath ever beene a Thing Civill, and well taken even in Monarchies; So it be without too much Pompe or Popularitie. But the most Honourable Kinde of *Following,* is to be Followed, as one that apprehendeth, o advance Vertue and Desert in all Sorts of Persons. And yet, where there is no Eminent Odds in Sufficiencie, it is better to take with the more Passable, then with the more Able. And besides, to speake Truth, in Base Times, Active Men are of more use, then Vertuous. It is true, that in Government, it is Good to use Men of one Rancke equally: for to countenance some extraordinarily, is to make them Insolent, and the rest Discontent; Because they may claime a Due. But contrariwise in Favour, to use Men with much Difference and Election, is Good; For it maketh the Persons Preferred more Thankfull, and the Rest more officious; Because all is of Favour. It is good Discretion, not to make too much of any Man, at the first; Because One cannot hold out that Proportion. To be governed (as we call it) by One, is not safe: For it shewes Softnesse, and gives a Freedom to Scandall and Disreputation: For those that would not Censure, or Speake ill of a Man immediately, will talke more boldly of Those; that are so great with them, and thereby Wound their Honour. Yet to be Distracted with many is Worse; For it makes Men, to be of the Last Impression, and full of Change. To take Advice of some few Frends is ever Honourable; *For Lookers on, many times, see more than Gamesters;*

And the Vale best discovereth the Hill. There is Little Frendship in the World, and Least of all betweene Equals, which was wont to be Magnified. That that is, is between Superiour and Inferiour, whose Fortunes may Comprehend, the One the Other.

Source: Bacon, Francis. (1907). "Of Followers and Friends." In W. Aldiss Wright (Ed.), *Bacon's Essays.* London: Macmillan and Co., pp. 198–200.

Understanding why people follow is important to leaders and followers alike. Knowing these motivations, one can design organizational environments to attract, accommodate, and retain followers. Leaders who understand their followers' motivations can respond to those motivations and avoid losing their followers.

Misunderstanding motivations can lead to disaster even when leaders have good intentions. For example, too many leaders believe that people follow a leader because of his or her charisma or vision. Thus, leaders will often expend great effort in trying to become charismatic or in shaping a vision. In reality, only some followers look for these characteristics. Others are motivated by their own personal vision, and many are wary of charisma. Instead, they prefer their leaders to be fellow adventurers who facilitate the achievement of a goal.

Why do people decide to forgo the leadership role? The followership paths people choose are characterized by different sets of motivations. As shown in Figure 13.2, a follower chooses one based on his or preferences on two points: first, whether the follower prefers self-expression or self-transformation, and second, whether the follower puts more emphasis on relationship bonding or on personal goals.

Followers choose certain followership paths in order to express themselves. Individuals who choose these courses are generally comfortable with their talents, lifestyle, and personal accomplishments. They are motivated by a desire to contribute their skills toward organizational goals.

Other paths help followers transform themselves. People who choose these routes are not satisfied with who they are; they want to become different and better people. For example, G. I. Gurdjieff (c. 1872–1949), the Russian philosopher and teacher, kept himself open to new ideas and belief systems so that he could continually transform himself. He traveled throughout Asia and Europe in search of teachers from whom he could learn, viewing rebirth as an essential part of living that should happen continually rather than as a onetime event.

Some followers appreciate the interpersonal involvement of followership. People who value these bonds follow people rather than goals or dreams. Others are more inwardly focused; they see followership not primarily as a relationship with others, but as a vehicle for achieving personal dreams. Many of the early NASA engineers worked together for ten years to put a person on the moon. But the goal, not their relationships with the leader, motivated them to follow.

Based on these two pairs of dimensions, seven major followership paths emerge: The apprentice's path, the disciple's path, the mentee's path, the comrade's path, the path of loyalty, the dreamer's path, and the lifeway path. Each person is likely to follow one or more of these paths during life; indeed, a person can travel down some of them simultaneously. The paths are not mutually exclusive.

The Apprentice's Path

Perhaps the most easily identified path is the one chosen by those aspiring to be leaders. They understand the need to learn the ropes and pay their dues. By proving themselves in the follower's role, they hope to win the confidence of peers and superiors. They accept the value of doing a good job in the role, studying leadership from the followers' perspective, and polishing followership skills, such as teamwork and self-management, that will always stand them in good stead. Many women residents of Jane Addams's Hull House, for example, saw Hull House as a community center where they could learn the professional skills necessary to launch careers in government, industry, and universities.

Figure 13.2   The Seven Paths of Followership

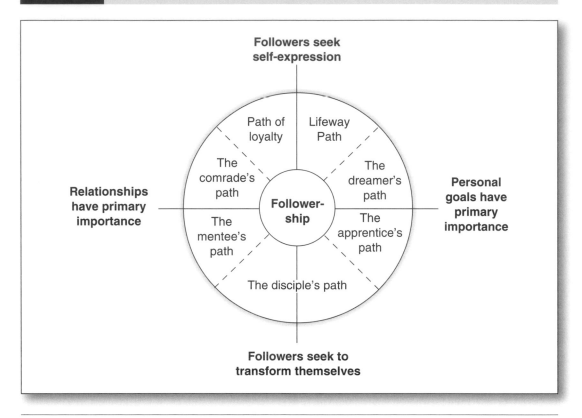

Source: Robert E. Kelley; used with permission.

In his *Politics,* Aristotle observed that Greece's would-be leaders, like many graduating students today, wanted to start at the top rather than work their way up. Decrying their power lust, Aristotle insisted that training as a nonleader was a necessary part of growing to leadership. He advised those who wanted to lead to learn first how to obey and to experience being a subject before becoming a ruler. In fact, most large bureaucracies treat followership as apprenticeship. In China's civil service, which dates back to the Han dynasty (206 BCE–220 CE), the candidate's ascent to leadership depended upon their performance in lower ranks. China's civil-service system became a model for other large bureaucracies that would follow it in history, indirectly influencing the U.S. military, where future leaders must spend time in the ranks, learning what it is like to be directed and commanded, before they are allowed to issue their own orders.

The Disciple's Path

Discipleship is seldom discussed in today's secular world, except when celebrity cults spill across the media headlines or religious fanaticism results in political fiascoes (as when the confrontation between the U. S. government and the Branch Davidian religious group in 1993 in Waco, Texas, resulted in the deaths of eighty-two Davidians). Nowadays associated almost exclusively with religion, discipleship conjures up images of crowds gathered at a master's feet, hanging on every word. Yet some remarkable followers in the secular world began as disciples. For example, having read Plato's dialogues, the seventeen-year-old Aristotle left his hometown for Athens to study in Plato's Academy. For the next twenty formative years, Aristotle worked and studied with a brilliant group of disciples under Plato's leadership.

> *Never follow the crowd.*
>
> —Bernard Baruch

The word *disciple* comes from the Greek. Its original meaning was "one who is learning from a teacher." Generally, it involved intellectual, not emotional or spiritual, development. Nor did it involve indoctrination in any set of beliefs. Although Aristotle clearly loved and was greatly influenced by Plato, he felt free to criticize him, and did.

Over time, discipleship took on another dimension. It moved beyond learning to mean "one who believes." It implies an act of conversion to a certain viewpoint. This conversion moves beyond intellectual judgment to an emotional commitment and obedience, where one breaks old ties and adheres exclusively to the new. It also leads to witnessing—that is, spreading to others what has been learned.

Although discipleship is generally placed in the context of religion, it permeates many fields. For example, Sigmund Freud (1856–1939) attracted disciples to his psychoanalytic theories and practices, and disciples of John Maynard Keynes (1883–1946), a champion of social welfare economics, argue with the disciples of Milton Friedman (b. 1912), a proponent of free-market economics. Disciples often represent the leader, serving as missionaries who carry the message to others.

The psychology behind this form of followership is identification. Followers want to bond with and emulate the leader. They are willing to become a part of something that is bigger, better, or more important than they are individually. Disciples give up their current persona to take on a new one—one that the followers feel enlarges them.

The Mentee's Path

Mentoring is different from apprenticing in that it involves an intensive one-on-one relationship between mentor and follower, which enables the follower to mature. Mentees entrust themselves, emotionally and developmentally, to someone who perhaps perceives them as a "diamond in the rough." The mentor helps shape the diamond so that it sparkles. The mentor in this case often directs the mentee's talents toward goals that will bring him or her great satisfaction.

The psychological readiness of an individual to benefit from this form of followership depends upon the individual's ability to surrender to the mentor's influence. Often, some experience in life—the death of a loved one, getting fired from a job—triggers this readiness.

Like apprentices, mentees choose to be followers so that they can transform themselves. Whereas the goal of apprenticeship is mastery of skills, however, the goal of mentoring is personal maturation. People who follow a mentor do so for personal benefit. But the followers who seek out mentors are not always trying to become leaders. They may simply see the mentoring relationship as a way of bettering themselves. Mentees hope to be better people, which will then allow them to be better contributors.

The Comrade's Path

Sometimes being part of a community shapes followership. The reason for following may have nothing to do with getting ahead, personal growth, or intellectual development. Instead, it may be about the intimacy and social support that develop when people bond.

Comradeship is found in any endeavor that requires the effort and talents of more than one person, whether sports, orchestral performances, or the construction of a supercomputer. People also band together as a way of coping with stress. The bonds formed in study groups that help members get through the first year of law school last long after graduation. In these situations, people follow for mutually reinforcing reasons: your feeling of good-will toward the group and the belief that survival is more likely if you collectively share and watch out for one another.

Nor is comradeship forged only during stressful times. Sometimes it happens when people are working together for a good cause. For example, Jane Addams, Julia Lathrop (1858–1932), and Florence Kelley (1859–1932) formed the inner circle of Hull House during the early years. Unlike the disciples and apprentices who gathered around Addams, Lathrop and Kelley were comrades-in-arms. They addressed each other in their letters as "Dear Sister" and developed a sense of camaraderie, of dedication to an ideal that was based on respect, commitment, and love.

The psychology behind comradeship is one of intimacy that comes from belonging. Once you feel part of something, you transcend feelings of isolation and even feelings of self. This explains why people follow rather than seek personal glory, and why they give their all so that their comrades can succeed.

The Path of Loyalty

Some people follow out of personal loyalty to the leader. Leonard Peikoff (b. 1933), the protector of objectivism, the individualistic philosophy of Ayn Rand (1905–1982), proudly described himself as the "feudal serf" of Ayn Rand's cause.

For some, this loyalty is an inherent obligation of existence. Fierce loyalty was expected of Japan's samurai. In the code of Bushido—the "way of the warrior"—loyalty is of paramount importance. Chinese Confucian ethics made obedience to parents the primary human duty, but Japanese Bushido gave precedence to loyalty to the leader.

The path of loyalty, like that of comradeship, requires emotional commitment to another. Deep within, you choose to follow this leader. You give your word. Unlike comradeship, the bond is one to one—follower to leader. Unlike in mentoring relationships, the follower motivated by loyalty is not concerned with personal maturation. The primary characteristic of the path of loyalty is commitment, willingly given and unshakable from the outside. Only the two people can tear it asunder.

The Dreamer's Path

Many of the best followers are committed to their personal dream rather than to a particular leader. They are so focused on achieving their dream that it does not matter whether they are in the leader or follower role. These people may follow a leader not because of who the leader is but because the leader embodies the idea or the cause. David Newell, a longtime follower of Fred Rogers,

the creator of the children's television program *Mister Rogers' Neighborhood,* summarized the reason that he and others there followed.

"Most people think we're in the TV business. But we're not. We're in the child development business. Our goal is to help children and families grow. Everything we do has the message at its core. That's what has kept me here for so long. If Fred or this organization ever moved away from these, then that's when I'd probably leave" (Kelley, 1992, 75). This follower is interested in the message first and the leader second. The dream is the guiding force.

William Broyles describes how, during the Vietnam War, the Viet Cong saw the war with the United States as the transcendent challenge. In their mind, they were fighting for a great goal, one worth dying for. They had traded in the rice paddy and were riding on the wind of history.

When people follow because of their dream, the psychology is called internalization. Followership occurs because individual goals are the same as the organization's or leader's goal. In other words, follower and leader believe in the same thing and want to make the same things happen. These followers control their ego drives and accept another's authority in their overriding desire to accomplish the goal. However, when the bond created by the dream withers, these people cease to play the follower role and the leader has no power over them.

The Lifeway Path

A final type of followership is taken by those who follow out of a conviction that no other lifeway is as rewarding. These people follow out of personal preference or because followership is compatible with their personal make-up. For example, they may be inherently altruistic or naturally skilled at following. Or, the follower role may be most consistent with their outlook on life.

For some, following is a way of serving, harking back to the original definition of the word follower. Unlike followers who are pursuing a particular dream, these followers make helping others their goal. Today's Peace Corps volunteers, who are trying to be of service to their Third World neighbors, are examples of the latter; their predecessors, who were following the dream articulated by John F. Kennedy, were examples of the former. Of course, someone could have a dream of having a lifeway of followership, but for the most part, these are different paths. Kelley has related this "servant followership" to "servant leadership," as described by Robert Greenleaf (1904–1990), the founder of the Center for Applied Ethics (now the Greenleaf Center for Servant-Leadership).

Others consciously decide that they are better suited to play the follower role all or part of the time. They are uncomfortable being leaders. They don't like being the one that everyone looks to for a vision, for inspiration, or for the final judgment. Being Number Two suits them much better that being Number One. It is the doing, not the directing, that they enjoy.

An intriguing subset of lifeway followers are those who have leadership instincts and skills but choose the follower role in certain circumstances. They may be leaders in other fields who do not have the time or emotional energy to take on a new leadership role but who still want to contribute. Some are leaders who know how important star followership is to them, and so they return the favor when they follow. In some cases their leadership talents are simply not suited to a particular situation, as when a corporate leader feels out of place in government meetings. These individuals are followers because they have rationally decided that following is what they want to do. They realize that they will be happier and the outcome will be more positive if they complement rather than compete with the leader.

External Factors Affecting Followership

As described above, followership style is highly affected by personal motivation and skill set. However, at least three external factors also come into play: leadership styles, rewards, and culture.

Leadership Styles

When the political theorist Bertrand de Jouvenal (1903–1987) said that a nation of sheep will bring about a government of wolves, he expressed dramatically how leadership and followership styles interact with each other, with cause and effect going in both directions. Autocratic leaders direct their followers without consulting them. They give orders that are not to be questioned, only implemented. Autocratic leaders are most likely to attract or encourage those followership styles that look to the leader for thinking and guidance, namely, the yes-people and the sheep. Likewise, those types of followers will either search for or elicit autocratic leadership. In essence, they demand it, even if the leader might prefer a different leadership style.

In a similar way, leaders can interact with the follower's chosen path. For example, appeal to those followers seeking transformation, such as those following the disciple's, the mentee's, or the apprentice's paths. If followers and leaders understand each other's styles and motivations, then they are more likely to understand their own behavior and more likely to pair off correctly.

Rewards

Followers, like leaders, respond to rewards. If yes follower behavior is expected by the leader and rewarded by the organization, then people are likely to fulfill the followership role using that style. It is not unusual for organizations undergoing difficult economic times to lay people off. In the face of this economic uncertainty and sense of betrayal by the organization—essentially the removal of rewards—many followers migrate to the pragmatic style.

Culture

The terms *follower* and *leader* carry strong cultural connotations. Various cultures view them differently and have different expectations for them. In the United States, leadership is considered better than followership. The U.S. culture encourages leadership development from a very early age, and sends negative signals about followership. In other countries, such as Japan, followership is strongly reinforced, while leadership is given less societal weight.

Ethics of Followership: Courageous Conscience

In the traditional leader-follower dynamic, the leader makes the decisions and sets the ethical framework for the group, while the follower is expected to do as told. But that is not how it works with the best followers. Instead, star followers spend considerable time and effort worrying about the ethics of their actions.

In some cases, leaders are forced to choose from among a series of bad options. Or, they are forced to make their decisions under enormous pressures that followers don't have. In such situations, ethics is seen as just one of many factors that must be considered in the final decision; it may get short shrift. But that is precisely why conscience is included in the range of skills that make up star followership. Even though there are times when it can be very inconvenient, leaders need their star followers to act as ethical watchdogs. The organization's future can depend on how effectively followers heed their consciences.

Star followers exhibit courageous conscience. Having courageous conscience means they have the ability to judge right from wrong and the fortitude to take steps toward what they believes is right. It involves both conviction and action, often in the face of strong pressures to abstain from acting.

Some followers are faced with a leader who asks them to do something they believe is wrong or to stop doing something they believe is good for the organization. In most cases the request will not be extreme; it will not jeopardize people's lives or constitute a gross legal violation in which millions of dollars are at stake. Rather, it will be something more ordinary, like altering a time sheet, withholding relevant information from another department in the company, padding a customer's bill, or producing products that have not been thoroughly tested for safety. Or they may have been working on a product to which they were personally committed, only to have the boss kill the project and reassign them to something else.

Under these circumstances, the best followers follow the dictates of their courageous conscience. When people talk about ethical conduct, they first think of one side of the ethical coin—avoiding or correcting existing wrongs.

So, when the boss asks subordinates to do something unethical, star followers take steps to help the leader see that it is wrong or, failing that, will refuse to carry out the order. But the courageous conscience goes beyond acknowledging and correcting wrong. The flip side motivates them to make positive contributions—for example, championing a new idea in the face of strong organizational resistance, dealing with a problem before it grows into a crisis, or arguing for the reinstatement of a worthy program that has been cut. Their courageous conscience may put their position at risk, but it is risk required of star followers.

The Changing Context of Followership

In 1977 a review of literature on followership turned up only three articles on the topic. In 2003, a Google Internet search on the term *followership* produced 10,589 hits, and *followership research* produced 3,930 hits. While not all of these hits will be completely relevant to the topic, it is still clear that in a little over twenty-five years, the field has changed substantially. Followership is now considered an important part of the followership-leadership equation.

Further Reading

Broyles, W. (1986). *Brothers in arms: A journey from war to peace.* New York: Alfred A. Knopf.

Burns, J. M. (2003). *Transforming leadership.* New York: Atlantic Monthly Press.

Kelley, R. E. (1988, November-December). In praise of followers. *Harvard Business Review, 66* (6), 142–148.

Kelley, R. E. (1992). *The power of followership.* New York: Doubleday.

Kelley, R. E. (1999). *How to be a star at work.* New York: Random House.

Klein, E.B., Gabelnick, F., and Herr, P. (Eds.). (1998). *The psychodynamics of leadership.* (pp. 27–53). Madison, CT: Psychosocial Press.

Leadership and Followership Focus Group. (1997). *KLSP: The balance of leadership and followership.* College Park, MD: Academy of Leadership Press.

CHAPTER 14

Empowerment

Lynn Offermann

George Washington University

In organizational contexts, empowerment typically involves sharing of power, whereby a hierarchically superior leader gives some of the authority and decision-making latitude previously in his or her purview to one or more followers, thus expanding the follower's sphere of influence. Once "empowered," the follower can engage in decision making within the expanded boundaries without the need to check back with the leader for permission to act.

True empowerment increases the follower's sense of self-worth and provides personal fulfillment. Leaders can delegate without empowering, either by delegating only menial tasks that will produce no increment in the follower's sense of mastery or purpose, or by inappropriately giving tasks to followers who are not able to succeed at them. Research on psychological empowerment suggests that four key components determine whether people feel empowered: meaning (consistency with values or ideals; care about the work), self-determination (behavioral choice or autonomy), self-efficacy (self-confidence about one's ability to perform well on a task), and the belief in the prospect of significant impact on the work or organization. Although many leaders feel that it is their job to control, and resist empowering their staffs, research is accumulating on the value of leaders sharing power through the psychological empowerment of followers.

Why Should Leaders Share Power?

The ability to speed up certain processes by allowing decisions to be made at hierarchically lower levels can have some distinct advantages for staff, organizations, and leaders.

Greater education, capabilities, and expectations of staff. As the education levels of staff rise, options for empowerment increase. Research indicates that most leaders will not delegate to incompetent staff, nor would their organizations want them to. But many leadership theories have suggested that talented and motivated staff members do not require the same kinds of leadership guidance as unskilled and uninterested staff, and, in fact, respond negatively to too much leadership

Source: From G. R. Goethals, G. J. Sorenson, and J. M. Burns (Eds.), *Encyclopedia of leadership* (pp. 434–437). Thousand Oaks, CA: Sage. © 2008 Sage Publications, Inc. Used by permission.

structure as "micromanagement." Having professional staff substitutes for the need to have a structuring leader, and such staff often expect to be empowered to act within the bounds of their skills. Leaders who fail to empower skilled staff risk losing their talents, motivation, and commitment.

Increase in knowledge and service sector employment. As the U.S. economy increasingly depends on the expanding knowledge and service sectors, empowerment becomes even more vital. Knowledge and information demands require the involvement and commitment of all staff members, not just leaders. Service quality occurs at the point of service contact, where the customer or client interacts with staff. The inability of staff to satisfy customer demands promptly and without "checking with a manager" yields customer dissatisfaction and the potential loss of return business. Empowering staff within predetermined limits allows them maximum flexibility to provide a satisfying customer experience.

Freedom for the leader to focus on broader strategic issues rather than primarily day-to-day management. Although leaders are often wary of sharing power, in fact it is the primary way that they can expand their own ability to focus on how to really add value to their organizations. Freed from a myriad of time-consuming actions now under staff oversight, the leader can focus more on strategic vision, on new and creative business options and prospects, and on expanding their client base and profit margins. They must also focus on coaching and developing staff to succeed in their newly empowered roles.

Thus, for both leaders and staff, successful empowerment can result in increased motivation, satisfaction, and learning, while organizations benefit from increased flexibility, superior client service, and better job performance. Unfortunately, these benefits are not always realized in practice.

Why are Leaders Reluctant to Share Power?

Implementing empowerment initiatives has proved more difficult than many organizations expected.

Numerous organizational attempts at empowerment have failed because of a leader's unwillingness or inability to engage in appropriate empowering behaviors. Research suggests that one reason for this may be a self-enhancement bias: leaders have a higher regard for work that they control or in which they have high input, even if others see no quality difference with or without leader input. Further, when leaders exert more control, they attribute greater success to themselves than to staff, and may denigrate subordinates as incapable. This self-fulfilling prophecy of perceived staff failure then leads to increased leader resistance to empowering staff, since the leader fears that lower quality work may result.

Even leaders who sincerely want to develop and empower their subordinates may find it difficult to do so. Empowerment can change the entire leader–follower relationship from one of hierarchical superiority/inferiority to a more egalitarian relationship built on mutual trust and support. For leaders, there is an element of risk: If subordinates can do what the leader used to do, what then is the leader's role? Empowerment does not just change the follower's job, but it changes the leader's job as well. And unless leaders are confident about their own abilities to move forward into a new and expanded role, it is likely that they will continue to do what they know how to do—at least some of which should now be their subordinate's job.

Becoming an Empowering Leader

Delegation is often one of the hardest leadership behaviors to execute well. At one extreme, leaders are reluctant to give up influence to staff, and either fail to delegate meaningful work or interject themselves unnecessarily with staff for whom delegation is appropriate and desired. On the other extreme, some staff complain that "delegation" means desertion, where a project is dumped on them with little discussion of parameters or expectations before a leader completely removes him or herself from further involvement, even as a consultant or monitor. Neither extreme will produce feelings of psychological empowerment in followers. Effective empowerment requires an accurate assessment of staff capabilities and "growing" staff into positions of increasing responsibility. It means providing inspiring goals as well as needed resources and information, removing organizational constraints, encouraging participation in decision making, and rewarding staff initiative and accomplishment. Leadership becomes less about direction and control, and more about making full use of subordinate capabilities in service of organizational goals.

> *Give us the tools, and we will finish the job.*
>
> —Winston Churchill

Effective empowering leaders must learn new roles as visionaries, coaches, team builders, champions, and facilitators, to name a few. They need to determine the boundaries of staff autonomy, and work with staff over time to expand those boundaries as staff competence and confidence grows. Ideally, empowerment begins with top-level leaders, who model empowering behaviors for lower-level leaders and support leaders in their efforts to master empowering behaviors. Some companies have gone so far as to virtually mandate empowerment by expanding the leader's areas of responsibility to the point that the leader cannot succeed without delegating and empowering staff. In these situations, leaders either empower others or face personal exhaustion and ineffectiveness. Investing in training for empowered staff—including leaders—can be of significant value. Dealing with supervisory fear of job loss and clarifying new leader role expectations can help allay fear that empowering others means losing one's own job.

Cautions About Empowerment

Despite its attractions, empowerment is not for every subordinate. First of all, not everyone wants to be empowered; some people may be perfectly content to have others make all the decisions, and dislike taking on more responsibility. Unfortunately, some leaders seem to overestimate the number of such empowerment-averse staff, and underestimate the percentage of staff who would welcome additional challenge and responsibility in their jobs. Nonetheless, individuals need to be ready to be empowered, both in terms of their skills and

their motivation levels, and leaders need to ensure that important goals are being achieved in an ethical and effective manner. Part of an empowering leader's job is to develop staff to the point of their being able to assume increasing responsibility with the leader's confidence and support.

In order to effectively empower staff, the organizational system itself needs to embrace and support empowerment. Specifically, research suggests that empowerment is most appropriate for skilled professional staff with high needs for achievement, who work on complex and non-repetitive tasks, in decentralized, less formalized, more flexible organizations that emphasize individual learning and participation. The core values of the organization must be clear to all employees, whose empowered actions then operate within the bounds of those values. The relationship between leaders and their empowered staff needs to be characterized by mutual trust and respect in order for empowerment to grow and flourish.

Cultural differences need to be considered as well. Employee reactions to particular managerial or leadership practices, including empowerment, may vary depending on cultural background. In terms of empowerment, a recent study by Robert et al. (2000) predicted that empowerment would be a better fit in more egalitarian societies (low on the cultural dimension of power distance) than in societies in which unequal power for different members of society is both accepted and acceptable (high power-distance cultures). Since high power-distance societies endorse hierarchical structures and members expect decisions to be made by those in higher-level positions, empowerment in high power distance societies may be seen as weak leadership. The authors found that empowerment was negatively associated with job satisfaction only in the highest power-distance society studied, India, while positively associated with satisfaction in the United States, Mexico, and Poland. Although the mechanism needs further study, this and other cross-cultural research does support the contention that it is dangerous to assume that empowerment will always be seen as a good thing by all followers in all cultures.

Finally, there is an ethical issue surrounding what has been called bogus empowerment, where leaders promise more responsibility than they actually give staff. Past research on participative management has suggested that many leaders consider themselves to be more participative than their subordinates do. Bogus empowerment is quickly discerned by staff, with negative results. True empowerment requires the moral courage to change the power relationship that leaders have with followers, and an acknowledgment that empowerment does not necessarily mean agreement. And what a leader promises in terms of empowerment, he or she needs to be prepared to deliver.

Empowerment can result in new opportunities for both leaders and followers, as well as increased organizational productivity and satisfaction when it is used appropriately with staff who are ready for it, by leaders who truly embrace it and are willing to expand their own roles as well as those of their staffs. In learning to unleash the creative power of staff through empowerment, modern leaders can discover the wisdom of ancient Chinese philosopher Lao-Tzu (cited in Bynner 1976, p. 46): "But of a good leader who talks little, when his work is done, his aim fulfilled, they will all say, "We did this ourselves."

Further Reading

Alpander, G. G. (1991). Developing managers' ability to empower employees. *Journal of Management Development, 10,* 13–24.

Block, P. (1996). *Stewardship: Choosing service over self-interest.* San Francisco: Berrett-Kohler.

Bradley, G. L., & Sparks, B. A. (2000). Customer reactions to staff empowerment: Mediators and moderators. *Journal of Applied Social Psychology, 30,* 991–1012.

Bynner, W. (1976). *The way of life according to Lao Tsu.* New York: Berkeley Publishing Group.

Ciulla, J. B. (1996). Leadership and the problem of bogus empowerment. In *Ethics and leadership working papers* (pp. 43–67). College Park, MD: Academy of Leadership Press, University of Maryland.

Dess, G. G., & Picken, J. C. (2000). Changing roles: Leadership in the 21st century. *Organizational Dynamics, 28(3),* 18–34.

Howard, A. (1998). The empowering leader: Unrealized opportunities. In G. R. Hickman (Ed.), *Leading organizations: Perspectives for a new era* (pp. 202–213). Thousand Oaks, CA: Sage.

Kerr, S., & Jermier, J. M. (1978). Substitutes for leadership: Their meaning and measurement. *Organizational Behavior and Human Performance, 22,* 375–403.

Kirkman, B. L., & Shapiro, D. L. (2001). The impact of team members' cultural values on productivity, cooperation, and empowerment in self-managing work teams. *Journal of Cross-Cultural Psychology, 32,* 597–617.

Lawler, E. E., III (1992). *The ultimate advantage: Creating the high involvement organization.* San Francisco: Jossey-Bass.

Offermann, L. R. (1998). Leading and empowering diverse followers. In G. R. Hickman (Ed.), *Leading organizations: Perspectives for a new era* (pp. 397–403). Thousand Oaks, CA: Sage.

Pfeffer, J., Cialdini, R. B., Hanna, B., & Knopoff, K. (1998). Faith in supervision and the self-enhancement bias: Two psychological reasons why managers don't empower workers. *Basic and Applied Social Psychology, 20,* 313–321.

Robert, C., Probst, T. M., Martocchio, J. J., Drasgow, F., & Lawler, J. J. (2000). Empowerment and continuous improvement in the United States, Mexico, Poland, and India: Predicting fit on the basis of the dimensions of power distance and individualism. *Journal of Applied Psychology, 85,* 643–658.

Simons, R. (1995, March–April). Control in an age of empowerment. *Harvard Business Review,* 80–88.

Spreitzer, G. M. (1997). Toward a common ground in defining empowerment. *Research in Organizational Change and Development, 10,* 31–62.

Stewart, G. L., & Manz, C. C. (1997). Understanding and overcoming supervisor resistance during the transition to employee empowerment. *Research in Organizational Change and Development, 10,* 169–196.

CHAPTER 15

Leadership and the Problem of Bogus Empowerment

Joanne B. Ciulla

University of Richmond

Empowerment conjures up pictures of inspired and confident people or groups of people who are ready and able to take control of their lives and better their world. The empowered are the neighbors in a community who band together and take action to drive out drug dealers; the longtime welfare mother who gets a job and goes on to start a business; the child who learns to read and to ride a bike. Power is a relationship between people with mutual intentions or purposes.[1] Empowerment is about giving people the confidence, competence, freedom, and resources to act on their own judgments. Hence, when a person or group of people are empowered, they undergo a change in their relationship to other people who hold power and with whom they share mutual goals. In a community, empowering citizens changes their relationship to each other and to other holders of power such as business and government. In a business, empowering employees changes their relationship to each other, management, and the work process.

You can hardly pick up a business book today without seeing the words *leadership, empowerment, trust,* or *commitment* either on the cover or in the text. Gone are the bosses of the industrial era. Organizations have entered a new age where employees are partners and part of the team. Not only are managers supposed to be leaders, but all employees are leaders in their own way. This is good. It's democratic. It shows respect for persons, and it sounds very ethical. So why isn't everyone happy? Why do business leaders worry about trust and loyalty? Why are employees cynical? One reason is that people are less secure in their jobs because of downsizing, technology, and competition from the global labor market. The other reason, and focus of this chapter, is that in many organizations, promises of empowerment are bogus. The word *bogus* is often used by young people to express their anger, disappointment, and disgust over hypocrisy, lies, and misrepresentations. This is how people feel when they are told that they are being empowered, but they know that they are not. When leaders promise empowerment, they raise the moral stakes in their relationship to followers. Failure to deliver can lead to even greater cynicism about leadership, alienation, and abdication of moral responsibility by employees and/or citizens.

When you empower others, you do at least one of the following: you help them recognize the power that they already have; you recover power that they once had and lost; or you give them power that they never had before. In his study of grass-roots empowerment, Richard Couto says there are two main kinds of empowerment. The first kind he calls psycho-political empowerment. It increases people's self-esteem and results in a change in the distribution of resources and/or the actions of others. In other words, empowerment entails the confidence, desire, and—most important—the ability of people to bring about real change. This is probably what most people think of when they think of empowerment. Couto calls the second form of empowerment psycho-symbolic empowerment. It raises people's self-esteem or ability to cope with what is basically an unchanged set of circumstances.[2] More often than not, leaders promise or appear to promise the first kind of empowerment but actually deliver the second.

In this chapter I argue that authentic empowerment entails a distinct set of moral understandings and commitments between leaders and followers, all based on honesty. I begin by looking at the cultural values behind the idea of empowerment, particularly as it applies in the workplace. My primary focus is on business organizations, but much of what I have to say about the moral aspects of empowerment applies to leaders and followers in community, nonprofit, and political contexts as well. I briefly outline how the idea of empowerment has evolved over the past fifty years of management theory and practice. Critical analysis of this history and the ways in which empowerment is manipulative and unauthentic then helps me talk about the moral aspects of empowerment and their implications for leadership.

Part I. The Social Values Behind Empowerment

The idea of empowerment has its charm. Americans treasure democracy and its accompanying values of liberty and equality. If democracy were the only goal of empowerment, Americans would have the most democratic workplaces in the world, but they don't. As Tom Wren points out, ever since American independence, there has been a conflict between the values of equality and authority.[3] This tension is clearly evident in all organizational life. However, there are other values in our culture that shape the leadership and values of the workplace. Charles Taylor identifies three values of the modern age that he says cause tremendous personal anxiety and social malaise: individualism, instrumental reason (which causes disenchantment with the world), and freedom (which people seem to be losing because of individualism and instrumentalism).[4] Ideally empowerment is what makes humans triumph over the anxiety they have over these values and provides the antidotes to the social malaise.

In the workplace are constant tensions among individualism, freedom, and instrumental value and/or economic efficiency (I count these as two aspects of the same value). In a society where people value individualism and freedom, the challenge of leadership in organizations is the challenge of leading a flock of cats, not sheep.[5] This means that leaders have to use more powerful means of control than they would in a culture where people live in accepted hierarchies. For example, Americans were first smitten with Japanese management because it was effective and seemed so democratic. What they failed to realize was that the Japanese could afford to be democratic because the social controls imposed by hierarchy and community were internalized in workers, hence requiring less overt control by managers. American business leaders face the challenge of maintaining control without overtly chipping away at individualism and democratic ideals. This is why the language of empowerment is so attractive.

Economic efficiency and instrumentalism are the most powerful and most divisive values in the workplace. They trump all other values, and our current faith in the market makes it difficult to sustain plausibly any other ethical values in an organization. The market is a mean, ruthless boss. Instrumentalism or the value of getting the job done is more important than the means and people used to get it done. Business leadership is effective if it gets results. Leaders and their organizations are successful if they make the most amount of money or do the most amount of work in the least amount of time. Not only are the ends more important than the means, but there is little if any room for things that have intrinsic but noninstrumental value in business. The greatest of all impediments to empowerment in business, and increasingly in all areas of life, is economic efficiency. It acts on rules that refuse to take into account special circumstances.

In addition to the values of instrumentalism, individualism, and freedom, I add a fourth social value that I call "niceness." It might sound strange to say that our culture values niceness at a time when there seems to be little civility. Niceness is not civility. Historian Norbert Elias traces the origin of civility to the sixteenth-century Dutch philosopher Erasmus. His book *De Civilitate Morum Puerilium (On Civility in Children)* is dedicated to a prince's son. It chronicles the proper behavior of people in society with a special emphasis on outward physical behavior. In short, it is an etiquette book about properly blowing one's nose, eating at the table, and relieving oneself. Published in 130 editions and translated into English, French, Czech, and German, Erasmus's book established the concept of civility as behavior that was considerate of other people in a society.[6] Kant later points out that civility is not morality (because it doesn't require a good will), but the similitude of morality—an outward decency.[7] Civility is the behavior that citizens should have toward their fellow citizens. It includes an obligation of citizens to be polite and respectful of the private rights of others.

Whereas the concept of civility develops as a form of outward consideration for others (for example, not picking your nose in public), niceness is used as a means of gaining the favor and trust of others by showing a willingness to serve. Niceness fits the description of courtly behavior, from which we get the term *courtesy*. This selection from the *Zeldler Universal Lexicon of 1736* captures the basic elements of commercial niceness:

The courts of great lords are a theater where everyone wants to make his fortune. This can only be done by winning favor with the prince and the most important people of his court. One therefore takes all conceivable pains to make oneself agreeable to them. Nothing does this better than making the other believe that we are ready to serve him to the utmost capacity under all conditions. Nevertheless we are not always in a position to do this, and may not want to, often for good reasons. Courtesy serves as a substitute for all this. By it we give the other so much reassurance, through our outward show, that he has a favorable anticipation of our readiness to serve him. This wins us the other's trust, from which an affection for us develops imperceptibly, as a result of which he becomes eager to do good to us.[8]

There are other distinctive facets of niceness that are embedded in the observations of social critics since the mid-twentieth century. The first element of niceness is the belief that social harmony means lack of conflict. In *An American Dilemma* Gunnar Myrdal explains one facet of niceness. He argues that American social scientists derived their idea of social harmony from liberalism based on the Enlightenment ideal of *communum bonum* or common good. Radical liberals wanted to reformulate corrupt institutions into places where natural laws could function. The radical liberal, who could be a communist, socialist, or anarchist, wanted to dismantle power structures of privilege, property, and authority. In the utopia of the radical liberal, the concept of empowerment would not be useful. People wouldn't need to be given power or made to feel powerful, because the restraints that institutions had on their lives would in theory be removed. However, the dominant view in the social sciences (and certainly among those who were management theorists) was conservative liberalism. The conservative liberal took society as it was and, under the influence of economics, adopted the idea of social harmony as stable equilibrium.[9] The social scientists studied empirically observable situations and terms such as balance, harmony, equilibrium, function, and social process. They pretended that these terms gave a "do-nothing" valuation of a situation, but behind these words carry a veiled set of value judgments. Myrdal notes: "When we speak of a social situation being in harmony, or having equilibrium, or its forces organized, accommodated, or adjusted to each other, there is almost inevitable implication that some sort of ideal has been attained, whether in terms of 'individual happiness' or 'the common welfare.'"[10]

Traditionally, management theorists have tacitly accepted the valuations behind these terms. Empowerment, like harmony, is assumed to be a good that brings about individual happiness. Social harmony in an organization meant accommodating and adjusting to people. Conflict or disharmony was a sign of failed leadership. Niceness comes out of this one-dimensional picture of stable equilibrium and harmony. If no one complains and yells at work, then there is social harmony. Furthermore, the "do-nothing," value-free stance of social scientists is in part responsible for some of the manipulative theories and practices in management.

David Riesman captured another root of niceness in his 1950 description of the emerging American character. In *The Lonely Crowd* Riesman described inner-directed people who can cope with society because they are directed by internal, general goals implanted in them by their elders. Riesman observed that these people are becoming few and far between. Inner-directed people have less need for empowerment because they have what they need built in. The more prevalent character type identified by Riesman is the other-directed person. These people are shallower, friendlier, and more uncertain of themselves.[11] Other-directed people take more of their clues on values and goals from the outside: They want to be liked and have a strong need to belong.

In his book, Riesman described a society dominated by other-directed people, in which manipulative skill overshadows craft skill and expense accounts overshadow bank accounts. Business is supposed to be fun, and managers are supposed to be glad-handers who joke with secretaries and charm their bosses and clients. Most important, Riesman noted the trend that continues today of rewarding highly skilled people with management positions and power over other people. Hence the skilled engineer who gets promoted has to become a skilled glad-hander. The growth of the service industry shaped this character type into the model leader-manager and employee. To be successful in a service, one has to be friendly, likable, and nice. Since Riesman's day, bank accounts matter more and expense accounts are smaller. What remains the same is the powerful value of the glad hand. Our society may be less civil, and perhaps because of it niceness has been commercialized into the courtly norm of friendly bosses, bankers, and waiters all intent on gaining favor with customers and superiors in order to facilitate a smooth transaction.

As practiced in business, niceness consists of not getting into conflict and behaving in a commercially friendly fashion. Because people don't seem to behave this way naturally, we need the help of the therapist to attain niceness. In *The Triumph of the Therapeutic* Philip Rieff says that truth has become a highly personal matter he calls "psychic truth."[12] He thinks that therapeutic effectiveness has replaced the value of truth in our culture. Truths that make people feel better and help them adjust and fit in are far more desirable than truths that rock the boat. If our culture places more importance on psychic truths than on real truths, and if some "truths" or therapeutic fictions are effective because they make people happier, then leaders only have an obligation to make people feel empowered. They don't have to give them actual power.

It is obvious why niceness, as based on therapeutic lies, conflict-free environments, and the kind of bland friendliness that we experience when we go to the store or a bank, is one of the values that lurk behind the history of empowerment in business. Leaders often prefer the nice kind of empowerment over the kind that leads to chaos and loss of control. As I have said, there is empowerment and bogus empowerment. I describe bogus empowerment as the use of therapeutic fictions to make people feel better about themselves, eliminate conflict, and satisfy their desire to belong (niceness); so that they will freely choose to work towards the goals of the organization (control of individualism), and be productive (instrumentalism). Leaders who offer bogus empowerment are unauthentic, insincere, and disrespectful of others. They believe that they can change others without changing themselves.

Part II. Empowerment and the Organization Man

C. Wright Mills offers one of the clearest articulations of bogus empowerment: "The moral problem of social control in America today is less the explicit domination of men than their manipulation into self-coordinated and altogether cheerful subordinates."[13]

Mills believed that management's real goal was to "conquer the problem of alienation within the bounds of work alienation."[14] By this he meant that the problems of the workplace had to be defined and solved in terms of the values and goals of the workplace itself. By controlling the meanings and the terms under which alienation was conquered and satisfaction found, employers could maintain control without alienating workers. William H. Whyte echoed Mills's concern about psychological manipulation in *The Organization Man,* only Whyte zeroed in on people's need to belong. The workplace of the late 1950s is both radically different from and strikingly the same as today's workplace. Whyte criticized the social ethic that makes morally legitimate the pressure of society against the individual. The social ethic rationalizes the organization's demand for loyalty and gives employees who offer themselves wholeheartedly a sense of dedication and satisfaction. The social ethic includes a belief that the group is a source of creativity. A sense of belonging is the ultimate need of the individual, and social science can create ways to achieve this sense of belonging.[13]

Whyte feared that psychologists and social engineers would strip people of their creativity and identity. He attacked the use of personality tests to weed out people who don't fit in. He also challenged the notion that organizations should be free from conflict. The critique of the workplace in Whyte's book is similar to the critiques that liberals have of communitarianism. Community-oriented life looks good, but it is ultimately oppressive and authoritarian. In the 1950s social critics worried about the conformity of people to institutions and the values of suburban life. Today we worry about lack of consensus about values and the breakdown of urban and suburban communities. There is an increasing effort in the workplace to build teams and emphasize the value of groups. No one seems worried about loss of creativity and submission of individual identity to group identity. Managers care more about the problem of the individual who isn't a team player, and a majority of management theorists today believe that groups and teams are the foundation of all that is good and productive.

Whyte says, "The most misguided attempt at false collectivization is the attempt to see the group as a creative vehicle."[16] Contrary to popular management thinking today, Whyte does not believe that people think or create in groups. Groups, he says, just give order to the administration of work. Whyte describes

an experiment done at the National Training Lab on leaderless groups. Theoretically, when the group "jelled," the leader would fade into the background, to be consulted for his expertise only. These groups resulted in chaos, but as Whyte puts it, the trainers hoped that the resulting "feeling draining" of the group would be a valuable catharsis and a prelude to agreement.[17] According to Whyte, the individual has to enter into the process somewhere. If everyone wants to do what the group wants to do, and nothing gets done, then the individual has to play a role in the process. However, Whyte wonders if we should openly bring individuals into the process or "bootleg" it in an expression of group sentiment. Basically, he sees the leaderless group as intellectual hypocrisy. The power and authority of groups simply mask the real power and authority of leaders.

Whyte urges people to cheat on all psychological tests given during job interviews and at the workplace. He takes a strong stance against the organization and what he sees as the social scientist's coercive idea of belongingness. Another famous illustration of the struggle against the organization is in Sloan Wilson's novel *The Man in the Gray Flannel Suit,* published a year before Whyte's book. In the novel a personnel manager asks the main character, Tom Rath, to write an autobiography in which the last line reads, "The most significant thing about me is. . . ." Rath, revolted by the exercise, debates whether to say what the company wants to hear (the therapeutic lie) or write about his most significant memory, concerning a woman he met during the war. Caught between truth and fiction, Rath holds on to his dignity by stating the facts—his place of birth, his schooling, and the number of children in his family. He writes that the most significant thing about him is the fact that he is applying for the job. He also says that he does not want to write an autobiography as part of his application.[18]

Rath draws a fine line between himself and the organization. Whyte misses the moral in the first scene of Wilson's book: Telling the truth strikes a much stronger blow for individual dignity than beating the organization at its own game. Wilson's novel resonates with students today because all of them at some time will have to decide how truthful they have to be in a job interview or with an employer and how much of themselves they are willing to give to an organization. It is sometimes hard to tell the truth when you want someone to like you. The thin line is not about the amount of hours or work one does. It is the boundary that people draw between their inner self and the parts of them needed to do their job. It is the line that allows a person to be both an individual and part of a group. In the modern workplace it isn't always easy to draw this line; some workplaces use programs with the language of leadership and empowerment in them to erase the line between the two parts.

The Race for the Worker's Soul

In the 1960s the centralized bureaucratic organization of the 1950s gave way to the sensitive approach to management. The National Training Labs developed sensitivity training and T-Groups to transform bossy managers into participative ones. After much crawling around on the floor together and getting in touch with their inner feelings, few managers were transformed. During the 1970s and 1980s, management fads designed to capture the souls of workers bombarded the workplace. Fueled by global competitive pressures, managers were ready to try anything to get people to work hard and be productive. In 1981, William Ouchi's *Theory Z* and Richard Pascal and Anthony Athos's *The Art of Japanese Management* were best-sellers. The "new" idea from Japan was job enrichment and quality circles—after all, it worked for the Japanese. In 1982, the mystical Eastern touch of these two books gave way to Thomas J. Peters and Robert H. Waterman's blatantly evangelical *In Search of Excellence.* Peters and Waterman realized outright that the role of a manager is to make meaning for employees and create excitement. They argued that excellent organizations do not produce the conformist described by Whyte. They assure us that "In the very same institutions in which culture is so dominant, the highest levels of true autonomy occur. The culture regulates rigorously the few variables that do count, and it provides meaning." Nonetheless, in these organizations "people are encouraged to stick out, to innovate."[19] If a strong culture provided meaning, it could reach to the very souls of employees, hence allowing for great freedom and creativity within the boundaries of the culture and the meanings provided by the culture. This kind of organization is designed to foster Mills's cheerful subordinates.

Popular books on management and leadership exert more influence on the way organizations are run than do most studies done by scholars in the fields. Another 1982 best-seller was Kenneth Blanchard's *The One-Minute Manager.* Blanchard's adult fairy tale portrayed a kindly and therapeutic manager who inspired fealty and commitment. It makes the manager into a combination Mr. Rogers–Captain Kangaroo. Some companies required all of their managers to read it; it sold over three million copies. In the 1990s, real softies can regress and read what Winnie the Pooh has to say about management.[20] The fairy-tale format continues to be popular. Books such as *Zapp! The Lightning of Empowerment* and *Heroz: Empower Yourself, Your Coworkers, Your Company* by William C. Byham and Jeff Cox take the form of heroic and inspiring fables.[21] The fables include knights and dragons and demonstrate how sharing power with workers can revitalize a company. Stephen Covey is the top evangelical crusader of leadership literature in the 1990s. A recent article described "Coveyism" as "total quality management for the character, re-engineering for the soul."[22] Covey preaches that businesses have to focus on making employees "feel good" about the organizational structures in which they work.

In the 1980s and 1990s the word *leadership* began taking the place of the word *management* in business books. The semantic change is also a conceptual change from the idea of a manager as a boss who commanded and controlled the process of production to the leader who inspires people to work towards mutual goals. Joe Rost says that in the old industrial paradigm, leadership was nothing more than good management.[23] Empowerment is at least implied in most recent articulations of leadership in business books today. What is confusing about this literature is that it continues to be written for people who usually hold the position of manager. In ordinary discourse people talk about managers who lead and managers who manage. The carefully crafted distinctions made in the scholarly leadership literature are not always present in popular discourse. What we do see in ordinary discourse is that leadership has positive connotations and is sometimes used as an honorific, whereas management is either neutral or slightly negative.

The management fads of the 1980s and 1990s have appealed to business leaders (and those who aspire to be business leaders) because they make them feel powerful, inspiring, adventuresome, and lovable all at the same time. The lovable leader is an attractive image, especially given the lack of respect and trust for authority figures in our society. Lovable leaders are nice because they are democratic and they do not openly exert power over others. Practicing lovable leadership requires some therapeutic fictions. CEOs of large corporations have spent fortunes on consultants and training programs. The goal of most of the programs has been to make work more enjoyable and participatory and to push power relationships between employees and management into the background. All of this is done in hope of creating a more competitive business. Sometimes these programs have backfired.

In 1987, the California Public Utilities Commission asked Pacific Bell to stop its leadership-development program. The program intended to move away from the old AT&T culture, empower low-level managers and give them more responsibilities, cut middle managers, and become more customer-focused. At Pacific Bell twenty-three thousand of sixty-seven thousand employees took the two-day training.[24] Charles Krone created the Leadership Development program that came to be called "Kroning." This New Age program aimed at getting all employees to use the same language and think at all times about the six essentials of organization health: expansion, freedom, identity, concentration, order, and interaction. The program was based vaguely on the Armenian mystic Gurdjieff's Law of Three, which teaches that there are no constraints that can't be reconciled.[25]

After a two-month investigation of this $40 million training program, the commission reported that employees complained of brainwashing. An employee survey turned up repeated descriptions of the program as Big Brother, thought control, and mind restructuring. Employees also claimed that the Krone program used obtuse language and unnecessary concepts that made some people feel stupid. The irony was that the investigation discovered that a large majority of employees expressed a love of and commitment to Pacific Bell and mistrust of its management.[26] A Meridian survey of two thousand Pacific Bell employees concluded that top managers at Bell "blame the employees for the lack of productivity and are trying to make them think better. However, the Pacific Bell workforce already knows how to think."[27]

Thirty years after *The Organization Man,* corporations spent $30 billion dollars on training. Most of the training was in skills, but in 1986 about $4 billion went to programs such as Krone's and Werner Erhard's rehashed EST franchise called Transformation Technologies Inc. In 1987, *California Business* surveyed five hundred corporate owners and presidents and found that half their companies used some form of consciousness-raising.[28] These programs focused on the same themes espoused today: empowerment, leadership, and positive thinking. They are distinctive because they used such unorthodox training techniques as meditation, biofeedback, and hypnosis. For example, a company called Energy Unlimited escorted executives across hot coals as a means of empowering people. Although many of these programs now look silly to the outsider, they gained serious followers among corporate managers. Their impact on other employees is unclear. We rarely hear about cases in which employees complain about a company motivational program. That's why the Kroning scandal is so interesting. Most employees are a captive audience: Their success in the organization is contingent on buying into these programs. Motivational human potential courses often create a short-lived sense of euphoria among employees and/or a Hawthorn effect. They raise the expectation that employees will be enriched and empowered. However, after the dust settles, everything seems the same until the next initiative.

Did these attempts to redistribute power and responsibility in the organization succeed? On the one hand, employees were being promised more power and control over their work; on the other hand, some felt that they were being manipulated by the training programs. The standard answer given today is that programs to empower employees often failed because supervisors and line managers did not want to give up power.

Empowerment and Participation

Discussions of worker participation, including such issues as empowerment and the team approach, derived from two sources: industrial relations research and management research (largely based on organizational behavior). On the industrial relations side, discussion in the 1970s focused on workplace democracy. Admirable models of workplace democracy included democratic worker councils employed at the time in Yugoslavian industries. These councils allowed workers to play an active part in all facets of the business. Employees even elected their own managers. Other researchers in the 1960s and 1970s studied worker cooperatives in hopes of finding clues to constructing new forms of truly democratic organizations.[29] The workplace-democracy advocates wanted employees to have control of the organization as a whole and to discover new possibilities for organizing work.[30] Behind their thinking was the idea that participation was central to democracy, where citizens had a say in all significant institutions, including family, school, and work.[31] Worker participation fit Couto's model of psycho-political empowerment. However, back in the Cold War era, real democracy in the workplace was considered un-American.

Researchers on the management side focused on quality of worklife and job enrichment and motivation. They were interested in giving employees more discretion over the actual task that they performed, not over the organization itself. A major emphasis was on making the employee feel good about work. This approach, which is the one usually emphasized in business schools, aimed towards therapeutic effectiveness and tended to fall into Couto's category of psycho-symbolic empowerment. One of the biggest problems with empowerment schemes is that the language used often raises unrealistic expectations about how much power and control employees actually gain over their work. They also fail to see any change in their relationship to other power holders. When employees discover the limits of their participation, they are disappointed. (One also wonders if people have addictive and/or insatiable desires for power.) For example, people in a quality circle could suggest changes on the production line, but not changes in their work hours. Many managers were ambivalent about giving away their own supervisory power. The Japanese never had these problems because supervisors usually headed up quality circles.[32]

It is useful to compare the impetus for and terms of participatory schemes in other countries with those in the United States. In his study of the macropolitics of organizational change, Robert E. Cole tells us that in the 1960s Japan, Sweden, and the United States gave small groups more discretion to make work more interesting, attract employees looking for satisfying work, and motivate employees. The Japanese called innovations such as

quality circles *decentralization of responsibility.* These small-group structures did not challenge the hierarchical structure of the organization. Sweden, in contrast to Japan, challenged the hierarchy of managerial authority and cast the early debate over these innovations in the political terms of *joint influence* and *democratization.* In the United States, while there were some union supporters of industrial democracy, discussion of empowerment was categorized in terms of *participation, quality of worklife, leadership,* and *employee involvement.*

Cole's study compares the amount of control given the workers and the success of the programs in different countries. The study concludes, "The Swedish tried more and accomplished less, while the Japanese tried less and accomplished more. By contrast, the Americans tried still less and accomplished very little."[33] The Japanese and the Swedes were clear about the boundaries of employee involvement. In Japan the aims were aesthetic: to give workers autonomy to make their work more challenging and enjoyable. The Swedes wanted to bring real democracy into the workplace. The Americans had goals similar to those of the Japanese. However, the language used by Americans, their adversarial labor climate, and cultural values of individualism and freedom made the scope of these programs appear to reach beyond the aesthetic aspects of work and hint at a greater say in the organization. Most participatory schemes were really benevolent ways of motivating people by making work more satisfying. What wasn't clear was whether a boring job in a democratic workplace was better than an interesting job in an undemocratic one. Americans tended to assume that the latter was the case.

The 1935 Labor Relations Act recognized the need to protect workers from bogus empowerment of participatory programs. Under it, quality circles and other similar participatory schemes are illegal unless employees have the right to choose their representatives and have a genuine voice in decisions. The act prohibited "sham unions" or in-house unions formed by employers attempting to keep out real unions. Because it is obvious to most people today that employers have to forge a cooperative partnership with employees to be competitive, the 1935 act looks like an atavism that ought to be eliminated. However, the law recognized that companies prefer cooperation and participation of their employees on their own terms. Most important, companies fear the loss of control that would come with unionization. In most businesses, empowering employees does not change the balance of power within the organization. Unions are still the only institution in history that ever addressed the asymmetry of power between employers and employees. Unions can be a strong form of empowerment because they give employees an independent voice that terrifies most employers. Businesses have always had such an intense fear of unions that one has to question what they mean when they talk about empowerment.

Teams and Quality

Management language in the 1990s is a continuation of terms that started in the 1960s. *Empowerment* replaces terms such as *worker involvement*. The emphasis on power gets at what managers failed to deliver despite their claims over the past thirty years. What has become abundantly clear in research done on productivity is that workers do a better job when they have a say in the way they do their work, the redesign of their jobs, and the introduction of technology into the workplace. Yet, over the past twenty years managers have been constantly amazed by this phenomenon, which tells us something about the respect they have had for their employees.

The twentieth century began with scientific management with its physical control over production. It will end with Total Quality Management (TQM) and its social control over production. They are two sides to the same coin. Scientific management separated the mind from the body of the worker to mass-produce goods. TQM puts workers together in teams to produce quality goods and services. Both systems assert a high level of control at all phases of production (albeit using different means of control), and both systems have been extremely successful at improving production of goods and services.

Teams are a powerful form of social control. Peer pressure from the group keeps everyone in line and pulling his or her weight. Teams affect the individual more directly than does the larger culture of the organization. If the group puts out a measurable product, it can "keep score," which makes it accountable and allows for direct feedback and reinforcement. Hence, it is not surprising that along with excitement over teams some

businesses engender a religious fervor for Total Quality Management. Originating from statistical quality control, TQM pieced together quality circles, team approaches, and leadership into a new philosophy that required leaders "to accept TQM as a way of life."[34]

In his book on leadership and TQM, Richard Pierce advises front-line supervisors to act like leaders and become "more participatory and less authoritarian." According to Pierce, participatory means listening to employees' ideas and, when appropriate, implementing their ideas. The author goes on to say that employees, too, have to change. They need to know "that improved quality performance on their part, while vital, may bring no added compensation ('What's in it for me?'), but in the long run, productivity and quality improvement are necessary for survival."[35] Behind TQM is the idea of reinstating a craft ethic in workers, which includes pride in workmanship and the intrinsic value of a job well done. Though this is a positive and rewarding model of work, it cannot be isolated from the context in which a job is done and the kind of work that is done. In this setting the manager does not want employees to behave as if they are engaged in an economic transaction. Yet the employer bases most of his or her decisions regarding the employee on economic considerations. This is a good example of a therapeutic fiction: Everyone pretends that work is not guided by the values of instrumentalism and economic efficiency.

A great attraction of TQM for business leaders is that it gives the impression that they are giving up control and being democratic (and nice), but they end up with more control. Furthermore, TQM has been very effective in improving the quality of goods and services. However, TQM theorists are not satisfied at stopping with improved quality. They assert that quality is a matter of ethics and that quality requires ethical leaders at the top giving customers what they want. One writer concludes that "companies have a moral obligation to live up to the promises they have made in advertisements, product brochures, and annual reports."[36] Ethical commitment in TQM focuses largely on a company's obligations to customers. True believers assume that TQM is intrinsically ethical because employees are empowered to participate in decisions and management listens to their employees. This is a fairly thin description of an ethical arrangement. The key issue here is the relationship of employees to management.

Listening to employees and allowing them to participate in decisions does not mean that their relationship to management or each other has changed, especially if the listening and participation takes place between parties of unequal power. Furthermore, TQM says that managers should treat employees like customers. This is a therapeutic fiction. Can a business really treat employees like customers? It's a nice idea, but it breaks down in practice.

In a recent book documenting the wonders of teamwork in various organizations, Kimball Fisher emphasizes the importance of authenticity. He says that the key values of a team leader are belief in the importance of work, a belief that work is life, a belief in the "aggressive" development of team members, and a conviction to "eliminate barriers to team performance." Team leaders have to be themselves, or authentic, Fisher quotes a manager as saying. "The distinction between the work person and the family person is unhealthy and artificial."[37] In today's volatile economic environment, rhetoric like this rings false because, as Robert Frost said, "Home is the place where, when you have to go there, /They have to take you in."[38] We don't have many workplaces that do that. Team leaders also know that no matter how hard they or their team work, it may still not be enough. Kimball is right that authenticity is a fundamental part of leadership, but unauthentic in his denial of the distinction between work and the family. People may choose to lead lives with no distinction between work and home, but this choice is up to the individual and often rests on the nature of his or her work.

Part III. What Makes It All Work

Sincerity and Authenticity

At this point, some readers may be irritated by the unkind portrayal of management practices that most people consider a vast improvement over scientific management and traditional bureaucratic forms of work. Clearly there are sincere and committed business leaders all over America who really care and do their best to make work more rewarding for employees. I am not claiming that all the management theories and programs of the past fifty years have been designed to fool the American worker, nor am I saying that all of the

social scientists behind these theories and the consultants who develop these programs are evil manipulators. Yet I do ask the irritated reader to consider the irony of the effort put into empowerment programs in an era of downsizing, when the ultimate fate of workers is not decided by business leaders but by the invisible hand. I have painted this dark picture to underscore the bankruptcy of empowerment without the honesty necessary for authentic empowerment. Clearly not all empowerment programs are intended to manipulate people, and some leaders really do want to empower their followers. However, to do so, they must be sincere and authentic.

In his book *Sincerity and Authenticity,* Lionel Trilling tells us that the public value of sincerity, like the concept of civility, emerged during the sixteenth century, a period of increasing social mobility in England and France. The art of acting with guile and expressing certain false emotions publicly became a tool for taking advantage of new social opportunities. Trilling says that sincerity was devalued when mobility and acting became accepted behaviors in a mobile society. People considered the sincere person stupid and unsophisticated. Audiences were no longer interested in seeing plays about "hypocrite-villains and conscious dissemblers."[39] It was more interesting to read or watch plays about people who deceived themselves. Authenticity replaced the notion of sincerity as a subject of dramatic interest.

The question of authenticity takes us back to Mills, Whyte, and Wilson's *Man in the Gray Flannel Suit.* Mills believed that people had to sell their personalities to work in bureaucratic organizations; Whyte was concerned with the toll of conformity on the individual; and in the opening scene of Wilson's novel, Tom Rath is both sincere, in that he tells the truth, and authentic, in that he tries to come to grips with who he is. Nevertheless, the remainder of the novel is really about his struggle to be truthful to himself. It's ironic that the phrase "man in the gray flannel suit" has come to characterize a boring conformist organization man. Tom Rath is anything but that. He is a man wrestling with the organization and struggling to be honest with himself and others.

According to Trilling, we have deprecated the value of sincerity by treating it as such a common commodity in society and the market place. If this is true, then the really valuable emotional commodities are authenticity and "true" emotions. Thus, either people who serve customers will require even better acting skills, or training will have to dig even deeper into the employee to evoke the appropriate real emotions. If training programs could get at people's real feelings, find the "hot buttons," employees would either no longer have to act, or they could engage in "deep acting." This may be the real reason for the use of intrusive motivational programs like EST and the Krone program. It also lurks in the background of the ideology of strong cultures. Make the workplace your family and carry to it all the sense of caring and responsibility that you feel naturally for family members. Although this sounds sinister, it is true that most organizations want their employees to have a certain "genuine" feeling about their work, the people whom they work with, and the organization. At Pacific Bell, employees really cared and were concerned about the company. Perhaps one thing that we learn from the Krone case is that attempts at engineering appropriate attitudes and emotions can actually undercut genuine feelings for a company. If a workplace is run honestly, people do care and are friendly; however, their emotions have to be free to be real. Nonetheless, the broader issues at stake remain the line between motivation and manipulation of emotions, and the claims that an organization can make on the inner self and emotions of an employee.

The principle of authenticity applies to organizations as well as individuals. Often motivational programs and leadership programs are just polite lies within a company. Quality of worklife and employee involvement programs and redesigned jobs benefit employees by making their work more interesting. They intend to make employees feel empowered and feel that the organization cares about their development. Nonetheless, there is a difference between feeling empowered and really being empowered. One wonders if employees willingly buy into the fiction of empowerment because of their own need to believe that they have power and control. If so, symbolic empowerment works because employees are unauthentic.

Reality and Truth

The obvious difference between authentic and bogus empowerment rests on the honesty of the relationship between leaders and followers. Honesty entails a set of specific practical and moral obligations and is a necessary condition for empowerment. In the beginning I outlined three social values behind empowerment: individualism; freedom; and instrumentalism and economic efficiency. The fourth value, which encompasses the first three, I have called niceness. I characterized the value of niceness as a kind of self-interested social harmony, commercial friendliness, and therapeutic truth. All the values color the way that people view the context of their work. To empower people, leaders must take into account the social and economic conditions under which they operate.

The issue for most businesses is not democracy in the workplace or the workers' need for self-esteem or self-fulfillment. Plainly and simply, it is competitiveness. According to today's conventional wisdom, businesses of the twenty-first century have to be lean, mean, and flexible. This condition requires a flatter organization structure and employees willing to learn and change with the changing demands of their job, the market, and technology. Companies must innovate constantly, which means workers need the flexibility and work ethic of the old craft guilds.[40] This is what TQM tries to do and why there is so much discussion about commitment.

In this new business environment, in a sense employees already have more power than they had in the past and employers have less. Information is a source of power. On the one hand, the use of and access to information technologies in the workplace give employees far more power than they had in the past. On the other hand, computerized control systems can impose even stricter discipline on workers and replace layers of management. Competition is the reality of company life, and the market rules the lives of business leaders. Business leaders, especially those who are responsible to stockholders, have significantly less power and control over their firms than in the past. The decisions of even those with the best of intentions are dominated by the demands of the market.[41] Internal power shifts occur not necessarily because one group intentionally gave up power, but because the demands of technology and economic efficiency required a new distribution of power. Power also decreases in organizations because of flattened organizational structure. Why does this matter? It matters because empowerment requires good faith. It is a kind of giving. You don't tell people that you are giving them power that they have already gotten through structural and technological changes.

Perhaps the greatest obstacle to empowerment today is downsizing, despite low unemployment figures. Although most workers remain unaffected by it, downsizing strikes fear into the hearts of all workers because it reminds them of the fundamental way in which they are totally powerless over their lives when business leaders act as if they are powerless to do anything but downsize. It would seem virtually impossible to empower people in organizations that do not make a strong commitment to keeping their workers employed through good times and bad. In their enthusiasm for downsizing, some companies may discover that they have demoralized workers who lack the security necessary to produce the creative and innovative products needed to be competitive in the world market.

The second requirement for empowerment in the workplace is a commitment by employers to go to great lengths to protect employees' jobs. For example, consider the case of Maiden Mills. On December 11, 1995, the factory burnt down. Owner Aaron Feuerstein distributed Christmas bonuses. Furthermore, for the next three months he continued to pay his employees their full salaries while the factory was being repaired. If job security is related to empowerment, there is a sense in which Feuerstein's workers felt more empowered than those who took part in the AT&T and Xerox leadership programs that same year. One can write this off as old-fashioned paternalism, but I doubt that any company initiative could produce in employees the trust, commitment, and self-esteem of the employees at Maiden Mills. Many companies try smoke and mirrors, but moral action is stronger and longer lasting than any therapeutic intervention. The great moral leaders of business choose moral commitment to people and society over economic efficiency. When they come out ahead, they demonstrate to other business leaders that when employees really are the most important resource, ethics really pays.

Empowerment as a Reciprocal Moral Relationship

When leaders really empower people, they give them the responsibility that comes with that power. But this does not mean that with less power, leaders have less responsibility. This point is often misunderstood. Perhaps one of the most ethically distinctive features of being a leader is responsibility for the actions of one's followers. For example, transformational leaders don't have less responsibility for their followers when they transform them; the followers have chosen to take on more. Couto offers a good example of a bogus empowerment relationship. Couto says he listened in amazement as a hospital administrator "told federal health-policy makers about her hospital's patient advocacy program that empowered low-income patients to find means to pay their hospital bills."[42] Is the administrator really giving people power, or is she simply unloading the hospital's moral responsibility on them? In the workplace, employees can only take full responsibility if they have the power and access to resources to influence outcomes. Empowerment programs that give employees responsibility without control are cruel and stressful. Authentic empowerment gives employees control over outcomes so that they can be responsible for their work.

When empowering employees, leaders must keep their promises. The best way to do this is to make promises that they can keep. When leaders empower employees, they need to be clear about the extent of that power and avoid the temptation of engaging in hyperbole about the democratic nature of the organization. An organization can always give employees more responsibility, but employees feel betrayed when they discover that they have been given less than the leadership's rhetoric implied. A leader who keeps his or her promises establishes the dependability necessary for trust.

Modern leadership consists of two ideals, trust and power, that often conflict with each other.[43] Trust has taken over from authority as the modern foundation of leadership. The moral concepts behind empowerment—responsibility, trust, respect, and loyalty—are reciprocal moral concepts: that is, they only exist if they are part of the relationship between followers and leaders. Like all the other moral principles that I have been examining in relationship to leadership and empowerment, they are related to truth and honesty. Honesty is one way to resolve the tension between power and trust. It is morally wrong to lie because lying shows lack of respect for the dignity of a person. This is why bogus empowerment is so devastating. Employees are made to feel foolish about falling for inflated claims and undelivered promises. Leaders lose credibility and respect because they have blatantly failed to respect their employees. Business leaders often overlook the reciprocal nature of these moral concepts, particularly the notion of loyalty or commitment. If leaders don't demonstrate in substantive ways that they are loyal and committed to their employees through good times and bad, they simply cannot expect employees to be loyal to them; and therapeutic interventions will be short-lived at best.

Last, if leaders are to establish a moral relationship with employees that allows for authentic empowerment, they need to think about reapplying constructively the traditional values behind empowerment. They must consider how to protect individualism even in team settings. Individualism has taken a beating by the communitarians in recent years, but there are some ethically important aspects to individualism, such as recognition and tolerance of difference and diversity.[44] Teamwork without tolerance of difference in opinion, gender, racial, or cultural background is unacceptable. Morally imaginative business leaders will challenge the dogma of instrumentalism and economic efficiency that sometimes mindlessly dominates all business decisions. It is difficult to say whether employees are more or less free on the job today then they were in the past. Though many are liberated from harsh physical toil and a dictatorial boss, others are caged in by competition, insecurity, and peer pressure. Empowerment means more than discretion on the job. It also requires freedom to choose and freedom from emotional manipulation.

To empower people authentically, business leaders have to be ready to overthrow some of the aspects of niceness. The truth is not always pleasant. It can disrupt the harmony of an organization and introduce conflict. When you really empower people, you don't just empower them to agree with you. Employees don't always feel good when they hear the truth, and leaders don't like to deliver bad news. As a result of the therapeutic fictions that are part of niceness, managers aren't forth-right in their assessment of employees' work and teachers aren't forth-right about the quality of their students' work. Assessment inflation makes people feel good in the short run, but it does not build the self-esteem necessary for empowerment in the long run.

I close with the notion of authenticity. Leaders cannot empower people unless they have the moral courage to be honest and sincere in their intention to change the power relationship that they have with their followers. If leaders want to be authentic about empowering people, they must first be honest with themselves. Too many leaders are not authentic. They talk about empowerment and participation and even believe that they are participatory, but in practice they lead in autocratic ways. Employees are "empowered" to organize their work, but when they do, management steps in and tells them how to do it their way.

James MacGregor Burns points to Franklin Roosevelt's decision to support the Wagner Act as an example of authentic empowerment. According to Burns, Roosevelt knew that the act gave a substantial amount of power to the people. He didn't necessarily like this fact; nevertheless, he supported the act.[45] Authentic empowerment requires leaders to know what they are giving away and how they are changing the relationship between themselves and their followers. This is the only way that they can commit to keeping their part of the empowerment relationship. It is difficult for leaders to give away their own power and even more difficult for them to take away power from others.

Leadership is a distinct kind of moral relationship between people. Power is a defining aspect of this relationship. Whenever there is a change in the distribution of power between leaders and followers, there is a change in the specific rights, responsibilities, and duties in the relationship. Both sides have to be honest when they make these changes and have to understand fully what they mean. Bogus empowerment attempts to give employees or followers power without changing the moral relationship between leaders and followers. Empowerment changes the rights, responsibilities, and duties of leaders as well as followers. It is not something one does to be nice in order to gain favor with people. Over the past fifty years business leaders have tried to harness the insights of psychology to make people feel empowered. These attempts have often failed and led to cynicism among employees because business leaders have ignored the moral commitments of empowerment. Without honesty, sincerity, and authenticity, empowerment is bogus and makes a mockery of one of America's most cherished values, the freedom to choose.

Notes

1. James MacGregor Burns, *Leadership* (New York: Harper and Row, 1978), 13.

2. Richard Couto, "Grassroots Policies of Empowerment," paper given at the annual meeting of the American Political Science Association, Sept. 1992, 13.

3. J. Thomas Wren, "Historical Background of Values in Leadership," Kellogg Working Papers, 1996.

4. Charles Taylor, *The Ethics of Authenticity* (Cambridge, Mass.: Harvard University Press, 1991), 2–9.

5. James O'Toole, *Leading Change* (San Francisco: Jossey-Bass, 1994).

6. Norbert Elias, *The History of Manners* (New York Pantheon Books, 1978), 53–55.

7. Immanuel Kant, "Idea for a Universal History with a Cosmopolitan Intent," *Perpetual Peace and Other Essays,* translated by Ted Humphrey (Indianapolis: Hackett Publishing, 1983), 31–32.

8. Elias, 9.

9. Gunnar Myrdal, *An American Dilemma,* vol. 2 (New York: Harper and Row, 1962), 1046–47.

10. Ibid., 1055.

11. David Riesman, *The Lonely Crowd* (New Haven: Yale University Press, 1950), 14–21.

12. Philip Rieff, *The Triumph of the Therapeutic* (New York: Harper and Row, 1966), 137. A similar point is made in Robert Bellah et al., *Habits of the Heart* (Berkeley, Calif.: University of California Press, 1985), chapter 2.

13. C. Wright Mills, "Crawling to the Top," *New York Times Book Review,* Dec. 9, 1956.

14. C. Wright Mills, *White Collar* (New York: Oxford University Press, 1951), 232–37.

15. William H. Whyte, Jr., *The Organization Man* (New York: Simon and Schuster, 1956), 6–7.

16. Ibid., 51.

17. Ibid., 54.

18. Sloan Wilson, *The Man in the Gray Flannel Suit* (New York: Arbor House, 1955), 14.

19. Thomas J. Peters and Robert H. Waterman, Jr., *In Search of Excellence* (New York: Warner Books, 1982), 105.

20. Roger E. Allen, *Pooh on Management* (New York: Dutton, 1994).

21. William C. Byham and Jeff Cox, *Zapp! The Lightning of Empowerment* (New York: Harmony Books, 1990); *Heroz: Empower Yourself. Your Coworkers. Your Company* (New York: Harmony Books, 1994).

22. "Confessor to the Board Room," *The Economist,* February 24, 1996.

23. Joseph C. Rost, *Leadership for the Twenty-First Century* (New York Praeger, 1991).

24. *Telephony,* June 22, 1987, p. 15.

25. Annetta Miller and Pamela Abramson, "Corporate Mind Control," *Newsweek,* May 4, 1987.

26. Ibid., 6.

27. Ibid., 70.

28. *Venture,* March 1987, p. 54.

29. Two good studies of cooperatives are Joyce Rothschild and Allen Whitt, *The Cooperative Workplace* (New York: Cambridge University Press, 1986); and Edward S. Greenberg, *Workplace Democracy* (Ithaca: Cornell University Press, 1986).

30. For example, see Martin Carnoy and Derek Shearer, *Economic Democracy: The Challenge of the 1980s* (Armonk, N.Y.: Sharpe, Inc., 1980); and Gerry Hunnius, G. David Garson, and John Case, eds., *Workers' Control* (New York: Vintage Books, 1973).

31. See Carol Pateman, *Participation and Democratic Theory* (London: Cambridge University Press, 1970).

32. Robert E. Cole, "The Macropolitics of Organizational Change: A Comparative Analysis of the Spread of Small-Group Activities," in Carmen Sirianni, ed., *Worker Participation and the Politics of Reform* (Philadelphia: Temple University Press, 1987), 39–40.

33. Ibid., 40.

34. See Richard S. Johnson, *TOM: Leadership for the Quality Transformation* (Milwaukee: ASQC Quality Press, 1993).

35. Richard J. Pierce, *Leadership. Perspective and Restructuring for Total Quality* (Milwaukee: ASQC Quality Press, 1991), 11.

36. Ibid., 13.

37. Kimball Fisher, *Leading Self-Directed Work Teams* (New York: McGraw-Hill, 1993), 105–9.

38. "The Death of the Hired Man," in *The Poetry of Robert Frost,* ed. Edward C. Lathem (New York: Holt, Rinehart and Winston, 1979), 38.

39. Lionel Trilling, *Sincerity and Authenticity* (Cambridge, Mass.: Harvard University Press, 1972), 13.

40. This description comes from Michael J. Piore and Charles F. Sable, *The Second Industrial Divide* (New York: Basic Books, 1984), 282–307.

41. Anthony Sampson, *Company Man* (New York: Times/Random House, 1995), 260.

42. Couto, 2.

43. See Francis Sejersted, "Managers as Consultants and Manipulators: Reflections on the Suspension of Ethics," *Business Ethics Quarterly* 6, no. 1 (January 1996): 77.

44. Taylor, 37.

45. My thanks to James MacGregor Burns for this example and for his other helpful comments on this chapter.

CHAPTER 16

Leading Teams

Imperatives for Leaders

J. Richard Hackman

Harvard University

When we think about a great team, the image we conjure up almost always includes a great leader. A surgical team flawlessly executes a risky and demanding procedure. The lead surgeon emerges from the operating room to receive the gratitude of the patient's family. An industrial team regularly sets new plant production records. The team leader receives an award and soon thereafter is promoted. An airplane encounters serious problems, but the crew finds a way to work around them and lands safely. All applaud the captain. The final chords of Mahler's Resurrection Symphony reverberate in the concert hall. The conductor, exhausted but beaming, turns to accept the applause of the audience.

Our tendency to assign to the leader credit or blame for successes or failures that actually are team outcomes is so strong and pervasive that I'm tempted to call it the "leader attribution error." It occurs for unfavorable as well as favorable outcomes—the standard remedy for an athletic team that experiences a string of losses is to replace the coach,

for example, and it is the conductor who is excoriated in newspaper reviews of a poor orchestral performance. Moreover, it is not just outside observers of bosses who make the error. Team members themselves, the people who worked together to generate the collective product, also are vulnerable. Organizational psychologist Richard Corn asked members of a diverse set of teams, ranging from community health groups to a mutual fund company to military units, to identify the "root cause" of their team, performance. For teams that were performing well, over 60 percent of the explanations had something to do with someone's personality or behavior—and that someone frequently was the team leader. For teams that were performing poorly, 40 percent of the initial attributions were about personality or behavior.[1]

Even *inaction* by a leader is often viewed as causing what transpires in a team. For example, members of self-analytic groups (i.e., groups whose purpose is to help members learn from analysis of their own group experiences) generally hold their leader responsible for

---

Source: Imperatives for Leaders, pp. 199-232 in *Leading Teams: Setting the Stage for Great Performances*, 2002, by J. Richard Hackman. Reprinted with permission of Harvard Business School Publishing.

the rocky start that they invariably experience. In most such groups, the leader remains silent for the first few moments to ensure that all behaviors that occur are spontaneously generated by—and therefore owned by—group members themselves. The leader attribution error is so strong that the leader's silence itself often is viewed by members as the main cause of what transpires. Only gradually do they come to accept and explore their own responsibility for the behaviors they have generated.

Highly trained and experienced professionals, people who perform demanding team tasks as part of their daily work, are as vulnerable to the leader attribution error as anyone else. A player in a top symphony orchestra, describing to me an extraordinary performance by the orchestra reported that the conductor had "pulled out of us a performance I didn't know we had in us." A player in a different orchestra, explaining an unsatisfactory concert, complained that the conductor "just couldn't get us to play beyond the notes on the page." Only when there is significant ambiguity about whether a team's performance was a success or a failure is the leader attribution error muted.[2]

Sometimes, of course, a team leader's actions really do spell the difference between team success and failure. That fact, reinforced by the leader attribution error, has fueled a steady flow of tests, surveys, and educational programs intended to help organizations select and train great group leaders. That flow persists despite the rather poor track record, discussed next, of team leader selection tools and training programs.

Leader Traits and Styles

Clearly, some people are better than others as leaders of teams. It is quite reasonable, therefore, to try to identify the traits that distinguish naturally good leaders from those who consistently fail to get the best out of the people with whom they work. Literally hundreds of research studies have attempted to do exactly that, measuring a panoply of leader traits (e.g., intelligence, sociability, self-confidence, and dozens more) to see which ones predict leadership effectiveness. As long ago as the 1950s, it had become clear that research would not succeed in identifying any set of universal traits that could reliably distinguish good from poor leaders.[3]

Many different attributes of individuals were found to be modestly associated with rated leader effectiveness and (especially) with who would be chosen to occupy leadership positions. But the practical usefulness of those lists was limited, both because they were so long (a dozen desirable attributes provide less clear guidance for action than does a handful) and because the size of the empirical relationships obtained was usually so small.

Contemporary research has not been much more successful in identifying the traits of superb team leaders than that done decades ago.[4] Neither hope nor the leader attribution error dies easily, however, and the commonsense belief that a leader's personal traits somehow determine his or her effectiveness in leading teams continues to guide both research and practice. The power of such thinking is perhaps best exemplified by the readiness of many members of the management community, as well as the general public, to accept the claim that a leader's "emotional intelligence" is the key determinant of team and organizational effectiveness. The irony is that many of the skills that are grouped under the emotional intelligence label are learnable. But use of the word *intelligence* as part of the label implies that whatever it is that emotionally intelligent leaders possess is at least an enduring personal attribute and perhaps even innate. It is bad enough that analytic intelligence, the kind of thing often referred to as "IQ," is so widely viewed as wired in at birth; it is even more troublesome that learnable leadership and interpersonal skills are labeled in a way to suggest that they are as well. Next, I suppose, someone will suggest that it is one's genetic endowment that determines how effective he or she can be as a team leader.[5]

There is a potentially optimistic implication of the rather pessimistic conclusions just drawn. If traits are not controlling, then perhaps *anyone* can be a good team leader as long as he or she learns the right ways to behave. If it could be established that certain leadership styles are better than others for leading teams, then leaders could be trained to exhibit those styles no matter what their personalities or demographic attributes happen to be. This was the approach taken in a training course for airline flight crews that I once observed. Each pilot-student took a paper-and-pencil test that, when scored, revealed his or her characteristic style of operating in teams. Instructors then suggested that certain styles were better than others for promoting crew effectiveness. Students were taught, for example, that captains should foster task accomplishment and interpersonal harmony simultaneously, and that they should avoid both autocratic and relentlessly democratic leadership styles. And they learned that first officers and flight engineers should be assertive with their captains (but not excessively or unpleasantly so) when they notice something that concerns them. The hope was that the styles taught in the classroom would be used to good effect when the pilot-students returned to their regular flying duties.

Although the pilots, like others who take tests measuring leadership style, found them interesting and informative, I have a number of concerns about such devices.[6] For one thing, research has shown that there is no one leadership style that works well across all situations.[7] A style that may be just what is needed when working with competent, trusted colleagues to develop a team work plan may fall badly when a newly formed team encounters an emergency situation that requires a rapid, decisive collective response. For this reason, research on leader styles has evolved from a search for the one best style to contingency models that specify which styles should be used in different circumstances. Such models identify those attributes of the situation and of the group being led that determine what leader behaviors are likely to work best, and they provide research-based guidance about how leaders ought to behave in various circumstances.[8] Contingency models necessarily become quite complex as research identifies more and more contingencies that moderate the relationship between leader behavior and team outcomes. In that inevitability lies the rub: The more complete and complex a contingency model, the more it requires of leaders a level of online cognitive processing that can exceed human capabilities.[9]

A second problem with leadership styles derives from our everyday assumption that leader behavior is the *cause* of member behavior and team dynamics. In fact, a leader's style may in many circumstances be as much a consequence of members' behaviors as it is a cause of that behavior.[10] If, for example, a leader is charged with managing a team of subordinates who are both competent and cooperative, the leader is likely to use a considerate, participative leadership style. But if team members are obviously not competent in carrying out the work and, moreover, exhibit hostility in their interactions with the leader, a much more structuring, directive, and autocratic style is likely to be exhibited. A team leader's style is not fixed. Just as a parent's style of interacting with a child often is more an effect of how that child is acting at the moment (tougher when the child is behaving poorly, democratic when the child sweetly suggests an after-dinner family conference to reconsider bedtime conventions) than a consistent expression of one's preferred style of parenting, a leader's behavior often is driven as much by how team members are acting as by the leader's espoused or preferred style. Finally, there is the problem of getting newly learned styles transferred from the training setting back to the workplace. Leaders almost always like, and feel helped by, well-run training programs that seek to improve their styles. Moreover, training settings are explicitly designed to encourage participants to experiment with new behavioral styles, and to reinforce improvements in their existing styles. The problem comes when a participant leaves the supportive training environment and returns to his or her regular workplace where colleagues may have become quite expert in dealing with the "old" style of the leader—and therefore may be quite unreceptive to the new style the boss developed while away at training. In a contest between a fresh and still somewhat fragile style learned in school, with the demands and expectations of the trainee's regular work setting, the new style almost always comes out the loser.

Indeed, those times when a newly learned style might be most valuable (eg., when there is extremely important work to be accomplished under considerable stress or time pressure) are precisely the times when that style is *least* likely to appear. When a person becomes highly aroused (as typically happens under stress), he or she reverts to well-learned behaviors, exhibiting whatever response is dominant for that person in that situation.[11] Dominant responses rarely are displaced by what is taught and learned in a leadership training course; they are too deeply ingrained for that. To return to our pilot-trainees, even the best students in the seminar are likely to revert to their old, tried-and-true behaviors when a highly stressful situation such as an engine fire or the loss of all generators is encountered in line flying. A story told by Captain Reuben Black of Delta Airlines illustrates. Some years ago, an instructor was attempting to get his students to memorize the thirteen steps that were to be taken in the event of a heater fire on a certain aircraft. The students were having trouble committing the list to memory, but the instructor persisted. Finally one veteran captain captured the essence of the problem when he exploded, "How the hell do you expect me to remember all this shit when I'm *scared?*" How, indeed?

So what is going on here? On the one hand, we all tend to overattribute responsibility for collective outcomes to the team leader. Although that tendency is often exaggerated to some extent—the leader attribution error—there is no doubt that what a team leader does (and doesn't do) is highly consequential for team effectiveness. On the other hand, researchers have been unable to generate usable knowledge about either the traits that characterize great leaders or their characteristic behavioral styles.

Is it just that we need to try harder to identify and measure the right personal attributes and behavioral styles of team leaders to be able to select and train them well? Management scholar Chris Argyris, who I believe shares my pessimism about the efficacy of existing leader selection and training technologies, proposes that any substantial improvement in leader effectiveness requires a fundamental recasting of leaders' "theories in use," which are the perceptual templates and behavioral programs that people rely on in planning and executing their actions.[12] If one seeks to create enduring improvements in leaders' behavioral styles, Argyris's strategy of essentially reprogramming their personal cognitive models may well be warranted. But is there another approach to the development of competent team leadership, one that does not require such fundamental change in leaders' personal styles of acting and interacting?

I believe there is. That alternative, which is explored in the rest of this chapter, involves a change of focus, from *who* the leader should be (leader traits) and *how* the leader should behave (leader behavioral style) to *what* the leader does and *when* in the life of a team it is done.

What Effective Leaders Do

Effective leaders attend first to the basic conditions that foster team effectiveness—the features of the team and the organizational context that have been discussed in this book. First of all, they make sure that they have created a real work team that will have some stability over time. They provide the team with a compelling direction. They fine-tune the structure of the team so it fosters rather than impedes teamwork. They tweak the organizational structures and systems so they provide teams with ample support and resources. And they arrange for, or themselves provide, expert coaching to help teams take full advantage of their favorable performance situation. Effective leaders do these things in their own way, using the idiosyncratic behavioral styles and strategies that they have found to work best for them. And they attend carefully to timing, moving quickly and decisively when opportunities for action open, but never trying to force an intervention when the time for it is not right.

Stacking the Deck

Great team leaders do not rely on any single strategy for promoting work team effectiveness. Instead, they stack the deck by getting all of the conditions we have been discussing aligned and pulling in the same direction, thereby reinforcing the impact of their own hands-on coaching. We saw in the previous chapter that good coaching helps a team in three ways. First, by building the level of *effort* that members apply to the work. Second, by increasing the task appropriateness of their *performance strategies*. And third, by helping members use well their pool of *knowledge and skill*. As Figure 16.1 shows, each of these three performance processes also is strengthened by a compelling direction, an enabling structure, and a supportive context.

A compelling direction carries a team a long way. It energizes team members, promoting collective effort. It orients members' attention and action, which provides the basis for making good choices among alternative performance strategies—or for inventing an entirely new strategy that is uniquely attuned to task requirements and opportunities. And it engages members' full complement of talents as they pursue collective aspirations that are of great consequence for the team or those the team serves.

Even good direction is insufficient, however, if the team is not well structured—if it has a poorly designed

Figure 16.1	How Team Design Shapes Team Performance Processes

Compelling direction		Enabling team structure		Supportive organizational context		Team performance processes
Energizes	+	Team Task Design	+	Reward System	→	Effort
Orients Attention	+	Norms of Conduct	+	Information System	→	Performance Strategy
Engages Talents	+	Team Composition	+	Educational System	→	Knowledge and Skill

task, if norms of conduct are absent or dysfunctional, or if the team itself is poorly composed. Each of the three components of a good structure has an important role in enabling a team to take advantage of good direction. A well-designed task promotes member motivation and effort. Norms of conduct that explicitly promote active environmental scanning and strategy planning increase the chances that the team will develop and implement a performance strategy fully appropriate for the task being performed. A well-composed team is small enough, and diverse enough, to facilitate the development and efficient use of member talents.

Finally, a supportive organizational context smoothes the path to team excellence. When a team has ample resources and support, members are able to keep moving toward their collective objectives without having to divert time and energy to surmount organizational impediments or circumvent bureaucratic roadblocks. A reward system that recognizes and reinforces excellent group performance fosters high and sustained team effort. An information system that keeps the members up to date about environmental demands and opportunities increases the chance that the team will develop and deploy performance strategies that are both efficient and appropriate. And an educational system that provides timely training and technical consultation increases the likelihood that the team will bring to the task the maximum possible level of task-relevant talent.

If a work team were in a boat on a river, having a compelling direction, an enabling structure, and a supportive organizational context would metaphorically allow members to row with the river's flow—simultaneously lessening the labor they must expend and hastening their arrival at the team's destination. If one or more of these conditions were *not* present, however, teamwork might well feel like rowing upstream against a strong, unpredictable current. The team might eventually get to its destination, but it would involve a lot more work and be a lot less certain than if the basic performance conditions were favorable.

Getting the Order Right

A *New Yorker* cartoon some years ago, as I recall it, depicted a bleary-eyed man sitting on the side of his bed, looking at a sign he had posted on the bedroom wall. The sign read: "First slacks, *then* shoes." Direction, structure, and context are the slacks. Coaching is the shoes. Unfortunately, coaches sometimes are called on by their organizations to do the shoes first, to try to salvage a team that operates in a performance situation that is fundamentally flawed. Even first-rate coaching can make little constructive difference in such circumstances—and may even do more harm than good by distracting members' attention from more fundamental aspects of their design or context that they ought to be addressing.[13]

For example, consider a team working on a mechanized assembly line where inputs are machine paced, assembly procedures are completely programmed, and performance operations are simple and predictable. How could a coach help that team? Not by encouraging members to work harder or more efficiently, because the amount of work processed is under control of the engineers who pace the line, not the team. Not by helping them develop more task-appropriate performance strategies, because the way the work is to be done is completely prespecified. And not by helping them develop or better use members' knowledge and skill, because the required operations are so easy that an increase in team talent would merely mean that an even smaller proportion of the team's total pool of talent would be used. In this situation, team performance processes are so severely constrained and controlled that the team has almost no leverage to improve them. For the same reason, there is little that even a great coach can do in working with the team to better its performance. Through no fault of the members, the team is essentially uncoachable.

Two questions come to the fore when one encounters an uncoachable team. First, can the performance situation be fundamentally restructured so the team *can* have a meaningful level of control over its own performance processes? And, if that is not possible, should the team exist at all? There are some kinds of work for which teams are a wholly inappropriate design choice, and some organizational settings in which teams can never succeed. It is never a good idea to "force" a team in such circumstances.

Even when a performance situation is not as team-unfriendly as the one just described, the quality of a team's design strongly conditions the impact of leaders' coaching interventions, as was documented by Ruth Wageman in a study of self-managing field service teams.[14] For each team studied, Wageman obtained independent assessments of the team's design, the coaching behaviors of its leader, the team's level of self-management, and its objective performance. She predicted that a team's design features would make a larger difference in both level of team self-management and its objective performance outcomes than would the leaders coaching behaviors, and she was right. Design was four times as powerful as coaching in affecting a team's level of self-management, and almost forty times as powerful in affecting team performance.[15] Clearly, design features do have causal priority over leader coaching in shaping team performance processes and outcomes.

Perhaps the most fascinating finding of the Wageman study turned up when she compared the effects on team self-management of "good" coaching (e.g., helping a team develop a task-appropriate performance strategy) with those of "bad" coaching (e.g., identifying a team's problems and telling members exactly what they should do to fix them). Figure 16.2 shows these effects for good coaching (the left panel of the figure) and bad coaching (the right panel). Good coaching significantly helped well-designed teams exploit their favorable circumstances, but made almost no difference for poorly designed teams. Bad coaching, on the other

Figure 16.2   How Team Design and Leader Coaching Jointly Affect Team Self-Management

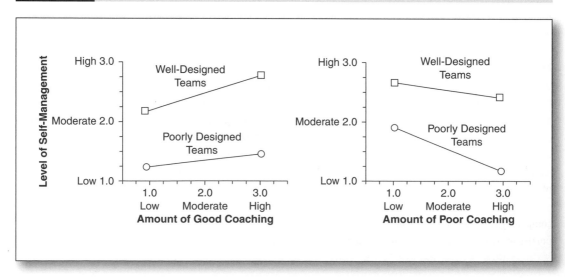

hand, significantly compromised poorly designed teams' ability to manage themselves, worsening an already difficult situation, but did not much affect the self-management of teams that had an enabling team structure and a supportive organizational context.

We seem to have here yet another instance in which the rich get richer (well-designed teams are helped most by good coaching) and the poor get poorer (teams with flawed designs are hurt most by bad coaching). Great coaching can be enormously valuable to a team in exploiting the potential of a fundamentally sound performance situation, but cannot reverse the impact of poor direction, a flawed team structure, and an unsupportive organizational context. The key to effective team leadership, then, is first to ensure that the team's performance situation is sound and then to help team members take the greatest possible advantage of their favorable circumstances.

How Effective Leaders Do It

Question: How do great leaders create the conditions that promote team effectiveness?

Answer: Any way they can.

Hidden within that brief, unhelpful question-and-answer dialogue are a number of imperatives that can guide leaders in improving the effectiveness of almost any organizational work team. So let us take the question and answer apart, phrase by phrase, and explore what lies inside.

. . . great leaders

As you read the words "great leaders," what came to mind? Did the leader attribution error do its work, prompting an image of an individual person who occupies a formal leadership role? My choice of the plural form in the section title was deliberate, to signal that team leadership can be—and, at its best, often is—a *shared* activity. Anyone and everyone who clarifies a team's direction, or improves its structure, or secures organizational supports for it, or provides coaching that improves its performance processes is providing team leadership. An external manager may be well positioned to do some of these things, such as setting a direction for the team that is well linked to broader organizational purposes, or securing organizational resources and supports. Other things are better done by leaders who work more closely with team members, such as tailoring a team's direction to its particular circumstances, fine-tuning the team's structure, and helping members learn how to use well the organizational supports the team enjoys. And it is the regular, rank-and-file members of the team who may be best able to provide the kind of peer coaching that can focus and refine team performance processes, thereby helping teammates work together in ways that minimize process losses and generate synergistic process gains. The question, then, is not so much who provides team leadership but rather how much the team is getting. So long as the focus of leadership activities is on creating conditions that enhance team performance, the more leadership the better.

. . . create the conditions

When we plan an action intended to make a difference in some part of our world, we almost always think in cause-effect terms. Hit the nail with the hammer and it goes into the wood. Compliment a colleague and that person will be pleased and maybe even like *you* better. Flash your headlights thrice just after someone has passed you at high speed and the other driver is almost certain to slow down (and, as a bonus, may experience that special sinking feeling that comes with realizing that one may have just sped by an unmarked police car).

Cause-effect thinking is so pervasive and useful that it sometimes can mislead us into behaving in inappropriate or self-limiting ways. We saw a few pages ago that leader style, which commonly is viewed as one of the main causes of subordinate behavior, is itself shaped by how competently and cooperatively those subordinates are behaving. In such cases, the usual direction of the causal arrow between leader and subordinate is reversed, from subordinate behavior to leader style rather than vice versa. That is useful information to have, but it raises a more fundamental question: If not the leader's style, what *does* determine how subordinates act? And what are the implications of that for the behavior of those who provide leadership to a team?

Team behavior is shaped, often in unseen and nonobvious ways, by the task and organizational conditions that characterize the performance setting. Leaders often are most helpful to teams, therefore, when they back off a bit from direct interventions intended to keep a team on a good course minute by minute and focus instead on creating and maintaining performance-enhancing organizational conditions. Even hands-on coaching, which would seem to be an instance when the leader's style has direct and immediate effects on team behavior, actually serves a larger and more general purpose—namely, to gradually build the team's capability to manage itself well.

Leaders always behave in accord with some model, even if implicit and even if incorrect, that specifies what actions are likely to yield what results. To replace a cause-effect model with one that focuses on the creation of enabling performance conditions is a significant change of orientation, and one that has implications for leader behavior at all stage's of a team's life. Whether one is launching a new team, assisting a team that has encountered performance problems, or helping an already well-performing team do even better, the same diagnostic questions apply. Is the team a *real* team, bounded and stable over time, that requires members to work interdependently to achieve some common purpose? Is the team direction clear, consequential, and challenging? Does the team's structure—its task, composition, and norms—facilitate good performance processes? Does the organizational context—the reward, information, and educational systems—provide the team with the supports that the work requires? And is there expert coaching available to the team to help members minimize the inefficiencies in their performance processes and instead harvest the potential synergies of teamwork?

Leaders, whether those who have formal responsibility for a team or others (including team members themselves) who seek informally to help the team do well, can refer to this simple checklist repeatedly during the life of a team. Almost always the answer to one or more of the diagnostic questions will point to some structural or contextual problem, or to an unexploited opportunity for strengthening the team's performance circumstances.

There is no way to "make" a team perform well. Teams create their own realities and control their own destinies to a far greater extent, and far sooner in their lives, than we generally recognize. After a team has launched itself on a particular track, its own actions create additional new realities which then guide members' subsequent behavior, which can set in motion either a cycle of ever-increasing competence and commitment or a downward spiral that ends in collective failure. Once members have established their shared view of the world and settled into a set of behavioral routines, there is not a great deal that leaders can do to change the team's basic direction or momentum.[16] What leaders *can* do (and a big job it is) is make sure the team is set up right in the first place—that it is well supported organizationally, and that members have ready access to the kind of coaching that can help them exploit the team's potential to the fullest extent possible. To ask a leader to do more than that is to ask too much—and, in the bargain, to impede the team's own development into a truly self-managing performing unit.

. . . that promote team effectiveness

Here, we rely upon a three-dimensional conception of team effectiveness. Effective teams, in this view, generate products, services, or decisions that are fully acceptable to those who receive or use them. *And* they become more capable as performing units over time. *And* their members find in the work of the team more learning and fulfillment than frustration and disillusionment. A team that is significantly and consistently subpar on any of these three criteria would not be viewed as effective.

Unfortunately, teams sometimes slip into a pattern of behavior that focuses too intently on one or two of the three criteria to the detriment of the others. In the course of my research, I have seen instances in which each of the three has become so dominant that a team's long-term effectiveness has been compromised. Most common, of course, is when meeting customer or client requirements captures virtually all of the team's attention and energy. Members focus intently and relentlessly on getting the work out, and if they even notice that the well-being of the team and its members is being overlooked, they defer such matters until "later, when we have a little breathing room." But later may not arrive until, perhaps, the team and its members have become so depleted that an operational breakdown occurs. At that point, the team may be unable to recover precisely because the resources that were being expended were never replenished. This phenomenon, surely, contributed to the collapse of some dot-com startups whose members enacted the "14/7" ethic with a vengeance and, in the process, depleted their collective resources to the point that they eventually had none left to deal with one more crisis, not even a relatively small one.

Organizational psychologist Edy Greenblatt observed a similar phenomenon in a setting where one might least expect to see it—namely, a vacation resort where the work done by organizational staff involved doing things that we usually define as play.[17] All day, every day, teams of staff members led guests in recreational activities ranging from dancing to diving, from singing to sailing. The level of emotional labor involved in presenting a relentlessly happy collective face to guests was extraordinary but that was what needed to be done— and that was what the staff did, day after day, week after week. Burnout in this happy vacation setting was much higher than one might have predicted, especially among those who kept their attention so intently focused on guests' pleasure that they neglected to find ways of restoring, let alone enriching, their stores of personal and collective resources.

Sometimes the imbalance is in the opposite direction. Leaders can become so focused on training and team building that they lose sight of a team's purposes and customers. I once visited the startup of a plant whose managers were extraordinarily proud of their programs to train new employees intensively in state-of-the-art production technologies and to build robust self-managing teams to operate those technologies. The training and team-building programs were indeed impressive and showed real promise of providing a model that eventually could be diffused throughout the parent corporation's existing, more traditionally managed plants. Unfortunately, plant managers and employees became so captivated by their innovative human resource strategy that they lost their focus on the plant's reason for being—namely, to produce high-quality products at the lowest possible cost for the company's customers. In part because of the high and continuing investments made in the plant's people and teams, labor costs were higher than budgeted and production targets remained just beyond reach. About a year after startup, an economic downturn hit the parent corporation particularly hard and the new plant was closed. Because plant managers had focused so intently on the second

and third components of effectiveness, we will never know whether the heavy investment they had made in developing the plant's people and teams eventually would have paid off for its customers and shareholders.

Actively managing trade-offs among the three components of effectiveness spawns many benefits for work teams. The team is less likely to fall victim to the hidden costs that almost always accompany an exclusive focus on any single aspect of overall effectiveness. Members are likely to be more attentive and thoughtful in planning what the team will do, thereby lessening the risk that they will reactively respond only to the most salient or immediate demands that press upon them. The team's purposes will remain at the center of members' attention, reducing the risk that the team will experience the dysfunctions that can surface when members focus more on their procedures than their goals.[18] Over time, the team surely will become a more flexible and effective self-managing performing unit than otherwise would be the case.

Team leaders are uniquely well positioned to help teams manage these trade-offs, for several reasons. The team leader often is in closer touch than team members with a team's broader context, including its links with other organizational units and with customers or clients, and therefore is in a good position to alert members if they start to overlook the interests of any one of the team's constituencies. Ideally, he or she will be less wrapped up in the hurly-burly of dealing with the demands and pressures that a team encounters in its daily work, and therefore more likely to notice if a team begins to slip toward an overemphasis on one or another of the components of effectiveness. And, finally, the team leader role usually carries some special legitimacy for raising questions about the focus of a team's work activities, thereby providing an opportunity for constructive interventions of a kind that come from members themselves only in the most mature self-managing teams. Even so, helping a work team recognize that its long-term well-being involves active management of trade-offs among the three components of effectiveness can be quite challenging, since team members may not always welcome or see the wisdom of interventions that appear to raise questions about how they are allocating their attention and energies. The challenge is worth taking on, however, because when well and sensitively met it can significantly strengthen the self-management capabilities of almost any organizational work team.

. . . *any way*

A while back, I needed to get from Boston to New York for a research meeting. There were multiple ways I could have accomplished that—by airplane, by train, by bus, even by driving my own car five hours to the meeting site. Each mode of transportation had distinctive advantages and disadvantages in terms of cost, convenience, vulnerability to weather delays, and the possibility of working while traveling. Still, each and every one of them would eventually have gotten me to New York. That fact exemplifies for individual choice what systems theorists call *equifinality.*[19] According to the principle of equifinality, there are many different ways that an open system such as a person, team, or organization can behave and still achieve the same outcome—in this case, to get to New York.

I drove. Driving was a little cheaper than the other options, but it took more time and offered zero possibility of getting work done en route. A colleague, surprised at my choice, used the phrase "really dumb" to characterize it. But I *like* to drive. Even more, I like having the flexibility of leaving the instant I am ready to go, and having choice about the route I will take. So I picked a way to get to New York that suited me just fine. My colleague would have made a different choice—but also would have gotten to New York. That is what is meant by equifinality.

As I write this, I am starting to think about the first meeting of a new research group that I will convene next month. How should I handle the first few minutes of that meeting? Should I begin by telling members the main objectives of the research project? Or should I ease into the purposes of the project gradually, perhaps starting out by inviting each member to talk briefly about his or her own research interests? Or should I prepare a read-ahead handout describing the project and open the meeting by asking members for their reactions and questions? Should I strike a formal, task-oriented tone, or be more casual and interpersonally oriented?

Once again, there is no right answer to those questions, no one best way for me to act as I launch my team. What *is* important is that somehow I get conditions established that help the group get off to a good start. As we have seen in previous chapters, this involves three activities: helping the team come to terms with its immediate task and ensuring that all understand how it is linked to the team's broader purposes; bounding the group as a performing unit so all members understand and accept that we, collectively, are the people responsible for the project; and establishing the basic norms of conduct that will guide member behavior in the initial phase of the group's life. Those are the things I must accomplish in that first meeting. But I have enormous latitude in *how* I accomplish them.

In fact, my actual behavior at the first meeting will be significantly shaped by the circumstances of the moment: Is everybody present when the meeting is supposed to start? Do all members already know one another? How much enthusiasm do they seem to have for the project? My behavior also will depend on my own preferred style of operating: Am I more comfortable taking an active, assertive leadership role, or do I prefer to solicit input from others and then summarize and integrate their ideas? Do I generally lead using a matter-of-fact style, or do I like to liven things up with humor? Am I someone who can describe a project in a way that engenders shared excitement in a group, or am I better at helping each member identify the particular aspects of the work that he or she personally finds most engaging? These and other considerations too numerous to mention—and certainly too complex to preprogram even with the most complicated decision tree—together will shape the actual behaviors I exhibit at the research group meeting. There are many different ways that I can create the conditions for a good team launch, and no particular style of leading is necessarily better than others for getting those conditions in place.

The principle of equifinality applies even in settings where much of what a leader must do is technologically determined or dictated by required procedures. The airline flight deck is one such setting. Because small deviations from proper procedures by a cockpit crew can spawn highly adverse consequences, much of the behavior of the crew leader, the captain, is highly standardized. Members can count on each new captain conducting some kind of briefing before the first flight begins, for example, because that is required by most airlines. What captains actually *do* in those briefings, however, is mostly up to them. But do captains who are viewed by their peers as excellent team leaders behave differently in their initial crew briefings than do those who are seen as only so-so team leaders?

To find out, researcher Robert Ginnett asked flight standards staff, who regularly fly with the airline's pilots to ensure that the highest standards of professionalism are maintained, to identify captains who all were fine pilots but who they considered to be either excellent or marginal team leaders. He then selected a number of captains in each of these two groups and, without knowing whether the nominators had placed a given captain in the excellent or marginal category, observed that captain's briefings of two different crews on two different occasions. Ginnett captured everything that happened from the moment pilots and flight attendants began to arrive in the briefing area—where they sat or stood, the content and style of the leader's remarks, how much other crew members participated, how long the briefing lasted, and more.

His first pass through the data revealed enormous variation among captains in both groups in the length, style, and content of their briefings. Closer inspection, however, showed that all of the captains who had been nominated as excellent team leaders accomplished, in their own idiosyncratic way, three things. First, they established the *legitimacy of their authority* as crew leader. They exhibited neither a laissez-faire nor fully democratic approach in conducting the briefing. They communicated their own authority and competence by unapologetically specifying what they sought and expected from the crew—but they also identified without embarrassment or apology the matters about which they needed information or assistance from others. Second, they established the *boundaries* of the crew, taking special care to ensure that all members, pilots and cabin crew alike, recognized that they shared responsibility for the flight and for the flying experience of their passengers. And third, they affirmed the *norms of conduct* that would guide crew behavior, that is, their expectations about how members would act and interact, particularly regarding how they would communicate and coordinate with one another.[20]

It is noteworthy that the captains gave less attention in their briefings to the *task* that the crew would perform than has been observed for excellent leaders of other types of work teams.[21] In airline operations, individual and collective tasks are defined and engineered in such

detail that there is little need for the captain to clarify or reinforce what the crew is there to accomplish. Even so, the excellent captains often did give special reinforcement to the importance of keeping safety in the forefront of everyone's attention—and, once again, did so in their own idiosyncratic ways.

The great diversity of styles used by team leaders in launching their crews is seen not just when a team first comes together, but also in how leaders establish and maintain the other conditions that foster team effectiveness—clarifying a team's direction, getting its structure right, arranging for contextual supports, and ensuring that the team receives competent coaching at the appropriate times.

The leader of a university computer support team I once observed used an entirely different strategy. This leader, who we will call Frieda, had solid credibility with senior university officials. Perhaps because her formal supervisors also were clients of her team, as well as being the people who occasionally had to field complaints from faculty who wanted their malfunctioning e-mail immediately fixed, they were highly motivated to do anything they could to help Frieda's team succeed. When she needed additional resources or support from the central university administration, Frieda would prepare a careful analysis of her team's present situation and of the future demands it was likely to face. Then she would calmly present the results of these analyses, along with her recommendations for action, to appropriate university officials—who almost always would accept her proposals. What Frieda wanted for her teams, Frieda usually got.

There is no one right way to provide leadership to a work team. Let me hasten to add, however, that there also are many *wrong* ways to go about creating the conditions for team effectiveness—strategies or styles that backfire or whose short-term benefits are negated by long-term liabilities. One way to get it wrong is to mislead or lie to those who are in a position to provide teams with the structures, resources, or supports they need in their work. Beyond the moral problems of lying, disingenuous strategies destroy the credibility of those who use them when, as inevitably happens, others discover that what is claimed cannot be trusted.

Another way to get it wrong is to ape someone else's style, or to follow prescriptions from a textbook or training course that specify how good leaders are supposed to act. It always is embarrassing to observe someone trying to enact a leadership style that is not the person's own—such as the junior manager who admiringly adopts the style of the charismatic, chief executive but succeeds only in calling attention to the enormity of their difference in competence. The junior manager would be better advised to cease practicing in front of a mirror and instead to spend that time and effort identifying and honing his or her *own* best style of leading.[22] It can be just as embarrassing to observe someone who has learned from a textbook or management training course how good leaders behave, and who then attempts to act that way back at work. "What happened to Charlotte at that training course?" team members ask one another. "Well, let's just wait it out; she'll probably be back to normal soon." And indeed she will.

The third way to get it wrong is to relentlessly enact one's preferred manner of leading even in the face of data that it is not working very well, to keep on keeping on with a style that is indeed one's own and with which one may be quite comfortable but that consistently yields unanticipated and unfavorable results.[23] Some leaders, for example, are most comfortable with what can be called a "command and control" style of leadership. They issue orders about what is to be done—not just by the team they are leading but also by their peers and even bosses, Sometimes command and control is fully appropriate—for example, among airline captains when a potentially catastrophic event such as an engine fire requires immediate and decisive action. On those occasions, the leader will be reinforced for using that style: "Immediate action was required, I issued the orders, team members did what I told them, and it worked out fine." But other times, such as in launching a team or exploring the implications for the team's performance strategy of a changing external environment, that style may be inimical to what needs to be accomplished. The leadership problem becomes severe when the leader does not recognize that his or her actions are not having the intended effects—or, worse, when the leader sees that things have not gone well but blames either the situation ("Nobody could have turned that around—it was wired for failure") or team members ("They just wouldn't do what I told them—they need to shape up real soon"). In such cases, there is no opportunity for the leader to self-correct because he or she is not open to data that might suggest that the leader's own actions contributed to the poor outcome.

Ginnett observed this inability (or unwillingness) to self-correct among those captains in his study who had been nominated by their peers as marginal team leaders. Although there was as much variation in briefing style among the marginal captains as among those who were viewed as excellent team leaders, there were two major differences between the two groups. First, no matter what style they used in conducting their crew briefings, the marginal captains failed to establish the conditions needed for a good team launch. Second, all of them, again in their own ways, exhibited significant problems with *control* that made it nearly impossible for them to use their experiences to become more effective. Some of these captains were persistently overcontrolling, not asking for input from other team members and ignoring or diverting any suggestions that members did manage to make. Others were persistently undercontrolling, so democratic or laissez-faire in conducting their briefings that crew members were left uncertain about how the team was supposed to operate. Worst of all were captains who vacillated between overcontrolling and undercontrolling in ways and at times that could not be anticipated, which in some cases nearly incapacitated team members in carrying out their own parts of the work. Ginnett's observations documented that even though these captains' briefings did not go well, they either did not recognize the dysfunctional effects of their style or they were unable (or unwilling) to alter it. How they led was how they led, no matter what consequences ensued. Excellent team leaders, by contrast, are aware of their natural styles—they know what they like to do, what they can do easily and well, and what they can accomplish only with difficulty if at all. They learn over time how to exploit their special strengths and preferences, and how to contain or circumvent their weaknesses. They attend carefully to the circumstances of the moment, and vary their behavior in real time to exploit unanticipated leadership opportunities and circumvent obstacles that risk blunting their initiatives. They may never have heard of the principle of equifinality, but they behave in accord with it. And, most important of all, they are continuously alert for signs that their actions may not be having their intended effects. For great leaders, expanding and strengthening their repertoire of leadership behaviors is a lifelong learning project.

. . . they can.

Some organizations provide team leaders with so little latitude for tailoring their leadership to the circumstances of the moment that to say, as I have said, that "great leaders create the conditions that promote team effectiveness any way they can" has no practical significance. Just as there is little point to having a work team if all performance processes are dictated by technology or prespecified operating procedures, so too there is little point to having someone occupy the role of team leader if he or she has no room to maneuver.[24] It is the difference between a jazz musician and a section player in a symphony orchestra: The former has lots of room to improvise, whereas the latter must follow exactly a detailed score—and do so under the direct and constant supervision of a conductor. Team leaders should be more like jazz musicians.

Not everyone can do it, not even when they have lots of latitude and support. Although I am chastened by the modest findings from researchers' decades-long search for leadership effectiveness traits, it nonetheless seems to me, based on my and my colleagues' studies of teams, that there are a handful of personal qualities that do distinguish excellent team leaders from those for whom team leadership is a struggle. Specifically, I suggest that effective team leaders have the following four qualities: (1) they know some things, (2) they know how to *do* some things, (3) they have *emotional maturity* sufficient for the demands of the leadership role, and (4) they have a good measure of personal *courage.*[23]

Know Some Things. The first attribute listed—knowledge about conditions that foster team effectiveness and the skill to create those conditions—is something that people who are "naturals" as team leaders know implicitly.

Fortunately, knowledge about the conditions that foster team effectiveness can be taught. This book seeks to do just that, and it also can be done in university courses and in management training seminars. A training course could, for example, help team leaders understand the importance for team effectiveness of having a clear, engaging, and consequential direction by using case analyses of effective and ineffective teams, or could teach them about the importance of timing in coaching interventions by analysis of videotapes of team coaches in action. Similar pedagogical devices could be used to teach team leaders about the other conditions discussed here. If a team leader does not already know what it takes to promote team effectiveness, he or she can readily learn it.

Know How to Do Some Things. It is not sufficient for those who lead work teams merely to know about the conditions for effectiveness; they also need to know how to create and maintain those conditions—in a word, they need to be *skilled* in leading teams. Two kinds of skills are critical to team leadership: skill in diagnosis, and skill in execution.

Effective team leaders carefully target their interventions, aiming them at those aspects of a team's interactions, its structure, or its context where the contemplated action is both feasible and likely to make a substantial and constructive difference. To choose intervention targets wisely requires *diagnostic skills.* Effective leaders are able to extract from the complexity of the performance situation those themes that are diagnostically significant (as opposed to those that are merely transient noise or that are of little consequence for team behavior). These themes, which summarize what is happening in the group or its context, are then compared with what the leader believes *should be* happening to identify interaction patterns or organizational features that are not what they could be. Only then is the leader in a position to craft interventions that have a reasonable chance of narrowing the gap between the real and the ideal. Natural team leaders do all of this intuitively and seemingly without effort. The rest of us may have to go through the diagnostic process step by step until, eventually, it becomes natural for us as well.

Beyond their excellence in diagnosing work situations and team dynamics, effective team leaders also are skilled in executing actions that narrow the gap between a team's present reality and what could be. Leaders who have a rich and diverse portfolio of *execution skills* are better able to do this than leaders who have but a few things they can do well. Richard Walton and I attempted to identify the execution skills that are most critical to team leader effectiveness; what we came up with is reproduced in Table 16.1. Even though moderately long, the list necessarily is incomplete. There always are new skills to be acquired by those who lead teams. Leaders who keep on with that learning

Table 16.1   Execution Skills of Team Leaders

Envisioning Skill

The ability to envision desired end states and to articulate and communicate them to others.

Inventive Skill

The ability to think of numerous nonobvious ways of getting something done.

Negotiation Skill

The ability to work persistently and constructively with peers and superiors to secure resources or assistance that is needed to support one's team.

Decision-Making Skill

The ability to choose among various courses of action under uncertainty, using all perspectives and data that can be efficiently obtained to inform the decision.

Teaching Skill

The ability to help team members learn both experientially and didactically.

Interpersonal Skill

The ability to communicate, listen, confront, persuade, and generally to work constructively with others, particularly in situations where people's anxieties may be high.

Implementation Skill

The ability to get things done. At the simplest level, knowing how to make lists, attend to mundane details, check and recheck for omitted items or people, and follow plans through to completion. At a more sophisticated level, the ability to constructively and assertively manage power, political relationships, and symbols to get things accomplished in social systems.

Source: From Hackman and Walton (1986). Leading groups in organizations. In P. S. Goodman (Ed.), *Designing effective work groups* (pp. 72-119). San Francisco: Jossey-Bass. This material is used by permission of John Wiley & Sons, Inc.

continuously expand the options they have available for helping the teams they lead.

Once again, some individuals are naturally talented in doing the right thing at the right time and in the right way to help their teams succeed, but others require training to develop their skills in taking action. Much is known about training procedures that can help people develop new skills or hone existing ones, and one of the things that is known is that skills cannot be mastered by reading books, listening to lectures, or doing case analyses.[26] Instead, skill training involves observation of positive models (i.e., people whose behavior illustrates highly competent execution of that which is being taught) coupled with repeated practice and feedback. Training in execution skills is necessarily personalized and for that reason is expensive and time consuming. But it is a critical ingredient in the mix that makes for a great team leader.[27]

Even with extensive training, not everyone is able to master the execution skills that can spell the difference between excellent and poor team leadership. Much is implicitly revealed about an organization by noting how senior managers deal with that fact.

Consider the training of pilots who fly commercial aircraft. The technical training of pilots, whether in a civilian flight school or in the military, is demanding and stringent. Those who cannot master the skills of safely flying an aircraft wash out and do not become pilots. The decision rule is more forgiving, however, once a pilot has logged enough years of service to be upgraded to captain, to move from being a team member to a team leader. Although captain upgrade courses in most commercial airlines do include leadership training, I am aware of no otherwise qualified pilot who was refused promotion to captain because of an inability to demonstrate mastery of leadership skills. This was advantageous for Bob Ginnett, whose research design required him to observe a number of captains who, although well qualified technically, were shaky as leaders of their teams. But the failure of airlines to insist that captains be superb leaders as well as superb pilots is surely less advantageous for the younger pilots they lead and, perhaps, for those who fly on the aircraft they command.

Emotional Maturity. The inability of some people to master leadership skills may have less to do with their cognitive capabilities than with their emotional make-up. Leading a team is an emotionally demanding undertaking, especially in dealing with anxieties— both one's own and those of others. Leaders who are emotionally mature are willing and able to move toward anxiety-arousing states of affairs in the interest of learning about them rather than moving away to get anxieties reduced as quickly as possible.

Competent team leadership often involves inhibiting impulses to act (e.g., to correct an emerging problem or to exploit a suddenly appearing opportunity) until more data have become available or until the time is right to make an intervention. Sometimes it even is necessary for leaders to take actions that temporarily *raise* anxieties, including their own, to lay the groundwork for subsequent interventions that seek to foster team learning or change.

Imagine that you have formed a task force that has one month to come up with an important new organizational policy. A full week has passed, and there is little

apparent progress. Various policy proposals have been offered and debated, but members' views are not coalescing and you are concerned that no momentum is developing. Two task force members come to you individually and privately to express their concern about how things are going and to suggest that you "do something" to get the task force moving. To do what the members ask would reduce their and your anxieties, but could undermine the development of the task force as a self-managing team. Moreover, it may be too early to intervene—the task force is still logging experience, and it might be better to let the tensions continue to build in hopes of a creative release at the group's midpoint. How do you respond to the members' pleas? The temptation to act is strong, but there also are good arguments for holding off for the moment, letting anxieties continue to build a while longer. To make a wise decision in this case requires not just knowledge of the life-cycle dynamics of time-bounded work teams but also the ability to manage one's own anxieties and emotions.

Another example. You lead a team in a municipal agency that manages the assessments of residential properties and provides data to those who prepare homeowners' tax bills. Your team relies heavily on a large database in carrying out its work, as do workers in several other municipal departments. This morning you received a memo from the senior manager of information technology announcing that the city had contracted with a vendor to convert its database of housing stock to a new system that will provide greater centralized control of the data and therefore reduce errors. The senior manager's memo states that the database will be unavailable for five days beginning the first of the next month while the vendor accomplishes the changeover, and thereafter all data changes will be submitted to staff in his department rather than be handled directly by end users. When you finish reading, you are furious. You were not consulted about either the new system or how the changeover will be handled. The first of each month, when the database will be temporarily unavailable, is exactly the time when your team most needs it. And, most infuriating of all, the new requirement to submit change requests to information technology staff will significantly compromise your team's ability to manage its work in its own way and on its own schedule. How do you respond to the memo? My own impulse, stronger than I wish it were, would be to craft a scorching reply to the information technology manager, with copies to the city manager and the mayor. That would be emotionally satisfying, to be sure. But would it be the most likely to ensure that my team would continue to have the information technology tools and support it needs in its work?

The impulse to get things taken care of sooner rather than later, or to strike back when one feels threatened or abused by others' actions, can be almost irresistible. It takes a good measure of emotional maturity for a leader to resist such impulses, to find ways to deal with one's anxieties and emotions that neither deny their reality and legitimacy nor allow them to dominate one's behavior.

Courage. The king of Asteroid 325 in Antoine de Saint-Exupéry's *Little Prince* found an excellent way to be a successful leader—he discerned what his subjects wished to do and then decreed that they do precisely that. Political candidates, these days, seem to have taken their cue from that king: Pollsters tell them what the people want, and the candidates promise to provide it. Such strategies may help one get elected, remain in favor with one's subordinates, or even hold onto one's job, but they are not *leadership* strategies.

Leadership involves moving a system from where it is now to some other, better place. It means that one often is at the margins of what people presently like and want, working close to the edge of what is acceptable rather than at the center of the collective consensus. To help a team address and modify dysfunctional group dynamics, for example, a leader may need to challenge existing group norms and disrupt established routines—and most likely will incur some anger from group members in doing so. To improve a team's contextual supports or to increase the resources available to it, a leader may need to rock the organizational boat—and may risk a loss of esteem with his other peers and superiors in doing so. To redirect a group from its traditional purposes to new ones that better reflect a changed external reality or revised organizational values, a leader may engender resistance so intense that it places his or her own job at risk. Such behaviors require courage.[28]

Leaders differ in how prepared they are to step up to these challenges, as is seen in the behavior of two executive team leaders described to me by Jim Burruss, a senior consultant at Hay McBer who works extensively with such teams. One of the leaders joined an organization that needed both trimming and redirection. The trimming would unfortunately involve a reduction in staff, but the redirection offered the prospect of an attractive new beginning. The manager informed his executive team that he planned to move simultaneously and immediately on both fronts by informing a significant number of staff that their present jobs no longer existed but that they were free to apply for new positions in the reconfigured organization. Executive team members were worried that their leader might be attempting too much too quickly. The manager heard them out but decided to proceed anyway—the worst that could have happened, he later said, was that he could have failed and lost his job.

The second leader regularly needed to have his backbone stiffened by his executive team. "You just *have* to take a stand on that issue," members would tell him. And, after hearing their arguments, he would agree to do so. But whenever one or another of his team members would speak to him later about the possible downside of the action he had agreed to take, he would back off to give the matter "additional thought." The strong actions that the organization actually needed, Jim reports, never happened.

In these examples, the leader who behaved courageously kept his job and prospered, and the one who could not muster his courage did not. It often is the other way around. Leaders who behave courageously are indeed more likely than those who do not to make significant and constructive differences in their teams and organizations—but they often wind up paying a substantial personal toll.[29]

What Can Be Learned. The four qualities just discussed are differentially amenable to training—and in the order listed. It is relatively straightforward to help team leaders expand what they *know* about the conditions that foster team effectiveness. It is more challenging, but with sufficient time and effort entirely feasible, to help them hone their *skills* in diagnosis and execution. To foster team leaders' *emotional maturity* is harder still, and is perhaps better viewed more as a developmental task for one's life than as something that can be taught.[30] *Courage* may be the most trait-like of the four attributes. Although there indisputably are differences in courage across individuals, it is beyond me to imagine how one might help leaders become more willing than they already are to take courageous actions with their teams, peers, and bosses to increase the chances that their teams will excel.

Because of the paucity of proven educational strategies for developing the emotional maturity and courage of would-be team leaders, the best present strategy for assuring they have these resources may be to carefully select for leadership roles those persons who have already exhibited them. Simply electing someone from the group as "team leader" or choosing as leader the member who has demonstrated the greatest *task* competence, for example, often will result in the wrong person occupying what can be a critical role for a work team. Leader selection processes, in this way of thinking, would rely more on direct evidence of behavioral competencies than on either standard personality measures or off-the-shelf tests of verbal and analytic ability.[31]

The personal attributes I have suggested here as key to team leader effectiveness may seem strange to those who are accustomed to thinking of leadership qualities mainly in terms of personality traits or behavioral styles, and I have offered my views in a speculative spirit. But it is nonetheless true that the superb team leaders I have observed over the years have most, if not all, of these very qualities. It may be worthwhile to give new thought to old questions about how team leaders might be selected, assessed, and trained on these difficult-to-measure but potentially significant attributes.

Getting It Done

There are nontrivial implications for organizational practice in the question with which the previous section began ("How do great leaders create the conditions that promote team effectiveness?") and in its answer ("Any way they can"). The main work of team leaders is to do whatever needs to be done to ensure that the handful of conditions that foster team effectiveness are in place—and stay there. Is the work team a *real* team, or just a collection of individuals who go by that name? Does it have a clear, engaging, and consequential direction? Does the team's structure enable, rather than impede competent teamwork? Does the team's organizational context provide the supports and resources that the team needs in its work? And does the team have available ample and expert coaching to help members get over rough spots and take advantage of emerging opportunities?

As we have seen, some of these conditions are best created before the team even meets for the first time, others at its launch meeting, others around the midpoint of its work, and still others when a significant piece of work has been completed. Serendipity and history play important roles in determining when the enabling conditions can be created or strengthened, how that might best be accomplished, and how hard it will be to do so. Sometimes most of the conditions will already be in place when a team is formed, and fine-tuning them will not pose much of a leadership challenge; other times, such as in an established organization that has been tuned over the years to support and control *individual* work, it can take enormous effort and ingenuity to establish even the basic conditions required for competent teamwork.

We also have seen that there is no one best strategy or style for accomplishing this kind of leadership work, nor any one person who is mainly responsible for getting it done. Instead, team leadership involves inventing and competently executing whatever actions are most likely to create and sustain the enabling conditions. Anyone who helps do that, including both external managers and team members who hold no formal leadership role, is exercising team leadership. What is important is that the key leadership *functions* get fulfilled, not who fulfills them and certainly not how they go about doing it.[32]

The richer the set of leadership skills held by team members and organizational managers, the greater the number of options available for getting the enabling conditions in place. It is like the difference between driving and taking the train. I pointed out earlier that when driving there are always alternative routes to the destination if one road is blocked. A train, however, has but one set of tracks. If there is an obstruction on the tracks, the train cannot proceed until the obstruction is removed. Relying on any single person to provide leadership is the equivalent of taking the train.

By contrast, having multiple individuals with diverse skills pitching in to help create and sustain the enabling conditions gives a team lots of room to maneuver. If one strategy for moving forward is blocked, perhaps by a recalcitrant manager or by technological constraints that would be enormously expensive to change, there are other strategies that also could work.

The more members who are contributing to the real work of leadership (that is, helping to create, fine-tune, and exploit the benefits of the enabling conditions), the better. Still, it usually is a good idea to have one person identified as the "leader" of even a self-managing work team to facilitate communication and coordination among members. Who that person is can rotate from time to time and even can be selected by members themselves. But making sure that things do not fall between the cracks and that information finds its way to the people who need it are activities usually handled most efficiently by a single individual who has overview of the entire work process.

One of the main objectives of this chapter has been to offer for consideration a nontraditional model of how leaders can help their teams and organizations do well, a model that focuses more on the functions that leaders fulfill than on anything about their personalities or styles. This approach to team leadership differs from commonsense notions, which posit that influence flows dominantly from the person identified as "leader" to the team rather than in all directions—upward to bosses and laterally to peers as well as downward from formal leaders to regular members. It differs as well from leadership theories that focus mainly on the personal characteristics of good leaders, or that specify the best leadership styles, or that lay out in detail all the major contingencies that researchers have documented among traits, styles, and situational properties.

There can be no useful theory of leadership without an accompanying theory that specifies what is required for systems to achieve their main purposes. I have tried to provide here a way of thinking about team leadership that integrates what we know about the conditions that foster work team effectiveness with what has been learned over the last several decades of research about leadership. This approach is more complex than any list of "principles of good management" or "one-minute" prescriptions. Yet it also is simpler (there are just a few key conditions) and more usable (create and sustain those conditions any way you can) than either contingency models of leadership or those that require fundamental reprogramming of leaders' personal models of intervention.

The present approach also is more optimistic than some others—for example, those that claim that leaders make no substantial difference, that they are but pawns in a larger drama driven by external forces,[33] or others that posit that high-status leaders should keep their distance from the group that is performing the work so they do not unduly influence members' deliberations.[34] Instead, I have attempted to lay out a way of thinking about leadership that empowers both formal and informal leaders so that, through their behavior, they have a reasonable chance of helping a team evolve into a performing unit that meets the legitimate expectations of its clients, becomes stronger over time, and contributes positively to the personal learning and well-being of its members.

Notes

1. For details, see Corn (2000).

2. See Meindl, Erlich, and Dukerich (1985); for a discussion of the mechanisms that drive leader attributions, see Meindl (1990).

3. Influential and pessimistic early reviews of research findings on leader traits were published by Stodgill (1948) and by Mann (1959), the latter focusing on the personality traits of *group* leaders. For reviews of more contemporary research on leadership traits and assessments of the present state of leadership research more generally, see Hogan, Curphy, and Hogan (1994), Hollander (1985), and the integrative books by Bass (1990), Chemers (1997), and Yukl (2002).

4. Among the most promising contemporary research streams on leader personality and collective performance identified by Hogan, Curphy, and Hogan (1994) are the studies of "charismatic" leaders by Robert House and his colleagues (e.g., House, 1977; House, Spangler, & Woycke, 1991) and research by Robert Helmreich and his colleagues on the role of airline captains' personalities in shaping crew dynamics and flight safety (e.g., Chidester, Helmreich, Gregorich, & Geis, 1991).

5. This possibility has been at least hinted at recently by one commentator (Nicholson, 2001).

6. My credibility on this topic may be lessened somewhat by what happened when I participated as a guest in one airline's training program. I took the test that was offered and, upon plotting my scores, discovered that my characteristic behavioral style was most similar to that of "housewife." This category was not viewed by other participants as among the most desirable. Although they acknowledged that a university professor might well fall into it, a real *pilot* surely would not. We laughed about the episode, but I could not help wondering about the feelings of those pilot participants who shared the category with me.

7. See, for example, Bass (1990) and Fleishman (1973).

8. For a review of contingency models of leadership, see Yukl (2002, chap. 8); for an example of a contingency model that focuses on leaders' cognitive resources, see Fiedler and Garcia (1987); for one that provides carefully drawn implications for leader behavior, see Vroom and Jago (1988).

9. Humans are quite limited in their ability to process multiple contingencies in making decisions about their behavior (Gigerenzer, 1999; Simon, 1990). Recognizing this, one distinguished contingency theorist had an electronic device constructed to guide leaders' decisions about their behavior. The leader sets various switches in accord with the characteristics of the decision situation, pushes a button, and has electronically revealed the course of action that, according to this scholar's contingency theory, should be followed. The device has not been marketed (indeed, its construction was something of a lighthearted enterprise), but it nicely symbolizes the difficulty of using complex contingency theories as guides for leader behavior.

10. See, for example, Farris and Lim (1969) and Lowin and Craig (1968).

11. Zajonc (1965). See Fiedler and Garcia (1987) for additional evidence about how a leader's ability to use his or her cognitive resources is compromised in stressful circumstances.

12. See, for example, Argyris (1993).

13. For further discussion of how the impact of coaching is conditioned by a team's direction, structure, and context, see Hackman and Wageman (2001).

14. For details of this study, see Wageman (2001). Design factors are likely to moderate the impact of almost any process-focused intervention, not just leader coaching. For example, consider the effects of "brainstorming" interventions on group creativity. As noted by Hargadon (1999), research evidence provides little support for brainstorming as a means for enhancing creativity. Would that conclusion hold if the groups researched had been superbly designed? Hargadon's own findings suggest that if brainstorming groups have both an information-rich context and a set of collective norms that actively support use of that information, the intervention may indeed promote creativity.

15. In statistical language, design features controlled 40 percent of the variation in team self-management, compared with 10 percent for leader coaching. For performance outcomes, design features controlled 37 percent of the variation, compared with less than 1 percent for leader coaching.

16. For discussion of the factors that make it difficult for a team to change course once members have established a standard mode of operating, see Gersick and Hackman (1990).

17. For details, see Greenblatt (2001).

18. For evidence about the risks of an overemphasis on procedures, see Woolley (2001).

19. See Katz and Kahn (1978, chap. 2).

20. For a detailed report of these findings, see Ginnett (1987, 1993).

21. See Hackman and Walton (1986) for a discussion of the special issues that arise for different types of teamwork.

22. The temptation to mimic the style of the master is a significant risk of the "apprenticeship" model of professional education. The risk is encountered in numerous domains. In schools of education, students may be so intent on mimicking the style of master teachers with whom they are working that they shortchange the development of their own unique talents as educators. In conservatories, talented young players may defer the development of their own musical voices in favor of learning to play in the style of the master with whom they are studying. Even in research training, apprentices may learn well how to design and conduct studies in the fashion of the senior scientist with whom they are working—but depart their training a pale copy of that scientist: "He's quite good," the letter of recommendation says, "but not as good as his professor." There is much to be learned from masters, but the best learning occurs when what the master has to offer is incorporated into the novice's evolving personal style of teaching, performing, researching—or leading.

23. The recovery community has an only slightly tongue-in-cheek aphorism that captures this phenomenon: "Insanity is doing the same thing over and over again, and expecting different results."

24. One airline that participated in our research went to great lengths to impress upon captains that their behavior was critical in helping the airline weather the difficult economic and operational times it had encountered. "If there is a delay before pushback," captains were told, "get out of the cockpit and see if you can help resolve the problem. You may be the one person who can really do something about it." It is ironic that these same captains, exhorted to exercise their authority to deal with problems formally beyond the bounds of their own job, found their latitude in doing their *real* work ever more limited.

25. These attributes closely parallel those previously identified in joint work with Richard Walton (Hackman & Walton, 1986).

26. See, for example, Campbell (1988), Goldstein (1991), and Goldstein and Sorcher (1974).

27. Schools of management generally are excellent in helping their students develop diagnostic and analytic skills, but most of them provide little or no training in the execution skills that would help management students *use* to good effect

what they have learned. This state of affairs may reflect the fact that it is much more labor intensive to help students develop leadership skills than it is to teach them concepts and analytic techniques. Or it may be that educators assume that leadership skills are best developed informally on the job. In either case, not to provide management students the opportunity to practice the skills they will need to enact team leadership roles is to significantly shortchange them. I am reminded of a cartoon depicting the first day of work of a freshly minted M.B.A. He has been given a tour of the facilities by his boss, and finally has arrived at his new office. "That was all very interesting," he says. "But now it's time to get to work. Where's the case?"

28.   For an exploration of managerial courage, including strategies for keeping one's job while exhibiting it, see Hornstein (1986).

29.   If courage is required of those who hold formal leadership roles, that quality is needed even more by regular members of teams who have no special obligation to lead but who nonetheless elect to take leadership initiatives. Official team leaders generally have some resources that regular members do not. They have at least modestly more formal power and more ready access to information, resources, and managerial colleagues. And they usually have a positive balance of what Hollander (1958) has termed "idiosyncrasy credits," the latitude to deviate from established group norms without incurring the corrections or sanctions that would be applied to other team members. Without these role-conferred advantages, it can be quite risky for a team member to courageously take an action or raise a question about matters that others have come to accept as "the way things are done here."

30.   Organizations do, however, differ enormously in the degree to which they provide a context that supports the emotional development of their members. In some, reflection on and thoughtful exploration of emotional issues is an accepted and valued part of organizational life. Other organizations are more like emotional playrooms for perpetual adolescents.

31.   The case for focusing on competence rather than "intelligence" in selecting among candidates is persuasively made by David McClelland (1973). Based on McClelland's work, the Hay McBer consulting firm has developed competence-based models for identifying leaders and composing senior management teams. Research now being conducted by Ruth Wageman of Tuck School at Dartmouth College and Mary Fontaine of Hay McBer is seeking to identify those team leadership competencies that are helpful to a team so long as they are held by any team member, regardless of role, versus those that are helpful only if they are held by the formal team leader.

32.   For further exploration of the functional approach to leadership, see Hackman and Walton (1986) and McGrath (1962). For an application of a functional approach to group decision-making processes, see Hirokawa (1985).

33.   The debate about how much difference leaders actually make has addressed mainly the impact of CEOs on corporate performance. This literature is reviewed by Wasserman, Nohria, and Anand (2001), who conclude that the question "Does leadership matter?" is unlikely ever to be satisfactorily answered. A more tractable and useful question, they suggest, is "*When* does leadership matter?"

34.   The proposal that leaders should keep their distance is among the recommendations offered by Janis (1982) to minimize the chances of "groupthink."

Bibliography

Abramis, D. J. (1990). Semiconductor manufacturing team. In J. R. Hackman (Ed.), *Groups that work (and those that don't)* (pp. 449–470). San Francisco: Jossey-Bass.

Alderfer, C. P. (1976). Boundary relations and organizational diagnosis. In H. Meltzer & F. R. Wickert (Eds.), *Humanizing organizational behavior* (pp. 109–133). Springfield, IL: Thomas.

Alderfer, C. P. (1977). Group and intergroup relations. In J. R. Hackman & J. L. Suttle (Eds.), *Improving life at work* (pp. 217–296). Santa Monica, CA: Goodyear.

Alderfer, C. P. (1980). Consulting to underbounded systems. In C. P. Alderfer & C. L. Cooper (Eds.), *Advances in experiential social processes* (Vol. 2, pp. 267–295). New York: Wiley.

Alexander, J. A., Lichtenstein, R., & D'Aunno, T. A. (1996). The effects of treatment team diversity and size on assessments of team functioning. *Hospital and Health Services Administration, 41,* 37–53.

Allen, T., Katz, R., Grady, J. J., & Slavin, N. (1988). Project team aging and performance: The roles of project and functional managers. *R&D Management, 18,* 295–308.

Allison, G. T. (1971). *Essence of decision: Explaining the Cuban missile crisis.* Boston: Little, Brown.

Allmendinger, J., & Hackman, J. R. (1995). The more, the better? A four-nation study of the inclusion of women in symphony orchestras. *Social Forces, 74,* 423–460.

Allmendinger, J., & Hackman, J. R. (1996). Organizations in changing environments: The case of East German symphony orchestras. *Administrative Science Quarterly, 41,* 337–369.

Allmendinger, J., Hackman, J. R., & Lehman, E. V. (1996). Life and work in symphony orchestras. *The Musical Quarterly, 80,* 194–219.

Amabile, T. (1993). Motivational synergy: Toward new conceptualizations of intrinsic and extrinsic motivation in the workplace. *Human Resource Management Review, 3,* 185–201.

Amason, A. C. (1996). Distinguishing the effects of functional and dysfunctional conflict on strategic decision making: Resolving a paradox for top management teams. *Academy of Management Journal, 39,* 123–148.

Ancona, D., & Caldwell, D. F. (1992). Bridging the boundary: External activity and performance in organizational teams. *Administrative Science Quarterly, 37,* 634–665.

Ancona, D., & Chong, C. L. (1999). Cycles and synchrony: The temporal role of context in team behavior. In R. Wageman (Ed.), *Groups in context* (pp. 33–48). Stamford, CT: JAI Press.

Argote, L., Insko, C. A., Yovetich, N., & Romero, A. A. (1995). Group learning curves: The effects of turnover and task complexity on group performance. *Journal of Applied Social Psychology, 25,* 512–529.

Argote, L., & McGrath, J. E. (1993). Group processes in organizations: Continuity and change. *International Review of Industrial and Organizational Psychology, 8,* 333–389.

Argyris, C. (1976). *Increasing leadership effectiveness.* New York: Wiley.

Argyris, C. (1985). *Strategy, change and defensive routines.* Boston: Pitman.

Argyris, C. (1993). Education for leading-learning. *Organizational Dynamics, 21* (3), 5–17.

Argyris, C., & Schon, D. A. (1996). *Organizational learning II: Theory, method, and practice.* Reading, MA: Addison-Wesley.

Arrow, H., & McGrath, J. E. (1995). Membership dynamics in groups at work: A theoretical framework. *Research in Organizational Behavior, 17,* 373–411.

Arrow, H., McGrath, J. E., & Berdahl, J. L. (2000). *Small groups as complex systems.* Thousand Oaks, CA: Sage.

Atkinson, J. W. (1958). Motivational determinants of risk-taking behavior. In J. W. Atkinson (Ed.), *Motives in fantasy, action, and society* (pp. 322–339). Princeton, NJ: Van Nostrand.

Atkinson, J. W., & Litwin, G. H. (1960). Achievement motive and test anxiety conceived as motive to approach success and to avoid failure. *Journal of Abnormal and Social Psychology, 60,* 52–63.

Bailyn, L. (1985). Autonomy in the industrial R&D lab. *Human Resources Management, 24,* 129–146.

Bandura, A. (2000). Exercise of human agency through collective efficacy. *Current Directions in Psychological Science, 9,* 75–78.

Barrick, M. R., Stewart, G. L., Neubert, M. J., & Mount, M. K. (1998). Relating member ability and personality to work-team processes and team effectiveness. *Journal of Applied Psychology, 83,* 377–391.

Bass, B. M. (1990). *Bass and Stogdill's handbook of leadership* (3rd ed.). New York: Free Press.

Belbin, R. M. (1981). *Management teams: Why they succeed or fail.* Oxford: Heinemann.

Bell, B. S., & Kozlowski, S. W. J. (in press). A typology of virtual teams: Implications for effective leadership. *Group and Organizational Management.*

Benbasat, I., & Lim, L. (1993). The effects of group, task, context, and technology variables on the usefulness of group support systems: A meta-analysis of experimental studies. *Small Group Research, 24,* 430–462.

Bennis, W., & Nanus, B. (1985). *Leaders: The strategies for taking charge.* New York: Harper-Collins.

Berlew, D. E. (1979). Leadership and organizational excitement. In D. A. Kolb, I. M. Rubin, & J. M. McIntyre (Eds.), *Organizational psychology* (3rd ed., pp. 343–356). Englewood Cliffs, NJ: Prentice-Hall.

Bettenhausen, K., & Murnighan, J. K. (1985). The emergence of norms in competitive decision-making groups. *Administrative Science Quarterly, 30,* 350–372.

Bion, W. R. (1961). *Experiences in groups.* London: Tavistock.

Blauner, R. (1964). *Alienation and freedom.* Chicago: University of Chicago Press.

Boettger, R. D., & Greer, C. R. (1994). On the wisdom of rewarding A while hoping for B. *Organization Science, 5,* 569–582.

Bowers, C. A., Pharmer, J. A., & Salas, E. (2000). When member homogeneity is needed in work teams: A meta-analysis. *Small Group Research, 31,* 305–327.

Brehm, J. W. (1966). *A theory of psychological reactance.* New York: Academic Press.

Brodbeck, F. C. (1996). Criteria for the study of work group functioning. In M. A. West (Ed.), *Handbook of work group psychology* (pp. 285–315). Chichester, England: Wiley.

Brooks, F. P., Jr. (1995). *The mythical man-month* (2nd ed.). Reading, MA: Addison-Wesley.

Brown, J. S., & Duguid, P. (2000). *The social life of information.* Boston: Harvard Business School Press.

Buckley, K. (2001). *Virtual teams: Structure, process, and culture as predictors of effectiveness.* Manuscript submitted for publication.

Campbell, D. (1990). *If you don't know where you're going, you'll probably end up somewhere else.* Allen, TX: Thomas More Publishing.

Campbell, J. P. (1988). Training design for performance improvement. In J. P. Campbell & R. J. Campbell (Eds.), *Productivity in organizations: New perspectives from industrial and organizational psychology* (pp. 177–215). San Francisco: Jossey-Bass.

Campion, M. A., Medsker, G. J., & Higgs, A. C. (1993). Relations between work group characteristics and effectiveness: Implications for designing effective work groups. *Personnel Psychology, 46,* 823–850.

Cannon-Bowers, J. A., Saks, E., & Converse, S. A. (1993). Shared mental models in expert team decision-making. In N. J. Castellan, Jr. (Ed.), *Current issues in individual and group decision-making* (pp. 221–246). Hillsdale, NJ: Lawrence Erlbaum.

Carky, K. (1991). A theory of group stability. *American Sociological Review, 56,* 331–354.

Chatman, J. A., & Flynn, F. J. (2001). The influence of demographic heterogeneity on the emergence and consequences of cooperative norms in work teams. *Academy of Management Journal, 44,* 956–974.

Chemers, M. M. (1997). *An integrative theory of leadership.* Mahwah, NJ: Lawrence Erlbaum.

Cheng, P. W., & Novick, L. R. (1991). Causes versus enabling conditions. *Cognition, 40,* 83–120.

Chidester, T. R., Helmreich, R. L., Gregorich, S. E., & Geis, C. E. (1991). Pilot personality and crew coordination. *International Journal of Aviation Psychology, 1,* 25-44.

Clark, R. C. (1986). *Corporate law.* Boston: Little, Brown.

Cohen, M. D., & Bacdayan, P. (1994). Organizational routines are stored as procedural memory. *Organization Science, 5,* 554-568.

Cohen, S. G. (1994) Designing effective work teams. *Advances in Interdisciplinary Studies of Work Teams, I,* 67-102.

Cohen, S. G., & Bailey, D. E. {1997). What makes teams work: Group effectiveness research from the shop floor to the executive suite. *Journal of Management, 23,* 239-290.

Cohen, S. G., & Denison, D. R. (1990). Flight attendant teams. In J. R. Hackman (Ed.), *Groups that work (and those that don't)* (pp. 382-397). San Francisco: Jossey-Bass.

Cohen, S. G., & Ledford, G. E., Jr. (1994). The effectiveness of self-managing teams: A quasi-experiment. *Human Relations, 47,* 13-43.

Cole, R. E. (1985). The macropolitics of organizational change: A comparative analysis of the spread of small-group activities. *Administrative Science Quarterly, 30,* 560-585.

Cooper, H. S. F., Jr. (1976). *A house in space.* New York: Holt, Rinehart & Winston.

Cordery, J. L., Mueller, W. S., & Smith, L. M. (1991). Attitudinal and behavioral effects of autonomous group working: A longitudinal field study. *Academy of Management Journal, 34,* 464-476.

Corn, R. (2000). *Why poor teams get poorer: The influence of team effectiveness and design quality on the quality of group diagnostic processes.* Unpublished doctoral dissertation, Harvard University.

Cummings, J. N. (2001). *Work groups and knowledge sharing in global organizations.* Unpublished doctoral dissertation, Carnegie-Mellon University.

Cusumano, M. A. (1997, Fall). How Microsoft makes large teams work like small teams. *Sloan Management Review,* 9-20.

David, P. (1986). Understanding the economics of QWERTY: The necessity of history. In W. Parker (Ed.), *Economic history and the modern historian* (pp. 30-59). London: Blackwell.

Davis-Sacks, M. L. (1990a). Credit analysis team. In J. R. Hackman (Ed.), *Groups that work (and those that don't)* (pp. 126-145). San Francisco: Jossey-Bass.

Davis-Sacks, M. L. (1990b). The tracking team. In J. R. Hackman (Ed.), *Groups that work (and those that don't)* (pp. 157-170). San Francisco: Jossey-Bass.

Davis-Sacks, M. L., Denison, D. R., & Eisenstat, R. A. (1990). Summary: Professional support groups. In J. R. Hackman (Ed.), *Groups that work (and those that don't)* (pp. 195-205). San Francisco: Jossey-Bass.

Deci, E. L. (1975). *Intrinsic motivation.* New York: Plenum.

De Dreu, C. K. W, & Van Vianen, A. E. M. (2001). Managing relationship conflict and the effectiveness of organizational teams. *Journal of Organizational Behavior, 22,* 309–328.

Delbecq, A. E., Van de Ven, A. H., & Gustafson, D. H. (1975). *Group techniques for program planning: A guide to Nominal Group and Delphi processes.* Glenview, IL: Scott, Foresman.

Deming, W. E. (1986). *Out of the crisis.* Cambridge, MA: MIT Center for Advanced Engineering Study.

Dentler, R. A., & Erikson, K. T. (1959). The functions of deviance in groups. *Social Problems, 7,* 98–107.

Devine, D. J., Clayton, L. D., Philips, J. L., Dunford, B. B., & Melner, S. B. (1999). Teams in organizations: Prevalence, characteristics, and effectiveness. *Small Group Research, 30,* 678–711.

DiMaggio, P. J., & Powell, W. W. (1983). The iron cage revisited: Institutional isomorphism and collective rationality in organizational fields. *American Sociological Review, 48,* 147–160.

Dixon, M. B., & Smith, J. A. (1995). *Anne Bogart viewpoints.* Lyme, NH: Smith and Kraus.

Donnellon, A. (1996). *Team talk: The power of language in team dynamics.* Boston: Harvard Business School Press.

Dowell, A. M., & Hendershot, D. C. (1996, November). *No good deed goes unpunished: Case studies of incidents and potential incidents caused by protective systems.* Paper presented at the meeting of the American Institute of Chemical Engineers Loss Prevention Symposium, Houston.

Drazin, R., & Sandelands, L. (1992). Autogenesis: A perspective on the process of organizing. *Organization Science, 3*, 230–249.

Druskat, V. U., & Kayes, D. C. (1999). The antecedents of team competence: Toward a fine-grained model of self-managing team effectiveness. In R. Wageman (Ed.), *Groups in context* (pp. 201–231). Stamford, CT: JAI Press.

Druskat, V. U., & Wheeler, J. V. (2001). *Managing from the boundary: The effective leadership of self-managing work teams.* Manuscript submitted for publication.

Dunnigan, J. F., & Nofi, A. A. (1999). *Dirty little secrets of the Vietnam war.* New York: St. Martin's Press.

Edmondson, A. E. (1999). Psychological safety and learning behavior in work teams. *Administrative Science Quarterly, 44*, 350–383.

Eisenberg, E. M. (1984). Ambiguity as strategy in organizational communication. *Communication Monographs, 51*, 227–242.

Eisenstat, R. A. (1984). *Organizational learning in the creation of an industrial setting.* Unpublished doctoral dissertation, Yale University.

Eisenstat, R. A. (1990). Fairfield systems group. In J. R. Hackman (Ed.), *Groups that work (and those that don't)* (pp. 171–181). San Francisco: Jossey-Bass.

Ely, R. J., & Thomas, D. A. (2001). Cultural diversity at work: The effects of diversity perspectives on work group processes and outcomes. *Administrative Science Quarterly, 46*, 229–273.

Emerson, R. M. (1962). Power-dependence relations. *American Sociological Review, 27*, 31–40.

Farris, G. R., & Lim, F. G., Jr. (1969). Effects of performance on leadership, cohesiveness, influence, satisfaction, and subsequent performance. *Journal of Applied Psychology, 53*, 490–497.

Feldman, M. S., & March, J. G. (1981). Information in organizations as signal and symbol. *Administrative Science Quarterly, 26*, 171–186.

Fiedler, F. E., & Garcia, J. E. (1987). *New approaches to effective leadership: Cognitive resources and organizational performance.* New York: Wiley.

Fleishman, E. A. (1973). Twenty years of consideration and structure. In E. A. Fleishman & J. G. Hunt (Eds.), *Current developments in the study of leadership* (pp. 1–37). Carbondale: Southern Illinois University Press.

Foushee, H. C., Lauber, J. K., Baetge, M. M., & Acomb, D. B. (1986). *Crew factors in flight operations: III. The operational significance of exposure to short-haul air transport operations* (Technical Memorandum No. 88342). Moffett Field, CA: NASA Ames Research Center.

Freeman, J. (1973). The tyranny of structurelessness. In A. Koedt, E. Levine, & A. Rapone (Eds.), *Radical feminism* (pp. 285–299). New York: Quadrangle Books.

Freud, S. (1959). *Group psychology and the analysis of the ego* (J. Strachey, Trans.). New York: Norton. (Original work published 1922).

Furnham, A., Steele, H., & Pendleton, D. (1993). A psychometric assessment of the Belbin Team-Role Self-Perception Inventory. *Journal of Occupational and Organizational Psychology, 66*, 245–257.

Gergen, K. J. (1972, May). Multiple identity. *Psychology Today,* 31–36, 64–66.

Gersick, C. J. G. (1988). Time and transition in work teams: Toward a new model of group development. *Academy of Management Journal, 31*, 9–41.

Gersick, C. J. G. (1989). Marking time: Predictable transitions in task groups. *Academy of Management Journal, 31*, 9–41.

Gersick, C. J. G. (1990). The bankers. In J. R. Hackman (Ed.), *Groups that work (and those that don't)* (pp. 112–125). San Francisco: Jossey-Bass.

Gersick, C. J. G. (1991). Revolutionary change theories: A multilevel exploration of the punctuated equilibrium paradigm. *Academy of Management Review, 16*, 10–36.

Gersick, C. J. G., & Hackman, J. R. (1990). Habitual routines in task-performing teams. *Organizational Behavior and Human Decision Processes, 47*, 65–97.

Giacalone, R. A., & Rosenfeld, P. (Eds.). (1989). *Impression management in the organization.* Hillsdale, NJ: Lawrence Erlbaum.

Gibbard, G. S., Hartman, J. J., & Mann, R. D. (Eds.). (1974). *Analysis of groups.* San Francisco: Jossey-Bass.

Gibson, C. B., & Cohen, S. G. (Eds.). (in press). *Creating conditions for effective virtual teams.* San Francisco: Jossey-Bass.

Gibson, C. B., & Zellmer-Bruhn, M. E. (2001). Metaphors and meaning: An intercultural analysis of the concept of teamwork. *Administrative Science Quarterly, 46*, 274–303.

Giddens, A. (1984). *The constitution of society.* Berkeley: University of California Press.

Gigerenzer, G. (1999). Fast and frugal heuristics: The adaptive toolbox. In G. Gigerenzer & P. M. Todd (Eds.), *Simple heuristics that make us smart* (pp. 3–34). New York: Oxford University Press.

Gillette, J., & McCollom, M. (Eds.). (1990). *Groups in context.* Reading, MA: Addison-Wesley.

Ginnett, R. C. (1987). *First encounters of the close kind: The formation process of airline flight crews.* Unpublished doctoral dissertation, Yale University.

Ginnett, R. C. (1990). Airline cockpit crew. In J. R. Hackman (Ed.), *Groups that work (and those that don't)* (pp. 427–448). San Francisco: Jossey-Bass.

Ginnett, R. C. (1993). Crews as groups: Their formation and their leadership. In E. L. Wiener, B. G. Kanki, & R. L. Helmreich (Eds.), *Cockpit resource management* (pp. 71–98). Orlando, FL: Academic Press.

Gladwell, M. (1997, April). Just ask for it: The real key to technological innovation. *The New Yorker*, 45–49.

Gladwell, M. (2000, February 24). True grit. *The New York Review of Books*, 30–33.

Glaser, R., & Klaus, D. J. (1966). A reinforcement analysis of group performance. *Psychological Monographs*, 80 (Whole No. 621), 1–23.

Gleick, J. (1987). *Chaos: Making a new science*. New York: Viking.

Goffman, E. (1967). *Interaction ritual: Essays on face-to-face behavior*. Chicago: Aldine.

Goldstein, A. P., & Sorcher, M. (1974). *Changing supervisor behavior*. New York: Pergamon.

Goldstein, I. L. (Ed.). (1991). *Training and development in organizations*. San Francisco: Jossey-Bass.

Goodman, P. S., Devadas, R., & Hughson, T. L. G. (1988). Groups and productivity: Analyzing the effectiveness of self-managing teams. In J. P. Campbell & R. J. Campbell (Eds.), *Productivity in organizations* (pp. 295–327). San Francisco: Jossey-Bass.

Goodman, P. S., & Leyden, D. P. (1991). Familiarity and group productivity. *Journal of Applied Psychology*, 76, 578–586.

Goodman, P. S., & Shah, S. (1992). Familiarity and work group outcomes. In S. Worchel, W. Wood, & J. Simpson (Eds.), *Group process and productivity* (pp. 276–298). London: Sage.

Greenblatt, E. L. (2001). *A paradox in paradise: Depletion and restoration of personal resources, emotional labor, and burnout in an idyllic total institution*. Unpublished doctoral dissertation, Harvard University.

Greenough, H. (1958). *Form and function: Remarks on art, design, and architecture*. Berkeley: University of California Press.

Gruenfeld, D. H. (Ed.). (1998). *Research on managing groups and teams: Composition*. Stamford, CT: JAI Press.

Gruenfeld, D. H., & Hollingshead, A. B. (1993). Sociocognition in work groups: The evolution of group integrative complexity and its relation to task performance. *Small Group Research*, 24, 383–405.

Haas, M. (2002). *Organizing knowledge work: A study of project teams at an international development agency*. Unpublished doctoral dissertation, Harvard University.

Hackman, J. R. (1969). Toward understanding the role of tasks in behavioral research. *Acta Psychologica*, 31, 97–128.

Hackman, J. R. (1984). The transition that hasn't happened. In J. R. Kimberly & R. E. Quinn (Eds.), *New futures: The challenge of managing corporate cultures* (pp. 29–59). Homewood, IL: Dow Jones-Irwin.

Hackman, J. R. (1985). Doing research that makes a difference. In E. E. Lawler, A. M. Mohrman, S. A. Mohrman, G. E. Ledford, & T. G. Cummings (Eds.), *Doing research that is useful for theory and practice* (pp. 126–149). San Francisco: Jossey-Bass.

Hackman, J. R. (1986). Group level issues in the design and training of cockpit crews. In H. H. Orlady & H. C. Foushee (Eds.), *Proceedings of the NASA/MAC workshop on cockpit resource management* (pp. 23–39). Moffett Field, CA: NASA-Ames Research Center.

Hackman, J. R. (1987). The design of work teams. In J. Lorsch (Ed.), *Handbook of organizational behavior* (pp. 315–342). Englewood Cliffs, NJ: Prentice-Hall.

Hackman, J. R. (1990). *Groups that work (and those that don't)*. San Francisco: Jossey-Bass.

Hackman, J. R. (1992). Group influences on individuals in organizations. In M. D. Dunnette & L. M. Hough (Eds.), *Handbook of industrial and organizational psychology* (Vol. 3, pp. 199–267). Palo Alto: Consulting Psychologists Press.

Hackman, J. R. (1993). Teams, leaders, and organizations: New directions for crew-oriented flight training. In E. L. Wiener, B. G. Kanki, & R. L. Helmreich (Eds.), *Cockpit resource management* (pp. 47–69). Orlando, FL: Academic Press.

Hackman, J. R. (1999). Thinking differently about context. In R. Wageman (Ed.), *Groups in context*. Stamford, CT: JAI Press.

Hackman, J. R., Brousseau, K. R., & Weiss, J. A. (1976). The interaction of task design and group performance strategies in determining group effectiveness. *Organizational Behavior and Human Performance*, 16, 350–365.

Hackman, J. R., & Lawler, E. E. (1971). Employee reactions to job characteristics. *Journal of Applied Psychology Monograph*, 55, 259–286.

Hackman, J. R., & Morris, C. G. (1975). Group tasks, group interaction process, and group performance effectiveness: A review and proposed integration. In L. Berkowitz (Ed.), *Advances in experimental social psychology* (Vol. 8, pp. 45–99). New York: Academic Press.

Hackman, J. R., & Oldham, G. R. (1980). *Work redesign*. Reading, MA: Addison-Wesley.

Hackman, J. R., & Vidmar, N. (1970). Effects of size and task type on group performance and member reactions. *Sociometry*, 33, 37–54.

Hackman, J. R., & Wageman, R. (1995). Total Quality Management: Empirical, conceptual, and practical issues. *Administrative Science Quarterly,* 40, 309–342.

Hackman, J. R., & Wageman, R. (2001). *A theory of team coaching.* Manuscript submitted for publication.

Hackman, J. R., Wageman, R., Ruddy, T. M., & Ray, C. R. (2000). Team effectiveness in theory and practice. In C. Cooper & E. A. Locke (Eds.), *Industrial and organizational psychology: Theory and practice* (pp. 109–129). Oxford, England: Blackwell.

Hackman, J. R., & Walton, R. E. (1986). Leading groups in organizations. In P. S. Goodman (Ed.), *Designing effective work groups* (pp. 72–119). San Francisco: Jossey-Bass.

Hansen, M. T., & Haas, M. R. (2001). Competing for attention in knowledge markets: Electronic document dissemination in a management consulting company. *Administrative Science Quarterly,* 46, 1–28.

Hapgood, F. (1994, August). Notes from the underground. *The Atlantic Monthly,* 34–38.

Hargadon, A. B. (1999). Group cognition and creativity in organizations. In R. Wageman (Ed.), *Groups in context* (pp. 137–155). Stamford, CT: JAI Press.

Hayek, F. A. (1988). *The fatal conceit: The errors of socialism.* Chicago: University of Chicago Press.

Heifetz, R. A. (1994). *Leadership without easy answers.* Cambridge, MA: Harvard University Press.

Helmreich, R. L., & Foushee, H. C. (1993). Why crew resource management? Empirical and theoretical bases of human factors training in aviation. In E. L. Wiener, B. G. Kanki, & R. L. Helmreich (Eds.), *Cockpit resource management* (pp. 3–45). Orlando, FL: Academic Press.

Helmreich, R. L., & Merritt, A. C. (1998). *Culture at work in aviation and medicine.* Aldershot, England: Ashgate.

Hirokawa, R. Y. (1985). Discussion procedures and decision-making performance: A test of a functional perspective. *Human Communication Research,* 12, 203–224.

Hirschman, A. O. (1989, May). Reactionary rhetoric. *The Atlantic Monthly,* 63–70.

Hoffman, L. R. (1965). Group problem solving. In L. Berkowitz (Ed.), *Advances in experimental social psychology* (Vol. 2, pp. 99–132). New York: Academic Press.

Hogan, R., Curphy, G. J., & Hogan, J. (1994). What we know about leadership. *American Psychologist,* 49, 493–504.

Hollander, E. P. (1958). Conformity, status, and idiosyncrasy credit. *Psychological Review,* 65, 117–127.

Hollander, E. P. (1985). Leadership and power. In G. Lindzey & E. Aronson (Eds.), *Handbook of social psychology* (3rd ed., Vol. 2, pp. 485–537). New York: Random House.

Hornstein, H. A. (1986). *Managerial courage: Revitalizing your company without sacrificing your job.* New York: Wiley.

House, R. J. (1977). A 1976 theory of charismatic leadership. In J. G. Hunt & L. L. Larson (Eds.), *Leadership: The cutting edge* (pp. 189–207). Carbondale; Southern Illinois University Press.

House, R. J., Spangler, W. D., & Woycke, J. (1991). Personality and charisma in the U.S. presidency: A psychological theory of leadership effectiveness. *Administrative Science Quarterly,* 36, 364–396.

Hutchins, E. (1991). The social organization of distributed cognition. In L. B. Resnick, J. M. Levine, & S. D. Teasley (Eds.), *Perspectives on socially shared cognition* (pp. 283–307). Washington, DC: American Psychological Association.

Ilgen, D. R. (1999). Teams embedded in organizations: Some implications. *American Psychologist,* 54, 129–139.

Jackson, J. (1965). Structural characteristics of norms. In I. D. Steiner & M. Fishbein (Eds.), *Current studies in social psychology* (pp. 301–309). New York: Holt.

Jackson, P. R., Mullarkey, S., & Parker, S. (1994, January). *The implementation of high-involvement work teams: A four-phase longitudinal study.* Paper presented at the British Psychological Society Occupational Psychology Conference.

Jackson, S. E. (1996). The consequences of diversity in multidisciplinary work teams. In M. A. West (Ed.), *Handbook of work group psychology* (pp. 53–75). Chichester, England: Wiley.

Janis, I. L. (1982). *Groupthink: Psychological studies of policy decisions and fiascoes* (2nd ed.). Boston: Houghton Mifflin.

Jehn, K. A. (1995). A multimethod examination of the benefits and detriments of intragroup conflict. *Administrative Science Quarterly,* 40, 156–282.

Jehn, K. A., & Mannix, E. A. (2001). The dynamic nature of conflict: A longitudinal study of intragroup conflict and group performance. *Academy of Management Journal,* 44, 238–251.

Jehn, K. A., Northcraft, G., & Neale, M. (1999). Why differences make a difference: A field study of diversity, conflict, and performance in work groups. *Administrative Science Quarterly,* 44, 741–763.

Jensen, M. C. (1993). The modem industrial revolution, exit, and the failure of internal control systems. *Journal of Finance,* 48, 831–880.

Jensen, M. C. (2000). Value maximization, stakeholder theory, and the corporate objective function. In M. Beer & N. Nohria (Eds.), *Breaking the code of change* (pp. 37–57). Boston: Harvard Business School Press.

Jones, E. E., & Pittman, T. S. (1982). Toward a general theory of strategic self-presentation. In J. Suls (Ed.). *Psychological perspectives on the self* (Vol. 1, pp. 231–262). Hillsdale, NJ: Lawrence Erlbaum.

Juran, J. M. (1974). *The quality control handbook* (3rd ed.). New York: McGraw-Hill.

Kahn, W. A. (1990). University athletic teams. In J. R. Hackman (Ed.), *Groups that work (and those that don't)* (pp. 250–264). San Francisco: Jossey-Bass.

Kahn, W. A., & Kram, K. E. (1994). Authority at work: Internal models and their organizational consequences. *Academy of Management Review, 19,* 17–50.

Kaplan, R. E. (1979). The conspicuous absence of evidence that process consultation enhances task performance. *Journal of Applied Behavioral Science, 15,* 346–360.

Katz, D., & Kahn, R. L. (1978). *The social psychology of organizations* (2nd ed.). New York: Wiley.

Katz, N. (2001). Sports teams as a metaphor and model for workplace teams. *Academy of Management Executive, 15* (3), 56–67.

Katz, R. (1982). The effects of group longevity on project communication and performance. *Administrative Science Quarterly, 27,* 81–104.

Katz, R., & Allen, T. J. (1982). Investigating the Not Invented Here (NIH) syndrome: A look at the performance, tenure, and communication patterns of 50 R&D project groups. *R&D Management, 12,* 7–19.

Katzenbach, J. R., & Smith, D. K. (1993). *The wisdom of teams.* Boston: Harvard Business School Press.

Klein, J. A. (1994). The paradox of quality management. In C. Heckscher & A. Donnellon (Eds.), *The-post-bureaucratic organization* (pp. 178–194). Thousand Oaks, CA: Sage.

Klein, J. A., & Kleinhanns, A. (2001). *Maximizing the contribution of diverse voices in virtual teams* (Paper 01-3, Program on Negotiation). Cambridge, MA: Harvard University.

Knight, D., Durham, C. C, & Locke, E. A. (2001). The relationship of team goals, incentives, and efficacy to strategic risk, tactical implementation, and performance. *Academy of Management Journal, 44,* 326–338.

Komaki, J. L. (2000, April). *An operant conditioning approach to team coaching.* Paper presented at the annual meeting of the Society of Industrial and Organizational Psychology, New Orleans.

Komaki, J. L., Desselles, M. L., & Bowman, E. D. (1989). Definitely not a breeze: Extending an operant model of effective supervision to teams. *Journal of Applied Psychology, 74,* 522–529.

Kozlowski, S. W. J., & Bell, B. S. (in press). Work groups and teams in organizations. In W. C. Borman, D. R. Ilgen, & R. J. Klimoski (Eds.), *Comprehensive handbook of psychology: Industrial and organizational psychology* (Vol. 12). New York: Wiley.

Kozlowski, S. W. J., Gully, S. M., Salas, E., & Cannon-Bowers, J. A. (1996). Team leadership and development: Theory, principles, and guidelines for training leaders and teams. In M. Beyerlein, D. Johnson, & S. Beyerlein (Eds.), *Advances in inter disciplinary studies of work teams: Team leadership* (Vol. 3, pp. 251–289). Greenwich, CT: JAI Press.

Langeler, G. H. (1992, March–April). The vision trap. *Harvard Business Review,* 4–11.

Langer, E. J. (1989). *Mindfulness.* Reading, MA: Addison-Wesley.

Latane, B., Williams, K., & Harkins, S. (1979). Many hands make light the work: The causes and consequences of social loafing. *Journal of Personality and Social Psychology, 37,* 822–832.

Lawler, E. E. (1969). Job design and employee motivation. *Personnel Psychology, 22,* 426-435.

Lawler, E. E. (1978, Winter). The new plant revolution. *Organizational Dynamics,* 31–39.

Lawler, E. E. (1999). Creating effective pay systems for teams. In E. Sundstrom (Ed.), *Supporting work team effectiveness* (pp. 188–212). San Francisco: Jossey-Bass.

Lawler, E. E. (2000). *Rewarding excellence: Pay strategies for the new economy,* San Francisco: Jossey-Bass.

Lawler, E. E. (in press). Pay systems for virtual teams. In C. Gibson & S. G. Cohen (Eds.), *Creating conditions for effective virtual teams.* San Francisco: Jossey-Bass.

Lehman, E. V., & Hackman, J. R. (2001). The Orpheus Chamber Orchestra: Case and video. Boston: Kennedy School of Government, Harvard University.

Lepper, M. R., & Greene, D. (1978). *The hidden costs of reward.* Hillsdale, NJ: Lawrence Erlbaum.

Lepper, M. R., Greene, D., & Nisbett, R. E. (1973). Undermining children's intrinsic interest with extrinsic reward: A test of the "overjustification" hypothesis. *Journal of Personality and Social Psychology, 28,* 129–137.

Levine, J. M., & Moreland, R. L. (1998). Small groups. In D. T. Gilbert, S. T. Fiske, & G. Lindzey (Eds.), *The handbook of social psychology* (4th ed., Vol. 2, pp. 415–469). New York: McGraw-Hill.

Liang, D. W., Moreland, R., & Argote, L. (1995). Group versus individual training and group performance: The mediating role of transactive memory. *Personality and Social Psychology Bulletin, 21,* 384–393.

Liebowitz, J. (1993, Winter). Self-managing work teams at PPG. *Self-Managed Work Teams Newsletter,* 1–4.

Lipton, M., & Lorsch, J. (1992). A modest proposal for improved corporate governance. *Business Lawyer, 48,* 5977.

Locke, E. A., & Latham, G. P. (1990). *A theory of goal setting & task performance.* Englewood Cliffs, NJ: Prentice-Hall.

Locke, E. A., Soari, L. M., Shaw, K. N., & Latham, G. D. (1981). Goal setting and task performance: 1969–1980. *Psychological Bulletin, 90,* 125–152.

Louis, M. R., & Sutton, R. I. (1991). Switching cognitive gears: From habits of mind to active thinking. *Human Relations, 44,* 55–76.

Lowin, B., & Craig, J. R. (1968). The influence of level of performance on managerial style: An experimental object-lesson in the ambiguity of correlational data. *Organizational Behavior and Human Performance, 3,* 440–458.

Maitlis, S. (2001). *Variations on a theme: Forms of organizational sensemaking.* Manuscript submitted for publication.

Mankin, D., Cohen, S. G., & Bikson, T. K. (1996). *Teams and technology.* Boston: Harvard Business School Press.

Mann, J. B. (2001). *Time for a change: The role of internal and external pacing mechanisms in prompting the midpoint transition.* Unpublished honors thesis, Harvard University.

Mann, R. D. (1959). A review of the relationships between personality and performance in small groups. *Psychological Bulletin, 56,* 241–270.

Manz, C. C., & Sims, H. P., Jr. (1993). *Business without bosses: How self-managing teams are building high-performing companies.* New York: Wiley.

Margolis, J. D. (2001). *Dignity in organizations.* Manuscript submitted for publication.

Mathieu, J. E., Heffner, T. S., Goodwin, G. R., Salas, E., & Cannon-Bowers, J. A. (2000). The influence of shared mental models on team process and performance. *Journal of Applied Psychology, 85,* 273–283.

McClelland, D. C., (1973). Testing for competence rather than intelligence. *American Psychologist, 28,* 1–14.

McGrath, J. E. (1962). *Leadership behavior: Some requirements for leadership training.* Washington, DC: U.S. Civil Service Commission.

McGrath, J. E. (1984). *Groups: Interaction and performance.* Englewood Cliffs, NJ: Prentice-Hall.

McGrath, J. E., & Hollingshead, A. B. (1994). *Groups interacting with technology.* Thousand Oaks, CA: Sage.

McGrath, J. E. & Kelly, J. R. (1986). *Time and human interaction: Toward a social psychology of time.* New York: Guilford Press.

McGrath, J. E., & O'Connor, K. M. (1996). Temporal issues in work groups. In M. A. West (Ed.), *Handbook of work group psychology* (pp. 25–52). Chichester, England: Wiley.

McLeod, P. L., Lobel, S. A., & Cox, T. H. (1996). Ethnic diversity and creativity in small groups. *Small Group Research, 27,* 248–264.

Meindl, J. R. (1990). On leadership: An alternative to the conventional wisdom. *Research in Organizational Behavior, 12,* 159–203.

Meindl, J. R., Erlich, S. B., & Dukerich, J. M. (1985). The romance of leadership. *Administrative Science Quarterly, 30,* 78–102.

Melville, H. (1993). *Typee: A peep at Polynesian life.* London: J. M. Dent. (Original work published 1846.)

Meyer, A. D., Goes, J. B., & Brooks, G. R. (1993). Organizations reacting to hyperturbulence. In G. P. Huber & W. H. Glick (Eds.), *Organizational change and redesign* (pp. 66–111). New York: Oxford University Press.

Miller, D., & Friesen, P. H. (1980). Momentum and revolution in organizational adaptation. *Academy of Management Journal, 23,* 591–614.

Moreland, R. L. (2000). Transactive memory: Learning who knows what in work groups and organizations. In L. Thompson, D. Messick, & J. Levine (Eds.), *Shared cognition in organizations* (pp. 3–31). Mahwah, NJ: Lawrence Erlbaum.

Moreland, R. L., Argote, L., & Krishnan, R. (1998). Training people to work in groups. In R. S. Tindale et al. (Eds.), *Theory and research on small groups* (pp. 37–60). New York: Plenum.

Moreland, R. L., & Levine, J. M. (1988). Group dynamics over time: Development and socialization in small groups. In J. E. McGrath (Ed.), *The social psychology of time: New perspectives* (pp. 151–181). Newbury Park, CA: Sage.

Moreland, R. L., & Levine, J. M. (1992). The composition of small groups. *Advances in Group Processes, 9,* 237–280.

Morrison, R. (1991). *We build the road as we travel.* Philadelphia: New Society Publishers.

Myers, J. A., & Norris, R. E. (1968). *Summary of results: B-737 crew complement evaluation.* Elk Grove Village, IL: United Airlines.

National Center for Employee Ownership (1991). The benchmark companies: Lessons from leading employee ownership firms. *Employee Ownership Report, II* (6), 1–5.

National Transportation Safety Board. (1982). *Aircraft accident report* (NTSB Report No. AAR-82-8). Washington, DC: Author.

National Transportation Safety Board. (1994). A *review of flightcrew-involved major accidents of U.S. air carriers, 1978 through 1990.* Washington, DC: Author.

Nemeth, C. J., & Staw, B. M. (1989). The tradeoffs of social control and innovation in groups and organizations. In L. Berkowitz (Ed.), *Advances in experimental social psychology* (Vol. 22, pp. 175–210). San Diego: Academic Press.

Neuman, G. A., & Wright, J. (1999). Team effectiveness: Beyond skills and cognitive ability. *Journal of Applied Psychology, 84,* 376–389.

Newman, K. (1980). Incipient bureaucracy: The development of hierarchies in egalitarian organizations. In G. M. Britan & R. Cohen (Eds.), *Hierarchy and society* (pp. 143–163). Philadelphia: Institute for the Study of Human Issues.

Nicholson, N. (2001, Spring). Gene politics and the natural selection of leaders. *Leader to Leader,* 46–52.

O'Reilly, C. A., III, Williams, K. W., & Barsade, S. (1998). Group demography and innovation: Does diversity help? In D. Gruenfeld (Ed.), *Research on managing groups and teams: Composition.* Stamford, CT: JAI Press.

Osburn, J. D., Moran, L., Musselwhite, E., & Zenger, J. H. (1990). *Self-directed work teams: The new American challenge.* Homewood, IL: Business One Irwin.

Osterman, P. (1994). How common is workplace transformation and who adopts it? *Industrial and Labor Relations Review,* 47, 172–188.

O'Toole, J. (1977). *Work, learning, and the American future.* San Francisco: Jossey-Bass.

Paletz, S. B. R., & Maslach, C. (2000, August). *The effect of agreeableness on group creative writing.* Poster presentation at the annual meeting of the American Psychological Association, Washington, DC.

Pascale, R. T. (1990). *Managing on the edge.* New York: Simon and Schuster.

Powell, W. W. (1990). Neither market nor hierarchy: Network forms of organization. *Research in Organizational Behavior,* 12, 295–336.

Poza, E. J., & Marcus, M. L. (1980, Winter). Success story: The team approach to work restructuring. *Organizational Dynamics,* 3–25.

Pritchard, R. D., Jones, S. D., Roth, P. L., Stuebing, K. K., & Ekeberg, S. E. (1988). Effects of group feedback, goal setting, and incentives on organizational productivity. *Journal of Applied Psychology,* 73, 237–358.

Pritchard, R. D., & Watson, M. D. (1992). Understanding and measuring group productivity. In S. Worchel, W. Wood, & J. A. Simpson (Eds.), *Group process and productivity* (pp. 251–275). Newbury Park, CA: Sage.

Rand, G. (1998, December). MD-88 crew pairing test results. *Up Front* (published by Delta Air Lines), 19–22.

Rhodes, L. (1982, August). The un-manager. *Inc.,* 2–10.

Roethlisberger, F. J., & Dickson, W. J. (1939). *Management and the worker.* Cambridge, MA: Harvard University Press.

Romanelli, E., & Tushman, M. L. (1994). Organizational transformation as punctuated equilibrium: An empirical test. *Academy of Management Journal,* 37, 1141–1166.

Saglio, J. H., & Hackman, J. R. (1982). *The design of governance systems for small worker cooperatives.* Somerville, MA: Industrial Cooperative Association.

Salas, E., Rozell, D., Mullen, B., & Driskell, J. E. (1999). The effect of team building on performance: An integration. *Small Group Research,* 30, 309–329.

Salzman, M. (1994). *The soloist.* New York: Vintage Books.

Schein, E. H. (1988). *Process consultation* (Vol. 1). Reading, MA: Addison-Wesley.

Schneider, B. (1987). The people make the place. *Personnel Psychology,* 40, 437–453.

Schneider, B., Goldstein, H. W., & Smith, D. B. (1995). The ASA framework: An update. *Personnel Psychology,* 48, 747–773.

Schultheiss, O. C., & Brunstein, J. C. (1999). Goal imagery: Bridging the gap between implicit motives and explicit goals. *Journal of Personality,* 67, 1–38.

Schumacher, E. F. (1973). *Small is beautiful.* New York: Harper & Row.

Schutz, W. C. (1958). *FIRO: A three dimensional theory of interpersonal behavior.* New York: Rinehart.

Schwarz, R. M. (1994). *The skilled facilitator.* San Francisco: Jossey-Bass.

Schweiger, D. M., & Sandberg, W. R. (1989). The utilization of individual capabilities in group approaches to strategic decision-making. *Strategic Management Journal,* 10, 31–43.

Scott, K. D., Bishop, J. W., & Casino, L. S. (1997, August). A *partial test of Hackman's normative model of group effectiveness.* Paper presented at the annual meeting of the Academy of Management, Boston.

Scott, W. R. (1991). Unpacking institutional arguments. In W. W Powell & P. J. DiMaggio (Eds.), *The new institutionalism in organizational analysis* (pp. 164–182). Chicago: University of Chicago Press.

Seifter, H., & Economy, P. (2001). *Leadership ensemble.* New York: Henry Holt.

Shipper, R., & Manz, C. C. (1992, Winter). An alternative road to empowerment. *Organizational Dynamics,* 48–61.

Simon, H. A. (1990). Invariants of human behavior. *Annual Review of Psychology,* 41, 1–19.

Simons, T. L., & Peterson, R. S. (2000). Task conflict and relationship conflict in top management teams: The pivotal role of intragroup trust. *Journal of Applied Psychology,* 85, 102–111.

Sinclair, A. (1992). The tyranny of a team ideology. *Organization Studies,* 13, 611–626.

Smith, K., Johnson, D. W., & Johnson, R. T. (1981). Can conflict be constructive? Controversy versus concurrence seeking in learning groups. *Journal of Educational Psychology,* 73, 651–663.

Smith, K. A., Salas, E., & Brannick, M. T. (1994, April). *Leadership style as a predictor of teamwork behavior:*

Setting the stage by managing team climate. Paper presented at the ninth annual conference of the Society of Industrial and Organizational Psychology, Nashville, TN.

Smith, K. K. (1983). An intergroup perspective on individual behavior. In J. R. Hackman, E. E. Lawler, & L. W. Porter (Eds.), *Perspectives on behavior in organizations* (pp. 397–408). New York: McGraw-Hill.

Smith, K. K., & Berg, D. N. (1987). *Paradoxes of group life.* San Francisco: Jossey-Bass.

Snook, S. A. (2000). *Friendly fire.* Princeton, NJ: Princeton University Press.

Spreitzer, G. M., Noble, D. S., Mishra, A. K., & Cooke, W. N. (1999). Predicting process improvement team performance in an automotive firm: Explicating the roles of trust and empowerment. In R. Wageman (Ed.), *Groups in context* (pp. 71–92). Stamford, CT: JAI Press.

Staw, B. M. (1975). Attribution of the "causes" of performance: A general alternative interpretation of cross-sectional research on organizations. *Organizational Behavior and Human Performance, 13,* 414–432.

Staw, B. M., & Boettger, R. D. (1990). Task revision: A neglected form of work performance. *Academy of Management Journal, 33,* 534–559.

Staw, B. M., Sandelands, L. E., & Dutton, J. E. (1981). Threat-rigidity effects in organizational behavior: A multilevel analysis. *Administrative Science Quarterly, 26,* 501–524.

Steiner, I. D. (1972). *Group process and productivity.* New York: Academic Press.

Steinhardt, A. (1998). *Indivisible by four: A string quartet in pursuit of harmony.* New York: Farrar Straus & Giroux.

Stevens, M. J., & Campion, M. A. (1994). The knowledge, skill, and ability requirements for teamwork: Implications for human resource management. *Journal of Management, 20,* 503–530.

Stogdill, R. M. (1948). Personal factors associated with leadership: A survey of the literature. *Journal of Personality, 25,* 35–71.

Strang, D., & Macy, M. W. (in press). "In search of excellence": Fads, success stories, and adaptive emulation. *American Journal of Sociology.*

Sundstrom, E. (Ed.). (1999). *Supporting work team effectiveness.* San Francisco: Jossey-Bass.

Sundstrom, E., McIntyre, M., Halfhill, T., & Richards, H. (2000). Workgroups: From the Hawthorne studies to the work teams of the 1990s. *Group Dynamics, 4,* 44–67.

Torbert, W. R., & Hackman, J. R. (1969). Taking the fun out of outfoxing the system. In P. Runkel, R. Harrison, & M. Runkel (Eds.), *The changing college classroom* (pp. 156–181). San Francisco: Jossey-Bass.

Traub, J. (1996, Aug. 26/Sept. 2). Passing the baton: What C.E.O.s could learn from the Orpheus Chamber Orchestra. *The New Yorker,* 100–105.

Trist, E. L. (1981). The evolution of sociotechnical systems as a conceptual framework and as an action research program. In A. H. Van de Ven & W. F. Joyce (Eds.), *Perspectives on organization design and behavior* (pp. 19–75). New York: Wiley.

Tschan, F., Semmer, N. K., Naegele, C, & Gurtner, A. (2000). Task adaptive behavior and performance in groups. *Group Processes and Intergroup Relations, 3,* 367–386.

Tuckman, B. W. (1965). Developmental sequence in small groups. *Psychological Bulletin, 63,* 384–399.

Tyler, L. E. (1983). *Thinking creatively: A new approach to psychology and individual lives.* San Francisco: Jossey-Bass.

Tyre, M. J., & Orlikowski, W. J. (1993, Fall). Exploiting opportunities for technological improvement in organizations. *Sloan Management Review,* 13–26.

Tziner, A., & Eden, D. (1985). Effects of crew composition on crew performance: Does the whole equal the sum of its parts? *Journal of Applied Psychology, 70,* 85–93.

Vroom, V. H., & Jago, A. G. (1988). *The new leadership: Managing participation in organizations.* Englewood Cliffs, NJ: Prentice Hall.

Wageman, R. (1995). Interdependence and group effectiveness. *Administrative Science Quarterly, 40,* 145–180.

Wageman, R. (Ed.). (1999). *Groups in context.* Stamford, CT: JAI Press.

Wageman, R. (2000). The meaning of interdependence. In M. E. Turner (Ed.), *Groups at work: Advances in theory and research.* Hillsdale, NJ: Lawrence Erlbaum.

Wageman, R. (2001). How leaders foster self-managing team effectiveness: Design choices versus hands-on coaching. *Organization Science, 12,* 559–577.

Wall, T. D., Kemp, N. J., Jackson, P. R., & Clegg, C. W. (1986). Outcomes of autonomous workgroups: A long-term field experiment. *Academy of Management Journal, 29,* 280–304.

Waller, M. J. (1996). Multiple-task performance in groups. *Academy of Management Proceedings,* 303–306.

Walton, R. E. (1980). Establishing and maintaining high commitment work systems. In J. R. Kimberly & R. H. Miles (Eds.), *The organizational life cycle: Issues in the creation, transformation, and decline of organizations* (pp. 208–290), San Francisco: Jossey-Bass.

Walton, R. E. (1985). From control to commitment: Transformation of workforce management strategies in the United States. In K. B. Clark, R. H. Hayes, & C. Lorenz (Eds.), *The uneasy alliance: Managing the productivity-technology dilemma* (pp. 237–265). Boston: Harvard Business School Press.

Walton, R. E., & Hackman, J. R. (1986), Groups under contrasting management strategies, In P. S. Goodman (Ed.), *Designing effective work groups* (pp. 168–201). San Francisco: Jossey-Bass.

Walton, R. E., & Schlesinger, L. S. (1979, Winter). Do supervisors thrive in participative work systems? *Organizational Dynamics*, 24–38.

Wasserman, N., Nohria, N., & Anand, B. (2001). *When does leadership matter?* Manuscript submitted for publication.

Watson, W., Michaelsen, L. K., & Sharp, W. (1991). Member competence, group interaction, and group decision making: A longitudinal study. *Journal of Applied Psychology*, 76, 803–809.

Watson, W. E., Kumar, K., & Michaelsen, L. K. (1993). Cultural diversity's impact on interaction process and performance: Comparing homogeneous and diverse task groups. *Academy of Management Journal*, 36, 590–602.

Wegner, D. M. (1987). Transactive memory: A contemporary analysis of group mind. In B. Mullen & G. R. Goethels (Eds.), *Theories of group behavior* (pp. 185–205). New York: Springer-Verlag.

Weick, K. E. (1993). Sensemaking in organizations: Small structures with large consequences. In J. K. Murnighan (Ed.), *Social psychology in organizations* (pp. 10–37). Englewood Cliffs, NJ: Prentice Hall.

Weick, K. E., & Roberts, K. H. (1993). Collective mind in organizations: Heedful interrelating on flight decks. *Administrative Science Quarterly*, 38, 357–381.

Weingart, L. R., & Weldon, E. (1991). Processes that mediate the relationship between a group goal and group member performance. *Human Performance*, 4, 33–54.

Weiss, H. M., & Ilgen, D. R. (1985). Routinized behavior in organizations. *Journal of Behavioral Economics*, 114, 57–67.

Weldon, E., & Weingart, L. R. (1993). Group goals and group performance. *British Journal of Social Psychology*, 32, 307–334.

Wells, W. P., and Pelz, D. C. (1976). Groups. In D. C. Pelz & F. M. Andrews (Eds.), *Scientists in organizations: Productive climates for research and development* (Rev. ed., pp. 240–260). Ann Arbor: Institute for Social Research, University of Michigan.

Wetlaufer, S. (1994, November-December). The team that wasn't. *Harvard Business Review*, 22–38.

Wheatley, M. J. (1999). *Leadership and the new science: Discovering order in a chaotic world.* San Francisco: Berett-Koehler.

Whyte, W. R., & Whyte, K. K. (1988). *Making Mondragon: The growth and dynamics of the worker cooperative complex.* Ithaca, NY: ILR Press, Cornell University.

Wicker, A. W. (1979). *An introduction to ecological psychology.* Monterey, CA: Brooks-Cole.

Wiener, E. L., Kanki, B. G., & Helmreich, R. L. (Eds.). (1993). *Cockpit resource management.* Orlando, FL: Academic Press.

Williams, R. (1986, October 27). FYs reject graded group projects. *HARBUS News*, 3, 5.

Williamson, O. E. (1975). *Markets and hierarchies.* New York: Free Press.

Wood, J. D. (1990). New Haven Nighthawks. In J. R. Hackman (Ed.), *Groups that work (and those that don't)* (pp. 265–279). San Francisco: Jossey-Bass.

Woodman, R. W., & Sherwood, J. J. (1980). The role of team development in organizational effectiveness: A critical review. *Psychological Bulletin*, 88, 166–186.

Woolley, A. W. (1998). Effects of intervention content and timing on group task performance. *Journal of Applied Behavioral Science*, 34, 30–49.

Woolley, A. W. (2001, August). *The unanticipated consequences of clear work procedures on shared goal priorities.* Paper presented at the annual meeting of the Academy of Management, Washington, DC.

Wruck, K. H. (1994). Financial policy, internal control, and performance: Sealed Air Corporation's leveraged special dividend. *Journal of Financial Economics*, 36, 157–192.

Yeatts, D. E., & Hyten, C. (1998). *High-performing self-managing work teams.* Thousand Oaks, CA: Sage.

Yorks, L., & Whitsett, D. A. (1989). *Scenarios of change: Advocacy and the diffusion of job design in organizations.* New York: Praeger.

Yukl, G. (2002). *Leadership in organizations* (5th ed.). Upper Saddle River, NJ: Prentice Hall.

Zajonc, R. B. (1965). Social facilitation. *Science*, 149, 269–274.

Zaleznik, A. (1997, November–December). Real work. *Harvard Business Review*, 5–11.

Zander, A. (1971). *Motives and goals in groups.* New York: Academic Press.

Zenger, T. R., & Marshall, C. R. (2000). Determinants of incentive intensity in group-based rewards. *Academy of Management Journal*, 43, 149–163.

Zucker, L. G. (1977). The role of institutionalization in cultural persistence. *American Sociological Review*, 42, 726–743.

CHAPTER 17

E-Leadership

Surinder S. Kahai

State University of New York at Binghamton

Bruce J. Avolio

University of Washington

The proliferation of information technology (IT) is creating a new context for leadership. Leaders must be proactive in the implementation and management of IT; to realize the benefits of IT deployment most fully, changes may be required in leadership style, corporate culture, and organizational structure. Challenges and opportunities are arising as organizations' stakeholders obtain, store, categorize, retrieve, and use information in new and faster ways. Customized relationships with stakeholders, made possible by advances in IT, are pressuring leaders to be more selective about their stakeholders and more responsive to them. The increasing use of electronic communication in organizations is also affecting leadership. Virtual teams, whose members communicate electronically because they work at a distance from one another—sometimes even on different continents—are increasingly common. While the basic functions of leadership found in conventional teams are not altered, the locus, relative importance, and performance of these functions are different in virtual teams.

In this entry, e-leadership is defined as a process of social influence that takes place in an organizational context where a significant amount of work, including communication, is supported by IT. That process of social influence is aimed at producing a change in attitudes, emotions, thinking, behavior, or performance. Let us consider e-leadership in five areas that Fred Dansereau and Francis Yammarino, experts in the field of organizational behavior and leadership, have identified as important in the study of leadership.

The first area, fundamental human processes, covers the set of psychological and related processes without which leadership would not be possible or, perhaps, relevant. It includes basic affective, cognitive, interpersonal, group, collective, and communication processes and factors. The second area, leadership core processes, covers what a leader does to exercise leadership. The third area, leadership outcomes, covers the ways in which leadership core processes are put together;

Source: From G. R. Goethals, G. J. Sorenson, and J. M. Burns (Eds.), *Encyclopedia of leadership* (pp. 417–423). Thousand Oaks, CA: Sage. © 2008 Sage Publications, Inc. Used by permission.

examples include team building, delegation, and participatory decision making. The fourth area, second-level leadership outcomes, covers the effects of leadership core processes on performance, satisfaction, absenteeism, and turnover, among other variables. The last area, substitutes for leadership, presents enhancers, neutralizers of, or replacements for the leadership core processes.

E-Leadership and Fundamental Human Processes

IT proliferation is changing when, how, and with whom organizational members, including leaders, communicate, as well as who can access what information at what time, how, and from where, and who has access to information media.

Communication Processes

Thanks to the increased communication that IT offers, leaders can spread their messages more easily. For instance, the CEO of Cisco Systems, John Chambers, doubled the number of Cisco employees who view his quarterly address by making it available on employees' desktops via Cisco's intranet (internal computer network). Communication flexibility is also making geographic, time, and organizational boundaries fuzzier, as seen in the growth of virtual teams. Such teams provide new challenges to leaders. The lack of face-to-face contact in virtual teams severely restricts a leader's ability to monitor and regulate members' performances, implement solutions to problems, and perform typical mentoring and developmental functions. Therefore, in virtual teams a leader must share these functions with the team itself.

Virtual teams are also challenging for leaders because they operate within an altered social context. Members from different cultures meet electronically; in the absence of prior interaction, the initial level of cohesion and trust among team members is typically low. These conditions make it challenging for a leader to maintain unity and cohesiveness and to motivate team members to achieve a common goal.

Leaders of virtual teams are also challenged by the variation in technology skills among team members, by the inherent difficulty in coordinating electronic messages that appear at different times, and by the consequent lack

of a sequential build-up of ideas. Leaders will be more effective if they display appreciation for the technical challenges team members face and if they create suitable processes for dissemination and collection of ideas.

While the use of electronic communication systems such as e-mail is increasing, leaders need to reflect on whether electronic communication is appropriate for the purpose at hand. Electronic communication is considered to lack richness because of its relative lack of nonverbal cues and its inability to provide rapid feedback. Accordingly, it is recommended for situations that lack a socioemotional component and are relatively clear. Rich communication is suggested for relationship-building or for issues that are complex, ambiguous, or equivocal. It is worth noting, however, that the richness of communication may not be determined entirely by the communication system employed—the context in which communication takes place may also play a role. For instance, prior use of e-mail with someone over a long period of time may make e-mail suitable for resolution of ambiguous issues. Leaders need to consider the fit between the context, the communication issue, and the communication medium when considering the use of a computer-mediated communication system.

Another good reason for the leader to exercise control over electronic communication is that electronic communication can be easily stored and circulated over the Internet—as many leaders who are not discreet in their electronic communication have discovered to their dismay. Drawn by the convenience of e-mail, a leader may e-mail remarks that he or she would otherwise reserve for private situations.

Access to Information

Access to information is affecting power dynamics within organizations. Open-access databases allow members of the organization to access useful information easily. While quick and easy access to a greater amount of information has put a greater onus on leaders to adjust rapidly and frequently to changes, it has also enabled them to have a complete view of what is going on in their organization, thereby altering their power vis-à-vis their followers. For instance, Lorenzo Zambrano, the CEO of Mexico's Cemex (a cement manufacturer), logs on to the corporate database at least once or twice a week and checks the oven temperatures at Cemex's nearly fifty plants, because a faulty kiln means lost business. When Zambrano sees something wrong, he skips several layers of executives and shoots an e-mail directly to the plant manager, questioning the problem. While this type of oversight can be effective, leaders have to exercise it carefully because followers who feel under constant scrutiny may become alienated.

The other side of the coin is that leaders are challenged by their followers' greater access to information. A senior industry leader in Singapore recently said to one of the authors of this article "How can I lead when everyone else has the same information that I have, and oftentimes sooner than me?" Consider another example. Military leaders who brief their staff in the early morning often find themselves contradicted by one of the many web-based news sources by lunchtime. The inconsistent information received can cause a soldier to question whether he or she has the latest mission-related details. And this doubt places a burden on the military leadership system to disseminate accurate information as quickly as possible and to verify that the disseminated information has been received. It also has changed the command system to one in which military officers are trained to communicate the intent underlying a commander's order. What is happening in the military needs to happen in every organization facing a dynamic environment. Employees need to be aware of their leader's intent, while having the flexibility to make independent decisions at the point of contact with their customers.

Leaders are in a quandary over how much access to the Internet to give to workers. While unfettered access is believed to contribute to worker learning, it is also believed to reduce productivity, as workers are tempted to access their e-mail frequently, to go to sites unrelated to work, or to copy their e-mails unnecessarily. To curb loss of productivity caused by employees' e-mail use, in the mid-1990s Charles Wang, CEO of Computer Associates, mandated that company e-mail had to be shut down at specified times during the day.

Access to Information Media

Greater access to information media is accelerating the trend towards networked organizational structures in which employees at lower levels and stakeholders such as customers and investors have an increased

leadership role. Online support groups emerge almost spontaneously today, enabling groups to organize a challenge to powerful leaders who in the past could have kept individuals in these groups apart. The site www.companycommand.com was created by U.S. army officers in 2000 who felt they needed additional support as they assumed new command positions. This spontaneous effort, which was eventually adopted by the U.S. Army, is being used as a model for promoting organizational learning and cultural change.

Today, a dissatisfied employee can take action much more easily than in the past. With a few clicks of the mouse, the employee can contact the top management team or send a message with a story to the entire organization or the local media. Technology savvy employees may even set up gripe websites. Message boards that are shared by customers, investors, and employees are proliferating, and organizational leaders need to keep an eye on them to get a sense of the stakeholders' pulse and act quickly to quell any misinformation. There are so many channels through which information flows today, however, that leaders can no longer control releasing the most important information.

E-Leadership and Leadership Core Processes

When work is supported to a significant extent by information systems, what core leadership processes are important? To answer this question, let us consider how a leader's actions can complement the application of information technology, how they can affect the assimilation and management of information systems, and how they can improve the functioning of technology-supported teams.

Complementary Processes

Successful IT assimilation requires complementary changes in an organization's leadership, culture, rewards, and structure. If the complementary changes do not occur, there will be little or no gain from IT investments. With increasing IT deployment, leaders need to be willing to delegate and let the organization be less hierarchical. Because knowledge work tends to accompany IT deployment and it becomes difficult to know whom to credit when it comes to knowledge creation, leaders may have a hard time motivating employees through the use of rewards. Rewarding some players and not others may also lead to mistrust among the stakeholders involved. In such circumstances, leaders will need to focus more on team building and goal alignment and less on offering rewards to motivate beneficial behaviors.

Assimilation and Management of IT

Leaders can affect IT assimilation and management in several ways. By offering a vision for the organization and explaining how IT fits into that vision, they can make IT assimilation meaningful. By believing in IT, participating in IT strategy and projects, and using IT, leaders can be role models and legitimize participation in IT projects and adoption of IT. Finally, leaders can issue mandates and policies requiring IT adoption and use.

It seems that senior leaders' perceptions and attitudes concerning IT determine progressive use of IT to a greater extent than their actual participation in IT planning, development, implementation, and maintenance.

Virtual Teams

The way in which a leader helps the functioning of a virtual team depends on the nature of the team. A leader is most likely to need to manage performance by initiating structure and coordinating communication if team members are temporally distributed, team membership is dynamic, members hold multiple roles, and the team itself is temporary. In such teams, the performance management function becomes critical because the leader receives information from members on a delayed basis and risks losing touch with—and influence over—events. On the other hand, when a virtual team's members are working synchronously in time with each other, membership is stable, members hold single roles, and the team has a lengthy life cycle, a leader will invest more energy on the team's development. Teams of this type are more likely to be able to manage and regulate themselves, reducing the leader's need to manage performance and increasing the time the leader can spend on developing cohesion and

effective long-term relationships among members—which will enable the team to sustain itself and perform effectively over its lengthy lifecycle.

Conventional Teams

Conventional teams may be supported by communication technologies known as group support systems (GSS). These systems are designed to overcome such barriers to communication as fear of evaluation or domination of the team by a few members. They do so by providing features that enable team members to offer comments or messages anonymously (allowing for more open and honest communication than might be given in a face-to-face meetings) and enabling more than one member to communicate at the same time. They may also include features such as agenda setting and suggestions for sequences of steps that the team should follow. When GSS are employed, leaders play a crucial role in facilitating the use of all their complex features. Leaders must decide whether use of GSS will be restrictive (that is, only a fixed sequence of activities based on GSS features will be allowed) or adaptive (such that GSS features are applied flexibly depending on how the group's interaction is emerging).

E-Leadership Outcomes, Second-Level Outcomes, and Substitutes

The relationship of leadership processes to outcomes in the form of IT assimilation and management was implicitly presented in the last section. It appears to be the case that no studies have systematically examined the outcomes of complementary leadership processes in the area of IT deployment or of leadership in virtual teams. There are, however, a number of studies that report outcomes of leadership processes in teams aided by GSS. We divided those studies into two groups based on whether or not they manipulated leadership behavior.

GSS Studies of Group Leaders without Leadership Manipulation

In these studies, leaders were either elected by group members or designated by the researchers. These studies indicate that the presence of leaders in groups aided by GSS, by itself or in interaction with GSS features, can affect participation, attempts to exercise influence, satisfaction with the process, decision quality, agreement among members, and willingness to disclose information. Though GSS tend to promote equality of participation and attempts to exercise influence in leaderless groups, they do not stop a leader from participating or exercising influence to a greater degree than others. In one study, the presence of a leader was associated with higher-quality decisions. In another study, assigned leadership reduced the level of agreement in the group in the presence of statistical feedback provided by the GSS. In a study in which a team was assigned a task involving negotiations between members with different motives, the presence of a leader lowered the willingness of group members to disclose information. Leadership had mixed effects on satisfaction; the mixed results may have been due to the interaction of leadership with GSS features, which were dissimilar across studies.

Because these studies did not manipulate leadership behaviors systematically, they offer little guidance in prescribing leadership behavior that would be helpful for groups making use of GSS. They do, however, suggest that GSS features may interact with leadership and, in some cases, substitute for leadership. For instance, the process structure provided by a GSS in the form of a normative set of steps to follow may undermine a leader by rendering the process structure provided by the leader redundant.

GSS Studies of Group Leaders with Leadership Manipulation

Researchers at the Center for Leadership Studies (CLS) at Binghamton University in Binghamton, New York, have conducted several experiments with groups whose members were present in the same place and communicated at the same time to examine the effects of participative, directive, transformational (the leader offers followers a transcendent purpose and encourages consideration and intellectual stimulation), and transactional (the leader views leadership as a transaction with followers) leadership styles in a GSS context. In one of the studies comparing the consultative form of participative leadership to directive leadership, they

found that for a task requiring creativity and in which participants provided input anonymously, participants made more supportive remarks when guided by participative leadership. Furthermore, participative leadership generated more solution proposals for a semistructured problem, while directive leadership generated more solution proposals for a more highly structured problem. In another study, transformational leadership led to higher levels of group potency—that is, the group's collective belief that it can be effective—than transactional leadership. Group potency in turn was positively associated with group effectiveness. Transformational leadership's superiority over transactional leadership in producing group potency diminished when there was anonymity in the group's brainstorming phase, which relied on individual effort, but increased when there was anonymity in the report generation phase, which required collective effort.

Two other studies produce similar findings that suggest that anonymity may enhance the effects of transformational leadership by creating a condition that is consistent with the transformational leader's emphasis on the collective. In one study, transformational leadership was found to limit social loafing—that is, decline in task-oriented activity—by encouraging all members to work for the good of the group. In another study, flow (a psychological state characterized by high levels of concentration, enjoyment, and intrinsic motivation) mediated team perceptions of transactional and transformational leadership only in the anonymous condition: Anonymity led to marginally more positive associations between perceptions of transformational leadership and flow.

In a study of the effects of transformational leadership on creativity, higher levels of transformational leadership were associated with higher levels of elaboration and originality. In groups whose members were identified, higher levels of transformational leadership were associated with greater flexibility. Under conditions of anonymity, however, leadership effects disappeared, probably because anonymity substituted for leadership by encouraging flexibility of thinking.

When examining the effects of components of transformational and transactional leadership in another study, the CLS researchers found that both transactional goal setting and inspiring leadership had a positive impact on group creativity. Intellectual stimulation and individualized consideration had negative effects on group creativity. Participants may have perceived the leader's intellectual stimulation as critical or judicial and therefore curbed their input or became more cautious in generating ideas.

The above studies suggest that leadership style indeed does make a difference in a GSS context. Anonymity interacts notably with the transformational and transactional leadership styles to influence group outcomes.

E-Leadership as an Emerging Area of Study

It appears that traditional patterns of leadership effects do not necessarily hold up in IT-supported contexts. We are beginning to learn more about the IT-enabled context, but a lot of ground remains to be covered in the future. We expect that future work in this area will begin to address such questions as these:

- How do increasing virtuality and greater use of mobile technologies influence the effects of e-leadership?
- Will e-leadership lead us into conflicts more quickly due to the rapid exchanges IT technologies make possible across complex issues and problems?
- How will new generations of employees respond to leadership that is more virtual than face to face?

Finally, the overarching question is whether the human element in organizations will be able to keep up with these advances and use them to achieve greater effectiveness.

Further Reading

Avolio, B. J., Kahai, S., & Dodge, G. E. (2000). E-leadership: Implications for theory, research, and practice. *The Leadership Quarterly, 11*(4), 615–668. Bell, B. S., & Kozlowski, S. W. J. (2002). A typology of virtual teams: Implications for effective leadership. *Group and Organization Management, 27*(1), 14–49.

Dansereau, F., & Yammarino, F. J. (1998). A multiple-level leadership mosaic: One way to put the pieces together. In F. Dansereau, & F. J. Yammarino (Eds.), *Leadership: The multiple-level approaches (Part B: Contemporary and alternative)* (Vol. 24, pp. 327–349). Stamford, CT: JAI.

Gill, J. (2001, November 16). *The tech-savvy CEOs: CEOs who have vital data at their command.* Retrieved March 27, 2003, from http://www.businessweek.com/technology/content/sep2001/tc2001096_876.htm

Hart, R. K., & McLeod, P. L. (2003). Rethinking team building in geographically dispersed teams: One message at a time. *Organizational Dynamics, 31*(4), 352–361.

Hitt, L. M., & Brynjolfsson, E. (1997). Information technology and internal firm organization: An exploratory analysis. *Journal of Management Information Systems, 14*(2), 81–101.

Jarvenpaa, S. L., & Tanriverdi, H. (2003). Leading virtual knowledge networks. *Organizational Dynamics, 31*(4), 403–412.

Kahai, S., Avolio, B., & Sosik, J. (1998). Effects of source and participant anonymity and difference in initial opinions in an EMS context. *Decision Sciences, 29*(2), 427–460.

Kahai, S., Sosik, J., & Avolio, B. (1997). Effects of leadership style and problem structure on work group process and outcomes in an electronic meeting system environment. *Personnel Psychology, 50,* 121–146.

Kahai, S., Sosik, J., & Avolio, B. (in press). Effects of leadership style, anonymity, and rewards on creativity-relevant processes in an electronic meeting system context. *The Leadership Quarterly.*

Kayworth, T., & Leidner, D. (2001–2002). Leadership effectiveness in global virtual teams. *Journal of Management Information Systems, 18*(3), 7–40.

Romei, L. K. (1996). Overload, overboard, overdone, out of control. *Managing Office Technology, 41*(6), 8.

Sosik, J., Avolio, B., & Kahai, S. (1997). Effects of leadership style and anonymity on group potency and effectiveness in a GDSS environment. *The Journal of Applied Psychology, 82*(1), 89–103.

Sosik, J. J., Kahai, S. S., & Avolio, B. J. (1998). Transformational leadership and dimensions of creativity: Motivating idea generation in computer-mediated groups. *Creativity Research Journal, 11*(2), 111–121.

Sosik, J. J., Kahai, S. S., & Avolio, B. J. (1999). Leadership style, anonymity, and creativity in group decision support systems: The mediating role of optimal flow. *Journal of Creative Behavior, 33*(4), 227–256.

Zigurs, I. (2003). Leadership in virtual teams: Oxymoron or opportunity? *Organizational Dynamics, 31*(4), 339–351.

CHAPTER 18

Leadership in the 21st Century

Kathleen E. Allen

Kathleen Allen and Associates

Juana Bordas

Mestiza Leadership International

Gill Robinson Hickman

University of Richmond

Larraine R. Matusak

LarCon Associates

Georgia J. Sorenson

University of Maryland

Kathryn J. Whitmire

Kathryn J. Whitmire Consulting

F or years scholars have been trying to define or describe the nature of leadership. Today, driving forces exist that suggest that the purpose of leadership in the 21st century, rather than the definition, must be the focal point of our leadership studies. Therefore, recognizing the context of these changing

Source: Leadership in the 21st Century by Kathleen E. Allen, Juana Bordas, Gill Robinson Hickman, Larraine R. Matusak, Georgia J. Sorenson, and Kathryn J. Whitmire. In *Leading Organizations: Perspectives for a New Era*, Gill R. Hickman (Ed.). Copyright © 1998 Sage Publications.

times, we propose that the *purpose of leadership* in the 21st century is

- To create a supportive environment where people can thrive, grow, and live in peace with one another;
- To promote harmony with nature and thereby provide sustainability for future generations; and
- To create communities of reciprocal care and shared responsibility—one where every person matters and each person's welfare and dignity is respected and supported.

Upon reflection it is easy to recognize that this approach to leadership will be confronted with many challenges. Among these challenges are some prominent trends that appear to be shaping thought and action for the future. A few of these challenges can be presented as dynamic trends. These are

1. Globalization

2. Increasing stress on the environment

3. Increasing speed and dissemination of information technology

4. Scientific and social change

Our human consciousness and capacities mutually shape these trends. They illustrate the point that leadership in the future will need to be anchored in a purposeful set of assumptions that are intended to advance human capacity and consciousness. The following narrative is intended to provide a framework for understanding the implications for leadership; it is obviously not all-inclusive.

Prominent Trends

Globalization. There is an increasing global consciousness in all sectors and societies of the world. This shift in thought and action has affected all sectors of society. Instead of focusing merely on the United States, the marketing of U.S. consumer goods, manufacturing, and even entertainment has drastically expanded to worldwide status.

This globalization of manufacturing, marketing, and competition has created multinational organizations designed to compete in the broader economic playing field. The economy itself has become global. The economic challenges of Mexico, Great Britain, or any country affect the global economy. The stock markets are interdependent.

Increasing stress on the environment. Issues related to the environment and its ability to support the world's populations in the future are becoming increasingly challenging. While the United States may lead the world in pollution control, environmental problems do not stay within the boundaries of any one nation. Struggles between economic interests and environmental interests continue all over the world. We see this exhibited in the debate over the use of old growth forests, wetland preservation, fishing rights, and legislation on chemicals that effect the atmosphere. Concerns about our fresh-water table will probably increase as industrial runoff and other such violations challenge us. Landfills continue to be overloaded with waste, triggering increased pressure for recycling. Toxic waste, land development, and complex environmental phenomena all contribute to issues of health education and human and animal welfare.

Increasing speed and dissemination of information technology. Mass communication has connected the world in ways that were unheard of 50 years ago. While the Pentium chip may be the latest addition to computers this year, just around the corner is the advent of nanotechnology. Nanotechnology will allow the application of techniques in every discipline from microbiology to political science that will drastically decrease the size of equipment and increase the capacity of processing and disseminating information. Today, electronic bits of information are transferred almost instantaneously. Information is rapidly disseminated throughout the world via the Internet, CNN, and major news networks. The result is that we know what has happened halfway around the world almost instantaneously. It is nearly impossible to keep information private.

Information technology is made up of "bits," and "bits" do not behave like consumer goods. Consumer goods can be stopped at country borders and their worth can be declared. "Bits" travel electronically across borders with little possibility of control. This may explain why we now have permeable boundaries among our organizations, communities, and individuals. For example, when the Chinese students were protesting in Tiananmen Square, they were also communicating by fax and other media to the rest of the world. The immediate information was very difficult, if not impossible, for the Chinese government to control. There are numerous similar examples.

Scientific and social change. The recent announcement of the cloning of a sheep heralds the shape of things to come from genetic engineering. Genetic engineering is just one of the scientific changes that will reshape our lives. Biomedical technology will not just continue to reveal the secrets of the gene code, but it will radically change the way we cure diseases and produce and grow our food. Social change will require new political, social, educational, and organizational structures. The perceptions of gender roles will also be reshaped and communicated widely. All of these changes will mingle with one another with little time delay.

These four trends are mutually shaped by, and interact with, the ethical and spiritual dimension of human beings. The challenge and questions for leadership then become, Can humans develop the self-discipline to choose how they currently interact with each other and the environment? Can we develop the ability to live in peace with each other? Can we learn to live in harmony with nature? Can we increase the speed at which we learn about complex, dynamic challenges and problems? Will the human race develop and support the required diversity to match and surpass the complexity of the dynamic system of the future? How far does our current consciousness extend? What is the effect of our current human capacity on the challenges of today and of the future?

While any one of these four dynamic trends could be more than enough to deal with, they cannot be treated as separate issues. They are highly interdependent and because of this it is difficult to discuss them as discrete identities. As they interact, they create an interesting set of implications that will have a powerful effect on how we practice leadership in the future.

Implications for Leadership

1. *Increasing diversity in our daily lives.* Globalization has not only affected our traveling, markets, and

perspective, it has also stimulated immigration and along with it population growth. This phenomenon creates a significant increase in diversity in our communities and in the workforce. Increased diversity in our lives will continue to challenge the assumptions many organizations have used to shape standards of practice. Leadership practices that recognize diversity as a positive asset of organizations and communities will need to be employed. New systems thinking will be required to design processes that increase inclusiveness and diversity in decision making.

2. *Increasing change.* The magnitude and speed of change will continue (Conner, 1992, *Managing at the Speed of Change*). The discomfort of having a decreasing amount of time to respond to change will be experienced. The complexity of change events will increase. Because the total system will be more interconnected, the number of facets that need to be considered will also increase. This will require leadership to design, support, and nurture flexible, durable organizations and groups. It will also require a systemic understanding in order to respond positively to the change events.

3. *Complexity.* As stated above our world is composed of a wide variety of infrastructures that are becoming increasingly complex and interwoven. Each one of the dynamic trends mentioned above is a complex system in and of itself. However, they all interact with one another creating a large, dynamic nonlinear system with smaller nonlinear dynamic systems nested within them. In these systems, sequential cause and effect are much more difficult to track and predict. Leadership will need to pace and intuit the changing complexity of the system. Complexity challenges every individual's capacity to fully understand or intuit the many interrelated systems. For this reason, complexity requires shared leadership and multiple perspectives.

4. *Interdependence.* This complex, changing system is also interdependent. Interdependence shapes complexity and complexity shapes interdependence. The dynamic trends of ecological stress, information technology, globalization, and scientific and social change all demonstrate the impact of interdependence and demand a total systems approach. The challenge and implication for leadership will be to initiate and practice a systems perspective.

5. *Increasing tensions around value differences.* There will be more tensions between individual rights and the common good of the larger community. We will be faced with the ethical ramifications of our organizations decisions as they influence not just the individual organization or corporation but also the community and the world. This will require that leadership be practiced with a significant ethical dimension that focuses on sustainable principles.

6. *Increasing gap between the rich and poor.* There will be continuing tension between the rich and the poor. This will affect both individuals and nations. This tension will include both economics and natural resources. This widening gap will require a leadership that recognizes justice and equity issues as well as economic and ecological concerns.

7. *Increasing requirement for continuous learning.* As stated repeatedly, these dynamic trends are continuously changing and interacting. The implication for leadership is the responsibility to encourage the speed at which individuals learn and to provide opportunities for these individuals to grow in understanding how this learning can be brought into the changing relationship with the community or organization.

Recognizing the trends that have been articulated here as powerful forces that demand a new form of leadership, and focusing on the purpose rather than the definition of leadership, leads us to assert that a shared, collaborative form of leadership will be the most successful approach in the next century.

Shared/Collaborative Leadership

This new leadership paradigm has been called by a number of different names: shared, participatory, collective, collaborative, cooperative, democratic, fluid, inclusive, roving, distributed, relational, and post-heroic. While consensus on the name of this "new leadership" has not been reached, there is a growing understanding that the patterns of hierarchical leadership that served us in the past are not well suited to the global complexity, rapid change, interdependency, and multifaceted challenges described above.

In the information age, the primary challenge will be to encourage the new, better-educated work force to be committed, self-managing, and lifelong learners. This "people focused" leadership has its roots in democratic traditions. It is founded on the belief that in the complex future "answers are to be found in community" (Wheatley) in group-centered organizations where "everyone can learn continually" (Senge). Followers are being transformed into partners, coleaders, lifelong learners, and collaborators.

As the demand for this new leadership grows, the command and control leaders at the top of the pyramid are being challenged to change. They are expected to become leaders who are facilitators, stewards, coaches, designers, and teachers (Senge). They are being challenged to become leaders who "walk their talk" and model the way, inspiring others, delegating and serving. Effective leaders are recognizing that every person has leadership qualities that can and must be recognized and used.

The new leadership paradigm, therefore, is restructuring our conceptual framework of what the practice of leadership is and our understanding of what effective leaders do. It is transforming the role of "followers" and revolutionizing the design of organizations for the 21st century.

A recent brochure from the Robert Greenleaf Center on Servant-Leadership captures this spirit: "The old organizational pyramids of the nineteenth century are crumbling, being replace by upside-down pyramids and circles and connections."

The term *collaborative and reciprocal leadership* is used here to describe the process that is at the heart of this change. Since collaborative leadership is more adaptable and fluid, focusing on relationships and the needs of people, so too, our intention is not to fixate on a definition or a set concept that describes the "new leadership." What is more important is to assist people to acquire the understanding and skills of the purpose of the new leadership and to describe for them how collaborative leadership principles can work for them in the context in which they choose to lead.

Evolution or progress requires the integration of past, present, and future. In the midst of unceasing change in an interdependent world, this recognition provides the solid ground from which to move into the uncertainty of tomorrow with an assurance that collaborative structures have served people well in the past and can show the way to collectively shape the future.

Principles of Collaborative/Reciprocal Leadership

A basic premise of collaborative leadership is recognition that no one person has the solutions to the multifaceted problems that a group or organization must address. Leadership in this context requires a set of principles that empower all members to act, and employ a process that allows the collective wisdom to surface. These principles must be based on an understanding that people have the knowledge and creativity to respond to the problems they face. They encourage the development of organizations that support collective action based on shared vision, ownership, and mutual values.

The evolution of collaborative leadership has been deeply influenced by the natural sciences as well as history. The Newtonian concept of a mechanistic world where people followed directions and where repetitive, learned responses were sufficient has given way to an organic, systems-oriented, and dynamic understanding of how people, groups, and organizations operate. This systems perspective requires nonlinear, holistic and multifaceted approaches to leadership that stress interactive participation, open communication, continuous learning, and attention to relationships.

The function of leadership then becomes the creation of systems, structures, and environment where this interaction and learning can occur. As Wheatley has stated, "Leadership is making sure you have the right patterns in place." Senge refers to this as fashioning an environment "where everyone takes on the responsibility for learning."

While change and adaptability are key aspects of a systems approach, there are core principles that nurture the interaction and learning that are essential to collaborative leadership. Following are seven of these principles:

1. *Promoting a collective leadership process.* "Post-heroic" leadership moves away from the theory that the "great man" has the answers to a shared, distributed, and fluid concept of leadership. This is based on the belief that depending on the need, situation, and requirements, different people assume the leadership role and that everyone has leadership potential. Collaborative leaders create supportive and open environments that encourage initiation, facilitate the sharing of information, and value each person's contribution. At the same time, individuals are encouraged to learn and stretch their leadership potential. Leadership, therefore, is assisting people to grow and learn.

In Scott Peck's work on building community, for example, the "leader" is a facilitator whose role is to create and hold the "safe space" where people can discover themselves and learn to relate to one another authentically. The focus is shifted from the individual leader to the group, community, or organization. In fact, at times, the nominal leader may not even be visible.

2. *Structuring a learning environment.* An organization or group that is learner focused supports continuous self-development and reflection. Practices such as listening, promoting open-mindedness, seeking constructive feedback, sharing ideas, and viewing conflict as an opportunity for growth are embedded in the culture. People closest to the problem or opportunity are encouraged to interact and find solutions or innovative approaches. To do this, Senge believes the group must function "in a mode of inquiry, knowing that nobody knows and everybody can learn continually."

As the group or organization practices learning together, open communication, mutual trust, shared meaning, and a sense of collective ownership emerge. Senge refers to this as "communities of commitment where people are continually learning how to learn together." Thus, people can venture out of their comfort zones and take the risks inherent in managing change.

3. *Supporting relationships and interconnectedness.* In collaborative leadership, the relationships and interconnectedness of people become a primary dynamic. Values such as respect, honesty, expecting the best from others, and the ability to exercise personal choice lay the foundation for covenant relationships to emerge. These relationships are based on trust and mutual responsibility. Collaborative leadership focuses attention on building the individual's and group's capacity to live these values, to benefit from their interdependence, and

to recognize that conflict and differences can foster growth and creativity.

Relationships are also strengthened through the development of a shared vision that allows people to set common directions, have mutual goals, and rise above self-interest. Shared vision and values function as a governing force where people can organize and manage themselves thereby getting the job done without the need for control or rigid policies and procedures.

4. *Fostering shared power.* For leadership to be collaborative or shared, power and ownership must be distributed throughout the organization. Shared power implies that everyone has responsibility for leading, decision making, and learning. Groups and teams are often used to make decisions sometimes with a consensus format. Accountability and responsibility are based on individual integrity and peer agreements.

As people collaborate around common goals, partnerships and coalitions evolve resulting in lateral networks of mutual influence (Rost and Nirenberg). Jill Janov in *The Inventive Organization* describes this process as multiple relationships acting in a flexible, flattened structure based on partnerships, self-regulation, and interdependence.

In *Re-Inventing the Corporation,* Naisbitt and Aburdene refer to this as a lattice or grid where power is found in the center, not at the top. Hierarchical structures are thus replaced by crisscrossing networks, overlapping, changing, and fluid boundaries. This web-like structure supports optimum participation, interaction, and empowerment.

5. *Practicing stewardship and service.* Stewardship is the cornerstone of reciprocal or shared leadership because it turns hierarchical leadership upside down. Stewardship focuses on ensuring that other people's needs are being served and not on exercising privilege, power, and control. According to Block, stewardship chooses partnership over patriarchy or hierarchy; empowerment over dependency; and service over self-interest. Thus, the leader is "in service, rather than in control."

In his landmark work *The Servant as Leader,* Robert Greenleaf describes this commitment as "wanting to serve first. Then conscious choice brings one to aspire to lead." The litmus test of collaborative leadership is based on whether people's needs are being served. As

people feel respected and valued as partners they can create a community of shared responsibility.

6. *Valuing diversity and inclusiveness.* For people to respect each other, build trust, and communicate openly, they must learn to accept and value individual differences. Valuing diversity is the rich soil that nurtures relationships, partnerships, and collaborative networks. This is reflected in the Scott Peck statement, "Perhaps the most necessary key to the achievement of community is the appreciation of differences."

Respecting each person's perspective and personal style frees them to contribute their ideas and talents so that people can learn together. Furthermore, this inclusiveness is a key aspect of transforming followers into stakeholders and nurturing collective ownership. It is an understanding that creativity and excellence are enhanced through diversity. Fostering authentic diversity can be accomplished by respecting different perspectives, fostering open-mindedness, practicing dialogue, and listening with attention and empathy.

7. *Committing to self-development.* The movement to collaborative or shared leadership is at its heart a personal transformation that is fueled by "a commitment to work on yourself first." Greenleaf believed that the motivation to serve was based on the desire for one's "own healing."

The understanding that one's inner life *reflects* positively or negatively on one's leadership can serve to bring authenticity and humility to the leadership process. By working on personal learning and growth, leaders model the way for others to focus on their own personal mastery and proficiency.

This authenticity and the ability to actually "live" the principles of collaborative leadership is reflected in Wheatley's statement, "We must be what we want to become, we must in every step of the way, embody the future toward which we are aiming." This resonates with the words of Mahatma Gandhi, who recognized that personal transformation was the heartbeat of leadership: "We must be the change we wish to see in the world." With the proper understanding, education, and training, every individual can begin to use the leadership gifts that they possess.

So, if these are the principles of collaborative leadership, then what are the practices or functions that collaborative leaders must practice? Based upon the premises we have stated in this document, namely,

- that as we approach the 21st century we must focus on the purpose rather than the definition of leadership,
- that the new leadership paradigm is collective and reciprocal, and
- that there are powerful trends moving us in this direction

We make the following recommendations for leadership practices for the 21st century.

Collective Leadership Practices in the 21st Century

Practices are activities, customs, and ways of operating used by an individual, group, organization, or community. We view practices as an integral component of organic or natural living systems and the means by which collective leadership is exercised. Embedded and articulated in the statement of purpose and leadership practices are our values and beliefs. We think that successful leadership will model the following collective leadership in the 21st century.

Purpose of Leadership in the 21st Century

To create a supportive environment where people can thrive and grow and live in peace with one another.

Collective Leadership Practices

1. Develop structures and processes to support collective leadership by
   a. holding shared vision and core values in trust and operationalizing them
   b. generating and supporting interdependent and interdisciplinary group processes
   c. establishing and sustaining inclusiveness of stakeholders
   d. creating and maintaining a free flow of information
   e. facilitating fluidity and flexibility in group processes and structures
   f. sharing and distributing power and authority among all group members
   g. building a system of peer responsibility and accountability
   h. demonstrating equity
   i. cultivating ritual and celebration

2. Foster human growth and development through
   a. engaging in continuous self-development and reflection
   b. enhancing and using intuition
   c. strengthening and sustaining spirituality
   d. coaching and nurturing the development of others
   e. creating opportunities for people to experience success (efficacy)
   f. promoting group and community capacity building and progress
   g. expecting the best from people
   h. celebrating individual and group success

3. Facilitate learning by
   a. creating learning communities
   b. including diverse individuals and perspectives
   c. fostering and demonstrating open-mindedness
   d. developing meaning and insight through individual and collective reflection
   e. seeking feedback and critique to enhance development
   f. developing creative and intuitive abilities
   g. sharing ideas through engaging in dialogue
   h. practicing deep listening
   i. using creative tension to foster change and new ideas
   j. acknowledging and using "mistakes" as opportunities to learn, reflect, and forgive

To promote harmony with nature and thereby provide sustainability for future generations.

4. Enhance the quality of life and preservation of nature by
   a. understanding the interdependent relationship between human and natural systems and working to enhance their viability

b. practicing "enoughness" (bigger or more is not always better)

c. achieving balance in emotional, spiritual, and physical aspects of life

d. using a long-term perspective thereby creating viability for current and future generations

e. generating and supporting systems thinking (wholistic thinking) as a basis for action

f. facilitating self-organizing, self-regulating, and self-renewing systems

g. using natural conflict to foster growth and change

h. recognizing and promoting the spiritual connectedness of all life

i. generating and sustaining peace among ourselves and aiding peace efforts globally.

To create a community of reciprocal care and shared responsibility—one where every person matters and each person's welfare and dignity is the concern of us all.

5. Create caring communities of leaders and participants through

a. developing trusting relationships

b. attending to the well-being basic needs and human rights) of others and providing opportunities for them to sustain themselves

c. supporting basic freedom for others and providing opportunities for them to maintain freedom for themselves

d. maintaining opportunities for people to make choices for themselves that are not harmful to others, and honoring the choices they make

6. Demonstrate courage by

a. taking risks

b. tackling the difficult issues

c. serving others

d. challenging others when they depart from core values held in trust

e. initiating change, transforming self, groups, and institutions

7. Model integrity and authenticity by

a. showing mutual respect

b. carrying out responsibilities

c. being accountable for one's actions

d. modeling integrity and authenticity (walk the talk)

e. being honest with self and others

f. demonstrating equity

g. practicing inclusiveness

Transition From Positional to Collective Leadership

Creating an environment where collective leadership is practiced starts with a *shared vision* supported by a set of specific values or beliefs which are integrated into the person's behavior (Wheatley & Kellner-Rogers, 1996). Some "inner work" is required for a person who wants to practice this form of leadership. Without this inner work, the practice of authentic collective or shared leadership does not occur. This inner work starts with values and beliefs. People who practice shared leadership believe that all people have the capacity to lead themselves. Further, they believe that the gifts and resources needed to accomplish a task can be found in the members of the group, not in a single leader. Therefore, the goal of positional leaders is not to direct or tell but to provide a structure that allows people to lead themselves.

This means that positional leaders distribute or *share the "power"* of their position. In this way, they enable groups to assume the responsibility and discover their own capacity to work together, decide, plan, and act. They are willing and able to share the power of their position to the maximum degree possible under the given circumstances. Their personal power remains evident, but they share their positional power. They may substitute or transmute the need for positional power into the joy of seeing the group evolve as a learning organization or community.

Another major element, after weaving the shared vision, is *modeling*. There is integrity in their vision of shared leadership that is reflected in the way they structure and respond to the development of the group. This integration of practice, vision, and modeling gives group members confidence that leaders "walk their talk" as reflected in their belief in each individual and their collective action.

Collective/reciprocal leaders spend time *structuring the environment* as a learning environment. This may include establishing the expectation of success. Then, the group is encouraged to take risks and challenge the way things have always been done. Group members are even encouraged to challenge their own beliefs about what they can or cannot accomplish without specific direction from a positional authority.

Risk taking is supported by the creation of a safety net. The safety net creates an environment where group members believe that it is safe to challenge and exercise personal choice in achieving the mutually stated goals. Peter Block once said that people trade sovereignty or freedom of choice for safety. A step in the critical passage to the new paradigm of shared leadership requires the members of the group to practice the freedom of choice that comes with being responsible and accountable to themselves and each other (Chaleff, 1995; Kelley, 1992).

Information is shared with all group members so that they have adequate knowledge and understanding about the task to make an enlightened decision (Wheatley & Kellner-Rogers, 1996). Positional leaders need not be the primary source of the information. In most cases, the members need to rely on each other and on their ability to gather accurate information rather than on a positional authority. This shift in the source of information triggers greater self-sufficiency and greater interdependence. By receiving power, choice, and information, members begin to believe that they can influence the situation and the outcome. This belief is reinforced by the subsequent accumulation of actual successes.

The interdependent structures and relationships help to ensure an understanding of the distribution of different talents among group members. This facilitates the acceptance by the group of different points of readiness to practice this combination of individual responsibility and shared leadership and accountability. It also helps members discover that they can both learn with, and depend upon, each other.

These interdependent structures support group members as they work together to successfully accomplish the specified task. As groups learn this new behavior, they need the assurance that the ambiguity or the anxiety they may be experiencing due to this different way of operating is normal and that their feelings are a part of group transformation. A group often experiences ambiguity, frustration, disorientation, fear, insecurity, and a frantic desire for the positional leaders to rescue them. All this shifts the role of leaders to that of facilitators, supporters, consultants, and sometimes teachers. For group members, the result of this experience is excitement, ownership of the process and product, confidence and competence, and better ideas and learning.

All these practices, and perhaps others of which we are not aware, are needed to meet the challenges of the future as we practice collaborative leadership.

References

Block, P. (1993). *Stewardship: Choosing Service Over Self-Interest.* San Francisco: Berrett-Koehler.

Chaleff, I. (1995). *The courageous follower: Standing up to and for our leaders.* San Francisco: Berrett-Koehler.

Conner, D. (1995). *Managing at the speed of change: How resilient managers succeed and prosper where others fail.* New York: Villard.

Greenleaf, R. K. (1991). *The Servant as Leader.* Indianapolis: The Robert K. Greenleaf Center.

Janov, J. (1994). *The Inventive Organization: Hope and Daring at Work.* San Francisco: Jossey-Bass.

Kelley, R. E. (1992). *The power of followership: How to create leaders people want to follow, and followers who lead themselves.* New York: Doubleday/ Currency.

Naisbitt, J. & Aburdene, P. (1986). *Re-Inventing the Corporation.* New York: Warner Books.

Peck, M. S. (1987). *The Different Drum: Community Making and Peace.* New York: Simon & Schuster.

Rost, J. C. (1994). "Leadership Development in the New Millennium." *The Journal of Leadership Studies,* 1(1), 91-110.

Senge, P. M. (1990). *The Fifth Discipline: The Art and Practice of a Learning Organization.* New York: Doubleday.

Wheatley, M. J. (1992). *Leadership and the New Science: Learning About Organizations From an Orderly Universe.* San Francisco: Berrett-Koehler.

Wheatley, M. J., & Kellner-Rogers, M. (1996). *A simpler way.* San Francisco: Berrett-Koehler.

PART IV

Impetus for Organizational Leadership

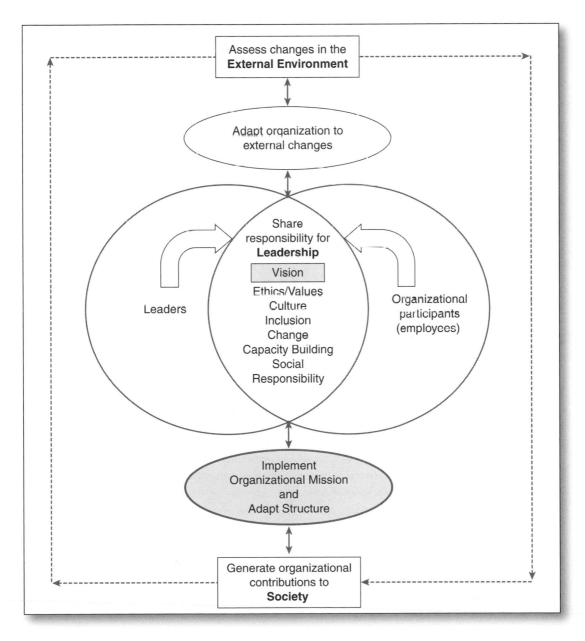

Overview

Vision and mission provide the impetus for organizational leadership. These factors give life, purpose, and direction to organizations. Based on a review of organizational vision literature by Sooksan Kantabutra (Chapter 19), vision can be described as a "mental model" or "conceptual representation" of an organization's future, which is used to understand and guide its actions. Research on this topic is relatively sparse even though visions or vision statements are widely used in organizations. Neither scholars nor practitioners agree on a common definition of vision, but Kantabutra found several shared characteristics among the definitions: Vision is about the future, it induces people to act toward a common goal, it provides a sense of direction, and it is important for strategy and planning. He examined research on both the attributes and content of organizational visions and found seven interdependent factors that comprise vision. These attributes include brevity, clarity, future orientation, stability, challenge, abstractness, and desirability or ability to inspire. There is no standard content for visions; they vary depending on the type of organization, the competitive environment, and how an organization wants to position itself strategically. Kantabutra also found that responsibility for creating and supporting a vision is shared among the organizational members and is not the responsibility of one central leader.

Organizational members use vision in the strategic planning process to help determine the organization's future direction. How can they discover whether their vision is consistent with the future? João Boaventura and Adalberto Fischmann (Chapter 20) developed a method of testing organizational visions based on concepts from the field of future studies. They propose a means of checking the content and consistency of visions using a simplified and improved technique for scenario building. The main purpose of scenario building is to construct several alternative futures and the respective paths for the organization. Basic components of building scenarios entail trends, uncertainties, and the relationships that govern the present environment. Boaventura and Fischmann use stakeholder analysis to identify key variables in the organization's external environment and compare these variables with the organization's vision. Organizational members can use this method to add variables that are absent and discard variables that are less important. Although this approach to scenario building cannot guarantee that an organization's vision will be totally consistent with the future, it can improve the likelihood of success.

Linda Williams (Chapter 21) examines the scholarship on organizational mission statements. Based on a review of definitions from several scholars, she asserts that one definition captures the essence of all the others—a mission statement tells two things about a company: who it is and what it does. Like vision statements, organizations are encouraged to address several factors in the content of their mission statement, including information about customers or clients, products or services, location and markets, technology, concern for survival, philosophy, self-concept, concern for public image, and concern for employees. Some researchers propose adding content about the organization's commitment to quality of life (QOL) goals and corporate ethos (that is, the way a corporation wants to be perceived by its internal and external constituencies). Williams concludes that mission statements have served as common organizational reporting tools for more than 30 years, and they will continue to matter in the future.[1]

A number of research studies, including a study by Williams,[2] have attempted to link the content of mission statements with the financial performance of organizations. These studies imply that the content of mission statements in high-performing companies is somehow linked to successful financial performance. If this link exists, why has the financial performance of some formerly profitable companies dropped precipitously in cases where there has been no change in their mission statement? This topic requires continued research to discover whether the link between mission statements and high performance can be substantiated and, if so, under what circumstances.

Are mission statements more than words? Are the actions of organizations actually consistent with their statements? Research by Barbara Bartkus and Myron Glassman (Chapter 22) goes beyond prescriptive or descriptive information about mission statements to examine the issue of whether organizations convert their words into actions. They explain that organizational mission statements have evolved from simple statements of purpose to public disclosures of organizations' promises and commitments to primary stakeholders (employees, customers, and the community). Even though organizations commonly list stakeholders in their mission statements, often because prescriptive literature recommends that they include them, Bartkus and Glassman conclude that the listing of stakeholders in the mission statement has limited impact on the actions of the organization (that is, actions that address stakeholders' issues). Conversely, organizations that include certain social issues (i.e., encouraging diversity and protecting the environment) in their mission statements were likely to take actions to address these issues. This finding is notable given that social issues such as diversity and protecting the environment are not included in the prescriptive literature.

Implementing an organization's mission requires effective organizational structure and design. N. Anand and Richard Daft (Chapter 23) note that, over the last 30 years, organizational design has moved through three eras: Era 1, self-contained organizational designs consisting of functional structures, divisional structures, and horizontal overlays and matrixes; Era 2, horizontal organizations designed with team- and process-based emphases; and Era 3, the opening of organizational boundaries using the hollow organization, modular organization, and virtual organization. There is no single design that will succeed for all new-era organizations. Organizational members will need to understand the design principles of each structure, weigh its strengths and weakness, and select the structure most appropriate for delivery of the organization's mission.

Notes

1.   Williams, L. S. (2008). The Mission Statement: A Corporate Reporting Tool With a Past, Present, and Future. *Journal of Business Communication, 45*(2), 118.

2.   The results of Williams's study are not included in this chapter. They are available in the complete article cited in the previous footnote.

CHAPTER 19

What Do We Know About Vision?

Sooksan Kantabutra

Mahidol University, Bangkok, Thailand

Introduction

Since the 1980s, the focus on leadership has shifted from traits and leader behaviors to the need for leaders to articulate visions to their followers, particularly those in organizations undergoing major change (e.g., Bass, 1990; Conger, 1991; Conger & Kauungo, 1987; Lucey, Bateman & Hines 2005). Shared vision also is said to be fundamental to network organizations of the future (Avery, 2004). In the changing context, vision refers to a cognitive image of a desired future state (Bennis & Nanus, 1985). It has alternated from being construed as a faddish and trendy concept, to being viewed as a fundamental attribute of effective leadership and a basis of one's power to lead (e.g., Kouzes & Posner, 1987; Zaccaro & Banks, 2004). Clearly, the importance of vision has been emphasized by leadership scholars in both theoretical discussions (e.g., Maccoby, 1981; Peters, 1987; Slater, 1993) and research (e.g., Kotter 1990; Larwood et al., 1995; Westley & Mintzberg, 1989). In particular, researchers (e.g., Hamel & Prahalad, 1989) have asserted that an organization with a well-articulated vision can achieve sustained competitive advantage over those organizations lacking such a vision. Time and time again, if a corporate leader is successful, his or her vision is cited as the cause and lauded as the foundation of the leader's greatness (Humphreys, 2004).

Given the criticality of vision in the leadership literature, the purpose of this paper is to identify the current knowledge about vision through a review of the theoretical and empirical literature. It starts with a theoretical background on early concepts of vision, vision definitions, and then vision components, followed by relevant empirical evidence. Finally, future research directions are proposed to advance our knowledge about vision.

Source: Kantabutra, S. (1992). What Do We Know About Vision? *Journal of Applied Business Research,* 24(2), 127–138. Reprinted by permission of the author.

Theoretical Background

In this section, early concepts of vision, the theoretical literature on vision definitions, attributes and content is discussed, followed by a review section of the empirical literature.

Early Concepts of Vision

Since charisma and vision concepts are closely related in the literature, it is unavoidable to discuss both in tracing back early concepts of vision. *Charisma* is a Greek word which means "divinely inspired gift" (Gove & Webster, 1993). This "divinely inspired gift" is, for example, an ability to perform miracles or predict future events. The sociologist Max Weber (1947) used charisma as a term to describe a form of influence which is not based on tradition or formal authority, but rather on follower perceptions that the leader is endowed with exceptional qualities. Weber pointed out that charisma occurs during a social crisis in winch a leader with exceptional personal qualities emerges with a radical vision that provides a solution to the crisis and attracts followers who believe in the vision and perceive the leader to be extraordinary.

While Plato's view of leadership was that a leader must be a man of power with a sincerely-truth-seeking vision (Takala, 1998), his point of view comes close to that of Weber because the Weberian concept of charisma is that a charismatic leader is self-ordained and self-styled with a "mission" which claims that his action is his destiny (Weber, 1947). Plato asserted that a leader must have charisma, the gift of grace, to be successful in his actions (Takala, 1998). In Plato's view, charisma is so important that, without it, a leader is not able to do his job, to be the head of a group. According to Plato, charisma is mystical and cannot be obtained by force of training (Takala, 1998). It is of divine origin.

"Charisma" and "vision" were long introduced in religions and political leadership. Espousing a vision within religious institutions is common (Thomas & Thomas, 1959). Mohammed and Jesus Christ are two examples of a religious leader who had a powerful "vision". What is particularly important about them is the "vision" they shared with their followers (Thomas & Thomas, 1959;

Viney, 1999). Both offered people a new and radical belief system. Jesus offered forgiveness of sins, life ever after, and everlasting love from his God (Thomas & Thomas, 1959). Mohammed's "vision" made him the Arab God's standard-bearer on earth (Thomas & Thomas, 1959; Viney, 1999). The role of the devil was significantly reduced, and followers could look forward to heaven, a very sensual place. By communicating their visions, Jesus and Mohammed offered people hope, a sense of aspiration, a sense of certainty, and a sense of being special (Thomas & Thomas, 1959). There is little wonder that their visions have been immensely portable. Islam moved far beyond the Arab people and traveled to Asia (Thomas & Thomas, 1959; Viney, 1999), while Christianity also traveled to many parts of the world (Adair, 1989; Thomas & Thomas, 1959; Viney, 1999). Obviously, both Jesus's and Mohammed's visions inspire followers across many different cultures, although they operated quite locally in their lifetimes.

In the political arena, the writer of Proverbs asserted several thousand years ago that vision is critical to people's lives (Stevenson, 1949; Wallis, 1994). Alexander the Great is a good example of a political leader with a vision. With his vision of conquering the world, he showed the way ahead, held the Greek army of some 30,000 foot soldiers together as a group, and encouraged individuals by example and word to keep going, notwithstanding the hardships and dangers of travel (Adair, 1989). Later on, no one would dispute the transformational power of visionary, political leaders such as Adolf Hitler, Abraham Lincoln, Mahauna Gandhi, and Nelson Mandela (Adair, 1989). These political leaders have inspired their followers to work toward their visions.

Before the 1980s, vision was mostly a concept of researchers who studied political leadership, and the leadership of social or religious movements. It was rarely considered within the leadership literature. Only in the past couple of decades has vision been extensively discussed in the leadership discipline. In this context, the use of vision has been widely exhorted as one of the main characteristics of "effective" leaders (e.g., Bass, 1985; Bryman, 1992; Conger & Kanungo, 1987; Humphreys, 2004). The leader creates a picture of a future world, which is frequently referred to as a vision (e.g., Hamburger, 2000). He/she then inspires his/her followers by communicating a positive and attractive image of the future, lifting people out of day-to-day existence and putting meaning into their lives (Hamburger, 2000). Not only is vision an idea or image of a desirable future, but the right vision can also actually jump-start the future by mobilizing people into action toward achieving it (Nanus, 1992). The motivational value of a clearly articulated vision comes mainly from the sense of broader purpose and meaning that the vision provides. One observation here is that both the business vision concepts and those in the political and religious leadership share the notion that leaders attempt to influence and engage their followers through his/her desired future state, still to a large extent a top-down approach to leadership.

There is no doubt, however, that many leadership scholars have seen vision as important to leadership, strategy implementation, and change (Collins & Porras, 1994; Doz & Prahalad, 1987; Humphreys, 2004; Hunt, 1991; Kotter, 1990; Robbins & Duncan, 1988; Sashkin, 1988). Although some managers dismiss visions as irrelevant to organization performance (see Rynes, Colbert & Brown, 2002), businesses need a purpose (Avery, 2005). Supporting this view, Handy (2002) argues that the purpose of a business goes beyond making a profit, to something "better", a higher-level purpose. Bryman (1992) argues that charismatic leaders have a vision or a higher-order purpose that they are capable of communicating to their followers in such as way as to ensure that followers will enthusiastically commit themselves to it. The leader's role then is to empower people to carry out the vision, and to structure the organization and its culture according to the vision. In trying to integrate the fragmented field of Leadership, Avery (2004) names a paradigm of leadership "Visionary Leadership", in which a leader espouses a vision to bring about superior performance outcomes through involving follower emotional commitment to the vision. This underlines the important role that vision plays.

The early concepts of vision in both political and religious leadership suggest a new sense of direction, and often involve a transformation of a group of followers, similar to the concepts of contemporary vision in the leadership literature. In political, religious and business leadership, where the top-down approach to management can be found, vision is developed and used by a leader to inspire followers to work toward a common goal.

Vision Definition

Despite its obvious importance, vision is still not defined in a generally agreed upon manner, which is critical because empirical research on vision may be affected by the various ways in which vision has been defined. Moreover, practitioners may also be confused as to which definition to adopt. Hunt (1991) and Sashkin (1988) suggest that vision is a form of leadership in which a visionary leader transforms an organizational culture to bring organization members to understand, accept and carry out his/her plan for the organization. Quite differently, Pearson (1989) and Phillip and Hunt (1992) have viewed vision as one of the required tasks top managers perform. Sashkin (1992) later on have viewed vision as a demonstration of leadership competencies. Considerable disagreement also exists over whether terms like mission, goals, core values, strategy, and organizational philosophy differ from vision. For example, much confusion exists between vision and mission. In an educational setting, Hallinger and Heck (2002) pointed out that an organizational mission is indeed a vision shared by organizational members. According to them, mission or shared vision exists when personal visions of a critical mass of people cohere in a common sense of purpose within a community. Here, vision is a purpose. On the other hand, Levin (2000) suggested that mission instead provides a statement of the purpose of an organization's existence, while vision is a statement of direction. Endorsing Levin's view, O'Brien and Meadows (2000) concurred that mission is a statement of purpose, although others prefer to define mission as an often-inseparable component of a business' vision. Lipton (1996), among others, defined vision as a combination of mission, strategy, and culture. In Lipton's view, mission was defined as the purpose of an organization, strategy as a basic approach to achieving the mission, and culture as the values of an organization that support purpose and strategy. Collins and Porras (1994) suggested two different components of vision: "core identity" and "envisioned future." To them, a good vision builds on the interplay between these two complementary forces. The vision defines "what we stand for and why we exist" that does not change (the core ideology) and sets forth "what we aspire to become, to achieve, to create" that will require significant change and progress to attain (the envisioned future). Therefore, a vision here indicates both purpose and direction.

Adopting a different view, other scholars stated that vision needs to come first in order to subsequently drive development of mission and strategy (e.g., Hay & Williamson, 1997; Parikh & Neubauer, 1993; Zaccaro & Banks, 2004). Therefore, vision, mission and strategy are three separable components. In addition to the confusion between mission and vision, vision is also seen as closely related to organizational goals and strategy (e.g, Levin, 2000; Schoemaker, 1992).

Philosophy and vision are also frequently confounded, probably because both are inspirational and idealistic. However, Levin (2000) argued that visions should go well beyond statements of philosophy by describing those values and ideals in action, including a description of how these ideals are practiced, what that experience is like for those affected, and a link between these preferred behaviors and successful performance. It seems that a vision here paints a picture of how it looks like and feels like when a vision is attained. Therefore, as opposed to many concise vision statements preferred by other scholars (e.g., Locke et al., 1991), Levin's notion of vision provides for more lengthy vision statements.

From a view of New Science that means exciting breakthroughs especially in quantum physics that are overturning centuries-old, Newtonian models of science, Wheatley (1999) suggested that vision is a field which leaders can use as a formative influence. Creating a vision means creating a power, not a place; an influence, not a destination. This field metaphor would help leaders to understand that they need congruency by matching visionary messages with visionary behaviors. Leaders also would know that vision must permeate through an entire organization as a vital influence on the behavior of all stakeholders. Leaders would also feel genuinely threatened by incongruous acts, because leaders would understand their disintegrating effects on what they dream to accomplish. Their organization would become an organization of integrity, where their words would be translated into action.

Despite the definitional confusion, a comparison of the various definitions of vision suggests that they share a similar set of characteristics (see Table 19.1).

Essentially, scholars agree that vision is about the future, induces people to act towards a common goal, provides a sense of direction, and is important for strategy and planning. Regardless of these commonly shared characteristics resulting from attempts to define vision, there is little agreement among academics as to what "vision" is. The situation does not appear very different among practitioners, as they are equally confused with the titles of mission, vision, values, beliefs, principles and strategic intent/direction (Baetz & Bart, 1996), Raynor (1998) suggested that these concepts are so tied together that to speak of one was to involve them all. Van der Heijden (1996) introduced the term "Business Idea", possibly as a way out, which he defined as an organization's mental model of forces behind its current and future success.

Taking a pragmatic approach to resolve the definitional confusion, Baum, Locke and Kirkpatrick (1998) chose to define the term vision as each leader defines it, because it is the leader's actual vision that guides his/her choices and actions. However, it appears that Baum et al. (1998) adopted the top-down approach to leadership in defining a vision. Baum et al.'s (1998) definition might not be practical in networked organizations of the future, in which vision emerges from all organizational members (Avery, 2004). Indeed, the focus on vision has shifted from a vision as proclaimed by a single central leader to a vision as proclaimed by all organizational members. Avery (2004) provides a reason for this by suggesting that a vision developed by a leader may not be the most effective as the business environment becomes more heterogeneous, highly complicated and dynamic. In the past where a business was locally defined and predictable, a vision from the traditional single leader was enough to provide a "right" direction. In such a dynamic and unpredictable context, leadership will need to operate more through vision and values permeating the culture (Avery, 2004), which will become or replace the single guiding vision (Drath, 1998). In this environment, each member of the organization shares the vision and values, being able to respond effectively, innovatively and timely to environmental changes. Avery (2005) also asserts that leaders that espouse a vision will be able to sustain their corporate performance in the long run.

More appropriately dealing with the definitional issue and the changing context, Mumford and Strange

Table 19.1   Commonly Shared Vision Characteristics

Item	Shared Characteristics	Theorists
1	Vision is always about a desirable future.	e.g., Collins & Porras, 1994; Kotter, 1997; Lipton, 1996; Sashkin, 1988, 1992; Senga, 1990
2	Vision is considered as necessary for leadership, a process of inducing others to act toward a common goal.	e.g., Bennis, 1990; Locke et al., 1991; Phillips & Hunt, 1992; Quigley, 1993; Sashkin, 1992; Wheatley, 1999
3	Vision provides a sense of direction for organizational members to proceed.	e.g., Collins & Porras, 1994; Davis & Meyer, 1998; Hunt, 1991; Jacobs & Jaques, 1990; Kotter, 1997; Levin, 2000; Lipton, 1996; Sashkin, 1988, 1992; Seeley, 1992; Senge,1990
4	Vision is seen as important for business strategy and planning.	e.g., Collins & Porras, 1994; Hay & Williamson, 1997; Parikh & Neubarex, 1993; Schoemaker, 1992; Senge, 1990; Vandemtewe, 1995

(2005) suggest that vision is ultimately a cognitive construction or specifically a mental model, a conceptual representation used to both understand system operations and guide actions within the system. I agree with Mumford and Strange's vision definition because a vision, defined as a mental model, can accommodate both the top-down and bottom-up approaches to leadership.

Vision Attributes

Senge (1990) argues that two types of vision exist: positive and negative visions. According to Senge, a positive vision emphasizes change and aspirations for growth, while a negative vision emphasizes continuing the status quo, even under changing environments. Despite the diverging views on how to define a vision, many leadership scholars appear to agree with Senge by providing different attributes seen to be necessary for a vision to be "positive". Among various opinions, Locke et al. (1991) view that an effective vision is inspiring, abstract, brief, stable and motivating. On the other hand, Conger (1989) suggests that an effective vision is strategic and well-communicated while Kouzes and Posner (1987) and Jacobs and Jaques (1990) assert that long-term and focus should be included. Sashkin

(1988) and Sims and Lorenzi (1992) proposed that effective visions are inspirational, widely accepted, and integrated with visions of others. A large group of scholars also argues that an effective vision should have clarity, because the degree of clarity or precision of the vision statement influences how well the vision is understood and accepted (e.g., Jacobs & Jaques, 1990, Locke et al., 1991; Nanus, 1992; Sashkin, 1988; Sims & Larenzi, 1992). Concurring with this view, Nanus (1992) suggested that effective visions should be clearly understood and act to direct effort. Other scholars have posited that effective visions should be inspiring and challenging to energize employees around a shared value system (Locke et al., 1991; Sashkin, 1988; Sims & Lorenzi, 1992).

Though many leadership theorists have postulated different attributes of vision, there are some commonly shared attributes among them, as shown in Table 19.2, which includes definitions derived from Baum (1994), Baum et al. (1998) and Locke et al. (1991) who are among a few scholars studying the commonly shared vision attributes.

Although vision is emphasized as a core issue in the prevailing vision-based leadership theories (Bass, 1990; Conger, 1989; Conger & Kanungo, 1987; Tichy & Divanna, 1986; Westley & Mintzberg, 1989), and many characteristics of effective vision have been introduced,

Table 19.2 Vision Attributes

Item	Shared Characteristics	Definitions
1	Brevity	A vision statement should be brief, but brevity should not overrule the endeavor to state the vision definitely.
2	Clarity	A vision statement should be clear and precise in such a way that it is understood and accepted. Clarity makes the overarching goals understandable to everyone.
3	Future orientation	A vision statement should focus on the long-term perspective of the organization and the environment in which it functions. It should guide the organization far into the future.
4	Stability	A vision statement should be general and abstract enough that it is not affected by most of the changes in the market or in technology.
5	Challenge	A vision statement should motivate people to work toward a desirable outcome. Visions challenge people to do their best.
6	Abstractness	A vision statement should represent a general idea as opposed to a specific achievement. It is not a narrow, one-time goal that can be met, then discarded.
7	Desirability or ability to inspire	A vision statement should represent an ideal that is worth working toward for the followers. If followers do not perceive the vision as an attractive goal, they will never commit themselves to achieving it.

none of the prevailing theories has exhaustively explained how each characteristic might create an impact on organizational performance. In his effort to develop a vision theory to fill in the gap, Kantabutra (2003) asserted that the seven vision attributes mentioned above interact to create a positive impact on overall organizational performance initially through follower satisfaction. A vision that is too brief will not positively impact overall organizational performance unless it is clear to followers what needs to be done, or it may not appear to challenge followers to do their best. A clear vision will not positively influence follower satisfaction because it may be too lengthy, preventing a leader to communicate it massively and frequently. It also may be too abstract, therefore possibly creating conflicts among groups with different specific purposes and not allowing for individual creative interpretation among followers. A too specific vision makes it difficult

to form an effective group to carry out the vision. Moreover, abstractness reflects stability in the vision because it implies no radical change over time. An unstable vision suggests to followers a serious lack of managerial integrity and commitment to the vision, negatively affecting follower morale. A vision that is brief, clear, abstract, challenging and stable will not draw follower commitment in working toward the vision unless the vision is also inspiring or desirable. In addition, when a vision is not inspiring or desirable, it is unlikely to develop and nurture a shared vision, which is critical to organizational performance. An inspiring vision that is clear, brief, abstract, challenging, and stable will not be able to attract affective commitment from followers unless it offers a compelling view of a better future. Without a desirable future picture, a leader is unlikely to be able to draw followers from where they presently are to work toward the vision.

Therefore, vision characterized by the seven vision attributes can improve the vision's effectiveness.

Vision Content

Literature on vision content is sparse. Andrews, Boyne and Walker (2006) draw from their study of one hundred and nineteen English local authorities to suggest that measures of strategy content must be included in valid theoretical and empirical models of organizational performance in the public sector because strategy content impacts organizational performance. Baum et al. (1998) argued that the content or core of a vision needs to be addressed because it is important to organizational growth. In a healthcare context, Williams-Brinkley (1999) argued that the focus of a healthcare vision should always be on patients, their families, and staff. In a public school setting, Kantabutra (2005a) argued that vision content should contain reference to teacher and student satisfaction, student achievement, and efficiency. Kantabutra (2005b) also argues that a vision should contain reference to corporate sustainability for a corporation to succeed in the long run. To be specific, such vision content should contain reference to moderation, reasonableness, the need for "self-immunity" mechanisms, knowledge, and morality to be able to sustain a business (Kantabutra, 2006).

A possible reason for the existence of many vision content proposals is that what should be included in vision content depends on the types of business and competitive environments in which they operate. If there is indeed common vision content across organizations, whether and how organizations can be developed, compete and sustain their strategic advantage are in serious doubt. Scholars appear to agree with this conclusion. For example, Westley and Mintzberg (1989) suggest that the strategic content of a vision may focus on products, services, markets, organizations, or even ideals, with this strategic component being the central image that drives the vision. Moreover, Collins and Porras (1994) suggest that vision content need not be common across different visionary organizations. This is consistent with Pearson's view (1989) that a successful vision takes into account industry, customers, and the specific competitive environment in identifying an innovative competitive position in the industry.

In conclusion, what should be included in vision content depends on how a business wants to position itself strategically, given that vision is ultimately defined as a cognitive construction or mental model used to both understand system operations and guide actions within the system (Mumford & Strange, 2005). This proposed vision definition appears to gain support from Westley and Mintzberg (1989) who suggest that vision process and content are blended together in accounts of visionary leadership. Though vision content and process, and visionary leadership, are distinctly different, it is clear that these aspects relate to one another in some complex ways. In theory, an effective vision should also be brief, clear, abstract, future oriented, stable, challenging and desirable or inspiring because these characteristics can enhance vision's effectiveness.

Empirical Background

Overall, research has demonstrated significant contributions of visions to organizational effectiveness (Zaccaro, 2001). Lack of vision also appears to be associated with failed attempts to manage organizational change (e.g., Collins & Porras, 1994; Lucey, Bateman & Hines, 2005) and attention to vision was found to be a key strategy employed by 90 leaders who enlisted others in a common vision (Bennis & Nanus, 1985). Visions offer a value-based direction for the company and provide a rationale for strategic decision making. While most of the previous research into vision was conducted at the individual level, as opposed to the level of the business-unit or organization-level, vision has been studied as a blend of charismatic leadership in a wide variety of samples and industries, with generally positive findings between this kind of leadership and followers' performance, attitudes, and perceptions.

Previous empirical studies range from laboratory subjects using students (e.g., Howell & Frost, 1989; Kirkpatrick, 1992; Puffer, 1990), military leaders (e.g., Curphy, 1990; Yukl & Van Fleet, 1982), national leaders (e.g., Bass, Avolio & Goodheim, 1987; House, Spangler & Woycke, 1991), corporate leaders (e.g., Baum et al., 1998; Bennis & Nanus, 1985; Kantabuira, 2003), educational leaders and administrators (e.g., Roberts, 1985; Roberts & Bradley, 1988; Sashkin 1988), to hospital leaders (e.g., Bryant, 1990; McDaniel & Wolf, 1992). In addition, no published studies have reported a negative or non-significant relation between charismatic leadership and individual performance, possibly because negative or non-significant findings are rarely published.

Not only is vision found to be associated with bringing about competitive performance, it is also found to be critical to sustaining it. Avery (2005) discovered that vision is important to sustainable enterprises. It was found that European sustainable enterprises adopted the long-term perspective in managing their enterprises. This long-term perspective allows the organizations more time for a vision to be communicated and take effect. Another possible explanation for the impact of vision on corporate sustainability is that espousing a vision provides a cognitive map that underpins how resources are to be used and combined within the organization (Avery, 2004). To that extent, the vision channels organizational competencies in the direction of the organization's goals, which takes time. Avery's (2005) research also pointed out that although all sustainable enterprises in her study had a vision, not all have articulated vision statements. For example, BMW did not have an explicit vision statement for many years. Rather, the vision appeared to stem from the brand. The BMW brand drives employees to maintain the high quality and excellence associated with it. This finding also supports the proposed vision definition of a cognitive construction or mental model that guides organizational actions discussed above.

Research on vision itself has generally focused on four aspects: development, articulation, communication, and implementation (e.g., Nanus, 1992; Quigley, 1993; Robbins & Duncan, 1988; Sashkin, 1992; Wall, Solum & Sobol, 1992; Westley & Mintzberg, 1989), Little is known about what constitutes an effective vision. Baum et al. (1998) were among the first who found positive relationships between vision attributes of brevity, challenge, future orientation, aspiring, abstractness, clarity, stability and vision content, and organizational performance in entrepreneurial firms. The researchers surveyed CEOs of architectural woodwork firms, and found that vision attributes and vision content were directly related to venture growth, as measured by sales, profits, employment, and net worth in these entrepreneurial firms. These vision attributes were strongly related to venture growth through their effects on vision communication. Visions characterized by the attributes of brevity, clarity,

abstractness, challenge, future orientation, stability, and desirability or ability to inspire have also been found to indirectly relate to customer satisfaction and directly relate to staff satisfaction in Australian apparel retail stores (Kantabutra, 2003). Findings from the two studies appear to endorse Kantabutra's (2003) proposed theory of vision that the seven attributes interact to improve vision's effectiveness.

Similarly, empirical evidence on vision content is scanty. Larwood et al. (1995) published the first large sample empirical study of vision content. In this study, chief executives in one national and three regional samples participated in a study of content and structure of their business visions. They were asked to describe their visions in one sentence and to evaluate their visions along twenty-six content dimensions. Vision content ratings appeared in clusters found to relate to rapidity of firm change, amount of control the executives exercised over firms, and type of industry. The study did not, however, associate vision content with performance, a critical missing piece. Later on, Kirkpatrick and Locke (1996) found that vision statements that emphasized product quality were related to increased trust, leader-follower goal congruence, and inspiration. In a recent study by Dvir, Kass and Shamir (2004), vision formulation, content of social-oriented values, and assimilation were positively related to affective commitment to the organization, and unrelated to continuance commitment among one hundred and eighty three high-tech employees. This finding indicates the positive relationships of a balanced transcendental and realistic content of the vision and a high level of "sharedness" in vision assimilation processes to affective organizational commitment. This makes sense because people need to know where they need to head from the vision content before they agree with the direction and commit to it.

In Australia, Kantabutra (2003) found that store manager visions containing reference to customer and staff satisfaction were significantly correlated to customer and staff satisfaction in Australian apparel stores. Sales, customer, employee and leadership were four frequently mentioned vision content elements in this study, which is not surprising because all are strategically important to acquire or maintain a leadership position in the market. Moreover, Rafferty and Griffin (2004), drawing upon their study of a large Australian public sector organization, suggest that visions do not always create a positive impact on follower attitudes, and that one should distinguish between "strong" and "weak" visions as well as vision content to see their effectiveness. This suggestion gains support from Senge's (1990) view of negative and positive visions discussed earlier.

Given a wide range of what to be included in a vision in the theoretical literature, it is interesting to find that some of the best visions were not brilliantly innovative and all too often had an almost mundane quality, usually consisting of ideas that are already well-known (Kotter, 1999). This finding suggests that there may be a limitation to effective vision content. In addition, the seven vision attributes and vision content are related in some sophisticated ways. For example, for a vision to be challenging and inspiring, the vision's content must contain challenging and inspiring references. Similarly, for a vision to be abstract, its content must be very broad so that it could cover all organizational interests. When a vision suggests such a broad meaning, it often becomes very simple. This might be an answer to why successful visions regularly had an almost mundane quality, usually consisting of ideas that are already well-known (i.e., to be the world's leader, to be the best, to die leading).

Another widely discussed assertion about vision is that vision must be shared between leader and followers to bring about superior performance outcomes, which has supporting empirical evidence. Kantabutra and Avery (2005) found that visions characterized by the attributes of brevity, clarity, stability, abstractness, future orientation, challenge, desirability and ability to inspire, and containing customer and staff satisfaction imagery, when shared by leader and followers, were correlated with enhanced organizational performance as measured by customer and staff satisfaction. Interestingly, shared visions directly created a positive impact on overall organizational performance through customer and staff satisfaction, taking into account manager efforts at empowerment and motivation, and staff use of vision to guide daily operations. Indeed, shared vision is inherent in staff performance, therefore creating an impact on customer satisfaction. More recently, Avery (2005) reported that there is plenty of evidence that shared vision, values, and corporate philosophy are operating among sustainable enterprises in Europe. This evidence underlines a role of vision in ensuring long-term organizational success.

In terms of realizing vision, Kantabutra (2003) found that visions characterized by the seven attributes of brevity, clarity, stability, abstractness, future orientation, challenge, desirability and ability to inspire played a significant role in realizing vision in Australian apparel retail stores. Using such vision, retail store managers could improve the effectiveness of their vision communication and attempts at motivation, empowerment and organizational alignment.

One mystery about vision is how people form viable visions. Among a very few researchers, Mumford and Strange (2005) found that vision formation requires descriptive models, reflection, and abstraction of key goals and/or key causes. Moreover, they also concluded that visioning involves a prescriptive model constructed through reflection and abstraction, and that visioning and planning should be treated as distinct constructs.

Supporting the theoretical literature, the empirical review reveals that vision is still critical to broader organizational success and sustainability. However, there are few reported studies on the critical components of effective visions and/or how such visions are formed. These few studies nevertheless indicated positive relationships between vision attributes and content, and organizational performance, supporting the previously discussed theoretical literature that "effective" visions are critical to organizational success. It also appears that the vision attributes findings lend support to Kantabutra's (2003) proposed Vision theory.

Conclusions and Future Research Directions

The literature review suggests that vision has been critical to managing people to achieve a goal since antiquity. Although the concept of vision has its critics, the empirical review suggests that effective visions do make a positive impact on performance outcomes in practice, directly and/or indirectly. Vision will continue to play a critical role in improving and sustaining organizational performance, despite the trend that the approach to leadership seems to shift from top-down to bottom-up. Given the definitional confusion and need to define vision for researchers and practitioners, I agree with Mumford and Strange that vision is ultimately defined as a cognitive construction or specifically a mental model, a conceptual representation used both to understand system operations as well as guide actions within the system.

Our knowledge on what an effective vision looks like and thus how such vision is formed is still limited. The literature suggests two components of vision: attributes and content. An attempt has been made to develop a vision, theory, proposing that effective visions are brief, clear, stable, challenging, future-oriented, desirable or inspiring, and abstract. This proposed vision theory appears to have broad support from the empirical literature. Similarly, our knowledge on the content of effective visions appears scanty. However, unlike vision attributes, there may not be a standard for vision content since vision content is strategic, depending on the type of business and its specific competitive environment.

Clearly, the literature suggests many areas for future vision research, including looking at what a vision is, the components of an "effective" vision, identifying the attributes and content of visions associated with competitive performance. This is essentially a critical area for both academics and practitioners that we know so little about. Accordingly, the following propositions are advanced for future research to further enhance our understanding about vision.

Proposition 1: Visions that bring about desirable performance outcomes and ability to sustain them are cognitive constructions or specifically mental models, conceptual representations used both to understand system operations and guide actions within the system.

Proposition 2: Visions characterized by the seven vision attributes bring about better performance outcomes and ability to sustain them than those not characterized by the seven vision attributes. The seven attributes interact to create the results.

Proposition 3: Visions containing strategic references bring about better performance outcomes and ability to sustain them than those not containing strategic references. These strategic references usually consist of ideas that are already well known.

Proposition 4: Visions characterized by the seven vision attributes and containing strategic references bring about better performance outcomes and ability to sustain them than those not characterized by me seven vision attributes and containing strategic

references. Both vision attributes and content interact to create such results.

References

Adair, J. (1989) *Great Leaders.* England: Talbot Adair Press.

Andrews, R., Boyne, G.A. & Walker, R.M. (2006) Strategy content and organizational performance: An empirical analysis, *Public Administration Review* 66(1), 52-63.

Avery, G.C. (2004) *Understanding Leadership.* London: Sage.

Avery, G.C. (2005) *Leadership for Sustainable Futures.* Northampton, MA: Edward Elgar.

Baetz, M.C. & Bart, C.K. (1996) Developing mission statements which work, *Long Range Planning* 29, 526-533.

Bass, B.M. (1985) *Leadership and Performance Beyond Expectations.* New York: Free Press.

Bass, B.M. (1990) *Bass & Stogdill's Handbook of Leadership: Theory, Research, & Managerial Applications* (3rd ed.). New York: Free Press.

Bass, B.M., Avolio, B.J., & Goodheim, L. (1987) Biography and the assessment of transformational leadership at the world class level, *Journal of Management,* 13, 7-19.

Baum, I.R., Locke, E.A. & Kirkpatrick, S.A. (1998) A longitudinal study of the relation of vision and vision communication to venture growth in entrepreneurial firms, *Journal of Applied Psychology,* 83, 43-54.

Baum, J.R. (1994) The Relations of Traits, Competencies, Vision, Motivation, and Strategy to Venture Growth, Doctoral dissertation, University of Maryland.

Bennis, W. (1990). Managing the dream: Leadership in the 21st century, *Training: The Magazine of Human Resource Development,* 27(5), 44-46.

Bennis, W. G. & Nanus, B. (1985) *Leaders: The Strategies for Taking Charge.* New York: Harper & Row.

Bryant, M.A. (1990) Relationship Between Nurse Managers Perceived Transformational versus Transactional Leadership Styles and Staff Nurse Turnover. Unpublished master's thesis, University of Arkon, Akron, OH.

Bryman, A. (1992) *Charisma and Leadership in Organizations.* London: Sage.

Collins, J.C. & Porras J.I. (1994) *Built to Last: Successful Habits of Visionary Companies.* London: Century.

Conger, J. A. & Kanungo, R.N. (1987) Toward a behavioral theory of charismatic leadership in organizational settings, *Academy of Management Review,* 12, 637-647.

Conger, J. A. (1991) Inspiring others: The language of leadership, *Academy of Management Executive,* 5(1), 31-45.

Conger, J.A. (1989) *The Charismatic Leader: Beyond The Mystique of Exceptional Leadership.* San Francisco: Jossey-Bass.

Curphy, G.J. (1990) An Empirical Study of Bass' (1985) Theory of Transformational and Transactional Leadership, Unpublished Doctoral Dissertation, The University of Minnesota.

Davis, S. & Meyer, C. (1998) *Blur: The Speed of Change in the Connected Economy.* San Francisco: Addison-Wesley.

Doz, Y.L. & Prahalad, C.K. (1987) A process model of strategic redirection in large complex firms: The case of multinational corporations, in: Pettigrew, A. (Ed.) *The Management of Strategic Change,* pp 63-88. Oxford, England: Basil Blackwell.

Drath, W. H. (1998) *Approaching the Future of Leadership Development.* Greensboro, NC: Center for Creative Leadership.

Dvir, T., Kass, N. & Shamir, B. (2004) The emotional bond: Vision and organizational commitment among high-tech employees, *Journal of Organizational Change Management,* 17(2), 126-143.

Gove, P. B. & Webster, M. (1993) *Webster's Third New International Dictionary.* Springfield, MA: Merriam-Webster Inc.

Hallinger, P. & Heck, R. (2002) What do you call people with visions? The role of vision, mission and goals in school leadership and improvement, in: Leithwood, K., Hallinger, P. & Colleagues (Eds.) *The Handbook of Educational Leadership and Administration,* pp 9-40. Dordrecht: Kluwer.

Hamburger, Y. A. (2000) Mathematical leadership vision, *Journal of Psychology,* 134(6), 601-611.

Hamel, G. & Prahalad, C.K. (1989) Strategic intent, *Harvard Business Review,* 89(3), 63-76.

Handy, C. (2002) What is a business for?, *Harvard Business Review,* 80(12), 48-55.

Hay, M. & Williamson, P. (1997) Good strategy: The view from below, *Long Range Planning,* 30, 651-664.

House, R.J., Spangler, W.D. & Woycke, J. (1991) Personality and charisma in the U.S. presidency: A psychological theory of leadership effectiveness, *Administrative Science Quarterly,* 36, 364-396.

Howell, J.M. & Frost, P. J. (1989) A laboratory study of charismatic leadership, *Organizational Behavior and Human Decision Processes,* 43(2), 243-269.

Humphreys, J. (2004) The vision thing, *MIT Sloan Management Review,* Spring, 96.

Hunt, J.G. (1991) *Leadership: A New Synthesis.* Newbury Park, CA: Sage.

Jacobs, T. O. & Jaques, E. (1990) Military executive leadership, in Clark, K.E. & Clark, M.B. (Eds.) *Measures of Leadership,* pp 281-295. West Orange, NJ: Leadership Library of America.

Kantabutra, S. (2003) An Empirical Examination of Relationships between Customer and Staff Satisfaction in Retail Apparel Stores in Sydney, Australia. Unpublished

Doctoral Dissertation, Macquarie Graduate School of Management, Macquarie University, Sydney.

Kantabutra, S. (2005a) Improving public school performance through vision-based leadership, *Asia Pacific Eduction Review,* 6(2), 122-134.

Kantabutra, S. (2005b) Leadership for sustainable organizations: A proposed model, *Sasin Journal of Management,* 11(1), 59-72.

Kantabutra, S. (2006) Relating vision-based leadership to sustainable business performance: A Thai perspective, *Kravis Institute Leadership Review,* 6(Spring), 37-53.

Kantabutra, S. & Avery, G.C. (2005) Essence of shared vision: Empirical investigation, *New Zealand Journal of Human Resources Management,* 5, 1-28.

Kirkpatrick, S.A. (1992) Decomposing Charismatic Leadership: The Effects of Leader Content and Process on Follower Performance, Attitudes, and Perceptions, Unpublished Doctoral Dissertation, University of Maryland, College Park.

Kirkpatrick, S. & Locke, E. (1996) Direct and indirect effects of three core charismatic leadership components on performance and attitudes, *Journal of Applied Psychology,* 84(1), 36-51.

Kotter, L.P. (1990) *A Force for Change: How Leadership Differs from Management.* New York: Free Press.

Kotter, J. P. (1997) Leading by vision and strategy, *Executive Excellence,* 14(10), 15-16.

Kotter, J. P. (1999) *What Leaders Really Do.* Cambridge, MA: Harvard Business Review Books.

Kouzes, J.M. & Posner, B.Z. (1987) *The Leadership Challenge: How To Get Extraordinary Thing Done in Organizations.* San Francisco: Jossey-Bass.

Larwood, L., Falbe, C. M., Kriger, M, R. & Miesling, P. (1995) Structure and meaning of organization vision, *Academy of Management Journal,* 85, 740-769.

Levin, M.L. (2000) Vision revisited, *The Journal of Applied Behavioral Science,* 36, 91-107.

Lipton, M. (1996) Demystifying the development of an organizational vision, *Sloan Management Review,* 37(4), 83-91.

Locke, E. A., Kirkpatrick, S., Wheeler, J.K., Schneider, J., Niles, K., Goldstein, H., Welsh & Chah, D.O. (1991) *The Essence of Leadership.* New York Lexington Books.

Lucey, J., Bateman, N. & Hines, P. (2005) Why major lean transitions have not been sustained, *Management Services,* 49(2), 9-13.

Maccoby, M. (1981) *The Leader.* New York: Simon & Schuster.

McDaniel, C. & Wolf, G.A. (1992) Transformational leadership in nursing service, *Journal of Nursing Administration,* 22(2), 60-65.

Mumford, M.D. & Strange, J.M. (2005) The origins of vision: Effects of reflection, models, and analysis, *Leadership Quarterly,* 16, 121-148.

Nanus, B. (1992) *Visionary Leadership: Creating A Compelling Sense of Direction for Your Organization.* San Francisco, CA: Jossey-Bass.

O'Brien, F. & Meadows, M. (2000) Corporate visioning: A survey of UK practice, *Journal of the Operational Research Society,* 51, 36-44.

Parikh, J. & Neubauer, F. (1993) Corporate visioning, in Hussey DE (Ed.) *International Review of Strategic Management* 4. pp 105-116. Wiley: Chichester.

Pearson, A.E. (1989) Six basics for general managers, *Harvard Business Review,* 67(4), 94-101.

Peters, T. (1987) *Thriving on Chaos.* New York: Harper & Row.

Phillips, R.L. & Hunt, J.G. (1992) Strategic leadership: An introduction, in Phillips, R.L. & Hunt, J.G. (Eds.) *Strategic Leadership: A Multiorganizational-level Perspective,* pp 2-14. Westport, CT: Quarum.

Puffer, S.M. (1990) Attributes of charismatic leadership: The impact of decision style, outcome, and observer characteristics, *Leadership Quarterly,* 1(3), 177-192.

Quigley, J.V. (1993) *Vision: How Leaders Develop It, Share It, and Sustain It.* New York: McGraw-Hill.

Rafferty, A.E. & Griffin, M.G. (2004) Dimensions of transformational leadership: Conceptual and empirical extensions, *Leadership Quarterly,* 15, 329-354.

Raynor, M.E. (1998) That vision thing: Do we need it? *Long Range Planning,* 31, 368-276.

Robbins, S.R. & Duncan, R.B. (1988) The role of the CEO and top management in the creation and implementation of strategic vision, in Hambrick, D.C. (Ed.) *The Executive Effect: Concepts and Methods for Studying Top Managers,* pp 137-152. Greenwich, CT: JAI Press.

Roberts, N. (1985) Transforming leadership: A process of collective action, *Human Relations,* 38, 1023-46.

Roberts, N.C. & Bradley, R.T. (1988) The limits of charisma, in Conger, J.A. & Kammgo, R.N. (Eds.) *Charismatic Leadership: The Elusive Factor in Organizational Effectiveness,* pp 253-275. San Francisco: Jossey-Bass.

Rynes, S.L., Colbert, A.E. & Brown, K..G. (2002) HR professionals' beliefs about effective human resource practices: Correspondence between research and practice, *Human Resource Management,* 41, 149.

Sashkin, M. (1988) The visionary leader, in Conger, J.A. & Kanungo, R.N. (Eds.) *Charismatic Leadership: The Elusive Factor in Organizational Effectiveness,* pp 122-160. San Francisco: Jossey-Bass.

Sashkin, M. (1992) Strategic leadership competencies: An introduction, in Phillips, R.L. & Hunt, G. (Eds.) *Strategic Leadership: A Multiorganization-level Perspective,* 139-160. Westport, CT: Quorum.

Schoemaker, P.J.H. (1992) How to link strategic vision to core capabilities, *Sloan Management Review,* Fall, 67-81.

Seeley, D. S. (1992) Visionary Leaders for Reforming Public Schools, paper presented at the Annual Meeting of the American Educational Research Association, San Francisco, CA.

Senge, P.M. (1990) *The Fifth Discipline: The Art & Practice of the Learning Organization.* New York: Currency Doubleday.

Sims, H.P., Jr. & Lorenzi, P. (1992) *The New Leadership Paradigm: Social Learning and Cognition in Organizations.* Newbury Park, CA: Sage.

Slater, R. (1993) *The New GE: How Jack Welch Revived an American Institution.* Homewood, TX: Business One Irwin.

Stevenson, B. (1949) *The Home Book of Bible Quotations.* New York: Harper & Row.

Takala, T. (1998) Plato on leadership, *Journal of Business Ethics,* 17(7), 785-798.

Thomas, P.I. & Thomas, D. L. (1959) *Living Biographies of Religious Leaders.* New York: Garden City Books.

Tichy, K.M. & Devanna, M.A. (1986) *The Transformational Leader,* New York: Wiley.

Van der Heijden, K. (1996) *Scenarios: The Art of Strategic Conversation.* Wiley: Chichester.

Vandermerwe, S. *(1995)* The process of market driven transformation, *Long Range Planning,* 28(2), 79-91.

Viney, J. (1999) *Drive: What Makes A Leader in Business and Beyond.* London: Bloomsbury Publishing.

Wall, B., Solum, R.S. & Sobol, M.R. (1992) *The Visionary Leader.* Rocklin, CA: Prima.

Wattis, J. (1994) *The Soul of Politics: A Practical and Prophetic Vision for Change.* New York: Orbis Books.

Weber, M. (1947) *The Theory of Social and Economic Organizations,* translated by Parsons, T. New York: Free Press.

Westley, F. & Mintzberg, H. (1989) Visionary leadership and strategic management, *Strategic Management Journal,* 10, 17-32.

Wheatley, M. J. (1999) *Leadership and the New Science: Discovering Order in a Chaotic World* (2nd). San Francisco: Berrert-Koehler.

Williams-Brinkley, R. (1999) Excellence in patient care demands a clear vision in action, *Health Care Strategic Management,* 17(1), 18-19.

Yukl, G.A. & Van Fleet, D.D. (1982) Cross-situational, multimethod research on military leader effectiveness, *Organizational Behavior and Human Performance,* 30, 87-108.

Zaccaro, S. J. (2001) *The Nature of Executive Leadership: A Conceptual and Empirical Analysis of Success.* Washington DC: APA Books.

Zaccaro, S. J. & Banks, D. (2004) Leader visioning and adaptability: Bridging the gap between research and practice on developing the ability to manage change, *Human Resource Management,* 43(4), 367-380.

CHAPTER 20

Is Your Vision Consistent?

A Method for Checking, Based on Scenario Concepts

João M. G. Boaventura

Universidade Paulista

Adalberto A. Fischmann

Universidade de São Paulo

1. Introduction

There is close consensus among the studies published in the literature that the future is an essential aspect of strategy, as has been stressed by various authors in the area of strategy. Chandler ([1], p. 13), Ackoff ([2], p. 29), Hofer and Schendel ([3], p. 204), Andrews ([4], p. 36), and Hamel and Prahalad ([5], p. 26) all emphasize that strategy should focus on the future. To connect strategy and future, several authors have recommended using scenario planning. Porter, for example ([6], p. 447), states that scenarios constitute a major tool for considering the future in strategic planning. Among other advantages, scenario techniques allow planners to draw up consistent visions of the future.

However, as Mercer [7] indicated, the traditional scenario construction methods are criticized for being very complex in their implementation, a factor that limits their broad implementation in organizations. Whether or not an organization makes use of scenario techniques, it nevertheless uses visions of the future to orient its strategies. But what happens if a vision is not consistent with the future?

On the basis of this problem, the present study describes a method to check the content and consistency of visions of the future and, if necessary, to provide further information for improving it. One important point is that the method should be simple enough to be understood and applied by other individuals interested in this same problem. It is also expected

Source: Is Your Vision Consistent? A Method for Checking, Based on Scenario Concepts, by Joao M. G. Boaventura and Adalberto A. Fischmann, *Futures* Vol. 40, 2008, pp. 597-612, © 2007 Elsevier. Reprinted with permission by Elsevier.

that the proposed method will contribute to the development of new means of improving and using scenario techniques as part of a method for making strategic decisions, a real requirement, as emphasized by Chermack [8] and Postma and Liebl [9].

The method described here is grounded on theoretical concepts used in scenario techniques and was tested on a real case in order to check its operational feasibility. The description of this test may also be also useful to illustrate how the method is applied. For this purpose, a company in the field of information technology was chosen, specifically, a manufacturer of POS (Electronic Point of Sale Equipment) in the Brazilian retail automation sector.

2. Theoretical Conceptualization

It would be interesting to explain the theoretical concepts and operational definitions used in the method being proposed, which is centered on testing and refining the vision of the future used, by organizations in their processes of formulating strategies.

2.1. Vision, or Strategic Vision, or Vision of the Future

Some authors, including Johnson and Scholes ([10], p. 13), simply define vision, or strategic vision, as a desired state for organizing the future. However, according to other authors, such as Wilson [11], strategic vision must analyze a company's future environment before defining what business might be possible in the future.

In this present study, the terms *vision, strategic vision,* and *vision of the future* are used interchangeably and consist of a set of two basic components: (A) a future configuration desired for the organization and (B) a future environment where this configuration can be successful. This concept of vision, which should link the future environment with the state in which the organization wishes to be in the future, is also defended by other authors [12-14].

Figure 20.1 illustrates the concept of vision used in this study.

2.2. Scenarios

Mannermaa [15] holds that scenario means research of the future, and this concept is based on the notion that the future is unpredictable. The main purpose of scenario building is to construct several different alternative futures and the respective paths that lead to them. According to van der Heijden et al. [16], the importance of scenario thinking lies in its ability to help overcome limitations on thinking, by developing multiple futures. Many authors (e.g., [17,18]) understand scenarios as mental models about the future environment and/or an organization in its future environment.

In the sense used in the field of futures studies the definitions of scenario are not controversial, although there are different methods for scenario planning. Most definitions consist of stories about what the future might be like, with each story describing an end state in the future and an internal consistent sequence of steps to move from one state to the other.

2.3. Basic Components of a Scenario

Trends, uncertainties, and the relationships that govern the present environment are basic components for building scenarios. Several scenario methods seek to describe how these components may condition the future environment. Examples can be seen in the methods of SRI [19], GBN [20], Future Mapping [21], Battelle [22], La Prospective [23], CSM [24], and Trend Impact Analysis [19].

The proposed method to check a vision of the future also considers trends, uncertainties, and the relationships that govern the environment, as the basic components of the method's process. The concept of how these basic components interact in the method proposed can be better understood by referring to Figure 20.2, adapted from Schoemaker [25].

In the method proposed here, both trends and uncertainties are the seeds of change in the present that lead to the future. Hence, they are called change drivers. In this regard, the concept of key variables should also be mentioned. According to Godet [26], key variables have the greatest power to influence the

Figure 20.1   Concept of Vision

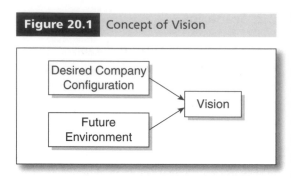

2.4. Key Variables

Throughout this article, all the elements of a scenario, such as trends and uncertainties, are referred to as variables, and those that have greater influence over the environment than others are termed key variables. The concept of key variables used here is that defined by Godet [23] in reference to environmental variables with greater power to influence the system.

system being studied, and they may consist of either trends or uncertainties.

The concept of trends mentioned above consists of a continuous, incremental change over a long period. But the concept of uncertainties discussed here is based on the proposal described by Ayres and Axtell [27] and consists of an event where the variables are known but their probability is not.

The rules of interaction shown in Figure 20.2, immediately following the consideration of trends and uncertainties, are designed to prevent nonplausible futures from being considered in the analytic process.

2.5 Trends and Contrasting Scenarios

According to Masini and Vasquez [28], a trend scenario describes the prolongation of the present situation, whereas contrasting scenarios describe different situations, starting off from the variations of certain key variables, and they are quite opposite to the trend scenario. The contrasting scenarios also focus on discovering relationships between facts that may not be sufficiently visible.

Figure 20.2   Basic Components of a Scenario

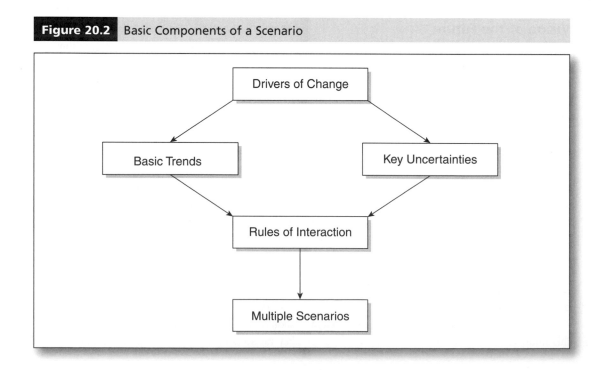

2.6. Future

In this study, the future is considered multiple, a view that is held by several other authors [15,19,26]. The term *future* is a concept adopted by scenario techniques where the future is expected to be the result of the combination of the various possible developments of events. On the basis of this concept, then, one cannot consider the future as the result of a projection that will lead to a single possible future state. In other words, it cannot be predicted.

The illustration shown in Figure 20.3, adapted from Ringland [19], gives an idea of this concept of a multiple future and implies that the future cannot be projected on the basis of current trends and strengths of the environment. Consequently, predicting the future by using forecasting techniques has serious drawbacks, which make them unfit for long-term planning. Several authors have held this position, including van Vught [29], Schwartz [20], Georgantzas and Acar [24], and Ayres and Axtell [27].

Another concept used is that of consistent future, in other words, a future that is described in a plausible scenario. Godet and Roubelat [30] define plausible scenarios as those found within a broader set of possible scenarios after restrictions have been considered. These restrictions consist of the elimination of unfeasible combinations of future situations, and these are only possible depending on the set they comprise. Some sets form feasible combinations and are therefore called plausible,

whereas others are considered unfeasible. Figure 20.4, adapted from Godet [26], is intended to illustrate this concept. The relevance of a scenario consistency is defended by many authors (e.g., [16,31,32]).

Scenario development methods use a number of techniques to avoid the creation of implausible scenarios. Among such methods are the "development steps" described in the Trend Impact Analysis Method [19], and "morphological analysis" in the La Prospective method [13]. The method proposed here for checking the consistency of a vision uses a technique similar to the "correlation matrix" used by Schoemaker [25] and was originally developed by Kirkwood and Pollack [33].

2.7. The Environment

One possible approach for analyzing an organization's external environment, which is used in the method proposed here, is stakeholder analysis, introduced by Freeman [34]. According to this approach, an organization's environment is strongly influenced by its stakeholders, and various authors have developed methods of stakeholder analysis based on this concept (e.g., [35-38]).

Another researcher, Mitroff [39], who also developed a method for stakeholder analysis, pointed out the need to identify the various characteristics of each major stakeholder, such as its motivations, intentions, interests, reasons, power, and knowledge. According to Mitroff and Emshoff [40], this method does not consider the

Figure 20.3 Multiple Futures

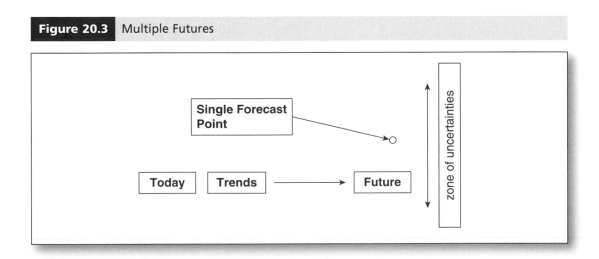

Figure 20.4 Possible, Plausible, and Desired Scenarios

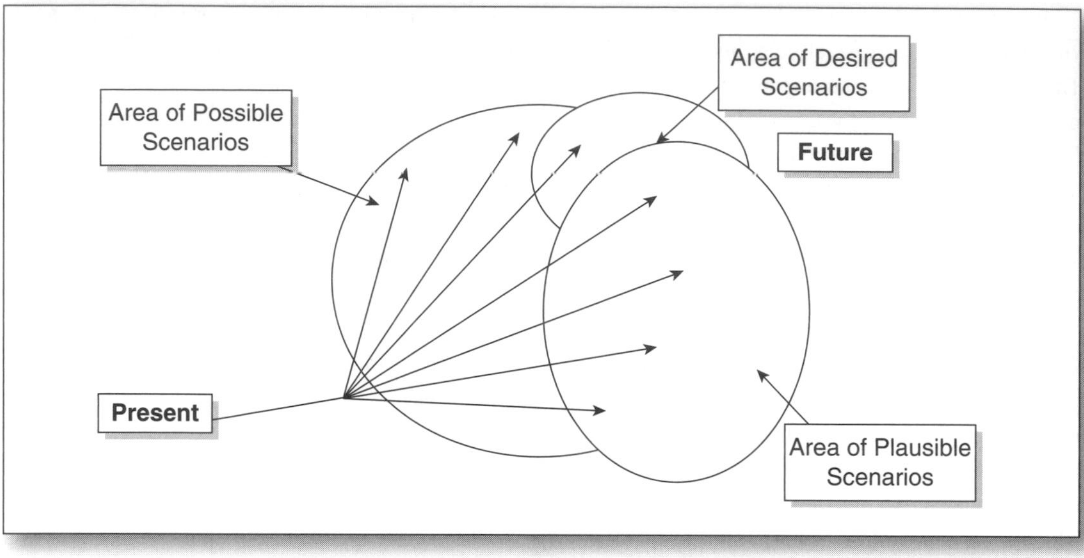

macroenvironment as a stakeholder, strictly speaking (SEPT—Social, Economical, Political and Technological), in contrast to the models proposed by Carroll and Buchholtz [38] and by Svendsen [36].

In one way or another, stakeholder analysis methods consider aspects of the macroenvironment (SEPT) in their processes, as does the method for checking the vision of the future proposed here. For the proposed method, the environment comprised stakeholders and the variables present in the macroenvironment that influence the organization. An idea of this concept can be seen in Figure 20.5.

3. The Proposed Method

The method proposed here has the objective of checking two pertinent aspects of the vision of the future. The first aspect is to ascertain whether the vision of the future being analyzed has taken into account the existence of the key variables of the sector under analysis. In this study, this first checking procedure is referred to as checking the contents of the vision. The second is to check whether or not the conditions assumed in this vision of the future are consistent, that is, whether they

present any mutual incompatibility. This second procedure is referred to here as checking the vision's consistency. As a subproduct of this checking, the method shows possible weak points related either to the absence of key variables or to incompatibilities among variables assumed. The vision of the future can be refined on the basis of this information.

The method absorbs theoretical concepts developed in the field of futures studies, especially those used in the scenario methods mentioned in this text. It is nevertheless useful to apply a test in order to check its operationality. One should recall that many scenario methods are criticized because, due to their complexity or cost, they are hard to operationalize, and this limitation is undesirable in the proposed method.

Figure 20.6 presents a flow sheet of the proposed method.

The proposed method for checking a vision of the future is structured into five stages: (1) analysis of the stakeholders and the macroenvironment (2) selection of the key variables (3) extraction of the environmental variables (4) checking the contents, and (5) checking the consistency.

The data are gathered through structured in-depth interviews. The interviewees are specialists in the

Figure 20.5 The View of Stakeholder and Environmental Forces

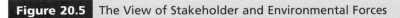

Figure 20.5 The View of Stakeholder and Environmental Forces

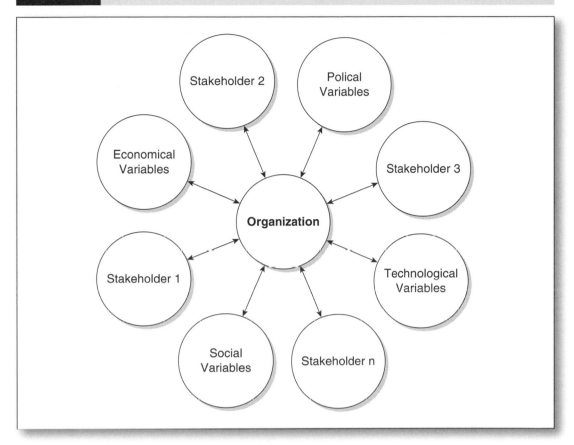

economic sector being appraised, but they belonged to different stakeholder groups. It is interesting to point out that stakeholder input is increasingly used in today's scenario projects, as observed by van Notten et al. [41]. The criterion for choosing the specialists is that they be key respondents, a concept described by both Fetterman [42] and Mackillip [43], meaning specific individuals capable of providing detailed information, including historical data, nuances, and/or relationships present in the environment.

3.1. Stage 1: Environmental Analysis

In Stage 1, the respondents are asked whom they consider to be the main stakeholders and what they consider the main forces in the macroenvironment in their respective economic sector. A list suggesting the typical stakeholders and the main forces in the macroenvironment is presented as a stimulus for discussion. The respondents are then asked to explain how the stakeholders and the forces in the environment influence the economic sector being analyzed. In this method, every type of influence on the sector resulting from the action by a stakeholder or by the macroenvironment becomes a variable. Since a single variable may be indicated by more than one respondent, all the variables obtained are consolidated after the first stage of data gathering.

A second round of interviews with the specialists is also held in Stage 1. This time the respondents judge the list of consolidated variables in terms of the degree of

Figure 20.6   Flow Sheet of the Proposed Method

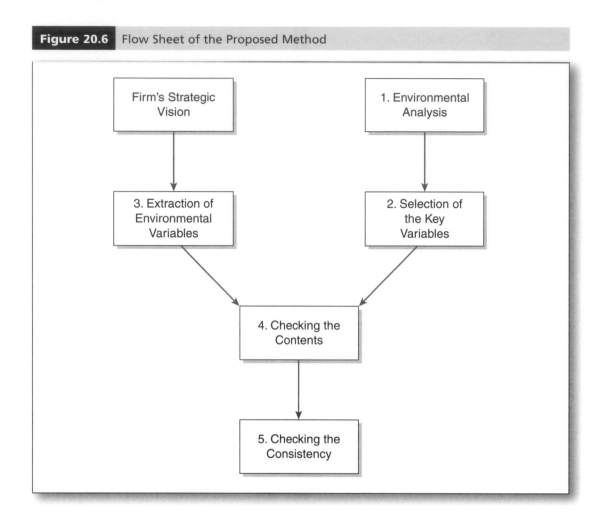

influence and the uncertainty of each variable. This procedure resulted in a graph originally used by Mitroff and Emshoff [40] in an assumption analysis method. After the data is gathered from the second round of interviews, the variables are tabulated, and those with the highest degree of importance in terms of their power to influence the respective sector are chosen for the next stage of the method.

3.2. Stage 2: Selection of Key Variables

In Stage 2, a third and last round of interviews with the specialists is held with the objective of selecting the key variables. The degree of dependence among the variables must therefore be checked and a more precise process of evaluation of the power to influence the variables in the sector must be carried out. This step consists of a comparison of pairs of variables. Using the results of this stage, a graph of the influence and dependence among the variables can be drawn up. The graph, first proposed by Godet [26], is then used to choose the key variables.

3.3. Stage 3: Extraction of Environmental Variables

Stage 3 serves the purpose of detecting the environmental variables considered in an organization's strategic vision. However, it is first advisable to ascertain whether the desired information is explicit in the documents used in the organization's strategic planning process. If it is not, the information must be obtained in interviews with managers who participated in the strategic process.

Stage 3 is similar to Stage 1, with two basic differences. First, the respondents are not specialists in the specific economic sector involved, but rather managers in the company being studied. Second, since scenario planning might not have been used to generate a vision of the future, the organization risks seeing the future environment as the only possible one, and therefore, different from that developed if one assumes that the future is multiple. In the case at hand, the variables of the uncertainty category were not considered as such but were assumed as one of the possible states of the future, a particularity that the questionnaires should be designed to reveal.

3.4. Stage 4: Checking the Contents

Stage 4 generates the method's first results, showing whether the key variables, those of greatest importance in the sector being studied, were or were not considered in the vision of the future being appraised. If they were, the organization's strategic vision is considered complete; otherwise, it is deemed incomplete. This information is useful for the organization because if there is a vision with incomplete contents, the organization can then consider the variables absent in the vision in order to evaluate whether the vision will remain consistent.

3.5. Stage 5: Checking the Consistency

The objective of Stage 5 is to discern whether the vision of the future is consistent or not in terms of the conditions assumed for the environment. This process takes place by applying what is described here as the consistency matrix, where the variables are arranged in rows and columns, and the possibility of coexistence among them is checked. When two variables can coexist in the future environment, then a *plus sign* (+) is placed in the respective cell in the matrix, otherwise a *minus sign* (−) should be placed there.

The result indicates whether the future considered in the organization's vision is plausible or not and, if not, why not. As in the preceding stage, the reasons for any lack of plausibility are included in the information the organization can use to refine its vision of the future.

4. The Test

The application test to check the method proposed has two purposes: the first and most important being to ascertain whether it is functional. The second purpose is to detect how it is implemented, in order to obtain a clearer understanding of its operation.

The strategic vision evaluated in the test is that of a leading manufacturer in the Brazilian POS (Electronic Point of Sale Equipment) segment. There is a large sector in Brazil that produces computerized equipment to be used at points of sale. This equipment handles not only credit card operations, but is also used by the federal government for controlling sales and purchases, for tax collection purposes. The government inspects the equipment through authorized compliance testing laboratories. Let first be defined the limits of this test.

The first limit is with regard to the sector being studied. Since the company is a manufacturer of POS equipment, the study is limited to Brazilian producers of this type of equipment.

Another limit of the study is the focus established by POS companies in Brazil regarding POS manufacturers. For this reason, participants in this sector other than manufacturers, such as distributors, system integrators, as well as manufacturers of accessories (bar code readers and electronic scales) and office supplies (paper and labels), were considered stakeholders in the industry, but they were not the central focus of analysis.

A third limit refers to the temporal dimension: the data were gathered between March and September 2003. A fourth limit consists of the proposed time horizon. For example, when the respondents to this test were asked to make suggestions and judge the variables, they were oriented to think in terms of the next five years.

The test used two methods of study. Stages 1 and 2 consist of a structured in-depth exploratory study for gathering data. Stages 3, 4, and 5 consist of a case study, the object of which was not the POS manufacturer but the test of the proposed model. Yin [44] explains that the case study method can be used to describe an intervention and a context where it takes place. In this test, the intervention consists of the application of the proposed method, and the context is the company studied, its vision, and the retail automation market in Brazil.

4.1. Stage 1: Environmental Analysis

The specialists were chosen according to the theoretical recommendation of the proposed method, and they belonged to different groups of stakeholders. These specialists were:

1. The commercial director of a POS manufacturer.

2. The commercial director of a manufacturer of bar code readers.

3. The director of development at a retail automation software manufacturer.

4. The president of the Brazilian Association of Retail Automation Companies.

5. The president of a Brazilian retail storeowners' association.

6. A journalist specialized in retail automation.

7. The commercial director of a distributor of retail automation equipment.

8. A tax inspector for the São Paulo State Government and member of the Automation Inspection Commission.

9. The president of a credit card company in Brazil.

10 A professor and researcher in the automation retail sector.

Figure 20.7 shows a perspective of the various types of stakeholders in this sector who were consulted.

The data gathered in Stage 1 generated 146 variables. After a process of consolidation by which these variables were filtered through a process of vocabulary unification, 69 different variables remained. Since each of the specialists identified an average of only 14.6 variables, the choice of such an eclectic group of specialists proved to be an efficient way to explore the universe of possible variables. As might be expected, it became clear during the in-depth interviews that even though all the specialists had an overall view of the sector, each one had more specific knowledge of certain aspects and variables of the system. Not only did the specialists identify different variables, they also did perceive the existence of different stakeholder groups in the sector.

Table 20.1 shows the different stakeholder groups identified by the specialists as belonging to the retail automation sector.

To answer the second questionnaire of Stage 1, the respondents used a scale ranging from −5 to +5 in order to judge both the influence and the uncertainty of the variables. After the evaluation had been tabulated, it was seen that most of the variables were classified as trends and only a few as uncertainties. In addition, statistical analysis indicated a negative correlation between the average score of the question about the uncertainty of each variable and its respective standard deviation. This indicates that the specialists show greater agreement in their opinions about trends than about uncertainties.

The statistical analysis also showed that there is a positive correlation between the average score of the variables and their respective standard deviations. This indicates that the specialists agree more often about which variables exert greater influence than about those that exert less.

To conclude Stage 1, the most important variables for Stage 2 were chosen. The criterion was to use the variables classified in the fourth quartile of the influence values, resulting in a group of 18 variables. Figure 20.8 shows the distribution of these variables as a function of the questions on influence and uncertainty.

The variables were named according to codes for their origin, category of stakeholder, and segment in the macroenvironment. These factors constituted a prefix followed by a sequential number, called the suffix.

Figure 20.7	Stakeholders Consulted

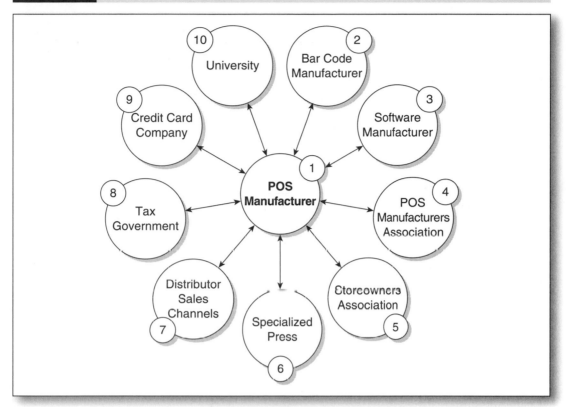

Each prefix was followed by a sequential number, which we call the suffix.

Table 20.2 shows the list of variables chosen for Stage 2.

4.2. Stage 2: Selection of Key Variables

In Stage 2, the specialists were asked once again to judge the influence of the variables on the system. However, this time the judgment applied only to the 18 most important variables, which had been chosen in Stage 1. In addition, a more precise process was used by making comparisons between pairs of variables. At the same time that the specialists evaluated the power of influence of each pair of variables, they also judged the relationship of dependence among them.

The first 18 variables selected generated 153 different combinations of pairs of variables to be judged. The evaluations were tabulated and later normalized in order to plot the influence-dependence graph. Figure 20.9 demonstrates this situation.

The influence-dependence graph, as described by Godet ([26], p. 95), has five different sectors:

- Sector 1. Essential variables: these high-influence and low-dependence variables are the explanatory variables that condition the rest of the system.
- Sector 2. Transmission variables: these high-influence and high-dependence variables are unstable by nature; any shifts in them have repercussions on the others.
- Sector 3. Resulting variables: these low-influence and high-dependence variables are influenced by those of Sectors 1 and 2.

Table 20.1 Stakeholders Indicated by the Specialists

Stakeholders	Experts									
	01	02	03	04	05	06	07	08	09	10
End user	X		X	X	X		X	X		X
Distribution channels	X	X		X	X	X	X	X	X	X
Software manufacturers		X	X	X	X		X	X		
Suppliers		X			X			X		
Unions							X			
Trade associations	X	X	X		X	X	X	X	X	X
Capital investors		X			X			X		
High-tech firms		X			X	X	X		X	
Competitors	X	X		X	X	X	X	X	X	X
Institutes of technology					X	X	X	X		X
Banks				X	X	X	X			X
Government	X	X	X	X	X	X	X	X	X	X
Public opinion institutes		X					X			
Contractors (technical assistance)								X		
Credit card companies									X	X

Figure 20.8 Influence × Uncertainty

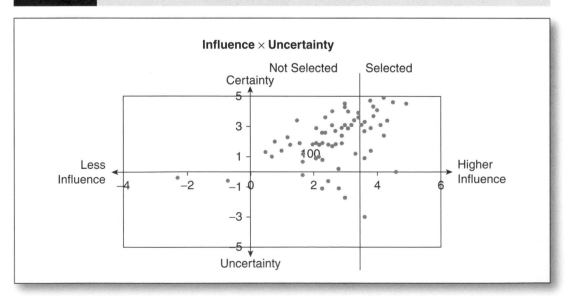

Table 20.2 Variables Chosen for Stage 2

Variable Name	Variable Description	Category
GOVERNMENT-3	Generates a law-based demand for fiscal POS	Trend
POLITICS-2	Tax reform influences demand for fiscal POS: If reform exerts tax control at place of final purchase, demand will increase; otherwise, demand will fall	Uncertainty
ECONOMICS-6	US$ exchange rate influences demand for fiscal POS; the lower the price of the US$, the higher the demand, and vice-versa	Uncertainty
SOFTWARE MANUF-2	Pressure for higher quality products	Trend
CREDIT CARD ASSOC-1	Resist the fiscal POS model	Trend
COMPETITORS-1	Pressure-aggressive marketing policies	Trend
POS MANUF ASSOC-1	Political actions in favor of the fiscal POS	Trend
COMPETITORS-7	Pressure for better infrastructure for technical assistance	Trend
COMPETITORS-6	Pressure for better performance From POS products	Trend
CREDIT CARD COS.-I	Resist the fiscal POS model	Trend
SOCIAL-1	New generation of storeowners will increase demand for fiscal POS	Trend
DISTRIB CHAN-2	Pressure for POS features that meet customers' needs	Trend
SOCIAL-3	Consumer behavior influences demand for fiscal POS. If consumers ask for invoices, there will be higher demand	Uncertainty
ECONOMICS-7	Abrupt changes in US$ rate reduces demand	Trend
POLITICS-4	Tax reform influences demand for fiscal POS. If tax control is exerted by the municipalities, demand for POS will fall, and vice versa	Uncertainty
COMPETITORS-3	Pressure for continuous technological updating	Trend
COMPETITORS-8	Pressure for fewer stages along sales channels	Trend
COMPETITORS-4	Pressure to decentralize distribution logistics	Trend

- Sector 4. Low-influence and low-dependence: these variables consist of market trends or of factors that are relatively unrelated to the system, having only a weak relationship with it.
- Sector 5. Variables of medium influence and dependence: nothing is known about these

variables a priori; they are of the "middle cluster" type.

The variables in Sector 1 were considered the key variables of the system and are listed in Table 20.3.

Figure 20.9 Influence × Dependence

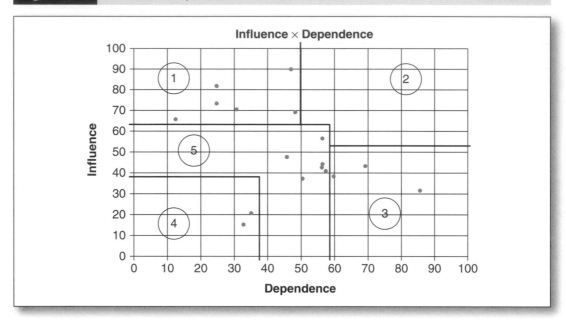

Table 20.3 Key Variables

Variable Name	Variable Description	Sector	Uncertainty/Trend
GOVERNMENT-3	Generates a law-based demand for fiscal POS	1	Trend
P0LIT1CS-2	Tax reform influences demand for fiscal POS. If tax control is exerted at place of final purchase, demand will increase; otherwise, demand will fall.	1	Uncertainty
ECONOMICS-6	US$ exchange rate influences demand for fiscal POS; the higher the price of the US$, the lower the demand, and vice-versa	1	Uncertainty
SOCIAL-3	Consumer behavior influences demand for fiscal POS. If consumers ask for invoices, there will be increased demand for fiscal POS and vice-versa; otherwise, demand will fall	1	Uncertainty
ECONOMICS-7	Abrupt variations in the US$ reduce demand for POS	1	Trend
POLITICS-4	Tax reform influences demand for fiscal POS. If control is exerted by the municipalities, demand for POS will fall; otherwise, it will rise	1	Uncertainty

4.3. Stage 3: Extraction of Environmental Variables

The first source of information used to investigate the vision of the future of the company being studied consisted of documents generated by the strategic planning process. These documents indicated that the vision of the future was defined by the company's

1. Being a global company,

2. Being present in each Brazilian retail company,

3. Competing in the various segments of automation.

Although the vision of the future was explicit and showed what the company would like to be in the future and how it plans to attain these objectives (2008), the documents failed to explain what the environment of this sector would be like in 2008. Asked about how they imagined what the sector would be like in 2008, company managers that participated in the strategic planning process said that there had been no discussion on this point during the planning process. Since the information on the environmental variables of the vision of the future was not explicit, the organizers of the study then resorted to interviews.

Considering that the description of the future environment was not explicit and had never been a topic for discussion in the planning process, the company managers were very likely to have different ideas on the topic. In fact, it would be surprising if the participants in the strategic planning process shared one converging idea of something so complex and with so many variables. In addition, the purpose of the test was not to see if the managers of the company being studied had the same information, but to test the operational feasibility of the proposed model. A pre-supposition was established at this point in the test: the company's vision of the future would be that which was in the mind of its Chief Executive Officer.

The CEO of the company being studied was a respondent for Stage 3 and referred to 15 different variables as influencers of the retail automation sector, a number that was virtually average of 14.6 indicated by the specialists. Thirteen of the 15 variables indicated by the company president were already on the list of those identified by the specialists, and two were new,

designated as COMPETITORS-9 and COMPLIANCE TESTING LABS-1.

Table 20.4 shows the result of the classification of these variables into trends and uncertainties.

4.4. Stage 4: Checking the Contents

Stage 4 consists of a simple process of checking to ascertain whether the key variables identified by the proposed method are present or not in the vision of the future of the company being studied. Although this is a simple procedure, the results are important and generated useful information for refining the vision of the future.

The test showed that four key variables were absent from the company's vision of the future, namely, GOVERNMENT-3, ECONOMICS-6, SOCIAL-3, and ECONOMICS-7. Therefore, as defined by the proposed method, the vision of the future of the company being studied cannot be considered complete.

Another aspect related to the four key variables absent from the vision of the future was that two were trends and two were uncertainties. As stressed by Masini and Vasquez [28], changes in the key variables are the seeds of the contrasting scenarios, which latter are able to describe conditions that strongly influence the organization in various ways. This implies that the absence of the two key variables in the uncertainty category brings about significant and different scenarios not considered in the vision of the future of the company being studied.

4.5. Stage 5: Checking the Consistency

To draw up the consistency matrix, not only must the correct variables be chosen, but they must also receive adequate treatment, consisting of the following procedures:

1. The key variables absent from the vision of the future were added.

2. Trend-type variables that the specialists classified as less important (Sectors 3 and 4 of the influence-dependence graph) were discarded.

Table 20.4 Classification and Vocabulary Harmonization of Variables

	Vocabulary Harmonization of Variables	
Generated Variable	*Variable Description*	*Uncertainty/Trend*
GOVERNMENT-2	Pressure for standardized products	Trend
COMPLIANCE TESTING LABS-1	Create barriers against new products	Uncertainty
ECONOMICS-1	Sales growth with economic growth	Uncertainty
CUSTOMERS-1	Resist fiscal POS model	Trend
COMPETITORS-9	Pressure for lower prices	Trend
CUSTOMERS-3	Pressure for more economical systems	Trend
CUSTOMERS-2	Pressure for equipment with better performance	Trend
COMPETITORS-8	Pressure for fewer stages along sales channels	Trend
SOFTWARE MANUF-2	Pressure for higher quality POS products	Trend
DISTRIB CHAN-1	Push profit margins down	Trend
STOREOWNERS ASSOC-1	Resist fiscal POS model	Trend
SUPPLIERS-1	Force continuous technological product updating	Trend
POS MANUF ASSOC-1	Political pressure in favor of fiscal POS	Trend
POLITICS-2	Tax reform influences demand for fiscal POS. If taxes are levied at place of final purchase, demand will increase; otherwise, it will fall	Trend
SOFTWARE MANUF-1	Pressure for standardized interface	Trend

3. In cases of disagreement between the specialists and the company CEO in classifying the variables as trend or uncertainty, the specialists' judgment prevailed.

After the above considerations, the variables presented in Table 20.5 were established.

The number of consistency matrices depends on the number of possible combinations of the different final states that each key variable of the uncertainty type can assume. Each uncertainty can take on at least two possible final states. In the study in question, with four key variables of the uncertainty type, 16 consistency matrices were generated.

The first matrix, the judgment of which has already been established, is shown in Table 20.6, below. In this matrix, all the combinations tested were compatible with one another, so all the matrix cells are marked with a plus sign (+).

The analysis of the consistency matrices showed that there are potential incompatibilities in the vision of the future of the company being studied. They arose as the result of the following situations:

1. When the GOVERNMENT-2 variable assumed its final state of "not forcing the standardized POS products," it was seen to be incompatible with the COMPLIANCE TESTING LABS-1, ECONOMICS-1, and POS MANUF ASSOC-1 variables.

Table 20.5	Variables Chosen for Checking Consistency	

	Vocabulary Harmonization of Variables	
Generated Variable	*Variable Description*	*Uncertainty/Trend*
GOVERNMENT-2	Pressure for standardized products	Uncertainty
COMPLIANCE TESTING LABS-1	Create barriers against new products	Uncertainty
ECONOMICS-1	Sales growth with economic growth	Uncertainty
CUSTOMERS-1	Resist fiscal POS model	Trend
COMPETITORS-9	Pressure for lower prices	Trend
SOFTWARE MANUF-2	Pressure for higher quality POS products	Trend
POS MANUF ASSOC-1	Pressure politically in favor of fiscal POS	Trend
POLITICS-2	Tax reform influences demand for fiscal POS. If taxes are levied at place of final purchase, demand will increase; otherwise, demand will fall	Uncertainty

2. When the POLITICS-2 variable took on its final state of "not defining tax control over destiny," it was seen to be incompatible with the ECONOMICS-1 and POS MANUF ASSOC-1 variables.

5. Conclusions

At the first level, the test showed that the proposed method for checking the vision of the future is operationally feasible. Through a relatively simple process—and simplicity is an important characteristic in the implementation of strategic management tools—the method proposed was capable of analyzing the vision of the future of the company being studied and indicating its shortcomings and points of inconsistency.

Second, with reference to the POS manufacturer's vision of the future, it became clear that there were variables which strongly influenced the system in the retail automation sector besides those considered in the vision of the future. There were also certain inconsistencies intrinsic to the company's vision. The key variables, forgotten in the vision of the future, were those related to the government and to aspects of the economic and social environment.

The primary stakeholders in the retail automation sector in Brazil were seen to be the government, the competitors, the distribution channel, and the credit card companies. The main uncertainties in the sector are related to the evolution of the fiscal reform currently underway in Brazil, the effects of variations in the exchange rate between the local currency and the US dollar, and changes in consumer behavior.

6. Recommendations

Although the test was applied to only one case—therefore, few, if any, of the conclusions can be generalized—there are indications that choosing an eclectic group of specialists from different categories of stakeholders is more effective for generating the variables for a study of a sector than consulting individuals who represent a single stakeholder category. Some strategic management models suggest using company managers for this type of study. As can be observed in the test, the specialists came up with an average of 14.6 variables each, although a total of 69 different variables were found. In addition, the specialists were not unanimous in determining what the main stakeholders were and had different levels of knowledge about the various characteristics of the environment. This reinforces the recommendation that an eclectic group of specialists should be used to generate the environmental variables.

Table 20.6 Consistency Matrix

MATRIX 01	COMPLIANCE TESTING LABS-1 Create barriers for new products	ECONOMICS-1 Sales growth with economic growth	POLITCS-2 Tax reform drives POS demand	CUSTOMERS-1 Resist the fiscal POS model	COMPETITORS-9 Pressure for lower prices	SOFTWARE MANUF-2 Pressure for higher quality POS products	POS MANUF ASSOC-1 Political action in favor of POS
GOVERNMENT-2 Pressure for standardized products	+	+	+	+	+	+	+
COMPLIANCE TESTING LABS-1 Create barriers against new products		+	+	+	+	+	+
ECONOMICS-1 Sales growth with economic growth			+	+	+	+	+
POLITICS-2 Tax reform influences demand for POS				+	+	+	+
CUSTOMERS-1 Resist the fiscal POS model					+	+	+
COMPETITORS-9 Pressure for lower prices						+	+
SOFTWARE MANUFAC-2 Pressure for higher quality POS products							+

References

[1] A.D. Chandler Jr., Strategy and Structure: Chapters in the History of the Industrial Enterprise, MIT Press, Cambridge, MA, 1962.

[2] R.L. Ackoff, Redesigning the Future, Wiley, New York, 1974.

[3] C.W. Hofer, D. Schendel, Strategy Formulation, West Pub., Saint Paul, MN, 1978.

[4] K.R. Andrews, The Concept of Corporate Strategy, third ed., Irwin, Homewood, IL, 1987.

[5] G. Hamel, C.K. Prahalad, Competing for the Future, Harvard Business School Press, Boston, MA, 1994.

[6] M.E. Porter, Competitive Advantage, Free Press, New York, 1985.

[7] D. Mercer, Simpler scenarios, Management Decisions 33 (4) (1995) 32–40.

[8] T.J. Chermack, Improving decision-making with scenario planning, Futures 36 (2004) 295–309.

[9] T.J.B.M. Postma, F. Liebl, How to improve scenario analysis as a strategic management tool?, Technological Forecasting and Social Change 72 (2005) 161–173.

[10] G. Johnson, K. Scholes, Exploring Corporate Strategy: Text and Cases, fifth ed., Prentice-Hall, New York, 1999.

[11] I. Wilson, Realizing the power of strategic vision, Long Range Planning 25 (5) (1992) 18–28.

[12] C.W. Ashley, L. Hall, Nonextrapolative strategy, in: J.S. Mendell, F.J. Pessolano (Eds.), Nonextrapolative Methods in Business Forecasting—Scenarios, Vision and Issues Management, Quorum Books, Westport, CT, 1985, pp. 61–76.

[13] M. Godet, Creating Futures—Scenario Planning as a Strategic Management Tool, Economica, Paris, 2001.

[14] P.J.H. Schoemaker, Profiting from Uncertainty: Strategies for Succeeding no Matter What the Future Brings, Free Press, New York, 2002.

[15] M. Mannermaa, In search of an evolutionary paradigm for futures research, Futures 23 (1991) 349–372.

[16] K. van der Heijden, R. Bradfield, G. Burt, G. Cairns, G. Wright, The Sixth Sense: Accelerating Organizational Learning with Scenarios, Willey, Chichester, UK, 2002.

[17] K. van der Heijden, Scenarios—the Art of Strategic Conversation, Willey, Chichester, UK, 1996.

[18] T.J. Chermack, Studying scenario planning: theory, research suggestions, and hypotheses, Technological Forecasting and Social Change 72 (2005) 59–73.

[19] G. Ringland, Scenario Planning—Managing for the Future, Willey, Chichester, UK, 1998.

[20] P. Schwartz, The Art of the Long View, Doubleday, New York, 1991.

[21] D.H. Mason, Scenario-based planning: decision model for the learning organization, Planning Review 22 (2) (1994) 6–11.

[22] W.R. Huss, E.J. Honton, Scenario planning: what style should you use?, Long Range Planning 20 (4) (1987) 21–29.

[23] M. Godet, A caixa de ferramentas da prospectiva estrategica, CEPES, Lisboa, 2000.

[24] N.C. Georgantzas, W. Acar, Scenario-Driven Planning: Learning to Manage Strategic Uncertainty, Quorum Books, Westport, CT, 1995.

[25] P.J.H. Schoemaker, Scenario planning: a tool for strategic thinking, Sloan Management Review 36 (2) (1995) 25–40.

[26] M. Godet, From Anticipation to Action, Unesco Publishing, Paris, 1993.

[27] R.U. Ayres, R. Axtell, Foresight as a survival characteristic: when (if ever) does the long view pay?, Technological Fore Social Change 51 (1996) 209–235.

[28] E.B. Masini, J.M. Vasquez, Scenarios as seen from a human and social perspective, Technological Forecasting and Socia (2000) 49–66.

[29] F.A. van Vught, Pitfalls of forecasting: fundamentals problems for the methodology of forecasting from the philosophy Futures 19 (1987) 184–196.

[30] M. Godet, F. Roubelat, Creating the future: the use and misuse of scenarios, Long Range Planning 29 (2) (1996) 164–171.

[31] P.J.H. Schoemaker, Twenty common pitfalls in scenario planning, in: L. Fahey, R.M. Randall (Eds.), Learning from Wiley, New York, 1998, pp. 422–431.

[32] P.P.M.A.R. Heugens, J.V. Oosterhout, To boldly go where no man has gone before: integrating cognitive and physical scenario studies, Futures 33 (2001) 861–872.

[33] C.W. Kirkwood, S.M. Pollock, Multiple attribute scenarios, bounded probabilities, and threats of nuclear theft, Future 545–553.

[34] R.E. Freeman, Strategic Management: a Stakeholder Approach, Pitman, Boston, MA, 1984.

[35] D.J. Wood, Business and Society, Harper Collins, Boston, MA, 1990.

[36] A. Svendsen, The Stakeholder Strategy: Profiting from Collaborative Business Relationships, Berrett-Koehler Publi Francisco, CA, 1998.

[37] J.W. Weiss, Business Ethics: a Stakeholder and Issues Management Approach, second ed., Dryden Press, Forth Worth, TX.

[38] A.B. Carroll, A.K. Buchholtz, A.K. Business & Society: Ethics Stakeholder Management, fourth ed., South-Wester Publishing, Cincinnati, OH, 2000.

[39] I.I. Mitroff, Stakeholders of the Organizational Mind: Toward a New View of Organizational Policy Making, Jossey-Bass, San Francisco, CA, 1983.

[40] I.I. Mitroff, J.R. Emshoff, On strategic assumption-making: a dialectical approach to policy and planning, Academy of Management Review 4 (1) (1979) 1–12.

[41] P.W.F. van Notten, J. Rotmans, M.B.A. van Asselt, D.S. Rothman, An updated scenario typology, Futures 35 (2003) 423–443.

[42] D.M. Fetterman, Ethnography, in: L. Bickman, D.J. Rog (Eds.), Handbook of Applied Social Research Methods, Sage Publications, Thousand Oaks, CA, 1998, pp. 473–504.

[43] J. Mackillip, Need Analysis: Process and Techniques, in: L. Bickman, D.J. Rog (Eds.), Handbook of Applied Social Methods, Sage Publications, Thousand Oaks, CA, 1998, pp. 261–284.

[44] R.K. Yin, Case Study Research: Design and Methods, second ed., Sage Publications, Thousand Oaks, CA, 1994.

CHAPTER 21

The Mission Statement

A Corporate Reporting Tool With a Past, Present, and Future

Linda Stallworth Williams

North Georgia College and State University

Although more than 30 years have now passed since "a furor over mission statements swept over corporate America" (Morphew & Hartley, 2006), mission statements still serve as common corporate reporting tools. Their long-term use by corporations has been characterized by significant change, however, especially in the format and delivery of these statements. For example, they are often found on corporate Web sites now. The purposes for this reporting genre have also increased and diversified, leading to some differences in the content and strategy of these statements.

Literature Review

The extensive literature pertinent to this study includes the following: (a) scholarship that defines the mission statement genre or makes recommendations for its content, (b) scholarship that provides a theoretical basis for expecting an effective mission statement to be associated with successful financial performance, and research to determine whether that connection can be supported by data, (c) scholarship that develops relevant rhetorical theories or discusses applications of those theories to corporate communication, including mission statements, and (d) studies of the mission statement as a strategy for creating a strong corporate ethos.

Mission Statement: Definitions

A mission statement "tells two things about a company: who it is and what it does" (Falsey, 1989, p. 3). A number of others offer a similar definition (Abrahams, 1995; Bart, 2000; Bart, Bontis, & Taggar, 2001; Collins & Porras, 1991; David, 1989; Drucker, 1973; Ireland & Hitt,

Source: The Mission Statement: A Corporate Reporting Tool With a Past, Present, and Future by Linda Stallworth Williams. *Journal of Business Communication*, Vol. 45, No. 2, April 2008, p. 94–19. Published by Sage Publications, on behalf of Association for Business Communication. Copyright © by the Association for Business Communication.

1992; Pearce, 1982), and this definition holds true regardless of whether a corporation refers to this statement as a "mission statement," a "mission," a "credo," "our philosophy," "core values," or something else (Abrahams, 1995; Collins & Porras, 1991; David, 2007; Ireland & Hitt, 1992; Pearce & David, 1987). These statements often address multiple audiences, or stakeholders, including a firm's management, employees, customers or clients, shareholders, and other residents of the communities, countries, and world where it does business (Abrahams, 1995; Amato & Amato, 2002; Bart, 1999, 2000; Collins & Porras, 1991; Klemm, Sanderson, & Luffman, 1991).

In addition to conveying a corporation's nature and reason for being, this statement may also outline where a firm is headed; how it plans to get there; what its priorities, values, and beliefs are; and how it is distinctive (Abrahams, 1995; Collins & Porras, 1991; Falsey, 1989; Ireland & Hitt, 1992; Klemm et al., 1991; Pearce & David, 1987). Bartkus, Glassman, and McAfee (2000) define a narrower focus for a mission statement: "We view a mission statement solely as a communication tool" (p. 29). They add that

> most firms would be better off if they narrowed the purpose of the mission statement to that of realistically communicating product and market objectives to stakeholders. The best mission statements simply define the company's business and suggest a future goal. (p. 29)

Their caution about overextending the scope of mission statements is shared by other practitioners and scholars (Bart, 2000; Collins & Porras, 1991; Ireland & Hitt, 1992).

Mission Statement: Recommendations for Content

A host of resource materials have been created to assist corporations and other organizations with drafting the perfect mission statement. Surprisingly, these guides offer somewhat similar advice about suggested content for these statements, even if they do not agree about the labels they assign to content components. For example, in an article often cited in mission statement literature, Pearce and David (1987) identify "eight key components of mission statements," a list that is modified slightly and expanded to nine

components by David (1989, 2007). A corporation is encouraged to provide information about its customers or clients, employees, products or services, markets, technology, self-concept, desired public image, philosophy, and strategies for growth and survival (David, 1989, 2007).

Other authors have renamed, expanded, narrowed, or redefined the suggested components (Bart & Baetz, 1998). For instance, specifying a company's commitment to QOL (quality of life) goals has been cited as important (Amato & Amato, 2002), a commitment that others might place under the categories of a firm's general philosophy, its concern for its employees, or its concern for its public image. In addition, organizational purpose and financial goals have been studied as content components (Bart & Baetz, 1998); however, some researchers consider an organization's purpose to be a subset of its philosophy and its financial goals to be a subset of its strategies for growth and survival. Two studies note that anywhere from 10 to 25 different mission statement components have been suggested or used (Bart, 1997; Bart & Baetz, 1998). Although authors usually provide rationales for the components and labels they use, the resulting variations in terminology and definitions limit the comparability of some studies with others and decrease the long-term benefits realized when earlier studies can be conclusively replicated. Therefore, although this serious flaw in the corpus of mission statement literature has been identified before (e.g., Bart et al., 2001; Peyrefitte & David, 2006), it has not yet been remedied.

Mission Statement Content and Performance: Theory

Corporations are urged to create mission statements for many reasons: to assert leadership (Klemm et al., 1991), to inform employees about the company's goals and unify their efforts toward accomplishing them (Bart, 1998; Ireland & Hitt, 1992; Klemm et al., 1991; Pearce & David, 1987), to serve as an effective public relations tool (Bart, 1998; David, 2007; Falsey, 1989), to provide a rationale for allocating resources (Bart, 1998; Bart et al., 2001; David, 2007), "to guide current, critical, strategic decision making" (Drohan, 1999), and to inspire enthusiasm about the firm (Bartkus et al., 2000; Collins & Porras, 1991; Ireland & Hitt, 1992).

The belief that mission statements can serve some or all of these purposes provides a commonly accepted theoretical basis for expecting corporations with a mission statement to be more successful than those without one. In addition to specific benefits that are said to accrue from having such a statement, successfully completing the mission statement process demonstrates that a firm can think reflectively, plan carefully, work collaboratively, and make informed decisions. Therefore, it is logical to think that this demonstrated expertise will contribute to overall success for a corporation.

Mission Statement Content and Performance: Research

Empirical evidence to support a link between corporate mission statements and performance is not plentiful or conclusive (Bart & Baetz, 1998; Bart et al., 2001; Peyrefitte & David, 2006). When the financial performance of firms with and without a mission statement was compared, three studies found no significant differences (Bart & Baetz, 1998; David, 1989; Klemm et al., 1991). In contrast, two other studies found that firms with mission statements did perform better (Rarick & Vitton, 1995; Stone, 1996), but the latter study cited anecdotal evidence only.

Despite this scarcity of persuasive empirical data, mission statements continue to be developed, disseminated, and valued, and researchers continue to be interested in studying them.

Some researchers have pursued the possible link between the content of mission statements and financial performance. In these cases, researchers have analyzed content to determine whether some components lead to greater results than others, and this line of inquiry is important to this study. One of the earliest studies compared the content of the statements of high-performing *Fortune* 500 firms to the content of those of low-performing ones, and the researchers found that the high-performing firms included three of the components—corporate philosophy, self-concept, and concern for public image—significantly more often (Pearce & David, 1987). However, they did not find significant differences between the two groups' inclusion of the other five components: customers or markets, product or service, geographic domain, technology, and concern for survival.

Based on a later study, researchers also concluded that effective content caused mission statements to be

positively associated with financial performance. They analyzed the content of mission statements belonging to firms randomly selected from the 1994 *Business Week* 1000 list and determined that the return on common shareholder equity for firms with "high content" statements was 26.2%, whereas the return for the firms with "low content" statements was 13.7% (Rarick & Vitton, 1995, p. 12). A "high content" mission statement included more of the following components: concern for public image; concern for quality; commitment to survival, growth, profitability; identity of customers and markets; identity of products and services; statement of company philosophy; and differentiation from competition. Using a different sample of industrial firms and a method other than content analysis, somewhat similar results were reported by Bart (1997). He surveyed CEOs and presidents from 44 industrial corporations, asking them to identify which of 25 different content components were clearly specified in their firms' mission statements. After tabulating their responses, Bart compared the "performance of the industrial firms based on each mission component" and found that 13 of the 25 components had a "positive relationship with performance" (p. 377). Four of these components—purpose, values, self-concept, and desired public image—had been identified as significant by Pearce and David (1987) as well, although Bart (1997) used different labels in some cases (e.g., purpose and values rather than philosophy). The other nine components that Bart found to be positively associated with performance were general corporate goals, concern for customers, concern for employees, concern for suppliers, concern for society, concern for shareholders, statement of vision, concern for survival, and competitive strategy.

The purpose and values components were again found to be associated with performance when mission statements from 136 large Canadian firms were collected and analyzed: "Significant positive differences in performance were found to be associated with mission statements which contained no financial goals, identified a firm's values/beliefs, defined a firm's purpose, and were relatively short" (Bart & Baetz, 1998, p. 845). Finally, by studying data collected from 83 large Canadian and U.S. firms with mission statements, researchers found that statements with sound content, ones with clearly specified ends and means, "can affect financial performance" (Bart et al., 2001, p. 29). These content components had not been specifically identified or studied before, but some of the previous researchers could have categorized ends and means as information belonging to the goals, competitive strategy, philosophy, or concern for survival and profitability components.

Mission Statement Content and Corporate Ethos: Rhetorical Theory

None of the literature reviewed thus far has used the term *corporate ethos* in connection with mission statements. Instead, other terms (e.g., *image, public image, identity*) have been used to describe the way that a corporation wants to be perceived by its constituencies. However, increasing numbers of scholars and researchers are choosing to use the term *corporate ethos* because rhetorical theory provides a sound theoretical basis for understanding the concept of ethos and why it matters to communicators who wish to persuade their audiences (e.g., Beason, 1991; Cross, 1991; Hyland, 1998; Kallendorf & Kallendorf, 1985; Stoddard, 1985; Swales & Rogers, 1995). As Cross (1991) points out, "Persuasion, the ability to win over an audience and inspire action is, after all, the underlying goal of most corporate correspondence, whether it's trying to create an image, keep goodwill, or collect an overdue bill" (p. 3). Mission statements are decidedly persuasive: If corporate communicators cannot persuade their constituencies to read their mission statements and respond to them appropriately— whether that means faithfully working for the corporation, buying its stock or products, or believing it is a contributing member of a community or society—then the efforts of those communicators have been wasted.

The term *ethos* originated with Aristotle, one of the earliest authorities on persuasion: "In his *Rhetoric,* written some 2,000 years ago as a guide to persuasive public speaking, he describes techniques that remain essential to persuasion and that offer important guidelines in the modern age" (Cross, 1991, p. 3). Aristotle aimed to educate the individual communicator, of course, rather than an organizational entity such as a modern corporation. Nevertheless, the process of carefully shaping and communicating an admirable and appealing character is similar whether the communicator is an individual or a group. In Book I of his *Rhetoric,* Aristotle discusses ethos as one of three appeals available to a communicator who wishes to persuade. The other two appeals are logos—strategies to reason with people—and pathos—strategies to stir their emotions. Although going to great lengths to explore logos and pathos, Aristotle considered ethos to be the most important of these appeals, and it is the most pertinent to this study.

Aristotle (1932) identifies three components of ethos: "intelligence, character, and good will" (p. 92). He stresses the importance of intelligence (i.e., knowledge, good sense, and expertise) because of its crucial impact on credibility. As a rule, communicators are not taken seriously if an audience perceives that they are uninformed, for whatever reason. Therefore, Aristotle discusses a number of strategies for formulating arguments that influence audiences. The kind of logically developed arguments that Aristotle prescribes are almost never included in mission statements because this genre rarely provides support or evidence for the general pronouncements and claims made (Swales & Rogers, 1995). However, when a mission statement provides accurate and timely information about the products or services a firm sells, about the qualifications of its management and employees, or about methods and procedures it uses to gain a competitive edge, it is providing evidence of its expertise. In addition, the writing style, organization, and visual rhetoric of a mission statement can show a firm's knowledge and skills (Stoddard, 1985).

When discussing character, the second aspect of ethos, Aristotle (1932, p. 91) says that a communicator should "evince the right character." Doing so requires that communicators understand the differences between virtues and vices and that they know the "characteristics and qualities that are valued by an audience and community" (Beason, 1991, p. 330). Applying this principle to corporate communicators suggests that including in a mission statement the values considered most important to a corporation and its audiences can strengthen a corporation's ethos. Collins and Porras (1991) delineate the kinds of information that might be included:

Core values and beliefs are the organization's basic precepts about what is important in both business and life, how business should be conducted, its view of humanity, its role in society, the way the world works, and what is to be held inviolate. (p. 35)

The starting point should be to articulate values and beliefs that the corporation already considers important or commits to adopting before deciding to showcase the values and beliefs it shares with its audiences (Collins & Porras, 1991). Otherwise, the corporation's ethos will suffer if its pronouncements are determined to be hollow and insincere (Collins & Porras, 1991).

As part of an extended discussion of contemporary applications of Aristotelian theory, Stoddard (1985) reminds us that ethos is not situated exclusively in corporate discourse (or discourse from any source) but relies on the audience's cooperation in meaning-making. Therefore, capable corporate communicators have the power of words and other rhetorical strategies at their disposal when attempting to create "the right character," but these strategies must be carefully chosen based on a clear assessment of all parts of the rhetorical situation, including the characteristics of the audience, the purpose for the communication, the specific context or environment, and so on (Stoddard, 1985). For instance, ethics scandals in recent years have heightened the public's concerns about corporate honesty and ethics. Therefore, a corporation can strengthen its ethos by stating in its mission statement that it values integrity and honors ethical standards on a daily basis. In addition, a manufacturing firm that must dispose of toxic wastes can help to dispel the fears of residents living near that business by pledging the firm's commitment to safe practices that protect the people and environments where it does business, thereby portraying itself as a corporation with a good conscience.

Furthermore, carefully shaping the presentation of the character of a corporation in keeping with the values of its audiences can appeal to "similitude" (Beason, 1991, p. 331). When communicators "point out similarities between themselves and their audiences," benefits often result because "almost all people are more likely to accept and trust a communicator who is perceived as being 'one of them' since such commonality gives the impression that communicator and audience share backgrounds, goals, and values" (Beason, 1991, p. 331).

Using "we" (or other first-person-plural pronouns) is a way to join a communicator and audience, thereby "claiming group membership with that audience" (Beason, 1991, p. 331).

Building on the same theoretical basis that supports the concept of similitude, other scholars focus on the use of first-person-plural pronouns to encourage internal stakeholders—employees—to identify with a corporation (Cheney, 1983; Swales & Rogers, 1995). Drawing on Kenneth Burke's "rhetoric of identification," Cheney (1983) explains how the identification process works within organizations like corporations:

> While an individual has the ability to identify spontaneously with an organizational target, the "move" is often encouraged by the organization in dealing with the member. Simply put, an individual who is inclined to identify with an organization (or an organizational subunit) will be open to persuasive efforts from various sources within that unit. The organization "initiates" this inducement process by communicating its values, goals, and information (i.e., the organization's own stated "identifications" in the form of guidelines for individual and collective action; the member may then "complete" the process by adopting or adapting the organization's interests, doing "what's best" for the organization, and perhaps even developing a salient identification with the organization as a target. (pp. 146–147)

The mission statement is a corporate guideline that definitely encourages identification because it is "rhetorically designed in order to ensure maximum employee 'buy-in'" (Swales & Rogers, 1995, p. 223).

Some scholars extend the scope of identification to include external stakeholders, thereby influencing a corporation's image and its identity. For example, Bartkus et al. (2000) state,

> Mission statements . . . enable current and potential employees, managers, suppliers, customers, and investors to self-select into the firm (to determine whether they want to get involved with it). . . . Ultimately, if stakeholders are able to align their individual objectives with those of the firm,

the result would more likely be an intrinsically motivated shareholder group. (p. 29)

A review of published mission statements shows that the stakeholders considered most important to a firm can differ depending on the nature of its business:

Companies in mining and construction are keen to stress a responsible attitude to the environment, newly privatized companies emphasize profitability and shareholders' interests and companies dependent on key skilled workers make sure that their value is mentioned in the statements. (Klemm et al., 1991, p. 75)

In all of these cases, the firms' statements reflect their understanding of their own contexts and audiences.

As a third aspect of ethos, Aristotle says that speakers should portray themselves as people of goodwill who show good intentions toward their audiences. Because of the effect of a speaker's demonstrated goodwill on the goodwill reciprocated by the audience, Aristotle discusses this concept in Book II as a part of a lengthy discussion of human emotions. In many cases, he says, the emotional state of a person is caused by an unfulfilled need. Cross (1991) supports Aristotle's assertion: "One of the most powerful motivations, and here Aristotle and modern psychology are in agreement, is an offer to satisfy a reader's needs, particularly emotional needs" (p. 5). Therefore, a communicator who wishes to alter the state of mind of his or her audience should first identify needs that the audience has and then craft a message that satisfies those needs in some way (Cross, 1991).

Applying this principle to corporations, Amato and Amato (2002) see goodwill as an important strategy for "cultivating and maintaining a corporate good guy image in the eyes of various stakeholders" (p. 72), and the benefits of this strategy are illustrated by a true example that Kallendorf and Kallendorf (1989) relate. In response to the public relations crisis faced by U.S. oil companies during the "oil crisis" in the early 1970s, Shell Oil Company mounted a public relations campaign to provide facts and information that would demonstrate that they were not "greedy price-gougers

who, at best, took unfair advantage of [oil] shortages and, at worst, actually caused the shortages" (p. 62). Three different attempts by Shell to use logic-based strategies failed to calm the anger felt by the public; in fact, using "logical argumentation" actually made the public angrier and more hostile (p. 62). However, when Shell shifted to an ethos-based approach, one aimed at generating goodwill, better results were achieved. A series of advertisements, the "Shell Information Series" and informative booklets, "Come to Shell for Answers," were highly successful because they helped to placate the public's anger and to repair Shell's damaged ethos.

Mission Statement Content and Corporate Ethos: Research

In 1985, Stoddard noted that Aristotle's theory had been confirmed by empirical research to determine the effects of ethos, although most of these studies had been

conducted in the contexts of communication theory and social psychology. . . . In the triangular model of discourse, communication theory substitutes the term "source" for rhetoric's "speaker" or "writer." Thus "source credibility" becomes an operational term for the classical concept of ethos. (p. 233)

Since 1985, research that tests the effects of ethos and labels it that way has increased (e.g., Beason, 1991; Livesey, 2002; Shenk, 1995; Swales & Rogers, 1995), and a few studies have investigated the links between mission statements and corporate ethos. One study analyzed these statements to identify character-building strategies and concluded that they "tend to stress values, positive behavior and guiding principles within the framework of the corporation's announced belief system and ideology" (Swales & Rogers, 1995, p. 227). These authors based their conclusions on a linguistic and textual analysis of a large collection of mission statements and a contextual and intertextual analysis of three mission statements from two different U.S. companies. Their close textual analysis of these three statements enabled them to identify specific linguistic features the corporations used to "foster [employees'] affiliation and identification," such as the frequent use of first-person-plural pronouns (p. 231).

Other studies have analyzed the ethos-building strategies in mission statements to determine which audiences were targeted and to learn whether the primary audiences were internal or external. In 1991, managers in 50 U.K. companies included on the *Times* 1000 index were surveyed to find out whether they saw mission statements as more important to the firms' identity (internal ethos) or image (external ethos), and the researchers concluded that "mission statements are seen by managers as more important internally than externally" (Klemm et al., 1991, p. 77), especially when these statements include company values because they enhance management's leadership within organizations.

Then, in 1997, mission statements found in the annual reports of companies on the *Business Week* 1000 list were analyzed to determine which stakeholder groups—customers, employees, suppliers, and shareholders—were targeted and what kinds of information—benefits, values, image, and focus—were conveyed to each group (Leuthesser & Kohli, 1997). They found that customers were addressed often, whereas suppliers were addressed rarely. In addition, these researchers found that "two-thirds of the mission statements included assertions addressing employees— second only to customers. Among these, value statements were the most prevalent" (p. 63).

Identity (internal ethos) and image (external ethos) were also studied in 2002 when the mission statements for firms included in the *Forbes* Best Small Business and *Fortune* 200 lists were analyzed to determine whether the inclusion of individual and societal QOL dimensions affected a corporation's ethos (Amato & Amato, 2002). They found that the mission statements belonging to the large firms addressed four of the seven societal dimensions (economic, social, institutional, and ecological) and three of the five individual dimensions (physical, safety, and esteem) significantly more often than the mission statements belonging to the small firms did. Although they found a link between size and some QOL dimensions, they found no link between profitability and QOL dimensions.

References

Abrahams, J. (1995). *The mission statement book: 301 corporate mission statements from America's top companies.* Berkeley, CA: Ten Speed Press.

Amato, C. H., & Amato, L. H. (2002). Corporate commitment to quality of life: Evidence from company mission statements. *Journal of Marketing Theory and Practice, 10*(4), 69–87.

Aristotle. (1932). *The rhetoric of Aristotle* (L. Cooper, Trans.). Englewood Cliffs, NJ: Prentice Hall.

Bart, C. K. (1997). Industrial firms and the power of mission. *Industrial Marketing Management, 26,* 371–383.

Bart, C. (1998). Mission matters. *CPA Journal, 68*(8), 56–57.

Bart, C. (1999). Making mission statements count. *CA Magazine, 132*(2), 37–39.

Bart, C. K. (2000). Lasting inspiration. *CA Magazine, 133*(4), 49–51.

Bart, C. K., & Baetz, M. C. (1998). The relationship between mission statements and firm performance: An exploratory study. *Journal of Management Studies, 35*(6), 823–853.

Bart, C. K., Bontis, N., & Taggar, S. (2001). A model of the impact of mission statements on firm performance. *Management Decision, 39*(1), 19–35.

Bartkus, B., Glassman, M., & McAfee, R. B. (2000). Mission statements: Are they smoke and mirrors? *Business Horizons, 43*(6), 23–29.

Beason, L. (1991). Strategies for establishing an effective persona: An analysis of appeals to ethos in business speeches. *Journal of Business Communication, 28*(4), 326–346.

Cheney, G. (1983). The rhetoric of identification and the study of organizational communication. *Quarterly Journal of Speech, 69,* 143–158.

Collins, J. C., & Porras, J. I. (1991). Organizational vision and visionary organizations. *California Management Review, 34*(1), 30–52.

Cross, M. (1991). Aristotle and business writing: Why we need to teach persuasion. *The Bulletin, 54,* 3–6.

David, F. R. (1989). How companies define their mission. *Long Range Planning, 22*(1), 90–97.

David, F. R. (2007). *Strategic management: Concepts and cases* (11th ed.). Englewood Cliffs, NJ: Prentice Hall.

Drohan, W. (1999). Writing a mission statement. *Association Management, 51,* 117.

Drucker, P. F. (1973). *Management: Tasks, responsibilities, and practices.* New York: Harper & Row.

Falsey, T. A. (1989). *Corporate philosophies and mission statements: A survey and guide for corporate communicators and management.* Westport, CT: Greenwood.

Hyland, K. (1998). Exploring corporate rhetoric: Metadiscourse in the CEO's letter. *Journal of Business Communication,* 35(2), 224–245.

Ireland, R. D., & Hitt, M. A. (1992). Mission statements: Importance, challenge, and recommendations for development. *Business Horizons,* 35(3), 34–42.

Kallendorf, C., & Kallendorf, C. (1985). The figures of speech, ethos, and Aristotle: Notes toward a rhetoric of business communication. *Journal of Business Communication,* 22(1), 35–50.

Kallendorf, C., & Kallendorf, C. (1989). Aristotle and the ethics of business communication. *Journal of Business and Technical Communication,* 3(1), 54–69.

Klemm, M., Sanderson, S., & Luffman, G. (1991). Mission statements: Selling corporate values to employees. *Long Range Planning,* 24(3), 73–78.

Leuthesser, L., & Kohli, C. (1997). Corporate identity: The role of mission statements. *Business Horizons,* 40(3), 59–66.

Livesey, S. M. (2002). Global warming wars: Rhetorical and discourse analytic approaches to ExxonMobil's corporate public discourse. *Journal of Business Communication,* 39(1), 117–148.

Morphew, C. C., & Hartley, M. (2006). Mission statements: A thematic analysis of rhetoric across institutional type. *Journal of Higher Education,* 77(3), 456–471.

Pearce, J. A., II. (1982). The company mission as a strategic tool. *Sloan Management Review,* 23(3), 15–24.

Pearce, J. A., & David, F. (1987). Corporate mission statements: The bottom line. *Academy of Management Executive,* 1(2), 109–116.

Peyrefitte, J., & David, F. R. (2006). A content analysis of the mission statements of United States firms in four industries. *International Journal of Management,* 23(2), 296–301.

Rarick, C. A., & Vitton, J. (1995). Mission statements make cents. *Journal of Business Strategy,* 16(1), 11–12.

Rogers, P. S., & Swales, J. M. (1990). We the people? An analysis of the Dana Corporation policies document. *Journal of Business Communication,* 27(3), 293–312.

Shenk, R. (1995). Ethos at sea. *Business Communication Quarterly,* 58(1), 5–11.

Stoddard, E. W. (1985). The role of ethos in the theory of technical writing. *Technical Writing Teacher, 11*(3), 229–241.

Stone, R. A. (1996). Mission statements revisited. *SAM Advanced Management Journal, 61*(1), 31–37.

Swales, J. M., & Rogers, P. S. (1995). Discourse and the projection of corporate culture: The mission statement. *Discourse & Society, 6*(2), 223–242.

CHAPTER 22

Do Firms Practice What They Preach?

The Relationship Between Mission Statements and Stakeholder Management

Barbara R. Bartkus

Myron Glassman

Old Dominion University

Introduction

"Practice what you preach." "Walk your talk." "Actions speak louder than words." These are all phrases commonly used to describe the expectation that words should match behaviors. It is generally acknowledged that firms should be truthful in advertising, and publish accurate annual financial statements and reports. Misrepresentation is met with harsh criticism and sometimes legal penalties. Similarly, there is an expectation that publicized statements such as missions are consistent with organizations' actions. However, recent scandals suggest that an organization's actions are not always aligned with the promises made in mission statements. For example, actions by Enron executives contrasted sharply with phrases in the firm's mission about the importance of integrity, respect, and communication. HealthSouth's accounting scandal occurred at a time when their mission stated "trust and integrity to be essential" (Plender, 2003). This anecdotal evidence begs the question: how common is the misalignment between what is "preached" in mission statements and the actions that firms "practice"? Our article reports on a study that investigates the alignment of mission statements with decisions and actions regarding stakeholders and social issues.

Although the literature on mission statements is fairly abundant, most is either prescriptive (e.g., Ireland and Hitt, 1992; Pearce and Roth, 1988) or descriptive (e.g., Bart, 1997a; David, 1989; Leuthesser and Kohli,

Source: Bartkus, B. R., Glassman, M. Do Firms Practice What They Preach? The Relationship Between Mission Statements and Stakeholder Management. *Journal of Business Ethics 83*, pp. 207–216. Copyright © 2008 Springer.

1997). Studies tend to focus on the elements that should be included or the elements that are commonly included in missions. Some authors (e.g., Bart, 1997b; 1998; Bart and Baetz, 1998; Bart et al., 2001; Bart and Hupfer, 2004; O'Gorman and Doran, 1999; Pearce and David, 1987) have extended the research by investigating if mission statements are associated with a more effective (i.e., higher performing) firm.

Most firms publish their missions. Typically, these statements are now public declarations which suggest that Drucker's (1973) original recommendation that a mission should be a simple statement of purpose has either been supplemented or replaced with the mission as a marketing or public relations tool directed at stakeholders. Thus, the mission statement has become an important part of managing the organization-stakeholder relationship—it communicates the firm's identity to stakeholders (Leuthesser and Kohli, 1997). It is likely that stakeholders expect the publicized mission to be a clear and correct portrayal of the organization. However, some have suggested that a mission statement is not always an accurate self-report (Ashforth and Gibbs, 1990; Waddock and Smith, 2000; Wright, 2002). A false or misleading mission statement can damage a firm's reputation. The reason is that reputation is built on credibility and "credibility is the believability of an entity's intentions at a particular moment in time... credibility is whether a company can be relied on to do what it says it will do" (Herbig and Milewicz, 1995, p. 21). If Mahon and Wartick (2003) are correct, that credibility and reputation are important issues in stakeholder management, then the accuracy of mission statements may be critical to effective stakeholder management and subsequent organizational success. Despite the importance of this issue, it appears that no one has investigated the accuracy of mission statements in regard to stakeholder issues. Thus, our study seeks to determine if mission statements are accurate self-reports of organizational stakeholder-related actions. That is, do firms practice what they preach?

Our article is organized into five parts. First, we look at mission statements as an important component of stakeholder management. Next, we present an argument that mission statements are likely to be accurate portrayals of the firm's actions. Third, we submit an alternative view, that missions are merely the result of institutional pressures that result in symbolic statements that are not related to action. Our methodology and statistical analysis follow in the fourth part. Finally, we discuss the implications of our results and present suggestions for additional study.

Mission Statements and Stakeholder Management

Corporate missions, originally simple statements of purpose (Bailey, 1996; Drucker, 1973; Ireland and Hitt, 1992), have evolved into public disclosures of organizations' promises to external constituencies regarding firms' commitments to stakeholders. The literature on mission statements emphasizes not only the importance of a stakeholder emphasis, but includes recommendations on the inclusion of specific elements (e.g., Ireland and Hitt, 1992; Pearce and David, 1987; Vogt, 1994). Indeed, empirical research indicates that mission statements frequently include primary stakeholders (see Bart, 1997b; Bart and Hupfer, 2004; Leuthesser and Kohli, 1997) and emphasize the organization's social responsibility (David, 1989).

The inclusion of primary stakeholders and social issues in mission statements suggests that some stakeholder groups are more salient to managers (Mitchell et al., 1997). These primary stakeholders, frequently holding both power and legitimacy (Mitchell et al., 1997), have their own goals that may impact the organization's long-term survival. As such, issues that are important to stakeholders, who directly or indirectly control needed resources (see Pfeffer and Salancik, 1978), may need to be publicly addressed. A firm that wishes to access stakeholder-controlled resources may need to, at the least, pay lip service to these issues. As such, research indicates that corporate phrasing in publications has shifted from "profit speak" (Fairfax, 2006, p. 692) to a public acknowledgment that stakeholders matter. Fairfax notes that 88% of the top 50 firms in the Fortune 500 include "stakeholder rhetoric" in the annual report and 86% include "stakeholder rhetoric" in the firm's website. Moreover, most firms affirm positive relationships with stakeholders and society in general in their publications (Fairfax, 2006) and mention specific stakeholder groups in their missions (Bart, 1997a; Bartkus et al., 2004; Leuthesser and Kohli, 1997).

The general use of "stakeholder rhetoric" supports Donaldson and Preston's (1995) argument that most managers recognize the importance of stakeholder management. Public declarations such as mission statements are created to convey a message to stakeholders about the way the organizations (i.e., executives, upper level management) want the firm to be perceived. As such, executives may include "politically correct" and/or socially acceptable phrases because the firm needs to acknowledge a responsibility to specific stakeholders and social issues. Such public declarations imply that the firm actually engages in behaviors that benefit these stakeholders. That is, the firm wants stakeholders to accept the mission as an accurate indicator of the organization's priorities and actions. However, because substantive management is expensive, difficult, and time-consuming, many managers may prefer symbolic mission statements (Ashforth and Gibbs, 1990). Symbolic management can appear to be "consistent with social values and expectations" (p. 180) but has the advantage of "[preserving] flexibility and resources" (Ashforth and Gibbs, 1990, p. 182).

We view stakeholder management as a broad concept that includes specific decisions and actions of the firm that affect stakeholders (see Hillman and Keim, 2001) *and* public relations communiqués designed to improve the firm's image. Thus, we offer two perspectives on mission statements and stakeholder management. One is that mission statements are written to guide and/or reflect policies and procedures within the organization, and therefore are accurate descriptions of the firm's stakeholder management practices. Alternatively, mission statements are stakeholder management tools that have little resemblance to the organizations' actual actions or decisions.

Mission Statements as a Guide/Motivator of Behavior

Our first perspective posits that mission statements are accurate portrayals of firms' stakeholder management actions. This argument is based on two factors. First, the mission statement is written as an internal policy or guide for employees and managers to direct behaviors and decision making, and second, the mission statement is an externally directed message that is part of an auto-communication or self-talk process (i.e., it reflects back to the organizational membership and thereby helps to control behavior).

A mission is the "foundation upon which decision makers can build corporate strategic planning processes" (Pearce and Roth, 1988, p. 39). This suggests that the mission is the basis for internal policies and procedures. As such, the mission statement is expected to guide and direct employees and managers (Campbell, 1997; Drucker, 1973; Ireland and Hitt, 1992). Research indicates that including clarity and specifics in missions is important if the mission is to be the backbone of policy. According to Bart et al. (2001), clearly written mission statements are more likely to be aligned with a firm's internal policies and systems, and better alignment is more likely to result in an effective guide for employees.

Although many missions may be directed at external constituencies, they are a form of auto-communication (see Christensen, 1997). Morsing (2006) argues that even when corporate communications are directed at an external audience (as are many mission statements), an important part of the communication is received internally. That is, the mission statement is a form of self-talk "through which the organization recognizes and confirms its own images, values and assumptions" (Christensen, 1997, p. 199). Although the publicized mission statement "[pretends] to inform external critical stakeholders about corporate actions and intentions . . . the primary purpose of the corporate messages is an efficient disciplining of the corporate body" (Morsing, 2006, p. 177). This suggests that the publicized promises included in the mission statement increase the social pressures on executives and employees to make decisions that are aligned with the firm's mission, even if the purpose of the phrasing in the mission is only to gain the approval of external stakeholders. This suggests that mission statement content should be a reliable indicator of the organization's stakeholder management.

Therefore, if the mission was written specifically to be a guide to behavior, or if the mission was written to appease stakeholders, we would expect organizational decisions to be aligned with mission statement content. However, some inconsistencies may be present because external issues (e.g., political pressures, regulations, competitive forces) may intervene and affect the end result. Nonetheless, we believe that if most decisions and policies are aligned with the mission statement's goals, we should find a positive relationship between mission statement content and stakeholder management actions.

H1: Firms with mission statements that include stakeholder issues are more likely to successfully address these issues in practice than firms with missions that omit these issues.

It is possible that the mission statement is not used as the foundation for decision making. Rather, the firm's current strategies, actions, decisions, policies, and reputation become the source of the information used to create the publicized mission. That is, the policies are written first and then the mission is written to reflect the policies and the resulting decisions. So, if the firm has been a good social performer in the past, the mission statement will reflect that and, as such, the mission is an accurate indicator of the firm's prior social performance. However, because a firm with a poor record of stakeholder management is not likely to boast about it, we take the position that an organization with a good stakeholder management record is more likely to include its accomplishments in its mission than a firm with poorer social performance.

H2: Firms with mission statements that include stakeholder issues are more likely to have successfully addressed these issues in the recent past than firms with missions that omit stakeholder issues.

Mission Statements as Impression Management

Another rationale for mission statements is that firms are *expected* to have mission statements. "Mission statements are popular because they are popular" (Krohe, 1995, p. 17). The creation and publicizing of missions may be largely the result of institutional pressures (see Meyer and Rowan, 1977) to gain moral legitimacy (Suchman, 1995). That is, organizational missions are created to give an impression that the firm has appropriate and publicly acceptable objectives. Accordingly, most mission statements suggest that the firm desires a positive relationship with stakeholders—a majority of mission statements include a phrase that

indicates concern for employees, society, and customers (Bart, 1997a; Leuthesser and Kohli, 1997). Moreover, many mission statements also include phrases that indicate that the firm is concerned with its public image and social policy issues (David, 1989). Similarly, Kaptein's (2004) study found that most firms include stakeholder concerns and social responsibility issues (e.g., discrimination, environment, product quality) in their corporate codes.

However, the inclusion of stakeholder concerns in the mission may not indicate the firm's actual objectives and guidelines for decision making (Bartkus et al., 2000). According to Campbell and Alexander (1997), developing realistic short-term and mid-term objectives based on a mission statement is fraught with problems. It is "[difficult to incorporate] the values that might be articulated at the Mission Statement stage, into the ethos and culture of the organisation [sic] and its day-to-day operations" (Moore, 1993, p. 55). Also possible is that the mission itself may have been crafted to "give off a false appearance of conformity to societal ideals" (Suchman, 1995, p. 588). In either case, Wright's survey (2002) supports the disconnect between mission statements and their value as a guide to decision making: 60% of managers believed that their organization's mission statement was not realistic.

We assert that firms create these misleading mission statements because they *need* to atone for their lack of positive stakeholder management *actions*. A socially acceptable mission statement is easier to craft than developing and implementing policies that meet stakeholder expectations. Thus, mission statements may be purely symbolic and be used instead of substantive management (Meyer and Rowan, 1977; Ashforth and Gibbs, 1990). As Suchman (1995, p. 195) states, "organizations often put forth cynically self-serving claims of moral propriety and buttress these claims with hallow symbolic gestures." Thus, our next hypothesis is based on Ashforth and Gibbs (1990, p. 185) proposition: "The protestation of legitimacy will be greatest for organizations with low legitimacy (as perceived by constituents)" and Suchman's (1995, p. 588) assertion: "at the extreme, because organizational goals often serve primarily as rationales for existence rather than as technical directives, managers can cynically revise even their core mission statements in order to give off a false appearance of conformity to societal ideals."

H3: Firms with mission statements that include stakeholder issues are less likely to successfully address these issues than firms with missions lacking these issues.

Method

Sample

The firms in our sample were the top 100 firms listed in the Fortune 500 published in 2001 (www .fortune.com). We were unable to locate a mission statement for 32 firms (these firms either did not have a mission statement in 2001, or did not publish their missions on the web or in their annual reports in 2001.

Variables

Dependent Variable. We define the dependent variable, the *ability to address stakeholder issues,* as a firm's actions and behaviors involving stakeholders. We limit our study to nonowners that are the primary stakeholders most common to mission statements, i.e., customers, employees, and the community (see Bart, 1997b; Leuthesser and Kohli, 1997). This definition is consistent with Mitchell et al.'s (1997) perspective that stakeholder primacy is based on power, legitimacy, and urgency. We find that the stakeholder groups mentioned in missions fit Mitchell et al.'s (1997) "dominant" category, possessing both power and legitimacy.

We followed Hillman and Keim's (2001) lead and used KLD's social issue ratings to measure stakeholder management actions. We looked at five broad areas of stakeholder management actions reported by KLD. Two define and evaluate the firm's actions toward specific stakeholder groups (employees and customers). The other three define and evaluate the firm's actions toward a wider part of society: the community, the environment, and diversity.

KLD Research & Analytics collects and organizes corporate social responsibility data. Evaluations are provided for positive actions (strengths) and negative actions (concerns). The employee relations category includes a firm's strengths in its relationships with unions, profit sharing, participative management, and strong retirement benefits. Employee concerns include problems with union relations, safety issues, downsizings, and underfunded retirement plans.

We operationalized the customer category as KLD's product evaluations. Strengths include quality, R&D, innovation, and products provided to the economically disadvantaged; concerns include problems with product safety, marketing, and antitrust controversies.

We combined the KLD human rights ratings with the community ratings for our "community, society, world" group. KLD's community category includes charitable giving and other community activities as strengths; concerns include investment and economic controversies. The human rights strengths include positive relationships with indigenous peoples near the firm's operating plants, transparent disclosure about overseas sourcing, and good union relationships in other countries; concerns include operations or investment in Burma, problems with labor issues in other countries, and controversies involving indigenous peoples.

KLD's environment category includes positive ratings for beneficial products and climate-friendly policies (reducing pollution, recycling, using alternative fuels). Environmental concerns include problems with hazardous waste, regulatory problems, ozone depleting chemicals, emissions, and fuel revenues associated with oil or coal combustion.

Independent Variable. Our independent variable is *mission statement content.* Each firm's web site and annual report was checked for the firm's 2001 mission statement. Since some academics and practitioners have used the terms mission, vision, philosophy, values, and goals interchangeably (see David, 1989; Levin, 2000), we defined "mission statement" broadly, similar to Leuthesser and Kohli's definition (1997), and included equivalent company descriptions and value statements that listed the same elements. Decisions were based on Ireland and Hitt's (1992) and Pearce and Roth's (1988) description of a mission statement. Thus, statements that included some of the following elements: purpose, goals, productmarkets, and values/philosophical views were included in our study. For some firms, we found value statements adjoining the firm's mission statement. In these cases, due to the focus of the study (public declarations of social responsibility in missions), we examined both the value statement and the firm's mission.

We read each mission statement to see if it included phrases that referred to the following stakeholders and/or social issues: community, society, world, environment, diversity, employees, and customers. Since many firms refer to the importance of the community in their missions, but may use different yet similar words such as "the world" or "society," we viewed all of these terms as "community." Similarly, we used the terms "associates" and "employees" as referring to the firm's employees. We also looked for specific terms in the mission that referred to customers, environment, and diversity. We created dummy variables for each of the stakeholder groups and social issues included in missions.

Statistical Methods. We used *t*-tests to look for differences between firms that included a specific element in the mission and firms with a mission that lacked the element. We used Levene's test for equality of variances to determine which *t*-ratio to examine to determine statistical significance. For Hypothesis 1 and Hypothesis 3, we examined whether there were significant differences in KLD's 2001 identification of strengths and concerns for firms that included specific elements in their 2001 missions as compared to firms that omitted those elements. If the mission statement was used as a guide to control behavior and decision making, we expected that we would find significantly more KLD strengths (for each element/issue) in firms that included the relevant elements in the mission statement and significantly fewer KLD concerns. To test Hypothesis 2, we looked at the 2000 KLD social performance ratings and the elements included in the 2001 mission statements. This allows us to test our hypothesis that past social performance is reflected in the mission.

Results

Frequencies and t-test results are presented in Tables 22.1 and 22.2. Table 22.1 shows the relationship between the content of the 2001 mission and 2001 KLD data, which allows us to test if missions are indicators of current stakeholder management practices (Hypotheses 1 and 3). We present the results for mission statements as indicators of past stakeholder management actions (i.e., 2001 missions and 2000 KLD data), in Table 22.2.

Hypothesis 1 predicted that firms with mission statements that include stakeholder issues would be more likely to successfully address these issues in practice than firms with missions that omit these issues. Therefore we expected significantly more KLD strengths in firms that included the relevant elements in the mission statement and significantly fewer KLD concerns. We found mixed support for this hypothesis. As shown in Table 22.1, KLD ratings on most of the stakeholder/social issues do not differ for firms that include the relevant element in their mission as compared to firms that omit the element. We found no significant differences among firms that included a reference to employees in the mission statement compared to firms that did not mention employees in their missions. The relationship between the inclusion of customers in the mission and product-related strengths or product-related concerns was not significant. However, in support of Hypothesis 1, our findings indicate that firms that include diversity in the mission statement have significantly fewer diversity concerns ($p < 0.000$). Our results also indicate that firms that include the environment in their mission statement have more environment-related strengths than firms that do not include this element in their mission ($p < 0.002$). However, the environmental concerns difference between firms that mention environment and firms that do not mention environment in the mission was not significant.

Hypothesis 3 predicted that firms that included stakeholder issues in their missions would be less likely to successfully address these issues than firms that omitted stakeholder issues. We found no support for Hypothesis 3.

Table 22.2 shows the results of our test of Hypothesis 2, the perspective that mission statements are more likely to be written "after the fact" and, as such, are descriptions of what the firm has done in the recent past. We found no significant differences for firms that include customers or employees in the mission and firms that do not mention these stakeholders. We did, however, find that firms that had more diversity-related concerns were less likely to emphasize diversity in their mission statement ($p < 0.000$).

Discussion

Mission statements have become a public disclosure that concisely describes the firm *as executives want the firm to be perceived.* Originally simple statements of the

| Table 22.1 | Mission Statement Content and Stakeholder Management Actions (H1 and 3) |

Mission (frequency of term in mission)	Stakeholder management actions in 2001	Mean difference	t-value	Signif. (2-tailed)
Customer (63%)	Product strengths	0.07	0.528	0.599
	Product concerns	0.03	0.096	0.924
Employee (34%)	Employee strengths	0.06	0.278	0.782
	Employee concerns	0.12	0.666	0.508
Diversity (19%)	Diversity strengths	−0.10	−0.194	0.846
	Diversity concerns[a]	−0.43	−6.717***	0.000
Environment (13%)	Environment strengths	0.79	3.267***	0.002
	Environment concerns	0.49	0.910	0.366
Community, society, world (31%)	Society strengths[b]	0.24	0.847	0.400
	Society concerns[c]	0.42	1.406	0.179

[a]Unequal variances; used signif level for unequal variances.
[b]Society strengths = community strengths + "non us str" [human rights].
[c]Society concerns = community concerns + "non us con" [human rights].
*$p < 0.05$, **$p < 0.01$, ***$p < 0.001$.

organization's purpose, missions now include commitments to social issues (protecting the environment, encouraging diversity, supporting the community). Our study indicates that the most commonly included elements in missions (i.e., mentioning specific stakeholder groups) are the least likely to have a significant impact on firm actions. However, elements that are not included in the prescriptive literature (social issues such as diversity and environment), are significantly related to stakeholder management actions.

We found that firms that include diversity in the mission statement had significantly fewer diversity concerns or conversely, firms that omitted diversity-related issues in their missions had more diversity concerns. Since the issue of diversity is not a typical part of a firm's *mission*—diversity does not describe the product market, or the strategy, or identify particular stakeholders as a priority—we surmise that diversity was part of the *mission statement* because diversity issues

were also included in the organization's day-to-day operating directives. This perspective has additional support considering the finding that firms with a recent history of diversity concerns omitted mentioning diversity in their missions in the following year. Although we have no earlier data for comparison, diversity may have been included in some mission statements as a reaction to the discrimination problems in the 1990s in firms such as Denny's Restaurants, the Coca-Cola Company, and Texaco. These firms and others were forced to include specific goals, and institute internal monitoring procedures and auditing systems as part of the settlement in these cases (see McKay, 2000; Schafer, 2000; Segal, 1999). It appears that positive stakeholder management actions regarding diversity are both a cause of mission statement content and an effect.

An interesting finding is that relatively few firms mentioned the environment in their mission statement, but the firms that do include a reference to the environment

Table 22.2   Mission Statement Content as an Indicator of Prior Stakeholder Management (H2)

Mission (frequency of term in mission)	Stakeholder management actions in 2000	Mean difference	t-value	Signif. (2-tailed)
Customer (63%)	Product strengths	0.08	0.629	0.532
	Product concerns	0.17	0.590	0.557
Employee (34%)	Employee strengths	0.04	0.174	0.863
	Employee concerns	0.12	0.718	0.476
Diversity (19%)	Diversity strengths	−0.35	−0.642	0.523
	Diversity concerns[a]	−0.31	−4.915***	0.000
Environment (13%)	Environment strengths	0.40	1.182	0.268
	Environment concerns	0.59	1.030	0.307
Community, society, world (31%)	Society strengths[b]	−0.07	−0.231	0.818
	Society concerns[c]	0.49	1.672	0.117

[a]Unequal variances; used signif level for unequal variances.
[b]Society strengths = community strengths + "non us str" [human rights].
[c]Society concerns = community concerns + "non us con" [human rights].
*$p < 0.05$, **$p < 0.01$, ***$p < 0.001$.

have more environmental strengths. Thus, with respect to the environment, there is a connection between missions and firm action. It is important to note that our findings refer to a positive relationship among environmental *strengths* (as measured by KLD) and mission content. We found no relationship between environmental *concerns* and mission content. This suggests that our finding is not industry-related. If firms in environment-unfriendly industries were more likely to include environment in the mission, we would have expected a significant relationship between environmental concerns and the inclusion of a reference to the environment because KLD's environmental concerns include companies operating in industries that are likely to have a negative impact on the environment such as manufacturers of ozone depleting chemicals, pesticides, chemical fertilizers,

coal and oil producers, utilities, transportation companies, automobile and truck manufacturers, etc. Environmental strengths are only associated with mission statement content in the same year. We are unable to determine if the relationship is because the mission statement was meant to be a guide to management decision making, or if the mission statement was intended purely as a public relations maneuver but influenced executives and employees through auto-communication.

We found that references to specific stakeholder groups (employees, customers, and community) were not related to stakeholder management actions. Mentioning stakeholders in missions may be an attempt to publicly acknowledge the importance of stakeholders, but our findings suggest that they are not included to guide decision-making, nor are they included as attempts to whitewash or cover-up negative actions or counter negative publicity. Including specific stakeholder groups in missions may be a public kindness in a world in which legally, stockholders are still the primary group to be satisfied. Such public gestures may be largely symbolic. Due to the conflicts among fulfilling stakeholder needs and limited resources, many managers may prefer symbolism (see Ashforth and Gibbs, 1990). Although there is a temptation to explain the disconnect between the mention of specific stakeholder groups in missions and organizational action as a result of top management's attempt to persuade or manipulate the public into believing that the firm is highly stakeholder-oriented, Suchman (1995, p. 588) asserts "the argument that organizations insincerely manage symbolism in order to dupe naive audiences may be somewhat overdrawn. Occasionally, audiences will actually desire a symbolic response, in order to further their own cultural or political objectives." This suggests that everyone feels a little better when included in the mission statement, even with full knowledge that their inclusion does not really make a difference.

The finding that stakeholder groups were more commonly included in missions but had no relationship to firm actions lends support for a symbolic and institutional perspective (Meyer and Rowan, 1977), particularly because the less commonly included issues were associated with firm action. Most of the previous research has focused on the most common elements of mission statements, with mixed results from the studies that investigated relationships between elements of mission statements and firm performance. Perhaps, it would be more fruitful to look at the more unusual mission statements. Firms with mission statements that do not closely follow the norm might also have missions that influence firm financial and social performance. Additional studies are also needed to investigate if accuracy in mission statements leads to a better reputation and therefore improved financial returns.

Returning to our initial question, "Do firms practice what they preach in their mission?" the answer is "sometimes." With respect to the stakeholders we studied, employees, customers, and society, the answer is "no." Firms do not "walk the talk." These elements are relatively common in mission statements, suggesting that these stakeholders are mentioned because it is expected (i.e., institutional reasons). With respect to the

two social issues we investigated, diversity and the environment, there are a number of possible reasons why we found evidence that firms "walk the talk." First, the inclusion of these issues is not prescribed. No one can be faulted if they are not included. This suggests that there are specific policy-related reasons that some social issues are woven into company mission statements. Second, because various groups and the government scrutinize firm performance in these areas, a firm that makes an untrue statement is likely to attract more attention. Thus, if the firm has internal guidelines that would oppose positive actions in these areas, the logical and credible course is "avoid the talk"—not mentioning an issue when performance is poor.

This study offers a new look at missions: their alignment (or misalignment) with firm actions. As such, it is somewhat preliminary in nature. Our findings indicate that some content areas of missions are based on institutional pressures while others are related to actions. Longitudinal studies would be helpful to determine if stakeholder management actions changed as mission statements were revised or altered, or if missions have a long-term effect (positive or negative) on firm actions.

A limitation is that some divisions of firms have separate (additional) mission statements, as do some departments and functional areas. These operational-unit missions may not be as publicized (or not publicized at all) and may reinforce the organizational mission, be unrelated to the organizational mission, or counteract the organizational mission.

References

Ashforth, B. E. and B. W. Gibbs: 1990, 'The Double-edge of Organizational Legitimation', *Organization Science* **1**(2), 177–194.

Bailey, J. A.: 1996, 'Measuring Your Mission', *Management Accounting* **44**(3), 44–47.

Bart, C. K.: 1997a, 'Sex, Lies, and Mission Statements', Business Horizons **40**(6), 9–18.

Bart, C. K.: 1997b, 'Industrial Firms and the Power of Mission', *Industrial Marketing Management* **26**(4), 371–383.

Bart, C. K.: 1998, 'Mission Matters', *CA Magazine* **131**(2), 31–34.

Bart, C. K. and M. C. Baetz: 1998, 'The Relationship Between Mission Statements and Firm Performance: An Exploratory Study', *The Journal of Management Studies* **35**(6), 823–853.

Bart, C. K., N. Bontis and S. Taggar: 2001, 'A Model of the Impact of Mission Statements on Firm Performance', *Management Decision* **39**(1), 19–35.

Bart, C. K. and M. Hupfer: 2004, 'Mission Statements in Canadian Hospitals', *Journal of Health Organization and Management* **18**(2), 92–110.

Bartkus, B. R., M. Glassman and R. B. McAfee: 2000, 'Mission Statements: are They Smoke and Mirrors?', *Business Horizons* **43**(6), 23–28.

Bartkus, B. R., M. Glassman and R. B. McAfee: 2004, 'A Comparison of the Quality of European, Japanese and U. S. Mission Statements: A Content Analysis', *European Management Journal* **22**(4), 393–401.

Campbell, A.: 1997, 'Mission Statements', *Long Range Planning* **30**(6), 931–932.

Campbell, A. and M. Alexander: 1997, 'What's Wrong with Strategy?', *Harvard Business Review* **75**(6), 42–49.

Christensen, L. T.: 1997, 'Marketing as Auto-Communication', *Consumption, Markets, and Culture* **1**(1), 197–228.

David, F. R.: 1989, 'How Companies Define Their Mission', *Long Range Planning* **22**(1), 90–97.

Donaldson, T. and L. E. Preston: 1995, 'The Stakeholder Theory of the Corporation: Concepts, Evidence and Implications', *Academy of Management Review* **20**(1), 65–91.

Drucker, P. F.: 1973, *Management: Tasks,* Responsibilities, Practices (Harper & Row, New York).

Fairfax, L. M.: 2006, 'The Rhetoric of Corporate Law: The Impact of Stakeholder Rhetoric on Corporate Norms', *Journal of Corporation Law* **31**(3), 675–718.

Herbig, P. and J. Milewicz: 1995, 'To Be or Not to Be . . . Credible That Is: A Model of Reputation and Credibility Among Competing Firms', *Marketing Intelligence & Planning* **13**(6), 24–33.

Hillman, A.J. and G. D. Keim: 2001, 'Shareholder Value, Stakeholder Management, and Social Issues: What's the Bottom Line?', *Strategic Management Journal* **22**(2), 125–140.

Ireland, R. and M. Hitt: 1992, 'Mission Statements: Importance, Challenge and Recommendations for Development', *Business Horizons* **35**(3), 34–43.

Kaptein, M.: 2004, 'Business Codes of Multinational Firms: What do They Say?', *Journal of Business Ethics* **50**(1), 13–31.

Krohe, J., Jr.: 1995, 'Do You Really Need a Mission Statement?', *Across the Board* **32**(7), 16–21.

Leuthesser, L. and C. Kohli: 1997, 'Corporate Identity: The Role of Mission Statements', *Business Horizons* **40**(3), 59–67.

Levin, I. M.: 2000, 'Vision Revisited', *The Journal of Applied Behavioral Science* **36**(1), 91–107.

Mahon, J. F. and S. L. Wartick: 2003, 'Dealing with Stakeholders: How Reputation, Credibility and Framing Influence the Game', *Corporate Reputation Review* **6**(1), 19–33.

McKay, B.: 2000. 'For Coke's Big Race Lawsuit, a New Wild Card—a Flamboyant Lawyer Known for Winning Big Awards Joins the Fray for Plaintiffs', *The Wall Street Journal,* April 14, B1.

Meyer, J. W. and B. Rowan: 1977, 'Institutionalized Organizations: Formal Structure as Myth and Ceremony', *American Journal of Sociology* **83**(2), 340–363.

Mitchell, R. K., B. R. Agle and D. J. Wood: 1997, 'Toward a Theory of Stakeholder Identification and Salience: Defining the Principle of Who and What Really Counts', *Academy of Management Review* **22**(4), 853–886.

Moore, G.: 1993, 'The Demise of Ethical Schizophrenia?', *Business Strategy Review* **4**(1), 53–66.

Morsing, M.: 2006, 'Corporate Social Responsibility as Strategic Auto-Communication: On the Role of External Stakeholders for Member Identification', Business Ethics: A European Review **15**(2), 171–182.

O'Gorman, C. and R. Doran: 1999, 'Mission Statements in Small and Medium-Sized Businesses', *Journal of Small Business Management* **37**(4), 59–66.

Pearce, J. A. and F. R. David: 1987, 'Corporate Mission Statements: The Bottom Line', *Academy of Management Executive* **1**(2), 109–116.

Pearce, J., II and K. Roth: 1988, 'Multi Nationalization of the Mission Statement', *SAM Advanced Management Journal* (Summer), 39–44.

Pfeffer, J. and G. R. Salancik: 1978, *The External Control of Organizations, a Resource Dependence Perspective* (Harper and Row, New York).

Plender, J.: 2003, 'Lights Flash', *Financial Times,* March **31,** 26.

Schafer, S.: 2000, 'Coke to Pay $193 Million in Bias Suit; Black Employees Sought Damages', *The Washington Post,* November 17, Final A01.

Segal, D.: 1999, 'Denny's Serves Up a Sensitive Image: Restaurant Chain Launches PR Drive to Show Minorities It Has Changed Its Ways', *Washington Post,* April 7, Final E01.

Suchman, M.: 1995, 'Managing Legitimacy: Strategy and Institutional Approaches', *Academy of Management Review* **20**(3), 571–610.

Vogt, J.: 1994, 'Demystifying the Mission Statement', *Nonprofit World* **12**(1), 29–32.

Waddock, S. and N. Smith: 2000, 'Corporate Responsibility Audits: Doing Well by Doing Good', *Sloan Management Review* **41**(2), 75–83. Cambridge. Winter 2000.

Wright, J. N.: 2002, 'Mission and Reality and Why Not?', *Journal of Change Management* **3**(1), 30–44.

CHAPTER 23

What Is the Right Organization Design?

N. Anand

IMD, Lausanne

Richard L. Daft

Vanderbilt University

Introduction

A start-up company in Florida, called World Response Group (WRG), developed an unusual woven mat for the horticulture industry that was made from all-natural fibers. Horticulture growers in the U.S. produce hundreds of millions of potted plants each year. The product, called Smart-Grow, dramatically reduced weed growth in potted plants and simultaneously provided important nutrients—all with no chemicals. Smart-Grow raw materials and manufacturing expertise were available in China and India. As the company grew, the managers and board members talked frequently about organization structure. Two schools of thought emerged. One group wanted to import raw materials into the U.S. for manufacturing by WRG and thereby have direct control over manufacturing, marketing, and sales. These functions would be departments within WRG. The second group wanted to import already manufactured and packaged products from overseas, outsource marketing to an agency, and hire a horticulture distribution company to handle sales. The second group pushed the concept that no one within the company would ever touch the product. Nor would there be functional departments for manufacturing, marketing, and sales.

That discussion of structure within WRG would not have occurred 30 years ago when Robert Duncan published his seminal article, "What is the Right Organization Structure?" in *Organization Dynamics* in 1979. At that time, organizations were thought to be self-contained, and structure defined the reporting relationships among internal functional departments.

Source: What Is the Right Organization Design? By N. Anand and Richard L. Daft, *Journal of Organizational Dynamics*, Vol. 36, No. 4, pp. 329-344. Copyright © 2007 Elsevier Inc.

Duncan's article provided important insights about the conditions under which different internal arrangements would achieve a company's mission. His insights are still referenced in management textbooks today.

The purpose of this article is to present key developments in organization structure and design that have occurred since Duncan's article and describe when each can be used for greatest effect. We will briefly review the important structural designs from 30 years ago and then describe key developments since that time. The concepts are organized into three eras, which reflect substantive changes in management thinking from vertical organization to horizontal organizing to open boundaries via outsourcing and partnering.

Era 1: Self-Contained Organization Designs

The first era of organizational design probably took hold in the mid-1800s, and was dominant until the late 1970s. In Era 1, the ideal organization was self-contained. It had clear boundaries between it and suppliers, customers or competitors. Inputs arrived at the organization's gate, and after a transformation process, left as a completed product or service. Almost everything that was required during the transformation process was supplied internally. Design philosophies from this era emphasized the need to adapt to different environmental and internal contingencies and the ability to control the different parts of the organization through reporting relationships in a vertical chain of command.

The structure of self-contained organizations can be thought of as: (1) the grouping of people into functions or departments, (2) the reporting relationships among people and departments, and (3) the systems to ensure coordination and integration of activities both horizontally and vertically. The structures of this era, including functional, division, and matrix designs, rely largely on the vertical hierarchy and chain of command to define departmental groupings and reporting relationships.

Functional

In a functional structure, activities are grouped together by common function from the bottom to the top of the organization. Each functional activity—accounting, engineering, human resources, manufacturing, etc.—is grouped into a specific department. Most small companies use this structure, as do many large government organizations and divisions of large companies.

Divisional

The divisional structure occurs when departments are grouped together based on organizational outputs. The divisional structure is sometimes called a product structure or profit center. Most large companies have separate divisions that use different technologies or serve different customers. People within each division have more product focus, accountability, and flexibility than would be the case if they were part of a huge functional structure. For example, United Technologies Corporation (UTC), which is among the 50 largest U.S. industrial firms, has product divisions for air-conditioning and heating (Carrier), elevators and escalators (Otis), aircraft engines (Pratt & Whitney), helicopters (Sikorsky), and aerospace (Hamilton Sundstrand), among others. Each division acts like a stand-alone company, doing its own product development, marketing, and finance.

Horizontal Overlays and Matrix

Few organizations can be successful today with a pure functional structure, because the resulting functional or divisional silos inhibit the amount of coordination needed in a changing competitive environment. Organizations break down silos by using a variety of horizontal linkage mechanisms to improve communication among departments and divisions. These coordination relationships are often drawn on organization charts as dotted lines. Many organizations use full-time product managers, project managers, or brand managers, to coordinate the work of several departments. The brand manager for Planters Peanuts, for example, serves as an integrator by coordinating the sales, advertising, and distribution for that product. General Motors Corp. has brand managers who are integrators responsible for marketing and sales strategies for each of GM's new models.

Organizations that need even stronger horizontal coordination may evolve to a matrix structure. The matrix combines a vertical structure with an equally strong horizontal overlay. While the vertical structure provides traditional control within functional departments, the horizontal overlay provides coordination across departments to achieve profit goals. This structure has lines of formal authority along two dimensions, such as functional and product or product and region. Some employees report to two bosses simultaneously. For example, after a regional marketing promotion went $10 million over budget, Nike Inc. managers engineered a matrix structure that assigned dual responsibility by product and region to manage the introduction of new products each year. Headquarters establishes which product to push. Then product managers determine how to do it, but regional managers have authority to modify plans for their regions. Nike's matrix provides a counterbalance between product manager and regional manager ambitions.

Era 2: Horizontal Organization Design With Team- and Process-Based Emphasis

The second era of organizational design started in the 1980s. As the world grew increasingly complex, organizations of Era 2 experienced the limits of traditional designs. Coordination between departmental silos within the organization became more difficult, and vertical authority-based reporting systems often were not effective in creating value for customers. At the same time, information processing capacity of organizations improved greatly, due to the availability of personal computers and networks. Design philosophies of this era emphasize the need to reshape the internal boundaries of the organization in order to improve coordination and communication.

The horizontal organization emphasizes reengineering along workflow processes that link organizational capabilities to customers and suppliers. While traditional self-contained organizations of Era 1 embodied the need for hierarchical control and separate functional specializations, the horizontal organization advocated the dispensing of internal boundaries that are an impediment to effective business performance. If the traditional structure can be likened to a pyramid, the

metaphor that best applies to the horizontal organization is a pizza—flat, but packed with all the necessary ingredients.

Examples

New product development is one context in which the horizontal organization design is most appropriate. Take the example of Ford Motor Co.'s Escape gas-electric hybrid sport utility vehicle (SUV), conceived in response to consumer demand and competition from rivals such as Toyota Motor Corp. and Nissan Motor Co. Ford adopted the horizontal organization design, which involved creation of a cross-functional team to handle the entire workflow for developing and launching a new automobile model. The team included highly accomplished individuals from research and product engineering—two groups that are traditionally in separate silos in Ford. There were two team leaders, one with experience in product development and another with expertise in launching vehicles in the market on time. In the development phase, the team invested a considerable amount of time learning about customer requirements firsthand, by talking to potential owners in addition to relying on market research reports. The research scientists and engineers shared a common office space, discussed emerging issues over group lunches, and improved product design through hallway chats. The team was sheltered from the rest of the organization and provided with resources rapidly as and when required. For example, when discussions with the Japanese battery supplier were stalling because of language difficulty, the Ford corporate office dispatched an engineer fluent in Japanese to help the team out. Once the prototype vehicle was developed, the team shifted into launch mode in order to get it ready for production. The team started working more intensively with outside suppliers that provided critical parts for the new vehicle and were always around to solve manufacturing problems. The Escape Hybrid SUV was launched on time and is regarded by industry experts as a successful product for Ford.

Other firms that have used the horizontal organization for new product development include Xerox Corp., Lexmark Printers, and Eastman Kodak Co. Another domain in which this design works effectively is in back-office tasks of financial services firms that involve handoffs to multiple departments. Barclays Bank in the U.K. uses the horizontal design for its mortgage services, incorporating legal and relocation services in addition to traditional tasks such as loan sanctioning and credit assessment.

The design features of the horizontal organization are summarized in Table 23.1.

Design Principles

Five principles govern the design of a horizontal organization. First, organize around complete workflow processes rather than departments. The key is to move away from a traditional department-centered mindset of breaking things down by functions. Instead, think about how different pieces of work are holistically accomplished in the organization. For example, at Progressive Casualty Insurance Company, adjusters and claims personnel are organized into teams that handle the entire claims process from beginning to end. Departmental boundaries are eliminated, and the claims response takes a few hours rather than a week. Second, diminish hierarchical differences and use teams to carry out the work, which is what Progressive does. The use of team structure empowers employees, decentralizes decision-making, and allows for greater learning across the organization. Third, appoint team leaders to manage the internal process in addition to coordinating the work. It is important to realize that monitoring the team's processes is as important as taking care of expected outputs. In the Escape Hybrid team, one individual took the lead role during development and adopted a relaxed and exploratory mindset, while another individual took on a more task-oriented and deadline-driven role during the launch phase. Fourth, allow team members to interact with customers and suppliers directly, so as to adapt and respond quickly if required. Direct contact allows members to keep abreast of changes in the environment more quickly. Finally, provide required expertise from the outside as and when requested by the team. A good team realizes that it does not have all the answers, and therefore it should not be shy about asking for help when needed.

Advantages

There is rapid communication among team members with different functional backgrounds, resulting in reduction in the time for getting workflows completed. Members of a team develop a broader perspective and become adept at solving problems that have the potential to hinder the effectiveness of the entire organization. Employees become more flexible in terms of skill and competence by being aware of the roles of others, and thus feel more empowered to make decisions. Being part of the team also guarantees some recognition and social support. Overall, the level of learning within the horizontal organization increases tremendously compared with the traditional pyramid structure, because of close contact with both customers and suppliers at either end of the workflow. For example, Ford executives used the horizontal approach to customer service for the Escape SUV. Several horizontally aligned groups were responsible for core processes such as parts supply and logistics, vehicle service programs, and technical support. As the processes took hold, learning and responsiveness increased sharply.

Disadvantages

As with any design option, the horizontal organization has its fair share of drawbacks. First, the identification of complete and self-contained work processes within an organization can be problematic. It may be difficult to separate workflows from departmental tasks in a straightforward manner. Strong departments within a firm might fight hard because they might perceive a loss of "turf." Even where the identification is done well and in a politically astute manner, there can be a short-run increase in costs while transitional arrangements are perfected and as employees adjust to the lack of direction. Second, there is the Cinderella problem: employees belonging to parts of the organization that have not been earmarked as horizontal might feel relatively neglected. The emphasis on cross-disciplinary teamwork and immediate customer gratification could stand in the way of deeper technical specialization that can result

| Table 23.1 | Design Features of the Horizontal Organization |

Features	Horizontal Organization
Figure	Core processes in the firm are organized cross-functionally.
What is it?	Breaking down internal boundaries and vertical silos to make subunits work together *horizontally*.
Design principles	1. Organize around complete workflow processes rather than tasks. 2. Flatten hierarchy and use teams to manage everything. 3. Appoint process team leaders to manage internal team processes. 4. Let supplier and customer contact drive performance. 5. Provide required expertise from outside the team as required.
Advantages	1. Rapid communication and reduction in cycle time of work done. 2. Individuals working together on teams develop broader perspective, more flexible and empowered roles. 3. Rapid organizational learning is facilitated. 4. Improved customer responsiveness.
Disadvantages	1. Separation of business activities into processes and non-process functions may be problematic. 2. Cinderella problem: non-process bits of the organization could feel neglected. 3. Teamwork could get in the way of functional specialization. 4. Traditional departments may instigate turf battles.
When to use	When the organization can create better value by improving internal coordination to enable greater flexibility and tailored responses to fit customer needs.

in innovative products. Finally, managers in entrenched departments may feel a loss of turf and may act politically to stymie attempts at effective horizontal collaboration.

When to Use

The horizontal design is best when the organization can create better customer value by improving internal coordination so as to be flexible and responsive to customers' needs. By creating key workflow processes and defining support tasks, there is a better line of sight to customers. This design should be used when the organization is able to move to the mindset of a team-based structure without great difficulty, and also when it is able to trade off the short-term losses incurred in making the new structure work against the gains that eventually accrue from it.

Era 3: Organizational Boundaries Open Up

The third era of organizational design came into its own in the mid-1990s, with rapid improvements in communication technology in the form of the Internet and mobile phones. Era 3 also coincides with the rise of emerging economies such as China and India, where there is a great pooled of skilled expertise in performing very specific tasks such as low-cost manufacturing and software development. The external and internal boundaries of the organization opened up as never before. Managers became increasingly comfortable with the idea that their organization could not efficiently perform all of the tasks required to make a product or service. In the early years of the era, large and bloated organizations shed a lot of tasks that were completed internally, and this led to a difficult period of adjustment. Later on, start-up organizations were designed at the outset to be more lightweight by having a number of tasks performed externally.

Hollow Organization

The biggest trend in the design of organizations in Era 3 has been, without doubt, the outsourcing of various pieces of work done internally to outside partners. The phenomenon became most noticeable in the shifting of the manufacturing function from the U.S. to cheaper areas of production in Asia. In 1986, a *Business Week* article noted that a number of industries—including auto, steel, machine tools, consumer electronics, and semiconductor chips—were shifting their production elsewhere, and hence could be characterized, in contrast to traditional manufacturers, as "hollow corporations." More than 20 years later, business commentators recognize that adopting the hollow organization design form has led to more value creation, because U.S. firms now focus on honing profit-making functions such as design and marketing.

Examples

There are now few industries that remain untouched by the hollow organization design option. Take the case of the U.S. military. Faced with contradictory demands—for greater troop deployment to fight terrorism around the world and pressure to cap the number of active personnel and reservists who are called up—the military has turned towards ever increasing use of private military company (PMC) contractors to provide all services except the core one of fighting battles and securing defensive positions. For instance, Kellog Brown & Root, a subsidiary of the Haliburton Corporation, builds and maintains military bases that have been deployed in Iraq and also provides for all catering and cleaning requirements, and its employees (comprising engineers, architects, logistics experts, cooks, and cleaners) live and work alongside servicemen and women in many active theatres around the world. Much of the sophisticated weaponry used by the military—such as the F-117 fighters, the Patriot missile, and the Global Hawk drone—is maintained on site by PMCs. A study of the use of PMCs by the military in Bosnia showed that outsourcing had reduced troop numbers by 24% and cut operational costs by 27%. As this illustration shows, the hollow design form allows for more flexibility, better use of specialist external technology, and greater efficiency.

More conventional examples of the hollow design abound. Sneaker companies Nike and Reebok Ltd. pioneered outsourcing of manufacturing to Southeast Asian contractors more than 20 years ago, and showed how profitability could be improved by adopting a hollow design. More recently, much of the mundane work of the financial services industry—such as processing insurance claims, approving mortgage loans, and analyzing financial statements of companies—has been accomplished by outsourcing partners located more than halfway across the globe. Another area is customer service work, from simple tasks such as confirming bank or credit card balances to sophisticated ones such as providing technical support for computer users. Rapid developments in communication technologies have allowed work that would have previously been kept in-house to migrate abroad. This trend has affected large and small companies alike. For example, Fluor Corp., a medium-sized California-based architectural services company, outsourced much of the work of generating blueprints and specifications for a multi-billion dollar Saudi Arabian petrochemical complex to a team of 200

Filipino architects employed by partner firm in Manila. Likewise, solo architects working in the U.S. can make use of freelance architectural contractors based in Hungary (where there is an abundance of trained architects) to render plans into three-dimensional specifications. The design features of the horizontal organization are summarized in Table 23.2.

Design Principles

There are three principles governing the design of the hollow organization. First, determine core and non-core business processes in the organization. Typically, core processes share these characteristics: they are critical to business performance, they create current or potential business advantage, and they are likely to drive future growth and rejuvenation. All other processes can be deemed non-core and are likely candidates for being outsourced. For example, in building the Cayenne SUV, Porsche retained critical processes such as engine production, transmission manufacturing, and final assembly—contributing to just about 10% of the finished automobile as core—and outsourced everything else. Second, harness market forces to outsource non-core processes. With increasing globalization and installation of high-touch informational technology systems, it is possible to offshore work to places that are not only cheaper, but also of higher quality. Big tax and audit firms, for example, routinely outsource the filing of individual and corporate tax returns to India-based firms such as MphasiS where highly qualified local accountants complete the task at a fraction of the price that an equivalent U.S. employee would cost. Third, write an effective and flexible contract to align incentives between the firm and the outsourcing provider. One sensitivity issue in using PMCs in war zones is that such firms are ultimately accountable to shareholders rather than the U.S. military, and therefore incentives have to be put in place to ensure continued cooperation.

Advantages

The main advantage of the hollow organization is in the cost savings that comes from utilizing a lesser amount of capital expenditure and in carrying a less administrative overhead. This design also provides greater organizational flexibility by allowing the use of higher quality inputs at less cost. Firms can focus on what they do best, while tapping into the best sources of specialization and technology that outsourcers can bring with them. The growing market for outsourced services, in turn, makes providers more competitive and innovative, thereby adding more to the bottom line of the hollow organization.

Disadvantages

There are several downsides to using the hollow design option. There is a loss of in-house skills, and with that possibly the reduced capacity to innovate. The costs of transitioning to a hollow state are high, and include intangibles such as reduced employee morale. Also, if the supplier is distant both geographically and culturally, then there may be additional costs in terms of increased monitoring or switching to another supplier. Hollow organizations have less control over the supply of their products because of dependence on outsourcing partners, and there is even a threat of being supplanted by suppliers. To illustrate, Motorola Inc. hired BenQ, a Taiwanese manufacturer, to design and develop handsets for its American markets; BenQ then used the expertise gained to create a market for itself in mainland China.

When to Use

The hollow design is usually considered when an organization faces heavy price competition, and consequently, pressure to cut costs. This prompts managers to see what processes can be done cheaper outside the organization. In order to avoid being held hostage to a single supplier, there has to be enough of a market to stimulate efficiency in the performance of outsourced processes.

Modular Organization

The modular organization was another design that was popularized in the early 1990s. The image that it

Table 23.2 Design Features of the Hollow Organization

Features	Hollow Organization
Figure	 Firms B and C supply internal organizational processes to Firm A.
What is it?	Outsourcing internal organization *processes* that support an organization's mission

Design principles	1. Determine non-core processes—those that are *not*
	  a. critical to business performance,
	  b. creating current or potential business advantage,
	  c. likely to drive growth or rejuvenation.
	2. Harness market forces to get non-core processes done efficiently.
	3. Create an effective and flexible interface through a contract that aligns incentives.

Advantages	1. Cost savings due to less capital expenditure and overhead. 2. Tapping into best sources of specialization and technology. 3. Market discipline that leads to supplier competition and innovation. 4. Flexibility in using lower cost and higher quality inputs.
Disadvantages	1. Loss of in-house skills. 2. Possible decrease in internal innovation capacity. 3. Costs of transitioning to hollow state. 4. Higher monitoring to align incentives. 5. Reduced control over supply. 6. Competitive threat of being supplanted by suppliers.
When to use	When there is heavy price competition with pressure to cut costs and there is enough of a market outside the organization to perform required processes.

presents of the organization is one of a collection of Lego bricks that can snap together or be hived off as necessary. The design is similar to the hollow organization in its use of outsourcing. Crucially, however, what is different and distinctive about this form is that outsourcing conforms to pieces of the product rather than outsourcing organizational *processes* (e.g., human resources, warehousing, and logistics) in the hollow form. The assembly of decomposable product chunks provided by internal and external subcontractors is the defining feature of modular organization design.

Examples

The making of Bombardier's Continental business jet shows how flexible modular organizations can be.

The jet can fly eight passengers comfortably from coast to coast in the U.S. without stopping to refuel. Bombardier has broken up the design of the aircraft into 12 large chunks provided by internal divisions and external contractors. The cockpit, center, and forward fuselage are produced in-house, but other major parts are supplied by manufacturers spread around the globe: tailcone (Hawker de Havilland, Australia), stablizers and rear fuselage (Aerospace Industrial Development, Taiwan), engines (General Electric Co., U.S.A.), wing (Mitsubishi, Japan), fairings to improve aerodynamics (Fischer, Austria), landing gear (Messier-Dowty, Canada), and avionics (Rockwell Collins, U.S.A.). It takes just four days for employees in Bombardier's factory in Wichita, Kansas to snap the parts together. There were a number of upsides for Bombardier in using the modular design. The firm was able to share development costs with its partners, slash the cycle time required to launch a new product, and enter the market at a price point that was about $3 million less than its nearest competitor.

Other industries in which modular organizations tend to be prevalent include automobile manufacture, bicycle production, consumer electronics, household appliances, power tools, computing products, and software.

The design features of the horizontal organization are summarized in Table 23.3.

Design Principles

Four principles govern the design of modular organization. First, break products up into separable modules that can be made on a stand-alone basis. Second, design interfaces that allow different modules to work with each other. If this aspect is poorly done, then it can cause tremendous headaches down the line. Bombardier learned this principle from tough experience while outsourcing modules for aircraft that it developed before the Continental jet. Third, outsource product chunks that can be made more efficiently by external contractors. PalmOne Inc., the manufacturer of personal digital assistants, uses modularity in the product to focus on developing the software while outsourcing various hardware modules to subcontractors such as HTC of Taiwan. Finally, enable the organization to focus on assembling the different chunks of the product created in-house and outside.

Advantages

The prime advantage of the modular structure is its efficiency and speed of response. Nissan operates the most efficient automobile plants in the U.S., thanks to its modular organizational design. Parts such as the frame, dashboard, and seats are built by contractors and shipped to the assembly line. Modular design also allows firms to take advantage of competence beyond their own boundaries. By partnering with HTC, PalmOne was able to reduce defects by 50%. Firms can experiment with the use of different suppliers that focus on being the best in their class. Another advantage for modular firms is the increased ability to innovate through the recombination of modules in different ways. Nissan, for example, can use its assembly line to build many more different models of autos than rivals, thanks to its greater modularity.

Disadvantages

One key issue that limits applicability of the modular organization design is the fact that not all products or production processes are amenable to chunking into modules. Second, poorly designed interfaces can hinder modules from working with each other and lead to costly rework. DaimlerChrysler adopted a highly modular design for its two-seater Smart Car, but the launch was beset with a number of problems because various parts of the car would not snap into place as planned and required extensive debugging. Finally, firms have to manage partner firms as if they were part of one large coalition—and this is where the modular design differs significantly from hollow. Innovation has to occur concurrently across a chain of partner firms in order to create a new generation of products, and laggards can hold up the entire development cycle.

When to Use

The modular design is used when it is possible to break up the organization's product into self-contained modules, and where interfaces can be specified such that the modules work when they are joined together.

Table 23.3   Design Features of the Modular Organization

Features	*Modular Organization*
Figure	Firm A assembles product modules produced by Firms A, B, and C.
What is it?	Assembling decomposable *product chunks* (*modules*) provided by internal and external subcontractors
Design principles	1. Break products into manageable modules. 2. Design interfaces that allow different chunks to work together. 3. Outsource product chunks that are produced more efficiently by others. 4. Design the organization to focus on assembling and distributing chunks created in-house and outside.
Advantages	1. Cost savings and speed of responsiveness. 2. Take advantage of competence beyond one's boundary. 3. Scope to experiment with different suppliers that focus on improving their own part. 4. Increased ability to innovate through recombination of modules in different ways.
Disadvantages	1. Not all products may be amenable to chunking into modules. 2. Poorly specified interfaces that hinder modules from work can hamper assembly. 3. Laggards can hold up innovation that occurs concurrently across a chain of collaborators.
When to use	When it is possible to specify the nature of product modules and to design interfaces that allow them to join up and function.

Virtual Organization

Few of today's companies can go it alone under a constant onslaught of international competitors, changing technology, and new regulations. Organizations around the world are embedded in complex networks of relationships: competing fiercely in some markets while collaborating in others. Collaboration or joint ventures with competitors usually takes the form of a virtual organization—a company outside a company created specifically to respond to an exceptional market opportunity that is often temporary. The metaphor for this design comes from virtual memory in a computer, which makes it act if there were more storage capacity than actually present.

Examples

When Marks & Spencer (M&S), the venerable British retail chain, suffered dramatically declining sales in its core product of women's clothing, it turned to a one-time rival for help. George Davies is a serial entrepreneur who has previously set up two companies that have competed successfully with M&S. Together they created a virtual organization called Per Una, with the objective of getting younger women interested in a range of fashionable but reasonably priced clothing. The arrangement was unusual for M&S, which is famously insular and likes to keep all its branding and merchandising in-house. In launching Per Una, M&S provided only retail shelf space and marketing support. Davies contributed everything else, including apparel and accessories, logistics, and sales training. M&S benefited from increased traffic into its stores, while Davis retained a major share of the profits. Per Una proved to be a big hit and helped revive M&S' business fortunes, and was later absorbed completely into M&S. This example illustrates the key features of the virtual organization—willingness to collaborate with unlikely partners, capitalizing on market opportunity, and dissolving the virtual entity when it has served its purpose.

Virtual organization design is very prevalent in the high-technology industry where concurrent competition and cooperation is rife. For example, Symbian Ltd., a software developer for mobile phones, is a virtual organization set up by a consortium of competitors for handsets, including Nokia AB Oyj, Sony Ericsson, Samsung Electronics Co., Panasonic, and Siemens AG. Large and mature companies also use virtual organization design to respond swiftly to a commercial opportunity. For example, rivals P&G and Clorox have recently collaborated with each other to create a new generation of plastic wrap, Glad Press 'n Seal, to compete with market leader Saran.

The design features of the horizontal organization are summarized in Table 23.4.

Design Principles

There are four principles governing the design of the virtual organization. First, create boundaries around a temporary organization with external partners. The organization may look like a separate entity as in a joint venture. Second, use technology to link people, assets, and ideas. Often the virtual organization is not tangible in terms of separate offices, facilities, and other types of infrastructure. It exists in people's minds. What makes it coherent is the sense of purpose and resources that are dedicated to achieving goals. For example, Billable Hour, a small business specialty wristwatch and greeting card retailer, relies on a far-flung network of partnerships, linked by technology, to produce its goods. Third, each partner brings its domain of excellence to bear. Fourth, disband or absorb once the opportunity evaporates. For example, at the height of the dot-com boom, Procter & Gamble Co. used technology partners to create a virtual organization called Reflect.com, with the aim of selling cosmetics online. After the boom faded away, P&G disbanded the organization and absorbed the learning from the experience into a more traditional cosmetics division.

Advantages

The virtual organization provides firms with the ability to move nimbly to exploit a favorable market opportunity. Virtual design also allows a firm to provide a product extension that would have been impossible otherwise, and also to jointly leverage organizational assets that are distributed across partnering firms. In the Glad joint venture, for example, the wrap was invented in P&G labs but marketed under Clorox's well-established Glad brand name. Since then, the two companies have continued the collaboration with the introduction of Glad Force Flex trash bags, which make use of a stretchable plastic also invented in P&G labs. Finally, another advantage of the virtual form is that it can be easily disbanded or absorbed once the opportunity for collaboration goes away, or it can be made into a stand-alone entity if the opportunity becomes larger.

Table 23.4 Design Features of the Virtual Organization

Features	Virtual Organization
Figure	 Firm A and B collaborate (ab) to supply Firm A and/or firms.
What is it?	Creating a *company-outside-a-company* to respond to an exceptional (often temporary) opportunity
Design principles	1. Create boundaries around a temporary organization with external partners. 2. Use technology to link people, assets, and ideas. 3. Each partner brings its domain of excellence. 4. Disband or absorb once the opportunity evaporates.
Advantages	1. Ability to move nimbly to respond to market opportunity. 2. Allows a firm to provide product extension or one-stop-shop service. 3. Leverage organizational assets distributed across partners forming the virtual firm. 4. No commitment to keeping the organization going after initial opportunity vanishes.
Disadvantages	1. Increase in the load of communication to ensure there is no duplication or redundancy. 2. Lack of trust could break down communication and coordination. 3. Employees in the virtual entity may have partisan or weak organizational identification.
When to use	When it is possible to explore a fleeting market opportunity by partnering with other organizations.

Disadvantages

The major downside of virtual organization design is that it requires a tremendous amount of communication and understanding to keep it going. Partners need to talk to each other to avoid duplication and redundancy. One recurring problem with the Per Una organization was that some of its apparel was strikingly similar to what M&S had designed. Another problem is that lack of trust or misalignment of incentives could break down communication and coordination. In the Per Una case this problem manifested itself in terms of M&S's indefinite return policy—customers can bring in goods that they are dissatisfied with any time; George Davies, on the other hand, wanted a time limit on when customers could come back in to claim a refund or exchange, so as to protect the profitability of the operation and also its reputation for fair commercial exchange. A final drawback is that employees in the virtual entity may have partisan or weak organizational identification, and this, in turn, may reduce their commitment.

When to Use

The virtual design is used when it is possible to explore a fleeting market opportunity by partnering with complementary organizations. In such situations, typically one organization does not have the necessary capability to respond, and it is necessary to look around to see what other organizations (including competitors) can offer. The design works best when there is clear understanding among partnering organizations as to their rights and obligations.

New Demands on Managers and Organizations

The shifting emphasis from vertical designs to horizontal designs to partnership designs has reshaped the roles of managers. The biggest change has been from having direct control over resources required for performance toward dependence on others over whom there is no direct control. Even with more dependence and less control under newer structural designs, managers are still responsible for performance outcomes. For a manager who is used to a traditional top-down approach, it is hard to let go of control. The late business guru Peter Drucker once noted that the problem with large company managers is that they are used to giving orders and not to working with a partner—a totally different proposition.

A nice example is provided by the transition of Strida, a U.K.-based company that sells lightweight foldable bicycles, from a functional design, vertically integrated manufacturer to a completely hollow form. In 2001, Strida received a large order from an Italian customer, willing to buy at a price that was below the cost of producing the bicycles in the U.K. The CEO of the company, Steedman Bass, immediately began investigating ways of making the organization more efficient. First, he decided to shut down the in-house production plant and identified a manufacturing partner in the Far East who could make the bike at lower cost. He used expert contractors to continue developing new bicycle models, to design the owner's manual, to design the company's Web site. He used various Web-based software services to ensure smooth communication between the designers and the manufacturer, to manage accounts, materials and documents. He then turned to a long-time vendor to take over the back-end operation of the company—including warehouse management, order fulfillment, inventory control, customer service, inbound container management, and accounts generation. The company has low overhead and is now structured to ramp up and down quickly in response to market fluctuations. Bass focuses almost exclusively on managing the various relationships that make up the business. Bass had loved making his own bikes, and therefore the biggest barrier in making the transition was in his willingness to find, trust, and hand over that responsibility to someone else that could do it more efficiently.

A study of the fit between executive style and executive roles by the Hay Group distinguished between *operations roles* and *collaborative roles*. Operations roles have traditional line authority and are accountable for business results, typically through direct control over people and resources. Successful operations managers set goals, establish analyses, take risks, and are intensely focused on results. Collaborative roles, however, lack direct authority over horizontal colleagues or partners, and are nonetheless accountable for key business results. Successful managers in collaborative roles are extremely flexible and proactive, achieve outcomes through personal communication and influence tailored to people and situations, and assertively seek out needed information.

The old way of managing was to defend the unit's boundaries and oversee its performance by emphasizing operations roles. However, collaborative roles are more common in new organizational structures. The key manager demands for succeeding with newer structural designs are as follows.

Get the Right Partner on the Bus

In a hollow or modular design this means spending time to get to know a potential partner's strengths, weaknesses, and goals. For routine, commodity-type sourcing, due diligence is less important. But for a significant partnership, trust in the partner is essential. Check for gaps in skills and competency to assess whether the partner can deliver what your business needs. It is good to investigate prospective partners by talking to other companies they've partnered with and to develop a sense of how well suited their culture and priorities are to your own. For hollow and modular designs, it is good to understand the process being outsourced and what to expect from the partner. When the partner takes it over, your control will be gone. The partner will get most of the benefit from improvements, innovation, and efficiencies.

Select People With Lateral Organizing Skills

Lateral organizing skills refers to the ability to work with people across organizations, including those with whom lines of responsibility and accountability are a little fuzzy. People who are part of a horizontal team or who work with outside partners must have excellent coordination, personal influence, and negotiation skills. Soft skills dominate hard skills in the newer organization designs. A process owner or a partner cannot simply order a change. It's about influence, influence, and influence to adjust the relationship to serve new demands. Managers with lateral organizing skills may also act as evangelists, convincing people to give up their own needs for the greater good of collaboration for customer satisfaction.

Seek Clarity, Not Control

As relationships move from vertical to horizontal and from work that can be observed to work performed elsewhere, much time has to be devoted to the front end of the relationship-setting expectations and creating structure. Every conceivable issue must be discussed and probably written down in contracts with outside partners. Memos of understanding are effective for process teams. The respective goals, incentives, and desired outcomes should be defined in advance. During the relationship, problems surely will arise and changes will be made, but clarity in the beginning is essential. Steedman Bass of Strida says that careful negotiation beforehand is critical. "Good contracts are important. They may be time-consuming, but taking the time to write and negotiate good contracts that work for both parties is essential. You're placing a lot of reliance on people, and it has to work. We did our homework up front, thinking of how we wanted the relationships to work, and that has probably eliminated 98% of the potential misunderstandings on either our part or theirs." Bass also emphasized, "I had never used contracts to sue or punish partners; I used them to mutually establish the playing field and rules of the game."

Design Coordination Mechanisms

Some amount of mutual control with partners can be asserted through explicit collaboration mechanisms. For an outside partner, example mechanisms might include a Leadership Governance Board of senior executives that meets quarterly, or monthly meetings of team leaders, or periodic visits to each others' sites to see the work, build relationships, and discuss results. Scheduled periodic discussions of metrics, performance results, and written reports should also be part of the coordination process with internal or external partners.

Conclusion

After much debate, the managers at WRG, the start-up horticulture supply company referred to at the beginning of this chapter, decided to adopt a hollow rather than a functional organization design. It was a learning process for managers and board members because the team's experience had been in traditional structures. A manager and board member made trips to India and China to meet and build personal relationships with suppliers. The product had to be supplied in bulk for horticulture nurseries, and in appealing individual packages for retail sales. The time and travel overseas was only a fraction of the cost of buying machines and building a small manufacturing plant. Building strong relationships with sales distributors and a marketing agency was more challenging. These businesses were focused on their own needs more than on a partnership. Moreover, the board member who worked with distributors had something of an autocratic temperament, which made it hard to connect with the prospective partners. The CEO, however, had a knack for building horizontal relationships with growers and university researchers for testing product efficacy. The science supporting the superior efficiency of SmartGrow was thereby accomplished at minimal cost. After some trial and error, the hollow organization form proved a boon to WRG.

The movement from Era 1 to Era 3 has vastly expanded the array of organization design choices available to managers. The new designs—particularly variations of the horizontal and hollow forms—that have evolved in the past three decades offer a number of advantages, but as we have noted, each has particular challenges as well. The shift from vertical to horizontal thinking and behavior can be difficult. The implementation of a horizontal or sourcing design has its own challenges. Realigning a large company along horizontal processes can require a wrenching change in people and culture. Adopting a hollow form may require less change in culture, but a new manager paradigm will be needed, with special focus on finding suitable external partners and building relationships that serve both partners. Maintaining external collaboration requires its own expertise. With increasing global competition, managers have to be astute and realistic about the organization design that provides them with competitive advantage and their customers with greatest value.

Selected Bibliography

Robert Duncan's original article titled "What Is the Right Organization Structure? Decision Tree Analysis Provides the Answer," *Organizational Dynamics*, 1979 (winter), 59–80, provides a brief overview of functional, divisional, and matrix structures. Stewart A. Clegg's book *Modern Organizations* (Sage, 1990) traces the evolution from traditional to contemporary organization designs. The classic reference on divisional structures is *Strategy and Structure* (MIT Press, 1962) by Alfred Chandler. *Matrix* (Addison-Wesley, 1979) by Stanley Lawrence and Paul Davis is the definitive introduction to the topic. Jay Galbraith's *Designing Complex Organizations* (Addison-Wesley, 1973) provides a brief yet comprehensive description of Era 1 designs.

In their book *Reengineering the Corporation* (HarperBusiness, 1993) Michael Hammer and James Champy discuss how reengineering horizontal processes can cut costs and improve customer value. John A. Bryne's "The Horizontal Corporation," *Business Week*, 20 December 1993, 76–81, provides a number of original illustrations of companies that have adopted the horizontal design. The principles of team-oriented organization design are succinctly articulated by Albert Cherns in "The Principles of Sociotechnical Designs," *Human Relations*, 1976, 29, 783–792. The Ford Escape SUV example used in the article is adapted from Chuck Salter's article "Ford's Escape Route," *FastCompany*, October 2004, 106–110. Frank Ostroff's book *The Horizontal Organization* (Oxford University Press, 1999) is a comprehensive exposition of that design option. A wonderful firsthand report of an organization moving from predominantly Era 1 vertical lines of command to Era 2 horizontal processes can be found in Mary Walton's *Car* (W.W. Norton, 1999).

Norman Jonas's 1986 article "The Hollow Corporation," *Business Week*, 3 March, 57–59, attracted widespread attention to the growing trend in outsourcing. The key principles of the hollow form are summarized by Simon Domberger in *The Contracting Organization* (Oxford University Press, 1998). Examples of the hollow form can be found in the following articles: Anthony Bianco and Stephanie Anderson Forest, "Outsourcing War," *Business Week*, 15 September 2003, 42–49; Pete Engardio, Aaron Berstein, and Manjeet Kripalani, "The New Global Job Shift," *Business Week*, 3 February 2003, 36–48; and Pete Engardio and Bruce Einhorn, "Outsourcing Innovation," *Business Week*, 21 March 2005, 86–94. More generally, John Hagel III and Marc Singer discuss the Era 3 philosophy of design in their aptly titled article "Unbundling the Corporation," *Harvard Business Review*, March-April 1999, 133–141.

The article titled "The Modular Corporation" by Shawn Tully and Tricia Welsh, *Fortune*, 8 February 1993, 106–115, helped spread awareness of this Era 3 option to a wide business audience. A comprehensive discussion of the modular form can be found in Carliss Y. Baldwin and Kim B. Clark, *Design Rules: The Power of Modularity v.1* (MIT Press, 2000). Academic articles discussing the key features of the modular form include the following: Ron Sanchez and Joseph T. Mahoney, "Modularity, Flexibility, and Knowledge Management in Product and Organizational Design," *Strategic Management Journal*, 1996, 17, 63–76; and Melissa A. Schilling and Kevin T. Steensma, "The Use of Modular Organizational Forms: An Industry Level Analysis," *Academy of Management Journal*, 2001, 44, 1149–1168. Examples of the modular form can be found in Philip Siekman's "The Snap-Together Business Jet," *Fortune*, 21 January 2002, 104A–104H; and David Welch's "How Nissan Laps Detroit," *Business Week*, 22 December 2003, 60–62.

William Davidow and Michael Malone's book *The Virtual Corporation* (HarperCollins, 2003) provides a good introduction to the opportunities and challenges of the virtual form. A framework that considers when the virtual form should be favored is provided by Henry Chesbrough and David Teece in their article "When is Virtual Virtuous? Organizing for Innovation," *Harvard Business Review*, January-February 1996, 65–73. Shona Brown and Kathleen Eisenhardt theorize the virtues of temporary organizations in their book *Competing on the Edge* (Harvard Business School Press, 1998). The P&G-Clorox virtual organization example was drawn from Patrica Seller's article "Teaching an Old Dog New Tricks," *Fortune*, 31 May 2004, 166–180.

Transitioning from a traditional organization design to a more contemporary option can be challenging. A number of books provide guidance on how the redesign challenge can be met, including Bruce Pasternack and Albert Viscio's *The Centreless Corporation* (Simon & Schuster, 1998); David Nadler and Michael Tushman's *Competing by Design* (Oxford, 1997); Henk Volbreda's *Building the Flexible Firm* (Oxford, 1998); Jay Galbraith's *Designing Organizations* (Jossey-Bass, 2002); and Michael Goold and Andrew Campbell's *Designing Effective Organizations* (Jossey-Bass, 2002).

PART V

Culture

The Organization's DNA

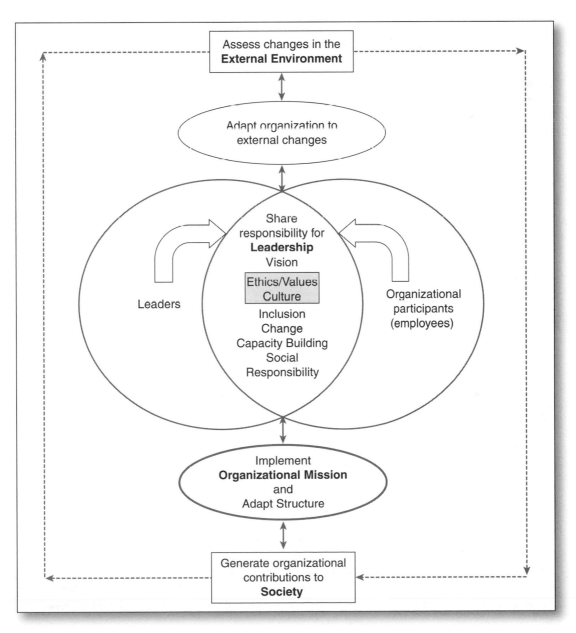

Overview

Culture

Culture is the life force of an organization. In organizations, much as in society, culture is where the real values and underlying beliefs, practices and behavioral norms, symbols, ceremonies, and customs exist. Gary Yukl (Chapter 24) cites a definition of culture by Edgar Schein, the leading scholar on organization culture, which identifies the culture of a group or organization as shared assumptions and beliefs about the world and the group's place in it, the nature of time and space, human nature, and human relationships. Yukl explains that underlying beliefs representing the culture of a group or organization are learned responses to problems of survival in the external environment and problems of internal integration. Leaders can influence culture through leader behavior—such as espoused values and visions, role modeling and attention, and reactions to crises—and the programs, systems, structures, and cultural forms that leaders implement. He indicates that culture in mature organizations is much more difficult to change than that in new organizations. Yukl also cites vision (discussed in Part IV) as a major influence on the organization's culture.

Schein (Chapter 25) emphasizes the importance of learning cultures and learning leaders. He maintains that the environment of new era organizations is different, more complex, more fast paced, and more culturally diverse than that in previous eras. As a result, the learning culture must have in its DNA a "learning gene," in the sense that members must hold the shared assumption that learning is a good thing worth investing in and that *learning to learn* is itself a skill to be mastered. Schein acknowledges that the learning culture will require shared leadership and learning because leaders will not know all the answers and will not be in control; therefore, they must learn to embrace trial-and-error learning and become supportive of the learning efforts of others. He describes the role of learning leaders and participants in different organizational situations, including growing organizations with founding leaders, midlife organizations, mature and declining organizations, mergers and acquisitions, and partnerships, joint ventures, and strategic alliances.

Ethics and Shared Values

The challenges involved in establishing values in an organization are intricately related to ethics. Al Gini (Chapter 26) proclaims that ethics is about the assessment and evaluation of values, because all of life is value laden, including work life. Ethics in organizations, as in other areas of life, compel leaders and participants to take into account the impact of their actions in relation to others. Gini contends that leaders and participants are required to ask the question, "What ought to be done in regard to the others we work with and serve?" Thus ethics in organizations is about how all of the organization's stakeholders are treated, including employees, customers or clients, and the community. Without ethics, the organization's culture might ingrain self-serving values to clone its own rather than sustain moral agents who engage in critical reflection.

Gini believes the responsibility of leadership is to raise the important questions continuously, engage in the assessment of how decisions and actions may affect self and others, and consider the potential consequences of alternative courses of action. Most important, leaders need to model moral behavior and create an organizational culture in which ethical behavior permeates the entire organization.

How do organizations build and sustain ethical cultures? Research by Alexandre Ardichvili, James Mitchell, and Douglas Jondle (Chapter 27) found five clusters of characteristics that differentiate ethical cultures. These cultures are mission and values driven; they balance the issues and needs of multiple stakeholders; their leaders role-model ethical standards and behaviors; the organization's processes are fair and demonstrate integrity; and the decision makers maintain a long-term perspective rather than emphasizing short-term gains.

Ethical Leadership Challenges

Some forms of leadership are dysfunctional and harmful to the organization and its participants. In these cases, leaders have a responsibility to engage in truthful self-reflection and self-correction; participants have a responsibility to themselves and their organizations not to become victims of poor, unethical, or abusive behavior. We look to organizational leaders to model ethical behavior, but, regrettably, there are examples of leaders not rising to the occasion. With the increase in shared leadership in new era organizations comes shared responsibility by leaders and participants to uphold ethical behavior in the organization. Mary Uhl-Bien and Melissa Carsten (Chapter 28) raise the question, "What if leaders *do not* behave ethically—who is responsible for ethics then?" They propose a framework called *upward ethical leadership*, which they define as leadership behavior enacted by individuals who take action to maintain ethical standards in the face of questionable moral behaviors by higher-ups. They identify several approaches that employees can use to respond actively to unethical conduct by leaders, and they describe practices that organizations can use to support the development of upward ethical leadership. For instance, Uhl-Bien and Carsten suggest ways for employees to increase their sources of personal power so that they are less dependent on the organization and more capable of exercising upward and horizontal influence. One major recommendation for organizations is that they move away from bureaucratic command-and-control cultures so that leadership can become a process of mutual influence and accountability.

Jean Lipman-Blumen (Chapter 29) warns of the damaging effect of toxic leaders. She defines *toxic leaders* as a global label for leaders who engage in numerous destructive behaviors and exhibit certain dysfunctional personal characteristics. The behaviors and qualities of toxic leaders can inflict serious and enduring harm on their followers and their organizations. Participants have a responsibility not to tolerate toxic leaders or allow themselves to be exploited by them, and hiring officials have a responsibility not to select and retain these leaders. Lipman-Blumen implores individuals and organizations to free themselves of toxic leaders and learn how to select constructive leaders who foster autonomy and freedom.

Barbara Kellerman (Chapter 30) describes a phenomenon she calls *bad leadership*. She explains that bad leadership falls into two categories: bad as in ineffective (unsuccessful) and bad as in unethical (failure to distinguish between right and wrong). Both leaders and participants are complicit in this form of leadership. Kellerman outlines a typology of bad leadership that comprises seven groups: incompetent, rigid, intemperate, callous, corrupt, insular, and evil. She provides descriptions and examples of these seven types of bad leadership, with the intention of helping individuals to avoid becoming entangled as bad leaders and bad followers.

Terry Price (Chapter 31) argues that ethical failures in leadership are primarily cognitive—that is, they are based on mistaken moral *beliefs* and *justifications* leaders make for their unethical behavior—rather than occurring from intentional choices to put self-interest ahead of moral requirements. He makes several crucial claims about ethical failures. Leadership encourages preoccupation with collective ends, sometimes to the neglect of other important moral considerations. For example, the means leaders use to achieve collective goals do not always consider parties in the moral universe other than those in the leader-follower relationship. As a result, leaders may seek collective goals using means that result in ethical failures because they believe they are justified in excepting themselves from the moral requirements that they would normally expect of others. Price warns that leaders need to restrict the exceptions they make of themselves and publicize their reasons for deviating from the requirements of morality.

CHAPTER 24

Influencing Organization Culture

Gary Yukl

University at Albany–State University of New York

Large-scale change in an organization usually requires some change in the organization culture as well as direct influence over individual subordinates. By changing the culture of an organization, top management can indirectly influence the motivation and behavior of organization members. Research on organizational culture provides further insight into the dynamics of transformational leadership and the processes by which a leader's charisma may become institutionalized.

Nature of Organization Culture

Schein (1992, 2004) defines the culture of a group or organization as shared assumptions and beliefs about the world and their place in it, the nature of time and space, human nature, and human relationships. Schein distinguishes between underlying beliefs (which may be unconscious) and espoused values, which may or may not be consistent with these beliefs. Espoused values do not accurately reflect the culture when they are inconsistent with underlying beliefs. For example, a company may espouse open communication, but the underlying belief may be that any criticism or disagreement is detrimental and should be avoided. It is difficult to dig beneath the superficial layer of espoused values to discover the underlying beliefs and assumptions, some of which may be unconscious.

The underlying beliefs representing the culture of a group or organization are learned responses to problems of survival in the external environment and problems of internal integration. The primary external problems are the core mission or reason for existence of the organization, concrete objectives based on this mission, strategies for attaining these objectives, and ways to measure success in attaining objectives. Most organizations have multiple objectives, and some of them may not be as

---

obvious as others. Agreement on a general mission does not imply agreement about specific objectives or their relative priority. Schein (1992, p. 56) provides an example of a company with consensus about having a line of winning products but disagreement about how to allocate resources among different product groups and how to market the products:

> One group thought that marketing meant better image advertising in national magazines so that more people would recognize the name of the company, one group was convinced that marketing meant better advertising in technical journals, one group thought it meant developing the next generation of products, while yet another group emphasized merchandising and sales support as the key element in marketing. Senior management could not define clear goals because of a lack of consensus on the meaning of key functions and how those functions reflect the core mission of the organization.

All organizations need to solve problems of internal integration as well as problem of external adaptation. Objectives and strategies cannot be achieved effectively without cooperative effort and reasonable stability of membership in the organization. Internal problems include the criteria for determining membership in the organization, the basis for determining status and power, criteria and procedures for allocating rewards and punishments, an ideology to explain unpredictable and uncontrollable events, rules or customs about how to handle aggression and intimacy, and a shared consensus about the meaning of words and symbols. The beliefs that develop about these issues serve as the basis for role expectations to guide behavior, let people know what is proper and improper, and help people maintain comfortable relationships with each other.

A major function of culture is to help us understand the environment and determine how to respond to it, thereby reducing anxiety, uncertainty, and confusion. The internal and external problems are closely interconnected, and organizations must deal with them simultaneously. As solutions are developed through experience, they become shared assumptions that are passed on to new members. Over time, the assumptions may become so familiar that members are no longer consciously aware of them.

Ways to Influence Culture

Leaders can influence the culture of an organization in a variety of ways (Deal & Kennedy, 1982; Schein 1992, 2004; Trice & Beyer, 1993; Tsui, Zhang, Wang, Xin, & Wu, 2006). The different types of influence can be grouped into two broad categories (see Table 24.1). One approach involves direct actions by the leader, and the other involves creation or modification of formal programs, systems, organization structure, facilities, and cultural forms. The effects of leaders on culture are stronger when the two approaches are consistent.

Leadership Behavior. Leaders communicate their values when they articulate a vision for the organization, make statements about the values and ideals that are important, and formulate long-term objectives and strategies for attaining them (see guidelines later in this chapter). Written value statements, charters, and philosophies can be useful as supplementary forms of communication, but they have little credibility unless they are supported by leader actions and decisions. One way for leaders to communicate values and expectations is by actions showing loyalty, self-sacrifice, and service beyond the call of duty. In their daily activity, leaders also communicate

Table 24.1	Ways to Influence Organizational Culture

Leadership Behavior
- Espoused values and visions
- Role modeling and attention
- Reactions to crises

Programs, Systems, Structures, and Cultural Forms
- Design of management systems and programs
- Criteria for rewards and personnel decisions
- Design of structure and facilities
- Symbols, rituals, ceremonies, and stories

their priorities and concerns by their choice of things to ask about, measure, comment on, praise, and criticize. In contrast, by not paying attention to something, a leader sends the message that it is not important.

Because of the emotionality surrounding crises, a leader's response to them can send a strong message about values and assumptions. A leader who faithfully supports espoused values even when under pressure to take expedient actions inconsistent with them communicates clearly that the values are really important. For example, one company with lower sales avoided layoffs by having all employees (including managers) work fewer hours and take a pay cut; the decision communicated a strong concern for preserving employee jobs.

Programs and Systems. Formal budgets, planning sessions, reports, performance review procedures, and management development programs can be used to emphasize some values and beliefs about proper behavior. Orientation programs can be used to socialize new employees and teach them about the culture of an organization. Training programs designed to increase job skills can also be used to teach participants about the ideology of the organization. Other approaches for socialization of new members include use of formal mentors who are selected because they are able to model and teach key values, and the use of internships, apprenticeships, or special assignments to work in subunits of the organization where the culture is strong (Fisher, 1986).

Criteria for Rewards and Personnel Decisions. The criteria used as the basis for allocating tangible rewards signal what is valued by the organization. Formal recognition in ceremonies and informal praise communicate a leader's concerns and priorities. Failure to recognize contributions and achievements sends a message that they are not important. Finally, differential allocation of rewards and status symbols affirms the relative importance of some members compared to others. For example, in comparison to companies in the United States, Japanese companies use far fewer status symbols and privileges of rank such as large offices, special dining rooms, and private parking spaces. The criteria emphasized in recruiting, selecting, promoting, and dismissing people provide another way to communicate

values. The effect on culture is stronger if the organization provides realistic information about the criteria and requirements for success, and the personnel decisions are consistent with these criteria.

Design of Organization Structure and Facilities. The design of organization structure may reflect values and beliefs about people and processes. A centralized structure reflects the belief that the leader can determine what is best, whereas a decentralized structure or the use of self-managed teams reflects a belief in individual initiative and shared responsibility. The design of facilities may also reflect basic values. Providing similar offices and having the same dining facilities for all employees is consistent with egalitarian values.

Cultural Forms. Cultural values and beliefs are also influenced by cultural forms such as symbols, slogans, rituals, and ceremonies (Trice & Beyer, 1993). Many different changes are possible, including elimination of existing cultural forms that symbolize the old ideology, modification of existing cultural forms to express the new ideology, and creation of new cultural forms. The following description of changes in the U.S. Postal Service provides some examples (Biggart, 1977).

When Winton Blount became the new Postmaster General in 1972, he initiated a number of changes to signal a new ideology which emphasized efficiency, competitiveness, and self-sufficiency rather than service at any cost and dependence on Congress. Changes in symbols included a new name for the post office, a new logo (an eagle poised for flight rather than Paul Revere riding a horse), new postal colors, and a new typeface for publications. The employee newsletter was drastically changed from a media for disseminating trivial information to a vehicle for advocating the new ideology and celebrating the success of local post offices that achieved the new efficiency standards. An advertising office was created to promote a new image for the postal service, and a training institute was established to train thousands of postal supervisors each year in management procedures consistent with the new ideology.

Rituals, ceremonies, and rites of passage can be used to strengthen identification with the organization as well as to emphasize core values. In many organizations new members are required to make a public oath of allegiance, to demonstrate knowledge of the ideology, or to undergo an ordeal to demonstrate loyalty. Also common are ceremonies to celebrate a member's advancement in rank, to inaugurate a new leader, and to acknowledge the retirement of a member. Rituals and ceremonies may also involve the communication of stories about important events and dramatic actions by individuals. However, stories and myths are more a reflection of culture than a determinant of it. To be useful the story must describe a real event and convey a clear message about values.

Culture and Growth Stages of Organizations

The influence of a leader on the culture of an organization varies depending on the developmental stage of the organization. The founder of a new organization has a strong influence on its culture. The founder typically has a vision of a new enterprise and proposes ways of doing things that, if successful in accomplishing objectives and reducing anxiety, will gradually become embedded in the culture. However, creating culture in a new organization is not necessarily a smooth process; it may involve considerable conflict if the founder's ideas are not successful or other powerful members of the organization have competing ideas. To succeed, the founder needs an appropriate vision and the ability and persistence to influence others to accept it. If the founder does not articulate a consistent vision and act consistently to reinforce it, the organization may develop a dysfunctional culture reflecting the inner conflicts of the founder (Kets de Vries & Miller, 1984).

One of the most important elements of culture in new organizations is the set of beliefs about the distinctive competence of the organization that differentiates it from other organizations. The beliefs are likely to include the reason why the organization's products or services are unique or superior and the internal processes that account for continued ability to provide these products and services. Implications for the relative status of different functions in the organization and the strategies for solving crises differ depending on the source of distinctive competence. For example, in a company that is successful due to its development of innovative products, the research and development function is likely to have higher status than other functions, and the likely response to a recent decline in sales is to introduce some new products. In a company that has been able to provide a common product at the lowest price, manufacturing will have higher status, and the response to a decline in sales is likely to involve the search for ways to reduce costs below those of competitors.

The culture in young, successful organizations is likely to be strong because it is instrumental to the success of the organization, the assumptions have been internalized by current members and transmitted to new members, and the founder is still present to symbolize and reinforce the culture. In such an organization, the culture will evolve slowly over the years as experience reveals that some assumptions need to be modified. Eventually, as the organization matures and people other than the founder or family members occupy key leadership positions, the culture will become more unconscious and less uniform. As different subcultures develop in different sub-units, conflicts and power struggles may increase. Segments of the culture that were initially functional may become dysfunctional, hindering the organization from adapting to a changing environment.

In general, it is much more difficult to change culture in a mature organization than to create it in a new organization. One reason is that many of the underlying beliefs and assumptions shared by people in an organization are implicit and unconscious. Cultural assumptions are also difficult to change when they justify the past and are a matter of pride. Moreover, cultural values influence the selection of leaders and the role expectations for them. In a mature, relatively prosperous organization, culture influences leaders more than leaders influence culture. Drastic changes are unlikely unless a major crisis threatens the welfare and survival of the organization. Even with a crisis, it takes considerable insight and skill for a leader to understand the current culture in an organization and implement changes successfully.

References

Baum, R. J., Locke, E. A., & Kirkpatrick, S. (1998). A longitudinal study of the relation of vision and vision communication to venture growth in entrepreneurial firms. *Journal of Applied Psychology,* 83, 43-54.

Bennis, W. G. (1959). Leadership theory and administrative behavior: The problem of authority. *Administrative Science Quarterly,* 4, 259-260.

Berson, Y., Shamir, B., Avolio, B. J., & Popper, M. (2001). The relationship between vision strength, leadership style, and context. *Leadership Quarterly,* 12, 53-73.

Biggart, N. W. (1977). The creative-destructive process of organizational change: The case of the post office. *Administrative Science Quarterly,* 22, 410-426.

Conger, J. A. (1989). *The charismatic leader: Behind the mystique of exceptional leadership.* San Francisco, CA: Jossey-Bass.

Deal, T. E., & Kennedy, A. (1982). *Corporate cultures.* Reading, MA: Addison Wesley.

Fisher, C. D. (1986). Organizational socialization: An integrative review. In K. M. Rowland & G. R. Ferris (Eds.), *Research in Personnel and Human Resources Management,* vol. 4, pp. 101-145. Greenwich, CT: JAI Press.

Kets de Vries, M. F. R., & Miller, D. (1984). *The neurotic organization: Diagnosing and changing counter-productive styles of management.* San Francisco: Jossey-Bass.

Kotter, J. P. (1996). *Leading change.* Boston: Harvard Business School Press.

Kouzes, J. M, & Posner, B. Z. (1987). *The leadership challenge: How to get extraordinary things done in organizations.* San Francisco: Jossey-Bass.

Kouzes, J. M., & Posner, B. Z. (1995). *The leadership challenge: How to keep getting extraordinary things done in organizations,* 2nd ed. San Francisco: Jossey-Bass.

Larwood, L., Falbe, C. M., Kriger, M. P., & Miesing, P. (1995). Structure and meaning of organizational vision. *Academy of Management Journal,* 38, 740-769.

Nadler, D. A., Shaw, R. B., Walton, A. E., & Associates. (1995). *Discontinuous change: Leading organizational transformation.* San Francisco, Jossey-Bass.

Nanus, B. (1992). *Visionary leadership: Creating a compelling sense of direction for your organization.* San Francisco: Jossey-Bass.

Peters, T. J. (1987). *Thriving on chaos.* New York: Harper Collins.

Peters, T. J., & Austin, N. (1985). *A passion for excellence: The leadership difference.* New York: Random House.

Richards, D., & Engle, S. (1986). After the vision: Suggestions to corporate visionaries and vision champions. In J. D. Adams (Ed.), *Transforming leadership.* Alexandria, VA: Miles River Press, pp. 199-214.

Schein, E. H. (1992). *Organizational culture and leadership,* 2nd ed. San Francisco: Jossey-Bass.

Schein, E. H. (2004). *Organizational culture and leadership,* 3rd ed. San Francisco: Jossey-Bass.

Strange, J. M., & Mumford, M. D. (2002). The origins of vision: Charismatic versus ideological leadership. *Leadership Quarterly,* 13, 343-377.

Strange, J. M., & Mumford, M. D. (2005). The origins of vision: Effects of reflection, models, and analysis. *Leadership Quarterly,* 16 (1), 121-148.

Thomas, B. (1976). *Walt Disney: An American tradition.* New York: Simon & Schuster.

Tichy, N. M. & Devanna, M. A. (1986). *The transformational leader.* New York: John Wiley.

Trice, H. M., & Beyer, J. M. (1993). *The cultures of work organizations.* Englewood Cliffs, NJ: Prentice Hall.

Tsui, A. S., Zhang, Z., Wang, H., Xin, K. R., & Wu, J. B. (2006). Unpacking the relationship between CEO leadership behavior and organizational culture. *Leadership Quarterly,* 17, 117-137.

CHAPTER 25

The Learning Culture and the Learning Leader

Edgar II. Schein

Massachusetts Institute of Technology, Emeritus

I n this chapter I want to focus on normative infer ence. There is much speculation nowadays about the direction in which the world is heading and what all of this means for organizations and leadership. My sense of this is that the various predictions about globalism, knowledge-based organizations, the information age, the biotech age, the loosening of organizational boundaries, and so on all have one theme in common—we basically do not know what the world of tomorrow will really be like, except that it will be *different*, more *complex*, more *fast*-paced, and more *culturally diverse* (Hesselbein, Goldsmith, and Somerville, 1999; Global Business Network, 2002; Schwartz, 2003; Michael, 1985, 1991). This means that *organizations and their leaders will have to become perpetual learners.*

When we pose the issue of perpetual learning in the context of cultural analysis, we confront a paradox. Culture is a stabilizer, a conservative force, a way of making things meaningful and predictable. Many management consultants and theorists have asserted that "strong" cultures are desirable as a basis for effective and lasting performance. But strong cultures are by definition stable and hard to change. If the world is becoming more turbulent, requiring more flexibility and learning, does this not imply that strong cultures will increasingly become a liability? Does this not mean, then, that the process of culture creation itself is potentially dysfunctional because it stabilizes things, whereas flexibility might be more appropriate? Or is it possible to imagine a culture that, by its very nature, is learning oriented, adaptive, and flexible? Can one stabilize perpetual learning and change? What would a culture that favored perpetual learning and flexibility look like?

To translate that question into leadership terms, what is the direction in which the leaders of today should be pushing cultural evolution to prepare for the surprises of tomorrow? What sort of characteristics and skills must a

---

Source: The Learning Culture and the Learning Leader by Edgar H. Schein, p. 393-418, *Organizational Culture and Leadership*, 3rd ed. by Edgar H. Schein. Copyright © 2004 John Wiley and Sons, Inc. Reprinted with permission of John Wiley and Sons, Inc.

leader have to perceive the needs of tomorrow and to implement the changes needed in order to survive?

What Might a Learning Culture Look Like?

The hypotheses spelled out in this chapter have resulted from many conversations with the late Donald Michael (1985, 1991) and with Tom Malone (1987), and Peter Senge (1990) about the organization of the future. They reflect a bringing together of what Michael sees as the learning needs of the future, what Malone sees as the theory and practice of coordination in the information age, what Senge visualizes as the art and practice of the learning organization, and my own thoughts about culture and innovation (Schein, 1990). Combining these ideas leads to a first attempt to describe the characteristics of a learning culture in terms of relevant dimensions and positions on those dimensions.

1. A Proactivity Assumption

A learning culture would have to assume that the appropriate way for humans to behave in relationship to their environment is to be proactive problem solvers and learners. If the culture is built on fatalistic assumptions of passive acceptance, learning will become more and more difficult as the rate of change in the environment increases. It is not clear how this kind of assumption works out in those cultures in which fatalistic acceptance is a central assumption. I would speculate that in those cultures a differentiation will take place between domains such as religion, in which the old assumption will hold, and business, in which new assumptions concerning active problem solving will come to coexist with the old assumptions. A good example of that kind of evolution is seen in Singapore's spectacular economic success, based on combining Asian and Western assumptions (Schein, 1996).

The learning leader must portray confidence that active problem solving leads to learning, thereby setting an appropriate example for other members of the organization. It will be more important to be committed to the learning *process* than to any particular solution to a problem. In the face of greater complexity, the leader's

dependence on others to generate solutions will increase, and we have overwhelming evidence that new solutions are more likely to be adopted if the members of the organization have been involved in the learning process. The *process* of learning must ultimately be made part of the culture, not just the solution to any given problem.

2. Commitment to Learning to Learn

The learning culture must have in its DNA a "learning gene," in the sense that members must hold the shared assumption that learning is a good thing worth investing in and that learning to learn is itself a skill to be mastered. Learning must include not only learning about changes in the external environment but also learning about internal relationships and how well the organization is adapted to the external changes. For example, one way of understanding the failure of DEC is to note that they were committed to continued technological innovation—that is, learning in the technology area—but there was very little reflection or commitment to learning how their own organization was creating destructive inter-group competition. DEC did not learn that achieving truth through debate could only work at the interindividual level. Once the debate became an intergroup debate, truth seeking was undermined by the need to protect turf and people.

The key to learning is to get feedback and to take the time to reflect, analyze, and assimilate the implications of what the feedback has communicated. A further key to learning is the ability to generate new responses; to try new ways of doing things and to obtain feedback on the results of the new behavior. This takes time, energy, and resources. A learning culture must therefore value reflection and experimentation, and must give its members the time and resources to do it.

The learning leader must both believe in the power of learning and personally display an ability to learn, by seeking and accepting feedback and by displaying flexibility of response as conditions change.

3. Positive Assumptions About Human Nature

Learning leaders must have faith in people and must believe that ultimately human nature is basically good and, in any case, malleable. The learning leader must believe that humans can and will learn if they are provided the resources and the necessary psychological safety. Learning implies some desire for survival and improvement. If leaders start with assumptions that people are basically lazy and passive, that people have no concern for organizations or causes above and beyond themselves, they will inevitably create organizations that will become self-fulfilling prophecies. Such leaders will train their employees to be lazy, self-protective, and self-seeking, and they will then cite those characteristics as proof of their original assumption about human nature. The resulting control-oriented organizations may survive and even thrive in certain kinds of stable environments, but they are certain to fail as the environments become more turbulent and as technological and global trends cause problem solving to become increasingly more complex.

Knowledge and skill are becoming more widely distributed, forcing leaders—whether they like it or not—to be more dependent on other people in their organizations. Under such circumstances a cynical attitude toward human nature is bound to create, at best, bureaucratic rigidity and, at the worst extreme, counterorganizational subgroups. In either case, the learning process will be fatally undermined.

Given this hypothesis, one might speculate about why McGregor's (1960) insight into this problem in terms of Theory X (cynical mistrust of people) and Theory Y (idealistic trust of people) still has not taken hold, more than forty years after it was first promulgated. One hypothesis is that he was proposing the more idealistic Theory Y at a time when control-oriented bureaucracies were still working fairly effectively. The real relevance of Theory Y may well be to the learning organization of the future. It is inconceivable to me how a learning-oriented leader could have anything other than Theory Y assumptions about human nature and how an organization in which knowledge and skill are widely distributed can work on any basis other than mutual trust. And this takes us all the way back to Kurt Lewin's classic studies of classrooms under autocratic or democratic leaders (1947). The autocratic classes could match and even outdo the democratic ones in performance when the teacher was present, but if the teacher left, the autocratic ones fell apart, whereas the democratic ones reorganized and continued to perform.

4. The Assumption That the Environment Can Be Dominated

A learning culture must contain in its DNA a gene that reflects the shared assumption that the environment is to some degree manageable. An organization that assumes that it must symbiotically accept its niche will have more difficulty in learning as the environment becomes more turbulent. Adaptation to a slowly changing environment is also a viable learning process, but I am assuming that the way in which the world is changing will make that less and less possible. The more turbulent the environment, the more important it will be for leaders to argue for and show that some level of control over the environment is desirable and possible.

5. Commitment to Truth Through Pragmatism and Inquiry

A learning culture must contain the shared assumption that solutions to problems derive from a deep belief in inquiry and a pragmatic search for truth. The inquiry process itself must be flexible and reflect the nature of the environmental changes encountered. What must be avoided in the learning culture is the automatic assumption that wisdom and truth reside in any one source or method.

As the problems we encounter change, so too will our learning method have to change. For some purposes we will have to rely heavily on normal science; for others, we will have to find truth in experienced practitioners because scientific proof will be impossible to obtain; for still others, we will collectively have to experiment and live with errors until a better solution is found. Knowledge and skill will be found in many forms, and what I am calling a clinical research process—in which helpers and clients work things out together—will become more and more important because no one will be expert enough to provide an answer. One might say that in the learning organization one will have to *learn how to learn*.

The toughest problem for learning leaders is to come to terms with their own lack of expertise and wisdom. Once we are in a leadership position, our own needs and the expectations of others dictate that we know the answer and be in control of the situation. Yet if we provide answers, we are creating a culture that will inevitably take a moralistic position in regard to reality and truth. The only way to build a learning culture that continues to learn is for leaders themselves to realize that there is much that they do not know and must teach others to accept that there is much that they do not know. The learning task then becomes a shared responsibility.

It is also worth noting that in many cultures, notably Western ones, the assumption that one knows and is in control is particularly associated with masculine roles. It is quite possible that women will find it easier, as leaders, to accept a whole range of methods for arriving at solutions and will therefore be more able to function in a learning role. It is also worth noting that required sabbaticals and career development systems that require cross-functional and geographic rotational assignments were probably invented to maximize the learning potential of individual leaders, while the practice of limiting the term of office of leaders was invented to maximize the organization's ability to bring in new points of view and new modes of inquiry.

I am often asked how to make someone more sensitive to culture. My short answer is "*Travel* more." It is through giving ourselves more varied experiences in more different kinds of cultures that we learn about cultural variation and develop cultural humility. The learning leader should make it a point to spend a lot of time outside his or her organization and travel to as many other cultures as is practical.

6. Orientation Toward the Future

The optimal time orientation for learning appears to be somewhere between the far future and the near future. One must think far enough ahead to be able to assess the systemic consequences of different courses of action, but one must also think in terms of the near future to assess whether or not one's solutions are working. If the environment is becoming more turbulent, the assumption that the best orientation is to live in the past or to live in the present clearly seems dysfunctional.

A similar argument can be made about assumptions about optimal units of time—should we think primarily in terms of minutes, hours, days, months, quarters, years, decades? This will, of course, depend on the task and the kind of learning that is going on, but the optimal

assumption is that one should pick medium-length time units for assessment: enough time to test whether a proposed solution is working but not so much time that one persists with a proposed solution that is clearly not working.

For any given task, the learning leader will have to make an instant diagnosis of what a medium length of time is, and that will vary from situation to situation. As the world becomes more complex we will be less and less able to rely on standard time units such as quarters or years. Because time has so many symbolic meanings and is so central to our daily conduct, the learning leader must be very conscious of her or his own assumptions about time and make these explicit for others.

7. Commitment to Full and Open Task Relevant Communication

The learning culture must be built on the assumption that communication and information are central to organizational well-being and must therefore create a multichannel communication system that allows everyone to connect to everyone else. This does not mean that all channels will be used or that any given channel will be used for all things. What it does mean is that anyone must be able to communicate with anyone else and that everyone assumes that telling the truth as best one can is positive and desirable.

This principle of openness does not mean that one suspends all the cultural rules pertaining to face and adopts a definition of openness equivalent to the proverbial "letting it all hang out"—there is ample evidence that such interpersonal openness can create severe problems across hierarchical boundaries and in intercultural settings. It means, rather, that one must become sensitive to *task-relevant information* and be as open as possible in sharing that. One of the important roles for the learning leader will be to specify, in terms of any given task, what the minimum communication system must be and what kind of information is critical to effective problem solving and learning. More information is not necessarily a good thing, because the more we know the more questions we develop about what we don't know. However, if a fully connected network ends up overloading everyone with information, certain channels can be voluntarily closed on a temporary basis. But the assumption that it is, in principle, possible and all right for anyone in the system to communicate with anyone else must remain in place.

A fully connected network can only work if high trust or at least high functional familiarity exists among all the participants. High trust is partly a function of leader assumptions that people can be trusted and have constructive intent. High functional familiarity is a function of the leader bringing interdependent people and units together often enough to allow them to become familiar with each other.

Creating an effective communication structure has implications for assumptions about space. The arrangement most likely to support learning is probably a flexible space structure that can be designed and redesigned as communication requirements change (Steele, 1973, 1986).

8. Commitment to Diversity

The more turbulent the environment, the more likely it is that the more diverse organization will have the resources to cope with unpredicted events. Therefore, the learning leader should stimulate diversity and promulgate the assumption that diversity is desirable at the individual and subgroup levels. Such diversity will inevitably create subcultures, and those subcultures will eventually be a necessary resource for learning and innovation.

For diversity to be a resource, however, the subcultures must be connected and must learn to value each other enough to learn something of each other's culture and language. A central task for the learning leader, then, is to ensure good cross-cultural communication and understanding throughout the organization. Creating diversity does not mean letting diverse parts of the system run on their own without coordination. Laissez-faire leadership does not work, because it is in the nature of subgroups and subcultures to protect their own interests. To optimize diversity therefore requires some higher-order coordination mechanisms and mutual cultural understanding.

9. Commitment to Systemic Thinking

As the world becomes more complex and interdependent, the ability to think systemically, to analyze fields of forces and understand their joint causal effects on each other, and to abandon simple linear causal logic in favor of complex mental models will become more critical to learning. There are many variations of systemic thinking, such as "systems thinking" as promulgated by Senge (1990) and Sterman (2000), systemic thinking in biology, systemic thinking in family therapy, and so on. The learning leader must believe that the world is intrinsically complex, nonlinear, interconnected, and overdetermined in the sense that most things are multiply caused.

10. Commitment to Cultural Analysis for Understanding and Improving the World

The learning culture must understand the concept of culture and the learning leader must be willing and able to work with culture, as will be illustrated in the following case example.

CASE EXAMPLE: SAAB COMBITECH

An excellent example of cultural intervention in the service of organizational learning is the 1997 seminar run by Saab Combitech, the R&D arm of the Saab company and its leader Per Risberg. Combitech consisted of seven separate research units working with different technologies such as developing complex training systems, military hardware, marine electronics, aerospace technology, and space exploration technology. These units had created their own subcultures based on their

(Continued)

(Continued)

tasks, technologies and the occupations of their employees. The units were friendly to each other, but did not understand each other well enough to discover how they could all improve if they shared more of their technological and organizational insights.

Risberg recruited me to help him design an intervention that would teach the hundred or so members of these groups about culture and help them to become more familiar with each other's cultures. The groups were required to read portions of my culture book before the seminar and to write me a letter in which they were to compare themselves to DEC and Ciba-Geigy and write out some observations on their own culture.

On the first day I introduced the culture model, gave them more examples, and reviewed their self-analyses. We then had each group volunteer two of its members to become "anthropologists" who would go into one other group to learn what its culture was like. I provided some dimensions of the sort covered in Chapters Five through Nine and gave them several hours to visit, observe, and inquire about the group's artifacts, espoused values, and tacit assumptions. On the second day these observations were reported in a plenary session so that each group heard how it was perceived by its two anthropologists and we all became highly aware of both the communality and diversity of assumptions across the groups.

The third day was devoted to a systematic exploration, in the plenary session, of the ways in which the research units were interdependent and how they could help each other by sharing more of their technology and know-how. That evening Risberg hosted the attendees and their spouses at a final banquet, which began with formal cocktails and a sit-down dinner at long tables. It was very awkward because many of the Combitech people did not know each other very well; the spouses were uncomfortable and we all chafed at the prospect of a long dull evening.

However, after the first course Risberg asked us all to go to our rooms and follow instructions that we would find there. We found a box with some new clothing—tie-dyed shirts, loose pants, slippers, and headbands! We were to put on these clothes and report to the parking lot, where we found a huge audio setup. We were then instructed to line up for dance lessons provided by an instructor—several simple steps that all of us could master. The leader then played some rhythmic music and we practiced our steps until we were able to really do the dance and enjoy it. We could feel ourselves relaxing and getting to know each other at this more primitive level, so that by the time we had danced for twenty minutes and were instructed to go back into dinner, we were all chatting amicably.

Dinner was a big Indian buffet that required much moving around and further loosening up. By the end of the evening there was laughter, backslapping, exchanges of cards, and commitments to get together in the future. Risberg had created a "cultural" event that reinforced beautifully his intention of having his research groups get to know each other and work more with each other. Not only did the group learn about culture as a concept, but the design of the workshop used culture creatively by having the groups play at being "anthropologists."

Having us all change into informal "hippie clothes" and dance together was similar in intent to what Ciba-Geigy did when, during our annual meeting, we would all have to shoot crossbows or engage in some other sport that brought us all down to the same level. Risberg had realized that even though his organization had existed for many years, the members were not well acquainted with each other and needed some event to build commonality.

How Relevant Are Other Dimensions?

Many other dimensions could be analyzed from the point of view of what would aid or hinder learning. With respect to most of those, the conclusions are not clear. For example, with respect to the dimension of individualism and groupism it would appear that both kinds of systems can learn, but perhaps the best prescription for learning is to accept the notion that every system has both elements in it, and the learning culture will be the one that optimizes individual competition and collaborative teamwork, depending on the task to be accomplished. A similar argument can be made around the dimension of task versus relationship orientation. An optimal learning system would balance these as required by the task rather than opting for either extreme.

With respect to degree of hierarchy, autocracy, paternalism, and participation, it is again a matter of what kind of task, what kind of learning is required, and the particular circumstances. In the Alpha Power example we saw that knowledge of environmental hazards and how to deal with them was initially learned in a very autocratic, top-down training program, but as experience in the field accumulated, the learning process has shifted to local innovation, which is then circulated to the rest of the organization. Innovative solutions to environmental, health, and safety issues are captured in videotapes and circulated throughout the organization. Monthly award lunches are held, at which successful teams meet with senior management and each other to share "how they did it" and to communicate solutions to other teams.

In the end we have to recognize that even the concept of *learning* is heavily colored by cultural assumptions and that learning can mean very different things in different cultures and subcultures. The dimensions I listed above reflect only my own cultural understanding and should therefore be taken only as a first approximation of what a learning culture should emphasize.

As we do more research at the national, organizational, and subgroup levels, other dimensions will surface. It does seem obvious, however, that some conceptual clarity about how we get organizations to learn and—to learn faster—is becoming a priority issue, and that we cannot get such clarity without tackling the difficult conceptual problem of how a culture itself can be a perpetual learning system.

To summarize, the learning culture must assume that:

- The world can be managed
- It is appropriate for humans to be proactive problem solvers
- Reality and truth must be pragmatically discovered
- Human nature is basically good and in any case mutable
- The best kind of time horizon is somewhere between far and near future
- The best kinds of units of time are medium-length ones
- Accurate and relevant information must be capable of flowing freely in a fully connected network
- Diverse but connected units are desirable

And finally, the learning culture must assume that the world is intrinsically a complex field of interconnected forces in which multiple causation and overdetermination are more likely than linear or simple causes.

The role of learning-oriented leadership in a turbulent world, then, is to promote these kinds of assumptions. Leaders themselves must first hold such assumptions, become learners themselves, and then be able to recognize and systematically reward behavior based on those assumptions in others.

Programs such as total quality management can be assessed in terms of whether or not they operate on the assumptions outlined above. The overt and espoused values that are stated for such solutions often hide assumptions that are not, in fact, favorable to the kind of learning I have described. If leaders are not aware of the cultural underpinnings of what they are doing or the assumptions of the group on which they are imposing new solutions, they are likely to fail. Learning leaders must be careful to look inside themselves to locate their own mental models and assumptions before they leap into action.

The Role of the Learning Leader in Different Organizational Situations

Having described the generic characteristics of a learning culture and the implications in general for the learning leader, I now turn to some additional factors that affect the different stages of organizational evolution. The learning dilemma will be different at different cultural stages.

Leadership in Culture Creation

In a growing organization, leaders externalize their own assumptions and embed them gradually and consistently in the mission, goals, structures, and working procedures of the group. Whether we call these basic assumptions the guiding beliefs, the theories-in-use, the mental models, the basic principles, or the guiding visions on which founders operate, there is little question that they become major elements of the emerging culture of the organization.

In a rapidly changing world, the learning leader/ founder must not only have vision, but also be able both to impose it and to evolve it further as external circumstances change. Inasmuch as the new members of an organization arrive with prior organizational and cultural experiences, a common set of assumptions can be forged only by clear and consistent messages as the group encounters and survives its own crises. The culture creation leader therefore needs persistence and patience, yet as a learner must be flexible and ready to change.

As groups and organizations develop, certain key emotional issues arise, concerning dependence on the leader, peer relationships, and how to work effectively. At each of these stages of group development, leadership is needed to help the group identify the issues and deal with them. During these stages leaders often have to absorb and contain the anxiety that is unleashed when things do not work as they should (Hirschhorn, 1988; Schein, 1983, Frost, 2003). The leader may not have the answer, but he or she must provide temporary stability and emotional reassurance while the answer is being worked out. This anxiety-containing function is especially relevant during periods of learning, when old habits and ways must be given up before new ones are learned. And if the world is becoming more changeable, such anxiety may be perpetual, requiring of the learning leader a perpetual supportive role.

This anxiety-containing function is especially relevant in entrepreneurs and founders of companies. The traumas of growth appear to be so constant and so powerful that unless a strong leader plays the role of anxiety- and risk-absorber, the group cannot get through its early stages of growth and fails. It helps to be in an ownership position, since everyone then realizes that the founder is in fact taking a greater personal financial risk, but ownership does not automatically create the ability to absorb anxiety. As Frost (2003) has shown so cogently, all organizations create toxins as part of their normal functions, so leaders must provide or create the toxin absorption and elimination function if their organizations are to be capable of learning.

The difficult learning agenda for founder leaders is how to be simultaneously clear and strong in articulating their vision and open to change as that very vision becomes maladaptive in a turbulent environment.

Leadership at Organizational Midlife

Once the organization develops a substantial history of its own, its culture becomes more of a cause than an effect. The culture now influences the strategy, the structure, the procedures, and the ways in which the group members will relate to each other. Culture becomes a powerful influence on members' perceiving, thinking, and feeling, and these predispositions, along with situational factors, will influence the members' behavior. Because it serves an important anxiety-reducing function, culture will be clung to even if it becomes dysfunctional in relationship to environmental opportunities and constraints.

Midlife organizations show two basically different patterns, however. Some, under the influence of one or more generations of leaders, develop a highly integrated culture even though they have become large and diversified; others allow growth and diversification in cultural assumptions as well and therefore can be described as culturally diverse with respect to their business, functional, geographical, and even hierarchical subunits. How leaders manage culture at this stage of organizational evolution depends on which pattern they perceive and which pattern they decide is best for the future.

Leaders at this stage need, above all, the insight and skill to help the organization evolve into whatever will make it most effective in the future. In some instances this may mean increasing cultural diversity, allowing some of the uniformity that may have been built up in the growth stage to erode; in other instances it may mean pulling together a culturally diverse set of organizational units and attempting to impose new common assumptions on them. In either case the leader needs to (1) be able to analyze the culture in sufficient detail to know which cultural assumptions can aid and which ones will hinder the fulfillment of the organizational mission and (2) have the intervention skills to make desired changes happen.

Most of the prescriptive analyses of how to bring organizations through this period emphasize that the leader must have certain insights, clear vision, and the skills to articulate, communicate, and implement the vision, but they say nothing about how a given organization can find and install such a leader. In U.S. organizations in particular, the outside board members probably play a critical role in this process, but if the organization has had a strong founding culture, its board may be composed exclusively of people who share the founder's vision. Consequently, real changes in direction may not become possible until the organization gets into serious survival difficulties and begins to search for a person with different assumptions to lead it.

Leadership in Mature and Declining Organizations

In the mature organization, if it has developed a strong unifying culture, that culture now defines even what is to be thought of as leadership, what is heroic or sinful behavior, and how authority and power are to be allocated and managed. Thus, what leadership has created now either blindly perpetuates itself or creates new definitions of leadership, which may not even include the kinds of entrepreneurial assumptions that started the organization in the first place. The first problem of the mature and possibly declining organization, then, is to find a process to empower a potential leader who may have enough insight and power to overcome some of the constraining cultural assumptions.

Leaders capable of such managed culture change can come from inside the organization, if they have acquired objectivity and insight into elements of the culture. However, the formally designated senior managers of a given organization may not be willing or able to provide such culture change leadership. If a leader is imposed from the outside, he or she must have the skill to diagnose accurately what the culture of the organization is, which elements are well adapted and which are problematic for future adaptation, and how to change that which needs changing.

Conceived of in this way, leadership is, first of all, the capacity to surmount one's own organizational culture, to be able to perceive and think about ways of doing things that are different from what the current assumptions imply. To fulfill this role adequately, learning leaders therefore must be somewhat marginal and somewhat embedded in the organization's external environment. At the same time, learning leaders must be well connected to those parts of the organization that are themselves well connected to the environment—the sales organization, purchasing, marketing, public relations, legal, finance, and R&D. Learning leaders must be able to listen to disconfirming information coming from these sources and to assess the implications for the future of the organization. Only when they truly understand what is happening and what will be required in the way of organizational change can they begin to take action in starting a learning process.

Much has been said of the need for vision in leaders, but too little has been said of their need to listen, to absorb, to search the environment for trends, and to build the organization's capacity to learn. It is especially at the strategic level that the ability to see and acknowledge the full complexity of problems becomes critical. The ability to acknowledge complexity may also imply the willingness and emotional strength to admit uncertainty and to embrace experimentation and possible errors as the only way to learn (Michael, 1985). In our obsession with leadership vision, we may have made it difficult for the learning leader to admit that his or her vision is not clear and that the whole organization together will have to learn. And, as I have repeatedly argued, vision only helps when the organization has already been disconfirmed and members feel anxious and in need of a solution. Much of what the learning leader must do occurs before vision even becomes relevant.

Leadership and Culture in Mergers and Acquisitions

When the management of a company decides to merge with or acquire another company, it usually makes careful checks of the financial strength, market position, management strength, and various other concrete aspects pertaining to the health of the other company. Rarely checked, however, are those aspects that might be considered cultural: the philosophy or style of the company, its technological origins, its structure, and its ways of operating—all of which may provide clues as to its basic assumptions about its mission and its future. Yet if culture determines and limits strategy, a cultural mismatch in an acquisition or merger is as great a risk as a financial, product, or market mismatch (Buono and Bowditch, 1989; COS, 1990; McManus and Hergert, 1988).

For example, at one point in its history General Foods (GF) purchased Burger Chef, a successful chain of hamburger restaurants; but despite ten years of concerted effort, GF could not make the acquisition profitable. First of all, GF did not anticipate that many of the best Burger Chef managers would leave because they did not like the GF philosophy. Then, instead of hiring new managers with experience in the fast-food business, GF assigned some of its own managers to run the new business. This was its second mistake, since these managers did not understand the technology of the fast-food business and hence were unable to utilize many of the marketing techniques that had proved effective in the parent company. Third, GF imposed many of the control systems and procedures that had historically proved useful for it; these drove the chain's operating costs up too high. The parent company's managers found that they could never completely understand franchise operations and hence could not get a feel for what it would take to run that kind of business profitably. Eventually GF sold Burger Chef, having lost many millions of dollars over the course of a decade.

Another example highlights the clash of two sets of assumptions about authority. A first-generation company, run by a founder who injected strong beliefs that one succeeds by stimulating initiative and egalitarianism, was bought by another first-generation company, which was run by a strong autocratic entrepreneur who had trained his employees to be highly disciplined and formal. The purchasing company wanted and needed the new managerial talent it acquired, but within one year of the purchase most of the best managers from the acquired company had left because they could not adapt to the formal autocratic style of the parent company. The autocratic entrepreneur could not understand why this had happened and had no sensitivity to the cultural differences between the two companies.

What is striking in both of these cases is the acquiring company's lack of insight into its own organizational culture; its own unconscious assumptions about how a business should be run.

In a third example, we see a case of cultural misdiagnosis. A U.S. company realized that it was about to be acquired by a larger British firm. The company conducted an internal audit of its own culture and concluded that being taken over by the British company would be highly unpalatable. It therefore instituted a set of procedures that made their company unattractive (such as poison pills) and waited for a situation that looked more promising. A French company came onto the scene as a potential buyer; it was perceived to be a much better cultural match, so the company allowed itself to be bought. Six months later the French parent sent over a management team that decimated the U.S. company and imposed all kinds of processes that were much less compatible than anything the U.S. company had imagined. But it was too late.

After mergers, acquisitions, or diversifications have run into trouble, managers frequently say that cultural incompatibilities were at the root of it, but somehow these factors rarely get taken into account during the initial decision-making process. What then is the role of leadership in these situations? Four critical tasks can be identified:

1. Leaders must understand their own culture well enough to be able to detect potential incompatibilities with the culture of the other organization.

2. Leaders must be able to decipher the other culture; to engage in the kinds of activities that will reveal to them and to the other organization what some of its assumptions are.

3. Leaders must be able to articulate the potential synergies or incompatibilities in such a way that

others involved in the decision process can understand and deal with the cultural realities.

4. If the leader is not the CEO, he or she must be able to convince the CEO or the executive team to take the cultural issues seriously.

Members of planning groups or acquisition teams often develop the cross-cultural insights necessary to make good decisions about mergers and acquisitions, but lack the skills to convince their own senior managers to take the culture issues seriously. Or, alternatively, they get caught up in political processes that prevent the cultural realities from being attended to until after the key decisions have been made. In any case, cultural diagnosis based on marginality and the ability to surmount one's own culture again surfaces as the critical characteristic of learning leaders.

Leadership and Culture in Partnerships, Joint Ventures, and Strategic Alliances

Joint ventures and strategic alliances require cultural analysis even more than mergers and acquisitions, because in today's rapidly globalizing world, cross-national boundaries are increasingly involved. Deciphering differences between two companies in the same national culture is not as difficult as deciphering both national and company differences when one engages in a partnership or joint venture across national boundaries (Salk, 1997). One of the special difficulties is determining whether the differences that are perceived are attributable to national or organizational cultures, yet it is important to make this determination because one must assume that the likelihood of changing national characteristics is very low.

The role of learning leadership in these situations is much the same as in mergers and acquisitions, except that leaders must even surmount their national identities. For example, Essochem Europe, the European subsidiary of Exxon, could never find local managers to put on their board because they were all "too emotional." They never came to terms with their own stereotype of managers as intrinsically unemotional sorts of people,

and never realized or accepted that this was based on their U.S. assumptions. Many organizations make international assignments a requirement for a developing general manager, with the explicit notion that such experiences is essential if potential leaders with broader outlooks are to surface. In other words, the learning leader must become marginal not only with respect to the organizational culture, but even with respect to national and ethnic culture.

Implications for the Selection and Development of Leaders

To summarize at this point, our analysis of organizational culture makes it clear that leadership is intertwined with culture formation, evolution, transformation, and destruction. Culture is created in the first instance by the actions of leaders; culture also is embedded and strengthened by leaders. When culture becomes dysfunctional, leadership is needed to help the group unlearn some of its cultural assumptions and learn new assumptions. Such transformations sometimes require what amounts to conscious and deliberate destruction of cultural elements, which in turn requires the ability to surmount one's own taken-for-granted assumptions, to see what is needed to ensure the health and survival of the group, and to make things happen that enable the group to evolve toward new cultural assumptions. Without leadership in this sense, groups would not be able to adapt to changing environmental conditions. What, then, is really needed to be a leader in this sense?

1. Perception and Insight

First, the leader must be able to perceive the problem, to have insight into the culture and its dysfunctional elements. Such boundary-spanning perception can be difficult because it requires one to see one's own weaknesses, to perceive that one's own defenses not only help in managing anxiety but can also hinder one's efforts to be effective. Successful architects of change must have a high degree of objectivity about themselves and their own organizations; such objectivity results from spending portions of their careers in diverse settings that permit them to compare and contrast different cultures. In the development of future leaders, many organizations are therefore emphasizing international experience.

Individuals often are aided in becoming objective about themselves through counseling and psychotherapy. One might conjecture that leaders could benefit from comparable processes, such as training and development programs that emphasize experiential learning and self-assessment. From this perspective one should also note that one of the most important functions of outside consultants or board members is to provide the kind of counseling that produces cultural insight. It is therefore far more important for the consultant to help the leader figure himself or herself out than to provide recommendations on what the organization should do. The consultant also can serve as a "cultural therapist," helping the leader figure out what the culture is and which parts of it are more or less adaptive.

To become learning oriented, leaders also need to acknowledge their own limitations. As the world becomes more turbulent, it will be more and more difficult to develop clear visions. Instead, leaders will have to admit to not knowing the answer, to admit to not being in control, to embrace trial-and-error learning, and to become supportive of the learning efforts of others.

2. Motivation

Leadership requires not only insight into the dynamics of the culture but also the motivation and skill to intervene in one's own cultural process. To change any elements of the culture, leaders must be willing to unfreeze their own organization. Unfreezing requires disconfirmation, a process that is inevitably painful for many. The leader must find a way to say to his or her own organization that things are not all right and must, if necessary, enlist the aid of outsiders in getting this message across. Such willingness requires a great ability to be concerned for the organization above and beyond the self, to communicate dedication or commitment to the group above and beyond self-interest.

If the boundaries of organizations become looser, a further motivational issue arises in that it is less and less clear where a leader's ultimate loyalty should

lie—should it be with the organization, the industry, the country, or some broader professional community whose ultimate responsibility is to the globe and to humanity in some broader sense?

3. Emotional Strength

Unfreezing an organization requires the creation of psychological safety, which means that the leader must have the emotional strength to absorb much of the anxiety that change brings with it as well as the ability to remain supportive to the organization through the transition phase, even if group members become angry and obstructive. The leader is likely to be the target of anger and criticism because, by definition, he or she must challenge some of what the group has taken for granted. This may involve such powerful symbolic acts as closing down a division in the company that was the original source of the company's growth and the basis of many employees' pride and identity. It may involve laying off or retiring loyal, dedicated employees and old friends. Worst of all, it may involve the message that some of the founder's most cherished assumptions are wrong in the contemporary context. It is here that dedication and commitment are especially needed to demonstrate to the organization that the leader genuinely cares about the welfare of the total organization even as parts of it come under challenge. The learning leader must remember that giving up a cultural element requires one to take some risk—the risk that one will be very anxious and, in the end, worse off, yet must have the strength to push into this unknown territory.

4. Ability to Change the Cultural Assumptions

If an assumption is to be given up, it must be replaced or redefined in another form, and it is the burden of learning leadership to make that happen. In other words, leaders must have the ability to induce "cognitive redefinition" by articulating and selling new visions and concepts or creating the conditions for others to find these new concepts. They must be able to bring to the surface, review, and change some of the group's basic assumptions. At Ciba-Geigy this process had only begun in the redirection project described in Chapter Eighteen. Many managers were beginning to doubt that the organization's commitment to science-based technical products could sustain the company in the long run. But so far no strong leader had emerged to convince the organization that consumer goods marketed through strong customer-oriented organizations could be a source of pride for the company.

5. Ability to Create Involvement and Participation

A paradox of learning leadership is that the leader must be able not only to lead but also to listen, to involve the group in achieving its own insights into its cultural dilemmas, and to be genuinely participative in his or her approach to learning and change. The leaders of social, religious, or political movements can rely on personal charisma and let the followers do what they will. But in an organization, the leader has to work with the group that exists at the moment, because he or she is dependent on the people to carry out the organization's mission. The leader must recognize that, in the end, cognitive redefinition must occur inside the heads of many members of the organization, and that will happen only if they are actively involved in the process. The whole organization must achieve some degree of insight and develop motivation to change before any real change will occur—and the leader must create this involvement.

The ability to involve others and to listen to them also protects leaders from attempting to change things that should not be changed. When leaders are brought in from the outside this becomes critical, because some of the assumptions operating in the organization may not fit the leader's own assumptions yet may still be critical to the success of the organization.

Summary and Conclusions

I have tried to articulate in this chapter the characteristics of a *learning culture* and the implications for leadership of the realities of creating such a culture in an increasingly turbulent and unpredictable world. I reviewed the culture change issues at the major stages of

organizational development and focused on the leadership role in developing strategy, in mergers and acquisitions, and in joint ventures and strategic alliances.

It seems clear that the leader of the future must be a perpetual learner, which will require (1) new levels of perception and insight into the realities of the world and into him- or herself; (2) extraordinary levels of motivation to go through the inevitable pain of learning and change, especially in a world with looser boundaries in which one's own loyalties become more and more difficult to define; (3) the emotional strength to manage one's own and others' anxiety as learning and change become more and more a way of life; (4) new skills in analyzing and changing cultural assumptions; and (5) the willingness and ability to involve others and elicit their participation.

Learning and change cannot be imposed on people. Their involvement and participation is needed in diagnosing what is going on, in figuring out what to do, and in actually bringing about learning and change. The more turbulent, ambiguous, and out of control the world becomes, the more the learning process must be shared by all the members of the social unit doing the learning.

In the end, we must give organizational culture its due. Can we recognize—as individual members of organizations and occupations, as managers, as teachers and researchers, and sometimes as leaders—how deeply our own perceptions, thoughts, and feelings are culturally determined? Ultimately, we cannot achieve the cultural humility that is required to live in a turbulent culturally diverse world unless we can see cultural assumptions within ourselves. In the end, cultural understanding and cultural learning starts with self-insight.

References

Buono, A. F., & Bowditch, J. L. (1989). *The human side of mergers* and acquisitions. San Francisco: Jossey-Bass.

COS (Centre for Organizational Studies) (1990). *Mergers and acquisitions: Organizational and cultural issues.* Barcelona, Spain: COS/Foundation Jose M. de Anzizu.

Frost, P. J. (2003). *Toxic emotions at work.* Boston: Harvard Business School Press.

Global Business Network (2002). *What's next? Exploring the new terrain for business.* Cambridge, MA: Perseus Books.

Hesselbein, F., Goldsmith, M., & Somerville, I. (Eds.). (1999). *Leading beyond the walls.* San Francisco, CA: Jossey-Bass.

Hirschhorn, L. (1988). *The workplace within: Psychodynamics of organizational life.* Cambridge, MA: MIT Press.

Lewin, K. (1947). Group decision and social change. In T. N. Newcomb & E. L. Hartley (Eds.), *Readings in social psychology.* New York: Holt, Rinehart and Winston.

Malone, T., et al. (1987). Electronic markets and electronic hierarchies. *Communications of the ACM,* 30, 484–497.

McGregor, D. M. (1960). *The human side of enterprise.* New York; McGraw-Hill.

McManus, M. L., & Hergert, M. L. (1988). *Surviving merger and acquisition.* Glenview, IL: Scott Foresman.

Michael, D. N. (1985). *On learning to plan—and planning to learn.* San Francisco, CA: Jossey-Bass.

Michael, D. N. (1991). Leadership's shadow: The dilemma of denial. *Futures,* Jan./Feb., 69–79.

Salk, J. (1997). Partners and other strangers. *International Studies of Management and Organization,* 26(4), 48–72.

Schein, E. H. (1983). The role of the founder in creating organizational culture. *Organizational Dynamics,* Summer, 13 28.

Schein, E. H. (1990). Innovative cultures and adaptive organizations. *Sri Lanka journal of Development Administration,* 7(2), 9–39.

Schein, E. H. (1996). *Strategic pragmatism: The culture of Singapore's Economic Development* Board. Cambridge, MA: MIT Press.

Schwartz, P. (2003). *Inevitable surprises.* New York: Gotham Books.

Senge, P. M. (1990). *The fifth discipline.* New York: Doubleday Currency.

Steele, F. I. (1973). *Physical settings and organization development.* Reading, MA: Addison-Wesley.

Steele, F. I. (1986). *Making and managing high-quality workplaces.* New York: Teachers College Press.

Sterman, J. D. (2000). *Business dynamics: Systems thinking and modeling for a complex world.* New York: McGraw-Hill/Irwin.

CHAPTER 26

Moral Leadership and Business Ethics

Al Gini

Loyola University Chicago

Those who really deserve praise are the people who, while human enough to enjoy power nevertheless pay more attention to justice than they are compelled to do by their situation.

—Thucydides

onventional wisdom has it that two of the most glaring examples of academic oxymorons are the terms "business ethics" and "moral leadership." Neither term carries credibility in popular culture and when conjoined constitutes a "null-set" rather than just a simple contradiction in terms. The reason for this is definitional, but only in part. More significant is that we have so few models of businesses and leaders operating on ethical principles. Simply put, the cliché persists because of the dearth of evidence to the contrary. At best, both these terms remain in the lexicon as wished-for ideals rather than actual states of being.

A *New York Times/CBS News Poll* conducted in 1985 revealed that 55% of the American public believe that the vast majority of corporate executives are dishonest, and 59% think that executive white-collar crime occurs on a regular basis. A 1987 *Wall Street Journal* article noted that one-fourth of the 671 executives surveyed by a leading research firm believed that ethics can impede a successful career, and that over one-half of the executives they knew bent the rules to get ahead.[1] Most recently, a 1990 national survey published by Prentice Hall concluded that the standards of ethical practice and moral leadership of business leaders merit at best a C grade. Sixty-eight percent of those surveyed believed

---

that the unethical behavior of executives is the primary cause of the decline in business standards, productivity, and success. The survey further suggested that because of the perceived low ethical standards of the executive class, workers feel justified in responding in kind— through absenteeism, petty theft, indifference, and a generally poor performance on the job. Many workers openly admitted that they spend more than 20% (eight hours a week) of their time at work totally goofing off. Almost half of those surveyed admitted to chronic malingering on a regular basis. One in six of the workers surveyed said that he or she drank or used drugs on the job. Three out of four workers reported that their primary reason for working was "to keep the wolf from the door"; only one in four claimed to give his or her "best effort" to the job. The survey concluded that the standard equation of the American workplace is a simple one: American workers are as ethical/dutiful in doing their jobs as their bosses and companies are perceived to be ethical/dutiful in leading and directing them.[2]

Sadly, ample evidence suggests that this mutually reinforcing thesis often starts long before one enters the confines of the workplace. Recently one of the teacher/coaches in the Chicago public school system not only encouraged his high school students to cheat in the city-wide Academic Decathlon contest, he fed them the answers. According to the 18-year-old student captain of the team: "The coach gave us the answer key. . . . He told us everybody cheats, that's the way the world works and we were fools to just play by the rules."[3] Unfortunately, just as workers often mirror the standards set by their bosses, these students followed the guidance of their teacher.

As a student of business ethics, I am convinced that without the continuous commitment, enforcement, and modeling of leadership, standards of business ethics cannot and will not be achieved in any organization. The ethics of leadership—whether they be good or bad, positive or negative—affect the ethos of the workplace and thereby help to form the ethical choices and decisions of the workers in the workplace. Leaders help to set the tone, develop the vision, and shape the behavior of all those involved in organizational life. The critical point to understand here is that, like it or not, business and politics serve as the metronome for our society. And the meter and behavior established by leaders set the patterns and establish the models for our behavior as individuals and as a group. Although the terms

"business ethics" and "moral leadership" are technically distinguishable, in fact, they are inseparable components in the life of every organization.

The fundamental principle that underlies my thesis regarding leadership and ethical conduct is age old. In his *Nichomachean Ethics,* Aristotle suggested that morality cannot be learned simply by reading a treatise on virtue. The spirit of morality, said Aristotle, is awakened in the individual only through the witness and conduct of a moral person. The principle of the "witness of another," or what we now refer to as "patterning," "role modeling," or "mentoring," is predicated on a four-step process, three of which follow: (1) As communal creatures, we learn to conduct ourselves primarily through the actions of significant others; (2) when the behavior of others is repeated often enough and proves to be peer-group positive, we emulate these actions; (3) if and when our actions are in turn reinforced by others, they become acquired characteristics or behavioral habits.

According to B. F. Skinner, the process is now complete. In affecting the actions of individuals through modeling and reinforcement, the mentor in question (in Skinnerean terms, "the controller of the environmental stimuli") has succeeded in reproducing the type of behavior sought after or desired. For Skinner the primary goal of the process need not take into consideration either the value or worth of the action or the interests or intent of the reinforced or operant-conditioned actor. From Skinner's psychological perspective, the bottom line is simply the response evoked.[4] From a philosophical perspective, however, even role modeling that produces a positive or beneficial action does not fulfill the basic requirements of the ethical enterprise at either the descriptive or normative level. Modeling, emulation, habit, results—whether positive or negative—are neither the sufficient nor the final goal. The fourth and final step in the process must include reflection, evaluation, choice, and conscious intent on the part of the actor, the because ethics is always "an inside-out proposition" involving free will.[5]

John Dewey argued that at the precritical, prerational, preautonomous level, morality starts as a set of culturally defined goals and rules which are external to the individual and are imposed or inculcated as habits. But real ethical thinking, said Dewey, begins at the evaluative period of our lives, when, as independent agents, we freely decide to accept, embrace, modify, or deny these rules.

Dewey maintained that every serious ethical system rejects the notion that one's standard of conduct should simply and uncritically be an acceptance of the rules of the culture we happen to live in. Even when custom, habit, convention, public opinion, or law are correct in their mandates, to embrace them without critical reflection does not constitute a complete and formal ethical act and might be better labeled "ethical happenstance" or "ethics by virtue of circumstantial accident." According to Dewey, ethics is essentially "reflective conduct," and he believed that the distinction between custom and reflective morality is clearly marked. The former places the standard and rules of conduct solely on habit; the latter appeals to reason and choice. The distinction is as important as it is definite, for it shifts the center of gravity in morality. For Dewey, ethics is a two-part process: it is never enough simply to do the right thing.[6]

In claiming that workers/followers derive their models for ethical conduct from the witness of leaders, I am in no way denying that workers/followers share responsibility for the overall conduct and culture of an organization. The burden of this chapter is not to exonerate the culpability of workers, but rather to explain the process involved: the witness of leaders both communicates the ethics of our institutions and establishes the desired standards and expectations leaders want and often demand from their fellow workers and followers. Although it would be naive to assert that employees simply and unreflectively absorb the manners and mores of the workplace, it would be equally naive to suggest that they are unaffected by the modeling and standards of their respective places of employment. Work is how we spend our lives, and the lessons we learn there, good or bad, play a part in the development of our moral perspective and the manner in which we formulate and adjudicate ethical choices. As a business ethicist I believe that without the active intervention of effective moral leadership, we are doomed to forever wage a rearguard action. Students of organizational development are never really surprised when poorly managed, badly led businesses wind up doing unethical things.

Ethics and Business

Jean-Paul Sartre argued that, like it or not, we are *by definition* moral creatures because our collective existence

"condemns" us continuously to make choices about "what we ought to do" in regard to others.[7] Ethics is primarily a communal, collective enterprise, not a solitary one. It is the study of our web of relationships with others. When Robinson Crusoe found himself marooned and alone on a tiny Pacific atoll, all things were possible. But when Friday appeared and they discovered pirates burying treasure on the beach, Crusoe was then involved in the universe of others, an ethical universe. As a communal exercise, ethics is the attempt to work out the rights and obligations we have and share with others. What is mine? What do I owe you?

According to John Rawls, given the presence of others and our need of these others both to survive and to thrive, ethics is elementally the pursuit of justice, fair play, and equity. For Rawls, building on the cliché that "ethics is how we decide to behave when we decide we belong together," the study of ethics has to do with developing standards for judging the conduct of one party whose behavior affects another. Minimally, "good behavior" intends no harm and respects the rights of all affected, and "bad behavior" is willfully or negligently trampling on the rights and interests of others.[8] Ethics, then, tries to find a way to protect one person's individual rights and needs against and alongside the rights and needs of others. Of course, the paradox and central tension of ethics lie in the fact that while we are by nature communal and in need of others, at the same time we are by disposition more or less egocentric and self-serving.[9]

If ethics is a part of life, so too are work, labor, business. Work is not something detached from the rest of human life, but, rather, "man is born to labor, as a bird to fly."[10] What are work and business about? Earning a living? Yes. Producing a product or service? Sure. Making money or profit? Absolutely. In fact, most ethicists argue that business has a moral obligation to make a profit. But business is also about people—the people you work for and work with. Business is an interdependent, intertwined, symbiotic relationship. Life, labor, and business are all of a piece. They should not be seen as separate "games" played by different "rules." The enterprise of business is not distinct from the enterprise of life and living because they share the same bottom line—people. Therefore, as in the rest of life, business is required to ask the question, What ought to be done in regard to others?

While no one that I am aware of would argue seriously against the notion of ethics in our private lives, many would have it that ethics and business don't or can't mix. That is, many people believe that "business is business," and that the stakes and standards involved in business are simply different from, more important than and, perhaps, even antithetical to the principles and practices of ethics. Ethics is something we preach and practice at home in our private lives, but not at work. After all, it could cost us prestige, position, profits, and success.

Theologian Matthew Fox maintains that we lead schizophrenic lives because we either choose or are forced to abandon our personal beliefs and convictions "at the door" when we enter the workplace. The "destructive dualism" of the workplace, says Fox, separates our lives from our livelihood, our personal values from our work values, our personal needs from the needs of the community. Money becomes the sole reason for work, and success becomes the excuse we use to justify the immoral consequences of our behavior.[11] This "dualism" produces and perpetuates the kind of "occupational schizophrenia" recently articulated by nationally known jurist Alan Dershowitz: "I would never do many of the things in my personal life that I have to do as a lawyer."[12]

According to ethicist Norman E. Bowie, the disconnection between business and ethics and the dualism of the workplace stem from the competing paradigms of human nature of economists and ethicists. Economics is the study of the betterment of self. Most economists, says Bowie, have an egoistic theory of human nature. Their analyses focus on how an individual rationally pursues desired tastes, wants, or preferences. Within the economic model, individuals behave rationally when they seek to strengthen their own perceived best interests. Individuals need only take the interests of others into account when and if such considerations work to their advantage. Economics, Bowie claims, is singular and radically subjective in its orientation. It takes all taste, wants, and desires as simply given, and does not evaluate whether the economic actor's preferences are good or bad. The focus remains on how the individual can achieve his/her wants and desires.

Ethics, on the other hand, is nonegoistic or pluralistic in nature. Its primary paradigm of evaluation is always self in relation to others. The ethical point of view, says Bowie, requires that an actor take into account the impact of his/her action on others. If and when the interests of the actor and those affected by the action conflict, the actor should at least consider suspending or modifying his/her action, and by so doing recognize the interests of the other. In other words, ethics requires that on occasion we "ought to act" contrary to our own self-interest and that on occasion a person "ought to" act actively on behalf of the interests of another. Economists ask, What can I do to advance my best interests against others? Ethicists ask, In pursuing my best interests, what must I do, what "ought" I to do in regard to others? Whereas economics breeds competition, ethics encourages cooperation.[13]

For R. Edward Freeman, these competing paradigms are firmly entrenched in our collective psyches, and give rise to what he calls "The Problem of the Two Realms." One realm is the realm of business. It is the realm of hard, measurable facts: market studies, focus groups, longitudinal studies, production costs, managed inventory, stock value, research and development, profit and loss statements, quantitative analysis. The other realm is the realm of philosophy/ethics. This is the soft realm, says Freeman. This is the realm of the seemingly ineffable: myth, meaning, metaphor, purpose, quality, significance, rights, values. While the realm of business can be easily dissected, diagnosed, compared, and judged, the realm of philosophy is not open to precise interpretation, comparison, and evaluation. For Freeman, in a society that has absorbed and embraced the Marcusian adage "the goods of life are equal to the good life," these two realms are accorded separate but unequal status. Only in moments of desperation, disaster, or desire does the realm of business solicit the commentary and insights of the realm of ethics. Otherwise, the realm of business operates under the dictum of legal-moralism: Everything is allowed which is not strictly forbidden.

For Freeman the assertion that "business is business" and that ethics is what we try to do in our private lives simply does not hold up to close scrutiny. Business is a human institution, a basic part of the communal fabric of life. Just as governments come to be out of the human need for order, security, and fulfillment, so too does business. The goal of all business, labor, and work is to make life more secure, more stable, more equitable. Business exists to serve more than just itself. No business can view itself as an isolated entity, unaffected by the demands of individuals and society. As such, business is required to ask the question, What ought to be done in regard to the others we work with and serve? For Freeman, business ethics, rather than being an oxymoron, a contradiction in terms, is really a pleonasm, a redundancy in terms.[14] As Henry Ford, Sr., once said: "For a long time people believed that the only purpose of industry is to make a profit. They are wrong. Its purpose is to serve the general welfare."[15]

What business ethics advocates is that people apply in the workplace those commonsensical rules and standards learned at home, from the lectern, and from the pulpit. The moral issues facing a person are age old, and these are essentially the same issues facing a business—only writ in large script.[16] According to Freeman, ethics is "how we treat each other, every day, person to person. If you want to know about a company's ethics, look at how it treats people—customers, suppliers, and employees. Business is about people. And business ethics is about how customers and employees are treated."[17]

What is being asked of the business community is neither extraordinary nor excessive: a decent product at a fair price; honesty in advertisements; fair treatment of employees, customers, suppliers, and competitors; a strong sense of responsibility to the communities it inhabits and serves; and a reasonable profit for the financial risk-taking of its stockholders and owners. In the words of General Robert Wood Johnson, founder of Johnson & Johnson:

> The day has passed when business was a private matter—if it even really was. In a business society, every act of business has social consequences and may arouse public interest. Every time business hires, builds, sells or buys, it is acting for the . . . people as well as for itself, and it must be prepared to accept full responsibility.[18]

Leadership

According to Georges Enderle, business leadership would be relatively simple if corporations only had to produce a product or service, without being concerned about employees; management only had to deal with concepts, structures, and strategies, without worrying about human relations; businesses just had to resolve their own problems, without being obligated to take the interests of individuals or society into consideration.[19] But such is not the case. Leadership is always about self and others. Like ethics, labor and business leadership is a symbiotic, communal relationship. It's about leaders, followers, constituencies, and all stakeholders involved. And, like ethics, labor and business leadership seems to be an intrinsic part of the human experience. Charles DeGaulle once observed that men can no longer survive without direction than they can without eating, drinking, or sleeping. Putting aside the obvious fact that DeGaulle was a proponent of "the great-person theory" of leadership, his point is a basic one. Leadership is a necessary requirement of communal existence. Minimally, it tries to offer perspective, focus, appropriate behavior, guidance, and a plan by which to handle the seemingly random and arbitrary events of life. Depending on the type of leadership/followership involved, it can be achieved by consensus, fiat, or cooperative orchestration. But whatever techniques are employed, leadership is always, at bottom, about stewardship—"a person(s) who manages or directs the affairs of others . . . as the agent or representative of others." To paraphrase the words of St. Augustine, regardless of the outcome, the first and final job of leadership is the attempt to serve the needs and the well-being of the people led.

What is leadership? Although the phenomenon of leadership can and must be distinguishable and definable separately from our understanding of what and who leaders are, I am convinced that leadership can only be known and evaluated in the particular instantiation of a leader doing a job. In other words, while the terms "leadership" and "leader" are not strictly synonymous, the reality of leadership cannot be separated from the person of the leader and the job of leadership. Given this caveat, and leaning heavily on the research and insights of Joseph C. Rost,[20] we can define leadership as follows: Leadership is a power and value-laden relationship between leaders and followers/constituents who intend real changes that reflect their mutual purposes and goals. For our purposes, the critical elements of this definition that need to be examined are, in order of importance: followership, values, mutual purposes, and goals.

Followership

As Joseph Rost has pointed out, perhaps the single most important thesis developed in leadership studies in the last 20 years has been the evolution and now *almost* universal consensus regarding the role of followers in the leadership equation. Pulitzer prize-winning historian Garry Wills argues that we have long had a list of the leader's requisites—determination, focus, a clear goal, a sense of priorities, and so on. But until recently we overlooked or forgot the first and all-encompassing need. "The leader most needs followers. When those are lacking, the best ideas, the strongest will, the most wonderful smile have no effect."[21] Followers set the terms of acceptance for leadership. Leadership is a "mutually determinative" activity on the part of the leader and the followers. Sometimes it's cooperative, sometimes it's a struggle and often it's a feud, but it's always collective. Although "the leader is one who mobilizes others toward a goal shared by leaders and followers," leaders are powerless to act without followers. In effect, Wills argues, successful leaders need to understand their followers far more than followers need to understand leaders.[22]

Leadership, like labor and ethics, is always plural; it always occurs in the context of others. E. P. Hollander has argued that while the leader is the central and often the most vital part of the leadership phenomenon, followers are important and necessary factors in the equation.[23] All leadership is interactive, and all leadership should be collaborative. In fact, except for the negative connotation sometimes associated with the term, perhaps the word "collaborator" is a more precise term than either "follower" or "constituent" to explain the leadership process.[24] But whichever term is used, as James MacGregor Burns wrote, one thing is clear, "leaders and followers are engaged in a common enterprise; they are dependent on each other, their fortunes rise and fall together."[25]

From an ethical perspective, the argument for the stewardship responsibilities of leadership is dependent upon the recognition of the roles and rights of followers. Followership argues against the claim of Louis XIV, *"L'état, c'est moi."* The principle of followership denies the Machiavellian assertions that "politics and ethics don't mix" and that the sole aim of any leader is "the acquisition of personal power." Followership requires that leaders recognize their true role within the commonwealth. The choices and actions of leaders must take into consideration the rights and needs of followers. Leaders are not independent agents simply pursuing personal aggrandizement and career options. Like the "Guardians" of Socrates' *Republic,* leaders must see their office as a social responsibility, a trust, a duty, and

not as a symbol of their personal identify, prestige, and lofty status.[26] In more contemporary terms, James O'Toole and Lynn Sharp-Paine have separately argued that the central ethical issue in business is the rights of stakeholders and the obligation of business leaders to manage with due consideration for the rights of all stakeholders involved.[27]

In his cult classic *The Fifth Discipline,* management guru Peter Senge has stated that of all the jobs of leadership, being a steward is the most basic. Being a steward means recognizing that the ultimate purpose of one's work is others and not self; that leaders "do what they do" for something larger than themselves; that their "life's work" may be the "ability to lead"; but that the final goal of this talent or craft is "other directed."[28] If the real "business of business" is not just to produce a product/service and a profit but to help "produce" people, then the same claim/demand can be made of leadership. Given the reality of the "presence of others," leadership, like ethics, must by definition confront the question, What ought to be done with regard to others?

Values

Ethics is about the assessment and evaluation of values, because all of life is value-laden. As Samuel Blumenfeld emphatically pointed out, "You have to be dead to be value-neutral."[29] Values are the ideas and beliefs that influence and direct our choices and actions. Whether they are right or wrong, good or bad, values, both consciously and unconsciously, mobilize and guide how we make decisions and the kinds of decisions we make. Reportedly, Eleanor Roosevelt once said, "If you want to know what people value, check their checkbooks!"

I believe that Tom Peters and Bob Waterman were correct when they asserted, "The real role of leadership is to manage the values of an organization."[30] All leadership is value-laden. And all leadership, whether good or bad, is moral leadership at the descriptive if not the normative level. To put it more accurately, all leadership is ideologically driven or motivated by a certain philosophical perspective, which upon analysis and judgment may or may not prove to be morally acceptable in the colloquial sense. All leaders have an agenda, a series of beliefs, proposals, values, ideas, and issues that they wish to "put on the table." In fact, as Burns has suggested, leadership only asserts itself, and followers only become evident, when there is something at stake—ideas to be clarified, issues to be determined, values to be adjudicated.[31] In the words of Eleanor's husband, Franklin D. Roosevelt:

> The Presidency is . . . preeminently a place of moral leadership. All our great Presidents were leaders of thought at times when certain historic ideas in the life of the nation had to be clarified.[32]

Although we would prefer to study the moral leadership of Lincoln, Churchill, Gandhi, and Mother Teresa, like it or not, we must also evaluate Hitler, Stalin, Saddam Hussein, and David Koresh within a moral context.

All ethical judgments are in some sense a "values vs. values" or "rights vs. rights" confrontation. Unfortunately, the question of "what we ought to do" in relation to the values and rights of others cannot be reduced to the analog of a simple litmus-paper test. In fact, I believe that all of ethics is based on what William James called the "will to believe." That is, we choose to believe, despite the ideas, arguments, and reasoning to the contrary, that individuals possess certain basic rights that cannot and should not be willfully disregarded or overridden by others. In "choosing to believe," said James, we establish this belief as a factual baseline of our thought process for all considerations in regard to others. Without this "reasoned choice," says James, the ethical enterprise loses its "vitality" in human interactions.[33]

If ethical behavior intends no harm and respects the rights of all affected, and unethical behavior willfully or negligently tramples on the rights and interests of others, then leaders cannot deny or disregard the rights of others. The leader's world-view cannot be totally solipsistic. The leader's agenda should not be purely self-serving. Leaders should not see followers as potential adversaries to be bested, but rather as fellow travelers with similar aspirations and rights to be reckoned with.

How do we judge the ethics of a leader? Clearly, we cannot expect every decision and action of a leader to be perfect. As John Gardner has pointed out, particular consequences are never a reliable assessment of leadership.[34] The quality and worth of leadership can only be measured in terms of what a leader intends, values, believes in, or stands for—in other words, character. In *Character: America's Search for Leadership*, Gail Sheehy argues, as did Aristotle before her, that character is the most crucial and most elusive element of leadership.

The root of the word "character" comes from the Greek word for engraving. As applied to human beings, it refers to the enduring marks or etched-in factors in our personality, which include our inborn talents as well as the learned and acquired traits imposed upon us by life and experience. These engravings define us, set us apart, and motivate behavior.

In regard to leadership, says Sheehy, character is fundamental and prophetic. The "issues [of leadership] are today and will change in time. Character is what was yesterday and will be tomorrow."[35] Character establishes both our day-to-day demeanor and our destiny. Therefore, it is not only useful but essential to examine the character of those who desire to lead us. As a journalist and longtime observer of the political scene, Sheehy contends that the Watergate affair of the early 1970s serves as a perfect example of the links between character and leadership. As Richard Nixon demonstrated so well, says Sheehy, "The Presidency is not the place to work out one's personal pathology."[36] Leaders rule us, run things, wield power. Therefore, says Sheehy, we must be careful about whom we choose to lead, because whom we choose is what we shall be. If, as Heraclitus wrote, "character is fate," the fate our leaders reap will also be our own.

Putting aside the particular players and the politics of the episode, Watergate has come to symbolize the failings and failures of the people in high places. Watergate now serves as a watershed, a turning point, in our nation's concern for integrity, honesty, and fair play from all kinds of leaders. It is not a mere coincidence that the birth of business ethics as an independent, academic discipline can be dated from the Watergate affair and the trials that came out of it. No matter what our failings as individuals, Watergate sensitized us to the importance of ethical standards and conduct from those who direct the course of our political and public lives. What society is now demanding, and what business ethics is advocating, is that our business leaders and public servants should be held accountable to an even higher standard of behavior than we might demand and expect of ourselves.

Mutual Purposes and Goals

The character, goals, and aspirations of a leader are not developed in a vacuum. Leadership, even in the hands of a strong, confident, charismatic leader remains, at bottom, relational. Leaders, good or bad, great or small, arise out of the needs and opportunities of a specific time and place. Leaders require causes, issues and, most important, a hungry and willing constituency. Leaders may devise plans, establish an agenda, bring new and often radical ideas to the table, but all of them are a response to the milieu and membership of which they are a part. If leadership is an active and ongoing relationship between leaders and followers, then a central requirement of the leadership process is for leaders to evoke and elicit consensus in their constituencies, and conversely for followers to inform and influence their leaders. This is done through the uses of power and education.

The term "power" comes from the Latin *posse:* to do, to be able, to change, to influence or effect. To have power is to possess the capacity to control or direct change. All forms of leadership must make use of power. The central issue of power in leadership is not will it be used, but rather will it be used wisely and well. According to James MacGregor Burns, leadership is not just about directed results; it is also about offering followers a choice among real alternatives. Hence, leadership assumes competition, conflict, and debate, whereas brute power denies it.[37] "Leadership mobilizes," said Burns, "naked power coerces."[38] But power need not be dictatorial or punitive to be effective. Power can also be used in a noncoercive manner to orchestrate, direct, and guide members of an organization in the pursuit of a goal or series of objectives. Leaders must engage followers, not merely direct them. Leaders must serve as models and mentors, not martinets. Or to paraphrase novelist James Baldwin, power without morality is no longer power.

For Peter Senge, teaching is one of the primary jobs of leadership.[39] The "task of leader as teacher" is to empower people with information, offer insights, new knowledge, alternative perspectives on reality. The "leader as teacher" is not just about "teaching" people how "to achieve their vision." Rather, it is about fostering learning, offering choices, and building consensus.[40] Effective leadership recognizes that in order to build and achieve community, followers must become reciprocally coresponsible in the pursuit of a common enterprise. Through their conduct and teaching, leaders must try to make their fellow constituents aware that they are all stakeholders in a conjoint activity that cannot succeed without their involvement and commitment. Successful leadership believes in and communi-

cates some version of the now famous Hewlett-Packard motto: "The achievements of an organization are the results of the combined efforts of each individual." In the end, says Abraham Zaleznik, "leadership is based on a compact that binds those who lead with those who follow into the same moral, intellectual and emotional commitment."[41] However, as both Burns and Rost warn us, the nature of this "compact" is inherently unequal because the influence patterns existing between leaders and followers are not equal. Responsive and responsible leadership requires, as a minimum, that democratic mechanisms be put in place which recognize the right of followers to have adequate knowledge of alternative options, goals, and programs, as well as the capacity to choose among them. "In leadership writ large, mutually agreed upon purposes help people achieve consensus, assume responsibility, work for the common good, and build community."[42]

Structural Restraints

There is, unfortunately, a dark side to the theory of the "witness of others." Howard S. Schwartz, in his radical but underappreciated managerial text *Narcissistic Process and Corporate Decay*,[43] argues that corporations are not bastions of benign, other-directed ethical reasoning; nor can corporations, because of the demands and requirements of business, be models and exemplars of moral behavior. The rule of business, says Schwartz, remains the "law of the jungle," "the survival of the fittest," and the goal of survival engenders a combative "us-against-them mentality" which condones the moral imperative of getting ahead by any means necessary. Schwartz calls this phenomenon "organizational totalitarianism": Organizations and the people who manage them create for themselves a self-contained, self-serving worldview, which rationalizes anything done on their behalf and which does not require justification on any grounds outside of themselves.[44] The psychodynamics of this narcissistic perspective, says Schwartz, impose Draconian requirements on all participants in organizational life: do your work; achieve oral goals; obey and exhibit loyalty to your superiors; disregard personal values and beliefs; obey the law when necessary, obfuscate it whenever possible; and deny internal or external discrepant information at odds with the stated organizational worldview.

Within such a "totalitarian logic," neither leaders nor followers, rank nor file, operate as independent agents. To "maintain their place," to "get ahead," all must conform. The agenda of "organizational totalitarianism" is always the preservation of the status quo. Within such a logic, like begets like, and change is rarely possible. Except for extreme situations in which "systemic ineffectiveness" begins to breed "organization decay," transformation is never an option.

In *Moral Mazes*, Robert Jackall parallels much of Schwartz's analysis of organizational behavior, but from a sociological rather than a psychological perspective. According to critic and commentator Thomas W. Norton, both Jackall and Schwartz seek to understand why and how organizational ethics and behavior are so often reduced to either dumb loyalty or the simple adulation and mimicry of one's superiors. While Schwartz argues that individuals are captives of the impersonal structural logic of "organizational totalitarianism," Jackall contends that "organizational actors become personally loyal to their superiors, always seeking their approval and are committed to them as persons rather than as representatives of the abstractions of organizational authority." But in either. case, both authors maintain that organizational operatives are prisoners of the systems they serve.[45]

For Jackall, all American business organizations are examples of "patrimonial bureaucracies" wherein "fealty relations of personal loyalty" are the rule and the glue of organizational life. Jackall argues that all corporations are like fiefdoms of the Middle Ages, wherein the lord of the manor (CEO, president) offers protection, prestige, and status to his vassals (managers) and serfs (workers) in return for homage (commitment) and service (work). In such a system, advancement and promotion are predicated on loyalty, trust, politics, and personality as much as, if not more than, on experience, education, ability, and actual accomplishments. The central concern of the worker/minion is to be known as a "can-do-guy," a "team player," being at the right place at the right time and master of all the social rules. That is why in the corporate world, asserts Jackall, 1,000 "atta-boys" are wiped away with one "oh, shit!"

Jackall maintains that, as in the model of a feudal system, employees of a corporation are expected to become functionaries of the system and supporters of the status quo. Their loyalty is to the powers that be, their duty is to perpetuate performance and profit, and their values can be none other than those sanctioned by the organization. Jackall contends that the logic of every organization (place of business) and the collective personality of the workplace conspire to override the wants, desires, and aspirations of the individual worker. No matter what a person believes off the job, said Jackall, on the job all of us to a greater or lesser extent are required to suspend, bracket, or only selectively manifest our personal convictions.

> What is right in the corporation is not what is right in a man's home or his church. What is right in the corporation is what the guy above you wants from you.[46]

For Jackall the primary imperative of every organization is to succeed. This logic of performance, what he refers to as "institutional logic," leads to the creation of a private moral universe; a moral universe that, by definition, is totalitarian (self-sustained), solipsistic (self-defined), and narcissistic (self-centered). Within such a milieu, truth is socially defined and moral behavior is determined solely by organizational needs. The key virtues, for all alike, become the virtues of the organization: goal preoccupation, problem solving, survival/success, and, most important, playing by the house rules. In time, says Jackall, those initiated and invested in the system come to believe that they live in a self-contained world which is above and independent of outside critique and evaluation.

For both Schwartz and Jackall, the logic of organizational life is rigid and unchanging. Corporations perpetuate themselves, both in their strengths and weakness, because corporate cultures clone their own. Even given the scenario of a benign organizational structure which produces positive behavior and beneficial results, the etiology of the problem and the opportunity for abuse that it offers represent the negative possibilities and inherent dangers of the "witness of others" as applied to leadership theory. Within the scope of Schwartz's and Jackall's allied analyses, "normative" moral leadership may not be possible. The model offered is both absolute and inflexible, and only "regular company guys" make it to the top. The maverick, the radical, the reformer are not long tolerated. The "institutional logic" of the system does not permit disruption, deviance, or default.

The term "moral leadership" often conjures up images of sternly robed priests, waspishly severe nuns, carelessly bearded philosophers, forbiddingly strict parents, and something ambiguously labeled the "moral majority." These people are seen as confining and dictatorial. They make us do what we should do, not what we want to do. They encourage following the "superego" and not the "id." A moral leader is someone who supposedly tells people the difference between right and wrong from on high. But there is much more to moral leadership than merely telling others what to do.

The vision and values of leadership must have their origins and resolutions in the community of followers, of whom they are a part, and whom they wish to serve. Leaders can drive, lead, orchestrate, and cajole, but they cannot force, dictate, or demand. Leaders can be the catalyst for morally sound behavior, but they are not, by themselves, a sufficient condition. By means of their demeanor and message, leaders must be able to convince, not just tell others, that collaboration serves the conjoint interest and well-being of all involved. Leaders may offer a vision, but followers must buy into it. Leaders may organize a plan, but followers must decide to take it on. Leaders may demonstrate conviction and willpower, but followers, in the new paradigm of leadership, should not allow the leader's will to replace their own.[47]

Joseph C. Rost has argued, both publicly and privately, that the ethical aspects of leadership remain thorny. How, exactly, do leaders and collaborators in an influence relationship make a collective decision about the ethics of a change that they want to implement in an organization or society? Some will say, "option A is ethical," while others will say, "option B is ethical." How are leaders and followers to decide? As I have suggested, ethics is what "ought to be done" as the preferred mode of action in a "right vs. right," "values vs. values" confrontation. Ethics is an evaluative enterprise. Judgments must be made in regard to competing points of view. Even in the absence of a belief in the existence of a single universal, absolute set of ethical rules, basic questions can still be asked: How does it affect the self and others? What are the consequences involved? Is it harmful? Is it fair? Is it equitable? Perhaps the best, but by no means most definitive, method suited to the general needs of the ethical enterprise is a modified version of the scientific method: (a) observation, the recognition of a problem or conflict; (b) inquiry, a critical consideration of facts and issues involved; (c) hypothesis, the formulation of a decision or plan of action consistent with the known facts; (d) experimentation and evaluation, the implementation of the decision or plan in order to see if it leads to the resolution of the problem. There are, of course, no perfect answers in ethics or life. The quality of our ethical choices cannot be measured solely in terms of achievements. Ultimately and ethically, intention, commitment, and concerted effort are as important as outcome: What/why did leaders/followers try to do? How did they try to do it?

Leadership is hard to define, and moral leadership is even harder. Perhaps, like pornography, we only recognize moral leadership when we see it. The problem is, we so rarely see it. Nevertheless, I an convinced that without the "witness" of moral leadership, standards of ethics in business and organizational life will neither emerge nor be sustained. Leadership, even when defined as a collaborative experience, is still about the influence of individual character and the impact of personal mentoring. Behavior does not always beget like behavior in a one-to-one ratio, but it does establish tone, set the stage, and offer options. Although to achieve ethical behavior an entire organization, from top to bottom, must make a commitment to it, the model for that commitment has to originate from the top.[48] Labor Secretary Robert Reich recently stated, "The most eloquent moral appeal will be no match for the dispassionate edict of the market."[49] Perhaps the "witness" of moral leadership can prove to be more effective.

Notes

1. Maynard M. Dolecheck and Carolyn C. Dolecheck, "Ethics: Take It From the Top," *Business* (Jan.-March 1989): 13.

2. James Patterson and Peter Kim, *The Day America Told the Truth* (New York: Prentice Hall Press, 1991), 1, 20, 21, 22.

3. "Quotable Quotes," *Chicago Tribune Magazine*, January 1, 1996, 17.

4. B. F. Skinner, *Beyond Freedom and Dignity* (New York: Alfred A. Knopf, 1971), 107, 108, 150, 214, 215.

5. Stephen R. Covey, *The Seven Habits of Highly Effective People* (New York: A Fireside Book, 1990), 42, 43.

6. John Dewey, *Theory of the Moral Life* (New York: Holt, Rinehart and Winston, 1960), 3-28.

7. Jean-Paul Sartre, *Existentialism and Human Emotions* (New York: The Wisdom Library, n.d), 23, 24, 32, 33, 39, 40, 43, 44.

8. John Rawls, "Justice as Fairness: Political not Metaphysical," *Philosophy and Public Affairs* 14 (1985): 223-251.

9. The academic issue of which system of ethics best answers the question "what we ought to do" is a moot point and may in fact be an artificial one. However, the reality is, whichever way one decides to answer the question, "what we ought to do" is an endemic requirement of the human condition.

10. Pope Pius XI, *Quadragesimo Anno* (On Reconstructing the Social Order) in David M. Byers, ed. *Justice in the Marketplace: A Collection of the Vatican and U.S. Catholic Bishops on Economic Policy*, 1981-1984 (Washington, D.C.: United States Catholic Conference, 1985), 61.

11. Matthew Fox, *The Reinvention of Work* (San Francisco: Harper San Francisco, 1994), 298, 299.

12. "Tempo" section, *Chicago Tribune*, Feb. 1, 1995, 2.

13. Norman E. Bowie, "Challenging the Egoistic Paradigm," *Business Ethics Quarterly*, vol. 1, no. 1 (1991): 1-21.

14. R. Edward Freeman, "The Problem of the Two Realms," Speech, Loyola University Chicago, The Center for Ethics, Spring, 1992.

15. Henry Ford, Sr., quoted by Thomas Donaldson, *Corporations and Morality* (New Jersey: Prentice Hall, 1982), 57.

16. Ibid., 14.

17. Freeman, "The Problem of the Two Realms."

18. General Robert Wood Johnson, quoted by Frederick G. Harmon and Gary Jacobs, "Company Personality: The Heart of the Matter," *Management Review* (Oct. 1985): 10, 38, 74.

19. Georges Enderle, "Some Perspectives of Managerial Ethical Leadership," *Journal of Business Ethics*, 6 (1987): 657

20. Joseph C. Rost, *Leadership for the Twenty-First Century* (Westport, CT: Praeger, 1993).

21. Garry Wills, *Certain Trumpets* (New York: Simon & Schuster, 1994), 13.

22. Ibid., 17.

23. E. P. Hollander, *Leadership Dynamics* (New York: Free Press, 1978), 4, 5, 6, 12.

24. In a recent article, Joseph Rost made a change in his use of the word *followers:* "I now use collaborators when I write about leadership in the postindusirial paradigm. This is a change from *Leadership in the Twenty-First Century*, in which I use the word *followers* all the time. The reason for the change is the unanimous feedback I received from numerous professionals throughout the nation.... After trying several alternative words, I settled on the word *collaborators* because it seemed to have the right denotative and connotative meanings. In other words, collaborators as a concept fits the language and values of the postindustrial paradigm of leadership." See Rost, "Leadership Development in the New Millennium," *The Journal of Leadership Studies*, vol. 1, no. 1 (1993): 109, 110.

25. James MacGregor Burns, *Leadership* (New York: Harper Torchbooks, 1979), 426.

26. Al Gini, "Moral Leadership: An Overview," *Journal of Business Ethics* (1996): to be published.

27. James O'Toole, *Leading Change* (San Francisco: Jossey-Bass, 1994); Lynn Sharp-Paine, "Managing for Organizational Integrity," *Harvard Business Review* (March-April 1994): 106-117.

28. Peter M. Senge, *The Fifth Discipline* (New York: Double/Currency Books, 1990), 345-352.

29. Christina Hoff Sommers, "Teaching the Virtues," *Chicago Tribune Magazine*, September 12, 1993, 16.

30. Thomas J. Peters and Robert H. Waterman, Jr., *In Search of Excellence* (New York: Harper & Row, 1982), 245.

31. Burns, chapters 2, 5.

32. Ibid., xi.

33. William James, *The Will to Believe* (New York: Dover Publications, 1956), 1-31, 184-215.

34. John W. Gardner, *On Leadership* (New York: Free Press, 1990), 8.

35. Gail Sheehy, *Character: America's Search for Leadership* (New York: Bantam Books, 1990), 311.

36. Ibid., 66.

37. Burns, 66.

38. Ibid., 439.

39. For Senge, the three primary tasks of leadership include: leader as designer; leader as steward; leader as teacher.

40. Senge, 353.

41. Abraham Zaleznik, "The Leadership Gap," *Academy of Management Executives*, vol. 4, no. 1 (1990): 12.

42. Joseph C. Rost, *Leadership for the Twenty-First Century*, p. 124.

43. Howard S. Schwartz, *Narcissistic Process and Corporate Decay* (New York: New York University Press, 1990).

44. Howard S. Schwartz, "Narcissistic Process and Corporate Decay: The Case of General Motors," *Business Ethics Quarterly*, vol. 1., no. 3: 250.

45. Thomas W. Norton, "The Narcissism and Moral Mazes of Corporate Life: A Commentary on the Writings of H. Schwartz and R. Jackall," *Business Ethics Quarterly*, vol. 2, no. 1: 76.

46. Robert Jackall, *Moral Mazes* (New York: Oxford University Press, 1988), 6.

47. Wills, 13.

48. Dolecheck and Dolecheck, 14.

49. William Pfaff, "It's Time for a Change in Corporate Values," *Chicago Tribune*, Jan. 16, 1996, 17.

CHAPTER 27

Characteristics of Ethical Business Cultures

Alexandre Ardichvili

University of Minnesota

James A. Mitchell

Douglas Jondle

Center for Ethical Business Cultures

Problem Statement and Research Question

Research on business ethics, organizational culture, and organizational leadership suggests that ethical or unethical behavior in organizations is a function of both individual characteristics and contextual factors (Meyers, 2004). Among these contextual factors, organizational culture is considered to be one of the most important influences (Cohen, 1993; Meyers, 2004; Trevino, 1986). In recent years, a number of research studies have attempted to link various attributes of organizational cultures to ethical behavior (Frederick, 1995; Trevino and Nelson, 2004). However, to our knowledge, none of the published studies propose comprehensive models of characteristics of ethical corporate cultures. Therefore, the goal of the reported study was to identify characteristics attributed to ethical business cultures by business practitioners. In this paper, we first briefly summarize the results of our review of literature on ethical corporate cultures and formulate the research question. Second, the study design, methodology, and sample are explained. Next, we present and discuss the study findings, including the list of attributes of ethical corporate cultures. Finally, implications for further research and business management practices are discussed.

In anthropological literature, culture is defined as accepted behavioral standards within the confines of a specified group as guided by a pattern of shared learned beliefs, traditions, and principles (Bolman and Deal, 1997; Trevino, 1990b). Schein defines organizational culture as learned responses where "basic assumptions and beliefs that are shared by members of an organization . . . define in a basic 'taken-for-granted' fashion an organization's view of itself and its environment" (1985, pp. 5–6). For the purposes of this article, ethical business culture encompasses for-profit organizations comprised of individuals working reciprocally with internal and external stakeholders. Though the objective of this study is to identify components of ethical business culture, from a holistic perspective, an ethical business culture fosters an organizational environment guided by shared values and beliefs (Trevino, 1990b). Furthermore, it is an environment where employees are not only expected to discern right from wrong, a basic minimum, but also more importantly are expected to go beyond the minimum to explore and implement ethical decisions when all choices seem right.

Organizational cultures are complex combinations of formal and informal systems, processes, and interactions (Cohen, 1993). Formal organizational culture components are comprised of leadership, structure, policies, reward systems, socialization mechanisms, and decision processes among other things. Informal culture components include implicit behavioral norms, role models, rituals, historical anecdotes, and language (Cohen, 1993; Frederick, 1995; Schein, 2004; Trevino, 1990a; Trevino and Nelson, 2004). Organizations possessing ethical cultures create and maintain a shared pattern of values, customs, practices, and expectations which dominate normative behavior in the organization (Trevino, 1990a).

Leadership is often mentioned as one of the most important elements of an organization's ethical culture (Brown and Trevino, 2006; Trevino, 1990a). Leaders who are perceived as being able to create and support an ethical culture in their organizations are those who represent, communicate, and role model high ethical standards (Brown et al., 2005), emphasize attention to goals other than economic, engage in "ethics talk" (Bird and Waters, 1989), and maintain a long-term view of relationships within and outside the organization. These top managers create and maintain an ethical culture by consistently behaving in an ethical fashion and encouraging others to behave in such a manner as well.

An ethical culture is associated with a structure that provides for equally distributed authority and shared accountability. It also has policies such as an ethical code of conduct that is clear, well communicated, is specific about expected procedures and practices, thoroughly understood, and enforced (Trevino et al., 1999). In addition, incentive systems are deliberately and clearly tied to behaving in concert with the code of ethics and accomplishment of non-economic goals in addition to economic outcomes (Trevino and Weaver, 2001). The socialization process of an organization with an ethical culture reinforces the practice of the values in a mission statement on a daily basis; so behavior is focused on issues of health and safety of employees, customer and community responsiveness, and fairness. In fact, employee perceptions of fairness or justice in an organization have been found to have central importance in creating an ethical culture (Trevino and Weaver, 2001). In addition, the decision-making processes in an ethical culture are designed to consider the ethical ramifications of business decisions instead of cost-benefit analyses alone.

The informal elements of a cultural system are less tangible aspects of organizational behavior. Such aspects include norms for behavior that are consistent with the ethical standards or the code of conduct, mission, and decision-making processes (Trevino and Brown, 2004). Consistent role modeling of such behavior forms the basis for a strong culture where everyone understands what is appropriate for the company. Other elements of the informal culture include the communication and belief in heroes and role models, along with myths and stories about how ethical standards of the organization have been upheld and revered by members (Trevino, 1990a). Such heroes and stories transcend the formal organizational culture and inspire others to behave in an ethical fashion. Organizational rituals also help bolster this informal culture by sustaining the ethical values of the members over time. Finally, the language used by organizational members plays a crucial role in shaping behavior in the informal ethical culture. Use of moral or ethics "talk" to address problem-solving and decision-making situations creates an awareness of the ethical dimension of such processes. Ethical cultures have leaders and members who engage in ethics talk regularly in pursuit of organizational activities.

In summary, various research studies have found that ethical cultures are based on alignment between formal structures, processes, and policies, consistent ethical behavior of top leadership, and informal recognition of heroes, stories, rituals, and language that inspire organizational members to behave in a manner consistent with high ethical standards that have been set by executive leadership. However, the above-mentioned studies were exploring only one or two dimensions of ethical organizational cultures (e.g., decision making, or leadership), and none of the studies attempted to create a comprehensive list of attributes of ethical cultures, based on the perceptions of business practitioners and/or executives. Therefore, the main research question driving the present study is:

What are, as perceived by study participants, the most important characteristics of ethical business cultures?

Research Design

This study was designed based on the grounded theory approach (Creswell, 1998). Grounded theory studies are focused on discovering a theory or a framework, describing or explaining a phenomenon under investigation, by analyzing data collected via field investigations. In the grounded theory approach, researchers are not making an attempt to develop a set of testable hypotheses or propositions. Instead, only a general question about the phenomenon is formulated with a goal of leaving sufficient space for the emergence of patterns, which could be used in formulating a new explanation of the phenomenon (Grbich, 2007). While grounded theory provides a general framework for designing studies, specific data collection and analysis methods can vary depending on preferences and expertise of individual researchers.

In this particular study, data collection was based on qualitative key informant interview method proposed by Kumar et al. (1993), and the data analysis was based on qualitative data clustering method developed by Miles and Huberman (1994). According to Kumar et al. (1993), key informant interviews are used when the researchers intend to obtain the data not from a random sample, but from a purposefully selected sample of individuals, who are likely to possess the most relevant information due to their key positions, experience, or expertise in industries or organizations of interest to the researcher. For the purposes of this study, the key informants were defined as top-level business executives, who were likely to have in-depth knowledge of practices (including ethics-related practices) of a variety of business organizations. A number of prominent academics, specializing in business ethics research, were included in the key informant group. The initial group of key informants for the study was nominated by members of the Board of Directors of the Center for Ethical Business Cultures. Subsequent nominations were obtained through snowballing technique, when study participants were asked to provide additional names of qualified individuals. In addition, some interviews were conducted at a national business ethics conference by one of the researchers and several associates of the CEBC.

Overall, 67 individuals participated in the study. They included 54 business executives, representing a wide range of industries, and 13 academics (See Table 27.1 for details).

Participants were asked to think about business organizations they would classify as having exemplary ethical business practices. Then, participants were asked to generate a list of statements descriptive of these organizations' ethical practices and behaviors. Overall, participants nominated 86 companies from nine industry sectors (see Table 27.2) and generated 389 descriptive statements.

Data analysis included clustering of the 389 statements with a goal of generating a short list of major clusters and representative statements under each cluster. As suggested by Miles and Huberman (1994), "Clustering is a tactic that can be applied at many levels to qualitative data: at the level of events or acts, of individual actors, of processes. . . . In all instances, we are trying to understand a phenomenon better by grouping and then conceptualizing objects that have similar patterns or characteristics" (p. 249). In addition to using specific suggestions for clustering, provided by Miles and Huberman, the researchers utilized a modified Delphi method to coordinate their work and to come up with a final list of clusters and statements. First, each of the three researchers worked independently and developed their own clusters and representative statements.

Table 27.1	Industry Affiliation of Study Participants

Industry affiliation	No. of participants
Consulting and information services	5
Energy sector	7
Finance and insurance	18
Health sector	2
Law firms	3
Manufacturing	8
Non-profits, foundations, churches	6
Retail	5
Academia	13

Table 27.2	Nominated Companies by Industry Sectors

Industry sectors	No. of nominated companies
Basic materials and commodity	5
Conglomerates	2
Consumer goods	18
Financial services	12
Health care	6
Manufacturing and technology	18
Service and retail	27
Transportation	4
Utilities	1

Next, they exchanged their lists, discussed the lists and rationale for the inclusion of individual items, and based on this review and discussion, each developed a next iteration of clusters/lists. This process was repeated three times.

Results

The final list of clusters and statements, associated with each of the clusters, is presented in Table 27.3. The five clusters that have emerged are: Mission- and Value-Driven, Stakeholder Balance, Leadership Effectiveness, Process Integrity, and Long-Term Perspective. Each cluster is represented by five to seven descriptive statements. Many of these statements are taken verbatim from interviews with study participants. Others are a result of rewording or combining statements made by different participants, but which had essentially similar meaning.

Discussion and Recommendations for Practice

The purpose of this study was to identify general characteristics attributed to ethical organizational cultures. Our research identified five clusters of characteristics that infer a comprehensive model; a model that can be engaged to influence operational practices in creating and sustaining an "organizational culture that encourages ethical conduct and a commitment to compliance with the law" (United States Sentencing Commission, 2004). In our opinion, a business *culture* with these characteristics will far exceed the minimal baseline requirements of the law.

The five characteristics of the model (see Figure 27.1) identified above are: Mission and Values Driven, Stakeholder Balance, Leadership Effectiveness, Process Integrity and Long-Term Perspective. The accompanying descriptive statements bind and link the model together, add clarity and resilience to its meaning, and create actionable guidance in its application.

Based on the study results, the keystone of the model is the characteristic Mission and Values Driven. It represents the lifeblood of the organization. For an organization to both survive and thrive, mission and values must be an integral

Table 27.3   Characteristics of Ethical Organizational Cultures: Clusters and Statements

Mission- and Values-Driven:

"Clarity of mission and values, reflected in ethical guidelines and behavior"

"Institutionalizes ethical values"

"Build relationships of trust and respect"

"Strong culture that actively eliminates people who don't share the values"

"Corporate values are sustained over long periods of time"

Stakeholders Balance:

"Balance all stakeholders (e.g., customers, employees, owners and community) in all their decision-making, consistently"

"Deal with all stakeholders on a consistently ethical and value-oriented basis"

"Good balance of customer value and profit"

"Giving back to the community in which the company does business"

"Work to be a good corporate citizen in a global economy"

"Respectful treatment and fair compensation for employees at all levels"

Leadership Effectiveness:

"Ethical culture starts at the top and is conveyed by example"

"Senior management demands ethical conduct at every level of the company"

"CEO and senior management live their lives with great personal integrity"

"When ethical issues arise, CEO does not 'shoot the messenger,' but gathers facts and takes action"

"Do what they say they're going to do"

Process Integrity:

"Dedication to Quality and Fairness in its people, processes, and products"

"Invest in ongoing ethics training and communication throughout the organization"

"Values are reinforced in performance appraisals and promotions"

"Values are reinforced in every-day execution"

"Excellent corporate governance processes, supported by Board quality and independence"

"Noble mission is internalized in company processes and behavior"

"Transparent decision-making by the people closest to the question"

Long-term Perspective:

"Place mission above profit and long-term over short-term"

"Acting in the best interests of customers, over the longer term"

"Board takes long view in managing shareholder value"

"Connect environmental sustainability, social responsibility, and profit"

"CEO says he's building an institution that he hopes will be here in 50 years"

| Figure 27.1 | Five Clusters of Characteristics of Ethical Business Cultures |

component of an organization's strategic focus. They must be aligned to foster a high performance culture and flow freely and systemically throughout the organization to become the genesis of operational norms (i.e., codes of conduct and ethics) that drive desired behavior.

Our research demonstrates that respondents place significant importance on the concept of driven behavior where "*clarity of mission and values, reflected in ethical guidelines and behavior*" is driven by an organization that "*institutionalizes ethical values*" and "*build[s] relationships of trust and respect.*" In a corporate culture, where core business functions are aligned with organizational processes, an environment is nurtured "*that actively eliminates people who don't share the values*" and sustainability over "*long periods of time.*" This implies an existence of mechanisms that select for fitness between organizational

values and individual values, a form of natural selection, which gleans deleterious behavior from the ethical organization.

Repeatability within the dataset of the suggestion of a relationship between ethical culture and the long-term led to identification of the Long-Term Perspective as a separate foundational characteristic of ethical organizational culture. Responses categorized by this characteristic brought into sharp relief the question, "what is the purpose of business?" Is it to maximize shareholder value or is it the responsibility of business to balance the need of various stakeholders? A typical response elicited was "*[placing] mission above profit, and long-term over short-term.*" What was of particular interest in responses categorizing this characteristic was the consistency of responses linked to Stakeholder Balance and Leadership Effectiveness.

The linkage implies model congruency and its iterative cohesiveness between characteristics.

Stakeholder Balance and long-term concerns were addressed by "*acting in the best interests of customers*" and taking the "*long view in managing shareholder value.*" Respondents recognized that, because employees are the ones who deliver service to customers, all employees need to receive "*respectful treatment and fair compensation.*" Respondents also expressed concern for the environment and the desired role and responsibility of organizations to its safeguard. They believe organizations must "*connect environmental sustainability, social responsibility, and profit.*" Linkage with Leadership Effectiveness was demonstrated by responses focused on survivability and longevity of the organization (i.e., the "*CEO says he's building an institution that he hopes will be here in 50 years*"). Respondents felt the responsibility of leadership was to establish a strategy focused on consistent long-term growth and not be influenced by short-term growth and gains.

In the stakeholder theory, business and business managers have a fiduciary responsibility to various stakeholder groups who, in themselves, have a vested interest in the success of the organization (Freeman, 1994). The countervailing theory espoused by Milton Friedman is stockholder centric, where the "one and only one responsibility of business [and corporate executives] is to increase its profits" (Friedman,1970).

The stockholders, or owners, are the risk takers. Therefore, they alone are entitled to benefit from the returns. Respondents in general did not agree with this perspective on profit distribution. They consistently referred to the responsibility an organization has to its numerous stakeholders and their interests in "*respectful treatment and fair compensation.*" Thus, Stakeholder Balance was identified as a key characteristic of an ethical culture.

The term Stakeholder Balance suggests that a tension exists between multiple stakeholders. Focusing too long and too much on any one stakeholder has the potential to create an environment of distortion and imbalance that can lead to ethical lapses. The model does not suggest that the tensions between stakeholders will disappear all together for the ethical organization. It does, however, create a forum for discussion and consideration of various stakeholder groups of an organization to work toward maintaining a "*balance [of] all stakeholders (e.g., customers, employees, owners, and community) in all [its] decision-making*" and to "*deal with all stakeholders on a consistently ethical and value-oriented basis.*" In addition, an underlining theme voiced by respondents was a redefining of the purpose of business. That is, the purpose of business is not to just make money. Rather, it is to provide a "*good balance of customer value and profit*" and "*giving back to the community in which the company does business.*" Furthermore, respondents expanded the definition of community to include the global community. The expressed belief was that an organization must "*work to be a good corporate citizen in a global economy.*"

Effective organizations have effective leaders. In an ethical business organization, effective leaders "talk the talk" and "walk the walk." In describing Leadership Effectiveness, the overarching theme was that "*ethical culture starts at the top and is conveyed by example,*" the "*CEO and senior management live their lives with great personal integrity*" and they "*do what they say they're going to do.*" Leadership, most notably senior management, must embody the organization's values in their own behavior and must articulate those values in a way that is compelling for employees and all other stakeholders. Ethical organizational culture is a nonstarter if senior management refuses to engage and function as role models for the rest of the organization. Another critical aspect of leadership in an ethical culture is the issue of retaliation. Respondents expressed a belief that an ethical culture is "*when ethical issues arise, [the] CEO does not 'shoot the messenger', but gathers facts and takes action.*" However, building and sustaining an ethical culture is also a two-way street. It depends on "*senior management [demanding] ethical conduct at every level of the [organization].*" It must permeate throughout all aspects of the business from top management to the frontline employee and throughout all functional systems of the firm.

The characteristic, identified as Process Integrity, was described as internalizing the company's mission "*in company processes and behavior.*" It includes the key functional units of the business, e.g., recruiting, hiring, firing, evaluating, compensating, promoting, and communicating. Numerous challenges exist, including establishing desired behavior standards and aligning the systems to encourage behavior and monitoring behavior. A key theme emphasized by the data was the importance of the company's values reinforced in "*performance appraisals and promotions*" and "*every-day execution*." This focused the attention on the necessity for alignment of processes to mediate confusion and the need for "*transparent decision-making by the people closest to the [issue].*" Specific attention was paid to the "*dedication to quality and fairness in its people, processes, and products*" and ongoing investment in "ethics, training, and communication throughout the organizations." Beyond management functional areas, the data emphasized "*excellent corporate governance processes, supported by Board quality and independence.*" This indicates a heightened awareness amongst the respondents to the importance of governance and its role and responsibilities in fostering ethical business cultures.

Future Research

The reported findings are based on a limited in size sample of respondents, identified through a convenience sampling procedure. Therefore, to provide recommendations applicable to a wide variety of businesses, the next logical step would be to develop a survey instrument that can be used in a large-scale quantitative study. The purpose of this next stage would be to validate the list of characteristics of ethical business cultures and to confirm the validity of five identified clusters. The study would involve a statistically representative sample of business executives and managers from a cross-section of industries.

References

Bird, F. and J. Waters: 1989, 'The Moral Muteness of Managers', *California Management Review* 32(1), 73–88.

Bolman, L. G. and T. Deal: 1997, *Reframing Organizations: Artistry, Choice and Leadership*, 2nd Edition (Jossey-Bass, San Francisco, CA).

Brown, M. and L. Trevino: 2006, 'Ethical Leadership: A review and Future Directions', *The Leadership Quarterly* 17(6), 595–616.

Brown, M., L. Trevino and D. Harrison: 2005, 'Ethical Leadership: A Social Learning Perspective for Construct Development and Testing', *Organizational Behavior and Human Decision Processes* 97(2), 117–134.

Cohen, D.: 1993, 'Creating and Maintaining Ethical Work Climates: Anomie in the Workplace and Implications for Managing Change', *Business Ethics Quarterly* 3(4), 343–358.

Creswell, J.: 1998, *Qualitative Inquiry and Research Design: Choosing among Five Traditions* (Sage Publications, Thousand Oaks, CA).

Frederick, W. C.: 1995, *Values, Nature, and Culture in the American Corporation* (Oxford University Press, New York).

Freeman, R. E.: 1994, 'The Politics of Stakeholder Theory: Some Future Directions', *Business Ethics Quarterly* 4(4), 409–421.

Friedman, M.: 1970, 'The Social Responsibility of Business is to Increase its Profits', *New York Times Magazine* September 13, 1970.

Grbich, C.: 2007, *Qualitative Data Analysis: An Introduction* (Sage Publication, Thousand Oaks, CA).

Kumar, N., J. Anderson and L. Stern: 1993, 'Conducting Interorganizational Research Using Key Informants', *Academy of Management Journal* 36(6), 1633–1641.

Meyers, C.: 2004, 'Institutional Culture and Individual Behavior: Creating an Ethical Environment', *Science and Engineering Ethics* 10(2), 269–276.

Miles, M. and M. Huberman: 1994, *Qualitative Data Analysis: An Expanded Sourcebook*, 2nd Edition (Sage, Thousand Oaks, CA).

Schein, E. H.: 1985, *Organizational Culture and Leadership* (Jossey-Bass, San Francisco, CA).

Schein, E. H.: 2004, *Organizational Culture and Leadership*, 3rd Edition (Jossey-Bass, San Francisco, CA).

Trevino, L.: 1986, 'Ethical Decision Making in Organizations: A Person-Situation Interactionist Model', *Academy of Management Review* 11(3), 601–617.

Trevino, L.: 1990a, 'A Cultural Perspective on Changing Organizational Ethics', in R. Woodman and W. Passmore (eds.), *Research in Organizational Change and Development* (Jai Press, Greenwich, CT), pp. 195–230.

Trevino, L. K.: 1990b, 'Developing and Changing Organizational Ethics: A Cultural Approach', *Research in Organizational Change and Development* 4, 195–230.

Trevino, L. and M. Brown: 2004, 'Managing to be Ethical: Debunking Five Business Ethics Myths', *Academy of Management Executive* 18(2), 69–83.

Trevino, L. and K. Nelson: 2004, Managing *Business Ethics: Straight Talk About How to Do it Right* (Wiley, New York).

Trevino, L. and G. R. Weaver: 2001, 'The Role of Human Resources in Ethics/Compliance Management: A Fairness Perspective', *Human Resource Management Review* 11(1), 113–134.

Trevino, L., G. R. Weaver, D. Gibson and B. Toffler: 1999, 'Managing Ethics and Legal Compliance: What Works and What Hurts', *California Management Review* 41(2), 131–150.

United States Sentencing Commission: 2004, '2004 Federal Sentencing Guidelines: Effective Compliance and Ethics Program', November 27, 2007 (available at http://www .ussc.gov/2004guid/ 8b2_1.htm).

CHAPTER 28

Being Ethical When the Boss Is Not

Mary Uhl-Bien
Melissa K. Carsten

University of Nebraska–Lincoln

Too many people who thought something "didn't feel right" failed to raise a red flag for a variety of reasons: They wanted to win a contract, they feared retaliation, they just didn't want to rock the boat, or they lacked the courage to speak up in a command-and-control culture. (Speech by Boeing CEO Jim McNerney, Conference Board, April 27, 2006)

I n 2003, a congressional investigation concluded that the Boeing Corporation had used illegal measures to win a military contract worth $21 billion. The contract, which was open to public bid, was granted to Boeing after the chief financial officer (CFO) offered up the position of vice president to a top acquisitions official in the U.S. Air Force. This came shortly after Boeing had been accused of stealing trade information from competitors and tampering with satellite launch information from China. Whereas the company was able to survive these scandals better than many of their unethical counterparts (e.g., WorldCom Inc. or Enron Corp.), Boeing was left with a damaged reputation, plummeting morale, and the hard-hitting fact that its unethical climate needed a major overhaul. As John Lockard, vice president and general manager at Boeing, observed, "when a handful of Boeing employees made wrong decisions, the impact was felt by all of our employees."

The major ethical scandals of the past decade (e.g., Enron, WorldCom, Tyco International, Arthur Andersen, HealthSouth Corp.) have shown all too

Source: Uhl-Bien, M. Carsten, M. K. Being ethical when the boss is not. *Organizational Dynamics,* 2007 Vol. 36, No. 2 pp. 187–201. Copyright © 2007 Elsevier Inc.

painfully that unethical behavior leaves few untouched. The devastation incurred by the Enron scandal is still being felt in the form of lost employee pensions, damaged relationships, and the residual demise of Arthur Anderson. Given the widespread impact and potential for harm that ethical scandals invoke, we would expect that in discussions of ethics, the strong sentiment would be that *all* organizational members are charged with upholding ethical and moral principles. Yet, this is often not the case. Instead, the predominant message we see conveyed in ethics discussions is that the responsibility for ethics lies primarily with organizational leaders. As articulated by Jim McNerney, chief executive officer (CEO) of Boeing: "We also realize it all starts with leadership. If an organization's leaders don't model, encourage, expect and reward the right behaviors, *why should anyone else in that organization exhibit those behaviors?*"

We worry about the message implied by this statement. What if leaders *do not* behave ethically—who is responsible for ethics then? Managerial leaders have been the prime culprits of many major ethical scandals, and excluding employees from discussions of ethical leadership leaves a vacuum in ethical enforcement and a greater likelihood that unethical actions of managers will go unchallenged.

Therefore, in this article we propose a framework for incorporating employees into the heart of discussions of ethical leadership. This framework, which we label *upward ethical leadership*, expands leadership beyond top-down models grounded in hierarchy and authority to a view of leadership as a mutual influence process that occurs among active participants. We define upward ethical leadership as leadership behavior enacted by individuals who take action to maintain ethical standards in the face of questionable moral behaviors by higher-ups. In this view, employees are not passive, powerless followers at the mercy of unethical leaders but rather power-holding participants in the leadership processes of the organization.

To explain this, we begin with a discussion of how the "problem of following" is a direct result of our socialization into hierarchical models of leadership, and how new views of leadership offer a way of framing leadership as a process of mutual influence and accountability. We then present a model of upward ethical leadership that illustrates how these new concepts can be applied in an ethical context to produce more active (rather than passive) responses among employees to unethical behavior by leaders. While we acknowledge that speaking up about managerial wrongdoing in an unethical climate is one of the most difficult predicaments employees can face, we suggest that by helping employees to establish their personal power and develop upward leadership skills we can better prepare them to be able to contribute to the enforcement of ethical behavior in the workplace. Overall, we propose that by expanding our view of leadership to recognize the power that both parties hold in the process (managers and subordinates), we can broaden the capabilities for ethical leadership in organizations and highlight the key role of *employees* in maintaining ethical climates.

The Problem With Following

The dilemmas presented by unethical behaviors of managers are particularly problematic for employees because of the nature of hierarchy in organizations. From a young age we are socialized into hierarchy, taught to respect others with higher status, obey authority, and take a subordinate role to those in superior positions. The traditional belief is that social order requires certain individuals (leaders) to be in charge, providing direction and establishing rules, and others (followers) to comply by implementing the direction and initiatives of those above. If followers do not comply with directives from leaders they are seen as "insubordinate," risking punishment in the form of sanctions, disregard (even ostracization) by others, or expulsion from the organization.

Silence

While this system of control clearly works, it has drawbacks. Hierarchy and obedience to authority create role expectations that influence whether employees choose to speak up about issues they are concerned about or defer responsibility and remain silent. All too often, hierarchical role expectations cause employees to assume they should not speak up for fear of being blamed and attacked for problems or issues they raise (e.g., "kill the messenger"). For example, in research on silence and voice, Frances Milliken and colleagues found that at least 85% of their sample (35 of 40 people) expressed that they had felt unable to raise an issue or concern to their bosses on at least one occasion, even though they felt the issue was important. The reasons employees gave for not speaking up primarily revolved around futility and fear—the feeling that speaking up will not make a difference and the concern that speaking up will cause them to be viewed as a troublemaker (complainer or tattletale), damage a relationship (loss of trust or acceptance), or experience retaliation or punishment (e.g., losing a job, not getting promoted). As described by one participant in their study:

> A coworker was being phased out, and it was unclear to those around why this was happening. I did not feel that I could speak honestly and openly to his bosses despite my strong working relationship with them. I felt that I would be fired or fall out of favour if I spoke up. I felt it was a moral imperative to act, but in the end, I did nothing. (Male, financial services firm)

This norm of silence can also be fostered by coworkers who feed fear climates by spreading anxiety and telling stories about how employees have been reprimanded or mistreated by leaders who attack them in response to something they said:

> I knew that someone else had spoken to the boss about it and was told: "You got what you deserved. Don't expect any more." Based on that vicarious experience, I knew that I wouldn't get anywhere and would only lose out in terms of being seen negatively. (Female, financial services firm as reported in study by Milliken et al.)

Once such fear climates begin to spread they are hard to contain. They present a problem not only in terms of loss of valuable information to managers but also in low morale, and eventually psychological withdrawal, among workers.

Obedience

Hierarchical thinking is also flawed in its assumption that leaders are the ones who make decisions and

that followers are to go along. As described by Charles Heckscher in his work on postbureaucracy, "An essential assumption of bureaucracy is that the top managers can get into their heads all the necessary information and make the best possible decisions . . . [and then] delegate pieces of implementation to people who are not so gifted." This bureaucratic premise again drives those lower in the hierarchy to take a passive role in organizational decision-making, believing that leaders know best and it is not their role to question.

The eye-opening results of the Milgram studies of authority in the early 1960s show the pervasiveness of this dynamic. These studies, which have received widespread attention from both social scientists and the general public, demonstrate that individuals are willing to inflict negative, even harmful, treatment on others simply at the request of an authority figure. Milgram found that when individuals see another as an authority figure (in a position of power) and/or having expertise the individual does not have, they will blindly obey commands—even those that lead to blatant negative consequences, such as inflicting shocks strong enough to kill someone. The consequences of such blind obedience are exemplified in horrific historical examples, including the Holocaust in Nazi Germany, or the Jonestown Massacre, in which individuals poisoned their children and then themselves at the directive of cult leader Jim Jones. However, this also plays out on a daily basis when employees fail to openly communicate with or question their bosses, leading to outcomes such as the Space Shuttle Challenger disaster, in which employees were well aware of the problems with the O-ring but did not communicate it to those in charge.

New Views of Leadership

Given the problems with the assumptions of the bureaucratic model and its emphasis on authority and obedience, some scholars are beginning to explore new ways of conceptualizing leadership that are not premised in hierarchy and authority. Such models, including shared leadership, relational leadership, and postindustrial leadership, are expanding the definition of leadership beyond downward actions of those in formal positions (e.g., managers) to behavior that can occur anywhere and in any direction in the organizational system. From this view, leadership is a behavior that can be enacted by anyone who uses influence to create change in a system. For example, employees who constructively question directives and decisions from above, offer suggestions for improvement or volunteer to lead improvement initiatives, or generate enthusiasm for a new idea, project, or action plan, could all be considered leaders (i.e., engaging in "upward leadership") even though they are in a subordinate role.

In this way, leadership is recognized as two-way influence—where the individuals who would traditionally engage in "following" are now active and committed participants in the leadership process. This does not mean they usurp the "authority" of the manager. Instead they work to collaborate with the leader in achieving the goals of the organization:

> In an organization I worked in, the corporate HR head of this well-known company (who was also my mentor), used to write detailed e-mails to his CEO (who is a pretty strong and well-known leader), describing to the CEO where he thought the CEO was going wrong, and where he needed to improve. It requires courage to tell your boss that he is wrong, and the reasons why you feel so. (Shabbir Merchant, Executive VP, Grow Talent LTD, May 1, 2006)

It is important for us to be very clear that this view does not promote disorder or "rampant noncompliance." Rather it promotes responsible leadership and accountability for leadership by *all* employees, not just managers. It does not see leadership as a prerogative of a manager. Instead, it purports that for organizations to be successful and maintain ethicality in today's complex business environment, organizations need to draw on all their resources. As noted by John Lockard, vice president and general manager of Boeing in a speech on business ethics and conduct (June 2, 2005): "When we say leadership, we're not just talking about the people who sit in the corner offices. We're talking about all of our people and all of our partners."

The Promise of Action

To illustrate how these ideas can be applied in the context of unethical behavior by higher-ups, in the

sections below we lay out a model that depicts the psychological reactions employees experience in the face of ethical misconduct by managers and why it will often lead to passive responses (e.g., silence, obedience). We then show how organizations and employees can create environments that promote the more active responses we label *upward ethical leadership*. We see upward ethical leadership as moving away from the problems of following and toward the promise of action.

Employee Reactions to Managerial Misconduct

The model in Figure 28.1 depicts a situation in which an employee is faced with unethical behavior by a manager. Unethical behavior could include lying to senior leaders or customers, falsifying reports or financial records, or directing employees to engage in these behaviors. For example, the illegal financial reporting of WorldCom was the result of senior managers coercing employees to alter financial documents, and in some cases, doing so themselves. Such situations create moral distress in employees who are aware of the unethical conduct but feel constrained from taking action to correct it. Depending on their sense of powerlessness (high or low), employees make a choice about how they will respond. They can respond actively (i.e., upward ethical leadership) by taking a stand against their manager, questioning the legality or ethicality of the action, or simply rejecting solicitations to assist with the unethical conduct. Or, they can respond passively (i.e., following) by remaining silent while the unethical activity occurs or complying with unethical requests and being obedient to authority.

Moral distress and unethical climates. At the heart of employees' reactions to managerial misconduct is the feeling of moral distress. As described by Professor Wendy Austin and her colleagues, moral distress is a term used to describe a reaction in which an individual believes he/she knows the right thing to do but does not do it, either due to internal weaknesses or failures or external constraints or barriers. It arises when an individual recognizes a moral responsibility but does not act upon it. This results in a feeling of great pain, anxiety or sorrow. In extreme cases, the pain can be acute, causing physical or mental suffering:

Figure 28.1 Employee Reactions to Ethical Misconduct by a Manager (Higher-Ups)

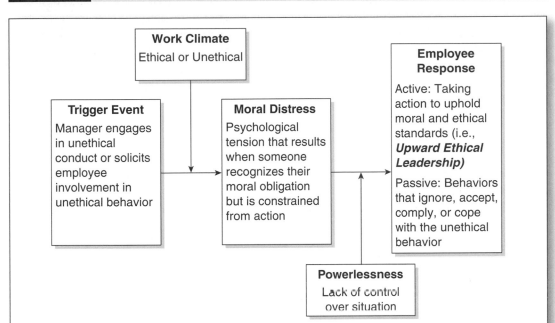

The lead interrogator of the Division Interrogation Facility had given me specific instructions: I was to deprive the detainee of sleep during my 12-hour shift by opening his cell every hour, forcing him to stand in a corner and stripping him of his clothes. Three years later the tables have turned. It is rare that I sleep through the night without a visit from this man. His memory harasses me as I once harassed him . . .

These lines were written by Eric Fair in a column submitted to *The Washington Post*. Mr. Fair was a civilian interrogator sent to Falluja in 2004 to assist the 82nd airborne division in the interrogation of Iraqi prisoners. Called into service because of his facility with the Arabic language, Fair believed his work would help obtain information from Iraqi prisoners that would contribute to ending the insurgency. Instead, he found himself in a situation previously (and currently) unimaginable to him: When ordered to inflict unspeakable treatment on Iraqi prisoners to draw out information about the insurgency, he complied. Believing he had no option but to follow directives from his commanders, he went along with orders and engaged in

torture tactics that haunt him to this day. The moral distress caused by this experience is so deep that he seeks outlets to make amends for his wrongs, such as writing columns to newspapers publicly confessing the immorality of his acts and his inability to take a stand when in the context of the situation. As the interrogator put it, "While I was appalled by the conduct of my friends and colleagues, I lacked the courage to challenge the status quo."

As illustrated in this example, moral distress arises when an individual feels constrained from taking moral or ethical action in an unethical situation. In order for moral distress to occur, the observer must acknowledge his or her moral responsibility for acting in the face of unethical conduct. In addition, he or she must perceive barriers to action which are internal (lack of courage, lack of power, etc.) and/or external (no neutral or anonymous outlet to report wrong doing) to the individual.

There are a number of reasons why employees might perceive they are unable to act in unethical situations. In addition to the obvious reasons, such as status differentials and the threat of being ostracized or terminated, there is also the issue of whether or not employees feel they have an appropriate outlet for reporting wrongdoing. In our model this is depicted as ethical versus unethical climates. Ethical climates are defined here as those in which established ethical standards and norms are consistently and pervasively communicated and maintained by organizational leaders and employees. Ethical climates are exhibited through strong ethical codes of conduct, easily accessible venues and hotlines for employees to report incidents of unethical behavior, and strict assurance that retaliation against employees who come forward will not be tolerated. For example, The Home Depot Inc.'s Ethical Code of Conduct states, "Associates have a duty to report suspected wrongdoing and should do so without fear of retaliation. The company will not tolerate any retaliation or threats of retaliation against anyone who reports in good faith a violation of the law, company policy, or this code of ethics."

Unethical climates are the opposite. They are characterized by questionable or even outright unethical behavior by managers and/or employees, with little action taken to redress this behavior, and in some cases (e.g., Enron), active condoning of inappropriate activities. In these climates employees have no obvious ways to report what they are seeing and experiencing, and cannot be assured that their efforts to demonstrate the courage and take a stand against unethical behavior will be appreciated (even worse, they may result in retribution).

Employees may experience unethical climates in only small pockets of an organization—for example, work units where employees feel a manager is behaving unethically but there is no apparent way for them to report this behavior or get the manager to change. Alternatively, unethical climates may characterize the organization more broadly and be accompanied by a command-and-control culture. Reports from WorldCom and Boeing suggest that individuals were rewarded for their "loyalty," defined as the willingness to go along, not question the decisions of superiors, and only speaking to higher-ups about positive things that were occurring in the organization. Employees may also report unethical climates when professional norms of conduct conflict with institutional realities, such as nurses who report moral distress when they do not have adequate resources for patient care due to hospital administration (e.g., low staffing levels, limited time available to spend with patients, inaccessibility to certain medical procedures).

In sum, when employees experience unethical behavior by a manager we expect them to feel some level of moral distress, simply due to the nature of hierarchy (e.g., manager seen as boss, socialization to obey authority, fear of speaking up). However, this distress will likely be much greater in unethical climates, because the options available to employees for taking moral action are much more limited. The experience of distress is important, because as described in the next section, it will be related to how employees decide to respond—whether they are willing to take an active stand relative to the unethical behavior or choose a more passive response, such as remaining silent or complying with unethical commands.

Powerlessness and choice of response (active or passive). Moral distress can lead employees to engage in various behaviors in an effort to relieve their negative psychological state. For example, employees may respond by remaining silent, taking a stance, acting secretively, sustaining themselves through work with clients, seeking support from colleagues, and exiting the organization. We can characterize these responses as active or passive. Active responses are displayed when employees take action to uphold moral and ethical standards (including speaking up, taking a stand, refusing to comply with unethical requests, surreptitiously reporting or rebelling against the unethical behavior, trying to identify alternatives to unethical behavior, or leaving the organization). Passive responses include behaviors that ignore, accept, comply, or cope with the unethical behavior (e.g., silence, participating in unethical behaviors, complying with orders to take an inappropriate action, or seeking support from others or solace from the positive elements of one's work to cope with personal feelings of distress).

Whether an employee chooses an active or passive response will depend on many personal and situational characteristics, which we include under the label of powerlessness. Powerlessness is a term we use to describe a sense of lack of control, over oneself and with others, in a situation. It can be seen as the expectancy or probability held by an individual that one's own behavior cannot determine the occurrence of desired outcomes.

When powerlessness is experienced, it creates a sense of hopelessness that anything can be done to resolve the situation. This hopelessness creates dissonance, or anxiety due to the inconsistency between what one believes should occur and what one is able to do. A mechanism that can be used to relieve the dissonance and the guilt invoked by high moral distress is a "flight from responsibility." In examining the experiences of nurses involved in the killings in Nazi Germany, researchers have found that many of these nurses dealt with the deliberate killing of patients by trying to avoid any concrete knowledge of what was happening, even as patients died before their eyes. Said one nurse, "I tried to soothe my conscience by telling myself that the doctor alone bears the responsibility." Therefore, high feelings of powerlessness are expected to lead to passive, rather than active, responses. When employees feel a sense of powerlessness they perceive a lack of options.

This feeling of powerlessness may be associated with differences in personality or individual characteristics. For example, individuals who are high in obedience to authority or low in self-esteem may never consider that there may be an opportunity to take a stand or speak up to higher authority, even in the best of situations. This tendency to defer to authority would also be characteristic of individuals from high power-distance cultures, in which less powerful individuals expect others to wield larger amounts of power than themselves. Others, for example those with proactive personalities, may consider action as the first option, and adopt a passive approach only in very extreme situations. Individuals high in proactive personality are characterized by a consistent tendency to "make things happen." These individuals exercise personal influence over their surroundings, and see the environment as jointly determined by both the person influencing the situation and the situation influencing the person. Since individuals who are proactive tend to demonstrate proactive behaviors across a wide range of situations, we would expect them to be less likely to assume powerlessness in the face managerial unethical conduct.

A feeling of powerlessness may also be manifest by the environment. For example, employees may perceive that they have no one to turn to, as in the case of Lucent Technologies Inc. employees who knew about revenue irregularities but did not have a trusted adviser or someone with whom they could discuss the situation. Moreover, employees may perceive that the consequences of not complying or taking a stand are too great, either personally or professionally, to risk an active response. These feelings are likely to be stronger in command and control cultures (e.g., Boeing) or those with high performance-based demands (e.g., Enron).

Consistent with our model, then, individuals who are higher in powerlessness are more likely to adopt passive responses. The feeling of powerlessness will vary by individuals and situations. For some individuals, taking an ethical stand when a manager's behavior is morally questionable will engender fear and distress *even in an ethical climate*. Hence, the thought of taking an active stand in an *unethical* climate may be unimaginable for most individuals.

Key to our framework, however, is our suggestion that individuals will be more willing and able to respond in an active manner *when they experience a lower sense of powerlessness*. In other words, individuals will be more likely to choose to respond actively if they perceive greater power to deal with the situation. Therefore, what we need to understand is: (a) how individuals can increase their sense of power and (b) how organizations can reduce employees' feelings of powerlessness. This is at the core of upward ethical leadership, and is the topic to which we turn next.

Empowering Action: Upward Ethical Leadership

Upward ethical leadership describes leadership behavior by employees who act to maintain ethical standards in the face of questionable moral conduct by higher-ups. It is important in cases where employees experience an ethical violation by a manager(s) and have no obvious venue, such as an ethics officer or ethics hotline, for reporting it. In these situations, employees must make a decision about whether they "risk" taking action or adopt a "flight from responsibility." The sections below help illustrate how, by training employees to develop personal power and upward leadership skills, we can prepare them to be more capable of choosing an active approach in the situation where they must make a decision about how to respond to managerial wrongdoing.

Power and dependence. Building on the discussion above, an important element of preparing employees to adopt an upward ethical leadership approach is getting them to understand their sources of power. Power is a sense of control over oneself and others, and the perceived probability that one can influence the occurrence of desired outcomes. From classic studies on power we know that power is based on dependencies. When one feels dependent on another, the other has power "over" them—the greater the dependency, the greater the power. For example, many employees feel their organizations have tremendous power over them because they are overly dependent on the organization for employment. This makes them feel they have no option but to comply with what the organization (or their manager) tells them to do (i.e., powerlessness).

To the extent that individuals can reduce this dependence, for example by making themselves more marketable, they reduce the power the organization holds with them. This is one of the outcomes of the downsizing craze in the 1990s—many employees became aware that they were at the mercy of one organization for employment. Since then, many workers have adopted a new approach to career management that involves making themselves more broadly marketable and more willing to change organizations if better options come along. The nature of dependency also explains why money is a tremendous source of power. When individuals have enough, they do not have to rely on anyone else to obtain it (they are "independent").

Individuals can also enhance their power by increasing others' dependence on them. For example, employees can make themselves more valuable to the organization. In the power literature, the latter is referred to as making oneself nonsubstitutable, making oneself central to the organization's mission, and increasing one's visibility. Top salespeople or highly respected managers, for example, have learned to capitalize on these capabilities by making themselves key contributors to the organizational mission, relatively hard to replace, and on the radars (highly visible) of others in the organization. They have power with the organization because the company does not want to lose them (which is also good for the company, as it gives them a skilled workforce).

Understanding dependence is integral to upward ethical leadership because engaging in such leadership behavior may involve making the decision to remove a higher-up's (e.g., a manager's) power over you. In other words, individuals who feel powerless because of a dependency on the manager who is behaving unethically (for a promotion, a raise, a preferred work schedule or assignment, a job) have the option to reduce this sense of powerlessness by removing the dependence. For example, the employee has to say to him/herself, "I realize there may be a cost to this behavior in that the manager may not give me the promotion, but I am willing to bear that cost to do what I think is morally right." While this choice is obviously not preferred and more likely to be necessary in situations of highly unethical climates, for employees to be able to engage in upward ethical leadership they will need to maintain this option.

The choice to remove the manager's power over them is made easier if the employee has managed her employability (e.g., marketability) to keep her options open. In such a case an employee does not have to suffer the consequences of refusing to go along with unethical behavior, but can choose to go elsewhere for the promotion. This concept involves remembering that, except in rare cases of totalitarianism or dictatorship, power is a choice: Individuals can choose to give it, or they can choose to remove it. People who understand how to effectively manage power always keep their options open so that they have the personal choice to act consistently with their personal values and beliefs, even when faced with situations such as ethical misconduct by managers.

Personal power. In addition to understanding the nature of dependence, upward ethical leadership involves recognizing that power is not just authority. Authority is one base of power, and can be a potent one, but it is certainly not the only, or even the most effective, power source. Moreover, authority is reserved to managers and therefore not available (typically) to subordinates; instead, subordinates must learn to establish their personal power (and organizations should encourage them to develop it as well).

Personal power is the ability to influence others to do something that you would like done, and is an informal power source that emanates from the individual and how he/she interacts with their environment (rather than power vested in a position). Individuals carry their personal power with them in the form of relationships, reputation, credibility, networks, competence, information, leadership skills, and expertise. Martin Luther King, for example, had tremendous personal power in the civil rights movement, even though he had no authority that gave him this power. Personal power is built over time and through interactions with others, and gives one a sense of confidence in his/her ability and/or capability. Most important to this discussion, it can be developed and used by subordinates because it does not require that one be in a formal position of power.

The types of personal power available to subordinates for upward ethical leadership are listed in Table 28.1. In addition to maintaining employability, which was discussed above, one of the most important sources of personal power in these situations is relationships. When individuals have established effective relationships with others they can draw upon these relationships in times of need, such as when a manager acts unethically. If individuals have not established effective networks of relationships, they have no one to whom they can turn. As Glenn Ebersole, an independent executive coach and founder of two consulting practices has stated, "There have been instances where I have been approached by unethical prospects and clients and was fortunate enough to have had strong mentors and supervisors, managers and owners that supported my actions to turn away from unethical requests."

These relationships can be with managers, coworkers, or colleagues/peers, and can be inside or outside the organization. Though the effort may be complicated by situations where the immediate manager is committing unethical behavior, individuals who have established solid work relationships with the manager may be more willing to approach the manager with concerns or to refuse to comply with the unethical behavior. Moreover, if they have effective relationships with their coworkers, they may be able to rally others to join them in expressing their concerns or refusing to comply with unethical directives, thereby minimizing the spread of the ethical misconduct.

Table 28.1 Power Sources Available for Upward Ethical Leadership

Source of Personal Power	Why Is It a Source of Power?	How Can You Use it?
Employability	Reduces dependence on the organization	Remove other's power over you (by being willing to leave) so you are free to act in accordance with your ethical principles and moral values
Relationships/networks • With manager • With coworkers/peers • With higher-ups • Outside the firm	Ability to influence others and draw support from your network	Allows for consultation with immediate manager or higher-ups. Employee can use their relationships to test the legitimacy of an unethical request or report the unethical conduct to a higher-up. Provides opportunity to secure the support of peers or coworkers (i.e., power in numbers)
Competence/reputation	Ability to influence others because you are respected	Employee can use their credibility as a source of strength, making it more likely others will listen if they speak up
Communication skills	Ability to influence with credibility and strength	Employee can use this skill to create a message that will be heard by others. Enhances ability to influence with confidence and without fueling conflict
Proactive problem-solving	Enhances self-control over situation by expanding options (reduces sense of powerlessness)	Employee can think of alternative ways to actively take a stand or generate ideas for considering wider range of possibilities for responding

Some of the most useful relationships in the case of unethical managerial behavior are those that individuals have established with "higher-ups"—managers at higher levels in the organization who are not their bosses. These individuals serve not only as an outlet for reporting unethical actions but a source of guidance and advice for the employee in deciding how best to deal with the situation.

Employees who are "connected" in such ways can be a valuable resource for organizations in maintaining ethical standards, because they have the power to respond actively to unethical conduct and are more likely to do so than those who have not established these relationships. An example of this can be seen by one WorldCom manager who, when asked to release money from an accrued account, called a top executive to make sure that the request was legitimate and to ask for advice on handling the situation.

Another key source of personal power is competence and reputation. These are important because they enhance an employee's credibility if he or she chooses to disclose the ethical misconduct. Speaking up or taking a stand will often pit the employee against the manager—hence the risk to the employee. If the employee has a solid reputation and is perceived as highly credible, however, others will be less likely to automatically disregard the individual and instead give the employee's concern legitimate consideration. For example, when a Hewlett-Packard Co. board member became suspicious about the internal methods used to investigate a media leak, he was able to convince the board, as well as some senior executives, to look more deeply into the matter. What resulted was evidence that the company had been engaging in "pretexting," or the act of obtaining personal information under false pretenses. Without a strong reputation of credibility, this board member may have experienced resistance to the insinuation that something illegal was occurring within the company.

Upward leadership skills. Organizations can also prepare employees for engaging in ethical leadership by helping them to develop their upward leadership skills. Key upward leadership skills for dealing with ethical misconduct by managers include understanding how to use supportive communication principles and the ability to engage in proactive problem-solving. These skills help individuals to approach the situation with the intent of trying to resolve the situation in a noninflammatory and proactive manner.

Supportive communication skills focus on approaching a communication situation with a problem-solving orientation, meaning the individual addresses the other with a statement such as "I have a problem and I would like to discuss it with you" (in essence, engaging the other in solving one's problem). The individual then frames all of the communication in such a way to avoid defensiveness (i.e., putting the other on the defensive) and disconfirmation (i.e., putting the other person down). Specific techniques include focusing on the problem and not the person (e.g., not "you are unethical" but "I am concerned that your behavior may be unethical") and being specific and not global (e.g., not "you always behave unethically" but "your asking me to falsify the numbers in the report yesterday was against the ethical code of conduct").

Supportive communication skills are designed to help individuals arm themselves to deal with difficult communication situations involving conflict (thereby empowering them to overcome the pervasive inclination to avoid conflict). They are particularly suited for upward ethical leadership because such situations naturally involve conflict. If not managed properly, communications can quickly break down and problems escalate.

Proactive problem-solving is taking the initiative to identify novel ways to approach problem situations. It is important to upward ethical leadership because it encourages individuals to be creative in thinking about ways to deal with the situation, rather than just assuming they can do nothing. In some cases this may involve expanding the options available for responding to the unethical action (e.g., using one's network to test the legitimacy of a behavior that is seemingly unethical). In other cases, employees may be able to provide managers with alternative approaches that attain objectives in an ethical, rather than unethical, manner (e.g., suggesting that a team be assembled to talk through a problem or devise a plan of action).

Summary. In sum, the discussion above illustrates how helping employees to establish their personal power and develop upward leadership skills can better prepare them to take action if they are faced with unethical behavior by managers or higher-ups. A focus on upward ethical leadership reframes thinking about leadership away from it being the sole responsibility of managers and toward it being a process that can be engaged in by organizational members more broadly. In this way, employees are important members of the group called "organizational leaders" who are responsible for enforcing and maintaining ethical standards and principles in businesses. Finally, we would also like to note here that, although these ideas are consistent with Ira Chaleff's framework for "Courageous Followership," we have intentionally chosen to call this behavior leadership because we do not think it involves following. Rather, it involves being a responsible participant in the leadership process.

Conclusions and Recommendations

An assumption of practitioners and ethics researchers is that managers are responsible for being role models for ethical behavior, establishing ethical climates, and enforcing consequences for employees who behave unethically. However, we know that in many organizational situations employees are witness to unethical actions by managers, with no apparent recourse for reporting this behavior. Therefore, missing in this discussion of ethics is the question of what employees can and should do in the context of unethical climates where it is the managers who are behaving unethically.

Managers who engage in, or solicit their employees' help with, unethical conduct create circumstances that limit employee action. Employees may feel trapped, obligated to comply, or perceive that there are no outlets for reporting the wrongdoing to individuals who can take corrective action. In the opening quote to this article, the CEO comments on employees' failure to speak up. As we have shown, in the face of managerial misconduct with no effective outlet for reporting such behavior, employees will likely feel a sense of powerlessness and a lack of responsibility (due to the nature of hierarchy) that causes them to choose a passive response, such as silence or obedience. Upward ethical leadership is premised on the proposition that, by helping employees to establish their personal power and develop upward leadership skills, we can reduce this sense of powerlessness and enable employees to feel capable of effectively addressing problems of ethical misconduct by higher-ups.

We suggest that organizations can foster upward ethical leadership by creating and supporting cultures that

recognize the value of employee leadership and reward individuals who demonstrate the courage to speak up. Some ways in which organizations can do this include:

- Move away from command-and-control cultures. Command-and-control cultures are top-down and fuel the problems of following (described above). Instead, organizations should encourage all employees to become active partners in the leadership process.
- Promote ethical climates. Create an atmosphere where ethical standards and norms are consistently and pervasively communicated and maintained by organizational leaders and employees. Establish strong ethical codes of conduct, easily accessible venues and hotlines for employees to report incidents of unethical behavior, and strict assurance that retaliation against employees who come forward will not be tolerated.
- Rethink how you see leadership. Not all managers are leaders and not all leaders are managers. Recognize that leadership can occur at any level of the organization and by anyone who works to effect productive change in a system (being a leader does not require being in a managerial position).
- Foster climates of responsibility rather than hierarchy. Don't restrict responsibility solely due to hierarchy. All employees should be empowered and be accountable for promoting ethical behavior that helps the organization be successful.
- Value upward leadership. Don't reward blind obedience and don't "kill the messenger." Encourage and reward questions and well intended push-back (be grateful to for employees who provide honest feedback, even if it is not easy to hear). Provide training in upward leadership skills (e.g., communication, proactive problem-solving).

Employees can also proactively prepare themselves for upward ethical leadership. As described above, this involves managing personal power and upward leadership skills. For example, as an employee you can work to:

- *Establish your personal power.* Knowing how you bring value to the organization can reduce your feelings of dependency. In addition, establishing strong networks of relationships can produce power in numbers and source of advice and support.

- *Know when it is right to question authority.* Trust your moral compass to tell you when something is not right. If you feel something is wrong, gather evidence and talk to your network to help you decide on a course of action.
- *Develop your upward leadership skills.* Pushing ideas or concerns up may require a different set of skills. Learn to communicate so your concerns will be heard. Don't discount your ethical responsibility—learn to think about problems and solutions in proactive ways.
- *Don't succumb to fear climates.* Be willing to "break the norm" of silence—usually the fears are unfounded. Knowing how to communicate information in nonoffensive ways will often resolve the problem.
- *Continually work to uphold your reputation and credibility.* Having credibility will add leverage to your concern and increase the likelihood that you will be heard.

In conclusion, when organizational leaders engage in ethical misconduct, the usual means for redressing the violation—managerial action—is no longer viable. Previous examples have shown us that employees are often aware of the misconduct, and in some cases, even asked to participate in it. To stop unethical behavior in these situations, we need to have employees who are willing and capable to take a stand, not only in terms of rejecting solicitations for collusion, but by actively addressing and containing the misconduct. We also need organizations to recognize and reward employees who engage in ethical leadership—the potential harm of ethical scandals promulgated by organizational leaders is too great to restrict responsibility for ethics only to managers.

Selected Bibliography

You can find information on Milgram's obedience studies in his 1974 book titled *Obedience to Authority: An Experimental View,* published by Harper and Row, NY, NY. Moreover, the book titled *Obedience to Authority: Current Perspective on the Milgram Paradigm,* edited by Thomas Blass and published by Jossey-Bass (2000) is an

excellent source for research that has been conducted on this topic in the past 35 years.

For more information on the postindustrial model of leadership, see *The Post-Bureaucratic Organization: New Perspectives on Organizational Change* edited by Charles Heckscher and Anne Donnellon (Sage Publications, 1994) and Joseph Rost's *Leadership for the Twenty-First Century* (Praeger, 1993). For models of shared and relational leadership, see Craig Pearce and Jay Conger's edited book *Shared Leadership: Reframing the Hows and Whys of Leadership* (Sage, 2003); Wilfred Drath's *Deep Blue Sea: Rethinking the Sources of Leadership* (Jossey-Bass, 2001); and Mary Uhl-Bien's chapter on "Relationship Development as a Key Ingredient for Leadership Development" in Susan Murphy and Ron Riggio (Eds.) *The Future of Leadership Development* (Lawrence Erlbaum Associates, 2003), 129-147. In addition, valuable resources on power and dependence and sources of personal power may be found in John Kotter's article on "Power, Dependence, and Effective Management," *Harvard Business Review,* July-August, 1977, and J. French and B. Raven's book chapter titled "The Bases of Social Power" in D. Cartwright's edited book *Studies of Social Power,* published by the Institute for Social Research, Ann Arbor, MI.

Further information on voice and silence in organizations can be found in a number of works by Francis Milliken and colleagues such as their 2003 article titled "An Exploratory Study of Employee Silence: Issues that Employees Don't Communicate Upward and Why," published in a special issue of *Journal of Management Studies* on Voice and Silence in Organizations, 40, 1453-1476. Similar work on voice, silence, and moral distress can be found in a 2005 article by Wendy Austin and colleagues titled "To Stay or To Go, To Speak or Stay Silent, To Act or Not To Act: Moral Distress as Experienced by Psychologists," *Ethics and Behavior,* 15, 197-212.

Two important works on followership include Ira Chaleff's 1998 book titled *The Courageous Follower: Standing Up To and For Our Leaders* (Berrett-Koehler Publishers, San Francisco, CA) and Robert E. Kelley's work, including a 1991 book chapter titled "Combining Followership and Leadership into Partnership" which is published in Ralph Kilmann and Ines Kilmann's *Making Organizations Competitive: Enhancing Networks and Relationships across Traditional Boundaries* (San Francisco, CA, Jossey-Bass).

CHAPTER 29

Toxic Leaders

They're Plentiful

Jean Lipman-Blumen

Drucker School of Management

> I am bewitched with the rogue's company. If the rascal have not given me medicines to make me love him, I'll be hanged.
>
> —*Falstaff in Shakespeare's* Henry IV

> Ah, mon cher, for anyone who is alone, without God and without a master, the weight of days is dreadful. Hence one must choose a master, God being out of style.
>
> —*Albert Camus,* The Fall

Falstaff is not the only follower who has ever felt bewitched by a toxic leader. Many of us succumb to their allure. Falstaff, for his part, was openly besotted with Prince Hal, the rebellious, youthful leader-in-waiting.[1] More often, however, we followers deny how truly enchanted we are. We may grouse about toxic leaders, but frequently we tolerate them—and for surprisingly long periods of time.

Tolerate, in fact, may be far too weak a word to describe the complex relationship between toxic leaders and their followers. These intriguing leaders first charm but then manipulate, mistreat, undermine, and ultimately leave their followers worse off than they found them. Yet many of these followers hang on. I do not speak merely of the leader's immediate entourage—the leader's close-in staff and advisors. I am speaking also

Source: Toxic Leaders: They're Plentiful, pp. 3–24. From *The Allure of Toxic Leaders: Why We Follow Destructive Bosses and Corrupt Politicians—and How We Can Survive Them* (2004) by Lipman-Blumen, Jean. Reprinted by permission of Oxford University Press, Inc.

of the larger mass of supporters (employees, constituents, volunteers) who only glimpse their toxic leader through a glass darkly—perchance through a window of the executive suite or on the television screen. More surprisingly perhaps, even those groups charged with keeping leaders under the microscope and on the straight and narrow—the media and boards of directors—fall under their sway.

Followers of toxic leaders often do much more than simply tolerate them. They commonly adulate, abet, and actually prefer toxic leaders to their nontoxic counterparts. That astonishing choice occurs everywhere that leaders strut their stuff—in business, politics, the nonprofit world of education and religion, athletics, the family, and all the other arenas of human action. During their heyday, Enron's Kenneth Lay and Jeffrey Skilling, WorldCom's Bernard Ebbers, ImClone's Samuel Waksal, Tyco International's L. Dennis Kozlowski, Sunbeam's Al Dunlap, HealthSouth's Richard Scrushy, Adolph Hitler, Boston's Roman Catholic cardinal Bernard Law, TV evangelist James Bakker, and Texas Tech basketball coach Bobby Knight, for starters, enjoyed—and many still enjoy—enthusiastic support from their followers.

One historical example from the corporate world: Not long after a jury convicted Michael R. Milken, the "junk bond king" of investment firm Drexel Burnham Lambert, of securities fraud, a large group of former DBL employees appeared on Phil Donahue's TV talk show. To a person, the still unemployed stockbrokers and administrative assistants spoke glowingly of their former boss, despite the fact that Milken's illegal actions led to the closure of the firm and the loss of their jobs.

Another historical example from the political arena: In 1904, while serving a sixty-day jail term for impersonating a constituent at a federal postal exam, Boston's Ward 17 boss, James Michael Curley, won an alderman's seat.[2] According to the *Boston Irish Reporter*, Curley explained, "I felt I had done a charitable thing for a man who needed a job, so he could support his wife and four children."[3]

Then in 1945, after decades of a "colorful career" and while under indictment for mail fraud, Curley was handily elected mayor of Boston.[4] In 1946, a jury convicted the "rascal king." The day the verdict came down, the middle-aged saleswomen in Filene's Basement, a venerable Boston institution for bargain hunters, wept disconsolately. Curley ran the mayor's office from his jail cell for five months, until President Harry S. Truman commuted his sentence in 1947. In 1950, Truman pardoned him.

Here's a more recent example: When I first began writing this, Vincent "Buddy" A. Cianci Jr., the mayor of Providence, Rhode Island, for twenty-one years, was on trial for graft. Cianci was accused of "heading a criminal enterprise [whose purpose] was to enrich himself personally and politically," according to prosecutor Richard W. Rose.[5] Nonetheless, the New York Times reported that the six-term mayor "remains popular despite the charges." Subsequently a federal jury found Cianci guilty of a felony. In December 2002, Cianci began serving a five-year, four-month sentence in a federal penitentiary in Fort Dix, New Jersey.[6] Following Cianci's sentencing, one female constituent wistfully complained, "I wish he'd get away with it."[7] Robert Barrera, a businessman from North Smithfield, lamented, "This is an event that people will remember like 9/11 and when Kennedy was shot. [Cianci] was such a positive influence you hate to see this."[8]

Where Are the Saints?

Do not look for saints among formal leaders. Saints rarely seek elected or appointed office. They seldom enter the rough-and-tumble of politics or the corporate world. Nor are we likely to encounter saintly leaders in the spit and polish of the traditional military. And, certainly, we'll be hard pressed to find them in the more arcane halls of academia. Oftentimes they are even absent from the sacred assemblies of the church, as the sexual abuse scandal within the Catholic Church has so poignantly revealed.

If saints did frequent such locales, there would be little need to consider why followers knowingly tolerate, seldom unseat, frequently prefer, and sometimes even create toxic leaders.

We are more likely to discover saintly leaders outside of formal organizations, taking up the burdens of unsung leadership. We might spot such leaders in the streets feeding the homeless or on the hustings among the voiceless, where social movements are fomented.

Still, formal organizations are not totally devoid of decent leaders. You can find them in steady, sometimes little-known companies that provide an honest service or produce a dependable product, or in the clinics that treat the undernourished and the impoverished, or in schools that care about knowledge, truth, and integrity. For example, by all accounts, Aaron Feuerstein of Malden Mills brightens the corporate firmament, even as he suffers financial setbacks.

Not everyone, of course, will agree on the saintliness of these leaders. In fact, their opponents frequently perceive them as rabble-rousers or worse. For example, when Mohandas Karam-chand Gandhi left South Africa after two decades of organizing the poorly treated Indian minority into a nonviolent political movement, "his greatest Afrikaner adversary, General Jan Smuts, was relieved enough to write to a friend, 'The saint has left our shores, I hope, forever.'"[9]

So we can all see at the outset that the topic of toxic leadership is vexing at best, given that my toxic leader may be your hero and vice versa. Even Hitler, most reviled of twentieth-century leaders, still has admirers. Historian Robert Gellately reports an interview with a survivor of the Nazi era:

> One . . . woman, wife of a prominent historian of Germany, neither of whom incidentally were Nazi Party members, . . . remembers . . . [that] "there were certainly eighty per cent who lived productively and positively throughout the time . . . We also had good years. We had wonderful years."[10]

Even Exemplary Leaders Have Some Toxic Chinks

Nor are leaders who are widely applauded as exemplary necessarily without their occasional toxic chinks. Numerous corporate leaders whose missteps were visible only to those in the inner circle have led their businesses to great financial success. Sometimes the toxicity is an act of commission, at other times one of omission. Lee Iacocca, as CEO of Chrysler, revived that nearly moribund company, yet stumbled into several ill-advised actions, including subsequent harsh treatment of the unionized employees who had contributed mightily to the automaker's resuscitation.

Some exemplary not-for-profit leaders have stepped over the line in their zeal to reach their laudable goals. Political leaders, too, some among the most admired—such as Franklin D. Roosevelt, Harry S. Truman, and even Abraham Lincoln—occasionally have acted in ways that we'd be hard pressed not to label "toxic."

Even the saints are not completely "toxic free." According to Christopher Hitchens, Mother Teresa blithely accepted a donation from financier Charles Keating, of the savings and loan scandal. Subsequently, the founder of the Order of the Missionaries of Charity wrote to presiding judge Lance Ito, attempting to intercede on Keating's behalf in the sentencing phase of his trial.[11] So let's be realists and remember that even beloved icons of leadership can display human frailties.

Public, Private, Not for Profit: Indulgence Reigns

In the last few years, the corporate stage has been littered with tattered integrity, limitless greed, lust for power, corrosive cynicism, and deliberately peddled illusions of the leader's omnipotence. From Victor Posner of corporate raider infamy to Dynegy's Chuck Watson, Sotheby chairman A. Alfred Taubman, Warnaco's Linda Wachner, and Gary Winnick of Global Crossing—and this far from exhausts the list—the corporate world has produced a bumper crop of toxic leaders.

The not-for-profit world boasts its own mother lode of candidates, including William Aramony of the United Way, who served seven years in the federal prison camp at Seymour Johnson Air Force Base in North Carolina. Aramony was convicted on twenty-five counts, including "conspiracy to defraud, mail fraud, wire fraud, transportation of fraudulently acquired property, engaging in monetary transactions in unlawful activity, filing false tax returns and aiding in the filing of false tax returns."[12]

The U.S. Olympic Committee, too, has had more than its fair share of toxic leaders. (We'll come to the International Olympic Committee shortly.) Some, such as former president Sandra Baldwin, who admitted lying on her resumé, have been forced to resign. Others, including CEO Lloyd Ward, who failed to disclose his conflict of interest in promoting his brother's and a childhood pal's firm to supply backup power for the Dominican Republic's games, received a genteel tap on the wrist from the board. In another toxic twist, the board ousted Baldwin's replacement, president Marty Mankamyer, after she revealed Ward's conflict of interest. The board of directors "blam[ed] her for infighting within the organization and claim[ed] she conspired with a staff member to try and force CEO Lloyd Ward from his job."[13] Through all this, Ward seemed to be hanging on. Not until after Mankamyer's ouster did the media drumbeat finally force Ward's departure.

Across the religious spectrum as well, we witness toxic leaders: TV evangelist James Bakker, convicted of twenty-four counts of fraud and conspiracy; Bishop Thomas O'Brien, former head of the Roman Catholic Diocese of Phoenix, involved in a deadly hit-and-run accident as well as the cover-up of child molestation by priests; the faceless ranks of pedophiliac priests in the United States and abroad; the late Rabbi Meir Kahane, New York urban terrorist turned member of the Israeli Knesset; and the 1930s demagogic radio priest Father Charles E. Coughlin.[14] The list goes on.

Toxic Leadership Crosses Geographical Borders in a Single Leap

Geographical borders do not impede the appearance of toxic leaders—political and corporate—who undermine, manipulate, terrorize, sabotage, diminish, and even eliminate their followers. From Josef Stalin in the Soviet Union to Augusto Pinochet in Chile, Richard Nixon in the United States, Indira Gandhi in India, Pol Pot in Cambodia, Ferdinand Marcos in the Philippines, Alberto Fujimori in Peru, Saddam Hussein in Iraq, Slobodan Milosevic in Yugoslavia, and Charles Ghankay Taylor in Liberia, we see that toxic leadership offers a multicultural, multiracial, multiethnic equal-opportunity career path.

Nor should we interpret all these political examples to mean that the political arena has a headlock on toxic leadership. In fact, media mogul Silvio Berlusconi, subsequently the prime minister of Italy, adroitly managed to plant a foot in both camps. As sitting prime minister, Berlusconi, the wealthiest man in Italy, was put on trial for allegedly attempting to bribe judges eight years earlier. With the trial nearing a verdict, Berlusconi convinced his political allies in Italy's lower house of parliament to pass an immunity bill suspending the trial until after his term of office. That move cleared the way for Berlusconi to assume the presidency of the

European Union, which was imminently scheduled to rotate to Italy.

During the trial, in a scene worthy of Woody Allen's directorial genius, Berlusconi testified that he had engaged in the shady business deal on which the trial centered at the urging of then Italian prime minister Bettino Craxi, who "urged him to do so for the good of Italy."[15] "I had no direct interest, and Craxi begged me to intervene because he believed that the operation damaged the state," Berlusconi insisted.[16] According to Berlusconi, his political adversary Romano Prodi intended to allow a state-controlled food company to be sold at a fire-sale price to one of Berlusconi's corporate competitors. (Incidentally, at the time of the trial Prodi was president of the European Commission.)

Moving unequivocally into the corporate arena, Jean-Marie Messier, chief executive of French media group Vivendi Universal, finally stepped down after a whirlwind tenure that left the shell-shocked company with an 80-percent decline in its value. The media had repeatedly predicted the departure of the former "darling of the Paris financial community" as he made one dramatic misstep after another. Nonetheless, the cosmopolitan CEO seemingly managed to keep his balance on that tightrope, at least until the major North American shareholder maneuvered his ouster.[17]

Across international borders, the not-for-profit world wallows in its own problems. Although some observers have diagnosed the Catholic Church's sexual abuse scandal as an "American affair," reports from other parts of the globe belie such oversimplification. A cover story in the National Catholic Reporter noted that in Sicily, Father Margarito Reyes Marchena, a Honduran immigrant, came under fire for allegedly abusing four Italian children. Father Vincenzo Noto, vicar general of the Diocese of Monreale, where Reyes had subsequently moved, declared, "The true victim is this 59-year-old priest." To aid the accused cleric, Father Noto started a collection and initiated a petition supporting Reyes.[18]

Let's consider one last set of international examples from the not-for-profit world of amateur athletes. First, the 1998 Tour de France earned the gold medal of scandal when Grenoble police arrested racers, trainers, and officials in a series of raids that "uncovered systematic use of the banned endurance-boosting hormone EPO."[19] The authorities detained Willy Voet, Festina team assistant, for "smuggling a carload of drugs across the Franco-Belgium border."[20] In addition, "authorities arrested the squad's manager and doctor."[21] That these toxic leaders had misled their charges was demonstrated by the fact that the Tour disqualified France's premier team and its top rider.

Second, in the 2002 Winter Games in Salt Lake City, Marie-Reine Le Gougne, a French Olympic skating judge, allegedly "favored a Russian couple in [the] pairs skate to ensure a gold medal for the French in the [subsequent] ice dancing competition."[22] In this winter wonderland soap opera, Le Gougne claimed that French figure-skating federation president Didier Gailhaguet had insisted that she vote for the Russians, but later retracted her confession.

The third example involves none other than the president of the International Olympic Committee, Juan António Samaranch. Samaranch was accused of numerous improprieties, from indulging in an overly opulent lifestyle on the committee's tab to turning a blind eye to the Salt Lake City "gifts for votes" effort to become the site of the 2002 Games. Add to that Samaranch's nepotistic maneuver: The IOC president proposed his son for life membership in the IOC. These charges did not prevent the IOC from awarding Samaranch the IOC's most coveted honor, the gold Olympic Order, and honorary life presidency of the IOC when he stepped down after twenty-one years at the helm of the beleaguered organization. Presumably because that didn't say it all, more than one hundred IOC delegates voted to rename the Olympic Museum, in Lausanne, Switzerland, the Samaranch Museum. To put the cherry on the banana split, the committee then voted to invite Samaranch to all future meetings of the ruling executive board. Clearly, Falstaff was not the only one enamored of a toxic leader.

Toxic Leadership Proves Historically Durable

Nor is toxic leadership a recent historical phenomenon. As the Old Testament suggests, it has been around since King David bedded Bathsheba and sent her husband to certain death in battle. It probably also figured prior to recorded history, along with the wooly mammoth. Wherever we look, we see ample evidence of toxic leaders, some more extreme than others. Many nevertheless manage to retain both their followers and hagiographers for a surprisingly long time.

From one historical period to another, more often than we might want to admit, we accept and applaud leaders who exhibit various degrees of toxicity—some simply incompetent, some cowardly, others morally myopic, some cynical and venal, still others downright evil—while occupying formal leadership positions. Centuries apart, British monarch Henry VIII and American industrialist Henry Ford wielded toxic power.

Sometimes we recognize leaders' toxicity only after they leave their institutions in disarray and their hapless followers in despair. Worse yet, we frequently perceive the inadequacies of toxic leaders in real time but do little to stop them. These toxic leaders too often have their way with us and depart in their own good time under their own steam. Not until J. Edgar Hoover, director of the FBI for nearly half a century, died in office was his malignant leadership revealed to the public, yet many Washington insiders had long been aware.[23] During his lifetime, however, presidents, the press, and ordinary citizens lionized Hoover, even as he perpetrated some of his most reprehensible acts, including blackmailing presidents and railroading innocent people to protect FBI informants.[24] At this writing, the FBI building in Washington, D.C., still proudly bears his name.[25]

Enter the Whistle-Blower

Even when whistle-blowers, such as the FBI's Coleen Rowley, WorldCom's Cynthia Cooper, and Morton Thiokol's Roger Bois-joly, step forward at great risk to name and career, rarely do their courageous efforts result in punishment of the toxic leaders they unmask.[26] True, the general public and the media often acclaim whistle-blowers. To wit, *Time* magazine anointed Cooper, Rowley, and Enron's Sherron Watkins "Persons of the Year" in 2002. (Sherron Watkins acknowledges that she inadvertently became a whistle-blower only after "a Congressional investigator for the House Committee on Energy and Commerce stumbled across her memos [to Enron CEO Ken Lay] among thousands of subpoenaed documents."[27] Nonetheless, FBI director

Robert Mueller commended Marion "Spike" Bowman, who headed up the FBI's National Security Law Unit, for "exceptional service." Bowman's unit was the very division that, in August 2001, denied the request of Rowley's Minneapolis office to search the apartment and computer of Zacarias Moussaoui, a suspect in the September 11 World Trade Center attack. Moreover, despite public recognition, Rowley and her co-whistle-blowers have been pushed aside in their own organizations. According to *Time*, one of Rowley's colleagues at the Bureau informed her that "high-level FBI agents in Washington had been overheard discussing possible criminal charges against her."[28] Once identified, whistle-blowers predictably suffer various forms of backlash in their organizations.

Although it is hard to believe, we tend to prefer toxic leaders for a host of tantalizing reasons. When we don't have them, we go to great lengths to create them. The staggering numbers of such leaders in every arena, documented in the daily news, give ample evidence of our predilection for these problematic figures.

The Paradox of Cynicism: The Leader's Longevity

Paradoxically, at the same time that we yearn for them, we also feel deeply cynical about toxic leaders. In fact, a recent poll suggested that the American public's expectations for the morality of congressional leaders fell markedly below those for ordinary citizens. Following the Enron, Andersen, and Global Crossing debacles, the public image of corporate leaders is probably not much better. Still, our cynicism is often tinged with just enough fascination to keep us from casting them out altogether.

Sometimes we ignore toxic leaders' obvious faults because their charisma blinds us, at least until the leader is publicly unmasked. One former assistant to the charismatic but corrupt president of a small private college, who eventually retired on his own schedule, confided to me, "I know our new president is an honest, intelligent, and kind man, but I really miss Dennis's charm. He was so much fun to be around."

True, a few toxic leaders, such as Buddy Cianci, have been overthrown, imprisoned, or otherwise done in, but they tend to be the exceptions. Most toxic leaders

achieve surprising longevity, even those without armies or secret intelligence forces to intimidate potential dissidents. Overthrowing such leaders is no mean feat. As we've just seen, Juan António Samaranch headed the International Olympic Committee for twenty-one years.

Let's also remember that Ferdinand Marcos, Slobodan Milosevic, and Saddam Hussein are only three among the more recent toxic political leaders who held on for years, notwithstanding considerable opposition. And Hussein's ouster came not at the hands of his own citizens but through an external coalition. A jobless Yugoslav lawyer interviewed in the final days of Milosevic's administration dejectedly described how both she and her husband had simply "kept their heads down" during the previous ten years because "the time was not right" to resist the leader's abuses.

Prominent supporters, from political parties to boards of directors who help catapult the leader into office, assiduously protect their leaders' power—tied, as it is, to their own self-interest. Many influential supporters collude willingly, others follow blindly, and still others are drawn unwittingly into compromising actions that hand the leader a club to hold over them.

As for the great mass of rank-and-file followers, despite their complaining around the copy machine, they, too, routinely accept the domination of poor leaders, even when they greatly outnumber them. The multiple reasons that prompt followers to put up with and even seek out toxic leaders stem from many sources—our psyches and those of the toxic leaders, the complex world in which we live, and the experiences followers have in that world.

The Media's Myopia

Even the media have difficulty resisting the seductive appeal of wily leaders. For example, historical accounts of Fidel Castro's early presidential days exemplify how enthralled the media worldwide can become with an intriguing leader, notwithstanding signs of nascent toxicity. In the corporate sector, ITT's Harold Geneen, Henry Ford and his grandson Henry Ford II, and arbitrageur Ivan Boesky held center stage as media superstars, despite their clearly noxious impact.

Business Week's cover story of the downfall of Tyco's L. Dennis Kozlowski made a rare admission of media myopia. In its analysis of how and why Kozlowski raided the Tyco coffers without restraint for close to a decade, the analysts candidly shared the blame they attributed to lawyers, accountants, executives, and the board of directors: "The press, including *BusinessWeek*, also bears some blame for generally portraying Tyco as a lean and mean profit machine."[29]

In many cases, corporate leaders who ravage their companies, along with thousands of employees, become the darlings of the media and financial analysts. Such was the case with former Enron CEO Kenneth Lay. At least that was so before he openly displayed strong poster boy credentials for toxic leadership by urging Enron employees to purchase company stock even as Enron was imploding.

Al Dunlap's earlier performance at Scott Paper, which markedly increased shareholder value, made him downright irresistible to Sunbeam's board. No matter that the human costs were great. No matter that Scott Paper ultimately ceased to exist. During Dunlap's tenure as Sunbeam's CEO, dozens of fawning articles appeared in the press. In fact, echoing Falstaff, John A. Byrne described Dunlap's appeal:

> The bewitching power that Al Dunlap exercised over Wall Street came from an embellished track record as a corporate tough guy. . . . Dunlap, his record showed, did not shy from either conflict or adversity. . . . If Wall Street could have invented an executive that perfectly suited its style and its preferences, it would have created Al Dunlap. In a way, it did.[30]

Rather sadly, at the peak of Dunlap's rampage, *Fortune* magazine reported a poll of Cornell MBA students in which 60 percent said they admired the self-labeled "Chainsaw Al" for his slash-and-burn strategy. They saw it as "results oriented."[31] Eventually Sunbeam was forced into bankruptcy proceedings. Later the Securities and Exchange Commission accused Dunlap of directing a "huge accounting fraud" during his Sunbeam heyday.[32] Subsequent investigations revealed he had engaged in similar illegal behavior in previous posts.

As long as these corporate titans paint the bottom line black, the media as well as boards of directors, not to mention eager stockholders, generally remain in their thrall. Unfortunately, the media's assessment of these leaders as "rising stars," "gurus," or "fallen angels"

infiltrates the public consciousness, significantly shaping the attitudes of impressionable leaders-in-waiting, who mistake them for role models.

Not all toxic leaders behave toxically all of the time. Like Ken Lay in his civic philanthropist's role, they can act nonmalignantly, even constructively, in some contexts and in a toxic way in others. Sometimes, however, the apparently benign behavior simply creates a smoke-screen or serves as the means to other toxic action. Of course, when leaders hang out their incompetence, moral myopia, corruption, or unmitigated evil for all to see, the media have no trouble flip-flopping almost instantaneously from fawning to feeding frenzy.

Corporate leaders are not the only ones who catch the media's eye. Leaders in all sectors—religious, political, and educational, for starters—are fair game once they expose their toxic colors. In the Roman Catholic Archdiocese of Boston, Cardinal Bernard Law's long-term devotion to social causes, as well as his efforts to reach out to Israel and Cuba, led many observers to predict he would become the first American pope. Yet this much-admired cleric eventually found himself in the eye of the sexual abuse hurricane within the Church. Once the media exposed his thirty-year cover-up of pedophiliac priests, they kept the story on the front burner.

Clearly, this was a scandal long in the making. For three decades, His Eminence had continued to reassign priests accused of molesting young parishioners to new parishes where they preyed (no pun intended) on other unsuspecting victims. Amid calls from angry Catholics for Law's resignation, a substantial segment of the Boston laity nonetheless continued to support the beleaguered cleric. In this case, the media's late but unrelenting attention ultimately aroused enough whistle-blowers and appalled enough Catholics to bring down the intransigent cleric.

In every arena, we have multiple examples of the media feeding off the toxic behavior of leaders. Two factors—the media's legitimate watchdog function and its profit motive—increase the Fourth Estate's attention to toxic leaders once they are unmasked.

The Distorted Lens on Leaders

Traditionally, many, if not most, books on leadership concentrate on leaders rather than on followers. They view leaders through a distorted lens, emphasizing their strengths and minimizing their failings. These admiring accounts burnish the leader's charismatic facets to blinding brightness and inflate their images to Herculean proportions. It is not surprising, then, that James MacGregor Burns observed in his pathbreaking book, *Leadership*, that "leadership is one of the most observed and least understood phenomena on earth."[33]

This genre of leadership studies commonly softens the dark shadows cast by seemingly superhuman leaders. Then, of course, the autobiographies of leaders paint their authors, like former Sunbeam CEO Al Dunlap and Chrysler's Lee Iacocca, only from their most flattering angle. Such tales of glory inspire us to emulate these grandiose figures or at least to warm ourselves in their reflected glow.

Lest the reader think I am engaging in the countersin— a shortsighted view of good leaders—let me be clear: I do, of course, recognize that positive leaders exist and frequently contribute much to society. Václav Havel, Nelson Mandela, Mohandas K. Gandhi, and Martin Luther King Jr. stand out on the world's political stage as exemplary leaders who led in turbulent times. Warren Buffett of Berkshire Hathaway, Aaron Feuerstein of Malden Mills, Herb Kelleher, former CEO of Southwest Airlines, Anita Roddick, founder of the Body Shop, and Marcy Carsey, cochair and executive producer of the Carsey-Werner Company, come to mind on the corporate side, plus many more unsung business leaders. In fact, the great benefits that good leaders can bring make us want to invest all leaders, deserving or not, with these constructive attributes.

Yet the topic of bad leaders, particularly as individuals, has its own following. Clearly, there has been no shortage of bad leaders to chronicle. Library shelves groan with such studies. Leadership books that train less distorted lenses on the leader's obvious toxicity appear mostly after their subjects are safely dead. Then we tend to perform psychological autopsies, searching for the disease that poisoned the leader's lives, along with our own.

For some time now, a sizeable market has flourished in posthumous profiling of incompetent, feckless, and cynical, not to mention evil, political and corporate leaders. These biographies detail their cradle-to-grave exploits. Half a century after his death, Hitler remains the top choice of political biographers. A search of Amazon.com reveals that between 1944 and 2003, biographers churned out no less than 2,067 books about Hitler, evidence of a feverish production schedule averaging more than thirty-five volumes per year.

Toxic leaders in the corporate world have also been subjected to biographical exhumations. John D. Rockefeller, ITT's Harold Geneen, and Henry Ford, founder of the Ford Motor Company, head a long list of business leaders admired in life only to be defrocked in death. During his lifetime Ford was revered as a corporate hero for his innovative assembly line and the unprecedented wages he paid his workers. Only later did posthumous biographies document the otherwise harsh treatment the automobile tycoon meted out to his employees, as well as his antiunion sentiments, his Nazi leanings, and his anti-Semitic activities and writings.[34]

Researchers Examine the Toxic Entrails

Beyond biographical research, the social and behavioral sciences have trained their lenses on human behavior associated with toxic leadership. Deeply affected by invasions in Europe, World War II, and the Holocaust, a small set of social and behavioral scientists— such as psychoanalyst Erich Fromm[35] and cultural anthropologist Ernest Becker[36]—sought to understand how civilized human beings could engage in such despicable behavior.

Experimental social psychologists, including Solomon Asch,[37] Leon Festinger,[38] and Muzafer Sherif,[39] designed experiments to determine how group pressures encouraged or discouraged conformity in group members, but by and large they did not explicitly link their important work to toxic leaders per se. In a major study stimulated by the phenomenon of Nazi leadership, Theodor Adorno and his colleagues developed the F-scale (F for fascism).[40] They sought to identify individuals with authoritarian personalities, people who were likely both to obey authority and to enjoy exercising it over others. Their focus, however, was largely upon that specific personality type.

Yale University researcher Stanley Milgram studied obedience to authority in a set of infamously disturbing experiments.[41] Indirectly, Milgram was exploring obedience to a toxic leader. Here, the toxic leader appeared in the guise of a "scientist" clad in a white lab coat, who instructed participants to administer what they believed to be electric shocks—some presumably "very dangerous"—to other "volunteers" engaged in the experiment. Milgram's research demonstrated that a surprisingly large percentage of individuals can be intimidated into obeying a malevolent authority, even when all the so-called authority does is wear scientific garb and intone, "The experiment must go on." Milgram's experiments did not, however, focus on why the participants were intimidated or why, even without intimidation, many of us yearn for, are attracted to, and sometimes prefer toxic leaders.

Some authors have examined why specific individuals or groups carried out the directives of a particular toxic leader. Hannah Arendt's landmark treatise on Adolf Eichmann scrutinized Hitler's notorious henchman, responsible for the murder of millions of Jews in Nazi death camps.[42] In that work, Arendt explored why an individual obeyed the orders of one specific evil leader, causing the implementer, too, to spiral into the "banality of evil." More recently, historians Daniel Goldhagen[43] and Robert Gellately[44] have looked backward to study the masses that supported, even implemented, Hitler's demonic strategies.

Leaders and Followers: Action, Interaction, and Inaction

Biographers and historians have explored the dark psychological spaces of toxic leaders to discern what made them tick. With rare exceptions, some we've already noted, seldom do they plumb the deep forces that make the followers tick. Leadership is often treated as action by the leader directed toward or against others. More appropriately, we should view leadership as interaction between leaders and their followers. What goes on between leaders and their supporters is perhaps far more significant for the course of history than simply what leaders do to followers.

Not only do we fail to dissect the interaction between leader and follower, but we often completely ignore the followers. We allow their inaction in the face of toxic leadership to fall below our angle of vision. Thus we rarely investigate what influences followers to tolerate—sometimes for decades—leaders who deceive, denigrate, and even destroy them.

Toxic Leaders: How Shall We Recognize Them?

"How do we recognize toxic leaders?" is a question worth a multivolume encyclopedia of its own. I am talking neither about garden-variety incompetents nor about insensitive bosses, whom most American workers love to hate but who don't do much serious damage. Rather, I am concerned with leaders who have toxic impact.

The dictionary defines toxic as "acting as or having the effect of a poison." Toxic leaders do indeed have poisonous effects that cause serious harm to their organizations and their followers, but the multiple toxins they can dispense create varying degrees of impairment. (And, of course, let's not forget that beyond individual toxic leaders, organizations qua organizations can yield their own toxins. They do so through detrimental policies and practices—including setting unreasonable performance goals, promoting excessive internal competition, and creating a culture of blame—that transcend any individual toxic leader.)[45]

To capture the complexity of toxic leaders, we need a multidimensional framework, one that delineates their actions, their character, their intent, and their impact on followers. It is not always easy to separate the actions of toxic leaders from their character. For example, when leaders consistently deceive their supporters, where do we draw the line between the act of lying and the embedded character flaw that sees no problem with misusing the truth? Intent and impact are similarly intertwined.

Followers suffer poisonous effects when leaders place their own well-being and power above their supporters' needs. Followers and the organizations they inhabit also endure great harm when leaders act without integrity by dissembling and engaging in various other dishonorable behaviors. Corruption, hypocrisy, sabotage, and manipulation, as well as other assorted unethical, illegal, and criminal acts, are part of the poisonous repertoire of toxic leaders. And, of course, in admittedly rare instances, toxic leaders move to the furthest point of the toxic spectrum and perpetrate downright evil. Nor is this the whole of a very complex picture.

Crafting even a rough definition of toxic leaders is a major challenge. Nevertheless, let's take a stab at it to help followers recognize harmful leaders before they allow themselves to be done in by them. Yet defining the gradations of toxic leaders or creating a primer on toxic leaders per se is not my central concern. In fact, toxic leaders provide only the backdrop for the focus I wish to keep on their followers.

Although I want to fasten our attention squarely on followers, still, it's important to define early on what we mean by "toxic leaders" so that we can appreciate the dimensions of the problem their followers confront. Let's undertake this critical task so that we may also understand exactly what kinds of leaders and what types of behavior the followers are willing to endure. In this context, the term "toxic leaders" covers a multitude of leadership sins.

Here, we shall use "toxic leaders" as a global label for leaders who engage in numerous destructive behaviors and who exhibit certain dysfunctional personal characteristics. To count as toxic, these behaviors and qualities of character must inflict some reasonably serious and enduring harm on their followers and their organizations. The intent to harm others or to enhance the self at the expense of others distinguishes seriously toxic leaders from the careless or unintentional toxic leaders, who also cause negative effects.

The degree and complexity of toxic behavior may differ among individual leaders; so may the range of their undesirable personal qualities. My goal, remember, is not to calibrate a given leader's thermometer of toxicity or to compare degrees of toxicity exhibited by different leaders. Nor do I want my readers to get hung up on how much of which behavior or characteristic constitutes toxicity. That would only distract us from our primary purpose.

Instead, our focus here is specifically on the dynamics that entrance the toxic leader's followers or at least help keep them in line. I want to explore what prompts us to accept and promote bad leaders and what often renders us lethargic, intimidated, reluctant, and inept at overturning them. To do so, however, requires first that we share a common general understanding of how toxic leaders act and what they are like.

Toxic Behaviors: How Toxic Leaders Act

For purposes of this book, let us categorize as toxic those leaders who engage in one or more of the following destructive behaviors. These behaviors range from deliberate, conscious engagement in despicable acts to unintentional, unconscious toxic behavior, such as failing to recognize their own or others' seriously harmful incompetence.

The characteristic destructive behaviors of toxic leaders include:

- Leaving their followers (and frequently nonfollowers) worse off than they found them, sometimes eliminating—by deliberately undermining, demeaning, seducing, marginalizing, intimidating, demoralizing, disenfranchising, incapacitating, imprisoning, torturing, terrorizing, or killing—many of their own people, including members of their entourage, as well as their official opponents

- Violating the basic standards of human rights of their own supporters, as well as those of other individuals and groups they do not count among their followers

- Consciously feeding their followers illusions that enhance the leader's power and impair the followers' capacity to act independently (e.g., persuading followers that they are the only one who can save them or the organization)

- Playing to the basest fears and needs of the followers

- Stifling constructive criticism and teaching supporters (sometimes by threats and authoritarianism) to comply with, rather than to question, the leader's judgment and actions

- Misleading followers through deliberate untruths and misdiagnoses of issues and problems

- Subverting those structures and processes of the system intended to generate truth, justice, and excellence, and engaging in unethical, illegal, and criminal acts

- Building totalitarian or narrowly dynastic regimes, including subverting the legal processes for selecting and supporting new leaders

- Failing to nurture other leaders, including their own successors (with the occasional exception of blood kin), or otherwise improperly clinging to power

- Maliciously setting constituents against one another

- Treating their own followers well, but persuading them to hate and/or destroy others

- Identifying scapegoats and inciting others to castigate them
- Structuring the costs of overthrowing them as a trigger for the downfall of the system they lead, thus further endangering followers and nonfollowers alike
- Ignoring or promoting incompetence, cronyism, and corruption

As you can readily see, this list starts at the intentionally negative end of the spectrum, where toxic leaders set out to dominate, even eliminate, their own followers, as well as people and groups beyond their own constituencies. At the other end of the spectrum, where incompetence becomes salient, the leader's toxicity is not necessarily deliberate. Yet the threat that unintended harm poses to followers is no less real, since followers may be in danger of losing their jobs, their homes, their life savings, and sometimes their very lives.

There are still other toxic behaviors by which we can recognize toxic leaders. For example, some toxic leaders use scarce resources to build monuments to themselves, rather than to meet their followers' basic needs. Some use corporate jets, decorate opulent executive suites, and draw multimillion-dollar salaries as their firms undergo serious downsizing. Saddam Hussein maintained a multibillion-dollar palace construction program while his people went hungry and sick.[46] Another measure of toxicity is the shabby treatment accorded those at the bottom of the followers' heap, while the elite receive white-glove treatment.

Not infrequently, some leaders who live exemplary public lives act privately in ways that evoke even their followers' disdain and undercut their own moral authority. Former U.S. president Bill Clinton, for example, would earn high marks for his brilliance as a policy analyst and political strategist in the first term of his administration. Nonetheless, Clinton's private behavior so lamentably lacked a moral compass that its consequences virtually immobilized him during his second term.

Toxic Qualities: What They're Like

There are numerous dysfunctional personal qualities or characteristics that feed toxic leadership. For example,

some leaders earn their toxic stripes through their cynicism, greed, corruptibility, moral blind spots, and stupidity. Narcissism, paranoia, grandiosity, and megalomania drive still other toxic leaders. Then there are leaders whom we recognize as toxic because their actions spring from malevolence, even evil intent. Still other leaders may be toxic through sheer cowardice.

High on this list of qualities are the following dysfunctional personal characteristics of toxic leaders:

- Lack of integrity that marks the leader as cynical, corrupt, hypocritical, or untrustworthy[47]
- Insatiable ambition that prompts leaders to put their own sustained power, glory, and fortunes above their followers' well-being
- Enormous egos that blind leaders to the shortcomings of their own character and thus limit their capacity for self-renewal
- Arrogance that prevents acknowledging their mistakes and instead leads to blaming others
- Amorality that makes it nigh impossible for them to discern right from wrong
- Avarice that drives leaders to put money and what money can buy at the top of the list
- Reckless disregard for the costs of their actions to others as well as to themselves
- Cowardice that leads them to shrink from the difficult choices
- Failure both to understand the nature of relevant problems and to act competently and effectively in leadership situations

Worst of all, perhaps, there are toxic leaders who combine several, or occasionally all, of these negative attributes and behaviors.

Readers probably have their own favorites that would augment this less-than-exhaustive inventory. Still, this varied set of behaviors and personal qualities exhibited by toxic leaders paints the background against which we can view the larger forces that make us suffer them.

Range and Levels of Toxicity Factors: How Much Is Too Much?

Sometimes these toxic behaviors and qualities cluster in groups. For example, Michael Milken, wunderkind leader of the junk bond operation at now-defunct Drexel Burnham Lambert, didn't reserve his brutal avarice and aggression for his competitors. He also undermined many of his own staff through terror tactics.[48] Moreover, Milken held his clients financially hostage when he needed to leverage their resources to complete whiz-fast megadeals. Nonetheless, former employees remark upon Milken's sincere devotion to children—his own and others'.

At other times, however, the leader's toxic behavior is far more circumscribed. In such cases, the leader may exhibit only one or two toxic behaviors and perhaps some less lethal ones, along with a more limited set of toxic qualities.

Even essentially effective nontoxic leaders, as noted earlier, occasionally engage in the milder forms of toxicity, but without causing great or enduring harm. Perhaps a substantially effective leader is the most we can reasonably expect from our fellow human beings. Let's remember, I am not prescribing a plaster-saint model of leadership. We shall simply slide down the theoretical rabbit hole if we are unwilling to recognize that leaders are human, like the rest of us, with their own reasonably limited sets of unsightly but nonmalignant warts.

To complicate matters, leaders may exhibit higher or lower levels on any of these qualities. Just how much deceit, cynicism, corruption, or ineptitude a leader must demonstrate to qualify as toxic is difficult to specify. Context, too, introduces an important muddying agent. In some historical moments, such as major crises, the same arrogance and ego that we commonly associate with toxicity can goad the leader to seemingly heroic efforts. During Britain's bleakest days in World War II, Winston Churchill's immense ego and unflagging ambition helped fuel his monumental success as the faltering nation's leader. In his earlier career, however, from the Dardanelles fiasco right up to World War II, these very same qualities made Churchill the butt of his political rivals' scorn.[49]

Thus under certain circumstances, even seemingly toxic leaders can either deploy those negative behaviors and qualities for more positive purposes or transform themselves to lead in a more constructive fashion. Clearly, context counts. As James Allen remarked, "Circumstance does not make the man, it reveals him to himself."[50] I would add, "and reveals him or her to others."

With respect to leaders' toxic behavior, the same issues of range and complexity apply. Some leaders behave badly from start to finish, while others behave pretty well at the outset but eventually lose their way. And, as the Churchill case illustrates, some grow from toxicity to grandeur or find themselves and their strengths in times of crisis.

At what point does the nontoxic leader step over the line into the toxic or even highly toxic zone? Let's not forget that President Franklin D. Roosevelt saw little wrong with packing the Supreme Court or herding Japanese-American citizens into internment camps during World War II.

What part do needy followers play in pushing nontoxic leaders over the boundary into toxic territory? New York mayor Rudolph Giuliani, egged on by anxious followers grateful for his stunning leadership performance following 9/11, almost crossed the line by attempting to extend his administration beyond the legal two-term limit.

Can we identify those forces or combinations of circumstances that move followers to downgrade their opinion of the leader from acceptable to unacceptable? Or vice versa, for that matter? Can we determine what conditions and what level of toxicity will finally goad followers into action?

Sometimes it takes damning public revelations about leaders for enraptured followers to pry the scales from their eyes. I recall a colleague from the former Soviet Union describing the deep disillusionment of her parents, both ardent Communists, which set in only long after Josef Stalin's death. Not until official documents unequivocally confirmed the whispered horrors of the Stalinist era, which they had steadfastly refused to believe, did the shaken parents finally recognize the Soviet dictator's toxicity.

Clearly, the nature of toxic leadership per se is both complex and compelling. Nonetheless, it is simply background to our major concern.

The Central Question

That brings us to our central question: What are the forces that propel followers, again and again, to accept, often favor, and sometimes create toxic leaders?

Isn't it high time to come to grips with why we usually let toxic leaders mistreat us and depart when it suits their purposes? With the recent revelations about toxic corporate leaders, our patience seems to be ebbing, at least temporarily. True, there are the occasional whistleblowers, such as WorldCom's Cynthia Cooper and former Morton Thiokol engineer Roger Bois-joly (of O-ring fame), who risk their careers, if not their very lives, to expose toxic leaders. At some tipping point, followers may revolt and attempt to bring down bad leaders. Still, the majority of followers stay the course, many because the barriers to escape seem much too strong, be they financial, political, social, psychological, or existential—or, worse yet, some overwhelming combination of these formidable obstacles.

Let me be very clear: Blaming the victim is not my intent. Rather, my hope is to liberate entrapped followers by laying bare the web of forces that tempts us to accept leaders who play havoc with our businesses, our governments, our schools, our communities, our societies, and possibly our lives. By exploring why and how toxic leaders entice us into seeing them through Falstaff's eyes, I believe we can take a giant step toward extricating ourselves from their grip. Then, perhaps, we can select better leaders and face up to the challenge of confronting our own leadership potential.

Notes

1. Shakespeare portrayed the initial relationship between the young, recalcitrant Prince Hal and the comic Falstaff as one of mutual infatuation. Early on, it is almost difficult to discern who is leading whom. Eventually, after Prince Hal ascends to the throne, forsaking his youthful toxicity, he rejects Falstaff.

2. Some accounts use the date 1903. Curiously reflecting Mayor Curley's "colorful" life, most of the "factual" information about Curley, including dates of his political and prison terms, varies considerably across sources.

3. Mike Ryan, "Boston's Irrepressible James Michael Curley," *Boston Irish Reporter,* November 1999, available at http://web.archive.org/web/20021021195940/ http://www .bostonirish.com/jmcurley.html.

4. Jack Beatty, *The Rascal King: The Life and Times of James Michael Curley (1874-1958)* (Cambridge, MA: DaCapo Press, 2000).

5. Associated Press, "Corruption Trial Starts for Mayor of Providence," *New York Times,* April 24, 2002, A16.

6. Associated Press, "What's Providence Like Without Buddy?" June 24–25, 2003, available at http://www.turnto 10.com/news/2290095/detail.html.

7. Alan Ehrenhalt, "The Paradox of Corrupt Yet Effective Leadership," *New York Times,* September 30, 2002, A23.

8. W. Zachary Malinowski, "Cianci Found Guilty of Racketeering Charge," *Providence Journal,* June 25, 2002, A1.

9. Pankaj Mishra, "Ex-Father of the Nation," *New York Times Book Review,* April 15, 2001, 12.

10. Robert Gellately, *Backing Hitler: Consent and Coercion in Nazi Germany* (New York: Oxford University Press, 2001), 3.

11. Christopher Hitchens, *The Missionary Position: Mother Teresa in Theory and Practice* (New York: Verso, 1995).

12. Matthew Sinclair, "William Aramony Is Back on the Streets," *NonProfit Times,* March 1, 2002.

13. Tim Dahlberg, "Top USOC Leaders Seek Mankamyer's Resignation," *Scoreboard,* January 21, 2003, available at http://www.evaa.nu/document/dunton/2003/ jan22.html.

14. Gordon Witkin, "Can Jim and Tammy Make a Comeback?" *U.S. News and World Report,* October 19, 1987, 21.

15. Frank Bruni, "Italian Leader, in a First, Testifies at His Own Bribery Trial," *New York Times,* May 6, 2003, A6.

16. Ibid.

17. BBC News, "Vivendi's Messier Steps Down," July 2, 2002, available at http://news.bbc.co.uk/l/hi/business/ 2075948.stm.

18. John L. Allen Jr., "Italian Church Rocked by Its Own Scandals," *National Catholic Reporter,* May 31, 2002.

19. Slam! Cycling, "Killy Report to IOC on Tour de France Scandals," August 20, 1998, available at http://www .canoe.ca/TourDeFrance/aug20_kil.html.

20. BBC Online Network, "Cleaning Up the Problem," June 27, 1999, available at http://news.bbc.co.uk/2/hi/sport/ tour_de_france/371200.stm.

21. Ibid.

22. Associated Press, "French Twist: Skating Judge Denies She Made a Deal for Scores," February 18, 2002, available at http://sportsillustrated.cnn.com/olympics/2002/figure_skating/ news/2002/02/18/french_judge_ap/.

23. Curt Gentry, *J. Edgar Hoover: The Man and the Secrets* (New York: W. W. Norton, 1991).

24. Joseph Salvati served thirty years in prison for murder after an FBI agent deliberately testified falsely against him. Documents that would prove Salvati's innocence had been hidden by FBI agents. J. Edgar Hoover's initials appear on documents in Salvati's file, indicating that the FBI director was aware of the details. See Brian McGrory, "For Feds, It's All Hard Time," *Boston Globe,* June 24, 2003, B1.

25. See, for example, Anthony Summers, *Official and Confidential: The Secret Life of J. Edgar Hoover* (New York: Orion, 1993). See also Gentry, *J. Edgar Hoover.*

26. Paul Krugman, "The Good Guys," *New York Times,* December 24, 2002, 23.

27. Mimi Swartz with Sherron Watkins, *Power Failure: The Inside Story of the Collapse of Enron* (New York: Doubleday, 2003), 345.

28. Amanda Ripley and Maggie Sieger, "The Special Agent," *Time,* December 30, 2002–January 6, 2003, 37.

29. Anthony Bianco, William Symonds, and Nanette Byrnes, with David Polek, "The Rise and Fall of Dennis Kozlowski: A Revealing Look at the Man Behind the Tyco Scandal," *Business Week,* December 23, 2002, 65–77.

30. John A. Byrne, *Chainsaw: The Notorious Career of Al Dunlap in the Era of Profit-at-Any-Price* (New York: HarperCollins, 1999), 20.

31. "New MBAs: Nasty by Nature," *Fortune,* February 17, 1997, 127.

32. Floyd Norris, "S.E.C. Accuses Former Sunbeam Official of Fraud," *New York Times,* May 16, 2001, A1.

33. James MacGregor Burns, *Leadership* (New York: Harper and Row, 1978).

34. See, for example, Neil Baldwin, *Henry Ford and the Jews: The Mass Production of Hate* (New York: Public Affairs, 2001).

35. Erich Fromm, *Escape from Freedom* (New York: Holt, 1991).

36. Ernest Becker, *Escape from Evil* (New York: Free Press, 1975).

37. Solomon E. Asch, "Effects of Group Pressure Upon the Modification and Distortion of Judgments," in Harold Guetzkow, ed., *Groups, Leadership, and Men* (Pittsburgh: Carnegie Press, 1951); Solomon E. Asch, "Studies on Independence and Conformity: A Minority of One Against a Unanimous Majority," *Psychological Monographs* 70, 9 (1956).

38. L. Festinger, H. W. Riecken, and S. Schacter, *When Prophecy Fails* (Minneapolis: University of Minnesota Press, 1956).

39. Muzafer Sherif, *The Psychology of Social Norms* (New York: Harper and Brothers, 1936).

40. T. W. Adorno, Else Frenkel-Brunswik, D. J. Levinson, and R. N. Sanford, *The Authoritarian Personality* (New York: Harper and Brothers, 1950).

41. Stanley Milgram, *Obedience to Authority: An Experimental View* (New York: Harper and Row, 1974).

42. Hannah Arendt, *Eichmann in Jerusalem: A Report on the Banality of Evil* (New York: Viking, 1963).

43. Daniel Jonah Goldhagen, *Hitler's Willing Executioners: Ordinary Germans and the Holocaust* (New York: Vintage, 1997).

44. Robert Gellately, *Backing Hitler: Consent and Coercion in Nazi Germany* (New York: Oxford University Press, 2001).

45. Peter Frost and Sandra Robinson, "The Toxic Handler: Organizational Hero—and Casualty," *Harvard Business Review,* July–August 1999, 96–106.

46. Adel Darwish, "Iraq: The Secret of the Palaces," December 2, 2001, available at http://web.archive.org/web/20030610105519/http://www.foreignwire.com/palaces.html.

47. In a study of 6,500 employees at seventy-six Holiday Inn hotels in the United States and Canada, the estimated cost of hotel employees' awareness of their managers' lack of integrity was calculated at $250,000 per hotel. Tony Simons, "The High Cost of Lost Trust," *Harvard Business Review,* September 2002, 18–19.

48. Connie Bruck, *The Predators' Ball* (New York: Penguin, 1988).

49. Piers Brendon, *Winston Churchill: A Brief Life* (London: Pimlico, 2001); Dennis Kavanagh, *Crisis, Charisma and British Political Leadership: Winston Churchill as the Outsider,* Sage Professional Papers in Contemporary Political Sociology, 06-001 (London and Beverly Hills: Sage, 1974).

50. James Allen, *As a Man Thinketh* (Camarillo, CA: De Vorss, 1983).

CHAPTER 30

Making Meaning of Being Bad

Barbara Kellerman

Harvard University

In a talk I once gave to the New Haven Jewish community, I referred to Hitler as a bad leader. The words were hardly out of my mouth when a member of the audience rose to differ. "Hitler may have been 'bad' as in 'ethically bad,'" he said. "But he was a good leader in that he was very effective."

The man was right. Given the ideology of National Socialism and the particulars of the Nazi agenda from 1933 to 1941 (when Germany made the mistake of invading the Soviet Union), Hitler's political and military strategies were nearly impeccable. Moreover, even between 1941 and 1945—the period leading up to Germany's defeat—at least one of Hitler's most cherished objectives, the annihilation of European Jewry, was realized with astonishing efficiency. Does this make Hitler a "good" leader?

If the lines of demarcation between effective and ethical blur for a leader as obviously evil as Adolph Hitler, it is no wonder that judging other leaders, less extreme, is harder. Was Ronald Reagan a good president? In many ways he was effective, much more effective than his Hollywood career might have predicted. But to liberal Democrats, who even in retrospect detest his domestic agenda in particular, to label Reagan a "good" president seems absurd.

The lack of clarity about what exactly defines a good leader, and how to distinguish a good leader from a bad one, is mirrored in the follower. Consider this question: Should followers follow the leader, or the dictates of their consciences? On the one hand, a strong argument can be made that to maintain order and get work done, followers should go along with their leaders except in dire circumstances. On the other hand, followers are not sheep, nor should they necessarily be part of any herd.

When Argentines took to the streets in early 2002 to protest the parties and politicians who had been discredited by the country's economic collapse, one might say that by noisily insinuating themselves into the

---

Source: Making Meaning of Being Bad, by Barbara Kellerman. pp. 29–38 in *Bad Leadership: What It Is, How It Happens, Why It Matters*, by Barbara Kellerman, 2004. Reprinted with permission of Harvard Business School Publishing.

political process they were being disruptive. Or one might take the opposite view: that by speaking out for what they believed, they were doing what good followers should do.

In an infamous case, Sherron Watkins, at the time vice president of corporate development at Enron, sent Kenneth Lay, Enron's CEO, a six-page memo in 2001 detailing her fears that the company would implode in a wave of accounting scandals. At first glance Watkins appears to be a good, even a very good, follower. But a closer look suggests that the picture is more complex. After the scandal broke and Watkins testified before Congress, some saw a traitor, a woman who was flagrantly disloyal to former colleagues at every level and indeed to Enron itself.

If we ask whether the end justifies the means, we further complicate the conversation. A letter sent anonymously to the president of a major university complained about the coach of the women's basketball team. The coach, a woman, was described as abusive to the point of creating an "extremely unhealthy and unproductive team environment." Specifically, her "primary leadership tools" were "criticism, public humiliation, demands of compliance, screaming and yelling, pitting players against one another, and other 'old-school' boot camp techniques."[1] Here's the question: Should the coach be judged on the basis of her performance, or that of her team?

The same issue arose with regard to Bobby Knight, once the legendary basketball coach at Indiana University (since 2000 he has been at Texas Tech University). Although as individuals his players were at the mercy of his frequent verbal and infrequent physical abuse, his team as a whole did brilliantly. How should Knight be judged? He got the end part right: His team was a winner. But his means were questionable: He browbeat undergraduates. So, finally, our assessment of a coach or leader, such as Knight, is bound to be subjective, personal, and value-driven. You might not like the idea of anyone ever striking a twenty-year-old. But given Knight's remarkable record as a winning coach, I might not find it so objectionable.

Clearly, means versus ends issues are like good versus bad issues: impossible to sort out with precision. No wonder the leadership industry simplifies things. No wonder it defines leaders simply as "people who do the right thing."[2]

But as we know, sometimes leaders do the wrong thing. Even the best and brightest aren't precluded from being seduced by power. Some of the twentieth century's most eminent intellectuals fell for really bad leaders in a really big way. The great German philosopher Martin Heidegger joined the Nazi Party because he longed to "return to some imaginary pre-modern idyll." Other Europeans of high repute, such as the leading French writer and philosopher Jean-Paul Sartre, became enamored of Stalin because there was nothing they hated so much as bourgeois capitalism.[3] Nor were Americans exempt from such foolish flirtations, especially, again, with Stalin. Out of willful ignorance and misguided optimism, writers such as Lillian Hellman and John Steinbeck spent years making excuses for the Soviet despot, apparently believing that all would be right in the end.

I do not underestimate the challenge of explaining followers like these, nor do I minimize the task of explaining bad leadership more generally. But if we have any hope of moving from bad leadership to better leadership, we must strike a balance between looking at the light and seeing in the dark.

Ineffective Leadership Versus Unethical Leadership

Bad leadership falls into two categories: bad as in ineffective and bad as in unethical. This distinction is not a theoretical construct. Rather, it is based on the empirical evidence. Look around and you will see that all bad leadership is bad in one, or sometimes both, of these ways.

The distinction between ineffective and unethical brings us back to the question of means and ends. Let's assume that Bill and Hillary Clinton's ambitious health care proposal was a well-intentioned initiative that, initially at least, had the support of most of their followers. But the means used—the ways in which the president and the first lady tried to get the American body politic from point A to point B—were inadequate to the point of being hapless. By the time the proposal was dead, even many of its early supporters had abandoned it. We can say, then, that at least in the area of health care policy, President Clinton was not a good leader. His good intentions notwithstanding, he was ineffective. Even his supporters would have to admit that his strategies and tactics were not up to the task, and so the job never got done.

By the same token, sometimes leaders and followers deploy effective means to unethical ends. It has become clear that for many years Boston's Cardinal Bernard Law (along with others in the Roman Catholic hierarchy) considered it his main mission to protect the good standing of the church. The problem was that this mission took precedence over the more immediate and humane one: to shield parishioners from predatory priests. Finally, the wrongdoing that kept the clergy's misconduct hidden from public view—the transfers, the payments, and the cover-ups—undermined the very church that the Cardinal wanted so badly to secure.[4]

Ineffective Leadership

Ineffective leadership fails to produce the desired change. For reasons that include missing traits, weak skills, strategies badly conceived, and tactics badly employed, ineffective leadership falls short of its intention.

One way to think about an ineffective leader is to reverse the ideal: If the ideal leader has traits such as intelligence, persistence, flexibility, and an even disposition, the leader who lacks many of these will likely run into trouble. The same holds for leadership skills. If the ideal leader is able to communicate, mobilize, collaborate, and make good decisions, leaders who are unwilling or unable to employ such skills are less likely to perform well than their better-disposed and better-endowed counterparts.

The rule for followers is analogous: Ineffective followers lack, or do not demonstrate, the traits and skills necessary for good followership. Robert Kelley found that the best followers were "strong, independent partners with leaders. They think for themselves, self-direct their work, and hold up their end of the bargain. They continuously work at making themselves integral to the enterprise, honing their skills and focusing their contributions, and collaborating with their colleagues."[5] By these measures, ineffective followers are weak and dependent, and they refuse in any significant way to commit or contribute to the group.

A final point: Leaders are generally judged ineffective because of the means they employ (or fail to employ) rather than the ends they pursue. Most leaders set goals that seem reasonable to at least a substantial minority of their constituents. But not many leaders and followers have the capacity to reach these goals. To be sure, the deck is often stacked against them. Context matters a great deal, and the challenges they face are, objectively, difficult. But in many cases leaders and their immediate followers simply lack the traits and skills required to surmount the long odds.

By all accounts Gray Davis, California's erstwhile governor, was in a situation fraught with political peril. The state was faced with formidable challenges, in areas ranging from deficits to demographics, and the citizens were restless. Even though no one complained that Davis was unethical, the impression gradually became widespread that he and his team were ineffective—so ineffective that in a special recall election he was unceremoniously dumped.

Unethical Leadership

Unethical leadership fails to distinguish between right and wrong. Because common codes of decency and good conduct are in some way violated, the leadership process is defiled.

I take issue with James MacGregor Burns's definition of the word *leadership,* in which leadership is, necessarily, an ethical act. Let me now return to the exact way that Burns uses the word, particularly in the phrase "transforming leadership." For Burns, leadership is implicitly ethical in that it "is done to realize goals mutually held by leaders and followers." In his view, transforming leadership goes a step further; it's even better. "Such leadership occurs when one or more persons engage with others in such a way that leaders and followers raise one another to higher levels of motivation and morality."[6]

In Joanne Ciulla's collection of essays *Ethics: The Heart of Leadership*, Burns takes yet another cut. Here he distinguishes among three types of leadership values: ethical values, moral values, and end values. Although he does not so group them, Burns is writing, on the one hand, about the leader's private self (the leader is honest, kind, and so on) and, on the other hand, about the leader's public self (the leader furthers the common interest).[7]

Burns goes on to suggest the following.

- Ethical leaders put their followers' needs before their own. Unethical leaders do not.

- Ethical leaders exemplify private virtues such as courage and temperance. Unethical leaders do not.
- Ethical leaders exercise leadership in the interest of the common good. Unethical leaders do not.

Most contemporary leadership scholars agree that the first principle is critical. Robert Greenleaf's "servant leader" leads because of a desire to serve others.[8] Joseph Rost sees leadership as "noncoercive influence" that leaves followers free to decide for themselves whether to go along.[9] And Edwin Hollander is content to bestow on leaders benefits, such as money and prestige, if in turn the leaders are accountable to followers.[10]

The second principle might seem new, and especially pertinent in a time of relentless media intrusion into the private lives of leaders such as Bill Clinton and Jack Welch. Although in recent years the question of whether a leader's private behavior impinges on public performance has been a hot topic, political philosophers have been interested in the issue for centuries. In general, the tolerance for moral fallibility, even if evident only behind closed doors, has been low. Confucius declared, "He who rules by virtue is like the polestar, which remains unmoving in its mansion while all the other stars revolve respectfully around it." In response to a question from Lord Ji Kang ("What should I do in order to make the people respectful, loyal, and zealous?"), Confucius urged him to be what today we call a role model: "Approach them with dignity and they will be respectful. Be yourself a good son and a kind father, and they will be loyal. Raise the good and train the incompetent, and they will be zealous."[11]

To act in accordance with the third principle is to exercise power, authority, and influence in the interest of the public welfare. To be sure, the contemporary literature on democratic theory argues that each of us, every citizen, bears the individual burden of assessing "the moral authority of political mandates."[12] But a good case can be made for the proposition that political leaders have a special responsibility to support the government and uphold the law only if they can do so in good conscience. If they cannot—if they are expected, for example, to uphold what they consider an unjust law—they are morally obliged to try to change course. One need hardly add that corporate, nonprofit, and military leaders should be held similarly accountable.

Ciulla argues that "leaders who do not look after the interests of their followers are not only unethical but ineffective."[13] At the same time, she takes the position that the standards to which we hold leaders should be the same as those we hold for everyone else—no lower and no higher. How then might this translate? If we accept Aristotle's dictum that virtues such as honesty and justice are acquired by practicing them, then leaders should do as Aristotle instructed: They should practice virtue because they want and intend to be virtuous.[14]

Nor are followers exempt. Like leaders, they are accountable for what they do.

- Ethical followers take the leader into account. Unethical followers do not.
- Ethical followers exemplify private virtues such as courage and temperance. Unethical followers do not.
- Ethical followers engage the leader and also other followers on behalf of the common good. Unethical followers do not.

Kelley found that followers were more troubled by ethical issues than were leaders. It's common for followers to be faced with an ethical dilemma: a situation in which they feel obliged by authorities to behave in ways that make them uncomfortable. Kelley writes that exemplary followers address the problem by demonstrating a "courageous conscience." Such followers have "the ability to judge right from wrong and the fortitude to take alternative steps toward what they believe is right."[15] Followers who lack a courageous conscience, particularly those who do not act even when something is obviously and egregiously wrong, are unethical.

Kelley is not, of course, suggesting that followers take on leaders freely and easily. In fact, his work supports the first principle, which clearly implies that leaders cannot be effective without cooperative followers. But followers are more obligated to the community as a whole than they are to any single individual, including the leader.

Kelley's research was conducted in the corporate sector. In contrast, John Rawls's seminal volume *A Theory of Justice* is about public life. Here too followers—citizens—are obliged to resist if resistance, rather than acquiescence, is in the common interest. Rawls describes civil disobedience as a "public, nonviolent, conscientious yet political act contrary to law usually done with the aim of bringing about a change in the law or policies of the government."[16]

Note that if a protest such as this one is successful, followers become leaders. Consider first the followership and then the leadership of Martin Luther King, Jr.—a subtle transition he described in a letter. "As the weeks and months unfolded," King wrote from his Birmingham, Alabama, jail cell in 1963, "we [Negroes] realized that we were the victims of a broken promise. The signs remained. Like so many experiences of the past we were confronted with blasted hopes, and the dark shadow of a deep disappointment settled upon us. So we had no alternative except that of preparing for direct [nonviolent] action, whereby we would present our very bodies as a means of laying our case before the conscience of the local and national community."[17]

The mixture of the ineffective and the unethical in bad leadership can never be known or measured precisely. This is a truth of the human condition. The important tasks then are to develop a greater awareness of the dynamics of bad leadership, and a better understanding of the different ways that leaders' actions can be both ineffective and unethical. Thus, I propose a typology of bad leadership that will highlight and distinguish the various ways in which we lead badly.

Types of Bad Leadership

After looking at hundreds of contemporary cases involving bad leaders and bad followers in the private, public, and nonprofit sectors, and in domains both domestic and international, I found that bad leadership falls into seven groups, which I have typed as follows:

- Incompetent
- Rigid
- Intemperate
- Callous
- Corrupt
- Insular
- Evil

To posit a typology is to invite argument. No less an expert than Max Weber, the German sociologist whose three types of authority—rational-legal, traditional, and charismatic—continue to influence leadership scholars some eighty years after his death, was wary of

his critics. "The fact that none of these three ideal types . . . is usually to be found in historical cases in 'pure' form, is naturally not a valid objection to attempting their conceptual formulation in the sharpest possible form," Weber wrote. "Analysis in terms of sociological types has, after all . . . certain advantages which should not be minimized."[18]

Let me echo Weber's defense and provide a few cautionary notes about this typology in particular:

- These types are no "purer" than any other types, including Weber's.
- The range is wide. Some leaders and followers are very bad; others are less bad. Moreover, in some cases the consequences of bad leadership are major, in others minor.
- Opinions change. When Harry Truman left office in 1953, his approval rating was a dismal 32 percent. But in 2000, historians rated him among the greatest of American presidents, just behind Lincoln, Franklin Roosevelt, Washington, and Theodore Roosevelt.[19]
- Views differ. About Thomas Krens, controversial director of New York's Guggenheim Museum, two contrasting questions were asked. Was Krens "an egomaniac who squandered the museum's resources on a quest to expand his empire"? Or was he instead a "brilliant, misunderstood radical who inherited an institution with a relatively small endowment and stagnant program and wanted to try something more daring than mounting the umpteenth Picasso show"?[20]
- As it is used here, the word *type* does not mean personality type, nor do I intend to suggest that to be rigid, for example, is a personal trait in evidence at every turn. Rather, rigid refers to a set of behaviors in which leaders and followers mutually engage and that results in bad leadership.

Nevertheless, dividing the universe of bad leadership into seven types gives us, as Weber says, certain advantages. First, the ability to distinguish among the ways of being bad orders an untidy world, where the idea of bad leadership is as confusing as it is ubiquitous. Second, the seven types serve a practical purpose. They make it easier to detect inflection points—points at which an intervention might have stopped bad leadership or at least cut it short. Finally, the types make meaning of being bad. They enable us to know better and more clearly what bad leadership consists of.

Before I describe the seven types, two additional notes. First, the first three types of bad leadership tend to be bad as in ineffective, and the last four types tend to be bad as in unethical. I set up a continuum in which the first type of bad leadership, incompetence, is far less onerous than the last type of bad leadership, evil. But of course the lines blur: Sometimes leaders and followers are ineffective and unethical. For this reason I simply describe the seven types of bad leadership in sequence. Second, although one of my themes is that bad followers are as integral to bad leadership as are bad leaders, in the following section the brief examples allude only to the leader.

Incompetent

Bernadine Healy served effectively as dean of the Ohio State University Medical School and as the first woman director of the National Institutes of Health. But during her brief tenure (1999–2001) as head of the American Red Cross, Healy lost her touch. She was a driven professional, determined rapidly to change the deeply ingrained Red Cross culture, with which she was unfamiliar. In short order, members of the staff, as well as the fifty-member Red Cross board, decided that Healy was too assertive, too critical, and too pitiless. Once she compounded her errors by presiding over a debacle involving donations accumulated in the wake of the attack on the World Trade Center, she was dismissed. In short, whatever Healy's previous successes, and for whatever reasons, as leader of the Red Cross she was incompetent.[21]

> Incompetent Leadership—the leader and at least some followers lack the will or skill (or both) to sustain effective action. With regard to at least one important leadership challenge, they do not create positive change.

Incompetent leaders are not necessarily incompetent in every aspect. Moreover, there are many ways of being incompetent. Some leaders lack practical, academic, or emotional intelligence.[22] Others are careless, dense, distracted, slothful, or sloppy, or they are easily undone by uncertainty and stress, unable effectively to communicate, educate, or delegate, and so on. Note also that the impact of incompetent leadership is highly variable. Sometimes, as in the case of pilot error, it leads to disaster. At other times it amounts to mere bungling.[23]

One case of incompetent leadership is that of Juan Antonio Samaranch, president of the International Olympic Committee from 1981 to 2000. His accomplishments were considerable, but toward the end of his tenure something went badly wrong. During his final years in office, Samaranch and his close followers ignored and thus implicitly sanctioned widespread corruption in the Olympic movement, thereby disgracing the very games they were supposed to honor as well as sustain.

Rigid

As soon as he took office, Thabo Mbeki, who succeeded Nelson Mandela as president of South Africa in 1999, took issue with the West and its approach to AIDS. Mbeki maintained that HIV did not cause AIDS, that leading AIDS drugs were useless and even toxic, and that poverty and violence were at the root of his country's rapidly growing problem with the lethal disease.

As a result of his hostility to the West and his notoriously unyielding quest for an African remedy, Mbeki continued to withhold from HIV-positive pregnant women the antiretroviral drugs that would have cut in half the transmission of the disease to their babies.[24]

> Rigid Leadership—the leader and at least some followers are stiff and unyielding. Although they may be competent, they are unable or unwilling to adapt to new ideas, new information, or changing times.

Mbeki can be described by Barbara Tuchman's phrase "wooden-headed"—a leader who consistently refuses to be "deflected by the facts."[25] Rigid leaders can be successful up to a point. But if they refuse to change with the changing wind, the result will be bad leadership.

One case of rigid leadership is that of financial analyst Mary Meeker. During the 1990s, while the prices of technology stocks skyrocketed, Meeker rode high. But when the market changed, she did not. Unable or unwilling to acknowledge that the party was over,

Meeker and her like-minded collaborators told her legions of listeners to hold on to their stocks even as the market tanked.

Intemperate

Russian President Boris Yeltsin, an alcoholic, was often intoxicated in private and in public, much to the embarrassment of his government and the Russian people. In 1999, to take only one example, Yeltsin was too drunk to get off a plane to greet the visiting prime minister of Ireland, who was left cooling his heels on the tarmac.[26] Alcoholism is a disease. But Yeltsin's failure to treat his problem affected his capacity to serve as Russia's head of state.

> **Intemperate Leadership**—the leader lacks self-control and is aided and abetted by followers who are unwilling or unable effectively to intervene.

In their book *Leadership on the Line,* Ronald Heifetz and Marty Linsky cautioned leaders to control their impulses: "We all have hungers that are expressions of our normal human needs. But sometimes those hungers disrupt our capacity to act wisely or purposefully."[27] Because we live in a time when all top leaders are grist for the media mill, the risk of such disruption is far greater than it was in the past.

One case of intemperate leadership is that of Marion Barry, Jr. Although Barry was elected mayor of Washington, D.C., no fewer than four times, almost throughout his time in office he lived a life of excess. In the end, his own inability to control his various hungers, particularly for crack cocaine, and his followers' inability to get him the proper help, dearly cost him as well as the city he had been elected to govern.

Callous

Most Americans who have any interest in such matters know the story of Martha Stewart. She has become rich and famous by figuring out that homemaking—cooking, gardening, sewing, entertaining, cleaning, indeed every conceivable domestic chore—could reflect artistry as well as drudgery.

But even before her indictment on charges stemming from insider trading, Stewart had acquired a bad reputation. Although she is a brilliantly accomplished and hard-working businesswoman, nearly from the start of her career she has been rumored to be unpleasant and unkind, particularly to employees. How many of these personal attacks are the consequence of Stewart's being a woman in a man's world is difficult to say. Most observers would agree that the rules for women at the top of the corporate hierarchy are different from the rules for men. Most would likely also agree that if Stewart is not exactly a monster or a sociopath, she can be mean. Described variously as a harridan, an uncaring mother, and nasty to those in her employ, Stewart has made bad manners part of her legend: "Neighbors and acquaintances said she was aloof, inconsiderate, and selfish. Employees said she was 'hot-tempered and unreasonable and left them little time to cultivate a garden of their own.' It was as if she created a vision that none around her could live in."[28]

> **Callous Leadership**—the leader and at least some followers are uncaring or unkind. Ignored or discounted are the needs, wants, and wishes of most members of the group or organization, especially subordinates.

Al Dunlap, the former CEO of Sunbeam Corporation, is a case of callous leadership. Brought in 1996 to turn around the fortunes of the appliance maker, Dunlap, through his abrasiveness, instead depleted morale and impaired the company's ability to function. As Sunbeam continued its downward spiral, Dunlap, with the support of his closest followers, cut himself off from the company and willfully ignored its ignominious descent. By the end of his tenure in 1998, Sunbeam had filed for bankruptcy.

Corrupt

In 1983, Michigan mall developer A. Alfred Taubman bought Sotheby's, the legendary auction house known, along with Christie's, for having cornered the market on the sale of fine art, jewelry, and furniture. Because the auction business had become increasingly competitive, by the mid-1990s Taubman and his

Christie's counterpart, Sir Anthony Tennant, were illegally conspiring to raise commission rates.

A few years later the scheme was discovered, and in 2001 Taubman was found guilty of price-fixing, sentenced to a year and a day in prison, and ordered to pay a $7.5 million fine. In addition, Sotheby's and Christie's were ordered to settle class action suits with more than one hundred thousand customers for $512 million.[29]

Taubman did not act alone: For her part in the price-fixing scheme, Sotheby CEO Diana (Dede) Brooks was sentenced to six months of home detention, three years of probation, and one thousand hours of community service. Brooks, a Yale-educated former Citibank executive whose tenure at Sotheby's had been viewed as highly successful, was spared a more severe sentence only because she cooperated with government investigators to provide evidence against Taubman.

> **Corrupt Leadership**—the leader and at least some followers lie, cheat, or steal. To a degree that exceeds the norm, they put self-interest ahead of the public interest.

Corrupt leaders are usually motivated by power or greed—by the desire, in any case, to acquire more of a scarce resource. For example, to make more money, corrupt leaders take bribes, sell favors, evade taxes, exaggerate corporate earnings, engage in insider trading, cook the books, defraud governments and businesses, and in other ways cut corners, bend rules, and break the law.

The story of William Aramony, once the highly respected head of United Way of America, is not unfamiliar: It is about the head of a large organization caught lying, cheating, and stealing. But it is at odds with how we think about charitable organizations and those who lead and manage them.

Insular

When the streets of Monrovia began to run with blood, Liberians begged President George W. Bush to intervene, to stop the conflict by sending troops. At first he dithered, siding for a time with those who said, in effect, "Our hands are too full to rescue a distant people determined to murder one another."[30]

Those who chose to differ, Secretary of State Colin Powell among them, argued for intervention on the grounds of national interest and because they considered it the right thing to do. "Liberia is not just another African country," one interventionist argued. "It is an American creation, founded by former slaves 150 years ago, reflecting our image and legacy."[31]

In terms of American foreign policy this might be considered yet another debate between isolationists and interventionists. But as far as the quality of leadership is concerned, the debate over whether or not to intervene in Liberia reflected the tension between those who believe that leaders are responsible only to their own constituencies and those who consider that they have a broader mandate—one that includes trying to stop large numbers of men, women, and children from being hacked to death, even in a distant land.

> **Insular Leadership**—the leader and at least some followers minimize or disregard the health and welfare of "the other"—that is, those outside the group or organization for which they are directly responsible.

Bill Clinton is the exemplar of insular leadership. Although the president knew of the genocide in Rwanda, he paid it little attention. Having been burned by his experience in Somalia in particular, Clinton, along with the rest of his foreign policy team, made the decision to steer clear of a calamity that was taking place far from home.

Evil

In 1991, Foday Sankoh, an itinerant photographer and army corporal with a primary school education, gathered a group of guerillas and started a civil war in Sierra Leone. Sankoh was known for his extraordinary charisma. But his followers, many of them poor boys from the countryside, were notorious above all for their brutality. They killed, raped, and spread terror across the small West African nation by chopping off the hands, arms, and legs of innocent civilians—men, women, and children alike. Sankoh was unperturbed. In fact, when some of his close associates spoke out against the flagrant abuses and violations of human rights, they were summarily executed.[32] In 2000, Sankoh was captured by British troops operating under the auspices of the United Nations; later he was turned over to the Special Court for Sierra Leone. The seventeen-count indictment charged him with crimes against humanity, including murder, rape, and extermination. Foday Sankoh died in custody in July 2003.

> **Evil Leadership**—the leader and at least some followers commit atrocities. They use pain as an instrument of power. The harm done to men, women, and children is severe rather than slight. The harm can be physical, psychological, or both.

Evil leaders are not necessarily sadistic. But some experts argue that our notion of evil should include the intent not only to terrorize but also to prolong suffering. They believe that all evildoers derive some sort of satisfaction from hurting others.[33]

As Bosnian Serb president during the early and mid-1990s, Radovan Karadzic, along with his followers, was responsible for the rape, murder, and pillaging of thousands of Bosnian Muslims and Croats, and for the infamous massacre in Srebrenica.

The Heart of Darkness

Making meaning of being bad is difficult. Consider this confusion: The *American Heritage Dictionary of the English Language* properly refers to Hitler as an "absolute dictator." But, perhaps because he was a wartime ally, the same dictionary describes Stalin only as a "Soviet politician who was general secretary of the Communist Party and premier of the U.S.S.R." This, even though we now know that Stalin was directly responsible for the deaths of some twenty million people.[34]

Moreover, like all typologies, the one in this book raises questions just as it provides answers. It's fair to ask, for example, whether leaders should be considered incompetent if the demands on their time preclude attention to all matters of importance. Similarly, one might reasonably wonder whether leaders are intemperate if they are not monogamous but still not promiscuous. The questions pertain to followers as well. Are you corrupt if you cheat, ever so slightly, on your taxes, knowing that many others are doing the same thing? Am I evil if my leader compels me to commit evil acts?

To avoid as far as possible the inevitable pitfalls of the inevitable complexities, I use only cases in which the evidence of bad leadership is overwhelming. In other words, because I recognize that even generally competent leaders are sometimes incompetent and that even generally kind leaders are sometimes callous, the examples of bad leadership used in this book are at the extreme—virtually indisputable.

The paradoxes of leadership—leaders who are, for example, corrupt and effective at the same time—further complicate the difficulty of making meaning of being bad. In 2000, Vincent A. (Buddy) Cianci, Jr., the mayor of Providence, Rhode Island, was sentenced to five years and four months in jail after being convicted of soliciting bribes for city contracts. But before being thrown into prison, Cianci had "transformed Providence from a grimy industrial backwater into the liveliest, most appealing city in New England."[35]

New York mayor Rudolph Giuliani presents a different kind of paradox. In the wake of 9/11, Giuliani was hailed as a hero, a leader worthy of comparison to Churchill. But before his appointment with history, Giuliani's approval ratings had been low. The mayor's rigid refusal to reach out to members of New York City's minority communities, particularly to people of color, meant that in at least one important way, he was inadequate, a bad leader.

Finally, problems of objectivity and subjectivity inevitably muddy the water. In all but the most egregious cases, opinions will differ about who deserves to be called a bad leader and why. As far as possible I head off this argument by choosing to focus on cases of bad leadership on which there is broad consensus.

The heavy lifting notwithstanding, we know three important things:

1. Sometimes leaders, and followers, make a difference.

2. Sometimes this difference is significant.

3. Sometimes the outcome is bad.[36]

The seven types of bad leadership, incompetent, rigid, intemperate, callous, corrupt, insular, and evil, are about the dark side—about how we get caught in webs we ourselves spin. It is my hope and intention that by discussing and distinguishing among the primary forms of bad leadership, we may ourselves avoid becoming entangled, both as bad leaders and as bad followers.

Notes

1.   Letter dated 9 December 2001 to the president of a leading West Coast university.

2.   Warren Bennis and Burt Nanus, *Leaders: The Strategies for Taking Charge* (New York: Harper & Row, 1985), 21. Bennis and Nanus were making a distinction between managers "who do things right" and leaders "who do the right thing."

3.   Mark Lilla, interviewed by Eric Alterman, "Q & A: Why Are Deep Thinkers Shallow About Tyranny," *New York Times* (10 November 2001), A15.

4.   For a full accounting of how the investigative staff of the *Boston Globe* uncovered this story, see Investigative Staff of the *Boston Globe, Betrayal: The Crisis in the Catholic Church* (Boston: Little, Brown, 2002).

5.   Robert E. Kelley, *The Power of Followership: How to Create Leaders People Want to Follow and Followers Who Lead Themselves* (New York: Doubleday, 1992), 166.

6.   James MacGregor Burns, *Leadership* (New York: Harper & Row, 1978), 18, 20.

7.   James MacGregor Burns, foreword to Joanne B. Ciulla, *Ethics: The Heart of Leadership* (Westport, CT: Praeger, 1998), x.

8.   Robert K. Greenleaf, *Servant Leadership: A Journey into the Nature of Legitimate Power* (New York: Paulist Press, 1977).

9.   Joseph C. Rost, *Leadership for the Twenty-First Century* (Westport, CT: Praeger, 1991), 82.

10.   Edwin P. Hollander, "Ethical Challenges in the Leader-Follower Relationship," in Ciulla, *Ethics: The Heart of Leadership,* 49–61.

11.   Confucius, *Analects of Confucius* (New York, Norton, 1977), 6, 8.

12.   Arthur Isak Applebaum, "Democratic Legitimacy and Official Discretion," *Philosophy and Public Affairs* 21, no. 3 (1992): 240. Also see Dennis F. Thompson, "Moral Responsibility of Public Officials: The Problem of Many Hands," *American Political Science Review* 74 (1980): 905–915.

13.   Joanne B. Ciulla, "Carving Leaders from the Warped Wood of Humanity," *Review Canadienne des Sciences de l'Administration* (Montreal) 18, no. 4 (December 2001): 313.

14.   Aristotle, *The Ethics* (London: Penguin, 1953), 91.

15.   Kelley, *The Power of Followership,* 168.

16.   John Rawls, *A Theory of Justice* (Cambridge, MA: Harvard University Press, 1971), 364.

17.   Martin Luther King, Jr., "Letter from a Birmingham Jail," in *Blessed Are the Peacemakers,* by S. Jonathan Bass (Baton Rouge: Louisiana State University Press, 2001). The letter is dated 16 April 1963.

18.   Max Weber, *The Theory of Social and Economic Organizations* (New York: Free Press, 1947), 329.

19.   "Presidential Rankings," 2000 poll from C-Span survey of historians, CNN, 21 February 2000.

20.   Deborah Solomon, "Is the Go-Go Guggenheim Going, Going . . ." *New York Times Magazine,* 20 June 2002.

21.   For an excellent description of Healy's tenure at the Red Cross, see Deborah Sontag, "Who Brought Bernadine Healy Down?" *New York Times Magazine,* 23 December 2001, 32.

22.   Daniel Goleman, *Working with Emotional Intelligence* (New York: Bantam, 1999), 317. For an interesting exchange about leadership and practical intelligence, see Robert Sternberg and Victor Vroom, "The Person Versus the Situation in Leadership," *The Leadership Quarterly* 13, no. 3 (June 2002): 301–321.

23.   For example, the failure by South Carolina governor Jim Hodges to communicate during Hurricane Floyd resulted in a monumental traffic jam. "Traffic Backs Up for Miles as Coastal Dwellers Flee Island," *St. Louis Post-Dispatch,* 16 September 1999, A9. See also Leigh Strope, "Hodges Said He Should Control Emergency Response," Associated Press State and Local Wire, 1 October 1999; and David Firestone, "Hurricane Floyd: The Overview," *New York Times,* 16 September 1999, A1.

24.   "S. African Leader Claims AIDS Drug Is Unsafe," *St. Louis Post-Dispatch,* 3 November 1999, A5; Barton Gelman, "S. African President Escalates AIDS Feud: Mbeki Challenges Western Remedies," *Washington Post,* 19 April 2000, A1; Samson Mulugeta, "S. Africa: A Country in Denial—AIDS Victims Suffer in Silence, President Dismisses Problem," *Newsday,* 21 August 2001, A16; Rachel Swarns, "In a Policy Shift, South Africa Will Make AIDS Drugs Available to Pregnant Women," *New York Times,* 20 April 2002, A8. In 2002 Mbeki's position on antiretroviral drugs softened slightly, at least in part because of the intervention of Canadian Prime Minister Jean Chretien. For a fuller description of Mbeki's rigid intransigence, see Samantha Power, "The AIDS Rebel," *New Yorker,* 19 May 2003.

25. Barbara Tuchman, *The March of Folly: Troy to Vietnam* (New York Ballentine, 1984), 7.

26. Fred Hiatt, "Ex-Aides Raise Questions about Yeltsin's Drinking," *Washington Post,* 8 October 1994, A21.

27. Ronald A. Heifetz and Marty Linsky, *Leadership on the Line: Staying Alive Through the Dangers of Leading* (Boston: Harvard Business School Press, 2002), 164.

28. "Image and Reality for Martha Stewart," *Greenwich Time,* 10 June 2003. See also Jerry Oppenheimer, *Just Desserts: The Unauthorized Biography of Martha Stewart* (New York: William Morrow, 1997), especially 236 ff. and 308 ff.; and Christopher M. Byron, *Martha, Inc.: The Incredible Story of Martha Stewart Living Omnimedia* (New York: John Wiley & Sons, 2003).

29. Peter Watson, "Under the Hammer," *The Guardian,* 7 December 2001, 2; Carol Vogel and Ralph Blumenthal, "Ex-Chairman of Sotheby's Gets Jail Time," *New York Times,* 23 April 2002, B1.

30. Nicholas D. Kristof, "Hearing Liberia's Pleas," *New York Times,* 29 July 2003, A23.

31. Chester Crocker, "A War Americans Can Afford to Stop," *New York Times,* 1 August 2003, A21.

32. James Traub, "The Worst Place on Earth," *New York Review of Books,* 29 June 2000, 61–65. The quotation is from Somini Sengupta, "African Held for War Crimes Dies in Custody of Tribunal," *New York Times,* 31 July 2003, A6.

33. Psychiatrist Michael Weiner has this view of evil, as cited by Sharon Begley, "The Roots of Evil," *Newsweek,* 21 May 2002, 32.

34. Sidney Goldberg, "Learning Lexicons: Dictionaries Call Castro a 'Leader' and Stalin a 'Statesman,'" 5 July 2002, *Wall Street Journal Online,* www.opinionjournal.com/taste/?id=110001946 (accessed 5 July 2002).

35. Alan Ehrenhalt, "The Paradox of Corrupt Yet Effective Leadership," *New York Times,* 30 September 2002, A25.

36. For example, in a 2002 presentation titled "Crisis in Corporate Governance," Bill George estimated that corrupt leaders at Global Crossing, Enron, Qwest, Tyco and WORLD-COM cost shareholders $460 billion

CHAPTER 31

Understanding Ethical Failures in Leadership

Terry L. Price

University of Richmond

I. The Main Argument

This chapter articulates the intuition behind the charge that leaders think that they are special, that ordinary rules do not apply to them, and that followers should be expected to do as the leader says, not as the leader does. My central thesis is that ethical failures in leadership are fundamentally cognitive, not volitional. In arguing for this thesis, I reject the standard view that leaders behave unethically simply because they are selfish. Leader immorality is more a matter of belief and knowledge than a matter of desire and will. As such, the unethical behavior of leaders cannot be fully understood in terms of self-interest and the choices leaders make to put self-interest ahead of what they know to be the requirements of morality. So, for example, leadership ethics is not just about adjudicating between the interests of leaders and followers. An account of ethical failures in leadership must assign a primary role to mistaken moral beliefs.

The argument for the cognitive account of ethical failures in leadership appeals directly to the beliefs leaders hold about the importance of their ends. Of course, we all believe that our ends are important; otherwise we would not have them as ends. Leaders are no different in this respect, but the collective nature of the ends to which leaders are committed gives added justification to these ends. This is what makes leadership ethics distinctive. Leaders can believe, based on the importance of the collective ends they seek to achieve, that they are justified in making exceptions of themselves and in excluding others from the protections of morality. On the account offered in this book, ethical failure is a straightforward consequence of the way we think about leadership and the way leaders think about themselves.[1]

It might be expected that a book on ethical failures in leadership would begin with a moral theory to work from. Relying on an explicit statement of the requirements of morality, I could then infer what constitutes an

---

Source: Excerpts from the Introduction, pp. 1–6. In *Understanding Ethical Failures in Leadership* by Terry L. Price (2005). Reprinted with the permission of Cambridge University Press.

ethical failure in leadership, thereby putting myself in a position to discern its causes. It is not my aim, however, to offer a direct specification of moral leadership, let alone to begin with one. In fact, this book is better characterized as an analysis of the challenges to determining what morality demands of leaders, especially as this determination is made from the distinctive perspective of leaders. If I am right, such cognitive challenges to morality preclude any kind of foundationalist analysis of ethical failures in leadership. Ultimately, the question is addressed of how leaders ought to act, given that they do not always know what morality requires of them. To this end, I offer practical normative responses to the fact that justification is not always transparent to leaders.[2] Leaders should, among other responses, restrict the exceptions they make of themselves to the pursuit of inclusive ends, and publicize their reasons for deviating from the requirements of morality.

Given the nature of leadership itself, leaders are especially likely to face cognitive challenges to ethical behavior. Leadership is not only goal oriented but privileges the goals of the parties to the relationship. In other words, leadership is characterized by both consequentialism and partiality. Accordingly, it encourages preoccupation with collective ends, sometimes to the neglect of other important moral considerations. First among these considerations is that there are ethical constraints on the means used to achieve group, organizational, or societal goals, even when goal achievement is in the interests of followers.[3] Second, there are other parties in the moral universe besides those individuals in the leader-follower relationship. So, even if it is true that leaders should always put their interests second to the interests of followers, we cannot conclude that so doing is sufficient for ethical success in leadership. Given these two considerations, volitional pressures on leaders to privilege self-interest are a much smaller part of the story than cognitive pressures on leaders to put the interests of the group ahead of the interests of individual followers and the interests of outsiders.

II. The "Hitler Problem"

One approach to ethics in leadership has been to use normative considerations to delimit the subject matter

itself. On this approach, since leadership is moral by definition, unethical behavior by those in power must be something other than leadership. The temptation to resort to definitions has been particularly strong in leadership studies, in part because of basic epistemological commitments that characterize standard social scientific research in this field.[4] But the definitional approach to ethics in leadership goes back at least to Plato, who argues that "every kind of rule, insofar as it rules, doesn't seek anything other than what is best for the things it rules and cares for, and this is true both of public and private kinds of rule."[5] Plato's view that *true* leadership is concerned with the good of the led, not the good of the leader himself, finds twentieth-century expression in the work of James MacGregor Burns, who goes so far as to deny that Adolf Hitler was a leader because "[l]eadership, unlike naked power-wielding, is . . . inseparable from followers' needs and goals," and Hitler was "an absolute wielder of brutal power."[6]

Must leadership be ethical to be leadership at all? This question is important to consider at the beginning of a book on understanding ethical failures in leadership. If the definitional approach to leadership is defensible, then there would seem to be no ethical failures in *leadership* for us to understand! I think we can admit that normative considerations help to mark off the domain of inquiry in leadership studies without undermining the book's purpose. Consider, for instance, that completely coercive relationships hardly count as leadership. Because the behavior of coerced agents is involuntary, the relationship between the coercer and the coerced is closer to the relationship between master and slave than that between leader and follower. Still, there is a large gap in reasoning between recognition of this conceptual point and the conclusion that behavior that deviates from morality is not leadership at all. Even if we assume that the relationship of leadership implies minimal agency on the part of followers, it would not follow that leadership always shows sufficient respect for the agency of followers or, for that matter, their well-being. Nor would it follow that leadership always puts the agency of followers to work in the service of ethical ends. Accordingly, we are left with many important moral problems that cannot be easily assumed away.

Joanne Ciulla contends that definitional approaches to leadership conceal particular normative commitments regarding the nature of the relationship between leaders and followers.[7] In effect, the definitions are misguided attempts to specify what constitutes good leadership, where *good* means both "morally good and technically good or effective."[8] This distinction helps us understand what Ciulla calls the "Hitler problem."[9] Burns and others who contend that Hitler was not a leader exploit the ambiguity in the question of whether he was a *good* leader. Since Hitler was at most technically good or effective, he can have been a good leader in only one sense of the term. Understanding the Hitler problem is therefore a prerequisite to beginning work in leadership ethics. Articulating particular normative commitments about leadership is the real task ethicists have faced all along. Simply calling some individuals *leaders* and others by a different name does not get around the fact that people in power sometimes engage in unethical behavior. Regardless of what we call these people, we want to be able to understand their behavior and help them to avoid it.

Commentators who make their normative commitments explicit by offering recommendations for how leaders ought to behave most often identify morally good leadership with what the definitional approach holds is necessary for leadership itself—namely, concern for the good of followers. It is on these grounds that thinkers from Aristotle to Machiavelli separate good and bad rule.[10] Contemporary observers of leadership have been no less inclined to make the opposition between concern for self and concern for others the defining distinction in leadership ethics.[11] This commitment to a volitional understanding of ethical failures in leadership makes for a sharp contrast with the cognitive account. Although it is not my aim to offer a direct specification of what morality requires of leaders, my argument for the cognitive account of ethical failures in leadership directly challenges the ascendancy of the view that it is enough that leaders forgo the claims of self-interest so that they might serve group, organizational, or societal goals. Service to these goals can promote mistaken beliefs by leaders that they are justified in making exceptions of themselves and in excluding others from the protection of morality's requirements. In these cases, their ethical failures are primarily cognitive, not volitional, in nature.

Notes

1. My approach is consistent with that of Howard Gardner, who writes, "Our understanding of the nature and processes of leadership is most likely to be enhanced as we come to understand better the arena in which leadership necessarily occurs—namely, the *human mind*. Perhaps this characterization should be pluralized as *human minds*, since I am concerned equally with the mind of the leader and the minds of the followers. . . . By focusing on the mind and invoking the word *cognitive*, I make deliberate contact with an approach to the study of mind that has developed rapidly in the last few decades. In contrast to the behaviorists, who have focused only on overt actions, and the psychoanalysts, whose interest has been directed chiefly at personality and motivation, cognitive psychologists examine how ideas (or thoughts or images or mental representations) develop and how they are stored, accessed, combined, remembered, and (all too often) rearranged or distorted by the operations of the human mental apparatus" (*Leading Minds: An Anatomy of Leadership* [New York: Basic Books, 1995], pp. 15–16).

2. See Allen E. Buchanan, "Social Moral Epistemology," *Social Philosophy and Policy* 19 (2002): 126–152.

3. For example, adherents of Immanuel Kant's moral philosophy would hardly be impressed by deception and manipulation by a leader whose goal was to advance the interests of followers. Though this kind of behavior can be perfectly altruistic, it can nevertheless fail to show morally appropriate respect for follower agency. In other words, the claim that a leader's deceptive and manipulative behavior was for the good of followers does not answer the charge that he did not engage properly their rational agency.

4. Given the empiricist assumption that, as David Hume puts it, all knowledge is about "relations of ideas" or "existence and matter of fact," ethics quickly becomes a matter of definition for social scientists (*A Treatise of Human Nature*, 2nd edition, ed. L. A. Selby-Bigge [Oxford: Oxford University Press, 1978], p. 458). After all, no amount of empirical data will give us the ethical facts, as opposed to people's ethical perceptions.

5. Plato, *Republic,* trans. G. M. A. Grube (Indianapolis: Hackett Publishing Company, 1992), p. 21 [345d–e].

6. James MacGregor Burns, *Leadership* (New York: Harper and Row Publishers, 1978), pp. 19, 27.

7. This paragraph and the one that follows it draw from Terry L. Price, "Ethics," in George R. Goethals, Georgia Sorenson, James MacGregor Burns, eds., *Encyclopedia of Leadership* (Thousand Oaks, CA: Sage Publications, 2004),

pp. 462–470, copyright © 2004 Berkshire Publishing Group. Reprinted with permission of Berkshire Publishing Group.

8. Joanne B. Ciulla, "Leadership Ethics: Mapping the Territory," in Joanne B. Ciulla, ed., *Ethics, the Heart of Leadership* (Westport, CT: Praeger, 1998), p. 13. See also James O'Toole, *Leading Change: The Argument for Values-Based Leadership* (New York: Ballantine Books, 1996); and John W. Gardner, *On Leadership* (New York: Free Press, 1990), ch. 7. O'Toole writes, "But that necessary factor of effectiveness turns out to be insufficient. . . . The values-based leadership advocated in these pages is different, therefore, from the prevailing modes in that its calculus includes the factors of *morality*"(p. xii).

9. Ciulla, "Mapping the Territory," p. 12. According to John Gardner, "We say that we want effective leadership; but Hitler was effective. Criteria beyond effectiveness are needed" (*On Leadership*, p. 67).

10. Aristotle distinguishes correct from deviated constitutions, claiming that "[w]henever the one, the few, or the many rule with a view to the common good, these constitutions must be correct; but if they look to the private advantage, be it of the one or the few or the mass, they are deviations" (*The Politics*, trans. T. A. Sinclair [New York: Penguin Books, 1981], pp. 189–190 [1279a28–1279a30]). Aquinas, appealing to God's exhortation in Ezekiel 34:2, "Woe to the shepherds of Israel who have fed themselves," similarly makes concern for the good of followers both sufficient and necessary for good leadership: "[I]f a ruler should direct a community of free persons for the common good of the people, there will be a right and just regime, as befits free persons. And if the governance of a ruler be ordained for the private good of the ruler and not for the common good of the people, there will be an unjust and wicked regime" (*On Kingship, To the King of Cyprus*, in Michael L. Morgan, ed., *Classics of Moral and Political Theory*, 3rd edition [Indianapolis: Hackett Publishing Company, 2001], p. 398). Even Machiavelli, who is known for the amoralism of *The Prince*, defends a historical cycling

between good and bad leadership in his *Discourses*, with the former being characterized by leaders who "[put] their own interests second and the public good first" (*The Prince*, eds. Quentin Skinner and Russell Price [Cambridge: Cambridge University Press, 1988]; and *Discourses on the First Ten Books of Titius Livius*, in Michael L. Morgan, ed., *Classics of Moral and Political Theory*, 3rd edition [Indianapolis: Hackett Publishing Company, 2001], p. 472.)

11. Robert K. Greenleaf recommends a form of leadership on which the leader "is servant first. . . . That person is sharply different from one who is *leader* first, perhaps because of the need to assuage an unusual power drive or to acquire material possessions" (*Servant Leadership: A Journey into the Nature of Legitimate Power and Greatness* [New York: Paulist Press, 1977]p. 13). Jane Howell and Bruce Avolio come to this same conclusion about the ethical use of power by way of an appeal to David McClelland's distinction between *personalized* and *socialized* power motives, suggesting that leaders should be motivated by a concern for the common good. (See Jane M. Howell and Bruce J. Avolio, "The Ethics of Charismatic Leadership: Submission or Liberation?" *Academy of Management Executive* 6, 2 [1992]: 43–54; and David C. McClelland, *Human Motivation* [Glenview, IL: Scott Foresman and Company, 1985].) Indeed, some leadership scholars believe that altruism makes a leader's behavior both ethical and effective and thus that the Hitler problem is not so problematic after all. According to Rabindra N. Kanungo and Manuel Mendonca, "Because the 'other'—that is, the organization and its members—is the raison d'etre of the leader's efforts, the altruistic motive becomes the only consistent motive for the leader's role" (*Ethical Dimensions of Leadership* [Thousand Oaks, CA: Sage Publications, 1996], p. 35). On this view, "[L]eadership effectiveness is ensured only by altruistic acts that reflect the leader's incessant desire and concern to benefit others despite the risk of personal cost inherent in such acts" (Kanungo and Mendonca, *Ethical Dimensions of Leadership*, p. 35).

PART VI

Inclusion

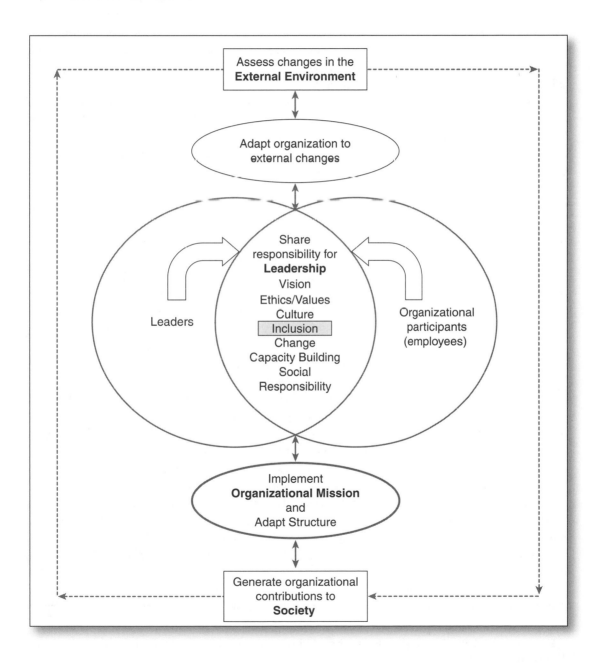

Overview

Inclusive Perspectives

In recent years, the term *inclusion* has been added to or replaced the dialogue about diversity. Inclusion and diversity are distinct yet related concepts. "Diversity focuses on organizational demography [that is, workforce composition, including race, sex, disability, ethnicity, and so on], whereas inclusion focuses on the removal of obstacles to the full participation and contribution of employees in organizations."[1] Real inclusion entails bringing people with varied backgrounds and unique perspectives into the organization and creating a climate in which they can thrive, learn, and contribute their capabilities to the organization's processes and outcomes. An underlying assumption of inclusion is that the human community—in this case, an organizational community—has a greater chance of understanding key issues, engaging in creative or innovative work, and creating effective, sustainable change by involving heterogeneous stakeholders in a mutual problem-solving arena.[2] As a result, inclusion enriches the organization's culture and builds its capacity.

Flannery Stevens, Victoria Plaut, and Jeffrey Sanchez-Burks (Chapter 32) favor "all-inclusive multiculturalism" (AIM) as a means to real inclusiveness. Stevens et al. assert that an AIM workplace approach strengthens inclusiveness by incorporating and respecting nonminorities, simultaneously fostering inclusion and respect for minorities. These researchers argue that colorblind approaches satisfy nonminorities but leave minorities feeling excluded. Alternatively, multicultural approaches are attractive to minorities, yet they can produce skepticism and resentment from nonminorities. Stevens, Plaut, and Sanchez-Burks state that the AIM method encourages positive intergroup relations, which result in increased participation by members and better organizational performance.

Research on inclusion of cross-cultural or cross-national employees is especially critical in new era organizations where leaders and participants from different countries work together. Yi-feng Chen, Dean Tjosvold, and Sofia Fang Su (Chapter 33) studied the interaction between foreign managers and local Chinese employees. They tested the theory of cooperation and competition during their investigation of how foreign managers and their Chinese employees deal with work-related controversy. Their findings confirmed that cooperative, rather than competitive or independent, goals help foreign managers and Chinese employees engage in constructive controversy (productive discussion of opposing views in a cooperative context) that in turn results in innovation and employee job commitment. Their respondents indicated that shared goals, common tasks, complementary roles, shared rewards, and trusting attitudes develop cooperative goals. Many cultural studies focus on how leadership differs in various cultures and countries, but there is a critical need for more studies like this one that examine how leaders and members in cross-cultural groups can work together more effectively, with mutual trust and respect.

Alice Eagly and Linda Carli (Chapter 34) address inclusion of women leaders at the top of organizations. They contend that even though women occupy a small percentage of executive level positions (6% of the Fortune 500 companies), the presence of a small number of women indicates that barriers to the top are no longer absolute. It is time to change the metaphor for women's climb to the executive suite, according to Eagly and Carli, from "the glass ceiling" (an invisible barrier to top-level positions) to "the labyrinth" (a complex journey toward a goal worth striving for). They indicate that routes to the top exist, but women will need to navigate the expected and unexpected twists and turns of the labyrinth. They identify various obstructions that women encounter (such as vestiges of prejudice and resistance to women's leadership) and propose actions that women can take (e.g., reaching a balance between communal and agentic qualities) and interventions that their organizations can implement (e.g., changing the long-hours norm or providing line management

---

1. Roberson, Q. M. (2006). Disentangling the Meanings of Diversity and Inclusion in Organizations. *Group & Organization Management, 31*(2), 217.

2. See Hickman, G. R. (2010). *Leading Change in Multiple Contexts: Concepts and Practices in Organizational, Community, Political, Social, and Global Change Settings.* Thousand Oaks, CA: Sage.

positions with appropriately demanding assignments) to help women reach the executive suite.

Research by Dana Wilson-Kovacs and colleagues (Chapter 35) draws parallels between disabled individuals in leadership positions and women or other marginalized groups in leadership positions. They indicate that persons with disabilities and women are often placed in highly precarious roles, referred to as the "glass cliff," that involve leadership positions in organizations or units that have recently experienced a consistent pattern of poor performance. Placement in these leadership positions puts individuals at a greater risk of failure than nondisabled or male counterparts. As a result, issues that pertain to disabled leaders and professionals in the workplace require organizational leaders and members to address three areas of inclusion: discrimination-and-fairness, access-and-legitimacy, and integration-and-learning.

Participants in Wilson-Kovacs and colleagues' study cited support from "inspirational individuals" rather than organizational or institutional support as contributing to the success of individuals with disabilities who occupy leadership positions. To bring about real inclusion, respondents recommended that they be regarded first and foremost in a professional capacity; they be allowed to take risks for the purpose of professional development and career progression; and human resource departments and organizational leaders facilitate equal opportunity, demonstrate a willingness and ability to understand disability, and implement effective administrative procedures to overcome barriers to sustaining and advancing their careers.

Meaningful support for lesbian, gay, and bisexual (LGB) employees is another vital area of inclusion in new era organizations. Ann Huffman, Kristen Watrous-Rodriguez, and Eden King (Chapter 36) found that the form of support needed by LGB employees is a multidimensional construct comprising supervisor, coworker, and overall organizational support. These factors represent three different but related constructs—that is, supervisor support is more strongly related to job satisfaction, coworker support is strongly related to life satisfaction, and organizational support has a strong relationship with outness. Huffman, Watrous-Rodriquez, and King confirm that all three components are important, and therefore organizations should attempt to create a climate in which each form of support is available to LGB employees.

The Society for Human Resource Management (SHRM) (Chapter 37) indicates that for the first time in history, four generations—Traditionalists, Baby Boomers, Generation X, and Millennials/Generation Y—work together in many organizations. These generations represent both similarities and differences in their expectations in the workplace. Employees in all four generations value achievement, work-life balance, and responsibility, and they want credible, trustworthy leadership. Each generation brings different assets to the workplace. For instance, Traditionalists are hard-working, stable, loyal, thorough, detail oriented, focused, and emotionally mature. Baby Boomers bring a team perspective, dedication, experience, knowledge, and a service orientation. Generation Xers are independent, adaptable, creative, techno-literate, and willing to challenge the status quo. Millennials are optimistic, able to multitask, tenacious, technologically savvy, driven to learn and grow, team oriented, and socially responsible. SHRM encourages organizations to create inclusive climates that capitalize on the assets of each generation for competitive advantage, taking care not to stereotype individuals based on their generation.

Douglas Hicks (Chapter 38) addresses the topic of religious diversity in the workplace. He contends that in contemporary America, the workplace is one of the principal places in which people encounter religious and other forms of difference. Now more than ever, employees non-compartmentalize their lives; that is, they bring their identity, problems, and beliefs to work. Hicks explains that for many employees, religious or spiritual beliefs and practices are an essential and inseparable part of their lives. He proposes a "respectful pluralism" framework that involves a set of ideas for creating mutual respect amid diversity and encourages coworkers of multiple perspectives and worldviews to communicate with each other and to work together in relative harmony. Three limiting norms provide parameters for respectful pluralism: *nondegradation*, a moral commitment to uphold the dignity of each employee and prohibit disrespectful speech, symbols, or messages directed at coworkers; *noncoercion*, which means employees must not use their position or proximity to colleagues or individuals they supervise to impose their religious, spiritual, or political values or subject them to unwanted invitations; and *nonestablishment*, which applies to organizations as institutions and asserts that it is morally unacceptable for an organization to endorse, or in any way promote, one particular religious or spiritual worldview over others. Using the tenets of inclusion and limiting norms, Hicks provides several scenarios that illustrate respectful pluralism in practice; for example, permitting Muslim women to wear the *hijab* in the workplace and not proselytizing to coworkers.

The tenets of respectful pluralism are applicable to each category of inclusion described in this section, encompassing race, gender, sexual orientation, culture, disability, multiple generations, and religion. Developing inclusive climates and practices in the workplace is not easy, but it represents one of the most significant tests of effectiveness, responsibility, and ethical behavior in new era organizations.

CHAPTER 32

Unlocking the Benefits of Diversity

*All-Inclusive Multiculturalism
and Positive Organizational Change*

Flannery G. Stevens

University of Michigan

Victoria C. Plaut

University of Georgia

Jeffrey Sanchez-Burks

University of Michigan

The U.S. workforce, owing to the steady increase of demographic minority entrants, is in a rapid state of change. Populations typically underrepresented in organizations, particularly ethnic minorities and women, have become an integral part of the workforce.[1] Leveraging this diversity has important implications for the promotion of positive organizational change through its facilitation of both individual and organizational performance (e.g., Brief, 2008; Earley & Mosakowski, 2000; Williams & O'Reilly, 1998). The need to create organizational environments receptive to diversity is therefore greater than ever. We argue that workforce diversity—if approached in a way that maximizes inclusion and minimizes resistance—presents organizations with opportunities to create change that fosters the positive human potential of their employees.

Source: Stevens, F. G., Plaut, V. C., and Sanchez-Burks, J. (2008). Unlocking the benefits of diversity: All-inclusive multiculturalism and positive organizational change. *Journal of Applied Behavioral Science* 44(1), 116–133. Published by Sage Publications on behalf of NTL Institute.

Numerous organizations have recognized and attempted to respond effectively to the demographic shifts in the workforce by launching diversity initiatives, hiring diversity consultants, and offering an array of diversity training programs (Kalev, Dobbin, & Kelly, 2006). A similar focus on these demographic trends and their implications for organizations is found among academic researchers, as seen in more than 450 articles on "diversity in the workplace" just since 2000. Scholars and practitioners have not, however, reflected sufficiently on whether—and to what extent how—organizational approaches to diversity promote employee receptivity to these initiatives. We posit that this lack of critical reflection has curtailed the effectiveness of diversity efforts. The current article complements and extends existing theory on how organizations manage demographic diversity in an effort to gain competitive advantage (e.g., Richard, 2000; Wright, Ferris, Hiller, & Kroll, 1995), specifically through their attempts to foster positive organizational change. We do so by reexamining fundamental cultural assumptions within organizations about how best to create a positive climate at work (Cameron, Dutton, & Quinn, 2003; Dutton & Ragins, 2006; Gittell, Cameron, Lim, & Rivas, 2006), particularly by drawing on diversity as a resource (Ely & Thomas, 2001).

In contrast with a problem-focused approach (typical of organizational development and change initiatives), viewing diversity as an opportunity rather than as a threat creates possibilities for increased organizational understanding (e.g., Jackson & Dutton, 1988) and positive, organization-wide change (Cooperrider & Sekerka, 2003). The current article focuses on the potential of workplace diversity as a catalyst for positive organizational change, a broad concept that includes analyzing and exemplifying instances of positive deviance (e.g., Cameron et al., 2003; Spreitzer & Sonenshein, 2003), virtuousness (e.g., Cameron, 2003) and endorsing an affirmative bias, or strengths-based orientation (e.g., Cameron et al., 2003; Clifton & Harter, 2003). We articulate a new organizational premise that heightens the potential for diversity to provide fertile ground for organizational change. Specifically, we explicitly address aspects of diversity as a "positive core" of organizational life—a key component of positive change (Cooperrider & Sekerka, 2003). In doing so,

we explicate how, if approached inclusively, diversity creates a context in which individuals can create high-quality relationships across difference (Davidson & James, 2006) and approach the best of the human condition.

In the current article, we discuss the two dominant approaches used by organizations attempting to change their climate surrounding diversity—colorblindness and multiculturalism—and how well these approaches address the unique needs of both minorities and non-minorities to affiliate with the organization.[2] In doing so, we briefly review extant research concerning diversity in the workplace as well as the benefits and limitations of the colorblind and multicultural approaches. We also discuss the implications of these two diversity perspectives for organizational functioning and for the individuals embedded within these organizations. Our discussion reveals a stark fundamental paradox in these two approaches that appears to limit their effectiveness. To reconcile the limitations of both the colorblind and multicultural approaches to diversity, we introduce a novel approach to managing organizational diversity—what we refer to as all-inclusive multiculturalism (AIM). As we describe in the following, this approach offers organizations a way to overcome the limitations of the colorblind and traditional multicultural ideologies by cultivating feelings of employee inclusion and thus provides a starting point for positive organizational change. Finally, we discuss implications for practice and describe a specific empirical agenda intended for future research.

Diversity in Organizations

Research over the past 50 years has shown little consensus about what constitutes diversity or how it affects organizational processes and outcomes (for a review, see Williams & O'Reilly, 1998). A common definition of diversity refers to the degree to which a workgroup or organization is heterogeneous with respect to personal and functional attributes (Jehn, Northcraft, & Neale, 1999). The extant literature on organizational diversity has produced inconsistent results on effects of diversity, with some researchers finding beneficial effects, such as increased creativity, productivity, and quality (e.g.,

Earley & Mosakowski, 2000; Ely & Thomas, 2001; Polzer, Milton, & Swann, 2002; Swann, Kwan, Polzer, & Milton, 2003; Watson, Kumar, & Michaelsen, 1993), and others finding a detrimental influence on organizational outcomes—particularly through process losses, increases in conflict, decreases in social integration, and inhibition of decision-making and change processes (e.g., Chatman, Polzer, Barsade, & Neale, 1998; Jehn et al., 1999; Morrison & Milliken, 2000; Westphal & Milton, 2000; for a review, see Mannix & Neale, 2006). Following from such inconsistencies, diversity has been dubbed a "double-edged sword" for organizations (Williams & O'Reilly, 1998).

In our discussion of diversity, we focus on the distribution of race and ethnicity among interdependent members of a work unit (Jackson, Joshi, & Erhardt, 2003; Pelled, Eisenhardt, & Xin, 1999),[3] whether a work group, department, or organization. In doing so, some of the heretofore mixed results of workplace diversity and its influence on organizational functioning are resolved. Specifically, the current article focuses on ways in which racial and ethnic diversity can be drawn on as a resource for building on employees' strengths; cultivating a climate that fosters respect, compassion, and openness; and ultimately, gaining a competitive advantage through generating feelings of inclusion of both minority and nonminority employees.

Previous research has emphasized how individuals utilize social categorizations based on demographic differences to make sense of their diverse environments (e.g., Hogg & Terry, 2000; Polzer et al., 2002), which in turn undercuts social cohesion and integration and leads to dysfunctional conflict (Polzer et al., 2002). Creating a positive diverse work environment is indeed quite challenging, but organizations need not be at the mercy of changes in the demographic composition of the workforce and the conflict that often accompanies these changes. Rather, in line with a strengths-based approach (Clifton & Harter, 2003), organizations can take charge by creating an environment conducive to embracing and fostering the benefits of such diversity, starting with the implementation and subsequent institutionalization of best practices that center on the self-affirmation and inclusion of all employees. Specifically, by creating a backdrop against which interracial interactions are interpreted as opportunities for learning, as opposed to being tense and filled with discord, employees have the chance to build supportive, enduring, and resilient relationships (e.g., Davidson & James, 2006). We posit that by fostering such relationships, an all-inclusive work environment promotes individual thriving, defined as "a sense of progress or forward movement in one's self development" and comprised of two dimensions of personal growth—learning and vitality (Spreitzer, Sutcliffe, Dutton, Sonenshein, & Grant, 2005, p. 538).

Diversity Approaches and Initiatives

Organizations cultivate and manage diversity in a variety of ways. Many organizations institute daily practices that demonstrate their commitment to fostering diversity at work through a series of what can be referred to as "diversity initiatives," whereas other companies eschew these multicultural initiatives in favor of a "colorblind" approach to diversity.[4]

The colorblind approach. The colorblind approach to organizational diversity is intertwined with American cultural ideals of individualism, equality, meritocracy, assimilation, and "the melting pot" (Markus, Steele, & Steele, 2000; Plaut, 2002; D. A. Thomas & Ely, 1996; K. M. Thomas, Mack, & Montagliani, 2004) and focuses on ignoring cultural group identities or realigning them with an overarching identity (Hogg & Terry, 2000). This "realignment" is achieved by placing emphasis on a superordinate goal or identity, such as a common affiliation with the broader organization, which typically increases an individual's organizational identity while decreasing the salience of individual differences (Chatman & Flynn, 2001). For example, an organization can structure rewards that foster greater nonminority-minority collaboration, bringing important deep-level characteristics to the foreground while pushing demographic differences, such as racial and ethnic diversity, to the background (Harrison, Price, & Bell, 1998). The irony in this practice is that diverse employees are discouraged from acting and thinking in the unique ways associated with their social categories, which does not allow them to utilize fully the viewpoints of their distinctive social group memberships.

The colorblind approach appears as a dominant model for diversity in mainstream American culture and organizations (Plaut & Markus, 2007; D. A. Thomas & Ely, 1996). This approach stresses individual accomplishments and qualifications over any other factor, such as diversity, and preserves the preference for unity and cohesion. Nonminorities who believe strongly in individual merit or have a high need to belong are likely to identify highly with an organization that espouses colorblindness (Plaut, Sanchez-Burks, Buffardi, & Stevens, 2007). In turn, these individuals are more likely to remain with the organization once employed as their identification with the organization's approach to diversity grows into identification with the organization as a whole (e.g., Dutton, Dukerich, & Harquail, 1994).

Although the colorblind perspective in principle is grounded in the ideals of meritocracy and equality—in essence, "treating all people the same" (Plaut, 2002)—evidence suggests that this approach is commonly interpreted by minorities as neither colorblind nor color neutral but rather as exclusionary (Markus et al., 2000). Members of the majority group typically endorse a colorblind approach to diversity because it is perceived as more inclusive of their group; minorities on the other hand distrust colorblind initiatives because they are perceived as being exclusive of their group. Moreover, minority distrust of colorblind ideals is exacerbated in cases where organizations do not appear to be especially diverse in the first place (Purdie-Vaughns, Steele, Davies, & Crosby, 2006). Within organizations perceived to ignore or devalue racial differences, frustration, dissatisfaction, and conflict will likely ensue, particularly for minority members high in racial identity (Chrobot-Mason & Thomas, 2002). These negative effects on organizational attachment are not surprising given that a colorblind perspective is also associated with higher levels of racial bias (Richeson & Nussbaum, 2004) and a tendency to ignore processes that perpetuate differential outcomes for nonminority and minority groups (Schofield, 1986). A colorblind perspective does not reliably indicate a prejudicial organizational stance but rather, may reflect an attempt by the organization to frame their diversity practices using an ideology that has traditionally appealed to nonminority groups. Although a colorblind ideology may appeal to nonminorities, this approach to diversity also may alienate minority employees and allow a culture of racism to develop (Bonilla-Silva, 2003).

The multicultural approach. The multicultural approach to diversity emphasizes the benefits of a diverse workforce and explicitly recognizes employee differences as a source of strength (Cox, 1991). Organizations promoting initiatives premised on a multicultural ideology are particularly attractive to minorities because diverse backgrounds are recognized as being different, and group identities, such as race, ethnicity, and religious affiliation, are retained and acknowledged (e.g., Plaut & Markus, 2007; Purdie-Vaughns et al., 2006; Verkuyten, 2005). Organizations employ a variety of strategies to emphasize diversity. For example, multicultural initiatives range from networking and mentoring programs, which provide additional resources for demographically underrepresented groups of employees, to corporate "diversity days" where employees' backgrounds are celebrated, diversity luncheons where food of different nations is served, and workshops or seminars that focus on aspects of diversity (e.g., Kidder, Lankau, Chrobot-Mason, Mollica, & Friedman, 2004; Linnehan & Konrad, 1999). Still, other companies may require—or strongly encourage—employees to attend diversity training, which is designed to diminish bias and increase cultural awareness among nonminority employees (Paluck, 2006).

Whereas multiculturalism should ideally foster a lasting organizational climate of inclusion and acceptance, multicultural diversity initiatives often fade, fall short of their goals, or fail completely because they are widely met by nonminorities with noncompliance and resistance (Brief et al., 2005; Kalev et al., 2006; Mannix & Neale, 2006; K. M. Thomas, 2008). Ironically, despite their overt attempt to foster inclusion in the workplace, multicultural initiatives can produce skepticism and resentment on the part of some groups—in particular nonminorities—who represent overlooked, yet critical, stakeholders in diversity issues (cf. James, Brief, Dietz, & Cohen, 2001). Many nonminority critiques of multiculturalism center on the claim that it excludes nonminorities and threatens unity (Plaut et al., 2007). This skepticism—perhaps even contempt—is echoed by Schlesinger's (1992) commentary on multiculturalism:

> "Multiculturalism" arises as a reaction against Anglo- or Eurocentrism, but at what point does it pass over into an ethnocentrism of its own? The very word, instead of referring as it should to all cultures, has come to refer only to non-Western,

nonwhite cultures. . . . When does obsession with differences begin to threaten the idea of an overarching American nationality? (p. 74)

To the extent that nonminorities experience identity threats from multicultural initiatives (Verkuyten, 2005), they are likely to engage in identity management strategies, ranging from devaluing out-groups (i.e., resisting diversity) to reducing their motivation to identify and affiliate with an organization that supports multiculturalism. Indeed, efforts to enhance workplace diversity through a multicultural approach have generated significant backlash (Linnehan & Konrad, 1999). This backlash is manifested at the individual level in biased language, discrimination, silence regarding inequities, avoidance of difference, and discrediting of ideas and individuals and at the organizational level in discriminatory human resource policies and practices, cultures of silence, and delays in diversity initiatives (K. M. Thomas & Plaut, 2008).

Moreover, exposure to multicultural ideology is associated with cognitions and behaviors that could further prevent organizations from realizing the potential of diversity. For example, nonminorities exposed to a multicultural statement subsequently show more activation of stereotypes associated with minorities and also are more likely to use individuals' category memberships, such as race, in making judgments about them (e.g., Cox, 1993; Wolsko, Park, Judd, & Wittenbrink, 2000). The multicultural perspective seemingly triggers group-based processing among nonminorities, which, if not properly managed, could exacerbate existing prejudices in the workplace. Research also has shown that nonminorities support general equal employment opportunity (EEO) policies but oppose affirmative action (AA) practices that focus on specific demographic criteria, such as race, in human resources decision making (Kleugel, 1985).

More recently, James and colleagues (2001) found that as potential job applicants, nonminorities reported less positive attitudes toward promotion opportunities and less attraction to an organization when policies were specifically framed as benefiting minorities than when the policies were more generally framed. In a follow-up study, these researchers surveyed employees in a large communications company and found, once again, that nonminorities reported significantly less positive job-related attitudes when exposed to EEO/AA

policies benefiting minorities. This is in stark comparison to the empirical research that shows consistent, positive relationships between minority attraction to organizations and a variety of techniques used by organizations to signal their value of diversity: recruiter characteristics, such as race (e.g., K. M. Thomas & Wise, 1999); diversity-related information portrayed in advertisements and brochures, such as EEO/AA policies (e.g., James et al., 2001); the representation of minorities within the organization (e.g., Avery, 2003; Perkins, Thomas, & Taylor, 2000); and the diversity initiative endorsed by the organization (Plaut et al., 2007).

The Aim Approach: Toward an All-Inclusive Workplace

Our review shows that organizations are faced with a serious challenge in responding to the increasingly diverse nature of the workforce: Neither the colorblind nor the multicultural approach to organizational diversity is received by all employees as a positive affirmation of their belongingness in the organization (see Baumeister & Leary, 1995). Nonminorities feel excluded in organizations espousing a multicultural approach and feel more comfortable with a colorblind approach. For these employees, who interpret multicultural initiatives as applying only to minority group members, such initiatives pose a threat to their social identity (Verkuyten, 2005) and may decrease their desire to affiliate with the organization. The reverse pattern emerges among minorities, who experience exclusion in workplaces that espouse colorblindness. For organizations to bring their positive core to the forefront, thus stimulating positive change, they need an alternative approach to diversity that does not face resistance from either nonminority or minority organizational members.

We propose that an AIM approach meets this need, emphasizing that diversity includes all employees— that is, both minorities and nonminorities alike. On one hand, the AIM approach recognizes the importance of differences and acknowledges such differences, which is essential for gaining minority support. On the other hand, the AIM approach explicitly acknowledges the important role that nonminorities play in workplace diversity, addressing their concerns of exclusion and disadvantage. Essentially, the AIM approach addresses deficiencies in the standard multicultural ideology without reverting to colorblindness. Whereas AIM acknowledges that the demographic groups to which people belong have important consequences for individuals, it also explicitly endorses this vision equally across members of all groups, including nonminorities. Given the pervasiveness of American values of equality and egalitarianism, which drive individualist ideology, this equal emphasis on groups is less of a mismatch for nonminorities. Moreover, AIM lifts perceived threats to unity that may form in reaction to multicultural policies (e.g., Schlesinger, 1992). Indeed, the AIM approach is consistent with approaches to intergroup relations that foster the maintenance of subgroup identities within the context of an overarching identity (see Hogg & Terry, 2000).

There is emerging empirical evidence of the positive effects that can be gained from this approach. For example, in our recent work, we and our colleagues (Plaut et al., 2007) had 35 nonminority undergraduate students participating for partial course credit (54% male; M age = 19.3 years) read a fictitious one-page newspaper article titled "Diversity Efforts Blanket Nation" about the spread of multiculturalism in corporations and universities across the United States. Participants randomly assigned to the control condition read this article, whereas participants assigned to the AIM condition read the same article with an additional paragraph describing multiculturalism as inclusive of everyone, including European Americans. Participants subsequently completed a computerized implicit association test (IAT) designed to gauge the strength of association of multiculturalism (vs. colorblindness) with exclusion (vs. inclusion). On the IAT, participants in the control condition showed significantly faster reaction times (i.e., stronger implicit associations) pairing multiculturalism with exclusion than multiculturalism with inclusion. This association, however, was absent for participants in the AIM condition. In short, by explicitly affirming the inclusion of nonminorities within a general multiculturalism ideology, the association of diversity with exclusion was significantly reduced. Notably, these findings further show that the perception that whites are included in multiculturalism were significantly stronger in the AIM condition (61%) than in the control condition (24%), but dropping participants who did not complete this manipulation check as expected

did not alter the results. In other words, the power of the AIM manipulation operated implicitly, regardless of whether participants were able to explicitly report inclusion of their group.

The findings that associations of multiculturalism with exclusion were attenuated with the AIM model points to its potential to enhance, rather than impede, positive intergroup relationships, as well as individual and organizational performance. Previous research shows that social exclusion is linked to aggressive behavior and decrements in intelligent thought (Baumeister, Twenge, & Nuss, 2002; Twenge, Baumeister, Tice, & Stucke, 2001). Moreover, research on self-affirmation has shown that affirming the self decreases defensiveness and prejudice (see Sherman & Cohen, 2006). In terms of personal growth, workplaces that foster identity safety may give individuals a better chance to flourish (Markus et al., 2000). We propose that only an all-inclusive approach allows all groups to fully develop and maintain identities that are either explicitly or implicitly important to them. To the extent that AIM policy helps diminish perceptions of social exclusion and affirms individuals' social identities, employee relationships with each other and with the organization should be strengthened.

Proposition 1: Implementing an AIM approach will promote a sense of inclusion among all employees and foster greater feelings of connectedness to one another, the organization, and its goals.

The AIM approach also helps organizations deal with the increasing complexity of a diverse workforce, including the challenge of how employees within diverse organizations interact with one another. Because organizations are increasingly diverse, social categorizations—for instance, along the lines of gender and race—become particularly salient in employees' daily interactions (Hogg & Terry, 2000). A key component in the creation of a truly inclusive climate is moving beyond surface-level tactics that display an appreciation of diversity and inspiring individuals to integrate diversity into their work lives through self- and other-appreciation within their organizational context (e.g., Davidson & James, 2006; D. A. Thomas & Ely, 1996). The foundation for developing an all-inclusive organization is in focusing on the formation of high-quality relationships among dissimilar others—that is, relationships that engender positive affect, encourage ongoing learning, are resilient, have longevity, and create "the capacity for individuals to engage, challenge, and support one another with clarity and confidence" (Davidson & James, 2006, p. 139).

With the AIM approach to diversity, employees are able to thrive and reach their fullest potential because there is a climate that encourages open communication and learning, affording individuals the opportunity to move past social categorizations and build mutually supportive and resilient relationships (Spreitzer et al., 2005). Such relationships are precluded in organizations with colorblind and multicultural diversity initiatives because of the feelings of exclusion engendered by each. Because the all-inclusive organization recognizes—and celebrates—the contextually salient identities of its employees, like race, opportunities for learning are created rather than squandered. By fostering an environment where individual differences are not ignored, as with the colorblind approach, or where feelings of inclusion are cultivated, in contrast with the exclusion of nonminorities engendered by multiculturalism, employees can engage each other in open, honest conversations about their differences. The AIM approach, through its facilitation of learning, promotes the formation of authentic relationships among diverse individuals and eschews the prejudice and stereotyping typically associated with diversity (e.g., Davidson & James, 2006; Wolsko et al., 2000).

> *Proposition 2:* High-quality relationships will emerge within organizations that implement the AIM approach, as indicated by increased empathetic understanding of others, social and emotional support, and sharing of information.

Implementing AIM

Practitioners and scholars alike have commonly espoused goals of greater diversity, yet neither have been able to unlock its potential benefits without being stymied by its major drawbacks. We propose AIM as a way to benefit from organizational diversity as opposed to falling victim to its potential shortcomings, which has implications for practice and research. In this section, we address ways an AIM climate can be fostered in organizations and how this approach to diversity will likely influence organizational functioning, as well as individuals within the organization. We then suggest new avenues for research and theory building.

Communication and language. Creating an AIM workplace involves crafting environments that are considered more inclusive by all employees. Developing a climate of inclusion in which minorities and nonminorities feel like they belong can begin with communicating these changes to its internal and external constituents. Drawing on our research manipulating the inclusiveness of multiculturalism in newspaper articles (Plaut et al., 2007), we propose using AIM-based language in narratives about the organization's stance on diversity. For example, word choices in an organization's diversity materials (e.g., mission statement, corporate brochures, etc.) that communicate the inclusion of all employees in diversity initiatives indicate a potential ideological stance that appeals to minorities and nonminorities alike. By explicitly including nonminorities in the concept of diversity, this ideological perspective makes it clear that these groups will enjoy the same recognition and respect as minority groups.

Another example of AIM-based communication involves avoiding language that appears exclusive. Typically, soliciting employee participation for multicultural activities involves asking them to submit ethnic recipes, suggest resources for learning about a particular culture, or simply attend and enjoy multicultural festivities. To capitalize on an AIM approach, requests for participation might employ statements of inclusion to increase nonminority acceptance of the initiative. For example, when asking for recipes for a multicultural picnic or cookbook, the invitation might mention interest in "family recipes from all employees" rather than "ethnic recipes reflecting your heritage." This avoids the trap of nonminorities feeling excluded on the assumption that "ethnic" does not include them (e.g., Devos & Banaji, 2005). Relatedly, organizations using an AIM approach could avoid using words like *diverse* to refer to ethnic minorities and instead communicate that all employees are included in the term *diversity*.

Building on work by James et al. (2001) on the effects of framing policies as generally benefiting employees, we suggest that organizations use AIM when communicating organizational policies related to hiring, promotion, mentoring, and networking programs. In most cases, policies and initiatives can be framed as benefiting everyone, as opposed to just one group of people (e.g., women, blacks, gays, and lesbians). When a practice does not directly benefit everyone, employees can be reminded that such practices promote professionalism and collegiality and are part of a greater effort to create a far stronger workplace environment for everyone (see K. M. Thomas, 2005).

Organizational structures and policies. Cultivating an all-inclusive, multicultural workplace also requires organizations to "put their money where their mouth is" and implement changes at the structural level (Kalev et al., 2006). For example, fostering both minority and nonminority leadership and involvement in diversity initiatives is fundamental to the AIM approach. Organizations can ensure that the unit responsible for diversity demographically reflects the inclusion they claim to promote. Diversity task forces, councils, and resource groups also should be comprised of minorities and nonminorities. Mentoring and social networking initiatives can practice AIM by including cross-race groupings (e.g., see Ragins, 1997, for an analysis of "diversified mentoring"). By-products of such efforts include not only career development benefits for protégés but also increased intercultural competence. Finally, organizations using AIM can design policies that not only purport to benefit all employees but actually do benefit all employees (see also Meyerson & Fletcher, 2000).

Proposed Benefits of AIM

We propose that through the facilitation of high-quality relationships across difference, an AIM approach allows organizations to realize promised benefits of diversity. An AIM workplace approaches diversity in a way that decreases conflict and resistance by allowing nonminorities to feel included and respected while simultaneously fostering minorities' feelings of inclusion and respect. By encouraging employees to feel included and valued, the AIM approach fosters organizational commitment and trust, internal motivation, and satisfaction for both minorities and nonminorities alike (Morrison & Milliken, 2000). It also allows individuals,

freed from concerns about inclusion, to innovate, flourish, and reach their fullest potential. Furthermore, an environment of inclusion and receptiveness serves as a backdrop against which employees subsequently interact with one another across demographic lines. Because no single demographic group is valued more than another—leaving no group marginalized—employees are more freely able to engage and challenge each other yet be supportive at the same time. In other words, an AIM approach fosters positive intergroup relations that result in heightened engagement and individual and organizational performance.

An AIM workplace also promises potential benefits for recruitment and retention. The posturing of its diversity policies to appeal to the widest range of people partially determines whether an organization attracts a talented, diverse workforce in the first place. Candidates of all demographic backgrounds use the organization's diversity policies in deciding whether or not to join its workforce (Edwards, Watkins, & Stevens, 2007; Rau & Hyland, 2003). How attractive an organization appears based on its diversity policies may be a significant factor in whether a new employee forms a strong identification with that organization (Dutton et al., 1994). An organization can increase its chances of attracting the most qualified candidates from all backgrounds by adopting diversity messages that appeal to minorities while not alienating nonminority candidates. Furthermore, because perceptions of an organization's diversity climate affect retention (McKay et al., 2007), utilizing an AIM approach to foster a truly inclusive climate should also result in retaining employees across demographic backgrounds.

While many organizations have implemented diversity policies and initiatives, few seem to have used AIM principles. A 2007 report on white male engagement sponsored by Mattel suggests that only 41% of companies surveyed had white males represented on diversity teams and only 3% included a white male resource or affinity group (Diversity Best Practices, 2007). An example of an organization that has successfully utilized aspects of the AIM approach is IBM. D. A. Thomas's (2004) case study of IBM's diversity strategy highlights the formation of eight task forces that analyzed personnel trends and market opportunities. Notably, the task force groupings represented many social identity groups, including white males, and each task force benefited from an executive sponsor who was not necessarily a constituent of that group. Thus, IBM both included a group typically left out of diversity initiatives (i.e., nonminorities) and promoted cross-race interaction. As would be expected of an AIM approach, the initiative resulted in development of cross-cultural competence, deeper knowledge of major markets, and attraction, development, and retention of employees.

Another company that illustrates an AIM approach to diversity is PepsiCo. Similar to IBM, PepsiCo organized affinity groups sponsored by executive committee members typically from a different social identity group (e.g., a black male sponsor of a white male group and a white female sponsor of a women of color group). PepsiCo also went a step further, charging sponsors with mentoring employees in their group. PepsiCo has since been named on several "top companies" lists for minorities including those of *Fortune*, Black Enterprise, and DiversityInc. In addition to gaining reputation as an employer, according to PepsiCo, the company has also experienced substantial revenue growth, which it attributes in part to new products inspired by these and other diversity efforts (Hymowitz, 2005).

Implications of AIM for Research and Theory

The practical implications of an all-inclusive workplace abound, as do future research questions regarding how AIM establishes a foundation for positive organizational change. For example, we posit that an AIM approach requires careful attention to workplace characteristics such as interdependent work and diversity cues. Furthermore, proper implementation of AIM entails recognition of important symbolic interaction and sense-making processes.

Interdependent work and diversity cues. Interdependent work and diversity cues are two mechanisms by which an AIM approach can positively influence organizational change. When employees must coordinate their activities because of highly interdependent work (e.g., on diversity councils and task forces, in mentoring and social networking programs, and in employees' work roles), there is greater necessity for interaction among demographically dissimilar individuals. According to Harrison and colleagues (1998), with this

increased interaction, individuals' tendencies to categorize their coworkers based on demographic characteristics dissipate, and as deep-level characteristics become more apparent, the value of diversity in facilitating organizational processes such as decision making, creativity, and innovation becomes evident (Chatman & Flynn, 2001; Earley & Mosakowski, 2000; Harrison et al., 1998; Pelled et al., 1999).

In addition, the extent to which employees subscribe to and engage in an AIM ideology depends on diversity cues that indicate the acceptance of employees' social identities (Steele, Spencer, & Aronson, 2002). For example, the distribution of diversity throughout the organization provides a signal to employees about the value of diversity. For minorities in particular, seeing that they are underrepresented in middle- and upper-management positions makes it more likely for them to discount the principles of the diversity initiative and conclude that the organization does not value people like themselves (e.g., Avery, 2003; Purdie-Vaughns et al., 2006). For nonminorities, not seeing themselves represented in diversity and inclusion structures leads to the perception that they are not valued and included. Future theorizing on diversity should therefore examine how to foster interdependent work and diversity cues that contribute positively to individual and organizational functioning.

Symbolic interactions. Importantly, although contextual factors (e.g., wording of diversity-related information) influence the development of an inclusive organizational environment, such objective features of the workplace are not the sole determinants of such an environment. Following a symbolic interactionist perspective of climate (Blumer, 1969; Schneider & Reichers, 1983), we posit that a climate for diversity emerges from a process of collective sensemaking (Weick, 1995), whereby employees together try to derive meaning about ways in which diversity is, or is not, valued in their organization. From this perspective, the value of diversity is not a "given," nor can it be mandated from upper management; rather, this value arises from interactions among the individuals within the organization (Ashforth, 1985; Schneider, & Reichers, 1983). Importantly, individuals form beliefs both about the value of diversity and about their organization's stance on diversity (Mor Barak, Cherin, & Berkman,

1998). Both play a role in individuals' active construction of diversity climate in an organization.

Future theorizing on diversity could therefore reveal how an organization's climate for diversity results from its social construction through employee interactions and communication, which in turn can be a powerful determinant of behavior over and above individual needs or motivational states (McKay et al., 2007; Schneider & Reichers, 1983). Employees do not interact with their dissimilar coworkers in a vacuum. Rather, they take part in these interactions while making sense of their organizational environment in an ongoing manner (Weick, 1995). As such, the consistency of organizational messages concerning diversity, particularly those supporting the AIM approach (e.g., through all-inclusive language), plays a large role in whether—and to what extent—employees view the organization as truly valuing its diverse workforce. In line with several properties of sensemaking (Weick, 1995), the social context is integral in setting the stage for cues, such as diversity-related practices (e.g., inclusion of all groups in diversity activities), to become salient and provide the basis for sensemaking. It is against the backdrop of all-inclusive multiculturalism that the organization can enact an environment conducive to positive organizational change. Integral to fostering positive change is the affirmation of each employee's personal identity, comprised of his or her unique characteristics and attributes, upon which the AIM approach is built.

Further examination of the role of individual differences in the all-inclusive workplace is also needed. In an effort to understand employees' reactions to diversity initiatives, other research (e.g., Plaut et al., 2007) has examined aspects of identity, such as the need to belong (Baumeister & Leary, 1995) and organizational identification (Dutton et al., 1994). We strongly encourage the coupling of organizational features with individual differences in future attempts to uncover mechanisms underlying employee reactions to diversity initiatives.

Conclusion

We have proposed that an AIM approach to diversity resolves problematic issues with traditional colorblind and multicultural approaches to diversity in organizations and increases perceptions of inclusiveness among employees. Our preliminary research findings suggest that an AIM approach does indeed decrease the association of multiculturalism with exclusion among nonminorities (Plaut et al., 2007). The AIM approach therefore promises to enhance positive relationships across difference, resulting in heightened employee engagement and individual and organizational performance. Organizations can develop an AIM workplace environment by infusing employee and prospective employee communication with all-inclusive language and by including all groups in diversity structures and policies. By fostering positive interdependent work and diversity cues and the construction of a positive climate for diversity through symbolic interaction, organizations can shape an environment conducive to positive organizational change.

In sum, taking small steps toward creating an AIM environment has the potential to enable substantial positive, organization-wide change, particularly through the development of feelings of inclusion and high-quality relationships across difference. In creating an all-inclusive, multicultural environment, organizations can create workplaces in which employees feel safe to innovate, knowing that their unique experiences and contributions are valued, and in which the generation of positive human relationships is facilitated, especially across demographic lines. Such relationships create a host of positive outcomes for individuals, organizations, and even the communities in which they are embedded (Cameron et al., 2003; Dutton & Ragins, 2006; Gittell et al., 2006), such as higher levels of physical and psychological well-being (Ryff & Singer, 2001), facility of the transfer of knowledge and coordinated action (Nahapiet & Ghoshal, 1998), and economic vitality (Cameron & Caza, 2004; Dutton, 2003).

Notes

1. The U.S. workforce (generally ages 25 to 64) is in the midst of a sweeping demographic transformation. From 1980 to 2020, the white working-age population is projected to decline from 82% to 63%. During the same period, the minority portion of the workforce is projected to double (from 18% to 37%), and the Hispanic/Latino portion is projected to almost triple (from 6% to 17%). Women are projected to

comprise 47% of the total labor force in 2014. They will also account for 51% of the increase in total labor force growth from 2004 to 2014 (Bureau of Labor Statistics, 2007).

2. Several different terms have been used in the literature to describe the concept of diversity approaches: perspectives (Ely & Thomas, 2001), ideologies (Wolsko, Park, Judd, & Wittenbrink, 2000), models (Plaut, 2002), and paradigms (D. A. Thomas & Ely, 1996). Although we will sometimes rely on these terms somewhat interchangeably, we will favor the term approaches because of this article's concern with organizational approaches to managing change.

3. Our focus here is on the racial and ethnic minorities typically underrepresented in organizations, such as blacks, Latinos, and Asians, although the arguments presented here have clear implications for organizational diversity beyond racial and ethnic lines (e.g., gender, sexual orientation, etc.). We use race and ethnicity jointly to reflect the U.S. Census Bureau's designation of these demographic variables.

4. Perhaps the best-known example of organizational involvement in diversity issues are affirmative action hiring practices, where demographic categories are considered in the hiring process and allow organizations to set goals for the fair representation of women and minorities (e.g., James, Brief, Dietz, & Cohen, 2001). These practices can be informed by either multicultural or colorblind ideologies, depending on how they are enacted.

References

Ashforth, B. E. (1985). Climate formation: Issues and extensions. *Academy of Management Review, 10*, 837–847.

Avery, D. R. (2003). Reactions to diversity in recruitment advertising: Are differences black and white? *Journal of Applied Psychology, 88*, 672-679.

Baumeister, R. F., & Leary, M. R. (1995). The need to belong: Desire for interpersonal attachments as a fundamental human motivation. *Psychology Bulletin, 117*, 497–529.

Baumeister, R. F., Twenge, J. M., & Nuss, C. (2002). Effects of social exclusion on cognitive processes: Anticipated aloneness reduces intelligent thought. *Journal of Personality and Social Psychology, 83*, 817–827.

Blumer, H. (1969). Symbolic interactionism: Perspective and method. Upper Saddle River, NJ: Prentice Hall.

Bonilla-Silva, E. (2003). *Racism without racists: Color-blind racism and the persistence of racial inequality in the United States.* Lanham, MD: Rowman & Littlefield.

Brief, A. P. (Ed.). (2008). *Diversity at work.* Cambridge, UK: Cambridge University Press.

Brief, A. P., Umphress, E. E., Dietz, J., Burrows, J. W., Butz, R. M., & Scholten, L. (2005). Community matters: Realistic group conflict theory and the impact of diversity. *Academy of Management Journal, 48*, 830–844.

Bureau of Labor Statistics. (2007). Demographic characteristics of the labor force (current population survey). Retrieved March 2007, from www.bls.gov/

Cameron, K. S. (2003). Organizational virtuousness and performance. In K. S. Cameron, J. E. Dutton, & R. E. Quinn (Eds.), *Positive organizational scholarship: Foundations of a new discipline* (pp. 48–65). San Francisco: Berrett-Koehler.

Cameron, K. S., & Caza, A. (2004). Exploring the relationships between organizational virtuousness and performance. *American Behavioral Scientist, 47*, 766–790.

Cameron, K. S., Dutton, J. E., & Quinn, R. E. (Eds.). (2003). *Positive organizational scholarship: Foundations of a new discipline.* San Francisco: Berrett-Koehler.

Chatman, J. A., & Flynn, F. J. (2001). The influence of demographic heterogeneity on the emergence and consequences of cooperative norms in work teams. *Academy of Management Journal, 44*, 956–974.

Chatman, J. A., Polzer, J. T., Barsade, S. G., & Neale, M. A. (1998). Being different yet feeling similar: The influence of demographic composition of organizational culture on work processes and outcomes. *Administrative Science Quarterly, 43*, 749–780.

Chrobot-Mason, D., & Thomas, K. M. (2002). Minority employees in majority organizations: The intersection of individual and organizational racial identity in the workplace. *Human Resource Development Review, 1*, 323–344.

Clifton, D. O., & Harter, J. K. (2003). Investing in strengths. In K. S. Cameron, J. E. Dutton, & R. E. Quinn (Eds.), *Positive organizational scholarship: Foundations of a new discipline* (pp. 111–121). San Francisco: Berrett-Koehler.

Cooperrider, D. L., & Sekerka, L. E. (2003). Toward a theory of positive organizational change. In K. S. Cameron, J. E. Dutton, & R. E. Quinn (Eds.), *Positive organizational scholarship: Foundations of a new discipline* (pp. 225–240). San Francisco: Berrett-Koehler.

Cox, T., Jr. (1991). The multicultural organization. *Academy of Management Executive, 5*, 34–47.

Cox, T., Jr. (1993). *Cultural diversity in organizations: Theory, research, and practice.* San Francisco: Berrett-Koehler.

Davidson, M. N., & James, E. J. (2006). The engines of positive relationships across difference: Conflict and learning. In J. E. Dutton & B. R. Ragins (Eds.), *Exploring positive relationships at work: Building a theoretical and research foundation* (pp. 137–158). Mahwah, NJ: Lawrence Erlbaum.

Devos, T., & Banaji, M. R. (2005). American = white? *Journal of Personality and Social Psychology, 88*, 447–466.

Diversity Best Practices. (2007, April). White male engagement: Inclusion is key. *CDO Insights, 1*(1).

Dutton, J. E. (2003). *Energizing your workplace: Building and sustaining high-quality relationships at work.* San Francisco: Jossey-Bass.

Dutton, J. E., Dukerich, J. M., & Harquail, C. V. (1994). Organizational images and member identification. *Administrative Science Quarterly, 39*, 239–263.

Dutton, J. E., & Ragins, B. R. (Eds.). (2006). *Exploring positive relationships at work: Building a theoretical and research foundation.* Mahwah, NJ: Lawrence Erlbaum.

Earley, P. C., & Mosakowski, E. (2000). Creating hybrid team cultures: An empirical test of transnational team functioning. *Academy of Management Journal, 43*, 26-49.

Edwards, B. D., Watkins, M. B., & Stevens, F. G. (2007). *It's not black and white: Differential applicant reactions to targeted recruitment efforts.* Unpublished manuscript, Auburn University.

Ely, R. J., & Thomas, D. A. (2001). Cultural diversity at work: The effects of diversity perspectives on work group processes and outcomes. *Administrative Science Quarterly, 46*, 229–273.

Gittell, J. H., Cameron, K. S., Lim, S., & Rivas, V. (2006). Relationships, layoffs, and organizational resilience. *Journal of Applied Behavioral Science, 42*, 300-329.

Harrison, D. A., Price, K. H., & Bell, M. P. (1998). Beyond relational demography: Time and the effects of surface- and deep-level diversity on work group cohesion. *Academy of Management Journal, 41*, 96–107.

Hogg, M. A., & Terry, D. J. (2000). Social identity and self-categorization processes in organizational contexts. *Academy of Management Review, 25*, 121–140.

Hymowitz, C. (2005, November 14). The new diversity. *The Wall Street Journal*, p. R1.

Jackson, S. E., & Dutton, J. E. (1988). Discerning threats and opportunities. *Administrative Science Quarterly, 33*, 370–387.

Jackson, S. E., Joshi, A., & Erhardt, N. L. (2003). Recent research on team and organizational diversity: SWOT analysis and implications. *Journal of Management, 29*, 801–830.

James, E. J., Brief, A. P., Dietz, J., & Cohen, R. R. (2001). Prejudice matters: Understanding the reactions of whites to affirmative action program targeted to benefit blacks. *Journal of Applied Psychology, 86*, 1120–1128.

Jehn, K. A., Northcraft, G. B., & Neale, M. A. (1999). Why differences make a difference: A field study of diversity, conflict, and performance in workgroups. *Administrative Science Quarterly, 44*, 741–763.

Kalev, A., Dobbin, F., & Kelly, E. (2006). Best practices or best guesses? Assessing the efficacy of corporate affirmative action and diversity policies. *American Sociological Review, 71*, 589–617.

Kidder, D. L., Lankau, M. J., Chrobot-Mason, D., Mollica, K. A., & Friedman, R. (2004). Backlash toward diversity initiatives: Examining the impact of diversity program justification, personal and group outcomes. *International Journal of Conflict Management, 15*, 77–102.

Kleugel, J. R. (1985). If there isn't a problem, you don't need a solution. *American Behavioral Scientist, 28*, 761–784.

Linnehan, F., & Konrad, A. M. (1999). Diluting diversity: Implications for intergroup in organizations. *Journal of Management Inquiry, 8*, 399–413.

Mannix, E. A., & Neale, M. A. (2006). What differences make a difference? The promise and reality of diverse teams in organizations. *Psychological Science in the Public Interest, 6*, 32-55.

Markus, H. R., Steele, C. M., & Steele, D. M. (2000). Colorblindness as a barrier to inclusion: Assimilation and non-immigrant minorities. *Daedalus, 129*, 233–259.

McKay, P. F., Avery, D. R., Tonidandel, S., Morris, M. A., Hernandez, M., & Hebl, M. R. (2007). Racial differences in employee retention: Are diversity climate perceptions the key? *Personnel Psychology, 60*, 35-62.

Meyerson, D. E., & Fletcher, J. K. (2000). A modest manifesto for shattering the glass ceiling. *Harvard Business Review, 78*(1), 126–136.

Mor Barak, M. E., Cherin, D. A., & Berkman, S. (1998). Organizational and personal dimensions in diversity climate: Ethnic and gender differences in employee perceptions. *Journal of Applied Behavioral Science, 34*, 82–104.

Morrison, E. W., & Milliken, F. J. (2000). Organizational silence: A barrier to change and development in a pluralistic world. *Academy of Management Review, 25*, 706–725.

Nahapiet, J., & Ghoshal, S. (1998). Social capital, intellectual capital and the organizational advantage. *Academy of Management Review, 23*, 242–266.

Paluck, E. L. (2006). Diversity training and intergroup contact: A call to action research. *Journal of Social Issues, 62*, 577–595.

Pelled, L. H., Eisenhardt, K. M., & Xin, K. R. (1999). Exploring the black box: An analysis of work group diversity, conflict, and performance. *Administrative Science Quarterly, 44*, 1–28.

Perkins, L. A., Thomas, K. M., & Taylor, G. A. (2000). Advertisement and recruitment: Marketing to minorities. *Psychology and Marketing, 17*, 235–255.

Plaut, V. C. (2002). Cultural models of diversity: The psychology of difference and inclusion. In R. Shweder, M. Minow, & H. R. Markus (Eds.), *Engaging cultural differences: The multicultural challenge in a liberal democracy* (pp. 365–395). New York: Russell Sage.

Plaut, V. C., & Markus, H. R. (2007). *Basically we're all the same? Models of diversity and the dilemma of difference.* Unpublished manuscript, University of Georgia.

Plaut, V. C., Sanchez-Burks, J., Buffardi, L., & Stevens, F. G. (2007). *What about me? Understanding non-minority aversion to diversity initiatives in the workplace.* Unpublished manuscript, University of Georgia.

Polzer, J. T., Milton, L. P., & Swann, W. B., Jr. (2002). Capitalizing on diversity: Interpersonal congruence in small work groups. *Administrative Science Quarterly, 47,* 296–324.

Purdie-Vaughns, V., Steele, C. M., Davies, P., & Crosby, J. (2006). *Identity contingency threat: How contextual cues affect African-Americans' trust in diverse settings.* Unpublished manuscript, Yale University.

Ragins, B. R. (1997). Diversified mentoring relationships in organizations: A power perspective. *Academy of Management Review, 22,* 482–521.

Rau, B. L., & Hyland, M. M. (2003). Corporate teamwork and diversity statements in college recruitment brochures: Effects on attraction. *Journal of Applied Social Psychology, 33,* 3465–3492.

Richard, O. C. (2000). Racial diversity, business strategy, and firm performance: A resource-based view. *Academy of Management Journal, 43,* 164–177.

Richeson, J. A., & Nussbaum, R. J. (2004). The impact of multiculturalism versus color-blindness on racial bias. *Journal of Experimental Social Psychology, 40,* 417–423.

Ryff, C. D., & Singer, B. (2001). *Emotion, social relationships and health.* New York: Oxford University Press.

Schlesinger, A. M. (1992). *The disuniting of America.* New York: Norton.

Schneider, B., & Reichers, A. E. (1983). On the etiology of climates. *Personnel Psychology, 36,* 19–39.

Schofield, J. W. (1986). Causes and consequences of the color-blind perspective. In J. F. Dovidio & S. Gaertner (Eds.), *Prejudice, discrimination, and racism* (pp. 231–254). San Diego, CA: Academic Press.

Sherman, D. K., & Cohen, G. L. (2006). The psychology of self-defense: Self-affirmation theory. In M. P. Zanna (Ed.), *Advances in experimental social psychology* (Vol. 38, pp. 183–242). San Diego, CA: Academic Press.

Spreitzer, G. M., & Sonenshein, S. (2003). Positive deviance and extraordinary organizing. In K. S. Cameron, J. E. Dutton, & R. E. Quinn (Eds.), *Positive organizational scholarship: Foundations of a new discipline* (pp. 207–224). San Francisco: Berrett-Koehler.

Spreitzer, G. M., Sutcliffe, K. M., Dutton, J. E., Sonenshein, S., & Grant, G. M. (2005). A socially embedded model of thriving at work. *Organization Science, 16,* 537–549.

Steele, C. M., Spencer, S. J., & Aronson, J. (2002). Contending with group image: The psychology of stereotype and social identity threat. In M. P. Zanna (Ed.), *Advances in experimental social psychology* (Vol. 34, pp. 379–440). San Diego: Academic Press.

Swann, W. B., Jr., Kwan, V. S. Y., Polzer, J. T., & Milton, L. P. (2003). Fostering group identification and creativity in diverse groups: The role of individuation and self-verification. *Personality and Social Psychology Bulletin, 29,* 1396–1406.

Thomas, D. A. (2004). Diversity as strategy. *Harvard Business Review, 82*(9), 98–108.

Thomas, D. A., & Ely, R. J. (1996). Making differences matter: A new paradigm for managing diversity. *Harvard Business Review, 74*(5), 79–90.

Thomas, K. M. (2005). *Diversity dynamics in the workplace.* Belmont, CA: Wadsworth.

Thomas, K. M. (Ed.). (2008). *Diversity resistance in organizations: Manifestations and solutions.* Mahwah, NJ: Lawrence Erlbaum.

Thomas, K. M., Mack, D. A., & Montagliani, A. (2004). Arguments against diversity: Are they valid? In F. Crosby & P. Stockdale (Eds.), *The Psychology and Management of Diversity in Organizations* (pp. 31–51). Malden, MA: Blackwell.

Thomas, K. M., & Plaut, V. C. (2008). The many faces of diversity in the workplace. In K. M. Thomas (Ed.), *Diversity resistance in organizations: Manifestations and solutions* (pp. 1–22). Mahwah, NJ: Lawrence Erlbaum.

Thomas, K. M., & Wise, P. G. (1999). Organizational attractiveness and individual differences: Are diverse applicants attracted by different factors? *Journal of Business and Psychology, 13,* 375–390.

Twenge, J. M., Baumeister, R. F., Tice, D. M., & Stucke, T. S. (2001). If you can't join them, beat them: Effects of social exclusion on aggressive behavior. *Journal of Personality and Social Psychology, 81,* 1058–1069.

Verkuyten, M. (2005). Ethnic group identification and group evaluation among minority and majority groups: Testing the multiculturalism hypothesis. *Journal of Personality and Social Psychology, 88,* 121–138.

Watson, W. E., Kumar, K., & Michaelsen, L. K. (1993). Cultural diversity's impact on interaction process and performance: Comparing homogeneous and diverse task groups. *Academy of Management Journal, 36,* 590–602.

Weick, K. E. (1995). *Sensemaking in organizations.* Thousand Oaks, CA: Sage.

Westphal, J. D., & Milton, L. P. (2000). How experience and network ties affect the influence of demographic minorities on corporate boards. *Administrative Science Quarterly, 45,* 366–398.

Williams, K. Y., & O'Reilly, C. A., III. (1998). Demography and diversity in organizations: A review of 40 years of research. In B. M. Staw & L. L. Cummings (Eds.), *Research in organizational behavior* (pp. 77–140). Greenwich, CT: JAI.

Wolsko, C., Park, B., Judd, C. M., & Wittenbrink, B. (2000). Framing interethnic ideology: Effects of multicultural and color-blind perspectives on judgments of groups and individuals. *Journal of Personality and Social Psychology, 78,* 635–654.

Wright, P., Ferris, S. P., Hiller, J. S., & Kroll, M. (1995). Competitiveness through management of diversity: Effects on stock price valuation. *Academy of Management Journal, 38,* 272–287.

CHAPTER 33

Goal Interdependence for Working Across Cultural Boundaries

Chinese Employees With Foreign Managers

Yi-feng Chen

Lingnan University

Dean Tjosvold

Lingnan University

Sofia Fang Su

Shanghai University of Finance and Economics

1. Introduction

Organizations are developing subsidiaries and joint ventures in foreign countries in order to exploit the opportunities to improve quality and lower costs (Buvik & Gronhaug, 2000; Charman, 2000; Cyr, 1995; Doz & Hamel, 1998; Hitt, Harrison, & Ireland, 2001; Inkpen & Beamish, 1997; Lane, Salk, & Lyles, 2001). But to capture the benefits of the global marketplace, the multinational managers must be able to work with local employees to create and implement innovations. Indeed, researchers have argued that productive interaction between managers and employees is critical for effective leadership (Boyd & Taylor, 1998; Brower, Schoorman, & Tan, 2000; Delugua, 1998; Graen & Uhl-Bien, 1995; House, Wright, & Aditya, 1997; Schriesheim,

This work has been supported by the Research Grants Council of the Hong Kong Special Administrative Region, China (Project No: LU3013/01H) to the second author.

Source: Goal interdependence for working across cultural boundaries: Chinese employees with foreign managers by Yi-feng Chen, Dean Tjosvold, and Sofia Fang Su, *International Journal of Intercultural Relations* 29 (2005): 429–447. Copyright © 2005 Elsevier.

Neider, & Scandura, 1998; Setton, Bennett, & Liden, 1996; Van Velsor, & Leslie, 1995). However, developing productive interaction between managers and employees is difficult, especially when they came from diverse cultures (Earley, & Gibson, 2002; Earley & Mosakowski, 2000). Cross-cultural researchers have recently argued for the need to develop a framework that can help diverse people overcome obstacles and work together productively (Bond, 2003; Leung, in press; Smith, 2003). This study examines the interactions that can affect the innovativeness and job commitment of foreign managers and local employees. Specifically, it proposes that foreign managers and Chinese employees with cooperative, but not competitive or independent goals, discuss their views openly and constructively. This in turn helps them develop job commitment and innovate.

1.1. Innovation for Foreign Operations

Subsidiaries and joint ventures in foreign countries offer the possibilities of developing strategic advantages in quality and cost. However, multi-national companies must adapt their approaches and combine them with the knowledge and opportunities of the local partner if they are going to realize these valuable innovations. The multi-national's business and technological expertise cannot simply be unilaterally applied but must also be adapted to local conditions and designed to exploit local opportunities (Hitt, Lee, & Yucel, 2002). They must engage in innovation—the planned and effective introduction of change—in order to develop advantages (Burpitt & Bigoness, 1997; West, 2002). This kind of continuous innovation requires the input and commitment of local employees. The relationship between foreign and local partners is considered the base for applying organizational abilities appropriately to yield successful foreign operations (Friman, Garling, Millett, Mattsson, & Johnston, 2002; Kale, Singh, & Perlmutter, 2000; Zaheer, McEvily, & Perrone, 1998).

The interface between foreign manager and local employee may then be a major engine for ongoing innovation in foreign operations. Foreign managers can bring their technical and business expertise, while local employees have knowledge and insight about how this expertise can be appropriately and effectively applied to the local situation. The foreign manager and local

employee can combine their different perspectives to implement innovations that include the technical and business expertise of the foreign manager along with the local knowledge of employees. However, the foreign managers and local employees must be able to discuss their views openly if they are going to combine their perspectives so that they can innovate and are committed.

1.2 Cross-Cultural Communication and Interaction

Interaction across diverse cultures generally presents a number of barriers and challenges (Adair, Okumura, & Brett, 2001; Rao & Hashimoto, 1996; Ratiu, 1983). Research is needed to understand and develop cross-cultural communication, especially as organizations are increasingly relying upon multicultural teams to innovate and to solve a wide range of problems (Wheelan, Buzalo, & Tsumura, 1998). People from diverse cultures are advised to become more aware of their own perspectives in how they communicate. Then they can learn to alter their behavior and develop trusting relationships with each other (Lam, 2000; Matveev & Nelson, 2004; Triandis & Singelis, 1998).

Although many researchers have investigated the barriers for cross-cultural communication (e.g. Kealey & Protheroe, 1996; Redmond & Bunyi, 1991; Samovar & Porter, 1991), an understanding of how to facilitate cross-cultural interaction is insufficiently developed. There is a need to develop knowledge that helps diverse individuals communicate and interact productively (Hofner Saphiere, 1996; Wiseman & Shuter, 1994).

Kimmel (2000) proposed that diverse people should develop a common platform that can serve as the basis for productive intercultural communication and interaction. This "micro-culture" should be developed through mutual adaptation and active engagement by the various cultures. Similarly, Leung (in press) has suggested that a common, mutually acceptable frame of reference, called *cultural tuning*, can facilitate effective intercultural interaction. Individuals consider their own norms, motives, and cognitive processes while also developing their shared, mutually acceptable understanding of how they can work together. They should also be prepared to reflect and learn from each other so that they refine their common platform.

Cross-cultural researchers have argued that studying actual intercultural interactions would develop relevant knowledge for diverse people. Smith (Leung, Smith, Wang, & Sun, 1996; Smith, Kruzela, & Groblewska, 2000) for example has investigated how diverse managers and employees manage "events" in order to identify mutually acceptable ways to deal with barriers. The present study tests the usefulness of the theory of cooperation and competition to investigate how foreign managers and their Chinese employees deal with specific situations and are able to innovate and strengthen job commitment.

1.3 Theory of Cooperation and Competition

This study proposes that the theory of cooperation and competition can identify conditions under which foreign managers and Chinese employees are able to create innovative solutions (Deutsch, 1973). Research has demonstrated that when participants emphasize their cooperative rather than competitive and independent goals they are able to discuss even divisive issues openly and constructively (Tjosvold, 1998).

According to Deutsch (1973), how goals are structured determines how individuals interact; their interaction patterns determine the outcomes (Johnson & Johnson, 1989). When a situation is structured cooperatively, individuals' goal achievements are positively correlated; individuals perceive that they can reach their goals if, and only if, the others also reach their goals. When a situation is structured competitively, individuals' goal achievements are negatively correlated; each individual perceives that when one person achieves his or her goal, all others with whom he or she is competitively linked to simultaneously fail to achieve their goals. With independent goals, individual achievements are unrelated.

Whether people see their individual goals to be cooperatively or competitively related critically affects their expectations, interaction, and outcomes (Johnson, Maruyama, Johnson, Nelson, & Skon, 1981; Stanne, Johnson, & Johnson, 1999). In cooperation, people believe that as one person moves toward goal attainment, others move toward reaching their goals. They understand that another's goal attainment helps them; they can be successful together. With cooperative goals,

people want each other to perform effectively because each person's competence contributes to each other's success. They interact in ways that promote mutual goals; in particular, they are able to discuss their views on various issues for mutual benefit.

1.4. Constructive Controversy

Experiments have documented that constructive controversy is a major dynamic by which people with cooperative goals are able to solve problems (Tjosvold, 1982, 1998; Tjosvold & Johnson, 1977). When decision-makers seek mutually acceptable solutions, they are more open to new and opposing information. Confronted with an opposing opinion, people tend to feel uncertain about the adequacy of their own positions. But with constructive controversy, they indicate their interest in the opponent's arguments and ask questions to explore the opposing views. They demonstrate that they know the other's arguments and understand the other's reasoning to examine the problem. They also take the information seriously and incorporate the other position into their own thinking and decisions. In this way, they develop a more complete awareness and appreciation of the complexity of the problem and create solutions that respond to the complete information. However, research in field settings is needed to document the extent to which foreign managers and local employees with cooperative goals are able to use constructive controversy to innovate.

In competition, people, believing that one's successful goal attainment makes others less likely to reach their goals, conclude that they are better off when others act ineffectively. When others are productive, they are less likely to succeed themselves. They pursue their interests at the expense of others. They are more likely to avoid open discussions or discuss issues in closed-minded ways in order to win the discussion. Independent goals have been found to have similar effects on interaction and outcomes (Johnson et al., 1981).

This study tests a model linking cooperative and competitive goals with constructive controversy, innovation and job commitment (Figure 33.1). Specifically, cooperative goals, in contrast to competitive and independent goals, among foreign managers and Chinese employees are expected to promote constructive

| Figure 33.1 | Hypothesized Models |

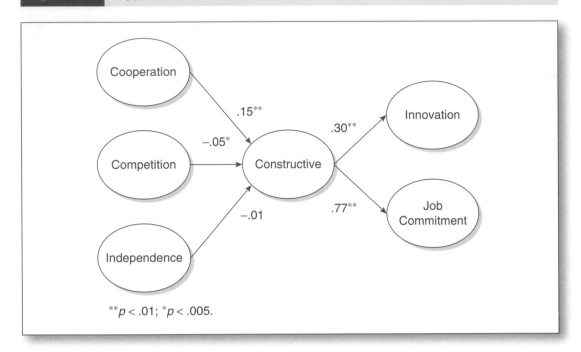

** $p < .01$; * $p < .005$.

controversy where they solve problems and innovate. These proposed relations are summarized in the following four hypotheses:

H_1. To the extent that foreign managers and Chinese employees develop cooperative goals, they engage in constructive controversy.

H_2. To the extent that foreign managers and Chinese employees develop competitive goals, they have low levels of constructive controversy.

H_3. To the extent that foreign managers and Chinese employees develop independent goals, they have low levels of constructivecontroversy.

H_4. To the extent that foreign managers and Chinese employees engage in constructive controversy, they innovate and develop job commitment.

2. Method

2.1. Participants

There were 111 interviewees who took part in the interview. There were 55 who had a Japanese manager and 56 who had an American manager. Of these interviewees, 73 were males; their average age was 29. Ninety-eight of them had worked with their manager for over 1 year.

The interviewees had different positions: 18 first-level managers, 23 middle-level managers, seven accountants, two finance specialists, 12 executive assistants, two secretaries, 16 office clerks, 13 engineers, 11 salesman, and seven persons in other positions. They worked in different departments: 14 in financial departments, 18 in sales departments, three in human resources departments, seven in production departments, 12 in executive departments, 38 in operations departments, 16 in technology departments, and three in other departments.

They came from different industries: 44 in manufacturing, 18 in wholesale, retail and catering, 12 in finance, 11 in social services, nine in transportation, storage, postal and telecommunications, nine in IT, two in education, culture, art, broadcasting, film and television, two in health care, sports and social welfare, and three in other fields.

2.2 Procedure

The critical incident technique (CIT) (Flanagan, 1954) was used to develop the interview structure.

CIT has been considered as "an observable human activity that is complete enough in itself to permit inferences to be made about the person performing the act" (Bitner, Booms, & Tetreault, 1990) and a particularly useful method when studying complex interpersonal phenomenon (Walker & Truly, 1992).

Interviewers informed the interviewees that the study was interested in how people in China work with their foreign manager. They were asked to provide a concrete example when they interacted with their boss as they worked on an issue. The interviewees were told that the example could be one where they worked successfully or one with which they had not worked successfully. Interviewees first described the story in detail about the incident, including the setting, what occurred, and the consequences. Then the interviewees were asked to rate specific questions on 5-point scales in order to analyze the incidents.

2.3 Interviewers

A Chinese researcher trained three university management students in Shanghai, China, to interview in a standard, non-suggestive manner and have the interviewees describe the interaction and respond to specific questions. They pledged to protect the confidentiality of the interviewees and carried out their interviews in Chinese Mandarin. The interview lasted one hour.

As the interview structure was originally written in English, three bilingual researchers translated it into Chinese. To ensure conceptual consistency, the questionnaires were translated back into English to check for possible deviation (Brislin, 1970). The questions were pre-tested to make sure that respondents clearly understood them. To prevent and eliminate potential concern about being evaluated, participants were assured that their responses would be held totally confidential.

3. Analysis

3.1 Goal Interdependence

Items for cooperative, competitive and independent goal interdependence were developed from a previous questionnaire study conducted in North America (Alper, Tjosvold, & Law, 1998). We used one-item scales to measure goal interdependence. The item for the cooperative goals was "How much would your reaching your objectives help the manager reach his objectives?" The item for competitive goals was "How much were your goals and the manager's goals structured so that they were win-lose?" The item for independence goals was "How much would your accomplishing your goal affect whether the manager achieved or did not achieve his goals?" Participants were asked to rate on a 5-point scale (1 = very little, 5 = very much) their degree of agreement to the three statements. (The rating was later reversed for the independent goals scale.) Appendix A has the items for these and other scales.

3.2 Constructive Controversy

Constructive controversy refers to the set of behaviors that have been found to develop from cooperative goal interdependence in problem-solving situations. Those who cooperated had been found to discuss opposing views openly, take each other's perspective, integrate them and seek a mutually beneficial solution. The nine-item scale was developed from a set of experimental studies (Tjosvold, 1998) and questionnaire studies (Tjosvold, Wedley, & Field, 1986). Subjects were asked to answer on a 5-point scale (1 = very little, 5 = very much) about their degree of agreement with the nine statements. A sample item from the scale was "How much did you and the manager use your opposing views to understand the problem better?" The coefficient alpha of the scale was .82.

3.3 Innovation

Interviewees were asked to rate the effect of innovation from the incident using a four-item scale developed by Burpitt and Bigoness (1997). Subjects were asked to answer on a 5-point scale (1 = very little, 5 = very much) about their degree of agreement with the four statements. A sample item was "How much did this interaction help you seek out information about new markets, products, and technologies from sources outside the organization." The scale had a Cronbach alpha of .81.

3.4 Job Commitment

Scales for job commitment were developed from previous research. Job commitment measured the extent to which interviewees described themselves as involved and motivated in their own assignments (Tjosvold, Hui, & Law, 1998a; Tjosvold, Sasaki, & Moy, 1998b). A sample item was "How much did this interaction help you feel very satisfied with your work?" Participants were asked to rate their degree of agreement to four statements on a 5-point scale (1 = very little, 5 = very much). The scale had a Cronbach alpha of .81.

4. Results

The incidents illustrate the role of goal interdependence. Correlations and structure equation analyses were used to examine the proposition that cooperative, competitive, independent goals and constructive controversy affect innovation and job commitment.

4.1. Incident Examples

The reported incidents support the theorizing that goal interdependence very much affects constructive controversy and innovation. An example of cooperative goals involved Mr. Li who worked in Yamei, a textile pattern company. With a large, urgent order, Mr. Li's Japanese supervisor decided to begin mass production without making a pattern first, although it violated company procedures. He wanted to satisfy the customers quickly and increase profit. Mr. Li was worried that this approach was too risky and the company would suffer considerably if problems arose. Li discussed his concerns with the manager openly and asked other colleagues to discuss with him too. Together the employees developed a number of ways to improve efficiency, including strengthening their relationship with the designer and worker and asking them to complete their work as soon as possible and improving production efficiency. After some discussion, the Japanese manager accepted those methods as he could see that they would improve company efficiency. With the cooperation of all employees, they increased the output with high quality

and delivered on time. Employees had the common goal to increase company profit, though they had different methods, and together achieved excellent results.

Ms. Bai is a project manager in charge of exhibition design for an American exhibition company. In designing a conference hall for a press release, she could not agree with her American boss about the background color. The supervisor thought white or black was appropriate while she suggested red. But the supervisor also wanted to have the best design and, rather than force her to follow his opinion, he asked her to elaborate upon her reasons. Ms. Bai told him that, in China, black and white are associated with funeral and interment, while red sets an auspicious atmosphere. Accepting the explanation, the supervisor agreed to use the red background. The design was very successful and the customer was very satisfied with the red background color.

Examples suggest that competitive goals interfere. Miss Lee worked in the human resource office of a real estate company and was involved in developing company rules for employees to improve productivity. Miss Lee's goal was to develop realistic rules that could be faithfully applied and implemented, otherwise the exercise was useless. But her Japanese manager had an incompatible goal that the regulations were just to show the boss that they did make something to regulate employees. They could not persuade each other despite efforts to do so. Miss Lee gave in and now the company has a set of elaborate, detailed rules that no one follows.

The results of independent goal incidents were typically counter-productive. Gao worked in an American hotel in Shanghai as an assistant for a human resource manager and was in charge of recruiting a new staff member. Mr. Huang, who was from the government's revenue department, recommended a specific person. After considering the candidate carefully, Gao concluded that he was suitable for their hotel and recommended him to his American boss, Delex. Delex rejected the candidate because he thought it would be difficult to manage someone who was recommended by Huang. Gao explained carefully about the situation in China and that *guanxi* (personal relationship) with a government officer was very important to the hotel. But Delex still did not agree. Gao thought recruitment should support the company as a whole, not whether the new recruit would make their managing more troublesome. He avoided the issue and Delex prevailed. But

Huang would not be as considerate of the hotel as before and guanxi with revenue were lost.

In another case of independent goals, Mr. Xiao was a marketing manager of a Japanese company, whose main business is transportation. The company had imported videos but the company needed a license to sell them legally. But his boss opposed getting the license because the goods had already been passed to the customer who had distributed its advertisements. Mr. Xiao was very concerned about the company's reputation and warned that they were operating against the law. However, the boss ignored his plea, as he was focused on providing service. Fortunately, the illegality was not detected, but the boss and his department lost reputation among their colleagues.

There were 56 cases in American companies of which 34 cases had largely cooperative goals, 13 competitive goals and nine independent goals. Of the 55 cases in Japanese companies, 27 had largely cooperative goals, 14 competitive goals, and 14 independent goals.

4.2. Correlations Among Variables

Correlations among the scales support the overall framework that goal interdependence and constructive controversy affected the innovation and job commitment (Table 33.1). Cooperative goals were positively correlated with constructive controversy ($r = .30, p < .01$) whereas competitive goals were negatively correlated with constructive controversy ($r = -.19, p < .05$). The correlation between independent goals and constructive controversy was negative, but not statistically significantly ($r = -.14$, $p = $ n.s.). As expected, constructive controversy was positively related to innovation ($r = .25, p < .01$) and job commitment ($r = .60, p < .01$).

4.3. Structural Equation Analysis

Structural equation analyses tested the model connecting goal interdependence, constructive controversy, innovation, and job commitment. The covariance structure analysis of the inter-relationship among these constructs was analyzed using EQS for Windows (Bentler & Wu, 1995).

We compared the indirect effects model that proposed the mediating effects of constructive controversy to the direct effects models. The direct effects models posited that cooperative, competitive, and independent goals impact outcomes directly whereas the indirect effects model proposes that constructive controversy mediates between goals and outcomes.

The χ^2 of the indirect effects model was 7.07 (df = 6) and the χ^2 of the direct effects models was 38.71 (df = 3) (Table 33.2). These results indicate that omission of the mediating effects of constructive controversy significantly deteriorated the indirect effects model. The NFI and CFI of the direct effects model were .43 and .39 whereas the indirect effects model had NFI and CFI of .94 and .99, respectively. Both fit indices of the indirect effects model were considered as indicating good model fit, given the usually accepted critical value of .90 (Bentler & Bonnett, 1980). Results of the causal model comparison suggest that the indirect effects model be accepted.

The path coefficients (Table 33.2) of the accepted model helped to explore the findings more specifically. Results indicated that cooperative goals had significant positive effects on constructive controversy ($\beta = .15, < .01$), competitive goals had significant negative effects on constructive controversy ($\beta = -.05, < .05$), independence goals had negative but not significant effects on constructive controversy ($\beta = -.01, p = $ n.s.). Finally, constructive controversy had significant positive effects on innovation ($\beta = .30, p < .01$) and job commitment ($\beta = .77, p < .01$).

4.4. Antecedents of Goal Interdependence

Results suggest the conditions that affect interviewees' conclusions about goal interdependence. After the respondents indicated the goal interdependence, they were asked to describe their reasoning that led them to make these conclusions.

Respondents indicated that shared goals, common tasks, complementary roles, shared rewards, and trusting attitudes developed cooperative goals. Chinese employees with American managers most frequently indicated that shared goals, trusting attitudes, and common tasks were the major reasons for cooperative goals; for Japanese managers, the most frequent reasons given were common tasks, complementary roles, and shared goals.

| Table 33.1 | Correlations Among Variables at the Team Level | | | | | | | |

	Mean	Std. deviation	(1)	(2)	(3)	(4)	(5)	(6)
(1) Cooperation	3.29	1.34						
(2) Competition	2.15	1.37	−.37**					
(3) Independence	2.60	1.32	−.38**	.33**				
(4) Constructive controversy	3.30	.76	.30**	−.19*	−.14	(.82)		
(5) Innovation	3.37	.91	.16	.09	−.04	.25**	(.81)	
(6) Job commitment	2.97	.98	.30**	−.15	−.11	.60**	.35**	(.81)

$N = 111$.
Values in bracket are reliability (coefficient alpha) estimates.
$*p < .05$, $**p < .01$.

The reasons for competitive goals mentioned by respondents were "outdo climate," independent tasks and mistrustful attitudes. The most frequent reason given by the respondents who had American managers was an independent task, while the most frequent reason provided by respondents who had Japanese managers was "outdo climate."

The reasons for independent goals mentioned by respondents were "outdo climate," independent tasks, and an independent attitude. Both groups regarded an independent attitude as the main reason.

5. Discussion

The foreign manager–local employee interaction may very much facilitate the adaptation and application of multi-national expertise to local conditions. But developing this productive interaction between managers and employees who are also culturally diverse may be particularly difficult (Earley & Gibson, 2002; Earley & Mosakowski, 2000). Findings support the proposition that the theory of cooperation and competition can provide a common framework for understanding the relationship and interactions that affects the extent to which foreign managers and Chinese employees work together to innovate. Specifically, results support the

study's overall model that cooperative, but not competitive or independent, goals help foreign managers and Chinese employees engage in constructive controversy that in turn results in innovation and employee job commitment. Managers and employees that employed cooperative goals were able to discuss their diverse views openly and constructively, thereby developing innovations and job commitment.

Although the findings support the hypotheses, the correlation of constructive controversy with innovation was modest compared to its correlation with job commitment. As suggested by the examples, the innovations actually accomplished between managers and employees may not be highly impactful. Indeed, this study focused on specific everyday interaction rather than on major events. However, even in these specific incidents, how managers and employees interacted appears to have affected their innovation.

Findings may seem contrary to the general conclusion that avoiding opposing issues is prevalent and culturally appropriate for China as a collectivist culture (Graham, Kim, Lin, & Robinson, 1988; Kirkbride, Tang, & Westwood, 1991; Tse, Francis, & Walls, 1994). Chinese people have been thought to promote harmony by avoiding discussing potential interpersonal problems (Hwang, 1996), However, Leung (1996, 1997) has argued that

Table 33.2   Parameter Estimates for Structural Model

Indirect effects model 1			Direct effects model 2		
Path from	Path to	Path coefficient	Path from	Path to	Path coefficient
Cooperation	Constructive controversy	.15**	Cooperation	Innovation	.15**
Competition	Constructive controversy	−.05*	Competition	Innovation	.11*
Independence	Constructive controversy	−.01	Independence	Innovation	−.01
Constructive controversy	Innovation	.30**	Cooperation	Job Commitment	.21**
Constructive controversy	Job commitment	.77**	Competition	Job commitment	−.04
			Independence	Job commitment	.02
Model χ^2	7.07			Model χ^2	38.71
df	6			df	3
NFI	.94			NFI	.43
CFI	.99			CFI	.39

*$p < .05$, **$p < .01$.

harmony motives in China can also refer to the desire to strengthen relationships and solve problems out of a genuine concern for harmony as a value in and of itself. Consistent with this reasoning, this study suggests that the constructive discussion of opposing views within a cooperative context can help foreign managers and Chinese employees to innovate and develop job commitment. Previous research has suggested that constructive controversy can be useful for Chinese managers and Chinese employees (Tjosvold et al., 1998a,b).

The theory of cooperation and competition, although developed in the West, proved useful for understanding leadership dynamics across cultures (Deutsch, 1973). Indeed, the theory appears to be useful in understanding the perspective of Chinese employees. Recent studies conducted in China also suggest the utility of the theory for understanding dynamics in Chinese organizations (Tjosvold et al., 1998a,b).

Results on the incidents themselves support the general model and provide understanding of the obstacles and how managers and employees overcame them. They suggest that foreign managers and Chinese employees find it difficult to voice their ideas directly so that the ideas are considered open-mindedly. Cooperative goals not only increase communication but also the willingness to incorporate each other's ideas. The examples also reaffirmed that shared goals, common tasks, trusting attitudes, and complementary roles can help Chinese employees and foreign managers believe their goals are cooperative. Independent tasks and an "outdo climate" give rise to competition, while independent attitudes promote independent goals.

As cross-cultural researchers have argued (Leung, in press; Smith, 2003), a common platform can help culturally diverse individuals work together. The theory of cooperation and competition can help develop this platform. Individuals with different cultures can combine their various norms, motives, and cognitive processes to strengthen cooperative goals and encourage constructive controversy (Leung, in press). They can also use the theory to reflect upon their interactions and work together more efficiently. Theories cannot be assumed to apply in other cultures but increasingly there is a need to develop theories that are relevant for more than one culture as the marketplace becomes more global.

Research has focused on developing maps of cultural differences (Smith, Dugan, & Trompenaars, 1996). As suggested recently by cross-cultural researchers, this study investigated how diverse people cope with specific events as they try to work together (Bond, 2003; Smith, 2003). Findings indicate that developing cooperative goals can provide a framework for diverse people who deal with barriers and obstacles to their effective collaboration.

Smith (Leung et al., 1996; Smith et al., 2000) has used event management that identifies central joint issues and then assesses how managers and employees deal with them together. This study shows how cross-cultural researchers can use the CIT to sample specific events and understand obstacles and ways diverse individuals overcome them. A methodological advantage of this approach is that participants recall and then report on a specific example and therefore have to engage in less generalization than the typical survey (Schwartz, 1999; Sudman, Bradburn, & Schwarz, 1996). The event management and CIT are complementary methods of directly studying cross-cultural interaction.

5.1. Limitations

The results of this study are of course limited by the sample and operations. The data are self-reported and subject to bias, and may not accurately describe the situations, although recent research suggests that self-reported data are not as limited as commonly expected (Crampton & Wagner, 1994; Spector, 1992). Respondents reported on specific events that should be less distorted and less subject to bias than questions that ask for generalizations (Podsakoff & Organ, 1986; Schwartz, 1999;

Sudman et al., 1996). Interviewees had the opportunity to recount the full example before they gave specific ratings. Recent evidence indicates that people often accurately perceive and report their social environment, especially when the purpose is for research rather than their evaluation (Balzer & Sulsky, 1992; Crampton & Wagner, 1994; Murphy, Jako, & Anhalt, 1992; Shraguer & Osberg, 1986; Spector, 1992; Sudman et al., 1996). Researchers have recently begun to use interviews as practical ways to help people report past events fully with accuracy (Goodman, Fichman, Lerch, & Snyder, 1995; Yukl, Kim, & Falbe, 1996). The study is also limited by common method problems but recent studies suggest that common method variance may not be as much of an artifact as commonly assumed (Spector, 1987). It could be useful to assess directly and compare the perspective of foreign managers as well as Chinese employees. Additional studies using different methods are needed to test and refine the propositions argued here (Spector & Brannick, 1995).

5.2. Practical Implications

In addition to developing theoretical understanding, continued support for the hypotheses can have important practical implications for structuring leadership and stimulating innovation in foreign operations. Foreign managers and local employees can develop shared goals, common tasks, trusting attitudes, and complementary roles that build cooperative goals (Tjosvold & Tjosvold, 1994, 1995). Foreign managers and local employees can also be trained in the skills of constructive controversy. They express their ideas and positions, ask each other for more information and arguments, and integrate their best ideas to create effective solutions. They stop defending their own views long enough to ask each other for more information and arguments. They put themselves in each other's shoes and see the problem from one another's perspectives. They agree to a solution that is most effective for all and implement it.

The interface between multi-national managers and local employees is critical for the success of foreign operations because managers and employees can combine their abilities and perspectives into practical innovations that they are committed to. However, cross-cultural interaction, especially between people with different status, can be particularly challenging. Foreign managers and Chinese employees were found to promote innovation and job commitment, provided that they had cooperative goals and were able to discuss their opposing views openly and constructively. The theory of cooperation and competition may be a basis for managers and employees developing a common approach to strengthening their leader relationship.

Appendix A

A.1. Goal Interdependence

(1) How much would your reaching your objectives help the manager reach his objectives?

(2) How much were your goals and the manager's goals structured so that they were win-lose?

(3) How much would your accomplishing your goal affect whether the manager achieved or did not achieve his goals?

A.2. Constructive Controversy

(1) How much did you and the manager express your views fully?

(2) How much did you and the manager consider each other's views open-mindedly?

(3) How much did you and the manager try to understand each other's concerns?

(4) Even when you and the manager disagreed, how much did you feel accepted by each other?

(5) How much did you and the manager use your opposing views to understand the problem better?

(6) How much did your manager show concerns for your rights as an employee in this situation?

(7) How much did your manager overcome his personal biases in the interaction?

(8) How much did your manager take steps to deal with you in a truthful manner in this situation?

(9) How much did your manager provide you with timely feedback about his decisions and implementation in this situation?

A.3. Impact on Innovation

(1) How much did this interaction help you seek out information about new markets, products, and technologies from sources outside the organization?

(2) How much did this interaction help you identify and develop skills that can improve your ability to serve existing business needs?

(3) How much did this interaction help you identify and develop skills that can help attract and serve new business needs?

(4) How much did this interaction help you seek out and acquire knowledge that may be useful in satisfying needs unforeseen by the client?

A.4. Job Commitment

(1) How much did this interaction help you feel very satisfied with your work?

(2) How much did this interaction help you feel committed to the goals of your work?

(3) How much did this interaction help you feel pleased with your job?

References

Adair, W. L., Okumura, T., & Brett, J. M. (2001). Negotiating behavior when cultures collide: the United States and Japan. *Journal of Applied Psychology, 86,* 371–385.

Alper, S., Tjosvold, D., & Law, S. A. (1998). Interdependence and controversy in group decision making: antecedents to effective self-managing teams. *Organizational Behavior and Human Decision Processes, 74,* 33–52.

Balzer, W. K., & Sulsky, L. M. (1992). Halo and performance appraisal research: a critical examination. *Journal of Applied Psychology, 77,* 975–985.

Bentler, P. M., & Bonnett, D. G. (1980). Significance tests and goodness of fit in the analysis of covariance structure. *Psychological Bulletin, 88,* 588–606.

Bentler, P. M., & Wu, E. J. C. (1995). *EQS for Macintosh user's guide*. Encino, CA: Multivariate Software Inc.

Bitner, M., Booms, B., & Tetreault, M. (1990). The service encounter: diagnosing favourable and unfavourable incidents. *Journal of Marketing, 54,* 71–84.

Bond, M. H. (2003). Cross-cultural social psychology and the real world of culturally diverse teams and dyads. In D. Tjosvold, & K. Leung (Eds.), *Cross-cultural foundations: traditions for managing in a cross-cultural world*. Aldershot, Hampshire, UK: Ashgate Publishing.

Boyd, N. G., & Taylor, R. R. (1998). A developmental approach to the examination of friendship in leader-follower relationships. *Leadership Quarterly, 9,* 1–25.

Brislin, R. W. (1970). Back-translation for cross-cultural research. *Journal of Cross-Cultural Psychology, 1,* 185–216.

Brower, H. H., Schoorman, F. D., & Tan, H. H. (2000). A model of relational leadership: the integration of trust and leader–member exchange. *Leadership Quarterly, 11,* 227–250.

Burpitt, W. J., & Bigoness, W. J. (1997). Leadership and innovation among teams. *Small Group Research, 28,* 414–423.

Buvik, A., & Gronhaug, K. (2000). Inter-firm dependence, environmental uncertainty and vertical coordination in industrial buyer-seller relationships. *Omega, 28,* 445–454.

Charman, C. D. (2000). A CEO Roundtable on Making Mergers Succeed. *Harvard Business Review, 37,* 145–154.

Crampton, S. M., & Wagner, J. A., III (1994). Precept–percept inflation in micro organizational research: an investigation of prevalence and effect. *Journal of Applied Psychology, 79,* 67–76.

Cyr, D. J. (1995). *The human resource challenge of international joint ventures*. Westport: Quorum Books.

Delugua, R. J. (1998). Leader-member exchange quality and effectiveness ratings. *Group & Organization Management, 23,* 189–216.

Deutsch, M. (1973). *The resolution of conflict*. New Haven, CT: Yale University Press.

Doz, Y. L., & Hamel, G. (1998). *Alliance advantage: the art of creating value through partnering*. Boston: Harvard Business School Press.

Earley, P. C., & Gibson, C. B. (2002). *Multinational work teams: a new perspective*. Mahwah, NJ: Erlbaum.

Earley, P. C., & Mosakowski, E. (2000). Creating hybrid team cultures: an empirical test of transnational team functioning. *Academy of Management Journal, 43,* 26–49.

Flanagan, J. C. (1954). The critical incident technique. *Psychological Bulletin, 54,* 327–358.

Friman, M., Garling, T., Millett, B., Mattsson, J., & Johnston, R. (2002). An analysis of international business business relationships based on the commitment–trust theory. *Industrial Marketing Management, 31,* 403–409.

Goodman, P. S., Fichman, M., Lerch, F. J., & Snyder, P. R. (1995). Customer–firm relationships, involvement, and customer satisfaction. *Academy of Management Journal, 38,* 1310–1324.

Graen, G. B., & Uhl-Bien, M. (1995). Relationship–based approach to leadership: development of leader-member exchange (LMX) theory of leadership over 25 years: applying a multi-level multi-domain perspective. *Leadership Quarterly, 6,* 219–247.

Graham, J. L., Kim, D. K., Lin, C., & Robinson, M. (1988). Buyer-seller negotiations around the Pacific Rim: differences in fundamental exchange processes. *Journal of Consumer Research, 15,* 48–54.

Hitt, M. A., Harrison, J. S., & Ireland, R. D. (2001). *Mergers & acquisitions: a guide to creating value for shareholders*. New York: Oxford University Press.

Hitt, M. A., Lee, H. U., & Yucel, E. (2002). The importance of social capital to the management of multinational enterprises: relational networks among Asian and Western firms. *Asia Pacific Journal of Management, 19,* 353–372.

Hofner Saphiere, D. M. (1996). Productive behaviors of global business teams. *International Journal of Intercultural Relations, 20,* 227–259.

House, R. J., Wright, N. S., & Aditya, R. N. (1997). Cross-cultural research on organizational leadership: a critical analysis and a proposed theory. In P. C. Earley, & M. Erez (Eds.), *New perspectives on international industrial/ organizational psychology* (pp. 535–625). San Francisco: The New Lexington Press.

Hwang, L. L. (1996). Conflict and interpersonal harmony among Chinese people: theoretical constructs and empirical studies. Unpublished doctoral dissertation, National Taiwan University (in Chinese).

Inkpen, A. C., & Beamish, P. W. (1997). Knowledge, bargaining power, and the instability of international joint ventures. *Academy of Management Review, 22,* 177–202.

Johnson, D. W., & Johnson, R. T. (1989). *Cooperation and competition: theory and research*. Edina, MN: Interaction Book Company.

Johnson, D. W., Maruyama, G., Johnson, R. T., Nelson, D., & Skon, L. (1981). Effects of cooperative, competitive and individualistic goal structures on achievement: a meta-analysis. *Psychological Bulletin, 89,* 47–62.

Kale, P., Singh, H., & Perlmutter, H. (2000). Learning and protection of proprietary assets in strategic alliances: building relational capital. *Strategic Management Journal, 21,* 217–237.

Kealey, D. J., & Protheroe, D. R. (1996). The effectiveness of cross–cultural training for expatriates: an assessment of the literature on the issue. *International Journal of Intercultural Relations, 20,* 141–165.

Kimmel, P. R. (2000). Culture and conflict. In M. Deutsch, & P. T. Coleman (Eds.), *The handbook of conflict resolution: Theory and practice* (pp. 453–474). San Francisco: Jossey-Bass.

Kirkbride, P. S., Tang, S. F. Y., & Westwood, R. I. (1991). Chinese conflict preferences and negotiating behavior: cultural and psychological influences. *Organization Studies, 12,* 365–386.

Lam, L. L. (2000). *Working with Chinese expatriates in business negotiations: portraits, issues, and applications.* Westport, CT: Quorum.

Lane, P. J., Salk, J. E., & Lyles, M. A. (2001). Absorptive capacity, learning, and performance in international joint ventures. *Strategic Management Journal, 22,* 1139–1161.

Leung, K. (1996). The role of harmony in conflict avoidance. *Paper presented in the Korean Psychological Association 50th anniversary conference,* June, Seoul, Korea.

Leung, K. (1997). Negotiation and reward allocations across cultures. In P. C. Earley, & M. Erez (Eds.), *New perspectives on international industrial/organizational psychology* (pp. 640–675). San Francisco: Jossey-Bass.

Leung, K. (2006). Effective conflict resolution for intercultural disputes. In: T. Garling, G. Backenroth-Ohsako, B. Ekehammar, & L. Jonsson (Eds.), Diplomacy and psychology: prevention of armed conflicts after the cold war. Cambridge: Cambridge University Press, in press.

Leung, K., Smith, P. B., Wang, Z. M., & Sun, H. (1996). Job satisfaction in joint venture hotels in China: an organizational justice analysis. *Journal of International Business Studies, 27,* 947–962.

Matveev, A. V., & Nelson, P. E. (2004). Cross cultural communication competence and multicultural team performance-perceptions of American and Russian managers. *International Journal of Cross Cultural Management, 14,* 253–270.

Murphy, K. R., Jako, R. A., & Anhalt, R. L. (1992). Nature and consequences of halo error: a critical analysis. *Journal of Applied Psychology, 78,* 218–229.

Podsakoff, P. M., & Organ, D. W. (1986). Self-reports in organizational research: problems and prospects. *Journal of Management, 12,* 531–544.

Rao, A., & Hashimoto, K. (1996). Intercultural influence: A study of japanese expatriate managers in Canada. *Journal of International Business Studies, 27,* 443–466.

Ratiu, I. (1983). Thinking internationally: a comparison of how international executives learn. *International Studies of Management and Organisation, 13,* 139–150.

Redmond, M. V., & Bunyi, J. M. (1991). The relationship of intercultural communication competence with stress and the handling of stress as reported by international students. *International Journal of Intercultural Relations, 17,* 235–254.

Samovar, L. A., & Porter, R. E. (Eds.). (1991). *Intercultural communication: A reader.* Belmont, CA: Wadsworth.

Schriesheim, C. A., Neider, L. L., & Scandura, T. A. (1998). Delegation and leader-member exchange: main effects, moderators, and measurement issues. *Academy of Management Journal, 41,* 298–318.

Schwartz, N. (1999). Self-reports. *American Psychologist, 54,* 93–105.

Setton, R. P., Bennett, N., & Liden, R. C. (1996). Social exchange in organizations: perceived organizational support, leader-member exchange, and employee reciprocity. *Journal of Applied Psychology, 81,* 219–227.

Shraguer, J. S., & Osberg, T. M. (1986). The relative accuracy of self-predictions and judgments by others in psychological assessment. *Psychological Bulletin, 90,* 251–322.

Smith, P. B. (2003). Meeting the challenge of cultural difference. In D. Tjosvold & K. Leung (Eds.), *Cross-cultural foundations: traditions for managing in a cross-cultural world.* Aldershot, Hampshire, UK: Ashgate Publishing.

Smith, P. B., Dugan, S., & Trompenaars, F. (1996). National culture and the values of organisational employees: a dimensional analysis across 43 nations. *Journal of Cross-Cultural Psychology, 27,* 231–264.

Smith, P. B., Kruzela, P., & Groblewska, B. (2000). Effective ways of handling work events in central and eastern Europe. *Social Science Information, 39,* 317–333.

Spector, P. E. (1987). Method variance as an artifact in self-reported affect and perceptions at work: myth or significant problem? *Journal of Applied Psychology, 72,* 438–443.

Spector, P. E. (1992). A consideration of the validity and meaning of self-report measures of job conditions. In C. L. Cooper, & I. T. Robertson (Eds.), *International review of industrial and organizational Psychology* (pp. 123–151). Chichester: Wiley.

Spector, P. E., & Brannick, M. T. (1995). The nature and effects of method variance in organizational research. In C. L. Cooper & I. T. Robertson (Eds.), *International review of industrial and organizational psychology* (pp. 249–274). Chichester: Wiley.

Stanne, M. B., Johnson, D. W., & Johnson, R. T. (1999). Does competition enhance or inhibit motor performance? A meta-analysis. *Psychological Bulletin, 125,* 133–154.

Sudman, S., Bradburn, N. M., & Schwarz, N. (1996). *Thinking about answers: the application of cognitive processes to survey methodology.* San Francisco, CA: Jossey-Bass.

Tjosvold, D. (1982). Effects of approach to controversy on superiors' incorporation of subordinates' information in decision making. *Journal of Applied Psychology, 67,* 189–193.

Tjosvold, D. (1998). Cooperative and Competitive Goal Approaches to Conflict: Accomplishments and

Challenges. *Applied Psychology: An International Review, 47*, 285–342.

Tjosvold, D., Hui, C., & Law, K. S. (1998a). Empowerment in the leader relationship in Hong Kong: interdependence and controversy. *Journal of Social Psychology.*

Tjosvold, D., & Johnson, D. W. (1977). The effects of controversy on cognitive perspective-taking. *Journal of Education Psychology, 69*, 679–685.

Tjosvold, D., Sasaki, S., & Moy, J. (1998b). Developing commitment in Japanese organizations in Hong Kong: Interdependence, interaction, relationship and productivity. *Small Group Research, 29*, 560–582.

Tjosvold, D., & Tjosvold, M. M. (1994). Cooperation, competition, and constructive controversy: knowledge to empower self-managing teams. In M. M. Beyerlein & D. A. Johnson (Eds.), *Advances in interdisciplinary studies of work teams*, Vol. 1 (pp. 119–144). Greenwich, CT: JAI Press.

Tjosvold, D., & Tjosvold, M. M. (1995). Cooperation theory, constructive controversy, and effectiveness: learning from crises. In R. A. Guzzo & E. Salas (Eds.), *Team effectiveness and decision making in organizations* (pp. 79–112). San Francisco: Jossey-Bass.

Tjosvold, D., Wedley, W. C., & Field, R. H. G. (1986). Constructive controversy, the Vroom–Yetton model, and managerial decision making. *Journal of Occupational Behaviour, 7*, 125–138.

Triandis, H. C., & Singelis, T. M. (1998). Training to recognize individual differences in collectivism and individualism within culture. *International Journal of Intercultural Relations, 22*, 35–47.

Tse, D. K., Francis, J., & Walls, J. (1994). Cultural differences in conducting intra- and inter-cultural negotiations: a Sino-Canadian Comparison. *Journal of International Business Studies, 24*, 537–555.

Van Velsor, E., & Leslie, J. B. (1995). Why executives derail: perspectives across time and cultures. *Academy of Management Executive, 9*, 62–72.

Walker, S., & Truly, E. (1992). The critical incident technique: philosophical foundations and methodological implications. In C. Allen & T. Madden (Eds.), *Winter educators' conference proceedings: marketing theory and applications*, Vol. 3 (pp. 270–275). American Marketing Association: Chicago, IL.

West, M. A. (2002). Sparkling fountains or stagnant ponds? An integrative model of creativity and innovation implementation in work groups. *Applied Psychology: An International Review, 51*, 355–424.

Wheelan, S. A., Buzalo, G., & Tsumura, E. (1998). Development assessment tools for cross-cultural research. *Small Group Research, 29*, 359–370.

Wiseman, R. L., & Shuter, R. (Eds.). (1994). *International and Intercultural Communication Annual, 18.* Thousand Oaks, CA: Sage.

Yukl, G., Kim, H., & Falbe, C. M. (1996). Antecedents of influence outcomes. *Journal of Applied Psychology, 81*, 309–317.

Zaheer, A. B., McEvily, B., & Perrone, V. (1998). Does trust matter? Exploring the effects of interorganizational and interpersonal trust on performance. *Organizational Science, 9*, 1–20.

CHAPTER 34

Women and the Labyrinth of Leadership

Alice H. Eagly

Northwestern University

Linda L. Carli

Wellesley College

I f one has misdiagnosed a problem, then one is unlikely to prescribe an effective cure. This is the situation regarding the scarcity of women in top leadership. Because people with the best of intentions have misread the symptoms, the solutions that managers are investing in are not making enough of a difference.

That there is a problem is not in doubt. Despite years of progress by women in the workforce (they now occupy more than 40% of all managerial positions in the United States), within the C-suite they remain as rare as hens' teeth. Consider the most highly paid executives of Fortune 500 companies—those with titles such as chairman, president, chief executive officer, and chief operating officer. Of this group, only 6% are women. Most notably, only 2% of the CEOs are women, and only

15% of the seats on the boards of directors are held by women. The situation is not much different in other industrialized countries. In the 50 largest publicly traded corporations in each nation of the European Union, women make up, on average, 11% of the top executives and 4% of the CEOs and heads of boards. Just seven companies, or 1%, of *Fortune* magazine's Global 500 have female CEOs. What is to blame for the pronounced lack of women in positions of power and authority?

In 1986 the *Wall Street Journal's* Carol Hymowitz and Timothy Schellhardt gave the world an answer: "Even those few women who rose steadily through the ranks eventually crashed into an invisible barrier. The executive suite seemed within their grasp, but they just couldn't break through the glass ceiling." The metaphor, driven

Source: Women and the Labyrinth by Alice H. Eagly and Linda L. Carli. Pp. 63–71 in *Harvard Business Review*, Sept. 2007. Reprinted with permission of Harvard Business School Publishing.

home by the article's accompanying illustration, resonated; it captured the frustration of a goal within sight but somehow unattainable. To be sure, there was a time when the barriers were absolute. Even within the career spans of 1980s-era executives, access to top posts had been explicitly denied. Consider comments made by President Richard Nixon, recorded on White House audiotapes and made public through the Freedom of Information Act. When explaining why he would not appoint a woman to the U.S. Supreme Court, Nixon said, "I don't think a woman should be in any government job whatsoever . . . mainly because they are erratic. And emotional. Men are erratic and emotional, too, but the point is a woman is more likely to be." In a culture where such opinions were widely held, women had virtually no chance of attaining influential leadership roles.

Times have changed, however, and the glass ceiling metaphor is now more wrong than right. For one thing, it describes an absolute barrier at a specific high level in organizations. The fact that there have been female chief executives, university presidents, state governors, and presidents of nations gives the lie to that charge. At the same time, the metaphor implies that women and men have equal access to entry- and midlevel positions. They do not. The image of a transparent obstruction also suggests that women are being misled about their opportunities, because the impediment is not easy for them to see from a distance. But some impediments are not subtle. Worst of all, by depicting a single, unvarying obstacle, the glass ceiling fails to incorporate the complexity and variety of challenges that women can face in their leadership journeys. In truth, women are not turned away only as they reach the penultimate stage of a distinguished career. They disappear in various numbers at many points leading up to that stage.

Metaphors matter because they are part of the storytelling that can compel change. Believing in the existence of a glass ceiling, people emphasize certain kinds of interventions: top-to-top networking, mentoring to increase board memberships, requirements for diverse candidates in high-profile succession horse races, litigation aimed at punishing discrimination in the C-suite. None of these is counterproductive; all have a role to play. The danger arises when they draw attention and resources away from other kinds of interventions that might attack the problem more potently. If we want to make better progress, it's time to rename the challenge.

Walls All Around

A better metaphor for what confronts women in their professional endeavors is the labyrinth. It's an image with a long and varied history in ancient Greece, India, Nepal, native North and South America, medieval Europe, and elsewhere. As a contemporary symbol, it conveys the idea of a complex journey toward a goal worth striving for. Passage through a labyrinth is not simple or direct, but requires persistence, awareness of one's progress, and a careful analysis of the puzzles that lie ahead. It is this meaning that we intend to convey. For women who aspire to top leadership, routes exist but are full of twists and turns, both unexpected and expected. Because all labyrinths have a viable route to the center, it is understood that goals are attainable. The metaphor acknowledges obstacles but is not ultimately discouraging.

If we can understand the various barriers that make up this labyrinth, and how some women find their way around them, we can work more effectively to improve the situation. What are the obstructions that women run up against? Let's explore them in turn.

Vestiges of prejudice. It is a well-established fact that men as a group still have the benefit of higher wages and faster promotions. In the United States in 2005, for example, women employed full-time earned 81 cents for every dollar that men earned. Is this true because of discrimination or simply because, with fewer family demands placed on them and longer careers on average, men are able to gain superior qualifications? Literally hundreds of correlational studies by economists and sociologists have attempted to find the answer.

One of the most comprehensive of these studies was conducted by the U.S. Government Accountability Office. The study was based on survey data from 1983 through 2000 from a representative sample of Americans. Because the same people responded to the survey repeatedly over the years, the study provided accurate estimates of past work experience, which is important for explaining later wages.

The GAO researchers tested whether individuals' total wages could be predicted by sex and other characteristics. They included part-time and full-time employees in the surveys and took into account all the factors that they could estimate and that might affect earnings, such as education and work experience. Without controls for these variables, the data showed that women earned about 44% less than men, averaged over the entire period from 1983 to 2000. With these controls in place, the gap was only about half as large, but still substantial. The control factors that reduced the wage gap most were the different employment patterns of men and women: Men undertook more hours of paid labor per year than women and had more years of job experience.

Although most variables affected the wages of men and women similarly, there were exceptions. Marriage and parenthood, for instance, were associated with higher wages for men but not for women. In contrast, other characteristics, especially years of education, had a more positive effect on women's wages than on men's. Even after adjusting wages for all of the ways men and women differ, the GAO study, like similar studies, showed that women's wages remained lower than men's. The unexplained gender gap is consistent with the presence of wage discrimination. Similar methods have been applied to the question of whether discrimination affects promotions. Evidently it does. Promotions come more slowly for women than for men with equivalent qualifications. One illustrative national study followed workers from 1980 to 1992 and found that white men were more likely to attain managerial positions than white women, black men, and black women. Controlling for other characteristics, such as education and hours worked per year, the study showed that white men were ahead of the other groups when entering the labor market and that their advantage in attaining managerial positions grew throughout their careers. Other research has underscored these findings. Even in culturally feminine settings such as nursing, librarianship, elementary education, and social work (all specifically studied by sociologist Christine Williams), men ascend to supervisory and administrative positions more quickly than women.

The findings of correlational studies are supported by experimental research, in which subjects are asked to evaluate hypothetical individuals as managers or job candidates, and all characteristics of these individuals are held constant except for their sex. Such efforts continue the tradition of the Goldberg paradigm, named for a 1968 experiment by Philip Goldberg. His simple, elegant study had student participants evaluate written essays that were identical except for the attached male or female name. The students were unaware that other students had received identical material ascribed to a writer of the other sex. This initial experiment demonstrated an overall gender bias: Women received lower evaluations unless the essay was on a feminine topic. Some 40 years later, unfortunately, experiments continue to reveal the same kind of bias in work settings. Men are advantaged over equivalent women as candidates for jobs traditionally held by men as well as for more gender-integrated jobs. Similarly, male leaders receive somewhat more favorable evaluations than equivalent female leaders, especially in roles usually occupied by men.

Interestingly, however, there is little evidence from either the correlational or the experimental studies that the odds are stacked higher against women with each step up the ladder—that is, that women's promotions become progressively less likely than men's at higher levels within organizations. Instead, a general bias against women appears to operate with approximately equal strength at all levels. The scarcity of female corporate officers is the sum of discrimination that has operated at all ranks, not evidence of a particular obstacle to advancement as women approach the top. The problem, in other words, is not a glass ceiling.

Resistance to women's leadership. What's behind the discrimination we've been describing? Essentially, a set of widely shared conscious and unconscious mental associations about women, men, and leaders. Study after study has affirmed that people associate women and men with different traits and link men with more of the traits that connote leadership. Kim Campbell, who briefly served as the prime minister of Canada in 1993, described the tension that results:

> I don't have a traditionally female way of speaking. . . . I'm quite assertive. If I didn't speak the way I do, I wouldn't have been seen as a leader. But my way of speaking may have grated on people who were not used to hearing it from a woman. It was the right way for a leader to speak, but it wasn't the right way for a woman to speak. It goes against type.

In the language of psychologists, the clash is between two sets of associations: communal and agentic. Women are associated with communal qualities, which convey a concern for the compassionate treatment of others. They include being especially affectionate, helpful, friendly, kind, and sympathetic, as well as interpersonally sensitive, gentle, and soft-spoken. In contrast, men are associated with agentic qualities, which convey assertion and control. They include being especially aggressive, ambitious, dominant, self-confident, and forceful, as well as self-reliant and individualistic. The agentic traits are also associated in most people's minds with effective leadership—perhaps because a long history of male domination of leadership roles has made it difficult to separate the leader associations from the male associations.

As a result, women leaders find themselves in a double bind. If they are highly communal, they may be criticized for not being agentic enough. But if they are highly agentic, they may be criticized for lacking communion. Either way, they may leave the impression that they don't have "the right stuff" for powerful jobs.

Given this double bind, it is hardly surprising that people are more resistant to women's influence than to men's. For example, in meetings at a global retail company, people responded more favorably to men's overt attempts at influence than to women's. In the words of one of this company's female executives, "People often had to speak up to defend their turf, but when women did so, they were vilified. They were labeled 'control freaks'; men acting the same way were called 'passionate.'"

Studies have gauged reactions to men and women engaging in various types of dominant behavior. The findings are quite consistent. Nonverbal dominance, such as staring at others while speaking to them or pointing at people, is a more damaging behavior for women than for men. Verbally intimidating others can undermine a woman's influence, and assertive behavior can reduce her chances of getting a job or advancing in her career. Simply disagreeing can sometimes get women into trouble. Men who disagree or otherwise act dominant get away with it more often than women do.

Verbally intimidating others can undermine a woman's influence, and assertive behavior can reduce her chances of getting a job or advancing in her career. Self-promotion is similarly risky for women. Although it can convey status and competence, it is not at all communal. So while men can use bluster to get themselves noticed, modesty is expected even of highly accomplished women. Linguistics professor Deborah Tannen tells a story from her experience: "This [need for modesty] was evident, for example, at a faculty meeting devoted to promotions,

at which a woman professor's success was described: She was extremely well published and well known in the field. A man commented with approval, 'She wears it well.' In other words, she was praised for not acting as successful as she was."

Another way the double bind penalizes women is by denying them the full benefits of being warm and considerate. Because people expect it of women, nice behavior that seems noteworthy in men seems unimpressive in women. For example, in one study, helpful men reaped a lot of approval, but helpful women did not. Likewise, men got away with being unhelpful, but women did not. A different study found that male employees received more promotions when they reported higher levels of helpfulness to coworkers. But female employees' promotions were not related to such altruism.

While one might suppose that men would have a double bind of their own, they in fact have more freedom. Several experiments and organizational studies have assessed reactions to behavior that is warm and friendly versus dominant and assertive. The findings show that men can communicate in a warm or a dominant manner, with no penalty either way. People like men equally well and are equally influenced by them regardless of their warmth.

It all amounts to a clash of assumptions when the average person confronts a woman in management. Perhaps this is why respondents in one study characterized the group "successful female managers" as more deceitful, pushy, selfish, and abrasive than "successful male managers." In the absence of any evidence to the contrary, people suspect that such highly effective women must not be very likable or nice.

Issues of leadership style. In response to the challenges presented by the double bind, female leaders often struggle to cultivate an appropriate and effective leadership style—one that reconciles the communal qualities people prefer in women with the agentic qualities people think leaders need to succeed. Here, for instance, is how Marietta Nien-hwa Cheng described her transition to the role of symphony conductor:

> I used to speak more softly, with a higher pitch. Sometimes my vocal cadences went up instead of down. I realized that these mannerisms lack the sense of authority. I strengthened my voice. The pitch has dropped. . . . I have stopped trying to be

everyone's friend. Leadership is not synonymous with socializing.

It's difficult to pull off such a transformation while maintaining a sense of authenticity as a leader. Sometimes the whole effort can backfire. In the words of another female leader, "I think that there is a real penalty for a woman who behaves like a man. The men don't like her and the women don't either." Women leaders worry a lot about these things, complicating the labyrinth that they negotiate. For example, Catalyst's study of *Fortune* 1000 female executives found that 96% of them rated as critical or fairly important that they develop "a style with which male managers are comfortable."

Does a distinct "female" leadership style exist? There seems to be a popular consensus that it does. Consider, for example, journalist Michael Sokolove's profile of Mike Krzyzewski, head coach of the highly successful Duke University men's basketball team. As Sokolove put it, "So what is the secret to Krzyzewski's success? For starters, he coaches the way a woman would. Really." Sokolove proceeded to describe Krzyzewski's mentoring, interpersonally sensitive, and highly effective coaching style.

More scientifically, a recent meta-analysis integrated the results of 45 studies addressing the question. To compare leadership skills, the researchers adopted a framework introduced by leadership scholar James MacGregor Burns that distinguishes between transformational leadership and transactional leadership. Transformational leaders establish themselves as role models by gaining followers' trust and confidence. They state future goals, develop plans to achieve those goals, and innovate, even when their organizations are generally successful. Such leaders mentor and empower followers, encouraging them to develop their full potential and thus to contribute more effectively to their organizations. By contrast, transactional leaders establish give-and-take relationships that appeal to subordinates' self-interest Such leaders manage in the conventional manner of clarifying subordinates' responsibilities, rewarding them for meeting objectives, and correcting them for failing to meet objectives. Although transformational and transactional leadership styles are different, most leaders adopt at least some behaviors of both types. The researchers also allowed for a third category, called the laissez-faire style—a sort of non-leadership that concerns itself with none of the above, despite rank authority.

Is It Only a Question of Time?

It is a common perception that women will steadily gain greater access to leadership roles, including elite positions. For example, university students who are queried about the future power of men and women say that women's power will increase. Polls have shown that most Americans expect a woman to be elected president or vice president within their lifetimes. Both groups are extrapolating women's recent gains into the future, as if our society were on a continuous march toward gender equality.

But social change does not proceed without struggle and conflict. As women gain greater equality, a portion of people react against it. They long for traditional roles. In fact, signs of a pause in progress toward gender equality have appeared on many fronts. A review of longitudinal studies reveals several areas in which a sharp upward trend in the 1970s and 1980s has been followed by a slowing and flattening in recent years (for instance, in the percentage of managers who are women). The pause is also evident in some attitudinal data—like the percentage of people who approve of female bosses and who believe that women are at least as well suited as men for politics.

Social scientists have proposed various theories to explain this pause. Some, such as social psychologist Cecilia Ridgeway, believe that social change is activating "people's deep seated interests in maintaining clear cultural understandings of gender difference." Others believe progress has reached its limit given the continuing organization of family life by gender, coupled with employer policies that favor those who are not hampered by primary responsibility for child rearing.

It may simply be that women are collectively catching their breath before pressing for more change. In the past century, feminist activism arose when women came to view themselves as collectively subjected to illegitimate and unfair treatment. But recent polls show less conviction about the presence of discrimination, and feminism does not have the cultural relevance it once had. The lessening of activism on behalf of all women puts pressure on each woman to find her own way.

The meta-analysis found that, in general, female leaders were somewhat more transformational than male leaders, especially when it came to giving support and encouragement to subordinates. They also engaged in more of the rewarding behaviors that are one aspect of transactional leadership. Meanwhile, men exceeded women on the aspects of transactional leadership involving corrective and disciplinary actions that are either active (timely) or passive (belated). Men were also more likely than women to be laissez-faire leaders, who take little responsibility for managing. These findings add up to a startling conclusion, given that most leadership research has found the transformational style (along with the rewards and positive incentives associated with the transactional style) to be more suited to leading the modem organization. The research tells us not only that men and women do have somewhat different leadership styles, but also that women's approaches are the more generally effective—while men's often are only somewhat effective or actually hinder effectiveness.

Another part of this picture, based on a separate meta-analysis, is that women adopt a more participative and collaborative style than men typically favor. The reason for this difference is unlikely to be genetic. Rather, it may be that collaboration can get results without seeming particularly masculine. As women navigate their way through the double bind, they seek ways to project authority without relying on the autocratic behaviors that people find so jarring in women. A viable path is to bring others into decision making and to lead as an encouraging teacher and positive role model. (However, if there is not a critical mass of other women to affirm the legitimacy of a participative style, female leaders usually conform to whatever style is typical of the men—and that is sometimes autocratic.)

Demands of family life. For many women, the most fateful turns in the labyrinth are the ones taken under pressure of family responsibilities. Women continue to be the ones who interrupt their careers, take more days off, and work part-time. As a result, they have fewer years of job experience and fewer hours of employment per year, which slows their career progress and reduces their earnings.

In one study of Chicago lawyers, researchers sought to understand why women were much less likely than men to hold the leadership positions in large law firms—the positions that are most highly paid and that confer (arguably) the highest prestige. They found that women were no less likely than men to begin their careers at such firms but were more likely to leave them for positions in the public sector or corporate positions. The reasons for their departures were concentrated in work/family trade-offs. Among the relatively few

women who did become partner in a firm, 60% had no children, and the minority who had children generally had delayed childbearing until attaining partner status.

There is no question that, while men increasingly share housework and child rearing, the bulk of domestic work still falls on women's shoulders. We know this from time-diary studies, in which people record what they are doing during each hour of a 24-hour day. So, for example, in the United States married women devoted 19 hours per week on average to housework in 2005, while married men contributed 11 hours. That's a huge improvement over 1965 numbers, when women spent a whopping 34 hours per week to men's 5, but it is still a major inequity. And the situation looks worse when child care hours are added.

Mothers provide more child care hours than they did in earlier generations—despite the fact that fathers are putting in a lot more time than in the past. Although it is common knowledge that mothers provide more child care than fathers, few people realize that mothers provide more than they did in earlier generations—despite the fact that fathers are putting in a lot more time than in the past. National studies have compared mothers and fathers on the amount of their primary child care, which consists of close interaction not combined with housekeeping or other activities. Married mothers increased their hours per week from 10.6 in 1965 to 12.9 in 2000, and married fathers increased theirs from 2.6 to 6.5. Thus, though husbands have taken on more domestic work, the work/ family conflict has not eased for women; the gain has been offset by escalating pressures for intensive parenting and the increasing time demands of most high-level careers.

Even women who have found a way to relieve pressures from the home front by sharing child care with husbands, other family members, or paid workers may not enjoy the full workplace benefit of having done so. Decision makers often assume that mothers have domestic responsibilities that make it inappropriate to promote them to demanding positions. As one participant in a study of the federal workforce explained, "I mean, there were 2 or 3 names [of women] in the hat, and they said, 'I don't want to talk about her because she has children who are still home in these [evening] hours.' Now they don't pose that thing about men on the list, many of whom also have children in that age group."

Underinvestment in social capital. Perhaps the most destructive result of the work/family balancing act so many women must perform is that it leaves very little time for socializing with colleagues and building professional networks. The social capital that accrues from such "nonessential" parts of work turns out to be quite essential indeed. One study yielded the following description of managers who advanced rapidly in hierarchies: Fast-track managers "spent relatively more time and effort socializing, politicking, and interacting with outsiders than did their less successful counterparts . . . [and] did not give much time or attention to the traditional management activities of planning, decision making, and controlling or to the human resource management activities of motivating/reinforcing, staffing, training/developing, and managing conflict." This suggests that social capital is even more necessary to managers' advancement than skillful performance of traditional managerial tasks.

Even given sufficient time, women can find it difficult to engage in and benefit from informal networking if they are a small minority. In such settings, the influential networks are composed entirely or almost entirely of men. Breaking into those male networks can be hard, especially when men center their networks on masculine activities. The recent gender discrimination lawsuit against Wal-Mart provides examples of this. For instance, an executive retreat took the form of a quail-hunting expedition at Sam Walton's ranch in Texas. Middle managers' meetings included visits to strip clubs and Hooters restaurants, and a sales conference attended by thousands of store managers featured a football theme. One executive received feedback that she probably would not advance in the company because she didn't hunt or fish.

Management Interventions That Work

Taking the measure of the labyrinth that confronts women leaders, we see that it begins with prejudices that benefit men and penalize women, continues with particular resistance to women's leadership, includes questions of leadership style and authenticity, and—most dramatically for many women—features the challenge of balancing work and family responsibilities.

It becomes clear that a woman's situation as she reaches her peak career years is the result of many turns at many challenging junctures. Only a few individual women have made the right combination of moves to land at the center of power—but as for the rest, there is usually no single turning point where their progress was diverted and the prize was lost.

What's to be done in the face of such a multifaceted problem? A solution that is often proposed is for governments to implement and enforce antidiscrimination legislation and thereby require organizations to eliminate inequitable practices. However, analysis of discrimination cases that have gone to court has shown that legal remedies can be elusive when gender inequality results from norms embedded in organizational structure and culture. The more effective approach is for organizations to appreciate the subtlety and complexity of the problem and to attack its many roots simultaneously. More specifically, if a company wants to see more women arrive in its executive suite, it should do the following:

Increase people's awareness of the psychological drivers of prejudice toward female leaders, and work to dispel those perceptions. Raising awareness of ingrained bias has been the aim of many diversity-training initiatives, and no doubt they have been more helpful than harmful. There is the danger they will be undermined, however, if their lessons are not underscored by what managers say and do in the course of day-to-day work.

Change the long-hours norm. Especially in the context of knowledge work, it can be hard to assess individuals' relative contributions, and managers may resort to "hours spent at work" as the prime indicator of someone's worth to the organization. To the extent an organization can shift the focus to objective measures of productivity, women with family demands on their time but highly productive work habits will receive the rewards and encouragement they deserve.

Reduce the subjectivity of performance evaluation. Greater objectivity in evaluations also combats the effects of lingering prejudice in both hiring and promotion. To ensure fairness, criteria should be explicit and evaluation processes designed to limit the influence of decision makers' conscious and unconscious biases.

Use open-recruitment tools, such as advertising and employment agencies, rather than relying on informal social networks and referrals to fill positions. Recruitment from within organizations also should be transparent, with postings of open positions in appropriate venues. Research has shown that such personnel practices increase the numbers of women in managerial roles.

Ensure a critical mass of women in executive positions—not just one or two women—to head off the problems that come with tokenism. Token women tend to be pegged into narrow stereotypical roles such as "seductress," "mother," "pet," or "iron maiden." (Or more colorfully, as one woman banker put it, "When you start out in banking, you are a slut or a geisha.") Pigeonholing like this limits women's options and makes it difficult for them to rise to positions of responsibility. When women are not a small minority, their identities as women become less salient, and colleagues are more likely to react to them in terms of their individual competencies.

Avoid having a sole female member of any team. Top management tends to divide its small population of women managers among many projects in the interests of introducing diversity to them all. But several studies have found that, so outnumbered, the women tend to be ignored by the men. A female vice president of a manufacturing company described how, when she or another woman ventures an idea in a meeting, it tends to be overlooked: "It immediately gets lost in the conversation. Then two minutes later, a man makes the same suggestion, and it's 'Wow! What a great idea!' And you sit there and think, 'What just happened?'" As women reach positions of higher power and authority, they increasingly find themselves in gender-imbalanced groups—and some find themselves, for the first time, seriously marginalized. This is part of the reason that the glass ceiling metaphor resonates with so many. But in fact, the problem can be present at any level.

Help shore up social capital. As we've discussed, the call of family responsibilities is mainly to blame for women's underinvestment in networking. When time is scarce, this social activity is the first thing to go by

the wayside. Organizations can help women appreciate why it deserves more attention. In particular, women gain from strong and supportive mentoring relationships and connections with powerful networks. When a well-placed individual who possesses greater legitimacy (often a man) takes an interest in a woman's career, her efforts to build social capital can proceed far more efficiently.

Prepare women for line management with appropriately demanding assignments. Women, like men, must have the benefit of developmental job experiences if they are to qualify for promotions. But, as one woman executive wrote, "Women have been shunted off into support areas for the last 30 years, rather than being in the business of doing business, so the pool of women trained to assume leadership positions in any large company is very small." Her point was that women should be taught in business school to insist on fine jobs when they enter the workforce. One company that has taken up the challenge has been Procter & Gamble. According to a report by Claudia Deutsch in the *New York Times*, the company was experiencing an executive attrition rate that was twice as high for women as for men. Some of the women reported having to change companies to land jobs that provided challenging work. P&G's subsequent efforts to bring more women into line management both improved its overall retention of women and increased the number of women in senior management.

Establish family-friendly human resources practices. These may include flextime, job sharing, telecommuting, elder care provisions, adoption benefits, dependent child care options, and employee-sponsored on-site child care. Such support can allow women to stay in their jobs during the most demanding years of child rearing, build social capital, keep up to date in their fields, and eventually compete for higher positions. A study of 72 large U.S. firms showed (controlling for other variables) that family-friendly HR practices in place in 1994 increased the proportion of women in senior management over the subsequent five years.

Allow employees who have significant parental responsibility more time to prove themselves worthy of promotion. This recommendation is particularly directed to organizations, many of them professional services firms, that have established "up or out" career progressions. People not ready for promotion at the same time as the top performers in their cohort aren't simply left in place—they're asked to leave. But many parents (most often mothers), while fully capable of reaching that level of achievement, need extra time—perhaps a year or two—to get there. Forcing them off the promotion path not only reduces the number of women reaching top management positions, but also constitutes a failure by the firm to capitalize on its early investment in them.

When the eye can take in the whole of the puzzle—the starting position, the goal, and the maze of walls—solutions begin to suggest themselves.

Welcome women back. It makes sense to give high-performing women who step away from the workforce an opportunity to return to responsible positions when their circumstances change. Some companies have established "alumni" programs, often because they see former employees as potential sources of new business. A few companies have gone further to activate these networks for other purposes, as well. (Procter & Gamble taps alumni for innovation purposes; Booz Allen sees its alumni ranks as a source of subcontractors.) Keeping lines of communication open can convey the message that a return may be possible.

Encourage male participation in family-friendly benefits. Dangers lurk in family-friendly benefits that are used only by women. Exercising options such as generous parental leave and part-time work slows down women's careers. More profoundly, having many more women than men take such benefits can harm the careers of women in general because of the expectation that they may well exercise those options. Any effort toward greater family friendliness should actively recruit male participation to avoid inadvertently making it harder for women to gain access to essential managerial roles.

Managers can be forgiven if they find the foregoing list a tall order. It's a wide-ranging set of interventions and still far from exhaustive. The point, however, is just that organizations will succeed in filling half their top management slots with women—and women who are the true performance equals of their male counterparts—only by attacking all the reasons they are absent today. Glass ceiling-inspired programs and projects can do just so much if the leakage of talented women is happening on every lower floor of the building. Individually, each of these interventions has been shown to make a difference. Collectively, we believe, they can make all the difference.

The View From Above

Imagine visiting a formal garden and finding within it a high hedgerow. At a point along its vertical face, you spot a rectangle—a neatly pruned and inviting doorway. Are you aware as you step through that you are entering a labyrinth? And, three doorways later, as the reality of the puzzle settles in, do you have any idea how to proceed? This is the situation in which many women find themselves in their career endeavors. Ground-level perplexity and frustration make every move uncertain.

Labyrinths become infinitely more tractable when seen from above. When the eye can take in the whole of the puzzle—the starting position, the goal, and the maze of walls—solutions begin to suggest themselves. This has been the goal of our research. Our hope is that women, equipped with a map of the barriers they will confront on their path to professional achievement, will make more informed choices. We hope that managers, too, will understand where their efforts can facilitate the progress of women. If women are to achieve equality, women and men will have to share leadership equally. With a greater understanding of what stands in the way of gender-balanced leadership, we draw nearer to attaining it in our time.

For a list of the sources the authors consulted, view the article at www.hbr.org.

CHAPTER 35

"Just Because You Can Get a Wheelchair in the Building Doesn't Necessarily Mean That You Can Still Participate"

Barriers to the Career Advancement of Disabled Professionals

Dana Wilson-Kovacs

Michelle K. Ryan

S. Alexander Haslam

Anna Rabinovich

University of Exeter

Introduction

Research shows that disabled people continue to be overrepresented in lower paid service jobs and underrepresented in better paid managerial and professional positions (Barnes and Mercer 2005; Goldstone and Meager 2002). Although disabled individuals often have educational achievement levels and years of experience that are equivalent to those of their non-disabled colleagues they have fewer opportunities for upward mobility in the workplace than non-disabled workers (Hyde 1998; Jones 1997) and there is clear evidence of

Source: "Just Because You Can Get a Wheelchair in the Building Doesn't Necessarily Mean That You Can Still Participate": Barriers to the Career Advancement of Disabled Professionals, by Dana Wilson-Kovacs, Michelle K. Ryan, S. Alexander Haslam, and Anna Rabinovich, *Disability & Society* 2008, Vol. 23, No. 7, pp. 705–717. Printed with permission of Taylor & Francis. This research was jointly funded by the European Social Fund (Project Reference 4130) and the ESRC (RES 062 23 0135).

vertical and horizontal segregation such that disabled employees are disproportionately represented in semi-skilled and unskilled occupations (Stevens 2002).

While the previous literature on disability in the workplace has invoked the concept of the glass ceiling to explain barriers to promotion (Braddock and Bachelder 1994), it has paid little attention to what happens once leadership positions are attained. Using the analysis developed in research on the "glass cliff"—which identifies the leadership positions or members of marginalized groups (e.g. women) as being highly precarious (Ryan and Haslam 2005, 2007)—this article examines the barriers that disabled professionals encounter as they advance in their careers. Our argument is developed in three parts. The first overviews the extant literature on disability and career development in relation to the glass cliff. The second introduces the present study and explores the circumstances in which our participants maintained higher level appointments. The concluding section considers the factors that led our participants to define their leadership positions as precarious and reflects on the characteristics of precariousness in relation to the experiences of disabled professionals.

Disability and Career Advancement

Past research into disability and employment has outlined a range of organizational and attitudinal barriers that disabled people face in seeking and maintaining employment and in advancing their careers. Employers in both the private (Stuart et al. 2002) and public sectors (Goldstone and Meager 2002) in the UK have been shown to have inadequate knowledge about disability, which can, in part, explain their resistance to hiring disabled workers. Employers often make assumptions about low productivity and the quality of output of such workers. Relative to other employees, employers are more likely to question the work ethic of disabled workers and their aspirations for career advancement while believing they are more prone to absenteeism, less committed to their work and less capable of getting along with others on the job (Cunningham, James, and Dibben 2004).

Stevens (2002) showed that employers think that disabled workers cost more to employ. This can be a reflection of: (a) the perceived costs involved in providing a working environment that caters to their specific needs and requirements; (b) the assumption that there is a greater possibility of disabled employees hurting themselves (leading to insurance claims); (c) the belief that related discipline and dismissal procedures are especially problematical. Together, these assumptions lead employers to believe that there is a greater risk in hiring and promoting disabled rather than non-disabled workers. For instance, organizational decision-makers are reluctant to assign disabled workers to projects that are visible and/or critical, because they consider these employees to be less likely than others to perform these tasks well (Hyde 1998). Such projects, however, are a precursor to career advancement (Morrison and Von Glinow 1990). Thus, by not being given the opportunity to perform in challenging roles, disabled professionals have limited opportunities to prove themselves. This lack of demonstrated competence in turn means that they are often passed over for promotion or for other opportunities to advance their career (Jones 1997). Along related lines, Stone and Colella (1996) demonstrated that disability may contribute to a perceived lack of fit and have a negative impact on individuals' acceptance into work groups, rates of promotion, assignment to challenging jobs and training and mentoring opportunities. Furthermore, tokenism in the workplace increases visibility and fosters isolation while at the same time restricting token employees' access to information and established networks of support. This appears to hold true for the career development of disabled professionals, who often lack role models, information about promotions and critical feedback (Braddock and Bachelder 1994; Levinson and Parritt 2005).

Given that disabled professionals tend not to receive the same outcomes (e.g. promotions, wage increases, mentoring, training opportunities, job opportunities) as their non-disabled counterparts, they may devalue them and hence decide not to pursue them (French 2004). Disabled employees may display self-limiting behaviours and decide voluntarily not to take advantage of career opportunities (Mowry and Anderson 1993) or go as far as refusing promotion (Roulstone et al. 2003).

While such explanations may seem to shift the blame on to disabled individuals, the self-limiting behaviour may be a coping strategy adopted to maintain a comfortable position, to keep work at a manageable level or to retain control (Shah 2005).

Nevertheless, despite organizational and individual barriers, disabled individuals have established successful careers and risen to positions of leadership. Those who succeed bring to their work innovative professional insights (French 2004; Levinson and Parritt 2005) and a strong work ethic (Shah 2005). To date, however, little is known about the challenges disabled professionals face in leadership roles and more research is needed in order to develop a comprehensive understanding of the structural obstacles they encounter. Although the number of such individuals remains small, the gap in existing literature could be seen to imply that difficulties cease as disabled individuals secure a professional career path or break through the glass ceiling. The present analysis examines whether this is the case using a framework informed by recent research on the experiences of members of other marginalized groups in leadership positions.

The Glass Cliff

Traditionally most writing on discrimination in organizations has focused on gender, and in particular on the difficulties women encounter when advancing in their careers (Kanter 1977). One timely addition to this literature comes from recent studies of women and leadership which suggest that female leaders are disproportionately represented in organizations that have recently experienced a consistent pattern of poor performance (Ryan and Haslam 2005). Being more likely to find themselves in charge of organizational units that are in difficulty, female leaders are also more likely to be exposed to unfair criticism and to be held responsible for negative events that were set in train before their appointment. In describing these dynamics the familiar "glass ceiling" metaphor is extended to suggest that these women tend to find themselves on a "glass cliff—such that their leadership positions tend to be more precarious and associated with a greater risk of failure than that of their male counterparts

(Ryan and Haslam 2007). In discussions of the glass cliff, precariousness is the result of a combination of factors, in particular a lack *of* formal and informal support from superiors and colleagues manifested in the absence of role models, mentoring and exclusion from professional networks, increased tokenism, isolation, alienation and prejudice (Ryan et al. 2007b). Likewise, a lack of resources to get the job done, a lack of information regarding the particular responsibilities of an appointment and a lack of time to accomplish duties make it more difficult for women to carry out their leadership roles and make their challenges harder to tackle and overcome. The existence of glass cliffs suggests that female leaders often have very different experiences in their leadership roles than men do, not least because these positions are associated with high levels of stress and can contribute to reduced organizational identification (Ryan et al. 2007a). Ongoing research reveals that the glass cliff is a relatively robust and widespread phenomenon (Ryan and Haslam 2007). While initial research into the glass cliff looked specifically at poorly performing companies, recent findings show that glass cliff positions are not restricted to top performing companies, or to women (Ryan et al. 2007b). Just as glass ceilings have been shown to exist across professions and to apply to a range of marginalized groups (Braddock and Bachelder 1994), so too do glass cliffs. Indeed, on this basis it seems likely that disabled individuals (as well as returning parents and people of different ethnic and religious backgrounds or sexual orientations) have leadership experiences that differ from, and are less optimal than, those of the majority. It is thus important to examine the ways in which disabled professionals define a position as precarious and the circumstances that contribute to identifying appointments as such.

Current Research and Methodology

The present paper reports the findings of a series of semi-structured interviews conducted as part of a wider programme of research that examined the barriers and opportunities women and other members of marginalized groups face once they attain leadership roles. The research aimed to: (a) gain a clearer view of the barriers and problems that members of marginalized groups encounter in the workplace; (b) document the ways in which these employees make sense of obstacles and opportunities; (c) understand whether and how the glass cliff might play itself out in these groups; (d) identify potential ways of dealing with the challenges faced by members of marginalized groups in advancing their careers. To this end, we examined each interviewee's career path, with particular emphasis on the critical events that shaped its direction. Participants were asked to reflect on who or what had most helped or hindered their progress and were invited to discuss the attitudes of key individuals, such as line managers, peers and subordinates, and to consider the level of support, formal or informal, that they received from their wider professional group. Precarious situations, such as those carrying a high possibility of failure, were identified by participants and examined in order to understand the forms risk takes in relation to career advancement in various professional environments.

As well as 58 one-to-one in-depth interviews, four focus groups were used as a method of data gathering over a period of 12 months in order to examine ideas of precariousness in relationship to work experiences and the impact of gender, disability, sexuality and ethnicity on work trajectories. This paper presents the testimonies of 14 participants with different physical impairments, including congenital, acquired and deteriorating conditions. Eight of the 14 were women—four in full-time employment as managers and executives in the Civil Service. Four men also worked full-time: two at senior levels in the Civil Service, one as a university lecturer and another as a senior personnel manager for a government training initiative. The remaining six participants had recently retired but continued to work on a voluntary basis. The professions and occupations represented included medicine, law, education and IT consultancy. All participants were, or had been, in senior management positions.

Our theoretical approach is guided by a social model perspective that understands disability as a phenomenon that is located within society, rather than the individual, and provides a grounded critical analysis of the experience of disability (Oliver 1990). In this view the category of impairment is seen as central to a medical model of disability and instrumental in the formulation of employment guidelines and social policy, but is unable to account for the social aspects of disability (Barnes and Mercer 2005; French 2004). Furthermore, our argument is based on a feminist approach that seeks to "denaturalize disability" and present it from the point of view of an individual's rights, within a framework of stigma, marginalization and exclusion (Garland-Thomson 2005, 1557). This allows a refined understanding of the tensions between government and organizational provisions, policy implementation and embodied experiences of disability.

We sought to capture voices rarely documented in the research literature and to offer an examination of discriminatory attitudes and practices (Shah 2005). As such, we provide a partial account that does not claim to draw any definitive conclusions, but instead highlights (a) the under the radar organizational behaviour that our interviewees encountered in their everyday working lives and (b) the ways in which they explained such behaviour in the light of their positions and career development. Based on a collaborative partnership between the researcher and the researched (Atkinson 1990), our study offered participants the opportunity to purposefully explore their working life trajectories and to reflexively address affective elements of this process (Heyl 2001). Data were analysed using a grounded theory approach (Glaser and Strauss 1967), where emerging themes were developed in relation to participants' stories.

Our qualitative approach allowed an investigation of the types of barriers encountered. As participants were self-selected, the views expressed here cannot be considered representative of all disabled professionals in leadership positions. The sample was neither random nor sufficiently large to draw generalizable conclusions. Nevertheless, the views presented below are indicative both of the kind of difficulties faced and of their pervasiveness. Furthermore, similarities between cases across professions and with other interviewed top ranking professionals from other marginalized groups point to generic obstacles in career advancement. Below we draw on the testimonies of disabled professionals to illustrate these obstacles and to highlight the factors that contribute to our participants' understandings of precariousness.

Lack of Opportunity

In contrast to the initial research into the glass cliff, which identified precariousness with a risk of failure and losing one's job (Ryan and Haslam 2005), our participants related precariousness primarily to a lack of opportunity in career advancement. Henry Walters (a pseudonym, as in all other examples below) is a 35-year-old health and safety executive in the Civil Service. Before a genetic illness affecting his eyesight and hearing was diagnosed he had had an exponential professional rise, achieving rapid promotion early in his career and entering senior management at the age of 27. Taking risks was seen as part of his professional advancement:

> Up until my experience of becoming disabled . . . there was a consistency in the way I decided to take developmental opportunity, to push in one direction against the other, to build new competence or new capability.

His view on risk taking changed after the diagnosis. He was willing to take "some risks," such as looking for new learning opportunities, but decided not to "work long hours" or seek "development where there's a risk of there being an impact on my health." However, the risk taking ethos of senior management did not allow for this shift in emphasis, as Henry observed:

> Whereas before the diagnosis the issue was about realizing potential, after the diagnosis the issue was about "well, you've only got half the capacity, therefore we do not believe there is any potential." It's that black and white.

As others attested, such an attitude has profound implications on the career advancement of disabled professionals. Steve Saunders is a 36-year-old senior personnel manager with achondroplasia, who worked in an organization that provides training and support for disabled people. Steve feels that his abilities were not stretched enough:

> You are not necessarily given the cutting edge stuff, you're often given the safer pieces of work rather

than cutting edge so you're not stretching and therefore because you're not stretching you're not necessarily learning.

Likewise, Monica King, a 41-year-old lawyer with dyslexia and dyspraxia, remarked:

> I wonder how much the work I do is important because it doesn't seem to kind of lead to kind of the other things I'd like it to lead to. . . . I don't feel that I've got that opportunity: to be pushed in my ability and to recognize the risk of it all going horribly wrong.

Both Steve and Monica hoped for a more dynamic work environment where they were encouraged to develop professionally, to take risks, fail and learn from their mistakes. Being allowed to take risks is associated with being able to "prove oneself," with realizing potential and with career progression. Learning means acquiring expertise that showcases one's abilities and is instrumental in promotion and new opportunities career-wise (Shah 2005). Other participants also commented on this lack of learning opportunities: some were "told to do the safe colouring" while their more able colleagues were "playing with the scissors," a vivid kindergarten metaphor which resonates throughout the sample.

Realizing one's full potential means having one's potential recognized in the first place. However, as Henry commented above, once disability is diagnosed such potential is ignored. Steve attributed this to a paternalistic working environment:

> If you can imagine the parent looking after a child, they don't want to stretch them too far and perhaps they don't praise their child enough but they don't overly criticize them even when perhaps they should do. I don't mean negative criticism, I mean "you could have done this better," "where do you think you went wrong," sort of thing, "how would you do it if it happened again."

While participants agreed that such an environment keeps positions "safe," they remarked on the absence of acknowledgment for their contribution to the organization, as well as on the lack of constructive feedback.

This lack of praise and criticism made judging and improving one's own performance difficult, if not impossible, and increased one's sense of uncertainty. The lack of opportunity also manifested itself in a lack of influence in making decisions. For instance, Steve found that he was the last one to be consulted, if at all, when important decisions were taken. He wished to be recognized as an equally knowledgeable peer and have his opinion considered, but felt that his token status overrode his professional capacity. Likewise, other participants felt that in the eyes of their peers and human resources departments they were anonymous quotas rather than equal members of the team: "the only reason I got where I am today is because they can tick the box" said Cynthia Brewer, a deaf 28-year-old management consultant. Thus, not being able to prove oneself, not being given feedback or being allowed to take part in the decision process amounts to a lack of opportunity that makes the career advancement of disabled professionals precarious, as they fail to be recognized as part of those who lead and make decisions.

Lack of Knowledge, Time and Other Resources

Research into the glass cliff has suggested that female professionals in leadership positions saw their positions as risky when they did not receive enough information to complete the given tasks appropriately (Ryan et al. 2007a). In our case there was a lack of information at the organizational level with regard to the different conditions of disabled employees. Henry emphasised this lack of knowledge within his human resources department:

> None of the [three core people within the department] are HR qualified, and they have no formal disability knowledge and skills, they don't understand disability as something permanent. . . . the diversity management process isn't really about preventing discrimination or creating equal opportunities, it's about administering a process which promotes equality rather than delivers it.

The lack of knowledge is particularly visible when the time and resources required to fulfil duties were overlooked. Similarly to the ways in which glass cliff research has shown that women leaders were not given sufficient time to carry out their responsibilities, our participants' experiences reveal that they were often not given the extra time they needed to perform tasks. This led to unreasonable expectations, unnecessary pressures and ultimately stress, as Cynthia reflected:

> I don't think my institution fully comprehended what was involved. And one thing I always say about my office is—I face discrimination, it's not through malice, it's through ignorance, and I think that very much comes into this, they didn't think, for example "if she's going to learn [another language] she might need some extra time because she's dyslexic." It just didn't occur to them.

Similarly, Henry stated:

> Unlike other diversity families or groups of people, certain ethnicities, sexual orientation, religion or sex, disabled people come with a price tag—to remove doors to let in a wheelchair costs money, it's part of the organizational maturity, so issues of resources have to be genuine and have to be really equal.

Several participants described how their workplace was not equipped in any sense to accommodate their career advancement. The lack of knowledge about different conditions was also related to a lack of resources to deal effectively with the needs of disabled employees. These can have immediate consequences for the ways in which one is expected to carry out everyday duties. Christopher Jenkins was a 54-year-old university lecturer whose childhood polio affected his mobility. He was proactive in making sure that his organization—in this case a higher education establishment—provided information to wheelchair users about building access. He recollected an incident where he was prevented from entering a building in which he was scheduled to teach:

> There was a lift there but I couldn't get my scooter into it because it was too small. It took about six months before somebody said to me, there's another lift but you're not meant to know about it.

In a different episode:

I had access to the car parking behind my own building but even though I was a disabled person and registered as a disabled person and had a university disabled sticker as well as my blue badge, that didn't entitle me to park in any other disabled car spaces in any other car park, I only had authorization on my swipe card to get into one car park.

In a similar vein, our participants reported how the adjustments needed to integrate them into the mainstream work culture were often ignored or executed awkwardly at the end of long bureaucratic battles. As Henry stated:

The only way you really get things as an individual is to argue in a reasonable way about what you want, and battle it out until the resources are provided, and in some cases it ends up in court, and if you're lucky you'll manage to have a good compelling argument up front and you eventually get it. It's not diplomatic and it's not very quick.

What is required, Henry observed, "is some extra thinking and some reorganization of the office for one individual to go in and work." Such a move will demonstrate that the organization is aware of its responsibility for the career advancement of disabled professionals and is committed to supporting them beyond the rhetoric of diversity (Hoque and Noon 2004). Moreover, appropriate support can only be provided through an understanding of the impact disability has on performance, an aspect largely ignored in the existing literature on disability and employment (Levinson and Parritt 2005). While information and resources are important, peer and organizational support is also needed in order to reduce the sense of precariousness felt by our participants.

Lack of Organizational and Peer Support

Similarly to the ways in which women experience glass cliffs, precariousness for our interviewees stemmed from a widespread lack of effective organizational support at both the formal and informal levels. This related to an absence of networks, mentoring and role models (Ryan et al. 2007b) and of specifically tailored programmes. Richard Travers, a 47-year-old IT management executive in the Civil Service who did not have the use of his hands or legs, noted how the lack of physical resources to deal with disability is only half of the problem: "I think that there are institutional barriers that are involved with disabled people. Just because you can get a wheelchair in the building doesn't necessarily mean that you can still participate."

Likewise, Henry remarked: "You don't get any structural support, it doesn't really exist. Because of the structural change required there is no formal system in place to do it." Support is needed in the form of clearer directives and guidelines. As Christopher's polio-related condition worsened he found himself unable to carry his teaching materials. He required regular breaks that his teaching timetable did not allow for. Upon consulting the Disability Rights Commission's guidelines he observed:

They need to be much more specific in what they're saying . . . if you read some of their publications about employing disabled people, it's very vague and very general, "make reasonable adjustments to work load" . . . the difficulty is, what is reasonable? And what is reasonable for one person, is not reasonable for another person. . . . Disability Rights Commission could be saying, "it is reasonable to give disabled people a coffee break, a lunch break," they don't have to say how long but just say, and then you can go back to your employer. I mean that was one of the things I had huge arguments about at the beginning, about my entitlement to have a coffee break.

Other participants talked about the uphill struggle of having their rights recognized. Andrea Hunt, a 45-year-old executive with MS, commented:

Employers don't understand reasonable adjustment, they don't understand the pressure, the different types of moves and changes because all injuries or disabilities we've got—no two people are the same.

In many cases there were increasingly hostile confrontations with the human resources departments, involving unions and court cases, as Andrea remarked: "I don't think there's any one of us that hasn't had to resort to legal action at some point, which is a very common thing." Often the employer suggests retirement because they cannot cope with the burden, as Christopher observed:

> The more physical problems you have in mobility, in getting around, in doing things, the more complicated that makes trying to hold down a job. In my instance, initial reactions from my employer were all-or-nothing. This is the job, you can either do it and if you can't do it, then you should retire. . . . But when you talk to people like Access to Work, who actually try and encourage people like myself to stay in work, they have a very different point of view.

Faced with these attitudes, our participants were prepared to challenge unsuitable provisions and be vocal and politically active in the organization, as Andrea explained:

> We needed the support, and we weren't getting it, and we decided, let's club together and try and get some kind of change. So that's worked quite well, in that it's got very high profile notice. We've brought pressure and we've had policies made, so that's great but you can only go so far. I can find lots of disabled people in my office but I can't find any of them who are talking about having a career as opposed to a job. I think we're taking a lot of support from each other and that we're all facing discrimination.

A lack of support was also found at the team level. When it came to pulling together as a team, disability and the sheltered position it projected could lead to animosity. Interviewees often reported being defined solely in terms of their condition, rather than in terms of their abilities. As a result, they were regarded as a liability with their workload and responsibilities being more likely to be passed to the rest of the team, as Christopher commented:

There are other colleagues who are not at all helpful, who consider that my capability to do less means more (work) for them, which they don't appreciate . . . so they don't go out of their way to be helpful.

Equally, the sheltered position may lead to tensions when internal restructuring took place and non-disabled colleagues felt their positions were threatened, while those of their disabled peers remained secure. Recognition, acceptance and inclusion at the simplest social level throughout the organizational hierarchy were identified by our participants as primary requisites in improving the situation. While the extent to which support was needed varied in relation to work environments, line of work, line managers and disability, our participants agreed that it should come from both the organization and peers. Often work cultures can hide deeply rooted prejudices, which both make evident and explain the lack of support at all levels. As Steve recalled:

> I had a team working for me and it went well, but there was one person in the team who really couldn't work for me, she could not work for a disabled person, openly admitted it, openly admitted that she couldn't work for a dwarf.

Effective support stems from understanding disability in specific contexts in order to effectively address the needs of their employees. It is also an indication that the organization is actively committed to their career advancement.

Discussion

It is apparent that the narratives presented above reveal two competing discourses: on the one hand, there is a story of success, encouragement, support and professional development, illustrated by the fact that those we interviewed had obtained positions "above the glass ceiling." On the other hand, there is evidence of rigid equal opportunities policies, ineffectual human resources departments and a lack of organizational knowledge in relation to disability. The treatment of disabled professionals is therefore paradoxical: on the one hand, they are defined in terms of their disability and treated paternalistically while, on the other hand, the support and resources they need in terms of continuing professional development and career advancement is ignored. Our participants acknowledged these competing discourses as illustrations of their precarious positions within organizations. Their experiences of precariousness related to organizational inadequacies that remained overlooked by diversity initiatives (Albiston 2005; Barnes and Mercer 2005; Hoque and Noon 2004).

Existing glass cliff research has demonstrated that precariousness and a related risk of failure represent the main characteristic of a glass cliff position (Ryan et al. 2007a). Precariousness stems from a lack of formal and informal support, a lack of knowledge about the circumstances in which appointments are made, a lack of information regarding the responsibilities of top ranking positions, a lack of material and human resources and a lack of sufficient time to carry out tasks (Ryan et al. 2007b). Fine tuning our understanding of the ways in which precariousness manifests itself at top management levels, the present findings demonstrate that there are significant parallels to be made between women's career advancement and that of disabled professionals in top ranking positions. They suggest that regardless of differences in working cultures, gender, disability and sexual orientation, both the definitions of precariousness and the barriers members of marginalized groups encounter in top ranking appointments are similar.

The stories presented here also suggest that precariousness is fostered by a paternalistic work culture. Such a work environment rarely recognizes one's contributions or provides feedback on existing performance. As acknowledgement and feedback are central to professional advancement, their absence jeopardizes chances to improve performance and therefore access to promotion. Moreover, this culture has an uninformed and unsupportive attitude to disability, which is not only detrimental to career progression but also conducive to discrimination and hostility.

Rather than associating precariousness directly with a risk of failure, the disabled professionals we interviewed related it to a failure to achieve one's potential, i.e., a lack of opportunity to have one's abilities

recognized, one's performance scrutinized and one's voice heard. Ryan and Haslam (2007) argued that despite the increased risk of failure, taking on challenging high ranking appointments is not necessarily perceived as inherently problematic. Indeed, in the present context taking risks is seen as an opportunity to demonstrate potential and prove oneself. It is also an essential element of professional development and career progression. The main difference here resides in being allowed to take risks and having the chance to do so. It is with disbelief, anger and resentment that our interviewees realized the degree of inflexibility shown by their organizations and talked about the difficulties they had encountered as they fought both to have their skills fully acknowledged and to have their condition understood by those working with them. In line with the existing literature on individual barriers to career progression (Mowry and Anderson 1993; Roulstone et al. 2003), such battles are likely to discourage disabled professionals from seeking to advance their careers. They are also likely to make survival in the organization an uphill struggle entailing greater stress, reduced organizational identification and, ultimately, organizational exit (Ryan et al. 2007a).

Our research suggests that while disabled professionals can break through the glass ceiling and attain top ranking positions, their being there is often viewed by peers and subordinates as a result of diversity quotas, rather than an acknowledgement of their true abilities. As with those at lower levels of professional hierarchies (Hyde 1998), they are judged on the basis of disability rather than their expertise (Levinson and Parritt 2005), which makes policy interventions unlikely to have the desired impact on the participation of disabled professionals in the workforce (Prime Minister's Strategy Unit 2005).

A further point on the efficiency of equal opportunities policies related to a lack of knowledge, time and resources needed to help disabled professionals. A lack of knowledge about conditions, and of provisions needed to facilitate career progression, was instrumental in their marginalization in the workplace (French 2004), as were the absence of physical and technological resources (such as wheelchairs, ramps, lifts and specialized software) and the lack of informed human resources personnel who can assist with the procurement of such resources. It is apparent here that organizational concerns over the cost of hiring disabled professionals continue to be present for those at higher levels of management (Cunningham et al. 2004; Stevens 2002).

Present evidence suggests that precariousness for our participants was also related to the level of formal and informal support available, as they felt that there was little genuine interest in how they might be helped. In line with the existing literature (Albiston 2005; Shah 2005), our participants acknowledged that their drive and skills were actively encouraged and practically supported by inspirational individuals, rather than by the organizations they were working for. Our participants emphasized that being regarded first and foremost in a professional capacity constituted an essential step towards facilitating equal opportunities. A willingness and an ability to understand disability and the implementation of effective administrative procedures are both necessary to overcome the barriers disabled professionals face in sustaining and advancing their careers. These findings are consistent with recent research which outlined discrepancies between the formal adoption of equal opportunities policies and their practical implementation across the public and private sectors (Barnes and Mercer 2005; Cunningham et al. 2004) and supports the observation that employers' knowledge of the employment provisions of the Disability Discrimination Act (1996) remains vague or inaccurate (Hoque and Noon 2004).

Conclusions

Existing writing on disability is notably silent on the experiences of disabled employees in top ranking positions. The focus on breaking through the glass ceiling (Braddock and Bachelder 1994) has led to an assumption that at higher levels of management dealing with disability raises fewer issues. Moreover, while past research into the glass cliff provided an overview of the barriers faced by members of marginalized groups in career advancement (Ryan and Haslam 2005, 2007; Ryan et al. 2007a, 2007b), it did not examine in detail the specific challenges encountered by disabled professionals. It is important to understand such difficulties

in order to bridge the gap in the literature on disability and career advancement and to provide a sound basis for policy implementation.

The testimonies presented above show how, regardless of equal opportunity policies, disabled professionals are likely to encounter numerous challenges in maintaining their positions. Our evidence suggests that while diversity measures may be enough in some cases to allow some individuals to break through the glass ceiling, they often fail to support career advancement in the longer term. Indeed, disabled professionals come across unanticipated obstacles, and are often unable to overcome them. This inability is due to the widespread unwillingness of human resources departments, immediate line managers and peers to understand, acknowledge and accommodate their needs. Appointments are defined as precarious as a result of a lack of opportunity and influence, of knowledge about disability, of appropriate resources and of formal and informal support. The critical character of a precarious position is specified by the combination of these problematical circumstances, which together tend to make poor performance and failure more likely. These factors are rarely experienced as momentary, isolated or unconnected events, especially at a senior level, where the pressure to prove oneself and perform is extremely high.

While not representative of the work experiences of all disabled professionals, our findings illustrate a number of important barriers met in different public sector organizations. Further documentation of the experiences of disabled individuals in senior positions who have not faced obstacles in their career advancement and of those in the private sector is required in order to gain a detailed and comprehensive understanding of the opportunities and challenges various work environments raise for disabled professionals. Nevertheless, our findings suggest both generic structural patterns in the career advancement of professionals from marginalized groups and complex differences in their manifestation. They demonstrate the continuing gap between equal opportunities policies and everyday work cultures and the pervasiveness of this gap at the highest level of management. For this reason, it essential that the ways in which precariousness manifests itself are not overlooked in our analyses of employment, disability and career progression. It is even more important that organizations review their approaches to diversity and incorporate and address specific requirements as they are raised by those who need them most.

References

Albiston, C.R. 2005. Bargaining in the shadow of social institutions: Competing discourses and social change in workplace mobilization of civil rights. *Law and Society Review* 39, no. 1: 11–49.

Atkinson, P. 1990. *The ethnographic imagination*. London: Routledge.

Barnes, C., and G. Mercer. 2005. Disability, work, and welfare: Challenging the social exclusion of disabled people. *Work, Employment and Society* 19, no. 3: 527–45.

Braddock, D., and L. Bachelder. 1994. *The glass ceiling and persons with disabilities*. Key Workplace Documents Federal Publications. Ithaca, NY: Cornell University Press.

Cunningham, I., P. James, and P. Dibben. 2004. Bridging the gap between rhetoric and reality: Line managers and the protection of job security for ill workers in the modern workplace. *British Journal of Management* 15: 274–90.

French, S. 2004. Disabled health and caring professionals: The experiences of visually impaired physiotherapists. In *Disabling barriers, enabling environments*, ed. J. Swain, S. French, C. Barnes, and C. Thomas. London: Sage.

Garland-Thomson, R. 2005. Feminist disability studies. *Signs: Journal of Women in Culture and Society* 30, no. 2: 1557–87.

Glaser, B.G., and A. Strauss. 1967. *The discovery of grounded theory*. Chicago: Aldine.

Goldstone, C., and N. Meager. 2002. *Barriers to employment for disabled people*, Department for Work and Pensions in-house report 95. London: Department for Work and Pensions.

Heyl, B. 2001. Ethnographic interviewing. In *Handbook of ethnography*, ed. P. Atkinson. London: Sage.

Hoque, K., and M. Noon. 2004. Equal opportunity policy and practice in Britain: Evaluating the "empty shell" hypothesis. *Work, Employment and Society* 18, no. 3: 481–506.

Hyde, M. 1998. Sheltered and supported employment in the 1990s: The experiences of disabled workers in the UK. *Disability & Society* 13, no. 2: 199–215.

Jones, G.E. 1997. Advancement opportunity issues for persons with disabilities. *Human Resource Management Review* 7, no. 1: 55–76.

Kanter, R.M. 1977. *Men and women of the corporation*. New York: Basic Books.

Levinson, F., and S. Parritt. 2005. Against stereotypes: Experiences of disabled psychologists. In *Disability and psychology*, ed. D. Goodley and R. Lawthom. Basingstoke, UK: Palgrave Macmillan.

Morrison, A.M., and M.A. Von Glinow. 1990. Women and minorities in management. *American Psychologist* 45, no. 2: 200–8.

Mowry, R.L., and G.B. Anderson. 1993. Deaf adults tell their stories: Perspectives on barriers to job advancement and on-the-job accommodations. *The Volta Review* 95: 367–77.

Oliver, M. 1990. *The politics of disablement*. London: Macmillan.

Prime Minister's Strategy Unit. 2005. *Improving the life chances of disabled people*. Prime Minister's Strategy Unit. http://www.cabinetoffice.gov.uk/strategy/work_areas/disability.aspx.

Roulstone, A., L. Gradwell, J. Price, and L. Child. 2003. *Thriving and surviving at work: Disabled peoples' employment strategies*. London: Policy Press.

Ryan, M.K., and S.A. Haslam. 2005. The glass cliff: Evidence that women are over-represented in precarious leadership positions. *British Journal of Management* 16: 81–90.

———. 2007. The glass cliff: Exploring the dynamics surrounding the appointment of women to precarious leadership positions. *Academy of Management Review* 32, no. 2: 549–72.

Ryan, M.K., S.A. Haslam, M.D. Hersby, C. Kulich, and C. Atkins. 2007a. Opting out or pushed off the edge? The glass cliff and the precariousness of women's leadership positions. *Social and Personality Psychology Compass* 1: 266–79.

Ryan, M.K., S.A. Haslam, D. Wilson-Kovacs, M.D. Hersby, and C. Kulich. 2007b. *The glass cliff: Precariousness beyond the glass ceiling*, a CIPD Executive Briefing. London: Chartered Institute of Personnel and Development.

Shah, S. 2005. *Career success of disabled high-flyers*. London: Jessica Kingsley.

Stevens, G.R. 2002. Employers' perceptions and practice in the employability of disabled people: A survey of companies in Southeast UK. *Disability & Society* 17, no. 7: 779–96.

Stone, D.L., and A. Colella. 1996. A model of factors affecting the treatment of disabled individuals in organizations. *Academy of Management Review* 21, no. 2: 352–401.

Stuart, N., A. Watson, J. Williams, N. Meager, and D. Lain. 2002. How employers and service *providers are responding to the Disability Discrimination Act 1995*, Department for Work and Pensions in-house report 96. London: Department for Work and Pensions.

CHAPTER 36

Supporting a Diverse Workforce

What Type of Support Is Most Meaningful for Lesbian and Gay Employees?

Ann H. Huffman

Northern Arizona University

Kristen M. Watrous-Rodriguez

St. Mary's University

Eden B. King

George Mason University

Nearly 1.2 million adults across 99.3% of counties in the United States self-identified as being in a same-sex cohabiting relationship in the 2000 census (D. M. Smith & Gates, 2001). Additionally, lesbian, gay, and bisexual (LGB) employees constitute between 4% and 17% of the American workforce (Gonsiorek & Weinrich, 1991), yet few studies have examined issues facing LGB employees (Clark &

Serovich, 1997). Research suggests that LGB individuals experience unique stressors associated with their sexual identity (e.g., Waldo, 1999) arising from the negative attitudes held by the heterosexual population regarding homosexuality. Heterosexism, which can be defined as "an ideological system that denies, denigrates, and stigmatizes any non-heterosexual form of behavior, identity, relationship, or community" (Herek, 1992, p. 89), results in stereotypes, prejudice, and discrimination toward LGB individuals in society as a whole, and in workplaces in particular (N. S. Smith & Ingram, 2004; Waldo, 1999).

Many LGB individuals spend the majority of their lives isolated from fellow minority group members, as they typically live and work in predominantly heterosexual environments (Meyer, 1995; Waldo, 1999). Additionally, LGB individuals' minority status is not visually obvious to members of the larger population in the same sense as other minorities' status (e.g., ethnic minorities' physical appearance). Because of their minority status and similarity to other minority groups, LGB individuals experience a unique form of psychological distress, termed *minority stress,* that results from the discordance between their values, culture, and experiences and those of the dominant culture (Meyer, 1995). This stress may be particularly high for LGB individuals due to the lack of an obvious minority status marker. People with whom LGB individuals interact are often unaware of the LGB individual's sexual orientation (i.e., minority status) and thus may express values or ideas that denigrate homosexuality, increasing the LGB individual's stress. Most individuals, regardless of minority status, spend the majority of their days in the workplace. The disconnect felt by minority individuals between their identity and others' expectations at work can lead to additional organizational stressors.

Research indicates that social support can alleviate the negative outcomes of work-related stress among primarily heterosexual samples (Witt & Carlson, 2006). Social support at work can lessen negative organizational outcomes such as absenteeism (e.g., Godin & Kittel, 2004; Lowe, Schellenberg, & Shannon, 2003) and turnover intentions (e.g., Acker, 2004; Leung & Lee, 2006; Lowe et al., 2003) and lead to positive organizational outcomes such as job performance (e.g., AbuAlRub, 2004; Shanock & Eisenberger, 2006), organizational commitment (e.g., Lowe et al., 2003; Redman & Snape, 2006), and job satisfaction (e.g., Acker, 2004; Redman & Snape, 2006). Unfortunately, most research is conducted on the heterosexual population because they constitute the majority. It is important, however, to understand the different experiences of minority members (e.g., LGB employees) and the impact of work stress on them. Receiving individualized social support from a supervisor or colleague may not be enough for

LGB employees. They may require a broader type of support from the organization as a whole to decrease the negative outcomes associated with their specific job demands. For example, a gay employee might feel that his boss is fair in work decisions, yet he may be uncomfortable bringing his personal life (e.g., picture of partner) to work. This lack of support for his sexual orientation may lead him to experience the negative organizational outcomes discussed above.

The purpose of this study is to help researchers and human resource managers gain a better understanding of the work environment and employee diversity. We extend previous research by examining how three types of work-related support (i.e., supervisor, coworker, and organizational) are relevant to one understudied but important minority group, LGB employees. Additionally, we examine how these types of support affect organizational and personal outcomes. As such, this research contributes to existing knowledge regarding sources of support in organizations. Moreover, by focusing on sources of support for an important and understudied population (i.e., LGB workers), this article offers empirical evidence guiding the development of HR practices that improve the experiences of diverse employees.

Support and the Work Environment

Schneider (1987) argued that "attributes of people, not the nature of the external environment" (p. 437) are key determinants of employee behavior. Social support is a "meta-construct" (Vaux, 1988) rooted in interpersonal interactions at work that includes emotional (e.g., listening to distressed workers), instrumental (e.g., helping employees achieve promotion), and structural assistance (e.g., providing flextime for personal days) provided by individuals (e.g., supervisor support) or organizations (e.g., organizational support). Social exchange theory (Blau, 1964) explains that organizational support affects the employee-organization relationship (e.g., Casper, Martin, Buffardi, & Erdwins, 2002) such that employees who support their supervisor or organization may expect that gesture to be reciprocated (Eisenberger, Huntington, Hutchison, & Sowa, 1986).

Support may be shown in many ways across different levels. Supervisors may provide support via tangible benefits (e.g., a year-end bonus) or organizations could be supportive through intangible efforts (e.g., culture, Thomas & Ganster, 1995; family-friendly work environment, Allen, 2001). Overall, studies on the general population have shown that both instrumental and psychosocial forms of support, provided by individuals and organizations, are negatively related to work stress (Abdel-Halim, 1982; AbuAlRub, 2004; Ganster, Fusilier, & Mayes, 1986; Hagihara, Tarumi, & Miller, 1998; Luszczynska & Cieslak, 2005; Viswesvaran, Sanchez, & Fisher, 1999).

Types of Support

Supervisor support is one of the most direct types of support. Research on the general (i.e., primarily heterosexual) population has consistently shown that supervisor support is related to important job attitudes such as job satisfaction (Thomas & Ganster, 1995). While supervisor support has been associated with important outcomes, to our knowledge no studies have examined the effect of supervisor support on LGB employees specifically. Researchers have examined broader conceptualizations of support for LGB employees that encompass multiple sources of support (e.g., supervisors, peers, subordinates, Griffith & Hebl, 2002; organizational support, King, Reilly, Hebl, & Griffith, in press), but have not examined each source of support independently. LGB employees may experience supervisor support differently than their heterosexual coworkers and may require different types of support (e.g., support for their sexual identity). This article will examine supervisor support of LGB employees, thus filling an important gap in the extant literature.

Another type of support that has received less attention is coworker support (Thompson & Prottas, 2005). Research on the general population suggests that coworker support is negatively related to work distress (Frone, Yardley, & Markel, 1997; Loscocco & Spitze, 1990). Ragins, Singh, and Cornwell (2007) recently found that coworker support was associated with job satisfaction, commitment, and turnover intentions for LGB employees. To our knowledge, no empirical studies have assessed the unique effect of coworker support for LGB employees independent of organizational and supervisor support. This is another important understudied area that will be addressed in the current article.

Surprisingly, very little research on the general population (or the LGB population) has compared supervisor and coworker support. Most research examines organizational support, which represents a more global form of support, or supervisor support alone. We propose that the origin of the support leads to differences in types of support. Supervisors, but not coworkers, hold power over the recipient of the support (Frone, 2000) and "represent an organization," so their support might be construed as being directed or supported by the organization and organizational policy (Rhoades & Eisenberger, 2002). In contrast, coworkers' support may be assumed to be more personal. While the same specific behaviors can represent either type of support (e.g., attentive listening, providing advice, or helping with a job), the message and its reception might vary. For example, because supervisors may be viewed as an extension of the organization, employees may view attentive behavior by a supervisor as organizationally driven, which might increase their job satisfaction. In contrast, it is unlikely that a coworker's attentive behavior would be viewed as an organizationally driven act. As such, it might increase employees' overall satisfaction (e.g., life satisfaction), but not the more specific component of job satisfaction. In summary, due to the source of each type of support, we suggest that supervisor support and coworker support are two unique constructs.

Researchers also have suggested that different groups may need different types of support (Wortman & Dunkel-Schetter, 1987). Wayment and Peplau (1995) propose that lesbians might value social support related to their personal identity more so than heterosexual women because it supports their feelings of self-worth. With this in mind, we contend that organizational support for LGB employees (i.e., the extent to which the organization as a whole provides instrumental and psychosocial support for LGB employees) captures a unique and important component of the work environment. Organizational support for LGB employees describes issues such as whether LGB employees need to be secretive about their sexual identity, whether they can display pictures of partners, and their comfort level with talking about their personal lives. Examples of organizational support for LGB employees include organizational-level nondiscrimination policies, diversity training, and support for LGB activities or groups.

Companies described as LGB-supportive organizations have rejected heterosexist policies and instituted "gay-supportive" policies that show support for and acceptance of sexual orientation diversity. Recent research indicates that the experience of heterosexist behavior might be mitigated by the policies, procedures, and practices of organizations (King et al., in press). The existence of such support (which also has been labeled "LGB-supportive climate") is associated with decreased perceptions of discrimination (Button, 2001; Griffith & Hebl, 2002; Ragins & Cornwell, 2001). In contrast, organizations that do not take instances of heterosexism seriously report more heterosexism (Waldo, 1999). As mentioned previously, LGB employees differ from majority group members due to the occurrence of minority stress (Meyer, 1995). Although employees may experience minority stress in a work environment, we suggest that an LGB-supportive organization will lessen the negative experiences of LGB employees.

Support is very important for LGB employees due to the unique stressors they experience. Yet surprisingly, we found only four studies that examined LGB support in the workplace. Results of these studies indicate that top management support (Day & Schoenrade, 2000) and an LGB-supportive climate (Griffith & Hebl, 2002) relate to LGB employees' job satisfaction and that the presence of LGB-supportive policies relate to fewer discrimination reports by LGB employees (Button, 2001; Ragins & Cornwell, 2001). One additional study (Wayment & Peplau, 1995) examined non-work-related social support among lesbian women and found that reassurance of worth was a more important type of support for lesbians than heterosexual women. These findings suggest that LGB-specific support at work might be an important variable for gay and lesbian employees. However, the extant literature is lacking with reference to LGB employees' experience of workplace support. The current article will attempt to fill that gap.

We have described three interpersonal factors in the workplace: supervisor, coworker, and organizational support for LGB employees. We suggest that each offers a different type of encouragement or buffering for the employee but that they also differ. First, they differ in their levels. Organizational support is a high-level, inclusive construct focusing on organizational functions and environments that are needed for success while supervisor and coworker support are more proximal measures

involving emotional, instrumental, and structural assistance for employees. Further, whereas positive organizational support includes both *formal and informal* practices and procedures, supervisor and coworker support focus primarily on the informal practices that assist and support employees. Second, the three constructs differ in the loci of support. While supervisor and coworker support originate from a specific individual, organizational support for LGB employees is more diffuse, as it is related to the organization as a whole. The final difference between these three constructs regards the receiver of the support. Supervisor and coworker support are directed at an individual employee, whereas organizational support is directed at an entire identity group. Thus, while supervisor and coworker support may alleviate personal stressors, organizational support may be necessary for mitigating more global stressors tied to an LGB identity at work.

Support and General Outcomes: Job and Life Satisfaction

We argue that the three types of support are distinct and relate differentially to satisfaction. Specifically, we posit that the strength of the relationship depends on the type of support involved (i.e., supervisor, coworker, and organizational support for LGB employees). The differences between the constructs are anticipated to affect the strength of the relationship between perceptions of the work environment and job and life satisfaction.

Job satisfaction describes an affective response to one's job. Much research has been conducted on this construct (see Spector, 1997). Life satisfaction, a less studied variable, is a general affective evaluation of one's life, detailing feelings about one's life, including one's job.

We draw on two psychological models to make predictions about the interrelations between type of support and type of satisfaction. First, the compatibility principle suggests that attitudes should match behavioral (and, by extension, attitudinal) criteria in level of abstraction (Ajzen & Fishbein, 1977). Two elements of attitudes specified by Ajzen and Fishbein are important in explaining the relationships between job and life satisfaction and our support variables: (1) target (i.e., focus of behavior) and (2) context (i.e., environment in which the behavior occurs). Further, predictive efficiency between constructs improves when these elements are similar. In terms of "target," attitudes toward the supervisor are more likely to relate to work outcomes (i.e., job satisfaction) than nonwork outcomes (i.e., life satisfaction). With this in mind, we posit that the most proximal type of support (i.e., supervisor support) would be most related to job satisfaction. Conversely, the more distal types of support (i.e., coworker and LGB support) would be more related to general satisfaction (i.e., life satisfaction). With this in mind, we posit that the most proximal type of support (i.e., supervisor support) would be most related to job satisfaction. Conversely, the more distal types of support (i.e., coworker and LGB support) would be more related to general satisfaction (i.e., life satisfaction).

Second, we use Frone's (2000) framework of interpersonal conflict and psychological outcomes to describe how different types of support affect job satisfaction. Drawing from Fiske's (1992) general theory of social relations, Frone suggested that coworkers' relationships can be described as communal sharing; coworkers focus on similarities and want to be liked by one another. In contrast, supervisor-subordinate relationships are based on authority ranking. The supervisor is seen as directly tied to the job, thus any negative interactions affect employees' feelings toward the job and organization. Frone's research supports his contention that interpersonal conflict with a supervisor negatively affects perceptions of the job, while conflict with coworkers negatively impacts perceptions of the self. Extending this logic, we expect that supervisor support will affect job attitudes (i.e., increase job satisfaction) to a greater extent than coworker support. Similarly, since organizational support is organization- rather than job-specific, we suggest that it would have less effect on job satisfaction than supervisor support.

H1a: Supervisor support is more strongly related to job satisfaction than coworker support or organizational support for LGB employees.

Regarding life satisfaction, we propose that since coworker support is more communal and not based exclusively on the job, it is more closely related to life satisfaction than supervisor support is. Organizational support for LGB employees offers a global affirmation of one's sexual identity so it likely extends beyond the specific job, meaning it also should demonstrate a stronger relationship with life satisfaction than supervisor support.

H1b: Coworker support and organizational support for LGB employees are more strongly related to life satisfaction than supervisor support.

Support and LGB-Specific Outcomes: Outness

Organizational research has focused on outness, one's willingness to disclose his or her sexual identity, due to the costs and benefits to the employee of disclosure (Ragins et al., 2007). Costs of disclosure include negative outcomes such as discrimination (e.g., Croteau & Lark, 1995), threats (Herek, 1995), and negative verbal exchanges (Bradford, Ryan, & Rothblum, 1994). Benefits include worker satisfaction (Day & Schoenrade, 1997; Griffith & Hebl, 2002) and organizational commitment (Day & Schoenrade, 1997, 2000; Ellis & Riggle, 1995). Research (e.g., Van Den Bergh, 1999; Wells & Button, 2004) indicates that outness also positively affects general wellbeing (e.g., mental, physical, and spiritual health), which can only serve to benefit the organization. Van Den Bergh (1999) stressed that "for lesbians and gay men to be the most productive at the workplace and the most involved within organizational cultures, it is critical that they feel safe in not hiding their sexual orientation" (1999, p. 23). Similarly, Wells and Button (2004) stated that being out at work "may combat isolation, bolster efficacy, engender social support for occupational goals, and allow the individual to contribute more fully to the organization's success" (2004, p. 151). While specific figures are difficult to calculate, Van Den Bergh (2003) reported that only 33% of lesbians and 62% of gay men were out. As such, we must ask, what can organizations do to allow employees to feel free to be "out"?

We believe the answer lies in support. In line with the extant literature, we propose that a supportive environment encourages sexual identity disclosure, thus enabling positive organizational attitudes (i.e., job satisfaction, organizational commitment) to occur. Indeed, research indicates that perceived workplace discrimination is related to sexual identity disclosure (Ragins & Cornwell, 2001); that LGB employees are more likely to disclose their sexual identity when nondiscrimination policies are in place (Ros-tosky & Riggle, 2002); and that employees in gay-supportive organizations are more likely to be out than those who are not (Griffith & Hebl, 2002; Waldo, 1999). It is important to note that these studies only examined organizational-level support for LGB employees; they did not examine different *types* of support. The present study will examine whether an overall supportive environment is required for LGB employees to be out or whether informal coworker and supervisor support is sufficient.

We propose that type of support should influence outness. Specifically, we argue that organizational support for LGB employees should have a stronger influence on outness than coworker support (e.g., workgroups in which coworkers cover for each other when one of them is absent) or supervisor support. LGB individuals employed in LGB-supportive organizations are protected by nondiscrimination policies and supported by gay-friendly policies. As such, they are more likely to feel comfortable disclosing their sexual orientation to fellow employees.

H2: Organizational support for LGB employees is more closely related to LGB outcomes (i.e., outness) than is supervisor support or coworker support.

Method

Participants

Participants (N = 99) who were employed and identified themselves as either gay or lesbian (95.7%) or bisexual (4.3%) were recruited for the present study. The average age was 36.5 (SD = 8.78) and 61.7% were male. Regarding race, 84.0% of participants identified themselves as white, 13.8% as Hispanic, 1.1% as African-American or black, and 2.1% as Asian.

Of our sample, 47.9% reported being involved in a long-term committed relationship and 14.9% had children. Concerning education, 2.1% of our sample reported having a high school degree or equivalent, 19.1% reported having completed some college, 40.4% reported having a college degree, and 38.3% reported completing some postgraduate coursework and/or a degree.

Procedure

Participants were recruited via two methods. First, researchers requested participation from patrons at gay-supportive establishments (e.g., restaurants, coffeehouses). Second, researchers solicited participants at a gay-pride event. Participants recruited at the gay-pride event were offered a chance to participate in a drawing for a gift certificate to a local restaurant in which two (out of 100 total) would win. Both data collections occurred in a large city in the southwestern United States. Of the individuals approached, the response rate was approximately 90%.

Measures

Sexual Identity

Participants were asked to identify their sexual orientation with the question, "What is your sexual identity?" with response choices of gay/lesbian, transgendered, bisexual, transsexual, and heterosexual.

Supervisor Support

Supervisor support was assessed with a revised Perceived Organizational Support Scale (Eisenberger et al., 1986; α = .93), which examines employees' perceptions of the extent to which their supervisor values the contribution of and cares about the well-being of his or her employees. The eight-item scale was accompanied by a five-point response scale (1 = strongly disagree, 5 = strongly agree). The full list of items is available from the first author upon request.

Coworker Support

Coworker support was assessed with the seven-item Coworker Support Scale (α = .90; Baruch-Feldman, Brondolo, Ben-Dayan, & Schwartz, 2002). Response items ranged from strongly disagree (1) to strongly agree (5). The entire scale is available from the first author upon request.

Organizational Support for LGB Employees

A revised version of Liddle, Luzzo, Hauenstein, and Schuck's (2004) Lesbian, Gay, Bisexual, and Transgendered Climate Inventory (LGBTCI) was used to assess participants' perceptions of the level of support for LGB employees in their workplaces ($\alpha = .96$). The LGBTCI is a 20-item scale with a response scale that ranges from (1) "does not describe at all" to (4) "describes extremely well." We conducted an exploratory factor analysis to ascertain whether the scale consisted of multiple factors and found that approximately 60% of the variance was accounted for with one factor (the second component was 7%). Further, we examined the factor loadings and found that all were over .57 for the first factor (.40 is the usual required cutoff; Hatcher, 1994), suggesting a unidimensional scale. Contact the first author for the full scale.

Job Satisfaction

Job satisfaction was measured with Cammann, Fichman, Jenkins, and Klesh's (1983) three-item measure of global job satisfaction. An example item is "In general, I like working here" ($\alpha = .90$). The scale uses a five-point response format ranging from strongly disagree (1) to strongly agree (5).

Life Satisfaction

Satisfaction with life was assessed using Diener, Emmons, Larsen, and Griffin's (1985) five-item measure. An example item is "The conditions of my life are excellent" ($\alpha = .88$). The scale is accompanied by a five-point response format, ranging from strongly disagree (1) to strongly agree (5).

Outness

Openness of sexual orientation was measured using a five-item scale that asked respondents to rate the degree to which they are open about their sexual orientation with coworkers, management, friends, family, and in life in general (Waldo, 1999). Response choices range from not at all (1) to completely open (5). We included the only two items from the scale that were specific to work (i.e., with coworkers and management in the workplace).

Discriminant Validity of the Three Support Variables

Since the support variables were similar, we wanted to determine if they were three distinct factors. We compared two theoretical models of the latent support construct using confirmatory factor analysis (CFA). A three-factor model (Model 1) conceptualized support as having three dimensions: supervisor, coworker, and organizational support for LGB employees. A simple one-factor model (Model 2) conceptualized support as one general construct. A CFA (Joreskog & Sörbom, 1979) was conducted to assess the difference in fit between the hypothesized three-factor model and the one-factor model. The chi-square value obtained from the three-factor model was contrasted with the chi-square value obtained from the one-factor model, and the results indicated that support is best measured as a multidimensional construct with three separate but related factors: supervisor, coworker, and organizational support for LGB employees (see Table 36.1). Additionally, the correlations between the organizational support factor and the other support factors suggested discriminant validity. Specifically, supervisor support and organizational support were moderately related ($r = .36$) and coworker support and organizational support were moderately related ($r = .45$), suggesting some discrimination between the constructs. We also examined correlation matrices to inspect differences between within-item and between-item relationships. Results showed that within-item coefficients were higher (coworker support ranged from .24 to .69; supervisor support ranged from .35 to .87; and organizational support ranged from .28 to .80) than between-item coefficients (supervisor-organizational ranged from .03 to .40; coworker-organizational ranged from .00 to .47; and coworker-supervisor ranged from .19 to .57).

Results

The means, standard deviations, and inter-correlations for all key variables are included in Table 36.2.

Hypothesis 1a proposed that supervisor support would be more strongly related to job satisfaction than coworker support or organizational support for LGB employees. We regressed the coworker support, supervisor support, and organizational support for LGB employees variables on job satisfaction and found that only supervisor support was significantly related to job satisfaction ($\beta = .43$, $p < .01$), thus supporting Hypothesis 1a (see Table 36.3).

Table 36.1	Chi-Square Test for Support Models				

Model	Observed χ^2	Df	$\Delta\chi^2$	Δ Df	Expected χ^2
3-Factor Model	1494.85	591			
1-Factor Model	2308.30	594			
			867.35*	3	7.82

*$p < .05$.

Table 36.2	Descriptive Statistics, Reliabilities (When Applicable), and Correlations

	M	SD	1	2	3	4	5	6
1. Supervisor Support	3.88	0.82	(.93)					
2. Coworker Support	4.02	0.69	.58**	(.90)				
3. LGB-Supportive Climate	3.01	0.75	.36**	.45**	(.96)			
4. Job Satisfaction	3.81	0.86	.52**	.38**	.25*	(.90)		
5. Life Satisfaction	4.65	1.38	.27**	.42**	.21*	.34**	(.88)	
6. Outness at Work	3.85	1.29	.18	.29**	.63**	.10	.20	(.84)

Notes: N = 98. Reliabilities (coefficient alphas) are along the diagonal in parentheses.
*$p < .05$, **$p < .01$.

Hypothesis 1b predicted that coworker support and organizational support for LGB employees would be more strongly related to life satisfaction than supervisor support. We regressed the coworker support, supervisor support, and organizational support for LGB employees variables on life satisfaction and found that only coworker support was significantly related to life satisfaction ($\beta = .39, p < .01$), offering partial support for Hypothesis 1b.

Hypothesis 2 stated that organizational support for LGB employees should be more closely related to LGB outcomes (i.e., outness) than supervisor support or coworker support. We regressed the coworker support, supervisor support, and organizational support for LGB employees variables on outness at work and found that only organizational support for LGB employees was significantly related to outness at work ($\beta = .63, p < .01$), in support of Hypothesis 2.

Discussion

Gay and lesbian employees are an integral part of the U.S. workforce (Van Den Bergh, 2003). It is both a responsibility and a strategic advantage for human resource managers to understand LGB workplace diversity. Results from the current study indicate that human resource practitioners should work to ensure that LGB employees feel supported by their supervisors, coworkers, and overall organization.

| Table 36.3 | Support Variables in Relationship to Job Satisfaction, Life Satisfaction, and Outness at Work |

	Job Satisfaction			Life Satisfaction			Outness at Work		
	B	*SE B*	*Adjusted R²*	*B*	*SE B*	*Adjusted R²*	*B*	*SE B*	*Adjusted R²*
Supervisor Support	.45**	.12		.06	.20		−.12	.16	
Coworker Support	.16	.15		.77**	.25		.10	.20	
LGB Support	.05	.12		.04	.20		1.09**	.16	
Model			.26			.15			.38

$N = 93$. **$p < .01$, *$p < .05$

Our results provide clear evidence that supervisor, coworker, and organizational support for LGB employees are similar yet unique constructs. We proposed these types of support would differ due to the level of the constructs, the loci of support, and the target of the support. Our results add empirical evidence to prior research that conceptualizes organizational support as a complex, multidimensional construct (e.g., Thompson & Prottas, 2005).

Moreover, we found that different types of support are differentially related to individual attitudes. Specifically, supervisor support was more strongly related to job satisfaction than either coworker or organizational support for LGB employees, and coworker support was more strongly related to life satisfaction than supervisor or organizational support. Our findings are consistent with Ajzen and Fishbein's (1977) compatibility principle. We found that job-specific attitudes (i.e., supervisor support) are more closely related to other job-specific attitudes (i.e., job satisfaction) than to general attitudes (i.e., life satisfaction). Conversely, general, non-job-specific attitudes (i.e., coworker support) are more strongly related to other general attitudes (i.e., life satisfaction) than specific attitudes (i.e., supervisor support).

Our results are also in line with Frone's (2000) framework of interpersonal conflict, as we found that supervisor support did affect job satisfaction. We should note, however, that our results failed to support the hypothesis that organizational support for LGB employees would be strongly related to life satisfaction. We propose two reasons for this nonsignificant finding. First, it could be a statistical power issue. Our small *N* size could have affected whether the relationship was statistically significant; however, the biserial correlation between these variables was .20, which represents a small to medium effect size ($d = .41$; Cohen, 1988). Second, organizational support may be just one aspect of LGB individuals' daily life. Following the level of abstraction argument (Azjen & Fishbein, 1977), it may be that life satisfaction is determined to a large extent by nonwork factors such as support from one's family of origin.

Finally, we found that organizational support for LGB employees had a stronger relationship with outness than supervisor and coworker support. This is in line with previous research showing that nondiscrimination polices (Rostosky & Riggle, 2002) and gay-supportive organizations (Griffith & Hebl, 2002; Waldo, 1999) are related to sexual identity disclosure.

Implications

Our results provide evidence that support encountered at work is positively related to work and personal outcomes. We examined the contribution that the support variables provide in explaining job and life satisfaction and found that supervisor, coworker, and organizational support for LGB employees explained 26% of the variability in job satisfaction, 15% in life satisfaction, and 38% in outness at work. It is obvious that all three types of support are important and, therefore, organizations should attempt to create an atmosphere in which each form of support is available to LGB employees.

In addition, organizations can focus efforts on particular outcomes by targeting particular types of support. For example, managers experiencing a decrease in job satisfaction can focus their energies on adequately supporting LGB employees, thereby increasing levels of the outcome of interest. Strategies to increase support such as leader modeling of supportive behaviors (Wayne, Shore, & Liden, 1997) and allowing individuals to participate in decision making (Rhoades & Eisenberger, 2002) are discussed in the literature.

Very little research has focused on organizational support for LGB employees. Our results suggest that it is important for organizations to develop an LGB-supportive workplace so that employees can be open regarding their sexual orientation. An LGB-supportive workplace likely maintains formal policies supporting LGB workers, such as same-sex partner benefits, nondiscrimination policies, and zero tolerance for heterosexist acts. In addition, LGB-supportive organizations would support employees with informal norms such as including same-sex partners in social events and using non-heterosexist language in company communication (see Ragins & Cornwell, 2001). This type of environment may be implemented through training programs, the institution of formal equity policies, or the creation of LGB networks.

The results of the present study could guide these efforts in several ways. First, the results suggest that LGB-supportive training programs might take a theoretical integrative approach to include support-based training. Specifically, training might focus on ways to be a fair and supportive employee, colleague, and/or supervisor. Additionally, such training could include a diversity element to educate employees about different perspectives and ways to be supportive of diverse individuals. Training and education should be implemented at all levels, including top management since their support affects employee job satisfaction (Day & Schoenrade, 2000).

Second, managers might create an atmosphere of acceptance by writing a statement affirming the organization's support for LGB employees (Button, 2001) that could be included in organizational information (e.g., website, pamphlets), increasing LGB applicants and employees in the organization. This statement also may increase outness among current LGB employees, which could increase worker satisfaction (Day & Schoenrade, 1997; Griffith & Hebl, 2002) and affective commitment (Day & Schoenrade, 1997). Finally, this act may increase acceptance of the organization and/or its products among the LGB population.

Third, organizations also could support informal or formal LGB networks (Button, 2001), offering employees a social network among the minority group. The provision of opportunities to network with similar others enables LGB employees to identify and socialize with individuals who share their experiences, which may lessen minority stress and alleviate their psychological distress (Meyer, 1995; Waldo, 1999). These networks could increase awareness of LGB employees and the organization's support for them, which could decrease heterosexism. Organizations would benefit from reduced heterosexism via the positive effects on psychological health (N. S. Smith & Ingram, 2004; Waldo, 1999), job anxiety (Griffith & Hebl, 2002), job satisfaction (Button, 2001: Griffith & Hebl, 2002), and organizational commitment (Button, 2001).

Fourth, organizations could conduct a survey to determine how supportive the organization's culture is by assessing whether the environment is hostile to LGB employees, whether people feel comfortable being openly gay, and whether there are openly gay individuals in management. This would provide a gauge of the current conditions and indicate what the organization needs to change or maintain.

In general, there are several ways that managers can influence the level of general and LGB support in their workgroup. We have suggested several in-depth ideas above and we also provide a list of suggested strategies in Table 36.4. These behaviors are actions that

Table 36.4	Managers' Actions to Promote a Supportive Environment		

Supervisor Action	Support Supervisor	Coworker Support	LGB Support
Provide mentoring opportunities (Triandis, Kurowski, & Gelfand, 1994; Van Den Bergh, 1999)	X		X
Plan social networking events (Button, 2001; Van Den Bergh, 2003)	X	X	X
Self-evaluate own actions concerning employees (Triandis et al., 1994)	X	X	X
Interact with employees from diverse group (Triandis et al., 1994)			X
Initiate Intercultural Training and Workshops for employees and managers (Button, 2001; Griffith & Hebl, 2002; Van Den Bergh, 1999, 2003)			X
Let job applicants know in interview process that organization is all-inclusive (Griffith & Hebl, 2002; Powers, 1996; Van Den Bergh, 2003)			X
Ask minority employees to point out current practices that are not supportive (Powers, 1996)			X
Welcome same sex partners to social events (Powers, 1996; Ragins & Cornwell, 2001; Van Den Bergh, 2003; Wells & Button, 2004)			X
Do not assume "majority/minority" status of any employee (Powers, 1996; Van Den Bergh, 2003)	X	X	X
Assess the climate for minority employees (e.g., surveys, Human Rights Campaign WorkNet)			X
Ask HR to include specific minorities (e.g., LGB) in content of current diversity training (Human Rights Campaign WorkNet, n.d.)			X
Schedule meetings with leadership/members of current LGB support group or list serve (Human Rights Campaign WorkNet, n.d.)			X
Become familiar with LGB organizations that monitor workplace discrimination and harassment (Van Den Bergh, 2003)			X
Allow employees time off for whoever the employee deems to be "family" (Van Den Bergh, 2003)	X		X
Use all inclusive language (e.g., partner versus spouse; Van Den Bergh, 1999) and respond negatively to homophonic statements (Powers, 1996)			X

Note: The X shows what type of the support is most strongly related to the supervisor behavior. We should note that all of the listed supervisor's behaviors are somehow directly or indirectly related to all three types of support.

managers have the power to enact (versus higher-level interventions such as same-sex benefits). Additionally, these behaviors can be directed toward any minority employee, not only LGB employees.

As mentioned previously, LGB employees lack an obvious minority status marker. Many other individuals experience invisible stigmas such as illness (e.g., mental illness, cancer), religious beliefs, being a sexual assault victim, or socioeconomic class (Ragins, in press). Our findings could be relevant to these groups. There may be some support-related factors that are common to these groups. Organizations may be able to develop an "umbrella of tolerance" that provides protection, support, and equality to individuals in all minority groups.

Finally, our findings are similar to those of other studies on minorities in the workplace. For example, Burke (1991) found that racial minorities employed in organizations that support and affirm racial diversity are more likely to be satisfied with their job.

Limitations and Future Studies

Although this study makes several important contributions, we also must acknowledge its limitations. First, the data were based on self-report measures that may be influenced by a tendency to respond in a socially desirable manner. Similarly, common method bias may be a concern since the study employed a cross-sectional design with all the variables coming from one single source (i.e., the survey). Second, our participants were surveyed at "gay-friendly" locations, most at a gay pride event, which is frequented by a very "out" population. These individuals may differ from less "out" LGB individuals in work attitudes and the processes related to them. Third, the sample consisted predominantly of white, educated males; thus, for the majority of our sample, the only minority status they experience is their sexual orientation. In contrast, many LGB individuals are members of racial or gender minority groups or are less educated than our sample, thus adding to their minority status. We cannot generalize our findings to less educated or more racially diverse LGB employees. Finally, we did not collect information concerning the organizations of our sample (e.g., diversity programs,

size of company, location). Future studies must find ways to include a more representative sample of LGB employees.

We included standardized support measures used in past research but we could have included additional measures and questions that would allow further explication of the context of the employee. For example, we did not include a general organizational support scale. Assessing perceptions of general organizational support would have allowed us to ascertain whether LGB-specific support is unique in predicting satisfaction. It also would have been helpful to know whether the participants' supervisor or coworkers were aware of the participant's sexual identity.

Although we found evidence of differences between types of support, we did not test *why* these types of support are different. We provided a framework to explain why we believe they are different (i.e., uniqueness in support is due to differences in the level of the constructs, the loci of support, and the target of support). It would be interesting to empirically test this framework to understand more about the processes involved in the different types of support. Future research should examine the experiences of other minority groups (e.g., racial or gender minorities) and determine the impact of support type on their workplace experiences and personal outcomes. In addition, future research should empirically test the relative efficacy of each of the strategies suggested for creating organizational support for LGB workers.

Conclusion

In the ideal workplace, there would be one organizational support construct that considers tolerance, respect, and support for *all* people from *all* groups. We would not have to designate a "family-friendly," "LGB-friendly," "race-friendly," or "age-friendly" culture, for it would be an "employee-friendly" or "people-friendly" culture. Unfortunately, the workforce is far from reaching such a lofty goal. We will have to continue to educate and train employees about specific minority populations, and continue to conduct research to assess how well we are faring in trying to achieve a bias-free, "people-friendly" workplace.

The reality is that in today's workforce a large number of employees are likely to come from disadvantaged social identity groups and, in most cases, their unique needs and experiences require understanding and respect. Results from the present study highlight the importance of acknowledging and understanding diverse employees and the issues they face in the workplace. For one minority group, LGB employees, support from coworkers, supervisors, and the overall organization differentially influences important outcomes such as job and life satisfaction and outness. Future research and practice must continue to be aware of sexual orientation diversity and its impact on organizational and personal outcomes.

References

Abdel-Halim, A. A. (1982). Social support and managerial affective responses to job stress. Journal of Occupational Behavior, 3, 281–295.

AbuAlRub, R. F. (2004). Job stress, job performance, and social support among hospital nurses. Journal of Nursing Scholarship, 36, 73–78.

Acker, G. M. (2004). The effect of organizational conditions (role conflict, role ambiguity, opportunities for professional development, and social support) on job satisfaction and intention to leave among social workers in mental health care. Community Mental Health Journal, 40, 65–73.

Ajzen, I., & Fishbein, M. (1977). Attitude-behavior relations: A theoretical analysis and review of empirical research. Psychological Bulletin, 84, 888–918.

Allen, T. D. (2001). Family-supportive work environments: The role of organizational perceptions. Journal of Vocational Behavior, 58, 414–435.

Baruch-Feldman, C., Brondolo, E., Ben-Dayan, D., & Schwartz, J. (2002). Sources of social support and burnout, job satisfaction and productivity. Journal of Occupational Health Psychology, 7, 84–93.

Blau, P. M. (1964). Exchange and power in social life. New York: Wiley.

Bradford, J., Ryan, C., & Rothblum, E. D. (1994). National lesbian health care survey: Implications for mental health care. Journal of Consulting and Clinical Psychology, 62, 228–242.

Burke, R. J. (1991). Work experiences of minority managers and professionals: Individual and organizational costs of perceived bias. Psychological Reports, 69, 1011–1023.

Button, B. (2001). Organizational efforts to affirm sexual diversity: A cross-level examination. Journal of Applied Psychology, 86, 17–28.

Cammann, C., Fichman, M., Jenkins, G. D., & Klesh, J. (1983). Michigan organizational assessment questionnaire. In S. E. Seashore, E. E. Lawler, P. H. Mirvis, & C. Camman (Eds.), Assessing organizational change: A guide to methods, measures, and practices (pp. 71–138). New York: Wiley.

Casper, W. J., Martin, J. A., Buffardi, L. C., & Erdwins, C. J. (2002). Work-family conflict, perceived organizational support, and organizational commitment among employed mothers. Journal of Occupational Health Psychology, 7, 99–108.

Clark, W. M., & Serovich, J. M. (1997). Twenty years and still in the dark? Content analysis of articles pertaining to gay, lesbian and bisexual issues in marriage and family therapy journals. Journal of Marital and Family Therapy, 23, 239–253.

Cohen, J. (1988). Statistical power analysis for the behavioral sciences (2nd ed.). Hillsdale, NJ: Lawrence Erlbaum Associates.

Croteau, J. M., & Lark, J. S. (1995). On being lesbian, gay or bisexual in student affairs: A national survey of experiences on the job. NASPA Journal, 32, 189–197.

Day, N. E., & Schoenrade, P. (1997). Staying in the closet versus coming out: Relationships between communication about sexual orientation and work attitudes. Personnel Psychology, 50, 147–163.

Day, N. E., & Schoenrade, P. (2000). The relationship among reported disclosure of sexual orientation, anti-discrimination policies, top management support and work attitudes of gay and lesbian employees. Personnel Review, 29, 346–363.

Diener, E., Emmons, R. A., Larsen, R. J., & Griffin, S. (1985). The satisfaction with life scale. Journal of Personality Assessment, 49, 71–75.

Eisenberger, R., Huntington, R., Hutchison, S., & Sowa, D. (1986). Perceived organizational support. Journal of Applied Psychology, 71, 500–507.

Ellis, A., & Riggle, E. (1995). The relation of job satisfaction and degree of openness about one's sexual orientation for lesbians and gay men. Journal of Homosexuality, 30, 75–85.

Fiske, A. P. (1992). The four elementary forms of sociability: Framework for a unified theory of social relations. Psychological Review, 99, 689–723.

Frone, M. R. (2000). Interpersonal conflict at work and psychological outcomes: Testing a model among young workers. Journal of Occupational Health Psychology, 5, 246–255.

Frone, M. R., Yardley, J. K., & Markel, K. S. (1997). Developing and testing an integrative model of the work-family interface. Journal of Vocational Behavior, 50, 145–167.

Ganster, D. C., Fusilier, M. R., & Mayes, B. T. (1986). Role of social support in the experience of stress at work. Journal of Applied Psychology, 71, 102–110.

Godin, I., & Kittel, F. (2004). Differential economic stability and psychosocial stress at work: Associations with psychosomatic complaints and absenteeism. Social Science and Medicine, 58, 1543–1553.

Gonsiorek, J. C., & Weinrich, J. D. (1991). The definition and scope of sexual orientation. In J. C. Gonsiorek & J. D. Weinich (Eds.), Homosexuality: Research implications for public policy (pp. 1–12). Newbury Park, CA: Sage.

Griffith, K. H., & Hebl, M. R. (2002). The disclosure dilemma for gay men and lesbians: "Coming out" at work. Journal of Applied Psychology, 87, 1191–1199.

Hagihara, A., Tarumi, K., & Miller, A. S. (1998). Social support at work as a buffer of work stress-strain relationship: A signal detection approach. Stress Medicine, 14, 75–81.

Hatcher, L. (1994). A step-by-step approach to using the SAS system for factor analysis and structural equation modeling. Cary, NC: SAS Publishing.

Herek, G. M. (1992). The social context of hate crimes: Notes on cultural heterosexism. In G. M. Herek & K. T. Berrill (Eds.), Hate crimes: Confronting violence against lesbians and gay men (pp. 89–104). Newbury Park, CA: Sage.

Herek, G. M. (1995). Psychological heterosexism in the United States. In A. R. D'Augelli & C. J. Patterson (Eds.), Lesbian, gay and bisexual identities over the lifespan? Psychological perspectives (pp. 321–346). New York: Oxford University Press.

Human Rights Campaign WorkNet. (n.d.). Introduction to Gay Issues in the workplace: Achieving a nondiscrimination policy that includes sexual orientation. [Brochure]. Washington, DC: Author.

Jöreskog, K. G., & Sörbom, D. (1979). Advances in factor analysis and structural equation models. Cambridge, MA: Abt Books.

King, E. B., Reilly, C. A., Hebl, M. R., & Griffith, K. (in press). The best and worst of times: Exploring dual perspectives of coming out at work. Group and Organization Management.

Leung, D. Y. P., & Lee, W. W. S. (2006). Predicting intention to quit among Chinese teachers: Differential predictability of the components of burnout. Anxiety, Stress and Coping: An International Journal, 19, 129–141.

Liddle, B. J., Luzzo, D. A., Hauenstein, A. L., & Schuck, K. (2004). Construction and validation of the lesbian, gay, bisexual and transgendered climate inventory. Journal of Career Assessment, 12, 33–50.

Loscocco, K. A., & Spitze, G. (1990). Working conditions, social support, and the well-being of female and male factory workers. Journal of Health and Social Behavior, 31, 313–327.

Lowe, G. S., Schellenberg, G., & Shannon, H. S. (2003). Correlates of employees' perceptions of a healthy work environment. American Journal of Health Promotion, 17, 390–399.

Luszczynska, A., & Cieslak, R. (2005). Protective, promotive, and buffering effects of perceived social support in managerial stress: The moderating role of personality. Anxiety, Stress and Coping: An International Journal, 18, 227–244.

Meyer, I. (1995). Minority stress and mental health in gay men. Journal of Health Sciences and Social Behavior, 36, 38–56.

Powers, B. (1996). The impact of gay, lesbian, and bisexual workplace issues on productivity. In A. L. Ellis and E. D. B. Riggle (Eds.), Sexual identity on the job: Issues and services (pp. 79–90). New York: Harrington Park Press.

Ragins, B. R. (in press). Disclosure disconnects: Antecedents and consequence of disclosing invisible stigmas across life domains. Academy of Management Review.

Ragins, B. R., & Cornwell, J. M. (2001). Pink triangles: Antecedents and consequences of perceived workplace discrimination against gay and lesbian employees. Journal of Applied Psychology, 86, 1244–1261.

Ragins, B. R., Singh, R., & Cornwell, J. M. (2007). Making the invisible visible: Fear and disclosure of sexual orientation at work. Journal of Applied Psychology, 92, 1103–1118.

Redman, T., & Snape, E. (2006). The consequences of perceived age discrimination amongst older police officers: Is social support a buffer? British Journal of Management, 17, 167–175.

Rhoades, L., & Eisenberger, R. (2002). Perceived organizational support: A review of the literature. Journal of Applied Psychology, 87, 698–714.

Rostosky, S. S., & Riggle, E. D. B. (2002). "Out" at work: The relation of actor and partner workplace policy and internalized homophobia to disclosure status. Journal of Counseling Psychology, 49, 411–419.

Schneider, B. (1987). The people make the place. Personnel Psychology, 40, 437–453.

Shanock, L. R., & Eisenberger, R. (2006). When supervisors feel supported: Relationships with subordinates' perceived supervisor support, perceived organizational support, and performance. Journal of Applied Psychology, 91, 689–695.

Smith, D. M., & Gates, G. (2001). Gay and lesbian families in the United States: Same-sex unmarried partner households. Retrieved April 12, 2007 from: http://www.urban.org/publications/1000491.html.

Smith, N. S., & Ingram, K. M. (2004). Workplace heterosexism and adjustment among lesbian, gay, and bisexual individuals: The role of unsupportive social interactions. Journal of Counseling Psychology, 31, 57–67.

Spector, P. E. (1997). Job satisfaction: Application, assessment, causes, and consequences. Thousand Oaks, CA: Sage.

Thomas, L. T., & Ganster, D. C. (1995). Impact of family-supportive work variables on work-family conflict and strain: A control perspective. Journal of Applied Psychology, 80, 6–15.

Thompson, C. A., & Prottas, D. J. (2005). Relationships among organizational family support, job autonomy, perceived control, and employee well-being. Journal of Occupational Health Psychology, 10, 100–118.

Triandis, H. C., Kurowski, L. L., & Gelfand, M. J. (1994). Workplace diversity. In H. C. Triandis, M. D. Dunnette, & L. M. Hough (Eds.), Handbook of industrial and organizational psychology (Vol. 4, pp. 267–313). Palo Alto, CA: Consulting Psychologists Press.

Van Den Bergh, N. (1999). Workplace problems and needs for lesbian and gay male employees: Implications for EAPs. Employee Assistance Quarterly, 15, 21–60.

Van Den Bergh, N. (2003). Getting a piece of the pie: Cultural competence for GLBT employees at the workplace. Journal of Human Behavior in the Social Environment, 8, 55–73.

Vaux, A. (1988). Social support: Theory, research and intervention. New York: Praeger.

Viswesvaran, C., Sanchez, J. I., & Fisher, J. (1999). The role of social support in the process of work stress: A meta-analysis. Journal of Vocational Behavior, 54, 314–334.

Waldo, C. R. (1999). Working in a majority context: A structural model of heterosexism as minority stress in the workplace. Journal of Counseling Psychology, 46, 218–232.

Wayment, H. A., & Peplau, L. A. (1995). Social support and well-being among lesbian and heterosexual women: A structural modeling approach. Personality and Social Psychology Bulletin, 21, 1189–1199.

Wayne, S. J., Shore, L. M., & Liden, R. C. (1997). Perceived organizational support and leader-member exchange: A social exchange perspective. Academy of Management Journal, 40, 82–111.

Wells, B., & Button, S. B. (2004). Workplace experiences of lesbian and gay employees: A review of current research. International Review of Industrial and Organizational Psychology, 19, 139–170.

Witt, L. A., & Carlson, D. S. (2006). The work-family interface and job performance: Moderating effects of conscientiousness and perceived organizational support. Journal of Occupational Health Psychology, 11, 343–357.

Wortman, C. B., & Dunkel-Schetter, C. (1987). Conceptual and methodological issues in the study of social support. In A. Baum & J. E. Singer (Eds.), Handbook of psychology and health (Vol. 5, p. 63–108). Hillsdale, NJ: Erlbaum.

CHAPTER 37

The Multigenerational Workforce

Opportunity for Competitive Success

HR Magazine

People of all generations and at all levels want their leaders to be credible, trustworthy, dependable, far-sighted, encouraging and good listeners.[1]

Introduction

For the first time in history, four generations work side-by-side in many organizations. The working generations span more than 60 years, including so-called Traditionalists, Baby Boomers, Generation X and Millennials/Generation Y. All bring different experiences, perspectives, expectations, work styles and strengths to the workplace. Despite the perceived "generation gap" from differing views and potential conflict, organizations—and especially HR—have the opportunity to capitalize on the assets of each generation for competitive advantage.

Predictions in *Workforce 2020* (published in 1997) focused on demographic change as a major global force shaping the world economy.[2] More than a decade later, SHRM's *2008 Workplace Forecast* upholds these predictions with key demographic trends: 1) the aging population, 2) retirement of large numbers of Baby Boomers, 3) generational issues and 4) a greater demand for work/life balance. At the same time, the loss of talent due to the retirement of older workers will likely drive an increased focus on skills, labor shortages and retention strategies for the current and future workforce.[3]

Source: The Multigenerational Workforce: Opportunity for Competitive Success. In *HR Magazine* 54, no. 3 (no author given), Mar. 2009, p. 1–9 *HR Magazine*. Published by Society for Human Resource Management.

Thus, in their respective industry sectors, HR leaders have the opportunity to create competitive success by strategically managing generational differences in terms of differing experiences, values and expectations. While not inclusive of all generational workplace issues, this article provides perspectives for HR and organizational leaders on selected key aspects of the multigenerational workforce and offers recommendations, primarily for U.S. organizations.

Today's Four Generations

Generally, the concept of a "generation" is attributed to social scientist Karl Mannheim from his work in the late 1920s.[4] Grounded in shared life experiences and defining historical and cultural events during individuals' formative years, each generation has different collective memories, expectations and values. As such, a generation is defined as an identifiable group that shares birth years and significant life events at critical developmental stages.[5] At the same time, it is very important to avoid stereotyping people from different generations. For example, research shows that people born at the beginning or end of a generation (referred to as "tweeners") can exhibit values and attitudes from two different generations.[6]

Generalities about generations can provide insight on values and expectations in the workplace. The oldest generation, Traditionalists (also known as Veterans, Matures, Depression Babies) grew up following the worldwide economic depression, with World War II as the major event in their childhood. They view work as a privilege and have a strong work ethic grounded in discipline, stability and experience.[7] The Baby Boom generation, born after World War II, is the largest generation in the United States and has had a significant impact on societies worldwide. Defining events of this generation include the space race, rock and roll, and women's liberation. Baby Boomers tend to be idealistic, driven and optimistic.[8]

Different experiences have shaped Generations X and Y. A much smaller generation than the Baby Boomers, Gen Xers were known as "latch-key children" with both parents working. They grew up during the time of high divorce rates and massive job layoffs of the 1980s. They are independent, creative, skeptical and distrustful of authority. In contrast, the younger generation (known as Millennials, Generation Y, Nexters) experienced terrorist attacks in their formative years, including September 11th, and technology has always been a part of their lives. They are confident, team-oriented, patriotic and social minded. Since their parents typically planned their activities, they are accustomed to having structured lives.[9]

An extensive study on generational differences found that leadership style preferences are reflected in selected admired leaders of each generation. Baby Boomers, for example, prefer leaders who are caring, competent and honest, as reflected in their choices of social leaders: Martin Luther King and Gandhi. Generations X and Y want leaders to challenge the system and create change: Ronald Reagan, Tiger Woods, Bill Gates. Each generation ranked honesty, competence and loyalty among the top leadership qualities, with honesty being the most important. For HR and organizational leaders, this means that firms need to recognize and understand the differences and similarities among generations regarding leadership qualities when it comes to the creation of leadership development programs for current and future leaders, for example (see Figure 37.1).[10]

Business Case

As highlighted by AARP in *Leading a Multigenerational Workforce*, intergenerational dynamics offer organizations a highly competitive advantage. That is, management can use different perspectives, strengths and unique values to positively influence the bottom line in key areas: corporate culture, recruitment, employee engagement, retention and customer service.[12]

Yet, while it is commonly held that each generation has highly different values, there are similarities. For example, in a groundbreaking research study, the Center for Creative Leadership surveyed more than 3,000 organizational leaders over a seven-year period to learn how organizations can effectively use similarities and differences among generations. A key finding of this research was that the top three values of all generations were family, love and integrity, although they demonstrated these values in various ways. From a

Figure 37.1   Four Generations in Today's Workplace

Generation	Percentage of Workforce	Assets in the Workplace	Leadership Style Preferences
Traditionalists Born 1922–1945 Ages 63–86	8%	Hard working, stable, loyal, thorough, detail-oriented, focused, emotional maturity.	Fair, consistent, clear, direct, respectful.
Baby Boomers Born 1946–1964 Ages 44–62	44%	Team perspective, dedicated, experienced, knowledgeable, service-oriented.	Treat as equals, warm and caring, mission-defined, democratic approach.
Generation X Born 1965–1980 Ages 28–43	34%	Independent, adaptable, creative, techno-literate, willing to challenge the status quo.	Direct, competent, genuine, informal, flexible, results-oriented, supportive of learning opportunities.
Millennials Born 1981–2000 Ages 8–27	14% and increasing rapidly	Optimistic, able to multitask, tenacious, technologically savvy, driven to learn and grow, team-oriented, socially responsible.	Motivational, collaborative, positive, educational, organized, achievement-oriented, able to coach.

Source: Author compilation from several sources.

managerial viewpoint, this information is very helpful in better understanding the root cause of differences, misunderstandings and conflict in the workplace.[13] In fact, studies in organizational and human behavior find that people seek similar factors in the workplace, and these commonalities can be leveraged to bond employees in support of a company's mission, vision and goals.[14]

Further, with skills shortages commonplace today, domestic and global organizations must focus on workforce optimization for bottom-line results. Predicted demographic changes highlight the importance of managing talent of all generations (see Figure 37.2). In the United States, for example, projections indicate there will be 10 million more jobs than workers by the year 2010. According to the Organization for Economic Cooperation and Development (OECD), working-age populations will decline by 65 million in the industrialized nations of OECD members, such as the European Union. At the same time, worker migration worldwide will likely create a highly competitive global labor

market at least until the year 2016, when all Millennials will have entered the workforce, alleviating worker shortage in the developed world.[15] According to the Pew Research Center, by 2050 in the United States, working-age adults will make up 58% of the population, down from 63% in 2005. Also, depending on economic factors, a greater share of workers ages 50 and older may stay in the workplace longer than in the past.[16] Thus, a renewed focus on training older workers will no doubt become a greater part of talent management. Projections such as these indicate that demographic changes will be substantial, requiring that HR and organizational leaders thoughtfully examine strategic optimization of their human capital.

Workplace Diversity

In recent years, the concept of generational differences as a legitimate workplace diversity issue has gained increasing

| **Figure 37.2** | Demographic Workforce Predictions |

Workforce 2000	Workforce 2020
The population and workforce will grow more slowly than at any time since the 1930s.	As retirement ages become increasingly less predictable, workforce planning will become more uncertain.
The proportion of women and minorities in the workforce will rise dramatically.	By 2020, according to the U.S. Census Bureau, the proportion of women in the workforce will have gradually increased to about 50%.
The average age of the population and workforce will rise, and the pool of young workers entering the labor market will shrink.	The continued presence of top-level older employees may cause dissension among their middle-aged subordinates eager for promotion.
The workforce is aging and thus becoming less willing to relocate, retrain or change occupations, yet the economy is demanding more flexibility.	Older workers will need different benefits, such as elder care programs.
Need to recognize the importance of a flexible workforce through company and national policies (e.g., flexible workforce programs, revised pension systems, promotion of retraining and lifelong learning).	To increase workforce participation, firms and governments will need to accommodate unconventional working arrangements to encourage people to return or remain in the workforce (e.g., parents, older workers).
Immigrants will represent the largest share of the increase in the population and the workforce since World War I.	The U.S. population and workforce will gradually become more ethnically diverse.

Source: Author compilation from several sources.

recognition. SHRM's director of diversity and inclusion initiatives, Shirley A. Davis, Ph.D., points out that in the United States, discussions of workplace diversity tend to focus on topics of race, ethnicity, gender, sexual orientation and disability. "However, in all parts of the world, there is another category of diversity that cannot be overlooked: multigenerational diversity. Today, there are greater numbers of workers from each age group that bring both new opportunities and challenges. If organizations want to thrive in this competitive environment of global talent management, they need employees and managers who are aware of and skilled in dealing with the four generations that make up the workforce."

The existence of four generations is a major factor in talent management. In its "Competitive Workforce" category, SHRM's Human Capital Leadership Awards Program recognizes organizations with workforce readiness efforts aimed at anticipating and meeting current and future business needs in a changing economic climate. In 2008, Sodexo, Inc. was a finalist in that category for its innovative strategies in multigenerational talent acquisition and engagement. Since recruitment and retention of a multigenerational employee pool are key to Sodexo's business strategy, HR leaders at the company's U.S. headquarters in Gaithersburg, Maryland, launched a multifaceted recruitment initiative. For example, Sodexo established a presence on social networking sites such as YouTube and LinkedIn to attract younger workers and created a new recruitment initiative aimed at veterans that translates military experience and skills into civilian jobs at the company. As a result, in 2007, there was a 24% increase in the number of job applicants, including a 38% rise in minority candidates and a 32% increase in gender diversity.[18]

"At Sodexo, understanding what drives each generation, and what their underlying experiences are, is the key to creating a cohesive work environment where our people feel valued and empowered to work together effectively," said Dr. Rohini Anand, Sodexo senior vice president and global chief diversity officer. "This appreciation of generational diversity, and initiatives customized to meet the needs of each generation, allows each group to fully contribute and be a part of the growth and success of the organization." Clearly, organizations that proactively use the strengths of different generations in the workforce are best positioned for success.

Ethics and Generational Differences

A recent SHRM white paper, *Ethics and Generational Differences: Interplay Between Values and Ethical Business Decisions*, examined how different generations approach questions of integrity and purpose. The authors point out that "with value systems and motivation at the heart of ethics—and divergent value systems seemingly inherent within the four generational groups—the existence of varied ethical perspectives among co-workers is not a surprise." They emphasize that understanding differing viewpoints on ethics in the workplace will help organizations make sound ethical business decisions.[19]

A common complaint among generations focuses on *work ethic*. Much of this conflict stems from how the term work ethic is defined and interpreted. Traditionalists and Baby Boomers may criticize the two younger generations about their lack of work ethic, with the oldest generation considering a strong work ethic as demonstrated by being part of the organization (and physically present in the office, in terms of actual hours) for long periods of time. Baby Boomers consider a combination of factors, such as collaboration, teamwork and meetings, as evidence of work ethic. In contrast, Generation X and Millennials see work ethic as working hard—often autonomously—and having a positive impact on the company, while also living a full life outside of their job. Views on the issue of respect also differ. Having "paid their dues," the two older generations expect respect from Generation X and Millennials—yet, the two younger generations consider that respect is earned by making a strong contribution, not by the passage of time.[20]

Despite these differences, research shows that no matter one's age, people value achievement, balance and responsibility and want credible, trustworthy leadership.[21] Such commonalities are important for HR to emphasize in the workplace. As highlighted in Figure 37.3, there are various actions that HR can take to help build stronger alliances in the workplace that both nurture and clarify ethical issues for workers of all generations.

Engaging the Millennial Generation

The Millennial generation challenges organizations, HR and managers on many levels. The literature points out that this generation can be "high maintenance," and yet, when companies provide the resources and flexibility to be creative, Millennials also can be highly productive. To attract, engage and retain Millennials, organizations must understand what types of work environment and learning experiences they want. If organizations do not adapt their corporate culture to fit the needs of this large generation, this may have detrimental results in terms of hiring, productivity and retention.

These "digital natives" quickly learn and multitask, prefer to work collaboratively with others and thrive on immediate feedback. Although Millennials do not want to be micromanaged, they want clear directions and managerial support and also demand freedom and flexibility to do work at their own pace and in their own way. They want increasing responsibility but need coaching on time management. They are committed to the company "long term"—meaning about a year or two. Such apparent contradictions can boggle the minds of managers from older generations. The key is to build solid relationships by getting to know them, listening and spending time with them. For this "education is cool" generation, managers will want to provide coaching and resources to meet employees' learning goals. From an HR policy and program viewpoint, it is best to avoid the "one-size-fits-all" philosophy. To attract and retain Millennials, organizations need to be willing to customize schedules, work assignments and career paths. Millennials will look to their managers to help them balance work and other commitments. Managers must focus on performance and consistently provide constructive feedback, praise, recognition and rewards.[22]

Companies that are successful in attracting Millennials are creative in their culture, HR policies, programs and work environment. A survey by Human Resource Executive, in partnership with the Great Places to Work Institute, identified "18 Great Companies for Millennials." Facets of corporate cultures sought include:

Figure 37.3	Ten Key Points for Ethical Business Management

1. Develop an internal campaign, with ethics as the #1 value for the organization and employees.

2. Avoid stereotyping employees according to their generation.

3. Clearly identify the priorities of the company and then link them to the priorities and values of employees to support business decisions.

4. When possible, learn the values and motivation of employees and then connect them to individual and organizational goals.

5. Focus on business results, not on methodology (as long as it is ethical). All groups want to contribute and achieve but may do so differently.

6. To make ethical guidelines relevant to everyone, establish ongoing training and support sessions.

7. Look for commonality among employees of different generations.

8. Embrace diversity of opinion and methodology.

9. Err on the side of more communication, such as using more types of media: face-to-face meetings, e-mail blasts, etc.

10. Remember to respect the dimensions of differing generations (age, technological savvy, alternative work experiences, innovation, etc.)

Adopted from: Guss, E., & Miller, M. C. (2008, October). *Ethics and generational differences: Interplay between values and ethical business decision* [SHRM White Paper]. Retrieved from www.shrm.org.

- Management's actions match its words.
- Employees are appreciated for good work and extra effort.
- Employees are involved in decisions that affect their jobs or work environment.
- Employees are treated as full members of the company, no matter the position.
- Promotions go to those who best deserve them, and the company culture is a team or family environment.

Marriott International Inc., for example, offers workplace flexibility—a benefit highly sought by young employees. In its "Teamwork Innovations" program, employees are encouraged to identify and eliminate redundant work. At one Marriott hotel, teams were able to cut 40% off the time that it took to turn over a shift and, with this time savings, were allowed to leave early. At the same time, Millennials like to work for "cool companies." In Portland, Oregon, the Umpqua Bank has internet cafés, coffee bars and couches where customers can relax and watch TV. Some branches even offer yoga and movie nights and have a water dish outside for dogs. The "cool factor" attracts both customers and young employees from high school and college.[24] As portrayed in these examples, organizations that strategically energize their company culture and effectively use the talents and drive of the Millennial generation will have a competitive edge.

HR Policies, Benefits, and Programs

Over time, the multigenerational workforce will influence the organizational work ethic, perceptions of organizational hierarchy, work relationships and ways of managing change. The literature suggests that as a result of differing experiences and perspectives, strongly held attitudes and diverse motivators, there will be an impact on two specific areas of human resource policy and employee development: retention and motivation.[25] To successfully retain and leverage talent of all generations, the following studies represent the growing foundation of evidence to make changes in company culture, HR policies, benefits and programs.

No matter which generation, the work environment tends to either attract or repel individuals. An exploratory study examined dimensions of employee fit with work environments and the impact of employee job satisfaction and turnover intention among different generations. The findings suggest that employees in the Baby Boom generation value work relationships as a contributor to employee satisfaction, whereas for Generations X and Y, the work environment fit (potential for career growth, decision-making opportunities, autonomy and job challenge) is a primary retention factor.[26]

Work/life balance is a key commonality among the four generations. A recent study that explored generational effects on work-family conflict in the United States suggests that changes reflect family and career stage differences. For example, "family interfering with work" has changed over time for Generation X and Baby Boomers but stayed at the same level for Matures, perhaps due to having fewer family demands (empty-nest family stage). Generation X and Baby Boomers value work/life balance, growth opportunities and positive work relationships. The implication is that managers and HR professionals will want to consider generational differences in work/life program design and monitor patterns of program use by different generational groups.[27]

In a study by the Boston College Center for Work & Family, thought leaders identified top trends that will affect the future of work/life: generational diversity, followed by global challenges, older workers, increasing stress levels and technology blurring. The increasing number of older workers is now a high-profile issue, with the aging workforce a challenge in the United States as well as in Western Europe and certain Asian countries, such as Japan. Companies must find ways to address the needs of various age cohorts based on their different life stages—for example, by keeping in mind different values and life experiences of the workforce when designing strategies that enable all employees to work together productively.[28]

Talent retention can be improved through different approaches to communicating and rewarding employees, using high-tech tools and employing a more high-touch approach where the manager-employee relationship is focused on more personalized rewards. By developing more unified and compassionate workplace cultures, organizations will be more attractive to people of all generations.[29] Such studies provide valuable insight and information to HR professionals to assess HR policies and programs for the multigenerational workplace (see Figure 37.4).

Global Generational Trends

Research reveals that comparable generations in countries outside of the United States have both similar and distinct generational workforce issues. As a result of technology, the world is smaller, with greater access to information, products and services, contributing to broadening world views. At a Boston College Global Workforce Roundtable, it was noted that there appears to be a global convergence of attitudes among people under the age of 30. These young people, who do not yet have an agreed upon identifying label (such as Millennials in the United States), have a global perspective, with a focus on quality of life, engagement in consumerism and a strong drive for personal and professional development.[31] Yet, this may not accurately portray attitudes of young people raised in rural and poor areas with limited exposure to global influences from television and the Internet.[32]

In contrast, the perspectives of older generations are strongly distinguished by local context. That is, these generations are highly influenced by culture, economics and events from their respective experiences, and they bring these viewpoints and values to the workforce. In China, for example, education was limited from 1966 to 1978 as a result of the Cultural Revolution. But for that event, many Chinese workers would likely be in senior leadership roles in organizations today; now, in contrast to their global peers, this group lacks education and experience. Cultural viewpoints also influence the workplace. In India, the concept of hierarchy has traditionally strongly influenced business decisions, such as strategy, promotions and communications. Yet, in today's Indian workplace, older workers view hierarchy as more important than do people of the younger generation.[33]

Additionally, it should be noted that the concept of the Baby Boom generation exists only in the developed world, with other nations not having the concerns resulting from this large generation. For example, many countries (e.g., Latino Christian, Arab, and African nations) did not have a significant reduction in fertility rates, nor did they embrace factors such as access to

Figure 37.4 HR Policies and Programs for the Multigenerational Workforce

HR Policies and Programs	Examples
Work/Life Benefits	Flexible hours, telecommuting, family leave, work/life balance policies, allowance for religious holidays, etc.
Rewards and Recognition	Compensation, rewards programs
Health Care	Long-term care, dependent care, elder care, EAPs, wellness programs
Training and Development	Professional development, mentorships, temporary work assignments, job sharing
Succession Planning	Formal leadership development programs, temporary work assignments

Sources: Author compilation from two sources.

contraception, the changing role of women in society and more recent focus on work/life balance.[34]

Finally, for the multigenerational workforce in Europe, the literature is rather limited. However, a new study from the *Journal of Managerial Psychology* explored workplace learning, organizational commitment and talent retention among European managers across generations. The results show that younger generations have stronger learning orientation and lower organizational commitment than older workers. Important practical HR insights include focus on offering leadership development, fostering learning goals and organizational commitment, and managerial emphasis on learning—all key retention factors for the younger generations.[35]

Three Key Management Strategies

Organizational communication: This key strategy is important to retain talent and avoid potential conflict. A SHRM survey revealed a number of ways to successfully work with a multigenerational workforce, with communicating information in multiple ways, such as oral and written, as the most successful. Different generations have varying levels of comfort with technology, such as e-mail, while others prefer face-to-face communication. Other approaches found to be successful include 1) collaborative discussion, decision-making or problem solving—providing an opportunity to express respect and inclusion of all employees; 2) training managers on dealing with generational differences; 3) team-building activities; and 4) creating mentoring programs to encourage workers of different generations to work together and share experiences.[36]

Succession planning: HR and organizational leaders must be aware of the internal talent pool, encompassing all generations, from which possible successors can be selected and developed. Regarding age-based demographics, HR needs to have a basic understanding of the different values and work attitudes of each generation—important information for cultivating and sustaining a preferred corporate culture.[37]

Mentoring: The goal of this strategy is to help ensure the transfer of knowledge from one generation to the next. As older workers look toward retirement, mentoring can be an effective vehicle to capture organizational knowledge. Structured mentoring programs are well suited for knowledge transfer. An important step is to survey the younger workers, learn their goals and developmental needs, and then pair them with more experienced employees. Also, using a variety of mentoring models is helpful. Examples include one-on-one mentoring sessions, senior leadership discussion panels, group mentoring programs and even "speed mentoring," where employees sit with organization experts and ask questions. Another model increasingly used is senior staff and leaders coaching younger employees in the onboarding process. This process begins in the hiring period and can last for up to a year, giving younger workers direct attention and professional development early in their career.[38] The following mini-case study presents a successful mentoring program.

Mini-Case Study: Mentoring Between Generations

Launched in 2001, the AARP award program "Best Employers for Workers Over 50" recognizes organizations with best practices and policies that address issues affecting the aging workforce and creating workplace opportunities for all. In 2008, the YMCA of Greater Rochester was ranked 4th out of 50 companies for this award.[39] In the last six years, the YMCA of Greater Rochester has had a formal mentoring program—Mentoring Across Generations—as part of its professional development curriculum. Vice president of human resources, Fernan R. Cepero, PHR, credits its success to the company culture, stating, "Throughout its 155 year history, the organization has focused on leaving a legacy and creating a legacy between generations."

The mentoring program enhances the professional development and personal growth of both the mentor and the mentee. It helps employees understand cultural nuances, gain expertise in a specific discipline and provide ideas and inspiration about career paths. It also exposes employees to different paths of the business and various management levels. As exemplified in the short example from the YMCA of Greater Rochester, mentoring—a critical component of succession planning—builds leadership capacity by increasing the professional strength of the organization's employees.

Dan Friday, a member of Generation Y and buildings and grounds director at the Monroe Family Branch, was new to his position. Tom Ward, buildings and grounds director at the West-side Family Branch and a Baby Boomer, volunteered to mentor Dan, remembering what it was like early in his own career. Over several months, their mentoring relationship developed. As Dan attests, "Tom has coached me on all sorts of issues—from mechanics to staffing. He introduced me to the Association of Facility Engineers, where I've met some very interesting building mechanics and learned about

construction projects that I am now considering for improvement to my facility." In fact, Tom has become much more than a mentor. He has helped Dan strip and wax floors, troubleshoot treadmill problems, and even filled in as pool operator when Dan was out for a week. At the same time, Tom has benefited from this relationship. As a subject matter expert, Tom has gained immense personal and professional satisfaction from seeing Dan grow and succeed in his leadership role.

As Mr. Cepero emphasizes, "Mentoring builds strong intergenerational working relationships, strategic use of intellectual capital and increased retention, and, at its core, ensures a continuous flow of knowledge management across generations."

In Closing

As HR professionals work to optimize talent in their respective organizations, research shows that it is critical to leverage the strengths of each generation. Whether in a domestic or global organization, HR has the unique opportunity to create a competitive advantage by guiding policy and program development and management strategies to increase attraction and retention of the four generations in today's workplace.

Endnotes

1.   Deal, J. J. (2007). *Retiring the generation gap: How employees young and old can find common ground*. San Francisco: Jossey-Bass and the Center for Creative Leadership.

2.   Judy, R. W., & D'Amico, C. (1997). *Workforce 2020: Work and workers in the 21st century*. Indianapolis, IN: Hudson Institute, Inc.

3.   Socety for Human Resource Management. (2008). *Workplace forecast*. Alexandria, VA: Author.

4.   Eyerman, R., & Turner, B. S. (1998). Outline of a theory of generations. *European Journal of Social Theory, 1*, 91–106.

5.   Kupperschmidt, B. R. (2000). Multigeneration employees: strategies for effective management. *The Health Care Manager, 19*, 65–76.

6.   Schewe, C. D., & Evans, S. M. (2000). Market segmentation by cohorts: The value and validity of cohorts in America and abroad. *Journal of Marketing Management, 16*, 129–142.

7.   AARP. (2007). *Leading a multigenerational workforce*. Washington, DC: Author.

8.   Glass, A. (2007). Understanding generational differences for competitive success. *Industrial and Commercial Training, 39*(2), 98+.

9. Ibid.

10. Arsenault, P. M. (2004). Validating generational differences: A legitimate diversity and leadership issue. *Leadership & Organization Development, 25*(1/2), 124+.

11. Author compilation from several sources: AARP. (2007). *Leading a multigenerational workforce.* Washington, DC: Author. Sabatini Fraone, J., Hartmann, D., & McNally, K. (2008). *The multigenerational workforce: Management implications and strategies for collaboration* [Executive Briefing Series]. Boston: Boston College Center for Work & Family. Zemke, R., Raines, C., & Filipczak, B. (2000). Generations at work: Managing the clash of veterans, boomers, Xers and nexters in your workplace. New York: American Management Association.

12. AARP. (2007). *Leading a multigenerational workforce.* Washington, DC: Author.

13. Deal, J. J. (2007). *Retiring the generation gap: How employees young and old can find common ground.* San Francisco: Jossey-Bass and the Center for Creative Leadership.

14. Whitacre, T. (2007, December). Managing a multigenerational workforce. *Quality Progress, 40*(1), 67.

15. Tucker, E., Kao, T., & Verma, N. (2005, July/August). Next-generation talent management: Insights on how workforce trends are changing the face of talent management. *Business Credit, 107* (7), 20–28.

16. Passel, J. S., & Cohn, D. (2008, February 11). *U.S. population projections: 2005–2050.* Washington, DC: Pew Research Center.

17. Author compilation from several sources: Johnston, W. B., & Packer, A. H. (1987). Workforce 2000: Work and workers for the twenty-first century. Indianapolis, IN: Hudson Institute, Inc. Judy, R. W., & D'Amico, C. (1997). Workforce 2020: *Work and workers in the 21st century.* Indianapolis, IN: Hudson Institute, Inc.

18. Johnson, E. (2008, November). 2008 SHRM human capital leadership awards—Finalists—Competitive workforce award. [*HR Magazine*] Alexandria, VA: Society for Human Resource Management.

19. Guss, E., & Miller, M. C. (2008, October). *Ethics and generational differences: Interplay between values and ethical business decision* [SHRM White Paper]. Retrieved from www.shrm.org.

20. Ibid.

21. Deal, J. J. (2007). *Retiring the generation gap: How employees young and old can find common ground.* San Francisco: Jossey-Bass and the Center for Creative Leadership.

22. Martin, C. A. (2005). From high maintenance to high productivity: What managers need to know about Generation Y. *Industrial and Commercial Training, 37*(1), 39–45.

23. Flander, S. (2008, April). Millennial magnets. *Human Resource Executive,* 22–29.

24. Ibid.

25. Glass, A. (2007). Understanding generational differences for competitive success. *Industrial and Commercial Training, 39*(2), 98+.

26. Westerman, J. W., & Yamamura, J. H. (2007). Generational preferences for work environment fit: Effects on employee outcomes. *Career Development International, 12*(2), 150+.

27. Beutell, N. J., & Wittig-German, U. (2008). Work-family conflict and work-family synergy for generation X, baby boomers, and matures: Generational differences, predictors and satisfaction outcomes. *Journal of Managerial Psychology, 23*(5), 507–523.

28. Harrington, B. (2008). *The work-life evolution study.* Boston: Boston College Center for Work & Family.

29. Tucker, E., Kao, T., & Verma, N. (2005, July/August). Next-generation talent management: Insights on how workforce trends are changing the face of talent management. *Business Credit, 107*(7), 20–28.

30. Author compilation from two sources: Jenkins, J. (2008, Winter). Strategies for managing talent in a multigenerational workforce. *Employment Relations Today, 34*(4), 19–26. AARP. (2007). *Leading a multigenerational workforce.* Washington, DC: Author.

31. Sabatini Fraone, J., Hartmann, D., & McNally, K. (2008). *The multigenerational workforce: Management implications and strategies for collaboration* [Executive Briefing Series]. Boston: Boston College Center for Work & Family.

32. AARP. (2007). *Leading a multigenerational workforce.* Washington, DC: Author.

33. Sabatini Fraone, J., Hartmann, D., & McNally, K. (2008). *The multigenerational workforce: Management implications and strategies for collaboration* [Executive Briefing Series]. Boston: Boston College Center for Work & Family.

34. Salt, B. (2008, September). The global skills convergence: Issues and ideas for the management of an international workforce. Australia: KPMG International.

35. D'Amato, A., & Herzfeldt, R. (2008). Learning orientation, organizational commitment and talent retention across generations: A study of European managers. *Journal of Managerial Psychology, 23*(8), 929–953.

36. Burke, M. E. (2004, August). *Generational differences survey report.* Alexandria, VA: Society for Human Resource Management.

37. Crumpacker, M., & Crumpacker, J. M. (2007, Winter). Succession planning and generational stereotypes: Should HR consider age-based values and attitudes a relevant factor or a passing fad? *Public Personnel Management, 36*(4), 349–370.

38. Jenkins, J. (2008, Winter). Strategies for managing talent in a multigenerational workforce. *Employment Relations Today, 34*(4), 19–26.

39. AARP. (2008, August). AARP best employers for workers over 50 program. Retrieved November 17, 2008, from www.aarp.org.

CHAPTER 38

Respectful Pluralism at Work

Douglas A. Hicks

Jepson School of Leadership Studies and University of Richmond

The analysis thus far has critically engaged with disparate approaches to addressing religious diversity, such as keeping religion and spirituality out of the workplace altogether, translating or reducing diverse religious beliefs and practices to a so-called common spirituality, or maintaining an era of Christian establishment. Building upon these earlier arguments, the remaining chapters construct an alternative perspective on how workplace leaders and followers can most adequately negotiate religion, in its various forms, in their organizations.

The central aim of this chapter is to provide a defensible and convincing explanation of and moral justification for respectful pluralism. I argue that this framework allows employees to express, within constraints to be outlined, their religious as well as political, cultural, spiritual, and other commitments within the workplace. In addition, no religious tradition should receive undue institutional preference or priority. In order to explain the constructive framework, the first section outlines the descriptive realities of the

contemporary workplace in which respectful pluralism would operate and to which it would respond. It also describes the nature of the moral argument I am making and how it can contribute to ongoing debate about religion and the workplace. The subsequent sections present the moral argument for respectful pluralism, including a concise statement of the framework's guiding principle and limiting norms. Finally, the framework is examined in practice vis-à-vis a number of real-life dilemmas that workplace managers and employees face. As a whole, the chapter offers a vision of how putting respectful pluralism into practice can help leaders—and religious adherents—to address religious diversity as well as other kinds of diversity at work.

Circumstances of the Contemporary Workplace

The framework begins by identifying those descriptive factors—*circumstances*—that contribute to the context

Source: Respectful Pluralism at Work. Pp. 159–183 in *Religion and the Workplace: Pluralism, Spirituality, Leadership* by Douglas A. Hicks. Copyright © 2003 Cambridge University Press. Reprinted with the permission of Cambridge University Press.

in which workplace organizations must navigate the myriad forms of religion.[1] These circumstances are not normative visions of how the workplace or society should be; rather, they account for the most relevant factors that workplaces currently confront. In that sense, these are not value-based claims. Of course, they do reflect certain values in the sense that all descriptive exercises reflect some *framing* of reality.[2] For example, compared to approaches advocating a generic spirituality at work, my account of the circumstances of the workplace places more emphasis on religious diversity. Each of the circumstances included here, then, depends upon a prior evaluation of which factors are significant in the current context.

The first circumstance of the contemporary workplace has received significant attention throughout the book: *a broad and increasing religious diversity among employees within organizations.* Diversities of various kinds (beliefs, traditions, practices, dress, speech) are fundamental elements that contribute to the need for a complex approach to religion and the workplace. If everyone in an organization held the same beliefs and engaged in the same practices, an institutional establishment of a specific religious or spiritual system of beliefs and practices would not be as morally or practically troubling as it is under the condition of diversity. (Even if such a situation did not exist, however, the institutional establishment of a particular religion in a workplace would still raise moral concerns.[3])

The second circumstance of the contemporary workplace is the descriptive understanding of *non-compartmentalization.* Stated in the framework of Hickman and other theorists of organizations, this simply refers to the phenomenon that, like it or not, employees bring their own identity, problems, and beliefs to work.[4] For many employees, religious or spiritual beliefs and practices are an essential and inseparable part of their life. Even in so-called secular workplaces, workers do not and cannot fully leave them behind. Hickman and others assert that workplaces that accommodate this fact are able to address the needs of their employees more efficiently and humanely.[5] The descriptive circumstance of non-compartmentalization has implications for various aspects of human resource management, including work–family policies and sick leave. It also pertains to how and how much religious and other

"personal" expression should be permitted at work. Many workplaces forbid explicitly religious speech or actions, but they cannot force employees not to think about, or to be influenced by, their religious commitments.

The third circumstance understands *workplaces as increasingly public sites in American society.*[6] Citing increased working hours and new technology that make workers available around the clock, social scientists assert that work has taken on a larger role in persons' lives in recent decades.[7] Employees spend more of their time and conduct more of their everyday lives in the workplace. Indeed, much of the current interest in spirituality and leadership can be attributed to this phenomenon, which often restricts people's involvement in traditional communities of faith.[8] In addition, through a process of transformation in the size and nature of firms, companies themselves have taken on an increasingly important role in American public life. Corporations hold a great deal of influence in terms of public policy, public opinion, and the shaping of civil society.[9] Moses L. Pava argues for calling corporations "quasi-public institutions," because they exercise a certain degree of power over employees, customers, and other citizens and they have a large public role in society.[10] In contemporary America, the workplace is one of the principal places in which people encounter religious and other forms of difference.[11] The ways in which employees from diverse religious backgrounds are either included or excluded in the corporate environment convey messages about who counts in public life. The public or quasi-public role of corporations also suggests that the workplace is a site in which employees might learn from one another.

The fourth circumstance that affects the contemporary workplace is *the complex and contested role of religion in public life.* This factor captures many roles that religion plays in American society. Scholarly and public discourse about the role of religion in the workplace does not occur in a vacuum but, rather, is informed by debates over the lingering Christian cultural establishment in public life, the realities of Christianity as the "religious preference" of a majority of Americans, the tradition of avowed secularism in the market sphere, and the recent interest in "spiritual leadership."[12] The first two of these elements serve as a reminder that any approach, including respectful pluralism, does not address a context in which adherents of all religious, spiritual, and other backgrounds have the same experience of expressing their religion at work and in public life; many employees who are Christians have received or do receive preferential treatment at work and in society. The current discussions of generic spirituality can marginalize atheists and some adherents of many religious backgrounds. At the same time, the secular understanding of modern society has pressured people of various religious and spiritual backgrounds to divorce some or all of their commitments from all aspects of their public lives.

The fifth and final circumstance considered here is the *for-profit nature of companies.* Workplace organizations in the so-called private sector are not (and should not be) religious institutions, and it bears restating that it is not their central purpose to serve as the principal religious site for employees.[13] My analysis assumes that, within the bounds of legality and morality, companies have the legitimate right to seek profits and to pursue the financial interests of the company. The Nobel laureate in economics Milton Friedman asserts that "the one and only social responsibility of business [is] to use its resources and engage in activities designed to increase its profits so long as it stays within the rules of the game."[14] It is not necessary to embrace Friedman's unconditional view in order to recognize the very important point that, within appropriate constraints, companies have a worthy and legitimate (instrumental) goal of profitability. Practical concerns require that, while moral concerns about employees and managers are fundamental, companies need to be profitable in order to exist as workplaces over the long term.

The Nature of Moral Argument in a Pluralistic Context

An argument for constructing respectful pluralism in the workplace should acknowledge that the reality of moral, philosophical, and religious disagreement among diverse perspectives applies not only to employees but to scholars as well. This section discusses the method and language used to construct that framework in subsequent pages.

Drawing upon Thiemann's "conditions of publicity,"[15] my book *Inequality and Christian Ethics* offers an extended account of how and why a variety of religiously based and other moral arguments should be allowed in public debates about contemporary economic issues.[16] I argue against a strict political liberalism that advocates a very narrow public sphere in which citizens can speak to one another only in terms of values reportedly held by all members of a society. Political liberals argue against welcoming appeals by some citizens to doctrines and worldviews that other citizens do not support and that they may not understand. Although these theorists' commitment to uphold equal respect of citizens is correct, their position unnecessarily impoverishes moral discourse, because it precludes citizens from drawing upon morally rich and imaginative perspectives. John Rawls, in his account of "public reason," offers one of the most articulate defenses of such liberal positions, though it is interesting to note that he substantially loosened the constraints he advocated for religious speech during the last ten years of his life.[17] In his argument for the use of public reason, Rawls rightly emphasizes that citizens have a duty to act with civility and should uphold the virtue of mutual respect toward fellow citizens. This helps guarantee that any power yielded by citizens to the state is justifiable to all citizens in language they understand. For Rawls, civility and respect can best be guaranteed when citizens speak to one another in terms that everyone holds in common. This position is problematic for a number of reasons, including the high level of confidence Rawls places on people's ability to concur on what values are commonly held as part of public reason. Further, his position does not adequately capture the importance of religion, and the difficulty of compartmentalizing it, in many citizens' lives.[18]

Rawls states that his argument for public reason applies only within the public political sphere, when citizens are deliberating matters of basic justice in a society. Rawls is not as concerned about the potential for coercion in institutions such as the workplace as he is when the state is involved. Pava, however, builds upon Rawls's framework and suggests that Rawls's account of public reason provides a helpful analogue for the workplace context as well. Managers should show respect toward their co-workers and subordinates by using language they can comprehend; however, "under appropriate and limited circumstances, [managers] may invoke and rely upon a religious, albeit private, worldview."[19] Employees, and especially corporations as institutions, have a moral obligation to justify their actions in terms that are as publicly accessible as possible.

My argument for how respectful pluralism should operate in the workplace attempts to broaden the liberal framework while upholding its concern that citizens (and employees) communicate to each other in ways that respect other citizens (and co-workers). I support Pava's contention that the corporation has tremendous public power and the capacity to influence employees' lives. After all, because corporations are major institutions of American public life, the explicit or implicit messages that companies send can strike at employees' overall sense of identity.

The political liberal position does not adequately recognize that people can communicate—on their own terms—across religious, spiritual, and moral divides. That is, I contend that workers can uphold mutual respect toward their co-workers even as they practice their particularistic religious commitments in the workplace. Does this mean that workers will constantly communicate with one another in religiously particularistic language as they go about the normal routines of their work? I do not believe so.[20] But I do mean to assert that employees should have the freedom to draw upon their religiously based ideas and symbols as they work; they should feel free to explain their beliefs to their co-workers and how their beliefs affect the way they approach their work. Like Pava's and Rawls's perspectives, however, the framework does contain a strong presumption against institutional use of religious language and symbols because of its potential to coerce or degrade employees from differing or minority backgrounds.

One factor influencing this pluralistic approach to moral conversation is my belief that there is no single "complete" language or set of values that is held in common by all citizens.[21] Otherwise stated, if citizens do hold in common a few values, such as freedom, equality, and toleration, these values are not "thick" enough to provide the resources to settle morally challenging leadership questions such as what role religion should play in the contemporary workplace. Attempts to translate religiously particular values into common spiritual or secular values are reductionistic at best and inaccurate at worst.[22] The framework also suggests, however, that citizens in the public sphere should welcome open discussion and debate of multiple perspectives in order that some level of agreement might be attained.

It is appropriate to specify more fully the kind of language I am employing to make the moral argument for respectful pluralism. While the aim of the argument is to suggest that organizations should allow religious, spiritual, and other forms of expression in the workplace, the moral argument of this book is not framed in the language of a particular religious or theological tradition.[23] The framework presented herein draws upon less comprehensive moral language, language that is typically, but not always, employed in leadership studies, religious studies, and business ethics.

As one possible objection to this part of my method, some scholars might argue that this position—like leadership ethics more broadly—lacks a coherent foundation, is not part of a community of discourse, or is an attempt to universalize values that are not universally held. Despite my own constructive critique of political liberalism, significant elements of that perspective inform respectful pluralism, and thus my framework is undoubtedly subject to some of the same criticisms directed against political liberalism.[24] I do *not* intend to claim that my perspective offers all of the moral resources for solving workplace dilemmas or that it should replace religious, philosophical, or other traditions of moral reasoning in the workplace or elsewhere. On the contrary, I am constructing an argument precisely in order to encourage pluralistic debate and the inclusion of multiple perspectives. I reject genetically spiritual frameworks that have the effect of reducing more substantive resources of religious traditions to common denominator beliefs. Respectful pluralism is an "incomplete" framework for settling issues in any given setting.

The framework of respectful pluralism is not, however, a purely procedural one, devoid of substantive claims. In order to construct respectful pluralism, I must appeal to substantive views concerning human dignity, equal respect, noncoercion, nondegradation, etc., that are not universally held. In Rawlsian language, an "overlapping consensus"[25] may or may not be reached on the substantive as well as procedural features of the approach. I offer the framework of respectful pluralism in the hope that some or many readers will find it convincing and that those who disagree will offer a superior approach that addresses the circumstances of the contemporary workplace.

The Moral Features of Respectful Pluralism

Dignity and Equal Respect

It is now possible to specify the moral features of respectful pluralism in organizations. This section views the circumstances of the contemporary workplace, discussed above, as the challenge to which respectful pluralism is a proposed response.

Constructing the framework begins not with the nature of the workplace, but with a series of basic assertions about the employee as a *human person*. The specific concerns and contextual factors of the workplace should fit within the general moral understanding of the human being. The most fundamental claim of the framework is that all persons possess an inviolable *human dignity*. There are many ways to ground such a basic assertion about dignity—that all humans are vulnerable or suffer pain, that they are all created by God, that all are in some sense sacred, etc. The debate about this justification of dignity is beyond the scope of this book.[26] Scholars and practitioners of various religious and other moral traditions will have different ways in which to ground the claim.

If the assumption that each person possesses human dignity is granted, the next claim is that every human being deserves to be accorded *respect*. It will be necessary, of course, to debate precisely what obligations people and institutions (including companies) owe to each human being based on that respect.[27] These fundamental assertions do not differentiate among human beings in terms of any feature that individuals possess that make them merit respectful treatment. Persons simply have dignity and deserve to be accorded respect because they are human.[28]

The third assertion is that all human beings possess *equal* dignity and thus deserve *equal* respect. Since the concept of human dignity is not based on human merit, or distinctive features of some people and not others, there is no justifiable reason to differentiate in the degree of respectful treatment due each person. Given that excluding any person would constitute a differentiation among persons, the scope of equality must extend to include all people. Some philosophers posit that equality (and the prior assertions) should be accepted as self-evident.[29] As Amartya Sen has argued, few if any contemporary moral philosophers (or citizens) debate whether moral equality exists among humans; they generally concur on that point. Rather, a central and contested moral question is, *Equality of what?*[30] In other words, while they agree that equal respect should be accorded to each human being, ethicists argue over precisely how moral equality should be guaranteed and what it demands. Respectful pluralism accepts the assertions regarding human dignity and equal respect outlined above and seeks to show what they require of companies and co-workers, given the circumstances of the workplace.

The comparative, critical analysis of religion in public life in India and Singapore suggests that some basic political and civil rights are owed to citizens prior to their entry into the workplace. Specifically, the framework of respectful pluralism takes as given, regardless of their workplace, that all employees (as citizens[31]) enjoy the basic freedoms of religious exercise, speech, assembly, press, and government petition that are guaranteed in the First Amendment to the US Constitution. Even as we debate how or if we can legitimately balance these rights within the instrumental market relationship, it must be assumed that these rights are part of the political structure in which employment occurs.

Respect, Voluntariness, and Coercion

Having identified these fundamental claims of human dignity and equal respect and some relevant political and civil rights, we can turn to consider the workplace. What conditions must be operative in the workplace relationship in order to guarantee equal respect for all employees and employers? A just society morally precedes and constrains the economic system. It should be seen as a precondition for the efficient operation of markets. Adam Smith, moral philosopher and founder of classical economics, states that "justice . . . is the main pillar that upholds the whole edifice" of society.[32] No relationship in the market sphere or any other sphere of life can justifiably violate the equal respect owed to each person. The basic human dignity of both employees and employers, by virtue of their status as human persons, constrains the profit-seeking activities of firms. As part of the fundamental moral guarantee to all persons undergirding economic relations, workers must be treated humanely and fairly. The specific conditions that guarantee humane and fair treatment, of course, must be determined in any given context. At a minimum, they must have commutative justice; the employment transaction (labor for salary) must be just.

For many ethicists, the essential justice of the transaction is seen in the *voluntariness* of both parties. People who enter into a market relationship of employment enter into a contract with a company. There is general agreement that deception or coercion should not be present in the labor contract. What other conditions ensure the voluntariness of such a contract? Under what conditions does a person give his or her genuine consent? The fact that a person accepts or enters into a work-for-pay relationship does not necessarily prove that that person has done so voluntarily. If there is no other reasonable choice—as in a monopolistic labor market—or if there is no reasonable option in which minimum dignity could be guaranteed and therefore laborers must accept an oppressive job over starvation, then it is difficult to say that the decision is truly based on free will. The knowledge that workers accept employment in sweatshops, for instance, does not attend adequately to the alternative options available (or not available) to potential workers when they accept that job. When potential employees have no other viable employment choices available to them, one of the basic conditions for a fair employment contract is violated.[33] Kurt Nutting writes:

The mere existence of expressed consent, or of alternatives, does not, of course suffice to show that there is no coercion. If the highwayman says, "Your money or your life," and I hand over my money, the existence of the alternative does not show that I have not been coerced into handing over the money. In general, to know if an agreement was reached noncoercively, we need to know if the agreement was between parties relatively equal in bargaining power—and this means that neither side faced a significantly "greater evil" than the other if the agreement could not be reached.[34]

Adam Smith noted that, in many cases, workers often face the greater evil (for example, starvation) in the relationship with an employer, who in the short term might face only the loss of production before another employee can be found.[35]

The market relationship of work involves, among other things, the operation of power among various parties. Nutting claims that the labor relationship always entails coercion,[36] but I differentiate between the morally justifiable power to influence, on the one hand, and coercion, which is the morally illegitimate use of power to influence, on the other. In my frame, coercion is a normative term that signifies inappropriate action or relationship. It is relevant to state that people of minority religious traditions—some who are immigrants to the US in recent years or decades, including Muslims, Hindus, and Latin American Catholics, Pentecostals, and evangelicals—often hold little socioeconomic power and arguably often do not enter into the labor market with the ability to make fully voluntary decisions about employment. They may not, therefore, be in a strong position to make requests for religious understanding or accommodation, not to mention salaries, benefits, and safety measures.[37]

The commitment to dignity and respect limits what demands a firm should make on its employees. To be sure, the work-for-pay relationship has a significant instrumental dimension to it but, at the same time, workers cannot be treated as other "inputs" to the production process, like capital or land, or simply as a means to some economic end.[38] Only while upholding the basic tenets of justice and protecting the dignity of workers can companies pursue profit. Instrumental relations are framed by a fundamental commitment to dignity and respect in a just society. Thus, we ask: what does a moral commitment to the dignity of persons require of companies and employees in terms of religious expression at work? When persons enter into a market-based relationship of work, how free and welcome are they to express themselves religiously (and in other ways)?

Working Conditions and Religious Expression

Recall that the second circumstance of the workplace assumes that work is a fundamental part of one's identity and that one's sense of dignity is significantly affected by one's work. Many Americans are self-employed and have significant control over their working conditions and ways in which they can express themselves while working. Even more Americans, however, labor as employees, working for companies large and small. In these organizations, what does upholding equal respect and human dignity require—and who is responsible for ensuring these requirements are met? In business ethics, attention to respect and dignity customarily focuses on the guarantee of fair wages and decent working conditions for employees. In legal terms, the latter commitment has been translated into minimum occupational safety and health standards, such as those enforced by OSHA (Occupational Safety and Health Administration) in the United States. In moral terms, some ethicists call for a fuller approach to ensuring that policies and cultures create a workplace in which the dignity of all is acknowledged and working conditions are humane and fair.[39]

Such conditions should be understood, I assert, within a wide view of health and well-being. Manuel D. Velasquez, citing Adam Smith's concern about the human costs of labor, argues that moral attention to working conditions should include a worker's mental as well as physical health.[40] Smith emphasized the ways in which the repetition of a few tasks, under the division of labor, could dull workers' minds and lead to lives of monotony.[41] In an effort to achieve morally acceptable working conditions and employee health, it is necessary to discuss the proper role of religious, spiritual, political, and cultural expression by individuals while at work.

At this point in the argument, a question arises: how vital to an individual's sense of human dignity is the freedom to express one's religious identity (or other aspects of one's identity) in the workplace? My moral argument depends upon the understanding—articulated in different ways by differing religious or philosophical traditions—that religious, spiritual, and cultural commitment is a constitutive part of one's identity that cannot be compartmentalized and should not be silenced from explicit expression during work hours. Earlier chapters have presented examples of how employees' fundamental beliefs and actions are evident in multiple kinds of expression.[42] I do not offer a universal account of "how religion is essential to identity in all spheres of life," because I do not believe there is one such account. Further, my argument for respectful pluralism cannot provide a definitive answer to the question of "how much" religion is appropriate in the workplace and what specific dimensions can be legitimately excluded. If the examples and cumulative discussion of earlier chapters are convincing, however, then they add support to my claim that workplace organizations should enable employees explicitly to express

their religious identity at work to a significant degree. Not to permit employees to do so in some measure would be a violation of their dignity. The possible contention that employees enter freely into a presumedly voluntary work-for-pay contract must be considered within the prior constraint of the need to guarantee each employee's human dignity. In situations of genuine voluntariness, employees would arguably be less likely than in many present situations to exchange their rights of explicit religious expression for wages.

This argument, based on the respect that is owed to workers and managers because they, as humans, possess dignity, has implications beyond the specific focus on religion and the workplace. Expression based upon other aspects of identity, including gender, race, ethnicity, age, and sexual orientation, similarly should be allowed at work. In addition, workplace rules about employee interaction should be subjected to the moral criterion of the respect due employees as persons.[43]

The argument for significant religious and other expression at work is not based upon the instrumental value of religion or spirituality for the company's level of motivation, quality of communication, or overall productivity. My analysis makes no claims about whether or not permitting such expression will make employees or companies more efficient or profitable. The features of respectful pluralism that invite, rather than repress, conflict may well contribute to efficiency, but I do not make that empirical claim. It is also reasonable to assert that allowing employee expression may well help with morale—but such a convenient overlap with efficiency is not necessary to make the policy a morally acceptable one.[44] Instead, the approach argues for a significant degree of employee expression based upon the prior moral obligation not to violate workers' dignity.

The Presumption of Inclusion, With Limiting Norms

The following paragraphs state, in the form of a principle and three norms, the essential framework of respectful pluralism. The principle and norms build upon the moral argument based upon the dignity and equal respect of all human beings and depending upon basic political and civil rights and commutative justice.

From that perspective, the principle and norms address the circumstances of the contemporary workplace— religious diversity, non-compartmentalization, the workplace as a public site, the contested place of religion in public life, and companies as for-profit enterprises.

The guiding principle of respectful pluralism is termed the *presumption of inclusion.* It can be stated as follows: To the greatest extent, workplace organizations should allow employees to express their religious, spiritual, cultural, political, and other commitments at work, subject to the limiting norms of noncoercion, non-degradation, and nonestablishment, and in consideration of the reasonable instrumental demands of the for-profit enterprise.

The term *presumption of inclusion* contrasts starkly with an understanding of the workplace as a secular sphere. Unlike that view, the principle assumes that non-compartmentalization holds true and that workers can properly bring their religious commitments to work. It places the moral burden of justification on policies that would limit personal expression. The framework does not, however, assert that any and every action by employees or managers is appropriate at work simply because an employee claims that it is a part of his or her identity. Rather, the essential criteria of inclusion and exclusion—the limiting norms—are the same, whether the expression is seen to be religious, gender based, cultural, political, or otherwise. The essential point is that the moral status of employees, possessing dignity and deserving respect, builds a presumption for a high degree of "personal" expression. Thus, even when workers are engaged in the market relationship of employment, it is generally permissible for them to express religious and other aspects of their identity. Note that this moral argument exceeds the legal minimums. Title VII of the Civil Rights Act (as amended) protects employees against discrimination and harassment based on many aspects of identity, including religion; but respectful pluralism is more expansive in calling for leadership that respects and allows employees to express their identity.

The first limiting norm is *nondegradation.* This norm prohibits coworkers from employing speech or symbols or otherwise conveying messages directed at particular individuals or groups of co-workers that show clear disrespect for them. As with other dimensions of the framework, this norm requires the exercise of judgment, by applying the moral commitment to uphold the dignity of each employee, in determining what types of expression are degrading or seriously disrespectful to other employees. Certainly, adherence to this norm has the potential to label many forms of religious, cultural, political, and other expression unacceptable.

The second limiting norm, *noncoercion,* suggests that, just as firms should not coerce employees in the employment relationship, employees must not use their power illegitimately to influence co-workers or subordinates. In particular, this norm suggests that employees should not use their position or proximity to colleagues or subordinates to impose their religious, spiritual, or political values on them or to subject them to unwanted invitations in ways that violate their co-workers' human dignity.

The third limiting norm, *nonestablishment,* addresses not individual employees but the workplace organization as an institution. It asserts that, given the circumstance of employee diversity, it is not morally acceptable for a company to endorse, or in anyway promote, one particular religious or spiritual worldview over others, even if that worldview is deemed "generic" or is intended to apply to all employees. Upholding the *equal* respect of each worker amidst diversity requires that individual employees be allowed to work within an environment in which leaders can apply the principle and limiting norms of respectful pluralism to all worldviews in a consistent manner. It is important to acknowledge, of course, that all organizations have an organizational culture; some scholars will call any such culture a functional equivalent of a religion. Respectful pluralism is itself a set of ideas for creating a culture that models, as the name suggests, mutual respect amidst diversity.[45] Thus, this criticism has merit. Yet respectful pluralism, while it depends upon substantive moral commitments, is not designed to offer a complete or an exclusive view of truth; rather, its purpose is to encourage co-workers of multiple perspectives and worldviews to communicate with each other and to work together in relative harmony. In short, the framework arguably meets its own criteria of noncoercion and non-degradation, and it respects the various aspects of identity that employees bring to work.

The other limiting consideration acknowledges the legitimate end of profit-seeking by companies. Accordingly, in addition to the moral constraints on personal expression, companies may place other reasonable constraints on expression, as long as they uphold the nonestablishment norm and do not degrade or coerce employees. As should be clear from the entirety of the framework, however, appeals to profitability cannot be made callously as an excuse to exclude all religious or spiritual expression. Further, a company may not make policies that grant the opportunity for one type of expression (for example, religious, spiritual, or political) but exclude another type.[46] Notice that one of the attractive features of respectful pluralism is that it does not require managers or others to determine whether an expression is driven by, or is seen by observers as having, religious, spiritual, or political motivations. Instead, managers and co-workers should apply the tenets of inclusion and limiting norms—which, admittedly, is no simple task. Employers retain legitimate rights to restrain personal expression of various kinds for legitimate safety or efficiency reasons, as long as they do so on an equal basis for all employees. The spirit of the presumption of inclusion, however, does suggest that managers need to have sound reasons to justify any decision not to allow personal expression. That is, the fundamental commitment to equal respect places the moral burden (but not necessarily the legal burden) on the company to show employees why a limit on personal expression is necessary. The legal limitations of Title VII and other federal and state laws are also in place as minimum guarantees against discrimination and harassment.

Respectful Pluralism in Operation: Permissible Expressions and Limitations

A few examples of workplace scenarios related to personal or institutional expression of religion (among other kinds of potential conflict) will give an idea of how respectful pluralism might look in operation.

When is it morally acceptable for employees to wear their religious garb at work? The presumption of inclusion suggests that respectful pluralism calls for a high level of understanding and flexibility on the part of the employer and co-workers toward religiously motivated dress. After September 11, 2001, Muslim women have faced tremendous problems in the workplace because of their religious obligation to wear *hijab*.[47] Respectful

pluralism's approach to such examples requires accommodation—on moral grounds—that goes beyond the standard *de minimis* interpretation of the legal framework required in Title VII of the Civil Rights Act.[48] Given that the workplace is a public or quasi-public institution, the company's decision to exclude women in *hijab* would not only send a message of exclusion to Muslim women, but it would reinforce the idea that Muslims' religious obligations place them outside of US public life. Muslim women who appear in *hijab* must be treated with the same respect accorded other employees; dress codes should be accommodated unless compelling dangers are demonstrated. As a practical matter, examples of suitable compromises abound in which religious persons were able to uphold their commitments while still meeting safety requirements.[49] In rare cases when genuine safety concerns prohibit a person in loose-fitting clothing to hold a position, corporations have a moral obligation beyond *de minimis* costs to find a suitable alternative position for the employee.

As a second example, consider an employee who wishes to hang a religious poster in his or her work area. For instance, a worker wishes to hang a poster that says, "Jesus Saves!" in his cubicle. A few other workers complain about the poster: "It has no place in the office" or "He shouldn't be declaring that his faith is better than mine." In a framework of respectful pluralism, this employee would be allowed to hang such a poster, as long as adherents of other religious and cultural groups are permitted to hang their own respectful posters as well. To be sure, some employees will find the Christian message to be disrespectful, at least in intention. In this author's judgment, this message in isolation is neither coercive nor degrading of persons of other faiths; but reasonable persons may disagree, and applications of respectful pluralism will have to be made in any particular setting. Indeed, the very discussion of whether or not something is perceived as coercive or degrading may well be a way to identify tension already latent among co-workers and to produce a beneficial outcome. Critics might say that this kind of debate is a distraction from work. I would make two kinds of argument in response to that criticism: first, I assert that conflicts will arise among workers whether explicit religious messages are allowed or not; second, I would reiterate my claim that, based upon respect for workers, it is impermissible to forbid religious and other expressions at work. Some limit on the number of posters, works of art, and plants, etc., could certainly be established, but those limits should be set and upheld for all persons, regardless of their rank and irrespective of the religious, political, or cultural tradition they reflect. It is not acceptable, however, to prohibit all employees from hanging any decorations or expressions in their work area.

As these examples show, it is incorrect to say that the substantive content of posters and other messages should not be evaluated. The general presumption of permitting religious, political, and other expression is limited morally by the three norms, in addition to relevant legal constraints, especially the legal limits placed on libelous or hate-inspiring speech. The norms of noncoercion and nondegradation require reflection on the substance of the message. It is not necessary, though, to ask whether a given expression is religious or spiritual in nature.

Contrast the Christian poster discussed above with a scenario in which an employee hangs a poster that states, "Homosexuals: repent and turn to Jesus Christ." This message entails a clear condemnation of certain persons' sexual orientation. Since sexual orientation is widely (though admittedly not universally) acknowledged as an important part of human identity, the poster's denigration of a personal identity violates the limiting norm of nondegradation. Whether or not a poster with such a message cites religious scripture (for example, biblical texts) should not make a difference in determining its inclusion or exclusion. An employer's personal view regarding homosexuality is not even relevant in this case; regardless of his or her personal view, an employer should forbid the display of such a poster on the grounds that many employees will interpret the poster's message as degrading to homosexuals. Respectful pluralism focuses on whether the content of the message itself reflects respect or disrespect for human dignity.

This example reveals that not all readers (or employers or employees) will agree with the framework of respectful pluralism. For some religious persons, homosexuality is incompatible with their (religiously, culturally, familially, or politically influenced) understanding of human nature and society. They might argue that respectful pluralism promotes (or is itself a form of) moral relativism because it allows theologically or morally unacceptable behavior to go unquestioned. The view of respectful pluralism does not require workplace leaders even to take a position on the

truth or falsity of the message, but, rather, it evaluates the actions and speech of employees in terms of the principle and norms.

The norms that limit the general presumption of inclusion of employee expression apply, in parallel fashion, to political messages as well as religious ones. For instance, employees are welcome to hang an American flag or a poster that states, "God bless America!" Similarly, workers should be allowed to hang flags of other nations as well.[50] It would not be permissible, however, for an employee to hang a poster (or wear a t-shirt or button) that says, "Foreigners, go home!" or, conversely, "Death to America!" Much like the religiously based case above, these messages are directed at a particular group of persons and suggest that their national identity is not welcome in the workplace. These messages fail the nondegradation test.

The second limiting norm within respectful pluralism prohibits situations in which co-workers, regardless of intention, have the effect of coercing other employees through their religious, spiritual, or other expression at work. On this point, consider cases of employees who wish to invite co-workers to religious events.[51] Supporters of the secular workplace would view the extension of *any* religious invitation at work as coercive, that is, as an illegitimate use of one's potential influence and proximity to put pressure on co-workers. Yet, given the importance of religion and the circumstance of non-compartmentalization, it is morally acceptable for employees to invite colleagues to religious events (or political rallies or cultural celebrations, for that matter) as long as they are willing to take no for an answer and then refrain from extending further unwanted invitations. After a person has indicated he or she does not want to receive such invitations, then it is, in fact, coercive (i.e., a violation of the norm of noncoercion) to continue making advances.[52] As with other examples, the line between invitation and proselytization is not always clear-cut, especially since co-workers might be unwilling to state their discomfort at being approached, but the co-worker's genuine ability to say no without fear of negative repercussions is a significant determining factor.

With coercion as with degradation, religious expression is not the only form of expression subject to debate. Selling Girl Scout cookies and other solicitations in the workplace provide illustrative examples. When an employee approaches a co-worker with the offer to buy some product, whether for a charitable cause or otherwise, that invitation need not necessarily be interpreted as coercive. Many employees might appreciate the opportunity to make a contribution to an organization or to buy the product. Others find the practice to be a terrible abuse of the goodwill of co-workers. As with religiously based invitations, when a boss or supervisor solicits employees to buy a product, the potential for coercion is even greater. Whether or not this is a violation of the noncoercion policy is dependent on the context but, once again, the guiding principle's presumption of inclusion and the ability of the person being approached to decline the offer are important guideposts.

The previous examples concern the first two limiting norms and deal with individual employees who seek to make religious or other kinds of "personal" expression while at work. The third norm, nonestablishment, applies to situations in which the expression is not merely individualistic but in some way reflects or suggests an undue institutional preference for a specific religious worldview. Leaders' individual religious beliefs and actions may easily be mistaken for institutionally supported expression. As a consequence, religious expression by formal leaders in any workplace is potentially more problematic than religious expression by employees who are not formal leaders. That is, because a leader has formal power, a leader's invitations, statements, or actions may be interpreted as unfair to employees of differing commitments, regardless of his or her intention. This point is admittedly a contentious one, especially since most of the spirituality and leadership literature focuses disproportionately on the faith of leaders.[53] The potential for coercion by bosses based upon their formal or positional power is often overlooked in these discussions. Both the Christian establishment view and the generic spirituality view tend to discount this problem, since in different ways each perspective supports the belief that employees generally hold the same set of values held by the manager.

Consider a manager who invites employees to a New Age ritual in her office before work once a week. The case would be essentially the same if the boss offered a Bible study class or a yoga session. Employees generally know about the weekly meeting, whether through word-of-mouth, e-mails, or bulletin board invitations. The boss or manager does not intentionally seek to exclude anyone—indeed, she would love for all to come—but she is unabashedly specific in presenting the content of her beliefs and practices. In other words, whether she is a Christian or Hindu or a New Age adherent, many employees would not recognize the meeting's religious/spiritual approach as reflective of their own beliefs and practices. Despite the fact that the manager makes efforts to assure that workers are neither rewarded for participating nor penalized for not attending, it is clear that she comes to know the regular attendees particularly well. Other employees feel they are losing access to her because they are not a part of this intimate circle.

This is a difficult situation, because managers, just like employees, should not have to sacrifice their faith or religious values when they enter the workplace. Yet, in order to avoid even the appearance of favoritism or coercion, the boss should find ways to hold or attend religiously based meetings in contexts other than the workplace. There are at least two possible alternatives. First, she could meet with employees, not in office space, but rather in a setting outside the workplace. (Holding such a meeting for subordinates in her home, however, might still create feelings of favoritism, though such a situation would still be preferable to meeting in her office.) A second alternative would be to attend meetings that lower-level employees hold in their own offices. Even this, however, would not dispel all of the questions about a preferred circle of employees.

This concern about institutional expressions of religion in the workplace also applies to religious symbols employed by companies themselves. The nonestablishment norm implies that neither the effective establishment of a religion nor the creation of a civil-corporate religion is compatible with respectful pluralism.[54] Consideration of an example of effective establishment and an example of civil–corporate religion will support this claim. First, consider a company that wishes to adopt a logo that includes the Christian symbol of a cross or a fish. After all, a member of the board of trustees states, the founder of the company was a strong Christian and believed in putting his faith to work. The company stands for care and service, board members reason, just as Christ embodied love and service. In addition, most of the workforce is Christian and no one objected when the company sponsored various Christian benevolence programs in the past. Surely, such a desire to reflect a religiously based value system can be well intentioned. Yet the practice violates the norm of nonestablishment. It does not attend adequately to the possible public impact that the effective Christian preference could have on the sense of place of non-Christians, particularly, but not exclusively, those in the workforce.

This reasoning applies not only to Christian or Jewish or Muslim expressions of religion. Consider a more generically spiritual approach that may be at least as potentially exclusive or coercive. I have in mind corporate continuing education seminars that require employees to meditate in order to "discover" their spiritual self at work. Leadership scholars have pointed out the potentially problematic nature of such "nontraditional" spiritual training programs, including their "high potential for psychological and legal fallout."[55] Because the framework of respectful pluralism does not depend on whether or not an argument is religious in order to be included or excluded, it is not necessary or relevant to determine whether a particular seminar takes a faith-based or secular approach to meditation, leadership, or professional development. The relevant question is whether or not the potential exists for employees to feel coerced or degraded in such training. In various cases, employees, including those from traditional religious backgrounds, have reported such negative effects. This practice violates the norm of nonestablishment and, in the process, probably violates the other two norms as well.

Conclusions

These examples do not settle or provide a definitive resolution to the myriad problems of diverse employee expressions in the workplace. Indeed, the framework of respectful pluralism is not meant to be a checklist with easy answers for any workplace. Particular contexts will require uniquely creative solutions to potentially divisive situations. It is also worth noting a few other limitations and further considerations of the framework. The commitment to acknowledge the human dignity of all workers and extend them equal respect—and hence grant employees the right to religious and other expression in the workplace—has implications beyond any one particular firm. Regarding issues of equitable pay or safe and healthy working conditions, the wider legal,

social, and cultural context affects the "deal" that individual employees and individual firms can negotiate. Analogously, the issue of employees' religious and other expression in the workplace demands a more comprehensive analysis of what opportunities are afforded employees in various workplaces, as well as in public life as a whole, to express aspects of their identity. This analysis should include attention to laws as well as to cultural norms and mores about religious expression. For instance, both the generic spirituality and the Christian establishment views continue to hold sway, not only in the workplace, but also in most aspects of American life today. The basic moral requirements of human dignity and equal respect should be discussed in various aspects of public life, including within religious communities. The attendant issues, then, do not merely call for workplace leadership, but also society-wide leadership concerning the appropriate role of religion in public life. Comparative analyses, such as my examination of India and Singapore, can also shed light on how the wider societal laws and norms impact religion's roles in the workplace.

Many (most) important philosophical and theological discussions about the nature of pluralism—and claims about truth and morality—are not answered by a framework for negotiating differences in the workplace. Indeed, on this point, my account of respectful pluralism seeks to minimize the number of situations in which managers must become theologians or must assess whether or not a religious claim is appropriately grounded or genuinely held. The presumption of inclusion and the limiting norms are designed to avoid making the workplace the context for settling philosophical or theological debates about the truth of religious (or political or cultural) expressions. I have emphasized, however, that the framework is not merely procedural and value-neutral. It is not. Coercion or degradation of employees, whether by the imposition of religious values or by the denial of employees' own religious expression, is unacceptable on moral grounds. The framework calls upon workplace leaders and the whole leadership process to put religious pluralism into practice in order to allow a diverse workforce to work together respectfully and even productively.

As with other forms of diversity, it is difficult to discuss religious expression predominantly in the negative terms of discrimination. (Analysis of discrimination is the most frequent, but not wholly satisfactory, mode of discussing race-based and gender-based diversity in the workplace.) In some cases, religious expression by employees does lead to discrimination against them in the workplace (for example, discrimination against Sikh men who wear turbans or Jewish men who wear the yarmulke). In other cases, however, religious expression by some can contribute to explicit or implicit discrimination against other employees (for example, institution-sponsored prayers at official workplace functions which fail to acknowledge employees from other traditions). In yet other instances, the relationship between religious expression and discrimination is ambiguous (for example, evangelical Christians who claim to experience discrimination because of their religious expression but in other ways enjoy the fruits of an effective Christian establishment in terms of the working calendar, etc.). My framing of respectful pluralism in constructive terms is intended to move beyond a merely defensive treatment of religion in the workplace. Religiously based and other commitments in a diverse workplace do create the potential for conflict—conflict that the framework of respectful pluralism is designed to orchestrate in ways that are positive for individual employees and the organization as a whole.

The approach of respectful pluralism also allows for a significant *pedagogical* component. That is, the presumption of inclusion of religious and other expression helps create a working environment in which people are able to share information about their religious, spiritual, and moral practices with others to a significant degree. As long as employees enter into the discussion (whether around the water cooler or in open lunchtime forums) in a spirit of respect and noncoercion, then they have an opportunity to learn from one another. The media tend to focus on the divisive nature of religion in public life (and, admittedly, the examples considered above may reinforce that view). The quieter, more mundane discussions at work, in which people share their own personal narratives, religious and otherwise, are less newsworthy but perhaps cumulatively more significant. The most basic point is that the leadership process should enable such conversations to take place on a level playing field that admits many points of view. The playing-field metaphor may be misleading, though, because the approach does not intend to generate competition in any sense.

The limiting norm of nonestablishment does not preclude efforts to create a workplace culture in which individual employees may express their religious commitments. Indeed, although the examples considered in this chapter have emphasized the negotiation of potential conflict among individuals, respectful pluralism offers a proactive approach to building a culture of mutual understanding. Consistent with the framework's presumption of inclusion, the overall approach assumes that, in many or most cases, religion is a healthy, central part of an individual's identity. Workplace organizations can address religious diversity in healthy ways, too.

Notes

1. This approach to understanding and responding to descriptive circumstances is parallel to John Rawls's attention (drawing upon David Hume) to the "circumstances of justice" as those conditions that necessitate a theory of justice. John Rawls, *A Theory of Justice* (Cambridge, MA: Harvard University Press, 1971), 126–30.

2. See Amartya Sen, "Description as Choice," *Oxford Economic Papers* 32 (1980).

3. Three kinds of problems would remain in that case, however. First, there would still be concern about potential coercion, viz., whether individuals are allowed to practice their religion on their own terms. Second, we would have to ask, why are adherents of other religious, spiritual, or moral backgrounds not included in the company?—and, will an employee from a different background who joins the company be respected? Third, there would still remain the issue of whether the workplace, through establishment, was inappropriately becoming, in itself, a *religious* institution.

4. See chs. 2 and 3 in *Religion and the Workplace: Pluralism, Spirituality, Leadership* by Douglas A. Hicks.

5. Note that non-compartmentalization can also be a normative claim—asserting that, since people should live integrated lives, they should be allowed to express themselves religiously and in other ways at work and elsewhere. Respectful pluralism makes such a moral argument. But it is based, in part, on the descriptive fact that it is difficult if not impossible for employees to keep the workplace free of personal "encumbrances" like religious commitment.

6. The term "private sector" is a misnomer; the business sector is only private in the sense of being non-governmental.

7. Juliet Schor, *The Overworked American: The Unexpected Decline of Leisure* (New York: Basic Books, 1992); Robert D. Putnam, *Bowling Alone: The Collapse and Revival of*

American Community (New York: Simon & Schuster, 2000). In Arlie Hochschild's language, managers have sought to make work more like home, even as home-life has become more like work. Arlie Hochschild, *The Time Bind: When Work Becomes Home and Home Becomes Work* (New York: Metropolitan Books, 1997).

8. See ch. 2 in *Religion and the Workplace: Pluralism, Spirituality, Leadership* by Douglas A. Hicks.

9. Patricia Werhane and Tara Radin, acknowledging the tremendous size and political and social power of corporations, suggest that corporate employees should receive due process rights in order to protect themselves from the potentially coercive influence of corporations—influence that is not recognized explicitly in standard views of work as "employment at will." Patricia H. Werhane and Tara J. Radin, "Employment at Will and Due Process," in *Ethical Theory and Business*, ed. Tom L. Beauchamp and Norman E. Bowie, sixth edn. (Upper Saddle River, NJ: Prentice Hall, 2001).

10. Moses L. Pava, "Religious Business Ethics and Political Liberalism: An Integrative Approach," *Journal of Business Ethics* 17 (1998). In particular, Pava notes that corporations: "A—create and sustain monopolistic markets, B—impose costs or externalities on non-contracting third parties, and C—lobby governmental official[s] for personal and corporate gain" (p. 1637). Pava chooses not to call corporations fully public because he notes, rightly, that the degree of coercion that a corporation can have on an employee is still not as great as that which a government can have on a citizen.

11. For one description of contemporary workplaces as a context for interreligious encounter, see Diana L. Eck, *A New Religious America: How a "Christian Country" Has Now Become the World's Most Religiously Diverse Nation* (San Francisco: Harper San Francisco, 2001), 316–20.

12. For a helpful framework for analyzing the multiple kinds and levels of context, see J. Thomas Wren and Marc J. Swatez, "The Historical and Contemporary Contexts of Leadership: A Conceptual Model," in *The Leader's Companion: Insights on Leadership through the Ages,* ed. J. Thomas Wren (New York: Free Press, 1995).

13. See ch. 6 in *Religion and the Workplace: Pluralism, Spirituality, Leadership* by Douglas A. Hicks.

14. Milton Friedman, *Capitalism and Freedom* (University of Chicago Press, 1962), 133.

15. Ronald F. Thiemann, *Religion in Public Life: A Dilemma for Democracy* (Washington, DC: Georgetown University Press, 1996), 135–41.

16. Douglas A. Hicks, *Inequality and Christian Ethics,* New Studies in Christian Ethics 16 (Cambridge University Press, 2000), 85–113. In that work I construct a Christian ethical approach to well-being and socioeconomic inequality.

17. Rawls's basic position is laid out in John Rawls, *Political Liberalism, The John Dewey Essays in Philosophy No. 4*

(New York: Columbia University Press, 1993), Lecture VI, pp. 212–54. He widened his perspective significantly in John Rawls, "The Idea of Public Reason Revisited," *University of Chicago Law Review* 64 (1997); specifically, he allowed for persons to appeal to religious reasons or to any other "reasonable comprehensive doctrine," as long as they also provided "proper political reasons" (for example, commonly held public political values) alongside the reasons of the more particular worldview (pp. 783–84). For a fuller discussion, see Hicks, *Inequality and Christian Ethics,* 93–101.

18. Hicks, *Inequality and Christian Ethics,* 97–101; this point relates to the second circumstance of the workplace, discussed above.

19. Pava, "Religious Business Ethics and Political Liberalism: An Integrative Approach," 1635.

20. Note that much of the expression of religious commitment (dress, symbols in one's work area, taking time off for prayers or holy days) is not about direct communication with co-workers at all.

21. Rawls employs the language of "completeness" in his analysis of public reason, asserting that public reason is complete when its "values alone give a reasonable public answer to all, or to nearly all, questions involving the constitutional essentials and basic questions of justice," in Rawls, *Political Liberalism,* 225.

22. See ch. 3 in *Religion and the Workplace: Pluralism, Spirituality, Leadership* by Douglas A. Hicks.

23. Surely my own perspective and training in Christian ethics, as I noted in the introduction, has influenced my argument in various ways.

24. I consider some of these criticisms in *Inequality and Christian Ethics,* ch. 5, esp. pp. 93–113. See also Thiemann, *Religion in Public Life.*

25. See Rawls, *Political Liberalism,* Lecture IV, pp. 133–72.

26. I have treated related questions in Hicks, *Inequality and Christian Ethics,* 20–23. In that work I go on to develop a Christian account of equality, based on human dignity and the claim that humans are created as equals by God.

27. It is important to note that this claim, that persons be treated with respect, pertains to the speech and actions that individuals and organizations should make toward persons. It does not, and cannot, require people to have moral respect, in a deeper (passive) sense, for individuals whose actions or beliefs do not accord with their own moral conception of the world. Indeed, to attempt to require people to hold an interior feeling or moral evaluation of respect for all other persons would be coercive. It is, rather, reasonable to ask persons to act with respect toward all persons because they are human beings, with dignity. It is possible for a workplace to fire an employee, or for the state to convict a criminal, by following laws and procedures that respect the person in that

process. My framework makes substantive claims about what respectful speech and actions are required in the diverse workplace. I am grateful to Jonathan Wight for discussions on this point.

28. Some scholars seek to ground dignity in the capacity to reason; but then persons with impaired reasoning or severe related disabilities may not be seen as having dignity. Such grounding cannot justify the fundamental assertion of human dignity of *all* persons and would thus be a *competing* moral conception to the ones based on that fundamental assumption.

29. For his part, Thomas Jefferson makes precisely this claim in the Declaration of Independence—"We hold these truths to be self-evident, that all men are created equal." Most modern scholars would agree with Jefferson's claim if the interpretation of the word "men" were broadened to include females as well as males and slaves as well as free persons.

30. This was the title of Sen's 1979 Tanner Lectures on Human Values. Amartya Sen, "Equality of What?" In *The Tanner Lectures on Human Values,* ed. S. McMurrin (Salt Lake City: Utah University Press and Cambridge University Press, 1980). See my discussion in Hicks, *Inequality and Christian Ethics,* 23–24.

31. It is vitally important to note that the assumption that all employees are citizens of the nation in which they work does not address directly the issue of the rights of migrant workers or immigrants—whether legal or illegal. For this moral argument, I am assuming that the civil and political rights of all persons, regardless of nationality, should be protected equally and that all persons are deserving of equal respect.

32. Adam Smith, *The Theory of Moral Sentiments,* trans. D. D. Raphael and A. L. Macfie, Glasgow Edition of the Works and Correspondence of Adam Smith (New York: Oxford University Press, 1976), II.ii.3.4, 86.

33. Manuel G. Velasquez, *Business Ethics: Concepts and Cases,* fifth edn. (Upper Saddle River, NJ: Prentice Hall, 2002), 460.

34. Kurt Nutting, "Work and Freedom in Capitalism," in *Moral Rights in the Workplace,* ed. Gertrude Ezorsky (Albany, NY: State University of New York Press, 1987), 102.

35. "Many workmen could not subsist a week, few could subsist a month, and scarce any a year without employment. In the long run, the workman may become as necessary to his master as his master is to him; but the necessity is not so immediate." Adam Smith, *An Inquiry into the Nature and Causes of the Wealth of Nations,* ed. R. H. Campbell, A. S. Skinner, and W. B. Todd, Glasgow Edition of the Works and Correspondence of Adam Smith, 2 vols. (New York: Oxford University Press, 1976), I.viii.12, 84.

36. Nutting, "Work and Freedom in Capitalism," 102–03.

37. The framework of respectful pluralism argues that all employees, regardless of their socioeconomic status, should be permitted to express their religious identity.

38. It is important to note that, in the market-based relationship of work, firms are not the only parties that have instrumental goals. Indeed, a variety of actors (or "stakeholders") have their own objectives. For instance, stockholders seek the long-term increase in the value of their stock. They certainly may also desire to contribute to society by making a product available for consumption or by creating employment opportunities for workers. Managers typically desire to maximize their own salary and benefits. Employees pursue a dependable and good salary. Managers and employees alike often seek to find meaningful or fulfilling work, not as a means, but as an end in itself. Indeed, employees often articulate their work in terms of living out their religious, spiritual, or moral obligations. Customers seek affordable, useful goods and services. Neighbors of the company hope that the presence of the business in their community will generate positive outcomes (e.g., employment, community relations, increased tax revenues) with a minimum of negative external effects (e.g., pollution, traffic congestion). For all of these parties, the protection of human dignity of all persons serves as a constraint on the legitimate objectives of market-based relationships.

39. Michael Boylan, *Business Ethics: Basic Ethics in Action* (Upper Saddle River, NJ: Prentice Hall, 2001), 215–17; Velasquez, *Business Ethics,* 457.

40. Velasquez, *Business Ethics,* 461–62.

41. Smith, *The Wealth of Nations,* V.i.f.50–54, 781–85. Smith's concern about dulled minds led him to call for public education for the "common people."

42. See esp. chs. 4 and 5 in *Religion and the Workplace: Pluralism, Spirituality, Leadership* by Douglas A. Hicks.

43. Instances of short periods of time on the job when conversation is not permitted may well be acceptable, but policies that forbid outright co-worker conversation during lengthy work shifts, such as those at some large retail department-store chains, are seriously suspect. Barbara Ehrenreich offers a first-hand account of her employment as a Wal-Mart employee and her encounter with such restrictive policies. Barbara Ehrenreich, *Nickel and Dimed: On (Not) Getting by in America* (New York: Metropolitan/Owl Books, Henry Holt and Company, 2001).

44. See ch. 9 in *Religion and the Workplace: Pluralism, Spirituality, Leadership* by Douglas A. Hicks.

45. Ibid.

46. Arguments based on legal reasoning have been successful in rejecting the exclusion of employees' expression

merely because it was religious. See examples in ch. 4 in *Religion and the Workplace: Pluralism, Spirituality, Leadership* by Douglas A. Hicks.

47. See chapter 4 in *Religion and the Workplace: Pluralism, Spirituality, Leadership* by Douglas A. Hicks for examples of discrimination against women based on their attempts to wear *hijab* at work.

48. Title VII of the Civil Rights Act (as amended) requires reasonable accommodation of religion by employers unless they show they would face "undue hardship" in doing so. The US Supreme Court decided in *TWA* v. *Hardison* (1977) that demonstrating such an undue hardship was not a high standard to meet. See Michael Wolf, Bruce Friedman, and Daniel Sutherland, *Religion in the Workplace: A Comprehensive Guide to Legal Rights and Responsibilities* (Chicago: Tort and Insurance Practice Section, American Bar Association, 1998), 104–34.

49. As one example, the Whirlpool Corporation's safety engineers gathered with Muslim women in its manufacturing plant to develop a mutually agreeable policy. James E. Challenger, "Firms Make Room for Different Religions," *Chicago Sun-Times,* May 14, 2000.

50. One difficult case is whether or not employees could hang a Confederate battle flag in their workspace. The framework of respectful pluralism objects to hanging that flag on grounds that, whatever the intentions of the employees who wish to display it, because of its historic ties to slavery and the segregationists who opposed the civil rights movement, the flag has come to signify disrespect for the human dignity of African Americans.

51. See ch. 4 in *Religion and the Workplace: Pluralism, Spirituality, Leadership* by Douglas A. Hicks for a discussion of recent legal cases that concern the issues of invitation and/or proselytization.

52. On this distinction, President Clinton's "Guidelines on Religious Exercise and Religious Expression in the Federal Workplace" offers a well-articulated position. William Jefferson Clinton, "Guidelines on Religious Exercise and Religious Expression in the Federal Workplace" (Washington, DC: The White House Office of the Press Secretary, 1997).

53. Much of the literature seems to suggest that, if religious values are going to come into the workplace, they will be introduced in a top-down fashion by the leaders. The literature tends to overlook the fact that lower-level employees also seek to live out their faith and often bring their religious identity into the workplace. This is a curious oversight.

54. Establishment religion and civil-corporate religion are discussed in detail in ch. 6 in *Religion and the Workplace: Pluralism, Spirituality, Leadership* by Douglas A. Hicks.

55. Mark Lipton, "'New Age' Organizational Training: Tapping Employee Potential or Creating New Problems?" *The Human Resources Professional* 3/2 (1991): 72.

PART VII

Capacity Building

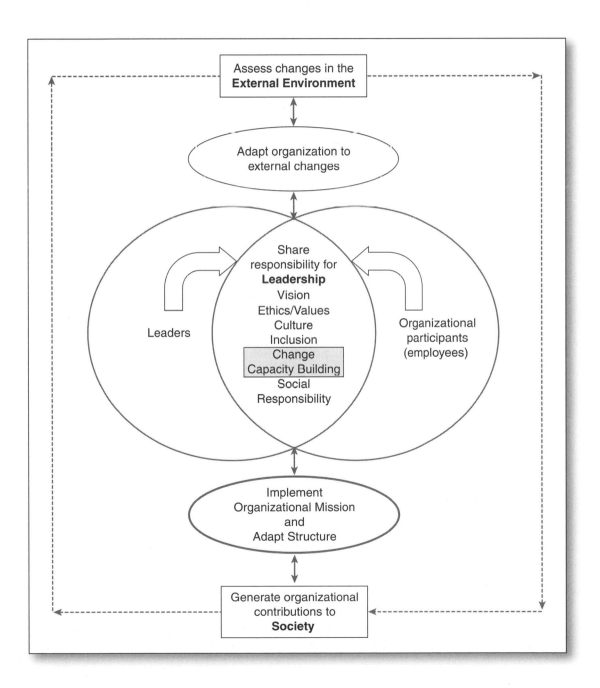

Overview

The organization's ability to meet new challenges from the external environment depends on its facility to build capacity among its members. The figure illustrates the interrelatedness among essential elements in the development of capacity. The chapters in this section contribute to understanding each of these interrelated components.

Adapting

The greatest demand on new era organizations is to face adaptive challenges. Ronald Heifetz (Chapter 39) contends that adaptive challenges demand leadership that can engage people in facing challenging realities and then changing at least some of their priorities, attitudes, and behavior in order to thrive in a changing world. Leadership in this context generates new cultural norms that enable people to meet an ongoing stream of adaptive challenges, which Heifetz calls "adaptive work." He describes seven requirements of this work:

1. Adaptive work is necessary in response to problem situations for which solutions lie outside the current way of operating.

2. Adaptive work demands learning—retooling the way one thinks and operates.

3. Adaptive work requires a shift in responsibility from authority figures and authority structures to the stakeholders themselves—responsibility taken by stakeholders.

4. Adaptive work requires people to distinguish what is precious and essential from what is expendable within their culture.

5. Adaptive work demands experimentation.

6. Adaptive work requires time—a longer time frame than technical problems.

7. Adaptive work is a normative concept—it involves the clarification of values and the assessment of realities that challenge the realization of those values.

Accordingly, adaptive work entails change, learning, taking responsibility, experimentation, time, conflict, and values clarification. Several of these themes are continued in this section of the book.

Leading Change

Change is an inherent component of capacity building in organizations and is a fundamental component of an organization's larger environment. Gill Hickman (Chapter 40) identifies several categories of organization change practices: collective or collaborative approaches, strategic planning and goal setting, stages of praxis, scenario building, appreciative inquiry, e-practices, and ethical practices. Collective or collaborative change involves institutionalized leadership and change practices that are embedded in the organization's essential systems; organizational learning that focuses on personal mastery, mental models, shared vision, team learning, and systems thinking; and shared power or empowerment, which entails delegating or distributing leadership, authority, responsibility, and decision-making power to individuals and teams throughout the organization. Strategic planning is rooted in strategic leadership and environmental scanning, described in Parts I and II.

Hickman compares Kurt Lewin's three-stage model of change with John Kotter's eight-stage model. Both models begin with establishing a sense of urgency, which initiates the change process, and move through to the final stage of anchoring new change in the culture. Scenario building, also discussed in Part I, advocates an eight-factor process that helps leaders and members use factual information and indicators of early trends to project alternative futures for the organization. Appreciative inquiry is a change process that uses successful processes and practices in the organization to build momentum and construct new realities for the future.

Leading change in virtual teams requires e-practices that combine select components of face-to-face leadership with technology, structured processes, clearly designated roles, frequent communication, and other factors. Finally, effective change processes require ethical practices consisting of authenticity, trust, and reciprocal care to sustain a healthy moral environment.

Collaborating

The opportunity for collaboration is present when the stakeholders recognize the potential advantages of working together for a mutual purpose.[1] Collaboration is enhanced by heightening the stakeholders' awareness of their interdependence, respecting and dealing constructively with differences, and assuming joint ownership of decisions and joint responsibility for future interactions.[2] The work of the Society for Organizational Learning (SoL) Sustainability Consortium illustrates essential processes of collaboration. Peter Senge and colleagues (Chapter 41) conducted research focused on several change initiatives in which cross-sector groups sought collaborative solutions to sustainability issues (social and ecological imbalances created by globalization). Researchers found three interconnected types of work involved in collaboration for systemic change: *conceptual*, making sense of complex issues; *relational*, far-reaching, unorchestrated dialogue for thinking, learning, and asking questions together; and *action driven*, building new change initiatives together. They summarized lessons learned from the three types of work that led to collaboration.

Developing Conflict Capital

Inevitably, learning, collaboration, and change depend on the ability of leaders and participants to use effectively the conflict that arises from differences. The beneficial outcome of such processes is *conflict capital*. Conflict capital (akin to other forms of capital) is a resource that results from discovering, understanding, and making use of differences among participants or stakeholders.[3]

Mark Gerzon (Chapter 42) identifies a form of leadership that draws on the constructive use of differences—the mediator. He posits that in multistakeholder situations, the mediator perspective allows individuals to transform differences into opportunities by serving as a steward of the whole rather than an owner of the parts. This leadership approach places conflict at the center of the process so that participants understand differing perspectives beyond superficial levels and use the complexity and scope of differences to generate original solutions. The mediator

approach does not require participants in the process to be conflict-resolution professionals. Instead, it provides a mediator perspective for leading in cross-boundary or diverse settings and incorporates practices to implement this approach. Gerzon synthesizes his and other colleagues' mediator practices into eight tools for leading through conflict: integral vision, systems thinking, presence, inquiry, conscious conversation, dialogue, bridging, and innovation. The challenge for actors in the change process is to create "a vision of what is possible"—that is, to imagine a situation in which the conflict has been transformed—then hold on to that vision throughout the process. The result of leading in this manner can produce substantial conflict capital.

Research by Donna Chrobot-Mason and colleagues (Chapter 43) identifies conflict resolution strategies for identity-based conflicts in organizations. These researchers explain that identity-based conflict involves disputes over the intrinsic value of groups with which individuals identify and that it often originates outside of the work context. Such disputes emerge as workers from various identity groups in conflict attempt to work together. As a result, conflicts embedded in society literally spill over into the organization. Chrobot-Mason et al. propose four leadership strategies for surmounting identity-based conflicts: *decategorization*, a strategy that uses person-based leadership strategy in which interactions are structured in ways that allow diverse groups or individuals to get to know one another as individuals; *recategorization*, a strategy that creates a new inclusive group identity that members share in common; *subcategorization*, an approach that allows members of both groups to have distinct but complementary roles that contribute toward a common goal and allow members to remain distinctive while working together in a cooperative fashion; and *cross-cutting*, a strategy that involves systematically or randomly selecting and placing individuals from different identity groups into project teams or task forces with relatively equal representation. The goals of these conflict resolution strategies are to facilitate deeper understanding and appreciation of perspectives among organizational members from different identity groups and to allow leaders and participants to move toward creating a common purpose.

Cultivating Democratic Processes

Capacity building through the use of democratic organizations looms in the distance for many organization members. Brook Manville and Josiah Ober (Chapter 44) maintain that organizational leadership structures are still firmly planted in the industrial age, despite enlightened rhetoric to the contrary. Organizational leaders in recent years have created partially flattened bureaucracies and narrowly distributed empowerment of employees. The leadership challenge for contemporary organizations is to determine how to transform industrial age bureaucracies into new era organizations that fully utilize the knowledge, intelligence, and capabilities of well-prepared organizational members. Manville and Ober recommend building an organization of citizens based on a democratic model inspired by ancient Athenians. They propose that organization members draw on Athenian democratic principles that supported the development of a community of citizens, because there are so few current models of democratic organizations. The framework that supports a community of citizens in an organization entails *participatory structures* for making decisions, resolving disputes, and managing activities; a set of *communal values* that defines people's relationships with one another; and practices of engagement that ensure the broad participation of the entire citizenry.

Congruent with Manville and Ober's analogy of Athenian democracy, Lynda Gratton (Chapter 45) offers six tenets that form the basis of a democratic enterprise. She asserts that (a) the relationship between the organization and the individual is adult-to-adult, (b) individuals are seen primarily as investors actively building and deploying their human capital, (c) individuals are able to develop their natures and express their diverse qualities, (d) individuals are able to participate in determining the conditions of their association, (e) the liberty of some individuals is not at the expense of others, and (f) individuals have accountabilities and obligations both to themselves and to the organization. Gratton applies a three-part litmus test to these tenets that consists of coherence, viability, and practicality.

The final chapter in this section addresses democratic value creation in organizations using a South African process of interactive forums called *umhlangano*, which means discussion/interaction. Mike Boon (Chapter 46) explains that the umhlangano is a community gathering within which participants can have deep discussions. These interactive forums bring together members of departments or sections that typically work with each other. According to Boon, rank and positional power have to be set aside and participants are asked to regard each other as human beings who bare their humanity and listen to each other with dignity. Facilitators from outside the group are often used in the beginning stages of an interactive forum. Democratic value creation occurs through a process of questioning, discussion, voting, and, preferably, consensus. The process is as important as the outcome, because the values of the organization, group, or section are generated and shared in a democratic manner, and values are not imposed by positional leaders.

Together, the processes, models, and leadership approaches in Part VII provide a foundation for capacity building in new era organizations. They can help organizational participants move from fearful to adaptive, crisis to change, insularity to collaboration, divisive conflict to conflict capital, and bureaucracy to democracy.

Notes

1. Gray, B. (1989). Collaboration: *Finding common ground for multiparty problems* (pp. 1–25). San Francisco: Jossey-Bass.

2. Ibid.

3. Definition originated by the editor.

CHAPTER 39

Adaptive Work

Ronald A. Heifetz
Harvard University

O ur language fails us in many aspects of our lives, entrapping us in a set of cultural assumptions like cattle herded by fences into a corral. Gender pronouns, for example, corral us into teaching children that God is a "he," distancing girls and women from the experience of the divine in themselves.

Our language fails us, too, when we discuss, analyze, and practice leadership. We commonly talk about "leaders" in organizations or politics when we actually mean "people in positions of managerial or political authority." Although we have confounded leadership with authority in nearly every journalistic and scholarly article written on "leadership" during the last one hundred years, we know intuitively that these two phenomena are distinct when we complain all too frequently in politics and business that "the leadership isn't exercising any leadership," by which we actually mean that "people in authority aren't exercising any leadership." Whether people with formal, charismatic, or otherwise informal authority actually practice leadership on any given issue at any moment in time ought to remain a separate question answered with wholly different criteria than those used to define a relationship of formal or informal authority. As we know, all too many people are skilled at gaining authority, and thus a following, but do not then lead.

Moreover, we assume a logical connection between the words *leader* and *follower*, as if this dyad (pair) were an absolute and inherently logical structure. It is not. The most interesting leadership operates without anyone experiencing anything remotely similar to the experience of "following." Indeed, most leadership mobilizes those people who are opposed or who sit on the fence, in addition to allies and friends. Allies and friends come relatively cheap; the people in opposition have the most to lose in any significant process of change. When mobilized, allies and friends become, not followers, but rather activated participants—employees or citizens who themselves often lead in turn by taking responsibility for tackling tough challenges, often beyond expectations and often beyond their authority. They become partners. When mobilized, opposition and fence-sitters become engaged with the issues, provoked to work through the problems of loss, loyalty, and competence embedded in the change they are challenged to make. Indeed, they may continue to fight, providing an ongoing source of diverse views necessary for the adaptive success of the business or community. Far from becoming "aligned" and far from having any

---

Source: From G. R. Goethals, G. J. Sorenson, and J. M. Burns (Eds.), *Encyclopedia of leadership* (pp. 8–13). Thousand Oaks, CA: Sage. © 2008 Sage Publications, Inc. Used by permission.

experience of "following," they are mobilized by leadership to wrestle with new complexities that demand tough trade-offs in their ways of working or living. Of course, in time they may begin to trust, admire, and appreciate the person or group who is leading, and thereby confer informal authority on the person or group, but they would not generally experience the emergence of that appreciation or trust by the phrase "I've become a follower."

If leadership is different from the capacity to gain formal or informal authority, and therefore different from the ability to gain a "following"—attracting influence and accruing power—then what can anchor our understanding of it?

Leadership takes place in the context of problems and challenges. Indeed, it makes little sense to describe leadership when everything and everyone in an organization are humming along just fine, even when processes of influence and authority will be virtually ubiquitous in coordinating routine activity. Leadership becomes necessary to businesses and communities when people have to change their ways rather than continue to operate according to current structures, procedures, and processes. Beyond technical problems, for which authoritative and managerial expertise will suffice, adaptive challenges demand leadership that can engage people in facing challenging realities and then changing at least some of their priorities, attitudes, and behavior in order to thrive in a changing world.

Mobilizing people to meet adaptive challenges, then, is at the heart of leadership practice. In the short term, leadership is an activity that mobilizes people to meet an immediate challenge. In the medium and long terms, leadership generates new cultural norms that enable people to meet an ongoing stream of adaptive challenges in a world that will likely pose an ongoing set of adaptive realities and pressures. Thus, with a longer view, leadership develops an organization's or community's adaptive capacity.

Adaptive work may be described in seven ways.

First, adaptive work is necessary in response to problem situations for which solutions lie outside the current way of operating. We can distinguish technical challenges, which are amenable to current expertise, from adaptive challenges, which are not. Although every problem can be understood as a gap between aspirations and reality, technical challenges present a gap between aspirations and reality that can be closed through applying existing know-how. For example, a patient comes to his doctor with an infection, and the doctor uses her knowledge to diagnose the illness and prescribe a cure.

In contrast, an adaptive challenge is created by a gap between a desired state and reality that cannot be closed using existing approaches alone. Progress in the situation requires more than the application of current expertise, authoritative decision making, standard operating procedures, or culturally informed behaviors. For example, a patient with heart disease may need to change his or her way of life: diet, exercise, smoking, and the imbalances that cause unhealthy stress. To make those changes, the patient will have to take responsibility for his or her health and learn a new set of priorities and habits. (See Table 39.1.)

Second, adaptive work demands learning. An adaptive challenge exists when the people themselves are the problem and when progress requires a retooling, in a sense, of their own ways of thinking and operating. The gap between aspirations and reality closes when they learn new ways. Thus, a consulting firm may offer a brilliant diagnostic analysis and set of recommendations, but nothing will be solved until that analysis and those recommendations are lived in the new way that people operate. Until then, the consulting firm has no solutions, only proposals.

Table 39.1 Technical and Adaptive Work

Kind of Work	Solutions and Problem Definition	Primary Locus of Implementation	Responsibility for the Work
Technical	Clear	Clear	Authority
Technical and Adaptive	Clear	Requires Learning	Authority and Stakeholders
Adaptive	Requires Learning	Requires Learning	Stakeholder > Authority

Source: R. A. Heifetz (1994, 76).

Responsibility Shift

Third, adaptive work requires a shift in responsibility from the shoulders of the authority figures and the authority structure to the stakeholders (people with an interest in an outcome) themselves. In contrast to expert problem solving, adaptive work requires a different form of deliberation and a different kind of responsibility taking. In doing adaptive work, responsibility needs to be felt in a far more widespread fashion. At best, an organization would have its members know that there are many technical problems for which looking to authority for answers is appropriate and efficient but that for the adaptive set of challenges, looking primarily to authority for answers becomes self-defeating. When people make the classic error of treating adaptive challenges as if they were technical, they wait for the person in authority to know what to do. He or she then makes a best guess— probably just a guess—while the many sit back and wait to see whether the guess pans out. Frequently enough, when it does not pan out, people get rid of that person in authority and go find another one, all the while operating under the illusion that "if only we had the right 'leader,' our problems would be solved." Progress is impeded by inappropriate dependency, and thus a major task of leadership is the development of responsibility taking by stakeholders themselves.

Fourth, adaptive work requires people to distinguish what is precious and essential from what is expendable within their culture. In cultural adaptation the job is to take the best from history, leave behind that which is no longer serviceable, and through innovation learn ways to thrive in the new environment.

Therefore, adaptive work is inherently conservative as well as progressive. The point of innovation is to conserve what is best from history as the community moves into the future. As in biology, a successful adaptation takes the best from its past set of competencies and loses the DNA that is no longer useful. Thus, unlike many current conceptions of culturally "transforming" processes, many of which are ahistorical—as if one begins all anew—adaptive work, profound as it may be in terms of change, must honor ancestry and history at the same time that it challenges them.

Adaptive work generates resistance in us because adaptation requires us to let go of certain elements of our past ways of working or living, which means to experience loss—loss of competence, loss of reporting relationships, loss of jobs, loss of traditions, or loss of loyalty to the people who taught us the lessons of our heritage. Thus, an adaptive challenge generates a situation that forces us to make tough tradeoffs. The source of the resistance that people have to change isn't resistance to change per se; it is resistance to loss. People love change when they know it is beneficial. Nobody gives the lottery ticket back when he or she wins. Leadership must contend, then, with the various forms of feared and real losses that accompany adaptive work.

Anchored to the tasks of mobilizing people to thrive in new and challenging contexts, leadership is not simply about change; more profoundly leadership is about identifying that which is worth conserving. It is the conserving of the precious dimensions of our past that makes the pains of change worth sustaining.

Improvisation

Fifth, adaptive work demands experimentation. In biology, the adaptability of a species depends on the multiplicity of experiments that are being run constantly within its gene pool, increasing the odds that in that distributed intelligence some diverse member of the species will have the means to succeed in a new context. Similarly, in cultural adaptation, an organization or community needs to be running multiple experiments and learning fast from these experiments in order to see "which horses to ride into the future."

Technical problem solving appropriately and efficiently depends on authoritative experts for knowledge and decisive action.

In contrast, dealing with adaptive challenges requires a comfort with not knowing where to go or how to move next. In mobilizing adaptive work from an authority position, leadership takes the form of protecting elements of deviance and creativity in the organization in spite of the inefficiencies associated with those elements. If creative or outspoken people generate conflict, then so be it. Conflict becomes an engine of innovation rather than solely a source of dangerous inefficiency. Managing the dynamic tension between creativity and efficiency becomes an ongoing part of leadership practice for which there exists no equilibrium point at which this tension disappears. Leadership becomes an improvisation, however frustrating it may be to not know the answers.

Sixth, the time frame of adaptive work is markedly different from that of technical work. People need time to learn new ways—to sift through what is precious from what is expendable and to innovate in ways that enable people to carry forward into the future that which they continue to hold precious from the past. Moses took forty years to bring the children of Israel to the Promised Land, not because it was such a long walk from Egypt, but rather because it took that much time for the people to leave behind the dependent mentality of slavery and generate the capacity for self-government guided by faith in something ineffable. (See Figure 39.1.)

Because people have so much difficulty sustaining prolonged periods of disturbance and uncertainty, people naturally engage in a variety of efforts to restore equilibrium as quickly as possible, even if it means avoiding adaptive work and begging the tough issues. Most forms of adaptive failure are a product of our difficulty in containing prolonged periods of experimentation and the difficult conversations that accompany them.

Work avoidance is simply the natural effort to restore a more familiar order, to restore equilibrium. Although many forms of work avoidance operate across cultures and peoples, two common pathways appear to exist: the displacement of responsibility and the diversion of attention. Both pathways work all too well in the short term, even if they leave people more exposed and vulnerable in the medium and long terms. Some common forms of

displacement of responsibility include scapegoating, blaming the persistence of problems on authority, externalizing the enemy, and killing the messenger. Diverting attention can take the form of fake remedies, such as the Golden Calf of the Bible's Book of Exodus; an effort to define problems to fit one's competence; repeated structural adjustments; the faulty use of consultants, committees, and task forces; sterile conflicts and proxy fights ("let's watch the gladiator fight!"); and outright denial.

Seventh, adaptive work is a normative concept. The concept of adaptation arises from scientific efforts to understand biological evolution. Applied to the change of cultures and societies, the concept becomes a useful, if inexact, metaphor. For example, species evolve, whereas cultures learn. Evolution is generally understood by scientists as a matter of chance, whereas societies will often consciously deliberate, plan, and intentionally experiment. Close to our normative concern, biological evolution conforms to laws of survival. Societies, on the other hand, generate purposes beyond survival. The concept of adaptation applied to culture raises the question, "Adapt to what, for what purpose?"

In biology the "objective function" of adaptive work is straightforward: to thrive in new environments. Survival of the self and one's gene-carrying kin defines the direction in which animals adapt. A situation becomes an

Figure 39.1 Technical Problem or Adaptive Challenge?

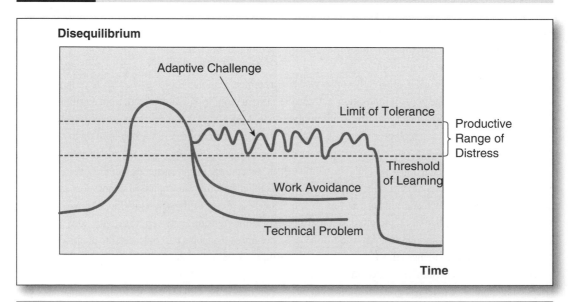

Source: Ronald A. Heifetz and Donald L. Laurie.

adaptive challenge because it threatens the capacity of a species to pass on its genetic heritage. Thus, when a species multiplies its own kind and succeeds in passing on its genes, it is said to be "thriving" in its environment.

Thriving is more than coping. Nothing is trivial in biology about adaptation. Some adaptive leaps transform the capacity of a species by sparking an ongoing and profound process of adaptive change that leads to a vastly expanded range of living.

In human societies "thriving" takes on a host of values not restricted to survival of one's own kind. At times human beings will even trade off their own survival for values such as liberty, justice, and faith. Thus, adaptive work in cultures involves both the clarification of values and the assessment of realities that challenge the realization of those values.

Because most organizations and communities honor a mix of values, the competition within this mix largely explains why adaptive work so often involves conflict. People with competing values engage one another as they confront a shared situation from their own points of view. At its extreme, and in the absence of better methods of social change, the conflict over values can be violent. The U.S. Civil War changed the meaning of union and individual freedom. In 1857 fulfilling the preamble to the Constitutional goal "to insure domestic tranquility" meant the return of escaped slaves to their owners; in 1957 it meant the use of federal troops to integrate Central High School in Little Rock, Arkansas.

Some realities threaten not only a set of values beyond survival, but also the very existence of a society if these realities are not discovered and met early on by the value-clarifying and reality-testing functions of that society. In the view of many environmentalists, for example, our focus on the production of wealth rather than co-existence with nature has led us to neglect fragile factors in our ecosystem. These factors may become relevant to us when finally they begin to challenge our central values of health and survival, but by then, we may have paid a high price in damage already done, and the costs of and odds against adaptive adjustment may have increased enormously.

Adaptive work, then, requires us to deliberate on the values by which we seek to thrive and demands diagnostic inquiry into the realities that threaten the realization of those values. Beyond legitimizing a convenient set of assumptions about reality, beyond denying or avoiding the internal contradictions in some of the values we hold

precious, and beyond coping, adaptive work involves proactively seeking to clarify aspirations or develop new ones, and then involves the hard work of innovation, experimentation, and cultural change to realize a closer approximation of those aspirations by which we would define "thriving."

The normative tests of adaptive work, then, involve an appraisal of both the processes by which orienting values are clarified in an organization or community and the quality of reality testing by which a more accurate rather than convenient diagnosis is achieved. For example, by these tests, serving up fake remedies for our collective troubles by scapegoating and externalizing the enemy, as was done in extreme form in Nazi Germany, might generate throngs of misled supporters who readily grant to charlatans extraordinary authority in the short run, but they would not constitute adaptive work. Nor would political efforts to gain influence and authority by pandering to people's longing for easy answers constitute leadership. Indeed, misleading people is likely over time to produce adaptive failure.

Further Reading

Foster, R. (2001). *Creative destruction: Why companies that are built to last underperform the market—and how to successfully transform them.* New York: Doubleday.

Freud, S. (1959). *Group psychology and the analysis of the ego.* New York: Norton.

Heifetz, R. A. (1994). *Leadership without easy answers* (p. 76). Cambridge, MA: Harvard University Press.

Heifetz, R. A., & Laurie, D. L. (1988). Mobilizing adaptive work: Beyond visionary leadership. In Conger, Spreitzer, & Lawler (Eds.), *The Leader's Change Handbook: An Essential Guide to Setting Direction and Taking Action.* New York: John Wiley and Sons.

Kuhn, T. A. (1962). *The structure of scientific revolutions.* Chicago: The University of Chicago Press.

May, R. (1975). *The courage to create.* New York: Bantam.

Pascale, R. T., Milleman, M., & Gioja, L. (2000). *Surfing the edge of chaos: The laws of nature and the new laws of business.* New York: Crown.

Selznick, P. (1957). *Leadership in administration.* New York: Harper & Row.

Tucker, R. C. (1981). *Politics as leadership.* Columbia: University of Missouri Press.

Wildavsky, A. (1984). *The nursing father: Moses as a political leader.* Tuscaloosa, Alabama: University of Alabama Press.

CHAPTER 40

Organizational Change Practices

Gill Robinson Hickman

University of Richmond

Which Practices Do We Employ to Implement Change?

The focus of considerable scholarship on leading change stems from studies of change practices in organizations. Researchers strive to determine which practices generate the most effective processes and outcomes. This section highlights several categories of practice—collective or collaborative approaches, strategic planning and goal setting, stages of praxis, and ethical practices—and links them to concepts of organizational change and leadership. Additionally, several practices including environmental scanning (periodic or continuous), scenario planning, and scenario building help to address several questions raised earlier in the chapter about the environment. Which primary factors or indicators in the environment are important to organizational well-being and survival? What are the indicators? How do organizational leaders and members proceed in this environment?

Collective/Collaborative Approaches

The literature on organizational leadership and change includes a small and diffuse body of research on collective or collaborative change approaches. Included in this category are institutionalized-leadership and change practices, organizational learning, and empowerment or shared power. These practices are interrelated and mutually reinforcing, as indicated in Figure 40.1. They function to support teleological, dialectical, and chaos/complexity change in conjunction with collective concepts of leadership.

Institutionalized-Leadership and Change Practices

O'Toole (2001) and his colleagues surveyed more than 3,000 leaders at various organizational levels in 10 large companies in Asia, Europe, and North America. They also interviewed 20–40 of the individuals who completed the survey from each company. O'Toole discovered that companies with the highest collective leadership capacity used systems that used institutionalized-leadership and change practices throughout their organizations. "We found that there is something palpably different about a company that emphasizes building enabling systems versus one that depends on a single personality at the top" (O'Toole, 2001, p. 168).

Source: Leading Change in Multiple Contexts. Thousand Oaks, CA: Sage. Copyright © 2009 Sage Publications, Inc.

| **Figure 40.1** | Collective/Collaborative Practices |

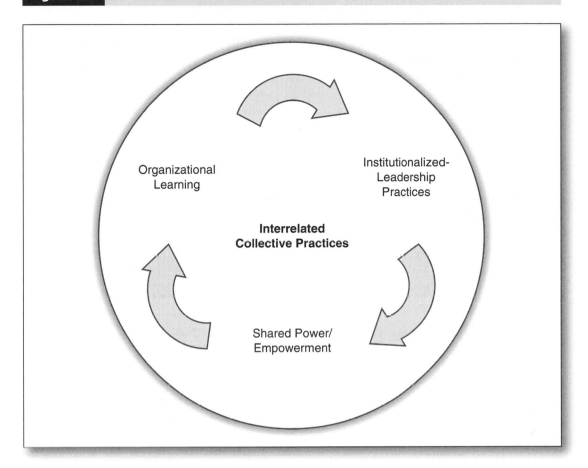

Similar to Kelley's (1988) description of effective or exemplary followers, O'Toole (2001) made the following discovery:

> [People throughout these companies] act more like owners and entrepreneurs than employees. . . . Take the initiative to solve problems. . . . Willingly accept accountability for meeting commitments and [living organizational values]. . . . Share a common philosophy and language of leadership. . . . [and] create, maintain, and adhere to systems and procedures designed to measure and reward . . . distributed leadership behaviors. (pp. 160–161)

Two major institutional practices when used together contributed to long-term success: coherence and agility. Coherence encompasses the common

behaviors that are found throughout an organization and that are directed toward achieving the organization's goals, and agility represents the organization's institutionalized ability to detect and cope with changes in the external environment, especially when the changes are hard to predict (O'Toole, 2001, p. 167). O'Toole found that the successful companies focused on building human capacity collectively rather than relying on a small number of individuals to lead and change the organization.

O'Toole (2001) measured each organization's effectiveness using 12 leadership systems:

- *Vision and strategy:* Extent to which corporate strategy is reflected in goals and behaviors at all levels.
- *Goal setting and planning:* Extent to which challenging goals are used to drive performance.
- *Capital allocation:* Extent to which capital allocation decisions are objective and systematic.

- *Group measurement:* Extent to which actual performance is measured against established goals.
- *Risk management:* Extent to which the company measures and mitigates risk.
- *Recruiting:* Extent to which the company taps the best talent available.
- *Professional development:* Extent to which employees are challenged and developed.
- *Performance appraisal:* Extent to which individual appraisals are used to improve performance.
- *Compensation:* Extent to which financial incentives are used to drive desired behaviors.
- *Organizational structure:* Extent to which decision-making authority is delegated to lower levels.
- *Communications:* Extent to which management communicates the big picture.
- *Knowledge transfer:* Extent to which necessary information is gathered, organized, and disseminated. (p. 165)

The highest-performing companies intentionally selected specific systems to emphasize and did not attempt to focus on all of the systems. To develop collective capacity throughout the organization, leaders and members had to ensure that their professional development, performance appraisal, and compensation systems foster coherent practices. These practices ensure alignment among systems so that a compensation system for project teams, for example, includes rewards for collaborative teamwork and does not unintentionally perpetuate competitive individual performance.

Organizational Learning

Organizational learning is a process that adapts the organization and its members to change in the external environment by encouraging experimentation and innovation, continually renewing structures and practices, and using performance data to assess and further develop the organization (London & Maurer, 2004, p. 244). The Technology Solutions case in Chapter 2 shows the company's emphasis on learning and continuous self-development in its employees through sharing ideas to spark new thoughts, seeking guidance from any member of the organization, and providing access to the newest and most innovative ideas possible.

Donald Schön (1971) was one of the early scholars to recognize the need for organizational learning as a process to foster change collectively. He made the following contention:

[Organizational participants] must become able not only to transform our institutions, in response to changing situations and requirements; we must invent and develop institutions which are "learning systems," that is to say, systems capable of bringing about their own continuous transformations. (p. 30)

Since Schön's initial work, organizational-learning systems have become an integral component of the change literature. Senge (1990) popularized organizational learning as a generative process that enhances the capacity of organizational participants to create. He stated that five essential elements must develop as an ensemble to create a fundamental learning organization:

- Personal mastery—continually clarifying and deepening personal vision, focusing energies, developing patience, and seeing reality objectively;
- Mental models—changing ingrained assumptions, generalizations, pictures, and images of how the world works;
- Shared vision—unearthing shared "pictures of the future" that foster genuine commitment;
- Team learning—aligning and developing the capacity of a team to create the results its members truly desire; and
- Systems thinking—integrating all the elements by fusing them into a coherent body of theory and practice. (pp. 6–10)

Several theories and concepts of leadership incorporate learning as a part of organizational development and change. Transformational, adaptive, and task-relations-and-change leadership encourage organizational learning by similar means, including challenging people to question assumptions; take risks; be innovative and creative; reframe problems and cultivate new approaches; analyze information about events, trends, and changes in the external environment; and then pursue new opportunities, meet unknown conditions or threats, and solve problems.

According to Berson, Nemanich, Waldman, Galvin, and Keller (2006), the literature on organizational learning implies that leadership can influence learning among organizational members and foster a learning culture. Individuals in leadership roles need to develop three essential organizational characteristics to facilitate a learning culture: participation—involvement of organizational members in processes such as decision making, learning, inquiry, challenge, and the creation of greater autonomy; openness—receptiveness to diverse ideas, tolerance, and free flow of information; and psychological safety—freedom to take risks, trust, and support (pp. 580–581).

Shared Power or Empowerment

Movement toward shared power or empowerment is a logical course of action as organizations place greater reliance on the collective or collaborative capabilities of their members to innovate and respond in turbulent or dynamic environments. Shared power or empowerment entails two components: delegating or distributing leadership, authority, responsibility, and decision-making power, formally vested in senior executives, to individuals and teams throughout the organization, and equipping organization members with the resources, knowledge, and skills necessary to make good decisions (Hughes, Ginnett, & Curphy, 2006, p. 537).

Senior executives must examine themselves to determine whether they are willing and ready to share power with employees as coleaders or partners in the process of leading change. Inauthentic attempts at empowerment can be more detrimental to organizational members than maintaining the status quo. Hughes et al. (2006) indicated that "empowered employees have latitude to make decisions, are comfortable making these decisions, believe what they do is important, and are seen as influential members of their team" (p. 539). The authors further described the following best practices for empowerment:

- having leaders in the organization decide whether the organization really wants or needs empowerment;
- creating a clear vision, goals, and accountabilities;
- developing others (through coaching, forging a partnership, developing knowledge and skills, promoting persistence, and transferring skills);
- delegating decision making to followers;
- leading by example; and

- making empowerment systemic—a strategic business practice that is reinforced in selection, performance appraisal, rewards, training, organizational structure, and so on. (pp. 539–542)

Strategic Planning

Executive leaders initiate strategic planning as a part of their overall design to adapt, change, and position the organization to thrive in a highly competitive and turbulent environment. Strategic planning generally originates from the top and involves members at various levels of the organization in certain components of the process. In business settings, companies use strategic planning to establish and sustain competitive advantage in their industry. Nonprofit and government agencies also use strategic planning to provide intentional direction to their organizations and adapt to external changes that affect their services and stakeholders.

Primary components of strategic planning include creating or updating the vision and mission, conducting an environmental scan, setting strategic direction using goals and strategies, and implementing and updating the plan. A vision, much like a compass, points an organization toward its desired end goal, or "true north." It is a realistic, credible, and appealing future for the organization that sets a clear direction; defines a more successful and desirable future; fits the organization's history, culture, and values; and reflects the aspirations and expectations of major stakeholders (Miller & Dess, 1996; Nanus, 1992; Yukl, 2006). A good vision links the present to the future, energizes people and garners commitment, gives meaning to work, and establishes a standard of excellence (Daft & Lane, 2005, p. 516). A mission is the tangible form of the vision that identifies the organization's purpose or reason for existing and identifies its uniqueness or distinctiveness (Miller & Dess, 1996, p. 9).

The vision and mission serve as a base or foundation for planning the organization's future (teleological change), whereas the strategic component involves specific positioning of the organization for competitive advantage or effective service delivery on the basis of factors outside the organization. Relying on multiple sources and multiple disciplines or inputs, leaders and members use environmental scanning to gather information about trends in the external environment:

- Stakeholder analysis—an assessment of the expectations, wants, and needs of all parties that have an interest or stake in the organization, including leaders, team members, managers, employees, customers/clients, recipients of services, and investors/shareholders, among others;
- Competitors' activities—knowledge of competitors' products, services, and methodologies through benchmarking and other information-gathering approaches;
- Demographic changes—changes in the age, ethnic composition, growth, or decline of the population;
- Social and lifestyle changes—women in the workforce, health and fitness awareness, erosion of educational standards, spread of addictive drugs, concern for the environment;
- Technological changes—advances in and use of all forms of technology;
- Economic changes—stock market indices, budget deficits, consumer-spending patterns, inflation rates, interest rates, trade deficits, unemployment rates;
- Legislative/regulatory and political changes—changes in crime laws, environmental protection laws, deregulation, antitrust enforcement, laws protecting human rights and employment; and
- Global changes—economic alliances, changes in consumer tastes and preferences, economic development, international markets, and poverty and disease rates. (Dess, Lumpkin, & Eisner, 2008, pp. 19, 44–50, 380)

The executive leadership team uses information from the environmental scan to determine the organization's opportunities and threats along with its strengths and weaknesses. On the basis of this analysis, the team identifies core competencies (capabilities that combine expertise and application skills) in the organization, evaluates whether there is a need for a major change in strategy, and identifies promising strategies along with possible outcomes of each strategy (Yukl, 2006, pp. 378–380). Frequently, a broad cadre of managers and members are invited to participate in the strategy formulation process. Strategies represent desired states of affairs that the organization wants to reach or end points toward which organizational efforts are directed (Daft & Lane, 2005, p. 526). They are the indicators of the organization's progress toward its vision, mission, and strategic direction.

Clearly, strategic leadership uses strategic-planning processes to bring about strategic change in organizations. Strategic planning is also compatible with teleological and dialectical change. As stated earlier, teleological change is constructed internally by leaders and members of the organization, yet this form of change cannot be fully effective without considering the kind of information that the environmental-scanning component of strategic planning highlights. Dialectical change can also benefit from the environmental-scanning component of strategic planning, even though strategic positioning may or may not be feasible in dialectical change.

Strategic planning is often a lengthy process in many organizations. With the increasing pace and unique patterns of change in society, organizations will need continuous scanning and highly participative processes with a broader base of members (beyond executive levels) to determine appropriate action in the short term while planning for the long term. The strategic-planning process may assume a different structure or different characteristics in a less-predictable and less-controlled environment of continuous change, experimentation, and learning. Some communication scholars and practitioners suggest that planning strategically may mean engaging in scenario planning—exploring possible outcomes of what could happen in the future and planning for those possibilities (Ströh & Jaatinen, 2001, p. 162). Scenario planning uses information from continuous-scanning processes to develop and plan for probable scenarios, while keeping plans flexible and adjustable.

Stages of Praxis

Kurt Lewin (1951) provided some of the earliest research on stages of praxis in organizational change. His force-field model identified three fundamental stages of change: unfreezing—the stage where organizational participants recognize that their old methods are no longer useful, often due to crises, threats, or new opportunities; changing—the phase where people seek new ways of doing things and choose new approaches; and refreezing—the stage in which leaders and participants implement the new approaches and establish them in the organizational culture (Yukl, 2006, p. 286). Lewin's earlier work provided a foundation for subsequent models (Kanter, 1983b; Kanter, Stein, & Jick, 1992; Kotter, 1996; Nadler, Shaw, & Walton, 1995) that expanded the stages, methods, and practices of organizational change. Figure 40.2 compares Lewin's three-stage model to a much later eight-stage model developed by John Kotter (1996). Kotter's model provides a fitting structure for examining praxis shared by other familiar models.

The Unfreezing Stage

The purpose of unfreezing old ways of doing things (Lewin, 1951), establishing a sense of urgency (Kanter et al., 1992; Kotter, 1996), or initiating a galvanizing event (an action or situation that requires a change response) (Kanter, 1983a, p. 22) is to draw attention to the critical need for organizational change. This sense of urgency or galvanizing event may stem from a current or impending crisis. Yet it is just as likely to come from the organization's inability to adapt—that is, the ability of its members to see and take action to address the gap between the current organization and its need to modify or change its culture, structure, behaviors, and responsibilities. According to Kotter (1996), this stage involves identifying and discussing crises, potential crises, or major opportunities that may galvanize or inspire change (p. 21). Crises include economic threats, competitive threats, changing markets, shifting demographics, or other changes in the external or internal environment. A galvanizing event may present a crisis or entail a new opportunity, such as launching new products; developing new markets, innovations, or services; and interacting with stakeholders in new ways, such as engaging in community volunteering or environmental sustainability programs.

Figure 40.2 Stages of Praxis

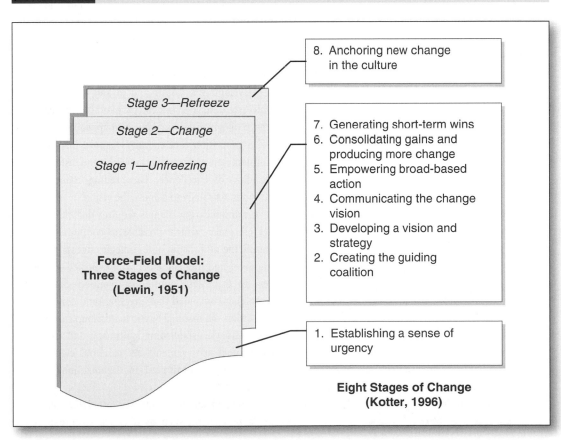

Both crises and opportunities can create fresh or revitalized momentum in an organization, especially when these crises or opportunities are acknowledged as authentic by members of the organization. Many people fear change and resist change efforts even in situations where a crisis or beneficial innovation is justified. There are multiple reasons why members of organizations resist change:

1. Lack of trust—distrust of the people who propose the change;

2. Belief that change is unnecessary—satisfaction with the status quo and no clear evidence of serious problems with the current way of doing things;

3. Belief that the change is not feasible—a view that the change is unlikely to succeed, too difficult, or likely to fail like some previous efforts;

4. Economic threats—fear that the change may benefit the organization but result in personal loss of income, benefits, or job security;

5. Relative high costs—concern that the cost of change may be higher than the benefits due to loss of resources already invested in the current approach or loss of performance as employees learn the new procedures and debug the new system;

6. Fear of personal failure—organizational members' reluctance to abandon known skills or expertise and their insecurity about mastering new ways of doing things;

7. Loss of status and power—fear of shifts in power for individuals or subunits that may result in loss of status in the organization;

8. Threat to values and ideals—resistance to change that appears incompatible with personal values or strongly held values embedded in the organization's culture; and

9. Resentment of interference—opposition of individuals to perceived control, manipulation, or forced change by others in situations where they have no choice or voice in the change. (Yukl, 2006, pp. 285–286)

Despite these fears, various organizations have implemented successful change processes by using the stages approach with effective forms of leadership and change.

The Changing Phase

Lewin (1951) referred to the next stage simply as the changing phase; later scholars (Kanter et al., 1992; Kotter, 1996; Nadler et al., 1995) defined several additional stages in the changing phase. Specifically, Kotter delineated six stages—creating the guiding coalition, developing a vision and strategy, communicating the change vision, empowering broad-based action, generating short-term wins, and consolidating gains and producing more change (p. 21).

Creating the guiding coalition involves putting together a group with enough power to lead the change and getting the group to work together as a team. This group could comprise the tags (members of the organization who lead with or without authority, often in a temporary capacity) to influence people and the processes of meaning making, cooperation, and action taking. They have the kind of influence that moves others to action through their facilitation of cooperation, interaction, and resonance among individuals involved in change or adaptive processes.

Developing a vision and strategy relates to the processes described in strategic planning or creating an image of a realistic, credible, and appealing future for the organization that energizes people, inspires commitment, gives meaning to work, and establishes a standard of excellence. The guiding coalition then develops a strategy to achieve the vision.

Communicating change[1] requires that change leaders use every vehicle possible to communicate constantly the new vision and strategies to organizational members and model the behavior expected of employees. In four case studies of planned change, the researcher concluded that "creating [and communicating] vision, maintaining buy-in to mission, sense-making and feedback, establishing legitimacy, and communicating goal achievement" are essential elements for maintaining commitment to organizational change (Lewis, 2000, p. 151).

Ströh and Jaatinen (2001) suggested that single incidents of change, such as a crisis, require different approaches to communication than do continuous changes (p. 159). They caution that technical communication channels, such as newsletters, electronic and face-to-face updates, or annual reports, are good but not sufficient in organizations where continuous change is a way of life. Effective communication channels need to be consciously embedded and facilitated in the continuous change process through dialogue, relationship building, diversity of ideas, and participative decision making for change (p. 159).

The use of dialogue, discourse, or conversation is a prominent theme in the literature on communicating change (Ford & Ford, 1995; Heracleous & Barrett, 2001; Jabri, 2004; Kellett, 1999). Kellett (1999) pointed out that creating collaborative learning through dialogue is one approach to generating continuous and intentional change in organizations (p. 211). Creating dialogic conversations is an intentional process with fundamental characteristics and guidelines:

- Dialogue provides a "container" for collective thinking with dedicated time to allow the process to emerge;
- The purpose of dialogue is to create thoughtful exchange, generate mutual understanding, make assumptions explicit, and take action with regard to the issues people care about and need to discuss;
- The spirit of inquiry is essential to dialogue and involves focusing on connections, embracing diverse perspectives, and allowing shared understanding to transform us;
- The process of reflective questioning relies on our ability to listen, value others, and address deep issues; and
- A dialogue is a practical approach for developing a meaningful vision or mission statement, understanding what needs to change and how the change aligns with other factors in the organization, and understanding and negotiating conflicts expressed in the dialogue process. (Kellett, 1999, p. 212)

Another key communication role in continuous change involves building relationships within and across the organization and building transorganizational relationships to develop networks and achieve creativity,

innovation, mutual problem solving, and shared meaning. Given this emphasis on relationships between entities, one researcher remarked, "Relationships are all there is to reality and nothing exists independent of its relationships with the environment" (McDaniel, 1997, p. 24).

Dialogue that encourages diversity of ideas is critical for continuous change in organizations. Yet diversity brings both conflict and cooperation, "marked by the struggle of multiple voices to be heard" (Kellett, 1999, p. 213). Dialectic communication is a process through which change occurs:

> In a change process, if there is an effective negotiation or resolution of core dialectics between the stakeholders, it is likely to be a collaborative change that is marked by a respect for difference. If, as Baxter and Montgomery say, "Relational well-being is marked by the capacity to achieve 'both/and' status" (p. 6), then "healthy" organizational change will be marked by talking through dialectics, or at least the respect for differences as they figure into change decisions. (p. 213)

Communication in continuous change environments is highly participatory by necessity. Organizations must facilitate dialogue within and across groups to generate and sustain a free flow of information, diversity of ideas, high levels of cooperation, and substantive involvement in decision making.

Empowering broad-based action requires getting rid of obstacles, changing systems or structures that undermine the change vision, and encouraging risk taking and nontraditional ideas, activities, and actions (Kotter, 1996, p. 21). Earlier in the chapter, empowerment was described as delegating or distributing leadership, authority, responsibility, and decision-making power and equipping organizational members with the resources, knowledge, and skills necessary to make good decisions. Empowerment can facilitate broad-based action in the change process when leaders and members fully endorse and incorporate it in their organizational values, culture, and practices. Organizational systems can be configured to reinforce empowerment in selection, performance appraisal, rewards, and training processes along with communication and work structures.

Generating short-term wins involves making change visible by recognizing, rewarding, and celebrating achievements along the way. This includes setting and achieving short-term goals that support the change initiative; recognizing and rewarding people who made the wins possible; demonstrating or showcasing completed projects and new products or services; publicizing new ventures, partnerships, or collaborative work arrangements; and recognizing monthly, quarterly, or annual accomplishments. Kotter (1996) identified three characteristics of a good short-term win—it's visible and large numbers of people can see it for themselves, it's unambiguous, and it's clearly related to the change effort (pp. 121–122). He pointed out that one possible drawback to acknowledging and celebrating short-term wins is the tendency of some people to lose momentum and motivation for completing the larger change. As a result, recognition of intermediate successes needs to be balanced with a realistic perspective that much more remains to be done. Clear or visible gauges of the work ahead are as important as indicators of successes to date.

Consolidating gains and producing more change occur when the guiding coalition, tags, and participants in change throughout the organization learn from and use the gains at each juncture to develop expertise and experience for producing more change. Because complex organizations function through interdependencies—people work in cross-functional and project teams across the organization and between organizations—change in one part of the system produces a kaleidoscope effect by changing all or most parts of the system. In other words, change in interconnected systems produces more change. This is a good outcome for the achievement and sustainability of the larger change, but it can be frustrating in the short run.

According to Kotter (1996), cumulative gains along the way provide increased credibility to change all systems, structures, and policies that no longer fit the transformation vision. Actions in this stage include hiring, promoting, and developing people who can implement the change vision and reinvigorating the process with new projects, themes, and change agents (pp. 21, 143).

Refreezing or Anchoring New Approaches in the Culture

This phase represents the last stage of change, as defined by Lewin or Kotter, respectively. Both Lewin and Kotter recognized this stage as the fitting time and place to establish or anchor new approaches and behaviors in the organizational culture (shared assumptions, beliefs, values, language, etc.). Many scholars (Deal & Kennedy, 2000; Kotter, 1996; Schein, 1992) acknowledge that culture is the most difficult element to change in an organization, and it is much more challenging to alter culture in mature organizations. Schein (1992) offered several primary and secondary ways to influence cultural change. Each of these factors reinforces the connection between new behaviors and organizational success:

- Primary ways to influence culture
  - *Attention*—the amount of attention leaders focus on certain issues or factors in the organization;
  - *Reactions to crises*—the values and assumptions expressed by leaders during crises;
  - *Role modeling*—the messages about values and expectations leaders communicate through their actions or through deliberate modeling such as coaching and teaching;
  - *Allocation of rewards*—the criteria used in the organization to allocate rewards; and
  - *Criteria for selection and dismissal*—values expressed through criteria for recruiting, selecting, promoting, and dismissing members of the organization.

- Secondary ways to influence culture
  - *Design of systems and procedures*—placing an emphasis on the new approaches or change in budgets, planning processes, reports, training programs, performance reviews, and so on;
  - *Design of organizational structure*—designing an organizational structure that facilitates the philosophy, working relationships or interdependencies, and flexibility needed to implement change and adapt to the environment;
  - *Rites and rituals of the organization*—the ritualization of certain types of behaviors can serve as a powerful reinforcer of leaders' assumptions;
  - *Design of facilities*—designing facilities that reflect the change in approach or philosophy such as open layouts; open access to conference rooms, dining facilities, and workout

spaces; or similar offices for all members of the organization;

- ○ *Stories, legends, and myths*—transmitting stories about actual events, people, or actions that exemplify the philosophy, values, and approaches that are important for change in the culture; and
- ○ *Formal statements*—conveying the new or modified philosophy, values, and approaches in organizational publications and other appropriate venues. (Schein, 1992, pp. 230–252; Yukl, 2006, pp. 290–293)

A final factor in refreezing or anchoring new change in the culture is developing a means to ensure ongoing leadership development. If change is dependent only on individuals currently serving in formal (chief executive officer) and informal (tags) leadership roles, then change processes will likely end when these individuals leave. This statement may seem obvious; however, lack of adequate leadership development has been the downfall of many promising attempts to generate organizational change. Individual and team leadership development along with O'Toole's (2001) concept of institutionalizing leadership in the people and systems of organizations provide the greatest potential for initiating, developing, and benefiting from change.

The practices identified in the stages-of-praxis category most often apply to teleological (intentional and constructed change) and strategic change. These stages can also facilitate evolutionary change when organizations need to adopt new structures, organizational types, or traits. They can apply to the maturity and revitalization phases of life-cycle change, especially as organizations face inertia or potential demise. Organizations in the maturity phase of life-cycle change have the hardest time embracing new opportunities or structures due to their entrenched organizational culture and history of success. Communicating a change strategy or vision among organizational members can foster dialectical change.

Different phases can require different forms of leadership. For example, charismatic leadership frequently succeeds in generating a sense of urgency by inspiring a motivating vision or purpose in the hearts and minds of organizational members. In the case of invisible leadership, however, the purpose itself may be the motivating factor (charisma of purpose) that drives organizational members to work toward a goal. Strategic leadership can help organizational participants shape the vision and strategies that will focus the change effort, and transactional and task-relations-and-change leadership may empower broad-based action to implement changes in behavior, work structures, or processes and generate short-term wins. Transformational leadership can operate during most stages of praxis; it may be particularly effective during the stage of consolidating gains and producing more change during the last phase involving anchoring new approaches in the culture. Coleadership or exemplary followership functions throughout the stages of praxis in a team effort to accomplish the common purpose of the change.

Scenario Building

Schwartz (1996) advocated an eight-step process of scenario building that helps leaders and members take a long view in a world of uncertainty (p. 3). He contended that scenarios are not predictions but mechanisms to help people learn. Scenario building involves more than guessing. It requires a process that uses factual information and indicators of early trends to project alternative futures. The eighth factor, which corresponds with Willis Harman's (1998) concept of "acting with feedback" (pp. 193–194), fosters ongoing learning and flexibility as leaders and participants move toward a desired common goal. Although scenario building is a method used most often in business or organizational settings, it provides a useful means for developing informed action in other settings, including nonprofit and government agencies.

Scenario building is especially useful for teleological change and strategic leadership due to its planned, constructed approach. However, it may also be relevant to dialectical change, including chaos and complexity theory and collective or collaborative forms of leadership, because it helps organizations prepare for multiple possibilities and identify early indicators in uncertain environments. In virtual or multichannel organizations, scenario building is highly compatible with e-leadership, which uses technology such as groupware to brainstorm and generate multiple responses simultaneously.

Appreciative Inquiry

Appreciative inquiry (AI) is an organizational change practice developed by Cooperrider and Srivastva (1987). It focuses on aspects of the organizations that are working well—the positive history and stories, best organization members, and the relationships that contribute to advancement—rather than on negatives, such as distrust, resistance, and barriers to positive possibilities. AI begins with and retains the "positive principle"—hope, excitement, caring, esprit de corps, urgent purpose, joy in creating something meaningful together—to sustain momentum throughout the process (Fitzgerald, Murrell, & Miller, 2003, p. 6). The process has five essential phases:

1. Choose the positive as the focus for inquiry.

2. Inquire into stories of life-giving forces.

3. Locate themes that appear in the stories and select topics for further inquiry.

4. Create shared images for a preferred future.

5. Find innovative ways to create that future. (Seo, Putnam, & Bartunek, 2004, p. 95)

AI uses a social constructionist approach to organizational change, a teleological model that focuses on the human ability to construct new realities for the organization through an intended process of change. Cooperrider and Srivastva's (1987) AI model departs from previous change approaches because it fully supports the idea that "organizational members have the capacity to create their own future," it rejects interventionist approaches that focus on problem-solving with a heavy emphasis on positivist methods, and it employs less linear methods, such as "stories, narratives, dreams, and visions that stimulate human imagination and meaning systems" (Seo et al., 2004, p. 96).

AI has received positive attention and considerable use by practitioners. Yet there has been little academic research conducted on this method. Future researchers need to raise and examine several methodological and organizational questions regarding AI: Do the methodologies and philosophy used in AI omit significant factors from the change process? For example, does the "positive only" approach of appreciative inquiry resolve underlying problems, conflicts, and mistakes in the organization or does it inadvertently mask or ignore them? Can positivist methodologies (survey research, experiments, etc.) in combination with AI methodologies (dialogues, interviewing, imagining) add or reveal vital information for organizational change that would not be apparent or available using AI methodologies alone? How does AI compare to other theories of change and organizational development? What are the comparative outcomes of AI in relation to other organizational change approaches over time?

E-Practices

Leading change in virtual teams requires some of the same practices as those used by face-to-face (FTF) teams, as well as some different practices. In a study of effective practices in virtual teams, Lurey and Raisinghani (2001) found that these teams, like their FTF counterparts, must have a shared purpose, their members must rely on each other to perform the work, and team leaders must facilitate positive group processes, generate team-based reward systems, and select the most appropriate team members for projects or change initiatives (p. 532). Virtual teams need additional factors to be effective:

- added connectivity among team members through more structured or formal processes including clearly developed and designated roles for team members and very explicit team goals; and

- more attention to communication issues that enhance personal contact and connection among team members such as facilitating face-to-face interaction when possible and identifying and using the most appropriate technology for the people and project. (p. 532)

Respondents in Lurey and Raisinghani's (2001) study used daily e-mail, personal telephone calls, and voice mail most frequently. Other means of communication, including group-telephone and online-computer conferencing, FTF interaction, groupware, shared databases, and videoconferencing, received less frequent use. The researchers suggested that the availability and use of videoconferencing may be effective in bringing together geographically dispersed team members.

To enhance successful e-practices, Zigurs (2003) made the following recommendations for virtual team leaders:

- provide training on participation in virtual teams;
- use team-building exercises in face-to-face processes, when possible;
- provide for both task and relational roles;
- establish standards for communication of contextual cues with each message;
- use process-structuring tools but build in adaptability for individual needs;
- use frequent communication and feedback to nurture emergent leadership and self-leadership that moves the team forward;
- put special and continuous emphasis on relational development; and
- anticipate unintended consequences and debrief the team's responses and approaches to these events. (p. 348)

Virtual organizations and multichannel corporations need the capacity to innovate, change, and respond quickly to meet the needs of customers or service recipients in a round-the-clock Internet environment. Change in virtual organizations and virtual divisions of multichannel organizations entails practices that are information rich and highly collaborative. Stace, Holtham, and Courtney (2001) suggested that these organizations base their design on principles of self-management, collaborative behavioral protocols, shared strategic intent, and equitable sharing of returns (p. 417). They advised that organizations base their e-practices on time spent in productive interchange, trust developed between people, and territory, defined as psychological space and a stake in outcomes (p. 417).

On the basis of current information, e-practices seem to apply to teleological (planned, constructed) and dialectical change, including chaos and complexity theory, in multichannel and virtual organizations. They align with virtual leadership, or e-leadership, and may be fitting for other collective forms of leadership, such as adaptive, team, and invisible. Research on effective virtual or e-practices is still developing. E-change may

ultimately constitute a new form of change with its own characteristics and processes.

Ethical Practices

Ethics require leaders and followers in organizations to take into account the impact of their actions in relation to others. Ethics are principles of right conduct or a system of moral values. The guiding question for ethical decisions and practices in leading change is, what ought to be done in regard to coworkers and customers (Gini, 2004, p. 28)? Gini (2004) pointed out that "ethics is primarily a communal, collective enterprise" (p. 28), which makes ethical practices especially relevant in this era of collective and collaborative approaches to leading organizational change, including adaptive, Ubuntu, Tao, invisible, team, and virtual leadership.

Critical issues for ethical practices in leading change consist of authenticity, trust, and reciprocal care, among others. Authenticity entails honesty—with one's self and others, between and among organizational leaders and members, and between organizational members and other partners, collaborators, and stakeholders. Authenticity is critically important in the practice of empowerment or shared power, which is a fundamental component of collective or collaborative leadership and change. Ciulla (2004) maintained that "the obvious difference between authentic and bogus empowerment rests on the honesty of the relationship between leaders and followers" (p. 76). She warned that it is not adequate for members of an organization to "feel" empowered; they must "be" empowered to make decisions, take action, and be accountable for their efforts on behalf of the organization (p. 76).

Leaders in positions of authority have a choice to share power with members of the organization or not, but bogus empowerment is both inauthentic and ineffective in the long run. Leaders must weigh the risk in each direction. If organizational leaders choose empowerment or shared power, they need to develop the training, resources, systems, and practices that support it. Most of all, senior leaders must have enough self-knowledge and introspection to know whether they are truly capable of sharing power or whether they fear that most organizational members are unable to handle shared power appropriately, and, therefore, members' mistakes will reflect negatively on leaders. If leaders decide not to empower members, they need to develop substantial capacity within the senior executive team to lead change in a dynamic environment. They must assess the potential impact on their competitive position or service delivery in relation to similar organizations with and without shared power among their members.

Authenticity is a significant factor in developing a sense of urgency or establishing a galvanizing event in the stages-of-praxis approach. Organizational members will likely become indifferent and highly suspect of any change effort when executive leaders attempt to revitalize an organization by "creating" a scare tactic to generate a sense of urgency. Instead, organizational leaders and members must build an honest, compelling case for revitalization on the basis of information, involvement, and commitment.

Openness, or transparency, is included here under the rubric of authenticity. Openness reinforces authenticity and trust by making processes, decisions, and information open and available to members of the organization. In the Technology Solutions case, members indicated that the company's transparency practices—a "no secrets" policy, free sharing of ideas, the open-door policy among all company members, and the discussions during company meetings—contribute to an open and innovative environment. Team members at Johnsonville Sausage performed budgeting and finance, hiring and firing, scheduling, and quality control. Processes, decisions, and information in the organization were transparent, enabling members to take appropriate actions. Members were fully aware of the company's financial status and competitive position in the market, and they knew whether cost cutting, layoffs, or downsizing were necessary for the company to thrive.

Tapscott and Williams (2006) discussed the idea that openness, or the new-era transparency, goes beyond disclosure of information to internal members of the organization. It includes a vast array of external collaborators. As a result, senior leaders need to decide whether they can honestly practice openness in the organization. If they decide to implement openness in the organization's innovations, processes, decisions, and information, then they need to develop systems and practices that support transparency along with procedures that protect some (but not all) confidential and proprietary information. If leaders decide not to practice full transparency, they still need to develop an organizational culture of trust where members experience authenticity and integrity in leader-member relationships. They also will need to evaluate the potential impact on their competitive position or service delivery of maintaining a highly proprietary and confidential organization.

Trust is the foundation of a relationship between and among leaders and members of an organization. Robert Solomon (2004) contended, "*Trust* characterizes an entire network of emotions and emotional attitudes, both between individuals and within groups and by way of a psychodynamic profile of entire societies" (p. 95). He characterized trust as a social role, a reciprocal relationship, a dynamic decision that makes leadership possible, something to be given that transforms a relationship at its most basic level (pp. 95–99). Honesty builds trust so that members have confidence in a leader's word that the need for change is authentic, that power is indeed shared, and that the member has true agency to effect change in the organization, while leaders have confidence that members can lead themselves, build competence, use their shared power to advance the change initiative, and sustain commitment to the organization's purpose.

Reciprocal care develops from a relationship of trust where "every person matters and each person's welfare and dignity is the concern of us all" (Allen et al., 1998, p. 57). Leading change in a collective or collaborative context creates greater interdependence and mutual responsibility between organizational leaders and members. The leader-follower relationship shifts from a traditional dynamic, where leaders assume responsibility for members, to a shared dynamic, where leaders and members assume responsibility for each other. This relationship involves reciprocal care for the rights, treatment, diversity, and well-being of leaders and members.

Leaders and members in organizations with ethical practices establish a "healthy moral environment," where ethical behavior and expectations are explicitly stated and conscientiously practiced and where ethical practices are not inadvertently undermined by contradictory messages in the organizations' environments (Ciulla, 1995, p. 494). The ethical practices of authenticity, trust, transparency, and reciprocal care apply to leadership and change concepts in this chapter and are necessary for collective or collaborative approaches.

They provide the essential underpinning for the communal, collective enterprise of ethics in the process of leading change.

Conclusion

There is no one approach or formula to choosing the most appropriate practices for leading change. Organizational members can inspire and generate change that allows their organizations to flourish in the midst of a turbulent environment when they consider and select mutually reinforcing forms of leadership, change, and practice. Intentional consideration of all three components of change—concepts of change, concepts of leadership, and change practices—is more than an analytical tool, though it definitely serves that purpose. It is a means of preparing people and their organizations for new ventures into the unknown, fueled by human innovation and advanced technologies.

Note

1. I am deeply indebted to my late colleague Fredric M. Jablin for his help in identifying articles and sources for the discussion on communication in this section.

References

Allen, K. E., Bordas, J., Hickman, G. R., Matusak, L. R., Sorenson, G. J., & Whitmire, K. J. (1998). Leadership in the 21st century. In B. Kellerman (Ed.), *Rethinking leadership: Kellogg leadership studies project 1994–1997* (pp. 41–62). College Park, MD: James MacGregor Burns Academy of Leadership.

Berson, Y., Nemanich, L. A., Waldman, D. A., Galvin, B. M., & Keller, R. T. (2006). Leadership and organizational learning: A multiple levels perspective. *Leadership Quarterly, 17,* 577–594.

Ciulla, J. B. (1995). Messages from the environment: The influence of policies and practices on employee responsibility. In J. T. Wren (Ed.), *The leader's companion: Insights on leadership through the ages* (pp. 492–499). New York: Free Press.

Ciulla, J. B. (2004). *Ethics, the heart of leadership* (2nd ed.). Westport, CT: Praeger.

Cooperrider, D. L., & Srivastva, S. (1987). Appreciative inquiry in organizational life. In R. W. Woodman &
W. A. Pasmore (Eds.), *Research in organizational change and development* (Vol. 1, pp. 129–169). Greenwich, CT: JAI Press.

Daft, R. L., & Lane, P. G. (2005). *The leadership experience* (3rd ed.). Mason, OH: Thomson/South-Western.

Deal, T. E., & Kennedy, A. A. (2000). *Corporate cultures: The rites and rituals of corporate life.* Cambridge, MA: Perseus Books.

Dess, G. G., Lumpkin, G. T., & Eisner, A. B. (2008). *Strategic management: Creating competitive advantages* (4th ed.). New York: McGraw-Hill/Irwin.

Fitzgerald, S. P., Murrell, K. L., & Miller, M. G. (2003). Appreciative inquiry: Accentuating the positive. *Business Strategy Review, 14*(1), 5–7.

Ford, J. D., & Ford, L. W. (1995). The role of conversations in producing intentional change in organizations. *Academy of Management Review, 20*(3), 541–570.

Gini, A. (2004). Moral leadership and business ethics. In J. B. Ciulla (Ed.), *Ethics, the heart of leadership* (2nd ed., pp. 25–13). Westport, CT: Praeger.

Harman, W. W. (1998). *Global mind change: The promise of the 21st century.* San Francisco: Berrett-Koehler.

Heracleous, L., & Barrett, M. (2001). Organizational change as discourse: Communicative actions and deep structures in the context of information technology implementation. *Academy of Management Journal, 44,* 755–778.

Hughes, R. L., Ginnett, R. C., & Curphy, G. J. (2006). *Leadership: Enhancing the lessons of experience* (5th ed.). Boston: McGraw-Hill.

Jabri, M. (2004). Team feedback based on dialogue: Implications for change management. *Journal of Management Development, 23*(2), 141–151.

Kanter, R. M. (1983a). *The change masters: Innovations for productivity in the American corporation.* New York: Simon & Schuster.

Kanter, R. M. (1983b). Change masters and the intricate architecture of corporate culture change. *Management Review, 72*(10), 18–28.

Kanter, R. M. S., Stein, B. A., & Jick, T. (1992). *The challenge of organizational change: How companies experience it and leaders guide it.* New York: Free Press.

Kellett, P. M. (1999). Dialogue and dialectics in managing organizational change: The case of a mission-based transformation. *Southern Communication Journal, 64*(3), 211–213.

Kelley, R. E. (1988). In praise of followers. *Harvard Business Review, 66*(6), 142–148.

Kotter, J. P. (1996). *Leading change.* Boston: Harvard Business School Press.

Lewin, K. (1951). *Field theory in social science: Selected theoretical papers.* New York: Harper.

Lewis, L. K. (2000). Communicating change: Four cases of quality programs. *Journal of Business Communication, 37*(2), 128–155.

London, M., & Maurer, T. J. (2004). Leadership development: A diagnostic model for continuous learning in dynamic organizations. In J. Antonakis, A. T. Cianciolo, & R. J. Sternberg (Eds.), *The nature of leadership* (pp. 222–245). Thousand Oaks, CA: Sage.

Lurey, J. S., & Raisinghani, M. S. (2001). An empirical study of best practices in virtual teams *Information and Management, 38*, 523–544.

McDaniel, R. R. J. (1997). Strategic leadership: A view from quantum and chaos theories. *Health Care Management Review, 22*(1), 21–37.

Miller, A., & Dess, G. G. (1996). *Strategic management* (2nd ed.). New York: McGraw-Hill.

Nadler, D., Shaw, R. B., & Walton, A. E. (1995). *Discontinuous change: Leading organizational transformation.* San Francisco: Jossey-Bass.

Nanus, B. (1992). *Visionary leadership : Creating a compelling sense of direction for your organization.* San Francisco: Jossey-Bass.

O'Toole, J. (2001). When leadership is an organizational trait. In W. Bennis, G. M. Spreitzer, & T. G. Cummings (Eds.), *The future of leadership: Today's top leadership thinkers speak to tomorrow's leaders* (pp. 158–174). San Francisco: Jossey-Bass.

Schein, E. (1992). *Organizational culture and leadership* (2nd ed.). San Francisco: Jossey-Bass.

Schön, D. A. (1971). *Beyond the stable state.* New York: Random House.

Schwartz, P. (1996). *The art of the long view: Paths to strategic insight for yourself and your company.* New York: Currency Doubleday.

Senge, P. M. (1990). *The fifth discipline : The art and practice of the learning organization.* New York: Doubleday/Currency.

Seo, M., Putnam, L., & Bartunek, J. (2004). Dualities and tensions of planned organizational change. In M. S. Poole & A. H. Van de Ven (Eds.), *Handbook of organizational change and innovation* (pp. 73–107). New York: Oxford University Press.

Solomon, R. (2004). Ethical leadership, emotions, and trust: Beyond "charisma." In J. B. Ciulla (Ed.), *Ethics, the heart of leadership* (2nd ed., pp. 83–102). Westport, CT: Praeger.

Stace, D., Holtham, C., & Courtney, N. (2001). E-change: Charting a path towards sustainable e-strategies. *Strategic Change, 10*, 403–418.

Ströh, U., & Jaatinen, M. (2001). New approaches to communication management for transformation and change in organisations. *Journal of Communication Management, 6*(2), 148–165.

Tapscott, D., & Williams, A. D. (2006). *Wikinomics: How mass collaboration changes everything.* New York: Portfolio.

Yukl, G. A. (2006). *Leadership in organizations* (6th ed.). Upper Saddle River, NJ: Prentice-Hall.

Zigurs, I. (2003). Leadership in virtual teams: Oxymoron or opportunity? *Organizational Dynamics, 31*, 339–359.

CHAPTER 41

Collaborating
for Systemic Change

Peter M. L. Senge
MIT Sloan School of Management

Benyamin B. Lichtenstein
University of Massachusetts

Katrin Kaeufer
SoL, Cambridge, Massachusetts

Hilary Bradbury
University of Southern California

John S. Carroll
MIT Sloan School of Management

For more than a century and a half, industrial growth has been weaving an ever-thickening web of interdependence around the world. Today, consumer choices on one side of the planet affect living conditions for people on the other side. Complex supply chains span the globe; for example, the average pound of food travels between 1,500 and 2,500 miles before it reaches an American consumer.[1] But these developments do not alter biological or social realities that have taken shape over thousands and millions of years. Consequently, businesses operating within this growing web are facing a host of "sustainability" problems: social and ecological imbalances created by this globalization, such as a widening social divide between

Source: Reprinted from Collaborating for Systemic Change by Peter M. Senge, Benyamin B. Lichtenstein, Katrin Kaeufer, Hilary Bradbury, and John S. Carroll. *MIT Sloan Management Review*, Winter 2007, Vol. 48, no. 2, p. 44-53. Copyright © 2007 by Massachusetts Institute of Technology. All rights reserved.

haves and have-nots, global climate change, exponentially growing chemical and material waste and loss of habitat and species.

Traditionally, businesses have thought such problems to be the result of economic externalities that require governments' attention. But while governments are a crucial part of lasting change, relying on governmental leadership to effectively deal with sustainability is questionable for many reasons. The first limitation is geography. Even the largest governmental institutions are limited by their borders and can't attack sustainability problems that are global in nature. The second limitation is time. Elected officials are limited by their election cycles and struggle to deal with problems that develop over decades and don't align with their time in office. Moreover, due to increased fragmentation in democratic societies, problems that transcend those of specialized interests tend to fall by the wayside.

For these and many more reasons, businesses are finding themselves compelled to exercise leadership around a host of sustainability issues. In particular, recognizing the limitations of what can be done in isolation, many business leaders have already formed collaborative initiatives like the World Business Council for Sustainable Development, the Coalition for Environmentally Responsible Economies and Societies and the Global Reporting Initiative. In spite of such initiatives, however, there are challenges we are just beginning to recognize.

For example, in 1991, Unilever—the consumer products giant based in London—initiated a worldwide collaborative effort toward creating a global certification regime for sustainable fishing involving fishing companies, distributors, retailers, local governments and nongovernmental organizations. Unfortunately, as soon as this Marine Stewardship Council was formed, it was immersed in controversy.[2] Environmental NGOs interpreted aggressive goals to certify major fisheries as a corporate drive to certify "business-as-usual" overfishing.[3] Conversely, NGO efforts to contest certification were criticized by the multinational corporations as stalling progress toward sustainability. One of the first projects of the MSC—to certify the Alaskan pollock fishery (the largest white fish fishery in the world)—became a multiyear legal battle. Similar difficulties have plagued other efforts to establish certification mechanisms in forestry, organic and nongenetically modified foods.

Two conclusions stand out from efforts like the MSC. First, recognition of the need for such collaboration is growing. Second, it is exceedingly difficult to engage a diverse group of partners in successful collaborative systemic change. Although some relevant research exists,[4] cross-sector collaboration at this scale is largely unexplored. The need is great, but the challenge is equally great.

The Society for Organizational Learning

Beginning in the late 1990s, organizational members of the Society for Organizational Learning began several initiatives focusing on collaborative solutions to a variety of sustainability issues.[5] The group's goals have included the application of systems thinking, working with mental models and fostering personal and shared vision to face these complex sustainability issues.[6]

Through its work, SoL has learned that successful collaborative efforts embrace three interconnected types of work—*conceptual, relational* and *action driven*—that together build a healthy "learning ecology" for systemic change. Failing to appreciate the importance of each is likely to frustrate otherwise serious and well-funded attempts at collaboration on complex problems. What follows are examples from particular projects in which this learning ecology provided an important foundation for substantive progress.

Conceptual Work: Framing Complex Issues

Making sense of complex issues like sustainability requires systems-thinking skills that are not widely shared. When effective collaboration is the aim, developing a shared conceptual "systems sense" is even more important.

Illustrative Conceptual Projects: Integrating Sustainability Frameworks

A dozen SoL organization members including Shell, Harley-Davidson, HP, Xerox and Nike formed the SoL Sustainability Consortium in 1999 to gain a better understanding of how learning tools could support their efforts to integrate sustainability concerns into their business practices.[7] One of the first conceptual projects that emerged in the consortium grew from the confusion of members about the many different sustainability frameworks and tools they encountered,[8] including the NaturalStep,[9] Natural Capitalism,[10] ISO 14001,[11] Zero Emissions Research Initiative,[12] biomimicry,[13] WBCSD Indicators,[14] ecological footprints,[15] life-cycle analysis,[16] and cradle to cradle.[17] (See "Describing Different Sustainability Frameworks," p. 530.)

This confusion became an issue because the proliferation of frameworks and tools was actually slowing progress toward sustainability rather than assisting it, especially because people were spending their time arguing about which framework was "right." In response the consortium frameworks group emerged—a subgroup of the consortium that included members from BP, Harley-Davidson, Plug Power, Visteon, MIT and U.S. Natural Step—that came up with two key ideas for integrating and relating different sustainability approaches.[18]

1. *There are three different worldviews that inform the notion of sustainability.*[19] These are *rationalism,* which recognizes the need for efficient utilization of resources through "meeting the needs of the present without compromising the ability of future generations to meet their own needs;"[20] *naturalism,* which recognizes the need to bring industrial systems into harmony with nature[21] by not depleting resources beyond their rates of regeneration; and *humanism,* which recognizes that sustainability depends on an intrinsic human desire to be part of healthy communities that preserve life for ourselves, other species and future generations.[22]

Each worldview provides a vital counterbalance to the others. For example, popular rationalistic concepts like eco-efficiency can help businesses waste less, but a growing economy can have an increasingly adverse environmental impact, even as it becomes more efficient in using natural resources. By contrast, naturalism addresses the total impact of industrial activity on nature, but unless it evokes a deep human desire to live within those limits, it doesn't necessarily motivate change. Similarly, humanism addresses the deeper motivations for sustainability but does not, by itself, lead to the practical tools and metrics for connecting business operations to sustainability outcomes.[23]

2. *Different sustainability frameworks relate to different levels in the management system.* Many frameworks focus on metrics. This is useful but narrow. Equally important is defining overall outcomes and having guidelines for shaping strategies. Organizational practices that include or go beyond metrics mediate between strategy and outcomes and constitute a critical aspect of any business.

Seeing different sustainability frameworks as working at different management levels clarifies their interdependency and potential complementarity. (See "Integrating Frameworks Across Levels," Table 41.1.) It also reminds us that management systems must be homegrown. Strategic guidelines and organizational metrics and practices must be tailored to the specific people, culture, market, technology and history of any enterprise. For example, NIKE Inc., a company that prides itself on innovation for vitality and more healthy personal life styles, naturally gravitated to biomimicry—innovation inspired by nature. Today, led by hundreds of independent designers who are part of Nike's larger network, the company is introducing a range of "biomimetic" innovations such as compostable cloth, shoes that are put together with biodegradable adhesives and an entire line of organic cotton athletic apparel. (Nike even helped to launch the Organic Cotton Exchange to bring more organic cotton onto the world market.) Translating general ideas into specific organizational strategies, practices and objectives takes imagination, courage, persistence, patience and passion. In its final report, the consortium subgroup concluded, "The sustainability challenge is fundamentally a learning challenge, a process that requires both 'outer changes' like new metrics and 'inner changes' in taken-for-granted assumptions and ways of operating."[24]

ABOUT THE RESEARCH

Data for this research were collected and analyzed by a team of four researchers who, over a six-year period, participated in more than a dozen meetings of the SoL Sustainability Consortium as well as being participant observers in all the collaborative projects. Using traditional ethnomethodology, researchers took extensive field notes of each of the consortium meetings and discussed these in post hoc research teleconferences. In addition, 42 semi-structured interviews with participants were conducted, recorded, and transcribed over a two-year period. Participants were asked about specific collaborative experiences, as well as their personal and business aspirations for the consortium as a whole. In order to gain a diversity of views, the research team chose individuals representing a range of organizational ranks (senior, mid-level, and junior) and attendance levels (core, frequent, and recent). Data were analyzed and coded for emergent themes, using inductive qualitative methods appropriate for exploratory research.[a] At the same time, individual case studies of collaborative projects were developed and compared in order to identify emergent routines and practices being transferred across projects.[b] We analyzed all these data for the presence of drivers and interaction patterns within the consortium as a whole, eventually developing a single system map that identified the three domains discussed here.[c]

The study has been guided by the principles of participatory action research[d] and community action research,[e] aiming to build a community that builds knowledge in a way that binds together the community. Thus, the researchers actively participated in meetings and projects and, in addition, they periodically presented interpretations from their research engaging participants, facilitators, and organizers in regular dialogues on its implications.

a. J.M. Corbin and A.I. Strauss, "The Articulation of Work Through Interaction," *Sociological Quarterly* 34, no. 1 (March 1993): 71-83; and M.B. Miles and A.M. Huberman, *Qualitative Data Analysis* (Thousand Oaks, California: Sage, 1994).

b. R.K. Yin, *Case Study Research: Design and Methods* (Beverly Hills, California: Sage, 1984); and K.M. Eisenhardt and L.J. Bourgeois III, "Building Theories From Case Study Research," *Academy of Management Review* 14, no. 4 (October 1989): 532-550.

c. H. Bradbury, D. Good, and L. Robson, "What Keeps It Together: Relational Bases for Organizing," in *Creating Collaborative Cultures*, ed. S. Shuman (San Francisco: Jossey-Bass/Wiley, in press).

d. P. Reason and H. Bradbury, "Introduction: Inquiry and Participation in Search of a World Worthy of Human Aspiration," in *Handbook of Action Research: Participative Inquiry and Practice*, ed. P. Reason and H. Bradbury (London: Sage Ltd., 2001), 1-14, and C.D. Argyris, B. Smith, and B. Putnam, *Action Science: Concepts, Methods, and Skills for Research and Intervention* (San Francisco: Jossey-Bass, 1985).

e. C.O. Scharmer and P. Senge, "Community Action Research," in *Handbook of Action Research: Participative Inquiry and Practice*, ed. P. Reason and H. Bradbury (London: Sage Ltd., 2001), 238-249.

Clarity must not come at the expense of oversimplification and trivialization of complex issues. Conceptual working groups can sometimes produce rousing action agendas that include little penetrating insight.

Lessons From the Conceptual Work

The learnings from conceptual work done on particular projects suggest the need for collectively built frameworks that create clarity without denying complexity.

Build community through thinking together and sharing. When faced with difficult conceptual tasks, it is faster and easier to leave the work to small groups of experts or to outsource it to consultants or academics. But doing so bypasses the collective intelligence embedded in diverse organizations and industries and can result in output for which there is neither deep understanding nor commitment. In contrast, when conceptual frameworks are developed collaboratively, the process builds community and fosters more extended application and testing. As one member reflected, "Working together to make sense of the different sustainability frameworks showed us that we were not the only company who was confused about sustainability and helped us communicate what sustainability meant in terms of outcomes and strategies in a way that worked in our culture."[25]

Achieve simplicity without reduction.[26] Clarity must not come at the expense of oversimplification and trivialization of complex issues. Conceptual working groups can sometimes produce rousing action agendas that include little penetrating insight; similarly, turgid analyses of complex issues can leave people better informed but no more able to take action. Nevertheless, tools like system dynamics[27] and stock-flow diagrams (see "Naturalism and Sustainability," p. 50) can help in digesting the complexity of a problem while communicating key features that guide action. Simple system models highlight key variables and key interrelationships.

Relational Work: Dialogue and Collaborative Inquiry

Success in any collaboration between organizations rests on the quality of relationships that shape cooperation, trust, mutuality and joint learning.[28] But supporting relationship building is not easy, given the competitive culture and transactional relationships typical in organizational life. Only rarely do groups move beyond "politeness" or win-lose debates into more authentic and reflective interactions characterized by candor, openness and vulnerability.

From its inception, members of the SoL Sustainability Consortium were committed to skills of reflective conversation and working with mental models as a way to build more productive relationships. As part of bringing new members into the community, a half-day, premeeting workshop introduced basic tools of organizational learning; specific ground rules for effective conversation were made explicit, including such things as confidentiality, radical respect for each other, the imperative to "listen, listen, listen" and inquiry balanced with advocacy. These steps were especially useful in ongoing projects in which people deepened their understanding of one another through genuine dialogue.

Illustrative Relational Projects: Women Leading Sustainability

The first Women Leading Sustainability dialogue was held in 2001 to explore the distinctive nature of women's leadership in sustainability initiatives. Over the years, participants developed a repository of the group's experiences, including stories about leading sustainability initiatives, reflections on personal challenges and lessons learned through the eyes of their children. In these ways, the group has lived the consortium's dedication to candor and cooperation.

The relational work of WLS has had tangible effects. For example, Simone Amber, founder of a corporate-funded, global Internet-based educational project called SEED, said that the honest dialogue of WLS helped her see how far sustainability efforts go toward helping others, especially those in developing countries. In WLS, participants' motivation for working on sustainability goes beyond business benefits by integrating work, family and self; and the members have developed a sense of purpose, fueled by a desire for their work to benefit others. These successes are embodied in the group's description of itself: "What matters most about this group is that we assert the importance of taking time for reflection so that our learning evolves through integrating action and reflection." Action and reflection are necessary for good decision making, yet in today's "just do it" culture, time for learning is rarely practiced or valued.

DESCRIBING DIFFERENT SUSTAINABILITY FRAMEWORKS

When the Society for Organizational Learning first organized in 1999, one of its first conceptual projects was to find a way to integrate and relate the existing sustainability tools and frameworks.

The Natural Step was founded by the Swedish research Karl-Henrik Robert in 1989, who developed the following scientifically based consensus definition of sustainability: In a sustainable society, nature is not subject to systematically increasing (1) concentrations of substances extracted form the earth's crust, (2) concentrations of substances produced by society, and (3) degradation by physical means, and in that society, people are not subject to conditions that systematically undermine their capacity to meet their needs.

Natural capitalism is a strategic framework based on four precepts: (1) radically increase the productivity of resource use; (2) shift to biologically inspired production (for example, biomimicry) with closed loops, no waste, and no toxicity; (3) shift business models away from the making and selling of "things" to providing the service that the "thing" delivers (thereby retaining ownership of products for recycling and manufacturing); and (4) reinvest in natural and human capital.

ISO 14001 was first published in 1996 and specifies the operational requirements for an environmental management system, providing generalizable objectives and goals with measurable metrics that can guide the environmental activities of organizations to most industries.

Zero Emissions Research Initiative was launched by the United Nations University/Institute of Advanced Studies in 1994 and was renamed Zero Emissions Forum in 1999. ZERI promoted the concept that all industrial inputs can be completely converted into a value-added inputs for another chain of production, in this context, the manufacturing line can be viewed as a series of production cycles and recycling system.

Biomimicry studies nature's models and imitates or takes inspiration from these designs and processes to create products and human processes. Based on research from multiple disciplines, biomimicry provides a framework for valuing not what we can extract from the natural world but what we can learn from it.

The World Business Council for Sustainable Development brings together 180 international companies in a shared commitment to sustainable development through economic growth, ecological balance, and social progress. The WBCSD has developed a set of eco-efficiency indicators to help measure progress toward economic and environmental sustainability in business.

"Ecological footprints" was first coined in 1992 by the Canadian ecologist William Rees and is used to manage the use of resources throughout the economy by measuring the total environmental impact of business.

Life-cycle analysis enables a manufacturer to quantify how much energy and raw materials are used and how much solid, liquid, and gaseous waste is generated at each stage of a product's life, from creations up to and including the end of its period of use.

Cradle to cradle articulates a set of principles that seek to transform manufacturing design from being purely opportunistic to focusing on the services that products provide. One key principle is the total elimination of waste in manufacturing: All components of manufactured goods would be recycled or reused, thus reversing the "cradle-to-grave" model that governs existing industry.

Table 41.1	Integrating Frameworks Across Levels

Different sustainability frameworks relate to different levels in the management system. Companies often develop customized or home-grown versions that combine elements of various frameworks.

Three Management Levels	Associated Sustainability Frameworks
Strategic guidelines	• The Natural Step • Natural Capitalism • Biomimicry • Cradle to Cradle

Organizational Practices
   • Operating policies
   • Metrics
	• ISO 14001
	• Life-Cycle analysis
	• Ecological Footprints

Organizational outcomes	• World Business Council Sustainable Development

Lessons From the Relational Work

The learnings from relational work done on particular projects suggest that the work must begin with far-reaching and unorchestrated dialogue that in turn sets the tone for systematic initiatives and practices.

Dialogue groups emerge from deep questions and longings. Although it is easy to focus on formal strategies and the mechanics of change, we shape our collective futures in "conversations that matter."[29] For example, the Women Leading Sustainability group explored how to connect their "inner" and "outer" lives, how to develop a career path that can provide leadership within the corporation while also being consistent with their core values and how best to engage stakeholders far beyond their organizations. Such conversations help clarify important issues and provide a "lived experience of how we naturally self-organize to think together, strengthen community, share knowledge and ignite innovation."[30]

Identifying powerful questions cannot be orchestrated or planned. They emerge over time with shifts in strategic context. The key is to recognize and engage them seriously in a spirit of dialogue and joint exploration. For example, John Browne, chief executive officer of BP p.l.c., has arguably done as much to legitimize the importance of climate change in the business world as anyone over the last decade. This started with a day-long meeting of climate scientists and a handful of BP top executives in 1996. "The very fact that we took a whole day on this issue was significant," says former BP chief scientist Bernie Bulkin. "Prior to that, this was a subject that might have gotten 20 minutes on a management team meeting agenda. But I remember Brown saying that 'We are grownups. We can think these things through on our own and find out what we really believe. Maybe we come to the same conclusion as the industry association, or maybe we come to a different conclusion.'" This "thinking together" eventually resulted in a historic speech Browne gave at Stanford University, in Stanford, California, in 1997, in which for the first time in public a CEO of a major oil company broke ranks with peers. He declared that it was sufficiently likely that climate change actually was occurring to warrant serious action, and he announced a series of initial commitments that BP would make unilaterally to reduce its emissions and begin investing in alternative technologies.

Nurturing relational space can be systematic and purposeful. Although the deep questions that drive dialogue cannot be overly planned, there are ways to encourage a relational ecology out of which initiatives will self-organize. For example, many of the founders of Women Leading Sustainability brought specific methods to the group, like personal check-ins and basic principles of dialogue and learning. The provision of free space is a must—and perhaps is the most challenging. Although it sounds simple, free space to simply explore what emerges is virtually nonexistent for today's busy managers.

Once it is recognized and legitimized, deepening relational space also infuses results-oriented work. Effective relational work encourages diverging conversations, asks difficult questions and helps confront dysfunctional practices and attitudes in our organizations and ourselves. Such capacities also benefit action-oriented change initiatives.

Action-Driven Work: Building Collaborative Change Initiatives

Conceptual and relational work are important for effective collaboration, but they are especially important as they come together to enable whole new levels of action. Effectively weaving together all three dimensions requires a new approach that is more personal *and* more systemic than traditional planned-change approaches.

Illustrative Action-Oriented Projects: Collaborating for Innovation in Food Systems

Although most consumers in wealthier countries are unaware of problems with global food systems, these are the largest drivers of poverty, social and political instability and local environmental deterioration worldwide. For example, falling prices for coffee have created a "crisis for 25 million coffee producers around the world, [many of whom] now sell their coffee beans for much less than they cost to produce."[31] Long-term trends of falling prices for major agricultural commodities— 40%-90% declines over the past 50 years for wheat, soy, maize, potatoes, dry beans and cotton—relentlessly drive down farmerincomes.[31] Whereas wealthy countries like the United States buffer farmers with over $500 billion in annual agricultural subsidies, developing countries do not have that luxury. As a result, the increasing production needed to meet demand and offset falling incomes leads to vast environmental degradation (for example, over 1.2 billion hectares of topsoil has been lost in the past 50 years—more than the area of China and India combined) as well as increasing worldwide water shortages, since 70% of water use is for agriculture. And yet, despite increases in production, 800 million people remain chronically underfed.

The Sustainable Food Lab project was organized around an innovative approach to weaving together conceptual, relational, and action spaces and included about 40 upper-middle and senior leaders.[33] These leaders were committed to a deeply personal action-learning process consisting of three phases: (1) cosensing in order to develop shared understanding of current and emerging realities, (2) coinspiring in order to share new knowledge and commitment, and (3) cocreating in order to design prototypes and pilot a small number of innovations conceived by the lab team. The process began with extended dialogues that brought out the different worldviews within the group, followed by five-day "learning journeys" to Brazil designed to immerse team members in the realities of the food system.[34] Time for reflection and dialogue offered windows into people's different views of reality.

In the midst of a subsequent eight-day retreat for reflection and planning, lab team members undertook two-day wilderness "solos" to catalyze deeper intuitions and commitments. "In many ways, the sustainability challenges stem from losing touch with the larger natural and social world, so these solos seem important," said project coordinator Hal Hamilton. In this case, when the work finally turned to formulating prototyping initiatives, the group discovered new levels of trust, commitment and energy. Eventually, eight different prototyping initiatives and associated teams formed, vetted their aims and wrote initial plans for getting to work. Several of these initiatives have evolved into ongoing action projects in three areas: (1) creating shared standards for sustainable food production so that farmers, buyers and the financial community can influence sound production practices, (2) restructuring specific supply chains to increase opportunities for small and mid-size farmers and fishermen, and (3) generating a "demand pull" for more sustainably produced goods and for policies that reward sustainability.

The overall success of this approach to developing action projects was summarized by one of the business participants in the following way: "It amazes me that you can take a group that has been doing individual things and build such a huge amount of trust."

Lessons From the Action-Oriented Work

The learnings from action-oriented work done on particular projects suggest the need to take time to gather input from all stakeholders so that true systemic thinking can give rise to sometimes radically innovative action.

It can take significant time to bring together the diversity of players needed for effective collaborative action. The initial founders of the Sustainable Food Lab—Unilever, Oxfam, the Kellogg Foundation and the Global Leadership Initiative—spent over two years gathering a sufficiently large and diverse network to undertake the project. While the scale of the challenge is huge, in this case "getting the system in the room"—meaning that the people who are present should represent all aspects and stake-holders of the problem being explored—is a common principle for all system-change processes. This is challenging not only because

of the time and effort involved but also because it includes people who will see the world very differently. By defining the project as a cross-sector, multistakeholder initiative, the founders not only signaled that it would take time to engage an appropriately diverse group of participants but also that it would take time to eventually generate action projects for which such diverse participants could truly collaborate.

The awareness of sustainability has been growing because systems thinking is enabling us to see more interdependences. It is reckless to think of commercial sustainability in isolation from social or environmental sustainability.

Systems thinking is essential for change, but it also can be messy and uncomfortable. According to Andre van Heemstra, a management board member at Unilever where the food lab was founded, "The whole awareness of sustainability (in the corporate world) has

---

Figure 41.1 Naturalism and Sustainability

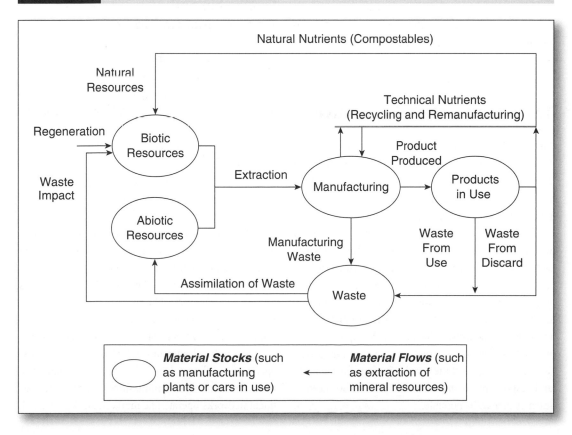

been growing because systems thinking, in different forms, is enabling us to see more interdependencies than we have seen in the past. It is those interdependencies that make you conclude that it is more than stupid—it is reckless to think of commercial sustainability in isolation of either social or environmental sustainability." As a conceptual tool, systems thinking can help to clarify interdependencies and complex change dynamics.[35] But at the same time, seeing systems *together* means allowing for different, sometimes conflicting views.

Radical methods are needed for collaborative action work. The basic toolbox from the organizational learning field—which includes systems thinking, building shared vision and working with mental models and dialogue—is a useful starting point in collaborating for systemic change, but it is just a starting point. New approaches for organizing complex change processes and for large-scale dialogue like the World Cafe[36]—a process for leading collaborative dialogue and knowledge sharing, particularly for larger groups—will also be needed. Traditionally, group and team dynamics approaches have sought to foster deep personal and interpersonal work, but much less is known about opening minds, hearts and wills across networks that cut across diverse organizational boundaries.

The Collaboration Imperative

Business as usual is reaching an evolutionary dead end. Efficiency improvements are useful but limited and, if extended too far, become counterproductive. It is hard to have healthy businesses, no matter how efficient, in unhealthy social and environmental systems.

Businesses, governments, and NGOs increasingly will confront complex sustainability problems for which isolated effort are inadequate. Transactional models for improvement (pay for performance, rewards and punishments, benefit-cost relationships, fear as the primary motivator) have never sufficed for dealing with transformational or "adaptive" change, which requires a new mandate for learning across organizations, industries and sectors. We are at the very beginning of recognizing and responding to this historic shift, and we need to learn as quickly as possible.

Distinct But Not Separate Approaches

Although it is convenient for analytic purposes to distinguish the conceptual, relational and action domains, our experience suggests that they interpenetrate each other in important ways. True systemic change means enacting new ways of thinking, creating new formal structures and, ultimately, transforming relationships. As Hal Hamilton of the food lab says, "The relationships among leaders across normal boundaries might be the most crucial ingredient to major change."

Interweaving conceptual, relational and action work is especially relevant for the cross-sector collaboration needed for many of the "big issues" confronting society. But there is little precedent for such collaboration—protagonists from different sectors often focus on building political leverage and power rather than creating new knowledge and possibilities together.[37] Only by integrating our thinking, relating and acting will projects like the food lab become more common and successful.

Leadership and Transactional Networks

While the limits of transactional ways of interacting are apparent, generating change at a scale that matters often requires engaging large communities of diverse participants with different motivations. Efforts like the food lab, by virtue of the deep personal and interpersonal work involved, have many members who share a strong commitment to the success of the enterprise as a whole. But specific projects also must involve a larger number of individuals and organizations in order to be viable. This means including people and organizations that are focused on narrower agendas and do not share the same sense of responsibility for the whole.

Leadership networks function like communities, transactional networks like markets. Markets are only viable when actors perceive that benefits exceed costs. By contrast, communities revolve around a larger purpose.

The resulting leadership and transactional networks operate on different logics. In effect, leadership networks function like communities, whereas transactional networks operate like markets. Markets are only viable when actors perceive that benefits exceed costs. From a transactional perspective, a collaborative effort is attractive when there is a compelling value proposition, a clear "business case." By contrast, the logic that binds communities revolves around a larger purpose that matters to people. It is not that they are indifferent to benefits and costs, but their primary motivation comes from a commitment to the transcendent aim of sustainable agriculture and its long-term strategic importance for their organizations.

Both types of networks matter for achieving large-scale systemic change. For example, articulating new industry norms that require direct competitors to work together also require enough participants who are genuinely committed to longer-term aims for the industry as a whole. Failing to discern and appreciate these differing motivations can result in stalled initiatives because of an overreliance on transactional players in the early going.

Three Recurring Questions

As we progress along this twofold path of collaborating to achieve practical changes and building learning communities capable of ongoing collaboration, we continue to wrestle with three questions.

1. How can we get beyond benchmarking to building learning communities? Benchmarking is a well-established form of cross-organizational learning, but a learning community involves much more than site visits or listening to PowerPoint presentations—it involves disclosure and vulnerability. Learning communities are most evident when people are openly discussing real problems and asking for help, and they grow as people offer help simply because they want to. Over time, they nurture common commitment and relationships based on respect and mutuality. Perhaps the biggest question is: Which people and organizations will be willing to move beyond more common transactional relationships to build the leadership networks from which such communities grow?

2. What is the right balance between specifying goals and creating space for reflection and innovation? Most collaborative efforts among businesses commence with explicit objectives. But initiatives like the SoL Sustainability Consortium and the Sustainable Food

Lab did not; rather, they organized according to a general intention to foster learning communities around broadly articulated sustainability issues. This created a good deal of anxiety but also provided space for exploration. Several short-term projects and dialogue groups materialized but did not achieve the critical mass to continue. On the other hand, no one would have predicted the long-term importance of the Women Leading Sustainability dialogue nor many of the Sustainable Food Lab initiatives aimed at radically shifting social and environmental conditions. These unforeseen developments and larger webs of collaborations would have been unlikely if the issues agenda were predetermined or driven from a central organizing group.

3. What is the right balance between private interest and public knowledge? There is much artistry in building collaborative systemic change initiatives, but at the same time, most of the key members of such networks are from for-profit businesses seeking competitive advantages. Commercial interests and proprietary know-how must be balanced with public interests when tackling systemic issues. SoL believes that balancing private and public interest means focusing on issues that are larger than individual organizations, improving the related systems that can benefit all and respecting that it takes healthy organizations to address these issues. In this sense, balancing public and private interests resembles the mantra of all great teams and healthy communities: It's up to each of us, and no one can do it alone.

Notes

1. B. Halweil, "Home Grown: The Case for Local Food in a Global Market," November 2002, www.worldwatch.org/pubs/paper/163.

2. See www.unilever.com/ourvalues/environmentand society/sustainability/fish/default.asp; www.msc.org; and B. May, D. Leadbitter, M. Sutton and M. Weber, "The Marine Stewardship Council (MSC)," in "Eco-labelling in Fisheries: What Is It All About?" ed. B. Phillips, T. Ward and C. Chaffee (Oxford: Blackwell Science, 2003), 14-33.

3. P.E. Steinberg, "Fish or Foul: Investigating the Politics of the Marine Stewardship Council" (paper presented at the Conference for Marine Environmental Politics in the 21st Century, Berkeley, California, April 30-May 2,1999), globetrotter .berkeley.edu/macarthur/marine/papers/steinberg-1.html.

4. S. Waddell, "Societal Learning and Change: How Governments, Business and Civil Society Are Creating Solutions to Complex MultiStakeholder Problems" (Sheffield, UK: Greenleaf Publishing, 2005).

5. See www.solsustainability.org; S. Schley and J. Laur, "The Sustainability Challenge: Ecological and Economic Development," The Systems Thinker 7, no. 7 (September 1996): 1-7; and C.O. Scharmer and P. Senge, "Community Action Research," in "Handbook of Action Research: Participative Inquiry and Practice," ed. P. Reason and H. Bradbury (London: Sage Publications, 2001), 238-249.

6. P.M. Senge, "The Fifth Discipline: The Art and Practice of the Learning Organization" (New York: Currency Doubleday, 1990/2006); P.M. Senge, A. Kleiner, C. Robers, R. Ross and B. Smith, The Fifth Discipline Field-book: Strategies and Tools For Building a Learning Organization" (New York: Currency Doubleday, 1994); G. Roth and P.M. Senge, "From Theory to Practice: Research Territory, Processes and Structure at an Organizational Learning Centre," Journal of Organizational Change Management no. 5 (February 1996): 92-106; and www.solonline.org.

7. P.M. Senge and G. Carstedt, "Innovating Our Way to the Next Industrial Revolution," MIT Sloan Management Review 42, no. 2 (winter 2001): 24-38; and J. Ehrenfeld, "Learning and Change in the SoL Consortium"(presentation at the Harley-Davidson Consortium meeting, Milwaukee, Wisconsin, April 9-11, 2003), www.solsustainability.org/toolkit.htm.

8. For a more comprehensive list and short analysis of 21 different frameworks, see J. Elkington, "Triple Bottom Line Reporting," 2003, www.ccc.govt.nz/ TripleBottomLine.

9. See http://www.naturalstep.org.

10. P. Hawken, A. Lovins and L. Hunter Lovins, "Natural Capitalism: Creating the Next Industrial Revolution" (Boston: Little, Brown, 1999).

11. See http://www.iso14000.com.

12. See http://www.zeri.org.

13. J.M. Benyus, "Biomimicry: Innovation Inspired By Nature" (New York: Morrow, 1997); and www.biomimicry.net.

14. H.A. Verfaillie and R. Bidwell, "Measuring Eco-Efficiency: A Guide to Reporting Company Performance" (Geneva: World Business Council for Sustainable Development, 2000).

15. Sturm, M. Wackernagel and K. Muller, "The Winners and Losers in Global Competition: Why Eco-Efficiency Reinforces Competitiveness: A Study of 44 Nations" (Zurich: Verlag Rüegger, 2000); and www.ecologicalfootprint.com.

16. See United Nations Environment Program/Society of Environmental Toxicology and Chemistry cooperation on best available practice in life-cycle assessment, www.setac.org/lca.html.

17. W. McDonough and M. Braungart, "Cradle to Cradle: Remaking the Way We Make Things" (New York: North Point Press, 2002).

18. B.J. Bulkin, J. Ehrenfeld, C. Gray, P. Morris, R. Saillant, T. Savino, T. Reese and P.M. Senge, "Integrating Frameworks For Sustainability," working paper, SoL Sustainability Consortium, Cambridge, Massachusetts, May, 2000 (revised, January 2002), www.solonline.org.

19. These three terms were influenced by the writings of John Ehrenfeld. For example, see J. Ehrenfeld, "Searching for Sustainability: No Quick Fix," Reflections 5, no. 8 (2004): 1-12.

20. World Commission on Sustainable Development; see www.un.org/esa/sustdev/csd/csd.htm.

21. J. Benyus, "Biomimicry" (New York: Morrow, 1997).

22. See www.un.org/Overview/rights.html.

23. A similar project is now underway among consortium members, seeking to clarify the social dimensions of sustainability. See SoL Societal Dimensions Workgroup, "Social Dimensions of Sustainability Frameworks Document" (presentation at SoL Sustainability Consortium, Brewster, Massachusetts, April 26-28, 2005), www.solsustainability.org.

24. The Working Group on Sustainability Frameworks, SoL Sustainability Consortium, Integrating Frameworks for Sustainability (Cambridge, Massachusetts, April 2001), www.solsustainability.org/toolkit.htm.

25. Anthony Reese, director of engineering planning, Harley-Davidson Motor Company, 2004.

26. This phrase is a favorite of Karl-Hènrik Robèrt, the Swedish oncologist and pioneer of The Natural Step framework.

27. G.P. Richardson, "Feedback Thought in Social Science and Systems Theory" (Philadelphia: University of Pennsylvania Press, 1991); and Senge et al., "Fifth Discipline Fieldbook," 1994.

28. Y.L. Doz and G. Hamel, "Alliance Advantage: The Art of Creating Value Through Partnering" (Boston: Harvard Business School Press, 1998); and L.C. Abrams, R. Cross, E. Lesser and D. Z. Levin, "Nurturing Interpersonal Trust in Knowledge-Sharing Networks," Academy of Management Executive, 17, no. 4 (2003): 64-77.

29. J. Browne and D. Isaacs, The World Cafe: Shaping Our Future Through Conversations That Matter" (San Francisco: Berrett-Koehler, 2005), 5.

30. Ibid.

31. Oxfam International, "Mugged: Poverty in Your Coffee Cup" (Oxford, United Kingdom: Oxfam 2002).

32. Food and Agriculture Organization of the United Nations, The State of Agricultural Commodity Markets," 2004, www.fao.org/docrep/007/y5419e/y5419e00.htm.

33. Business participants included Unilever, General Mills, Rabobank, SYSCO (the world's largest food distributor), Nutreco (the world's largest fish farming company) and Sadia (one of Brazil's few multinational food companies), along with

smaller food companies and farm cooperatives. Senior government officials from Europe and South America were involved, along with global NGOs like Oxfam, World Wildlife Fund, Consumers International and The Nature Conservancy and local NGOs from Suriname, Brazil, the United States, the Netherlands, Italy and Germany.

34. Scharmer describes the method-of-learning journey in CO. Scharmer, Theory U: Learning From the Future As It Emerges" (Cambridge, Massachusetts: SoL, in press).

35. Sustainability Institute Report, "Commodity Systems Challenges: Moving Sustainability into the Mainstream of Natural Resource Economics," (Hartland, Vermont: Sustainability Institute 2003); andwww.sustainer .org/tools_resources/pers.html.

36. Brown and Isaacs, "World Cafe"; and Senge, "Fifth Discipline," 357-360.

37. As a comparison, see R. Bouwen and T. Taillieu, "Multi-Party Collaboration As Social Learning For Interdependence: Developing Relational Knowing For Sustainable Natural Resource Management," Journal of Community and Applied Social Psychology 14 (2004): 137-153.

CHAPTER 42

Leading Through Conflict

The Mediator

Mark Gerzon
EastWest Institute

Leadership occurs when . . . leaders and followers raise one another to higher levels of motivation and morality.

—James MacGregor Bums

The conventional use of the term *mediator* refers to a person who serves as an intermediary to reconcile differences, particularly in political and military conflicts. If we scan the news headlines in any particular week, we often find the concept used in precisely this narrow professional context.

"European and Russian mediators return to Kiev for a fresh round of talks to help resolve the ongoing political crisis in the Ukraine"

"Mediators call key meeting on security in Darfur"

"Mideast mediators see no significant progress on the 'roadmap' to peace"

"Mediators urge Colombian Government to halt hostilities to enable release of kidnapped tourists"

"Brazil to send political mediators to Haiti"

But today the meaning of the term has exploded beyond its original use. If we reach past the headlines, we will encounter another, much wider dimension of mediation. These references go well beyond intervening in civil wars or international strife and apply to business, civic, educational, and family conflicts as well.

"The association of Canadian divorce mediators will meet in Ottawa this week to. . . ."

"The US-China Business Mediation Centre, the first joint conciliation institute between the two countries. . . ."

"After receiving twenty hours of training, student mediators become part of the pool of mediators at their campus"

Source: The Mediator, by Mark Gerzon. Pp. 47–58 in *Leading Through Conflict: How Successful Leaders Transform Differences Into Opportunities* (2006) by Mark Gerzon. Reprinted with permission of Harvard Business School Publishing.

"Community mediators brought leaders of both factions together to. . . ."

"Union leaders and airline officials meet with mediators to. . . ."

"The plaintiff consulted with mediators before filing his lawsuit against. . . ."

As even these few examples indicate, the professional role of the mediator applies to virtually every leadership terrain as well as our personal lives. Indeed, there are a growing number of signs pointing to the Mediator (with a capital *M*) as the emerging leadership archetype of our era.

Wherever we speak or teach around the world, my colleagues and I often ask participants in my classes or workshops to name "the person who symbolizes for you the kind of leadership that the world most needs today." They never name demagogic leaders who play on people's fears and prejudices to gain and maintain power, or managerial leaders who, while technically competent, limit their vision solely to their group, organization, or country. No, they always name leaders who are mediators. And the one they select most often is Nelson Mandela.[1]

Whether in Hong Kong or Hyde Park, Malaysia or Massachusetts, the name "Mandela!" is shouted from audiences around the world. Often without being able to articulate it, humanity evidently is recognizing together that his kind of leadership will lead to harmony rather than war, justice rather than oppression, sustainability rather than destruction, and respect rather than discrimination. In other words, it will lead to a world in which difference and conflict are recognized, as part of the natural order, and are seen as opportunities for learning and positive transformation in our relationships, enterprises, and institutions.

"I was born free," Mandela wrote in his autobiography. "Free to run in the fields near my mother's hut, free to swim in the clear stream that ran through my village." At first, Mandela recalls, he wanted freedom only for himself. Then he wanted it for "everyone who looked like I did." But then, during what he calls the "long and lonely years," his integrity evolved. As Mandela put it:

My hunger for the freedom of my *own* people became a hunger for the freedom of *all* people. . . . I knew as well as I knew anything that the oppressor must be liberated just as surely as

the oppressed. A man who takes away [another] man's freedom is a prisoner of hatred, and is locked behind the bars of his prejudice. . . . Both are robbed of their humanity. When I walked out of prison, that was my mission: to liberate the oppressed and the oppressor both.[2]

Mandela's vision shifted from being a champion for *black* South Africans, to being a champion for *all* South Africans regardless of racial or tribal identity, to being a champion for cross-boundary harmony everywhere. He became an advocate for the *whole* community—and, in microcosm, for the whole world. Although his focus was local and regional, his impact was global—which is why it continues to move people throughout the world.

During a recent visit to Robben Island off the coast of South Africa, when I looked through the bars on the window of Mandela's cell, I could see only the side of the towering walls surrounding Cell Block C. It was designed that way on purpose: to block Mandela's vision.

As it turned out, however, Mandela's vision was clear. It was his guards whose vision was impaired. During his quarter century behind bars, Mandela learned to see the future clearly. He had faith that the system of apartheid would end and that a new multiracial South Africa would be born. The prison, which was his university, is now ours. Paradoxically, we journey to this prison to learn about freedom.

In Mandela's prison, as in many other organizations, all three archetypes of leadership were present. Demagogues had created the system of apartheid and established the prisons to enforce it. Managers administered the system, diligently doing their jobs, obeying the rules, and maintaining the status quo. The gift of Mandela's leadership was that, as a mediator, he held a vision of the whole. He dedicated himself during his years in prison to creating a South Africa that would work not just for one "side" or the other but for everyone.

Mediators have the critical capacity to see the whole—and to act in its best interest (see Figure 42.1 for traits that characterize Mediators.) The potential for doing so is already part of each of us and part of our language. When we speak of someone seeing the "whole picture" or thinking "out of the box," we are referring to one of the prerequisites for leading through conflict. (Conversely, when we comment on "groupthink," "tunnel vision," and "myopia," we are referring to its absence.) Various researchers, who have studied it closely, have called this kind of leadership

Figure 42.1 The Mediator

The Mediator

- Strives to act on behalf of the whole, not just a part
- Thinks systemically and is committed to ongoing learning
- Builds trust by building bridges across the dividing lines
- Seeks innovation and opportunity in order to transform conflict

"integral," or "unitive," "Level 5," "third-side," and "second-tier."[3] But all of these diverse frameworks reach a common conclusion: *some leaders are not stopped by differences but can lead across them effectively.*

The Mediator is the focus of this chapter because this model of leadership is able to turn conflict into a positive force for achieving our larger purposes. This kind of leader transforms conflict from a force that can be destructive and divisive into one that is healing and connecting. Since we human beings urgently need to make conflict work *for* us rather than *against* us, those who can lead through conflict hold the key.

Perhaps no honor for leading through conflict is more widely known than the annual Nobel Peace Prize. Every year, the Norwegian award committee bestows this coveted prize on a person or an organization that represents values that, in their view, are truly universal. In recent years, for example, the award was bestowed on an Iranian woman fighting for human rights, a South African archbishop struggling against apartheid, an Irish woman who led the global campaign to eliminate land mines, and an American ex-president who tried to bring peace to the Middle East and to other war-torn countries. Nobel Peace Prize winners (with some notable exceptions) almost always share one common quality: they led through conflict.

Under ideal circumstances, leaders would always act according to what one of my colleagues, David Chrislip, calls the *collaborative principle:* "If you bring the *appropriate people* together in *constructive ways* with *reliable information,* they will create authentic vision and strategies for addressing the shared concerns of the organization or community."[4] The three elements identified in italics—which can be summarized as the *who,* the *how,* and the *what* of conflict prevention—are each vitally important. Leave out any one of them, and, sooner or later, conflict worsens. Incorporate them all, and conflict may be transformed.

Unfortunately, whether in organizations or communities, circumstances are rarely ideal. All the "appropriate people" are often not involved. Meetings are often not conducted in "constructive ways." Instead of "reliable information," incomplete and inaccurate data, with either intentional or accidental biases, is often used. Consequently, decisions are often biased, partisan, or otherwise flawed, and the result is conflicts like these:

Parents at your neighborhood school are polarizing around a proposal to close it. Some parents with younger children are determined to keep it open, while others are excited about the expanded, improved curriculum that will be available at the new, consolidated middle school. Rumors and accusations are rampant. When acrimony between the two groups reaches a boiling point, the school board calls a meeting. You decide to attend in order to find out more about the issue. But when you arrive at the meeting, friends on each opposing side approach you and make clear that they expect your support. What do you do?

Your team at work is under pressure to meet new goals, but progress is slow. You know the cause is that one person's behavior at meetings always derails the discussion. If you don't address this person, you are concerned that nothing will change, goals will not be met, and you will be held responsible. But if you do speak to him, you are afraid it might just turn him against you. Do you speak to him—or to your boss? Or do you just keep quiet?

You attend a town council meeting because you want to voice your opinion on an issue that affects you and your family. The meeting format allows you to have three minutes at a microphone if you stand in a line and wait your turn. You notice how ineffective most speakers are, since they are speaking in an arbitrary order and with so little time. Do you speak despite your misgivings about the format? Or do you just skip it and go home?

If you find situations similar to these to be confusing, even overwhelming, be patient with yourself. It simply means that you need to learn new skills for dealing with them. Each of us can learn to be Mediators simply by becoming apprentices and learning the tools of the trade. Anyone who sincerely and humbly studies all of these tools and applies them to his or her life—whether at work, in a community, or at home—will experience a remarkable, positive shift. Taken together, the tools of the Mediator can profoundly change our lives.

Tool 1: Integral Vision

A conflict erupts—and it involves you. You can't control it. You can't avoid it. But you are definitely *in* it. What is the first thing you need to do?

Nothing. That's right: absolutely nothing!

Unless violence or other immediate danger is involved, the first tool required in a conflict is not about *doing*. It is about witnessing—*seeing the whole*. So unless your physical safety, or someone else's, is at risk, it is better to look *before* you leap.

Integral vision is the commitment to hold all sides of the conflict, in all their complexity, in our minds and hearts. The dictionary defines *integral* as necessary to the *completeness* or the whole. As we will use the term here, integral vision is necessary to the *transformation* of the whole. Leaders who transform conflict have learned, often the hard way, not to strike out blindly at the first "bad guy" they encounter. They neither exacerbate the conflict through violence nor exploit it for narrow self-interest. On the contrary, Mediators make sure that before they take action, they have committed themselves to seeing as much of the larger picture as possible.

Two feuding tribes may build a wall through an orchard, separating it into two. But the fruit is still the same; the roots are still in the same earth; the same bees will pollinate the blossoms; the same sun will shine on their leaves. No matter how high we make these walls, how much we fortify them, how much we spend to hire guards with guns, how much barbed wire we place on top of them, or how deep the trenches we dig around them, our walls do not demarcate the end of the world. They simply mark the borders of our imagination.

Integral vision requires questioning any dividing line that separates "us" and "them." There are many lines, including ones made by nature ("shorelines, forest lines, sky lines, rock surfaces, skin surfaces and so on") and others made by human beings (e.g., Christian/heathen or Muslim/infidel). Integral vision prevents us from turning any of these lines into walls, and makes us aware of the webs that connect us.[5]

Tool 2: Systems Thinking

Once our intention is clearly focused on understanding the whole conflict, we naturally want to *think systemically:* to identify all (or as many as possible) of the significant elements related to the conflict situation and to understand the relationships between these elements. For example, in the following chapters, many conflict-transforming leaders deal with conflict by asking a question that helped them think more systemically.

- Why is this company riddled with conflict? asked CEO Gunther Thielin. What can I do to make the parts work together more effectively as one efficient enterprise?

- What is the social and political system that maintains apartheid in South Africa? asked Nelson Mandela. How can I, as a black person, change that system so that every person, black and white, is free?

- What aspects of the economy of Boston systematically prevent affordable housing from being built? asked William Edgerly. How can I, as president of a major bank, help make housing accessible to the city residents who need it?

- How can the United Nations operate in Baghdad so that we actually help the Iraqi people recover from this awful war? asked Nada al-Nashif, a key UN officer during postwar reconstruction. How do we as an institution enter this social system so that we do not "take sides" but bring the sides together to rebuild the country?

To deal with any of these conflicts requires learning to think about *all* the pieces of the puzzle. The success of these leaders, and their counterparts in scores of other professions, results in large part from their capacity to think systemically.

Tool 3: Presence

Transforming conflict requires more than just our minds; it requires our whole being. We can only be present to the whole conflict to the degree that we are actually present as our full selves. No matter how much we may want to see the whole and think about it systemically, we cannot do so if we are not right *here,* right *now. Presence* is an expression of our capacity to apply all our mental, emotional, and spiritual resources to witnessing and transforming the conflict.

Being present takes us beyond ordinary "thinking," which can be part of the solution—or part of the problem. Ordinary thinking, for example, can be used to bring antagonists to the peace table and end violence; but it can also be used to construct a bomb and as a strategy for detonating it in order to sabotage that peace agreement. Presence means that our entire selves are engaged, not just a disembodied "thinker." It is closely related to, but more than, mere self-awareness or emotional intelligence. It is bringing our being into the present moment of any leadership challenge we may face.

Some leaders develop presence by periods of solitude in the wilderness, while others seek coaching or 360-degree feedback from colleagues. Others cultivate it through meditation, through playing music or creating art, or through other forms of spiritual self-discipline. Although the methods for cultivating presence vary, their purpose is to optimize the most valuable resource any one of us possesses: our whole being.

This quality of presence, which often manifests itself as calmness or stillness, should not be misconstrued. Just like everyone else, leaders who transform conflict have strong opinions, feelings, reactions, and interests. When they are exposed to disputes, particularly those in which they themselves have played an active part, anger and anguish course through their bodies too. They feel all the emotions—fear, grief, sorrow, and even rage—that affect everyone at different times. But because they have vowed to transform conflict, this intention informs everything they say, and do, and feel—including how, and when, they speak.

In this sense, presence is the master tool. It is what gives us access to all the other tools for transforming conflict, and guides us as we decide which tool to use when, where, and how. The more deeply we develop this quality of presence, the more effectively we will use all the other tools.

Tool 4: Inquiry

No one can fully understand complex systems, or challenging conflicts, without asking questions. No matter how much knowledge we might have in our heads, sooner or later we need to draw on the wisdom of others. If we don't, our analysis will almost certainly be incomplete.

Inquiry is a way of asking questions that elicits essential information about the conflict that is vital to understanding how to transform it. In addition to learning what is inside the boundaries of their profession, or worldview, leaders must also learn what is beyond those boundaries. To paraphrase Albert Einstein's well-known statement: a conflict cannot truly be transformed effectively with the same mind-set that produced it in the first place. Inquiry permits us to examine the situation afresh. Now we can begin to ask, *Who* is involved in this conflict? *When* did it begin? *Where* is it stuck? *How* has it changed over time? *Why* have previous efforts failed? *What else* do I need to know before I engage?

Although experts in this field use terms such as stakeholder analysis, issue analysis, or conflict analysis, we will use the simpler word *inquiry* to refer to the related skills of asking generative questions—and then listening carefully to the answers. It is this process of inquiry that guides us in determining where we need to focus our attention. Whether as businesspeople or government officials, educators or citizen activists, Mediators keep digging deeper until they are convinced that they are approaching the heart of the matter. They ask challenging questions, even if it means being unpopular or taking risks. As U.S. Senator Robert Byrd put it during the prelude to the U.S.-led war in Iraq, "It is not now, nor was it ever, unpatriotic to ask questions."[6]

Because inquiry is such a pivotal tool, one of the most common characteristics of Mediators is their curiosity. Attend any gathering with them, and you will hear them probing—sometimes gently, sometimes pointedly. They rarely pontificate about their favorite theory but instead can be heard asking question after question until the pieces begin to fall slowly into place.

Since information is only useful if we listen to it, Mediators are also distinguished by their deep commitment to first hearing what others have to say. While they may be powerful speakers, what makes them so effective is not their tongues but their ears. They learn to hear the difference between truth and half-truth, and equally important, between the spoken and the unspoken.

Please note: these first four tools are almost entirely about process, not about outcomes. They are about preparation, not action. This is because a constructive, trust-building process is essential to achieving positive, lasting transforming of conflict. If you want to skip all this preparation and just go straight to "action" or "making a deal," go right ahead. But if your conflict was actually that easy to resolve, you probably would not be reading this chapter.

Tool 5: Conscious Conversation

At the heart of conscious conversation is choice. Mediators know how to support those involved in a conflict to become aware that they have a *choice* about how to communicate. The Mediator's challenge is to create an environment in which the antagonists experience their freedom to use language in other, more diverse and effective ways. The range of communication styles includes verbal brawling, debate, discussion, and presentation, as well as negotiation, council, dialogue, and, of course, silence. *Conscious conversation* is the practical application of the awareness that we are free to choose how we speak and listen.

By making participants in conflicts aware of this wide range of choices, the leader as Mediator has an immediate impact on the quality of conversation. Language starts to be used in new and more conscious ways. Reactive, mindless attacks and counterattacks give way to more creative, catalytic interchange. Before they know it, those in conflict are learning more about the situation, and about themselves.

Tool 6: Dialogue

Of all the forms of discourse Mediators use, we often focus on dialogue as a doorway to transformation. This is because *dialogue* is an inquiry-based, trust-building way of communicating that maximizes the human capacity to bridge and to innovate.

Particularly if there are two (or more) sides with different worldviews, dialogue enables them to meet face-to-face and begin to connect across whatever divides them. Within any negotiation or dispute settlement process, dialogue serves as a valuable catalyst for reducing attachment to "positions," creating greater awareness of deeper "interests," and paving the way for stronger relationships and new options.

The purpose of dialogue in conflict situations is not just to improve the quality of discourse but also to lay the foundation for transformative action. Because of the creative application of the preceding tools, including dialogue, the stakeholders are far less likely to act in habitual, one-sided ways that reinforce the cycle of conflict, and far more likely to act in collaborative ways that lead to genuine innovation.

Tool 7: Bridging

In conflict situations, transformation rarely occurs because of one individual's genius. Far more often, it results from collaborative, creative relationships that form a human bridge across divisive boundaries. Whether the bridge needs to be built between two divisions in a company or two ethnic groups in a community, that bridge is a precondition for transforming the conflict.

Bridging is the process of building partnerships and alliances that cross the divisions in an organization or a community. Sooner or later, verbal exchange, no matter how meaningful, is not enough. Participants want to *do* something together. To move through the conflict, they must change their behavior toward each other or their way of dealing with the conflict. They must build a bridge across whatever has separated them not a bridge of steel and metal cables but a bridge of cross-boundary leadership.

We have many words for the construction materials from which these invisible bridges are built—trust, social capital, respect, healing, empathy, understanding, courage, collaboration, caring, or even love. But however we name it, it comes down in the end to this fundamental and mysterious truth: *the energy between the conflicting parties must change in order for conflict to be transformed.* When this shift occurs, what was impossible before now becomes possible. The stage is now set for a breakthrough.

But innovations do not happen all at once. If one occurs, those who witness it will think they actually saw it happen. But, like the sprout breaking through the soil for the first time, the process began a long time before it became visible. It began weeks or months earlier. The names of the Mediators who long ago tilled the soil and planted the seed may have been forgotten. But the fruits of their labors may last forever.

Tool 8: Innovation

Innovation is the creative, social, or entrepreneurial breakthrough that creates new options for moving through conflicts. Such breakthroughs, if they occur, cannot be guaranteed in advance. (If they can, then they are not truly a breakthrough but rather someone's preconceived plan.) The breakthrough is an innovation, something that perhaps could be imagined but not achieved until now. This innovation—"something newly invented or a new way of doing things"—brings hope. It points the way toward resolving, or transforming, the conflict. For the first time, there is now "light at the end of the tunnel."

As this often-used phrase implies, however, the light is at the *end*. Whether we reach it or not depends on our navigating the tunnel. For a conflict to be "transformed" in an enduring way, all those involved must "own" the outcome. They must "buy in." The new idea, plan, or innovation needs to be adopted by most, if not all, of the key stakeholders. Otherwise, the innovation may look good on paper, but it will not take hold. Those involved in the conflict must take this new possibility and make it their own—if not wholeheartedly, then at least provisionally. They have to not only endorse it but also promote it to their respective constituencies. If this sense of ownership spreads, the innovation may become an enduring solution to the conflict. But only time will tell.

Think about it. How many peace treaties have been shredded by bullets? How many carefully drafted business contracts have ended up in court? How many strategic plans end up in the wastebasket because someone was not consulted? How many political compromises have been undone by the next election? (Even more sobering, how many passionate love affairs culminate years later in bitter divorce proceedings?)

Even when a conflict seems to be resolved and those involved support the outcome, it is still too soon to bring the curtain down on the drama of conflict. In fact, the most important part of the drama often takes place when everyone thinks it is "over." Only a novice will now uncork the champagne and declare victory. You can put up a banner emblazed with the words *Mission accomplished!* if you want—but do not be surprised if events prove otherwise. It is far better to celebrate your progress quietly; save the champagne for when the stakeholders have demonstrated the will to sustain it. Then and only then can you be confident (although never certain) that the agreements that were achieved will endure.

As useful as these tools are, never forget the power of your own purpose. One can swing a hammer for any reason—to wound or to heal, to build or to destroy—and it is still a hammer. But the tools outlined here are different. The impact of the Mediator's tools depends on the intentions of the leader who holds them in his or her hands. Unlike with ordinary tools in a carpenter's toolbox, not only do we use the Mediator's tools, *they* use *us*. As we use them to transform conflict, we may find that they transform us as well.

Notes

1. Other frequently mentioned names include Mahatma Gandhi, Martin Luther King, Jr., and sometimes Vietnamese Buddhist monk Thich Nhat Hanh, the Sri Lankan peacemaker Dr. A. T. Ariyaratne, former U.S. president Jimmy Carter, UN Secretary-General Kofi Annan, or Burmese democracy activist Aung San Suu Kyi.

2. Nelson Mandela, *Long Walk to Freedom* (Boston: Back Bay Books, 1995). I am grateful to Robert Gass and the Art of Leadership training program for drawing my attention to this passage.

3. Ken Wilber, *The Collected Works* (Boston: Shambhala, 2000). It is important to note that, from Wilber's perspective, systems thinking is a component of his "all quadrant–all level" model, which transcends and includes systems thinking. Readers are invited to explore Wilber's thinking more fully—for instance, *Integral Psychology* (Boston: Shambhala, 2000). Dr. Susanne R. Cook-Greuter, "A Detailed Description of the Development of Nice Action Logics in the Leadership Development Framework Adapted from Ego Development Theory" (manuscript, ca. 2002); Jim Collins, *Good to Great: Why Some Companies Make the Leap and Others Don't* (New York: HarperCollins Publishers, 2001); William Ury, *The Third Side* (New York: Penguin Books, 2003), http://www.thirdside.org; and Don Beck and Christopher Cowan, *Spiral Dynamics* (London: Blackwell Publishers, 1996).

4. For the most current explanation of this collaborative principle, see David D. Chrislip, *The Collaborative Leadership Fieldbook* (San Francisco: Jossey-Bass, 2002).

5. Quotations are from Ken Wilber, *No Boundaries: Eastern and Western Approaches to Personal Growth* (Boston: Shambhala Publications, 2001).

6. Brian Knowlton. "Democratic Leaders Lash Out at Bush," *International Herald Tribune*, September 26, 2002.

CHAPTER 43

Illuminating a Cross-Cultural Leadership Challenge

When Identity Groups Collide

Donna Chrobot-Mason
University of Cincinnati

Marian N. Ruderman
Center for Creative Leadership

Todd J. Weber
University of Nebraska–Lincoln

Patricia J. Ohlott
OMG Center for Collaborative Learning

Maxine A. Dalton
Hot Springs, NC

T he challenge of managing interpersonal and resource-based conflict in organizations has been well documented (e.g., Amason and Schweiger, 1997; Jehn, 1995; Rahim, 2001). However, an even more complex, intense and disruptive type of conflict seems to be emerging in the workplace as a significant challenge for organizational leaders. Identity-based conflicts, involving disputes over the intrinsic value of

Source: Illuminating a Cross-Cultural Leadership Challenge: When Identity Groups Collide by Donna Chrobot-Mason, Marian N. Ruderman, Todd J. Weber, Patricia J. Ohlott, and Maxine A. Dalton. *International Journal of Human Resource Management 18* (Nov 2007): 2011–2036. Published by Routledge, Taylor & Francis.

the social groups with which individuals identify, often originate outside of the work context, but they emerge as workers from various identity groups in conflict attempt to work together. The conflicts embedded in society literally spillover into the organization influencing work processes and practices. In this paper, we begin to illuminate the unique challenges leaders face in attempting to prevent identity-based conflicts from emerging and escalating.

Our work is based on a review of the literature and illustrated with examples from interviews with leaders conducted as part of a pilot study. Based on an examination of literature in the areas of intergroup conflict, workplace diversity, and social identity theory, we identified the critical constructs and models applicable to this leadership challenge. In the first part of this paper, we discuss four strategies identified by the social identity literature: decategorization, recategorization, subcategorization and crosscutting. In the second part, we discuss the relationship of these strategies to cultural differences. In doing so, we have identified a critical gap in the current literature. To date, there has been very little discussion of the role of cultural context in determining an appropriate and effective leadership strategy for preventing conflict between social identity groups. Therefore, our unique contribution to the leadership literature based on this multidisciplinary literature review is to offer research propositions for future work in this area as well as identify potential 'blind spots' such as the importance of taking cultural factors into account when managing social identity conflict in the workplace.

In addition to reviewing the literature, we spoke with 24 individuals in leadership positions in various countries to get their first hand accounts of what it is like to lead in the context of very salient social identity group differences. These stories are used in the paper for illustrative purposes only. Drawn from nine different countries, the interviewee accounts bring to life constructs discussed in the literature.

The Leadership Challenge

For decades now, researchers have been predicting that globalization, increased technology, civil rights legislation and changing demographics would create new challenges for leaders who must manage a diverse workforce (e.g., Chrobot-Mason, 2003; Jackson, 1992; Morrison, 1992). All of these factors have significantly increased the likelihood that workers from both genders, various nationalities and ethnic backgrounds, multiple races, and a variety of religions will be required to work together.

Robert House and Global Leadership (2004) argue that organizations must consider cultural differences as the globalization of business continues to increase. He states that 'as economic borders come down, cultural barriers go up, thus presenting new challenges and opportunities in business. When cultures come into contact, they may converge on some aspects, but their idiosyncrasies will likely amplify' (House and Global Leadership and Organizational Behavior Effectiveness Research Program, 2004: 5). In this paper, we examine conflicts that emerge due to historically deep-rooted boundaries and tensions between social identity groups, which create unprecedented leadership challenges in today's workplace.

Social identity conflicts can be distinguished from interpersonal disagreements by the *nature of the causal attributions made by the disputants and by the amplification of the event to a larger collective* (Simon and Klandermans, 2001). In other words, a disagreement may begin between two people but in a social identity conflict, at least one party attributes causality to the social identity and intergroup history of the players, not to individual differences. When at least one party attributes a conflict event to race, gender, religion, sexual orientation, nationality or ethnicity, and takes sides based on their own race, gender, religion, sexual orientation, nationality, or ethnicity, this is a social identity conflict.

Friedman and Davidson (2001) contend that it is important to consider identity groups within a social power structure and that not all groups hold equal status within a particular societal context. Whereas some social identity groups are privileged, others are systematically disadvantaged and hold a position of lower status and power within society. Due to the centrality of social identity, its importance to the development of a healthy self-concept, and the inequalities that exist between social identity groups in most societies, social identity conflicts are charged with emotion, difficult to resolve and often intractable. 'When identities are intertwined with shared ideologies, the stakes in a conflict are much greater and the costs of reaching a resolution are much higher than for conflicts not rooted in group membership' (Putnam and Wondolleck, 2003: 43). In general, intergroup conflict emerges either as a result of competition over scarce resources or a reaction to a perceived threat posed by an 'evil other' (Himes, 1980; Katz, 1964; Rothman, 1997). Unlike resource or interest-based types of conflict which are typically well-defined and may be resolved through compromise, identity-based conflicts involve disputes over the intrinsic value of the social group with which individuals strongly identify, and consequently the individual's own value is at stake (Cavey, 2000; Hicks, 2001). As a result of the importance of the conflict to the essence of the individual's existential value, these conflicts are usually resistant to resolution and can quickly escalate (Putnam and Wondolleck, 2003).

To illustrate these phenomena in the workplace, let us draw from an interview conducted in Mozambique. The story involves tension between Portuguese and Africans in a large multinational corporation. In the organization, the Portuguese still hold the majority of positions of power. For five centuries, Mozambique was a Portuguese colony. Liberation from Portugal took place in 1975 after a protracted war. This was followed by a civil war, famine and severe economic problems. Mozambique became a democracy with the 1990 constitution, giving rights to all. Racial tensions reflect this legacy of colonization and slavery. In addition, Mozambique has been drawn into the struggles against white rule in South Africa and Rhodesia.

The interviewee tells the story of a black receptionist who is approached by the wife of a white, Portuguese expatriate senior director. The white woman asks to see her husband, which violates a corporate policy forbidding employees to receive personal visits during work hours. The black receptionist refers to the policy and refuses the visit, which angers the white woman. She proceeds to phone her husband, who then angrily approaches the receptionist, yelling at her and using racial slurs to denigrate her. The interviewee then tells how the conflict escalates as black employees approach the white director to tell him he was wrong. The white director then proceeds to write a memo to another white senior vice president, who punishes the black receptionist for her behaviour. The conflict continues to escalate even further as another black staff member (a cleaner) takes the story to the media and the labour

authorities. Eventually, the department of foreign affairs intervenes. The interviewee describes this conflict as the 'tip of the iceberg' rather than an isolated event because there is a longstanding history of conflict between these two groups ever since the time the Portuguese ruled Mozambique. This story clearly depicts how a societal conflict between two identity groups can spill over into the work context such that group members begin to take sides and attribute the cause of the conflict to negative intergroup history rather than an isolated disagreement between two individuals.

To summarize, leaders face a unique challenge when members of social identity groups who have historically been deeply divided by race, ethnicity, religion, social class, region, etc. come together in the workplace and are divided as a result of some dispute in which the cause is attributed to social identity differences and the dispute is then amplified to a larger collective. In the next section, we review literature on Social Identity Theory (SIT), inter-group anxiety, faultlines and conflict escalation, to illustrate further the challenges leaders face when attempting to resolve a social identity conflict at work.

Literature Review

Social Identity Theory

Psychological theory and research suggest that people tend to have strong needs for both inclusion and differentiation (Brewer and Brown, 1998). Belonging to social groups seems to satisfy both needs by allowing the individual to belong to some larger collective as well as distinguishing oneself from members of other groups. Social identity theory may be used as a basis for understanding the positive and negative outcomes that result when members of different identity groups interact. Social identity theory presumes that an individual's self-concept is derived from membership in a social group together with the psychosocial value and emotional significance attached to that membership (Turner and Giles, 1981). The theory suggests that individuals engage in a cognitive process in which they classify themselves and others into categories or groups. This categorization process serves two functions: (a) it provides individuals with a systematic means of defining others, and (b) the individual is able to define him- or herself within the social environment (Ashforth and Mael, 1989). In general, these theories suggest that people evaluate the social groups to which they belong as positive and are motivated to maintain such evaluations in order to preserve a favorable self-image.

Inter-group Anxiety

The historical legacy of conflict between identity groups may strongly influence the extent to which conflict emerges in the workplace. For example, the intensity and duration of previous conflicts may influence the emergence of continued conflict between identity groups. This phenomenon, known as *intergroup anxiety* (Stephan and Stephan, 1985), is created by three sets of factors: prior intergroup relations (e.g., the amount and conditions of prior contact); prior intergroup cognitions (e.g., knowledge of the outgroup, stereotypes, prejudice, expectations and perceptions of dissimilarity); and situational factors that characterize the intergroup interaction (e.g., amount of structure, type of interdependence, group composition, relative status). The anxiety stems from the anticipation of negative consequences or comparisons as a result of having been in contact with the other group (Fisher, 1990; Stephan and Stephan, 1985). Consequences of intergroup anxiety may include avoidance of intergroup interaction, information processing biases (e.g., seeking information to confirm existing stereotypes), heightened emotional responses to outgroup members (e.g., overreaction to even slight provocations) and stronger positive ingroup bias that results from a perceived threat to self-esteem, all of which may increase the likelihood of identity-based conflict (Stephan and Stephan, 1985). Intergroup anxiety thus can be a primer for conflict within the organization and the more entrenched and historically volatile intergroup relations have been in the past, the more difficult it will be for the leader to bridge differences and manage social identity conflict effectively. In our previous example, the political history of the conflict between Portugal and Mozambique resulted in a generalized distrust between these two groups, serving as a primer for conflict within the organization.

Faultlines

Identity group representation or composition within the workplace may serve to 'activate' or evoke categorization and thus increase the potential for conflict between identity groups. Lau and Murnighan (1998) proposed a concept they call faultlines to examine the underlying patterns of group member characteristics that can be an important determinant of subgroup conflict. 'Group faultlines are hypothetical dividing lines that may split a group into subgroups based on one or more attributes' (Lau and Murnighan, 1998: 328). Gender faultlines, for example, divide a work group's members into male and female subgroups.

Faultlines in work groups are similar to faultlines in the earth's crust in that group members' many demographic dimensions resemble multiple layers, they may go unnoticed without the presence of external forces, and strong faultlines provide an opportunity for work groups to crack open, revealing the importance of their attributes. Faultlines may be activated by topics, issues or events that make certain social identities particularly salient (see Powell and Taylor, 1998, for an example). For example, affirmative action issues may activate racial divisions, political reform debates may activate liberal and conservative identities, and gender faultlines may be activated when workplace sexual harassment is discussed. However, recent research suggests that communication in work groups with strong faultlines may prove problematic even when the group's task and faultlines are unrelated (Lau and Murnighan, 2005). In other words, the mere presence of these social identity differences can make teamwork difficult.

The faultlines model (Lau and Murnighan, 1998) provides a useful analogy for understanding the challenges that leaders of demographic diversity must confront. When faultlines exist within the organization because of diversity, there is significant potential for social identity groups to polarize (Simon and Klandermans, 2001; Wetherell, 1987) such that battle lines will be drawn along those faultlines and work may be negatively impacted. Returning to our Mozambique example, it is easy to see how the intergroup anxiety between the Portuguese and Mozambicans sets the stage for group polarization and the racial slur activated the faultline between whites of Portuguese ancestry and blacks of African ancestry in the organization. In situations where there is a long history of distrust and contempt between groups in the society and intergroup anxiety is high, the mere presence of these faultlines may pose problems for the leader. For example, in Israel where there is a long and deeply rooted history of intense conflict between Palestinians and Israelis, faultlines in an organization might easily erupt into social identity based conflicts. One of our interviewees told a story about a strong Israeli/Palestinian faultline in a hospital workforce. The interviewee described the work environment as one in which the underlying conflict and tension was ever-present. In less extreme situations, for example where intergroup anxiety is moderate, faultlines in the organization may be activated by an external event that occurs in the society or an event occurring inside the organization, which serves to make identity group differences and intergroup anxiety salient and thus leads to group polarization. Once group polarization occurs, the scope of the leadership challenge depends largely on the extent to which the conflict escalates or dissipates.

Conflict Escalation

The process of escalation is well documented in the conflict literature. Northrup (1989) outlines a series of stages (threat, distortion, rigidification and collusion) in which he describes the role of identity in conflict escalation. During the first stage, an event occurs that is perceived as invalidating to the core sense of identity for group(s) involved, which is experienced as a serious threat. In the second stage, distortion, group members attempt to psychologically respond to the threat, often by denying or redefining the incident in order to maintain the core sense of identity. In the third stage, rigidification, perceptions of threat increase resulting in greater polarization where ingroup/outgroup distinctions become increasingly exaggerated and rigid, and dehumanization may result. During the final stage, parties collude in maintaining the conflict and the conflict becomes institutionalized such that the social identity of the group becomes interwoven with the conflict itself. At least some of these stages of conflict are apparent in our Mozambique example, beginning with the racial slur that is experienced as a threat by black employees, followed by greater polarization and intergroup distinctions as both black and white employees begin to take sides and involve others at higher levels in the organization.

Leading Across Social Identity Differences

When social identity conflicts emerge in the workplace, it seems that organizational members turn to leaders for help. In this paper, we define leaders as individuals with formal organizational authority who engage in processes and actions that lead to shared direction, alignment and commitment (O'Connor and Quinn, 2004; Van Velsor and McCauley, 2004). Employees expect leaders, persons with formal authority, to intervene when social identity conflicts emerge. One of our interviewees illustrates this point by saying, 'They look to us as the leadership of the program to create an environment that lessens that struggle, lessens that conflict.' Leaders' reactions to identity-based conflicts have the potential to either de-escalate the conflict situation or polarize social identity groups even further. Therefore, the role of the leader in such situations is particularly important. However, the leadership literature suggests that the role of the leader is particularly challenging, given that he/she is also a member of one of the social identity groups.

Haslam (2001) proposes that a particular group member will be perceived as prototypical of his/her group to the extent that the person is similar to members of his/her own group and different from members of other groups. Turner (1987) suggests that the group member who is most likely to exercise leadership and exert influence is the one who represents the strongest in-group prototype; that is, the one who is most representative of the shared social identity of the group. Research suggests that liking, or attraction, increases compliance with requests (Berscheid and Reis, 1998). The most prototypical person is able to influence because he or she is socially attractive to the other group members who are thus more likely to agree and comply with suggestions. Further, a cycle results in which the ability of the leader to influence the group increases as the attributions of leadership made by others increase. Through their compliance, the group publicly endorses the leader, imbues him or her with greater status and prestige, and thus increases the leader's power to influence (Hogg, 2001). In a conflict situation social identity becomes more salient (Tsui and Gutek, 1999) and members can be expected to confer leadership increasingly on those whom they perceive to best embody the position of their ingroup (Fielding and Hogg, 1997; Hogg, 1996).

Literature Review Summary and Workplace Implications

Based on the literature review and the interviews we conducted, we believe social identity conflicts are manifested in the work context in the following way. Anxiety between social identity groups exists in society due to historical and deeply rooted tensions. One of the few places in which these groups are forced to interact is the workplace. Faultlines that exist within the organization or within work teams become activated when external forces (e.g., identity conflict in society) make subgroup distinctions highly salient. Group members 'collide' when they find themselves having to work together on the same team or within the same organization. The anxiety and conflict originating in society has the potential to spill over into the organization (Lau and Murnighan, 1998; Simon and Klandermans, 2001), particularly when an event activates faultlines in the organization and social identity differences become salient.

Initially a conflict may erupt between two individuals, but if at least one party attributes the conflict to social identity group differences that resonate with historical tensions between groups and involve other people, the conflict becomes a social identity intergroup conflict. The higher the intergroup anxiety that currently exists because of the history of conflict between the two groups, the more likely it is that escalation will occur and people will begin to take sides. Escalation occurs as groups increasingly begin to polarize (i.e., in-group/out-group distinctions become more salient) and as attempts to communicate and/or resolve the conflict fail. When at least one group appears unwilling to change or acknowledge a problem and the other group is unwilling to concede, conflict resolution is likely to fail. Group members begin to involve outsiders (e.g., union representatives, the media) or attempt to push the issue up the chain of command within the organization.

Leadership intervention could occur at multiple points in time as the conflict escalates and more people become involved. Interventions may take the form of preventive or reactive measures. Preventive measures include actions taken to reduce the likelihood of conflict erupting or escalating and measures to reduce the potential negative impact of a future conflict. Reactive measures refer to those decisions made in the moment to ameliorate a conflict as it unfolds. Reactive measures may include apologies, group dialogue, separation of groups, education, coaching, punishments, etc. The earlier in the escalation cycle the leader can intervene, the more likely it is that conflict will be mitigated and negative implications for productivity and employee satisfaction will be minimized. In the next section, we review four strategies to prevent identity group conflicts based on Social Identity Theory: decategorization, recategorization, subcategorization and crosscutting.

Overcoming Identity-Based Conflict

Perhaps one of the most well known and oldest strategies for reducing intergroup conflict is the contact hypothesis (Allport, 1954). The contact hypothesis states that interaction between groups will improve intergroup relations under specific conditions. Some of the conditions that should promote more positive attitudes among majority group members (Devine and Vasquez, 1998) include: (a) contact between people of equal status; (b) co-operative rather than competitive interactions; (c) institutional support such that those in positions of authority endorse integration; (d) positive outcomes of contact; (e) contact between similarly competent others; and (f) contact with a non-stereotypic other. Although numerous studies have shown that intergroup contact under such conditions can reduce stereotyping, bias, and discrimination (Stephan, 1987), the contact hypothesis has serious practical limitations in that these conditions are extremely difficult to achieve in real-world intergroup situations (Devine and Vasquez, 1998). However, early research on the contact hypothesis served as a springboard to the development of several categorization strategies based on social identity theory (Brown, 2000). Social Identity Theory predicts that individuals classify themselves and others into social categories creating in-group/out-group distinctions that often lead to in-group bias, negative affect toward out-group members, and intergroup conflict. Researchers thus began to consider the application of social categorization processes to create the opposite effects and reduce bias and intergroup conflict.

Decategorization proposes that contact will be most effective when interactions between individuals are not category-based, but rather person-based (Brewer and Miller, 1984). Interactions should be structured to reduce the salience of category membership and allow participants the opportunity to get to know out-group members as individuals, to disconfirm stereotypes and perceptions of the out-group as homogeneous. In decategorization, personal identity is emphasized and group identity is de-emphasized. Research on decategorization has shown that personalization can alter intergroup stereotypes, but does not always reduce prejudice, perhaps because positive interpersonal experiences do not necessarily generalize to attitudes toward the whole group (Brewer and Brown, 1998).

Using a person-based leadership strategy is consistent with several related theories. For example, transformational leadership theory suggests that a key component of effective leadership is individualized consideration, in which the leader considers individual hopes, abilities, needs and goals, listens to individuals attentively, and fosters their development by coaching, teaching and advising (Avolio and Bass, 1995; Bass, 1997). The leader-member exchange (LMX) theory of leadership (Graen and Uhl-Bien, 1995) recommends that leaders relate to each follower as a unique individual. In Pettigrew's (1998) theory of the contact process, organizational members who are afforded the opportunity to get to know dissimilar colleagues as individuals rather than as members of the out-group may be more likely to develop close ties and empathy towards each other. The existing literature on social identity conflict, in addition to these related theories, supports the idea that decategorization can help to reduce social identity conflict.

Organizations using a decategorization strategy may try to promote positive experiences in a variety of ways. One simple way is with social gatherings or parties that include members of diverse social identity groups and provide employees with opportunities to get to know one another as individuals. Organizations may also implement decategorization strategies through the formal structure by creating an environment supportive of collegial relationships. Organizational tasks and reward structures may be configured to encourage mutually collegial relationships (Brickson, 2000). One of the interviews from a South African bank provides an example—a manager encouraging the black majority

and the white minority to socialize at company events for the purpose of learning how to better get along with one another.

Recategorization also attempts to alter group member perceptions of group boundaries, but suggests that this should be accomplished by creating a common or super-ordinate category in which both in-group and out-group members belong. Known as the common in-group identity model (Gaertner et al., 1993), this intervention is designed to minimize attention to category differences by creating a new inclusive group identity (Brewer and Brown, 1998). In a review of the literature, Dovidio et al. (2001: 433) conclude that recategorization of a person as an in-group member rather than as an out-group member has been demonstrated to produce greater perceptions of shared beliefs, to facilitate empathic arousal and to reduce blame for negative outcomes. They argue that 'recategorization reduces bias by extending the benefits of in-group favoritism to former out-group members'. Recently, Lau and Murnighan (2005) suggest that when strong faultiness exists, group members might require common goals or integrative tasks to overcome their divisive subgroup structures.

For example, one interviewee spoke about an environmental school in Israel that brings together Israeli and Palestinian teens to work together on preserving common natural resources. In essence, the participants are taught to recategorize each other as stewards of a shared natural resource. Another interviewee described how members from rival gangs worked together to carry food and medical supplies to a shelter housing victims from a natural disaster. Non-profit organizations often use their mission to 'save the world (or a part of it)' as a recategorization strategy. They emphasize that different groups are in this world together. In for profit organizations, concepts such as market share, winning the war for talent, and profits are often used to create a super-ordinate organizational goal. Tsui and Gutek (1999) suggest that one way to create a super-ordinate category in the workplace is to increase the salience, relevance, and importance of belonging to the organization as a social category for all organizational members. Thus, the organization itself becomes the all inclusive identity group.

The *subcategorization* strategy argues that intergroup contact should be structured so that members of both groups have distinct but complementary roles to contribute toward a common goal (Hewstone and Brown, 1986). Ideally, this approach allows members of both groups to meet the need for distinctiveness, but also work together in a cooperative fashion to accomplish a goal. Dovidio et al. (1998) found that when two groups were equal in status but contributed different experiences or expertise to the task, bias was eliminated. The authors conclude that group differentiation and super-ordinate goals may in fact complement each other by recognizing and drawing from both group differences and group commonalities.

Haslam and Ellemers (2005) argue subcategorization works best by first allowing subgroup members to engage in activities that promote identity and then bring different groups together to build a super-ordinate understanding. Haslam et al. (2003) have offered a process model to be used in organizational contexts. In the first stage of their model, organizations identify which social identities employees use to define themselves collectively. In the second phase, subgroup caucusing, relevant subgroups within the organization develop goals that are relevant to their identities before coming together as a super-ordinate group. A series of experimental studies by Eggins and colleagues demonstrated that more positive outcomes occurred when subgroups were provided the opportunity to caucus prior to coming together as a large group than when subgroups were not given these opportunities (Eggins et al., 2002).

One practice illustrating this strategy is the use of affinity groups in organizations (Jayne and Dipboye, 2004). Many large organizations have formal networks intended to recognize the distinctiveness of a particular social identity group. For example, there are groups for women and for the non-dominant racial or ethnic groups in the society. Organizational members given the opportunity to have voice and input as members of a particular social identity group or groups, and at the same time contribute and identify with the super-ordinate goals of the organization may be examples of the subcategorization strategy in practice.

Finally, Brewer (1995) argues that social categorizations external to the organization become problematic when they are equated with organizational subcategories. For example, social categories often overlap with functional groups within the organization such that employees may be categorized as male executives and female clerical staff, or white supervisors and black assembly line workers. Brewer (1995) suggests the use of *crosscutting* to minimize this problem and reduce intergroup conflict. This strategy involves systematically or randomly crossing work group roles with category membership. The thinking behind this strategy is that if social identity and function do not co-vary, then it is less likely that disruptive incidents that occur between people in the workplace will be attributed to social identity group membership. However, there are practical considerations in applying crosscutting strategies that limit its use. This strategy requires all employees to be qualified to work across all levels and functions within the organization and this suggests equal access to educational opportunities in society.

For example, consider an organization in South Africa described by Booysen (2005). In accordance with the South African constitution, this organization is trying to shift the distribution of occupations such that black Africans and Afrikaners engage in similar jobs in an organization. In this case, it is not working well because the skill sets of the two groups are not sufficiently similar. Pre-Apartheid educational strategies have made it difficult to use a crosscutting strategy in the post-Apartheid world. Although it may be difficult to use a crosscutting strategy when educational opportunities have been unequal, crosscutting may be highly effective in virtual work teams. Virtual teams composed of members who are geographically dispersed may be a way of facilitating crosscutting role assignments because they encourage networked structures and collaborative approaches to task completion among a large enough pool of workers to allow for an appropriate mix of skill level and social identity group membership (Armstrong and Cole, 1995). In one of our interviews, we learned of a crosscutting group in the US that was viewed by the organization as extremely successful. This group, composed of employees at all levels, social identity groups, and functions, acted in an advisory capacity to the HR Director with regard to benefits and other HR practices and policies. Creating this group served to reduce boundaries between the social identity groups and increased intergroup interaction.

What Is a Leader to Do?

In the Mozambique example, the individual with the formal authority to deal with the situation is the white

Senior Vice President who punished the black reception-ist for her behaviour. This caused the conflict to escalate and brought in the attention of the media and the government. What might have been a more effective course of action for the organization? Would any of the strategies drawn from the literature on self-categorization been of help in this collectivistic environment (Jackson, 2003)? Would implementation of these strategies have helped prevent the conflict in the first place?

Looking at the literature review from the perspective of this example illuminates a major omission in the current literature on resolving identity-based conflicts in the workplace, namely, a lack of consideration of the effectiveness of these strategies within various cultures or in culturally heterogeneous work groups. As societal-driven social identity conflict in the workplace is an international issue reflecting the local cultural-historical context, we propose that it is essential that leaders consider the cultural context in which they are attempting to bridge social identity differences (Kim et al., 2004; Triandis, 1996). Would these strategies, articulated largely by American, British and Australian authors, work in a more collectivistic environment such as sub-Saharan Africa? In fact, we consider the lack of under-standing about the cross-cultural appropriateness of the different strategies to be a significant gap in the existing literature and propose that certain strategies may be ineffective and counter productive in some cultures.

For example, consider this story of an organizational leader on an expatriate assignment in Zambia who unknowingly hired mostly members of the dominant tribe. Although none of her subordinates directly confronted her about this, she learned indirectly through conversation that some subordinates considered her a 'tribalist'. The interviewee, who was British, chose to handle this by approaching the head of the department in which she had done the hiring and subtly tried to show her ignorance of tribes by letting him know indi-rectly that she had no intent to favour the dominant tribe. When asked why she chose this strategy, she said that although her immediate reaction as a 'Brit' would be to tell someone 'hey this is nonsense, this has to stop', and confront the issue directly, she chose to handle the situation differently. 'In Zambia you just don't tackle things head on. . . . You need time to talk around the point rather than directly at the point.' This example illustrates the need to consider the cultural context

when examining effective leadership strategies for deal-ing with identity based conflicts in the workplace.

We predict that organizations may experience social identity conflicts in a variety of contexts in which cultural differences must be considered. For example, a leader from one culture who is asked to lead organiza-tional members from another culture may adopt a strategy considered unacceptable or inappropriate within the followers' culture. This may happen when a leader from a multinational firm assumes an expatriate assignment or becomes the leader of a multinational virtual team. Organizational problems may also arise when employees from different cultures with a history of intergroup conflict or tension are forced to work together (e.g., creation of multinational firms, through mergers and acquisitions, outsourcing, new markets, etc.) and the leader finds him/herself faced with com-peting expectations of acceptable leadership practices.

Therefore, in the remaining sections of this paper, we discuss cultural values that may affect employee perceptions of the effectiveness of leadership strategies and present research propositions reflecting the moder-ating role of culture in the effectiveness of various lead-ership strategies to overcome identity based conflicts.

Cultural Values

At the societal level, values may be defined as shared, abstract ideas of good and desirable goals that serve as guiding principles for human behaviour and that are expressed in the way social institutions (e.g., organizations) operate and function (Williams, 1968; Schwartz, 1999). The 'average value priorities of societal members reflect the central thrust of their shared enculturation, independent of individual differences due to unique experiences or heredity' (Smith and Schwartz, 1997: 95). Societal-level cultural values reflect basic human issues that all societies must confront in order to regulate human activity—the relationship of the individual to the group, the response to uncertainty, the response to social inequality; the need to assure responsible social behaviour; the balance between com-petition and action versus co-operation and adaptation in response to the natural and social world, and the ori-entation to time—the short-term present versus the long-term future. A number of theories has been devel-oped to identify, articulate and measure cultural values (e.g., Hofstede, 2001; House and Global Leadership and Organizational Behavior Effectiveness Research Program, 2004; Inglehart et al., 1998; Maznevski et al., 2002; Schwartz, 1990, 1999; Smith et al., 2002; Triandis, 1995; Trompenaars and Hampden-Turner, 1998) and there is a burgeoning literature discussing the merits of each.

Within the literature on cultural values, the relationship of the individual to the group has received considerable attention (see Earley and Gibson, 1998; Gelfand et al., 2004; Kagitcibasi and Berry, 1989; Oyserman et al., 2002; Schwartz, 1994 for reviews). Several theorists have examined the relationship between the individual and the group, including Kluckhohn and Strodtbeck (1961), Hofstede (2001), House and Global Leadership and Organizational Behavior Effectiveness Research Program (2004), Triandis (1995), and Schwartz (1994). In this paper, we will focus our attention on the relationship between the individual and the group, as defined by the constructs of individualism and collectivism.

There are some key concepts relating to individualism/collectivism that are particularly relevant to this paper. First, there are significant cultural differences in the salience of group membership and the number of groups with which an individual identifies. Members of collectivist societies identify strongly with fewer social identity groups and group membership is likely to be salient and relatively fixed (Su et al., 1999; Tsui and Gutek, 1999). Smith and Long (2006) suggest compared to individualist cultures, attachments to core identities in collectivist cultures are less fluid and options for self-categorization will fluctuate less because group affiliations are non-negotiable in such cultures. Additionally, group categories represent greater meaning and importance in some societies than others. For example, in India, religion is strongly related to status, and in China, the family is the primary basis of self-identity (Tsui and Gutek, 1999).

Second, members of collectivistic cultures are likely to make clearer distinctions between in-group and out-group members (Triandis, 1986). Chen et al. (1998) found evidence to suggest that people from individualistic cultures are mainly concerned with enhancing their personal sense of self and that in-group bias is based on peoples' desire for personal self-enhancement. In contrast, they found that in collectivist cultures, people exhibit in-group favouritism not as a means of enhancing their personal sense of self, but as an end in

its own right. Triandis (1994) argues that conflict with out-groups is to be expected in collectivist cultures because collectivists tend to be self-sacrificing toward in-group members and generally exploitative toward out-group members. Brewer (2001) also argues that intergroup comparisons will be less competitive in societies where individuals may ascribe to a variety of social identities, and thus have multiple avenues for meeting needs for inclusion and distinctiveness.

Finally, it is worth noting that collectivist cultures often develop in countries with relatively homogenous populations and, as a result, are likely to have homogenous organizations. However, such settings are not the area of interest for this paper, since we are concerned with social identity conflicts that occur as the result of employee interactions between in-group and out-group members (i.e., diverse social identity group interactions). Such conflict is likely to occur when there is at least a minimal level of heterogeneity in the organization. As a result, our discussions will focus on organizational settings in which employees from a diverse range of social identity groups meet each other, including some that may have a history of conflict within the larger society.

In the next section, we examine the impact of cultural differences on leader effectiveness in managing identity-based conflicts using the four strategies based on social identity theory. We will offer propositions to suggest that these strategies may be met with significant resistance and prove ineffective in certain cultural contexts. We rely on arguments from the cross-cultural literature which suggest that members of collectivist cultures hold an interdependent self-construal and members of individualist cultures hold an independent self-construal (Markus and Kitayama, 1991). Cultural differences in self-construals equate to an emphasis on unique individual characteristics, attributes, and preferences for individualistic cultures, and an emphasis on the group for collectivist cultures, in which the self becomes meaningful and complete only when it is considered in relationship to the collective. We also rely on arguments from the cross-cultural literature, which suggest that in-group/out-group distinctions and boundaries are more salient and less fluid in collectivist cultures than individualist cultures (Erez and Earley, 1993). This cultural distinction becomes important when leaders attempt to utilize categorization strategies that, by definition, focus on shifting in-group/out-group distinctions.

Decategorization

In the organizational literature, there has been a call for leaders of diverse work groups to purposefully engage in a leadership style that emphasizes decategorization, or person-based interactions rather than group-based interactions (Brickson and Brewer, 2001; Scandura and Lankau, 1996). Leaders using this strategy may focus their efforts on activities that emphasize individual identity and deemphasize group identity such as sponsoring events that encourage employees from different social identity groups to become acquainted with one another more personally or role modeling this strategy by taking time to interact personally with employees as unique individuals.

The strategy of decategorization is explicitly an individual focused approach since it strives to de emphasize group social identity. Therefore, this strategy is consistent with the 'normative imperative' in individualist cultures to express one's unique attributes and characteristics (Markus and Kitayama, 1991) and the emphasis placed on differences among employees in individualist cultures (Gelfand et al., 2004). In contrast, the preference in collectivist cultures is to express oneself in relation to others, interdependent with the larger collective group, and to place emphasis on the commonalities among organizational members. Although employees in collectivist societies tend to be highly relationship oriented and some researchers have found that personalized leadership strategies will be effective in collectivist cultures because of the preference for a relational self-concept (see Hogg et al., 2005), this strategy will likely only be effective with in-group members. Leadership strategies that attempt to promote and foster stronger relational ties with out-group members, particularly out-group members with whom there is a history of conflict and tension, will be met with strong resistance in collectivist cultures.

Hofstede (2001: 229) argues that, 'In a collectivist culture, who one's friends are is predetermined by existing group ties; in an individualist society, friendships have to be specifically cultivated.' Relationships between colleagues in collectivist cultures depend on whether the colleagues are seen as a member of the in-group versus the out-group. Colleagues who are in-group members are treated as family members and cooperation is expected, however, out-group members

are often treated with hostility (Hofstede, 2001: 244). Triandis (1989) has argued that in-group/out-group distinctions are vitally important in collectivist cultures and that the subjective boundary of one's in-group may be narrower in collectivist cultures. There is evidence to suggest that compared to Americans, Chinese show a greater tendency to fight with or avoid members of out-groups (Triandis et al., 1990).

In contrast, collegial relationships in individualistic cultures may be characterized as more independent of group identity, making it less likely that the strategy of decategorization would be threatening to employees. Leaders attempting to mitigate social identity conflict in collectivist cultures or with organizational members from collectivist cultures may experience significant resistance toward any strategy that attempts to de-emphasize group ties and familial-like relationships with coworkers and fosters or attempts to force personal relationships with out-group members (members from social identity groups in which there is a history of tension and anxiety). This may be perceived as a threat to existing and valued in-group/out-group distinctions in collectivist cultures.

> Proposition 1: Culture will moderate the negative relationship between decategorization and social identity conflict. Specifically, the decategorization strategy will be more effective at reducing social identity conflict with members of individualist cultures than members of collectivist cultures.

Recategorization

A recategorization strategy may be employed by a leader who attempts to use charisma and visionary leadership to evoke a higher sense of purpose (Bass, 1985) or to create a common enemy and thus facilitate an inclusive or super-ordinate identity among group members. Hogg and Terry (2000) argue that an effective leadership strategy is to increase social attraction and solidarity within the organization or work group by focusing on inter-organizational competition and emphasizing desirable attributes of the organization to provide positive distinctiveness (e.g., the organization's competitors in the market become the outgroup). When implemented successfully, the development of a super-ordinate identity proposed by the recategorization strategy may have very positive benefits. The creation of a common, inclusive, or super-ordinate identity involved in the recategorization strategy is consistent with the interdependent self-construal held by members of collectivist cultures. Members of collectivist cultures who hold more interdependent self-construals are motivated not by achieving separateness, but rather by serving the collective and thus more fully realizing one's connectedness (Markus and Kitayama, 1991). The GLOBE study contrasts cultures that are high on collectivism and individualism, suggesting collectivists emphasize relatedness with groups and are likely to put group goals ahead of personal goals (Gelfand et al., 2004). In collectivist societies, social units with common fate, common goals, and common values are centralized (Oyserman et al., 2002).

In contrast to decategorization, the emphasis on making a new more inclusive social identity salient makes recategorization fundamentally a collective process where new group boundaries are developed or boundaries that are more inclusive are encouraged and strengthened. Furthermore, conformity has been found to be higher in nations high on collectivism (Bond and Smith, 1996) and the leader is expected to play a paternalistic role and guide subordinate actions (Hofstede, 1980), therefore, members of collectivist cultures will likely conform to the super-ordinate goals set by the leader and/or organization. Assuming the super-ordinate identity is not perceived as a threat to existing social identity groups, we predict that employees from collectivistic cultures will generally be more receptive to this strategy because a collective approach encourages employees to look beyond their individual identities and needs and place the needs of the organization in the forefront. The practice of identifying with a larger group is consistent with the values of collectivist cultures, unlike the preferences of employees from more individualistic cultures in which greater emphasis and value is placed on distinguishing oneself from others.

Proposition 2: Culture will moderate the negative relationship between recategorization and social identity conflict. Specifically, recategorization will be a more effective strategy for reducing social identity conflict with members of collectivist cultures than members of individualist cultures.

Although in general, members of collectivist cultures will likely be more accepting of the recategorization strategy because it emphasizes the goals of the collective, there are circumstances in which recategorization would likely be met with resistance in collectivist cultures and acceptance in individualist cultures. For example, Haslam and Ellemers (2005) point out that the goal of the recategorization strategy is to encourage group members to cast aside their old group membership and embrace a new super-ordinate identity that is inclusive of members of both the in-group and out-group. It might be argued that a leader's attempts to unite employees through super-ordinate goals from social identity groups with a deeply rooted history of conflict and high intergroup tension will be met with resistance by members of collectivist cultures because in-group/out-group distinctions are more salient, fixed, and impermeable than individualist cultures (Erez and Earley, 1993). However, we would argue that recategorization will likely be accepted by members of collectivist cultures if employees identify with the organization and view the leader as a legitimate authority figure and agent of the organization.[1]

Sagiv and Schwartz (2000) contend that within collectivistic cultures, organizations function almost like extended families. Hofstede makes a similar argument, claiming that

In a collectivist society, the workplace itself may become an ingroup in the emotional sense of the word . . . The relationship between employer and employee is seen in moral terms. It resembles a family relationship, with mutual obligations of protection in exchange for loyalty.

(Hofstede, 2001: 237)

Gelfand et al., (2004) suggest that in collectivist cultures, organizational members view themselves as highly interdependent with the organization. They state that 'generally speaking, the sharing of the employees' identity with the organization would be so strong that the organization would become a part of members' self-identity' (Gelfand et al., 2004: 446). When organizational identity is high and the organization is viewed as an extension of the family, as is typically the case in collectivist societies, then super-ordinate goals set by the organization or the organizational leader will be embraced by members of collectivist cultures even when some proportion of employees in the work group or organization are viewed as social identity out-group members.

Additionally, recategorization may prove effective with members of individualist cultures to the extent that accomplishing super-ordinate goals yields individual rewards. As Haslam and Ellemers (2005) point out, people who primarily conceive of themselves as separate individuals can only be expected to direct their efforts toward the achievement of collective goals when this affects their individual outcomes. Therefore, the recategorization strategy will generally be more effective with members of collectivist cultures when the leader is perceived as a member of the in-group, and it will be more effective for members of individualistic cultures when collective and personal goals are congruent.

Subcategorization

Although there is support in the social identity literature for both the decategorization and recategorization strategies, recent research suggests (see Haslam and Ellemers, 2005) that subcategorization is preferable because members of different social identity groups may identify with a super-ordinate identity that also incorporates subgroup differences. In fact, some scholars have argued that neither decategorization nor recategorization will have long-lasting effects and are likely to invoke threat for non-dominant groups, but that a third approach which integrates the two strategies will be more effective in reducing intergroup conflict. Subcategorization (or the mutual intergroup differentiation model) involves the nesting of subgroup identities within a super-ordinate identity (Hewstone and Brown, 1986). The goal is to structure intergroup contact so that members of both groups have distinct but complementary roles to contribute toward a common goal (Hewstone and Brown, 1986).

Hornsey and Hogg (2000a: 143) present a model of subgroup relations in which they argue that 'social harmony is most likely to be achieved by maintaining, not weakening, subgroup identities, provided they are nested within a coherent super-ordinate identity.' Their research (Hornsey and Hogg, 1999, 2000b) provides evidence to suggest that intergroup bias may be reduced when subgroup membership is part of a larger super-ordinate category. They also found that bias was strongest when only the super-ordinate category was made salient. Lau and Murnighan (2005) suggest that their research findings support the subcategorization strategy and imply that managers need to select tasks that take advantage of groups' within-subgroup inclinations when strong faultlines exist in the workplace.

Rather than give up their identities, or assimilate into a larger, dominant identity group, many diversity scholars have argued that organizations should adopt a multicultural perspective for organizational integration so that members are not forced to sacrifice an important aspect of their identity in order to succeed in their jobs (Cox, 1993: 60). This leadership strategy is a hybrid, seeking to draw on the stability of existing subcategories while unifying efforts within a larger super-ordinate identity that reaches across any existing social identities. As a result, we do not expect this approach to be influenced systematically by either individualism or collectivism. This strategy allows both an interdependent and independent self-construal to exist and ideally rewards both. Additionally, we predict that perceived threat to identity will be low in both cultures. In collectivist cultures, perceived threat to the group will be low because organizational members are able to maintain their identity and are valued for their contributions made based on this group membership. In individualist cultures, perceived threat to the individual will be low as long as individual self-interests are met in concert with meeting the collective interests of the group through collaboration to accomplish a common goal.

Proposition 3: Culture will not moderate the negative relationship between subcategorization and social identity conflict. Subcategorization will be an effective strategy to reduce social identity conflict for members of both collectivist and individualist cultures.

The strategy of subcategorization provides a hybrid approach, preserving existing social identity groups while encouraging such groups to interact in a positive way. However, one major limitation of this approach is the conditions necessary for positive interaction, particularly if it is required that each group's area of expertise is equally valued (Dovidio et al., 1998). We were unable to think of many examples in history of social identity groups in conflict that are both separate and equal. We propose that this strategy will be effective in reducing social identity conflict in either individualistic or collectivistic cultures; however, it will be most effective if social identity conflict is moderate. If social identity conflict or intergroup anxiety and tension is high and power and status differences between groups is high, this strategy seems unlikely to decrease conflict because it is unlikely that group members will be capable of valuing the others' input.

Crosscutting

Another strategy that leaders may explore to ensure that subgroup identities are valued within the organization is the use of crosscutting. Brewer (1995) recommends crosscutting, systematically or randomly crossing work group roles with category membership, to ensure adequate representation from various subgroups within the organization. So, for example, a project team or task force that may include representatives from various functional groups and levels of the organization should have approximately equal representation based on gender, race, religion, and other demographic attributes. The leader may facilitate the task force or create it and then leave the group to manage itself, in order to foster greater buy-in and communication across groups in conflict.

In support of this approach, Marcus-Newhall et al. (1993) found that within crosscutting groups, group members were less likely to favor their own group on post-test ratings, and less likely to differentiate among the group categories than in groups that did not involve a crosscutting structure. Additionally, Bettencourt and Dorr (1998) report that crosscutting role assignments decrease in-group bias of both minority and majority group members, compared to convergent role assignment. This strategy may be effective because it serves to reduce faultline strength within work groups. Lau and Murnighan (1998) argue that faultline strength will be strong with moderate levels of diversity but weak with high levels of diversity. Crosscutting by design ensures highly diverse work groups.

Although this strategy has proven to be successful in some organizational contexts within the United States, its use in more collectivistic cultures may be less effective. An assumption in restructuring the work group so that members of various social identity groups and

levels of the organization work together is that the task is of primary importance and that in-group/out-group distinctions will be of secondary importance. However, as was mentioned above, in collectivist cultures, the personal relationship prevails over the task and over the company (Hofstede, 2001).

Furthermore, Hofstede writes that management in a collectivist culture is management of groups. In collectivist cultures, structuring work groups such that ethnic or other in-group members work together is considered an effective strategy to support work productivity (Hofstede, 2001: 45). Whereas in individualistic cultures, the composition of work groups is based on individual criteria and keeping in-group members together is often unwanted and considered an ineffective managerial strategy, Harrison et al. (2000) provide evidence to suggest that organizational members in collectivist cultures will have more difficulty 'adjusting to frequent shifts in workgroup and team membership, where such shifts involve the disruption and disestablishment of pre-existing in-groups formed over extended periods of time and based on friendship and other developed affiliations' (Harrison et al., 2000: 492).

Similar to the decategorization strategy, crosscutting places greater value on individual contributions and unique characteristics and therefore is more consistent with independent self-construals within individualist societies. Shifting group boundaries and attempts to create a new work group composed of both ingroup and outgroup members is likely to evoke perceptions of identity threat to employees from collectivist cultures.

> Proposition 4: Culture will moderate the negative relationship between crosscutting and social identity conflict. Specifically, the crosscutting strategy will be more effective at reducing social identity conflict for members of individualist cultures than members of collectivist cultures.

Conclusions and Implications for Research and Practice

From our discussion, many avenues for future study become apparent. Although we recognize some serious limitations in applying current research and theory on Social Identity Theory (SIT) to leadership interventions designed to prevent or mitigate the negative effects of identity-based conflict in the workplace, the literature does highlight some potential implications for leaders that are worth considering. Furthermore, we have argued for the importance of considering cultural context when adopting a categorization-based strategy to reduce social identity conflicts at work.

In Table 43.1, we attempt to summarize our propositions by making predictions about the effectiveness of four leadership strategies in cultures characterized as Collectivistic versus Individualistic. We believe that our integrated multidisciplinary literature review lays the foundation for a compelling research agenda.

In this chapter, we have focused on the moderating role of culture in determining the effectiveness of four categorization strategies identified in the social identity theory literature. Although research and theory on conflict reduction based on social categorization has a long history, this work has received considerable criticism with regard to its applicability to organizations. Research testing social identity theory has generally been conducted using laboratory experiments, often with student samples, and thus it has been criticized for its lack of generalizability to real world settings. Further, these strategies seem difficult to implement. In particular, the decategorization and recategorization strategies described above have been criticized because they involve the abandonment of subgroup identities, which may be psychologically and practically difficult to implement when real-life groups are involved (Brown, 2000).

Further, there is a significant lack of knowledge as to how leaders in positions of authority in actual organizations might use these strategies. Although there is some empirical support for the social identity theory of leadership (see Hogg, 2001, for a review), much of this research has also been conducted in laboratory settings with undergraduate student populations and thus needs to be tested in the field. Reicher and Hopkins (2003) suggest that most of the focus of social identity research on leadership has been on what leads people to be endorsed as leaders by others, and there has been little focus on what leaders actually do. Thus, we concur with Reicher and Hopkins (2003: 200) that there is an 'urgent need to analyze the active dimensions of leadership'. Research in this area should begin to develop a more complete understanding of leadership strategies that help minimize the negative effects of identity-based conflict on

information processing, employee commitment, work group cohesiveness, and ultimately performance.

Additionally, appropriate leadership strategies must be identified within specific cultural and societal contexts. In our paper, we have focused on cultural differences regarding the relationship between the individual and the group. Future research in this area should also consider the cultural dimension of power distance, which Hofstede (2001: 98) defines as, 'The extent to which the less powerful members of institutions and organizations within a country expect and accept that power is distributed unequally.' In high power distance cultures, the leader is likely not expected to resolve identity-based conflicts, but rather to rely on organizational policies and formal rules for maintaining order and productivity (Smith et al., 2002). Thus, power distance may be important to consider in examining when identity-based conflict will be perceived as a problem where the leader's role is to resolve the conflict, versus the perception that identity based conflict is a natural and normal occurrence.

In addition to cultural factors, other societal factors such as economics, political and legal systems may influence leadership as well. For example, are leadership strategies differentially effective in democracies and totalitarian societies? Do laws governing rights, obligations, and opportunities influence leadership approaches with respect to social identity differences? Does the relative wealth of a country influence leadership approaches for dealing with differences? These types of factors need to be explored in order to have a better understanding of how to deal with social identity conflicts in organizations. Organizational policies may have an impact on the management of social identity conflicts as well; for example, consider holiday, promotion and disciplinary policies. So might organizational climate. A climate emphasizing respect might have different dynamics than one emphasizing power. It is also important to look beyond the role of formal leaders and focus more generally on acts of leadership regardless of the positional authority of the person engaging in them. Finally, social identity conflicts may occur between group members who know each other well and have pre-existing friendships, or conversely, between social identity group members who do not know each other well (or perhaps at all prior to the conflict), but find themselves interacting with one another due to work demands. Even though faultlines may be activated by

Table 43.1 Summary of Propositions

Leadership strategy	Leader effectiveness in managing identity-based conflicts	
	Collectivistic cultures	*Individualistic cultures*
Decategorization (Person-based interactions)	Low effectiveness Social identity is salient, strong and less fluid; therefore, strategies that ignore or attempt to minimize group identity will be met with strong resistance and will influence leader effectiveness negatively in dealing with social identity conflicts.	High effectiveness Individual self-interests are given priority over collective interests and employees define themselves primarily based on unique characteristics and attributes. This strategy will likely be effective because it is focused on the individual.
Recategorization (Superordinate identity)	High effectiveness Accomplishing the goals of the collective group is consistent with the interdependent self-construal in a collectivist culture. This leadership strategy will be effective when employees identify with the organization and the leader.	Low effectiveness Since individual self-interest is of primary importance in individualistic cultures, leaders will likely only be effective using this strategy when the goals of the collective and personal goals are congruent.
Subcategorization (Nested subgroups)	High effectiveness This strategy will likely be effective (if social identity conflict is moderate or the strategy is used as a preventive measure) because group members are able to maintain their identity with the social group and are valued for their contributions based on this group membership.	High effectiveness This strategy will likely be effective (if social identity conflict is moderate or the strategy is used as a preventive measure) because individual contributions will be recognized and valued, which is consistent with an independent self-construal.
Crosscutting (Cross-group composition)	Low effectiveness This strategy will not be effective because shifting group boundaries are likely to evoke identity threat.	High effectiveness This strategy will be effective because greater emphasis and value is placed on individual contributions and unique characteristics.

external forces in both cases, it seems possible that conflict is less likely to escalate and more likely to be resolved when group members involved in the conflict have pre-existing friendships or close work relationships. Therefore, various types of work relationships should be examined as well in future research.

Although we chose to focus on identifying the negative work outcomes that result from identity-based conflict, additional work in this area may suggest that there are also positive outcomes. For example, organizational learning may occur as a result of having to navigate successfully through an identity-based dispute. Argyris (1976) refers to this as double-loop learning, that is, learning to change underlying values and assumptions to solve problems that are ill structured and complex. There may be much to learn from organizations that generalize what they have learned in the past to implement strategies successfully that prevent future identity conflict.

Given the complexity and sensitive nature of studying identity-based conflicts in the workplace, we believe a variety of tools, methods and theoretical approaches is required to study this phenomenon adequately. A combination of inductive and deductive approaches will likely be necessary (Lee, 1999). Van de Vijver and Leung (1997) further provide a thorough discussion of the methodological issues and concerns that need to be considered in conducting cross-cultural research. Based on their work as well as others conducting cross-cultural research, we would recommend the use of a triangulated approach to study leadership strategies in various cultures, including, but not limited to, questionnaires to assess responses to hypothetical situations, semi-structured interviews to obtain qualitative data detailing employee and leader experiences involving identity-based conflicts, and an organizational assessment to determine organizational practices and policies.

This review points to a variety of implications for the management of human resources. At a very basic level, the leadership challenge discussed will have a major impact on numerous human resource functions. Recruiting, retention, employee development, employee relations, compensation and training are all impacted by the growing likelihood of social identity conflicts in organizations that are becoming increasingly globalized (Herriot and Scott-Jackson, 2002). Human resource systems considered effective in earlier days are likely to be called into question in organizations that are bringing groups with histories of hostilities and

mistrust together in the work place. Organizations cannot underestimate the conflicts that may occur when people from different religious, national, political, ethnic and gender groups who previously have not had to work together come into contact in the workplace. These conflicts can generate serious threats to organizational effectiveness. It is in the best interest of the leader to recognize the impact of the legacies of societal conflict and distrust in the work place and take steps to manage identity based conflict.

There are two steps that organizational leaders may take to ameliorate social identity conflict in today's globalized environment. One step is simply to recognize that these conflicts may happen and to be prepared for them. Awareness is helpful because it can result in locally relevant preventive strategies such as the development of conflict resolution skills. Whether the approach is individual or collectivistic, organizations need to develop the capacity to deal with social identity conflict when it arises. Leaders need to recognize symptoms of the escalation of social identity conflicts and to recognize when a faultline is about to erupt. Preventive strategies may include policies and practices regarding the treatment of workers, decisions regarding the structure of work groups, or training in how to resolve conflict.

A second step organizational leaders may take is to develop the cultural intelligence of its members. Brislin et al. (2006) argue that cultural intelligence can be developed and that helping workers to understand what it is like to be from another identity group is one way to accomplish this. Thus, perspective taking around issues of social identity and developing an organization's ability to act in culturally intelligent ways may be a helpful way to start addressing social identity conflicts in organizations. From a human resource perspective, it is important that those in positions of leadership be able to deal with the challenge of social identity conflicts at work. Those in leadership positions will be more effective to the extent that they can adjust their behavior and approaches to reflect an understanding of the local context and feelings of different social identity groups.

In this chapter, we have reviewed the relevant literature and explored leadership in the context of social identity conflicts at work. When group identity conflicts occur in organizations, not only is work disrupted, but also group members experience substantial pain and distress that may only be remedied through significant and difficult changes in values, attitudes and behaviours. The task of leadership is to facilitate group members wrestling with these issues, such that a deeper understanding and appreciation of differences may lead group members toward a more complex view that both incorporates the diverse perspectives of the groups in question and allows the leader to move toward creating a common purpose to which all can subscribe. Thus, the organization may grow in its understanding of the needs, values, and potential contributions of employees representing various social identity groups within the organization because of the conflict. This may ultimately strengthen the organization's ability to value employee differences and to deal more effectively with identity-based disputes if or when they arise in the future.

Note

1. This assumption would be true for vertical collectivist cultures but likely untrue for horizontal collectivist cultures. In HC cultures, people emphasize common goal with others but do not submit easily to authorities (Gelfand et al., 2004).

References

Allport, G.W. (1954) *The Nature of Prejudice.* Reading, MA: Addison-Wesley.

Amason, A.C. and Schweiger, D.M. (1997) 'The Effects of Conflict on Strategic Decision Making Effectiveness and Organizational Performance'. In De Dreu, C.K.W. and Van de Vliert, E. (eds) *Using Conflict in Organizations.* London: Sage, pp. 105–15.

Argyris, C. (1976) *Increasing Leadership Effectiveness.* New York: Wiley.

Armstrong, D.J. and Cole, P. (1995) 'Managing Distances and Differences in Geographically Distributed Work Groups'. In Jackson, S.E. and Ruderman, M.N. (eds) *Diversity in Work Teams: Research Paradigms for a Changing Workplace.* Washington, DC: American Psychological Association, pp. 187–215.

Ashforth, B.E. and Mael, F. (1989) 'Social Identity Theory and the Organization', *Academy of Management Review,* 14(1): 20–39.

Avolio, B.J. and Bass, B.M. (1995) 'Individual Consideration Viewed at Multiple Levels of Analysis: A Multi-level Framework for Examining the Diffusion of Transformational Leadership. Special Issue: Leadership: The Multiple-Level Approaches (Part I)', *Leadership Quarterly,* 6(2): 199–218.

Bass, B.M. (1985) *Leadership and Performance Beyond Expectations.* New York: Free Press.

Bass, B.M. (1997) 'Does the Transactional-transformational Leadership Paradigm Transcend Organizational and National Boundaries?', *American Psychologist,* 52(2): 130–9.

Berscheid, E. and Reis, H.T. (1998) 'Attraction and Close Relationships'. In Gilbert, D.T., Fiske, S.T. and Lindzey, G. (eds) *The Handbook of Social Psychology,* 2 (4) New York: McGraw-Hill, pp. 193–281.

Bettencourt, A.B. and Dorr, N. (1998) 'Cooperative Interaction and Intergroup Bias: Effects of Numerical Representation and Cross-cut Role Assignment', *Personality and Social Psychology Bulletin,* 24(12): 1276–93.

Bond, R. and Smith, P.B. (1996) 'Culture and Conformity: A Meta-analysis of Studies Using Asch's (1952b, 1956) Line Judgment Task', *Psychological Bulletin,* 119(1): 111–37.

Booysen, L. (2005) 'The Leadership Challenges in Dealing with Cultural Identity Conflict in South Africa'. In Hannum, K. (Chair) (ed.) *Leadership Across Differences.* Symposium conducted at the meeting of the International Leadership Association Amsterdam, the Netherlands.

Brewer, M.B. (1995) 'Managing Diversity: The Role of Social Identities'. In Jackson, S.E. and Ruderman, M.N. (eds) *Diversity in Work Teams.* Washington, DC: American Psychological Association, pp. 47–68.

Brewer, M.B. (2001) 'Intergroup Identification and Intergroup Conflict: When Does Ingroup Love Become Outgroup Hate?'. In Ashmore, R.D., Jussim, L. and Wilder, D. (eds) *Social Identity, Intergroup Conflict and Conflict Resolution.* Oxford: Oxford University Press, pp. 17–41.

Brewer, M.B. and Brown, R.J. (1998) 'Intergroup Relations'. In Gilbert, D.T., Fiske, S.T. and Lindzey, G. (eds) *The Handbook of Social Psychology, Vol. 2* (4th edn). New York: McGraw-Hill, pp. 554–95.

Brewer, M.B. and Miller, N. (1984) 'Beyond the Contact Hypothesis: Theoretical Perspectives on Desegregation'. In Miller, N. and Brewer, M.B. (eds) *Groups in Contact: The Psychology of Desegregation.* New York: Academic Press, pp. 281–302.

Brickson, S. (2000) 'The Impact of Identity Orientation on Individual and Organizational Outcomes in Demographically Diverse Settings', *Academy of Management Review,* 25(1): 82–101.

Brickson, S. and Brewer, M.B. (2001) 'Identity Orientation and Intergroup Relations in Organizations'. In Hogg, M. and Terry, D. (eds) *Social Identity Processes in Organizational Contexts.* Philadelphia, PA: Psychology Press, pp. 49–65.

Brislin, R., Worthley, R. and MacNab, B. (2006) 'Cultural Intelligence: Understanding Behaviors That Serve People's Goals', *Group and Organization Management,* 31(1): 40–55.

Brown, R. (2000) 'Social Identity Theory: Past Achievements, Current Problems and Future Challenges', *European Journal of Social Psychology,* 30: 745–78.

Cavey, V. (2000) 'Fighting Among Friends: The Quaker Separation of 1827'. In Coy, P.G. and Woehrle, L.M. (eds) *Social Conflicts and Collective Identities.* Boston, MA: Rowman and Littlefield Publishers, Inc., pp. 133–48.

Chen, Y.R., Brockner, J. and Katz, T. (1998) 'Toward an Explanation of Cultural Differences in In-group Favoritism: The Role of Individual Versus Collective Primacy', *Journal of Personality and Social Psychology,* 75(6): 1490–502.

Chrobot-Mason, D. (2003) 'Developing Multicultural Competence for Managers: Same Old Leadership Skills or Something New?', *The Psychologist-Manager Journal,* 6(2): 5–20.

Cox, T.H. (1993) *Cultural Diversity in Organizations: Theory, Research and Practice.* San Francisco, CA: Berrett-Koehler Publications.

Devine, P.G. and Vasquez, K.A. (1998) 'The Rocky Road to Positive Intergroup Relations'. In Eberhardt, J.L. and Fiske, S.T. (eds) *Confronting Racism: The Problem and the Response.* Thousand Oaks, CA: Sage, pp. 234–62.

Dovidio, J.F., Gaertner, S.L. and Bachman, B.A. (2001) 'Racial Bias in Organizations: The Role of Group Processes in its Causes and Cures'. In Turner, M.E. (ed.) *Groups at Work: Theory and Research.* Mahwah, NJ: Lawrence Erlbaum Associates, pp. 415–44.

Dovidio, J.F., Gaertner, S.L. and Validzic, A. (1998) 'Intergroup Bias: Status, Differentiation, and a Common In-group Identity', *Journal of Personality and Social Psychology,* 75(1): 109–20.

Earley, P.C. and Gibson, C.B. (1998) 'Taking Stock in our Progress on Individualism-Collectivism: 100 Years of Solidarity and Community', *Journal of Management,* 24(3): 265–305.

Eggins, R.A., Haslam, S.A. and Reynolds, K.J. (2002) 'Social Identity and Negotiation: Subgroup Representation and Super-ordinate Consensus', *Personality and Social Psychology Bulletin,* 28(7): 887–99.

Erez, M. and Earley, P.C. (1993) *Culture, Self-identity, and Work.* New York: Oxford University Press, pp. 74–96.

Fielding, K.S. and Hogg, M.A. (1997) 'Social Identity, Self-categorization, and Leadership: A Field Study of Small Interactive Groups', *Group Dynamics: Theory, Research, and Practice,* 1(1): 39–51.

Fisher, R.J. (1990) 'Needs Theory, Social Identity and an Eclectic Model of Conflict'. In Burton, J. (ed.) *Conflict: Human Needs Theory.* New York: St Martin's Press.

Friedman, R.A. and Davidson, M.N. (2001) 'Managing Diversity and Second-order Conflict', *The International Journal of Conflict Management,* 12(2): 132–53.

Gaertner, S.L., Dovidio, J.F., Anastasio, P.A., Bachman, B.A. and Rust, M.C. (1993) 'The Common Ingroup Identity Model: Recategorization and the Reduction of Intergroup Bias'. In Stroebe, W. and Hewstone, M. (eds) *European Review of Social Psychology (Vol. 4).* Chichester: Wiley, pp. 1-26.

Gelfand, M.J., Bhawuk, D.P.S., Nishi, L.H. and Bechtold, D.J. (2004) 'Individualism and Collectivism'. In House, R.J., Hanges, P.J., Javidan, M., Dorfman, P.W. and Gupta, V. (eds) *Culture, Leadership, and Organizations.* Thousand Oaks, CA: Sage Publications, pp. 437–512.

Graen, G.B. and Uhl-Bien, M. (1995) 'Relationship-based Approach to Leadership: Development of Leader-member Exchange (LMX) Theory of Leadership Over 25 Years: Applying a Multilevel Multi-domain Approach', *Leadership Quarterly,* 6(2): 219–47.

Harrison, G.L., McKinnon, J.L., Wu, A. and Chow, C.W. (2000) 'Cultural Influences on Adaptation to Fluid Workgroups and Teams', *Journal of International Business Studies,* 31(3): 489–505.

Haslam, S.A. (2001) *Psychology in Organizations: The Social Identity Approach.* London: Sage.

Haslam, S.A., Eggins, R.A. and Reynolds, K.J. (2003) 'The ASPIRe Model: Actualizing Social and Personal Identity Resources to Enhance Organizational Outcomes', *Journal of Occupational and Organizational Psychology,* 76(1): 83–113.

Haslam, S.A. and Ellemers, N. (2005) 'Social Identity in Industrial and Organizational Psychology: Concepts, Controversies, and Contributions'. In Hodgkinson, G.P. and Ford, J.K. (eds) *International Review of Industrial and Organizational Psychology (Vol. 20).* Chichester: John Wiley, pp. 39–118.

Herriot, P. and Scott-Jackson, W. (2002) 'Globalization, Social Identities and Employment', *British Journal of Management,* 13(3): 249–57.

Hewstone, M. and Brown, R.J. (1986) 'Contact is Not Enough: An Intergroup Perspective on the Contact Hypothesis'. In Hewstone, M. and Brown, R. (eds) *Contact and Conflict in Intergroup Encounters.* Oxford: Blackwell, pp. 1–44.

Hicks, T. (2001) 'Another Look at Identity-based Conflict: The Roots of Conflict in the Psychology of Consciousness', *Negotiation Journal,* 17(1): 35–45.

Himes, J.S. (1980) *Conflict and Conflict Management.* Athens, GA: The University of Georgia Press.

Hofstede, G.H. (1980) *Culture's Consequences, International Differences in Work-related Values.* Beverly Hills, CA: Sage Publications.

Hofstede, G. (2001) *Culture's Consequences: Comparing Values, Behaviors, Institutions, and Organizations Across Nations.* Thousand Oaks, CA: Sage, pp. 209–78.

Hogg, M.A. (1996) 'Intragroup Processes, Group Structure and Social Identity'. In Robinson, W.P. (ed.) *Social Groups and Identities: The Developing Legacy of Henri Tajfel.* Oxford: Butterworth-Heinemann, pp. 65–93.

Hogg, M.A. (2001) 'A Social Identity Theory of Leadership', *Personality and Social Psychology Review,* 5(3): 184–200.

Hogg, M.A., Martin, R., Epitropaki, A., Mankad, A., Svensson, A. and Weeden, K. (2005) 'Effective Leadership in Salient Groups: Revisiting Leader-member Exchange Theory from the Perspective of the Social Identity Theory of Leadership', *Personality and Social Psychology Bulletin,* 31(7): 991–1004.

Hogg, M.A. and Terry, D.J. (2000) 'Social Identity and Self-categorization Processes in Organizational Contexts', *Academy of Management Review,* 25(1): 121–40.

Hornsey, M.J. and Hogg, M.A. (1999) 'Subgroup Differentiation as a Response to an Overly-inclusive Group: A Test of Optimal Distinctiveness Theory', *European Journal of Social Psychology,* 29(4): 543–50.

Hornsey, M.J. and Hogg, M.A. (2000a) 'Assimilation and Diversity: An Integrative Model of Subgroup Relations', *Personality and Social Psychology Review,* 4(2): 143–56.

Hornsey, M.J. and Hogg, M.A. (2000b) 'Subgroup Relations: A Comparison of Mutual Intergroup Differentiation and Common Ingroup Identity Models of Prejudice Reduction', *Personality and Social Psychology Bulletin,* 26(2): 242–56.

House, R.J. and Global Leadership and Organizational Behavior Effectiveness Research Program (2004) *Culture, Leadership, and Organizations: The GLOBE Study of 62 Societies.* Thousand Oaks, CA: Sage Publications.

Inglehart, R., Basâñez, M. and Moreno, A. (1998) *Human Values and Beliefs: A Cross-cultural Sourcebook: Political, Religious, Sexual, and Economic Norms in 43 Societies; Findings from the 1990–1993 World Value Survey.* Ann Arbor, MI: University of Michigan Press.

Jackson, S.E. (1992) *Diversity in the Workplace.* New York: Guilford Press.

Jackson, T. (2003) Management and Change in Africa: Key Results. Online at http://www.africamanagement.org (accessed 27 April 2006).

Javidan, M., Stahl, G.K., Brodbeck, F. and Wilderom, C.P.M. (2005) 'Cross-border Transfer of Knowledge: Cultural Lessons from Project GLOBE', *Academy of Management Executive,* 19(2): 59–76.

Jayne, M.E. A. and Dipboye, R.L. (2004) 'Leveraging Diversity to Improve Business Performance: Research Findings and Recommendations for Organizations', *Human Resource Management,* 43(4): 409–24.

Jehn, K.A. (1995) 'A Multimethod Examination of the Benefits and Detriments of Intragroup Conflict', *Administrative Science Quarterly,* 40(2): 256–82.

Kagitcibasi, C. and Berry, J.W. (1989) 'Cross-cultural Psychology—Current Research and Trends', *Annual Review of Psychology,* 40: 493–531.

Karim, A.U. (2003) 'A Developmental Progression Model for Intercultural Consciousness: A Leadership Imperative', *Journal of Education for Business,* 79(1): 34–9.

Katz, D. (1964) 'Approaches to Managing Conflict'. In Kahn, R.L. and Boulding, E. (eds) *Power and Conflict in Organizations.* London: Tavistock Publications.

Kim, K., Dansereau, F., Kim, I.S. and Kim, K.S. (2004) 'A Multiple-level Theory of Leadership: The Impact of Culture as a Moderator', *Journal of Leadership and Organizational Studies,* 11(1): 78–92.

Kluckhohn, C. (1951) 'The Study of Culture'. In Lerner, D. and Lasswell, H.D. (eds) *The Policy Sciences.* Stanford, CA: Stanford University Press.

Kluckhohn, F.R. and Strodtbeck, F.L. (1961) *Variations in Value Orientations.* Evanston, IL: Row, Peterson.

Lau, D.C. and Murnighan, J.K. (1998) 'Demographic Diversity and Faultlines: The Compositional Dynamics of Organizational Groups', *Academy of Management Review,* 23(2): 325–40.

Lau, D.C. and Murnighan, J.K. (2005) 'Interactions Within Groups and Subgroups: The Effects of Demographic Faultiness', *Academy of Management Journal,* 48(4): 645–59.

Lee, T.W. (1999) *Using Qualitative Methods in Organizational Research.* Thousand Oaks, CA: Sage.

Marcus-Newhall, A., Miller, N., Holtz, R. and Brewer, M.B. (1993) 'Crosscutting Category Membership with Role Assignment: A Means of Reducing Intergroup Bias', *British Journal of Social Psychology,* 32(2): 124–46.

Markus, H.R. and Kitayama, S. (1991) 'Culture and the Self: Implications for Cognition, Emotion, and Motivation', *Psychological Review,* 98(2): 224–53.

Maznevski, M.L., DiStefano, J.J., Gomez, C.B. and Noorderhaven, N.G. (2002) 'Cultural Dimensions at the Individual Level of Analysis: The Cultural', *International Journal of Cross Cultural Management,* 2(3): 275.

Morrison, A.M. (1992) *The New Leaders: Leadership Diversity in America.* San Francisco, CA: Jossey-Bass Publishers.

Northrup, T.A. (1989) 'The Dynamic of Identity in Personal and Social Conflict'. In Kriesberg, L., Northrup, T.A. and Thorson, S.J. (eds) *Intractable Conflicts and Their Transformation.* Syracuse, NY: Syracuse University Press, pp. 55–82.

O'Connor, P.M.G. and Quinn, L. (2004) 'Organizational Capacity for Leadership'. In McCauley, C.D. and Van Velsor, E. (eds) *The Center for Creative Leadership Handbook of Leadership Development.* San Francisco, CA: John Wiley and Sons, Inc., pp. 417–37.

Oyserman, D., Coon, H.M. and Kemmelmeier, M. (2002) 'Rethinking Individualism and Collectivism: Evaluation of Theoretical Assumptions and Meta-analyses', *Psychological Bulletin,* 128(1): 3–72.

Pettigrew, T.F. (1998) 'Intergroup Contact Theory', *Annual Review of Psychology,* 49(1): 65–85.

Powell, G.N. and Taylor, K.B. (1998) 'Beyond O.J.: Examining Race Relations in the Workplace', *Journal of Management Education,* 22(2): 208–17.

Putnam, L.L. and Wondolleck, J. (2003) 'Intractability: Definitions, Dimensions, and Distinctions'. In Lewicki, R.J., Gray, B. and Elliott, M. (eds) *Making Sense of Intractable Environmental Conflicts.* Washington, DC: Island Press.

Rahim, M.A. (2001) *Managing Conflict in Organizations (3rd edn).* Westport, CT: Quorum Books.

Reicher, S.D. and Hopkins, N. (2003) 'On the Science of the Art of Leadership'. In van Knippenberg, D. and Hogg, M.A. (eds) *Leadership and Power: Identity Processes in Groups and Organizations.* London: Sage.

Rothman, J. (1997) *Resolving Identity-based Conflict in Nations, Organizations, and Communities.* San Francisco, CA: Jossey-Bass.

Sagiv, L. and Schwartz, S.H. (2000) 'A New Look at Culture: Illustrative Applications to Role Stress and Managerial Behavior'. In Ashkanasky, N.N., Wiilderon, C. and Peterson, M.F. (eds) *The Handbook of Organizational Culture and Climate.* Newbury Park, CA: Sage.

Scandura, T.A. and Lankau, M.J. (1996) 'Developing Diverse Leaders: A Leader-member Exchange Approach', *Leadership Quarterly,* 7(2): 243–63.

Schwartz, S.H. (1990) 'Individualism-collectivism—Critique and Proposed Refinements', *Journal of Cross-Cultural Psychology,* 21(2): 139–57.

Schwartz, S.H. (1994) 'Beyond Individualism/ collectivism, New Cultural Dimensions of Values'. In Kim, U.H., Triandis, C., Kagitcibasi, C., Choi, S.C. and Yoon, G. (eds) *Individualism and Collectivism: Theory, Methods, and Applications.* London: Sage, pp. 85–119.

Schwartz, S.H. (1999) 'Cultural Value Differences: Some Implications for Work', *Applied Psychology: An International Review,* 48(1): 23–48.

Simon, B. and Klandermans, B. (2001) 'Politicized Collective Identity: A Social Psychological Analysis', *American Psychologist,* 56(4): 319–31.

Smith, P.B. and Long, K.M. (2006) 'Social Identity in Cross–cultural Perspective'. In Brown, R. and Capozza, D. (eds) *Social Identities: Motivational, Emotional, Cultural Influences.* London: Psychology Press.

Smith, P.B., Peterson, M.F., Schwartz, S.H. and colleagues (2002) 'Cultural Values, Sources of Guidance, and Their Relevance to Managerial Behavior: A 47 Nation Study', *Journal of Cross Cultural Psychology,* 33(2): 188 -208.

Smith, P. B. and Schwartz, S. (1997) 'Values'. In Berry, J.W., Segall, M.H. and Kagitcibasi, C. (eds) *Handbook of Cross-cultural Psychology. Vol. 3: Social Behavior and Applications.* Boston, MA: Allyn and Bacon, pp. 7-118.

Stephan, W.G. (1987) 'The Contact Hypothesis in Intergroup Relations'. In Hendrick, C. (ed.) *Group Processes and Intergroup Relations. Review of Personality and Social Psychology,* 9. Thousand Oaks, CA: Sage, pp. 13-40.

Stephan, W.G. and Stephan, C.W. (1985) 'Intergroup Anxiety', *Journal of Social Issues,* 41(3): 157–75.

Su, S.K., Chiu, C., Hong, Y., Leung, K., Peng, K. and Morris, M.W. (1999) 'Self-Organization and Social Organization: US and Chinese Constructions'. In Tyler, T.R., Kramer, R.M. and John, O.P. (eds) *The Psychology of the Social Self.* Mahwah, NJ: Lawrence Erlbaum Associates, pp. 193–222.

Triandis, H. (1986) 'Collectivism vs. Individualism: A Reconceptualization of a Basic Concept in Cross-cultural Psychology'. In Bagley, C. and Vernma, G. (eds) *Personality, Cognition, and Values.* London: Macmillan, pp. 60–95.

Triandis, H. (1989) 'The Self and Social Behavior in Differing Cultural Contexts', *Psychological Review,* 96(3): 506–20.

Triandis, H.C. (1994) *Culture and Social Behavior.* New York: McGraw-Hill, Inc, pp. 144–80.

Triandis, H.C. (1995) *Individualism and Collectivism.* Boulder, CO: Westview Press.

Triandis, H.C. (1996) 'The Importance of Context in the Study of Diversity'. In Jackson, S.E. and Ruderman, M.N. (eds) *Diversity in Work Teams: Research Paradigms for a Changing Workplace.* Washington, DC: American Psychological Association, pp. 225–33.

Triandis, H.C., McCusker, C. and Hui, C.H. (1990) 'Multimethod Probes of Individualism and

Collectivism', *Journal of Personality and Social Psychology*, 74(1): 118–28.

Trompenaars, F. and Hampden-Turner, C. (1998) *Riding the Waves of Culture: Understanding Diversity in Global Business (2nd edn)*. New York: McGraw-Hill.

Tsui, A.S. and Gutek, B.A. (1999) *Demographic Differences in Organizations: Current Research and Future Directions*. Lanham, MD: Lexington Books.

Turner, J.C. (1987) 'The Analysis of Social Influence'. In Turner, J.C., Hogg, M.A., Oakes, P.J., Reicher, S.D. and Wetherell, M.S. (eds) *Rediscovering the Social Group: A Self-categorization Theory*. Oxford: Blackwell, pp. 68–88.

Turner, J.C. and Giles, H. (1981) *Intergroup Behavior*. Oxford: Blackwell.

Van de Vijver, F. and Leung, K. (1997) *Methods and Data Analysis for Cross-cultural Research*. Thousand Oaks, CA: Sage Publications.

Van Velsor, E. and McCauley, C.D. (2004) 'Introduction: Our View of Leadership Development'. In McCauley, C.D. and Van Velsor, E. (eds) *The Center for Creative Leadership Handbook of Leadership Development*. San Francisco, CA: John Wiley and Sons, Inc, pp. 1–22.

Wetherell, M. (1987) 'Social Identity and Group Polarization'. In Turner, J.C. (ed.) *Rediscovering the Social Group: A Self-Categorization Theory*. New York: Basil Blackwell, Inc., pp. 142–70.

Williams, Jr, R.M. (1968) 'Values'. In Sills, E. (ed.) *International Encyclopedia of the Social Sciences*. New York: Macmillan, pp. 283–7.

CHAPTER 44

Beyond Empowerment

Building a Company of Citizens

Brook Manville

Saba Software

Josiah Ober

Princeton University

We live today in a knowledge economy. The core assets of the modern business enterprise lie not in buildings, machinery, and real estate, but in the intelligence, understanding, skills, and experience of employees. Harnessing the capabilities and commitment of knowledge workers is, it might be argued, the central managerial challenge of our time. Unfortunately, it is a challenge that has not yet been met. Corporate ownership structures, governance systems, and incentive programs—despite the enlightened rhetoric of business leaders—are still firmly planted in the industrial age. We grant ownership rights only to the providers of financial capital, not to the providers of intellectual capital. We govern through small management teams at the top of hierarchies. We motivate people through Pavlovian carrot-and-stick incentives.

It's true that business organizations have become less bureaucratic in recent years and that authority has been pushed down through the ranks. People at lower levels—unit managers, factory workers, customer service representatives—have greater autonomy today than they did a generation ago. But such "empowerment," as it's commonly called, is limited. Workers are able to make decisions about their immediate jobs or to participate in somewhat broader decisions about their own units, but they still have little or no voice in decisions about the direction of the overall company. They remain essentially disenfranchised. It should be no surprise, therefore, that many knowledge workers feel estranged from their organizations—their outlook distrustful, their attitude cynical, their loyalty tenuous.

At the heart of the problem is a lack of adequate models. Although we know how command-and-control management works in an industrial company, we have no working template for a truly democratic system of management—one suited to the knowledge worker's

---

Source: Beyond Empowerment: Building a Company of Citizens, by Brook Manville and Josiah Ober. *Harvard Business Review,* 2003, Jan 81 (1), pp. 48–53. Reprinted with permission of Harvard Business School Publishing.

need for and expectation of self-determination and self-government. But if a usable model for a democratic organization does not yet exist in the business world, history offers a compelling, if unexpected, prototype. Some 2,500 years ago, the city-state of ancient Athens rose to unprecedented political and economic power by giving its citizens a direct voice and an active role in civic governance. Although not without its flaws, the city's uniquely participative system of democracy helped unleash the creativity of the Athenian people and channel it in ways that produced the greatest good for the society as a whole. The system succeeded in bringing individual initiative and common cause into harmony. And that is precisely the synthesis that today's companies need to achieve if they're to realize the full power of their people and thrive in the knowledge economy.

An Ancient Model

It is the year 480 BC. Dawn is breaking over the small Greek island of Salamis, just off the coast of Athens. Thousands of Athenian citizens huddle on slender, wooden galleys, clutching weapons and oars. Facing them are hundreds of powerful, hulking warships, the majestic fighting navy of the Persian Empire. That force is poised to complete the Persian takeover of the Greek mainland and its prize jewel, the flourishing city of Athens. Across the narrow strait, on a commanding hill, sits the Great King of Persia himself, eager to witness the culmination of years of preparation. He expects that victory will come easily. After all, the Athenians are a ragtag bunch. They do not even have a king of their own to dispense orders.

Yet by the time dusk falls, the Persian king's grandiose plans are in ruins. The Athenians have successfully carried out a bold and innovative battle plan, using the agility of their lighter ships, together with their deep knowledge of local geography and weather, to outmaneuver and ultimately defeat their far more powerful foe. Spurred by a deep sense of civic duty, the Athenians have fought together with especial valor, and their superior ingenuity, motivation, and commitment carry the day. Against all odds, a small community of 30,000 citizens defeats a colossal, monarchic military machine.

In the years following their great victory at Salamis, the Athenians were quick to exploit their advantage, steadily expanding their influence across the Aegean Sea. Skillfully combining diplomacy and military might, and resiliently rebounding from setbacks, they built the first great Greek empire. They not only kept the Persians at bay, but swept pirates from the sea, making the Aegean a safer place to trade. Commerce boomed, and many individuals prospered. Private and public wealth soared, as the city-state collected the modern-day equivalent of billions of dollars in taxes and tributes from a rapidly expanding group of subject states.

At the same time, Athens spawned a cultural florescence the likes of which the world had never seen. The atmosphere of the democratic city was open, experimental and entrepreneurial. Philosophers, artists, scientists, and poets from across the Mediterranean world flocked to Athens's academies, workshops, and public squares. Not only was the great Parthenon built, but many other masterpieces of architecture and sculpture were created too. Moral philosophy came into being, the craft of history writing emerged, and drama became a great art form. Scientists developed new theories about everything from the atomic structure of matter to the relationship of the earth to heavenly bodies.

Underpinning all the achievements was a system of governance based on personal freedom, collective action, and an open, democratic culture. Athens was at heart a community of citizens—a "politeia," to use the Greek word—and each of those citizens had both the right and the obligation to play an active role in the society's governance. (Although the Athenian conception of democracy marked a historic leap forward in civic and political thinking, it is important to note that it did not extend to the enfranchisement of women or immigrants, much less the freeing of chattel slaves.) Our emaciated modern conception of democracy makes it difficult to understand the richness of the original Athenian concept. What we call "citizenship" today—an essentially passive legal status involving only minimal civic obligations and relying on a distant and entrenched governing elite—is but a shadow of the Athenian politeia.

The Architecture of Citizenship

What made the democracy of ancient Athens so successful, and why does it stand as a good model for businesses today? First, the system was not imposed on the Athenian people, but rather it grew organically from their own needs, beliefs, and actions—it was as much a spirit of governance as a set of rules or laws. Any managerial structure that is to have true meaning to knowledge workers must also emerge naturally from their own aspirations and initiatives. And second, the system was holistic—it was successful because it informed all aspects of the society, just as a productive corporate culture must inform all aspects of an organization and its management. The Athenian democracy encompassed *participatory structures* for making decisions, resolving disputes, and managing activities; a set of *communal values* that defined people's relationships with one another; and an array of *practices of engagement* that ensured the broad participation of the entire citizenry. By looking more carefully at this architecture of citizenship, we gain hints of what the business organization of the future might look like.

Participatory Structures. The Athenian system of governance had what might be called a radically flat organization—much flatter than even the leanest of corporate structures today. A set of clearly defined and universally understood processes and institutions—including councils, courts, assemblies, and executive offices—served to minimize hierarchy, inhibit the development of a ruling class, and engage citizens in governance and jurisprudence. In addition to taking part in local policy making, every adult male Athenian had the opportunity to attend the great citizen assembly, which met almost weekly to debate and vote on matters of importance, from financing the construction of a new road to fighting a war. The assembly was steered by a council of 500 citizens whose membership rotated annually. The councilors took turns setting the assembly's agenda and presiding over its deliberations.

To ensure that the decisions of the populace would be executed swiftly and well, the Athenian governance structure also included teams of "executives"—generals, administrators, managers—who were selected by election or lottery. Turnover in executive positions was systematic: At some point in their lives, most of Athens's 30,000 citizens had the opportunity to participate as a leader. Individual performance was carefully monitored, and outgoing executives were rewarded or punished accordingly—but only by their peers, the body of citizens themselves. The administration of justice was similarly open and participatory. Citizen arbitrators settled most conflicts, but when arbitration failed or the crime was particularly serious, juries representing the entire citizenry made the judgments and set the penalties.

Transparent procedural rules governed judicial and policy-making processes, keeping them simple, fair, and flexible. But the processes also allowed, even encouraged, passion and emotion. Many decisions made by the citizens were literally matters of life and death; no one was ejected from meetings for speaking loudly or heatedly—as long as the rights of others were respected. Expertise in technical matters was deeply valued, but the concept of professionalism played little part in the system. Amateur engagement was seen as preferable to professional management because it encouraged the constant sharing of fresh viewpoints and knowledge. It was expected that people with expertise in a particular area would come forward whenever their skills were needed, without becoming part of any standing bureaucracy. Laws and policies were stated in plain language; professional prosecutors and lawyers were unknown. Time limits on debate in courts and assemblies allowed each citizen to have his voice heard and prevented any bloc from dominating the proceedings. And voting on policy was open and mostly "by consensus," though secret ballots were employed for judicial decisions to ensure fairness.

People with expertise came forward whenever their skills were needed, without becoming part of any standing bureaucracy.

In combination, these democratic structures ensured that no obstacles or barriers would arise to separate the Athenians from their government. More important, they reflected the people's deep trust in their own ability to chart the course of their state. Think how different such a notion is from the beliefs that underlie corporate management structures today. In most companies, major decisions continue to be made by small, insular elites behind the closed doors of executive offices and conference rooms. Tightly scripted planning, budgeting, and approval processes deter rather than encourage free thinking and honest debate. The entire shape of the modern company reflects a fundamental distrust of its members—a distrust that, as recent American business scandals have shown, can all too easily give rise to a malignant arrogance.

Communal Values. Establishing democratic structures is not enough, of course. People do not walk miles to attend meetings, forsake precious time to play temporary executive roles, or risk their lives in wars merely for the sake of "structures." For ancient Athenians, as for knowledge workers today, motivation came from a higher purpose—from a sense of shared ownership in their community's destiny. A distinctive set of values made the personal communal and the communal personal. In most companies today, by contrast, there is a tension between the employee's individual will and the will of the organization. Management is forever arbitrating the bounds between personal freedom and the corporate interest. In Athens, there was no such tension. The interest of the citizen was indistinguishable from the interest of the government.

The society placed the highest possible value on individuality, diligently protecting each person's right to self-determination, equality of opportunity, and security. Every citizen was free to—and encouraged to—express himself publicly, debate and dissent, and participate actively in all decisions that would materially affect him. But he was also free to pursue his private interests; he was not expected to engage constantly in public matters, but to contribute only when his skills and perspectives were needed. All citizens were given an equal chance to fulfill their personal potential while making their greatest possible contributions to the society. Finally, each citizen was secure, protected from the physical coercion and verbal abuse that would have made it impossible to enjoy either freedom or equality. As members of a community devoted to the common good, citizens were expected to band together not only to guarantee their collective security from external threats, but to guarantee the security of each individual from vicious behavior on the part of any aberrant internal member or group. The public welfare depended on the protection of each of the community's members.

A second set of Athenian values, balancing those that focused on individuality, centered on community, on the belief that the people *are* the state. So deeply held was this concept that it was embedded in the language: "Athens" was only the name of a place; the name of the community was "the Athenians." The physical manifestations of the city paled in importance to its people. The historian Thucydides memorably quotes an Athenian general's address to the citizenry on the eve of a great battle: "Not ships, not walls, but men make our city." How many knowledge workers today, hearing a similar pronouncement from their company's top management, would believe it? How many would automatically embrace the company's interest as their own?

Critical to the day-to-day integration of individual and community was a third set of values having to do with moral reciprocity. The sense of moral reciprocity provided the all-important link between "What's in it for me?" and "What's in it for us?" Its essence was the shared belief that engagement in the life of the community was educational in the broadest sense: It gave each individual the chance to become better, to grow wiser, and to fully develop his talents. As a citizen, you owed the community your best effort; the community, in return, owed you every opportunity to fulfill your potential. By providing unfettered opportunity to each of its members, the society understood that it would arrive at the best solutions to problems facing everyone.

On the surface, moral reciprocity may seem like an ancient version of what in business has come to be called "the employability contract": An employer promises to further the employee's professional development (and thus career prospects) in return for the employee's commitment to perform at the highest possible level throughout his or her tenure. There are, however, two significant differences between the modern concept of employability and the Athenian concept of moral reciprocity. First, employability does not foster long-term loyalty—indeed, it envisions each worker's likely departure. Employability is a short-term bargain that assumes a conflict between the interest of the community and that of its individual members. Athenian citizens, by contrast, could not ordinarily be "fired" from their organization, nor were they likely to leave it for any but the direst of reasons. Whether modern global business can (or should) ever return to a goal of long-term employment remains to be seen. But the contract between the individual and community will be richer and more productive for both if it has a meaningful chance of durability.

How many knowledge workers today would automatically embrace the company's interest as their own?

The second difference between employability contracts and moral reciprocity is less obvious but perhaps more important. Whereas moral reciprocity is integrally tied to a broader dependency between the individual and the community, employability is simply a quid pro quo understanding about working and learning on the job. Without the chance to meaningfully participate in steering one's own destiny, without the opportunity to gain the sincere respect of one's peers, without an honest stake in making the community more successful through one's own work and ideas, employability can quickly decay into generic training programs or bogus choices among short lists of uninspiring assignments. Narrowly construed employability contracts will motivate knowledge workers only so far.

Practices of Engagement. The structure and values of Athenian democracy outlined above provided the framework for citizenship. Ultimately, however, citizenship must be expressed in action—in day-to-day practices—or it will quickly degenerate into bureaucracy, routines, and self-interest. An organization's practices define its culture, how work gets done. To the Athenians, though, the practices of democracy were not just about "doing citizenship" but also about "learning citizenship." They continually refined their understanding of the workings of democracy through their actions and interactions in public squares, in leadership roles, and in jury trials.

The practices that animated the Athenian system can be broken out into subgroups, though it is essential to think about them in their totality—and as embedded in the structures and values to which they gave life.

Practices of access ensured that every citizen had free and equal opportunity to participate in self-governance. Athenians volunteered in both making and executing decisions, sharing their knowledge by participating in forums and initiatives at both the local and statewide level. The rotation of roles was crucial to the dynamism of governance, enabling all citizens to have opportunities to lead, to assume executive positions, and in general to take turns at ruling and being ruled.

Practices of process were essential in ensuring that deliberations, decision making, and execution were carried out in ways that were consistent, fair, and timely. Citizens sought consensus, making decisions and judgments based on trust among well-intentioned individuals (the polar opposite of today's partisan politics). All governmental

and judicial processes were transparent, ensuring that every decision was based on information freely offered and supported by clearly expressed reasons. The populace also believed in making decisions swiftly; citizens maintained a sense of urgency in bringing debates to a conclusion. Finally, it was expected that all would support and, as necessary, assist in executing decisions, regardless of one's point of view prior to the final vote.

Practices of consequence ensured that citizens did not come to see process as an end in itself (a sure recipe for bureaucracy), but rather maintained a focus on achieving practical and concrete results. Fundamental to the society's emphasis on outcomes was the concept of merit; the people strove to ensure that every decision was based on the best argument, never on the position, privilege, or prejudice of those deciding. Another cherished concept was accountability—accepting personal responsibility for respecting the values of the citizen culture in all decision-making and executive settings, supporting those values in one's own conduct, and accepting peers' judgments about one's performance. Finally, the Athenians considered it an obligation to challenge the process—to seek to reverse misguided policies, appeal bad decisions, and call attention to, and act upon, misbehavior that threatened the community or any of its members.

Each of these three sets of practices was governed by an overarching group of *jurisdiction practices,* which ensured that every decision was made in the right place, by the right people, and at the right time. The community believed that decisions should be made by those with the greatest knowledge of the issues and the greatest stake in the consequences. This meant that technical decisions tended to be left to experts; decisions about battle strategy, for example, were reserved for generals. Decisions of great consequence, from levying taxes to declaring war, demanded full-scale debate by the society as a whole. Other, more mundane decisions—scheduling festivals or resolving disputes between neighbors, for example—were made locally. So precious was the possession of citizenship for Athenians that the entire citizen body had the jurisdiction to consider any proposal to confer citizenship upon a foreigner.

The culture of citizenship created by the Athenians—with its interplay of structures, values, and practices—encouraged every person to zealously pursue individual excellence and at the same time created, through shared processes of self-governance, an emotional commitment to efforts for the common good. This kind of "both/and" thinking has recently been promoted by Jim Collins and other management thinkers. It seeks to break the conflict between self-interest and corporate interest. Pericles, the Athenian statesman, expressed the essence of this attitude. Every citizen, he said, was "the rightful lord and owner of his own person," exhibiting "an exceptional grace and versatility." And, he went on, thanks to their politeia and their entire way of life, the citizens were collectively able to be a great and powerful community.

Indeed, this "school to the rest of Greece," as Pericles called his city, was the envy of and an object of fear to its enemies. One of Athens's rivals spoke in awe of how the motivation of its citizens yielded outstanding performance: "They regard their bodies as expendable for their city's sake, and each man cultivates his own intelligence, for doing something notable for the common cause. . . . Of the Athenians alone it may be said, they begin to possess something almost as soon as they desire it, so quickly are they able to act upon something once they have made a decision . . . and when they are successful, they regard that success as nothing compared to what they will do next."

Looking Ahead

The Athenian model of organizational democracy is just that—a model. It does not provide a simple set of prescriptions for modem managers. It does, however, offer a window into how sizable groups of people can successfully govern themselves with dignity and trust and without resorting to a stifling bureaucracy. Most important, it shows the need to combine structures, values, and practices in a coherent, self-sustaining system. Simply creating forums or processes for group decision making will not be enough—half-hearted measures will only amplify employee cynicism. Building and sustaining a company of citizens requires a genuine change in organizational and managerial culture.

Most of today's workers are familiar with the basic values and structures of democracy, and most have experience with some forms of communal action at work, whether it's serving on self-managed teams, reaching decisions through consensus building, or sharing leadership responsibilities. The idea of moving toward a more democratic structure should not, therefore, be a foreign one. Still, what we're talking about is a radical change in the corporate mind-set, and complications abound. Consider a few of the most obvious: Technological advances, demographic shifts, and the increasing globalization of markets have dispersed workforces, undermined traditional assumptions about job security and employee loyalty, and created far more open markets for tabor. The very definition of an "employee" has grown fuzzy, as companies rely increasingly on freelancers, contractors, and temporary workers.

One of the first hurdles a company will need to clear is simply to define what constitutes a "citizen." What are the benefits, rights, and responsibilities that go along with formal citizenship in an organization? Should limited citizenship be available, with lesser rights and responsibilities? Should contractors and partners be given some form of citizenship? How should different levels of citizenship be managed? How should ownership rights and other rewards be distributed? These are hard questions, and every company will need to answer them in its own way, taking account of its size, circumstances, and goals.

One thing, however, is certain: The practice of citizenship cannot be imposed from above. It must grow out of the actions and beliefs of the citizens themselves. The transition to a more democratic business organization will thus take time, requiring many experiments and many successes and failures. While an organization's managers will necessarily play key roles in establishing basic goals and values—as a series of great leaders did for Athens—they must also have the courage to take their turn in being led, as the self-confidence of the citizenry grows. It is a process that must never cease: The experience of democracy must continually refine the practice of democracy.

Pericles told his fellow Athenians that "future ages will wonder at us, even as the present age wonders at us now." Over two thousand years later, his bold prediction rings true. But our attention to Athens should not be limited to wonder. It should encompass emulation as well.

CHAPTER 45

The Tenets of the Democratic Enterprise

Lynda Gratton

London Business School

There has been an extraordinary diversity of democratic models, and no treatise on the Democratic Enterprise can claim to represent the definitive set of ideas. Rather, such a treatise can only amount to a set of suggestions, or what I have called tenets. I have constructed these tenets by looking at both the richness and depth of historic thinking, and at the present-day experience of democracy of our three citizens, Greg, Nina, and Stewart.

I have also applied three litmus tests to each tenet:

Coherence. The first is the condition of coherence, the capacity of the tenets to be mutually reinforcing, and to create a consistent system of thinking about an organization. The tenets are not intended to end debate, but rather to stimulate it, by presenting a set of unified, and unifying, principles to help frame and inform the ongoing decisions with which organizations are faced.

Viability. The tenets have been selected on the basis of economic viability. By this I mean they are within the economic structure and goals of both commercial and not-for-profit organizations. The reason for this criterion is simple: citizens can only exercise their rights if they are members of an economically viable business. For this to occur there must be an expansion of economic opportunity to maximize the availability of resources to individuals. If the exercise of citizen rights jeopardizes the long-term health of the company, these rights should not be upheld. The tenets of the Democratic Enterprise have been constructed to create value for the organization while maximizing human potential.

Practicality. The third condition is "practicality," that the tenet is capable of being operationalized in a company through a set of supporting practices and processes. In devising the tenets I have taken this notion further by specifying that they can be put to

---

work in most companies within a relatively short period of time. This is essentially the stance of the pragmatist, and I make no apologies for it. The long-term democratization of organizations is a legitimate conversation." But my concern is the realistic steps that can be taken now. My agenda is not entirely short term; rather, my expectation is that steps taken now will clear the way for discussions to follow, as democracy proves out both in benefits *and* practicality. In this way enterprise democracy is both a destination, and a journey.

With these selection criteria in mind, what do we mean when we talk of the Democratic Enterprise? There are many forms the democratization of work could take.

In its most structural form, the democratization would mirror the workings of the *demos* in ancient Athens, with the full participation of every citizen in decisions about general policy.[2] This would involve the senior team being accountable to the employees, obliged to justify their actions to the employees and, like leaders of ancient Athens, able to be removed by the employees. Further, the senior team would be chosen by the employees and would act in the interests of the employees. This form of democratization is the principle underpinning works councils in many continental European companies and will increasingly be contained within future legislation of the European Union. However, it has not been a dominant structure in Anglo-American companies, where rights of involvement are held primarily by the financial stakeholders of the company, not by employees without a financial stake. While the structural form of democracy is a legitimate form of democracy in organizations, it is not the form to which this book is addressed, as it fails to meet the third condition of selection: that is it can be made practical within a relatively short period of time.

The form of democracy which I believe has potentially the most impact on the working lives of individual employees, at least in the short term, is what David Held terms "Democratic Autonomy."[3] In this form the modern Democratic Enterprise would, like ancient Athens, provide the necessary conditions to enable citizens to pursue their own interests, and where the free development of all would be a common goal.

With this in mind, and drawing heavily on the discussion about state democracy, I have identified the tenets that form the basis of the Democratic Enterprise. I believe these six tenets, realistic rather than aspirational, could stand at the centre of successful organizations.

The Six Tenets of the Democratic Enterprise

1. The relationship between the organization and the individual is adult-to-adult.

2. Individuals are seen primarily as investors actively building and deploying their human capital.

3. Individuals are able to develop their natures and express their diverse qualities.

4. Individuals are able to participate in determining the conditions of their association.

5. The liberty of some individuals is not at the expense of others.

6. Individuals have accountabilities and obligations both to themselves and the organization.

The first two tenets have as a common framework the principle of autonomy. This principle provides the anchor point for both conceiving and building a robust model of the Democratic Enterprise. In Held's words:

> What is the status of the principle of autonomy? This principle ought to be regarded as an essential premise of all traditions of modern democratic thought . . . the capability of persons to choose freely, to determine and justify their own action, to enter into self-chosen obligations.
>
> Held, *Models of Democracy,* p. 303

Looking back at the stories of Greg, Nina and Stewart, it is striking the way they consider themselves and their organizations within the framework of autonomy. Think of Greg as he zigzags across BP: he understands himself, he knows what is important to him, and he is prepared to take action. Or Nina as she describes her plans for herself and for the life she wants to create at McKinsey. Pericles could have been describing Greg or Nina when he said:

> Each single one of our citizens, in all the manifold aspects of life, is able to show himself the rightful

lord and owner of his person, and do this, moreover, with exceptional grace and exceptional versatility.

Thucydides, *The Peloponnesian War*,
pp. 147–8

In attempting to capture the democratic ideal of autonomy within the day-to-day experiences of citizens such as Nina, Greg and Stewart, I have used two related constructs. The first is the idea of the adult-to-adult relationship, and the second is the metaphor of the individual as an investor. By using these concepts I am attempting to capture the reality of contemporary organizational life and to create clear boundaries in which to frame the tenets.

First Tenet: An Adult-to-Adult Relationship

At the heart of democracy is the nature of the relationship between the individual and the state. In classical democracy this relationship was manifest among members of the *polis,* each capable, and each believing the other capable, of entering decisions in a fair and thoughtful manner. This was echoed in John Stuart Mill's ideal of the educated, insightful citizen capable of entering into the day-to-day activity of the state.[4] This is an adult-to-adult relationship between citizen and state. With Marx and later Weber, however, we see the role of citizens diminished to the extent that they have to be protected by the state, while the role of active citizen is taken by the elected government. Here the metaphor for the relationship would be more parent–child, with the parent protecting the rights and needs of a child incapable of self-knowledge, or indeed action and volition.

The basis of the Democratic Enterprise is a relationship between the individual and the organization that is adult-to-adult.[5] It is firmly "Theory Y" rather than "Theory X." Greg, Nina and Stewart all view themselves as being in control of their lives, whatever that may mean. Think of Greg as he takes the helm of his career and tacks across the functions, businesses and countries of the BP organization. Or Nina as she reflects, "Self-governing pervades the way we think about ourselves." Or Nina again, taking accountability for times when she pushed too far, times when she lost her compass and belief in herself.

In the adult-to-adult relationship, responsibility for behaviour and changes in behaviour are shared by both parties; the needs of both parties are openly debated and considered, and there is freedom on the parts of both parties to act. The emphasis is on the autonomous employee, one capable of assuming both the self-insight and self-direction the role of adult entails.

Second Tenet: Individuals as Investors

In the second tenet I address the question of where ownership of a resource resides. To Marx and Engels, industrialization had created a system in which the capitalists owned the factories and technologies and the wage-labourers were without property. Under this scenario the position of the worker is incomparably weaker than that of his or her employer, who can not only sack the worker but can fall back on employing any number of other, undifferentiated workers in the event of a sustained conflict. Workers soon discover that the individual pursuit of interests is ineffective, and it is only through collective action that they can establish the conditions for a fulfilling life. Here the picture is of the employee as commodity, manipulated by the organization and required to enter into a confrontational mode to ensure remuneration for their labours.[6]

In the majority of contemporary organizations the human asset is not mere muscle, however, but brain, and the dominant activity is not the operation of machines but the generation of knowledge. And in the world of knowledge, ownership of resources is more complex.[7] In the factories where Marx made his observations, the withholding of labour could be actively observed, and indeed the role of the supervisor was to govern this process and maximize output.

But in the knowledge economy each of us can choose to give or withhold our knowledge and it is virtually impossible to detect when we are doing so. Hence the role of the supervisor becomes obsolete, and is taken by the creation of an organizational culture of trust and reciprocity in which employees *actively choose* to share their knowledge. This notion of active choice fundamentally changes the relationship between the organization and the individual. And, as the nature of the relationship changes, so does the transaction. In

Marx's world the employee is the *asset* to be controlled and manipulated. In the knowledge economy the employee is an *investor,* actively choosing to invest (or withhold) ideas, inspirations and skills.[8] Ownership of the talents and resources of the individual rests firmly with the individual.

In the words of Andy Grove, Chairman of Intel:

> No matter where you work, you are not an employee. You are in business with one employer—yourself—in competition with millions of similar businesses world-wide. Nobody owns your career. You own it as a sole proprietor.

The investor mindset is perhaps most clearly seen in Nina. Recall her words:

> I will have to make some decisions. What will be my unique proposition? I know I have lots of choices. In the next two weeks I have to work through the "Nina Bhatia strategy project" and then syndicate it with my colleagues and say "this is what I plan to do, and this is the help I need, what do you think?"

Nina places herself firmly into the investor mindset. Investors are individuals who take primary responsibility for both the creation of their talents and resources and the deployment and leverage of these resources. We can actively manage our personal and career resources just as we might manage our financial resources. Again, the emphasis is on personal autonomy, the capacity to be self-directed.[9]

For the condition of investor to be met, two tenets of the democratic relationship must be in place: that individuals are able to determine their conditions of association, and, by doing so, that they are able to develop and express their diverse qualities.

Third Tenet: The Expression of Diverse Qualities

Autonomy requires what Carl Jung called *individuation,* the capacity of each person to become themselves. Not what their parents want them to be, not what their teachers want them to be, not what their partners want

them to be—but what they want to be, and indeed what they can be.[10] What Nina wants to be, of course, is not the same as what Stewart wants to be, or indeed what Greg wants to be. Implicit in this freedom is the individual expression of diverse qualities.

John Stuart Mill described the expression of diverse qualities as a central aspect of liberty:

> Liberty of thought, feeling, discussion and publication (unburdening "the inward domain of consciousness"); second, liberty of tastes and pursuits ("framing the plan of our life to suit our own character"); and third, liberty of association or combination so long as, of course, it causes no harm to others.
>
> John Stuart Mill, *On Liberty,* pp. 71–2

To Marx and Schumpeter, expression of individual variety was lost beneath the heavy hand of mechanization and automation. In Marx's view "individuals" have limited choice; instead they are prisoners of their past, particularly of the social class and economic circumstances to which they are born. Similarly, Schumpeter viewed people as vulnerable to what he called "extra-rational" forces, capable of denying their capacity for growth and ensnaring their freedom to make choices about themselves.[11]

In contemporary democracy we have an opportunity to return to the spirit of Aristotle and John Stuart Mill in our embrace of *individuation.* We can re-cast democracy as a basis for tolerating and negotiating difference. After all, what makes for joy and meaning for one individual is not true for all individuals at all times. This speaks to both the individual, in his or her propensity for autonomous behaviour, and to the organization, in its capacity to deliver sufficient variety for diverse qualities to be expressed.

In these first three tenets we have set an agenda for the Democratic Enterprise. It specifies the relationship between the individual and the organization, speaks to the ownership of the resources held by the individual, and calls for the free expression of the diverse qualities of the individual. Each of these tenets has as its underlying expectation that each individual can become the best he or she can be. Thus, these tenets form an important base to creating the autonomy and inspiration which rests at the heart of the Democratic Enterprise, and which we observed in the stories of our three citizens.

But, while Nina, Stewart, and Greg are individual citizens, they are also colleagues, active participants in the performance of the companies in which they are members. John Stuart Mill captured the possible tension in his third element of liberty, "liberty of association or combination so long as, of course, *it causes no harm to others*" (my italics). The emphasis here is on "no harm to others." But for Nina, Stewart and Greg, their objective is not simply to create no harm; it is to actively and relentlessly contribute to the success of their work teams and their organizations. It is to the contribution of the individual to the organization that the final three tenets are addressed.

Fourth Tenet: Participation in the Determination of Conditions of Association

Participation in determining the conditions of association specifies the rights of individuals, the entitlement to pursue action and activity. Rights define spheres of independent action, enabling the creation of *space* for action. Without active determination of the conditions of association it is impossible for any employee to truly enter into an adult-to-adult relationship, or behave as an active investor. Within true participation, the individual is an active maker of choices.

We see participation running through the stories of our three citizens. How Nina has actively participated in finding roles and job experiences that would stretch her, yet still enable her to meet her obligations as a mother. How Stewart has actively participated in creating the boundaries of his job to manage his personal needs while still delivering on the BT's business goals. But active participation in the conditions of association was never an end in itself for any of our citizens; rather, participation was one of the life forces that kept them engaged in the company. These are the words of John Stuart Mill:[12]

When people are engaged in the resolution of problems affecting themselves or the whole collectively, energies are unleashed which enhance the likelihood of the creation of imaginative solutions and successful strategies. In short, participation in social and public life undercuts passivity and enhances general prosperity.

John Stuart Mill,
Considerations, pp. 207–8

What do "conditions of association" actually refer to within an organizational context? We return to these conditions in more detail when we look at the three building blocks of the Democratic Enterprise. But even now we can see these conditions at work in the stories of the citizens. For Nina participation is key to the allocation of projects and jobs and her allocation of time. Her ability to be the best she could be depends on her opportunity to participate in deciding the stretching roles she will take, and her participation in determining the hours she works. Participation in determining the hours of work is also important to Stewart at BT, along with the opportunity to participate in determining the location of his work.

In this fourth tenet the point of negotiation is primarily between the organization and the individual, but in the fifth tenet the arena is broadened to also include the relationship between the individual and his or her colleagues.

Fifth Tenet: The Liberty of Some Individuals Is Not at the Expense of Others

This is one of the fundamental tenets of the Democratic Enterprise, that choices made by some individuals are not at the expense of others. The determination of the conditions of association is based in part on "rights" of the space for action. But rights also constrain: they specify the limits on independent action so it does not curtail or infringe others. As we have discussed, autonomous individuals have different wants and values. And, as investors, they have differing amounts, and types, of resources to leverage. Democracy cannot be about dumbing down to the lowest common denominator. Nor can it be about the more powerful appropriating resources at the expense of the less powerful.

Within the Democratic Enterprise there are individual wishes and desires. But they do not occur in isolation from colleagues or company. For example, Nina's wish to spend less time in the evenings with clients has an impact on her immediate colleagues. Stewart's desire to work from home has a similar effect on his co-workers. In Greg's case, his capacity to build a broad portfolio of skills puts him in a very powerful position in remuneration negotiations: what stops him from exploiting his position to obtain a package that is unjust in comparison with others? (And what of senior executives with still more power than Greg?) This aspect of the relationship between citizens has always been a central dilemma for political theory: finding a balance between might and rights, powers and law, duties and rights[13]— and achieving fairness, if not equality, in compensation.

For Marx the issue was clear: the powerful would always exploit the weak and only through solidarity and action would the weak assume sufficient power to have their needs met and avert exploitation. The role of the state was to act in the interests of the majority, rather than in the interests of the most powerful. In contemporary democracy the balance between might and right is assumed by the government as the creator of laws that specify the distribution of opportunity and resources.

In a democratic state there will be areas of dispute, and opportunities for the choices made by the strong to be at the expense of those with less power and access to resources. The same is true of the Democratic Enterprise, and as a consequence the Democratic Enterprise must offer a just means of negotiating value differences that provides protection for the employee from the arbitrary use of authority and coercive power. Historically organizations have created mechanisms to negotiate differences and, in my account of the Democratic Enterprise that follows, I describe some of the ways this can occur. Central to this provision is the sixth tenet, the accountabilities and obligations of individuals to themselves, their colleagues and their organizations.

Sixth Tenet: Accountabilities and Obligations

The obligations of the citizen have always been central to democracy. In the classic democracy of Athens, each citizen had clear obligations to participate in the creation and nurturing of the common life. Athenian citizenship entailed taking a share in the functions of

the state by participating directly in the affairs of the state. Athenian democracy was marked by a general commitment to principles of civic virtue: dedication to the republican city-state and subordination of private life to public affairs and common good. The public and private were intertwined, and individuals could only fulfill themselves and live honorably as citizens through the *polis.*

In the Democratic Enterprise, accountabilities and obligations are crucial aspects of the relationship between the individual and the organization.[14] Nina at McKinsey, for example, is part of a complex web of obligations. She has obligations to herself (to be the best she can be, to develop breadth and depth). She has obligations to her clients (to deliver world-class expertise and advice) and to her team (to mentor, coach and support). At the same time, McKinsey has obligations to Nina: to support her desire to participate in a challenging range of roles and ensure she does not become too specialized. Nina has rights (for personal development, for market-based remuneration) but also responsibilities. It is the implicit contract of obligations that binds rights and responsibilities. Much of this contract is implicit, rich in assumptions rather than facts, uncertainties rather than predictability. One striking aspect of Nina's story is how adept her organization is at "contracting capability": the ability to make and keep strategically appropriate psychological contracts based on voluntary participation rather than control. The concept of obligations and accountabilities is particularly pertinent to the Democratic Enterprise, and forms a key aspect to the third building block.[15]

Notes

1. Much of the writing on the participate element of democracy does not meet the criteria of practicality. While I believe participate decision making is a legitimate aspiration, our research suggests that it is very far from practicality in most company. For a view of the possible mechanisms of participative democracy in contemporary organizations see, for example, McLagan, P. and Nel, C., *The Age of Participation.* San Francisco: Berrett-Koehler Publishers, 1995 and 1997; Purser, R.E. and Cabana, S., *The Self-Managing Organization.* New York: Free Press, 1998; Greenberg, E.S., *Workplace Democracy: The Political Effects of Participation.* Ithaca, NY: Cornell University Press, 1986.

2. The possible workings of participative democracy founded on ancient Athens is compellingly described in Manville, B. and Ober, J., *Company of Citizens: What The World's First Democracy Teaches Leaders about Creating Great Organizations.* Boston: Harvard Business School Press, 2002.

3. This form of democracy is described at length in ch. 9 of Held, D., *Models of Democracy.* Cambridge: Polity Press, 1996.

4. John Stuart Mill believed that it was the combination of liberty and democracy that created the greatest possibility for what he termed "human excellence" see, for example, Mill, J.S., "Considerations on Representative Government" in Acton, H.B. (ed.), *Utilitarianism, Liberty, and Representative Government,* London: Dent, 1951.

5. The categorization of parent/child and adult/adult is drawn directly from psycho-dynamics. See, for example, Harris, T.A., *I'm OK, You're OK.* London: Arrow, 1995.

6. This was the view described by Marx in Marx, K. and Engels, F., *The Communist Manifesto* in *Selected Works,* vol. 1. Moscow: Progress Publishers, 1969.

7. The significant differences associated with the knowledge-based economy and the organizations operating within it have been described by many. See, for example, Nonaka, I. and Takeuchi, H., *The Knowledge Creating Company.* New York: Oxford University Press, 1995 and more recently Eisenhardt, K.M. and Santos, F.M., "Knowledge-Based View: A New Theory of Strategy?" in Pettigrew, A., Thomas, H. and Whittington, R. (eds), *Handbook of Strategy and Management,* pp. 139–64. London: Sage Publications; 2002 and Cairncross, F., *The Company of the Future: How the Communications Revolution Is Changing Management.* Boston: Harvard Business School Press, 2002.

8. This notion of the asset and investor has been developed and described in Gratton, L. and Ghoshal, S., "Managing Personal Human Capital: New Ethos for the "Volunteer" Employee," *European Management Journal,* 21 (2003): 1–10.

9. The changing nature of the relationship between the individual and the organization has been described by a number of commentators, see, Cappelli, P., *The New Deal at Work: Managing the Market-Driven Workforce.* Boston: Harvard Business School Press, 1999.

10. Much of my thinking about individual autonomy comes from Jung's beliefs on the subject of the individual and the journey they take. Jung's concept of individuation is described by Edward Edinger in *The Creation of the Consciousness: Jung's Myth of Modern Man.* Toronto: Inner City Books, 1984. For the original see Jung's psychological factors in "Human Behavior, The Structure and Dynamics of the Psyche," *The Collected Works,* Vol. 8, Princeton: Princeton University Press, 1953–79. My own thinking has been enormously enriched by the work of the Jungian analyst James Hollis. All of his books bring insight to Jung's work, but perhaps most thought provoking is *Swamplands of the Soul: New Life in Dismal Places.* Toronto: Inner City Books, 1996. I used the metaphor of the "swamplands" to describe aspects of Nina's story. James Hillman has also acutely observed the world through the Jungian lens, see e.g., *The Soul's Code.* New York: Random House, 1996. The political philosopher, Anthony Giddens, has made a connection between Jung, and autonomy and democracy, from the perspective of modern relationships, in *The Transformation of Intimacy: Sexuality, Love and Eroticism in modern societies.* Stanford: Stanford University Press, 1992.

11. See Schumpeter, J., *Capitalism, Socialism and Democracy.* London: Allen and Unwin, 1976.

12. See Mill, J.S., "Considerations on Representative Government" in Acton, H.B. (ed.), *Utilitarianism, Liberty, and Representative Government.* London: Dent, 1951.

13. The concept of "rights" and "duties" has been a central aspect of the debate on the nature of democracy. See, for example, the debate in Burnheim, J., *Is Democracy Possible?* Cambridge: Polity Press, 1985.

14. There is a growing literature on accountabilities and obligations. For an overview of the foundational issues, see e.g. Etzioni, A., "The Responsive Community: A Communitarian Perspective," *American Sociological Review,* 61 (1996): 1–11.

15. We return at length to this issue of accountabilities and obligations later in the book. Much of my thinking on the topic evolved from interacting with the companies of the three citizens and from scholarly work on the nature of the relationship between individuals in organizations, see e.g. Burt, R.S., *Structural Holes: The Social Structure of Competition.* Cambridge, MA: Harvard University Press, 1992; Coleman, J.S., *Foundations of Social Theory Cambridge,* MA: Harvard University Press, 1990; and Granovetter, M.S., "Economic Action and Social Structure: The Problem of Embeddedness," *American Journal of Sociology,* 1985, 91 (1985): 481–510.

CHAPTER 46

The Path to Democracy and Sharing

Mike Boon

CEO, Vulindlela Network

Imagine you are lying on your deathbed. Gathered round are your family and your close friends. As you look around, you see the people whom you love and cherish most in life. Everything fades for a moment. The voices seem to echo. But there is one voice you can hear quite clearly. It has been asking questions persistently. It is your own voice.

Have you lived your life well? Have you lived life joyfully and given love freely? Have you come to the end of your life knowing what it is to be truly human?

What would your answers be? Do you give love—or is that too "soft" a question to be asking a disciplined and controlled pragmatist? Do you really know the joy of interacting with people who are close to you, and the joy of knowing they care about you?

Often we consciously or unconsciously hide behind a veneer of professionalism and intellect. We so easily fall into the trap of building great screens that shut out real contact with people. We can be wary of exposing ourselves to others, fearing the pain and anguish that deep and complete vulnerability can bring. So we mostly don't allow it, and prefer to bluff and bluster our way through life, positioning ourself as "the real success story," "the real professional everyone looks up to." But do people really look up to us and admire us, or are they merely flirting with the materialism we perhaps represent? After all, if one has managed to accumulate wealth, it is regarded as something to be proud of. Surely this is not all there is to life?

A short while ago, I had a discussion with a business associate. He is immensely successful and wealthy and involved in a range of businesses. He owns properties around the world, a yacht in the Mediterranean, a villa in Portugal, and another in France. Yet he is lonely. He feels that his life has no meaning. More than anything in the world, he wants to meet a special person who will make him feel happy and fulfilled. He wants to be married and have children, and have the time to develop deep and close friendships.

Source: The Path to Democracy and Sharing. Pp. 101–113 in *The African Way: The Power of Interactive Leadership*, by Michael Boon. Zebra Press & Oshun Books, a division of Random House Struik.

Sadly he is now suspicious that any potential partner is only interested in his wealth. But all his searching is outside of himself. He has not examined who he is to find the root cause of his unhappiness. He has lost touch with his own humanity. He uses all the right phrases, talks about care and family and emotion, but somehow it is all empty, and anyone listening to him will quickly sense this.

There is a way for him to experience real life, but this involves becoming vulnerable and cracking the veneer of being an efficient machine. He needs to share his loneliness with, among others, the people he works with and leads. Every manager and leader will be thinking to himself that this situation is in no way similar to his own. After all, he is not lonely—he is surrounded by lots of people who respect him. Dig deeper. How do your staff feel? How many of them can you honestly say would come to you with their deepest feelings? Perhaps this will tell you whether you are lonely or not.

In a survey in which directors and senior managers were asked whether or not they, as leaders, were lonely, 70 percent said they were. However, it is necessary to distinguish between the loneliness of making leadership decisions and loneliness caused by purposeful isolation from colleagues or community. Why are people lonely when they are surrounded by capable professionals? There may be several reasons, but one is almost certainly because they have lost the ability to share. Many of us no longer know how to share, because in Western culture vulnerability has come to mean weakness. Therefore managers often pursue and laud "rugged individuality."

Sharing involves trust, respect and honesty, and it presupposes that these values are in place in a viable workplace community.

Many leaders are lonely because they do not share anything, including leadership. For various reasons, they believe that, as the leader, they will make the best decisions. This may be true for purely professional issues, although even that could be argued. However, it does not hold for issues related to values. No person is capable of routinely responding to value challenges in the same way as a group would respond to them. For this reason, if the leader persists in taking value-related decisions alone, he will gradually alienate himself from the group—not because the group believes him to be bad, but because they see him as separate from and not representative of themselves.

It is fascinating to analyse and correct problems relating to values or, rather, as I prefer to put it, *value infringement*.

For all these reasons, it is important to be in a team with other people who share the same values. As a result, trust is built and decisions are easier to make. Everyone works and lives according to the same agenda. Even leaders can be human and share the concerns and pressures of life and leadership. But, more importantly, they can give those who follow the joy of discovering intrinsic capabilities and leadership potential within themselves.

How then can leaders go about creating values and becoming part of a noble and caring community without imposing a predetermined set of values on the team?

Interactive Forums— The *Umhlangano*

Before any system can be put into place, there has to be a structure through which it can be implemented. Discussion groups or "interactive forums" must be formed (I call these *umhlanganos*),[1] which gather and group departments or sections that work together. These groups, which in practice are natural work teams, involve everyone in the department, including managers and union officials. No one is exempt and nothing has greater priority. During these discussions, rank or positional power has to be set aside. All the participants must be asked to regard each other simply as human beings who bare their humanity and listen to each other with dignity.

In the past, a suit and tie was often regarded as authority, and authority meant trouble for the lower ranks. Try to find ways of breaking down this conditioning and the perception it conveys. Perhaps dressing more informally—especially on *umhlangano* days— and then raising this as a discussion point could help. It is a good idea to use an external facilitator to run at least the first few community forums or *umhlanganos*. This ensures that there will be no positional power at play in the session and that everyone, including the manager, can participate fully in all discussions. This facilitator need not be from outside the company, but could be drawn from an unrelated department. Simply put, you should look for someone who has reasonable facilitation skills and great integrity and maturity, who is respected, productive, and in no way influenced by the agendas and positional power of the group. Once people have attended a few *umhlanganos* and understood the process, the chairperson or facilitator need not be an external one. Facilitators can then be appointed by the members of that team. However, chairing or facilitating *umhlangano* sessions is not easy and, until the process is well entrenched, a suitably trained and strong external individual should remain in place.

The *umhlangano* is a community gathering, so its participants can have a lot of fun. But it is also a place where they can have deep discussions. More than perhaps anything else it is a mechanism that will drive personal accountability. The subjects for discussion in the initial sessions are issues on which no one person has licence. All human beings have a right to have their say about values. This is a forum in which opinions can be aired. The *umhlangano* can also make decisions. These must be by secret ballot, and achieved through consensus. However, the forum can only make decisions about issues for which it is responsible and accountable. As the upholding of values is something for which everyone is responsible and accountable, the forum can make decisions that affect values. Similarly, the rules of consensus should be determined by the *umhlangano*.

The *umhlangano* should meet for around two hours, once every four to six weeks (and more frequently in the beginning). Through these forums, the entire basis of *ubuntu* will be reflected in your business, perhaps for the first time. Remember: *Umuntu ngumuntu ngabantu* (a person is only a person because of other people). It must be emphasized that there is no rank at this forum—merely a group of human beings. Gradually, based on the clear foundation of shared values, people can be encouraged to raise any issue they like. Where there is a lack of congruence between values and behaviour, the community and each individual is accountable to take action. In accountability terms, doing nothing is doing something, so team members will hold each other accountable for inaction.

For example, a matter in which the strategic direction of the company is questioned could be raised.

Questioning is fine and should be encouraged, and the chief executive officer (CEO) must ensure that answers are forthcoming—even if it is to say the matter is confidential and to explain why this is the case. The forum cannot make decisions regarding company strategy, as it is neither responsible nor accountable for strategic issues. However, if the strategic path conflicts with values, the forum has a right to be directly involved and even to decide against accepting the strategy. Such a session would need to include the management personnel who are accountable for the strategy.

An example outside of the African environment was the United States's policy of involvement in Vietnam. The decision of the United States government (the national CEO and his management) to get involved in Vietnam conflicted with the values of the American people, who then had an ethical right to change the strategy. Protest and mass action eventually forced the government to listen to the people (the *umhlangano),* and to withdraw from Vietnam. The same can be said of the United States–led war in Iraq. The American people were led (by their CEO) to believe that they were in serious danger from Iraqi "weapons of mass destruction." When it was discovered that this was a fabrication, the people, initially fully supportive of their CEO, became divided, until eventually it was not a matter of whether to withdraw, but how to do so. The CEO statistically became "the most unpopular president in United States history."

But let's return to the *umhlangano.* It is important to make a few cultural and historical observations about an *umhlangano.* The system is based on the traditional concepts of *amandla* (ordinary strength or power) and *ibandla* (the strength that comes from many people). Traditionally, it was the *ibandla* that guided the king. It gave him the opportunity to read the consensus of his people.

The opposite of an *umhlangano* is an *umbango.*[2] In an *umhlangano,* maximum positive criticism and creative energy are generated. In the *umbango,* individuals criticize negatively to achieve their own ends—perhaps with the ultimate aim of dethroning the leader. In an *umhlangano,* criticism is voiced to strengthen the leader and one another. There is a very fine line between the two concepts. South Africans, in particular, because of relatively recent history, tend to have difficulty differentiating between the two. In the *umbango,* one argues for position; in the *umhlangano,* one argues to build and strengthen what is being created.

Various ways in which the *umbango* gains strength is by nullifying positive arguments, refusing to participate, and intimidating and undermining anyone whose thrust is towards openness and togetherness. This is achieved by creating subversive dissension and fear, by isolating the leaders of the positive thrust and attempting to discredit them. An effort is made to position the leaders as the enemies of the people.

In the past, one would often hear the word *impimpi*.[3] Roughly translated, this means "sell-out." It was and is sometimes still used to stop people from participating openly with one another and, more particularly, with management. In this way, one shifts from an *umhlangano* to an *umbango*. Forcing the openness of all procedures and discussions works directly against the *umbango*. Openness works against politicking and the formation of camps. In an open environment, the *umbango* will die.

Democratic Value Creation and First Steps Towards Starting a New *Umhlangano*

If we believe in democracy—the true spirit of democracy—then we should, of course, have no problem with democratic value creation. However, many businesses do not necessarily see the correlation between democratic principles, community and business. "Democracy in business?" many people will ask, and say, "Sure, as long as it's controlled!"

It is ironic that people who decry autocracy in government and go to extreme lengths to ensure that government is democratic and open, given half a chance, become absolute autocrats in business or the running of an organization.

If one believes that there are certain universal truths or principles that are core to all humanity, you will have no difficulty pursuing democratic value creation. It involves a process of questioning, discussion and voting on values. The questioning is not as simple as it sounds. Without trust, people will be suspicious of the motive behind the questions, and will not necessarily speak out. Patience and integrity must prevail, and, as people learn to trust the leader, they will open up and begin to participate.

But how does one go about democratically creating values? The first question from the facilitator to the

umhlangano participants is simple: What values are really important to you as an individual? Or, phrased differently: By what rules do you govern your life?

Encourage participants simply to call out words. No discussion should occur at this stage. Write down every word or phrase that is called out. From time to time, throw in your own words. Check whether the group accepts them and keep urging the group for more. Once participants appear to have exhausted their own list, let them go over it and check whether there are other values they would like to add. Don't rush. Bear in mind they are likely to have given you values, principles and behaviours. Don't intellectualize—simply write them down.

Now start with the first value on the list, initiate a discussion on what this value means to the group (see "Narrowing the Grey," p. 584). At the end of the discussion, everyone will have a clear understanding of what the particular value means to the group. If the culture of your organization is rather formal, vote (in secret) on whether the value should be accepted or not. You will have to discuss exactly what constitutes the motion being carried—perhaps 90 per cent of those present, or even more—before you vote. Use consensus rather than a simple majority for this crucial step in deciding on values. Once consensus is fully understood by everyone, you will not even need to vote, but this will take time and trust. Consensus is a reflection of the general leaning towards decisions and will meet with little resistance. If your culture is less formal, you may be able to dispense with the voting and use a sense of consensus alone. The decision should feel right to everyone present—even those who disagree. If it doesn't, people will complain loudly.

If the value is accepted, write it up on a separate overhead or flip chart for everyone to see. Now do the same for the next value. Start the discussion. Repeat this until every original word raised by the group has been covered. This process may take an entire session, or possibly several sessions, but at the end you will have developed a list of values the group believes are really important to them as individuals. Leaders, of course, are a part of that group and share in the process.

Examples of the types of values that may be important to people and that are frequently raised are shown in Table 46.1.

Now that the group has created a list of values, you need to ensure that the company combines its lists of

Table 46.1 Values		
English	*Sotho*	*Xhosa*
Care	Tsotello kappa khathallo	Ukukhathala
Understanding/Good interaction	Kutlwisisano	Ukuva/ukulandlela
Respect	Hlompho	Ukuhlonipha
Pride in what we do	Ho ikhantsha ka seo re se etsang	Ukuzingca
Openness	Ho Buleha	Ukuthetha phandle
Listen and hear	Ho utlwella le ho utlwa	Mamela yiva
Loyalty	Botshepehi	Thembeka
Proactive	Ho etsa	Ukunceda
Natural drive	Thahasello ya ho atamela	Ukufunda amanye to
Draw closer to other cultures	Haufi meetlo emeng	Amasiko
We are "of Africa"	Re ba Afrika	Singa ma-Afrika
Trust	Tshepa	Ukuthemba
Honesty	Botshepehi	Ukunyaniseka
No "them and us"	Re khannwa ke mphato eseng ("bona" le "rona")	Sibanye

values with this new list of values. Each value that the company raises must be put through the same process of scrutiny and discussion. You need to end up with only one list that is accepted by the entire company or community.

There is no reason for the company not to be in absolute agreement with the values listed. After all, the leadership participated in the creation process and had ample opportunity to argue for or against particular values. The process has, in fact, reduced conflict and brought various players closer together. It has done away with "them and us" and created a "we." If the value is on the list, it is because the majority of people believe it should be. And that's consensus democracy!

Through this shared value-creation exercise, everyone—including management, union and staff-has effectively agreed to buy into and uphold the values. Make sure this is stated categorically and that everyone agrees. Before we continue, we need to cover value negotiation, or "narrowing the grey."

Narrowing the Grey

When discussing values, I sometimes make use of a very simple model. From a leadership perspective it may be useful to offer this model as a basis of discussion around values. There are three areas one needs to be aware of when dealing with values (see Figure 46.1). The objective of leadership is to narrow the grey area or, if you prefer, to reduce dissonance. A cohesive team experiences minor dissonance in the shared values of the team. They experience different attitudes, but not different values.

That Which Is "Right"

The centre of the model—the core—is the area of value assessment that the individual regards as "right." There is a complete and unbending understanding of the value at stake, and any behaviour contravening this

Figure 46.1 Values Model

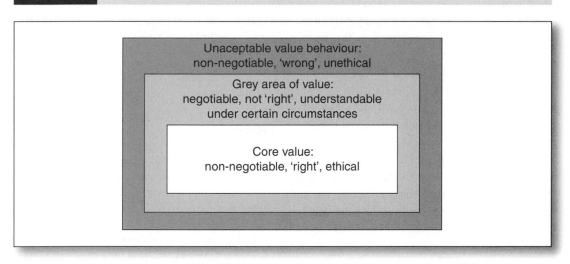

will be considered unethical. For example, a tenet of the value "honesty" is that one never steals. If you are among colleagues and you see a R100 note lying under someone's chair, you don't keep it, you hold it up and ask who has lost some money. This behaviour is considered "right" and displays the individual's understanding of the value "honesty."

That Which Is Negotiable

Surrounding the core is a grey "negotiable" area. Here, the value is constantly tested against a subliminal hierarchy of personal values. For example, although it was not right for the man to steal, he was stealing food for his starving children. In this instance the value of "care" for the children has greater weight than the value of "honesty." It doesn't make the theft honest, but it does make it understandable. Take care to let this discussion of grey areas focus on actual behaviours and not on intellectual concepts.

That Which Is "Wrong"

The third and final band is behaviour that the individual simply considers "wrong." This area represents the flip side of the core value area. An example of unacceptable or "wrong" behaviour may be: Someone has a

good job and lives well. However, he took a colleague's handbag and stole all her money. This person's behaviour is wrong, dishonest and not negotiable. Once again, ensure that the discussion focuses clearly on behaviours, not only on intellectual concepts.

Do not expect the value-creation exercise to be plain sailing. There will be disagreement, and this should be encouraged. At first, people in the team may try to avoid exposing themselves through discussion. But when they realize the process will continue regardless, they will, at the very least, participate in deciding whether or not to adopt a value. Indeed, if a secret ballot is used, the chairperson, with witnesses, must count the votes in full view of everyone. If he or she comes across a spoilt ballot, the counting must be stopped immediately and the whole voting process repeated. In other words, everyone in the *umhlangano* must vote either for or against an issue—this forces accountability. No one can be a spectator or a passenger in such a critical exercise.

The process is as important as the outcome. The group as a whole is "narrowing the grey," or gaining a clear understanding of what each value means to the group. The group determines each value's boundaries and defines acceptable and unacceptable behaviour regarding this value. Maximum discussion and participation is therefore crucial.

You may notice that people will attempt to gauge what the popular leaders think before committing themselves. It is important to keep pointing out that this is *ubuntu* at work. If an individual—be it the CEO or the most charismatic leader in the group—is followed blindly, the individuals in the community are not deciding for, and therefore leading, themselves. They are subtly avoiding their own accountability. Don't allow the process to be hijacked. If it is, all that happens is that centralized leadership shifts from the leader to another individual, and not to the group and each individual in it. The people will, in many instances, consciously or unconsciously, be trying to shift centralized leadership to another individual. Resist this by persuasively pointing out what is happening. I often mention to groups that we are in the process of empowering the group, and pursuing something the group wants. An individual or a few representatives cannot be allowed to take on that power. They are not the group, and the individuals must accept their accountability and responsibility.

There will probably be several sessions in which values will need to be discussed. Later discussions should be a lot easier than the first session, and people should be focused only on the values and what they mean. The process of narrowing the grey, in particular, should test each individual's core beliefs and paradigms. They will

have exposed themselves as individuals and become vulnerable, but you will start to notice a drawing together of the entire group. This gradual formation of a new, complete team, a new community with shared values created by all and agreed to by consensus has, in fact, simultaneously been creating trust.

Notes

1. *Umhlangano* (Nguni) = discussion/interaction.

2. This means a vendetta, or a family or tribal feud. It can even mean an instrument used to achieve witchcraft. However one defines it, there is no doubt that the gathering is negative, subversive and destructive.

3. The word *impimpi* originated in the early settler days, when white landowners ran large black labour forces. They often wanted to know what was going on among the ranks, and they would pay a particular individual, perhaps in brandy, to inform them. They would call this person their "pimp." A spy who was controlled by some form of blackmail became known as an *impimpi*. The term, therefore, is very derogatory and fear-laden. In later years, suspected *impimpis* were often necklaced or killed in barbarous ways.

PART VIII

New Responsibilities of Organizational Leadership

Social Activism

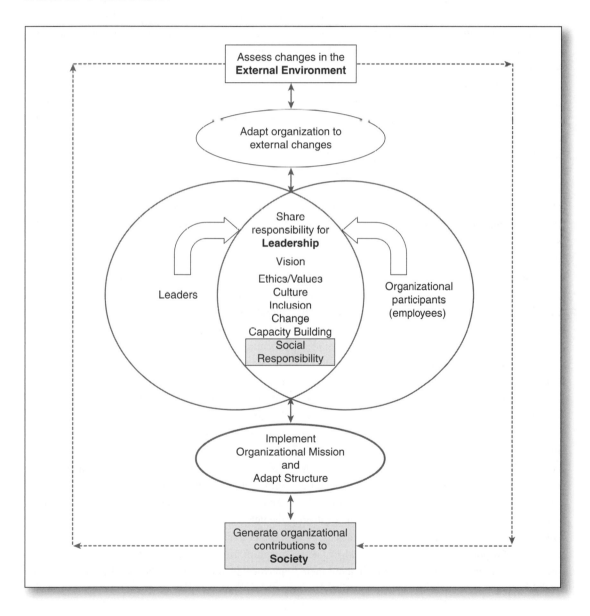

Overview

Organizations may be in the most advantageous position to facilitate unprecedented advances for society and solve highly complex problems based on their capacity to mobilize people, technology, and financial resources across communities and nations. Many organizational leaders and participants see their viability as inextricably linked to the viability of society. A steadily growing number of leaders and participants are incorporating social issues and social activism as important components of their organizational vision, mission, and values.

In the previous section, Manville and Ober proposed a model for building a community of citizens inside the organization. In this section, Sandra Waddock (Chapter 47) offers a framework for developing corporations, as entities, into fully integrated citizens of society. She situates corporations in an interdependent system where their visions, missions, values, and actions are linked to actors and institutions in the political, social, and ecological spheres. Organizations that aspire to become *leading* corporate citizens are expected to do far more than acknowledge discretionary responsibilities associated with doing social good. Waddock recommends that they pay attention to how fundamental responsibilities—some of which are those traditionally assumed by governments, such as labor and human rights, environmental sustainability, and anticorruption measures—are being met in all of the company's strategies and operating practices, as well as to the outcomes and implications of corporate activities.

Hannah Clark (Chapter 48) describes a new genre of companies called B Corporations—the B stands for "beneficial." To become a certified B Corporation, Clark explains that a company must amend its articles of incorporation to state that its leaders must consider the interests of employees, the community, and the environment instead of worrying solely about shareholders. This change allows companies to define themselves as socially responsible to consumers and investors and commit a certain percentage of the company's profits to social causes without being concerned that their values will be compromised by external investors or shareholders.

Since B Corporations are on the cutting edge of new organizational forms, there is no research about them and there are no legal challenges to their practices. Even

so, these pioneering companies represent a bold new experiment in corporate responsibility.

Frank Den Hond and Frank De Bakker (Chapter 49) look at the ideological influences of activist groups, such as the anti-sweatshop movement, on corporate social change activities. They argue that ideology (a shared worldview) matters in how activist groups seek to change the nature and level of corporate social change activities. Since the 1990s, activist groups have challenged companies directly rather than using indirect public policy routes. Moderate activists see companies as part of the problem but also believe they can be part of the solution, whereas radical activist groups do not see companies as part of the solution. These perspectives result in different tactics for influencing corporate social change. Moderate groups may use tactics such as petitions, marches, or boycotts/buycotts. Radical groups may engage in lawsuits, blocking entry gates, sabotage, or Internet activism (hacktivism). Den Hond and De Bakker suggest that the practical implications of their study for activists involve spending time and effort educating their constituencies on how to become effective instruments for change. Practical implications for companies entail taking stock of activist groups' ideological positions to understand the range of tactics they might employ.

In contrast to the actions of social movement groups to pressure companies into enacting social change, K. M. Thiagarajan (Chapter 50) presents a poignant case that illustrates the power of "doing well while doing good." He describes his efforts to rejuvenate the rural branches of a commercial bank in India by establishing a microcredit program for women in local villages. The venture began in the for-profit setting of a bank and developed into a nonprofit program within the bank. The Bank of Madura (now ICICI Bank) was losing money in its rural branches in poor villages. Thiagarajan decided to change the incentive system for attracting bank managers to rural branches by increasing their pay to the same level as urban managers and offering them the opportunity to initiate a social change program in the villages. He used the appeal of a powerful mission (also described in Part IV) to bring managers into the program. The bank managers recruited women into the microcredit program and helped them organize into self-help groups (SHGs). These managers provided women with the skills they needed to participate in the program.

Through the support of their SHGs, the village women taught other women the skills they learned and subsequently changed each other in ways that were unimaginable at the beginning of their venture. The bank's rural branches came alive and flourished, along with the bank managers. The rural branches began to overflow with village women entrepreneurs, who repaid their loans at impeccable rates.

The issues that all of the authors raise in this section go to the core of social activism on the part of organizations. If new era organizations want to become leading corporate citizens, leaders and members will need to become "transforming" in the sense that James MacGregor Burns intended originally when he applied this concept to the political and social movement context.[1] He stresses that leaders who aspire to be truly transforming must generate collective purpose and transforming processes that are ultimately linked to social change.[2] Based on these criteria, there are still questions that organizations must address. In these unstable economic times, can organizational leaders and members, especially in businesses, engage in true social change and sustain economic viability? Can their efforts make a *real* difference in the well-being of society?

Notes

1. See Chapter 6, "Transforming Leadership," by James MacGregor Burns, in Part II of this text.

2. Ibid.

CHAPTER 47

Leading Corporate Citizenship

Sandra A. Waddock

Boston College

I want to challenge you to join me in taking our relationship to a still higher level. I propose that you [corporate leaders] . . . and we, the United Nations, initiate a global compact of shared values and principles, which will give a human face to the global market.

Globalization is a fact of life. But I believe we have underestimated its fragility. The problem is this. The spread of markets outpaces the ability of societies and their political systems to adjust to them, let alone to guide the course they take. History teaches us that such an imbalance between the economic, social and political realms can never be sustained for very long. . . .

We have to choose between a global market driven only by calculations of short-term profit, and one which has a human face. Between a world which condemns a quarter of the human race to starvation and squalor, and one which offers everyone at least a chance of prosperity, in a healthy environment. Between a selfish free-for-all in which we ignore the fate of the losers, and a culture in which the strong and successful accept their responsibilities, showing global vision and leadership.

—Kofi Annan, former secretary-general of the
United Nations,[1] in a speech at the World Economic Forum, 1999

Corporations: Citizens of the (Natural and Human) World

Former United Nations secretary-general Kofi Annan's speech, delivered at a meeting of the world's business leaders in Geneva in 1999, sparked a firestorm of interest among executives attending, to the point that the United Nations launched the UN Global Compact as a formal organization two years later in 2001. By 2008, the UN Global Compact was the world's largest corporate citizenship initiative, with more than 5,600 signatories, over 4,300 of which were businesses, including many transnational corporations.[2] Annan's words highlight an important and often forgotten reality: Business is integrally connected to both the social context in which it operates and the natural environment on which we all depend. With his statement, Annan signaled new recognition of an important shift in the long-term relationships that businesses can expect to have with their many constituencies—their stakeholders as well as how they treat the natural environment.[3] As businesses have grown larger and more powerful, their attendant responsibilities to be good corporate citizens wherever they operate have also grown. Indeed, some argue that the rise of the very term *corporate citizenship* since the late 1990s came about in part because some companies in the process of globalization began to assume responsibilities formerly assigned solely to governments.[4] Today, expectations that businesses will play a constructive role in society are further enhanced by worries about global climate change.

Corporate citizenship is an integral part of the whole corporation as it exists in whole communities and whole societies, with whole people operating within. In this sense of wholes within other wholes, corporations are what philosopher Ken Wilber terms *holons*, that is, both wholes in and of themselves and parts of something larger. As holons, companies are embedded in and affect the web of relationships that constitutes societies, just as biological systems are also interrelated webs.[5] In administering some of the responsibilities of citizenship, companies are increasingly finding themselves held accountable for their impacts on society and social rights (e.g., not polluting or otherwise contributing to deteriorating environmental conditions, including global warming), on individual or civil rights (e.g., freedom from abusive working conditions), and on political rights (e.g., being held accountable when participating in countries whose governments do not uphold basic political and individual rights).[6]

The embeddedness of corporations in societies—that is, their existence as socially constructed holons in economic, political, and societal contexts—means that careful attention needs to be given to how they behave. Being or becoming a leading corporate citizen implies that companies must understand their relationships to

both primary and secondary stakeholders in society, must learn to treat those stakeholders as well as the natural environment respectfully, and must understand the global context in which businesses operate. Sustainability depends on these systemic understandings, whether it is the ecological sustainability so in question today according to many environmentalists, the sustainability of the societies and communities in which businesses operate, or the longevity of the business itself.

If we conceive of companies in terms of their relationships to stakeholders and the natural environment, then we come to the following definition of leading corporate citizenship:

> Leading corporate citizens are companies that live up to clear constructive visions and core values consistent with those of the broader societies within which they operate, respect the natural environment, and treat well the entire range of stakeholders who risk capital in, have an interest in, or are linked to the firm through primary and secondary impacts. They operationalize their corporate citizenship in all of their strategies and business practices by developing respectful, mutually beneficial relationships with stakeholders and by working to maximize sustainability of the natural environment. They are transparent about and responsible for their impacts and are willing to be held accountable for them.

Corporate citizenship by this definition involves far more than meeting the discretionary responsibilities associated with philanthropy, volunteerism, community relations, and otherwise doing "social good," which some people think is sufficient[7] and which constitutes corporate *social* responsibility.[8] This broad understanding of citizenship means paying attention to how fundamental responsibilities—some of which are those traditionally assumed by governments, such as labor and human rights, environmental sustainability, and anticorruption measures—are being met in all of the company's strategies and operating practices, as well as to the outcomes and implications of corporate activities. For many companies, it means developing a "lived" set of policies, practices, and programs that help the company achieve its vision and values. The decision to be a *leading* corporate citizen is, of course, still voluntary on the part of companies; however, companies do bear responsibility for the ways in which they treat their stakeholders and nature—and can be judged on their impacts—whether they proactively or interactively assume the role of "good corporate citizen." Furthermore, the imperatives of ecological sustainability, which have become apparent in recent years, mean that few companies or individuals today can afford to ignore the systemic consequences of a production system that is not focused on ecological sustainability as well as responsible practice.

Given the preceding definition of *leading corporate citizens,* let's start with a proposition: The core purposes of the corporation include but go far beyond generating shareholder wealth. Indeed, wealth and profits are simply important byproducts of the firm's efforts to create a product or service for customers that adds enough value that customers are willing to pay more than they would otherwise pay. Value-added goods and services are produced through the good offices of employees, managers, suppliers, and allies, using a wide range of forms of capital. Management thinker Charles Handy puts the issue straightforwardly:

> To turn shareholders' needs into a purpose is to be guilty of a logical confusion, to mistake a necessary condition for a sufficient one. We need to eat to live, food is a necessary condition of life. But if we lived mainly to eat, making food a sufficient or sole purpose of life, we would become gross. The purpose of a business, in other words, is not to make a profit, full stop. It is to make a profit so that the business can do something more or better. That "something" becomes the real justification for the business.[9]

Investments in businesses go way beyond those made by shareholders. Capital does, of course, include the important financial resources supplied by the owners or shareholders. Equally important, capital also encompasses the intellectual and human capital provided by employees, the trust and loyalty of customers that products or services will meet expectations and add value (for which they will pay), and various forms of social capital.

Furthermore, capital includes the infrastructure and social relations supplied by the communities and other levels of government in locations where the company has facilities. It encompasses the natural resources supplied by the ecological environment that go into the production and delivery of goods and services. It includes interdependent relationships developed among its business partners, suppliers and distributors, and it exists in the social contract written or unwritten by a range of local, state, and national governments, which have provided the social—and legal—contract and necessary physical infrastructure on which the firm's existence is premised.

All of these capitals are supplied to the firm by stakeholders. A stakeholder, generally, is any individual or group affected by or that can affect an organization.[10] Companies exist in relationship to and because of their stakeholders. Simply stated, despite the prevailing idea that the purpose of the firm is to maximize shareholder wealth (and though it is absolutely essential that companies do produce wealth to survive), because of their numerous impacts, corporations are considerably more than profit-maximizing efficiency machines. Corporations are inherently and inextricably embedded in a web of relationships with stake-holders that create the very context in which they do business and that enable the enterprise to succeed. Without its core stakeholders and a healthy natural environment, the corporation cannot survive long term, nor can it begin to make a profit, never mind maximize profits. In many ways, the corporation is nothing more and nothing less than its primary relationships. Indeed, recent legal scholarship suggests that there is, in fact, no legally mandated requirement in the United States for firms to "maximize" shareholder wealth, despite the common understanding that has spread widely around the world.[11]

Therefore, we begin with this premise: Profits are essential to corporate success and, indeed, corporate survival. Profits are critical to sustaining democratic capitalism, but they are in fact a byproduct of the many relationships on which a corporation—or any other organization—depends for its legitimacy, power, resources, and various kinds of capital investments. This perspective, which differs from the traditional economics perspective on the firm (which says that the one and only purpose of the firm is to maximize profits or shareholder wealth), is called the *stakeholder capitalism concept of the firm.*

In this stakeholder view, stakeholder relationships and the operating practices (policies, processes, and procedures) that support those relationships are the basis of leading corporate citizenship.[12] Much is being written about global corporate citizenship these days. The neoclassical economics model, which dominates much business thinking, suggests that the corporation should maximize wealth for one set of stakeholders: the owners or shareholders. Conformance to existing law and meeting ethical responsibilities come next, especially in the view of the late economist Milton Friedman, who espoused the neoclassical economics perspective. In his classic article against the concept of social responsibility, entitled "The Social Responsibility of Business Is to Increase Its Profits," Friedman argues that:

> the doctrine of 'social responsibility' is essentially a "collectivist doctrine" that differs only in that it asserts collectivist ends are possible without collectivist means. Furthermore, he believes social responsibility is a "fundamentally subversive doctrine" because in a free society, business has only one social responsibility—to use its resources and engage in activities designed to increase its profits so long as it stays within the rules of the game.[13]

The basis for Friedman's assertion, echoed by other economists, that shareholders are the only important stakeholder is that owners have taken a risk with their investments in the firm and are therefore owed a profit. But this view is too constricted to be useful in a world that increasingly recognizes that other stakeholders are equally important to the survival and success of the firm and that they too make significant investments in the welfare of the firm.

Stakes and Stakeholders

Let's start this journey into leading corporate citizenship by considering the definition of a *stake* and therefore a *stakeholder* in more detail. The word *stake* can have one of three different general meanings, each representing a different type of relationship between the stakeholder and the entity in which a stake exists (see Table 47.1). First, a stake is a claim of some sort, for example, a claim of ownership based on a set of expectations related to principles of ethics, such as legal or moral rights, justice or fairness, the greatest good for the greatest number, or the principle of care.

Second, a stake can signify that a stakeholder has made an investment, thereby putting some sort of capital at risk.[14] In this usage, a stake is an interest or share in some enterprise or activity, a prize (as in a horse race or other gamble), or perhaps a grubstake (for which the provider expects a return for the risk taken). Typically, the type of risk under consideration relates specifically to the type of capital invested. Thus, for example, owners invest financial capital in the firm, while communities may invest social capital—or relationships built on trust and association—in the firm's local presence or create infrastructure to support the firm's activities. Employees invest their human capital, their knowledge, and their intellectual energies—all forms of capital—in the firm. Customers invest their trust as part of the firm's franchise and hence their willingness to continue to purchase the goods and services produced by the firm. Suppliers may invest in specific technology, equipment, or infrastructure so that they can enhance their relationship to the firm over time and make the bonds tighter.

Third, the last meaning of *stake* is a bond, such as a tie or tether, something that creates links between two entities, including tangible links that bind the entities together (e.g., contracts, long-term relationships for purchasing supplies), as well as intangible relational links. Intangible bonds can come about because a stakeholder identifies in some way with the organization and therefore feels an association with the organization that potentially creates one of the other types of stakes, a claim or a risk.[15]

Stakeholder Relationships and the Public

Responsibilities of Management

Notice that each of the types of stakes identified in Table 47.1 creates a *relationship* between the stakeholder and the organization in which there is a stake.[16] For example, owners are clearly stakeholders. By making an investment, the stakeholder owner creates a

Table 47.1	The Types of Stakes

Stake as:	Stake Is Based on:
• Claim	• Legal or moral right
	• Consideration of justice/fairness
	• Utility (greatest good for the greatest number)
• Risk 1. Owner 2. Community 3. Employee 4. Customer 5. Supplier	• Investment of capital, including: 1. Financial capital 2. Social/infrastructure capital 3. Knowledge/intellectual/human capital 4. Franchise (trust) capital 5. Technological, infrastructure capital
• Bonds (tether, tie)	• Identification (process)
Each type of stake creates a relationship that, when constructive and positive, is:	
1. Mutual 2. Interactive 3. Consistent over time 4. Interdependent	

relationship with the organization, though as management thinker Charles Handy points out, most shareholders today do exactly that—hold shares—without much real semblance of ownership.[17] Similarly, the stakeholder who puts something at risk for possible benefit through an enterprise creates a relationship with that enterprise, as communities do when they invest in local infrastructure that supports a firm's activities or employees do when they invest their human or intellectual capital in their work. Bonds of identity also create ongoing relationships. The important point, then, is that whichever meaning we use for *stake*, being a stakeholder creates an ongoing and interactive relationship between the stakeholder and the enterprise or activity.[18]

Stakeholder relationships also create a boundary around managerial responsibilities so that corporations are responsible not for all of the problems of society but only for those that they create or those that affect them. Thus, when we think about corporate responsibility, we can think in terms of the public responsibility of managers, which is limited to the areas of primary and

secondary involvement of their enterprises. The principle of public responsibility, which was developed by scholars Lee Preston and James Post, comes about in part because companies are granted permission or charters (literally, incorporation papers) by the states in which they are established and in part as a result of the impacts that companies have on their various stakeholders and the natural environment and for which society wishes to hold them accountable.[19] It is notable that early corporate charters permitted companies to stay in existence only as long as their activities served a social benefit, and there is considerable discussion today about reviving this notion.[20]

The scope of managers' public responsibilities is quite wide given the resources that companies, particularly multinational companies, command; the geographical and product/service scope of many large companies; and the resulting power they hold. According to Preston and Post, management's responsibilities are limited by the organization's primary and secondary involvements (see Figure 47.1). Primary

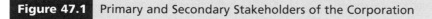

Figure 47.1 Primary and Secondary Stakeholders of the Corporation

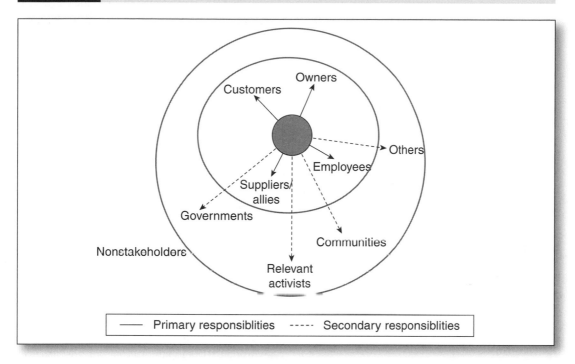

involvement arenas are related to the main business mission and purpose of the firm as it attempts to live out its vision in society. Thus, as Preston and Post state, "Primary involvement relationships, tested and mediated through the market mechanism, are essential to the existence of the organization over time."[21]

Primary involvement arenas are those that affect primary stakeholders, that is, those stakeholders without whom the company cannot stay in business.[22] For most companies, primary stakeholders include owners, customers, employees, suppliers, distributors, and partners. Although some people believe that the environment is a stakeholder, because it supplies the raw materials necessary to the company's existence,[23] we will take the perspective that the environment is not a stakeholder but rather an *essential underpinning* to all human civilization, an underpinning that needs to be healthy for human civilization to survive,[24] that in many instances is treated *as if* it were a stakeholder.[25]

Managerial public responsibilities do not end with primary involvement arenas; they extend also to arenas of secondary involvement, which include those arenas and relationships that affect or are affected by the firm's activities. Secondary stakeholders are those who affect or are affected by the company's activities indirectly or as a byproduct. Secondary stakeholders may not participate in direct transactions with the corporation or be necessary to its survival. Because they can affect the firm or are affected by the firm's activities, it is important that secondary stakeholders' needs and interests be taken into consideration in much the way that the needs and interests of primary stakeholders are.[26] Thus, the governments that create the rules of the game by which companies operate, as well as the communities that supply the local infrastructure on which companies depend, can be considered secondary stakeholders.

Stakeholders interact with—or in the case of primary stakeholders actually constitute—organizations; that is, they are in relationship to an organization or company. For example, activists may attempt to influence corporate environmental policy but may not be in a position to put the company out of business; thus, they are secondary stakeholders. Similarly, towns and cities located downstream from a company may feel the impact of its polluting a river that flows through them and thus are secondary stakeholders. Firms ignore these impacts at their peril, because secondary stakeholders can be demanding or dangerous when their needs are urgent; when, for a variety of reasons, they have power; or, if they are inactive, when they are awakened into action.[27]

Companies are typically started and financed by owners, who in the current thinking of many business leaders are considered the dominant (and sometimes only important) stakeholder. Other stakeholders are critical to the success of companies as corporate citizens because they too have placed various forms of their capital at risk, are invested in, or are tied in relationships to companies. For example, *employees* as stakeholders develop, produce, and deliver the company's products and services. A company's existence is also contingent on the goodwill and continued purchases of *customers.* Companies depend on the earth for raw materials (ultimately) and *suppliers and allies or partners,* who produce the raw materials necessary for the company to generate its own goods and services. Relationships with these stakeholder groups constitute any leading corporate citizen's *primary stakeholder relationships.*

There are also *critical secondary stakeholder relationships* without which most companies could not survive. For example, companies rely on *governments*—local, state/provincial, national, and increasingly international— to create rules of society that make trading, economic, and political relationships feasible over time. Corporate citizens rely on their local *communities* for an educated workforce and for the infrastructure that makes production of goods and services possible (e.g., roads, local services, zoning regulations). And there are other critical secondary stakeholders, depending on the particular circumstances of the company and the nature of its business (see Case 1).

Stakeholder Responsibility

Stakeholders also bear responsibility for their actions and impacts on companies, so the interaction is never a one-sided one. Just as we might argue that companies have sometimes unrecognized responsibilities, so too, it is increasingly clear, do the stakeholders who pressure companies for changes. Nongovernmental organizations (NGOs), employees and labor unions, activists and pressure groups, customers, and investors, among the other important stakeholders with which companies must contend, need to behave responsibly

and thoughtfully in their engagements with companies, just as they expect companies to do with them. Ethical practices apply to individuals in all organizations, not just businesses. It is important in a stakeholder engagement that all parties attempt to understand the perspectives, demands, and pressures that the others are facing. Thus, just as companies need to understand the social, human rights, ecological, and related concerns of civil society stakeholders, so too do stakeholders from those spheres need to understand the economic imperatives under which businesses are operating.

Corporate Responsibility and Citizenship

By defining *corporate citizenship* through the lens of a company's strategies and operating practices, we are taking a practice-based stakeholder view of the corporation, which significantly broadens understanding of the stakeholders to whom a firm is accountable. This view moves the conversation directly toward the quality and nature of the relationships that companies develop with stakeholders and an assessment of the impacts of corporate activities on those stakeholders, as well as on the natural environment, whose interests are frequently represented by environmental activists, though it is not itself a stakeholder.[28] Such a perspective moves our thinking away from a largely descriptive and even instrumental (or usefulness) perspective on stakeholder relationships. We move, in this book, toward a normative model, that is, a model of how, in the best of worlds, stakeholder relationships and company practices *ought* to be, as the opening quotation by Kofi Annan, former secretary-general of the United Nations, suggests.[29]

As noted, the UN Global Compact is the world's largest corporate citizenship initiative, with more than 5,600 members, 4,300 of which are corporations.[30] On its Web site, the Global Compact makes the case that "Business, trade and investment are essential pillars for prosperity and peace. But in many areas, business is too often linked with serious dilemmas—for example, exploitative practices, corruption, income inequality, and barriers that discourage innovation and entrepreneurship. Responsible business practices can in many ways build trust and social capital, contributing to broad-based development and sustainable markets."[31]

CASE 1. BOSS HOG

With a billion dollar business, North Carolina is the United States' number two producer of hogs. Swine production has experienced explosive growth under the stimulus of franchises offered by large meat-processing corporations, like Murphy Family Farms, which give growers a set price for the output of their mass production operations. Many of the estimated 10 million porkers who populate North Carolina's eastern lowland counties spend their lives confined to pens in huge, high-tech facilities that deliver food to the front and dispose of waste at the rear via conveyor belts. Because a hog produces four times as much waste as a human being, one corporate hog farm can generate a waste stream equivalent to that of a city of 250,000 people. A Web site entitled Hog Watch, posted by the Environmental Defense Fund (EDF), notes that North Carolina's hogs "produce a mind-boggling amount of waste: 19 million tons of feces and urine a year, or over 50,000 tons every single day. That's more waste in one year than the entire human population of Charlotte, North Carolina, produces in 58 years! To make matters worse, almost all of North Carolina's hogs are concentrated in the eastern coastal plain, an economically important and ecologically sensitive network of wetlands, rivers, and coastline." The traditional method for dealing with this prodigious outflow has been to dig a waste lagoon, followed by spraying the liquefied waste on nearby fields as an organic fertilizer.

By the mid-1990s, the growth of these swine factories in North Carolina was generating a political backlash against the externalities imposed on neighboring communities by corporate hog farm practices. Beyond the obvious "public bad" of a downwind stench and the incremental impact of acid rain from evaporating ammonia, the waste lagoon and field spray system create a nitrogen-rich effluent carried by rain into nearby streams. Excessive nitrogen in the streams feeds the bloom of algae, turning the streams emerald green. When this algae collects in wetlands near the ocean, it dies and sinks to the bottom. Bacteria, feeding on the dead algae, rob the water of oxygen, causing periodic fish kills near fishing and tourist areas. The failure of one industry to recognize and internalize its externality costs imposes an economic burden on other industries, while also negatively impacting society and the ecological system.

In the summer of 1995, public concern about the negative environmental impacts of corporate pig farming reached new heights in the soggy, smelly aftermath of Hurricane Floyd. Torrential rains in June swelled the state's more than 3,600 waste lagoons to near overflowing, weakening their retaining walls and threatening a deluge of liquid waste on downstream fisheries and communities. Many hog farmers illegally drained excess lagoon waste into streams and swamps to prevent a breach in their dikes. In the end, Hurricane Floyd washed out 50 waste lagoons and drowned more than 30,000 hogs. Defenders of corporate hog farm practices sought to divert public blame and political retribution by claiming that this environmental calamity was an act of God. A critic in the state legislature countered that this was a sign from God that conventional methods for dealing with the industry's societal mess were inadequate and had to change.

State politicians, previously concerned with promoting economic development and highly sensitive to the political clout and campaign contributions of "Boss Hog," responded to public pressure for increased regulatory controls and oversight In 1997, the general assembly imposed a temporary moratorium on new hog farms and stepped up regulatory oversight of swine operations. In 1999, Governor Jim Hunt decreed that existing waste lagoons must be phased out over 10 years. The following year, the Democratic state attorney general Mike Easley, in charge of the regulatory crackdown, ran for governor on a platform calling for more balance between the push for economic growth and the pull

(Continued)

(Continued)

for corporate accountability and environmental sustainability. In 2003, Easley established a successful moratorium on the construction of new hog farms in eastern North Carolina. By 2007, North Carolina had become the first state in the United States to pass a law banning new construction or expansion of lagoons or sprayfields in a bill entitled the Swine Farm Environmental Performance Standards Act. The search is on for a new, more sustainable swine waste processing technology, at an estimated cost to taxpayers and hog farmers of at least $400 million. The EDF has conducted a six-year study to evaluate five new technologies with less problematic ecological impacts. One of the most promising approaches is a bacterium that reduces the waste to amino acids that can be reconstituted as animal feed. In the end, the solution to this problem will be political rather than scientific. The EDF and a coalition of farmers reached an unprecedented agreement in 2007 to work together to implement some of the newer technologies and demonstrate a both/and solution to hog farming, in which farmers can still be profitable yet cause much less environmental damage.

Some have called on the government to promote a "systems solution" by creating a market for the processed swine waste, whether as compost, animal feed, or crab bait. This solution would give farmers some added income to cover the higher cost of managing manure. Many hog farmers have borrowed heavily to finance expansion at a time when overproduction has driven the price of pork bellies below the break-even point for many producers. A more sustainable industry may also be a smaller industry, with limits to growth to accompany limits on waste.

Discussion Questions

1. Take the perspective of different actors in this situation (e.g., farmers, local communities downriver and downwind of the hog farms, politicians, customers). How would being in these different situations shift your perspective on the viability and importance of keeping local pig farms operating?

2. What would be the best solution to this situation from each stakeholder's perspective? How can an overall solution be reached?

Sources: Jerry Calton, University of Hawaii, Hilo. This case is based on the *Raleigh News-Observer* investigative series entitled "Boss Hog," which won the 1996 Pulitzer Prize for public service journalism. For an in-depth look at this messy issue, go to http://www.nando.net/sproject/hogs. See also the Environmental Defense Fund, "Hog Watch," http://www.environmentaldefense.org/system/templates/page/subissue.cfm?subissue=10 (accessed March 16, 2004); North Carolina and the Global Economy, "History of North Carolina Hog Farming," http://www.duke.edu/web/mms190/hogfarming/ (accessed March 5, 2008); Environmental Defense Fund, North Carolina, 2007 Swine Farm Environmental Performance Standards Act http://www.edf.org/documents/6979_NC_Swine_Performance_Act.pdf (accessed March 5, 2008); "Cleaning Up Hog Waste in North Carolina," September 2007 Update, http://www.edf.org/page.cfm?tagID=68 (accessed March 5, 2008).

There has been a virtual explosion of interest in the issue of corporate citizenship and corporate responsibility since the mid-1990s. The growing global membership of the UN Global Compact attests to this growing interest. Increasing attention to issues of climate change and sustainability have only heightened the understanding of business's interdependence with the rest of society, its stakeholders, and the natural environment.

Another important initiative involves the chief executive officers of 200 of the world's largest companies, who formed the World Business Council for Sustainable Development (WBCSD), with members from some

35 countries representing 20 different industries. The WBCSD "provides a platform for companies to explore sustainable development, share knowledge, experiences and best practices, and to advocate business positions on these issues in a variety of forums, working with governments, non-governmental and intergovernmental organizations."[32] These organizations are representative of a wide range of relatively new businesses and multistakeholder associations that attempt to bring stakeholder engagement and dialogue, sustainability, and responsibility to the fore.

In other words, responsible leaders and managers, it has become clear, cannot operate blindly with respect to the impacts that their actions have on societies, on any and all of their stakeholders, or on the natural environment, especially if they hope to do well over the long term. Gaining the respect and commitment of employees, customers, suppliers, communities, and relevant government officials, as well as owners, is essential to productivity and performance. Because corporations are part of and interdependent with the communities and societies in which they operate, they need to engage actively with their stakeholders. Maintaining positive stakeholder relationships involves establishing constructive and positive relationships with them, as well as being constantly aware of both the status and the health of each stakeholder group. These relationships, then, are the essence of corporate citizenship.

Stakeholder Relationship Management

Respect for others is at the heart of good stakeholder relations. Although it is frequently true that companies have a great deal of power because they command significant resources, they also need to recognize the importance of maintaining good relationships with their stakeholders to experience outstanding long-term performance. Recent research, for example, shows that when companies score highly in *Fortune* magazine's reputational ratings, they are also consistently high performers with respect to their primary stakeholders.[33] Furthermore, companies that are responsible also appear to perform at least as well financially, with the possibility—when ethics and stakeholder relationships are added—of creating a virtuous circle.[34] That is,

companies that do well financially also appear to do well with respect to corporate citizenship, and vice versa.

Companies' stakeholder relationships can evolve in one of three ways: reactively, proactively, or interactively.[35] Good stakeholder relationships can be sustained only if the company takes an interactive stance.

Reactive Stance

When companies or their managers take a reactive stance, they may not be paying attention very much to what is going on outside the company's boundaries. They may deny their responsibility for establishing and maintaining positive policies toward stakeholders, engage in legal battles to avoid responsibility, or do the bare minimum to meet the letter but not the spirit of the law.[36] Reaction puts the company and its managers on the defensive rather than in a more positive mode. Because managers have failed to anticipate problems from stakeholders, they may find themselves wondering how things evolved in such a negative fashion.

Proactive Stance

Better, but probably still insufficient to establish truly positive stakeholder relationships, is the stance that companies sometimes take when they work proactively to anticipate issues arising from external stakeholders. They may do this by establishing one of any number of what are called boundary-spanning functions to cope with their external relations.

Boundary-spanning functions are those that cross organizational boundaries, either internally or externally, and attempt to develop and maintain relationships with one or more stakeholder groups. For example, modern multinational corporations typically have at least some of the following functions: public affairs, community relations, public relations, media relations, investor relations, employee relations, government relations, lobbyists, union relations, environmental officers, issues management, and, increasingly for corporate responsibility, corporate social responsibility, and corporate citizenship.

Interactive Stance

Even a proactive stance falls short of the ideal unless the company's boundary-spanning functions are managed interactively and with respect for the claims, risks, and bonds that stakeholders have. Because stakeholders exist in relationship to the firm, they are embedded in a network that makes them interdependent for their mutual success in activities in which their interests overlap. Thus, arguably the best stance for showing ongoing respect for the firm's stakeholders is a mutual and interactive one that is consistent over time and that acknowledges both the mutuality of the relationship and the interdependence of the two entities.

Such constructive and positive relationships between organizations and their stakeholders are built on a framework of interaction, mutual respect, and dialogue, as opposed to management or dominance. That is, progressive companies do not attempt to manage or dominate their stakeholders. Rather, they have recognized the importance of engaging with them in a relationship based on respect and dialogue or talking *with* each other in a dialogue rather than talking *at* each other, which is more one-sided. Building this relationship is not a one-time thing but rather an evolving long-term process that requires commitment, energy, a willingness to admit mistakes, and a capacity for both parties to change when necessary. Implicitly, this approach recognizes power on both sides of the conversation—and demands a willingness to acknowledge that mutuality.

Understanding the Spheres of Influence: The Ecological Underpinning

Even at present population levels, nearly a billion people go to bed hungry each night. Yet the soils on which we depend for food are being depleted faster than nature can regenerate them, and one by one the world's once most productive fisheries are collapsing from overuse. Water shortages have become pervasive, not simply from temporary droughts but also from depleted water tables and rivers taxed beyond their ability to regenerate. We hear of communities devastated by the exhaustion of their forests and fisheries and of people much like ourselves discovering that they and their children are being poisoned by chemical and radioactive contamination in the food they eat, the water they drink, and the earth on which they live and play.

As we wait for a technological miracle to resolve these apparent limits on continued economic expansion, some 88 million people are added to the world's population every year. Each new member of the human family aspires to a secure and prosperous share of the planet's dwindling bounty. . . . Bear in mind that population projections are produced by demographers based only on assumptions about fertility rates. They take no account of what the planet can sustain. Given the environmental and social stresses created by current population levels, it is likely that if we do not voluntarily limit our numbers, famine, disease, and social breakdown will do it for us well before another doubling occurs.[37]

Modern business activities occur in an intensely competitive, even hypercompetitive, and relatively newly globalized environment,[38] where issues of ecological sustainability have only relatively recently, if at all, begun to enter most managers' mind-sets. In this environment, change is a constant, and there is ever-increasing pressure for enhanced productivity and performance. For many businesses, growth and efficiency come by way of dog-eat-dog competition in which the winner takes all in terms of market share and supposedly maximized profits for shareholders.

Without diminishing the importance of competition—and competitiveness—for corporate success, we can add another perspective in a both/and rather than either/or logic. Consider that companies operate in a sphere or sector of activities we can call the economic (or market) sphere. This sphere has all of the imperatives of growth, efficiency, productivity, and competition inherent in the current capitalistic paradigm, which—with the fall of communism, the ascendance of developing or emerging nations, and the rapid evolution of e-commerce—now is operating at some level in most free societies in the world. We know, however, that the economic sector cannot operate independently of the rest of society, nor of its ecological underpinning. The economic system is a creature of society and one major sphere of influence.

There is more to society than economics. Living well—that is, living the good life, by almost anyone's definition—has important elements of long-term sustainability with regard to community (the civil society sphere) and ecological (the natural environment sphere) health, and also requires some form of governance, or government (the public policy sphere), to function well. Each of these spheres (which will sometimes be called sectors) intersects and overlaps to some extent with all the others; hence, they must be viewed together as a system, inextricably and unavoidably interwoven. The success of any one of these sectors requires that there be an appropriate balance of power and interests among all of them as well as with the ecological surroundings on which they depend.

To complete this picture and provide for an integrated view of what is frequently called the global village (i.e., the world of communities in which we all live and to which we are all connected), we must deeply understand the critical role of the ecological or natural environment. The ecological environment or sphere forms the essential foundation on which all else rests. Without the diversity inherent in the natural environment, without its sustaining resources (which provide raw materials for production), and without appropriate balance in human activities to protect those natural resources, industry and human society quite literally cannot sustain themselves. In that sense, we are dependent on this foundation of ecology and the web of life that it supports for our very existence.[39] Leading corporate citizenship needs to be understood as a system characterized by ecological interdependence and mutuality among entities operating in the different spheres (see Figure 47.2). The following are definitions of each of the spheres that form a core structure for understanding leading corporate citizenship:

1. The *economic* sphere encompasses the businesses, profit-generating enterprises, and associated supplier/distributor relationships that produce the goods and services in markets on which human civilization today depends.

2. The *political* or *public policy* sphere encompasses government bodies at the local, state, regional, national, and global (international) levels that create the rules by which societies operate and establish what is meant (within and among societies) by the public interest or common good.

3. The *civil society* or civilizing sphere encompasses all other organized forms of activity, such as nongovernmental organizations (NGOs), nonprofit enterprises, schools, religious organizations, political organizations, families, and civic and societal enterprises. This sphere generates the civilizing relationships and sense of community that characterize human society.

4. The *natural* or *ecological environment* underpins and supports all else, providing sources of raw materials for sustaining human civilization and healthy societies. A healthy ecology is essential to the long-term health of all of human civilization.

Understanding how these spheres intersect and influence one another necessitates a brief journey into system thinking, followed by a more in-depth look at the ecological sphere that underpins what we call society.

Systems Thinking: The Need to Integrate the Environment

Western philosophy and Western science underpin the capitalistic economic system in which we live today throughout much of the developed world. Western science, including the social science of economics, tends to approach its subjects by taking them apart and reducing them to their smallest elements—a linear process of atomization or fragmentation. Once the smallest elements or fragments have been understood, the Western approach hopes to reintegrate the subject and thereby figure out how it works as an integrated whole. This approach derives from thinkers like Descartes, is premised on Newtonian physics, and is empiricist in its orientation in that it seeks observable evidence in coming to its conclusions; it tends to assume that linear cause-effect relationships exist and can be explained scientifically.

But this approach, which essentially reduces things to their fundamental parts or atomistic elements, also separates the material elements (body) from nonmaterial aspects of the world like consciousness, emotions, aesthetic appreciation, and spirituality. In simple terms, Western thinking has largely separated and broken into fragmented parts the mind and body, with little mention at all of heart, spirit, community, or meaning, none of which are directly observable. It has, in some respects, done much the same thing to the environment,

Figure 47.2   Spheres of Influence: Economic, Political, Social, Ecological

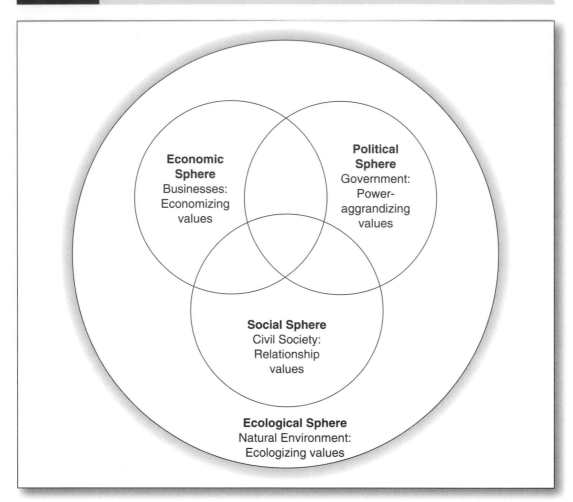

making some people forget (or ignore) our very human interdependency with the never-ending cyclicality of nature, a nonlinear set of relationships. Additionally, technological advances have sometimes made progress seem inevitable, as if a solution to whatever problems arise is always just around the corner. The Western approach has a major drawback in that it tends to lessen people's ability to think about the system as a whole, which also reduces their ability to think about systemic and ecological impacts of business actions.

The fragmented or atomistic approach has come under severe criticism in recent years, for reasons that management thinker Peter Senge highlights (see Note 1). Many people now believe that a more integrated approach, in part ecologically based and in part based

on an integration of mind and body (or material and nonmaterial), better speaks to the long-term needs of human beings and the communities and organizations to which they belong. Such an approach will be particularly critical in the technologically complex and ecologically resource-constrained future, during which issues of climate change and ecological sustainability will very likely begin to dominate many important business decisions, and an understanding of the impacts of one part of the system on the others will be increasingly necessary.

This systemic approach to leading corporate citizenship has been fueled by the development of chaos and complexity theories, which are shedding greater tight on the behavior of complex systems, a set to which human systems clearly belong. It has been further advanced by quantum physics, astrophysics, and biology's new understandings of the nature of matter and the interconnectedness among all living things, as well as between living and nonliving matter.[40]

Such developments have highlighted the need for a more integrated approach to understanding the impact of human beings, and the economic organizations they create, on the world and in particular on the natural environment. One seminal work emphasizing a systems approach to management is Peter Senge's influential book *The Fifth Discipline*.[41] Systems thinking emphasizes wholes or, more accurately, holons—whole/parts—and the interrelationships and interdependencies among

them.[42] A holon is anything that is itself whole and also a part of something else. Thus, for example, a neutron is an entity, a whole, and it is also a part of an atom. A hand is an entity in itself and also a part of an arm, which is part of a body, and so on. In social systems, an individual (whole) is part of a family (whole) that is part of a community, and so on. In organizations, individuals are part of departments, which are units of divisions, which are parts of the corporate entity, which are part of their industry whole, which in turn are parts of society. Holons are integrally linked to the other holons of which they are a part. When something shifts in one holon, the other holons are affected as well because all holons in a given system are interdependent.

NOTE 1: SYSTEMS THINKING

A cloud masses, the sky darkens, leaves twist upward, and we know that it will rain. We also know that after the storm, the runoff will feed into groundwater miles away, and the sky will grow clear by tomorrow. All these events are distant in time and space, and yet they are all connected within the same pattern. Each has an influence on the rest, an influence that is usually hidden from view. You can only understand the system of a rainstorm by contemplating the whole, not any individual part of the pattern.

Business and other human endeavors are also systems. They, too, are bound by invisible fabrics of interrelated actions, which often take years to fully play out their effects on each other. Since we are part of that lacework ourselves, it's doubly hard to see the whole pattern of change. Instead, we tend to focus on isolated parts of the system, and wonder why our deepest problems never seem to get solved.

Source: Peter Senge, *The Fifth Discipline: The Art and Practice of the Learning Organization*, revised edition (New York: Currency Doubleday, 2006), pp. 6–7.

We can think of holons as being nested within each other. Each holon is nested within the next level of holon, assuring their interconnectedness and interdependence. What this nesting means in system terms is that anything that affects one part of the system also affects (at some level and in some way) the whole system. Thinking about systems in this way changes our perspective on the corporation's role in society: No longer can we believe that a company operates independently of its impacts on stakeholders, society, or nature. Because companies are part of the larger holon of the communities, societies, and the global village in which

they are nested, these systems must, by this way of thinking, affect one another reciprocally.

For example, a company might think of itself as separate from a nonprofit organization to which it has given money in the past or from a supplier in its supply chain. When the company withdraws funding—cuts the nonprofit off or decides to use another supplier—the company's leaders may believe that they have ended their impact and responsibility. But the withdrawal of funding creates shifts in the financial stability of the nonprofit or the supplier and has multiple ramifications both within these enterprises and for the clients they serve. And while the company may believe that it is immune from these impacts, there may be subtle shifts in employee morale or important customer relationships that ultimately affect the business. All actions within holons have impacts. Indeed, quantum physicists now tell us that all actions have impacts on the whole system, though they may be subtle, and chaos theorists note that very small changes, or what Senge would call leverage points, can influence large system shifts over time.

The general approach in the Western world to support a given position has been to look for empirical evidence, that is, objective data. Rather than looking at subjectively (or in collective settings, intersubjectively) experienced realities, the typical Western approach is to focus on the material evidence that can be gathered to support the case. But thinkers like Senge (and ecologists like Gladwin, physicists like Capra, and theorists like Wheatley, among many others)[43] propose that it is important to incorporate not only the objective data but also the nonmaterial, that is, the elements of consciousness and conscience, of emotion and feelings, of meaning and meaningfulness, of spirit and indeed of spirituality, if the work of an enterprise is to be approached holistically

Philosopher Ken Wilber has worked to construct an integrative developmental framework for understanding the world's systems.[44] He notes that the Western tradition has focused almost exclusively on objective,

empirically observable elements of individual and collective systems. Wilber generates a two-by-two matrix (see Figure 47.3) in which he places individual and collective exterior elements (i.e., what is objective, observable, measurable) on what he terms the right-hand side. On the left-hand side, he places the individual and collective interior aspects of the world. Complete understanding of any system therefore encompasses (1) interior, or nonobservable, elements that we must ask about, such as thoughts, feelings, meanings, and aesthetic appreciation, and (2) exterior, or observable, elements. Additionally, both interior elements and external elements also contain individual and collective aspects. Wilber names three categories of holons—*I, we,* and *if*—by collapsing both individual and collective exterior elements into the single category of observable behaviors, namely, it/its.

Try to keep in mind that really understanding any system, including business decisions in the context of the organization and its environs, inherently requires dealing with all four ways of viewing the world (interior/individual, interior/ collective, exterior/individual, and exterior/collective). We are all familiar with traditional data-gathering efforts that focus on the importance of objective information, whether individual or group. For example, traditional financial measurement for both individuals (i.e., pay) and companies (i.e., profits) is a normal measure. At the same time, subjective individual

Figure 47.3   Wilber's Framework for Understanding Holons

	Left-Hand Side	Right-Hand Side
	Interior	**Exterior**
Individual	Subjective Intentional Realm of "I" experienced	Objective Behavioral Realm of it observed
Collective	Intersubjective Cultural Realm of "We" experienced	Interobjective Social Realm of "It(s)" observed

aspects—that is, how individuals experience their organizations or what the group experiences or its culture—are also meaningful in creating visionary organizations.

By taking an integrative and holistic systems perspective, we can reshape how we see our impact on the world and the world's on us. In the words of Peter Senge:

> Systems thinking is a discipline for seeing the "structures" that underlie complex situations and for discerning high from low leverage change. That is, by seeing wholes we learn how to foster health.... [Systems thinking and the related disciplines of personal mastery, mental models, shared vision, and team learning] are concerned with a shift of mind from seeing parts to seeing wholes, from seeing people as helpless reactors to seeing them as active participants in shaping their reality, from reacting to the present to creating the future.[45]

Starbucks (see Case 2) is one company that understands the importance of taking a systemic approach to its business and its many stakeholders—as well as one that recognizes the growing imperative of sustainability, which will be discussed in the next section of this chapter.

Natural Ecology: The Biological Basis for Citizenship

Why do some companies move toward sustainable ecological practices in addition to recognizing the importance of stakeholders throughout their supply, production/service delivery, and distribution chains? Let us begin by understanding the overall system in which businesses operate at their foundation: the natural environment. The Earth's population is now estimated at more than 6.6 billion and projected to reach 9 billion by 2050, which some observers believe is overstretching Earth's resources. For example, the Global Footprint Network's research indicates that humanity is already in "ecological overshoot," that is, using 1.2 times more resources than the Earth can supply (which is possible for a short period of time but not over an extended time period).[46]

In 2007, the Intergovernmental Panel on Climate Change (TPCC) released its Synthesis Report,[47] which warns that the scientific consensus is that "warming of the climate is unequivocal" and that all natural systems are being affected by these changes, which the panel attributes to humanity's impact on the natural environment. The IPCC report gives five important reasons for concern about climate change and its impacts on human civilization. First, there are risks associated with unique and threatened systems, including polar and high mountain ecosystems, increased risk of species extinction, and coral reef damage. Second, risks of extreme weather events, such as droughts, heat waves, and floods, can affect large geographical regions. Third, the distribution of impacts and vulnerabilities, as IPCC notes, features big regional differences in climate change impacts; the most vulnerable groups, like the poor and elderly, are likely to be worst affected, as are populations in low-latitude, coastal, and less developed regions. Fourth, there are aggregate impacts of climate change on economic stability and conditions, such as the costs associated with dealing with extreme weather patterns. Just witness the ongoing costs of cleaning up after Hurricane Katrina in 2005 in the United States, as an example of some of the kinds of costs incurred with extreme weather. Fifth, global warming over centuries might result in substantially rising sea levels from melting glaciers. With vast swaths of humanity now living in coastal areas, rising sea levels will prove costly in many different ways.

CASE 2. STARBUCKS'S MOVING TARGETS: SUSTAINABILITY, FAIR TRADE, AND SUPPLIER RELATIONS

Can a huge company with enormous retail clout, a company that dominates its industry, gain credibility with consumers and critics alike by promoting more ecologically sensitive shade-grown coffee for the environment, supply chain management, and fair trade pricing for its suppliers? That is

(Continued)

(Continued)

exactly what coffee giant Starbucks is trying to do, but not without criticism. As of 2008, Starbucks had 7,087 company-operated retail stores and 4,081 licensed stores in all 50 United States plus the District of Columbia, and it operated, licensed, or joint ventured more than 4,500 stores in 43 countries outside the United States. It also sells its coffee in a wide range of restaurants, businesses, airlines, hotels, and universities, as well as through mail order and online catalogs. Ubiquitous as it has become, Starbucks seems well on its way to achieving its goal of establishing itself as the most recognized and respected brand in the world. So how does a company that has achieved such market dominance by selling coffee (and related) products move toward ecological sustainability and fair treatment of its suppliers and their workers in its growing operations?

In 1992, Starbucks established its first environmental mission statement (see Exhibit 1). After being roundly and publicly criticized for its labor and sourcing practices, the company had, by 1995, developed its Framework for a Code of Conduct, becoming the first coffee company to acknowledge its responsibility for the working conditions, wages, and rights of coffee workers on the farms of its suppliers. By 1998, Starbucks had formed an ongoing partnership with Conservation International (CI) intended to support shade cultivation, which protects biodiversity, encourages the use of environmentally sustainable agricultural practices, and helps farmers earn more money. This partnership, which was renewed and upgraded in the summer of 2000, permits CI to work on five coffee-growing projects in Latin America, Asia, and Africa. Through a program called Conservation Coffee, Starbucks enables CI to help small farmers grow coffee in the buffer zone of the reserve under the shade of the forest canopy. Growing coffee in the shade helps protect the reserve's forests, streams, and wildlife while also providing substantial income benefits for the farmers. As a result of this collaboration, Starbucks was awarded the 2005 World Environment Center Gold Medal for International Corporate Achievement in Sustainable Development for its CAFE (Coffee and Farmer Equity) Practices. This recognition was the 21st annual such award given by the World Environment Center.

Exhibit 1   Starbucks's Environmental Mission Statement

Starbucks is committed to a role of environmental leadership in all facets of our business. We will fulfill this mission by a commitment to:

- Understanding of environmental issues and sharing information with our partners (employees).
- Developing innovative and flexible solutions to bring about change.
- Striving to buy, sell and use environmentally friendly products.
- Recognizing that fiscal responsibility is essential to our environmental future.
- Instilling environmental responsibility values.
- Measuring and monitoring our progress for each project.
- Encouraging all partners to share in our mission.

Source: http://www.starbucks.com/aboutus/envapproach.asp (accessed February 24, 2004).

In 2001, the company, still facing criticism about its percentage of purchased shade-grown coffee and increasing attacks on wages and working conditions on suppliers' farms, established a Preferred Supplier Program to "encourage continuous improvement in sustainable coffee production." This program established a point system in which suppliers could become preferred suppliers not only by meeting certain quality standards (a given for the quality-conscious company) but also by focusing on environmental impacts (e.g., soil management, water reduction, various waste management and conservation approaches); social conditions of workers (e.g., wages and benefits, health and safety, living conditions); and economic issues, especially economic transparency. By late 2003, the company's experience with this program had evolved into its Supplier Code of Conduct, which required suppliers to live up to Starbucks's own standards (see Exhibit 2).

Exhibit 2   Starbucks's Approach to Sustainable Trade

Our products are grown, produced and/or manufactured by a multitude of suppliers around the world. As our global supply chain operations expand and become increasingly complex, we recognize the importance of instituting an overarching framework that ensures ethical trading practices, increases transparency and continues to build a sustainable network of suppliers. Starbucks is working on many levels to implement such an approach.

Starbucks' Supplier Code of Conduct articulates our core values and the expectations we have of our suppliers. The Code includes social responsibility standards for both agricultural products and for manufactured goods.

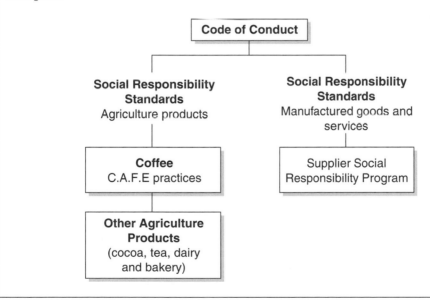

Source: http://www.starbucks.com/aboutus/supplier_code.asp (accessed March 6, 2008).

(Continued)

(Continued)

By 2007, *Fortune* magazine ranked Starbucks as number 2 in the top 20 "Most Admired" companies and made the following statement:

> For years now Starbucks has paid fair-market prices to Third World coffee farmers and helped develop ecologically sound growing practices. Starbucks is also a regular on FORTUNE'S annual list of the 100 Best Companies to Work For. It's green, it's humane, it's politically correct, it sells a popular product and provides a comfy place to hang out and consume same—what's not to like? Certainly investors have no complaints: If you had put $1,000 into Starbucks stock when the company went public in 1992, you'd have been $52,718.10 to the good at year-end 2006, versus just $3,515.30 for the S&P 500.

Starbucks consistently moves progressively forward in its efforts to establish a leadership position on environmental sustainability issues within the coffee industry. Using The Natural Step's sustainability framework (discussed in the next section of this chapter), Starbucks identified three primary areas of environmental impact on which to assess its ecological footprint: sourcing; transportation; and store design and operations, including energy, water, recycling, and waste reduction. In 2002, Starbucks president and chief executive officer Orin Smith accepted a Humanitarian Medal of Merit for Starbucks's leadership on sustainability from the Coffee Quality Institute.

Still, critics never seem to be satisfied with Starbucks's performance on human rights, labor, and ecological issues. The activist group Global Exchange, which has an ongoing campaign to pressure Starbucks to procure and promote more fair trade coffee, comments, "Coffee farmers are becoming even more impoverished, going further into debt and losing their land due to extremely low world coffee prices. Meanwhile coffee companies such as Starbucks have not lowered consumer prices but are pocketing the difference, even taking into account the quality premiums in the specialty industry. According to Fair Trade Labeling Organizations International, Fair Trade farmers sell only about 20% of their coffee at a Fair Trade price. The rest is sold at the world price, due to lack of demand. Demand can be created by large corporations selling Fair Trade." The activist group advocated that consumers exert pressure on Starbucks by requesting brewed fair trade coffee in retail shops and otherwise making their preferences known.

For Starbucks, the quest for credibility with its customers, activists, and investors presents a series of ever-new challenges around its supply chain management, environmental, and purchasing policies. These challenges over time have pushed the company in the direction of recognition of new and expanding responsibilities, in line with society's changing expectations for large and powerful companies.

Sources: Bart Slob and Joris Oldenziel, "Coffee and Codes: Overview of Codes of Conduct and Ethical Trade Initiatives in the Coffee Sector," http://www.somo.nl/html/paginas/pdf/Coffee_&_Codes_2003_Enhanced_NL.pdf (accessed March 6, 2008); Elliot J. Schrage, "Promoting International Worker Rights through Private Voluntary Initiatives: Public Relations or Public Policy," Report to the U.S. Department of State (Iowa City: University of Iowa Center for Human Rights, 2004); Starbucks, "About Us," http://www.starbucks.com/aboutus/ (and related links) (accessed March 6, 2008); "Fortune's Most Admired Companies, 2007," http://money.cnn.com/galleries/2007/fortune/0703/gallery.mostadmired_top20.fortune/2.html (accessed March 6, 2008); Starbucks, "Company Fact Sheet," http://www.starbucks.com/aboutus/Company_Factsheet.pdf (accessed March 6, 2008); Conservation International, "Agriculture and Fisheries, Starbucks Coffee Company," http://www.celb.org/xp/CELB/programs/agriculture-fisheries/starbucks.xml (accessed March 7, 2008); Global Exchange, "Starbucks Campaign," http://globalexchange.org/campaigns/fairtrade/coffee/starbucks.html (accessed March 7, 2008).

With all of this evidence about environmental damage now mounting, there is an increasing imperative to deal with the impact of human beings on the ecology that sustains humans in ways that are sustainable ecologically. One organization that has taken a creative and systemic approach to understanding ecological sustainability and business's role in it is the Swedish nonprofit organization The Natural Step (TNS).[48]

Founded in 1989 by Dr. Karl-Henrik Robert, TNS works to develop a consensus about the ecological environment, the role of humans in that environment, and the ways in which humans are threatening not only other forms of life on Earth but also themselves by engaging in activities that result in deteriorating natural conditions.[49] Robert, joined by a Swedish physicist, John Holmberg, defined a set of important system conditions based on the laws of thermodynamics and natural cycles that form TNS's framework for environmental sustainability.

Sustainability, as the biologist Humberto Maturana notes, is critical not just to the environment but also to human beings, and particularly to the natural environment's capacity to sustain human civilization. The environment, Maturana points out, will go on in one form or another, no matter what humans do to it. The real question is: Can human society survive major ecological changes?[50] TNS's framework is aimed at helping both individuals and organizations understand ecology systemically so that the use (and abuse) of natural resources can be reduced and newer sustainable approaches to production developed. In addition, TNS hopes to help focus the development of new, less resource-intensive technologies and to provide a common language and set of guiding principles for sustainable enterprise. TNS has relatively recently been introduced into the United States, Canada, the United Kingdom, Japan, and Australia; however, TNS is a household word in Sweden.

Thinking Systemically About Ecology: The Natural Step Framework[51]

TNS highlights some of the problematic aspects of human economic development on the ecology. Because of the impact of the 6.6 billion people currently alive on Earth, multiple ecological systems—including croplands, wetlands, the ozone layer, rain forests, fisheries, and groundwater—are facing serious trouble. Visible garbage is filling up landfills, while various pollutants accumulate less visibly in the atmosphere. Rain forests continue to be depleted with almost unimaginable impacts on world ecology, for not only do rain forests provide fresh water, but they also cleanse the atmosphere. Some ecologists believe that a sustainable number of people on Earth would be between 1 and 2 billion, well below current population levels. The Global Footprint Network estimates that by 2008, humanity's footprint was some 23 percent greater than the Earth's carrying capacity,[52] and increasing population will only place more stresses on the natural system.

According to environmentalist Paul Hawken, "We are far better at making waste than at making products. For every 100 pounds of product we manufacture in the United States, we create at least 3,200 pounds of waste. In a decade, we transform 500 trillion pounds of molecules into nonproductive solids, liquids, and gases."[53] Clearly, if we believe that the Earth's resources are limited and that demands on the system cannot be sustained at this rate of "progress," then a new approach to productivity—indeed, potentially a wholly new, more ecologically based system of production—is necessary. TNS's framework provides a set of system conditions that, according to the scientists who originally created the system in Sweden (and others where it is being replicated throughout the world), will be needed to prevent the world from hitting a wall of unsupportable demands on the natural environment. Note 2 lists the system conditions for sustainability as developed by TNS, which works with companies such as Home Depot, Bank of America, and McDonald's on implementing these conditions. The Natural Step takes the position that practices are not sustainable when society "mines and disperses materials at a faster rate than they are redeposited back into the Earth's crust" (e.g., mining raw materials like coal or oil), when "society produces substances faster than they can be broken down by natural processes" (e.g., producing toxins like dioxin), and "extracts resources at a faster rate than they are replenished (e.g., overharvesting trees or fish), or by other forms ecosystem manipulation" (e.g., soil erosion).[54]

The TNS system is aimed at sustainable development. Sustainable development was originally defined by the Brundtland Commission, in its 1987 report "Our Common Future," as "development that meets the needs of the present without compromising the ability of future generations to meet their own needs."[55] Sustainability also can be seen as "a process of achieving human development ... in an inclusive, connected, equitable, prudent, and secure manner," according to the ecological scholar Thomas Gladwin and his colleagues.[56] Gladwin has defined five elements that represent a set of constraints on human development, similar to those for the material world that TNS produced (see Table 47.2).

Inclusiveness connotes an expansive view of the space, time, and component parts of the observed ecology, embracing both ecological and human conditions in the present and the future. *Connectivity* means understanding the inherent interconnectedness and interdependence of elements of the world and problems in the world. *Equity* means a fair distribution of resources and property rights within and between generations. Putting connectivity and equity together suggests greater comprehension of the unavoidable links between, for example, creating better ecological health and efforts to reduce poverty or the gap between rich and poor.

NOTE 2: THE NATURAL STEP'S FOUR SYSTEM CONDITIONS FOR SUSTAINABILITY

The Natural Step system conditions, also called principles of sustainability, define the basic conditions that need to be met in a sustainable society. By looking at the three ways we are damaging nature, and then adding the word "not," The Natural Step has defined the three basic principles for an ecologically sustainable society. However, because we are talking about sustainability for people and for the planet, a basic social principle is also needed—that all people have the opportunity to meet their needs. From this assessment, we articulate four basic principles. In a sustainable society, nature is NOT subject to systematically increasing:

1. concentrations of substances extracted from the Earth's crust,

2. concentrations of substances produced by society,

3. degradation by physical means, and, in that society . . .

4. people are not subject to conditions that systematically undermine their capacity to meet their needs.

Source: Copyright © The Natural Step. Reprinted with permission. All rights reserved.

Prudence means taking care of the resources of the world, as suggested by the TNS constraints. In practice, being prudent means keeping ecosystems and socioeconomic systems healthy and resilient; avoiding irreversible losses of ecological or other resources; and, again as the TNS constraints indicate, keeping human activities within the earth's regenerative capacity. Finally, *security* focuses on the sustainability of human life, that is, ensuring "a safe, healthy, high quality of life

for current and future generations."[57] Sustainability is critical because, whereas nature in some form or another will survive whatever happens, human civilization's existence is dependent on a relatively narrow set of ecological conditions for its support. Straining the Earth's capacity beyond these conditions would prove costly in many ways.

What is important here is to recognize that systems thinking fundamentally means thinking in new ways

Table 47.2	Constraints on Sustainable Human Development
Inclusiveness	Expansive view of space, time, and elements of ecology (present and future)
Connectivity	Understanding inherent interconnectedness and interdependence of world's elements and problems
Equity	Fair distribution of resources and property rights (within and between generations)
Prudence	Taking care of world's resources so they are healthy and resilient
Security	Sustainability of healthy, high-quality human life for present and future generations

Source: Thomas N. Gladwin, James J. Kennelly, and Tara-Shelomith Krause, "Shifting Paradigms for Sustainable Development: Implications for Management Theory and Research," *Academy of Management Review* 20, no. 4 (October 1995), pp. 847–907.

about the relationships that exist among human beings, the enterprises they create, and the rest of the natural world.

Thinking about ecological sustainability may mean complementing traditional (Western) ways of viewing human beings' relationship to the natural world with more holistic perspectives. It may even mean shifting our perspective away from an anthropomorphic (human-centered) or technocentric (technologically oriented) worldview and beyond even an ecocentric (ecological) worldview.[58] It may mean a wholly integrative approach to economic development focused on sustainability.

A fully integrative perspective would synthesize the three critical spheres of civilization (economic, political, and societal) with the ecological and would also integrate the subjective and intersubjective elements of emotions, intuition, aesthetics, and culture, among others, into our perspective. The result would be a better understanding of the values that underpin each sphere of activity and their integration into an ecologically sustainable and holistic worldview.

The Need for Balance

Just as nature requires a balance among elements to sustain any healthy ecological environment, we must think about leading global and local corporate citizenship as

part of the social ecology. Balance among the interests of all three important sectors of human civilization is of paramount concern. In sustaining this balance among sectors and with the natural world, we must also marry competition and competitiveness with cooperation and collaboration, in the process that biologists call symbiosis. Competition *and* collaboration, with sustainability, are necessary and important to societal—and business—health and success. The physicist Fritjof Capra perhaps puts it best:

The recognition of symbiosis as a major evolutionary force has profound philosophical implications. All larger organisms [and organizations], including ourselves, are living testimonies to the fact that destructive practices do not work in the long run. In the end the aggressors always destroy themselves, making way for others who know how to cooperate and get along. Life is much less a competitive struggle for survival than a triumph of cooperation and creativity. Indeed, since the creation of the first nucleated cells, evolution has proceeded through ever more intricate arrangements of cooperation and coevolution.[59]

Mastering systems thinking is a critical element of creating continually improving and learning enterprises.[60] An integrative systems approach is essential if we are to conceive of operating businesses, as well as governments and civil society enterprises, in sustainable ways, giving due consideration to the seventh generation out, as our Native American ancestors would have noted.

Leading Challenges: A New Paradigm for Corporate Citizenship

Fundamentally, leading corporate citizenship cannot evolve into constructive stakeholder relationships without the active participation of effective, aware, and progressive leaders. Aware leaders have thought deeply about their own values and vision and, as a result, are prepared for the complex world they must face. Being prepared will not necessarily lessen the complexity or the difficulty of the decisions they must make, but awareness does help leaders make the right decisions when challenges are high, as they inevitably are in complex social and political environments. Particularly in an era in which activists and other stakeholders can mobilize nearly instantaneously and globally, awareness of and response to the demands of leading a corporate citizen is a must. In effect, this mobilization is what happened in 1999 when activists prevented the World Trade Organization from meeting in Seattle, in 2001 when terrorists struck the World Trade Center and the Pentagon, and since that time in the increasing antiglobalization sentiments expressed by activists around the world.

Endnotes

1. Kofi Annan, "Business and the U.N.: A Global Compact of Shared Values and Principles," World Economic Forum, Davos, Switzerland, January 31, 1999. Reprinted in *Vital Speeches of the Day* 65, no. 9 (February 15, 1999) pp. 260–61. For further information on the Global Compact, see http://www.unglobal compact.org.

2. Information on membership and the UN Global Compact can be found at http://www.unglobalcompact.org.

3. The classic references are R. Edward Freeman, *Strategic Management: A Stakeholder Approach* (New York: Basic Books, 1984), and William M. Evan and R. Edward Freeman, "A Stakeholder Theory of the Modern Corporation: Kantian Capitalism," in *Ethical Theory and Business,* ed.

T. Beauchamp and N. Bowie (Englewood Cliffs, NJ: Prentice Hall, 1998). Max Clarkson identifies stakeholders as primary and secondary, depending on the level of risk they have taken with respect to the organization. See Max B. E. Clarkson, "A Stakeholder Framework for Analyzing and Evaluating Corporate Social Performance," *Academy of Management Review* 20, no. 1 (1995), pp. 92–117. Freeman also recently updated his original book; see R. Edward Freeman, Jeffrey Harrison, and Andrew Wicks, *Managing for Stakeholders: Business in the 21st Century* (New Haven, CT: Yale University Press, 2007).

4. Dirk Marten and Andrew Crane, "Corporate Citizenship: Towards an Extended Theoretical Conceptualization," *Academy of Management Review* 29 (2004).

5. See the works of Ken Wilber, for example, *A Brief History of Everything* (Boston: Shambala, 1996); *Eye of the Spirit: An Integral Vision for a World Gone Slightly Mad* (Boston: Shambala, 1998); and *The Marriage of Sense and Soul: Integrating Science and Reason* (New York: Random House, 1998). For a discussion of the web that constitutes life and the ways in which all matter is interrelated, see Fritjof Capra, *The Web of Life* (New York: Anchor Doubleday, 1995).

6. Marten and Crane, "Corporate Citizenship."

7. Michael Porter's views on corporate (social) responsibility are characteristic of this perspective. See Michael Porter and Mark R. Kramer, "The Competitive Advantage of Philanthropy," *Harvard Business Review* 80, no. 12 (December 2002), pp. 56–69; see also Michael Porter and Mark R. Kramer, "Strategy and Society: The Link Between Competitive Advantage and Corporate Social Responsibility," *Harvard Business Review* 84 (December 2006), pp. 78–92.

8. Sandra Waddock, "Companies, Academics, and the Progress of Corporate Citizenship," *Business and Society Review* 109 (March 2004), pp. 5–42.

9. Charles Handy, "What's a Business For?" *Harvard Business Review* (December 2002). Reprinted by permission of Harvard Business Review. Copyright 2002 by the Harvard Business School Publishing Corporation; all rights reserved.

10. Freeman, *Strategic Management*; Freeman et al., *Managing for Stakeholders.*

11. See Lynn A. Stout, "Why We Should Stop Teaching *Dodge v. Ford,*" UCLA School of Law, Law-Econ Research Paper No. 07-11, available at SSRN: http://ssrn.com/abstract=1013744; Kent Greenfield, "A New Era for Corporate Law: Using Corporate Governance to Benefit All Stakeholders." 2007 Summit on the Future of the Corporation, paper series 19–28.

12. See, for example, James E. Post, Lee E. Preston, and Sybil Sachs, "Managing the Extended Enterprise: The New Stakeholder View," *California Management Review* 45, no. 1 (2002), pp. 6–29; James E. Post, Lee E. Preston, and Sybil

Sachs, *Redefining the Corporation* (New York: Oxford University Press, 2002).

13. Milton Friedman, "The Social Responsibility of a Business Is to Increase Its Profits," *The New York Times Magazine*, September 13, 1970. Copyright © 1970. The New York Times Company. Reprinted with permission.

14. See Clarkson, "A Stakeholder Framework," for an extended discussion of stakes. See also Ronald K. Mitchell, Bradley R. Agle, and Donna J. Wood, "Toward a Theory of Stakeholder Identification and Salience: Defining the Principle of Who and What Really Counts," *Academy of Management Review* 22, no. 4 (October 1997), pp. 853–86.

15. For a perspective on this point, see Tammy MacLean, "Creating Stakeholder Relationships: A Model of Organizational Social Identification—How the Southern Baptist Convention Became Stakeholders of Walt Disney," paper presented at the annual meeting of the Academy of Management, San Diego, CA, 1998.

16. Thanks are owed to Max B. E. Clarkson for providing a basis for thinking about corporate social performance in terms of stakeholder relationships. See Clarkson, "A Stakeholder Framework."

17. Handy, "What's a Business For?"

18. See, for example, Freeman, *Strategic Management*, and Evan and Freeman, "A Stakeholder Theory of the Modern Corporation." See also Clarkson, "A Stakeholder Framework," and, more recently, Mitchell, Agle, and Wood, "Toward a Theory of Stakeholder Identification and Salience."

19. The concepts of primary and secondary involvement come from Lee E. Preston and James E. Post, *Private Management and Public Policy: The Principle of Public Responsibility* (Englewood Cliffs, NJ: Prentice Hall, 1975).

20. See Kent Greenfield, "New Principles for Corporate Law," *Hastings Business Law Journal* 1 (May 2005), pp. 87–118; Greenfield, "New Era for Corporate Law."

21. Ibid., p. 95.

22. This definition comes from Clarkson, "A Stakeholder Framework," p. 106. However, the distinction goes back to Freeman, *Strategic Management*.

23. For example, see Mark Starik, "Should Trees Have Managerial Standing? Toward Stakeholder Status for Non-Human Nature," *Journal of Business Ethics* 14 (1995), pp. 204–17.

24. See, for example, Robert A. Phillips and Joel Reichart, "The Environment as a Stakeholder? A Fairness-Based Approach," *Journal of Business Ethics* 23 (January 2000), pp. 183–97.

25. For a theoretical explanation, see Duane Windsor, "Stakeholder Responsibilities: Lessons for Managers," in *Unfolding Stakeholder Thinking: Theory, Responsibility and Engagement*, Jörg Andriof, Sandra Waddock, Bryan Husted, and Sandra Sutherland Rahman, eds. (Sheffield: Greenleaf, 2002), pp. 137–54.

26. Clarkson, "A Stakeholder Framework," p. 107.

27. Mitchell, Agle, and Wood, "Toward a Theory of Stakeholder Identification and Salience." Mitchell, Agle, and Wood's model has been somewhat modified by Steven L. Wartick and Donna J. Wood, *International Business and Society* (Maiden, MA: Blackwell Press, 1998), in the fashion incorporated into this discussion.

28. See Duane Windsor, "Stakeholder Responsibilities."

29. For background on descriptive, instrumental, and normative branches of stakeholder theory, see Thomas Donaldson and Lee E. Preston, "The Stakeholder Theory of the Corporation: Concepts, Evidence, and Implications," *Academy of Management Review* 20 (January 1995), pp. 1, 65–91.

30. See http://www.unglobalcompact.org for background.

31. UN Global Compact, http://unglobalcompact .org/AboutTheGC/index.html (accessed December 9, 2007).

32. World Business Council for Sustainable Development, http://www.wbcsd.org/templates/TemplateWBCSD5/layout .asp?type=p&MenuId=NjA&doOpen=1&ClickMenu=LeftMenu (accessed December 9, 2007).

33. Note that this link is the basis of the instrumental argument for positive stakeholder relationships, as discussed by Donaldson and Preston, "The Stakeholder Theory of the Corporation."

34. See for example, Joshua D. Margolis and James P. Walsh, *People and Profits? The Search for a Link Between a Company's Social and Financial Performance* (Mahwah, NJ: Erlbaum, 2001); Joshua D. Margolis and James P. Walsh, "Misery Loves Companies: Rethinking Social Initiatives by Business," *Administrative Science Quarterly* 48 (2003), pp. 268–305; S. A. Waddock and S. B. Graves, "Quality of Management and Quality of Stakeholder Relations: Are They Synonymous?" *Business and Society* 36, no. 3 (September 1997), pp. 250–79; S. A. Waddock and S. B. Graves, "The Corporate Social Performance—Financial Performance Link," *Strategic Management Journal* 18, no. 4 (1997), pp. 303–19.

35. For a discussion of this framework, see Preston and Post, *Private Management and Public Policy*.

36. See Clarkson, "A Stakeholder Framework," p. 109. Clarkson's "postures" are different from the stances outlined here.

37. David C. Korten, *When Corporations Rule the World* (San Francisco: Berrett-Koehler, 1995), p. 21.

38. See Richard D'Aveni, *Hypercompetition: Managing the Dynamics of Strategic Maneuvering* (New York: The Free Press, 1994).

39. For a marvelous and accessible description of the interconnectedness of living and material entities, see Capra, *The Web of Life*.

40. For some insight into these topics, you can start with James Gleick, *Chaos: Making a New Science* (New York: Viking, 1987); Stuart Kauffman, *At Home in the Universe: The Search*

for the Laws of Self-Organization and Complexity (New York: Oxford University Press, 1995); Capra, *The Web of Life*; Humberto R. Maturana and Francisco J. Varela, *The Tree of Knowledge: The Biological Roots of Human Understanding*, rev. ed. (Boston: Shambala, 1998); and of course Peter Senge, *The Fifth Discipline: The Art and Practice of the Learning Organization*, revised edition (New York: Doubleday, 2006).

41. Senge, *The Fifth Discipline*.

42. The term *holon* is from Arthur Koestler and is extensively developed in Ken Wilber's work. Relevant works by Wilber include *Sex, Ecology, Spirituality: The Spirit of Evolution* (Boston: Shambala, 1995), *Eye of the Spirit*, and *A Brief History of Everything*.

43. Thomas N. Gladwin, James J. Kennelly, and Tara-Shelomith Krause, "Shifting Paradigms for Sustainable Development: Implications for Management Theory and Research," *Academy of Management Review* 20, no. 4 (October 1995), pp. 874–907; Fritjof Capra, *The Turning Point: Science, Society, and the Rising Culture* (New York: Bantam Books, 1983); Margaret J. Wheatley, *Leadership and the New Science: Learning about Organization from an Orderly New Universe* (San Francisco: Berrett-Koehler, 1992).

44. See Wilber, *Sex, Ecology, Spirituality; Eye of the Spirit*, and *A Brief History of Everything*.

45. Senge, *The Fifth Discipline*, p. 68.

46. Global Footprint Network, http://www.footprintnet work.org/gfh_sub.php?content=global_footprint (accessed December 19, 2007).

47. Intergovernmental Panel on Climate Change, Fourth Assessment Report, Climate Change 2007: Synthesis Report 2007, http://www.ipcc.ch/pdf/assessment-report/ar4/syr/ar4_syr_spm.pdf (accessed December 19, 2007). Information in this paragraph is taken from this report.

48. The Natural Step's U.S. Web site is http://www .naturalstep.org/com/nyStart/.

49. More information on The Natural Step can be found at http://www.naturalstep.org.

50. This paragraph is based on a talk by Humberto Maturana at the 1998 annual meeting of the Society for Organizational Learning (SoL). A version of this talk by Humberto Maturana Romesin and Pille Bunnell, entitled "Biosphere, Homosphere, and Robosphere: What Has That to Do with Business?" is available at http://www.solonline.org/res/wp/maturana/index.html (accessed June 29, 2004).

51. This section is partially based on The Natural Step Web site, http://www.naturalstep.org (accessed February 25, 2004, updated December 20, 2007).

52. Global Footprint Network, http://www.foot print network.org/gfn_sub.php?content=footprint_overview (accessed December 20, 2007). Much more information and a means of calculating your own ecological footprint can be found at http://www.foot printnetwork.org/index.php.

53. Ibid.

54. From The Natural Step Web site, http://www.natural step.org.nz/tns-f-system-conditions.asp (accessed December 20, 2007).

55. Brundtland Commission, "Our Common Future: Report of the World Commission on Environment and Development," 1987, http://www.un.org/documents/ga/res/42/ares42-187.htm (accessed November 28, 2007), p. 24.

56. Gladwin, Kennelly, and Krause, "Shifting Paradigms for Sustainable Development."

57. U.S. President's Council on Sustainable Development, quoted in Gladwin, Kennelly, and Krause, "Shifting Paradigms for Sustainable Development." Much of the discussion in these paragraphs is based on this article.

58. These terms are developed in Gladwin, Kennelly, and Krause, "Shifting Paradigms for Sustainable Development."

59. Capra, *The Web of Life*, p. 243.

60. Senge, *The Fifth Discipline*.

CHAPTER 48

A New Kind of Company

*B Corporations Worry About Stakeholders,
Not Just Shareholders*

Hannah Clark

Inc. Magazine

By almost any standard, Give Something Back is a thriving business. Launched in 1991 with $40,000 from two founders, the office products company generated $25 million in sales in 2006. Give Something Back, which donates more than half of its profits to charity, could have grown even faster if founders Mike Hannigan and Sean Marx were willing to take in outside investors. But though they get offers regularly, they've always said no. The reason: "We couldn't offer an investor an opportunity to invest in us and feel in any way that our social goals were protected," Hannigan says.

It's a problem that has long dogged socially responsible businesses. Public companies are legally obligated to maximize returns to shareholders, according to a widespread interpretation of corporate law. For private firms, it's more a matter of withstanding pressure from investors. Hannigan and Marx, for example, fear their social mission could be threatened if an investor changed his mind about Give Something Back's penchant for charity. They want to avoid the fate of ice cream maker Ben & Jerry's, which received a buyout offer from the Dutch conglomerate Unilever (NYSE:UL) in 2000. Founders Ben Cohen and Jerry Greenfield didn't want to sell, so Cohen assembled a group of investors to make a counteroffer. When they couldn't offer as much as Unilever, shareholders sued, and the company, then publicly traded, was forced to relent. In April 2000, Ben & Jerry's was acquired by Unilever for $326 million.

That's exactly the situation that B Lab, a new nonprofit organization, aims to prevent. The group is creating a new kind of company—the B Corporation.

Source: A New Kind of Company: B Corporations Worry About Stakeholders, Not Just Shareholders, by Hannah Clark. *Inc: The Magazine for Growing Companies,* July 2007. Published by Goldhirsh Group. Copyright © Mansueto Ventures LLC.

(The B stands for "beneficial.") It's less a legal designation than a certification system that will allow businesses to define themselves as socially responsible to consumers and investors. To become a certified B Corporation, a company must amend its articles of incorporation to say that managers must consider the interests of employees, the community, and the environment instead of worrying solely about shareholders. Those amendments, according to B Lab, will let entrepreneurs like Hannigan take on outside investors without worrying that their values will be compromised. "For us, this is a huge step forward," says Hannigan, whose company recently became one of about two dozen certified B Corporations.

B Lab's founders got the idea from Leslie Christian, president of Progressive Investment Management. In 2004, she co-founded a new venture, Upstream 21, a holding company in Portland, Oregon. Christian says she and her partners "wanted to be really clear that we wouldn't be doing something solely in the interest of shareholders." Upstream's attorney drafted the language, and earlier this year Upstream acquired its first company. "When you look at what makes a company successful, is it the absentee landlords? No, it's the people who work there," Christian says.

B Corporations must do more than simply edit their articles of incorporation. They have to pay B Lab one-tenth of 1 percent of revenue, and score at least 40 out of 100 on a survey B Lab developed after consulting with more than 150 entrepreneurs, investors, and academics. It's similar to the LEED certification system for green buildings or TransFair's certification of fair-trade businesses. Companies gain points for a number of practices, including democratic decision making, having good benefits, donating profits to charity, and being energy efficient. "We want to help consumers separate good companies from good marketing," says Jay Coen Gilbert, co-founder of the apparel company AND 1, who launched B Lab with Bart Houlahan, AND 1's former president, and Andrew Kassoy, a principal at private equity firm MSD Capital, which manages Michael Dell's money.

Certification, however, can be somewhat suspect; some organic farmers, for example, have said the organic certification system has actually weakened their movement by enabling the creation of organic factory farms. And some of the questions on B Lab's survey—"Are corporate events or team-building exercises held at least twice annually?"—have dubious social value. B Corporations can be strong in some areas (say, employee ownership) but weaker in others, such as environmental stewardship. But social entrepreneurs are clearly thirsting for standards, and B Lab is far from the only organization working to develop them. The nonprofit Natural Capital Institute is developing a standard for responsible business known as Wiser, and a labeling initiative called Reveal aims to launch soon as well.

B Lab is different from the others because of the articles of incorporation amendment it requires. But how it might play out in the courts is an open question. If a B Corporation were forced for economic reasons to lay off half its workers, would it risk being sued? Could Greenpeace take a company to court for not living up to its green goals? That depends, in part, on the state; 11 states have laws that would insulate directors from liability, says R. Todd Johnson, a partner with the corporate law firm Jones Day, who consults for B Lab. Some states don't even allow companies to add stakeholder interests to their articles of incorporation; only 31 have expressly permitted it by passing what are known as constituency statutes. Ultimately, however, whether the amendments are legally binding will be up for debate until they are tested in court.

It's also far from clear that the amendment is even necessary. Legal scholars are divided on whether companies are actually legally obligated to maximize returns to shareholders. Margaret Blair, a law professor at Vanderbilt University, calls the legal obligation a "mythology," and is surprised the owner of a private company would feel the need to amend its articles of incorporation, given that privately held businesses are not subject to hostile takeovers. In a widely cited 1986 case, *Revlon* v. *MacAndrews & Forbes Holdings,* the Delaware Supreme Court ruled that once a public company is soliciting buyout bids, it must accept the highest offer, though a company can simply refuse to put itself up for sale. But that decision is valid only for tender offers—often-hostile bids that bypass management and go directly to shareholders, according to Blair. "It just doesn't happen in the case of private companies," she says.

Coen Gilbert admits that B Lab is a work in progress. But the group already has lined up powerful supporters, including Adam Lowry, co-founder of Method Products, a popular maker of green soaps and cleaning products; Steve Voigt, CEO of King Arthur Flour; and Jason Salfi, co-founder of Comet Skateboards. Jeffrey Hollender, CEO of the consumer products company Seventh Generation, says he has considered participating in at least 10 rating systems and always rejected the idea—until now. He thinks a successful rating system is vital for the social responsibility movement to succeed. "There is a tremendous potential for the idea to lose credibility because of a lack of standards," Hollender says. "I don't want to say this is perfect, but this is desperately needed right now."

CHAPTER 49

Ideologically Motivated Activism

How Activist Groups Influence Corporate Social Change Activities

Frank Den Hond
Frank G. A. De Bakker

VU University Amsterdam

The nature and level of a firm's corporate social change activities can be understood as an expression of what that firm believes to be its social responsibilities. Such activities are expected or demanded by the firm's social constituencies, but they are beyond what is minimally required by law, and they may occur at a cost to the firm (Carroll, 1979). As the activities of corporations have become matters of public debate, pressure from activist groups has become more prevalent; consumer activism is one example (Klein, Smith, & John, 2004; Kozinets & Han-delman, 2004). This trend is likely to continue as, in many countries, the responsibility to address social issues, such as those relating to the natural environment, working conditions in developing countries, protection of consumers, and human rights, increasingly is being transferred from the state to firms and other private institutions (Matten & Crane, 2005). Activist groups present themselves as legitimate claimants in these matters and, accordingly, put pressure on firms to address such issues, occasionally with considerable success. For instance, dozens of companies ceased their activities in Burma when pressured by activist groups whose motivation was to stimulate democracy and peace in this country ruled by, arguably, an oppressive and brutal junta (Spar & La Mure, 2003). Likewise, activist groups in the anti-sweatshop movement keep exerting pressure on major brand producers in the apparel and shoe industries to improve working conditions and wages in the industries' international supply chains (Knight & Greenberg, 2002).

In the management literature the question of stakeholder tactics largely has been left unattended

---

Source: Den Hond, F., De Bakker, F.G.A. Ideologically Motivated Activism: How Activist Groups Influence Corporate Social Change Activities. *Academy of Management Review* 2007, Vol. 32. No. 3, pp. 901–924. Copyright © Academy of Management.

(Whetten, Rands, & Godfrey, 2002), despite the existence of a strong tradition in the social movement literature to study tactics and targets of activist groups. Nevertheless, even in the social movement literature, only recently have scholars attended to the question of how social movements shape corporate social change activities. This question is relevant for various reasons. As claimants of the firm, being motivated by ethical concerns rather than material self-interest (Knight & Greenberg, 2002), activist groups are secondary stakeholders in the sense that the firm's survival does not depend on their continuing support (Clarkson, 1995). They have a claim they consider urgent and legitimate, but they have little bargaining power against firms. Even so, many activist groups are not interested in solely affecting the level of social change activities in an individual firm but, rather, strive for field-level change (Lounsbury, Ventresca, & Hirsch, 2003). For example, during the Brent Spar episode, Greenpeace clearly indicated that its protest was not only directed against the intended disposal of this particular decommissioned oil storage platform but against the very principle that oil platforms could be sunk into deep-sea ridges; according to Greenpeace, the world's oceans are not dumping sites (Jensen, 2003). Finally, often a number of activist groups aim to affect the nature and level of corporate social change activities in a firm, but they do so from varying ideological positions. This brings in the issue of collaboration and competition among activist groups (Zald & McCarthy, 1980). For all these reasons, it is theoretically interesting and highly relevant for corporate executives to understand the sources of pressures for corporate social change, the mechanisms by which firms are pressured, and the role of activist groups therein.

In order to address the question of how activist groups influence corporate social change activities, we make use of institutional change and social movement theories. The relevance of institutional change theory (Greenwood, Suddaby, & Hinings, 2002; Tolbert & Zucker, 1996) is in highlighting the ends of activist groups' activities—that is, institutional change at the field level. Activist groups may use two complementary routes in stimulating field-level change. One is to work at the field level—for example, in demanding state regulation. The other is to work at the organizational level and

to hope that change in individual firms will eventually evoke field-level change. In this article we focus on the latter route, since this route is increasingly important. Institutional change theory, however, is less developed regarding the means that can be employed to further these ends. We therefore turn to the social movement literature, since this literature offers a rich and diverse tradition of research on the public expression of collective grievances (della Porta & Diani, 1999; McAdam, McCarthy, & Zald, 1996; Snow, Soule, & Kriesi, 2004). Moreover, it is increasingly being applied in organizational research (cf. Davis, McAdam, Scott, & Zald, 2005; Davis & Thompson, 1994; Hensmans, 2003; Rao, Morrill, & Zald, 2000; Van de Ven & Hargrave, 2004).

Rowley and Moldoveanu (2003) have made an important step forward in understanding some of the antecedents of corporate social change activities. Building on social movement theory, they argue that both the interests and the identity of what they call "stakeholder groups" matter in explaining *why* and *when* these groups act in pressuring companies. Rehbein, Waddock, and Graves (2004) tested Rowley and Moldoveanu's propositions in the context of shareholder activism and found that activists selectively target companies that are highly visible and whose practices raise specific issues of interest to society. Still, it remains unclear *how* different activist groups try to get their claims attended to. We suggest that the choice of protest tactics depends on the activist group's ideological position, rather than on its interests and identity.

To develop our argument, we first argue that activist groups with similar interests and identities operate differently, and we relate this to radical and reformative ideologies. Next, we consider the ultimate object of activist groups—institutional change—and explore how radical and reformative activist groups seek to encourage processes of deinstitutionalization and reinstitutionalization. We then present a typology of the various tactics that activist groups may employ and subsequently combine this typology with the institutional change process in order to derive a number of propositions on how radical and reformative activist groups seek to further institutional change. In doing so we investigate how institutional change and social movement perspectives can be productively combined to develop new theoretical insights on an important set of antecedents of corporate social change activities. We illustrate our argument with examples of activist groups that seek to affect the level and nature of firms' corporate social change activities. Finally, we reflect on the theoretical and practical implications and suggest some directions for future research. For the sake of the argument, we regard activist groups and firms as distinct actors that often have diverging interests. Reality may be more complicated, though, since there may also be movements within firms (Raeburn, 2004) or inside allies working together with external activist groups (Lounsbury, 2001).

Activist Groups and Ideology

We view activist groups as stakeholder groups that represent a social movement or that claim to do so. A starting point in defining a social movement is to regard it as a shared belief about a preferred state of the world (McCarthy & Zald, 1977), but one that is able to mobilize people into an organized collective effort to solve social problems or even to transform the social order (Buechler, 2000). People participate in social movements because of three interrelated motives: instrumentality, identity, and ideology (Klandermans, 2004). If their interests, identities, and ideologies sufficiently overlap, people may decide to cooperate in changing their circumstances and in expressing their identity and ideology. Activist groups then emerge out of the need for organization and coordination. They are *activist* in transforming shared ideals, concerns, or grievances into organized contention, and they are a *group* in the sense that a collective identity enables them to overcome the problem of collective action.

People may create activist groups by joining together into loosely organized networks (Diani & McAdam, 2003), or, depending on their ability to mobilize sufficient resources, they may create activist groups that are more like formal social movement organizations—highly professional and internally differentiated organizations that aim to shape and structure the social movement (McCarthy & Zald, 1977). Of course, both possibilities are extremes on a continuum, and activist groups may form at any point along this continuum.

Within a particular social movement, usually a number of activist groups operate, each with its own

organizational repertoire of arguments and tactics (Clemens, 1993). As Rowley and Moldoveanu (2003) have suggested, understanding their interests and identities helps in understanding *why* stakeholder groups become activist groups. The explanation may be similar for activist groups within the same social movement because of the considerable overlap in their interests and identity, but there may be significant differences in *how* these activist groups operate. Indeed, within social movements the question of how activist groups should operate is a recurrent topic for debate, and occasionally a point of cleavage. Although activist groups can change their goals and tactics over time (Zald & Ash, 1966), we suggest that looking at ideological connotations of activist groups can teach us a lot about the tactics these groups consider appropriate to invoke institutional change (Minkoff, 2001; Zald, 2000).

The concept of ideology comprises an interconnected set of beliefs and attitudes relating to problematic aspects of social and political topics that are shared and used by members of a group and that inform and justify choice and behavior (Fine & Sandstrom, 1993; Zald, 2000). This concept arises from the circumstances and experiences in that group's history. In some instances ideologies of social movements may be widely shared, elaborate, consistent, and encompassing, but they are not necessarily so, since in other cases they may be contested, partial, incoherent, and fragmented (Platt & Williams, 2002). Ideologies indicate "a sense of what is problematic" (Blee & Currier, 2005: 138) and can therefore start from a fairly vague discontent. They develop over time and in interaction with other activist groups in the same social movement (Platt & Williams, 2002; Zald, 2000).

Activist groups that campaign for the realization of similar goals can be distinguished according to their ideological stance, since "nearly all social movements divide into 'moderate' and 'radical' factions at some point in their development" (Haines, 1984: 31). Those activist groups that "offer a more comprehensive version of the problem and more drastic change as a solution . . . are normally called radical" (Zald & McCarthy, 1980: 8), whereas activist groups at the other end of the spectrum are considered moderate or reformative. In the context of corporate social change, reformative groups are taken to believe that although companies are part of the problem, they can also be part of the solution. In contrast, radical groups do not believe that companies can be part of the solution. Again, intermediate positions are possible. We focus on the degree of radicalism in the ideologies of activist groups as a significant dimension in the choice of particular tactics at the operational level.

At first sight, associating an activist group's ideological stance with its preference for particular tactics might look somewhat tautological. For example, radical activist groups tend to be organized non-hierarchically, to be non-bureaucratic, and to emphasize participatory democracy. They are ideologically anti-capitalistic, emphasize working outside the current political/economic system, and are multi-issue organizations. Due to their marginalized status, [they] tend to rely on innovative tactics as well as alternative forms of communication (Fitzgerald & Rodgers, 2000: 589).

However, the association between ideological stance and preferred tactics is not entirely rigid, as both anecdotal evidence and findings from empirical research show. One anecdote regards the case of a major Dutch animal rights protection organization (Dierenbescherming). Local branches of this reformative activist group were confirmed to have financially contributed to the violent and disruptive actions of a radical animal rights group (Dierenbevrijdingsfront, comparable to the American Animal Liberation Front). In addition, members of Dierenbescherming's national board even participated in several of the violent actions of Dierenbevrijdings-front *(NRC Handelsblad,* November 29, 2003, and December 13, 2003).

Conversely, radical groups may be involved in actions that by no means can be classified as disruptive or violent, such as buying shares of a contested firm in order to be admitted to speak at shareholder meetings. Another example is the "subvertising" that is applied in a campaign where airlines are contested for their involvement in the "deportation" of economic refugees out of Europe. "It is an image polluting campaign. It takes the typical images, logos, colors and ideas of a company and slightly changes their contents. . . . it should question the image as if something in this image is seriously flawed, a flaw which should be pointed out to the consumer" (No Border, 2005).

Apart from these anecdotes, evidence from systematic research is also available. Rucht, for instance, concludes that "informal groups can be moderate in their activities and formal groups can tend towards radical action" (1999:

166). Lustig and Brunner (1996) show that two American environmental organizations, the Environmental Defense Fund (EDF) and Citizen's Clearinghouse for Hazardous Wastes (CCHW), have radical stances on pesticides but differ in how they operate: CCHW uses nonconventional, disruptive tactics, but EDF does not. Further, Meyer suggests that even if the choice of a set of core tactics by a peace organization is best explained by the ideology of the organization, still "a number of organizations in the sample did not identify as protest movements, yet engaged in occasional acts of protest" (2004: 182). Finally, it should be noted that many of the disruptive, innovative, and non-conventional tactics explored by radical groups are adopted by reformative activist groups at later stages in the development of a social movement (Tarrow, 1983). Activist groups thus have a broader and more complex set of tactics at their disposal than would be suggested from looking at their ideology alone.

Activist groups are aware of the complex amalgam of more or less converging interests, identities, and ideologies that characterize the movement in which they operate. Ideological variety within a social movement can lead to "radical flank effects," which involve the consequences of the existence of radical factions on the ability of reformative factions to realize their goals (Haines, 1984). The existence of a radical group may affect the legitimacy of a reformative group as being representative of its constituency; it may increase public awareness of reformative groups, their definitions of the problem, and their access to decision makers; or it may affect their ability to attract resources.

On the one hand, movement characteristics thus restrain the choice of action of activist groups, their flexibility in tactical choices, their possible organizational form, and the level of accountability they must demonstrate toward their constituents (Dreiling & Wolf, 2001; Minkoff, 2001). But, on the other hand, activist groups can deliberately make use of these characteristics—for example, when influencing the broader movement's ideological stance through the specific framing of contested issues or when differentiating themselves from other activist groups in the movement with whom they compete for resources (McCarthy & Zald, 1977; Zald & McCarthy, 1980). Social movements can even make use of this effect strategically, for example, by having radical groups perform disruptive tactics to pave the way for the claims of reformative groups

(Haines, 1984). In this sense ideology and instrumental behavior are not opposites (Zald, 2000); ideology suggests how activist groups may operate instrumentally to effectively pursue their beliefs and interests, even to the extent that they—temporarily—denounce their identity. The specialization and differentiation among activist groups could allow the entire movement to operate more flexibly and to find a solution to the legitimacy dilemma by the loose coupling of the activities of radical and reformative activist groups.

Looking at different ideological positions as influencing activist groups' tactics to stimulate corporate social change therefore goes beyond Rowley and Moldoveanu's (2003) distinction between interest- and identity-based activism. In their model of stakeholder group mobilization, the interests and identity of individuals, as well as the characteristics of the group they belong to, are considered determinants of group mobilization toward the focal organization. Of course, identity and ideology are related concepts, but identity refers to social relations, whereas ideology refers to views and beliefs (Hunt & Benford, 2004; Snow, 2004).

In short, collective identity provides "a shared and interactive sense of 'we-ness' and 'collective agency'" (Snow, 2001: 2213), whereas ideology stabilizes the relationships among an actor (or a group of actors), its (their) adversary, and its (their) objectives (Kozinets & Handelman, 2004). Ideology "is assumed to provide the rationale for defending or challenging various social arrangements and conditions" (Snow, 2004: 396)—for instance, the level of corporate social change activities. Adding the notion of ideology as another influential factor of activism hence takes the discussion beyond the individual and its group, since this notion provides a link to the worldview the group adheres to. Ideology therefore provides a useful link to understanding activist groups' expectations and demands at the organizational and field levels and to the repertoire of tactics these groups consider legitimate and suitable for establishing corporate social change.

Activism and Institutional Change

Institutions can be defined briefly as "multi-faceted, durable social structures, made up of symbolic elements,

social activities, and material resources" (Scott, 2001: 49). They have isomorphic effects on the actors in an organizational field by constraining their behavior through coercive, normative, and cognitive forces (Scott, 2001), but they are simultaneously shaped by interaction among the actors in the field. Field frames (Lounsbury et al., 2003) provide order and stability in an organizational field, since they comprise the technical, legal, or market standards that define the normal modes of operation within that specific field (Lawrence, 1999). According to Lounsbury et al., the "notion of field frame is an intermediate concept that has the durability and stickiness of an institutional logic, but akin to strategic framing, it is endogenous to a field of actors and is subject to challenge and modification" (2003: 72). Some actors in the field, including activist groups, thus try to influence field frames, turning the field into an arena of power relations (Brint & Karabel, 1991). Activist groups employ various tactics in order to better align the prevailing field frame with the preference structure that characterizes the social movement they represent. Before we discuss how radical and reformative activist groups differ in this respect, we need to conceptualize institutional change.

Characteristics of Institutional Change

Institutional change comes in several forms, including the genesis of an institution, its elaboration, its decline or abandonment (deinstitutionalization), and its replacement by another institution (reinstitutionalization; Jepperson, 1991). No doubt, the ambition of activist groups is to significantly alter or even replace current institutions by others, but their efforts may have less dramatic consequences in that current institutions are only marginally modified or not even affected at all. Institutional change is constrained by the relatedness of a challenged institution and other institutions and by the mutually reinforcing systems of practices, interests, and ideas that are embedded in the challenged institution (Greenwood & Hinings, 1996; Holm, 1995; Jepperson, 1991). Hence, to change institutions, old institutions first need to become deinstitutionalized and disentangled before new or adapted ones can be reinstitutionalized (Greenwood et al., 2002; Tolbert & Zucker, 1996).

Theorization—the "justification of an abstract solution" (Greenwood et al., 2002: 60)—is an important condition for reinstitutionalization, since it "specifies why the potential adopter should attend to the behavior of one population and not some other, what effects the practice will have, and why the practice is particularly applicable or needed" (Strang & Meyer, 1993: 500). This institutional change process provides activist groups with several points of leverage to pursue corporate social change, notably in stimulating the deinstitutionalization and reinstitutionalization of field frames.

Figure 49.1 suggests that institutional change has taken place when a field frame, F_1 (at time t_1), has developed into another field frame, F_2 (at a later point in time, t_2). When F_1 has transformed into F_2, it can be argued, first, that F_1 has become deinstitutionalized and, subsequently, that F_2 has reinstitutionalized. The distinction is analytical, because in reality it may be very difficult to define an exact moment in time at which the transformation of F_1 into F_2 is completed. During some period of time, F_1 and F_2 are likely to coexist, and elements of F_1 are likely to be found as sediments in the practices informed by F_2 (Cooper, Hinings, Greenwood, & Brown, 1996). We nevertheless can distinguish activities aimed at the deinstitutionalization of current practices in F_1 from those aimed at the reinstitutionalization of preferred alternative practices in F_2, because different forms of legitimacy are invoked to justify them.

Moral legitimacy has been argued to be central in processes of deinstitutionalization, and pragmatic legitimacy in processes of reinstitutionalization (Greenwood et al., 2002; Lounsbury et al., 2003). However, we expect that radical and reformative activist groups will differ in how they invoke these different forms of legitimacy in striving for corporate social change. Differences will appear in the type of arguments they use, as well as in the level of activity they demonstrate.

Deinstitutionalization, Reinstitutionalization, and Legitimacy

Before F_2 can be reinstitutionalized, F_1 needs to be sufficiently destabilized for field players to even start thinking about alternatives to it. In the process of deinstitutionalization, moral legitimacy is central, because it

is related to an evaluation of whether the organization "effectively promote[s] societal welfare, as defined by the audience's socially constructed value system" (Suchman, 1995: 579). When striving for the deinstitutionalization of F_1, activist groups systematically invoke moral legitimacy. However, in doing so, radical and reformative activist groups use different arguments. This idea builds on a distinction between consequential and structural aspects of moral legitimacy (Suchman, 1995).

Actors may be granted moral legitimacy because of what they *do* (consequential) or because of what they *are* (structural). If a firm's activities—or the consequences thereof—are considered appropriate and effective in promoting societal welfare, the argument to grant moral legitimacy is said to be consequential. If, however, a firm receives moral legitimacy because it is considered an appropriate entity in itself, the argument is said to be structural. Reformative activist groups turn their judgment that the activities of a particular firm are not appropriate or effective in promoting societal welfare into a disavowal of this firm's activities; they use a consequential argument. In contrast, radical activist groups expand the moral judgment to discrediting the firm itself. They locate the firm in a "morally disfavored taxonomic category" (Suchman, 1995: 581), thus adding a structural argument to the consequential argument.

For example, radical branches of the animal rights movement categorically oppose farms that raise livestock for their meat and skins, because, they argue, animals have intrinsic rights that are violated when the animals are killed for consumption. Hence, they campaign against the very existence of such farms, and even the entire meat and fur industries. Reformative groups limit their campaign to improving the conditions under which the animals are raised (Jasper & Nelkin, 1992). Both groups are motivated by moral indignation, but they use different arguments.

> Proposition 1: In striving for the deinstitutionalization of an established field frame, reformative activist groups use consequential arguments, whereas radical activist groups supplement consequential arguments with structural arguments.

Theorization is a central activity in the reinstitutionalization of preferred practices, as articulated in F_2. To do so, activist groups use arguments based on moral

Figure 49.1 Types of Legitimacy Invoked in Processes of Frame Transformation

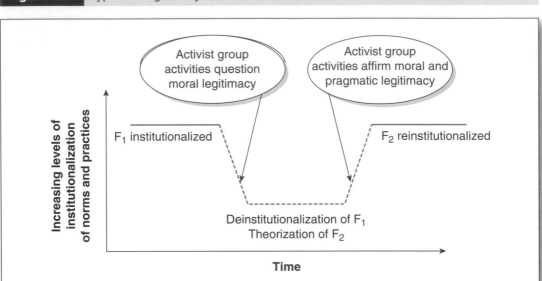

legitimacy. This is not surprising, since the alternative practices are preferred simply because of their expected consequences. However, theorization that solely builds on arguments of moral legitimacy is unlikely to provide a sufficient condition for diffusion, for to some extent firms may resist pressures for institutional isomorphism (Oliver, 1991). Additional arguments are needed before theorization can have the effect of "turning diffusion into rational choice" (Strang & Meyer, 1993: 500). Additional arguments can be found by invoking pragmatic legitimacy, which "rests on the self-interested calculations of an organization's most immediate audiences" (Suchman, 1995: 578). Again, reformative and radical activist groups are likely to differ in the extent to which they invoke arguments based on pragmatic legitimacy.

For instance, as Lounsbury et al. (2003) observed in their study of institutional change regarding recycling, reformers made use of appeals to both moral and pragmatic legitimacy when advancing recycling, whereas radicals solely used arguments connected to moral legitimacy. Pragmatic legitimacy is invoked because theorization is not only about the desirability but also about the viability of an alternative frame (Strang & Meyer, 1993; Tolbert & Zucker, 1996). However, whereas the pragmatic legitimacy of F_2 is very clear to the activist group—because adoption of F_2 by a challenged firm makes the activist group see the firm "as being

responsive to [its] larger interests" (Suchman, 1995: 578)—this legitimacy is not necessarily clear to the firm. The challenge to activist groups is to convince the firm of the interest it has in receiving pragmatic legitimacy from them. In order to do so, activist groups must seek to occupy a position in society that signals their relevance to this firm—they must increase their salience (Mitchell et al., 1997) in such a way that their involvement in adopting F_2 becomes relevant and valuable to the challenged firm and thus adds to this firm's self-interested calculations.

Activist groups may advance different types of arguments to contend why it would be in a firm's interest to receive pragmatic legitimacy. They may try to convince the firm that adopting F_2 is in its best interest because of material benefits to the firm; the argument could be that adopting F_2 enables the firm to explore attractive market opportunities or to benefit from lower costs. Alternatively, activist groups may allow the firm to make use of their reputation in bolstering its own reputation, which may help the firm to differentiate from its major competitors. Finally, activist groups may even allow the firm to be involved in their own internal decision making. For example, it has been reported that WWF[1] regularly accepts sponsorship from companies, and, in return, these companies may use the WWF logo or even obtain a seat on WWF's board—practices for which the organization is heavily criticized by other, more radical activist groups (Wilson, 2002).

The granting of pragmatic legitimacy thus implies a cooperative stance toward firms, increasingly so when the arguments used vary from pointing out business opportunities to allowing firms to have a say in whether and how the activist group's assets, such as its reputation, can be used to the firm's benefit. In light of the different ideologies of radical versus reformative activist groups, it is to be expected that only the latter groups will be inclined to use arguments based on pragmatic legitimacy in advancing the theorization of F_2. Because there is only limited space in the collective action frame of the most radical activist groups for firms and the current structures in which firms operate, their theorization of F_2 is unlikely to address the firm's self-interested calculation that is inherent to pragmatic legitimacy.

> Proposition 2: In striving for the reinstitutional-ization of their preferred field frame, radical activist groups use arguments based on moral legitimacy, whereas reformative activist groups supplement these with arguments based on pragmatic legitimacy.

Having examined the arguments invoked by activist groups, we now turn to their level of activity during different stages of the institutional change process. By granting pragmatic legitimacy, activist groups run the risk of being co-opted. Activist groups are likely to differ in their opinion about the risk of co-optation. Radical activist groups are less likely to call for cooperation, since this can be seen as a confirmation of existing structures; they would not want to be connected to other actors representing the very system they discredit.

For example, the involvement of a large number of reformative activist organizations in the establishment of the UN Global Compact has generated severe criticism from more radical activist groups. In the Global Compact activist groups, policy makers and businesses signed a set of principles concerning environmental protection, labor rights, and human rights that stimulate firms to voluntarily report on the progress they make in these domains (Kell, 2003). Radical activist groups contest the voluntary nature of the Global Compact, believing it offers insufficient incentives for firms to change their practices since it might shield participating firms from further governmental regulation. Moreover, these groups see their potential leverage over firms threatened, because the involvement of reformative groups might cause participating firms to be no longer willing to listen to noninvolved activist groups.

We therefore expect that radical activist groups will consider the risk of co-optation as greater, whereas reformative activist groups will assess this as less risky. For this reason radical activist groups are likely to devote a greater share of their time and resources to activities related to deinstitutionalization than to reinstitutionalization.

Conversely, reformative activist groups will be keener to engage in activities aimed at reinstitutionalization than deinstitutionalization. In deinstitutionalizing F_1 and reinstitutionalizing F_2, reformative activist groups focus their energy on the issue of how firms in general may convincingly show that they have established high levels of corporate social change activities. According to them, firms ought to be transparent and accountable, because under such conditions market forces will reward those firms exhibiting high levels of corporate social change activities and punish those that do not. They leave it to others to draw implications from what firms report.

For example, Consumers International (CI) campaigns to increase the levels of corporate social reporting, and it especially demands producer transparency and accountability (Scholte, 2004). Rather than challenging labor conditions in a specific firm's supply chain, the group posits that labor conditions in general should be in accordance with international standards, urging firms to demonstrate their compliance with such standards. Such information should allow consumers and investors to make their own choices regarding which firms' products to buy or in which stock to invest.

There is hardly any activity oriented toward deinstitutionalization to be observed in these campaigns. If firms were to be discredited in such campaigns, it would be because of their lack of transparency rather than because of the labor policies of their supply chain. Opposite radical activist groups, reformative groups hence show a higher level of activity aimed at reinstitutionalization than deinstitutionalization.

> Proposition 3: Reformative activist groups spend more of their resources and time on

activities aimed at reinstitutionalization than deinstitutionalization, whereas radical activist groups spend more of their resources and time on activities aimed at deinstitutionalization than reinstitutionalization.

Tactics for Institutional Change

There are many different tactics that activist groups may use, ranging from petitions and lobbying to confrontations and sabotage (Rochon, 1988) and reflecting the entire range of conventional, disruptive, and violent tactics (Tarrow, 1998). There is a long history of examples of material damage to firms caused by activist groups. For instance, between 1811 and 1816 the Luddites applied machine-breaking tactics, deliberately looking for opportunities to further their own interests (higher wages, job security), rather than acting out of an indiscriminate position against industrialization per se; they hit where it hurt (Hobsbawm, 1952). The activism of these Luddites, however, was different from present-day economic protest in democratic advanced capitalist societies, since the Luddites "were defending livelihoods under threat from new economic forces and could not campaign overtly without facing severe repression" (Plows, Wall, & Doherty, 2004: 200).[2]

Friedman (1999) provides another historical example, reporting that, since the 1880s, stand-ins and other obstructionist tactics, such as picket lines, were used to convince customers not to buy at particular stores—for example, if the owner would not hire African American labor. Shop owners were selectively put under pressure to comply with these demands by negatively affecting their turnover.

Current activist group protest tactics are believed to be increasingly supplemented by inflicting symbolic damage on companies, such as affecting a firm's reputation through the clever use of mass media, rather than bringing economic damage to firms (Friedman, 1999; Taylor & van Dyke, 2004). To understand the different tactics activist groups can employ vis-á-vis firms, we discuss two influence logics.

Although the tactics of activist groups have received ample attention in the social movement literature, the focus there is often on the political change these activist groups strive for (Taylor & van Dyke, 2004). Della Porta and Diani (1999: 174-ff.) discuss several mechanisms by which protest tactics can be effective in a public policy context. They suggest that collective action may be effective in forcing decision makers to change or abandon contested practices or policies if the protest raises the cost of continuing the contested practices or policies ("logic of material damage") or if the protest is supported by a large number of people ("logic of numbers").[3] We argue that these two logics can be elaborated in the corporate context.

Damage and Gain

The logic of material damage is based on economic calculation. By disturbing or slowing down the normal operational rhythm or by damaging the property of a decision maker—a government or a firm—protesters increase the cost the decision maker must bear to continue the contested decisions or policies. Ultimately, the cost will rise so high that the balance with the benefits to the decision maker will no longer be positive.

For example, a significant part of the persisting protests against nuclear energy plants in Germany focused on increasing the cost of nuclear energy. Strong demands for double security measures and concrete containment of reactors added to the investment cost. Also, antinuclear energy activists chained themselves to the railways, not only showing their dedication but also expecting that the cost of transport of nuclear materials—owing to loss of time, the use of special police forces, and so forth—would rise so high that, on balance, the economic feasibility of nuclear energy would disappear (Kolb, 2002).

Cost may rise because a challenged organization is required to spend time and resources in responding to the challenge, or because it needs to make organizational adjustments by creating new functions and departments (Rowley & Berman, 2000). Although the mechanism is likely to work in both public policy and corporate contexts, it is probably more effective in the latter because of the profit motive of firms (McWilliams & Siegel, 2001; Spar & La Mure, 2003). In practice, however, the cost added or the reduction of revenues needs to be substantial in order to have more than a marginal impact on a healthy firm (Spar & La Mure, 2003).[4] Making a significant impact on the firm's economic position is quite a challenge for activist groups, especially in the case of large firms that have ample slack resources.

The logic of material damage needs to be expanded in two ways to better fit the corporate context. First, material *gain* may also be effective in sustaining or bringing about corporate social change activities—for example, if consumers decide to preferentially shop at one company rather than another in order to reward it for its particular policies or practices ("buycott"; Friedman, 1999; Vogel, 2004). Second, gain and damage need not always be material but can also be *symbolic.* Morrill, Zald, and Rao (2003) point to Scott's (1989) distinction between material and symbolic aspects: "'material' forms focus on the subversion (and often the destruction, hampering, or appropriation) of organizational technologies and resources, whereas 'symbolic' forms attempt to subvert dominant meanings, ideologies, and discourses" (2003: 394). Protest results in symbolic damage if it is made clear that the decision maker is publicly typified as noncomplying with institutionalized rules, values, or categories.

Inflicting symbolic damage has become an option since the rise of mass media (Friedman, 1999). For example, large companies that operate in advertising-intensive consumer markets have become dependent on their reputation with critical constituents to maintain sales or to keep valuable members of their workforce (Fombrun & Shanley, 1990; Turban & Greening, 1997).

Several examples of protest have been reported where protesters quite ingeniously have made use of the vulnerability of such firms for reputation damage with consumers. By taking corporate symbols and logos out of context and transforming them, protesters aim to influence the mental association that consumers experience when viewing these symbols in another instance (cf. Bennett, 2004; Carty, 2002; No Border, 2005). Usually, there is no intention of inflicting immediate material damage. The ambition is to convince the public at large, and through them political decision makers, that the firm belongs to some morally disfavored taxonomic category. Doing so is a first step in creating sufficient public support, for example, for a boycott to succeed, even if some consumers, because of their changed perception of the firm, may already decide to shop elsewhere. Thus, symbolic damage contains a threat of inflicting material damage.

Conversely, symbolic gain may change to material gain, for example, when a reinforcement of the firm's reputation leads to increased turnover. The logic of material damage thus needs to be complemented by a logic of material gain, as well as by the logics of symbolic damage and symbolic gain.

Numbers

The logic of numbers is applied in different participatory forms of action, such as petitions, marches, boycotts, and other forms of grassroots mobilization. By showing their numbers, protesters collectively express that they no longer believe that the decisions or policies of a decision maker are desirable, proper, or appropriate. If a conflict escalates, the loss of legitimacy of decisions and policies may expand to negatively affect the legitimacy of the decision maker itself (Beetham, 1991). Of course, the larger the number of protesters, the greater this effect will be. This mechanism may work effectively in corporate situations if the decision maker depends on the support of the contesters. For instance, Frooman (1999) argues that when a firm's management depends on the continuing support of a particular stakeholder group, this group may use the threat to withdraw its support as a lever in negotiations. The salience of this particular stakeholder group increases if it can mobilize more supporters, all the more so if those supporters are publicly visible and highly reputed.

In their attempts to affect the level and nature of corporate social change activities, activist groups may thus choose to employ tactics based on participatory forms of action in order to increase their leverage over firms. However, it has been suggested that tactics based on the logic of numbers have decreased in importance. For several reasons, in the corporate context, consumer protest has changed in character over the past century, from being predominantly "marketplace oriented" to "media oriented" (Friedman, 1999). One reason is related to the opportunities that mass media—and more recently the internet—offer in the dissemination of relevant information and images (Illia, 2003; Taylor & van Dyke, 2004). Another reason can be found in the current difficulties that activist groups face in mobilizing the numbers of protesters required for this type of protest tactic to be successful. A third reason is related to the character of modern corporations: several remain invisible behind their subsidiaries that market different products, each under its own brand, whereas other corporations have been able to create strong customer loyalties (Friedman, 1999).

Other tactics may substitute for the numbers, however. Nonparticipatory protest tactics do not depend on a large number of protesters but on the quality of the resources that a small number of highly dedicated activists bring into the protest (Rucht, 1988). Examples of such resources are access to specialized knowledge and high-quality information, access to mass media, expertise in political lobbying, or expertise in court procedures. In terms of the tactics presented in Table 49.1, as much symbolic damage might be inflicted through a well-designed media campaign as through a rally or petition, but, in order to be effective, the latter must be massively attended while the former can be brought about by a small number of dedicated, ingeniously operating protesters.

On these theoretical bases we classify various protest tactics that activist groups may use vis-à-vis companies in Table 49.1. The left column contains the intended outcome of the use of tactics: material or symbolic. The other columns indicate to what extent the success of tactics depends on the participation of a large number of protesters: protest tactics can be participatory or nonparticipatory (mass participation versus elite participation). Having examined the ideology of activist groups, its repercussions for the type of arguments these groups use, and the level of activity they may develop in contributing to the deinstitutionalization of F_1 and, respectively, the reinstitutionalization of F_2, we now discuss the employment of tactics.

Application of Tactics

To consider how various forms of protest are actually used by activist groups that wish to advance corporate social change activities, we start from the assumption that the interaction between activist groups and firms is, at least partly, guided by an instrumental logic under resource constraints: for activist groups because of their change ambitions, for firms because of their profit motive. Cost and effectiveness then can be seen as two central characteristics of the tactics applied by activist groups. In relation to Table 49.1, we first argue that, in general, activist groups are likely to start their protest by choosing tactics that are nonparticipatory and that are aimed at having a symbolic impact, and, second, that as the interaction escalates or endures over time, radical activist groups will increasingly use tactics aimed at material damage, whereas reformative ones will be inclined to mobilize larger numbers of protesters.

Table 49.1	Typology of Tactics in the Interaction Between Social Movement Organizations and Firms

Intended Outcome of Use of Tactics	Dependence on Participatory Forms of Action Is High ("Mass Participation")	Dependence on Participatory Forms of Action Is Low ("Elite Participation")
Material damage	Boycott	Blocking of gates, sabotage, occupation of premises, internet activism ("hacktivism"), lawsuits
Material gain	Buycott	Cooperation
Symbolic damage	Writing letters/emails, petitions, marches, rallies	Shareholder activism, street theater, negative publicity, research
Symbolic gain	Voluntary action	Positive publicity, cooperation

Tactical Starting Position

The tactics in the lower right column of Table 49.1 are nondisruptive, and their resource intensity is relatively low. Therefore, they offer a common tactical starting position for both radical and reformative activist groups. Similar to the public policy context, it is to be expected that activist groups will begin to vent their dissatisfaction by informing the firm about their grievances and will demand corrective action to be taken. In the case of continuing unsatisfactory response or nonresponse by the firm, more radical or resource-intensive protest tactics will be used (della Porta & Diani, 1999; Tarrow, 1998), leading eventually to an escalation of the controversy. Why would, at least initially, tactics that bring about a symbolic impact be preferred over those aimed at making a material impact? To support our claim that the tactics in the lower right column of Table 49.1 are indeed likely to be a tactical starting position, we need to make it plausible that nonparticipatory tactics with a symbolic impact can be effective and are easier to organize than the other tactics presented.

Among participatory tactics, we contrast a boycott (material damage) with a letter writing campaign (symbolic damage). Both need to attract a large number of participants to be effective, but a boycott requires a continuing effort on the part of the participants, whereas letter writing merely demands a one-time effort. Letter writing campaigns have proven to be effective, if only through the appeal made on moral legitimacy. However, by writing a letter, participants indicate that they are willing to mobilize. Their willingness to make a one-time effort increases the chance they might also participate in more demanding or longer-lasting protest tactics—for example, by participating in a boycott.[5] If sufficient numbers of people participate in tactics aimed at inflicting a symbolic impact, a momentum may build that can be transformed into participation in tactics aimed at material damage. The anticipated consequences to the firm, if a large number of people indeed live up to their initial commitment, may be such that the firm does not dare to take the risk of neglecting the activism. Regarding material gain, a similar argument can be developed for a "buycott" versus the promise to do business with the firm. Among the range of participatory tactics, it is therefore easier, and potentially equally effective, for activist groups to employ those tactics that aim at having a symbolic rather than a material impact.

Likewise, in the case of nonparticipatory tactics, we contrast tactics intended at inflicting significant material damage, such as sabotage, with those intended at inflicting symbolic damage, such as a media campaign. When using tactics aimed at inflicting material damage, activist groups—especially reformative ones that depend to a greater extent on their numbers for efficacy—run the risk of alienating their constituency and losing potential allies, whereas publicly discrediting the firm in a media campaign may result in a reconsideration by other parties as to whether or not to continue to do business with the firm, at least under similar conditions as before. There may not be immediate material damage, but neglecting continued symbolic damage exposes the firm to the risk of material damage (Wartick, 1992). For example, investors may eventually increase the cost of capital to reflect increased risk perceptions. Adding significant material gain to the firm, in contrast, is equally risky to activist groups—especially to radical ones—since it may be interpreted by their constituents and (potential) allies as a sign of selling out or being co-opted, thus hampering their independence. In either case we therefore can presume that activist groups will initially seek to increase the efficiency of their efforts by keeping to tactics aimed at having a symbolic impact in which the threat of a material impact substitutes for a real impact.

Finally, resource efficiency arguments would also predict that activist groups prefer to adopt nonparticipatory rather than participatory tactics. After all, significant effort is required to mobilize the crowds that are needed to make the logic of numbers effective. Knowledge about and feelings of discontent and agreement with the cause are not sufficient conditions for individuals to participate in protest activities (Klein et al., 2004). Not only does the collective identity of the movement need to be incorporated into people's political consciousness before they can be mobilized (Gamson, 1992), but, to become participants in protest, individuals must also be linked to the movement's network. They must be convinced of the net benefits of participation both for themselves and for the protest event, while mundane practicalities such as illness or lack of transportation should not obstruct their participation (Klandermans, 2004).

It requires a large effort on the part of the organization to overcome such barriers. Regarding consumer boycotts, Vogel concludes that "it has proven very difficult to mobilize large numbers of consumers to avoid the products of particular companies for social or political reasons" (2004: 96). Still, both material and symbolic impacts can be brought about with a small number of dedicated and experienced persons through nonparticipatory tactics. Few people are needed to investigate a firm's contribution to social welfare, and only a well-written press release may be needed to inflict reputation damage if it is shown that this contribution is lower than generally assumed (Fombrun & Shanley, 1990). In addition, a handful of protesters may suffice to relate a firm to disavowed practices if adequate media coverage is secured. Protest is newsworthy if it involves many people, utilizes radical tactics, or is particularly novel (Rochon, 1988). The latter two criteria can well be met with a small number of dedicated people and are therefore easier to organize than the first one. Hence, in terms of cost and effectiveness, non-participatory tactics aimed at bringing about a symbolic impact are a prime choice for activist groups in many cases.

Proposition 4: Both radical and reformative activist groups employ nonparticipatory tactics aimed at making symbolic impacts when starting to influence the nature and level of corporate social change activities.

Diverging Tactics Under Escalation

Although the arguments presented above provide insight into activist groups' tactical starting positions, it remains to be explained *why* firms would respond to the arguments of activist groups. If a firm repetitively ignores, defies, refuses, or otherwise responds negatively to an activist group's demand, the conflict endures over time and may escalate. In addition to having compelling arguments, activist groups then need to increase their salience with the firm. One well-known strategy, used by both reformative and radical groups, is to increase the legitimacy of their demand and to strengthen their position in the organizational field by seeking support from other powerful and legitimate actors. Such actors can be found both within and

outside the broader social movement; other activist groups in the same movement, unions, large shareholder groups, social investors, or political parties are among potential allies (cf. Berry, 2003; Frooman, 1999; Keck & Sikkink, 1998; Rowley, 1997).

To operate beyond such indirect strategies, activist groups need a reputation for being able to mobilize large numbers of supporters or to bring damage or gain to the firm. In order to make the firm respond to their demands, they may feel the need to live up to their reputation. In this respect, moving from nonparticipatory to participatory tactics and moving from tactics aimed at having a symbolic impact to those aimed at having a material impact represent two options for activist groups to increase their salience with firms. How to increase salience is a relevant question in situations of both deinstitutionalization and reinstitutionalization that radical and reformative activist groups are likely to approach in different ways.

Deinstitutionalization. In general, deinstitutionalization is focused at opposing institutionalized practices in F_1. Both reformative and radical activist groups will invoke moral legitimacy in arguing why they disavow this practice within the organizational field, but radical activist groups will be more inclined to also challenge the moral basis of the current field structure of a contested industry (Proposition 1). Nonparticipatory tactics aimed at having a symbolic impact may suffice to underscore the consequential arguments used when invoking moral legitimacy (Proposition 4). Some escalation can be accomplished within this set of tactics. For example, substantiating the threat of recourse to law by starting a lawsuit makes the protest more vehement. Likewise, when aiming to inflict reputation damage in a negative media campaign, the phrasing of the claim and the images used may be more or less confrontational (Bennett, 2004). However, the different forms of inflicting symbolic damage still have the dual objective of delivering the claim to both the company and bystanders and convincing them that the practices under F_1 are wrong. Deinstitutionalization represents a situation of conflict in which further escalation would lead radical activist groups to adopt tactics intended to inflict material damage and reformative ones to adopt participatory tactics.

In normal situations people usually have little reason to discredit a decision maker, even if they do not agree with all the decisions made. In situations of enduring or escalating conflict, this may change (Beetham, 1991). At some point activist groups will start to use structural arguments related to moral legitimacy, but radical activist groups will be more likely to do so than reformative ones. Radical activist groups are more likely to challenge the structural position of a firm within an organizational field and to dispute the trustworthiness of firms in general—and challenged ones in particular. This leads them to see lower barriers for the application of nonconventional protest tactics. Consequently, they will be quicker to employ tactics of material damage, including bringing the firm's daily operations to a halt by blocking gates or even applying sabotage. Moreover, their radical position will make it even more difficult for them to mobilize sufficient numbers, beyond the normal difficulty of mobilizing support for participatory protest tactics. In attempting to strengthen their position vis-à-vis companies, radical activist groups will thus be more resource efficient in employing nonparticipatory protest tactics rather than mobilizing the relatively few people already convinced, especially since nonparticipatory tactics may also have the effect of increasing the number of people who support their position (Plows et al., 2004).

Alternatively, reformative activist groups will find it harder to justify the infliction of material damage during deinstitutionalization. If they try to inflict material damage on firms, they will face a considerable risk of alienating a substantial part of their constituency. This might lead to the erosion of the central resource that provides them leverage in their engagement with firms. In escalating situations, reformative activist groups therefore will find it more attractive to actually lever their constituency base—and, thus, to use participatory tactics—than to revert to tactics aimed at inflicting material damage.

Finally, because of the discrediting that is associated with deinstitutionalization, it is unlikely that tactics intended to provide symbolic or material *gain* will be found in this context. However, in the case of reformative activist groups, the analysis might be more complicated. As we argued before, collaborations between activist groups and firms may combine various stages in the process of institutional change, including deinstitutionalization and theorization. In this context, cooperation, as a nonparticipatory tactic that is based on the

provision of symbolic or material gain, may also be part of the efforts aimed at deinstitutionalization.

The partnership between WWF and Unilever to establish the Marine Stewardship Council (MSC) might serve as an example in this respect. The MSC was formed in 1997, when Unilever was concerned about its supply of seafood and WWF about the state of the oceans (Cummins, 2004). Both the firm and the activist group saw a need for change in institutionalized practices in the fishery industry. An important part of the activities of the MSC hence has been to discredit conventional fishery practices (Hernes & Mikalsen, 2002). The joint development of the MSC led to a viable alternative field frame F_2 regarding "sustainable fishing" that has gained prominence in the fishery industry over the years (Cummins, 2004).

> Proposition 5: As conflict escalates or endures over time, during deinstitutionalization, reformative activist groups increasingly will use tactics aimed at mobilizing larger numbers of protesters, whereas radical activist groups increasingly will use tactics aimed at material damage.

Reinstitutionalization. Reinstitutionalization implies the actual substitution of field frame F_2 for F_1. In order to accomplish this, reformative activist groups are likely to supplement arguments based on moral legitimacy with arguments based on pragmatic legitimacy, whereas radical activist groups will merely rely on moral legitimacy arguments (Proposition 2). Again, the question surfaces concerning what tactics might lever these different sorts of legitimacy, once nonparticipatory tactics aimed at having a symbolic impact do not suffice. Since reinstitutionalization is about generating support for new theorizations and about the diffusion of alternative practices throughout an organizational field, additional arguments and incentives are required beyond those that highlight the moral legitimacy argument.

To get their claims attended to—and, thus, to get support for the alternative practices they propose— reformative activist groups need to make them sufficiently relevant and valuable to the challenged organization. This approach is likely to result in tactics of material and symbolic gain. In the application of these tactics, an activist group may indicate benefits to the firm, or it might lend its reputation to bolster the firm's reputation. Using participatory tactics increases the benefits to the firm since it shows the potential value of adhering to the practices under F_2. The number of people involved in the tactics adds to the activist group's salience. Broadly supported tactics of material and symbolic gain therefore add to the reasons why a firm would adopt an alternative practice.

Radical activist groups, however, are less inclined to spend a large share of their resources on reinstitutionalization because they do not believe that firms can be part of the solution they aim for (Proposition 3). This seriously hampers the opportunity to grant pragmatic legitimacy, since this would require an activist group to make its claim relevant and valuable to the contested firm's objectives. Quite a few radical activist groups are likely to disband or reorient their energies during reinstitutionalization.[6] Nevertheless, radical groups may address issues of reinstitutionalization by invoking moral legitimacy, but they are likely to do so only under specific circumstances; the consequences of doing so then would have to fit in with their world view. Invoking moral legitimacy in reinstitutionalizing alternative practices might, for instance, imply a radical transformation in ownership structure and, to some extent, the development of an alternative economic entity. The influence tactics employed in such a situation then would be a combination of symbolic and material gain. Developing an alternative economic entity would be aimed at resulting in material gain to this alternative practice; activist groups' expressions of support for this practice could result in symbolic gain and, thus, strengthen the reinstitutionalization process. Of course, as a corollary, material damage to vested corporate interests within an organizational field might result (similar to a boycott), but this usually is not the main objective since radical activist groups dispute these interests anyway.

The support of local exchange trading systems (LETS) is an example of such an approach (Pacione, 1997), since these trading systems "operate as an alternative (local) market for the members' goods and services" (Crowther, Greene, & Hosking, 2002: 355). Consequently, LETS often are fairly limited in scale and based in local communities (Crowther et al., 2002). Participants deliberately place themselves and their transactions outside the normal economic order, causing material damage by withdrawing their expenditure from firms. It is likely that nonparticipatory tactics are chosen when radical activist

groups aim for such a specific reinstitutionalization; relatively small numbers of protesters can develop such systems, but it is their individual contribution to the LETS that is important for its success.

> Proposition 6: As conflict escalates or endures over time, during reinstitutionalization, reformative activist groups increasingly will use participatory tactics that are aimed at both material and symbolic gain within the prevailing field frame, whereas radical activist groups increasingly will use tactics aimed at material and symbolic gain within an alternative field frame.

Tactics for Field-Level Change

Although most of the interaction occurs between activist groups and firms, the activist groups' ambition ultimately would be to accomplish field-level change. There are two main routes for field-level change that are open to activist groups. One route is to work at the field level. Activist groups might try to affect the coercive, normative, or cognitive institutional pressures in the field—for instance, by lobbying with public authorities and business associations for regulation or standards or by raising public awareness. They might even try to establish a new organizational field, more or less independent from the one being challenged (cf. the LETS system). Indirect tactics have already been investigated (Berry, 2003; Keck & Sikkink, 1998; O'Rourke, 2003), so we do not further discuss this route here.

The other main route for activist groups to accomplish field-level change is by convincing individual field members one by one to change their practices. The question for activist groups then is what type of firms to focus on. The population of firms in a given field, around a particular issue, comprises a significant number of disinterested firms. Usually, however, a number of proactive firms that seek to manipulate their institutional context in anticipation of activist group demands can also be identified, as well as a number of laggard firms that seek to defy or avoid activist group pressure (Oliver, 1991). Both cases offer specific points of leverage for activist groups. Laggard firms can be discredited in public relatively easily, or they can be threatened by recourse to law. In contrast, proactive firms have already significantly moved to adopt practices under the alternative field frame F_2 or have indicated that they are willing to do so. To the extent that their proactiveness provides a differentiation advantage over competitors, these firms have an interest in maintaining such a proactive reputation. This makes them vulnerable to challenges to their reputation (Wartick, 1992). Also, if F_1 is sufficiently destabilized, early adopters of the new practices under F_2 might be considered by other firms in the field to have found a workable solution to the prevailing uncertainty that is worth mimicking, thus contributing to the diffusion of the new practices (DiMaggio & Powell, 1983).

Working at the level of the individual firm, we suggest that radical activist groups predominantly challenge proactive firms by applying tactics that increasingly aim at bringing about material damage. If they can convincingly show how even proactive firms are incapable of doing good, the consequence will be that laggard firms are viewed as even less able to do good, which, in turn, implies a clear need for fundamental change. For instance, the targeting of Nike in anti-sweatshop campaigns (Carty, 2002; Wokutch, 2001) is a case in which a highly visible firm—a leader in its industry—was targeted by activist groups to garner increased attention for their attempts to alter manufacturing practices field wide. When Nike moved to implement a code of conduct, protests continued, with the aim of showing that working conditions in the supply chain remained substandard.

The main thrust in such activism is to destabilize the current field frame, but this gives radical groups little influence over the overall direction of the development of corporate social change activities at the field level. If they wish to operate at the field level, radical groups, given their ideological stance, have little choice but to try establishing a different field frame, independent from prevailing ones, to further their own symbolic and material benefits (Proposition 6). For example, radical "culture jammers" promote "Blackspot sneakers" through their web site. Buyers of these shoes acquire a voting share in "The Blackspot Anticorporation," which operates a Portuguese union shop where the sneakers are made from organic, vegetarian, and recycled materials (Adbusters, 2005).

Reformative groups are less restrictive in their choice of targets when working at the firm level. They may both challenge laggard firms and work with proactive firms. By challenging laggard firms to raise their minimum level of corporate social change activities, the average standard in the entire organizational field will eventually be lifted. By stimulating proactive firms in their corporate social change policies and practices and by stimulating firms to become more proactive, reformative groups may try to expand the frontiers of corporate social change policies and practices in the organizational field. To achieve field-level change, these groups are therefore likely to trust in the diffusion of their preferred practices through processes of institutional isomorphism. They normatively present their preferred practices as good standards of professional behavior, and they hope for the unchecked spread of these practices as firms recognize them as worth mimicking (Propositions 2 and 6), or they work to get private standards, regulations, and codes of conduct accepted as field standards that can be enforced. Working at the field level, reformative activist groups thus either challenge laggard firms or cooperate with proactive firms.

> Proposition 7: To bring about field-level change, radical activist groups are more likely to challenge proactive firms, whereas reformative groups are more likely to challenge laggard firms and work with proactive firms.

Under conditions of escalation, both radical and reformative activist groups will seek to reinforce their position by forging coalitions among themselves, as well as with actors outside the social movement. However, given the diverging preferences for tactical choices owing to the different ideological orientations of radical and reformative groups—especially regarding the question of how to approach proactive firms (Proposition 7)—conflict can be expected to arise within the coalition, potentially leading to radical flank effects (Haines, 1984). To overcome their internal ideological differences, activist groups may try to diminish their internal conflict by creating coalitions that act as more or less independent organizations in working for field-level change. An example is the Clean Clothes Campaign (CCC), in which a variety of activist groups operate together. Often, CCC operates as an independent organization on behalf of its activist founders, but, occasionally, one or two founding groups operate independently from CCC. The Free Burma Coalition (FBC) is another example (Spar & La Mure, 2003).

Coordinated efforts across a broader movement could enhance its efficacy, since radical activist groups could thus indirectly engage in reinstitutionalization efforts that they could not easily support independently, their ideological position hampering most cooperation with firms. For reformative activist groups, coordination can be attractive because it reinforces their efforts for deinstitutionalization without risking their options for reinstitutionalization. Still, collaboration for deinstitutionalization is more likely to occur than collaboration for reinstitutionalization, since there is a common target during deinstitutionalization, whereas different preferences regarding the alternative field frame that is to be reinstitutionalized may limit the opportunities for collaboration during reinstitutionalization.

Proposition 8: The efficacy of joint efforts by radical and reformative activist groups in reinstitutionalization is enhanced if radical groups are constrained in applying tactics aimed at material damage.

Discussion and Conclusion

Questions of whether firms engage in corporate social change activities, and of what the nature of such activities is, are not only related to managers' wishes to do good or to improve their firm's competitive position but also to societal demand. Activist groups step forward to articulate societal preferences about the level and nature of corporate social change activities, and they challenge firms to comply with these preferences. The interaction between activist groups and firms is an antecedent of corporate social change activities that has received limited systematic attention in the literature to date. Our exploration in this realm gives rise to several implications and suggestions for further research.

Theoretical Implications

Our contributions to theory development are threefold: (1) we argue that ideology is a factor that

significantly influences which tactics activist groups employ vis-á-vis firms, (2) we identify a range of tactics that activist groups may employ in a corporate context, and (3) we link the tactics of different ideologically driven activist groups to their ambition of influencing the nature and level of corporate social change activities.

We first pointed out why ideology is an important characteristic of activist groups that needs to be considered in order to understand how these groups operate in a corporate context. Why and when activist groups move to act in such a context can be understood from their interests and identity (Rowley & Moldoveanu, 2003), but understanding *how* these groups act also requires considering their ideology. Although activism emerges from a social setting where people know and trust each other, it is their shared world view that affects how they act. Ideology links to the different types of legitimacy that play a role in the institutional change process by enabling activist groups to develop the abstract notions of legitimacy into arguments about what—in their view—is appropriate and justified to affect the level and nature of corporate social change activities in an organizational field. Looking at ideology is therefore a useful complement to merely considering interests and identity if we are to understand how activist groups try to influence firms.

We further proposed a typology to derive propositions on the choice of tactics by activist groups to enforce their ambitions at different stages of the institutional change process. The typology is based on the nature of damage or gain that activist groups aim to bring about (material, symbolic) and on the number of people that need to be involved for the tactics to be effective (participatory, nonparticipatory). It is an elaboration of the various logics identified by della Porta and Diani (1999) as to why social movement pressure might be effective in a public policy context. Translating and extending these logics to a corporate context constitutes the second contribution of this article. Having such a typology available for analyzing activism toward firms can contribute to our understanding of stakeholder tactics.

Our final and main contribution rests in combining these two points. We used insights from social movement studies and institutional change theory to explore how activist groups influence corporate social change activities. The ambition of activist groups in articulating their preferences can be regarded as setting in motion a process of aspired institutional change that involves both the deinstitutionalization of practices in the established field frame (F_1) and the reinstitutionalization of an alternative set of preferred practices in an alternative field frame (F_2). We argued that ideology matters in *how* activist groups seek to change the nature and level of corporate social change activities. In working to affect the deinstitutionalization of F_1 and the reinstitutionalization of F_2, radical and reformative activist groups use different legitimacy-based arguments, exhibit different levels of activity, and make different tactical choices. Building on these differences, we further suggested that radical and reformative groups differ in how they eventually work to bring about field-level change. The typology in Table 49.2 summarizes these differences.

Practical Implications

Practical recommendations can be formulated for activist groups and firms. For activist groups, an important implication of our argument concerns the involvement of their constituency. The pressure they exert on firms regarding the nature and level of corporate social change activities predominantly takes place in a private context over which public authorities deliberately have little direct influence. National governments and supranational bodies, such as the United Nations and the Organization for Economic Cooperation and Development, stress the voluntary character of corporate involvement in such issues as environmental protection and labor conditions beyond what is required by law. As claimants in these matters, activist groups have traditionally acted politically in trying to influence the diffusion, interpretation, and implementation of laws and regulations, as well as in lobbying for the formulation of new laws and regulations.

However, since the early 1990s, activist groups have increasingly challenged business firms *directly,* as opposed to the more established ways of *indirectly* challenging them through channels of public policy (cf. Berry, 2003; Spar & La Mure, 2003). Although their ambition of establishing field-level change remains the same, this direct route requires activist groups to approach their constituents differently. Whereas in the public policy context the constituency might be

enrolled as voters, the private policy context offers the opportunity to expand the constituency's role to that of consumers, who, by selectively using their consumer power on a daily basis—or by threatening to do so—may affect the level and nature of corporate social change activities. If activist groups wish to join this bandwagon of "political consumerism" (Micheletti, Follesdal, & Stolle, 2004), they will need to spend time and effort to educate their constituency on how to become an effective instrument for change. This is especially relevant for reformative activist groups, being more dependent on participatory tactics than radical groups.

Similarly, for firms, taking stock of activist groups' ideological positions is helpful in understanding the range of tactics they might expect, even if it is still not completely predictable when, where, and how activist groups might challenge them. If firms wish to keep or gain some control over the process, they will need to be involved in the shaping of new practices through theorization. Moreover, better insight into activist groups' tactics enables some level of anticipation regarding these tactics. An improved understanding of the types of activist groups, and the different tactics they might apply, offers firms insight into the conditions of starting a debate and its contents, including reasons why the more radical activist groups would be less interested in participating in such a debate. Hence, looking in greater detail at influence tactics that activist groups use in trying to shape corporate social change activities may help firms to understand some crucial societal dynamics that may either facilitate or impede these activities.

Implications for Further Research

One potentially fruitful avenue for further research would be to analyze how activist campaigns regarding individual firms build up to field-level change. Looking at the development of campaigns over time could provide insight into the different tactics that are applied at different stages of the institutional change process. This could be elaborated by taking into account, for instance, questions of whether activist groups have developed new tactics when orienting their focus toward challenging corporate behavior. Has this development resulted in a new cycle of protest (Tarrow, 1983) or in a different tactical repertoire (Clemens, 1993)? Analyzing protest

Table 49.2 Typology of the Level of Activity, the Arguments Used, and the Tactics Applied by Activist Groups in Their Interaction With Firms During Different Stages of Institutional Change

Institutional Process Aimed For	Ideological Stance			
	Radical		Reformative	
	Deinstitutionalization	Reinstitutionalization	Deinstitutionalization	Reinstitutionalization
Arguments used	Moral legitimacy: consequential + structural arguments	Moral legitimacy: consequential arguments	Moral legitimacy: consequential arguments	Moral legitimacy: consequential + structural arguments + pragmatic legitimacy
Level of activity	High	Low	Low	High
Tactics during escalation	Symbolic damage + material damage Nonparticipatory	Symbolic gain + material gain Nonparticipatory	Symbolic damage + symbolic gain Nonparticipatory + participatory	Symbolic gain + material gain Nonparticipatory + participatory
Field-level changes	Challenge proactive firms	Work to establish an alternative field	Challenge laggard firms	Work with proactive firms

events could be helpful in investigating these kinds of questions (Koopmans & Rucht, 2002).

Another relevant issue regards the role of cooperation and competition among different activist groups that work in a particular social movement. Do these groups work together, and, if so, how? Is there indeed some form of coordinated specialization and differentiation among activist groups that enhances their collective effectiveness in pursuing their institutional change ambitions, as suggested by the radical flank effect? Rowley and Moldoveanu (2003) expect that interest and identity overlap among stakeholder groups have differentiated effects on whether or not they take action. According to them, interest overlap increases the likelihood that stakeholder groups will mobilize, whereas identity overlap decreases this likelihood, since these groups would want to profile themselves. Yet, at the movement level, it can often be observed that activist groups with similar identities collaborate in working on the same cause, sometimes openly and sometimes disguised under umbrella organizations. For example, Schurman (2004) shows how radical and reformative

activist groups productively collaborate in the antibiotech movement. More work is needed to establish whether, or under what conditions, identity or ideology has stronger effects on collaboration between activist groups striving for institutional change.

Although we suggested a proposition on the efficacy of joint protest tactics by radical and reformative activist groups, a limitation of our research is that we did not consider the outcomes of activist groups' efforts in great detail. Such outcomes are notoriously difficult to measure (Gamson, 1990; Giugni, 1998). Addressing the question of whether activist groups actually succeed in changing the nature and level of corporate social change activities is a third topic for further research. It is unlikely, however, that such outcomes solely depend on activist groups' efforts; characteristics of the firm or the industry in which the firm operates will be another important set of factors. In this respect, one might speculate about the existence of an "industry opportunity structure" (Schurman, 2004), similar to the concept of "political opportunity structure" in social movement studies (Kriesi, 2004; Tarrow, 1983, 1998). Industry opportunity structures may be related to economic, organizational, and cultural features that constrain or enhance the ability of firms within an industry to change their behavior. They may include cost structures, the level of competition, customer preferences, typical board compositions, and capital and advertising intensities (Baron, 2001; McWilliams & Siegel, 2001; Schurman, 2004).

Firms' motives and objectives in corporate social change activities might also be relevant for the outcomes of the deinstitutionalization and reinstitutionalization of practices. Lounsbury (2001), for instance, shows how an environmental organization coordinated with ecological activists inside universities to facilitate the creation of recycling programs that became staffed with full-time ecologically committed recycling coordinators, thus contributing to the success of these programs. The interplay between internal and external activists might be an important element in such studies. However, to suggest that such factors are straight predictors of outcomes would be to reinforce the structural bias that the political process tradition in social movement studies has been criticized for (cf. Goodwin & Jasper, 1999). Since it is unlikely that structural conditions offer similar opportunities to different activist groups (Hilson, 2002), taking into account the different tactics that activist groups deploy remains highly relevant. This would expand the scope of research beyond the analysis of activist groups' tactics to also linking antecedents and consequences.

To conclude, we have shown that the social movement literature and institutional change literature have several interesting points to offer and could well be combined to study the role of activist groups in influencing the nature and level of social change activities in companies. Both theories highlight specific aspects of the processes activist groups try to influence. From the social movement literature, much can be learned about the way influence is exerted by activist groups, whereas institutional change theories can suggest the underlying field-level structures and the mechanisms required to alter these. In discussing the interchange between the two streams of research, McAdam and Scott (2005) propose viewing organizational fields as the fundamental unit of analysis, pointing to the roles of different actors during episodes of field-level change. Studies of field frames and institutional strategies provide useful starting points in this direction. Looking at the roles of different actors in such processes—individually and collectively—can

contribute to our understanding of how influence strategies within organizational fields work and, thus, of how corporate social change activities are being shaped. Investigating the concept of institutional entrepreneurship (cf. Dorado, 2005; Maguire, Hardy, & Lawrence, 2004) might be instrumental here. The exploration in this article, focusing on ideological positions, provides a relevant starting point for further theoretical and empirical research into how activist groups may influence the rules of the game, and maybe even overrule them.

Notes

1. WWF was formerly known as the World Wildlife Fund but now presents itself by just this abbreviation, sometimes explained as World Wide Fund for Nature.

2. We thank one anonymous reviewer for pointing out the possible interpretation of Luddite activism as an early example of activist group pressure on companies, aimed at increasing the level of corporate social change activities. In addition, in this article we highlight activist groups in a broadly democratic advanced capitalist society. After all, in defending livelihoods and facing severe repression, the Luddites might not differ that much from, for instance, the Ogoni people in the oil fields of Nigeria.

3. Della Porta and Diani (1999) also discuss a "logic of bearing witness," in which protesters show their dedication and commitment to the cause they support by deliberately running personal or financial risk. In our view this logic is mainly meant to increase the vehemence of protest and will often be used in combination with another logic; it works by supporting and enhancing the logics of material damage and numbers. Therefore, we do not consider the logic of bearing witness as a self-standing logic in the interactions between activist groups and firms regarding the level and nature of corporate social change activities.

4. As one reviewer rightfully indicated, there might be a difference in this respect between firms whose cost structure is dominated by fixed costs and those where variable costs dominate, but a full treatment of this question is beyond the scope of this article.

5. The mechanism resembles the so-called foot-in-the-door technique, in which agreement with a small request is followed by a larger request that is then more difficult to refuse (Burger, 2001; Freedman & Fraser, 1966). Although it is plausible that the mechanism also works in this particular context, we do not believe that this has been confirmed yet.

6. We thank an anonymous reviewer for raising this issue.

References

Adbusters. 2005. *Blackspot shoes.* http://adbusters.org/metas/corpo/blackspotsneaker/home.html, accessed June 26.

Baron, D. P. 2001. Private politics, corporate social responsibility, and integrated strategy. *Journal of Economics and Management Strategy,* 10: 7–45.

Beetham, D. 1991. *The legitimation of power.* Basingstoke, UK: Palgrave.

Bennett, W. L. 2004. Branded political communication: Lifestyle politics, logo campaigns, and the rise of global citizenship. In M. Micheletti, A. Follesdal, & D. Stolle (Eds.), *Politics, products, and markets: Exploring political consumerism past and present:* 101–125. New Brunswick, NJ: Transaction.

Berry, G. R. 2003. Organizing against multinational corporate power in cancer alley: The activist community as primary stakeholder. *Organization and Environment,* 16: 3–33.

Blee, K. M., & Currier, A. 2005. Character building: The dynamics of emerging social movement groups. *Mobilization,* 10: 129–145.

Brint, S., & Karabel, J. 1991. Institutional origins and transformations: The case of American community colleges. In W. W. Powell, & P. J. DiMaggio (Eds.), *The new institutionalism in organizational analysis:* 337–361. Chicago: University of Chicago Press.

Buechler, S. M. 2000. *Social movements in advanced capitalism.* New York: Oxford University Press.

Burger, J. M. 2001. Psychology of social influence. In N. J. Smelser & P. B. Baltes (Eds.), *International encyclopedia of the social and behavioral* sciences: 14320–14325. Oxford: Elsevier Science.

Carroll, A. B. 1979. A three-dimensional conceptual model of corporate performance. *Academy of Management Review,* 4: 497–505.

Carty, V. 2002. Technology and counter-hegemonic movements: The case of Nike Corporation. *Social Movement Studies,* 1: 129–146.

Clarkson, M. B. E. 1995. A stakeholder framework for analyzing and evaluating corporate social performance. *Academy of Management Review,* 20: 92–117.

Clemens, E. S. 1993. Organizational repertoires and institutional change: Women's groups and the transformation of U.S. politics, 1890–1920. *American Journal of Sociology,* 98: 755–798.

Cooper, D. J., Hinings, B., Greenwood, R., & Brown, J. L. 1996. Sedimentation and transformation in organizational change: The case of Canadian law firms. *Organization Studies,* 17: 623–647.

Crowther, D., Greene, A. M., & Hosking, D. M. 2002. Local economic trading schemes and their implications for marketing assumptions, concepts and practices. *Management Decision,* 40: 354–362.

Cummins, A. 2004. The Marine Stewardship Council: A multi-stakeholder approach to sustainable fishing. *Corporate Social Responsibility and Environmental Management,* 11: 85–94.

Davis, G. F., McAdam, D., Scott, W. R., & Zald, M. N. (Eds.). 2005. *Social movements and organization theory.* New York: Cambridge University Press.

Davis, G. F., & Thompson, T. A. 1994. A social-movement perspective on corporate control. *Administrative Science Quarterly,* 39: 141–173.

della Porta, D., & Diani, M. 1999. *Social movements: An introduction.* Oxford: Blackwell.

Diani, M., & McAdam, D. (Eds.). 2003. *Social movements and networks: Relational approaches to collective action.* Oxford: Oxford University Press.

DiMaggio, P. J., & Powell, W. W. 1983. The iron cage revisited: Institutional isomorphism and collective rationality in organizational fields. *American Sociological Review,* 48: 147–160.

Dorado, S. 2005. Institutional entrepreneurship, partaking, and convening. *Organization Studies,* 26: 385–414.

Dreiling, M., & Wolf, B. 2001. Environmental movement organizations and political strategy: Tactical conflicts over NAFTA. *Organization and Environment,* 14: 34–54.

Fine, G. A., & Sandstrom, K. 1993. Ideology in action: A pragmatic approach to a contested concept. *Sociological Theory,* 11: 21–38.

Fitzgerald, K. J., & Rodgers, D. M. 2000. Radical social movement organizations: A theoretical model. *Sociological Quarterly,* 41: 573–592.

Fombrun, C., & Shanley, M. 1990. What's in a name: Reputation building and corporate strategy. *Academy of Management Journal,* 33: 233–258.

Freedman, J. L., & Fraser, S. C. 1966. Compliance without pressure: The foot in the door technique. *Journal of Personality and Social Psychology,* 4: 195–202.

Friedman, M. 1999. *Consumer boycotts: Effecting change through the marketplace and the media.* London: Rout-ledge.

Frooman, J., 1999. Stakeholder influence strategies. *Academy of Management Review,* 24: 191–205.

Gamson, W. A. 1990. *The strategy of social protest* (2nd ed.). Belmont, CA: Wadsworth.

Gamson, W. A. 1992. The social psychology of collective action. In A. D. Morris & C. McClurg Mueller (Eds.), *Frontiers in social movement theory:* 53–76. New Haven, CT: Yale University Press.

Giugni, M. 1998. Was it worth the effort? The outcomes and consequences of social movements. *Annual Review of Sociology,* 24: 371–393.

Goodwin, J., & Jasper, J. M. 1999. Caught in a winding, snarling vine: The structural bias of political process theory. *Sociological Forum,* 14: 27–54.

Greenwood, R., & Hinings, C. R. 1996. Understanding radical organizational change: Bringing together the old and the new institutionalism. *Academy of Management Review,* 21: 1022–1054.

Greenwood, R., Suddaby, R., & Hinings, C. R. 2002. Theorizing change: The role of professional associations in the transformation of institutionalized fields. *Academy of Management Journal,* 45: 58–80.

Haines, H. H. 1984. Black radicalization and the funding of civil rights: 1957–1970. *Social Problems,* 32: 31–43.

Hensmans, M. 2003. Social movement organizations: A metaphor for strategic actors in institutional fields. *Organization Studies,* 24: 355–381.

Hernes, H. K., & Mikalsen, K. H. 2002. From protest to participation? Environmental groups and the management of marine fisheries. *Mobilization,* 7: 15–28.

Hilson, C. 2002. New social movements: The role of legal opportunity. *Journal of European Public Policy,* 9: 238–255.

Hobsbawm, E. J. 1952. The machine breakers *Past and Present,* 1: 57–70.

Holm, P. 1995. The dynamics of institutionalization: Transformation processes in Norwegian fisheries. *Administrative Science Quarterly,* 40: 398–422.

Hunt, S. A., & Benford, R. D. 2004. Collective identity, solidarity, and commitment. In D. A. Snow, S. A. Soule, & H. Kriesi (Eds.), *Blackwell companion to social movements:* 433–457. Oxford: Blackwell.

Illia, L. 2003. Passage to cyberactivism: How dynamics of activism change. *Journal of Public Affairs,* 3: 326–337.

Jasper, J. M., & Nelkin, D. 1992. *The animal rights crusade: The growth of a moral protest.* New York: Free Press.

Jensen, H. R. 2003. Staging political consumption: A discourse analysis of the Brent Spar conflict as recast by the Danish mass media. *Journal of Retailing and Consumer Services,* 10: 71–80.

Jepperson, R. L. 1991. Institutions, institutional effects, and institutionalism. In W. W. Powell & P. J. DiMaggio (Eds.), *The new institutionalism in organizational analysis:* 143–163. Chicago: University of Chicago Press.

Keck, M., & Sikkink, K. 1998. *Activists beyond borders: Advocacy networks in international politics.* Ithaca, NY: Cornell University Press.

Kell, G. 2003. The Global Compact: Origins, operations, progress, challenges. *Journal of Corporate Citizenship,* 11: 35–49.

Klandermans, B. 2004. The demand and supply of participation: Social-psychological correlates of participation in social movements. In D. A. Snow, S. A. Soule, & H. Kriesi (Eds.), *Blackwell companion to social movements:* 360–379. Oxford: Blackwell.

Klein, J. G., Smith, N. C., & John, A. 2004. Why we boycott: Consumer motivations for boycott participation. *Journal of Marketing,* 68(3): 92–109.

Knight, G., & Greenberg, J. 2002. Promotionalism and sub-politics: Nike and its labor critics. *Management Communication Quarterly,* 16: 541–570.

Kolb, F. 2002. *Soziale Bewegungen und politischer Wandel* [Social movements and political change]. Lüneburg: Deutscher Naturschutzring.

Koopmans, R., & Rucht, D. 2002. Protest event analysis. In B. Klandermans & S. Staggenborg (Eds.), *Methods of social movement research:* 231–259. Minneapolis: University of Minnesota Press.

Kozinets, R. V., & Handelman, J. M. 2004. Adversaries of consumption: Consumer movements, activism, and ideology. *Journal of Consumer Research,* 31: 691–704.

Kriesi, H. 2004. Political context and opportunity. In D. A. Snow, S. A. Soule, & H. Kriesi (Eds.), *Blackwell companion to social movements:* 67–90. Oxford: Blackwell.

Lawrence, T. B. 1999. Institutional strategy. *Journal of Management,* 25: 161–187.

Lounsbury, M. 2001. Institutional sources of practice variation: Staffing college and university recycling programs. *Administrative Science Quarterly,* 46: 29–56.

Lounsbury, M., Ventresca, M. J., & Hirsch, P. M. 2003. Social movements, field frames and industry emergence: A cultural-political perspective on U.S. recycling. *SocioEconomic Review,* 1: 71–104.

Lustig, S., & Brunner, U. 1996. Environmental organizations in a changing environment: Major U.S. environmental organizations in the 1990s. *Environmental Politics,* 5: 130–139.

Maguire, S., Hardy, C., & Lawrence, T. B. 2004. Institutional entrepreneurship in emerging fields: HIV/AIDS treatment advocacy in Canada. *Academy of Management Journal,* 47: 657–679.

Matten, D., & Crane, A. 2005. Corporate citizenship: Toward an extended theoretical conceptualization. *Academy of Management Review,* 30: 166–179.

McAdam, D., McCarthy, J. D., & Zald, M. N. (Eds.). 1996. *Comparative perspectives on social movements: Political opportunities, mobilizing structures, and cultural framings.* New York: Cambridge University Press.

McAdam, D., & Scott, W. R. 2005. Organizations and movements. In G. F. Davis, D. McAdam, W. R. Scott, & M. N. Zald (Eds.), *Social movements and organization theory:* 4–40. New York: Cambridge University Press.

McCarthy, J. D., & Zald, M. N. 1977. Resource mobilization and social movements: A partial theory. *American Journal of Sociology,* 82: 1212–1241.

McWilliams, A., & Siegel, D. 2001. Corporate social responsibility: A theory of the firm perspective. *Academy of Management Review,* 26: 117–127.

Meyer, M. 2004. Organizational identity, political contexts, and SMO action: Explaining the tactical choices made by peace organizations in Israel, Northern Ireland, and South Africa. *Social Movement Studies,* 3: 167–197.

Micheletti, M., Follesdal, A., & Stolle, D. (Eds.). 2004. *Politics, products, and markets: Exploring political consumerism past and present.* New Brunswick, NJ: Transaction.

Minkoff, D. C. 2001. Walking a political tightrope: Responsiveness and internal accountability in social movement organizations. In M. D. Montilla & E. J. Reid (Eds.), *Exploring organizations and advocacy: Governance and accountability:* 33–48. Washington, DC: Urban Institute.

Mitchell, R. K., Agle, B. R., & Wood, D. J. 1997. Toward a theory of stakeholder identification and salience: Defining the principle of who and what really counts. *Academy of Management Review,* 22: 853–886.

Morrill, C., Zald, M. N., & Rao, H. 2003. Covert political conflict in organizations: Challenges from below. *Annual Review of Sociology,* 29: 391–415.

No Border. 2005. *Campaigning against aviation companies.* http://www.noborder.org/avia/display.php?id14, accessed June 17.

Oliver, C. 1991. Strategic responses to institutional processes. *Academy of Management Review,* 16: 145–179.

O'Rourke, D. 2003. Outsourcing regulation: Non-governmental systems of labor standards and monitoring. *Policy Studies Journal,* 31: 1–29.

Pacione, M. 1997. Local exchange trading systems: A rural response to the globalization of capitalism? *Journal of Rural Studies,* 13: 415–427.

Platt, G. M., & Williams, R. H. 2002. Ideological language and social movement mobilization: A sociolinguistic analysis of segregationists' ideologies. *Sociological Theory,* 20: 328–359.

Plows, A., Wall, D., & Doherty, B. 2004. Covert repertoires: Ecotage in the UK. *Social Movement Studies,* 3: 199–219.

Raeburn, N. C. 2004. *Changing corporate America from inside out: Lesbian and gay workplace rights.* Minneapolis: University of Minnesota Press.

Rao, H., Morrill, C., & Zald, M. N. 2000. Power plays: How social movements and collective action create new organizational forms. *Research in Organizational Behavior,* 22: 237–281.

Rehbein, K., Waddock, S., & Graves, S. B. 2004. Understanding shareholder activism: Which corporations are targeted? *Business and Society,* 43: 239–267.

Rochon, T. R. 1988. *Between society and state: Mobilizing for peace in Western Europe.* Princeton, NJ: Princeton University Press.

Rowley, T., & Berman, S. 2000. A brand new brand of corporate social performance. *Business and Society,* 39: 397–418.

Rowley, T. J. 1997. Moving beyond dyadic ties: A network theory of stakeholder influences. *Academy of Management Review,* 22: 887–910.

Rowley, T. J., & Moldoveanu, M. 2003. When will stakeholder groups act? An interest- and identity-based model of stakeholder group mobilization. *Academy of Management Review,* 28: 204–219.

Rucht, D. 1988. Themes, logics, and arenas of social movements: A structural approach. In B. Klandermans, H. Kriesi, & S. Tarrow (Eds.), *From structure to action: Comparing social movement research across cultures:* 305–328. Greenwich, CT: JAI Press.

Rucht, D. 1999. Linking organization and mobilization: Michels's iron law of oligarchy reconsidered. *Mobilization,* 4: 151–169.

Scholte, J. A. 2004. Civil society and democratically accountable global governance. *Government and Opposition,* 39: 211–233.

Schurman, R. 2004. Fighting "Frankenfoods": Industry opportunity structures and the efficacy of the anti-biotech movement in Western Europe. *Social Problems,* 51: 243–268.

Scott, J. C. 1989. Everyday forms of resistance. In F. D. Colburn (Ed.), *Everyday forms of peasant resistance:* 3–33. Armonk, NY: M. E. Sharpe.

Scott, W. R. 2001. *Institutions and organizations* (2nd ed.). Thousand Oaks, CA: Sage.

Snow, D. A. 2001. Collective identity and expressive forms. In N. J. Smelser & P. B. Baltes (Eds.), *International encyclopedia of the social and behavioral sciences:* 2212–2219. Oxford: Elsevier Science.

Snow, D. A. 2004. Framing processes, ideology, and discursive field. In D. A. Snow, S. A. Soule, & H. Kriesi (Eds.), *Blackwell companion to social* movements:380–412. Oxford: Blackwell.

Snow, D. A., Soule, S. A., & Kriesi, H. (Eds.). 2004. *Blackwell companion to social movements.* Oxford: Blackwell.

Spar, D. L., & La Mure, L. T. 2003. The power of activism: Assessing the impact of NGOs on global business. *California Management Review,* 45(3): 78–101.

Strang, D., & Meyer, J. W. 1993. Institutional conditions for diffusion. *Theory and Society,* 22: 487–511.

Suchman, M. C. 1995. Managing legitimacy: Strategic and institutional approaches. *Academy of Management Review,* 20: 571–610.

Tarrow, S. 1983. *Struggling to reform: Social movements and policy change during cycles of protest.* Ithaca, NY: Cornell University Press.

Tarrow, S. 1998. *Power in movement: Social movements and contentious politics* (2nd ed.). Cambridge: Cambridge University Press.

Taylor, V., & van Dyke, N. 2004. "Get up, stand up": Tactical repertoires of social movements. In D. A. Snow, S. A. Soule, & H. Kriesi (Eds.), *Blackwell companion to social movements:* 262–293. Oxford: Blackwell.

Tolbert, P. S., & Zucker, L. G. 1996. The institutionalization of institutional theory. In S. R. Clegg, C. Hardy, & W. R. Nord (Eds.), *Handbook of organization studies:* 175–190. London: Sage.

Turban, D. B., & Greening, D. W. 1997. Corporate social performance and organizational attractiveness to prospective employees. *Academy of Management Journal,* 40: 658–672.

Van de Ven, A. H., & Hargrave, T. J. 2004. Social, technical, and institutional change: A literature review and synthesis. In M. S. Poole & A. H. Van de Ven (Eds.), *Handbook of organizational change and innovation:* 259–303. New York: Oxford University Press.

Vogel, D. 2004. Tracing the American roots of the political consumerism movement. In M. Micheletti, A. Follesdal, & D. Stolle (Eds.), *Politics, products, and markets: Exploring political consumerism past and present:* 83–100. New Brunswick, NJ: Transaction.

Wartick, S. L. 1992. The relationship between intense media exposure and change in corporate reputation. *Business and Society,* 31: 33–49.

Whetten, D. A., Rands, G., & Godfrey, P. 2002. What are the responsibilities of business to society? In A. Pettigrew, H. Thomas, & R. Whittington (Eds.), *Handbook of strategy and management:* 373–408. London: Sage.

Wilson, J. 2002. The sponsorship scam. In E. Lubbers (Ed.), *Battling big business: Countering greenwash, front groups and other forms of corporate bullying:* 44–52. Monroe, ME: Common Courage Press.

Wokutch, R. 2001. Nike and its critics. *Organization and Environment,* 14: 207–237.

Zald, M. N. 2000. Ideologically structured action: An enlarged agenda for social movement research. *Mobilization,* 5: 1–16.

Zald, M. N., & Ash, R. 1966. Social movement organizations: Growth, decay and change. *Social Forces,* 44: 327–341.

Zald, M. N., & McCarthy, J. D. 1980. Social movement industries: Competition and cooperation among movement organizations. *Research in Social Movements, Conflicts and Change,* 3: 1–20.

CHAPTER 50

Missionary Leadership

Harnessing the Power of the Mission

K. M. Thiagarajan

Microcredit Foundation of India

Nonprofit organizations often come into being to serve social causes that are not deemed to be profitable or viable in a market economy. Empowering poor rural women and providing them small loans, helping the disabled, educating the poor, preventing the spread of HIV, protecting the environment, upholding human rights, and the like are social causes that attract nonprofit organizations. The "mission" of such organizations is embedded in the "cause" that is sought to be served by them.

In the case of for-profit organizations, even when they have lofty ideals as their chosen mission, it is implicitly understood by all parties concerned—management, employees, shareholders, and the public—that the mission is subservient to the basic goal of maximizing shareholder wealth. It is only natural that the primary concern of an organization set up to earn profits should be precisely that: to earn profits and enhance shareholder wealth or market capitalization. Like all human endeavors, such organizations also serve various public purposes, such as producing goods and services needed by the society and providing employment, in the process of achieving their primary goals.

The social causes served by nonprofit organizations have the power to attract a special group of highly committed individuals who seek satisfaction from serving those causes. The mission also has the power to unite all those who subscribe to it and to unleash tremendous energy. Missionary leadership is the process whereby a leader uses the inherent power of the mission to attract highly committed individuals who want to serve the cause and then enables them to derive satisfaction from such service.

If this distinct character of a nonprofit organization that has a genuine, embedded mission is not understood, and if one deals with leadership in nonprofits in the same manner as in for-profit organizations, we would lose a crucial and powerful advantage that is unique to nonprofits. The consequences can be serious, not only for nonprofits but also for society as a whole.

The concept of "missionary leadership" evolved from my experience in initiating a program to extend microcredit to poor women in Indian villages. Ironically, this project was the result of my attempt to rejuvenate the loss-making rural branches of a commercial bank—a for-profit organization. A brief description of the project follows.

Case Study: Microcredit to Rural Women

In 1993, I became the chairman and chief executive of Bank of Madura, a commercial bank in the private sector in India. It was a tradition-bound, moderately profitable, regional bank with low levels of technology and productivity. In response to the economic liberalization initiated by the Indian government at that time and rapid changes in the market, a major restructuring effort was undertaken. Loss-making branches were merged with other branches or closed. New branches were opened across the country in cities with good profit potential. The operations were computerized and automated. New products and services were introduced. Profitability improved substantially.

The chink in the armor was the vast network of rural branches (102 out of a total of 275 branches) located in villages with small populations and low levels of economic activity. The rural branches were started more due to government policies and regulatory pressures than out of commercial considerations. Whereas the policy allowed closure of urban branches, closure of rural branches required various permissions, which were difficult to obtain. Gradually, after obtaining the necessary approvals, some of the branches were merged and the number reduced to seventy-seven. When the option of closure no longer existed, we had to deal with the real issue of how these branches could be revitalized.

At this point I learned about the tremendous work done by the Grameen Bank of Bangladesh, founded by Muhammad Yunus, a pioneer in the field of microcredit. Following his example, in November 1995 we established the Rural Development Division to provide microcredit to poor women in the villages where our branches were located.

In the Indian version of microcredit, which has evolved its own group formation and credit delivery models,

self-help groups (SHGs) are the basic unit to which the loan is given. Each SHG is composed of twenty women who voluntarily form the group and choose one another in the knowledge that they have to jointly guarantee the loan. During the first six months, they save a small amount each month (they determine the amount, based on their earnings), pool the savings, and deposit these funds in the bank. The monthly deposit is normally in the range of 50 cents to one U.S. dollar at the official exchange rate (although in buying power it is worth much more in India, especially in rural areas). They meet twice a month and receive training on how to organize their group meetings, start a bank account, and calculate interest and also learn about women's rights and other general issues. During the second six months, besides continuing to save, they begin to lend their savings to group members. The group decides the amount, rate of interest, priority of needs, and other procedures for lending. During this one year, the women become quite proficient in handling finance, understanding the implications of cooperating and pooling their savings, and the importance of repayment. They also gain self-confidence, become articulate, and understand the need for joint social action. At the end of the first year, the group becomes eligible to receive credit from the bank, subject to regularity in savings and repayment of internal loans by every group member. Normally, the loan is about U.S.$50 per person, but in the case of Bank of Madura, an individual could receive up to U.S.$200 to undertake small business activities like raising a milk cow, setting up a tailoring shop, or producing food items. Repayment is made every month, and the group collects the amount due and pays the bank. The loan is given without any collateral but is guaranteed by all of the SHG's members. The initial training, peer group pressure to be responsible, and mutual monitoring by the members all help considerably in the repayment rate, which is about 99.5 percent.

Normally, the self-help groups are formed by NGOs (nonprofits), and banks extend the loans. However, we decided to form the groups ourselves through our branches. This was an unusual move for a commercial bank, and to understand the process, we need to take a look at how banks work in India.

Rural branches are managed or administered by the head of a geographical division, which has many metropolitan, urban, and rural branches. Since the volume of business is very low in rural branches, the division heads do not pay attention to them. The executives and staff in banks, who are better educated and highly paid relative to those in many other segments, do not like to live in villages. Lack of modern amenities, good schools, health care facilities, and entertainment make villages unattractive to them and their families. To illustrate, many government banks have a policy of making the promotion of managers from grade I to grade II contingent on a stint in a rural branch. Such transfers are commonly known as "punishment postings." Most often, staff live in nearby towns and commute to the village. They spend very little time at the branch and do not interact with the villagers, who are poor, uneducated, and socially not their equals.

When the Rural Development Division was started, it became obvious that unless this issue was faced squarely, the division could not take off. As a first step, the management of all the rural branches was brought under the division irrespective of the branch locations. This move made rural branches gain legitimacy and gave a sharp focus to their activities. Next we decided to "attract" people from within the bank who wanted to get involved in rural development work on a voluntary basis instead of compelling people to work in these branches. Although the personnel department was skeptical, people did come forward. Instead of selecting all those who volunteered, we decided to select people on the basis of their commitment to the project and their willingness to live in the village. The candidates were also told that they should relate to people in the village, especially the women, as equals, without any gender, caste, class, or other biases.

Those who showed any hesitation in the interview were not selected. This move sent strong signals throughout the bank that senior management was committed to the concept of rural development through microcredit. Many individuals who were already in the division opted to stay; however, not all were retained. A thorough review of each person's background was made to ensure that he or she could be part of the new project. Those who were considered unsuitable were transferred out. The personnel policy was also amended to provide automatic transfer to an urban branch to anybody in the Rural Development Division, at any time, who requested this. Within a few months, a team of about 325 highly motivated individuals, from a total of 2,600 employees, was assembled.

The core team of senior executives, headed by the divisional manager, studied various microcredit projects in detail, visited many nonprofits involved in forming SHGs, received training from experts in the field, and met frequently to decide on a strategy. After an intensive two-day residential workshop without anybody from outside the division, the core team decided to form SHGs themselves without linking with nonprofits. This was a big surprise, but the decision was accepted.

This led to the birth of a "nonprofit" within the for-profit bank. The cost of starting, training, and monitoring SHGs, which is called "capacity building," is an expensive and time-consuming process. This cost is even higher when a bank promotes groups through its own personnel, whose salary levels are much higher than salaries in the nonprofit sector. Besides, the overheads of the bank are also high. This is why banks rely on nonprofits to undertake capacity building and only come in to provide credit.

The decision to directly promote SHGs was based on the reasoning that there would be no additional cost, since the cost of fixed overheads and salaries of individuals in the rural branches was already being incurred. A decision was also made that no increases in staff or overhead costs would be allowed in the Rural Development Division. The capacity of the division to promote SHGs without additional costs was pegged at fifteen hundred SHGs. It was also agreed by the core team of executives in the division that new methodologies to promote SHGs at lower cost would be found when the capacity of fifteen hundred groups was reached.

The new division was organized around five clusters of branches with a project manager heading each cluster. A training center was started that trained all the staff in the division on promoting, training, and monitoring SHGs. To begin with, the core team decided to go slow: start a few groups and evaluate the process. Since it takes one year before a group becomes eligible for a loan, it took time to evaluate the process. Thereafter, groups were started in larger numbers. Initially, the team faced hardships in working in the villages, promoting groups, and training women who were either not very educated or illiterate. These hardships vanished when they saw the difference they were making in the lives of the village women and the hospitability, friendship, and gratitude received from them.

In the year 2001, Bank of Madura merged with ICICI Bank, which is the second-largest financial institution in India. I continued with the bank for one year as adviser for the microcredit project before I went on to found the Microcredit Foundation of India in 2002. During the time I was adviser to the project, we selected two hundred women who were members of the SHGs promoted by the bank to start SHGs on their own. These women were well versed in the concept and had demonstrated leadership qualities. They were further trained by the bank personnel before they started forming groups. They were also remunerated for this work, but this cost is considerably lower than the cost of promoting groups by the bank. Now there are five hundred village women who are promoting groups under the supervision of bank personnel and linking them with the bank for credit. At last count, there were eight thousand SHGs, with a membership of 160,000 women. When this number and the credit portfolio grow further, the activity has the potential to become profitable.

Key Elements of Success

The employees of the bank who worked in other divisions and visitors to the Rural Development Division, especially from other banks, were amazed at the level of commitment, hard work, and satisfaction in their achievement shown by the employees of this division. Four key elements in this process can be identified:

1. *Presence of a powerful mission.* Although we never had a separate "mission statement" for this division, the mission became quite obvious. "Empowering poor women in villages through self-help groups and microcredit" was the unstated but obvious mission. It might be added that even though we had a "mission statement" for the bank that was widely publicized and also printed on pocket-sized laminated cards that were distributed to every employee, few could remember it. The employees' true commitment was to the mission of the SHG program, not to the bank's "manufactured" mission.

2. *Commitment to the mission.* The mission of this division did strike a chord in many individuals, and they were willing to work in villages, to be part of it, despite hardships and personal inconvenience. They had left a job and joined a mission.

3. *Motivation from within.* During my many interactions with people in the division, it was obvious that the source of motivation was coming from within and not from external stroking or rewards. The zeal they exhibited could be legitimately characterized as missionary. Once the key elements were in place, the members of the division were working for themselves and not for me, the divisional manager, or the bank.

4. *Cohesiveness as a team bound by a common cause.* There were fewer disputes in the division compared to the rest of the bank, and those that arose were easier to resolve. All that was needed was to answer the question, "What is best for this project, this cause?" There was an implicit understanding that the cause was greater than the individual.

I did not play an active day-to-day leadership role in this process as one might expect of the executive leader of an organization. My main contributions were the following:

- Identifying the activity or the "cause."
- Thinking of the idea of attracting "volunteers," rather than assigning work to people based on their educational qualifications, experience, or past performance, as is usually the case, and then thinking of ways to motivate them. These mission-driven workers provided their own motivation.
- Acting as a "gatekeeper" to ensure that individuals committed to the mission were selected and that others were not chosen.
- Giving everyone a lot of freedom.

The experience I have just described can be viewed as an instance of "transforming leadership" as conceptualized by James MacGregor Burns (1978) or "transformational leadership" as conceived by Bernard Bass (1985), and in fact, it can be made to fit into the framework of these theories. However, if one were to do that, much of the learning that can be gained from this experience would be lost. If the process can be looked at afresh, it might reveal significant differences that can perhaps add additional insights into leadership processes that transform organizations.

Missionary Leadership

The term *mission* is now commonly used in all organizations, and mission statements have become mandatory. However, the word *missionary* is still associated with people who seek the propagation of a faith. In the present context, the term *missionary leadership* is used in its generic sense to highlight the fact that nonprofits would require leaders who are themselves deeply committed to the mission and strive to fulfill it.

Concept of a Mission

The term *mission* is overused and therefore overburdened to the extent that the underlying concept itself may become trivialized. The idea of a mission whose votaries become missionaries and exhibit uncommon zeal and are willing to go to any length to uphold and fulfill the mission even at the cost of personal deprivation needs to be restored to its rightful place. Despite the devaluation of the term *mission*, as in the term *mission statement*, the power of the concept to motivate people is real.

The concept of "missionary leadership" is predicated on the presence of a genuine mission. The relationship between the leader and followers is based on their common, shared desire to serve the mission and is not purely relational. This would distinguish missionary leadership from leader-member exchange theory (Graen and Scandura, 1987), for example, or even transformational leadership, which focus primarily on the relationship between leader and follower.

Assembling a Missionary Team

Leadership theories tend to assume that the followers are a given and leaders proactively transform them or elevate followers from lower to higher levels of needs. However, a missionary leader is one who understands the power of the mission to attract committed individuals and deliberately assembles a team of dedicated people to fulfill it.

All individuals, at some level of their being and at different stages in their lives, respond to their inner needs, even if they do not always actualize them. This is true even when they are transactional in the context of their work, business, or other spheres. Thus at any given time, some individuals are more ready to serve causes and join a mission than others. They might do this by volunteering their services, joining the effort full time or part time, or supporting the cause from the outside by raising resources and giving moral support.

The success of a leader in a nonprofit organization will depend on the extent to which he or she can identify, attract, and retain individuals who can become missionaries for the cause the leader espouses. Conversely, success will also depend on the person's ability to avoid engaging contractual or transactional workers who have no commitment to the mission, even as unpaid volunteers.

In assembling the mission team, in addition to commitment, the team members also need competence, and the selection process has to be conscious of this. The ideal scenario would be to have a team that is highly committed and highly competent. Compared to for-profit companies, nonprofits can be weak in the areas of accounting and finance, administration, and management. However, it would be easier to provide training and support to a team of highly motivated missionary followers than to try to get a group of qualified and competent people who pursue their own personal agendas instead of being fully committed to the mission. Today, many managerial functions, including payroll, accounting, database management, external communication, and even fundraising, can be outsourced to professional firms who specialize in them. Nonprofits can consider this option so that they can focus their energies on the main purpose of the organization.

This aspect of carefully selecting and assembling a team of people who are committed to the cause is perhaps the most critical element in the success of missionary leadership. The alternative is the time-consuming and difficult process of getting a group of employees to buy into the vision or take ownership of the mission and trying to transact with them through rewards and punishments or transform them by raising their levels of motivation.

Motivation

The source of motivation of missionary followers is at the sublime level and not at the mundane, need-fulfillment level, which is often the case with contractual workers. Motivation at the mundane level is based on satisfying the material or ego needs of individuals in return for their work and contribution to the organization. Material needs based on desire are hard to satisfy because fulfillment creates new desires. Ego needs also expand with fulfillment. An important component of material and ego needs is the desire for differential gains, where satisfaction is obtained not only from what one gets but also from how much more one gets in relation to others. This leads to competition between members of a team, lack of trust, and a breakdown in communication and makes team building a difficult hurdle.

Motivation at the sublime level addresses issues that are internal to the individual—the need for personal growth and the desire to derive satisfaction from serving a cause. Serving a common cause binds individuals and promotes cooperation. The energies are focused on serving the cause.

The distinction between the two types of motivation—need fulfillment at the mundane level and inner fulfillment at the sublime level (see Exhibit 50.1) does not mean that people fall into either one category or the other. All individuals have material and ego needs, and they seek ways to satisfy these needs from their workplace, family, friends, and community. It is also true that all individuals have deeper, inner needs at a sublime level, where they seek satisfaction from serving a cause that benefits society and not themselves individually. Some people are more aware of this need in themselves than others. People may respond to these needs at different times in their lives. Typically, college students and retirees are keen to work with nonprofits. Many individuals pursue both types of needs at the same time.

The missionary leader has to be conscious of this distinction and respond to the inner needs of followers to seek satisfaction from serving the cause. In the process, the leader has to ensure that the other needs of the individuals, such as financial security and emotional support, are satisfied so that they do not detract these people from their goal of serving the cause.

Role of the Leader

Leadership theories generally revolve around the leader's qualities, such as charisma, and his or her ability to motivate followers. The theme of this chapter is that in nonprofits with a mission, the real source of motivation

is the power of the cause being served and the inner need of individuals to seek personal satisfaction at a sublime level from serving the cause. The leader is the medium that enables this process. The leader does not modify or transform the needs or motivational level of the followers but recognizes the deeper needs in the individuals that attracted them to the mission and offers them the opportunity to fulfill these needs.

The missionary leader also has to ensure that the powerful energies that can be unleashed are directed toward serving the cause and not dissipated on internal organizational issues such as communication, problem solving, or conflict resolution, which soak up organizational energy. If the leader can establish a culture where each member subscribes to the idea that the cause is greater than the individual or the team and builds consensus on how the team should work together focused on the achievement of the cause, the energies will be unified.

The leader of a nonprofit organization has the unique opportunity to focus the collective energy of a group of committed people on the cause instead of dissipating this powerful energy on motivational and organizational issues.

Conclusion

Missionary leadership can transform a nonprofit in pursuit of a genuine mission. The concept of missionary leadership proposed in this chapter is based on my own personal experience; it is not a theory based on data collection or research. If this chapter prompts discussion, analysis, and further study, my purpose in writing it will have been well served.

References

Baas, B. M. *Leadership and Performance Beyond Expectations.* New York: Free Press, 1985.

Burns, J. M. *Leadership.* New York: HarperCollins, 1978.

Graen, G. B., and Scandura, T. "Toward a Psychology of Dyadic Organizing." In B. Staw and L. L. Cummings (eds.), *Research in Organizational Behavior.* Vol. 9. Greenwich, Conn.: JAI Press, 1987.

Author Index

Subject Index

About the Editor

Gill Robinson Hickman (Ph.D., University of Southern California) is currently Professor of Leadership Studies in the Jepson School of Leadership Studies at the University of Richmond. Her previous experience includes Founding Dean in the School of Health at California State University, Acting Associate Dean at Virginia Commonwealth University, and Professor of Public Administration and Director of Human Resources for two organizations. She was also a founding partner in a small California retail business.

Dr. Hickman has published three books: *Leading Change in Multiple Contexts: Concepts and Practices in Organizational, Community, Political, Social, and Global Change Settings* (Sage Publications); *Leading Organizations: Perspectives for a New Era* (Sage Publications); and *Managing Personnel in the Public Sector: A Shared Responsibility* (with Dalton Lee). In addition, she has published a number of book chapters and articles on leadership studies. Her current research and book project with Dr. Georgia Sorenson focuses on the power of invisible leadership, which examines leadership in settings where dedication to a powerful purpose is the motivating force for people to take action.

Dr. Hickman has presented at the China Executive Leadership Academy Pudong (CELAP), Shanghai, China; the Leadership in Central Europe Conference at Palacky University in Olomouc, Czech Republic; the Salzburg Seminar in Salzburg, Austria; and the University of the Western Cape in South Africa. She has participated as a panel member at international conferences in Amsterdam, The Netherlands; Guadalajara, Mexico; and Vancouver and Toronto, Canada. At the Jepson School, she teaches courses on leading change, theories and models of leadership, leadership in organizations, and leadership in a diverse society.

Supporting researchers for more than 40 years

Research methods have always been at the core of SAGE's publishing program. Founder Sara Miller McCune published SAGE's first methods book, *Public Policy Evaluation*, in 1970. Soon after, she launched the *Quantitative Applications in the Social Sciences* series—affectionately known as the "little green books."

Always at the forefront of developing and supporting new approaches in methods, SAGE published early groundbreaking texts and journals in the fields of qualitative methods and evaluation.

Today, more than 40 years and two million little green books later, SAGE continues to push the boundaries with a growing list of more than 1,200 research methods books, journals, and reference works across the social, behavioral, and health sciences. Its imprints—Pine Forge Press, home of innovative textbooks in sociology, and Corwin, publisher of PreK–12 resources for teachers and administrators—broaden SAGE's range of offerings in methods. SAGE further extended its impact in 2008 when it acquired CQ Press and its best-selling and highly respected political science research methods list.

From qualitative, quantitative, and mixed methods to evaluation, SAGE is the essential resource for academics and practitioners looking for the latest methods by leading scholars.

For more information, visit **www.sagepub.com**.